A COUNTRY PILLOW BOOK
by
David Kavanagh

DramBooks

Published by Dram Books.
ISBN 0-9548567-1-6
Cover image:'The Wood' ©Gill Kavanagh.

For
*Genevieve
Niluka and
Richard*

CONTENTS (i)

CONTENTS (ii)

PIKE: how we caught the terror of the haunted pond

IF you're talking predatory freshwater fish, there's one that springs immediately to the fore; the King of the Killers; the great white shark of the local pond..*the pike*.

Built like an elegant Cruise missile with its fins set far back from its large, rapacious mouth, the pike is a real-life monster of the deep - especially for any careless minnow which makes the mistake of ambling into its larder.

Frogs, ducklings, water voles - in fact anything small enough to crush between those snapping jaws and swallow - need to take care when Mr Pike is on the prowl.

There are tales, probably not all apocryphal, of tiny dogs drowned by huge pike and pets as large as Alsations left injured. Even humans have suffered the odd nip or two.

Beautifully camouflaged to nestle unseen among the reeds, the pike operates by stealth for most of his hunt then strikes with fearsome speed.

It's little wonder that some anglers become so besotted with this magnificent fish that over time no other quarry will do and landing bigger and better pike turns into an obsession, a more elemental fight between Man and nature.

Unfortunately for Mr Pike, a gourmet of living flesh, his own flesh can also be quite tasty.

At the risk of making this sound like a cookery feature, there are many varied recipes for pike - one I possess even dates back to 18th Century Hungary: 'Pike Cooked in Horseradish Cream' (*Csuka Teifeles Tormaval*) serves eight and involves lashings of sour cream, butter, and flour, as well as piles of grated horseradish.

So the biter has been bit into on countless occasions. Not that this affects the mystique of this murderous fish.

I haven't been an active angler myself for years but the hairs on the back of my neck still prickle at the memory of how we - well, my brother actually - caught Starey Eyes, a large pike who earned his nickname from his frighteningly hypnotic gaze.

However, not many had seen him - least of all me.

Starey Eyes lived in a stinking, green slime-slicked pond flanked on one side by trees, on the other by an almost vertical embankment occasionally abused as a tipping area.

Hemmed in by rusting prams and old plastic toilet seats, no wonder Starey Eyes had starey eyes. He was angry. Very angry.

Who wouldn't be, surrounded by toilet seats all day ?

The ghastliness of this environment was further enhanced by rumours that the pond was haunted by the ghost of a young woman who had drowned herself there.

So it was with some trepidation that myself and my older brother settled down one day with a single fishing rod, line, and spinner between us to try to tempt Starey Eyes from the depths.

It wasn't a long wait, perhaps because by then there was so little natural prey left in the pond.

Within half an hour, we noted with odd squeaky voices that an ominous shadow was tracking our red and gold Veltic spinner as it traversed the narrowest, deepest section of the elongated pond.

Suddenly, a flash of silver in the water showed Starey Eyes had struck then instantly recoiled as the barbs dug into his mouth.

The rod was almost wrenched from my 12 year-old brother's grasp yet somehow, with maniacal zeal, he managed to reel in Starey Eyes.

Having brought no landing net, 15 pounds or so of furious, writhing pike finally dropped at our feet - just as the spinner jerked free of its mouth.

"*Catch it !*," my brother shouted.

I took one look at those savage teeth.

"*You catch it !*," I replied.

We compromised. Neither of us caught it and before my brother could find a branch to subdue him, Starey Eyes had flapped his mighty tail and powered himself back into the water.

We stood there quivering, watching the agitated surface of the pond slowly return to normal. Then we went home.

We still congratulated ourselves.

We really had caught Starey Eyes - at least for a few, unforgettable moments.

1

UGLY ROWS FLARED when pro and anti-hunt campaigners clashed again all over the country at traditional Boxing Day foxhunting meets.

But supporters from both camps were content to verbally attack each other for the most part whenever the factions squared up.

More than 1,000 people lined each side of the main street in Maldon, Essex, when about 80 members of the Essex Farmers and Union Hunt held their meet.

Police managed to keep both sides apart and said they were pleased that a potential riot was avoided.

The Maldon event, one of the biggest of about 300 normally scheduled across the country, was held on Bank Holiday Monday instead of Boxing Day, which this year fell on a non-hunting Sunday.

Hunt supporters cheered and applauded the Essex riders while anti-hunt campaigners vented their fury on them, calling them "cruel" and "perverted".

Labour MP Angela Smith joined the anti-hunt protesters.

She said: "It is high time hunting was ended. You can still have the red jackets and the hounds and ride across the countryside but let's not have a live quarry. Let's have drag hunting instead."

Conservative MP John Whittingdale, also at the hunt, said: "I don't hunt myself and I don't wish to. But I recognise that hunting does contribute a huge amount to this area.

"There is no question that the countryside would suffer if hunting were to be banned."

Dawn Preston, spokeswoman for the Hunt Saboteurs Association, said: "This season could and should be the last season when hunting with hounds is a legal activity.

"Thousands of animals will be hounded to death in this period, and their only hope will be the presence of hunt saboteurs who use non-violent direct action to disrupt hunting."

A NATIONAL SURVEY is underway into how birds use our gardens for breeding and nesting.

Heading the study is John Tully, from Bristol, a member of the British Trust for Ornithology Council.

He has dispatched questionnaires to thousands of people in a bid to pick up vital data, part of the BTO's ongoing Garden Bird Watch project.

Mr Tully particularly wants to discover if birds are happy to use the centres of our busy towns and cities to breed. Results of the survey are due to be released in March.

FARMERS' LEADERS HAVE been seeking urgent talks with the malting industry following the recent announcement of the closure of Paul's Maltings in Wallingford, Oxfordshire.

The news left farmers shocked and meant the whole of southern England would be without a domestic outlet for malting barley, according to the National Farmers Union.

NFU Cereals Committee chairman Richard Butler said: "This announcement has serious implications for malting barley in southern England.

"This closure means that there are now no maltings remaining in this area, which means the viability of growing malting barley in the south of the country is seriously threatened. Producers of this specialist crop have rightly expressed severe concerns.

"We will be seeking urgent meetings with maltsters and malting barley traders early in the New Year to see how we can protect our markets in the face of this development."

RURAL POST OFFICES, police stations and schools could be merged under one roof so that village communities don't lose them, it has been revealed.

Government planners currently looking at methods of revitalising villages across the country are studying a proposed scheme to put all three vital centres side by side.

The hope is that the merged services will remain stronger together and help maintain and improve quality of life for villagers living there.

For years many villages have suffered as local post offices, schools, and police stations closed one by one.

However, the new proposals are unlikely to be implemented without a fight. Already the National Federation of Sub Postmasters has announced its disappointment with the idea.

A TENANT FARMER was found guilty of permitting potentially damaging dredging work on the River Avon in Hampshire without giving the required notice to English Nature.

The farmer permitted vegetated silt and gravel to be removed from King's Stream and allowed the dredgings to be dumped on the banks of the stream affecting 800 metres of the Site of Special Scientific Interest, revealed English Nature.

The farmer's claim that he had a reasonable excuse was dismissed by a magistrates court which ruled that the proposed works should have been outlined to English Nature in accordance with the Wildlife and Countryside Act 1981.

But because the farmer believed, albeit wrongly, that his work was beneficial to the stream and he did not intend to break the law, he was given an absolute discharge.

"The River Avon is of both national and international importance to wildlife," said Ian Davidson-Watts, an English Nature conservation officer.

"The wetland habitats support rare species like the Desmoulins Whorl snail, otters, and water voles which cannot tolerate large scale river improvement operations.

"The damage caused to the SSSI by this operation will mean that many species may be unable to recolonise the area."

THE RSPB HAS been warning bird-friendly gardeners they could be killing with kindness this Christmas if they fail to observe basic safety and hygiene standards when feeding the birds.

Grahame Madge, RSPB press officer, said: "Every winter the nation's garden birds get a real boost from the two out of every three people who put food out for them. But the Society is concerned that, inadvertently, some birds may be put at increased risk from disease."

In the last week, concern had grown over the safety of some peanuts being sold as bird food.

Independent tests had shown that some consignments of two varieties of peanut from India and one from Argentina contained high levels of aflatoxins - poisons which were known to caused death in domesticated birds.

Aflatoxins were produced from the Aspergillus fungus which could thrive in the high humidity of peanut growing areas but, apart from stringent scientific tests, there was no way of identifying affected peanuts.

Mr Madge added: "The RSPB is advising the public that they should only buy peanuts from reputable suppliers who know the country of origin of their produce. Peanuts sold loose, especially those marked unfit for human consumption, are potentially likely to be the most problematic.

"But of course, there are alternatives to peanuts, and other high-calorie foods, such as sunflower seeds, suet and cheese. These will provide garden birds with a much-needed energy boost. People may be becoming more conscious of their waistlines but birds need the highest-fat foods to survive."

With large numbers of birds visiting some feeding stations, there could also be a build up of stale food and droppings.

Cleaning the surface regularly with dilute disinfectant would provide a safer environment and having several bird tables or feeders in a garden would reduce competition for food which causes high stress levels among some birds, particularly finches.

FRESH FEARS HAVE been raised that thousands of British beef eaters may still be at risk of developing the human strain of BSE.

New tests involving mice have apparently revealed that the cattle disease Bovine Spongiform Encephalopathy and new variant CJD are in all likelihood caused by the same infectious agent.

The results have increased concern that a large section of the UK's population may still be "at considerable risk."

WORKERS FROM THE Environment Agency worked flat out as heavy rain hit many parts of Cornwall, Devon and Somerset in the run-up to Christmas.

"Recent flood defence schemes in Cornwall proved their worth and helped avert flooding in Truro, Polperro, Perranporth and Porthleven," said a spokesman.

"The Agency's flood warning centre issued over 70 flood warnings as the worst hit areas saw 90mm of rain fall in 48 hours. At the height of the problem, 12 red warnings, 20 amber and 40 yellow flood warnings were all in force across the region.

"Flooding would have been much worse without the recent improvements to our warning systems and our new defences across the region have performed well, averting flooding in many areas.

"Some of the worst flooding occurred at Bude on the Neet and Gunnislake on the Tamar where levels rose to their highest level since 1979.

"In Bude, houses are thought to have been flooded as high levels on the canal and the river combined with excess surface water to overwhelm capacity.

"Overall, there have been reports of over 100 properties in Cornwall being flooded and there has been widespread flooding of minor roads with many becoming impassable.

"Many rural roads in Devon also became waterlogged as the rivers Torridge, Taw, Waldon and Dart all reached red warning levels. There have been reports, too, of flooding in the villages of Harbertonford, Yeoford and Umberleigh.

"There was extensive flooding across the Somerset Levels and Moors and both the River Isle and the Tone reached dangerously high levels."

At one point the River Tone was being closely monitored as it threatened to flood Taunton town centre, the spokesman added.

FRIENDS OF THE Earth has written to 20 farmers across the country, urging them to dig up what it calls "illegal crops."

The letters inform the farmers that "genetically modified winter oilseed growing at 24 sites - including three farm scale trials - are not covered by legal consent, and should therefore be dug up," said a spokesman.

The letters follow a recent court order from the High Court confirming that Government permission allowing the crops to be planted was illegal. The order, resulting from a successful legal challenge by FoE, was not contested by the Government.

In the letters farmers are told that "FoE...believes that these GM winter rape crops should not be in the ground and should not remain there. We respectfully urge you, as strongly as we can, to consider destroying them."

Liana Stupples, campaigns director for Friends of the Earth, added:"The High Court has confirmed that permission to plant these winter GM oilseed rape crops was unlawful. To allow them to stay in the ground would simply bring the law into disrepute.

"Our letter to these farmers notifies them of the situation and urges them to consider destroying these crops. Public confidence in GM crops is already at an all time low. Allowing these crops to grow will only let it sink even lower.The Government must also act to end this farcical situation."

THE VAST MAJORITY of people using quiet country lanes are now fearful of being hurt by traffic, according to a survey.

The findings by the Council for the Protection of Rural England show how dangerous our country roads now seem and how little peace of mind can be found along once tranquil routes.

Some 65 per cent of people questioned admitted that they felt threatened by traffic all or some of the time.

In total, more than 1,000 people were asked for the views, of which 95 per cent walked, cycled, or rode horses in the country.

More than 90 per cent were also motorists themselves.

Out of the whole group questioned, only three per cent now said they felt safe from traffic on country lanes and 91 per cent felt the current speed limit of 60mph on many roads should be reduced - down to 20mph, according to some respondents.

Of those who helped CPRE with its survey, 72 per cent felt that walkers, cyclists, and horse riders should have priority over motorists on quiet country lanes.

Comments collected during the survey included:

"Sometimes I get the feeling that car users think people should not be walking on roads, not even country lanes"- Avon respondent.

"Too many drivers seem to feel that four wheels dominate over two wheels, feet, hooves or anything else"- Cornwall respondent.

"It is dangerous to walk to neighbours or to the post box, even in daylight"- Essex respondent.

"The grass verges are quite steep in places. Where the lane narrows I have to scramble up the verge sometimes to get out of the way of the traffic" - Warwickshire respondent.

FIVE SCOTTISH LOCHS could get Europe-wide recognition for being vital to birds which arrive there when temperatures plunge too low in their native countries.

Greenland white-fronted geese, whooper swans, and Icelandic greylag geese arrive in such significant numbers at the Caithness lochs that the district looks set to be recognised as a European Special Protection Area.

Scottish Natural Heritage has been asked to consult landowners and residents about Loch Scarmclate, Loch Heilen, Loch Watten, Loch Wester, and Loch Calder.

The five lochs are said to represent an important staging post in the migrations of all three bird species which are protected under EU wild bird law.

FRANCE HAS BEEN accused of cynically 'twisting the knife' in Tony Blair's back over the beef crisis by playing off the new Scottish Parliament against the Prime Minister.

In a cosy fireside chat with British journalists, French Premier Lionel Jospin let slip the damaging revelation that Mr Blair had refused a compromise where France would accept Scottish grass-fed beef.

Politicians in Scotland were furious at the news and accused the Labour leader of squandering a deal that could have given Scots farmers £100million a year.

The Scottish National Party labelled the move "a betrayal of Scotland."

As the crisis deepened, British MEPs had staged a walkout at the European Parliament in a snub to French President Jacques Chirac while he opened a new building in Strasbourg.

Meanwhile, furious farmers have accused three British supermarkets of betrayal after it was revealed they were stocking French turkeys for Christmas.

The news that the supermarkets were selling the turkeys while Britain's dispute with France was still at its height angered the National Farmers Union.

But Somerfield, Safeway, and Sainsbury's defended the sales, saying not enough turkeys had been produced on the home market to support huge Christmas demand.

However, the NFU said the move gave completely the wrong impression to the French, who were already operating outside EC law by refusing to sell British beef despite scientific tests putting it in the clear.

Asda and Tesco announced they were not selling any French turkeys and had no plans to.

MOVES TO REGENERATE a grouse moor in North Wales have been given a boost by a ball at the southern end of the country.

The Welsh Grouse Ball, held at Cardiff's Angel Hotel, raised £8,000 towards the upkeep of Pale Moor in North Wales.

The Welsh Grouse Project "aims to demonstrate the management required to restore red grouse to Wales," revealed a spokesman for the Game Conservancy Trust.

The Trust itself is an independent wildlife conservation charity which carries out research into game and its habitats.

TWO TOP DRESSAGE trainers are to host The British Horse Society's national one-day instructors' convention next year.

The event, on March 28 at The College Equestrian Centre, Keysoe, Bedfordshire, features "the world renowned dressage trainer Christoph Hess and international dressage rider Nicole Uphoff," said a spokesman.

Mr Hess is currently director of training at the German National Centre in Warendorf.

"Nicole Uphoff is probably best known for her highly successful partnership with Rembrandt as a member of the German Olympic dressage team winning Olympic, World and European team and individual gold medals," added the spokesman.

The pair would work with UK riders on young dressage horses to reveal their training system.

The convention was aimed primarily at BHS instructors but dressage fans were welcome.

MORE THAN 15,000 dead or oiled birds have now been washed ashore since the oil tanker Erika broke up off the Brittany coast on December 12, according to the RSPB.

Large numbers of birds came ashore on Christmas Day with more than 7,000 birds found in the region of south Finistere and Morbihan, said a spokesman.

Oiled birds had been picked up from Finistere to Charente-Maritime along 400-500km of coastline.

Chris Harbard, of the RSPB, said: "This must be the worst oil spill for birds in this part of Europe - far worse than the Amoco Cadiz spill 20 years ago. Many of the birds out at sea in the Bay of Biscay region will be UK seabirds from colonies in the Irish Sea.

"We will never know exactly how many birds have died as only a small percentage are usually washed ashore. The final total of birds oiled or killed may reach hundreds of thousands."

Birds affected were mainly guillemots, razorbills, gannets and eiders with smaller numbers of puffins, shags and cormorants involved, he said.

Among the dead and dying guillemots were many carrying British rings indicating they come from breeding colonies in the UK.

The Ligue pour la Protection des Oiseaux in France was appealing for help from European welfare organisations, especially for expertise and facilities for cleaning oiled birds.

The numbers of oiled birds affected were now more than the French welfare groups could deal with and the cleaning centres were full, said the RSPB.

Help was coming from other countries including the UK, Belgium and the Netherlands. At least 600 guillemots were being flown to the UK for treatment by the RSPCA.

Philippe Dubois, of the LPO, said: "Thousands of birds have now been found dead and most others are in poor condition and have lost up to half of their body weight. The spill is far worse than the Amoco Cadiz spill in 1978 when only 5,000 birds were found in three months."

TOXIC SHEEP DIPS blamed for causing death and illness to farmers have finally been censured by the Government which has halted their sale.

The organophosphate dips will be removed under a move which recognises for the first time the risk they pose.

However, they could later be reinstated if companies can produce safer versions.

THE COUNTRYSIDE Alliance has attacked the Hunt Saboteurs Association's 1999 Christmas Card campaign, calling it "vindictive and spiteful."

The card itself, entitled 'A Christmas Wish', features a queue of huntsmen waiting to enter a job centre.

At the front, a hunt worker holds a copy of the Employment Service's help back to work leaflet.

The card was allegedly sent to a number of hunt kennels around the country.

The card campaign was launched "only a few weeks after hunt follower Bob Freeman, badly injured in a riding accident, was sent a sickening get well soon card as he lay in a coma in a Birmingham hospital," said an Alliance spokesman.

"The message in the card, believed to have been sent by an anti-hunt activist, read: 'Dear Bob. Delighted to hear of your fall. Hope you suffer in agony before dying, like the animals you kill.' The card arrived on the day he died."

BRITAIN'S BIRD OF the century is the red kite, according to a forthcoming book by expert ornithologist Chris Mead.

The red kite tops a list of bird success stories in The State Of The Nation's Birds, out next April, because of the way it has fought back from the brink of extinction with human help.

Behind the red kite in the top 10, comes the fulmar, followed by the blackcap, great skua, hobby, magpie, siskin, gannet, nuthatch, and guillemot.

The top 10 losers are the now extinct red-backed shrike in first place, lapwing, black grouse, corn bunting, turtle dove, snipe, grey partridge, skylark, wryneck, and spotted flycatcher.

THE LAST YEAR before the new Millennium saw a dramatic public reaction against GM food and ingredients, according to Friends of the Earth.

A spokesman said this included the canteen caterers at Monsanto's own UK HQ banning GM ingredients from food.

MPs in the House of Commons were now also being served food that avoided GM ingredients.

One FOE survey showed that most of the UK's top food chains, including McDonald's, Domino Pizza and Wimpy, had removed GM ingredients, with most getting rid of GM derivatives as well.

Supermarkets had also been forced to respond with all the leading stores removing GM ingredients from their own label food and phasing out GM derivatives, said the spokesman.

In addition, 24 of the top 30 food manufacturers operating in the UK said that they had either removed GM ingredients and derivatives, or were removing them.

Adrian Bebb, food campaigner for Friends of the Earth, added:"The public has made its concerns about GM ingredients very clear. It appears that even Monsanto's own catering firm has no confidence in this new technology."

GIANT SANDBAGS HAVE been brought in by the Environment Agency to defend the Somerset Levels from flooding.

The agency is preparing to pack bags that hold a cubic metre of sand each against the medieval Baltmoor wall to ensure it can withstand more rain, according to a spokesman.

BRITISH EGGS ARE in danger of vanishing from the shops because of a new EU directive, it has been claimed.

Home produced eggs could disappear from retail shelves over the next few years as firms leave the industry because they are unable to make the huge investment needed to meet the new directive, says the National Farmers Union.

A survey of egg producers by the union revealed that confidence was "at an all-time low.

"Crucially 60 per cent believe they will not be in egg production within the next decade," said a spokesman,"largely because of competition from imports and the cost of meeting the EU directive which sets new standards for cage, free range and barn egg systems.

"The industry, which is already being rocked by low incomes, will have to spend as much as £550 million to alter poultry housing because of the new rules which come into force from 2002."

Among main concerns expressed by producers in the survey were that cheaper eggs produced to lower animal welfare standards would flood into the EU without restriction, and that the rules would not be implemented fairly across Europe.

"The British market will be particularly vulnerable to imports of egg products used in processing," said the spokesman.

"In this situation consumers will have little chance to opt for eggs produced to high animal welfare standards because they will be just one ingredient in the product."

NFU deputy president Tim Bennett added:"It is crucial that our egg industry doesn't grind to a standstill as producers, through no fault of their own, find themselves in a complete no-win situation.

"Understandably, producers feel overwhelmed by the incredible expense that this new directive presents at a time when they can least afford it.

"Even those that decide to battle on fear that planning restrictions will block the alterations they need to make to their poultry units."

RAMBLERS HAVE a host of winter walks to choose from across the UK, including the Festive Five walk for anyone who wants to travel to Wales.

"Take to the hills and the Pembrokeshire coast to blow away those post-Christmas or Millennium cobwebs," urged a spokesman for The Pembrokeshire Coast National Park.

PRINCE WILLIAM'S foxhunting activities have come under the spotlight again following the death of a youth in a hunting accident.

The teenager, aged 17 like the prince, was killed as he rode out with the Cheshire Hunt which saw about 80 riders braving atrocious weather conditions.

An experienced member of the hunt, the dead youth was following the hounds when his horse apparently came to grief as it tried to jump a hedge.

It is believed the horse may have rolled onto him at the icy spot in Spurstow near Chester.

The League Against Cruel Sports was quick to criticise the Cheshire Hunt for allowing someone so young to take part.

However, a spokeswoman for the Hunt itself said the youth was a good rider and had been a keen member since he was a child.

Anti-hunt campaigners claim that the sport is too dangerous for young people and have underlined the fact that the dead youth was the same age as the prince.

Prince William himself was spotted out with the Beaufort Hunt again on the same day the youth died in Cheshire, sparking fresh calls for him to quit foxhunting.

FLUORESCENT FISH ARE set to become a weird new feature of the River Thames after the Environment Agency launched a scheme to keep tabs on fish stocks.

Agency fisheries staff re-stocked 10 sites on the lower freshwater Thames (between Marlow and Molesey) with 3,500 barbel.

The two-year-old fish, raised at the Agency's Calverton fish farm, were tagged using a technique being tried for the first time in the Thames.

"The fish will be identified with coloured fluorescent implant tags," said a spokesman. "The specially developed material is injected as a liquid into the tissue of the fish, later curing into a pliable solid. The fish are discreetly marked either in the head or ventral area.

"The marks should remain on the fish for years and the Agency hopes anglers will provide feedback on recapture of fish."

Information sheets detailing where and what to look for would be circulated to Thames angling clubs.

Routine Agency survey work should also provide additional recapture information.

"The collected data will be highly valuable in assessing the effectiveness of each site for stocking this species, and provide important information regarding fish movement within the Thames," added the spokesman.

A CLEAN-UP OPERATION is underway to help make life easier for trout and grayling trying to spawn in a river hit by silt deposits.

Workers from the Environment Agency are trying to retain and improve gravel spawning grounds in the River Rye at Harome.

"Gravel beds are excellent spawning grounds for brown trout and grayling but in the Rye their potential has become limited because large quantities of silt have built up on the gravels downstream," said a project spokesman.

"The Agency has now come up with a scheme to protect and retain these valuable spawning gravels by 'green engineering' of the riverbank, along with some tree planting."

MALLARD: cheery bird that saved me from a beating

I WAS feeding a couple of mallard ducks at my local pond the other day when it struck me just how much we take this most handsome of British birds for granted.

With the backdrop of the muddy pond water behind it, the bottle green head of the male seems almost as iridescent and stunning as a kingfisher's plumage.

The mallard is the commonest of our ducks and, fairly unusually for ducks, can nest in trees when the mood takes it.

Winter influx from abroad once boosted numbers to as many as 700,000 birds in this country with the average indigenous number put at 150,000 breeding pairs a few years ago.

But recently fears were raised that numbers are dwindling.

A researcher for the Wildfowl and Wetlands Trust told me:"*It's difficult to calculate mallard numbers compared to other ducks because they tend to live anywhere, not mainly on the big estuaries like other species. Gamekeepers also release them for hunting at various sites which complicates matters.*

"*Mallard often fly in from Russia and elsewhere during the winter. Populations fluctuate but I think we are seeing a slow but steady decline overall.*"

Seems a shame, if that's true. I've always had a soft spot for mallard ducks as they inadvertently saved me from a beating many years ago.

As a boy, I used to trek through woodland which surrounded a lake brooding with almost Gothic foreboding.

In the centre of this dark lake was a small wooded island upon which a modest band of cheery mallard nested each year.

One particular day, myself and a friend sauntered through some bushes beside the lake to come upon our worst nightmare - a local gang of toughs slumped semi-naked around a fire after swimming al fresco.

With little hope of successful retreat, we simply had to grin and bear our misfortune as these older boys glowered at us menacingly and spat threats.

In a desperate attempt to mollify them, I inquired why they had a clutch of blue-green mallard eggs sitting beside the fire.

"*Cookin' em. Gonna eat 'em,*" one of them sniffed, not in a very friendly way, it has to be said.

The path ahead was blocked by the gang so we sat down beside the fire.

It went quiet - worryingly quiet - as they glanced malevolently at each other and worked out what torture to inflict upon the interlopers.

Then one of the gang suddenly exclaimed:"*Eh 'oop! T'eggs are bloody 'atchin'.*"

A mood of wonderment swept over the gathering and we were temporarily forgotten as some of the eggs did, indeed, begin to hatch from the heat of the fire.

Within a minute, at least three ducklings were just visible through their broken shells.

I fully expected the gang leader to chortle merrily as he swallowed the choicest duckling whole, complete with shell. Amazingly, he didn't.

Even more amazingly, he dragooned the gang into plunging back into the lake, delicately holding the cracking eggs above their heads en route to the original nest.

"*'Urry up!, 'urry up!,*" he ordered as the swimmers covered some 20 metres to the island.

Enid Blyton could hardly have contrived a sweeter outcome.

However, not wishing to ride our luck any further, myself and my friend slipped away. Bunch of pansies, that gang, we decided - when we were safely out of earshot.

Sadly, I never found out if the chicks survived, but at least we did.

HUNT SABOTEURS CLAIM *they* were the victims of violent assaults from hunt supporters during traditional New Year's Day meets around the country.

The saboteurs, themselves often blamed for violence in the past, also alleged former Tory MP and Olympic gold medallist Sebastian Coe laid into them with his own verbal onslaught.

"You know the hype - the year 2000, a new millennium, a new start. Not so it appears for hunts and their supporters as hunt saboteurs attending the traditional New Year's Day meets found out," said a spokesman for the Hunt Saboteurs Association.

"Saboteurs at a meet of the Old Surrey, Burstow and West Kent Foxhounds in Kent were subjected to an unprovoked attack on both their vehicle and themselves by hunt supporters.

"A saboteur attending a meet of the Southdown and Eridge Foxhounds in East Sussex also had to seek hospital treatment after he was viciously attacked by a security guard hired by the hunt.

"Saboteurs present had just successfully prevented the hounds from killing a fox using non-violent direct action and it seems this was enough to spark off the unprovoked attack.

"Sebastian Coe was a surprise visitor at a meet of the Surrey Union Foxhounds near Dorking, Surrey, but what came as more of a surprise to saboteurs present were his threats that their vehicles would not be in the same pristine condition when they returned to them!

"Saboteurs in Cambridgeshire at a meet of the Fitzwilliam Foxhounds were equally surprised and appalled at the hunt's attempt to blame them for the 40ft fall of a hound after it fell off a bridge the hunt were crossing."

Dawn Preston, spokeswoman for the Hunt Saboteurs Association added: "It is the first day of a whole new year, a whole new century and on this day alone hunt saboteurs have suffered all the usual attacks, both verbal and physical, that we see so often."

A PLAGUE OF rats is reported to be threatening seabird numbers on Ramsey Island, off the Pembrokeshire coast.

Wildlife volunteers are using tonnes of poison to try to bring the situation under control before it proves too late for some species. Manx shearwaters are believed to be the worst affected by the rats, whose numbers have exploded and who regularly prey on chicks as well as taking eggs.

FRANCE MUST NOT be allowed to achieve its aim of blocking British beef imports simply because the legal case was now formally underway, farmers' leaders have announced.

The National Farmers Union spoke out as the European Commission submitted its case to the European Court.

. Welcoming the news that papers have been sent to the European Court, NFU president Ben Gill said that the union had asked the Commission to apply to the court for "interim measures." These would require the French Government to lift its ban pending a decision by the court on the Commission's case.

He said: "We know that the legal process can be a slow and lengthy one. Every day is a day too long for British farmers and this must be settled urgently.

"France is in flagrant breach of the law. Why should we now be forced to wait? The court case is simply not a solution to the problem."

A SURVEY BY a gardening magazine has revealed just how grumpy gardeners can be made by the hobby they profess to love.

Slugs and snails were the most loathed garden pests while the most hateful garden jobs were raking up leaves, mowing the lawn, cleaning the pond, cleaning tools, and washing pots, according to Amateur Gardening.

Most hated plants were the leylandii, ivy, dahlia, marigold, and pampas grass.

Most hated weeds were bindweed, dandelion, ground elder, hairy bittercress, and horsetail.

BRITAIN'S PORK INDUSTRY has been plunged into crisis thanks to massive over production of the meat around the world.

The news came as French pork pate imported into the country was taken off the shelves after causing a health scare and leaving two people dead in Europe.

British pig farmers are said to be losing £4million each week with estimated job losses throughout the industry expected to top 49,000.

A report jointly compiled by the Meat and Livestock Commission, the National Pig Association and the British Pig Executive, presses Government to give producers emergency payments.

These would help farmers survive what had been called the worst crisis in the industry for 50 years.

Mike Sheldon, chief executive of the National Pig Association, explained: "High production levels in Europe and the strength of sterling have made trading conditions for British pig producers extremely tough. But what has brought us to our knees is the £90 million we spend each year on animal welfare standards and BSE-related controls not applied elsewhere in the EU."

Meanwhile, French pork pate was dumped all over Europe after a newborn baby infected in the womb and an elderly woman both died of listeria poisoning.

Four other people fell seriously ill in the outbreak.

The Rillets pork pate and Langotines pork tongue pate, made by the Coudray factory in France, were sold in some delicatessens in Britain. A spokesman for the Health Department said of the pate:"If in doubt, chuck it out."

ROLLING STONES GUITARIST Keith Richards has joined villagers in Sussex who are battling developers aiming to build new properties in local woodland.

The legendary musician, whose hard-living lifestyle may seem at odds with his love of the British countryside, is reportedly furious at the threat to trees and wildlife near his West Wittering home.

Richards, 56, formed a partnership with Mick Jagger and the rest of the group that went on to fill acres of tree-based newspaper and magazine newsprint.

These days, the grizzled rocker is said to be a conservationist with a deep love of trees.

He lives in a £1.5million mansion close to the shoreline of the Manhood Peninsula and is reported to be a popular local figure, even taking part in "harvest blessing" ceremonies with friends.

Villagers became concerned about the future of the area when two businessmen bought up sections of woodland and began tree clearance.

The Rolling Stone and other locals gathered a petition to the local council to get the work to stop.

They succeeded but by then more than 50 trees were thought to have been lost, many over a century old.

Wildlife had also suffered as a result, according to a report commissioned by the campaigners.

However, the businessmen appear to be determined to build on the land.

A PLUM JOB is currently being offered by English Nature for a keen birdwatcher who is no bird brain .

"English Nature requires an ornithologist to provide expert advice to staff in local teams," explained a spokesman.

This involved "setting nature conservation objectives for internationally and nationally important bird sites."

It also entailed "development and communication of clear and concise guidance to a wide range of staff."

Only graduates need apply, according to the spokesman.

"The successful candidate would have a first or second class degree in a biological or environmental science, a sound knowledge of bird conservation issues and a good understanding of national and international habitat and species conservation legislation."

Starting salary is £16,500 per year.

Anyone wanting an application form should contact Hazel Hynds of the Uplands Team, English Nature

The closing date for completed applications is January 28.

Interviews will start from February 7.

LUXURY CAR FIRM Rolls Royce faces a bill for £14,000 after it was prosecuted for an oversight which could have threatened the environment close to its Derby factory.

The company was fined £10,000 and ordered to pay £4,000 costs at Derby Magistrates Court following prosecution by the Environment Agency.

An investigation had found that "a scrubber system serving a chemical treatment plant had not been operating correctly between February and May 1998," said an Agency spokesman.

The chemical process was part of the aerospace manufacturing operations.

While "no significant off-site effects were found", the Agency regarded the Rolls-Royce failure to maintain control of its operations as "a significant failure."

Following the Agency's enforcement action Rolls Royce has established procedures to prevent anything similar occurring in future.

Rolls-Royce plc pleaded guilty to failing to operate the plant in the manner authorised under the Environmental Protection Act 1990.

ANOTHER rise in interest rates announced by the Bank of England Monetary Policy Committee totally ignored the fears of world financial experts that the pound was substantially over-valued, claims the National Farmers Union.

High interest rates fed a high pound and NFU president Ben Gill said the 0.25 per cent increase would simply exacerbate the critical situation.

THE RAMBLERS ASSOCIATION has won its case in a legal row about a footpath that runs across the estate of millionaire Nicholas Van Hoogstraten.

"Lewes Magistrates Court found that on two occasions the footpath was illegally blocked by a barbed wire fence, a locked gate, refrigeration units and a barn," said a spokesman for the association.

"Rarebargain Ltd, the company currently registered as owner of the land over which the path runs, was charged by the 127,000-member association with obstructing a public highway. Their solicitor declined to give a defence.

"The association proved the 100-year-old footpath crossing the estate had been blocked by the various obstructions, rendering it impassable for over a decade."

Jerry Pearlman, RA member and solicitor in the case, added: "The ruling is a victory for the British public, which quite naturally expects that all public footpaths are kept open for people to enjoy.

"The footpath network is part of our common heritage and the Ramblers Association will do all in its power to defend the rights of the public."

Rarebargain Ltd was fined £1,600 for two counts of blocking the footpath illegally and was ordered to pay costs of £3,500.

CONTROVERSIAL legislation that will introduce the freedom to roam in England and Wales is expected to be published in late February.

The public will then be able to see how the Government is planning to introduce the new law.

The fresh legislation will be part of the wider Countryside Amenity and Conservation Bill announced last November.

9

BADGER LOVERS ARE launching a major public protest campaign against Government plans to kill thousands of the animals blamed for spreading TB among cattle.

The National Federation of Badger Groups claims the Government will be slaughtering badgers needlessly to avoid having to face up to real cattle welfare problems.

Protesters expect as many as 20,000 badgers to die during efforts to prove they infect cows with bovine tuberculosis.

Dr Elaine King, conservation officer for the NFBG, said: "Members of the National Federation of Badger Groups are not opposed to farmers or farming.

"We oppose the Ministry of Agriculture's failure to address this problem in an intelligent and sustainable way.

"Farmers themselves say that slaughtering wildlife is harming the public's perception of their industry. We are not the only ones who want a solution here. Farmers want it, too."

The NFBG was pressing for a new vaccine to protect cattle as well as for other new measures such as a clearer diagnosis programme to detect TB in cows.

MORE THAN 150,000 seabirds are now thought to have perished after the oil tanker Erika broke up off the Brittany coast last December - many of them from British breeding colonies.

The cost of the disaster, both to the birds themselves and to the pockets of welfare groups, has prompted the RSPB to call for new laws to make oil carriers safer.

Dr Euan Dunn, RSPB marine policy officer, said: "It is time to end a system where oil companies can gamble with safety at sea and the marine environment by chartering vessels at the lowest cost they can find.

"There is an urgent need for legislation which sets much more rigorous standards for charter vessels. Oil companies ducking these standards should face stiff penalties. At the same time, best practice - such as preferential use of double-hulled tankers - should be encouraged with incentives."

The disaster was the worst oil spill in terms of seabird mortality ever to hit Europe, according to the RSPB.

"The spill has killed an unprecedented diversity of birdlife with 50 species recorded so far," said a spokesman."Of the casualties 75 per cent are guillemots and a further 15 per cent are razorbills and puffins. Kittiwakes, gannets and even storm petrels have also been oiled.

"The oil has impacted on coastal species, too, such as grebes and herons, plus wildfowl like brent geese, common scoter and eider, as well as waders like dunlin, sanderling, redshank and grey plover.

"British rings recovered indicate that most of the victims are young guillemots from the Irish Sea, the west of Scotland, and possibly as far afield as Icelandic colonies. The RSPB anticipates major colony declines in the years ahead."

MOUNTAIN HARES LIVING in north Derbyshire are to be the subject of a survey after being introduced to moorland there more than 100 years ago.

Better know as natives of northern Scotland, a small number continue to survive in the English enclave and the Derbyshire Wildlife Trust hopes to count them.

The job might not be as hard as it sounds as mountain hare fur turns white in winter, making them highly visible as they bound away across snow-less moorland.

They are also markedly smaller and plumper than brown hares, apparently less skittish and more easily approached.

The study aims to discover whether they are in decline, as the common brown hare is across the whole of the country.

Foxes and stoats prey on the Derbyshire mountain hares but in the Scottish Highlands, their chief predator would be the golden eagle.

Initial estimates put the number of Derbyshire mountain hares at over 500, still tiny compared to the Scottish population of almost 40,000.

A MEMBER OF the Yorkshire Wildlife Trust is at the centre of controversy after admitting he shoots grey squirrels that plunder titbits he puts out for birds.

Police and RSPCA officials in Huddersfield have investigated the activities of local wildlife lover Brian Lucas and found his actions are not illegal.

But the situation has highlighted the different views held about grey squirrels, an imported species native to North America which has usurped the British red squirrel in many areas.

Bigger and more aggressive than the red, the grey squirrel is also responsible for eating the eggs and young of many garden birds.

Mr Lucas, an expert on wildlife, has angered some local people by shooting the squirrels with an air rifle.

However, the RSPCA admits that grey squirrels are classed as vermin, alongside mice and rats.

"People see squirrels as nice and fluffy," Mr Lucas said."But they are vermin. The other name for them is tree rats.

"As a naturalist I am more interested in looking after our own flora and fauna than feeding these animals which destroy our birds."

A spokesman for Yorkshire Wildlife Trust confirmed it was investigating complaints about Mr Lucas.

THE FELLING OF a 150-year-old oak tree may lead to prosecution for the makers of a TV history programme.

The oak tree was among almost two dozen mature trees allegedly chopped down in Bromley by the makers of popular Channel 4 history show Time Team.

Local heritage officials say all the trees were protected by a preservation order so the programme had no right to go ahead.

The felling work was apparently done to recreate an ancient wooden site on the Norfolk coast.

However, the TV show has hit back, saying a great deal of care was taken to select trees from a managed woodland that were going to be felled anyway.

THE WAY THAT timber from Welsh forests is harvested and marketed is to undergo a major overhaul to improve efficiency, says the Forestry Commission.

Forest Enterprise Wales, which manages Welsh forests on behalf of the National Assembly for Wales, has now set up WHAM - short for Welsh Harvesting and Marketing.

It is hoped that the reorganisation of one of the top industries in Wales will eventually provide timber buyers with a one-stop shop for the whole of the country.

At present, wood taken from Welsh forests is still harvested and marketed through five separate districts - Canolbarth, Coed y Cymoedd, Dolgellau, Llandovery, and Llanrwst.

WHAM production manager John Weir explained: "This is the way forward for harvesting the timber of the nation's forests. We are struggling in the global market, that's no secret. WHAM will make us more efficient and able to meet challenges ahead.

"Much of the equipment used in Welsh forests at the moment is over 15 years old. We aim to increase the quality of our contractor base by encouraging investment in machinery that is more efficient and kind to the environment."

Forest Enterprise Wales had been forced to reassess its procedures after a slump in the timber market left prices at a 30-year low.

All the key posts have now been filled and WHAM will be up and running from April 1 this year.

WHAM harvesting manager Chris Edwards added: "Efficiency is the key to this initiative. It is a vital development if the forests of Wales are to remain profitable and able to compete in the world marketplace."

FARMERS IN YORKSHIRE are meeting with Government representatives over the next few months in a bid to beat pollution.
Almost 250 farms, covering about 200 square kilometres in the Holderness Drain Catchment area, will be visited by inspectors .
The farmers have already been sent a question - naire to fill in and will be interviewed by environment protection officers.

ANGLERS HAVE BEEN warned not to try to fool investigators by sneakily obtaining back-dated licences to avoid prosecution after being caught fishing without them.

"The warning follows two cases in the past six months where people have been heavily fined for doing so," said an Environment Agency spokesman.

THE DRASTIC DECLINE in skylark numbers is largely the result of an EU-backed move from spring-sown to autumn-sown cereals by UK farmers, according to research by the RSPB.

A study involving 995 skylark nests, carried out between 1996 and 1999 across 24 farms in East Anglia, Oxfordshire and Dorset, discovered twice as many skylarks were found in spring-sown cereals compared to autumn-sown.

Spring-sown cereals allowed the stubble of the previous crop to be left unploughed, providing food and cover for skylarks over the preceding winter months.

POLICE ARE HUNTING a cruel gunman who apparently used swans at a wildlife sanctuary for target practise and ended up killing eight of the majestic birds.
The mystery attacker has been condemned by wildlife enthusiasts after the swans were found slaughtered at a sanctuary in Gloucestershire.
Police are investigating after the corpses of the birds were discovered littering the Cotswold Water Park near Cirencester.

AIR QUALITY IN rural areas has suffered a record decline, according to a disturbing report by Friends of the Earth.

Pollution figures for the countryside were the worst recorded in the last seven years and have prompted fresh health fears.

Asthma, heart disease and lung problems in the country are all believed to have escalated in direct response to the deterioration of air quality.

A spokesman for Friends of the Earth said the news would "embarrass the Government, which is backing down from Election promises to cut traffic levels on Britain's roads.

"Only five months ago, Deputy Prime Minister John Prescott hailed the 1998 figures as showing the biggest improvement in air quality since records began."

BREAKFAST IS GETTING a makeover by farmers' leaders in a bid to brighten up its image and boost traditional British fayre such as eggs, bacon and cereal.
"Breakfast - the first and most important meal of the day - is becoming a casualty as people lead ever busier lifestyles," explained a spokesman for the National Farmers Union.
Researchers found that a fifth of schoolchildren and 30 per cent of parents typically started the day without eating breakfast, mainly because of lack of time or oversleeping.

LADY MEMBERS OF the Haydon Hunt in Northumberland have created a stir by stripping off for a saucy calendar to raise hunt funds.

The ladies, aged 19 to 51, are proving so popular in a variety of poses that the initial print run of 350 copies has already sold out in their local town of Haydon Bridge.

Hunt secretray Val Jones, 43, posed as Miss May and the mother-of-two was sure she and the other amateur models had contributed to a tasteful document.

11

COW: mothering instinct puts our own baby in peril

DANGEROUS and unpredictable - not normally how you would describe that placid beast, the cow, but this was the picture painted after they were involved in two undeniably savage attacks.

In separate incidents weeks apart, one man was trampled to death and another left badly injured.

You rather expect such violence from bulls - but cows?

On each occasion - and here's the rub - the cows were accompanied by calves. Despite the tragedy of one man's death, I find it oddly comforting that centuries of domesticating cattle have failed to remove that implacable force...maternal instinct.

As a child I used to walk to primary school through fields full of cows in the summer months and never experienced a problem. But as an adult I have had the odd tricky moment with them, none worse than a few years ago.

Back then, a country walk briefly degenerated into turmoil and a little 'paternal instinct' came into play.

It all happened during an ill-advised ramble across unfamiliar countryside with my wife, our baby daughter, and two other adults.

Even a tiny tot gets heavy after a while and myself and my wife were soon lagging behind, cursing our decision to put our crying baby through this pointless ordeal.

Climbing over a stile, we suddenly found ourselves surrounded by a large herd of Friesian cows, some with calves.

Startled and agitated by the baby's cries, they moved in on us, lowering their heads and stamping aggressively.

By now, any escape route was cut off and we had no option but to press on through them, me holding our scream-ing baby tight, trying not to imagine what might happen if she was knocked from my grasp.

I shouted and lashed out with my boots to clear a path and, thankfully, the cows gave way.

But I was pretty relieved when we made it out of the field. It was an object lesson in how everyday circumstances can suddenly conspire against you.

Cows are fascinating animals and not just because they can be so physically imposing. Black and white Friesian cows originate from Denmark, though they are actually named after a Dutch region where they brought prosperity.

They give the highest UK milk yield at about 1,200 gallons following each calving. That's a lot of milk.

The light brown Jersey cow, probably the prettiest with its doe-like eyes, came here from the Channel Islands.

However, its ancestry is thought to be rooted in Asia and the breed's unusual tolerance of hot conditions is believed to be a throwback to those days.

Hereford cows are another common breed, known for their white faces and big reddish-brown frames.

As a journalist, I once covered a court case involving a Hereford bull which attacked a group of lady ramblers after it was illegally allowed to roam.

Bizarrely, in his defence, the farmer claimed it was not a bull which attacked them but a cow with a hormone problem.

One by one, the lady ramblers took the witness stand to describe their ordeal and each was asked to describe the (ahem) equipment of the animal that chased them. Some used the politest euphemisms they could muster.

All were eventually forced to concur with the prosecuting solicitor's more prosaic words, if only to establish legal clarity.

One woman even described a *"large, hanging gentile"* - which sounded like a religious slur on the poor animal.

Another court case involving cows springs to mind, one covered by a former colleague elsewhere.

Police staked out a field at night after a farmer complained his cows were being repeatedly disturbed.

When officers pounced, they found a young farm labourer - naked apart from Wellington boots - squatting on a bail of straw behind a snoozing cow.

He claimed to be sleepwalking.

BIRDS OF PREY kill far fewer pigeons and game birds than has previously been assumed by pigeon fanciers and gamekeepers, according to new research.

The results of a five-year study into the effects of birds of prey on other species have just been published.

The report, by the Raptor Working Group for the Department of the Environment, Transport and the Regions, concludes that birds of prey should remain fully protected because a range of other solutions are available to address local problems.

A spokesman said:"Regarding grouse moors, the Joint Raptor Study at Langholm concluded that it is extremely unlikely raptors were responsible for the long-term decline in grouse numbers there.

"The DETR commissioned research by the Hawk and Owl Trust on the numbers of racing pigeons taken by birds of prey. This found that peregrines take only about 3.5 per cent and sparrowhawks under 4 per cent of the UK racing pigeon population annually.

"Overall losses of racing pigeons to all causes are about 52 per cent each year, mostly to bad weather and collisions with pylons etc. This is similar to the natural mortality rates for woodpigeons.

"Regarding predation at pheasant release pens, the Group recommend wider dissemination of the results. But with up to 20 million pheasants being released for shooting each year, bird of prey predation is minimal.

"The Group also completed an extensive review of evidence for the effect of birds of prey on farmland birds such as skylarks but concluded that changes in agricultural practices have been the primary cause of declines in formerly common species. Songbird population changes have not differed between areas with or without sparrowhawks."

Graham Wynne, RSPB chief executive, said: "We now look forward to working with landowners, pigeon fanciers and others to develop techniques to deal with any local problems. Meantime, we ask the Government to strengthen legal protection afforded to raptors and act decisively against those who illegally persecute these splendid birds."

THE ENVIRONMENT AGENCY is hunting for eight new members to serve on two of its key committees. Three appointments are to be made to the Regional Environment Protection Advisory Committee and five to the Regional Fisheries Ecology and Recreation Advisory Committee.

ATTEMPTS TO BREED from a captive pair of red kites ended in disaster at a Yorkshire conservation centre when the female devoured the male.

The impromptu feast happened at The Yorkshire Dales Falconry and Conservation Centre which specialises in breeding rare and protected species.

Head falconer Paul Reeves explained:"We had been attempting to breed and release red kites. Unfortunately, the female ate its prospective mate. This is not usual behaviour in the wild as the birds would simply fly away from confrontation.

"Obviously, in captivity they can't. But we have to try a breeding programme to ensure the survival of the species."

Recently, the centre took receipt of two bald eagles from a Prague zoo but there were no plans to release their offspring in the UK, unlike the programme involving native species such as the buzzard and peregrine falcon.

ANGRY FARMERS BESIEGED a superstore warehouse in Bristol to protest at imports of "foreign" meat in the face of the country's livestock crisis.

A group estimated at more than 140-strong staged a temporary blockade outside the Safeway premises.

They said they had gathered to show their disgust at the store's policy on continuing to bring in New Zealand lamb while British lamb was rejected.

Their leaders claimed that Safeway had gone back on an earlier agreement to buy British lamb before any foreign meat was imported.

Store chiefs hit back saying they did support British meat but the New Zealand lamb gave customers more choice.

One sheep farmer said:"We are not after huge profits. We are just trying to make a living as best we can."

The blockade came shortly after the Government published its controversial report on rural economic and social conditions.

FRANCE FACES FRESH pressure over its illegal beef ban after British farmers' leaders formally started legal proceedings themselves.

As he presented a letter of claim to the French Embassy, NFU president Ben Gill said the union would seek an injunction against the French Government in the French courts if no action was taken to lift the ban.

The letter, for delivery to the French Prime Minister Lionel Jospin, sets out in detail the legal and factual reasons why the ban should be lifted immediately.

Mr Gill said: "The NFU is intent on pursuing a satisfactory outcome for British farmers who are still being hampered by France's illegal stance.

"The facts speak for themselves. With the legal arguments so much in favour of the ban being lifted, France cannot be allowed to continue this course.

"The longer that this episode continues to be unresolved, then the more that the sheer credibility of the EU Commission to enforce its own laws is pulled sharply into question, and the greater the damage to the British beef industry."

SCOTTISH FARMERS' LEADERS are going it alone in a bid to win Government backing for the future of their businesses.

The tartan branch of the National Farmers Union is preparing an in-depth strategic document to show what can be achieved with the right help.

Scottish farmers aim to persuade the Prime Minister that their agricultural industry may be of even greater importance to the local rural economy than it is in England.

Over the next few weeks, the leaders hope their different situation will help them win the kind of cash support that their counterparts in England have so far been unable to secure, according to the Scottish NFU.

The news comes after Tony Blair defended his Government's position on agriculture and the countryside, admitting there was a farming crisis but refusing to accept town and country were divided.

The Prime Minister said: "Let me state again, farming is in crisis. They need short-term help. We can put in investment and I have said I will talk to farmers' leaders about it. But it must be tied to reform.

"Yes, there are problems. Yes, some of these problems are specifically rural, like bus services and post offices.

"But there are villages, towns and cities in very rural parts of Britain that face the same problems as the rest of Britain. We aren't two nations - we are one nation. Same values. Same challenges. Often, though not always, there are common solutions."

Later, Mr Blair announced that struggling village post offices would get cashpoint machines installed in a bid to boost falling profits.

He revealed that the Post Office had struck a deal with banks so that 3,000 new machines would be installed up and down the country.

But critics have rounded on the Prime Minister for coming up with simplistic solutions to the grave financial crisis facing many people in the countryside.

A HI-TECH clean-up operation is being launched to recover an area of contaminated land in Dorset.

Cogdean Elms industrial site at Corfe Mullen has a long history of chemical activity with pollution there estimated to date back 40 years.

Specialist contractors have been brought in to treat the contamination and prevent further pollution of the Ashington Stream, a tributary of the River Stour.

Analysis of samples has confirmed that chlorinated solvents are seeping into the stream.

A SECLUDED SURREY village formerly known for its residents' fight to protect local badgers has hit the headlines for being the "cash capital of Britain."

Woldingham, which dates back to the 17th Century, has been found to have the highest percentage of millionaires living there - almost 17 per cent of its 1,488 adult residents.

The survey, which looked at the country's wealthiest postcodes, found Woldingham slightly ahead of the second richest spot, Gerrards Cross in Buckinghamshire.

Researchers from credit information company Experian took more than a year to compile the definitive list of where so many of the nation's wealthiest people choose to live.

Woldingham is hidden away in a National Trust forest with many people passing right by without knowing its secret - until now.

THE WAR BETWEEN hunt supporters and hunt saboteurs has carried on into the new Millennium following earlier clashes during Boxing Day and New Year meets.

Saboteurs trailed members of the Cheshire Forest Foxhounds during a recent hunt and claimed to have captured film of them "trespassing" on the high-speed Manchester to London train line near Knutsford.

In another confrontation involving the two sides near Maldon, violence broke out during a joint meet of the West Street Tickham Foxhounds (from Kent) and the Essex Farmers and Union Foxhounds.

The Hunt Saboteurs Association claims a female saboteur was taken to hospital with a suspected broken wrist and six arrests were made, five saboteurs and one huntsman.

BIRDS AND OTHER wildlife are being threatened by the activities of peat extraction workers around the country, according to the RSPB.

The society has called on the Government and the peat industry to speed up the ending of extraction work close to or on some of the country's most sensitive nature reserves.

Despite Government plans for gardeners to use substitutes instead of real peat by the year 2010, the RSPB says there is still no sign of a clear plan of action to achieve this.

According to the society, almost 90 per cent of peat extraction currently takes place on or near to an SSSI (Site of Special Scientific Interest).

The wetlands are a vital resource for many species of birds and insects, such as the dragonfly.

A spokesman for the RSPB said:"We are disappointed that the peat working group report does not go far enough in prescribing action to protect SSSIs, and also to encourage alternatives to peat.

"If the industry is serious about helping to protect wildlife, it should end extraction on SSSIs and find other ways to give gardeners and growers the products they need by putting more investment into peat alternatives.

"If the Government wanted to end peat extraction on SSSIs, it could do it tomorrow. The powers are there."

HARE COURSING HAS been at the centre of fierce debate again with pro and anti-hunt groups engaged in a war of words over the blood sport's most high-profile UK event.

Despite Government moves to ban all forms of hunting with dogs, the annual Waterloo Cup at Altcar near Southport still attracted widespread support.

Coursing is said to be one of the world's oldest blood sports and was formally endorsed in Britain by Elizabeth I who ordered rules and regulations drawn up.

But its detractors say it is barbaric and shames not only the owners of greyhounds that take part but onlookers who cheer the violent deaths of captured hares.

This year more than 60 dogs were booked to compete over several heats to find the winner of a £4,000 cheque and trophy.

Waterloo Cup steward Sir Mark Prescott has been hare coursing since he was a boy and is mystified by the feeling against it.

"People don't understand that coursing is about the speed and agility of the dogs," he said."It certainly isn't about killing hares."

Even so, about 15 hares were expected to be killed over the three-day competition from February 22 to 24.

Earlier, a campaign to ban hare coursing was launched in London with protesters boarding a barge on the Thames outside Westminster.

They called on MPs to attack the Waterloo Cup, claiming dozens of hares faced cruel deaths.

Douglas Batchelor, chairman of the Campaign for the Protection of Hunted Animals, said: "Hare coursing is a cruel sport and the Waterloo Cup is one of the worst examples.

"We want the Prime Minister to be true to his word and ban hunting with dogs."

RURAL REBELS IN Scotland may soon be sending letters without stamps to Prime Minister Tony Blair in a protest about the planned closure of a number of remote sub-post offices.

It was hoped the protest - not quite as fearsome as that epitomised by Mel Gibson in 'Braveheart' - would nevertheless drive home to the Premier the stark effect such closures would have on villagers.

Highland councillors came up with the idea as they discussed the impact of Government plans to do away with the need for sub-post offices by paying benefits directly into claimants' bank accounts.

Meanwhile, in a surprise development, it was announced subsidies may be made available to keep afloat struggling rural post offices after all.

The announcement of a cash lifeline by Trade Secretary Stephen Byers could see post offices, which often form the hub of village life, supported by central government or local councils.

MOLES ARE ON the march and could soon take over thousands of open spaces across Britain, gardeners have been warned.

A population explosion of the burrowing creatures is being predicted over the next few months.

Recent weather conditions have proven very favourable to the furry mammal with more than usual numbers of molehills already reported.

Areas worst hit have apparently recorded a 50 per cent rise on previous mole numbers with the population set to rocket further as the breeding season approaches.

Mole traps are being snapped up to deal with the rise in numbers with one Berkshire pest controller saying:"I know one company sold 500 traps in 10 days."

Among the most industrious of animals, moles cause fury among some farmers and gardeners by undermining fields and destroying lawns.

THE RSPB HAS welcomed new Government measures to crack down on egg thieves and wildlife criminals as announced by Environment Minister Michael Meacher.

The creation of a new National Wildlife Crime Unit will help police forces across the UK and the world to gather intelligence on wildlife criminals and take more co-ordinated action.

Graham Elliot, head of the RSPB wildlife investigations section, said: "Combined with the proposals to include custodial sentences for wildlife criminals in the forthcoming Countryside Amenity and Conservation Bill, these measures should provide a more secure future for our most vulnerable wildlife."

In 1998 the RSPB received 738 reports about wild bird offences.

RARE DOTTERELS ARE not quite as dotty when it comes to parenthood as first thought, according to new research into the beautiful Scottish mountain birds.

Once the eggs are laid by the more colourful female, they are incubated by the male - an almost bird-like equivalent of the human house husband.

However, even house husbands get cheesed off occasionally and it was feared the dotterel male often jeopardised the eggs by leaving them alone for long periods in freezing conditions.

Not so, according to the New Scientist magazine, which reveals how researcher Sue Holt discovered a hidden advantage the male was relying on.

This is an unusual ability by the embryos to survive frequent exposure of the eggs.

Ms Holt said one clutch still hatched successfully despite being deserted by the male 23 times over a period of 30 days, a fatal dereliction of duty for other species.

The researcher, who examined 47 dotterel nests in the Grampian mountains, found eggs survived even if abandoned for up to 10 hours at a time.

In Britain, the 22cm birds are virtually restricted to the Scottish Highlands where the cold climate appeals to them.

The distinctive waders are equally at home living in Siberia.

BRITISH FARMERS AND growers could be devastated by a new energy tax that could see many leaving the country to start afresh abroad, it has been claimed.

The National Farmers Union says the proposed Climate Change levy would be another heavy blow to the farming industry, with over 10,000 jobs at risk.

"The levy on gas, coal and electricity usage will cost the industry £20 million, and will hit horticulture especially hard," said a spokesman."Growers have already ensured they have achieved significant improvements in energy efficiency."

NFU president Ben Gill has warned the Government that without suitable exemption from the levy, the resulting lack of confidence and ability to compete on the world market would lead to large scale business closure or relocation abroad.

He stressed that Spain and Portugal currently had no plans for an energy tax, while Holland and Germany had adopted a cost-neutral scheme for horticulture.

Mr Gill added: "Sectors such as horticulture, which are exposed to the full realities of an unsupported marketplace, should not be penalised by this tax. Many of our competitors are exempting horticulture or at least lowering the tax rate.

"It is no wonder then that faced with the prospect of huge extra costs, many UK growers are now questioning the viability of remaining in this country.

"Surely the Government does not want to see much of British horticulture being taxed out of existence and driven abroad, especially when estimates show that this could lead to at least 10,000 job losses."

TWO BIG CATS could be prowling the Gloucestershire countryside following the sighting of a mystery animal days after a pet dog was savaged.

Police are investigating claims that a huge ginger coloured cat was spotted walking past a local woman's home close to midnight.

The animal, which sounded like a lynx from the description given, was said to have pointed ears and be much bigger than a fox.

This second incident follows the highly publicised attack on a pet collie dog in the area whose neck was ripped open to the bone, as if by a panther.

A large black cat had previously been glimpsed in the locality.

ENGLISH NATURE CLAIMS a deal struck with an international quarry firm will be of lasting benefit to over 40 country wildlife and heritage sites. The organisation has signed an agreement with international building materials firm Hanson Quarry Products Europe which, it says, should protect the Sites of Special Scientific Interest long-term.

RECORD LOW NUMBERS have been recorded for some of the country's best-known birds such as the song thrush, grey partridge and corn bunting, according to a new report.

The State of the UK Birds, which examines populations of regular breeding birds, also claims that the vast majority of Government conservation plans have little hope of success and further population declines are inevitable.

Dr Mark Avery, RSPB director of conservation, said: "Currently, only a handful of 26 Government biodiversity action plans for birds are likely to reach or exceed their targets.

"Generally, the most successful action plans are for the rarer species in the UK, including corncrake, cirl bunting and stone-curlew, where targeted on-the-ground action can deliver some immediate benefits, largely thanks to wildlife-friendly landowners and conservation groups."

BEER DRINKERS IN America will be hoping for an out-of-this-world experience when they sink a tipple made from English barley.

For the ale is being produced by a specialist US brewery using barley from the celebrated crop circles of Wiltshire.

Officials from Crop Circle Beer are used to tracking alleged alien activity around the world, concocting beers from crops apparently flattened by their landing craft.

So it was all in a day's work for a representative to visit local farmer Tim Carson with an invitation for him to boldly go into a new venture with them.

BADGER CULLING BY the Government has already turned into "an ill-contrived shambles", according to the National Federation of Badger Groups which points to damning findings in a new report.

"We are extremely alarmed by the report and extend our sympathies to the members of the Independent Scientific Group who had to write it," said Dr Elaine King, spokeswoman for the NFBG.

"The Group's frustration with the hopeless Ministry of Agriculture is palpable and the report confirms our predictions and worst fears.

"The so-called 'Krebs experiment' is proving to be unworkable and is already seriously delayed. Professor Sir John Krebs failed to take account of even the simplest practical realities on the ground at every stage, despite the strongest possible warnings from ourselves and others, including statutory conservation agencies."

WELSH FORESTRY AND its wood processing industry now support more than 4,400 full-time jobs and are worth £475m to the economy, according to a Forestry Commission report.

FARMERS' LEADERS HAVE attacked EU plans to stop farmers giving health boosting vitamins and minerals to their animals in any other form than compound feed.

The changes, proposed in the EU Draft Feeding Stuffs Regulations 2000, have been slammed as "unnecessary" and liable to "create animal welfare problems."

TAWNY OWL: face to face in a rain-drenched bush

FEW wild sounds are more quietly thrilling after dark than the mournful "*hoooo...huhooo*" of a tawny owl as its perches somewhere unseen, a lonely sentinel of the night.

It's the commonest of our owls whose adaptability has seen it thrive in some of our biggest towns and cities where small birds often replace the usual mice and voles on its menu.

Equally recognisable from its much sharper, almost screeching "*kewick*", this stubby chestnut and grey bird seems to have earned a unique place in the affections and folklore of the nation.

Any collection of wildlife nick-nacks or figurines seems incomplete without at least one tawny owl among them.

But make no mistake, despite its loveable image, the tawny owl is an assassin out of the top drawer.

Shakespeare probably had a tawny owl in mind when he wrote about the eerie night of King Duncan's murder in 'Macbeth':"*A falcon, towering in her pride of place, was by a mousing owl hawk'd at and kill'd.*"

In fact, Shakespeare was well aware of the dramatic power owls can wield in our subconscious and often included them in his plays. This again from Macbeth:"*It was the owl that shriek'd, the fatal bellman, which gives the stern'st good-night.*"

A tawny owl, like most other owls, is a master of camouflage and even in daylight can sit undisturbed in trees or bushes until some prying blue tit or sparrow disturbs it, raises the alarm, and sparks off a fit of mobbing.

Regular roosts are characterised by a sprinkling of pellets below and these regurgitated pods of fur and bone give a fascinating insight into the luckless creatures the bird has feasted on.

Unlike the barn owl, whose overall population has been decimated in recent decades, tawny owl numbers seem to have remained steady, which is heartening.

However, I might not hold quite so much affection for tawny owls had an incident some years ago not ended the way it did.

Back then I came, quite literally, face-to-face with a tawny owl and was probably lucky not to lose an eye, as others have done in similar encounters.

Those rapier talons that effortlessly snuff out the lives of countless mice and voles in a tawny owl's career can just as easily puncture a human eyeball.

On the day I got a little too close for comfort, it had started to pour with rain, an absolute downpour which even in woodland had me looking for better cover.

I found it in a thick collection of tall holly bushes, all growing side by side so that the overall shape resembled a large green bungalow.

I'd sheltered there before and, just as before, found the spacious central recess almost dry despite the deafening rattle of rain above and around me.

Obviously, it was quite dark and fairly prickly in there but I was virtually able to stand up straight while I waited for the worst of the rain to ease.

After a few minutes, it did, and rather than shuffle straight back out again, I decided to push a couple of branches away with my arm to try to peer outside.

Immediately, I was confronted by two enormous black eyes staring back at me just a foot or so away.

A tawny owl had been sitting there all the time. It's difficult to say who was the more startled, it or me.

Perhaps it had been snoozing or, faced with a soaking, had just decided to sit tight until the rain stopped.

Whatever, it now decided to act and went up vertically like a rocket through the 'roof' of the holly.

I took a couple of seconds to recover then crashed out of the bushes to try to spot it again.

It wasn't too difficult.

Despite soaring noiselessly to the top of a nearby birch tree, its sudden appearance had sparked outrage among other birds and it was quickly surrounded and mobbed.

I watched as it flew from tree to tree vainly trying to shake off its tormentors until it finally disappeared.

Sometimes, it's no fun being a predator.

FRENCH HUNTERS ARE in the firing sights of EU lawmakers after two million people objected to their potting well-known songbirds - many of them en route back to Britain.

The hunters, blamed by wildlife groups for the decline of songbirds returning to this country to breed, currently enjoy looser regulations on shooting than elsewhere in Europe.

The EU-wide petition collected to restrict their activities called for greater protection for wild birds flying through France.

Organised jointly by the Ligue pour la Protection des Oiseaux, BirdLife International, and France Nature Environnement in France, the petition was promoted in the UK by the RSPB, with support from WWF (UK), The Scottish Ornithologists Club, the Wildfowl and Wetlands Trust, The Wildlife Trusts and the Hawk and Owl Trust.

Half a million of the names on the petition were collected from the UK.

A spokesman for the RSPB said:"A French law, passed in 1998, allows hunters to start shooting birds as early as mid-July in some areas, continuing until the end of February. This makes France the only European country with a hunting season of seven and a half months - the European average is only five and a half months.

"The early start means some birds will still be nesting when shooting begins and the extra month of hunting during February occurs when many British birds are migrating back to breed.

"The French law is incompatible with the European Union Birds Directive which is designed to give protection to birds during the breeding season and during migration."

The European Commission had already initiated a case against France before the European Court of Justice - but French hunters are calling for the Birds Directive to be weakened to allow their law to stand.

The petition included almost 1,130,000 signatures from France itself.

WILDLIFE FRIENDLY FARMERS and landowners are being urged by The Wildlife Trusts to apply for "green cash" before it is too late.

"Funding through the Countryside Stewardship Scheme has dramatically increased in England from £35million in 1999 to £51million, but landowners will lose out if their applications are not received before May 31," warned a Trust spokesman.

POLICE AND WILDLIFE experts have been called in to investigate apparent sightings of a six-foot crocodile or alligator in a local lake.

Passers-by alerted the authorities to a large creature stalking the water at Heaton Park, Newcastle, and fears of a prank evaporated when the sightings continued.

The Reptile Trust, which recently revealed hordes of exotic pets were being released annually into the wild, was called in to help track down the beast.

From descriptions given the Trust believes the mystery animal may be a South American cayman.

Trust spokesman Peter Heathcote said:"We are taking the reports seriously and want anyone who sees it to contact us and not approach it themselves."

The release of an alligator into a local lake may not be as unusual on Tyneside as it first appears.

Three 3ft alligators were collected by the Trust last year after being abandoned by their owners in the region.

DELICATE TRIMMING WORK has been carried out by tree surgeons on a Scottish tree thought to be the oldest in Europe.

"Picts, Romans, Vikings and Normans - you name it and the Fortingall Yew has seen it all," said a Forestry Commission spokesman.

"But it needed some tender loving care if it was to see much more of the new millennium."

The Fortingall Yew is an ancient yew tree thought to be up to 9,000 years old that stands in a church-yard at Fortingall, near Aberfeldy, Perthshire.

"It now comprises only two remnants of its trunk, the rest having been destroyed by rot, fire and vandalism," revealed the spokesman.

The tree surgeons carried out careful work intended to help the yew survive as long as possible. They also took cuttings that would be grown on by scientists "to preserve the genetic qualities of this remarkable tree. "

One estimate of its age is based on studies by forestry scientist Alan Mitchell who considered it more than 5,000 years old.

But another expert, Alan Meredith, put its age at 9,000 years.

"Local legend has it that Pontius Pilate, the Roman Governor of Judaea who had Christ crucified, was born near the tree when his father, a Roman envoy, was visiting local Celtic chieftains," added the spokesman.

NEW LAWS BEING drawn up to protect special wildlife sites have been hailed by English Heritage as one of the most significant improvements in the fortunes of English wildlife in the last 20 years.

Responding to publication of the new Countryside and Rights of Way Bill, chairman Baroness Young said:"Sites of Special Scientific Interest take pride of place as our finest wildlife sites in England and fully merit the additional protection that this new legisla - tion will provide.

"The Countryside and Rights of Way Bill will mean proactive management, proper protection and positive thinking for SSSIs.

"Over 30 per cent of SSSIs are in unfavourable condition and we are pleased that the Government has given us the tools to improve their management."

DESPERATE DAIRY FARMERS are hoping a high-profile rally in Central London will awaken the public and MPs to their plight.

The current critical situation in the dairy industry with milk producers facing rock bottom prices is simply unsustainable, according to the National Farmers Union.

The union says its Fair Share of the Bottle campaign is currently raising consumer awareness of the raw deal suffered by dairy farmers up and down the country.

It was vital to put pressure on the rest of the milk supply chain to give farmers a fairer share of the end return.

NFU president Ben Gill said:"All of us must continue to play our part in keeping the public aware of the dire situation facing British dairy farmers. It is only with consumers on our side that we can turn this disastrous situation around.

"Things simply cannot continue as they are - the prices being received are simply laughable.

"Every effort possible is being made by the NFU to halt and reverse this appalling situation."

The London rally (on March 15) had been planned with the intention of giving farmers the chance to directly lobby MPs.

The price dairy farmers receive for their products has plunged by 27 per cent in three years to less than 10 pence per pint, while consumers paid an average of 34 pence per pint last year.

Farmers complain that the "massively inflated price of sterling", plus the fall in milk prices paid to farmers, are driving the dairy business to the wall.

Agrimoney compensation is available in Europe to compensate farmers and the NFU is pressing the Government to pay this.

THE FORESTRY COMMISSION has joined forces with the Motor Sports Association in a bid to give budding rally drivers "a step up into the hot seat of world class competition."

In a move certain to anger wildlife lovers already opposed to cars racing through countryside, the Commission is hoping to increase the number of young rally drivers.

A new funding arrangement will see two rounds of the British Rally Championship offering reduced entry fees for amateur drivers wanting to burn rubber on quiet forest tracks.

Chris Probert, of the Forestry Commission, said:"Our forests provide some of the most challenging terrain available in this country and we are keen that this resource is open to those who don't always have the financial backing to enter into top level competition."

BRITISH MEAT EATERS could now be at serious risk of contracting CJD in imported continental beef products, it has been revealed.

A new cattle test developed by Swiss scientists has found that as many as 100 BSE-infected cows may have been eaten in their native country last year.

Results of the post-mortem test suggest that many more herds than previously thought could be infected with BSE across Europe, raising the possibility of a continental outbreak of human variant CJD.

Dr Bruno Oesch, of the University of Zurich, has confirmed that all the infected Swiss animals had no links whatsoever to British herds.

He believed the test would also prove BSE was rampant in Germany and France - which has taken the high moral ground over British CJD cases and imposed an illegal ban.

A spokesman for the National Farmers Union said:"This just underlines our call for British customers to buy British every time. Our beef industry is now subject to the most stringent standards anywhere in the world."

THE BLAZE DEATH of country sports loving MP Michael Colvin has come as a hammer blow to rural groups which saw him as a leading spokesman in their fight to retain their way of life.

Members of The Countryside Alliance say they have been left stunned and saddened by the death of Mr Colvin and his wife Nichola in a fire at their country home.

The Tory MP was a former vice-chairman of one Alliance predecessor organisation, the British Field Sports Society, from 1987 to 1994.

He was also chairman of the Council for Country Sports from 1987 until 1997, when it was wound up following the formation of the Countryside Alliance.

Caroline Tisdall, a board member of the Countryside Alliance and near-neighbour of the Colvins in Hampshire, said: "Our thoughts are with their family at this very sad time. It is a great shock. Michael and Nichola worked so hard for the countryside over many years."

FORESTERS HAVE A new weapon in the fight to protect forests from devastation by high winds - a computer program.

Boffins at the Forest Research Agency say the new program "takes a lot of the guesswork out of predicting the risk of wind damage for conifer woodlands planted anywhere in Great Britain."

RAMBLERS ARE CELEBRATING publication of the new Countryside and Rights of Way Bill as the most important piece of countryside legislation in 50 years.

"The Bill will introduce a legal freedom to roam in England and Wales, marking the pinnacle of a 116-year campaign by countryside lovers nationwide," said a spokesman for the Ramblers Association.

"The legislation will give the public freedom to walk on specific, mapped areas of mountain, moor, heath, down and common land, with provisions to extend this to coastlines in the future."

The association also welcomed additional powers to force local authorities, which have a legal duty to keep footpaths clear, to take action against landowners guilty of obstructing paths.

FEARS OF A future Government crackdown on angling - similar to that still intended for foxhunting - appear to have been officially dismissed by New Labour.

Elliot Morley, Minister for the Countryside and Fisheries, revealed:"The Government is fully committed to the future of angling and believes it is an important sport and mass-participation leisure activity for all ages.

"Its contribution to the economy, particularly in rural areas, should not be underestimated.

"We have already taken some important measures by approving measures to conserve salmon and most recently ending the coarse fish close season on canals."

In a statement welcoming the report of the independent Salmon and Freshwater Fisheries Review Group, he added:"We will be consulting widely and inviting comments on the review group recommendations.

"I hope that all those interested in fish and fisheries, together with those concerned about the conservation of the freshwater environment, will take the opportunity to let us have their views."

Earlier, in a move to reassure both ramblers and landowners, Mr Elliot had spoken at a conference organised jointly by the Royal Agricultural Society of England and the Royal Forestry Society about the country's woodlands.

Greater access to woodlands would promote healthier living and enable more people to explore the countryside, he said.

He also underlined the importance of the new Countryside and Rights of Way Bill with its proposed new power enabling landowners to dedicate land voluntarily to public access.

FARMERS AND CONSERVATIONISTS have protested at a new EU rule that effectively penalises landowners for setting aside areas for wildlife.

Financial penalties may now be incurred on subsidies if farmers allow hedges or undergrowth to grow more than two metres into a field - perfect habitat for many creatures.

Dr Alan Woods, director of policy for the Country Landowners Association, said:"We are supporting conservation bodies in asking for the new rule - due to be applied from May 15 - to be delayed until 2001.

"This would enable a full environmental assessment to be carried out and for less damaging alternative rules to be investigated.

"The long-term aim must be to move progressively away from production-based subsidies towards explicit payments for the environmental services provided by farmers."

CRUCIAN CARP AND tench have been brought in to revitalise two Welsh lakes that have lost their lustre in recent years.

The Environment Agency Wales and Carmarthenshire County Council used the fish to complete a collaborative project to develop Cwmoernant Reservoirs.

The lakes at Tanerdy, on the outskirts of Carmarthen, have been developed as part of the agency's urban fisheries programme.

"Over two and a half thousand Crucian carp and tench were stocked in the two lakes earlier this month to ensure that anglers have good quality fish to catch in coming years," revealed an Agency spokesman.

"These stocks will be further boosted with over a thousand young tench from the Agency's coarse fish farm during the summer.

"Crucian carp have become increasingly scarce throughout the UK due to interbreeding with other species - particularly goldfish - and competition in the form of common and mirror carp. These are close but larger relatives of the Crucian carp and are regularly stocked by anglers.

"However, the lakes at Cwmoernant are ideal for Crucian carp as they like shallow, still waters with dense vegetation."

A 30-YEAR PLAN to build a new infants school is in turmoil because it would lie on a bee farm's flight path.

The bizarre problem was only discovered in the final stretch of campaigners' marathon fight for the Devon school.

The South Molton school looked certain to go ahead until it was revealed youngsters would walk beside local beekeeper Paddy Wallace's honey farm - home to a million bees.

Fears have now been raised that the plan would be too dangerous with the ever-present possibility of a swarm of angry bees descending on a luckless child.

Devon County Council has confirmed that the scheme had already been given outline planning consent.

An investigation is currently underway to see whether the building work can still go ahead.

A FARMER'S WIFE was shocked to find herself and her wooden shed being lifted skyward when a jet flew over.

Air turbulence from the low-flying jet is being blamed for the bizarre incident which left Tracey Mills terrified but unhurt.

Mrs Mills, whose husband Alan farms the land at Stour Row, Dorset, was working inside her office hut when the jet roared past.

The hut was momentarily jolted off its foundations before thudding back down.

An investigation has been launched into the incident which also left three cars damaged from steel roof sheets ripped from their fittings.

It appears that the jet had come from an RAF base in Somerset but the Ministry of Defence is conducting its own probe.

SCIENTISTS have confirmed that the death of 15-year-old Claire McVey, from Ilfracombe, North Devon, was caused by variant CJD - making her the UK's youngest victim.

CLEARER LABELLING ON meat and food packages has come a step closer in a campaign to boost British farmers and their produce.

Vague or misleading labels have been blamed for leaving patriotic shoppers confused when they pop into their local shops aiming to buy British.

Farmers from across the country travelled to London to show their support for a Bill calling for clearer labelling of food, attending the second reading of the private member's Bill brought by Conservative MP Stephen O'Brien.

The National Farmers Union and the National Pig Association also backed his call for labelling which identified country of origin and provided information about the standards of production.

NFU vice-president Richard Watson Jones said: "Customers have said they want to support our farmers and rural economy by buying British. Confusing labelling must not be allowed to cheat them of the choices they want to make at the check-out.

"This bill would be a huge help for consumers and British agriculture, which depends on the support of the public."

The NFU recently launched its own Label Watch campaign with about 3,000 farmers and their wives completing surveys designed to check that retailers are adhering to new Government guidelines on labelling that state origin labels on foods should be clear and unambiguous.

Meanwhile, members of the public and consumer organisations were given the chance to tell Food Safety Minister Baroness Hayman what they thought about food labelling at an Open Forum also held in London.

The meeting was part of the Better Food Labelling initiative launched by Lady Hayman last month.

FOXHUNTING SUPPORTERS have been boosted by new signals that Premier Tony Blair may be aiming to water down Government plans to ban the sport.

The Prime Minister is reported to be considering regulating foxhunting instead of pressing for an outright ban.

His change of stance in the face of fierce countryside opposition has been revealed by the cross-party Middle Way Group of MPs.

If true, it could mean that foxhunting will stay but be subject to tighter controls than it has previously seen - a move that would still infuriate anti-hunt campaigners and MPs.

CROOKS WHO RUSTLE wildflowers such as snowdrops and bluebells may soon face a less rosy future.

New get-tough measures are due to be unveiled by the Government to stop criminals lining their pockets at the expense of the countryside and the people who enjoy its beauty.

Recently, police circulated the details of known bulb rustlers to forces throughout the country in a bid to make life harder for crooks at the heart of what is now big business.

In January, two thieves were jailed after denuding a wood in Hertfordshire of 300,000 snowdrop bulbs estimated to be worth £60,000 when sold to unscrupulous garden centre bosses.

It was thought to be the harshest punishment yet for the crime.

However, such penalties could become more common when details of the Government crackdown are revealed.

A spokesman for Cambridgeshire Police said of bulb rustling:"We have evidence it is becoming an organised crime. People now go out in lorries with special tools to dig up bulbs.There is a lot of money to be made."

CORNISH COCKLES ARE in crisis with numbers showing a steep decline in recent years, according to the Environment Agency.

The agency has teamed up with local conservationists in a bid to preserve remaining stocks with a plea going out that smaller cockles be left undisturbed.

Before byelaws are passed to cover the crisis, the Environment Agency has appealed to the general public to leave smaller cockles alone so they have a chance to breed.

"The cockle breeding season runs from Easter to the end of September and the cockle populations are very susceptible to permanent damage," explained an Agency spokesman.

"Protecting the biodiversity of our rivers is of prime importance if we want to preserve our environment.

"All we are asking is for people to put back any cockles smaller than 2cm, or the size of a 20p coin. Hopefully, we can then reverse the fortunes of the humble Cornish cockle and help to maintain our prime estuary habitats."

Recently, the Agency joined conservationists in hosting a number of meetings at a local hotel to discuss the proposed byelaws.

AS IF THE mink was not bad enough, wildlife experts fear the British countryside faces invasion from thousands of other 'foreigners' - including pythons and boa constrictors.

Exotic pets are being released into the wild at an alarming rate, according to the Reptile Trust which now deals with about 2,000 cases each year.

Lizards such as giant iguanas are among pets which are thrown out when they grow too large for domestic premises, reveals the Trust.

Children are particularly at risk from hungry snakes, some of which can grow 20ft in length with the power to crush a man.

In America several toddlers have been killed by abandoned pets.

BADGER LOVERS HAVE expressed their dismay that two new trial areas are to be incorporated into the Government's cull of up to 20,000 badgers.

As with all the other sites - or triplets - badgers will be trapped in cages and shot.

Guy James, chairman of the National Federation of Badger Groups, said: "It is frustrating and deeply depressing to see MAFF preparing to sacrifice yet more badgers on the alter of political expediency.

"The badger culling trial is a complete waste of taxpayers' money and a costly diversion from finding a true solution to bovine TB in cattle.

"In the meantime, farmers continue to suffer the impact of the disease and to be misled into thinking that badgers are the problem.

"It is appalling that the Government is persisting with the trial despite great practical problems which are continuing to emerge. Killing badgers will not solve the TB problem."

Irene Brierton, chairman of the Mid-Derbyshire Badger Group, added: "We are extremely disappointed. This triplet seems to have been incorporated just to placate the NFU.

"We did not even consider Derbyshire to be a TB hotspot - there's simply no history to it. Derbyshire badger groups will campaign with all lawful means at our disposal."

Faye Burton, of the Staffordshire Badger Conservation Group, was equally upset.

She said:"We've been fighting this campaign for 25 years. MAFF simply shouldn't be pouring money down the drain like this."

THE SAME SCIENTISTS who controversially created Dolly the sheep have now announced the birth of five pig clones - said to be the first in the world.

PPL Therapeutics, based in Edinburgh, says it hopes the animals will help meet demand for pig organs if they are approved for use in human transplants.

The five piglets, which were born on March 5, have been named Christa, Alexis, Millie, Carrel and Dotcom.

PPL spokesman Dave Ayares said:"They're wonderful, they're healthy, they're bouncing around."

PPL said the piglets were created from adult cells using technology similar to that which led to the arrival of Dolly.

The company added:"This opens the door to making modified pigs whose organs and cells can be successfully transplanted into humans - the only near-term solution to solving the worldwide organ shortage crisis."

Clinical trials into the use of animal organs for human transplant could commence within four years.

MALARIA GRIPPED PARTS of the British countryside during what was one of the coldest periods in the country's history, a new study has revealed.

Writer Paul Reiter tells of the bizarre irony in 'From Shakespeare to Defoe: Malaria in England in the Little Ice Age'.

Despite bitterly cold winters in the 17th Century, records show mosquitoes were spreading malaria around the country.

Residents living close to Kent and Essex marshland were particularly susceptible with dozens dying as a result.

"The entire story took place in a period when temperatures were probably colder than in any other period in the past 10,000 years," said Mr Reiter.

AN ABANDONED WORLD War Two airstrip is the source of fresh hope for Britain's wildflower meadows.

The 235 hectare former Blakehill airfield near Cricklade in Wiltshire will be the site of the largest restoration of an ancient wildflower meadow in the UK, meeting 50 per cent of Government targets for restoring ancient meadows over the next decade.

Wiltshire Wildlife Trust bought the site with a grant of £868,500 from the Heritage Lottery Fund and support from North Wiltshire District Council.

"Its chequered history spans more than 700 years," said a Trust spokesman."It was once part of ancient Braydon Forest, the hunting ground for King John."

THE RSPB HAS attacked the Government for "failing to show the full picture" about environmental damage caused by farming.

Although it generally welcomed publication of a new report, the Society remained "highly critical of the exclusion of some sets of figures which would clearly demonstrate the environmental damage caused by current agricultural policy."

Matt Rayment, an RSPB economist, added: "Over the past three decades, changes in farming have had a directly damaging impact on the environment. The RSPB is disappointed these fundamental changes have not been measured in this report. Trends of farmland bird populations, including grey partridges, corn buntings and skylarks, are vital indicators on the health of the countryside."

A HUNT SABOTEUR sustained a suspected broken nose in ugly scenes involving Prince Charles' favourite Quorn Hunt, it has been claimed.

About 60 saboteurs attended the recent hunt at Wymeswold near Loughborough.

Police stepped in to "escort saboteurs to safety" when they came under attack, according to the Hunt Saboteurs Association.

A VISION OF of Scotland as "a land of fine trees, where people are proud of their trees, woods and forests" has been unveiled to the Scottish Parliament.

Scotland is already the most forested country in the UK, with more than 16 per cent woodland cover.

Its overall area of woodland has almost trebled over the past 100 years to 3,203,000 acres.

Plans for future development were contained in a draft Scottish Forestry Strategy that Forestry Minister John Home Robertson MSP presented.

BRITISH BATS HAVE been boosted by a "landmark victory" involving a local authority which damaged one of their roosts, it has been claimed.

Leicestershire County Council was fined £2,500, with £400 costs, after being found guilty of damaging a bat roost at a property owned by them.

A local company which carried out the roof work for the authority was fined £1000 with £225 costs, after also pleading guilty.

A spokesman for the Bat Conservation Trust said:"The result has massive implications. It is now clear that the onus is on local authorities to ensure that surveys for bats and other protected wildlife are conducted before proceeding with any work on buildings owned by them. They cannot leave the responsibility to their contractors."

It was the first time a prosecution had been brought under the Conservation Regulations 1994 to protect bats, says the Trust.

Trust conservation officer Gillie Sargent added: "I would like to congratulate Leicestershire Constabulary for bringing this prosecution. I am delighted with the outcome of the court case.

"It sends a very clear message to local authorities and their contractors that they need to take wildlife law seriously.

"Bat populations have declined dramatically over the past few decades mainly due to the loss of roosting sites and change in land use.

"Bats now rely heavily on man-made structures and buildings. People can make a significant contribution to their conservation by protecting roosts in their property.

"Bats have had a bad press in the past but they are, in fact, harmless, beautiful animals and are very beneficial to the environment."

THE BRITISH ARE a nation of walkers and rely on walking to stay fit and healthy, according to a survey commissioned by the Ramblers Association.

"The poll suggests that a staggering 77 per cent of the British population - up to 45 million people - walk for pleasure at least once a month," said an Association spokesman.

"And an amazing six out of 10 of those questioned said that walking is their main form of exercise.

"Of those who walk for pleasure, 37 per cent generally walk for less than two miles, 41 per cent for between two and four miles, and 21 per cent for more than four miles."

RA walks co-ordinator Murray Hatcher added: "Walking is good for your health. It is cheap and fun, so it is hardly surprising that over three quarters of the British population walk on a regular basis.

"And opportunities for walking in Britain are getting even better with the new Countryside Bill."

KILLER WHALES HUNTING off the Cornish coast are expected to become a magnet for British holidaymakers over the next few months.

The five or so whales, thought to be feeding on huge plankton-eating basking sharks, make an arresting sight as they power past fishing boats and thousands of tourists seem certain to converge on the region to try to catch a glimpse of them.

Tourists are also invited to play a part in attempts to identify the whales from markings on their bodies and dorsal fins.

These are likely to have been recorded somewhere around the globe already by whale watchers.

A spokesman at the National Marine Aquarium in Plymouth said he welcomed the arrival of the killer whales.

"Tourists will have every chance of bumping into one if they are in a boat off the Cornish coast this summer," he said.

"If people get film of them or take photographs, individual whales can be identified by their markings. Holidaymakers can play their part in helping us to unravel the mystery of where these killer whales have come from."

MORE THAN 30 new woodlands are to be created in Welsh national parks after the country won a green cash injection of £750,000.

The National Assembly's agriculture and rural development secretary, Christine Gwyther, said the Forestry Commission had earmarked the cash to help fund the creation of new woodlands in some of the most beautiful parts of the country.

She was delighted with the quality of the successful bids for the final round of grants and praised the support of private landowners for the project.

"These new areas of woodland will complement the valuable landscapes already within the national parks and enhance their value for woodland biodiversity," she said.

"This increase in woodland cover reflects the variety of woodland types found in Wales, including new upland ash and oak."

Snowdonia National Park will get 19 new wood-lands totalling 465 acres; Brecon Beacons National Park gets eight totalling 163 acres; and Pembrokeshire Coast National Park will get three totalling 30 acres.

TRYING TO TRACK down your nearest woodland has been made a lot simpler thanks to inclusion of woodlands on Ordance Survey Explorer maps for the first time.

The results of the Woodland Trust's 28-year campaign to protect ancient woods and create new native woods can now be clearly seen on the maps.

Trust chief executive, Mike Townsend, said: "With our woodlands being marked on these maps, it makes it much easier for people to see where their nearest, freely accessible woods are.

"It will now be easier for people to find, explore and enjoy our beautiful woods."

THREE PICNIC RECIPES by star cooks Sophie Grigson, Hugh Fearnley-Whittingstall and Marguerite Patten have been chosen to spearhead the Council for the Protection of Rural England's National Picnic Weekend in June.

ENGLISH NATURE HAS been waging war on thousands of voracious North American bullfrogs discovered in the heart of the British countryside.

More than 6,000 of the frogs - which devour any living creature small enough to go inside their huge mouths - have already been captured during the operation on the Kent-East Sussex border.

The bullfrogs, which can weigh two pounds and be as wide as a shovel, enjoy making a meal of native frogs, as well as ducklings, fish, and rodents that come too close.

The colony was uncovered last October when a farmer discovered the frogs inhabiting lakes on his land, laying waste to other wildlife species as they serviced their enormous appetites.

English Nature believes many frogs may have escaped their initial attempts to trap them and could be about to re-emerge from hibernation in the next few weeks.

Operation Bullfrog was set up to track down as many of the foreigners as possible before they disperse into the landscape and create a new ecological disaster.

SUPPORTERS OF DRAG hunting have been boosted by former Beatle Paul McCartney who made a plea to foxhunting groups.

The pop star appealed to foxhunters to switch to drag hunting in an impassioned letter published by the Daily Telegraph.

Sir Paul, in the news recently after admitting a relationship with one-legged model Heather Mills, called foxhunting a "barbarity".

"Studies show that foxhunting accounts for only four per cent of foxes killed on farms," he wrote.

"It seems hunting isn't an efficient form of control anyway."

He appealed to hunt groups to show compassion to the fox while helping to save rural jobs.

By laying a scent for hounds to follow, all the tradition and history of hunting could continue, he added.

BRITISH SHOOTERS HAVE welcomed new guidelines from the Home Office on firearm security which, they say, are less bullying than feared.

The Home Office issued the guidelines to help set "sensible standards as to how best to prevent firearms being stolen," according to a spokesman.

"It is not the intention of the Government to reduce the number of firearms held by certificate holders. The misuse of firearms mainly involves those in unlawful possession."

Pat Johnson, secretary of the British Shooting Sports Council, said: "The guidance stems from the determination of the shooting associations to ensure that the shooters' voice should be heard. The process firmly confirms the Home Office as the only body entitled to give definitive advice on such matters."

HERDING SHEEP WAS far less bother with a hovercraft when a farmer's trusty dog was temporarily out of action.

With faithful pet Fred recovering from an operation, Norman Barrow was faced with a dilemma of how to round up hundreds of sheep scattered across his fields.

It was a typical problem facing one of today's farmers but the solution owed more to technological wizardry than animal husbandry - a hovercraft.

Mr Barrow borrowed the air-propelled machine from an off-road driving centre near his farm in Gloucestershire.

He was already on good terms with the centre who use his fields for their courses.

And his verdict on going to work by hovercraft?

"Brilliant!," he said, although he was quick to point out that loyal Fred was still faster and kinder to the environment than the hovercraft.

ORGANIC EGG PRODUCTION could be one way struggling egg farmers try to crack the current slump in their fortunes.

Problems facing egg producers were discussed at a national conference in the West Midlands where delegates considered various money-making schemes, including organic egg production.

However, the National Farmers Union says capital investment is needed.

"The British egg industry has suffered two years of unprofitability, with neither egg producers nor the main supply companies covering production or operating costs," said an NFU spokesman.

"Over the same period the industry has invested more than £4 million to improve production and food safety standards to ensure British eggs are among the safest in the world. It has also spent £4 million per year on advertising.

"Now investment in the future is threatened as intense price competition between the major retailers has forced shop prices down to as low as 50p per dozen, a figure well below production, packing and supply costs."

NFU deputy president Tim Bennett added: "If the UK egg industry is going to remain viable and contin - ue to deliver the quality product we now expect, producers must be paid a fair price."

THE CLAMPDOWN ON exploitation of workers in the fruit and vegetable packing industry is being extended.

Agriculture Minister Elliot Morley has announced that the Government is to extend Operation Gangmaster to all parts of the country where gangmasters are active.

THE £200 MILLION lifeline handed by the Government to British farmers has received a cautious welcome following a make or break summit meeting in Downing Street.

But the Countryside Alliance immediately warned that the package of measures would only provide relief to rural communities if followed up with delivery.

Chief executive Richard Burge said: "This money has been a long time coming and is of course welcome. Let us be clear, however, that much of this aid is simply that which is due to farmers under EU rules, and is merely compensating them for the distorted trading conditions that they have faced."

HEN HARRIERS COME under fire in a new report which blames high numbers of the birds of prey for reducing grouse populations.

The study 'Raptors and Red Grouse: Conservation Conflicts and Management Solutions' was written by scientists from the Game Conservancy Trust, the Institute of Terrestrial Ecology and the Institute of Biology at the University of Stirling.

Its main author, Dr Simon Thirgood, of the Trust, said: "There is a major conflict that must be dealt with. On the one hand, heather moorland is one of our most important biological resources and management of this land for grouse shooting helps retain this habitat without government subsidy.

"However, high densities of hen harriers greatly reduce grouse numbers and shooting bags, thus reducing the incentive of landowners to invest in moorland management.

"The birds of prey themselves are frequently persecuted to reduce this risk. At the moment, it's a no-win situation which must be resolved urgently."

The report debates an earlier proposal by the Game Conservancy Trust that the distribution of harriers needs to be extended.

Reintroduction of harriers onto heather moorland where they were eliminated would also be helpful.

"Once new populations were established, steps could be taken to limit harrier predation on grouse," added a report spokesman.

A SCIENTIST DOING research on genetically modified crops for the Government is also being paid by industry to make the case for GM crops, claims Friends of the Earth.

The revelation has outraged the environmental watchdog group which has called on the Government to sack Dr Peter Lutman.

"Dr Lutman works at the Institute of Arable Crops Research (IACR), part of a consortium of research groups carrying out Government work on farm-scale trials," said an FoE spokesman.

"The consortium has contracts worth £3.3 million with the Government for this work. Dr Lutman is co-author of a report to the Government on progress on the trials.

"Dr Lutman is also at the heart of CropGen, a new initiative launched by the biotechnology industry to make the case for GM crops."

Two other scientists from IACR were also part of CropGen which had confirmed to FoE that scientists on the CropGen panel were paid for their work as panel members.

FoE food campaigner Pete Riley added:"This is outrageous. IACR seems to be happy that their scientists are paid by the biotech industry to make the case for GM crops while they are working on supposedly neutral scientific studies on the subject for the Government. This deprives IACR work on the trials of any credibility."

TERMITES HAVE TERMINATED the smooth running of a plan to build new houses close to the North Devon coastline.

Britain's only known termite colony has eaten away at the bid for homes at Saunton.

In an unusual move, the Forestry Commission has invoked legal powers to freeze the housing scheme while a programme of eradication remains unfinished.

Fears were raised that the termites would go on the march, colonising the new properties which would seem unaffected in the early stages.

Eventually, however, the gnawing insects would make a meal of the buildings' framework, putting them in danger of collapse.

Termites fed from a central point outwards, it was revealed, so by the time they were discovered it would already be too late.

A DOOMSDAY SCENARIO has been painted by farmers' leaders following Budget Day confirmation about the feared climate change levy.

The Treasury's announcement that farmers and growers would have to pay the tax would sound a death knell for many in the industry, claims the National Farmers Union.

"At a time of crisis throughout horticulture and agriculture, farmers and growers will be incensed that a further unilateral cost burden is being imposed upon them," said NFU president Ben Gill.

The NFU estimates that the levy - even with a discount - will cost the industry more than £5 million per year.

Mr Gill said: "While the Government has recog - nised that the new tax will have a negative impact and has offered us a 50 per cent discount for five years, it will not be enough to lessen what will be a devastating charge on farmers and growers.

"The Treasury clearly does not understand the full implications of this tax to an industry on its knees. Thousands of jobs are at risk and a whole industry could be exported because we have not been given a complete exemption."

A TREE HOUSE built by three young brothers is to get the chop.

The brothers have been told to pull down the construction that they took eight months to build at their home in Hordle, near Lymington, Hampshire.

The trio were in tears after the decision by New Forest District Council which said the tree house in their garden broke planning laws.

But the writing was already on the wall after planning officer Pat Aird wrote to the boys' parents, telling them that their only course of action was to get rid of the construction, or apply for retrospective planning permission - which had almost zero chance of success.

"It is unlikely planning permission will be granted because of the obstructive appearance of the structure due to its height, means of construction and proximity to the highway," she wrote.

"Any building in the garden of a house needs planning permission.

"Because it's permanently fixed to the ground it is development.

"The rules apply to a tree house just as they apply to a shed or to a conservatory."

RAT: shock in an African hut replaced by admiration

I MUST confess I have never much liked rats, especially since I was woken at 3am in a Moroccan mud hut by one brazenly sitting on my bare chest.

Even now, years later, I can clearly recall lying on a bed roll, feeling those small sharp claws digging into my hot skin as the rat sniffed around for food.

Squatting there on my solar plexus, it actually seemed quite heavy.

With no electricity in the huts, it was only by chance that my hand happened to be lying near the torch.

Finally waking, I scrabbled to switch it on, just in time to see the rat bounce away and streak up the wall into the thatched roof.

The most amazing aspect of the whole incident, however, was witnessing the speed of the human female following my shout of: "*Rat!*"

My partner went from deep sleep to a quivering, shrieking, standing position faster than an Olympic sprinter off his starting blocks.

I was lucky not to be bitten. Rats anywhere, but especially in Africa, carry a number of horrible diseases and I would not have rated my chances of enjoying the rest of my holiday very highly if that foraging rodent had sunk its teeth into my blood stream.

Mind you, it could have been worse. We were told that the previous year a German couple had flown home after finding a cobra slithering about in their hut - presumably seeking a tasty rat for its supper.

Although I don't really like rats, I can't help but admire them.

Their survival skills are second to none in the animal world, which is why there are now estimated to be five or so resident rats for every human being in Britain, the vast majority living unseen alongside us.

Crafty, resourceful, and stealthy, they are unlike other rodents such as rabbits in that their diet extends to meat, sometimes meat which they kill themselves.

Hungry rats commonly prey on mice or frogs and I once disturbed one lurking at the edge of a lake, waiting for the chance to snatch a tiny duckling among several passing by. (It was fairly easy not to confuse it with a harmless 'water rat' - which is really a vole - because of its sharper features and the fact it fled away from the water.)

The brown rat is now by far the commonest species in this country, having ousted the black rat from many of its old stamping grounds.

Bigger and more aggressive than the black rat, the brown is as likely to be found living in a country hedgerow or farm building as eking out an existence beneath the floorboards of the grandest Metropolitan mansion.

With many predators such as foxes, cats and owls to contend with, it's little wonder brown rats are super efficient breeders, giving birth to as many as 11 babies at a time.

That rats are intelligent will come as no surprise to anyone who keeps them as pets, the white pet shop version being a more placid derivation of the original brown rat. But it is still enthralling to see that intelligence at work.

I remember visiting a decrepit little railway station one afternoon, hoping to meet a friend off a train.

To get to the deserted platform, I had to walk down a flight of ancient steps which were strewn with assorted rubbish.

The train duly arrived and a couple of passengers got off and walked up those steps. My friend didn't.

Feeling a bit miffed as the train moved off, I decided to wait there for the next one to arrive in about 10 minutes and leant into a recess in the wall.

I was alone again now, the only sound the faint clink-clinking of the railway line measuring the train's departure until even that had petered out.

As soon as it did, I became aware of a faint rustling to my left.

I stuck my head out and saw five rats had appeared on the steps.

They were feasting' again on some food left in the rubbish.

It was quite obvious they had been waiting patiently to resume their meal.

I watched them until the railway line began to gently clink-clink again to herald the approach of the next train.

Immediately, almost as one, they vanished down a hole nearby.

Smart cookies, rats.

WETLAND WILDLIFE SITES dotted around the English coast are to have their futures insured against sea damage by Government cash.

Fears had been raised that many of the sites and their wildlife were gradually being lost to encroachment by the sea.

"Species of rare coastal birds including the bittern rely on these habitats, as well as important numbers of wading birds such as the avocet," said a Government spokesman.

Seaside plant life such as sea purslane, sea lavender and saltmarsh grass would also be threatened if erosion was not halted.

Six general areas had been identified as requiring the most urgent work to protect local habitats.

These were the Winterton Dunes, Norfolk; Suffolk coast and its estuaries; Essex coast and its estuaries; North Kent coast; Dungeness and Pett Levels in East Sussex; and the West Sussex and Hampshire coast.

"New funding arrangements put in place by the Ministry of Agriculture will ensure that habitats will be either saved or recreated," added the spokesman.

"Money for individual projects will come from the Ministry flood defence budget which has been increased by £23million over three years."

Schemes for the six areas would be formulated under the Coastal Habitat Management Plans.

Projects were due to be drawn up jointly by English Nature and the Environment Agency in close consultation with MAFF and the DETR.

FARMERS AND LANDOWNERS have scored a victory over a proposed Brussels directive that would have effectively penalised them for helping wildlife.

If passed, wildlife rich hedges around fields would have faced severe cutting back for owners to qualify for European grants.

The so-called "two-metre" rule, which was to be introduced on the insistence of the European Court of Auditors, would have penalised farmers if field margins exceeded two metres.

The EU has now agreed not to impose any ruling, at least for this year, following widespread protest.

A TERRIBLE PONG has prompted the Environment Agency to set up a new liaison group in Distington, Cumbria, aimed at sniffing out a solution.

"The role of the new group will be to consider the progress in resolving the odour problem in the area and to review, in public, the performance of two local waste operators, Cumbria Waste Management and Alco Waste Management," said an Agency spokesman.

Environment protection officer, Anne Jackson added: "Whilst both operators have undertaken a lot of work, the problem has not yet been eliminated."

BEAVERS ARE ON the way back in Scotland after the aquatic mammals were hunted to extinction there more than 400 years ago.

About 10 beavers will be released into a controlled environment within Forestry Commission land as part of a scheme to see if they can adapt to life there in the 21st Century.

A secluded site has been chosen for the pilot project which will be monitored by Scottish National Heritage to ensure that a population explosion does not occur - as has happened with other species which escaped into the wild.

However, the scheme is not without its critics with the Scottish Landowners Federation attacking it as foolish.

"After a gap of 400 years, former habitats are unrecognisable. We cannot simply recreate a bit of the past within the present demands on our countryside and expect this to be sustainable," said a spokesman.

All the beavers introduced will be of the European variety which, unlike their better known American cousins, do not make massive dams.

The World Wide Fund for Nature says water vole, otter, salmon and trout could all benefit from the beavers' grazing, coppicing, and modest dam building work.

THE HAND OF God may have played a role in blocking research into GM crops - or at least His earthly representatives could see it that way.

The Church of England's Ethical Investment Advisory Group has taken a stance against the controversial crops - a move welcomed by Friends of the Earth.

The Church says it will not allow GM crops to be grown on its land while too many questions about them remain unanswered.

"It is not yet appropriate to grant tenancies for crop trials on Church land given the uncertainties caused by the lack of an ethical framework," confirmed a spokesman.

Adrian Bebb, GM campaigner for Friends of the Earth, said:"We are delighted that the Church's ethical advisors want the Church to be a good neighbour and not grow GM crops while concerns and uncertainties remain.

"Farmers who have already agreed to take part in GM trials should also heed this advice. If they contaminate their neighbours' crops with GM pollution they may find themselves liable for the damage they have caused."

RAMBLER BOB HORNE is hoping to complete a marathon walk which might daunt much younger men.

Teacher Bob, aged 51, has just set out on the walk of a lifetime which will take him 2,000 miles across Europe after starting off at the north west tip of Scotland.

Bob will eventually end his journey in Nice, France.

"My motivation for the trek is the desire to fulfil a youthful dream before it's too late," he explained."When I was 18, a friend and I were going to walk from Land's End to John O'Groats. In the event, we spent two months digging holes in the roads around Halifax."

Family, career and other interests intervened and it was only now "on the verge of real decreptitude" that his long-standing ambition had been revived.

27

A FUTURISTIC FUEL hailed by conservationists and farmers alike has now been propelled into the limelight - willow.

"The first commercial crop of willow being grown in Britain to provide green electricity is being harvested," revealed a spokesman for the National Farmers Union.

"The harvest of this green fuel, which takes four years to establish, will be seen as a significant step forward in realising the potential power of alternative crops.

"It will provide the first supply of green fuel from an energy crop for the first wood-fired power plant of its kind in Europe when it comes on line this summer - a landmark for the increasingly important partnership between industry and agriculture in developing alternative energy in Britain."

The new power station near Selby, Yorkshire, should provide electricity for over 33,000 people and will have an annual demand for about 68,000 tonnes of willow.

"More than 600 hectares of the new green fuel, or Short Rotation Coppice, is being grown on farmland in Britain. A further 500 hectares of native willow will be planted by farmers this spring," added the spokesman.

Willow can grow to six metres in three years - four metres in the first 12 months - and it is this rapid growth which makes it "a fantastic supply of renewable energy and a fast-growing haven for wildlife."

Developers of the power plant hoped that more farmers could be encouraged to help grow another 900 hectares of willow.

A DAY OUT pheasant shooting was the top prize when more than 100 gamekeepers got together in London to try their luck at potting clays.

The Walter Cole-BASC gamekeepers' clay shoot was held at the West London Shooting Ground after being organised by Walter himself and BASC south east regional officer Angus Irvine.

"I am delighted that something that began as a fun day for my family and friends has grown to include so many keepers," confessed Walter."It was a great day."

The pheasant shoot prize will be enjoyed on the Venn estate with an additional day's wildfowling going to the top beater. In the Gamekeeper Classes, first prize went to Peter Searles, of Pembridge, Herefordshire. Open Class winner was John Smith, from Wantage, Oxon; Young Shot winner was Daniel Gibson, of Hitchin, Herts.

UNDERCOVER FISHERIES INSPECTORS used infra-red night sights to monitor the illegal activities of a man netting fish, a court heard.

The man was later fined £200 for fisheries offences at Llangefni Magistrates Court and ordered to pay £100 towards the costs of the Environment Agency which brought the prosecution.

CHASING A RABBIT soon wiped the smile off Smiler the greyhound's face when she fell more than 140ft off a cliff.

The ex-racing greyhound had been enjoying her usual daily walk near cliffs on the Isle of Wight when she spotted the rabbit.

Within seconds, she had sprinted in pursuit but ended up toppling over the cliff and coming to rest on a tiny ledge 200ft from the ground.

Owner Freda Pollard feared the worst after news of her pet's disappearance was broken to her by the shocked walker who had taken Smiler for her exercise.

But local residents heard the dog's yelps after she had spent a miserable night huddled on the ledge and the coastguard was alerted.

Climbers quickly rescued the animal.

MORE THAN 250 farmers attended the launch of a new supermarket scheme which could help break down rural hostility towards big business.

It is hoped that the initiatives by ASDA will lead to increased understanding between farmers and store bosses who have often been at loggerheads.

NFU vice-president Richard Watson Jones welcomed plans unveiled by ASDA to support British farmers when he attended a farming conference organised by the supermarket chain.

Speaking at the Growing Together event in Leeds, he said such initiatives would help strengthen the relationship between producers and retailers.

Link-saves on milk, an investment in farmers' markets at ASDA stores, and plans for a new free-milk-for-schools programme were all announced at the conference.

Mr Watson Jones said: "The NFU is pleased that ASDA continues to recognise the plight of British farmers. The long-term survival of British farming is vital to all parts of the food chain - including retailers.

"This conference is a good opportunity for farmers and retailers to discuss the real issues of concern affecting the food industry."

SHOOTERS SAY THE bid to ban foxhunting in Scotland has been plunged into disarray after they fired their own broadside.

Their sport would have been "crippled by the proposed law" as it stood, according to The British Association for Shooting and Conservation.

"Lord Watson has now proposed a string of amendments to his own anti-hunting Bill which he claims will remove the threat to shooting but BASC says this is not enough. The whole Bill should be thrown out," said a spokesman.

"BASC has now been asked to appear before the committee which will consider amendments to the Bill. Those proposed by Lord Watson appear to remove the need for licences for such shooting activities as deer stalking with a dog and driving foxes to standing guns. They also allow the use of a dog - or dogs - to flush foxes to protect game birds."

In a further concession, Lord Watson wanted to remove the section that would have made it an offence to feed a shot rabbit to a dog.

Dr Colin Shedden, director of BASC Scotland, added: "BASC Scotland will maintain its fundamental opposition to this Bill until shooting, gamekeeping and countryside management are unaffected."

THE RSPB IS appealing for information about migrant birds such as cuckoos and swallows in a bid to build up a picture about their likely survival rates in years to come.

Details gathered would be compared to results of previous RSPB surveys to see if migrant birds were arriving back any earlier to the UK from southern Europe and Africa.

Data from other sources suggested that some species were returning earlier because of the warmer spring temperatures resulting from climate change.

April was a key month for the arrival of many migrant species and thought to be a good starting point for people to keep watch.

Anyone seeing or hearing one or more of our most well-known migrant bird species should send the date and location (including a four figure OS map grid reference if possible) to: Flightpath 2000, RSPB, The Lodge, Sandy, Bedfordshire SG19 2DL.

The list of selected migrants to look out for was: wheatear, sand martin, blackcap, chiffchaff, willow warbler, common sandpiper, little ringed plover, yellow wagtail, common tern, house martin, cuckoo, reed warbler, swallow, garden warbler, sedge warbler, whitethroat, turtle dove, swift, hobby, spotted flycatcher.

Details could also be sent online via www.rspb.org.uk/youth.

Closing date for observations is June 30.

David Chandler, RSPB principal youth officer, said: "Flightpath 2000 is a great way for us to see if migrant birds are arriving back in Britain earlier than they have done in the past.

"While not a problem now, earlier arrival dates in the future could make some birds susceptible to unpredictable severe, cold and wet spring weather, which could reduce their numbers."

AN OBSESSIVE ORNITHOLOGIST who once walked 838 miles to see a museum's bird collection is in the spotlight again after his bird paintings went on display.

Sixty stunning, life-sized watercolours by Victorian scientist William MacGillivray are on display at the Natural History Museum in London until June.

MacGillivray's overwhelming fascination with birds originally led him to walk from Scotland to London to see the British Museum's bird collection.

It is the first time the paintings have been shown in public after the artist apparently hid them away during his lifetime following a fall-out with jealous science colleagues.

Besides being a painter, MacGillivray wrote five books about the history of British birds, as well as dissecting specimens to learn more about bird anatomy.

GM SUPER SALMON and trout could be heading for British fish farms within the year if the American firm behind them gets the go-ahead, it has been revealed.

The "transgenic" fish grow far faster and bigger than normal stocks because the US company AF Protein has inserted genes from different species of fish to accelerate the growth process.

At 18 months, a GM salmon will have grown 10 times faster than a normal salmon and be about five times as large.

But fears have been raised that tampering with natural salmon stocks for profit will eventually lead to the extinction of the Atlantic salmon.

Campaigners against GM food have been appalled by the news and say producing salmon this way is even more hazardous to the environment than farming GM crops.

Friends of the Earth explain this is because transgenic fish might easily escape, scatter, and breed with normal fish producing unknown consequences.

AF Protein president Elliot Entis has shrugged off criticism, saying there was no real difference between his company's fish and non-GM fish.

"We are confident there is a market," he added, confirming the fish would be offered to fish farms around the world in the next 12 months if the US Government cleared them for sale.

RURAL POSTMASTERS HAVE shown the extent of their anger with the Government through a national poll commissioned by the Countryside Alliance.

The NOP poll revealed "an overwhelming disillusionment with the Government's performance and grave fears for the future of the post office network," according to the Alliance.

"In England and Wales today only four per cent of postmasters believe the Government is doing a good job at protecting rural post offices," said a spokesman.

"The figure has decreased dramatically, down from 27 per cent in July 1999. The majority, 55 per cent, believe that the Government is doing a very bad job.

"Just five per cent of rural postmasters - down from 18 per cent - believe the Government understands the value of village post offices to the community well, and 87 per cent believe that the Government understands it badly."

The poll also revealed "major scepticism" among postmasters about the forthcoming policy of transferring benefit payments from cash at the post office to direct bank transfer.

Alliance chief executive Richard Burge added: "The Countryside Alliance is pledged to resist the disastrous policy of paying benefits via automated credit transfer. The policy will place benefit recipients in the uncaring hands of the banks."

A NEW VEAL operation has been backed by farmers' leaders in a bid to help British farmers compete with those abroad.

Veal is one of the foods most objected to by animal welfare campaigners but organisers of the new business say it will be produced in a "welfare friendly" way.

The scheme was launched at Kingsley Hill Farm, Heathfield, East Sussex.

FARMERS AND VILLAGERS across Britain have been outraged at the life sentence handed to farmer Tony Martin after he was convicted of murdering a 16 year-old burglar.

The 55 year-old farmer blasted Fred Barras with a shotgun after being woken in the night at his decrepit farmhouse in Norfolk. Fellow burglar Brendon Fearon was injured as he fled the scene.

Bachelor Martin, who is appealing against the verdict, faces years behind bars following the incident which was the culmination of a series of burglaries at his property.

Norwich Crown Court had heard how he had felt besieged by burglars and terrified on the fateful night he awoke to find two intruders downstairs.

But the jury found against him and police later warned that the case should be a lesson to people who took the law into their own hands - ignoring the fact that Martin had felt totally abandoned by local officers.

Thousands of letters of support have poured in for the farmer from across Britain, according to PR personality Max Clifford who became a friend during the case.

Law and order campaigner Peter Cadbury attacked the verdict as monstrous, adding:"The law is now entirely on the side of the intruder."

In a prepared statement Martin himself released during the case, he said:"We are supposed to live in a civilised society but that's not the way I have been treated. People are not aware of what it is like to live in the countryside.

"Criminals prevail and it cannot be right. It is not reasonable that people should live in fear."

BASKING SHARKS COULD go into decline in British waters after a move to offer them protected species status was blocked.

The giant plankton eating sharks, now so common off Cornwall that they attract predation from killer whales there, are a growing food source for Far Eastern gourmets.

The Government had called for an international restriction on trade in the sharks whose huge fins are prized for sharkfin soup.

But fellow delegates at the UN conference in Nairobi voted against the British move, which could now lead to an increase in global basking shark slaughter - and fewer visitors to our shores.

Tourists are expected to converge on the Cornish coast this summer to see a pod of killer whales hunting the sharks.

If conservationists' fears are realised, however, the sight of either species off Cornwall may once again become a rarity.

BRITAIN'S RING OUZELS appear to be in severe decline after a national survey into the 'mountain blackbirds' found numbers had plummeted.

An RSPB investigation has established that the current population of ring ouzels is now likely to be between just 6,000 and 7,500 pairs.

Rowena Langston, RSPB research biologist, said:"Until now, most of the evidence for a fall in numbers has arisen from the fact that this bird has simply disappeared from many previously known breeding haunts, like Bodmin Moor.

"We believe these contractions in its breeding range, especially in the Southern Pennines, the Southern Uplands, the Grampians, and the Western Highlands, and the possible disappearance of ring ouzels from Northern Ireland, mask a much more severe decline."

One of the country's least known songbirds, there were still elements of its behaviour that were not clearly understood, she added.

One poser was why ring ouzels had always seemed to disappear for a few weeks in late summer before the birds began their autumn migration to North Africa.

A UNIVERSITY RESEARCHER has come up with an idea to scale down fish farm cages by making the fish themselves behave more like homing pigeons.

The proposition by postgraduate student Jonathan Lovell involves sending out signals from a special underwater microphone which attract fish for feeding.

Species such as cod and whiting could also be trained to respond, he believes, after he conducted a series of experiments on fish in a Plymouth reservoir.

The 30 'trained' fish had learnt to respond to computer created mating sounds or feeding noises.

With the microphone helping the fish come volun - tarily to feeding points, there could be less need for cage systems currently employed by salmon farms, Jonathan says.

As well as attracting fish, the part-time lecturer believes the underwater microphone could be deployed to deter unwelcome species such as marauding sharks.

JUST TATTOO MUCH is how many farmers feel about a new EU-inspired directive that will force them to tattoo their sheep.

The bill for identifying the country's 44 million sheep is likely to top £6million but is a move that the EU has demanded so that no individual animal is anonymous in the system.

The Government has bowed to pressure from Brussels in passing on the order which has outraged sheep farmers, many with little or no spare funds left to pay for the work.

Under proposals announced by Agriculture Minister Nick Brown, each sheep will either be tattooed on its head or have a tag attached to its ear.

The Tory Opposition has already attacked the scheme as a waste of time, amounting to yet more bureaucratic bungling which will further pressure farmers.

Supporters of the plan say it will help trace outbreaks of disease back to the farm where affected sheep originate from.

Farmers who choose not to comply could be fined thousands of pounds.

ACTRESS JOANNA LUMLEY has been spearheading the launch of a new anti-cruelty film in a bid to get live exports of sheep to the Continent banned.

The film 'Some Lie Dying' draws together 18 months of undercover work by Compassion in World Farming investigators and was shown at the House of Commons.

The TV star called for an urgent end to live exports after the disturbing film showed the suffering of exported sheep.

Joanna, who was joined in her plea by Dover MP Gwyn Prosser, asked if the country really wanted to see its sheep and lambs being sent on long cruel journeys to continental abattoirs.

A CIWF spokesman said:"This Easter, lambs are being born on to hills and green fields throughout the country. From July onwards, as they reach slaughter weight, over a million will be exported for slaughter abroad.

"Many of the animals exported from Britain are sent on journeys of 40 or 50 hours or more to Italy, Greece and Spain, where often they are killed in abattoirs using cruel and illegal slaughter methods.

"The current law that is meant to protect animals being transported on the continent is the 1995 EU Transport Directive. When it was agreed, it was hailed by EU govern- ments, including our own, as a law that would end the suffering inflicted on animals by long journeys."

That law was patently not working, as the film showed.

"By the time they get to southern Europe many British lambs are in a heart-rending condition. They are exhausted, dehydrated and stressed. Some are injured, while others have collapsed. In the worst cases, many die."

SOPHISTICATED WEATHER MAPPING tech- nology has been used by scientists to explain the facts behind one of the most serious air pollution episodes to hit Britain in recent years.

During the incident, in September 1998, sulphur dioxide rose high above acceptable levels across a large part of the Midlands and South Yorkshire.

"The report shows that unusual weather condi- tions allowed sulphur dioxide to accumulate and create a band of pollution which moved in a south westerly direction, affecting parts of Yorkshire, Nottinghamshire, Derbyshire, Leicestershire, Staffordshire and the West Midlands," explained a spokesman for the Environment Agency.

"Peak sulphur dioxide concentrations up to six and a half times higher than the air quality standard were recorded for the period."

This was high enough for people to fall ill, particularly the already weak or vulnerable.

THE NEWLY LAUNCHED Food Standards Agency will play a major role in reassuring consumers about how safe their food is to eat, claim farmers' leaders.

The Agency's proposed early review of the Meat Hygiene Service was already good news, according to the National Farmers' Union.

NFU president Ben Gill said: "We welcome the decision by the FSA to look closely at not only the protection offered by the MHS but whether it is working in the most efficient way possible, and whether there is an opportunity to make changes that would bring about cost savings which would benefit our farmers."

The FSA has set a target to continue the reduction of salmonella in poultry cases by a further 50 per cent over the next five years.

Mr Gill revealed: "UK farmers are working relentlessly to eliminate salmonella in poultry. We welcome the opportunity to work with the FSA to ensure we can achieve this in the shortest time scale."

He also called on the FSA to honour its commitment to put imported food under equal scrutiny, saying it was vital that a level playing field on food safety standards was achieved to ensure consumer confidence in the food chain.

Mr Gill concluded: "The FSA will provide an independent body set up purely to offer indepen- dent, expert advice to consumers on the food they eat in the most open way. This has to be welcome in bringing much-needed balance to the debate."

GIN DRINKERS CAN toast a move by The Woodland Trust to safeguard a remaining stronghold of the juniper tree whose berries help produce the tipple.

The conifer is on the decline in Britain despite being part of the landscape for the last 10,000 years.

Thwaitestones Wood, a 37-acre site in North Yorkshire, has been boosted by £20,000 from the Forestry Commission so the Trust can put in place measures that will benefit the juniper.

Boundaries will be built to help protect smaller bushes from grazing by sheep and rabbits while berries are collected for planting in local nurseries. Resulting saplings will then be planted back in the woodland.

Heather Swift, northern regional manager for the Woodland Trust, said: "Juniper is a very distinctive plant. It is one of Britain's few native conifers and it only grows in remote upland areas.

"Our main concern is that it is not regenerating naturally and so is in danger of dying out forever. We haven't seen young new plants for about 10 years."

SNOWDONIA NATIONAL PARK chiefs are eager to see more than 465 acres of new native woodland after winning £400,000 of Government cash.

Chris Smith, forestry and woodlands officer for the park, said: "This is a real boost towards increasing native woodland coverage."

The cash has been allocated to a wide range of landowners.

Among successful applicants were Chris and Maryclare Davies, of Rhiw Goch, Penrhyndeu- draeth, who said: "We welcome the opportunity to return the hillside to its ancient wood status and provide a pleasant recreational extension for the local community and visitors alike."

MORALE AMONG RURAL police in Norfolk has been severely dented by public outrage over the jailing of farmer Tony Martin, it has been claimed.

Officers have been stung by ferocious criticism since a life sentence was handed to the 55 year-old farmer after he shot dead a teenage burglar at his ramshackle farm.

The Chief Constable of Norfolk fears morale among his force may never properly recover as a result of the national outcry over the case from all sections of society.

Ken Williams claims staff have been subjected to "grossly offensive and vulgar" telephone calls from members of the public making unfair accusations.

Meanwhile, to tens of thousands of people, the case appears to have become a symbol of everything that is rotten about the current justice system which often seems to favour the criminal over the victim.

During a week of escalating interest in the plight of the farmer - which saw one national newspaper attract 250,000 pledges of support for him - Tory leader William Hague sparked a political row by promising to change the law if he came to power.

From his prison cell where he is beginning a life-term, Martin himself told another newspaper:"I did not commit murder. I only did what anyone else would have done in the same circumstances.

"I was just trying to defend myself and my property. I am very moved by the support there has been for me from so many quarters.

"In the end, I believe it will be that public pressure which will win me justice and freedom."

THE VAST MAJORITY of Scottish people want their new Parliament to tackle rural issues such as poverty and the farming slump - not foxhunting.

In fact, only one per cent are interested in the fox-hunting debate, according to an independent survey welcomed by the Scottish Countryside Alliance.

Allan Murray, director of the Alliance in Scotland, said:"The Scottish people, in both town and country alike, want the Scottish Parliament to concentrate on real issues such as rural poverty and unemployment.

"Why should parliamentary time be wasted on a Bill that does nothing to address these?"

The survey also revealed that the majority of those questioned believed a foxhunting ban would have a detrimental effect on the rural economy.

THE HEADACHE OF tangled land tax problems could be soothed away by attendance at a rural tax planning conference now being organised for June.

Adrian Baird, chief taxation adviser to the Coun - try Landowners Association, is leading the 17th successive annual IBC conference on the theme 'Taxation of Agricultural and Rural Land'.

A LOCAL COUNCIL is in a flap over ducks and appealing for help to reduce numbers on an overcrowded pond.

So many ducks now inhabit the pond at Saffron Walden that hot-tempered drakes are killing ducklings, according to Uttlesford District Council leader Robert Chambers.

Other ducks were killed by cars as they spilled out onto a nearby car park so the public are being asked to step in.

Councillor Chambers wants duck lovers to bag ducks and take them to new homes far enough away that they will not fly back.

It is hoped that the pond will then return to being the peaceful wildlife haven it once was.

Anyone who wants to offer any of the ducks a new home should contact Councillor Chambers.

FARMERS' LEADERS WENT on a fact-finding tour of one of the country's most important agricultur - al hotspots - New Covent Garden Market in London.

NFU president Ben Gill and the delegation met traders at the 56-acre site where 300 stallholders have an annual turnover of more than £330m a year.

Mr Gill said: "New Covent Garden is an extremely valuable outlet for this country's smaller scale, high quality producers. It has a huge reputation for meeting this country's needs for fresh produce and provides an important gateway to London's leading restaurant sector.

"The tour looked at ways in which growers can boost sales for British produce and more effectively match demand by building effective supply relation - ships with traders on the shop floor."

Market authority chairman Leif Mills added: "The market has provided a reliable service to the nation's growers and producers for hundreds of years, in both hard times and good."

NEW SEASIDE HOMES could be at risk from flooding if a development company fails to heed advice, claims the Environment Agency.

In an unusual move, the Agency has openly expressed "grave concern" about the stance taken by the Sovereign Harbour Company over properties in Eastbourne.

"The Harbour Company undertook to move shingle around the harbour to maintain the beach to the east," explained an Agency spokesman.

"Despite pressure from the Agency, the company has not done this. Consequently, the foreshore has been eroded away by the waves and the land behind it is at risk."

The Agency had expressed concern about the East Sussex site several times.

"The defences still remain inadequate. Yet the Harbour Company is part of a group developing the coastal strategies," said the spokesman.

"Flooding of the area was only narrowly avoided last autumn by emergency works from the Harbour Company bolstering up the existing thin shingle bank. The present defences remain inadequate to protect a development projected to grow to over 2,500 dwellings, let alone the other low lying land.

"The Agency wishes to see a vibrant East-bourne but adequate sea defences must be provided by the developers so that the safety of the community can be assured."

Sovereign Harbour Company has pointed to previous agreements reached with the Agency about how the area would be strengthened.

FOX: hunt gives pause for thought as death comes slowly

FOXES are now so common in some of our cities that they can be spotted in broad daylight trotting along railway lines or relaxing in quiet gardens.

Urban foxes appear to have had little trouble adapting to much noisier, busier surroundings than those enjoyed by their rural cousins.

In fact, with generous portions of rich food provided regularly by city residents, it is not surprising some urban foxes can become pests.

Foxes are superb animals and we would be much poorer without them. However, I don't think I am unique in holding that view while also supporting foxhunting - with one or two reservations.

I have never hunted myself or been a member of any clubs that do. Despite the hunt ban, I still occasionally enjoy mingling with my local hunt during its Boxing Day "meets" outside a pub, admiring the horses and hounds, marvelling at the sheer spectacle on a freezing winter's day.

Nevertheless, I was always opposed to some aspects of hunting, largely because of an experience I'll come to.

My philosophy - naive and simplistic to many, no doubt - was that a fox should only be pursued above ground.

Then it could be caught and dispatched in seconds by the hounds.

What I never liked was digging out a fox safe in its hole or baiting it to death underground with a team of terriers.

Hardly fair, or sporting.

I remember once being out for a walk and coming across a knot of hunt followers on top of a hill.

As we talked, the hounds were being put to work sweeping through the valley below us.

One jolly, ruddy-cheeked individual - I think he said he was a lawyer - suddenly broke off, cupped his hands to his mouth, and began whooping like a man possessed.

The reason for this quickly became apparent. A big dog fox had been put up by the hounds from a tangle of bushes and was powering up the hill towards us.

The sudden hollering turned him back and sent him across a brook running parallel to the bottom of the hill.

By now the hounds had sighted the fox and were screaming with excitement, a curious sound.

From our vantage point on top of the hill we had a perfect view of the fox as he tore across the fields on the other side of the brook.

He was heroic in his determination to escape while the hounds were magnificent in their pursuit.

This happened to be a hunt on foot, without horses, so no riders careered into view to complicate the pulse-quickening scene.

By doing a large 'U' turn and snaking through a few dense hedgerows, the fox managed to shake off the hounds and leave them floundering.

I for one felt like cheering as he made it to safety in a dense patch of woodland. Except he wasn't safe. Not by a long shot.

Fifteen minutes later, myself and those hunt supporters - who had seemed to 'adopt' me - arrived at the site in the woods where the fox had gone to ground.

On one side, the frustrated hounds had been corralled by a whip man while the terrier men went to work.

Four vicious terriers were sent down the hole where the fox waited, trapped.

Someone said, rather too gleefully for my liking, that the hole led to a small underground stream but recent rain had swollen the stream and cut off any escape route there.

Meanwhile, two men with spades tried to dig down to the fox from above.

The drama dragged on and on.

Each terrier returned with its muzzle bloodied and torn but was sent back down again regardless.

Eventually, the muffled barks and shrieks of pain underground began to peter out.

For me at least, the thrill of the chase had long since evaporated but I still could not drag myself away.

If anything, the others were even keener to witness the inevitable outcome.

With a sense of growing unease, I noticed several children among them.

Then nothing. No more subterranean barks. All the terriers exhausted but unable to drag out the fox.

The huntsmen and their followers grew almost silent.

At last the two men digging reached the fox. One grabbed its tail and yanked it out.

It was dead all right. Drowned. Rather than face any more torment from the terriers it had pushed itself too far into the water so it could no longer breathe.

The bedraggled corpse was tossed to the hounds who broke it up in moments.

I walked away in a daze, feeling wretched.

POLICE ARE PROBING the death of one of the country's most threatened birds of prey which appears to have been blasted from the sky.

RSPB officials are also involved after the lifeless hen harrier was spotted on open land.

The female harrier's body was later recovered by the RSPB from land close to the society's Geltsdale nature reserve on the Cumbria/Northumberland border.

Officers from Cumbria Police are investigating reports that two men were seen carrying firearms in the vicinity before the harrier was killed.

Graham Elliott, RSPB head of investigations, said:"We are alarmed by this discovery and outraged that people may still be killing birds of prey illegally.

"There are only 12 nesting female hen harriers in England so the death of this one female is a major blow to the English population.

"It is particularly sad because this bird is likely to have had a nest and may have reared chicks successfully."

The RSPB says its reserve at Geltsdale is one of only two regular breeding sites in England for hen harriers.

Hen harriers were once widespread throughout the UK but the 19th Century saw them virtually eliminated from mainland Britain.

In the early part of the 20th Century the population only survived on Orkney and the Western Isles.

However, the population increased again from the 1940s onwards, spreading back to the mainland and often taking advantage of new forestry plantations or heather moorland.

Hen harriers have been blamed for reducing grouse numbers and have sometimes been persecuted by farmers and gamekeepers.

A COLONY OF BATS is poised to flutter onto the first rung of the property ladder after their very own des' res' was built for them on an exclusive estate.

The lesser horseshoe bats faced being homeless after their present roost on the site of a former Gloucester hospital was condemned to help make way for more than 30 new homes.

But the Gloucester Bat Group quickly stepped in and a wildlife expert designed a purpose built £40,000 bungalow which will nestle among all the other luxury homes.

Up to 50 bats are expected to use the 12-metre bungalow initially but numbers may grow to 200.

The bat bungalow will be monitored and looked after by The Vincent Wildlife Trust.

A spokesman said: "It is not usual for a roost to be incorporated into a development. We will make sure it remains secure and peaceful for the bats."

STUPID AND MISGUIDED were just two of the criticisms levelled at the Countryside Agency's recent report on rural life in a damning indictment by the Countryside Alliance.

The Alliance slammed the report from Countryside Agency as a "revisionist" view of rural life which distorted or downplayed the real issues.

Chief executive Richard Burge said that any 60-page report on "the state of the countryside" which devoted just 23 lines to the problems of rural crime and policing whilst devoting three whole pages to recreational access for visitors, either showed an absurdly misguided sense of rural priorities or the hand of Government interference in its drafting.

He also ridiculed as "fatuous and politically-motivated" the report's complete omission, from its analysis of the cultural and recreational life in the countryside, all mention of country sports including fishing - which was the biggest recreational pursuit in the country - as well as major recreational activities such as country and agricultural shows.

"The few sensible things in this report," Mr Burge added, "such as its focus on the problems of poverty and social exclusion in rural areas, have been spoiled by its disingenuously distorted take on how the countryside actually operates and how its people really live."

CORNWALL HAS HOSTED the start of the British 'early potato' season which will see 300,000 tonnes eventually harvested across the country.

The early, or new, potato is "one of the most looked forward to arrivals on the culinary calendar, with 86 per cent of people aware of the start of the season," according to a survey by the British Potato Council.

The National Farmers Union has joined forces with the BPC to raise awareness of this "best-loved and most versatile vegetable."

NFU vice-president Richard Watson Jones, a potato grower himself from Shropshire, said: "There are few foods we look forward to more than the arrival of the new potato.

"Piping hot early potatoes, drizzled with butter and topped with a sprig of mint offer the first real taste of British summertime."

Recipe cards offering details of how early potatoes can be incorporated into a variety of dishes will be made available.

'RATTY' THE WATER vole has taken an especially strong liking to Lincolnshire - although no-one seems to know why.

The county has remained a stronghold of the rodent made famous in 'The Wind In The Willows' while numbers elsewhere in Britain have plummeted to worrying lows.

The animal's liking for Lincolnshire emerged after a conference was organised by the Environment Agency aimed at helping it to continue to thrive there.

"While nationally the water vole has experienced a steep decline, water voles in Lincolnshire remain relatively abundant," confirmed an Agency spokesman.

"To help maintain this healthy population, an action plan for protecting water voles in Lincolnshire is due to be published."

Favourite habitats would be enhanced.

THE CAMPAIGN FOR safer rural roads has stepped up a gear with a new crusade by the Council for the Protection of Rural England and other groups.

Launched during UN Road Safety Week, the CPRE asserted that "new quiet lanes" should be given the green light across the country.

The international safety week focused on the needs of vulnerable road users such as walkers, cyclists and horse riders and coincided with local elections across England.

Paul Hamblin, CPRE's head of transport, said:"For too long the needs of the motorist on country lanes have been paramount. Quiet lanes recognise that minor rural roads should be available to be used by everybody - those on foot, bike, and horse, as well as in vehicles - without fear of intimidation from traffic.

"A few forward-looking authorities like Norfolk, Kent, Devon and Surrey are promoting quiet lanes but many more need to follow.

"Across the country, councillors will shortly be approving their five-year Local Transport Plans. These provide real opportunities to deliver new freedoms to those who have been driven off the road.

"Any prospective councillor who supports more walking and cycling, safer roads and improved quality of life, should be supporting the widespread introduction of quiet lanes. Does yours?"

The House of Commons was also due to debate the Government's Transport Bill, he added.

The CPRE - with support from Transport 2000, the Children's Play Council, the Local Government Association and 120 back-bench Labour MPs - was supporting an amendment to the Bill which would give new powers to local authorities to designate quiet lanes.

This would give legal protection to walkers, cyclists and horse riders.

SCRAPPING CHARGES TO farmers for dairy hygiene inspections has come a step closer thanks to the Food Standards Agency.

Farmers' leaders have welcomed the speed at which the Agency has acted to move forward plans to drop the charges.

Tim Bennett, NFU deputy president, said: "It is extremely encouraging that the consultation to enable the necessary legislative changes to be made has taken place so swiftly.

"What is more important, though, is that the final removal of the charges takes place with urgency - this will be a boost to the hard-pressed dairy sector."

The NFU also wanted the inspection regime itself streamlined.

DAZZLING DISPLAYS OF bluebells have been packaged into a helpful guide by The Woodland Trust, enabling fans to travel from one blooming site to another across the country.

Woods in England, Scotland, and Wales - where the best displays are expected - have been compiled into an online list by the Trust complete with individual map references for easy location.

"The British climate is perfect for bluebells," said a Trust spokesman. "They are particularly fond of old broadleaved woodlands where they can flower in the spring before the tree leaves block out most of the sunlight.

"However, the variety most often grown in gardens is a foreigner, the Spanish bluebell, which has flowers growing all round the stalk, rather than the classic lopsided British look.

"In many woods these days, hybrids of the British and Spanish varieties can be seen.

"The bluebell is also sometimes called the wild hyacinth and in some areas the name "bluebell" is given to the harebell, which has more bulbous bell-shaped flowers."

AN ELDERLY SHETLAND pony appears to have taken a 'toy boy lover' to produce a foal at the grand old age of 35 - more than a century in human years.

Peggy Blue became secretly pregnant after apparently enjoying a tryst with a pony aged just 12 months old which was put out to graze in a nearby field nearly a year ago.

As she quietly walked around her own field near Stockport, no-one suspected that Peggy Blue had more things on her mind than where her next lunch was coming from.

Producing the foal has left her owner George Mathers shocked but delighted - especially as he had been trying to mate her for three decades without success.

He explained that Peggy Blue did produce a single foal when still young but then lost all interest - until her mating instincts were patently reawakened by the much younger horse, Trigger.

Horse experts say they have never previously heard of a Shetland pony giving birth at such a late stage.

AN AROMATHERAPY MASSAGE was among treats lined up by footballing legend Jack Charlton to raise much-needed cash for the Game Conservancy Trust.

However, macho Jack has no plans to administer any scented treatments himself - the gentle pummelling was just one of the lots at an auction he agreed to host for the Trust.

Other lots to go under the hammer included a spot of salmon fishing and loan of a top-of-the-range Range Rover for a weekend.

'An Evening With Jack Charlton' at a Scottish hotel also promised 'tall tales' from the soccer giant whose real passion has always been fishing and outdoor pursuits.

Wine and a finger buffet were included in tickets for the night at the Craigmonie Hotel, Inverness.

CANAL BOAT USERS are being kept on the straight and narrow by the Environment Agency in Wales with a new scheme to cut pollution.

Working in partnership with the Shropshire Union Canal Society, the Agency is offering special oil absorbent pads to combat accidental oil spills.

35

LABOUR'S CLAIM THAT it cares about the countryside has suffered another major blow with most people agreeing country dwellers get a raw deal, according to a survey.

BBC Radio 4's Today programme and Country Life magazine commissioned the survey which saw 2,000 people canvassed for their views in both town and country.

Surprisingly, even the 'townies' felt that their rural neighbours were being treated unfairly by the present Government.

Some 61 per cent of people questioned believed the Government had got its stance on the countryside wrong and was misjudging the situation.

According to ICM Research, which conducted the poll, there was virtually no difference in replies from people who lived in towns compared to those who lived in the country.

This was thought to suggest that townsfolk cared just as much about the countryside - and were equally upset at Government meddling.

Just 27 per cent of people canvassed believed the Government genuinely understood the problems facing rural Britain.

Even more worrying for Labour, twice as many people think rural life has deteriorated rather than improved under its stewardship since Tony Blair came to power.

The findings are the latest shock for the party which has received unprecedented criticism from rural groups.

Huge Conservative gains during recent local elections were believed to be partly due to fears that the countryside is at greater risk under Labour.

FIVE RUNAWAY PEACOCKS have ruffled feathers among villagers enduring sleepless nights because of their twilight screeches.

The two males and three females quickly became the bane of residents' lives in Halberton, Devon, after arriving there out of the blue.

The gang apparently went on the run after pecking their way free of containers transporting them from an old people's home.

Recently, their screeches have been getting worse but a saviour may have arrived in the form of peacock expert Ian Sanders.

Mr Sanders, who keeps seven of the birds himself, has offered to catch the pesky peacocks and help send villagers back to the land of Nod.

TAKING A DIP in British coastal waters should be even safer this summer after the Environment Agency increased its number of pollution checks to safeguard health.

The Agency has been busy running checks on a record 481 sites across England and Wales for this year's bathing season.

THE COUNTRYSIDE IS fast becoming a more dangerous place to live because of cutbacks in rural police services, according to the Police Federation.

The peaceful image of living in remote countryside could be a risky illusion as vast areas go un-policed and residents are left at the mercy of burglars and other criminals, the Federation's conference in Brighton heard.

Lenient judges and soft ministers were blamed for allowing the shocking rise in rural crime which, in many places, has outstripped police officers' ability to cope.

John Harrison, spokesman for the sergeants' division of the Federation, said:"England's green and pleasant land might be pretty but it certainly is not peaceful any more."

He said the controversial jailing of farmer Tony Martin for killing a burglar had focused attention on the problem in a way no previous cases had.

"Tony Martin isn't a hero," he said."He isn't a martyr either. But up to the point where he fired the fatal shot, he was the victim. His home had been invaded. There was no prospect of the forces of law and order coming to his immediate assistance."

The public were rightly furious that the three crooks who came to burgle his property in the night had racked up over 150 previous convictions between them.

"The contrast between the sentence passed on the victim and the absurd leniency shown time and time again to those who attacked his home, sticks in our throats."

The fault often lay with Government which passed laws that helped criminals, such as by always allowing them bail despite their records, added Mr Harrison.

A DOG CHASING rabbits startled nudists sunning themselves on a secluded beach when it dropped in on them from 200ft.

The dog clattered down the cliff face in East Sussex after chasing a rabbit along the edge then overbalancing and plummeting to earth.

Nudists at the beach near Hastings were shocked by the incident which nevertheless left the animal suffering only minor injuries.

The dog's dramatic fall comes just weeks after a similar incident occurred further along the South Coast on the Isle of Wight.

Back then, Smiler the greyhound fell more than 140ft off a cliff but came to rest on a tiny ledge 200ft from the ground.

The exhausted ex-racing greyhound was rescued after originally being given up for dead.

DAIRY, BEEF AND sheep farmer Les Armstrong is undertaking a fact-finding tour of the South West to see other farmers' problems first hand.

Mr Armstrong, NFU Livestock Committee chairman, plans to meet farmers at Winsford livestock market near Bristol to listen to their own 'beefs' about the industry during a busy schedule.

He was also due to attend a beef and sheep strategy meeting jointly organised by the NFU and the MLC at Exeter Market.

Mr Armstrong, from Cumbria, said: "There are a vast number of issues that the NFU is tackling on behalf of the livestock sector. We also remain committed to a red tape review."

ANGLERS AND SHOOTERS have triumphed over what many people saw as a back-door bid to spoil their country sports.

Shooting and fishing have won protection after an attempt to extend the right to roam to riversides and woodlands was withdrawn.

Labour MP Gordon Prentice had promoted a new clause to the Countryside and Rights of Way Bill which would have extended access 'by order' to riversides and woodlands in England and Wales.

The Countryside Alliance explained: "Having alerted the angling and shooting communities to this threat and having detailed the problems posed by the amendment, the Alliance briefed MPs on the damage this proposal could cause to wildlife, sporting interests and the consequent knock-on effect for rural economies.

"A full cross-party debate was held, during which many MPs spoke against the proposal. Environment Minister Michael Meacher asked for the clause to be withdrawn on the grounds that the statutory agencies had deemed such an extension inappropriate."

Richard Burge, chief executive of the Alliance, added: "The extension of access to watersides would have damaged some of our most sensitive habitats and would have jeopardised the sport of over 3.4 million anglers as well as the legitimate interests of the shooting community.

"This decision will enable shooters to continue the practice of wildfowling - which has always been well regulated and, above all, a safe pursuit.

"We would far rather increase access voluntarily than by force.

"We have worked hard to highlight the serious shortcomings and lack of justification for this amendment and are delighted that common sense has prevailed."

A FLEEING COW caused consternation when it crashed through the window of a shoe shop after escaping from a cattle market in North Wales.

The runaway heifer initially wandered into the shop in Mold then panicked and decided to escape by jumping through the window - much to the dismay of staff and customers.

Some customers were terrified by the drama, according to the shop's manageress Joyce Simpson, who said that her premises were left a real mess with glass and hoof marks everywhere.

The heifer, which was later recaptured and sold at market, is thought to have become upset while standing in its trailer and made a break for freedom.

A parked car was also damaged but the animal itself sustained only minor cuts.

POOLS OF BLOOD found near a public footpath may at first have seemed like the leftovers from a vampires' convention.

But the grisly discovery which led to a full investigation and closure of the footpath at Red Ball, Devon, turned out to have a more mundane cause - leaving a company facing fines and costs of over £19,000.

Environment Agency officers called to the scene found "bloody waste" spread on a field, prompting a foul smell and allowing large amounts of blood to collect in pools.

"Bloody waste had pooled next to a public footpath. Other pools of blood were observed across the field, one very close to a pen housing livestock," said an Agency spokesman.

"The investigation revealed that the amount used was in excess of that which was necessary for agricultural benefit and had not been properly incorporated into the soil."

A Cheshire-based firm admitted depositing controlled waste on land where a licence authorising such a deposit was not in force, and pleaded guilty to disposing of controlled waste in a manner likely to cause pollution or harm to human health.

ONE OF BRITAIN'S rarest seabirds - the roseate tern - has been given a boost with the formation of a new human partnership aimed at improving its fortunes.

Northumbrian Water Environmental Trust is supporting RSPB work to safeguard the tern at its stronghold on Coquet Island in Northumberland.

The Trust will donate £54,000 to the RSPB to help finance an action plan for the tern - a vital part of which includes protecting its nesting colony on the island.

More financial backing for the project will come from TXU Europe Power, a long-term supporter of the Society, to take the cash available over £60,000.

"Coquet Island is located one mile off-shore from Amble on the Northumberland coast, and its lighthouse is a familiar coastal landmark," said a spokesman.

"The 14-acre island is owned by the Duke of Northumberland and managed by the RSPB."

FIVE SMELLY SHEEP pelts formed a key exhibit in a theft case against a family of three heard before Gloucester magistrates.

The magistrates were forced to inspect the defrosted skins one by one after they were laid out before them.

The trio were looking for markings on the pelts which would identify which farm they came from - a crucial part of the case but not the sweetest of tasks.

Each of the skins had been seized a year ago following a raid by trading standards officers at local premises.

In the end, despite the pelts being initially frozen and carefully handled, the markings were found not to be clear enough to support prosecution claims against the accused family.

The magistrates quickly delivered not guilty verdicts and the pungent pelts were removed.

MILK PRODUCERS ARE being invited to band together for extra strength in a newly-formed body called the Federation of Milk Groups.

It is hoped the companies will then be better able to face up to increasing financial pressures.

FARMERS' LEADERS WANT to see a crackdown on crime in rural areas following the controversial jailing of farmer Tony Martin for murder.

NFU president Ben Gill has called for better policing and security for people living and working in the countryside.

Mr Gill said: "There is a growing feeling of helplessness in rural communities - stemming from the inability of the legal system to deliver successful prosecutions.

"Without appropriate resources for police forces to cover these rural areas, many more farmers may be subjected to vandalism and mindless crime."

Recent cases such as that involving farmer Tony Martin had highlighted the way the legal system was unable to provide adequate policing and security, said Mr Gill.

He added: "Rural crime and the damage and threats caused by environmental activists and eco-warriors all too often seem to be uncontrollable. This cannot be allowed to continue any longer.

"There is a real and growing feeling in rural areas that the law works against the law abiding citizen and in favour of those who choose to behave as if the law did not exist."

THE STEEP DECLINE in numbers of the once common house sparrow has prompted a new survey to try to track down nesting birds.

The study, launched jointly by the RSPB and BBC, comes as fears increase for the perky little bird once taken for granted as a mainstay of British bird populations.

The RSPB says sparrow numbers were previously found to have fallen by "a staggering 64 per cent", a figure which involved an estimated loss of 9.6 million birds, particularly from farmland.

"Some anecdotal evidence suggests that there are now fewer sparrows in villages and towns," said an RSPB spokesman.

"The latest results of the Big Garden Bird-watch show there was an average of only four sparrows seen per garden, compared to a figure of eight in 1990.

"The RSPB is urging young people, their families and friends to look for their neighbourhood house sparrows, and to report the number and location of any nests seen."

COUNTRY TRIALS OF experimental GM crops have edged closer to chaos after it was revealed millions of British people may have unwittingly eaten food contaminated by genetically modified seeds.

The revelation saw the Government fiercely attacked by green campaigners who labelled the mistake "an environmental catastrophe".

The Ministry of Agriculture has admitted that hundreds of farms across the UK grew imported oilseed rape which included some batches of genetically modified seeds.

Oil from this crop has now apparently entered the food chain and been used in a variety of foods.

SCOTLAND IS THE latest battleground where country lovers are being recruited to help fight killer tree diseases.

Forestry Commission scientists are appealing for anyone with an interest in the Scottish countryside to help track down two diseases threatening local alder trees.

Ten per cent of riverside alders in England and Wales are now known to be dead or dying from a disease caused by a species of the Phytophthora fungus.

Alders in parts of Scotland are also affected by Phytophthora - and another condition known as 'crown dieback', the cause of which is unknown.

"However, our knowledge of the extent of these problems in Scotland is still incomplete. For that reason we want people who are out and about in the countryside this summer to tell us if they think they have come across any cases of Phytophthora disease or dieback," said Dr Steven Hendry, a pathologist with the Commission's Forest Research agency.

"We believe that many people who enjoy the countryside, such as anglers, ramblers and country sports enthusiasts, can be very helpful, because many of them are also good amateur naturalists."

Phytophthora disease is caused by a fungus that infects the roots of the tree and kills off the bark at the base of its stem. The dying bark produces a tarry or rusty fluid that oozes out to form spots on the trunk.

The first symptoms of crown dieback are the presence of dead and dying leaves or leafless twigs in the tree's crown during the summer.

LEAKED FINDINGS FROM the Government commissioned inquiry into foxhunting apparently suggest a downplaying of hunted foxes' pain.

If true, the conclusions from the Burns inquiry will dismay anti-hunt campaigners but cheer supporters who have long said foxes suffer minimum trauma until the final seconds.

The opinion of the committee headed by Lord Burns is said to be that there is no pressing evidence that foxes suffer fear and pain when pursued by hounds.

Confusingly, other aspects of the committee's investigation do appear to come down on the anti-hunt campaigners' side.

Overall, the apparent lack of a definite viewpoint is thought to make it less likely that new laws outlawing foxhunting will be passed in the short-term - at least not before the next election.

However, anti-hunt MPs are said to be ready to press on with plans for a Bill aimed at making fox-hunting illegal when the inquiry report is published.

A QUARTER OF Scotland may be covered in woodland by 2054, says Scottish Forestry Minister John Home Robertson.

The Minister made the claim during the annual dinner of the Royal Scottish Forestry Society at Crieff Hydro, where he also launched a website promoting the famous trees of Perthshire.

He recalled that a number of years ago the Society had called for a doubling of the area of Scotland "under some form of tree cover" to 25 per cent of the land area.

"I suspect we may well achieve this by your Society's bicentenary in the year 2054," he said.

HEDGEHOG: shy visitor with a taste for chip shop

WHEN it comes to violent yobs wanting to inflict grievous bodily harm on small, defenceless animals, the humble hedgehog is a pricklier proposition than most.

With about 5,000 spines to protect it and the amazing ability to curl itself into a ball, it stands a better than average chance of surviving the attentions of a marauding human.

I was quite cheered to read in a recent court case that a hedgehog had been left apparently unscathed after two idiots kicked it around for their own cruel amusement.

The spines cushioning the impact of those kicks are actually hairs which have evolved into defensive spikes, growing to about an inch in length and dropping out annually to be replaced by new ones.

In the wild, foxes and badgers don't have much of a problem preying on young hedgehogs whose spines are not so tough and whose muscles for curling into a ball are not fully developed.

An adult hedgehog is more difficult to tackle but is not totally safe against a badger's powerful claws or the teeth of a sly fox who drops it into water and waits for it to uncurl before launching an attack on its underside.

There's something about hedgehogs that makes them quite appealing to most of us. Perhaps it's because they have short, stubby legs and a rather clumsy, almost comical, way of getting about.

If you ever spot one in the garden, it will probably be rooting about for slugs and snails.

Birds' eggs are another favourite food, when it can reach them.

Thomas Hardy obviously realised you were most likely to see hedgehogs in the summer months when he wrote:"*Some nocturnal blackness, mothy and warm, when the hedgehog travels furtively over the lawn.*"

I saw one a few months ago as I drove down a winding, high hedge-flanked road at about 8pm.

I easily managed to avoid it since it was trundling along the gutter.

Yet I couldn't help but wince at its vulnerability in that environment, spines or not.

The flattened corpses of hedgehogs on our roads have become so numerous that car companies even joke about them in their TV adverts.

At one time, a well-known crisp company even offered '*hedgehog crisps*' - not flavoured by hedgehogs at all but withdrawn when the intended joke misfired.

I used to live at a house where a family of hedgehogs visited the patio each night and the big patio windows allowed perfect close-up viewing.

Back then I experimented with a wide variety of tempting fayre, including cat food, which is supposed to put hedgehogs in Hedgehog Heaven.

For some unknown reason, my visitors rather turned their pointy little noses up at this.

But they went potty for something else - the batter off cod bought from the local fish and chip shop.

They tore into this delicacy like demons, actually snorting, raising their spines, and challenging each other to 'bump-bump' fights in their efforts to snap up the smallest scraps.

So entertaining was this behaviour that for a while I put out the batter off my cod quite regularly.

The biggest of the group took to pouncing on the largest piece and dragging it whole towards the bushes.

Unfortunately, cod without batter lacks a certain something, and even the spectacle of a hedgehog struggling across the lawn with what looked like a giant hedgehog duvet was not enough to prolong this food source indefinitely.

Later in the year, when temperatures had dropped and the first frosts had decimated plants and flowers, I was shocked to see three puny juvenile hedgehogs wandering miserably around the garden.

There was no doubt what lay in store for them with insufficient fat stores to hibernate and little natural food left.

So I jumped up and found a bucket, aiming to capture them and rear them in the garage. Sadly, by the time I got outside, they'd vanished.

A day or so later, heavy snow fell. I never saw them again.

NEW FEARS HAVE been raised over contamination of British fields by GM seeds - this time involving maize.

With the confidence of farmers and the public at an all-time low in Government GM trials following the previous contaminated seeds blunder, the latest revelation seems certain to heap further scorn on the whole scientific enterprise.

According to claims from green campaigners, the European Seeds Assocation - which represents EU seed distributors - has information that as much as one per cent of the entire EU maize crop could be tainted.

While ESA itself has not confirmed the claims, it has agreed that it cannot guarantee that the maize is not contaminated. Nor could it say whether any contaminated crops were likely to have entered the food chain by now.

Recently, Friends of the Earth praised the actions of farmer John Sanderson in publicly ripping out 25 acres of GM tainted oilseed rape at his Suffolk farm.

Mr Sanderson was among 600 farmers facing up to the nightmare that they had been sold oilseed rape seeds contaminated by GM seeds.

FoE Real Food campaigner Pete Riley said:"This is a brave action by an individual farmer facing company pressure and Government indifference. But it is a disgrace that farmers have been put in this position.

"The Government has a duty to see that all the contaminated crops are removed from the ground at once, and that farmers are properly compensated for any losses they suffer.

"We have repeatedly warned the Government that the issue of liability for damage caused by GM crops is completely unresolved. Incidents like this are bound to happen if the headlong rush to commercial development of GM crops continues."

CONTROVERSIAL METAL SCULPTURE The Angel of the North now has a neighbouring piece of art to keep it company - a 50ft high goat.

Commuters travelling through the North East were originally stunned when the 208-tonne Angel first appeared on a Gateshead hillside in all its towering glory.

Now another artist has given vent to his lofty talent by constructing a giant goat on a hill in the Ouseburn Valley, Newcastle.

Unlike the 20-metre high Angel, however, the goat is merely pictured in sand by artist Martin Young but the effect on thousands of passers-by is just as dramatic.

Mr Young says he will cover the goat's outline with assorted materials throughout the year in a bid to make it fit in with its environment. Autumn could see it covered in leaves.

HUNDREDS OF BADGER cubs are starving to death because the Government has culled their mothers, according to a national badger welfare organisation.

The National Federation of Badger Groups is attempting to focus attention on the plight of the cubs after a single young animal was rescued recently "barely alive."

The cub was found wandering near Devizes in Wiltshire where MAFF has been conducting the latest phase of its controversial badger cull.

Dr Elaine King, conservation officer for the NFBG, said: "The discovery of this starving cub confirms our worst fears about MAFF killing badgers during the breeding season.

"Orphaned cubs are now either dying under-ground of starvation or are leaving the safety of the sett in a desperate attempt to find their mothers."

The NFBG says it warned the Government that trapping and shooting badgers at this time of year would result in the death of female badgers which were nursing dependent cubs under-ground.

Dr King added:"Starving badger cubs to death is cruel by any standards and a criminal offence. If this Government had any respect for animal welfare it would stop the badger cull now."

Pauline Kidner, an NFBG Trustee who is caring for the rescued cub, said: "At our centre we rehabilitate 30-40 badger cubs each year. It is clear that this pathetically thin cub was very close to death through starvation. With round the clock care, he has taken fluids and is just starting to eat."

The Government says culling would not be a worthwhile policy option if the closed season - February, March, April - lasted any more than three months.

ADVERTS PROMOTING BRITISH pork sparked a storm of protest across Europe from producers who claimed they were unfair and in bad taste.

The British Meat adverts, which showed a mother pig feeding her piglets, carried the line: "After she's fed them, she could be fed to them."

The adverts went on to explain: "On many farms across the world, pigs are fed meat and bone meal which partly consists of offal, bones, and other animal parts. Pigs could even be fed on meat and bone meal derived from their own mother.

"However, by buying pork, bacon, or ham carry-ing the British Meat Quality Standard mark, you can be sure you are not supporting this practice."

British pigs were reared on vegetable-based feed, the advert added, but other producers - includ-ing those of Danish bacon - hit back, saying their own welfare and hygiene standards were equally high.

FOUR IN FIVE Suffolk residents want their coun-ty council to improve its "dire footpath record" or reduce council tax for the area, according to a survey.

The NOP poll commissioned by the Ramblers Association follows claims that Suffolk has an estimated 1,300 problems on its footpath network.

An RA spokesman said:"Despite walking being the main form of exercise for more than half the population of East Anglia, the state of the county footpaths makes it impossible to take a short walk without encountering problems and Suffolk council has allowed many footpaths to become blocked and impassable."

A COUNTRY WI member sparked the dramatic protest which wrecked Prime Minister Tony Blair's carefully prepared speech at Wembley Arena and panicked the New Labour party machine.

The heckler, identified later as a widow from the Baldock and Clothall villages' WI group in Hertfordshire, stunned Mr Blair as she shouted:"This is getting political."

Slow handclaps, jeers, and walkouts soon followed as Mr Blair looked flummoxed and tried to laugh off the protest after 10,000 Women's Institute members had packed the Arena for their national conference.

Rural WI groups from all over the country were represented at the venue and - in line with tradition - expected the Prime Minister to deliver a non-political speech.

But many were dismayed by what was quickly seen as party political rhetoric aimed at cutting the Government free from its recent troubles.

Many in the audience were married to farmers, landowners, and other rural workers who feel their livelihoods are under greater threat since Labour came to power.

One woman later complained of apparent falsehoods contained in the Premier's speech, saying:"We are women from rural communities and we have seen our bus services go and our education system deteriorate despite him saying it has improved."

Following his disastrous speech to the rebellious WI, Mr Blair was attacked in the Commons by Tory leader William Hague who said he had abandoned Middle Britain and Middle Britain was now abandoning him.

The WI protest is seen as the strongest warning to the Government from the country's rural heartlands since thousands of country workers converged on London to campaign against the threat to their jobs and way of life

WETLAND LANDSCAPES FROM Africa to the Arctic have been reproduced on a 100-acre wildlife site - in the heart of London.

The £16 million Barn Elms reservoir sanctuary, close to Hammersmith Bridge, originally comprised four Victorian reservoirs which were abandoned after the building of the Thames Water Ring Main.

Sir David Attenborough, who helped launch the development, said: "It is wonderful that through an accident of development this huge area has been turned into wild countryside.

"Birds flying in from Russia and all over Europe will be disporting themselves in front of the citizens of London in a wonderful changing spectacle."

Birdwatchers can get close to birds in cleverly designed hides while children can pond dip, all just four miles from Westminster.

BUREAUCRATIC BUNGLING HAS been blamed for yet another episode in the sorry saga of GM crops - this time involving native bird life.

The RSPB in Scotland has discovered that seed distributed to farmers as part of a scheme to boost farmland bird numbers on Orkney contained genetically modified material.

A spokesman explained: "Worried at the decline of common species of farmland birds, the RSPB has been running schemes in conjunction with farmers to plant crops which are highly beneficial to birds at key sites.

"Eleven of these sites were on Orkney, including one on our own land at Durkadale. The scheme involved distributing seeds to farmers for planting in order to provide food for birds next winter.

"We have since discovered that the seed provided on Orkney contained Hyola 38 oilseed rape, contaminated with GM material, which has been at the centre of controversy.

"These seeds have now been planted at seven of the Orkney sites, including our own. But RSPB Scotland will act to plough in all of the crops before they have time to shed pollen or set seed.

"All unplanted seeds will be destroyed. We will then be seeking redress from those responsible for this situation."

Dr Mark Avery, RSPB director of conservation, added: "We have always maintained that rigorous scientific assesment of the possible impacts of GM crops on wildlife is crucial before they can be commercially released.

"It is deeply ironic that we should now be on the end of this bureaucratic bungling."

ENGLISH NATURE HAS called for more organic farming in a bid to reverse the loss of wildlife in the countryside.

Chairman Baroness Young said:"We know that in the past intensive farming practices have dramatical - ly reduced the wildlife in our countryside.

"We also know that organic farming is one of the farming systems that has great potential to increase both the distribution and number of farmland plants and animals like the corn buttercup and the skylark.

"UK consumers have demonstrated that they wish to buy organic food but at present most organic food is imported. Imported organic food does not help either British wildlife or British farmers.

"By increasing our organic production we can benefit both our own wildlife and our beleaguered farming community. We must have the political will and Government support to enable farmers who wish to convert to do so.

"Organic farming still only occupies about three per cent of the UK agricultural area and we want to see that increased."

EIGHT MAJOR RETAILERS have confirmed they will use the eye-catching British Farm Standard logo on food and goods to help patriotic customers buy British.

Asda, Co-op, Marks and Spencer, Safeway, Sainsburys, Somerfield, Tesco and Waitrose will all display the mark when it goes public on June 13 with a high profile launch.

NFU president Ben Gill said:"This is great news. Shoppers from Cardiff to Carlisle will only have to look for the little tractor to know that they are buying food they can trust."

41

FURIOUS HUNT SUPPORTERS are aiming to intensify their defence of foxhunting if the Government seeks a ban.

London could play host to more mass protests by country groups after it was revealed Home Secretary Jack Straw had prepared a new Bill.

The Bill will give MPs in England and Wales a variety of options which range from leaving things as they are to imposing a complete ban.

Labour MPs who oppose foxhunting are delighted by the new Bill but the Countryside Alliance has pledged to lead further campaigns to keep foxhunting legal.

Countryside Alliance chief executive Richard Burge said the Government was not giving the public enough time to consider the Burns report, due to be published in days.

He said: "What we want is a sensible and sane debate on the facts and decisions made by Parliament based on evidence and not prejudice.

"If that is not achieved, then I think the resolution of rural people, in the context of a massive decline in rural life, is even stronger than in 1998."

More than 200,000 people joined a pro-hunt rally in London two years ago when a private member's Bill passed a second reading in the Commons.

Liberal Democrat MP Lembit Opik, joint chairman of the cross-party Middle Way Group which wanted a compromise in the hunting debate, was dismayed by Mr Straw's action.

He said: "My worry is there is so much emotion and so little logic being applied to this issue that people will simply vote for the strongest ban - unless there is a safeguard to force a rational consideration of the Burns recommendations."

A SPIRIT OF adventure saved the bacon of Wilbur the piglet whose escapades melted the hearts of his owners in Devon.

The week-old piglet trotted off to freedom when he escaped from a farm, covering almost two miles from Lympstone to Exmouth.

Despite his puny size, the piglet negotiated a series of farm gates, four fields, hills, and two busy roads before he was found rooting through vegetables in a garden.

Police were alerted by the garden owner and swooped on the tiny porker, taking him back to the farm where he made his great escape.

Although the farm raises pigs for slaughter, the owners were so flabbergasted by Wilbur's feat that they have spared him from the chop.

He will now be kept as a pet - and is currently being bottle fed to help him regain his strength.

COUNTRYSIDE TRANQUILLITY IS vanishing at an alarming rate as noise from traffic and other sources gets worse, says a new report.

Anti-noise campaigners reveal that more and more rural lives are being made miserable by the steady rumble of traffic, barking dogs, loud music and aircraft.

Vast stretches of countryside - equivalent to the size of Wales - have been lost to England in the last four decades, according to the report by the Council for the Protection of Rural England.

Assistant director Tony Burton said: "Tranquillity, and the chance to get away from it all, are defining features of rural England.

"As rural tranquillity is shattered and it becomes harder to find peace and quiet in the countryside near towns, so the quality of life of the nation is diminished."

The CPRE report shows that the South East has been particularly badly hit due to a huge increase in road building and motorway construction.

Around London alone, an area of tranquillity twice the size of Oxfordshire is said to have disappeared in the last 30 years with a total of 222,912 acres of countryside built on.

BEEF LABELS WHICH reveal the sex of the animal being eaten would be an expensive nonsense if introduced by Brussels bureaucrats, say farmers' leaders.

The NFU claims a more realistic approach is needed in the on-going debate in Europe over beef labelling.

NFU deputy president Tim Bennett said:"The UK supports the proposal to make it compulsory to label beef with its country of origin.

"We are proud of our product and believe this would provide consumers with greater awareness of what they are buying and further evidence of product traceability.

"But labelling beef with the sex of the animal will impose huge costs on Britain's beef industry, provide information of limited use, and offer no further safeguards to consumers. The suggestion is, quite frankly, absurd."

Meat trade and farm union representatives aimed to press home their message when they met MEPs during a trip to Brussels.

A MOTHER TAWNY owl has been causing mayhem by attacking people who get too close to her offspring.

Five victims have included the Rev Kathy Collins who was set upon as she walked to a communion service in Bishop's Castle, Shropshire.

Only her thick anorak saved her from serious injury courtesy of the irate owl's talons, she believes, but others have been slashed and bruised.

One man was left stunned and bleeding after being flown at as he took his dog for a late night walk.

Another actually spotted one of the owl's chicks on the ground but was gashed on the scalp as he bent down for a closer look.

Nearby building work is believed to have panicked the mother bird and her chicks into leaving their nest.

Local residents have been warned to be on their guard until the owl calms down.

THE EYES OF rural Britain are on the Appeal Court in London as Tony Martin begins his fight to be released from prison.

The case of the Norfolk farmer convicted of murdering a teenage burglar created a national furore when he was jailed for life in April.

Martin, 55, was given the life term after being found guilty of murdering Fred Barras, 16, at his lonely, decrepit farmhouse.

Norwich Crown Court had heard that the dead teenager had been accompanied by two other petty crooks and the trio boasted scores of convictions between them.

Despite his claims to have been virtually abandoned by local police and feeling terrified when the fateful drama unfolded, Martin was convicted of murder by a 10-2 majority.

Farmers, landowners, and rural communities hit by constant crime were particularly incensed that Martin could be dealt with so severely when, in their view, he was the victim.

The image of rural policing in Norfolk was also severely dented by public outrage over the jailing of the farmer.

The Chief Constable feared morale among his force might never properly recover after a national outcry over the case from all sections of society.

Ken Williams said his staff had been subjected to "grossly offensive and vulgar" telephone calls from members of the public making unfair accusations.

The start of Martin's appeal is expected to pre-empt a fuller hearing later in the year when his fate will finally be decided.

ENGLISH WOODLAND COVER could be increased by an area almost as large as Birmingham by planting trees on brownfield sites, claims the Government.

"There is a real opportunity to create a new and green future for England's brownfield land," announced Elliot Morley MP, England's Forestry Minister, on publication of a joint Forestry Commission/National Urban Forestry Unit report.

Mr Morley added: "Whilst some of this land may be earmarked for other uses, if we planted new woodland on just 15 per cent of it we could increase England's woodland cover by over 25,000 hectares - an area almost equivalent to the size of Birmingham.

"New urban woodlands offer a quality environment and support healthier living, with access to open space for recreation. Woodlands in and around towns and cities really can make a difference to people's lives."

His announcement comes after Deputy Prime Minister John Prescott was attacked for aiming to relax Green Belt laws that currently prevent the countryside being consumed by housing.

THE IMPACT OF birds of prey on grouse numbers is much more severe than initially thought, according to new research.

Shooting was found to be unviable after raptors had halved stocks of grouse, says a report published in the Journal of Animal Ecology.

The paper 'Raptor Predation and Population Limitation in Red Grouse' was written by Dr Simon Thirgood and Nicholas Aebischer of the Game Conservancy Trust, along with colleagues Stephen Redpath and Peter Rothery of the Institute of Terrestrial Ecology.

Dr Thirgood, based in the Institute of Cell, Animal and Population Biology Unit at the University of Edinburgh, said: "Summer predation by harriers and peregrines halved autumn grouse densities and nearly 40 per cent of grouse chicks were killed by the end of August.

"These findings have extremely important implications for wildlife management and biodiversity conservation.

"If a grouse moor becomes unviable due to predation, then moorland management, which is so vital for biodiversity in the uplands, will cease."

COUNTRYSIDE CAMPAIGNERS HAVE been boosted by local councils' rejection of Deputy Prime Minister John Prescott's bid to build 43,000 houses a year in the South East.

The verdict by SERPLAN - the South East Regional Planning Authority - amounted to a severe snub for Mr Prescott after he planned to dramatically increase the number of homes.

Mr Prescott had been pressing for 860,000 new properties to be built before 2016 to cater for an increased population - but many countryside groups had attacked his scheme for threatening what was left of the region's green areas.

The Deputy Prime Minister, who has received thousands of protest letters from angry residents since he unveiled his scheme, can still order local authorities to build the homes.

But that would be a high risk strategy for Labour as the next General Election approaches and rural residents - many of whom voted for Labour last time - weigh up the pros and cons of voting again for a party already under fire for its rural policies.

Shadow Environment Secretary Archie Norman praised SERPLAN, adding:"The Government is committed to building the wrong homes in the wrong places."

A HEN WITH half its top beak missing has been returned to a girl who lost her beloved pet when her mother accidentally sold it.

Keighley Stranger, 14, was heartbroken when the chicken - named 'Hen' - vanished from her mother's farm near Whitchurch in Shropshire.

It soon became apparent that her pet had been snapped up by mistake after a man called to buy some chickens from the farm.

Keighley was particularly upset by the loss of Hen as she had cared and looked after the bird since it was an egg.

However, as the buyer had not left his details, an appeal for information was launched which ended with the safe return of the odd-looking pet.

The man spotted the appeal himself in a local newspaper and drove Hen back to the farm - straight into the arms of Keighley.

THE HIDDEN HAZARDS of camping in the countryside have been starkly brought home after a group of youngsters fell victim to an E-coli outbreak caused by infected sheep faeces.

Nearly 20 children were struck down by the potentially fatal bug which left one eight-year-old boy from their number seriously ill in a Scottish hospital.

The group picked up the bug after pitching tents at a scout camp site in Aberdeenshire where droppings had become host to the E-coli bacteria.

Environmental health investigators from the local council conducted a search of the site and tested droppings - all of which contained the bug.

However, nearby puddles were also infected with E-coli and it became apparent recent heavy rains had washed over the site and carried the bug across a far wider area.

A spokesman for Aberdeenshire Council said:"Clothes pick up wet faecal matter more easily so the rains were not helpful."

Tests for the bug had also been carried out on food and water supplies at the camp site but all had proven negative, he added.

The seriously ill victim first had kidney dialysis in hospital before undergoing more specialist treatment at another medical centre.

The other youngsters, boys and girls, were being cared for at their own homes.

Scout Association chiefs in Scotland launched an investigation into the incident and underlined the need for vigilance against possible future E-coli outbreaks at camps.

MORE THAN 800 pheasant chicks died when a blaze ripped through the shed where they were kept on a farm.

The chicks were believed to have had little chance of escaping the fire which gutted the shed near Wolverhampton.

An investigation revealed that a heater which had been used to keep the chicks warm may have been to blame for the incident after setting bedding alight.

Farmer Henry Duppa was left counting the cost of the disaster which could reach over the £1,000 mark.

He had raised the alarm after seeing smoke pouring from the shed.

Firemen took nearly an hour to quell the flames.

RECENT INTEREST IN European soccer has been used by the Environment Agency to kick out-of-date fishing licences into touch.

A spokesman said June 16 saw the start of the traditional coarse fishing season on rivers in England and Wales just as Euro championship soccer hooked the nation. The Agency was reminding all anglers hoping to strike on the riverbank that they must drop their old licence and ensure a valid one is included in their new season's kit.

A SWARM OF bees came to rest beneath the saddle of a woman's bicycle - leaving her to walk a mile home.

Grandmother Esther Mickleburgh was horrified to find the swarm in place when she went to collect her bike after work in Welwyn Garden City, Hertfordshire.

The baby clothes packer has a terror of stinging insects and was unwilling to try to dislodge the swarm, thought to number thousands of bees.

After she fled back inside her work place, colleagues at first believed she was joking - until they saw the buzzing evidence for themselves.

The bees stayed on the bicycle for 24 hours before flying away. Experts believe they were merely resting after becoming exhausted trying to find a new place to live.

HILL FARMERS NEED a simpler support payment scheme to help them eke out a living in harsh territories, according to farmers' leaders.

The scheme should be based on "an historic average area payment and environmental enhance - ments", says the NFU.

The union claims the rejection of initial Hill Farm Allowance proposals presented to the European Commission in January had been a huge setback.

It was urgently pressing the British Government and the European Commission to accept new proposals.

NFU Less Favoured Area Committee chairman Peter Allen said:"This alternative scheme provides a more secure future for hill farmers whilst meeting the sentiments of the Commission's legislative require - ments.

"The EU timetable for the approval of the new HFA scheme is very tight but it is vital that the purpose of this important mechanism is not lost in the rush for change."

A FRIESIAN COW has been named 'Lucky' after plunging 300ft off a cliff and escaping with a few cuts and bruises.

The animal went over the cliff near Exmouth in Devon after breaking through barbed wire close to the top in pursuit of some juicier grazing.

Farmer Mike Ellet said Lucky was discovered walking dazed around the beach below after a passer-by raised the alarm.

The heifer was indeed fortunate to be alive as her bulk somehow missed landing on an array of boulders at the foot of the cliff. A patch of mud is believed to have aided her survival.

The animal is now recovering from her ordeal back at the farm where another cow also took the same plunge in a previous drama.

Sadly, that cow was not so lucky and died from its injuries.

TV AND RADIO personality Chris Tarrant, a keen angler, saw his £140,000 fishing boat wrecked in a mystery blaze on the Thames near his Surrey home.

Mindless vandals have been blamed for the blaze which infuriated Tarrant - especially as his family often slept aboard the Ben Gunn and could have been killed.

Police are investigating the torching of the boat which Tarrant said had "horrified" and "disgusted" him.

RURAL CRIME BURST back into the headlines after a village postmaster stabbed an armed assailant to death just days after farmer Tony Martin began his appeal against murder.

Richard Watkins, 50, tackled the gunman with a knife he had been using to cut the strings on newspaper bundles at his quiet Worcestershire shop.

The would-be robber, who had hit Mr Watkins over the head with a shotgun, staggered out of the shop fatally wounded and was later found dead in a getaway car driven by an accomplice.

Although Mr Watkins was questioned by police, it seemed doubtful he would face charges like Mr Martin, whose case was reviewed at the Appeal Court in London .

Villagers in Wolverley rallied to the defence of Mr Watkins - described as a "gentle giant" - who was left shaken by the incident. A gash in his scalp required stitches.

It was believed to be the third robbery attack on the post office in recent years with villagers also suffering at the hands of burglars and thieves.

Mr Watkins, a bachelor who lives with his sister and elderly mother, is said to be a popular and well respected member of the village.

Following the drama, which happened just after 10am, he was interviewed by police who later revealed they were treating him as a victim in the case.

This was in stark contrast to the position taken by Norfolk Police when farmer Tony Martin blasted a teenage burglar to death with a shotgun.

Another farmer, Brian Ward, was also freed from court recently after an incident when he shot and wounded one of a group of trespassers on his land at night.

THE "ABSURDITY" OF the French beef ban has been pressed home by a British farming spokesman on French soil.

The NFU delegate told a seminar on BSE that it was not acceptable for France to assume the Presidency of the EU from July while continuing to ban British beef.

Animal Health and Welfare Committee vice-chairman Neil Cutler hammered home the message when he spoke at the French Senate Colloquium in Paris.

He said:"The EU independent Scientific Steering Committee - which includes eminent French scientists - has approved UK BSE controls. The beef export ban has been lifted by all EU countries except France. Member states simply cannot pick and choose the laws they will and will not obey, especially when they are holding the Presidency."

ANGLERS COULD BE on a violent collision course with animal rights saboteurs already boosted by Government moves to ban foxhunting.

The Campaign for the Abolition of Angling held a week of protests to coincide with the start of the coarse fishing season and pledged more would follow as it intensified its fight for the rights of fish.

But anglers, some of whose fishing has already been disrupted by stone-throwing protesters, seem unlikely to bow to increased pressure.

Millions enjoy what is said to be Britain's favourite outdoor sport which has none of the underlying 'class' implications that many believe lie behind Labour's move against foxhunting.

The Government has also appeared to rule out any new laws against angling, despite furious protests from campaigners who also want shooting banned.

A spokesman for the Campaign for the Abolition of Angling said:"We are dedicated to banning angling. We were established in 1981 following the publishing of the Medway Report which concluded that fish can feel pain and have the ability to suffer. Our work consists of publicity, education, and direct action."

They aimed to make their presence felt at the start of the fishing season to let anglers know how cruel they thought fishing was.

BRITAIN'S ANCIENT WOODLANDS face multiple threats which could see them wiped out unless urgent action is taken now, according to the Woodland Trust.

Broadleaved woodland, in particular, contains more globally threatened and rapidly declining species than any other UK habitat, says the conservation charity.

"Changes in environmental conditions, including higher temperatures, changes in rainfall patterns, drought and storm frequency will have a dramatic impact on ancient woodland," said a spokesman.

"Loopholes in the law and poor planning regula - tions exacerbate the fact that 85 per cent of ancient woodland has no legal protection. Intensive agricultural practices are also further isolating already fragmented woods.

"This is compounded by overgrazing by livestock and deer, arresting the growth of new trees and preventing ancient woodland from regenerating."

A RACEHORSE LEAPT into a Devon river and swam 500 metres downstream after throwing its jockey during a race.

Novice filly Norwey Lady had been competing in a National Hunt flat race at Newton Abbot when it suddenly dumped its jockey and leapt railings into the River Teign.

Despite its fitness, the horse got into difficulties and could have drowned if firemen had not been quickly on the scene.

A rowing boat was employed to get firemen out to the distressed horse which had become stranded on a sandbank in the centre of the river.

Later, the animal appeared to have made a complete recovery after being treated for shock and a cut to its leg.

No-one was any the wiser as to why it had suddenly decided to abandon its place in the race and go for a dangerous dip instead.

THE CONTROVERSIAL PROSPECT of farm animals being routinely used in experiments to aid human health has moved a step closer after a new breakthrough in cloning technology.

Scientists at Scottish biotech firm PPL Therapeutics have explained that their latest advance might help them breed herds of animals with in-built resistance to many diseases.

However, the same advance might also mean farm animals, particularly sheep, being employed as human gene carriers to test out treatments aimed at human health.

Such moves would mark a sophisticated step forward in the already hotly debated area of animal experiments.

Nature magazine revealed that the scientists had succeeded in creating the first genetically modified sheep clones, including two lambs called Diana and Cupid.

Dr Alan Coleman, research director at PPL Therapeutics, said animal models of human illnesses could be created for testing treatments.

"Mice are used if the model they present is a good one, but often you don't get the same symptoms humans have," explained Dr Coleman. "Sheep might be a much better model."

He gave the example of Cystic fibrosis which was associated with a particular gene variation.

The same variation had been introduced in mice but the animals failed to develop the condition as humans would.

Dr Coleman revealed that his company hoped to produce selectively modified pig clones within the next 12 months.

PPL Therapeutics recently announced that it had already succeeded in creating five pig clones - an even more difficult undertaking than producing sheep.

WATER SUPPLIES WOULD be overwhelmed by demand if proposed massive building development across the South East goes ahead, it is claimed.

The Environment Agency's view is another boost to countryside campaigners who have been opposing Deputy Prime Minister John Prescott's plans to vastly increase housing in the region.

The Agency says it is worried that proposed levels of growth in the South East would result in unacceptable damage to the environment.

A spokesman said:"The Agency is particularly concerned that there are insufficient water resources in areas such as the Thames Basin and Ashford in Kent to support planned development. It has also pinpointed towns such as Basingstoke, Ashford and Aylesbury where river water quality may be downgraded as sewage treatment works struggle to cope with increased volumes of effluent."

A DISPOSITION TOWARDS neatness has never been associated with cattle and sheep - so heads were scratched in North Wales when animals were spotted lying in a row.

Time and again, sheep and cows took up the same position in a field in Clwyd, baffling passers-by used to seeing animals scattered everywhere.

In the end, the explanation proved quite mundane - the animals were merely taking advantage of an underground pipe leaking steam and heating up the ground.

The field is situated next to council education offices and a probe found the leak may have been going on for a year.

Despite the animals enjoying the warm earth, the actual cost of the leak to the council has been estimated at £5,000.

ICELAND'S BIG MOVE into organic food has led the Soil Association to attack the Government for not supporting organic producers in this country.

Patrick Holden, director of the Soil Association, said: "This is a major embarrassment for the Government as yet another retailer seeks to expand its range of organic food.

"Most of the food will have to be imported - currently 70 per cent of organic food already is - to meet demand.

"The Soil Association has been calling on the Government for years to develop a strategy to increase the level of organic farming and food production in UK.

"With the closure of the Organic Farming Scheme last November, there is currently no money available to assist farmers in conversion until April 2001.

"We believe the Government needs to act now to provide the necessary resources so that the supply of UK grown organic produce can meet consumer demand."

ALMOST 700 PIGS and piglets perished in a blaze which swept through their piggery in North Yorkshire after an electrical fault developed at the premises.

Firemen who raced to the scene of devastation near Boroughbridge managed to save 600 other pigs which had also been trapped by the flames.

North Yorkshire Fire and Rescue Service said crews worked fast in difficult conditions to make sure the fire did not spread to other buildings.

Early indications were that the fire seemed to have been caused by an overloaded thermostat or wires that became overheated.

Assistant divisional officer Simon Gibson, who led firemen at the scene, warned farmers to take extra care with their buildings.

ENGLISH NATURE HAS launched an in-depth probe into the wildlife and environmental well-being of UK rivers.

It is hoped that information gleaned during the project will also be of use to other countries across Europe.

A spokesman said:"The impact of farming practices on rivers, the link between salmon and pearl mussels, what makes rivers good for otters, and how the harmful impact of river engineering can be reversed, will all be examined."

Data gathered would be used to develop conservation strategies.

THE PUBLIC BACKLASH over threatened closures of rural post offices is thought to be behind surprise Government moves to rescue them.

The frosty reception received by Prime Minister Tony Blair recently from Women's Institute members, as well as lobbying by rural campaigners and post office chiefs themselves, are all thought to be behind the U-turn.

Instead of being closed, many country post offices may now be revitalised by a Government package that will see them operating as banks with closer links to the internet.

The proposals by Trade and Industry Secretary Stephen Byers follow a report by the Cabinet Office into the future of British post offices.

Many rural post offices faced closure after being expected to lose up to a third of their business when benefits are paid directly into bank accounts starting in 2003.

The new proposals, which will involve post offices being collectively sub-titled a 'universal bank', will see them receive new technology by early next year.

Each post office will then be linked to the worldwide web as part of a move to expand services and keep the network strong.

A recent NOP poll of rural postmasters, commissioned by the Countryside Alliance, showed "an overwhelming disillusionment with the Government's performance and grave fears for the future of the post office network."

In England and Wales, only four per cent of those canvassed believed the Government was doing a good job at protecting rural post offices.

THE PROMOTION OF French markets in Britain by local authorities has been slammed as "indefensible" while the country maintains its illegal ban on British beef.

NFU president Ben Gill has written to the chairman of the Local Government Association's Rural Commission Gordon Keymer about the issue.

It follows complaints from farmers about French markets taking place in their local areas.

Mr Gill said: "In normal circumstances I would have no desire to interfere in decisions taken by local authorities on such matters.

"But I have to say that for many people in rural communities this kind of promotion is highly insensitive.

"At a time when the French authorities are maintaining their ban on British beef illegally and without any scientific justification, it is indefensible for local government to be encouraging the purchase of French goods."

THE COUNTRYSIDE ALLIANCE has issued a new clarion call to members and supporters to help it defeat moves to ban foxhunting.

Chief executive Richard Burge said the organisation's directors had laid out plans which would ensure that proposals in a hunting options Bill would never result in a ban becoming law.

"As of now, a sustained and escalating campaign of action begins. It will be relentless, implacable and prolonged," he pledged.

"It will be local and national, targeted not only at the media but at all members of Parliament looking towards re-election.

"It will lead up to and beyond the biggest peace time march that London has ever seen. Supporters, individuals or groups, are asked to stand by. A call to arms may be at short notice. It may require travel and it will certainly require dedication and commitment."

Alliance chairman John Jackson added:"Our battle is to persuade Government ministers and the Prime Minister himself to stand up against the illiberal attitudes and authoritarian prejudices of many of his backbenchers."

SALMON COULD SOON be making a clean breast of things by swimming up a Yorkshire river once labelled among the filthiest in Europe.

The fish are expected to make a reappearance in the River Don, swimming through Doncaster and up to Sheffield for the first time in 200 years thanks to an "innovative" flood defence scheme.

The newly completed scheme at Crimpsall Sluice, Doncaster, involves re-joining an old cut-off section of the River Don to the main river.

A spokesman for the Environment Agency explained:"It has removed the last remaining modern river obstruction to fish species migrating from the tidal Don into the heart of industrial South Yorkshire.

The new project also involved "a fish-friendly weir - a flood defence structure built as a rock chute for fish to swim over and reach previously unreachable parts of the River Don system."

The scheme has been described as a monumental step forward in reversing the trends of decades of industrial destruction of the region's urban rivers.

TREE SPARROWS ARE now thought to be extinct in Dorset, according to concerned local birdwatchers.

The little birds, closely related to better known house sparrows, appear to have deserted the area.

A talk about farmland birds given at Poole RSPB's AGM proved a depressing experience for all those present.

They heard that once common species including skylark, starling, grey partridge, lapwing and tree sparrow had declined "at an alarming rate".

Tree sparrows, in particular, were now "probably extinct" in the county while grey partridge numbers were down 75 per cent.

However, other species seemed to be holding their own.

Another Dorset wildlife group, The Friends of Broadstone Nature Reserve, is hoping to see nightjars on Corfe Hills at the end of the month.

WASP: two painful encounters with this small menace

SUMMER in this country often heralds one of our less welcome traditions as temperatures start to rise - getting ourselves bitten and stung.

In Africa, when some villagers aren't busy dodging lions and crocodiles, they still have poisonous spiders, snakes, and scorpions to contend with.

Then there's that killer of millions worldwide, the malaria-carrying mosquito.

In Britain, we generally face much gentler hazards in the great outdoors.

Even the adder rarely inflicts a fatal bite, while wasps, bees, ants and ticks are hardly in the same category as those African menaces.

Even so, these last four are still capable of putting the kibosh on what had previously been an enjoyable ramble or picnic.

Wasps are probably the most aggressive of this group, with the largest European strain - the hornet (vespa crabro) - inflicting a particularly painful sting.

However, Common or 'German' wasps are the two species most often encountered and are virtually identical.

Quite handsome in their black and yellow stripes, these characters are nevertheless 17-18 millimetres of pure spite when upset - and I should know. I've had two painful encounters with them.

The first occasion, when I was a child, was far worse.

Walking in woods with my older brother and his friend I'd begun to lag behind in a daydream.

I hadn't a clue that they'd discovered a wasps' nest up ahead and decided to play a rather mean prank on me.

As the entrance hole to the nest was situated beside the footpath, they simply jumped up and down on it before fleeing.

Seconds later, bemused by their actions, I stepped into a cloud of very angry wasps aiming to wreak revenge.

Not being Dr Doolittle, I could not explain that I was innocent of squashing their nice home.

What came next is largely a blur of pain and terror as I set off running, covered by wasps. Wasps in my ears, eyes, hair, down my chest and all over my hands.

I was stung about 30 times which, considering the number that attacked me, was probably a lucky escape.

Feeling guilty at the success of their dastardly trick, the two perpetrators rushed me to the friend's house where his mum ripped off my shirt and daubed me all over with something called 'dolly blue' - an antiseptic substance now long gone.

Dolly blue or not, for the next few years I would scarper if a wasp so much as buzzed anywhere near me.

My second close encounter came about in adulthood when I made the mistake of investigating an active wasps' nest in the attic.

Not quite sure where it was, I finally lifted up an old piece of carpet and the wasps rose en masse to greet me.

Although I was only stung once, my pride was sorely injured, especially as my partner never stopped giggling for three days.

Apparently, the sight of me fending off wasps while dextrously trying not to crash through the ceiling was the funniest thing she had ever seen. Oh, how I laughed.

Fortunately for me, neither incident brought on what seems to be an increasingly common condition these days - anaphylactic shock.

This is where an allergic reaction occurs to a bite or sting and victims go into a state of shock, sometimes so severe that an injection of adrenaline is needed to save their lives.

Ticks, meanwhile, are said to be a growing menace in the countryside but it's a pest I've not fallen victim to so far.

Although tiny when they attach themselves, these blood-sucking spider-like creatures can swell to the size of a baked bean.

They can also carry disease so must be taken seriously.

Found in woods and grassland they are none too choosy about their hosts and attach themselves to any passing animal - including us.

Medical experts advise using tweezers to remove them, rocking the body back and forth to ease the head free.

If this snaps off, the area is more likely to become infected.

Finally, bees and ants have never given me any great problems, though I've been stung and bitten by both.

But then I've never upset a whole bees' nest or encountered the wood ant at close quarters.

This ant carries an extra surprise in its armoury.

If you crouch down to prod it, you're liable to get a squirt of formic acid in your eye from its abdomen. Charming.

A MAJOR PROBE into Britain's insect life has been launched in a bid to find new natural ways to control crop pests and save farmers' cash.

Wildlife charity the Game Conservancy Trust has won a £312,000 research contract to discover how farmers can make the best use of beneficial insects - while helping the environment and their bank balances.

The Trust is taking part in the 3D Farming Project which will be funded to the tune of £1.1 million annually and last four years.

Dr John Holland, head of entomology for the Trust, said:"There's a whole army of insects out there that can be used to help the farmer and the environment.

"We need to thoroughly research ways of ensuring that these beneficial beetles and spiders have the best conditions for doing their job of gobbling up pests.

"For example, spiders tend to be attracted to certain areas within a crop and we need to know why so we can adapt our management of field boundaries accordingly."

The Trust will explore how insects can be used to destroy pests like aphids which damage cereal crops.

Research will also be done at the Institute of Arable Crops Research into how parasitic wasps can be manipulated by aphid sex pheromones to increase their effectiveness at destroying the pests.

Meanwhile, the Central Science Laboratory will look at whether wildflower strips can be used to encourage hoverflies - voracious aphid eaters - and spiders will have their diet investigated by researchers at Scottish agricultural colleges.

"The 3D project is so-called because it explores the three Ds - diversity, distribution and dispersal of beneficial insects," added a Trust spokesman.

COUNTRYSIDE UFO SIGHTINGS are back in the news after a Gloucester man filmed two unidentified flying objects above the Forest of Dean.

Richard Lewis captured the mystery objects on his video camera as he filmed from his home.

He revealed that he initially believed they were two hot air balloons.

However, they began to move rapidly around in a way impossible for a balloon.

Both objects were black, he said, and had suddenly disappeared from view, although there were almost no clouds to be seen.

He filmed the objects for about three minutes until they vanished and stills from the incident have now been published in his local newspaper for public debate.

SONG THRUSH NUMBERS have crashed across Britain leaving a notable hole in the dawn chorus for many people, according to the RSPB.

Intensive farming practices have been blamed for the dramatic decline of the once common bird which, nevertheless, remains as popular as ever.

Dr Mark Avery, the RSPB director of conservation, said:"The future of the song thrush in our countryside is a cause for grave concern. The birds are unable to maintain healthy populations in agricultural areas with very intensive farming. The national population is suffering severely as a result.

"The situation has become so critical that, in some rural areas, gardens now support over 20 times more nesting song thrushes than arable farmland."

Colleague Dr Will Peach, RSPB research biologist, added:"The biggest single cause seems to be the loss of favoured feeding habitats such as wet ditches, woodlands and damp grazed grassland.

"Song thrushes like to forage on soft damp ground where favoured prey, such as snails, are abundant."

MORE THAN 1,000 fish have been washed up dead after a mystery pollutant entered a river in Lancashire.

Environment Agency investigators have been trying to trace the source of pollution which killed the fish in Stock Beck, Barnoldswick.

"The fish include trout, bullheads and stone-loach," said an Agency spokesman."About half a mile of the river is affected, between Crow Nest Road, off the B6252 Skipton Road, and Greenberfield Lane.

"Water samples have been taken and will be analysed to identify the pollutant.

"The Agency will be speaking to local businesses and investigating drainage systems in the area in a bid to find where it came from.

"Although fish have been killed, investigations show insect life in the river is largely unaffected.

"Insects and invertebrates provide food for fish and their survival should ensure fish can return to the affected stretch of Stock Beck."

BLACKBIRDS HIT THE wrong note by causing a flap at an international music festival in North Wales.

Officials at the Llangollen International Musical Eisteddfod had their work cut out trying to keep a number of the birds from entering the main pavilion.

For some reason, the intruders decided the pavilion was perfect for roosting and made it their twilight home before the festival got underway.

This provided an unexpected problem for hard-pressed officials.

Instead of concentrating on readying the area for a massive daily influx of visitors, some eisteddfod workers were detailed to clean up blackbird droppings.

Chairs were regularly targeted by the birds, although organisers were sure that they would all scarper when the noisy week-long event eventually started.

THE ROYAL SHOW was the launch pad for a new plea to the Government to support desperate farmers whose businesses have been driven to the edge.

NFU president Ben Gill delivered a hard-hitting speech which, he said, revealed what farmers and growers wanted from New Labour as they walked an economic tightrope.

"Above all we need the Government to act on the recognition that farming IS the countryside," he said.

"To recognise and promote the reality that the countryside is not a benign frozen Constable water colour, but a vibrant, living and breathing, ever changing food chain where one species survives at the expense of another.

"To accept that all this needs positive management of the type that we have given for so long with seemingly little recognition. "This autumn, the Rural White Paper must address these and many other issues. It must be a realistic blueprint for the future of farming and Rural Britain based on knowledge and understanding. Our future remains at stake.

"There is much that is inspiring in our industry. I see it as I travel around the country. I have found a wealth of examples of how farmers and growers are developing innovative approaches to our current problems.

"All too often, though, they are frustrated by bureaucracy and unnecessary red tape; by a lack of joined-up Government; by an unbelievable level of commercial reality; and by a worrying lack of understanding about the countryside and what makes it tick. This has got to change."

He added at the Warwickshire show that farmers required clear and consistent messages from all levels of Government plus regulation in proportion to risk.

COUNCILS ACROSS BRITAIN will be studying the results of a legal battle over pigeons between a London authority and Railtrack.

Wandsworth Council has launched an unprecedented action against the rail company over pigeons being allowed to roost under a local railway bridge.

The pigeons' droppings create a nuisance, are a health hazard - and Railtrack is responsible, according to council chiefs.

Railtrack denies this.

The authority is seeking an injunction to get the firm to fill in or cover roosting sites within the bridge.

If successful, it is believed that local authorities across the country with similar pigeon problems could bring their own actions against Railtrack.

THE MILLIONAIRE LANDOWNER Nicholas Van Hoogstraten has agreed to allow walkers through his East Sussex estate following a long legal battle with the Ramblers Association.

Mr Van Hoogstraten, who has allegedly called walkers "riff-raff" and "the great unwashed", says he will pay for a new footpath that avoids the obstructions blocking a public path on his estate.

"Earlier this year the Association sensationally won a case at Lewes Magistrates Court which issued a fine of £1,600 after it was proved that the path had been illegally blocked by a barbed wire fence, a locked gate, refrigeration units and a barn," said an RA spokesman.

"East Sussex council issued an enforcement notice in March requiring companies connected with the site and the landowners to either clear the footpath or come up with an acceptable diversion.

"The council had the power to clear a way through the obstructions and reclaim the cost of the work.

"Now, as part of a diversion proposal submitted to the council, Mr Van Hoogstraten has agreed that he would pay for a new path as well as signposts and two new stiles."

A SHROPSHIRE PIG farmer found his delicious hog roast was not to everyone's taste at a best of British food festival - and was forced to move his stall after a Muslim taxi driver complained.

Half an hour after setting up the roast at the Heart of England festival in Telford, farmer Jon Hooper had to quit his pitch outside a shopping centre.

The rank, where several Muslim drivers park, was close by and a council spokesman approached the farmer and told him he was insulting their religion.

Mr Hooper was forced to relocate away from his former pitch outside McDonald's.

He was so angry that he attacked the event as a farce, pledging not to take part any more.

Mr Hooper and his wife, who run a pig farm near Telford, only set up their hog roast business recently.

The couple had decided to follow Government advice to diversify.

GREATER HORSESHOE BATS fly up to four times further to hunt than previously thought, according to new research by English Nature.

The rare bats travel as far as 16 kilometres per night from their roost sites to feast on insects, as revealed in a study of the creatures at Berry Head, near Torquay in Devon.

With a wingspan of 14 inches, the greater horseshoe is one of Britain's biggest bats and needs a large supply of insects, including moths, cockchafers and dung beetles.

Ideal locations for such insects are cattle grazed pastures and English Nature has been working with local farmers in Devon to re-establish grazing on suitable areas over which the bats feed.

English Nature's David Appleton said:"Our knowledge has increased considerably through this new research.

"We are delighted that we can now target measures to conserve and protect this rare species.

"There are just over 4,000 greater horseshoe bats in the UK.

"With this new information, we can hopefully increase their numbers."

NEW LABOUR IS reported to be heading for a battle with the House of Lords over the Countryside and Rights of Way Bill.

Deputy Prime Minister John Prescott is apparently preparing to invoke the Parliament Act to force the legislation through if it is blocked by the Lords.

The Bill, which received its Second Reading in the Lords recently, has been described by supporters as the most important piece of countryside legislation in 50 years.

The Ramblers Association explained:"It will create a legal freedom to roam on specific, mapped areas of mountain, moor, heath, down and common land, with provi- sions to extend this to coastlines in the future.

"It will also force local authorities to take action against landowners guilty of obstruct- ing paths on their land and come up with plans to improve rights of way networks.

"If the House of Lords attempts to block the legislation it will be seen as a huge challenge to the Government as the Bill introduces two key Labour election promises - opening up the countryside for walkers and protection for wildlife sites.

"It is a Parliamentary convention that the Lords do not reject manifesto commitments. The Parliament Act, which has only been used a handful of times, allows the Govern- ment to force through legislation one year after the Bill's original Second Reading."

The Bill faces strong opposition in the Lords, especially over night-time access, dogs, occupier liability and compensation.

During the Second Reading, Lord Moran attacked walkers saying:"Ramblers do not put anything into the countryside, unlike farmers or young volunteers who help the RSPB, the wildlife trusts, and those in the British Trust for Conservation Volunteers."

Other peers branded ramblers "arrogant" and "militant."

TENDER LOVING CARE is being handed out at a hospital site - to three pairs of rare cirl buntings.

Developers turning buildings at the old Devon hospital into homes have agreed to protect the buntings and have joined forces with wildlife experts.

Hundreds of metres of hedges will be planted and large tracts of grass left untouched at Exminster Hospital near Exeter to encourage insects that the buntings feed on.

Devington Homes, developers of the £11 million housing scheme, have liaised with the RSPB and local councillors to give the buntings every chance of further colonising the area.

The site is thought to be the most easterly outpost of cirl buntings in Britain and vital if they are to spread further across the country.

FOREIGN IMPORTS WILL continue to feed the rocketing demand for organic produce unless Britain's organic farmers get more Government support, warn farmers' leaders.

NFU deputy president Tim Bennett says that despite the rising popularity of organic food, the number of UK farmers applying to convert is levelling off, or even falling.

He said:"Unless significant changes to the public support system are made, imports will continue to supply the bulk of our organic market, particularly as producers in other member states have been better supported during conversion and afterwards.

"This has the obvious effect of enabling those in receipt of better support to be able to market their products at lower prices than UK producers, effectively undercutting UK production."

The Organic Farming Scheme had given a desperately needed boost to British farmers switching to organic production from 1998, he said, but this ran out of cash after four months and was subsequently closed.

"UK consumers would prefer to buy UK produced food," he added."We therefore need to determine whether we are prepared to invest in home production or continue our dependence on imports."

AN ANCIENT HILL fort in Wales which was home to a famous Roman prisoner has been revealed again for the first time in 60 years.

Forest Enterprise Wales has spent 10 years care- fully clearing trees and undergrowth from the 30 hectare ancient monument at Breidden Hill, near Newtown.

British chieftain Caractacus was captured there before being shipped to Rome and the story features in the work of Roman writer Tacitus.

Caractacus was credited with leading fierce resistance against the Romans before they took him away in chains.

While being led through Rome, he asked why the Romans were so cruel when they lived in such a beautiful city. Impressed by his bearing, they spared his life.

AN 'AUTOGRAPH WALL' will be among attractions at this year's CLA Game Fair, held in the grounds of imposing Blenheim Palace in Oxfordshire.

All visitors will be invited to scribble their signatures on the wall which should become a highly visible symbol of the popularity of country activities.

The game fair, from July 28 to 30, again sets out to offer something for everyone with a varied programme of events.

A spokesman said it encompassed "all aspects of country living with major shows and features, displays, international and national championships, and over 600 exhibitors. Whether you want to watch, participate, learn, browse, buy or socialise, the CLA Game Fair is the place to be.

"The Countryside Alliance area will have something of interest for everyone, including a farmers' market, where you can buy locally produced honey, cheese, meat, herbs, wine and other fresh produce direct from the primary producer. Book signings will also take place each day, giving you the opportunity to meet some of the best countryside authors."

DOG ATTACKS HAVE left 24,000 sheep dead or badly injured across Britain in the last year, according to figures just released.

The shocking tally marks an eight per cent increase in reported attacks compared to the previous year.

It has also prompted a new campaign to raise awareness of the problem.

The National Sheep Association has now joined forces with the RSPCA and NFU to send a joint message to dog owners to take more care of their pets.

The Livestock Worrying Campaign will use weatherproof warning signs that have been produced for use on rights of way and other footpaths.

Andrew Opie, the NFU's head of technical department, said:"This is a major initiative to try and make the public aware of the harm their dogs can cause.

"I would urge all livestock farmers to put signs up wherever the public are likely to be walking their dogs."

However, sheep are not the only farm stock at risk from dogs allowed to roam free by owners.

Poultry is equally vulnerable to attack, say organisers of the campaign which has been launched all over the country.

Cattle and horses could also be spooked and end up causing harm not only to themselves but to the dog itself and even its owner.

SPECIALITY FOODS, organic produce and farmers' markets point the way to the future of farming, according to the Council for the Protection of Rural England.

Kaley Hart, CPRE's rural policy officer, said:" Successful farm enterprises of the future will need to be about more than just producing crops and live - stock.

"They will also need to get income from managing the countryside for its beauty and diversity and adding value to their products.

"Local food initiatives are no longer a niche market. They are a bright spot in an otherwise bleak farming economy and contribute almost £5 billion to the economies of rural areas."

COMPENSATION RATES FOR those farmers sold hyola oilseed rape crops with GM impurities are now "fair" after weeks of intensive debate.

NFU officials have been in talks with Advanta since the announcement last month that a number of farmers had unwittingly planted GM-affected rape.

Advanta has revealed it will pay £337 per hectare for the 2000 crop and some 9.5 per cent more for growers north of the line between Newcastle and Carlisle, in recognition of their higher yields.

NFU president Ben Gill said:"We believe the affected farmers will see this as a fair settlement. It provides a speedy solution."

ELECTRIC STUNNING EQUIPMENT was used to rescue over 2,000 fish in a pre-planned operation at a reservoir near Darlington.

The reservoir, at Broken Scar, is used for storing river water and is being drained by Northumbrian Water for vital maintenance.

Fish including chub, dace, gudgeon, and roach could have been left high and dry so water chiefs called in the Environment Agency to help.

A team of fisheries officers used nets and electro-fishing equipment which temporarily stuns fish so that they float to the surface unharmed.

Richard Holmes, Agency fisheries officer for the Tees catchment area, said: "These fish had entered the reservoir as fry from the River Tees and grown well.

"They could not stay there due to this draining operation so we were happy to help out. Over 2,000 were successfully removed and returned to their rightful home in the Tees."

A RUNAWAY BULLOCK has been offered a home at an animal sanctuary after it dramatically escaped from an abattoir.

Bertie the bullock fled the abattoir in Dundee and caused traffic mayhem as it ran across a bridge.

Motorists swerved to avoid the bullock which was eventually brought under control after being darted by a transquilliser gun.

The animal's bid for freedom seemed to have come to nothing - until the sanctuary in Norwich heard about its plight.

Now Hillside Animal Sanctuary has contacted abattoir firm Mathieson Jess pledging to buy Bertie and pay the cost of transporting him.

MORE THAN 14,000 chickens perished in a blaze which swept through a farm in Hampshire.

The fire is believed to have broken out in a packing shed and scores of firefighters were called in to deal with it.

About 40,000 other chickens at the farm in Basingstoke escaped the flames and were looked after by the RSPCA. Some birds also fled from the fire ravaged shed itself.

Firemen called the fire an "inferno" and said the farmer had done everything he could to halt the blaze.

Over 70 firemen worked together to bring the fire under control, a task which took them about two hours.

The incident comes weeks after 700 pigs and piglets perished in a blaze which hit their piggery in North Yorkshire.

Firemen who raced to the scene of devastation there managed to save 600 other pigs which had become trapped by the flames.

BIRDWATCHERS HAVE been boosted by the reappearance in the wild of a species that has not nested here for hundreds of years - spoonbills.

The birds, so named because of their distinctive beaks, are related to herons and are believed not to have nested here for more than 300 years.

A pair of spoonbills has arrived at a wildlife reserve owned by the RSPB in Dumfriesshire and the birds appear to be settling in to stay.

Although spoonbills have been occasional visitors in the past, fingers are crossed that their latest appearance could be the start of a spoonbill renaissance in Britain.

BADGER LOVERS HAVE welcomed a decision not to pursue a national badger cull beyond the controversial action already being taken.

During a meeting of the TB Forum, the NFU, the Royal College of Veterinary Surgeons and the British Cattle Veterinary Association accepted that badger culling was not an appropriate way to solve the bovine TB crisis.

Dr Elaine King, conservation officer for the National Federation of Badger Groups, said:"For 25 years, MAFF, the NFU and the veterinary profession have claimed that badgers are the primary cause of bovine TB in cattle.

"Now they have accepted that cattle husbandry and health must be addressed in order to solve the problem.

"This important concession will allow farmers, vets, and conservation organisations to work together in finding solutions to bovine TB which meet the four key criteria laid down by the NFBG.

"The solutions must be practical for farmers, humane for livestock, caring for wildlife and acceptable to the public."

She said that farmers needed proper grant funding if husbandry measures were to be implemented successfully.

"We hope that by taking an holistic approach to cattle health, solutions will be found not only to bovine TB, but also to other cattle diseases, which are increasing at an alarming rate," she added.

"At the same time, we hope these solutions will help to maintain a diverse rural economy with support particularly directed at smaller family farms whose margins are most narrow."

BRITAIN'S HUMBLE COD is now being ranked alongside the tiger and panda as an endangered species by environmental pressure group the Worldwide Fund for Nature.

Also endangered are the jobs of the fishermen that depend on it - 15,000 full-time and 3,500 part-time across the UK.

Without action to save the cod, stocks could soon be fished out in British waters, says the WWF, and haddock could be next to go.

The group made the announcement to raise awareness of the plight of the UK's marine environment and send a warning to the fishing industry to take preventative action.

A spokesman said:"Cod and chips could be a thing of the past if we are not careful. But we are not just an organisation concerned with protecting the environment at any cost.

"The jobs in the fishing community are also of great concern to us."

GROWERS OF BRITISH summer fruits are being left in a jam because of a shortage of seasonal workers to harvest their fruit.

Thousands of tonnes of strawberries, raspberries and cherries are being allowed to rot - leaving foreign competitors to take a slice of the increase in demand, say farmers' leaders.

"Imports of strawberries rose 39 per cent in the three years to 1998, meaning British growers now supply less than half of the 72,000 tonnes bought in Britain each year," said a spokesman for the NFU.

"The problem is caused mainly by a lack of British casual workers due to current low unemployment levels.

"And growers looking to employ foreign students during their holidays are thwarted because the Government only allocates a limited number of work permits for students each year."

The NFU has now set up an email address to enable anyone who wants a summer job picking fruit to get in touch.

LAND USED TO turn out Army crackshots has been bought from the Ministry of Defence in a move to convert it into a premier wildlife site.

For 100 years soldiers were taught to shoot on Rainham Marshes on the outskirts of London but now the RSPB is setting its sights on fresh targets after paying more than £1million.

A spokesman for the RSPB said:"Almost 100 years of use as an Army rifle range has preserved this huge expanse of grazing marsh on the edge of London.

"Acquisition of the site has brought to an end the long history of development threats as London spreads down the Thames.

"The RSPB now faces the great challenge of creating a wetland nature reserve. This will include the essential task of removing any contamination and checking for unexploded ordnance, which will be arranged by the MoD."

TINY TRANSMITTERS HAVE been helping wildlife researchers learn more about one of Britain's rarest bats.

The transmitters were stuck to the backs of barbastelle bats, among the oddest looking of the species with squashed faces and thick ears which meet between their eyes.

English Nature and the National Trust joined forces in the study involving one of the largest known remaining UK colonies of barbastelles in Somerset.

The sophisticated transmitters were attached to about 15 of the bats and meant researchers could build a clearer picture of their feeding activities and social interplay.

As planned, all the transmitters fell off within a month - leaving the monitored bats free to carry on chasing moths undisturbed as before.

THE COUNTRYSIDE ALLIANCE says its membership is soaring following its recent "call to arms" to prevent a hunting ban.

The call was issued by the Alliance after it was revealed that an options Bill, which could include a ban on hunting, would be introduced in the next parliamentary session.

Since then, membership numbers have risen quickly - 1,600 applications since the start of July alone.

FARMERS' LEADERS HAVE called on the Department of Health to use best British produce in a new pilot scheme offering school children free fruit.

Michael Holmes, chairman of the NFU Horticulture Executive, said the introduction of fruit to the school timetable was a much-needed pro-active step in promoting the consumption of fruit among youngsters in the UK.

He believes the Department of Health should source locally-produced fruit as part of its initiative to benefit British growers and school children alike.

He said:"If every school child between the ages of four and six was given an English apple a day this would represent 40 per cent of our home-grown crop. It would be fantastic news for the industry."

Research into measures to increase fruit consumption and other pilot projects - funded largely by UK growers - were proving hugely successful, he added.

He hoped the department would liaise closely with the fruit industry when making arrangements to take its proposal forward.

Mr Holmes also welcomed another commitment by the Department of Health to fund a programme to increase fruit and vegetable consumption among the population in general.

Both projects were announced as part of the Government's programme of reform for the NHS - 'A Plan for Investment. A Plan for Reform.'

A QUARTER OF the methane gas released into the atmosphere comes from "belching" cows, MPs have heard.

The animals' digestive system is proving a potent polluter as it adds to the greenhouse effect behind global warming.

During the final question time of the summer, Labour MP Gordon Prentice told fellow members:"Belching cows are actually responsible for 25 per cent of the methane released into the atmosphere - a very powerful greenhouse gas."

He revealed a dietary supplement was available that could be introduced into cows' feed to reduce the problem.

Government Agriculture Minister Nick Brown conceded he was happy to investigate anything that might improve farmers' incomes.

ANYONE WANTING TO branch out on a new career might like to study the latest job opportunities offered by The Woodland Trust.

Woodland officers are urgently required in Hertfordshire, Essex, and Buckinghamshire with a £25,000 salary, car, and pension going to the lucky applicants.

Application forms are available.

DAMAGE TO THE countryside from pollution is still not being properly reflected in the fines handed out to guilty companies, says the Environment Agency.

And although regulation of industry is cutting hazardous emissions by thousands of tonnes, ongoing pollution across England and Wales is marring environmental gains.

In its report 'Spotlight on Environmental Performance - 1999', the Agency highlights big reductions in pollution from power stations, processing plants, and the chemical and mineral industries.

At the same time, over 500 companies and individuals were prosecuted for serious pollution offences which left the public and the environment exposed to a host of nasties, including asbestos, dangerous waste, chemical gas clouds and raw sewage.

Environment Agency chairman Sir John Harman said:"The Agency continues to be disappointed about the overall level of fines imposed on companies once they have been found guilty of an environmental crime.

"The Environment Agency believes the current average level of fines still does not reflect the long-term damage and strain forced on our precious environment through criminal neglect."

A REPLICA RIVER with associated wildlife was one of the star attractions at the CLA Game Fair in Oxfordshire.

The Game Conservancy Trust provided the eye-catching feature for the fair, which is believed to be the biggest and most popular of its type in Europe.

Thousands flocked to the three-day event held at historic Blenheim Palace which provided a huge array of countryside activities and attractions for visitors.

The Trust's stand was said to be its best and most innovative yet, including the replica river, fish tanks for children to dabble in, and an exhibition about the Trust farm at Loddington.

Live otters, duck decoy carving, gun engraving, and welfare techniques for game were among other attractions offered by the Trust.

The conservation charity also used the fair to flag up its latest fox and moorland research to help broaden visitors' knowledge of the countryside.

FORTY PER CENT of top English wildlife sites are in a poor or declining condition, according to the annual report of English Nature.

"The new Countryside and Rights of Way Bill cannot come a moment too soon," said chairman Baroness Young.

"The Bill is essential if we are to help improve these degraded wildlife sites. Positive management has been secured on many SSSIs across England through co-operation and genuine partnership with the many farmers, landowners and land managers who are responsible for them.

"Without this legislation, however, all the hard work to protect and manage these natural jewels can only have a limited effect.

"Many of the measures in the proposed Bill will really strengthen our ability to build on this positive partnership.

"Underpinning this, there will be powers to effectively address cases of deliberate damage and neglect including third party damage which is currently of concern for many SSSI owners."

HERON: an aristocrat makes a meal of some tiddlers

WITH his deadly sword-like beak, tall figure and imperious stalking manner, the heron has always seemed like an aristocrat among birds to me as he goes about his daily hunt for food.

Often a loner during hunts, he can stand motionless for hours on end in freezing water as he picks off fish, frogs, insects, small birds and mammals that come within striking distance.

Long legs and a long neck help herons reach an impressive 98 cms in height which is about the size of a Canada goose.

But a heron's more upright, rigid stance makes him seem even larger.

Occasionally, you can spot herons standing like scarecrows in open fields when their luck has run out at ponds or lakes and they turn their attentions to warmer-blooded prey.

This change of strategy, combined with a heron's eye-catching grey, white and black plumage can add up to a wonderful bonus for the casual bird-watcher strolling in open countryside.

It's usually quite difficult to get close to a sharp-eyed heron in the wild - or so I thought until I went on holiday to Ireland recently.

There, at an idyllic inlet about 30 miles south of Cork, I sat watching a heron fishing in shallow salt water just 20 feet away.

Boats bobbed around near a jetty and fishermen readied a trawler for another expedition close by.

But this particular heron seemed unconcerned.

Ruthlessly, relentlessly, he stalked and ate a succession of silvery tiddlers, snatching them up one after another.

I counted at least 10 victims so this bird obviously boasted a healthy appetite.

That beak is truly formidable and I can't remember my Irish heron missing with a single strike, such was the surgical precision of his technique.

Although herons are fairly evenly distributed across the whole of the British Isles, nesting herons are more difficult to pinpoint.

So I was fortunate as a child to live near a communal nesting site located in trees in the middle of a swamp.

During the frenetic breeding season, the big adult birds would flap in on mighty wings to feed their ravenous chicks and often tottered unsteadily on legs not best designed for perching in branches.

For someone who previously thought the heron solitary and elusive, this breeding colony was an eye-opener.

Noisy and smelly, you were aware of its existence from quite a distance.

However, so cleverly was it arranged in the centre of the swamp that there was no real danger from predators, at least not from the likes of foxes or stoats.

Perhaps a hawk or owl could have threatened the chicks from the air but it would have been a brave individual that was willing to risk a stab from a heron's murderous beak.

Even so, herons don't have it all their own way and I read of one bird that needed rescuing after falling foul of two swans.

These bigger, even more powerful birds brook no opposition during their own breeding time and it appeared the heron had simply strayed too close to their nest.

Battered and dazed in a furious onslaught, it was finally plucked to safety by a human rescuer before the swans could move in and finish it off.

Herons have also been cruelly treated by Man, usually as a result of ignorance.

So impressive are a heron's fishing skills that many people once believed the bird's legs must hold a magical allure, drawing fish helplessly within killing range.

Sadly, this mistaken belief backfired on the heron.

Many birds were trapped and dispatched so that their severed legs could be spread around local fishing areas for the benefit of human anglers - presumably to little effect.

COUNTRY CAMPAIGNERS ARE outraged by Government moves to launch GM crop trials at 25 new sites despite the whole programme running into a storm of criticism.

Prime Minister Tony Blair is apparently still keen to pursue the trials despite New Labour admitting contamination is inevitable and following recent exposure of worrying mistakes.

The Soil Association, which champions organic farming, has attacked Mr Blair for "blowing Clinton's pro-GM saxophone."

A spokesman said:"Apparently singing from the same pro-GM songsheet as the US President at the recent G8 summit in Okinawa, Mr Blair has shown himself to be dangerously out of tune with the British public's views on this crucial environmental and food safety issue.

"The Prime Minister's comments made no distinction between the wider use of biotechnology in medicine as opposed to the less rigorously tested and uncontained application of genetic modification in agriculture and food production.

"After stating in February this year that 'There is no doubt that there is potential for harm, both in terms of human safety and in the diversity of our environment, from GM foods and crops', Blair seems to have changed his tune for this duet with Clinton.

"Apparently supporting President Clinton's uncritical pro-industry position on GM food, Blair stated 'The science of biotechnology is going to be for the first half of the 21st Century what information technology was to the last half of the 20th Century'."

Soil Association GM-campaigner Harry Hadaway added:"Tony Blair seems to have been seduced by Bill Clinton's GM-sax appeal. This is particularly worrying given that the US Government's own scientists are warning about inadequate GM safety testing."

SEAGULLS AND PIGEONS causing the same sort of mess in Devon could meet with very different fates.

Teignbridge councillors have decided that while pigeons can get the chop for their dirty deeds, the seagulls will fly free.

Although both are guilty of despoiling local areas, only seagulls are a protected species while pigeons can be eliminated with a controlled cull.

The disparity is unlikely to wash with residents and holidaymakers who have felt the full force of a seagull's bowel movement.

"A seagull splattered me with what seemed like half a pint of the stuff as I waited for my wife outside a shop," recounted one disgruntled Devon holidaymaker."It took ages to clean off."

MORE PEREGRINE FALCONS than ever before are proving their adaptability by nesting in cities.

The predators, which can reach 200mph in a stoop, have been spotted in 40 urban nest sites across the country.

But besides setting up shop in the likes of Liverpool and Cardiff, the high-speed falcons have also been observed in the capital.

Ornithologist Chris Mead identified one of the birds hunting pigeons and other birds near London's Stock Exchange.

Peregrines have fought back from a severe decline in the last 60 years after gamekeepers, pesticides, and other hazards almost wiped them out.

Recently, the RSPB blamed disgruntled pigeon fanciers for a poisoning campaign being waged against the birds.

Despite this, numbers are now thought to have risen to about 1,300 pairs.

FRIENDS OF THE Earth says it "expressed quiet satisfaction" at what it saw as the failure of the Dump the Pump campaign to inspire widespread public backing.

In a move certain to anger supporters of the national petrol protest, FoE transport campaigner Tony Bosworth announced:"The Dump the Pump campaign will do nothing to help rural communities, poorer households, or the environment.

"That is why it has been widely ignored by people up and down the country. We hope the campaign will now meet a decent, quick and obscure end.

"The pressure must now be put on the Government to show that the money from fuel taxation is being spent on improving our trains, running more bus services, and helping make our streets safe for cyclists and pedestrians.

"Britain's transport crisis needs a green solution, not the simplistic slogan peddled by Dump the Pump."

FISH WERE SPOTTED desperately trying to outswim a mystery pollutant which had entered their river with devastating consequences.

Salmon, trout, pike and other species were among 10,000 fish later washed up dead when the unidentified pollution ran into the River Dee.

An investigation has been launched by environmental experts after a 20-mile stretch of the Dee was affected across the Shropshire/Welsh border.

Anglers have been shocked by the extent of the carnage and fear fish stocks might struggle to recover, especially if the source of the pollution is never found.

A spokesman for the Welsh Federation of Coarse Anglers, said:"Whatever went into the river seems to have run along the bottom first because the flat fish and eels got caught first. Then, within half an hour, other fish were dying.

"People have said they could actually see the fish trying to keep in front of the pollution, trying to race it."

SCOTS FISHERMEN ARE being urged to embark on shorter trips and catch fewer fish in a bid to boost the quality of remaining stocks.

The Scottish Fishermen's Federation says a change of mindset is vital to safeguard the industry and eventually give fishermen more power.

President Alex Smith revealed the objective when he opened the Fishing Co-operatives Exhibition at Fraserburgh.

HORRIFYING DEATHS CAUSED by 'drowning' in grain silos are the subject of a warning being put out to prevent further tragedies.

Farmers' leaders are reminding farmers and their families of the dangers posed by grain silos as this year's harvest gets into full swing.

"Moving grain acts like quicksand on a human body and every year one or two people are suffocated when they are dragged under grain in a silo," explained a spokesman for the NFU.

"When the outlet of a grain bin is opened, grain flows out through a small hole at the bottom of the pit creating a suction effect.

"Problems usually arise when the emptying switch is thrown accidentally while someone is standing on the grain."

The NFU is urging farmers to take some simple steps to minimise the dangers to themselves and others.

These includes educating everyone - especially children - to the dangers of silos; ensuring the grain pit has a strong grid at or near its surface; and fitting safeguards in each grain bin, such as a scaffolding pole or overhanging ladder.

NFU technical services committee chairman Marcus Themans added:"Too often farmers and farm workers are unaware of the dangers of moving grain in a silo.

"A person standing up to their knees in moving grain would be subjected to a massive suction effect, impossible to escape even with people attempting to pull you out.

"Knowledge of these potential hazards and cheap and easily fitted design features can reduce or even eliminate the dangers."

BASKING SHARKS HAVE been spotted powering up the Bristol Channel in force.

About eight of the plankton-eating giants were observed together off the north Devon coast, giving a visual treat to local residents and holidaymakers.

The sharks have become an increasingly common sight off South West beaches.

So much so that a pod of killer whales was drawn to Cornish waters earlier this year in pursuit of them.

Killer whales traditionally prey on basking sharks with their peg-like teeth making light work of blubbery bodies which can reach 30 feet in length.

Plymouth's National Marine Aquarium has been building up a database involving basking sharks and asking the public to send in photographs and data.

It is hoped the move will help with an international bid to protect the sharks, known for their gentleness towards inquisitive divers.

THE RAMBLERS ASSOCIATION has attacked a county council for what it sees as the betrayal of the public over a dispute involving a multi-millionaire landowner.

The Association has accused East Sussex County Council of conducting a sham public consultation regarding a blocked footpath on the estate of Nicholas van Hoogstraten.

An RA spokesman explained:"The 140-year-old public path on High Cross Estate, Uckfield, East Sussex, has been illegally blocked with a locked gate, barbed wire, refrigeration units and a barn for more than 10 years.

"The council has suspended a recent order to clear the route while it considers an application by the landowner to divert the path.

"But the Ramblers Association has learned that hundreds of people have already written to the council urging it not to accept the diversion and to clear the existing path instead.

"Now the council is washing its hands of a decision over the route of the path by saying it intends to pass the diversion proposal to a public inquiry."

Ramblers executive committee member Kate Ashbrook added:"The council consultation process has been a complete sham.

"We know that hundreds of people have written to object to the proposal, yet the council is still planning to go ahead with the unnecessary diversion.

"There is simply no need for a lengthy and expensive public inquiry in this case. The council clearly does not have the guts to make a decision on the path.

"Instead of passing the buck, it should listen to public opinion, reject the proposed diversion, and open up this ancient path for everyone to use."

ROAD RAGE MAY be a problem for motorists but anglers in Shropshire have their own phenomenon to deal with - RIVER rage.

A man in a speedboat has apparently brought terror to the once peaceful banks of the River Severn where anglers like to relax over their fishing.

Racing along, the mystery tormentor allegedly heads for anglers' fishing lines and deliberately snaps them before roaring away.

Telford and Wrekin Council is investigating the latest incident, said to be just one of a series which have left anglers angry and upset.

One angler lost 200 yards of line before it finally snapped and claimed to have heard the speedboat driver laughing in contempt as he made off.

BRITISH SHEEP FARMERS could be facing losses of £60 million as the industry questions whether the European Commission cares about it.

The NFU is openly doubting European commitment to the country's sheep farmers regarding the Basic Sheepmeat Price, the impact of exchange rates and the future of the Sheep Annual Premium scheme.

NFU deputy president Tim Bennett said:"We feel that the Commission has not taken into account the changing marketplace of the past few years which has rendered the Basic Price out of line with the current needs of the sheepmeat market.

"The NFU estimates that the overall effect of exchange rates could mean a loss of £3 per ewe, costing the UK sheep industry more than £60 million.

HATED BY MANY for their panoramic banality, bright yellow oilseed rape fields have nevertheless proven a surprising hit for one tiny resident - the linnet.

Fields full of oilseed rape have been credited with throwing a lifeline to what is one of the country's fastest declining songbirds - down 40 per cent in numbers over three decades.

Research in Oxfordshire by the RSPB and Oxford University has shown that adult linnets have been exploiting unripe oilseed rape seed from May onwards to feed their chicks.

This is because their traditional foods, such as seeds from weeds like charlock, have become scarcer in the countryside following the increased use of herbicides.

Vicki Swales, RSPB head of agricultural policy, said:"This research shows how the crops that farmers decide to grow can have an important bearing on the fortunes of farmland birds.

"Break crops, such as oilseed rape, provide a much-needed form of food for farmland birds, especially linnets."

Sadly, the linnet resurgence could be cut short as the trend for growing oilseed rape seems likely to decline along with a reduction in the oilseed rape subsidy paid to farmers.

Around 900 linnet nests were monitored on 10 farms by Oxford University student Darren Moorcroft who found a third of chicks starved to death in nests on a farm with no oilseed rape.

However, most chicks remained well fed in areas where the parent birds could take advantage of oilseed rape.

WOODLAND EDGES ARE probably the best areas for nurturing wildlife and plants, reveals a new Forestry Commission report aimed at woodland managers.

The report offers comprehensive new guidance to managers on the best ways to use boundaries and tracksides in lowland forests to maximise nature conservation.

A spokesman explained that in areas where direct sunlight could reach the forest floor a greater variety of plants, insects, birds and animals were encouraged compared to what happens in more shaded woodland.

Gordon Patterson, principal biodiversity adviser for the Commission, added:"Edge habitats in the forest have particular micro-climatic conditions that favour many species of conservation importance.

"For woodland managers who want to increase the nature conservation value of their forests, manipulation of light, micro-climate and vegetation succession are the keys to managing edges for creating diverse and species-rich habitats."

A RED KITE found dead in Buckinghamshire woodland has prompted an investigation by RSPB officials.

The probe should find whether the rare bird has been deliberately killed or died from eating poisoned vermin - a previous cause of fatalities.

The fork-tailed body of the rare bird was discovered in woods near Marlow by a man out for a stroll.

Although there were no obvious signs that it had been shot, it would not be the first kite to die by human hand recently.

The RSPB says another kite in the area was unlawfully killed within the last year.

The dead bird is thought to come from the Chilterns kite release programme which has seen 90 imported Spanish kites successfully bred to produce scores of offspring over the last decade.

About 300 red kites now live in and around the Chilterns while others have been transported elsewhere in the country to help replicate the programme there.

GROUSE ARE THE key to creating thriving moorland habitats for other wild birds, according to a study by two game conservation bodies.

'Conservation and Management on Grouse Moors' is a joint study by the Game Conservancy Trust and the National Gamekeepers Organisation.

"This dynamic little bird is the key to biodiversity and flourishing wildlife in a habitat which is unique to the UK and the landscape owes its very existence to grouse shooting," said a spokesman.

"Waders, including curlew, lapwing and golden plover, fare far better on grouse moors than on unmanaged moors.

"Golden plovers and lapwings are five times as abundant on grouse moors compared to other moors, and curlews are twice as common.

"Other birds found on grouse moors and associated mountain tops include twite, merlin, golden eagle, dotterel and ptarmigan.

"Heather moorland has been largely retained because of grouse shooting which is the main financial incentive for its conservation."

OTTERS ARE NOW thriving in Yorkshire and parts of the North East after years when they had virtually disappeared there.

The shy aquatic mammals have staged a remarkable comeback alongside other endangered wildlife, says a report just published by the Environment Agency.

The report, 'Focus on Biodiversity', reveals otters are flourishing throughout Yorkshire and Northumbria while salmon, sea trout, water voles and freshwater mussels are prospering in Northumbrian rivers.

Singled out for special mention is the once widespread but now endangered tansy beetle whose entire British population is believed to be confined to the banks of the River Ouse in York.

But with this habitat now under threat, English Nature has begun removing the beetles, storing them for relocation to ensure the species survives.

A WHEAT FIELD in Oxfordshire is providing a booming trade for a local pub after pranksters constructed a crop circle in it.

Takings at the Fox and Hounds pub in Uffington have soared since the intricate circle appeared - drawing hundreds of visitors.

ILLEGALLY DUMPED RUBBISH is a rocketing problem for the countryside with farmers and growers swamped by a rising tide of filth, a new report reveals.

Furtive fly-tippers now regularly use the countryside to offload assorted refuse such as old tyres, burnt-out cars, and ancient baths, according to an NFU survey.

"More than half the respondents said fly-tipping is a major on-going problem with more than a quarter of farmers and growers having seen a significant increase in fly-tipping over the past year," said a spokesman.

"With harvest now in full swing and many fields open for easy access, the illegal dumping of tonnes of waste material on farms is likely to increase further over the next few weeks.

"The volume of the material is often considerable - in one case recently eight tonnes of tyres were dumped in a field. And once waste has been dumped at one site, the offenders often return.

"Perpetrators are seldom brought to book for their actions because a substantial amount of evidence is necessary to successfully prosecute flytippers.

"In the absence of the offender, local authorities can take action against the landowner to remove the offending material."

NFU deputy president Tim Bennett added:"It is quite unacceptable that farmers are having to bear the brunt of the costs of clearing up a crime they did not commit.

"The problem has got much worse since the introduction of the Landfill Tax. Instead of encouraging people to recycle their rubbish, reducing the volume produced, it has had the effect of simply increasing the illegal dumping of waste."

THE ACCIDENTAL KILLING of wandering albatrosses was the topic used to launch this year's British Birdwatching Fair.

Saving the world's largest flying bird has become a campaign waged by BirdLife International and publicised during the three-day fair at the Egleton Nature Reserve, Rutland Water.

A spokesman for the RSPB said:"Hundreds of thousands of seabirds are killed every year, accidentally hooked on the longlines put out by fishing vessels, many of them fishing illegally.

"Approximately 60 species of seabirds have been recorded as being caught on longlines. Among these are 18 albatross species and the legendary wandering albatross is especially at risk.

"Nearer home, tens of thousands of North Atlantic seabirds, mostly fulmars, are drowned every year as they become ensnared on longlines fishing for cod, ling and tusk."

A RARE FISH has been spotted by Environment Agency scientists swimming in a once heavily polluted river in the north of England.

The shy 'allis shad', part of the herring and sardine family, was seen in the River Ouse in Yorkshire - the first time it has been identified at the location.

"Agency scientists stumbled on the fish during a recent survey near York," explained a spokesman.

"In the past both the allis and a second variety of shad found in domestic waters - the twaite - were fished in considerable numbers. But increased pollution in our estuaries has restricted the British population of both species."

However, measures to upgrade the tidal Ouse and Humber Estuary were now paying rich dividends.

Fishery science team leader Richard Jenkins added:"The return of the shad is a very important step for the Ouse system. Over recent years we have seen salmon and sea trout return - and now the shad.

"This is a result of major improvements and efforts to clean up the Ouse and the Humber Estuary over the last few years. With water quality improving further, we would hope to see more of these wonderful fish."

The shad is now classified both nationally and internationally as "rare and threatened" and is protected by legislation.

Usually, the allis shad ascends rivers in spring for nocturnal spawning over gravel beds before returning to the sea by late summer.

The fish itself is herring-like in appearance but deeper-bodied with a bluish cast.

COUNTRYSIDE CAMPAIGNERS ARE furious at a Government move to quash laws preventing unsightly billboards peppering country roads.

Deputy Prime Minister John Prescott is in the firing line again after relaxing laws stopping advertising hoardings in tranquil areas.

Although the Government says local councils will still have powers to prevent excessive advertising, the Council for the Protection of Rural England is angered by the move.

A spokesman said:"We now face the prospect of all kinds of billboards appearing along roads in some of our most beautiful rural areas."

It is hoped that Mr Prescott, in overall charge of the Environment, can be persuaded to change his mind and reverse the decision before big business can exploit the opportunity.

But the Government hopes farmers will benefit from renting out parts of their land to companies who want to advertise.

A PENSIONER IS at loggerheads with a council over its 100ft high willow trees which loom over his home, blocking out light.

As Gloucester City Council mulls over new Government proposals to allow it to cut down boundary trees causing neighbour disputes, Andrew Miles, 81, has accused it of hypocrisy.

The three willow trees stand about 20ft away from his property but Mr Miles claims the authority refuses to trim back their huge outlines.

He has branded the council a "neighbour from hell" and said it should examine its own behaviour before casting an eye at the new Government scheme.

BRITAIN'S THREE MILLION anglers now contribute a whopping £3.3billion annually to the nation's coffers, it has been revealed.

The revelation will be a severe blow to protesters wanting to stamp out country pursuits, particularly those supporting a growing campaign against the "cruelty" of fishing itself.

Details of the cash mountain provided by anglers were highlighted by the Environment Agency as it published its formal response to the recent Salmon and Freshwater Fisheries Review.

Dave Clarke, head of fisheries for the Agency, said:"We welcome the review group emphasis on developing the economic, recreational and social value of fisheries within a sustainable framework.

"In particular, we note that around three million people now fish each year, spending £3.3billion annually."

The overall thrust of the review accorded with the Agency's own views and concerns.

"We agree that fisheries need to be managed in the context of wider environmental and conservation concerns, as many of the problems affecting them stem from the wider uses of land and water," said Mr Clarke.

"Proper funding for protection is vital. Without healthy and sustainable fish populations, fisheries themselves cannot exist in the long term."

FEAR OF DISEASE jumping the species barrier and being passed to humans has led to the halting of a £12 million research programme into the use of pig organs for transplant.

Scientists at Edinburgh's Roslin Institute, famous for its cloning experiments, have put the brakes on a six-year research project just a third of the way in.

The move follows research elsewhere which proved that viruses carried by pigs could be transferred to humans and create an epidemic.

The decision to halt the Roslin research is being generally welcomed following previous scientific blunders that led to the outbreak of BSE in cattle and its human equivalent CJD.

THE RSPB HAS warned of the danger of complacency after welcoming Government moves to protect a further 82 English wildlife sites using European law.

The Society says many of the sites will remain highly vulnerable until they are more strongly protected under English law.

Dr Mark Avery, RSPB conservation director, said:"We are extremely pleased the Government has at last recognised the importance of these sites for wildlife. But the RSPB remains concerned this protection creates a false sense of security."

However, European law should now protect them from things like peat extraction.

SWINE FEVER COULD be spreading to new parts of the country despite desperate measures to clamp down on an outbreak in Suffolk and Essex.

Concerns have been raised that farms in Cheshire, Lincolnshire, and Derbyshire may also be affected by the outbreak which has already seen almost 10,000 pigs slaughtered.

Tests are now being conducted by Ministry of Agriculture vets in a race to ascertain whether thousands more pigs need to be killed.

Earlier, a backlash against the EC's devastating decision to ban export of live pigs from Britain appeared to be on the cards after supermarket Asda threatened to drop Belgian pate in protest.

British pig farmers, already put under the cosh by tough market conditions, were horrified by the Commission move to bar live pigs and pig semen following the outbreak of the disease.

An Asda spokesman said:"It will cost us money but we want to do it. We need an industry going forward. British pig farmers are going out of business every day."

A WOLF HAS apparently been sighted running free in Scotland - but no-one knows whether it has escaped from a wildlife park or is part of a secret release programme.

The animal was spotted in Clashindarroch Forest, near Huntly, by Gloucester lawyer Conrad Sheward who was on a shooting trip.

Mr Sheward, 62, was accompanied by a friend and his friend's teenage son when the trio chanced upon the animal, known for its ferociousness in the wild.

"At first I thought it was just a big fox," said Mr Sheward."It was grey with a whitish tail. But then I realised it was much too big for a fox. It was not a dog either."

He had previously seen wolves before up close in zoos and there was no doubt in his mind that this is what it was.

MANY COUNTRY VILLAGES are becoming "artificial husks" following the demise of local shops and stores which formed the focus of their communities, claims the Countryside Agency.

Today, a third of the UK's 14 million country population no longer have a local shop and have to trek into towns and cities to buy basic groceries.

"Villages which lose their shops quickly lose their identities as communities," said Margaret Clark, spokesman for the Government agency which identifies rural problems.

The steep decline in the fortunes of country shops is thought to be a knock-on effect from the widespread loss of rural sub-post offices.

Increased competition from supermarket chains is also believed to be a factor in the loss of shops, helping to drive any remaining vibrancy out of vulnerable communities.

FEARS HAVE BEEN raised among ramblers that the Countryside and Rights of Way Bill could be badly weakened or abandoned in its present form.

The Bill, praised by ramblers but opposed by many landowners, has been caught in a backlog of legislation at the House of Lords.

A spokesman for the Ramblers Association revealed peers had tabled more than 300 amendments which meant that the Bill had very little chance of progressing.

PRAYERS WILL MARK the massive but often unseen contribution of country women to British agriculture as part of a worldwide 'thankyou' for their work.

Farmers' leaders are to join church and religious groups in an international day of celebration to highlight the global contribution of rurally based wives, mothers, and daughters.

This will be the fourth time that the NFU has led UK celebrations of World Rural Women's Day, scheduled for Sunday, October 15.

Celebrations here will complement those already organised in other countries including China and the United States.

NFU president Ben Gill said:"World Rural Women's Day gives an opportunity for all involved in farming and rural communities to recognise the crucial role played by women in farming around the world.

"The industry welcomes the opportunity this day offers us all to say thank you."

This year the NFU will be working in conjunction with the Arthur Rank Centre and the Women's Food and Farming Union.

A special prayer, written by the Rev Gordon Gatward, of the Arthur Rank Centre in Stoneleigh, will be available to everyone taking part.

Rev Gatward said:"The Church has an acute awareness of the central role of women in the community and particularly in the more isolated areas of the country.

"I hope we can play a key part in raising awareness of their contribution by taking the celebration into the heart of our communities."

RURAL CRIME IS spiralling out of control with many criminals viewing the countryside as a soft touch compared to towns and cities, say the Conservatives.

While CCTV and tough policing continue to make inroads into urban crime, the countryside has seen an extra 70,000 offences committed in the last year.

This is a leap of six per cent, according to Shadow Home Office spokesman John Bercow.

To make matters worse, police officers are leaving rural police stations at twice the national average.

This makes it even easier for determined crooks to earn rich pickings - almost £170 million worth of ill-gotten gains last year.

Country areas in Essex, the Thames Valley, and Hampshire are among the worst hit places with some rural communities feeling under siege.

"This is further evidence that the Government has dumped rural Britain," claimed Mr Bercow.

"For those living in rural areas it is a tragedy."

SUPERMARKET BOSSES ARE being sent stark details of how little money Britain's farmers are making while supplying them.

Shocking figures comparing production costs for eggs and poultry meat with cash received by farmers have been dispatched to supermarket chiefs by the NFU.

This was meant to "graphically illustrate the threat facing production in Britain" according to a spokesman for the farmers' union.

"The figures show no sign of any let-up in the poor prices that have been endured by farmers for the last three years, with caged egg producers losing an average 17.6p per dozen and poultry meat barely covering its costs."

The NFU says it has sent the figures with a letter from its Poultry Committee Chairman Charles Bourns as a "wake up call" to retailers.

He reminds stores that real commitment is needed to protect the future of farmers who have invested heavily to meet their demands.

Such investments have included satisfying the requirements of farm assurance schemes, as well as expenditure on environmental and welfare legislation.

Egg producers now also need to make extra financial commitment to placate new EU calls for even higher welfare standards.

Mr Bourns said:"Producers have worked together to differentiate their product and raise standards. They deserve to see a fair return for their efforts."

A TOURIST IN Dorset ended up covered in blood when a seagull dropped a large whelk shell on her head.

The victim was stunned by the impact of the shell dropping an estimated 60ft onto her skull as she was enjoying her holiday at Lyme Regis.

Eyewitnesses said the bird had been aiming to break open the shell on rocks but misdirected the whelk, thought to weigh about six ounces.

The blow left a large gash on the woman's head, covering her in blood and prompting the harbourmaster's assistant to administer first aid.

Local residents say gulls often smash open whelks at the spot and the holidaymaker, from the Midlands, was just unlucky.

A SEARCH FOR crabs at a beach in Devon almost went with a bang for two youngsters when they discovered a live grenade.

The explosive, thought to date from the Second World War, was discovered beneath cliffs at Teignmouth as the pair crept around looking for crabs.

After they raised the alarm, bomb disposal experts raced to the scene but had to wait until the grenade was uncovered by the tide the following day before taking action.

They then carried out a controlled explosion as the grenade appeared to be in an unstable state and was too dangerous to move.

During the drama, a lifeboat crew patrolled the River Teign estuary to warn of the danger.

THE COUNTRYSIDE ALLIANCE's army of supporters should be marching on its stomach following a fund-raising event this autumn.

Hunting fans across the country are being urged to raise £100 for the campaign to keep hunting legal by charging 10 friends £10 a head for a roistering night dubbed 'Host a Roast' in October.

61

TWO OF SCOTLAND'S best known alpine birds will be among the first species to vanish if scientists' startling predictions about global warming come true.

The dotterel, an attactive mountain wader, and the grouse-like ptarmigan live in the northern danger zone where scientists say vast numbers of animal and plant habitats could be destroyed.

"Global warming means a horrifying future for nature," said Jennifer Morgan, director of the World Wide Fund for Nature climate change campaign.

"This is a wake-up call to world leaders - if they do not act to stop global warming, wildlife around the globe may suffer the consequences.

"They must give top priority to reducing levels of carbon pollution to prevent a catastrophe that could change the world as we know it."

On a brighter note, the organisation has just launched a dolphin watch in Dorset to monitor five bottlenose dolphins which visit the waters off Christchurch between summer and spring each year.

The dolphins - named Echo, Bob, Lumpy, Spot and Nick - have already been extensively tracked but the wildlife charity needs to learn more about their activities during winter.

Data collected about the pod will be used by the group's Ocean Recovery Campaign, contributing to general information about dolphin behaviour.

Already, researchers have received reports from Dorset of the dolphins riding the bow waves of boats and allowing people to stroke them.

WATER BUFFALO COULD help a farmer put his financial troubles behind him as he ploughs on with a new career venture.

Nick Griffin was so desperate to make more money that he ended up disposing of his 100 Friesian dairy cattle in preference for a herd of buffalo.

New calves have recently been born among the 120 animals at his Slapton farm on the Beds-Bucks border.

Now plans are afoot for large-scale milk production using a high-tech milking parlour.

Mr Griffin has joined only a handful of specialist farmers in the country keeping water buffalo.

He has picked up tips and information from Romania where the herd was bred.

With traditional British farming still under the cosh, he is staking everything on making his new business a success - on the back of an animal originating from Asia.

THE COUNTRYSIDE ALLIANCE has called on members to step up their campaign of lobbying MPs to help keep hunting legal.

A spokesman said:"Many of our opponents in Parliament are claiming to receive hundreds of letters and e-mails from those opposed to hunting.

"In the run-up to legislation this autumn, it is imperative that we counter this by lobbying hostile MPs.

"Constituency co-ordinators and hunts with hostile MPs must organise letter writing, e-mailing and surgery visits in a sustained way over the next few months.

"Many MPs claim to have received no letters in favour of hunting when we know this not to be the case.

"To help us attack these inaccurate claims, please copy all correspondence.

"We must act now to show MPs that the Burns Report does not justify a ban and that they have a responsibility to liberty and tolerance to oppose a ban."

WILD ORCHIDS AND Essex skipper butterflies are among species which have won better protection from vehicles at a nature site near Maidstone.

Boxley Warren is part of the Wouldham to Detling Escarpment SSSI that extends along the North Downs and is also the home of the nationally rare box tree.

Deputy Prime Minister John Prescott has now issued a Nature Conservation Order which will give the site better protection from scrambler motorbikes, cars, and fly-tipping.

English Nature conservation officer Teresa Bennett said:"For many years there has been a problem with vehicles causing damage and visible scarring.

"This Order is necessary to protect Boxley Warren which supports orchids, chalkhill blue and Essex skipper butterflies, and the yew woodland with all its associated wildlife."

MORE THAN 15,000 young trees have been planted to create a wood in memory of hundreds of soldiers slaughtered in a First World War battle.

The Woodland Trust joined forces with a local newspaper in Hull to guide residents in planting the trees at the site which was recently blessed by religious leaders.

Local people decided to call the site Oppy Wood after the battle of the same name fought in France in May, 1917.

On one fateful day, 200 Hull men were killed and 400 others injured, captured or recorded as missing in action.

A Trust spokesman explained:"It was believed bad planning was the main reason for the huge losses.

"The men were ordered to attack at night up a rise, which silhouetted them against the bright moon."

AN ENERGETIC POD of five or six killer whales was spotted close to shore in the Shetlands.

The black and white whales appeared to be hunting but it was unclear what their exact prey might be.

However, basking sharks, dolphins, seals, and a variety of fish are all on the menu.

GREY SQUIRREL: American import defeats British cat

WITH a vicious bite and seriously destructive habits, it's a little surprising that the grey squirrel has prospered so well in its adopted country.

Looking fluffy and cuddly has obviously helped this American import, which is now common throughout much of the UK after usurping our own native red squirrel in most areas.

Grey squirrels are certainly widespread in my neighbourhood and, unlike foxes or badgers, seem to relish living alongside Man without feeling the need to hide themselves away.

They often seem very brave or very reckless.

Only recently I was in a church hall when one paused on a fence right next to the window, casually stared in at me, then hopped on its way.

This is supposed to be a wild animal, I reminded myself.

Other times I have known them explore friends' houses and select some tasty titbit before departing.

Grey squirrels were introduced to this country in the 19th Century from hardwood forests in the United States.

Nuts and acorns are top of their menu but they also eat bark, tree buds and flowers, which can bring them into conflict with humans.

Additionally, squirrels take birds' eggs or even the chicks themselves, a practice which slightly undermines their cuddly image.

Nevertheless, while rats and mice are destroyed in their thousands, culling just a handful of squirrels is frowned upon in today's politically correct climate, as some councils have discovered from outraged local residents during pest control campaigns.

Squirrels nest either in a hole in a tree or build their own living quarters from a ball of twigs called a drey.

In summer, dreys can be quite flimsy but in winter, when the cold starts to bite, these are altogether more substantial constructions.

Being comparatively difficult for predators to catch, grey squirrels have been known to live for 10 years in the wild.

Keen eyesight and a powerful sense of smell give them great protection when allied to their natural athleticism and climbing ability.

Like cats, they have also been known to survive falls of up to 35ft without injury.

Talking of cats, I was once a neutral observer of a feud between a grey squirrel and a girlfriend's cat.

The cat, a particularly bad-tempered female, had come to hate this squirrel which regularly hopped around the garden fence, trespassing on her territory in the most provocative manner.

Each time it appeared, the cat would hiss, arch her back, then try to bring her teeth and claws to bear on the intruder, which wasn't easy.

The squirrel would angrily chatter back from its vantage point, flick-flick its tail in alarm, then scarper up a tree as the cat attacked.

This went on for weeks until the moment of truth dawned when the pair finally came together on the ground in a flurry of screeches and fur.

I think I was enjoying a glass of wine in the house at the time when a commotion outside suddenly interrupted.

Racing into the garden, I almost tripped over the terrified cat fleeing back to the house with an ugly gash on her forehead.

The wound, still dribbling blood, was the result of a savage bite from her arch enemy.

With the cat vanquished, the squirrel now sat quietly in the tree looking down.

If I didn't know any better, I would swear it was smirking.

That cat never chased a squirrel again.

FARMERS ARE BEING urged to take extra care not to pollute streams and rivers with toxic chemicals when they dip their sheep this autumn.

The Environment Agency says it wants to avoid a repeat of the disasters in 1997 and 1998 when widespread, serious pollution problems occurred after farmers had dipped or showered sheep to protect them.

Geoff Bateman, chairman of the Agency's Rural Land Use Group, revealed there had initially been a positive response by farmers and contractors to their campaign to raise standards.

"Last year there was a move away from using synthetic pyrethroid dips. As a consequence, very few pollution incidents were recorded," he explained.

"However, the situation this year is more difficult with the only available sheep dip compounds being based on synthetic pyrethroids which are enormously toxic to our environment. Already this year serious pollution problems have been recorded in Wales.

"We are urging the industry to build on last year's good record and minimise the impact of sheep dipping on the environment and rural economy."

To help farmers reduce the risk of pollution the Agency has just issued an information sheet containing various tips.

THE MYSTERY OF how two Baltic Sea sturgeon dropped onto a lawn in mid-Devon was solved following an appeal for information by a local newspaper.

Falling fish is not a new phenomenon but Tiverton gardener Mrs Thorven Smith was astounded when the six-inch fish - one still alive - were identified as starry sturgeon.

Frogs, fish, and other aquatic inhabitants are occasionally sucked up into the sky during extreme weather conditions before falling back to earth.

But the route the two fish used to find their way into Mrs Smith's garden was rather shorter than first imagined.

A neighbour told the newspaper he had bought the fish for his pond from a Somerset aquarium - and his cat Smudge had tried to make a meal of them.

GREY SEALS WILL be the star attraction for Welsh wildlife lovers as the pupping season arrives and parts of the coastline play host to new life.

Staff at the Pembrokeshire Coast National Park have been busy organising trial trips to see one of the main pupping beaches there.

A spokesman explained:"The grey seals of the Pembrokeshire seas take shelter as the pupping season approaches and offer a spectacular sight at a range of locations along the coast."

GROWERS OF TRADITIONAL English hazelnuts have cracked one of the most discerning markets for nuts - native red squirrels.

The NFU says that English growers have doubled their usual harvest this year with part of the bumper crop providing a treat for red squirrels which much prefer them to dried foreign versions.

"Up to 15 tonnes of fresh hazelnuts - some six million nuts - will be transported from where they are grown in the south of England," said a spokesman.

"They will be taken to animal reserves and estates in the north of England and Scotland to give the dwindling red squirrel population a crunchy feast.

"English hazelnuts, also called cobnuts, have been eaten as a human delicacy for years - now the squirrels have jumped on the bandwagon.

"They are marketed fresh, not dried like most other nuts, with a green husk and a white crunchy kernel. They are only available as a green nut from now until mid-October with stored brown nuts available until Christmas."

John Cannon, chairman of the Kentish Cobnuts Association, will sell some of his own crop in areas where red squirrels are prevalent.

He said:"Part of our harvest will go to specialist suppliers who will then sell them on to individuals and organisations keen to conserve red squirrels.

"They tell us that red squirrels prefer fresh English hazelnuts hands down over the dried nuts imported from countries like Turkey, Italy and France.

"Red squirrels have good taste - fresh English nuts are a hand-picked delicacy."

THE DECLINE OF the British barn owl has been halted - and the bird owes a debt of thanks to rats at the other side of the world.

Malaysian rats were only brought under control after local owls were encouraged to breed among them in special nest boxes on poles.

The scheme was so successful it was adapted to help our own barn owls whose numbers had plummeted, the British Association Annual Science Festival heard at London's Imperial College.

The Hawk and Owl Trust, which led the project, has since put up 1,000 pole nest boxes in suitable areas around the country.

As a result, the barn owl is moving away from extinction and numbers appear to be finally recovering.

Colin Shawyer, director of the Trust, said:"The decline has been stopped. The population has stabilised and, instead of the previous decline, we now have about 4,000 pairs."

FEMALE PIGEONS ARE being bamboozled in Brighton and Hove by having their real eggs swapped for china replicas which will never hatch.

The fiendish scheme also involves siting pigeon 'hotels' around the coastal towns, encouraging the birds to nest there rather than at random sites on rooftops.

The dovecotes and china eggs form part of a pioneering project to cut the problem of pigeon mess that afflicts towns and cities across the country. Other local authorities are expected to follow suit if it proves a success.

BULLFROGS ARE THE latest threat to the British countryside with English Nature asking the public for urgent help in tracking down fugitives now breeding in the wild.

The ravenous North American frogs devour our own frogs and small creatures, compete for habitat, and spread new diseases to which native wildlife has little resistance.

A spokesman for English Nature explained:"Despite a recent importation ban, the North American bullfrog has been found at a number of sites across England.

"Many were bought as pets but then escaped, or were released, into the wild. Breeding has now been confirmed at one site on the Kent-Sussex border.

"English Nature is taking this issue very seriously. We want to prevent the establishment of bullfrog populations. We are therefore asking for the public's help in tracking down any remaining bullfrogs.

"It is unlikely that there are very many bullfrogs in the wild, but we would like to know if you have seen or heard one."

Adult bullfrogs grew up to eight inches in length - much bigger than native species - with their tadpoles reaching 15cms and taking two to three years to develop into froglets as big as normal British frogs, he added.

"Britain is also home to a few other introduced frog species, especially in the South East, which may cause confusion. However, the bullfrog is the largest and is readily identified through its appearance and calls."

DUNG FROM HIGHLAND cattle could provide an extra boost to heather moors in Scotland by attracting more insects for game birds.

Dr Adam Smith, of the Game Conservancy Trust, told the Highland Cattle Society Conference in Perth that the benefits from cattle had been discovered in a controlled study involving plots grazed by cattle, by sheep, or left alone.

"Dung from the cattle supports high insect and other invertebrate numbers which provide potential food for grouse and wading bird chicks," he explained.

"Manipulating grazing pressure is an important tool to regenerate moorland but, as an alternative to traditional shepherding, preliminary studies indicate that stocking Highland cattle on upland and afforested areas may be an ecological and economic alternative.

"These cattle could have a lower impact on regenerating vegetation but a high impact on dense ground cover. Further, there is reduced damage over winter through browsing since cattle are usually wintered off exposed moorland.

"Game and wading bird species may benefit from cattle stocking because of nutrient cycling and the fragmentation of dense ground cover."

FARMERS ARE WARNING they will turn up the heat on the Government to beat its "unfair treatment" despite Premier Tony Blair saying he will not back down.

Farmers for Action UK said a symbolic blockade of an oil refinery in Cheshire to protest about high fuel prices was just a taste of things to come.

Later, members joined truckers in a spate of new protests.

More than 200 farmers took part in the initial blockade which was monitored closely by police and quickly parted to allow lorries through.

But thousands more were believed to be involved in fresh demos.

The protest has sparked alarm that petrol panic buying could result if the action spreads.

David Handley, chairman of the action group, said farmers felt they were being betrayed by the Government and big business.

He added:"We have decided to follow our counterparts in France. This is going to be an ongoing situation. I would suggest this is going to be a winter of unrest."

Farmers are protesting at crippling fuel prices - just the latest in a series of blows to hit the industry.

A BRAZEN FOX has used all his wily powers to ingratiate himself with soft-hearted players at his local golf club.

Now members of Milton Golf Club in Peterborough are so used to having their games interrupted by the animal that they stop to feed him treats.

Chocolate bars are top of the list of goodies that the fox is fed - a world away from foxes' more hard won natural diet in the wild which includes anything from rabbits to rats.

Even the club's chairman Roy Rome has developed a soft spot for the fox but is concerned that the chocolate-rich diet fed to him by fellow members might be doing more harm than good.

He is trying to make amends himself - by carrying a little bag around containing pet food when he tees off.

HUNT SABOTEURS HAVE been accused of rampaging through foxhunting kennels in West Sussex - terrorising a family and leaving a policeman injured.

Up to 30 masked saboteurs are reported to have descended on the Surrey and Burstow Foxhound Kennels in East Grinstead.

Manager Mark Bycroft said the shouting gang smashed windows and hurled insults as his pregnant wife and their toddler cowered inside.

Two policemen who had turned up to head off the violence were overpowered and one left injured in the fracas.

However, the Hunt Saboteurs Association claims their members came under violent attack from people wielding pickaxe handles after arriving at the scene to protest about an earlier incident.

A WOMAN IN Gloucestershire spent three hours vainly trying to rescue a duck snared by fishing wire in the middle of a lake.

In the end, passing nightclub bouncer Dean Greenhough came to her aid - stripping to his underpants and becoming a hero of the hour by rescuing the duck.

THE FUEL CRISIS has starkly revealed the growing gulf between the needs of Britain's farmers and the ambitions of the country's environmentalists.

Despite the vast majority of the public supporting farmers and hauliers in their protest, Friends of the Earth claimed high fuel costs were the only way forward.

Instead of backing farmers, FoE attacked Prime Minister Tony Blair for not explaining to the country well enough that high fuel prices were needed for both the economy and environment.

Roger Higman, the group's senior climate and transport campaigner, said:"Mr Blair should make it clear that high fuel prices are needed to tackle the terrible consequences of global climate change.

"This was the reason that the Conservative Party introduced the fuel price escalator in 1993, and why Gordon Brown continued the policy until last year.

"Mr Blair must make very clear that climate change is driving this policy and that, if western nations don't act, millions of people around the world will die or lose their livelihoods as a result of floods and hurricanes."

Any cut in fuel prices would also damage Britain's credibility in international climate negotiations due to take place in the Hague in mid-November, he added.

However, both the Countryside Alliance and the NFU have given their backing to the farmers, a move more in step with the mood of the country.

In an open letter to Tony Blair, NFU president Ben Gill said the protests reflected the scale of the anger and frustration being felt by farmers and growers in the countryside at large.

He said:"We have said over and over again to the Treasury that it was only a matter of time before farmers' patience on fuel taxes ran out - the current duty is nothing short of extortionate."

WILDLIFE RICH SALTMARSHES and mudflats are vanishing at an alarming rate from the nation's coastline, according to a new study by the RSPB.

However, the report 'Seas of Change' says new areas could also be created to turn back the tide in favour of wild birds and fish if financial incentives were offered to landowners.

"Areas of mudflat and saltmarsh are one of the nation's richest wildlife habitats and in winter support around two million birds, internationally-important concentrations of wading birds like black-tailed godwit, knot, grey plover and dunlin,"said a spokesman.

CANNIBALISM AMONG OTTERS has sparked fears that the aquatic mammals are being driven insane by environmental pressures.

Although the British otter population has recently shown signs of fighting back from dwindling numbers, the evidence of cannibalism and infanticide has shocked scientists.

According to a report in British Wildlife, researchers conducted post mortems on 200 otters and found that more than 30 had suffered serious attacks by other otters.

However, these were not put down to the normal territorial conflicts among males as the violent attacks had sometimes led to the death of the animal and females were also victims.

More disturbingly, one dead male otter was found to have eaten a young cub, the remains of which were still in its stomach.

Severe wounds were found all over the bodies of dead otters, with bites to the genitals and face quite common.

MYSTERY SURROUNDS THE vanishing and reappearing act accomplished by a small herd of Aberdeen Angus cattle in Hampshire.

Police were alerted after the bull and six cows disappeared from a field in Fareham leaving no clue as to their whereabouts.

Farmer Philip Paul was certain they had been stolen and ferried to a slaughterhouse where their meat could be sold on.

But he was amazed when all the cattle reappeared the following day in the same part of the field where he had last seen them.

Although they were unharmed by their ordeal, they seemed disturbed and ravenously hungry - prompting further questions about how or why they were taken in the first place.

RURAL COMMUNITIES WILL suffer badly because of BT's hike in call charges for public and private phones, it has been claimed.

Richard Burge, chief executive of the Countryside Alliance, said:" BT intends to double the minimum charge from public call boxes and increase the cost of local calls from telephones in the home. The telephone is a lifeline for rural people and this increase will hit them hard."

Mr Burge also attacked the present cost of using the internet - a facility that could make life easier for rural communities but is currently too expensive.

BT seemed determined to maintain its stranglehold and revenue from local calls.

"We hear so much about how the internet is going to revolutionise rural industry. Well, it will simply fail to happen unless we get unmetered access to the network," he warned.

CYANIDE IS BEING blamed for the sudden death of up to 5,000 fish found floating in a canal in the West Midlands.

The Environment Agency has launched an investigation into the incident at a canal at Birchills, near Walsall.

A spokesman said:"Following tests, it has been discovered that a small quantity of cyanide was present in the water. The affected stretch of water has been isolated to allow removal of the dead fish.

"Although there is no danger to the public in the surrounding areas, people are advised to avoid the canal itself and in particular to keep dogs away."

OPEN WARFARE IS feared between farmers and environmentalists following the judgement to allow anti-GM campaigners to go unpunished after wrecking crops.

The NFU reacted with anger and shock at the "perverse" not guilty verdict in the trial of protesters who trashed a field of genetically modified maize in East Anglia.

NFU president Ben Gill said the verdict at Norwich Crown Court amounted to declaring open season on British farmland.

He said:"This case was about criminal damage to a farmer's crop. It raises fundamental issues about the right of farmers to go about their lawful business.

"We find it extraordinary that, even with such clear evidence, a not guilty verdict was reached. This gives the green light to wanton vandalism and trespass."

Mr Gill said that if the trial sites were to be made public, better protection must be given to farmers lawfully taking part in the trials in future.

"I will be urgently writing to Jack Straw in advance of a scheduled meeting on this and other issues," he said.

"The NFU believes it is right that we learn as much as possible about GM crops before any decisions can be taken about whether they can be grown commercially.

"It is bizarre that those who are seeking to stop the trials from taking place are also saying there is insufficient evidence on GM crop safety to allow them to be grown."

Anti-GM crop protesters have hailed the not guilty verdict as a victory for common-sense in the face of widespread fears about GM crops contaminating the whole of the British countryside.

WASPS BROUGHT TERROR to a primary school cross country run when one pupil accidentally stepped on their nest.

About 14 youngsters from Clive Primary School in north Shropshire were stung - some several times - as the wasps vented their fury.

Hundreds of wasps were reported to have attacked the group, which included five adults, after their nest was disturbed.

Headteacher Mary Lucas was among adults taking part in the run and said wasps "just poured out of the nest" during the terrifying incident.

Fortunately, none of the group suffered an allergic reaction to multiple stings, she added, and pest control officers later destroyed the nest.

RAMBLERS HELD RALLIES all over the country in a show of support for the Government's beleaguered right to roam legislation.

Fears have been raised that controversial new laws opening up the countryside will effectively be blocked by landowners.

A DISCARDED HAM sandwich is being blamed for the outbreak of classical swine fever which saw more than 30,000 pigs slaughtered and cost the farming industry millions.

The amazing theory comes from Ministry of Agriculture investigators who claim to have traced the start of the outbreak to sow number 857Y at a farm near Quidenham in Norfolk.

A passing rambler is believed to have either dropped or thrown the sandwich to the pig which ate it and then went on to start the first swine fever outbreak in Britain for 14 years.

The virus, which only affects pigs, can survive for up to a year on ham products but causes no danger to human health while being fatal for pigs.

The in-depth probe has revealed that the infected sow later had a litter of 12 piglets but, within a week, eight of the piglets died. The other four recovered but were subsequently suckled by different sows.

As a result, the piglets began spreading the virus themselves while their mother infected other pigs before dying.

The swine fever strain, first identified in Switzerland eight years ago, is believed to have come from boar meat imported from eastern Asia.

The same type was also found in a consignment of meat illegally imported into Austria a year later.

A PET PARAKEET survived a week in the wild and was finally reunited with his Devon owner after chatting to him on the telephone.

Plymouth pensioner John Keily was devastated when his parakeet Bobby escaped, tramping miles around his home in a vain hope of spotting the bird.

Police and wildlife workers were alerted about the missing parakeet but no-one knew he had already flown into neighbouring Cornwall.

There, exhausted and lost, he was finally caught and taken to local couple Geoff and Jennifer Green who specialise in keeping exotic birds.

They put out a message on local radio asking for Bobby's owner to come forward - a message picked up by a chum of Mr Keily who relayed it to him.

Mr Keily then rang the Greens' bird centre , asked them to put Bobby on the phone, and wished him Good Morning - whereupon the parakeet exclaimed:"Good morning. Bobby's a good boy!" and proved his master's ownership.

GOLD MEDAL SUCCESS for shooting in Sydney has been hailed as a victory for Britain's rural sports despite constant Government interference.

A spokesman for the Countryside Alliance said:"What a marvellous effort from young Richard Faulds in the double trap shooting and from Ian Peel in the trap shooting category.

"One gold and one silver out of a team of six is not bad going, especially when you consider that our shooting team gets very little public funding - unlike many of our other higher profile but far less successful international sporting teams.

"The Alliance is proud to have made its own small contribution to the team's efforts with its sponsorship assistance through our Campaign for Shooting.

"And our shooting team's efforts are even more remarkable when you consider that the Government and politicians are, it seems, falling over themselves to put more and more obstacles in the way of nurturing our shooting talent."

67

TWO IMAGES OF the Labour Party Conference seem likely to be remembered the longest in the minds of rural campaigners - the peaceful protesters outside the hall, and the ranting of Deputy Prime Minister John Prescott as he attacked them.

Delighting delegates by apparently playing the class card, the former trade union official said the "contorted faces" of Countryside Alliance members only made him more determined to ban foxhunting.

Meanwhile, in another memorable outburst, Leader of the Lords Baroness Jay announced that she understood the problems of rural communities because she kept "a little cottage in the country".

Later, it emerged the cottage was located in a prime piece of Oxfordshire woodland and embroiled in a dispute with neighbours over the side effects of building work to expand it.

During the conference, NFU deputy president Tim Bennett had taken part in a parade involving more than 150 farmers and their tractors in a peaceful demo through the streets of the seaside resort.

As the march came to a halt outside the Brighton Centre, Mr Bennett accompanied a group of farmers inside to meet Agriculture Ministers Joyce Quin and Elliot Morley.

Mr Bennett said:"Farmers have been extolled by Government to help themselves out of the crisis.

"They are trying to do exactly that but all the time they are being hampered in their efforts by Government-made problems.

"Falling incomes, extortionate taxes and red tape are all threatening the desperate fight to survive."

Countryside Alliance chairman John Jackson called on members to continue exhibiting self-discipline in their protests despite emotions running high.

BITTERNS AND OTHER birds have been boosted by international protection being granted to two wildlife sites in London.

The sites - one in the Lee Valley and the other in south west London - comprise a number of former gravel pits, reservoirs, and sewage treatment lagoons vital for wintering waterbirds.

English Nature chairman Baroness Young said:"This announcement is great news. It will help safeguard over 1,200 hectares of the London area for important species of waterfowl."

The Lee Valley supports six per cent of Britain's wintering bittern population with other parts of the two sites important for wintering wetland ducks.

Each site now has two international designations - Special Protection Areas are a European designation to protect birds, while 'Ramsar' sites protect wetlands around the world.

THE HARDY EVERGREEN rhododendron may be a beauty in the garden but it's a beast in the forest, according to the Forestry Commission.

Anyone sick of the sight of it who wants to clear rhododendron from forests and woodlands can go along to a workshop to learn how best to do it in Scotland on November 1.

"Rhododendron was introduced into Britain in 1763 and planted extensively by the Victorians. In the United Kingdom it is an invasive weed species that thrives on acid soils in wetter parts of the country,"said a spokesman.

"It infests many areas but is particularly aggressive in woodlands where it can spread rapidly, preventing other species of natural vegetation from getting enough light and nutrients to survive.

"Woodlands invaded by rhododendron are difficult to regenerate naturally and eventually become dominated by an under-storey of dense, head-high rhododendron. Once established, it becomes very difficult to eradicate."

A SCOTTISH RIDER has won one of the toughest equestrian competitions in the world on a horse rescued from the knacker's yard.

The mare Mhairi caught the eye of David Hay-Thorburn when he was on the lookout for new blood for his stables at Brenfield.

At first he knew little about the background of the horse that only escaped death after a dealer gave her one last chance, but her attractiveness made her stand out from other sales animals.

Mr Hay-Thorburn paid just £200 for Mhairi and built her up until she became the undoubted star of a pony trekking business he runs.

But her strength and ability were so marked that he decided to enter her in a world famous Austrian competition which combines orienteering skills with horse riding.

Horse and rider have now become the first British pair to triumph in Le Trec - beating almost 50 other entrants.

NUMBERS OF BSE infections among British cattle have dropped dramatically while variant CJD among humans has leapt to at least 74 cases.

According to the latest report from the Ministry of Agriculture, Fisheries and Food, the BSE outbreak is now well under control.

Only 30 new cases are being found among cattle each month - a vast improvement on the 1,000 cases recorded each month seven years ago.

Tests show that almost two thirds of UK herds with adult breeding cattle have now never had a single case of BSE.

However, the human cost of variant CJD continues to rise - albeit at a slower rate than first predicted.

Some 63 people had died of it by the end of June this year with other cases investigated involving people still alive but expected to succumb.

FEARS HAVE BEEN raised that zombie farm animals could be created in future by GM companies.

Chickens or pigs bred to feel no pain could be the next target of big businesses, according to the new Agriculture and Environment Biotechnology Commis - sion.

It believes new laws are needed to stop GM technology creating a future filled with so-called Frankenstein Farmyards.

BADGER: mighty burrower needs to keep its head down

POWERFULLY built, yet shy and elusive, the badger is an animal which sparks almost as much controversy and debate in the countryside as the fox.

Strong claws, big forearms, and a muscular, streamlined body mean the badger is perfectly designed for digging and living unseen underground.

Its tendency to exist in large family groups has also added to its ability to thrive despite the urbanisation of much of the country.

Badger baiting - where victims are often maimed even before dogs are let at them for 'entertainment' - has long been a scourge.

But conservationists have been fighting back and most counties now have groups dedicated to protecting badgers, backed up by police and the RSPCA.

Unfortunately, badgers have recently been under threat again from official quarters.

Renewed fears about tuberculosis being spread from badgers to cattle recently sounded the death knell for thousands of twilight foraging 'brocks'.

Protesters, many of whom think badgers are innocent of the TB charge, are appalled that renewed slaughter of these handsome, hardy creatures has become a feature again of the British countryside.

Meanwhile, opinion among scientists themselves remains divided on how much, or even if, badgers are responsible for spreading TB among cattle.

But it is quite sad to reflect that some 4,500 badger setts were already wiped out using poisoned gas between 1975 and 1982.

When you consider that an average sett can contain up to 15 animals, parents and cubs, it is easy to imagine the scale of suffering involved.

Putting all that aside, it is not difficult to be charmed by a badger.

I have always looked upon them as mini-bears, although they are actually from the same evolutionary tree as stoats and weasels.

Nevertheless, they have many of the same mannerisms as bears and are also omniverous.

"They'll eat almost anything," one seasoned Home Counties badger watcher, Jean Beach, told me when I called in for a chat.

"I've taken out lots of different foods over the years, from peanuts to fish heads. They seem to love it all."

Worms are the staple diet. Yet badgers will also feast on fruit, birds' eggs, and small mammals, including - perhaps less endearingly - baby rabbits, dug from their burrows using those formidable claws.

Jean knew the precise locations of several setts.

However, not surprisingly, these were kept a closely guarded secret.

When we spoke, Jean told me the sows were preparing to give birth so the setts were quieter. Expectant mums often spent more time underground.

The best time to see badgers is when the youngsters emerge.

This is usually around mid-March, after a female has given birth to two or three cubs, with weaning starting at about 12 weeks.

The last occasion I saw a badger up close myself was not a happy experience.

It was curled up beside a road, very quiet and still. Dead, in fact.

Road accidents do account for a large number, usually males roaming the country-ide in search of new territories.

But roadside corpses can also have a more sinister history.

An RSPCA inspector told me that badger baiters occasionally disposed of the evidence this way, giving a false impression of how the animal met its end and preventing any awkward inquiries.

A carefully placed tyre tread might even reinforce the deception.

I was pretty certain the badger I found had not been baited as a close examination revealed no tooth marks.

It had few visible wounds on it at all so I think it must have died slowly from internal injuries, which seemed just as pitiful.

THE BATTLE FOR Britain's countryside between ramblers and landowners has resulted in the longest debate in the House of Lords since 1988.

Controversial proposals to give more freedom to roam led to an 18-hour debate which raged through the night and only came to a close when the nation was rising for breakfast at 8am the next day.

Lists of detailed amendments had to be discussed for the Countryside and Rights of Way Bill to progress - an exercise seen by supporters of the Bill as a classic blocking attempt by peers representing landowning interests.

But peers from both Labour and Tory camps attacked the Government for trying to include access after dark as part of any new legislation.

Conservative agriculture spokeswoman Lady Byford said night-time access prompted concerns over security and safety, as well as the environment.

Ramblers recently held rallies all over the country in a show of support for the Government's hotly contested right to roam legislation which protesters say will threaten wild species.

Thousands of people supporting the Bill gathered at 20 separate events across England and Wales.

Among those attending the rallies was the Deputy Leader of the Commons who spoke about the Government's desire to see the new law progress through Parliament.

At a rally in South Yorkshire, Paddy Tipping said:"The public has been campaigning for this legislation for over a century. This access is now finally within its grasp."

Nicky Warden, head of a ramblers freedom to roam campaign team, added:"We are delighted by the Government's determination to pass the legislation in its entirety this year."

BIG CAT EXPERTS are prowling the wilds of Leicestershire which has recorded more alleged sightings of the predators than anywhere else in Britain.

Investigators from the Exotic Animal Register in Bristol are conducting a serious probe of the region which has played host to more than 120 sightings this year alone - far more than elsewhere.

Leicestershire has been dubbed "big cat country" following a spate of recent incidents.

However, local people do not treat the sightings as a new phenomenon as huge cats were apparent - ly seen in the county as long ago as the 1950s.

Back then, one big cat made a special impression on terrified residents and was subsequently labled the Monster of Hinckley.

LABOUR VIEW THE countryside in the same way they view the Dome, according to Tory leader William Hague.

Addressing rural campaigners at the start of the Conservative conference in Bournemouth, he pledged a fairer deal for farmers if the electorate ditched Labour at the next election.

He said:"This Government only sees the countryside as a theme park, a rural version of the Dome. Farming and the countryside both deserve better."

He condemned what he labled "a metropolitan elite" who had no understanding of the country-side for imposing their will on rural communities.

He also blamed Labour for allowing a split to grow between residents in the country and those in the town. Tories would heal the rift, he pledged.

Mr Hague immediately came under attack from Labour who once again accused him of jumping on any bandwagon available to get elected.

SCOTTISH BOGS ARE the subject of a new exhibition which noisily celebrates their appeal with distinctive sound effects.

The interactive exhibition put on by Scottish Natural Heritage is called 'Wild, Wet and Wonderful' and aims to brush aside any visitor misgivings about boglands.

Despite their outward lack of appeal, bogs support a rich variety of wildlife, say organisers of the event at the Harestanes Countryside Visitor Centre near Jedburgh.

Scotland still has some of the finest wetland areas in the world while many other countries have disposed of their own boglands without even realising the cost.

BEAVERS MAY BE reintroduced soon in the Argyll area of Scotland after Scottish Natural Heritage unveiled plans involving the aquatic mammals.

The Mammal Society says the proposed site is in the Knapdale Forest which is owned by the Forestry Commission and managed by its agency Forest Enterprise.

"It is hoped to release around 12 European beavers in order to study their impact," said a Society spokesman.

"The field trial would run for five years, after which an informed decision would be made about whether a full reintroduction would be desirable.

"If, following a trial, it is decided that the species should not be reintroduced to Scotland, the project would be dismantled and all the animals removed."

A NEW REGISTER of companies still using compounds that can damage the countryside and its wildlife has been produced by the Environment Agency.

The register lists over 274 companies collectively holding almost 40,000 items of equipment such as transformers and capacitors which use harmful PCBs - polychlorinated biphenyls.

Paul Leinster, the Agency's director of environmental protection, said:"The phasing out of PCBs is good news for the environment. They accumulate in fatty tissues and can harm wild birds, river and sea fish and wild mammals.

"Many PCBs will have to be removed or decommissioned by the end of this year and nearly all use of PCBs will have ceased by 2010."

IMMEDIATE ACTION IS needed by the Government to save threatened farmland birds from extinction in parts of the country, says the RSPB.

The Society is urging MAFF to allow farmers and conservationists to protect some of our most threatened species which face being wiped out in arable areas.

The Ministry is currently evaluating the success of the arable stewardship scheme, an agri-environment project which has been piloted in only two English regions.

But because this evaluation may come too late for some birds, the RSPB is calling for the scheme to be rolled-out immediately to prevent species like skylarks, tree sparrows, and corn buntings from disappearing altogether in some areas.

MAFF is currently committed to turning round the declines of key farmland birds by 2020, as part of its Public Service Agreement.

Yet the RSPB believes that immediate roll-out of arable stewardship options involving 'winter stubble', 'conservation headlands' and 'wildbird seed mixtures' would be the first new step to help achieve this target.

Dr Sue Armstrong-Brown, RSPB agriculture policy officer, said:"The early roll-out of these measures will be a lifeline for farmland bird populations which are on a knife-edge in some areas. It is now up to MAFF to take action before its too late."

In addition, the RSPB is urging MAFF to quickly set up two special projects under the stewardship scheme to help two threatened upland bird species - black grouse and twite.

Earlier, RSPB chief executive Graham Wynne said Government rural policy was failing to deliver at all levels - social, economic and environmental.

DESPITE HIS UNROMANTIC surname, farmer Robert Clapp has been judged the winner in a national beauty contest aimed at finding the most attractive face of farming.

With his dashing good looks, 25 year-old Robert "romped home" in the NFU contest to unearth the country's "tastiest farmers" to help promote the new red tractor British food logo.

Robert, who farms in Somerset, beat 17 other entrants after proving his credentials before a London judging panel which included Cosmopolitan editor Lorraine Butler.

Seven regional winners were also selected in the contest, aimed at beefing up the British Farm Standard mark.

Ms Butler cooed:"Seeing these farmers has changed my perception of agriculture. I'm sure these new faces of farming will give the industry a new image and help to woo shoppers into buying British food."

POLICE SWOOPED ON homes across the South to arrest 18 people as part of a probe into an attack on a fox hunt's kennels last month.

More than 80 officers launched a series of dawn raids in Surrey, Sussex, Kent, Somerset, and London in an operation codenamed Tempo.

Eight women were among the people held during the swoop which was led by Surrey Police officers assisted by officers from four other forces.

Police are continuing their inquiries and further arrests could still be made.

About 50 anti-hunt protesters descended on the Old Surrey, Burstow and West Kent Fox Hound Kennels in Felbridge, Surrey, last September leaving a trail of destruction and terror.

The hunt kennels manager later told how his pregnant wife had been forced to flee with their 15-month-old daughter just before their home was attacked with rocks.

Mark Bycroft, 29, claimed the protesters had shown absolutely no respect for women, children, property or animals.

He also claimed hunt colleague Jeremy Wright was hit by a brick while a hail of stones smashed 17 windows after police alerted him the protesters were on their way.

The masked demonstrators screamed abuse at kennel staff and overpowered two policemen during their 15-minute protest.

The attack on the kennels followed an earlier incident which left a hunt saboteur seriously injured as he protested against a hunt meeting at Horsted Keynes, near Crawley, West Sussex.

HEDGEHOG LOVERS ARE feeling a little prickly at suggestions from birdwatchers that their favourite mammal is responsible for declining bird populations.

Even TV naturalist David Bellamy has been caught up in the row after reportedly calling for a national cull of hedgehogs to save ground nesting birds.

Officials from the British Hedgehog Preservation Society have sprung to the defence of the spiky animal which, nevertheless, appears to be polishing off birds' eggs on a massive scale.

They say the popular garden visitor cannot be viewed as vermin and should not face being wiped out in a similar way.

Warm weather has been blamed for a population surge among hedgehogs in recent years which has had a knock-on effect against bird populations in some areas.

A NEW BLUNDER within Government GM crop trials has sparked fresh fears about their safety after the production of sugar beet that refused to die.

A mix-up involving seeds used for the trials in Cambridgeshire and Oxfordshire meant that sugar beet produced to resist a certain weed killer could not be killed off using any other weedkillers.

The mistake is just the latest in a series of GM boobs which have left environmentalists, farmers, and country people worried.

Despite this, and in the face of widespread fears for the long-term health of the countryside, the Government has again moved to reassure the public.

A spokesman for the Department of the Environment, Transport and Regions insisted that neither human health nor the health of the countryside had been put at risk.

BRITISH BIRDS ARE at greater risk than ever before of being shot, poisoned, trapped or having their eggs stolen, according to a new report.

The RSPB survey on wildlife crime calls for new laws to prevent birds being illegally wiped out by human hand.

The report, Birdcrime '99, shows that last year 681 crimes against wild birds were reported across the country.

This included 153 incidents of shooting or destruction of birds of prey, 70 reported poisoning incidents, 245 nest robberies and 63 reports of illegal taking, possession or sale of wild birds.

Figures recorded so far this year already show a sharp rise in crime, particularly involving poisoned birds of prey - a tally which includes 14 red kites, 11 peregrine falcons, and three golden eagles.

Graham Elliott, head of the RSPB investigations unit, said the Society aimed to beef up the section of the Countryside and Rights of Way Bill dealing with wildlife crime.

He said:"In our submissions the RSPB has been calling for custodial sentences for the most serious offenders, which we believe would be a far greater deterrent to wildlife criminals than the current low levels of fines.

"Additionally, we have called for proposals to give police officers a power of arrest to prevent the destruction of evidence.

"Police have previously relied on arresting wildlife offenders for ridiculous offences such as the alleged possession of a stolen telephone directory or the suspected possession of a stolen car.

"From our regular dealings with the national network of Police Wildlife Liaison Officers, we know that these proposed measures would be popular with all those working hard to stamp out this shocking level of wildlife crime."

A SECOND GIANT wasps' nest has been found in Shropshire just three years after the county set a world record with one discovered at Telford.

Back in 1997, the world beater measured 4ft 8ins by 4ft 6ins and played host to thousands of wasps before its removal.

Now pest controllers have tackled another huge but slightly smaller wasp nest measuring more than 3ft by 3ft near Wem, north of Shrewsbury.

A spokesman for North Shropshire District Council said the county was obviously an area where exceptionally large wasps' nests could be found - though no-one knew why.

The latest monster, located in the attic of Houlston Manor, was still very active and would have got even larger had workmen not destroyed it.

BROWN TROUT HAVE been boosted on the River Avon in Wiltshire thanks to a joint effort between local anglers, a landowner, and the Environment Agency.

Surveys by the Agency's fisheries team have confirmed that work on the river two years ago has paid off with juvenile trout now flourishing in the river.

"For years the stretch of the Avon downstream of the village of Easton Gray was impounded by sluice gates at a former mill," explained an agency spokesman.

"This produced an unnatural, deep channel, choked with silt and reed, depriving the native brown trout of the clean, gravel riffles and pools they need to spawn."

Because of this the Agency joined forces with the landowner and the local angling syndicate to remove the gates and reinstate the river's natural features.

Latest research has found young trout well established, along with bullheads, native crayfish and a wide variety of invertebrates.

THE WOODLAND TRUST is co-ordinating a series of public tree planting events this autumn all over England, Wales, and Northern Ireland.

The Trust is urging tree lovers to take part in its Plant a Wood on your Doorstep campaign aimed at replacing greenery lost over successive decades.

A spokesman said:"You will need sensible footwear - wellingtons or boots,warm clothes, and a spade if you have one - although we will have some available. Come when you like and stay as long as you like. Bring lots of your family and friends.

"You may like to take advantage of our special offer on the day to dedicate the trees you plant. We will produce a special certificate and a card for you at a cost of £10 each. They make a good Christmas or birthday present."

MOST FARMERS ARE facing an average £4,000 loss next year as the crisis facing British agriculture escalates.

NFU president Ben Gill says a report by Deloitte and Touche confirms the desperate need for the Government to pay aid to farmers.

The union has expressed grave fears that the 22,000 job losses from farming in the 12 months to June last year will be exceeded in current census figures, to be released in December.

A SPONSORED SNOOZE TO help save badgers was one of the doziest ideas of last year's National Badger Day - and it actually worked.

A girl from Devon completed a sponsored 24-hour sleep which raised £50 towards protecting the popular creatures and lit a torch for some uninterrupted slumber.

Organisers of this year's National Badger Day, on October 28, want others with equally weird ideas to take part.

"Once you have decided what you are going to do, organise your event and get it publicised in the local press," advised a spokesman for the National Federation of Badger Groups.

"If you are under 16, get a responsible adult to help you.

"Whatever your age, make sure everybody who takes part will be safe."

COUNTRY CAMPAIGNERS have pledged that their second mass rally in London will be even bigger than their first as they unleash their full fury against the Government.

Protesters who gathered 300,000-strong in central London two years ago say their ranks will be swelled by thousands more country people demonstrating against a list of threats to rural life.

Details of the second demo, led again by the Countryside Alliance, were unveiled during a conference at the Royal Geographic Society in the capital.

Alliance chairman John Jackson says the countryside is seething with resentment at the way New Labour has ridden roughshod over rural communities.

The group, which supports foxhunting and other country pursuits, is pressing for a raft of rural concerns to be taken more seriously by ministers.

Top of these is the preservation of foxhunting but the list also includes provision of better rural public transport, and more support for embattled country shops and post offices.

The Alliance is also aiming to create a vast network of internet-linked members to strengthen its rural power base and make communication easier.

Meanwhile, in a separate development, farmers and transport chiefs have joined forces in a concerted effort to pressure the Government to lower fuel prices.

The NFU and Freight Transport Association have formed their own alliance to forge a submission to the Treasury calling for price cuts.

A CHINA CLAY firm in Cornwall has been ordered to pay fines and costs of almost £8,000 after polluting a local river with a massive spill of waste.

Environment Agency protection officers were called to the River Fal at St Stephens near St Austell in April after reports that it was running milky white.

They found a substantial part of a dam holding waste materials from clay workings had collapsed into the river with thousands of tonnes of waste stored behind it released into the water.

"This was a major pollution and it can take years for a river to fully recover from an incident of this size," said Rob Torr, for the Agency.

"As well as smothering spawning beds and destroying the chance for fish eggs to survive, clay particles cause problems for many plants and kill small invertebrates that are the staple diet for the river's fish."

Before Bodmin Magistrates, the St Austell firm pleaded guilty to causing polluting matter to enter controlled waters.

The company was fined £7,500 and ordered to pay £255 costs.

TRADITIONAL LIVESTOCK FARMS face being wiped out because of Government inaction, says the Soil Assocation.

Changes need to be made quickly to the current unfair system of charging for meat inspection or most such farms will go to the wall.

"Small and medium-sized abattoirs and cutting plants are being forced out of business by crippling, grossly unfair charges which are imposed nowhere else within the EU," said a spokesman.

"The situation is so serious that the Soil Association has joined forces with six organisations to help save the smaller abattoir sector which organic livestock producers and consumers of locally-produced organic meat depend upon."

Sir Julian Rose, a trustee of the Association, has presented a 120,000-strong petition to Downing Street asking the Prime Minister to take urgent action.

He added:"These small meat plants are fundamental to the development of a successful and diverse organic sector.

"Losing them affects both organic farmers and their customers who expect high animal welfare standards and short journey times for organic livestock."

A GREY SEAL pup is battling back to health after being rescued on the verge of death from a Devon beach.

The exhausted, underweight pup was thought to be just hours from death when a member of the public alerted Torbay Wildlife Rescue Service after spotting the animal in a cove at Brixham.

Estimated to be about seven weeks old, the pup weighed 13 kg - less than its probable birth weight and much less than the 50kg it should weigh by now.

It has been treated for a minor injury to a flipper by a local vet who plans to transfer it to the National Seal Sanctuary in Cornwall when it gets stronger.

Since its rescue, the pup has been named Bryher, after one of the northern Isles of Scilly.

THE VISUAL ALLURE of raging flood water increases the personal risks to people caught up in such dramas, according to the Environment Agency.

With thousands of homes and businesses hit across the South East recently and with more heavy rains predicted, casual sightseeing when floods hit is being actively discouraged.

A spokesman said:"The Agency urges people in areas with Severe Flood Warnings NOT to undertake any non-essential journeys or go out to view the flooding.

"Flood water can be fast-moving and very dangerous."

Residents forced to abandon homes are asked to always check first with emergency services or the authorities before returning because of possible lethal hazards from disrupted electricity or gas supplies.

Rubber gloves should also be worn when cleaning up after flood waters, adds the Agency, as the water is often contaminated with oil and sewage.

NFU MUTUAL HAS revealed that vehicle theft cost the farming community £73 million in 1998 while the bill for the theft of over 100,000 stock came to £4 million.

VIOLENT ATTACKERS ARE less likely to claim victims in the countryside than in towns and cities, says a report.

According to the British Crime Survey, a person living in the countryside stands an average 2.7 per cent chance of falling victim to violent crime - compared to 4.2 per cent nationally.

Burglary, too, appears more of a problem for urban dwellers with 4.3 per cent of homes nationally hit, compared to just 2.6 per cent of rural households.

In addition, car crime is less prevalent in rural areas with nine per cent suffering vehicle-related crime as against 12.6 per cent nationally.

But findings in the survey will be of little reassurance to isolated rural communities currently feeling beseiged by criminal activity.

Back in June, NFU president Ben Gill called for urgent Government action to combat a rising tide of crime in the country.

He wrote to Home Secretary Jack Straw about farmers and other rural residents left feeling vulnerable to crime with inadequate police protection - as in the Tony Martin case.

He said: "Lack of police officers protecting our countryside and a shortage of funds means British farmers are suffering a persistent wave of property crime in particular.

"Government policy needs to re-focus on diverting more resources - officers, money and equipment - to these areas."

PLAYING 'CHICKEN' AMONG traffic is usually a dangerous game - but not if you happen to be one of a group of hens in Norfolk.

These wily birds have set up home on a traffic roundabout in Ditchingham and councillors have just decided they can continue to live there.

The full weight of Norfolk County Council was brought to bear on the hens as it examined whether the birds posed a hazard to passing motorists.

In the end, the authority concluded that they did not - which was clucking good news for the hens as they find the roundabout rather a nice place to live.

Local residents are protective of the birds and delighted by the county's decision - but some feel warning signs should be put up so that visiting motorists do not get in a flap and cause an accident.

TV CELEBRITY CHEF Ross Burden will lead the Countryside Alliance's national dinner party fund-raising event later this month.

The flamboyant cook is spearheading the event on October 28 which could see thousands of people across the country sitting down to their own Host a Roast soirees.

"This is likely to be the largest dinner party the country has ever seen," said Ross.

A MAJOR ATTACK has been launched on the Government's Countryside and Rights of Way Bill in a new blow to its supporters.

Country groups said to represent more than half a million rural residents and businesses have united in highlighting major concerns about the Bill - itself backed by thousands of ramblers, dozens of MPs, and other organisations.

Together the Country Landowners Association, NFU, Countryside Alliance and Moorland Association have branded the proposed right to roam provisions "unbalanced and unworkable".

In its present form, the Bill could be a recipe for disaster, they say.

Rather than promoting harmony between landowner and rambler, it was more likely to spark disputes.

"This Bill will cause conflict, controversy and chaos in the countryside," said Anthony Bosanquet, president of the CLA.

"The Government must listen to the people who live and work in rural areas."

Rural groups were dismayed by Government reluctance to resolve some of the biggest areas of concern by amending the Bill.

Key areas of concern include abuse of access rights, occupier liability, night-time access, and dogs.

As far as dogs are concerned, protesters say the new right of access to "mountain, moor, heath, down and common land" is for people, not their dogs.

Dogs should be allowed only under stringent controls, they maintain.

"The Environment Minister recently stated he wanted a 'balanced Bill'. At the moment it is not," said Richard Burge, chief executive of the Countryside Alliance.

"Rural groups are not willing to pick up the pieces when the Bill fails on the ground."

Tim Bennett, deputy president of the NFU, added: "The Government has promised to strike a fair balance between the rights of walkers and land managers.

"But, as yet, the Bill fails to achieve this.

"Access must not disrupt or interfere with the operational needs of farm businesses."

A RIVER TRIBUTARY used as a bolt hole by fish during bad weather was polluted by housing developer Barratts, a court heard.

Barratts West Midlands Ltd, of Halesowen, pleaded guilty at Stafford Magistrates Court to one charge relating to the pollution of the Deepmore Drain, a tributary of the River Penk.

Following prosecution by the Environment Agency, the company was fined £5,000 and ordered to pay £485 costs.

Environment protection officer Dave Gribble said after the case: "Barratts failed to address the issue of containing contaminated drainage on site, allowing it to get into the wider environment.

"Suspended solids sink to the bottom of water courses, affecting aquatic life.

"I hope the fine sends a message to the construction industry that pollution prevention and control measures must be a priority rather than just being considered on an ad-hoc basis once problems have occurred."

Nick Mullen, acting for the company, apologised and said that heavy rainfall the previous evening had contributed to the problem.

PINE MARTENS COULD be reintroduced to their old hunting grounds in southern England years after the ferocious predators were wiped out there.

According to a report by English Nature and wildlife charity People's Trust for Endangered Species, it would now be possible to reintroduce pine martens to their historic habitats in England.

A spokesman for English Nature said:"About 150 years ago, pine martens were widespread throughout Britain. However, in a few short decades they were almost completely exterminated to protect game birds on large shooting estates.

"Today they are one of our rarest mammals with good populations restricted to Galloway and north-west Scotland.

"Fully grown, pine martens are about the size of a domestic cat and have chestnut-brown hair with a creamy throat. They live for up to 12 years and prefer to live in woodland with surrounding rough grassland.

"They mainly eat voles and mice, supplementing their diet in the autumn with berries. As with many predators, they will also consume small birds and birds' eggs."

The report, based on extensive research by Dr Paul Bright of the University of London, concluded that there was no practical reason why pine martens should not be reintroduced into the English countryside - provided people want them.

Dr Bright's team surveyed six wooded areas in Devon, Somerset, Dorset, Avon, East Sussex and Cumbria for suitable habitat.

They also asked local people about their attitudes to pine martens with an average 64 per cent of farmers, 65 per cent of gamekeepers and 90 per cent of local residents in favour of reintroduction.

THE PUBLIC HAVE been given a final chance to comment on plans by the Woodland Trust to enhance the largest remaining area of ancient woodland in the Chilterns.

Penn Wood, near Amersham in Buckinghamshire, was acquired by the Trust in 1999 after a huge national fund-raising campaign.

Local support was vital to prevent the wood being turned into a new golf course by developers.

Management plans now include the gradual removal of many non-native conifer trees and maintenance of old trees.

Coppicing and grazing by cattle will also be reintroduced to enable the Trust to restore the original wood pasture and grassland, providing habitat for a vast range of flowers, insects, birds and mammals.

FARMERS ARE NOW conserving water supplies more than ever before to cope with unpredictable weather and help the environment, a report reveals.

The NFU 'Water-wise' survey of 1,000 farmers was produced as part of a unique alliance with the Environment Agency and green groups, including the WWF and RSPB.

It found that nearly two thirds of farmers use water more efficiently than five years ago; almost 70 per cent have invested in reservoirs or storage facilities; 80 per cent test soil moisture to ensure irrigation water is not wasted; nearly 40 per cent collect rainwater or recycle it for use; and more than 80 per cent have taken steps to conserve wetland habitats.

NFU president Ben Gill said:"Farmers and growers are acutely aware of the importance of water to their industry and are key facilitators in meeting the needs of the environment.

"Despite the pressures on investment they have made huge strides to ensure they are making the most efficient use of supplies. Our 'Water-wise' campaign intends to build on this."

POLICE RACED TO the peaceful River Wye in Derbyshire following reports of a crocodile taking a dip there.

The RSPCA were also alerted and joined the hunt on a stretch of the river near Bakewell.

Finally spotting something in the water, an RSPCA man took his courage in both hands and plunged in.

Then the truth emerged as the 'crocodile' turned out to be nothing more savage than an inflatable toy.

Police, who said they were duty bound to investigate following a number of alarm calls from passers-by, admitted it would have been strange to find a crocodile living wild in the Peak District.

A KALEIDOSCOPE OF colour is set to sweep across the land, says the Forestry Commission, with a vintage year for autumn reds and golds predicted.

"Staff will be monitoring our key autumn hotspots in England, Scotland and Wales to find each week's most spectacular array of autumn colour," said a spokesman.

"As the first frosts begin to bite, the leaves are about to explode into a dizzying array of gorgeous golds, rich russets, burnished bronze and deep orange."

A free information pack to help people find Britain's top spots to enjoy autumn woodlands at their best is available from the Commission.

The pack has been designed to let people know the best woodlands to visit and what to see.

VILLAGERS in Cambridgeshire are in a flap about the pong from turkey droppings which forced many to remain indoors for weeks last summer.

Nearly 100 residents from Pymore have signed a petition saying the smell could drive them potty again if the wind turns.

A local haulier has been blamed for collecting turkey waste in his yard ready for transportation to a bio-mass burning power station.

But while the scheme may have environmental benefits, residents say their nostrils can detect no benefit at all.

Local councillors will soon decide whether the turkey dung scheme should trot off.

BLUE TIT: water pistol drives off marauding predators

SMALLER, but more cocksure and adventurous, perhaps it isn't surprising that the blue tit was recently found to have overtaken the sparrow as the commonest of our garden birds. This perky little character, with his jaunty blue 'cap' and tubby shape, is now believed to be the most frequent visitor to nut net or bird table in countless gardens nationwide.

I can still remember, as a child, the sudden arrival of that distinctive blue and yellow plumage in the bushes outside the window being a major event. By then, the usual hordes of plainer, drabber sparrows or much larger, noiser starlings had normally finished off any titbits provided.

Today, the tables have turned and numbers of sparrows, at least, seem to be in decline, although no-one seems certain as to why this might be.

Not that this would concern your average blue tit who just goes about his hunt for food with his usual frenetic pecking and dazzling acrobatics.

It's interesting to observe blue tits seeking caterpillars in the same bushes as bigger, more aggressive great tits. Although a blue tit, if it has any sense, always gives way to the great tit, its lighter frame and nimbler perching skills allow it to venture right to the edge of the tiniest twigs where a juicy insect or caterpillar might be hiding. So it is seldom without a meal.

Nesting blue tits produce a single brood of up to 13 chicks each year. This seems quite a high number but needs to be since so few will survive those first dangerous days out in the big wide world when many predators are lurking.

For two years, a blue tit - I'm sure it was the same one - nested in a bird box I put up above the kitchen window at a house where I used to live.

I often watched the mother or its partner return to the box with caterpillars when the chicks hatched, darting in and out of the hole so as to attract the least attention from prowling cats or magpies. One day I even disturbed a magpie, squatting on top of the box like an evil ghoul, trying unsuccessfully to reach the cowering chicks inside with its beak.

Outraged, I metamorphosed immediately from neutral observer to vigilante and from then on even kept a loaded water pistol handy.

Any magpies or drooling cats I discovered anywhere near the box were duly squirted.

I remember my daughter, aged about two back then, coming to me urgently one Saturday morning with a strange look in her eyes.

She led me out of the kitchen door into the back garden where one of the blue tit chicks lay motionless, its neck broken after falling seven feet onto concrete. It had obviously slipped, the victim of its own curiosity.

I picked up the soft, still-warm bundle with its lolling head and tight-closed eyes.

I think I had already launched into a heavy, reassuring speech before I realised my daughter was actually back in the kitchen scoffing her yoghurt. Each year, I managed to miss the dramatic moment when the fully fledged chicks finally burst out of the nest and scattered into surrounding bushes.

But I think I was probably only a few minutes late the last time around when one nervous juvenile actually stayed put for a while.

As you can imagine, the mother became quite frantic to eject it and tried everything, bar dragging it out by the scruff of its neck.

Eventually, junior took the plunge and shot into the nearest bush to hide.

I have no idea how many chicks survived but later in the day saw a neighbour's stealthy ginger tom lying drowsily in the grass next door.

He was licking his chops and paws with the satisfaction of one who had just enjoyed a gourmet meal.

HUNT GROUPS HAVE unveiled a raft of new proposals to beat off impending Government action to outlaw their controversial sport.

The 10 main associations have announced a joint package of measures to respond to the recommendations of the Burns Report which was published earlier this year.

"The measures, which beef up a number of checks and guidelines, are aimed at providing additional reassurance to the public and the authorities that the hunting process is properly regulated and stands up to rigorous scrutiny," said a spokesman for the Countryside Alliance.

"As the Scott Henderson Inquiry of 1951 and the Phelps Inquiry of 1997 both stressed, hunting has survived and prospered for so long only due to the goodwill that it enjoys in rural areas and from farmers in particular, and its ability to react responsibly to changing circumstances.

"The hunting associations are determined that public confidence should be maintained and enhanced whilst at the same time ensuring that hunting's practical benefits for and importance to rural communities are neither lost nor diminished."

Top of the list of new ideas is a bid to break down barriers between hunters and the general public with a push for more openness and accountability.

"All hunts will have their own interactive website live by the end of 2001. These websites will include maps, fixture cards, personality profiles and other general details in relation to all UK hunts," said the spokesman.

"They will enable the public to easily obtain more information about their local hunt and also have a secure and personal point of contact."

More than 300 UK hunts will now be out for between two and four days a week after the season got underway on November 1.

RSPCA INVESTIGATORS ARE baffled by a series of increasingly macabre animal deaths in Buckinghamshire.

Mutilated fox, rabbit and deer carcasses have been found strung up in trees in the countryside.

Decapitated badgers and duck remains have also been discovered while the latest find involves an emaciated young foal.

The foal, found near Flackwell Heath, had sustained wounds to the side of its head and had possibly been bludgeoned to death by its attacker.

Two years ago, the ritualistic slaughter of two rams in the Chesham area was blamed on Satanists by the farmer who lost them.

HORSE RIDERS HAVE been boosted by the opening of the first stretch of what could become a 120-mile bridle path.

The first 12-mile section of the route runs from Hertfordshire into Essex but it is hoped that over years the entire bridle path will stretch the whole distance around London.

Planners want it to stay close to the M25 motorway so the route can be better guided around the capital in as efficient way as possible.

The scheme has royal backing in the form of Princess Anne, the president of the British Horse Society, who will be following each new development.

The ambitious plan is just one way the BHS wants to better open up Britain to the country's estimated 2.4 million horse riders.

It is also pressing for new national routes to be planned by local authorities for the time when the Countryside and Rights of Way Bill finally becomes law.

GREYHOUND LOVERS ARE being urged to get out their diaries for a national event which aims to celebrate their favourite dog.

'Greyhound 2000, A Millennium Celebration' will enable visitors to "see at first hand the unique qualities and abilities of this noble breed," according to a spokesman.

The event aims to bring together all aspects of the greyhound world - showing, racing and coursing - for the first time in history.

Greyhound 2000 takes place from December 10 to 14 at Newmarket and a major feature will be the first ever 'Champion Greyhound of the Year' class held in this country under Kennel Club rules.

A 14-class Pedigree Greyhound Show is scheduled, along with an exhibition titled 'The Greyhound through the Ages'.

THE CORPSE OF a 16ft whale was among the more unusual items washed up on a Sussex beach lashed by recent gale-force winds.

The whale, believed to be a minke, was found by local resident Elaine Norman-Davis after coming to rest on shingle at Shoreham beach.

The luckless giant appeared to have been dead for some time because its skin was peeling and parts of the body were plainly decomposing.

The Environment Agency was alerted and planned to cut open the whale to examine internal organs for pollution levels, as well as studying its mouth for clues to its age.

However, before a team could join the whale at the location, the sea had reclaimed the creature and carried it away to another resting place.

THE RSPB HAS asked the Government to "seize the high ground" on managing water to create wildlife rich wetlands following repeated flood crises across the country.

Sarah Fowler, RSPB head of water policy, said:"There has been no fundamental reform of arrangements for flood defence for 70 years.

"While the priority for flood defence has shifted from protecting agricultural land to protecting urban areas, the legal and institutional arrangements have by and large remained the same.

"We must resist the determination to drive every drop of rain down the drains and out to sea and, instead, work with nature to reduce the threat of flooding."

FORTY MILLION SHEEP may now face slaughter in the latest terrible twist of Britain's BSE crisis, it has been revealed.

National sheep and lamb stocks could be decimated if tests prove that BSE has spread from cows to sheep, according to the Foods Standards Agency.

No genuine cases of BSE have yet been identified in sheep but news that the Government is preparing for such a possibility is a devastating blow to sheep farmers and consumers alike.

Many shoppers turned to lamb as soon as beef was deemed unsafe and thousands will have continued eating it and buying it for their families over the following years.

With a question mark now hanging over the safety of lamb, consumers everywhere will be even more mystified about which meat is the safest to buy.

Meanwhile, the fightback to restore the battered image of beef itself goes on with an NFU report putting a positive slant on the situation.

A spokesman revealed that 81 countries across the world had now lifted their ban on the import of British beef with France a notable exception.

The EC was maintaining legal action against France for this breach with the NFU also pursuing the issue through the courts.

Traditionally, France has represented the largest market, importing 61,400 tonnes in 1995.

"Figures show that the confidence of the British public in beef has returned to pre-BSE levels," said the spokesman. "Estimates for this year are that Britain has consumed 950,000 tonnes of beef, of which 204,000 tonnes were imported."

CRAYFISH HAVE BEEN plucked to safety from a northern English river to save them from a creeping disease.

The rare white-clawed crayfish faced being wiped out in the River Ribble after it became infected with crayfish plague.

More than 400 of the tiny lobster-like creatures were painstakingly collected by Environment Agency rescuers.

The crayfish will be returned to the Ribble after it is found to be clear of the fatal infection.

A BADGER SURVIVED after being caught in a snare attached to a fence post which it dragged around in agony at Biggin Hill, Kent.

A passer-by who spotted its distress alerted a local badger protection organisation which raced to the scene.

Once it had been rested and its damaged neck stitched, the hardy animal was released into the wild.

THE RSPB IS aiming to get tough with Cyprus over carnage caused to millions of birds migrating across the country each year.

The Society has called on the European Union to suspend Cyprus from EU entry negotiations until its government clamps down on illegal bird trapping - believed to account for the slaughter of up to 20 million migratory birds every year.

"RSPB investigators, working undercover on the island in recent days, have unearthed carnage on a massive scale," said a spokesman.

"Trappers using miles of wall-of-death nets and lime sticks ensnare millions of birds, including blackcaps, robins and song thrushes, to supply delicacies for island tavernas."

Graham Elliott, RSPB head of investigations, added: "The scale of the slaughter is sickening. Cyprus, at the eastern end of the Mediterranean, is on a major migration route with millions of birds pouring through the island in spring and autumn.

"Seeing the extent of the trapping, it is amazing any birds manage to get through at all.

"Bird trapping is totally illegal on Cyprus. Despite limited attempts by the local authorities to control trapping, the practice is still extremely widespread and in many areas is carried out blatantly in full public view as our investigations have proved.

"The RSPB will be writing to the European Union to call for a suspension of Cyprus from entry negotiations until the island authorities can stamp out this abhorrent practice. Bird trapping is outlawed by the European Birds Directive."

The RSPB is urging anyone who wishes to complain about bird trapping on Cyprus to write to: President Glafcos Clerides, Presidential Palace, Nicosia, Cyprus.

A GIANT TURTLE thought to be up to 100 years old has been rescued after becoming entangled in fishing nets off the Shetlands.

The 7ft leatherback turtle has been nicknamed 'Osiris' after an ancient Egyptian god saved from dying by his wife.

The turtle, whose head is bigger than a man's, was found exhausted and injured in the nets by fishermen checking lobster pots.

Because of the trauma it had endured, the turtle went into shock and sank into a semi-conscious state - prompting concern over its chances of survival.

However, efforts are being made to revive the one-tonne monster at a wildife sanctuary in the Shetlands.

EU RED TAPE has driven British farmers to the edge of bankrupcy because of a frantic adoption of petty regulations in this country, it has been claimed.

Tough enforcement by teams of inspectors was another thorn in the side of farmers already facing ruinous circumstances, according to a report commissioned by Prime Minister Tony Blair.

The report, compiled by the Better Regulation Task Force, confirms that most farmers are losing money and smaller producers face going out of business.

Even without the enforcement of EU regulations, a combination of factors had made this a terrible period for farmers trying to eke out a living.

But zealously enforced EU rules about how to carry on their businesses was making the situation even worse, the report says.

DEVASTATION WREAKED ON farms by recent flooding has been compiled into a "dossier of chaos" by farmers' leaders.

The NFU aims to present a heavy file to Agriculture Minister Nick Brown detailing the catastrophic impact that the weather has had on farmers up and down the country.

Major problems include extensive delays in the sowing of winter cereal crops; large areas of crops destroyed either by flooding or water-logging; and up to 50 per cent of potato crops going un-harvested across the country in sodden ground.

NFU president Ben Gill said:"With our report, we intend to give as clear a picture as possible to the Minister so that he can begin to consider what other practical steps can be taken to assist farmers.

"It is going to be impossible to detail the full impact of these storms for some time as reports are still coming in from all our regions but it is clear that damage and consequential losses will run into hundreds of millions of pounds.

"We will be trying to put a firmer figure on this as the days go by.

"Coming on top of the bad weather earlier this month, farmers are beginning to feel their problems are insurmountable."

The chaos dossier is being put together using local information from an NFU network of regional offices and will be given to the Minister by Mr Gill.

"I am pleased that Elliot Morley has announced some flexibility for those farmers whose crops have now been destroyed by floods and water-logged ground," he added.

The worst hit region appeared to be the South East.

THE SORRY STORY of how and why farmland birds have declined so much is described in a new booklet from the British Ornithologists' Union.

'Ecology and Conservation of Lowland Farmland Birds' contains written versions of talks given at a BOU conference at Southampton University.

The conference was the brainchild of Dr Nicholas Aebischer from wildlife conservation charity the Game Conservancy Trust.

He said:"There has been a catastrophic decline in numerous farmland bird species, and urgent action must be taken if the situation is to improve."

Dr Mark Avery, RSPB director of conservation, added:"The appalling declines in farmland bird populations are already well documented. This publication shows there is at least some light at the end of the tunnel.

"Set-aside and agri-environment schemes have helped some species, such as the corn bunting and stone-curlew, but more money is needed to help farmers turn round these declines."

BEEF SALES IN France have plunged by 40 per cent as the country's defiance over British beef imports comes back to haunt it.

Rumours that many French CJD cases have been covered up by the authorities have emerged as at least three people are confirmed to be suffering from the fatal disease.

One victim, aged 19, whose favourite food was beef hamburgers, is in a coma expected to prove fatal in weeks.

Now the public has been warned by health chiefs to expect dozens of victims as more French cows are found to be suffering from BSE.

The EC is maintaining legal action against France for refusing to lift its ban on British beef with the NFU also pursuing the issue through the courts. Traditionally, France has represented the largest market for British beef.

THE SECRETIVE STONE-curlew is staging a revival after numbers plummeted over recent decades, it has been revealed.

Farmers are being praised for their part in helping to bring the farmland bird back from the abyss by providing the right conditions for it to thrive.

Numbers had dropped as low as 160 pairs in 1985 but now the bird appears to be rapidly gaining ground again.

Robin Wynde, RSPB stone-curlew co-ordinator, said:"This year, stone-curlew breeding numbers are the most promising for many years. There were just over 250 nesting pairs, mainly confined to Wessex and Breckland, in East Anglia.

"Although the numbers of chicks these pairs reared was relatively low this year - largely due to the effects of high rainfall - the increasing population is a sign that these birds are thankfully responding to con - servation measures designed to boost their numbers. Farmers have played a vital role in this success."

LURCHER DOG OWNERS in Shropshire have been warned to be on their guard against a gang of 'dognappers'.

RSPCA officials issued the alert after a family pet was snatched and only released five days later after it was found to be lame.

The pet lurcher, called Blue, had been securely fastened outside a house in the Telford area before its mystery disappearance.

Investigators believe the pet had been used to hunt rabbits but was returned to the family home after it was revealed to be physically unfit.

The dog suffers from a permanent limp and originally came from a rescue centre which nursed it back to health from an emaciated state.

The RSPCA wants owners of similar pets to take extra precautions to ensure their dog does not disappear for good.

FRIENDS OF THE Earth has launched a fresh attack on the Government over the latest blunder involving GM food experiments.

The organisation acted after learning that laboratory tests found Phileas Fogg Tortilla Chips and own-brand tortilla chips sold by Asda and Safeway contained GM ingredients not licensed for sale in the UK.

With illegal GM traces also found in Tesco and Sainsbury tortilla chips, FoE is demanding tough action from the Government to properly protect the public from GM ingredients that have not passed EU safety requirements.

THE SLAUGHTER OF badgers in a Government-backed cull could go on until 2004 before any useful information is produced, it has been revealed.

The controversial programme of killing carried out under MAFF was given the go-ahead to determine whether fewer badgers would reduce the incidence of bovine TB in cattle.

But scientists in charge of the programme have now admitted to MPs that more time than expected is needed to formulate conclusions from the exterminations.

Members of the Independent Scientific Group admitted the delay in reaching the end of the slaughter when they came before the Agriculture Select Committee.

But Professor John Bourne, chairman of the ISG, said he believed the first stage cull in all 10 areas of the trial would be finished by the end of 2001.

Although they might have some "useful results" by 2002, it was looking more likely that these would only be achieved by 2004.

Scientists needed enough data to make reliable statistical conclusions, even though the programme would already have cost nearly £35million by the end of 2002.

The news has angered the National Federation of Badger Groups which has attacked the cull of up to 20,000 badgers from the start as muddled and cruel.

Spokesman Dr Elaine King said:"While the Government spends money on the trial, it cannot afford to develop solutions to bovine TB which are acceptable to the public, to wildlife, and practical for farmers."

Recently, the NFBG blasted organisers of the cull "for trying to conceal horrific cruelty to one of our best loved wild mammals" during the programme.

THE COUNTRYSIDE AGENCY has organised a raft of "eat the view" events across the country aimed at promoting local food and goods.

Richard Lloyd, head of farming and forestry for the Agency, explained:"If we are to be successful in conserving the countryside we enjoy today, it is vital that consumers are aware of how what they buy affects rural areas.

"The 'Eat The View' campaign will help consumers make the link between the landscapes and habitats they value and the products they buy.

"Consumers can help to protect the land and livelihoods of rural people now, and for future generations, by buying products from producers who manage their land in an environmentally conscious way and by limiting intensive farming practices."

Buying locally produced meats and cheeses was just one example of how people could "eat the view" in a practical way.

A BAN ON beagling could only have a negative impact on the countryside, says the Countryside Alliance.

Pointing to recent findings, a spokesman said:"The Government inquiry into hunting concluded that where hunting and coursing take place, hare numbers tend to be at high levels and that any ban would result in a decline in the hare population in those areas.

"On land where hunting is favoured, the ban may result in a loss of habitat suitable for hares which would have serious consequences for a number of birds and other animals."

As he spoke, more than 70 beagle packs from all over the country were preparing to take part in the fifth National Beagling Day at the weekend despite a proposed hunting ban.

"The event is an opportunity for regular supporters of beagling to introduce others to the enjoyment of one of the oldest forms of hunting in the world," he added."All that is needed is a good pair of boots and a bit of energy."

SPOONBILLS AND A little auk are among the more unusual birds blown off course by recent gale force weather which saw them fall to earth at a Devon wildlife sanctuary.

Great northern divers were also among the unexpected visitors to Dawlish Warren Nature Reserve, courtesy of the bad weather.

The first-time visitors are currently making themselves feel at home alongside the reserve's regular guests which include oyster catchers, dunlin, and teal.

Guided walks organised by reserve staff will ensure the public get a chance to see storm chased species.

The spoonbills in particular have been easy to spot - their exhausted figures were slumped around one of the reserve hides.

A BARRAGE OF criticism has been levelled at the leading fisherman who called for thousands of seals to be killed to preserve stocks of North Sea cod before the fishing industry collapses.

David Shiel, chairman of the Anglo-Scottish Fishermen's Association, says up to 50,000 grey seals should be wiped out in an organised cull with numbers then kept down with more annual culls.

His call has been condemned by animal welfare groups and conservationists whose efforts over the years have seen a dramatic revival in grey seal numbers.

Undaunted, Mr Shiel says seals are pests which take no notice of tough EU quotas.

MORE TIMBER FROM Scottish forests will be transported by rail and sea in future, according to Scotland's Deputy Minister for Rural Development, Rhona Brankin MSP.

The move is supported by the Forestry Commission as a means to help cut congestion on the roads and use transport more beneficial to the environment.

A spokesman for the Commission said: "Scotland's timber harvest is set to double over the next 15 years as forests planted in the 1960s and 1970s mature.

"Moves to minimise the number of timber lorries on public roads will be welcomed by those groups concerned about their potential impact on the environment, traffic congestion, rural communities and lightly constructed rural roads."

WILDLIFE RICH HEDGEROWS have been saved from the chop after farmers' leaders faced down Brussels bureaucrats.

The NFU is celebrating success in overturning an EU ruling that could have destroyed large areas of traditional habitat on Britain's arable farms.

The EU had threatened to dock subsidy payments if hedgerows, field margins, and ditches were more than two metres wide.

Farmers faced hacking down vast swathes of hedgerows - putting in peril a huge array of wildlife and plants which depend on these areas.

However, following in-depth submissions, the EU has ruled that the inclusion of boundary areas within the UK's IACS calculations can now continue.

NFU vice-president Michael Paske said the ruling came after intense lobbying by the union and hailed the result a victory for farmers and conservationists alike.

"The Commission has been made aware of the unique network of hedgerows, field margins and ditches that make up Britain's countryside and the huge importance placed upon them," he said.

"MAFF has also provided the assurances that UK farmers secure no advantage from this calculation and that to alter the system would have created many more losers in terms of the countryside and wildlife."

Meurig Raymond, vice-chairman of the NFU Cereals Committee, said he was pleased common sense had prevailed.

He added:"In the current climate for cereals producers, the prospect of being forced to rip out field boundaries at the behest of Brussels would have been one regulation too far."

NEWLY BORN SEAL pups are at risk after marine oil pollution hit Cornish beaches following recent stormy weather.

Old oil spills are thought to have been stirred up to swell new spills which have covered beaches and seeped into caves where the pups lie.

The remote caves are traditionally used by seal mothers to deliver their young but now many are believed to be contaminated by oil from slicks washed ashore.

The Cornwall Wildlife Trust says only preventive action can stop the problem arising again in future and wants tighter regulations on ships and boats.

It has called for a single European agency to monitor vessels for seaworthiness to head off crises such as that involving the Erika off Brittany earlier this year and the Torrey Canyon off Cornwall in 1967.

TREES AND WOODS that enhance urban living have been given short shrift in the newly published Urban White Paper, according to The Woodland Trust.

Although it welcomes other findings in the paper, the Trust says it is worried about the lack of importance given to trees in towns and cities.

Hilary Allison, Woodland Trust policy director, said:"The presence or absence of trees and woodland is central to people's perceptions of the quality of their local environment.

"One of the most successful Early Day Motions of the current Parliament was on the need for the Urban White Paper to address urban woods and trees. We are disappointed that the cross party consensus of over 170 MPs for this simple step seems to have been ignored.

"The issue has been scarcely acknowledged, buried instead in a very general section on urban environment. If we want people to choose to live in urban areas we must ensure they are not disenfranchised from an experience of nature."

POLICE SHOT DEAD an enraged bull in Shropshire after it had escaped from a local slaughterhouse.

The bull made its bid for freedom in Shrewsbury and managed to evade its pursuers for three days by fleeing into a field containing tall maize.

But the animal was reported to be becoming dangerous and had started thrashing about near a railway line.

A vet and RSPCA team at the scene had failed in their efforts to sedate the rampaging animal so it was left to a police marksman to destroy it.

Later, Shrewsbury police said the bull had to be killed because it posed a serious threat to the public.

ANIMAL RIGHTS GROUPS aim to speed up the disappearance of fur farming by staging protests at centres across the country.

A national week of demonstrations was co-ordinated by the Coalition to Abolish the Fur Trade whose members have labled the practice "barbaric".

The Fur Farming (Prohibition) Bill is scheduled to be on the statute book and get Royal assent in weeks.

All 11 mink farmers would then have until January 2003 to cease operating completely under the new laws.

One protest group made their feelings known outside a mink farm at Onneley in Staffordshire.

But owner Len Kelsall blasted the protest as a waste of time as he plans to shut down anyway after negotiations with the Government over proper compensation are complete.

GM FOOD FIRMS should be made legally responsible for their blunders, says Friends of the Earth.

Spokesman Adrian Bebb said of the growing list of GM blunders:"It is becoming increasingly clear that the biotech industry cannot control its products and Government regulation is pathetically lax. Little wonder that public confidence in the GM industry is so low.

"The Government must learn the lessons of BSE and ensure that our food is protected from illegal ingredients.This means setting up effective testing systems and making GM firms legally liable if things go wrong."

ENGLISH NATURE HAS vowed to "take the sting out of storms" through schemes to protect vulnerable storm-lashed coastlines.

In the past, coastal communities and wildlife have been regularly devastated by gales but the creation of new 'coastal habitat management plans' (CHAMPS) is intended to safeguard both.

"Climate change and sea level rise are putting pressure on our coastlines with flood and coastal defences undermined by storms," said a spokesman."The combined effect on natural inter-tidal habitats is one of erosion and loss.

"CHAMPS will enable us to forecast changes and let conservationists and engineers produce schemes that are sustainable and better value for money."

To this end, English Nature had awarded an initial 18-month contract for the production of six pilot CHAMP schemes to map out the future of local coastal habitats.

The first six schemes will centre on the Dungeness and Pett Levels; Essex coast and estuaries; Suffolk coast and estuaries; West Sussex and the Solent; north Kent estuaries and marshes; and the Wash and north Norfolk coast.

English Nature coastal expert Stephen Worrall added:"These are rapidly changing coasts. It is vital we adopt a long-term 'big picture' approach to planning how they are managed.

"Forecasting coastal evolution over the next 30 to 100 years will be the key to understanding the impact of coastal change.

"Acting now to deliver long-term policies is essential to achieving sustainable habitats and defences.

"CHAMPS bring a new perspective to how we plan our environment."

A TERRIFIED BULLOCK almost drowned after accidentally taking a dip in a private swimming pool in North Wales.

The animal was discovered floundering in the pool at Caerwys after crashing through the fence of a local farm.

Tangled up in tarpaulin that covered the outdoor pool, the animal became panicked and the emergency services were summoned.

Firemen realised the bullock was in danger of drowning as the pool is more than 7ft deep at its deepest end.

Using all their resources they managed to keep the animal in the shallow end until they could improvise a way out by piling up bricks to make a walkway.

The bullock finally managed to break free and was declared uninjured by a vet called to the scene.

CONTROVERSY OVER THE Queen wringing the neck of a shot pheasant has continued to rage with anti-bloodsport groups lining up to attack her.

Animal Action was among the first to blast Her Majesty after she deftly put the stricken bird out of its misery during a traditional shoot at Sandringham.

Protesters were furious not only with the wringing itself but with the ongoing support the Queen still gives to shooting and other country sports.

However, country groups have maintained their overwhelming support for what she did, saying it was the most humane action in the circumstances.

A spokesman at Buckingham Palace also defended the Queen.

He added:"The Royal Family's views on field sports are well-known.

"The Queen simply put the bird out of its misery as quickly as possible."

OYSTERS CAN GO on living unmolested in a Devon river in a new blow to local fishermen.

Government agency inspectors have refused to lift restrictions on the River Teign which have seen the shellfish escape harvesting for the last three years.

Problems with water quality meant that a ban was placed on selling local oysters for human consumption - and this will stay in place for the best part of another year.

But while the decision is good news for oysters, it is very bad news for local fishermen.

Many have seen a huge drop in income as a result and are struggling to make ends meet.

One, Wes Highgate, whose family has worked the river for generations, says he is facing ruin as a result of the ban by the Food Standards Agency.

But the Agency appears determined to keep the ban in place until concerns over the oysters' threat to human health have faded.

FOXHUNTING, FUEL AND farmers were three themes in a heated public debate held at the Institute of Education in London.

Organised by pro-democracy organisation Charter 88, an invited audience of 200 were able to put questions to a four-strong panel which included Countryside Alliance chairman John Jackson.

Mr Jackson told the audience that through the communications revolution, including the Internet, democracy was in better shape than it had been since the Second World War.

He asserted that people were better informed and more able to strive for civil liberties and democracy than ever before.

Soon the Alliance would be linking 500,000 rural people together through its communications initiatives, he added, and these residents would then be better placed to sustain their communities.

Also on the panel were George Monbiot from The Guardian, Peter Hitchens from the Daily Express, and Susan Kramer, who was the Lib Dem candidate for Mayor of London.

THE 40ft CORPSE of a rare fin whale has been dragged ashore by tug at Morecambe in Lancashire.

Investigators think the female giant may have been struck and killed by a ship.

TORIES HAVE POURED scorn on Deputy Prime Minister John Prescott's long-awaited plans to boost rural communities.

Shadow Environment Secretary Archie Norman was the first to attack Mr Prescott's much heralded Rural White Paper.

Labour had failed to appreciate the extent of the crisis facing farmers, to address the problem of rising rural crime, or to take seriously the mounting pressure on Green Belt areas, he claimed.

Launching the Paper, Mr Prescott said he wanted to see "a living countryside, with thriving rural communities and access to high quality public services; a working country-side, with a prosperous and diverse economy, giving high and stable levels of employment.

He also wanted "a protected countryside, in which the environment is sustained and enhanced, and a vibrant countryside which can shape its own future and whose voice is heard by government at all levels."

Mr Prescott told MPs in a Commons statement that the Government aimed to invest £192 million over the next three years on rural transport to boost an existing investment of £170 million.

A further £1 billion over the next 10 years would be spent on rural bypasses.

In addition, he announced a doubling of the existing Housing Corporation programme to enable thousands more affordable homes to be built in rural areas.

He also pledged to: continue to safeguard rural schools against closure, and invest to improve them; to connect all rural schools to the internet by 2002; to create more childcare and early education places; to increase resources for rural ambulances to cut response times; to improve GP services through mobile units; and to set up new one-stop primary health care centres, offering video and telelinks to specialist health advice without the need to travel far.

A GLOUCESTERSHIRE MAN kept quiet for a year after spotting a huge black cat prowling a local field - because he feared people would think him a drunk.

Pensioner John Hopewell has now revealed details of his own big cat sighting in a region where investigators are building up a dossier.

The puma-like creature has been spotted five times in the last two months alone by a variety of witnesses.

Despite his earlier reservations, Mr Hopewell's claims are being taken seriously and added to others compiled into a record.

The pensioner says he now wants local police to capture the mystery beast.

LANDOWNERS HAVE WARNED ramblers "do not start lacing up your boots yet" as the Country-side and Rights of Way Bill completes its passage through Parliament.

"All you have is an Act, a piece of paper," said Dr Alan Woods, of the Country Landowners Association, who led the team which worked on the Bill on behalf of 50,000 members.

Between them, the members own a massive 60 per cent of rural land in England and Wales.

"The real work starts now to sort out a Michael Meacher muddle," said Dr Woods.

"There is a huge amount of work to be done to flesh out the bare bones of the legislation.

"The Government knows there is plenty to do - its target for having the new right in place is the end of 2005.

"Mr Meacher has left an enormous amount of detail to be sorted out by the Countryside Agency before any foot can step, as of right, on mountain, moorland, heath, down or common land.

"All the land involved will have to be mapped first and go through a consultation and appeals procedure before the new right can be brought into effect on any of it."

DANGER TO FARMERS from dodgy tractors and other equipment has been addressed by new 'health check' guidelines.

The Vehicle Health Check Scheme was unveiled at the Royal Smithfield Show in London, the biennial machinery and livestock showcase for the industry.

An NFU spokesman explained:"The guidelines cover every aspect of vehicle safety from maintaining effective windscreen wipers to servicing.

"They are designed to help farmers comply with the Provision and Use of Work Equipment Regula - tions."

NFU Technical Services chairman Marcus The - mans added:"The safety of machinery and its safety in use is of paramount importance to farmers and growers. This scheme aims to assist farmers and growers who use such equipment."

A COW THAT died after a daring rescue operation has earned its rescuers something to remember it by - certificates of commendation.

So impressed were RSPCA chiefs with the derring-do of Devon firefighters that they decided to mark their efforts with the awards - despite the drama's unfortunate outcome.

The Sidmouth firemen had joined forces with an RAF helicopter crew in an exhausting battle to pluck the animal to safety after it plunged 100ft over a cliff.

The Friesian heifer was eventually sedated and lifted clear of the beach where it had become trapped last May.

The farmer who owned the cow was so delighted by the operation that he wrote to rescuers to express his gratitude.

Sadly, the animal had suffered serious internal injuries during its ordeal and had to be put down a few days later.

The firemen pondered on the fate of the stricken cow as they received their awards.

A WANDERING piglet has been named Wilma after being found abandoned in Liverpool.

The 10-week-old animal is being cared for at an animal rescue centre following its mystery appearance.

FROG: lake study leads to a sudden unwelcome dip

EACH spring, lakes and ponds across the country are decorated with that glutenous, jelly-like substance known as frogspawn - the starting point for a biological transformation that has fascinated children for generations. Before long, the unpromising black dots within each jelly mass swell and hatch to produce hundreds of frenetically wriggling tadpoles, which themselves slowly metamorphose into perfectly formed, fingernail-sized frogs.

Meanwhile, spawn laid in strings and sited in deeper water - less commonly seen - will result in offspring for the frog's cousin, the much scalier, less athletic toad.

The whole process seems to hold a special appeal for youngsters.

I myself studied and prodded frogspawn on countless occasions as a child, waiting for buckets of the translucent stuff laid at the edge of our small village lake to burst into life.

It seemed to take forever.

When armies of tadpoles did eventually emerge, I lay on my stomach on the bank with a hand and arm submerged up to the shoulder.

Nothing in the world seemed as thrilling at that moment as slowly paddling through dense clouds of the slippery creatures.

Occasionally, I would catch a few, studying their glistening bodies for a few seconds before releasing them back into the anonimity of their seething tadpole brethren.

I was doing this one year when I overbalanced and fell in.

The water was quite shallow but for a moment I failed to get my bearings and struggled to find a foothold.

Fortunately, an adult was fishing close by and rushed over.

I was soon dumped back on the bank, a spluttering, half-drowned wreck.

Oddly, the experience never put me off tadpoles.

If anything, it only made me keener on the little darlings.

April and May see tadpoles completing their development into frogs, deserting their ponds over June and July to hunt for food.

Most will end up being eaten themselves by a variety of predators.

Even blackbirds take their fair share as junior frogs desperately seek cover in grass and hedges.

By November, young and old frogs have started to hibernate, the males burrowing themselves into mud at the bottom of the pond.

These bottom dwelling frogs would obviously drown were it not for their amazing ability to breathe through their skin as the rest of the body shuts down.

Yet they might still suffocate to death if the pond freezes and stays frozen for any length of time.

You can prevent this happening yourself by breaking the ice.

Take care, though, as violent shockwaves can kill fish as well as frogs.

Better to site a kettle or pan filled with boiling hot water on top to gently melt the ice - not forgetting to attach a string, of course, if you want your pot back.

A female relative of mine has a phobia about frogs and will go into shock herself if one so much as hops into view.

As her garden has a long-established pond which attracts several frogs, she suffers regular shocks.

Despite the efforts of her husband to keep the pond clear of both spawn and frogs, the air is often rent by a scream as another marauding amphibian pops up unannounced.

Frogs, like many creatures, can be incredibly single-minded come the mating season.

A living, writhing 'ball' of frogs stacked one upon the other underwater are often so preoccupied by their Roman orgy that onlookers can get amazingly close, a fact which presents a convenient smorgasbord opportunity to any hungry heron or pike.

Goldfish are sometimes even killed by amorous male frogs who fail to find a mate and end up clamping their forelegs around the fish's gills, suffocating the poor wretch as they try to get their wicked way.

Nature can be cruel.

GROUSE MOOR OWNERS have been warned to stop the illegal slaughter of birds of prey on their land before some species are wiped out forever.

Hen harriers, in particular, are regularly killed and fears have been raised that the English population of harriers may shortly become extinct.

Only FIVE pairs of hen harriers nested successfully in England this year, athough the Game Conservancy Trust believes that the English uplands could support at least 230 nesting pairs.

In contrast, the Isle of Man, where persecution is almost unknown, supports around 50 pairs of the predators in a far smaller area.

Hen harriers, it seems, are being routinely killed on grouse moors because they eat red grouse before the start of the shooting season.

Julian Hughes, head of species policy for the RSPB, said:"Only those hen harriers which are given individual protection in England are allowed to nest successfully.

"Hen harriers attempt to nest on English grouse moors annually but have failed each year since 1997, whereas they are mostly successful on other moors. We believe that systematic shooting of adult birds and the destruction of nests is widespread.

"Long-term declines in grouse numbers have been caused by a loss in area and quality of heather moorland. Grouse stocks will only recover through enhanced habitat management, not by the illegal and unacceptable killing of raptors."

Peter Davies, spokesman for the Raptor Study Groups in the north of England, added:"For the sake of these impressive birds, we are calling on grouse moor owners and gamekeepers to call a halt to the year-on-year slaughter of hen harriers."

THE WOODLAND TRUST has called for urgent action to safeguard the future of Northern Ireland's devastated woods.

Julian Purvis, deputy chief executive of the Trust, said:"Northern Ireland's woods have been ravaged for thousands of years. Most recently, development pressures, poor planning regulations and intensive agriculture have meant that Northern Ireland, second only to Iceland, is now the most deforested region in Europe.

"Just six per cent of Northern Ireland is covered by trees, compared with the European average of 36 per cent.

"It is estimated that only 0.2 per cent of the landscape is covered by ancient woodland, our most important habitat for wildlife.

"The Woodland Trust aims to conserve, recreate and restore the country's native woodland and the wildlife it supports for the benefit of everyone."

MOUNTAINS OF ROTTING fruit which left farmers in despair over the summer may become a thing of the past after a move to increase the number of casual pickers.

Thousands of tonnes of fruit were discarded this year when the usual stream of students and casual workers dried up.

Now the Government has announced that it is to increase the number of work permits to allow overseas students to help out on British farms during their holidays following an awareness-raising campaign by the NFU.

Typical English fruits like strawberries and raspberries were left to rot because growers simply could not find enough workers to help pick them.

The NFU wrote to the Government highlighting the benefits that would be brought about by an increase in permits.

Officials then met representatives of various Government departments to continue to press the importance of the issue.

NFU Education and Employment Committee chairman Bob Fiddaman said:"This is extremely good news for the horticulture sector - large growers can need hundreds of people because summer fruits are all hand picked.

"It is also good news for those students wanting to come to here to learn about British horticulture. This is a classic example of how sustained lobbying really can achieve tangible benefits to farmers and growers."

The number of annual permits issued under the Seasonal Agricultural Workers Scheme has been increased from 10,000 to 15,200.

FREE THE DAWLISH 300 - not a rallying cry for the release of wrongly convicted prisoners but a request to a man who trapped 300 pigeons in Devon.

The birds were caught by a Dawlish Town Council waterfowl warden amid ongoing debate about how much mess they cause.

However, their capture sparked unease among local residents when they realised the birds could soon be for the chop.

Teignbridge District Council chief environmental health officer Ben Hosford subsequently requested the release of the birds and let it be known their capture had not been sought by his authority.

He is now working with the Pigeon Control Advisory Council to look at more humane ways to reduce problems caused by pigeons.

AGRICULTURE AND RELIGION have become embroiled in an unlikely clash over land in County Durham.

Ushaw Priest Training College has won initial backing from Derwentside District Council for a £5million development on local farm land involving a country hotel and 18-hole golf course.

The college, run by Roman Catholic priests, had to look at ways to develop the land because of a steep drop in numbers of young men wanting to become priests.

But a local tenant farm family have objected to the scheme which would see them forced to move away and are building up local support in their battle to overturn the proposals.

A spokesman for the college explained:"The college was built and expanded to cater for 400 students. We are now down to about 40, but we are using the same Grade II listed buildings."

THE GLORIOUS SPECTACLE of whales or dolphins powering by British beaches could soon become a thing of the past, according to a new report.

Porpoises, too, are among more than 20 aquatic species facing extinction from a combination of factors such as being caught in fishing nets or poisoned by sea-borne chemicals.

The Whale and Dolphin Conservation Society has moved to raise the alarm over an increasing threat to some of the best-loved visitors to our waters.

Mark Simmonds, spokesman for the WDCS, warned:"UK whales, dolphins and porpoises have been given plenty of 'paper protection' but little of this has any real effect.

"These problems need to be acknowledged and addressed urgently before it is too late for the UK's remaining whales and dolphins."

A more sinister hazard facing underwater mammals, reveals the WDCS, is the rising use of powerful low-frequency sounds by intelligence gathering units from opposing navies.

Such activity has been blamed in the past for playing a part in the rising number of whales beaching themselves for no apparent reason - often with fatal consequences.

In addition, the RSPCA calculates that 20,000 bottlenose dolphins have perished in British waters in the last six years - killed by fishing nets.

Hundreds of thousands of harbour porpoises have also fallen victim to gill nets which have been dubbed 'walls of death' because of their indiscriminate killing.

Despite all this, the Government has recently come under attack for failing to implement changes to fishing activities which many say could reverse the steep decline of marine species.

A HAMPSHIRE FAMILY will be tucking into beef on Christmas Day in deference to their honoured guest - a turkey.

In fact, it will be the fourth Christmas that Martina the turkey has joined in with a seasonal stuffing which is much to her liking.

The turkey is a pet which belongs to the Hickey family in Winchester where it enjoys strutting its stuff alongside their two dogs.

Local people have come to treat the bird as a celebrity and the attention appears to be going to the head that never gets lopped off come the festive season.

The preening bird, which often settles down to watch TV with the family, likes nothing better than to admire her own reflection.

THE COUNTRYSIDE ALLIANCE reacted with fury to claims in The Guardian that it was prepared to drop its hunting ban protest in return for more help in rural communities.

The Guardian story arose from a dinner which took place between senior Alliance figures and a small group of Labour MPs to discuss the Rural White Paper and other rural issues.

However, details reported were "grossly untruthful" and a complete fabrication of the facts, according to the Alliance.

Chief executive Richard Burge, who took part in the meeting himself at the House of Commons, said:"The Guardian's version of events is a mixture of pure fantasy.

"It is inconceivable that we would have said or implied the remarks attributed to us regarding our commitment to hunting. It is significant that this article fails to cite any relevant direct quote from us arising out of this meeting.

"The Burns Inquiry has shown that hunting is not inherently cruel and properly managed is as humane as the other legitimate ways of managing quarry species."

CANOEING HAS LITTLE or no impact on fish stocks, according to new research by the Environment Agency - but anglers still object to it.

"In recent years there has been an ongoing debate over the compatibility of angling and canoeing activities, particularly where these activities occur on the same stretch of water at the same time," said an Agency spokesman.

"The research found there is no empirical evidence linking canoeing with damage to spawning grounds and stocks.

"One outstanding area of conflict identified during the research between anglers and canoeists centred on the disturbance of angling activities by canoeists.

"Some anglers argue canoeists using the same stretches of water at the same time are devaluing anglers' licence privileges."

The Environment Agency says it wants to resolve friction between the two groups through better understanding and communication.

SPIN DOCTORING AN answer to the countryside's problems is no replacement for genuine help, says the Country Landowners Association.

CLA president Anthony Bosanquet explained:"The Rural White Paper has diagnosed many countryside problems and has prescribed the treatment.

"But continuing the spin-doctoring of politics will not deliver a cure.

"That will be achieved only when promises of the White Paper are turned into reality.

"There will be no weekend countryside for everyone to enjoy until those who bear the real responsibility for its long-term economic and environmental success are liberated from the shackles of regulation and recognised as equal citizens in our democracy.

"The Rural White Paper will make a difference only when it ceases to be a dream and becomes a reality."

Mr Bosanquet made his remarks during the Countryside Agency conference to debate the Rural White Paper following its unveiling by Deputy Prime Minister John Prescott.

HARE COURSING HAS been at the centre of fresh protests with animal rights campaigners staging demonstrations at the Greyhound 2000 event in Newmarket, Suffolk.

The sport, where pairs of dogs are marked against each other as they pursue a hare, has a long history and is said to be steeped in tradition.

Supporters say the whole point is to test the speed and agility of the dogs and the actual killing of hares - thought to happen in about one in eight chases - is incidental.

However, protesters such as the League Against Cruel Sports, claim that this is untrue and the killing of the hare forms an important part of the "repulsive and barbaric entertainment."

Greyhound 2000 has been billed as the best national showcase ever for greyhounds and lovers of greyhounds with a host of attractions for visitors besides hare coursing.

The League Against Cruel Sports made a formal stand against the hare coursing event by delivering a letter of protest to the National Coursing Club before the first dogs were released.

Organisers of Greyhound 2000 say that hares have the advantage in any chase because they live in the area, know the territory, and can easily go to ground in well located burrows.

In addition, their field of vision is so great that they can watch pursuing dogs closing in on them from behind and take evasive action at the crucial moment.

The NCC also staunchly defended the event, saying that hare coursing had survived four previous inquiries into whether it was too cruel to continue.

But Dave Ward, spokesman for the League Against Cruel Sports, asserted the sport was repulsive because it involved the hunting and killing of an animal which was not even a pest.

HEDGEHOGS ARE FINDING discarded ice cream cartons from the McDonald's burger chain a prickly problem, it has been claimed.

The RSPCA raised the alarm after receiving calls from the public alerting them to the fact that hedgehogs were often becoming trapped in the newly designed cartons.

Foraging hedgehogs are apparently imprisoned in increasing numbers thanks to their backward facing spines that allow them to easily push inside cartons but not so easily extricate themselves.

McDonald's is reported to be looking at ways to overcome the hazard, probably by redesigning the cartons to make them more hedgehog friendly.

THOUSANDS OF CHRISTMAS turkeys eaten in Britain will have been reared on food tainted by GM ingredients, claims Greenpeace.

The environmental group has published a list of outlets where, it says, shoppers can still buy turkeys reared on traditional feed and identified others where they are not.

A Greenpeace spokesman said:"Despite massive public rejection, GM is still being sneaked into our food by being used in the feed of animals like turkeys."

Safeway and Somerfield own-brand turkeys are among those reared with the addition of GM material in their feed, claims Greenpeace.

It says other big turkey sellers such as Tesco and Asda are committed to stopping GM addition to turkey feed.

However, the British Turkey Information Service says pressure groups often use turkeys as a vehicle to push their views at this time of year. Consumers had nothing to worry about.

BEEF CATTLE HAVE been swapped for badgers by a Devon farmer aiming to capitalise on a growing national interest in the natural world.

The BSE crisis put paid to Tiverton couple Kevin and Anne Atkinson's efforts to build up a herd of premium beef cattle.

But when they let go of their herd, they turned to another animal for salvation - the badger - pouring more than £10,000 into the construction of a hide on their land.

Now visitors are given commentaries on the British countryside before being led into the hide to await the popular burrowing creatures.

The couple's badger watching scheme is slowly gaining ground and they hope it will eventually become a full-time business.

MPs WHO VOTE for a complete ban on foxhunting would be helping to bring Parliament itself into disrepute, says the Countryside Alliance.

The Alliance has attacked the "astonishingly vindictive nature of the proposals which form the basis of Option Three in the Bill and which would give police draconian and intrusive powers against law-abiding ordinary people."

It adds:"If MPs are unwise enough to vote for Option Three it will cause huge anger amongst a large minority in the countryside and beyond and will bring Parliament into disrepute. Responsible people will not tolerate being stigmatised and oppressed as criminals.

"This matter no longer has to do with hunting but raises profound questions about personal liberty and the principle of tolerance for minorities in a fair democracy.

"It would clearly be perverse for Parliament to force through a ban on one single human activity regarding animals rather than ensuring a much-needed overhaul to tighten up animal welfare legislation in general.

"This would merely prove that MPs' obsession with hunting is based on prejudice against people rather than concern for animals' welfare."

SIX KILLER WHALES were observed close to shore off Unst in the north Shetlands.

The giant predators were seen around Haroldswick and were possibly hunting a group of harbour porpoises spotted in the same area.

FARMERS ARE JOINING forces with conservationists in a last-ditch bid to prevent the extinction of the humble tree sparrow and other birds, it has been revealed.

Almost 80 farmers are taking part in emergency measures to try to safeguard remaining tree sparrows, yellowhammers, and corn buntings with a special three-year bird-feeding project.

In a move to provide essential winter food, all the farmers taking part will leave some crops unharvested, plant special crops on set-aside land, and put waste seed from grain stores on open farm tracks.

Dr Mark Avery, RSPB director of conservation, said: "Some species of seed-eating farmland birds, particularly tree sparrows, yellowhammers and corn buntings, are disappearing from many areas.

"We believe that one of the most fundamental reasons for their decline is a lack of food over the winter.

"In particular, the switch from planting crops in the spring to planting in autumn has denied feeding opportunities to many seed-eating birds.

"The winter stubble fields, which were a feature after the autumn harvest, used to provide a seed-rich haven for clouds of birds.

"Sadly, these stubble fields, and their birds, are a distant memory in many areas. We strongly hope that this project, with farmers and conservationists working together, will provide a lifeline for birds, especially where they are most at risk."

Guy Smith, a farmer from East Anglia taking part in the scheme, said: "This project is an excellent new RSPB initiative which gives farmers an opportunity to understand how birds react to the way a farm is managed.

"Like many farmers, I care passionately about the wildlife on my farm and I can take just as much pleasure from seeing a flock of corn buntings foraging on my fields as I do from growing a good crop. "

BUTTERFLIES ARE FLOURISHING in Britain as a result of global warming making the climate milder and more to their liking, scientists have found.

Some dwindling national species are staging a revival while other species normally found abroad are making their way to UK shores in increasing numbers.

Even traditional migrant species are arriving earlier each year and staying on longer before flying out again, a conference on global warming organised by the RSPB heard.

One such species, the orange tip, now travels three weeks earlier to this country because it is no longer put off by freezing temperatures.

FARMERS' MARKETS HAVE become so successful they now provide a £65million lifeline each year for the struggling farming community.

The number of markets available has more than doubled since last Christmas with more than 300 now operating on a regular basis, reveals the NFU.

NFU president Ben Gill said:"I would encourage everyone to celebrate Christmas with a trip to their local farmers' market.

"Shoppers will be able to find a fabulous array of the finest local produce to stock up their larders for a traditional Christmas dinner.

"They will also be supporting the rural economy and helping farmers to protect and maintain the countryside we all love."

Thousands of customers are expected to shop at festive farmers' markets around the country in the run-up to Christmas.

A huge selection of local produce is being made available, from ultra fresh vegetables to home-cured hams, game and venison.

AN ENTIRE FAMILY of Scottish badgers is to be rehoused at a cost of £30,000 by a local authority after causing serious damage to a road.

Aberdeenshire Council took action after hearing how tunnelling work by the creatures was undermining the A97 Huntly-Banff road.

Workmen had been repeatedly called in to correct faults and strengthen the road near Aberchirder but councillors decided to act after more baby badgers were found.

An artificial sett comprising nine buried chambers is being built in a nearby field with an underground steel mesh barring the way back.

One councillor, Sydney Mair, said he found it incredible that the authority was willing to spend £30,000 relocating badgers.

He joked that any troublesome council tenants would simply be kicked out.

A POLL ON hunting with dogs indicated that more than half the general public want it to continue, according to a TV programme.

The independent NOP survey for ITN's Powerhouse programme on Channel 4 found that 51 per cent of the public do not want to see hunting with dogs banned.

Nigel Henson, director of communications for the Countryside Alliance, said:"Support for a ban has been in consistent decline and it is good to see that the statistical con-trick which has been perpetrated by the anti-hunting lobby - that '70 per cent' are in favour of a ban - is finally being rumbled."

But Mr Henson added that it was a preposterous notion that legislation which would involve the removal of civil liberties from a law-abiding minority could be justified on the basis of any opinion polls.

TREACHEROUS MUD ALMOST proved a fatal trap in the British countryside for a South African fossil hunter.

Liz Blumenthal had to be airlifted to safety by helicopter after becoming trapped near cliffs in Dorset.

The tourist's shoes and trousers had been torn off as she clawed her way from waist-deep mud - but she was too terrified to move further as more mud was all around. Luckily, her screams for help were heard and rescuers raced to her aid.

MORE THAN 350,000 dogs from foxhounds to working terriers would be penalised by a total ban on hunting, says the Countryside Alliance.

The figure was revealed as the fate of hunting with dogs raised the political temperature at Westminster again with MPs tearing into each other in the Commons.

Labour MPs appeared determined to vote for a ban on "barbaric" foxhunting despite a massive surge of protest from rural communities and urban sympathisers worried at the threat to thousands of country jobs.

However, Home Secretary Jack Straw favoured better regulation - not an outright ban.

The option to outlaw the ancient country sport was one of three in the Government Hunting Bill, debated in the Commons during its Second Reading before a final vote can be held.

The Countryside Alliance claimed 5,000 supporters of foxhunting had gathered in Trafalgar Square and 2,000 in Parliament Square during the debate.

The protesters had "attended a peaceful and spontaneous rally this afternoon to show their strength of feeling against the unnecessary hunting with dogs Bill," said a spokesman.

"A number of people had travelled to London with their family dogs to demonstrate that a ban on hunting with dogs would not only affect fox and stag hounds, but working terriers, greyhounds and lurchers numbering over 350,000 dogs in total.

"It could even, absurdly, affect family pets who, whilst out walking, might show the natural canine characteristic of chasing wild mammals such as rabbits and hares."

A WOMAN IN Ipswich was lucky to survive an unexpected encounter with a goose which flew into her face after taking off from a local pond.

The force of the blow knocked her semi-conscious and she began to choke after swallowing her tongue.

Fortunately, a passer-by trained in first aid rushed to help and, after being treated at hospital, the victim was taken home to recover.

A GOLD PENDANT thought to date back to Roman Britain has been unearthed by metal detector on farmland near Shrewsbury in Shropshire.

The pendant hangs on a necklace, is tubular in shape, and was apparently designed to hold a mystery substance.

An inquest into the find heard that the only other example of such a necklace dates back to the Fourth Century AD. However, experts think this item could be much older.

DEEP CONCERN HAS been expressed by conservationists at moves within the European Parliament to weaken protection given to birds migrating back and forth to Britain.

A 'declaration' proposed by an Italian MEP called for Member States to be allowed to set their own dates for hunting seasons according to the most recent scientific data available.

But the RSPB has condemned the idea.

A spokesman explained:"It may sound innocuous but experience shows that some EU governments, particularly the French, cannot even be trusted to implement the current legislation correctly.

"Only last week the European Court found France not to have respected opening and closing dates for hunting seasons, which would have protected migratory birds."

OTTERS HAVE BEEN among the worst-hit wildlife victims of flooding caused by rivers bursting their banks recently, it has been revealed.

Many are thought to have perished after being swept into traffic while young otters are believed to have drowned in their burrows.

In London, up to a third of the water loving mammals are feared to have died after their refuges along the Thames were gradually swamped.

ENGLISH NATURE HAS urged families to work off the Christmas pudding this year with a bracing visit to a National Nature Reserve.

"You have recycled your Christmas wrapping paper and put the vegetable peelings on the compost heap, but what next?," asked a spokesman.

"Get some fresh air and lose some of those extra calories by visiting a reserve or other local wildlife spot over the Christmas break.

"There is still a lot of wonderful winter wildlife to be seen in our countryside. But the best places to experience our hardiest plants and animals is on our National Nature Reserves."

David Arnold-Forster, English Nature chief executive, added:"Many of us forget the beauty of the countryside in winter when it is often easier to see wildlife."

THREE GOVERNMENT MINISTERS will be addressing delegates at the 12th Soil Association national conference on organic food and farming next month.

The conference, to be held at the Royal Agricultural College, Cirencester, from January 5-7 will be addressed by Michael Meacher, Nick Brown and Ritt Bjerraard, a Danish minister of agriculture.

Simon Brenman, Soil Association agriculture development director, said:"Consumer support for the use of pesticides, intensive livestock systems, and GM technology has never been lower and we are offering the nation a genuine alternative."

FREEZING WEATHER EXPECTED in most regions into the New Year has not stopped the Envi - ronment Agency issuing yet more flood warnings.

Director of operations, Archie Robertson, said while the critical situation on the coastlines was receding, people must continue to be on the alert.

"We are not out of the woods yet. People in flood affected areas must remain vigilant and prepared for flooding," he added.

PRO-HUNT GROUPS have hailed Boxing Day meets a huge success after more than 300,000 supporters turned out in defiance of the proposed ban.

Protesters aiming to ban hunting with dogs as "cruel and outdated" were believed to number a few hundred in comparison.

"Well over 325,000 people are reported to have supported the Boxing Day meets of their local hunts," said a spokesman for the Countryside Alliance.

"In nearly 300 venues spread across England, Scotland, Wales and Northern Ireland, support for hunting has been robust and a direct challenge to the options Bill.

"Despite extensive boasts by animal rights organisations that they would be mounting major counter-protests, only three venues were affected and protester numbers did not exceed 500 in total.

"The success of this year's Boxing Day meets clearly represents the final nail in the coffin of the anti-hunt lobby's 'Deadline 2000' campaign, launched at great expense in 1998 with the promise to secure a ban by the year 2000.

"Earlier this year the Government's own Inquiry into hunting with dogs, headed by Lord Burns, confirmed that hunting was an important part of the lives of many thousands of people and the report provides no case for a ban."

Sam Butler, chairman of the Alliance's Campaign for Hunting, added:"With the 'ban' option in the Government's Bill already the subject of considerable criticism for its vindictive and draconian nature, Deadline 2000 is dead and buried."

The massive turnout of support, he said, was visible proof of the strength of feeling in the countryside that a ban on hunting was unnecessary, unpopular and unenforceable.

However, anti-hunt groups such as the League Against Cruel Sports say the colour and festivity of Boxing Day meets can still be preserved without a fox being torn to pieces.

A BABY SEAL with a poor sense of direction crawled inland until it ended up exhausted on a coastal road close to a Scottish village.

The grey seal pup, thought to be about a month old, was finally rescued after it came to rest close to a tower used by the RAF at Rosehearty near Fraserburgh.

Conservationists were alerted and the pup was taken to the Grampian Wildlife Centre at New Deer where it was said to be recovering from its ordeal.

Later it will be taken to a seal sanctuary in Fife to be further built up before its expected release back into the wild.

PLASTIC STOPPERS IN wine bottles could cause the gradual destruction of some of Europe's best wildlife habitats, warns the RSPB.

Mass replacement of traditional cork stoppers with plastic ones might destroy the cork industry by 2015 and with it would go some of the continent's best-known birds.

"The RSPB Cork Report shows that the threat to wildlife from plastic stoppers is far greater than previously thought, " said a spokesman.

"In only five years, plastic has grabbed an estimated five to seven per cent of the £500-800 million global bottle-stopper market.

"At current growth rates, plastic stoppers are likely to have at least a 15 per cent share of the global market by 2015.

"Once this threshold is reached, the surplus of cork supply will be sufficient to trigger price falls of up to a quarter, resulting in cork farmers being forced out of business or having to grow less environmentally-friendly crops such as eucalyptus.

"Such a crash in the cork market will be disastrous for the wild birds which depend on the cork forests, and for the 80,000 people directly involved in cork production."

Many birds relied heavily on healthy cork forests for food and nesting sites, he added, and without a viable cork industry species such as the booted eagle, black kite and turtle dove could vanish forever from large areas of Spain and Portugal.

Hannah Bartram, RSPB agriculture policy officer, added:"It is an outrage that plastic stoppers are replacing natural cork - a truly sustainable product which benefits people and wildlife. We owe it to future generations to fight this short-sightedness.

"The Iberian cork forests have taken thousands of years to develop but it will take only a few years for them to disappear. We will continue to lobby retailers on this issue. In the meantime, we urge anyone that cares about wildlife to complain to the retailer if they find a plastic stopper in their wine bottles."

A DEVON WOMAN is planning to set up a sweet-smelling centre treating sick or injured horses using aromatherapy.

Showjumper Sandra Reeves hit on the idea after using alternative medicine to treat two sick horses in the past when traditional healing methods failed.

Sandra, 41, from Ottery St Mary, near Sidmouth, has had a lifelong passion for horses which spilled over into her interest in complementary medicine.

Four years ago she formed the Equine Aromatherapist Association with another woman after taking a diploma in alternative medicine.

Now she treats horses by allowing them to sniff or lick various oils and hopes to set up her specialist centre soon.

A FARMER WHOSE farm incorporates racehorse stables is hoping to race ahead of the turkey crowd this Christmas on the back of his fattened geese.

William Brisbourne, who farms with his brothers near Oswestry, Shropshire, is putting his money on roast goose becoming more popular than turkey.

He believes the time is ripe for a seasonal resurgence of goose and has ploughed his cash into meeting expected demand.

HARE: arriving in style by crashing through a hedge

BIG, sleek and fast, the hare is an impressive native of our countryside, though a creature which is spotted less and less as its normal habitats vanish under the property developer's bulldozer.

The destruction of much of our countryside has sounded the death knell for many ancient hare communities with the wide open spaces necessary for their survival gradually disappearing.

Anyone who has ever watched a hare going at full pelt across a field cannot fail to be impressed by the sight.

Much bigger and more athletic than the rabbit, the brown hare is usually a match for any pursuing fox or bird of prey with ambitions to feast on its tasty, high-speed flesh.

Baby hares - or leverets - are, of course, a different matter and many are taken by predators despite their inborn skill of lying motionless for hours on end in the centre of a windswept field.

Two or three leverets are born in each litter and, like their parents, must learn to survive the ferocious winds, rain, and freezing temperatures that blast the open fields.

Such conditions normally put other creatures to flight but a hare will stoically huddle down to see out the worst of the weather in the barest of cover.

Hares can clock up an impressive 35mph when they are disturbed or when vying with fellow hares for dominance during their annual Mad March period.

At this time of year, it is possible to watch male hares standing up on their hind legs 'boxing' with a fellow male or being 'boxed' back in return by a female - called a Jill - brushing off unwelcome advances.

In between these bouts of frenetic pawing, hares will streak around a field at a dizzying rate of knots, seemingly oblivious to onlookers.

I remember one day stopping my car in an anonymous country lane to check the engine and being diverted by the crazy activities of some hares in a nearby field.

I must have watched them for half an hour, marvelling at their sheer turn of speed and impressive jinking runs as they tried to shrug each other off.

Another time, I was enjoying a quiet country ramble when I was startled by a huge Jack hare which came crashing unannounced through the hedgerow to my left.

Grey-brown with orangey tufts of hair on his underside, he clattered to a halt in a ditch beside the footpath where I was walking.

For a couple of seconds, he lay there stunned, his enormous marble-like eyes staring straight at me.

Compared with a rabbit, the hare seems a much wilder, tougher creature altogether and the look in those eyes was uncompromising, almost fearless.

However, something seemed to have put him to flight.

It was possible that he had just shaken off a fox or perhaps another Jack hare, even bigger than himself, had got the better of him.

Whatever, in a moment, he was back on his feet and sprang across the path like a gazelle, disappearing into another hedgerow on my right and powering across the next field until he was out of sight.

For such a relatively large animal, the camouflage skills of the hare are also quite impressive.

Resting up in the middle of a field, a hare lies close to the ground with his big ears flat against his body.

From a distance, he appears like a small mound of earth and will often not move until anyone trudging by is within a few feet.

A rambler who walks in remote countryside, particularly someone who prefers open spaces to densely wooded areas, will probably put up a hare at some time.

It is often a shock to see that explosion of fur near your feet, a sensation generally replaced by admiration as the hare gracefully bounds away to find some peace and quiet elsewhere.

ANIMAL RIGHTS PROTESTERS appear to be dramatically stepping up their campaigns against hunting and anything else perceived as "cruel" - even at the cost of putting humans in peril.

Recent incidents have included letter bombs being posted in northern England to people working in the agricultural sector; the theft of almost an entire £100,000 beagle pack in the south; and a pledge to outlaw angling if hunting goes.

The push for a ban on fishing was made by the Hunt Saboteurs Association over the festive season and prompted the Countryside Alliance to call for unity in defending its future.

Charles Jardine, director of the Alliance's Gone Fishing campaign, said:"The angling community is finally coming around to the idea that the sport is under serious threat as a result of assertions from animal rights organisations such as the HSA and the Campaign for the Abolition of Angling.

"We are under no illusions as to the reach and tenacity of these people. We have consistently called for Britain's three million anglers to shake off the apathy usually shown in the face of these attacks on personal choice and liberty to fight for the future of their sport.

"It is clear that we must join together in unified support for all our chosen pastimes.

"It is of the utmost importance that anglers and angling supporters stand up and make their collective feelings known.

"None of us can imagine a world without angling and, if we stand united, hopefully we will never have to."

A BIG CAT believed to be a puma leapt a 5ft high hedge with ease after being spotted in Devon by a motorist.

The sighting is just the latest in a recent series and comes after a similar creature was noticed on the Queen's Sandringham estate over Christmas.

The leaping puma was clearly seen by mechanic Simon Cann as he drove along the A396 close to Tiverton.

Bursting out of bushes at the side of the road, it darted in front of his car then stopped momentarily at the hedge. Initially, Mr Cann thought the animal was a large dog until he got closer and the animal sprang over the hedge like a true cat.

Mr Cann told his local newspaper:"It was all over in a flash but there was absolutely no doubt about what I saw."

VOLUNTEERS are wanted by the RSPB in Buckinghamshire to help save one of the county's best-loved farmland birds - the lapwing.

Helpers will work alongside farmers over the spring and summer to save nests.

RAMBLERS ARE ON the warpath over moves to expand Army training in part of the North Pennines - barring walkers and farmers from one of the country's most beautiful areas.

A public inquiry starting on April 24 seems the only way to settle the row with local protesters forming themselves into an action group to take on the might of the Ministry of Defence.

"MoD proposals for training at Warcop in Cumbria would close the area to walkers for much of the year and also revoke farmers' grazing rights that date back to the 18th Century," explained a spokesman for the Ramblers Association.

"This will mean a loss of access to miles of footpaths and bridleways including routes that provide access to the Pennine Way. The number of visitors to the area will fall drastically.

"The MoD says farmers will be compensated and the extra training opportunities are needed to prepare troops properly. Alternative paths to those closed could be provided but campaigners say these are inadequate."

WOODPECKERS WHICH WRECKED a wood church tower in Essex have been offered a fake one erected nearby following restoration work on the original.

Residents in Great Henney raised £50,000 to build a new spire after woodpeckers had pecked the old one so badly it was in danger of toppling.

Locals hope the birds will be fooled when they start tapping out messages to each other in earnest come the spring.

IN HIS NEW Year message, farmers' leader Ben Gill remained optimistic that 2001 might not be as dire as 2000.

"Last year saw us full of optimism for a New Year, decade, century and millennium. In reality, it could not have turned out much worse for British farmers and growers," said the president of the NFU.

"The ravages of the over-valuation of sterling and continuing unnecessary red tape have been compounded by the dreadful weather.

"So what of 2001? In the face of the increasing globalisation and the opening up of world markets it is easy to feel like giving up.

"But there are glimmers of hope that at long last suggest we might have seen the worst."

SHOOTERS HAVE REACTED angrily to extra "administration costs" which have made their sport more expensive.

As of January 1, new pricings for firearms licences have been introduced for individuals and dealers.

The cost of being granted a shotgun licence has jumped by £7 to £50.

Meanwhile, the cost of renewing an existing licence has rocketed by £22 to £40.

For dealers, the cost of being granted a licence has jumped by £32 to £150 while the cost of renewing an existing licence has soared by £100 to £150.

The Campaign for Shooting says it is not satisfied that these changes reflect the true increase in "administration costs" or that this term is clearly defined.

It is also calling for the Home Office and Police Constabularies to be more open and consult more widely in future.

LONG-TAILED TITS appear to be fighting back from a steep decline in the 1970s by changing their feeding habits and becoming less shy of human contact, it has been revealed.

Once a rare visitor to the garden bird table, the long-tailed tit is now much more frequently sighted tucking into titbits provided by householders.

Initial results from a British Trust for Ornithology survey show a 25 per cent increase in the number of adult long-tailed tits caught and ringed in 2000 compared to 1999.

"It is likely that the recent mild winters have enabled long-tailed tits to survive well to the following year and good weather in the early spring has led to productive breeding seasons," explained a spokesman for the BTO.

"This increase is part of a longer-term trend - up 60 per cent between 1983 and 1996 - although it follows a steep decline in the late 1970s.

"In addition, the long-tailed tit has also changed its behaviour. It is now a regular visitor to gardens and has started using food, such as peanuts and fat balls, put out for other species."

The Trust says numbers of reed and sedge warblers, and whitethroat, have also increased.

"As these are summer visitors, the warmer winters in the UK cannot explain these changes and further work is needed to understand why their numbers are increasing," said the spokesman.

In contrast, three other warbler species - blackcap, garden warbler and willow warbler - had all shown significant declines in adult numbers. Continued monitoring would show whether these changes were the start of a long-term trend or just an annual blip.

FEARS OF A big cat prowling part of Scotland have prompted police to issue a warning to local farmers.

The alarm was raised after farmer James King found the remains of a lamb which had been stripped off all flesh as if by a large predatory cat.

Experts who examined the carcass near Huntly have now confirmed that the signs point to a big cat having slain and eaten the lamb.

Mr King himself is adamant that the way the lamb was slaughtered and the flesh stripped was unlike anything he had ever seen before - certainly nothing like the way dogs attack and kill.

Two farmers in the Grampian region have previously reported seeing a huge black cat stalking the area - something Mr King had paid little attention to until now.

Police have warned farmers to take care.

THE NEW YEAR was used as a platform by the Countryside Alliance to launch its new political advertising campaigning aimed at keeping hunting.

The campaign, launched on January 1, demands that Parliament "gets real" about the hunting issue in the face of so many other important issues facing politicians.

Campaign leader Sam Butler said:"This campaign will run up to and beyond the Livelihood and Liberty March in London on March 18 and, of course, the General Election.

"It highlights the need for politicians to get their priorities right. Get on with the real job of dealing with serious social problems, or continue with this obsession of seeking social revenge on law-abiding people.

"It seems now that even the Home Secretary realises there is no case to ban hunting, confirming the findings of the Government's own Inquiry into hunting earlier this year. It doesn't matter which party they represent, MPs must get real or get out."

PRACTICAL-MINDED FARMER Don Evett knew just what to do when he discovered a human skull on his land - he put it in a plastic carrier bag and took it to the police.

Mr Evett made the gruesome find while out walking with his dogs on his farm at Aston Clinton in Buckinghamshire.

The local councillor carefully picked up the skull and took it to his local police station, accompanied by his two sons and grandson.

Shocked officers later recovered the rest of the skeleton in the field, thought to have been separated from the skull by scavenging animals.

The bones are believed to belong to a man who went missing in the area several months ago.

Police are not treating the death as suspicious.

COUNTY COUNCILLORS IN Lincolnshire are being urged by the Ramblers Association to make a New Year resolution to improve the state of the county's paths in 2001.

RA spokesman Stuart Parker said:"The path network in Lincolnshire is in immediate need of attention. Although the county council has a legal duty to ensure all rights of way are open, during the year 2000 it consistently put a low priority on the path network.

"In the council budget for 2001 we want to see sufficient resources devoted to getting the footpath network into shape.

"As a major arable producer, the county also suffers from paths being ploughed up and overgrown with crops, which is why we are asking the council to publish its policy on dealing with those who flout the law.

"A new year always offers the opportunity for a fresh start, and we hope that Lincolnshire councillors will make a resolution now to improve the county path network in 2001."

BRITISH GROWERS FACE "hundreds of millions of pounds in extra costs" because of red tape, says the NFU in a new report.

'UK Horticulture:A Time for Understanding' highlights "a rash of current and planned 'green' red tape, including the Climate Change Levy, Waste Regulations and Water Bill which are squeezing the life out of the industry,"said a spokesman.

93

BADGERS ARE AT the centre of fresh conflict between farmers and conservationists as pressure grows for more widespread culling to halt the spread of TB in cattle.

Dr Elaine King, spokesman for the National Federation of Badger Groups, has attacked moves to increase the present scale of killing.

She said tens of thousands of badgers had already been exterminated in recent years even before the ongoing Krebs cull trials were launched with the aim of killing 12,500 more.

The badger was being used as a "scapegoat" by people in the agricultural sector over the rise of TB, she added.

However, farmers are said to be desperate to halt the spread of TB in their herds which is simply yet another problem driving them out of business.

The NFU has criticised a Select Committee report on TB and badgers which it says "skates over the very real problems being suffered here and now by Britain's cattle farmers."

The recent escalation of TB among badgers and cattle had not been taken into account, it claimed, nor had delays in the present Krebs cull which were proving disastrous to thousands of cattle farmers and their families.

Brian Jennings, chairman of the NFU Animal Health and Welfare Committee, said:"Cattle desperately need to be protected from a disease that is distressing, costly and hugely disruptive to farm businesses, and has led to the slaughter of almost 30,000 cattle since 1996.

"It is vital, therefore, that swift action is taken to reduce the incidence of TB and to ease the enormous hardship being endured by farmers."

THE LACK OF countryside knowledge among modern children is a problem about to be addressed in a new initiative.

And anyone who thinks there isn't a problem need look no further than a recent survey which found more than half the youngsters in a test group had no idea what "free range" meant.

Youngsters' understanding of countryside issues will be boosted by the formation of a new one-stop shop for rural education, says the Country Land and Business Association.

The CLA welcomed the merger of the Food and Farming Education Service with the NFU education programme to become the Food and Farming Education Trust.

CLA president, Anthony Bosanquet, said:"We look forward to working with FFET to improve young people's understanding of the countryside."

THE RURAL CHARACTER of much of the South West is the golden goose the Government risks killing with plans for more property sprawl, warns the Council for the Protection of Rural England.

Nigel Kersey, CPRE senior regional policy officer, spoke out after it became apparent the scale of Government proposals were 11 per cent higher than building numbers collectively proposed by local authorities.

He said:"This level of development exceeds the capacity of the South West's countryside and half the new housing will be built on greenfield sites. The Government plans have largely ignored the impact on the South West's uniquely rural character.

"The economic prosperity of the South West is largely dependent on the quality of its countryside and its predominantly rural character.

"While the Government has made a welcome shift towards prioritising rundown land in towns and cities, the threat from urban sprawl risks killing the goose that lays the golden egg."

Some 20,000 extra homes will be built annually throughout the region in the next 20 years if the plans go ahead, changing the appearance of the South West forever, he added.

JUST WHEN YOU thought Christmas was safely behind you, The Woodland Trust is urging a search and grab mission involving all those festive greetings cards.

New trees will be planted on the proceeds collected by recycling thousands upon thousands of Christmas and New Year cards, explains the Trust.

Local Government Minister Hilary Armstrong MP formally launched the national Christmas card recycling scheme in the first week of January.

"Whereas people will probably reuse Christmas decorations for years to come, people are less inclined to think of alternatives to the dustbin for our cards," said a Trust spokesman.

"Last year, we recycled less than 10 per cent of our cards."

Boots The Chemists has teamed up with the Trust to offer a Christmas card recycling service in all of their stores throughout the UK until February 28.

Last year, the scheme led to the recycling of over 400 tonnes of cards across Britain, helping the Trust to create 12 new woods.

PRIME MINISTER TONY Blair favours a complete ban on foxhunting despite the threat it will pose to rural jobs and traditions, it has been revealed.

MPs are due to vote on three options, one of which involves a complete ban on hunting with dogs - making it illegal and criminalising anyone trying to carry on the centuries-old sport.

Although his views have always been anti-hunt, Downing Street let it be known that Mr Blair would be voting for a complete ban himself.

The move has angered pro-hunters who fear thousands of jobs will be lost and thousands of horses and hounds put down after a ban.

Home Secretary Jack Straw has previously stated he prefers allowing hunting to continue but with tougher legislation in place.

Labour supporter and broadcaster Melvyn Bragg is leading his own campaign to try to keep foxhunting legal.

He says it could put farmers in his native Cumbria out of business.

A CONSTITUTIONAL NIGHTMARE is the prospect facing New Labour after MPs voted against foxhunting in the face of public opinion apparently defending it.

Despite recent polls pointing to a swing in favour of leaving hunters with dogs alone, a free vote saw the majority of MPs choosing to criminalise it with a complete ban.

However, the Bill to ban hunting with dogs stands little chance of becoming law before the next election as opposition in the House of Lords will be unrelenting.

The Bill also faces severe legal tests which could ultimately set Parliament against the law courts in an unprecedented wrangle.

In addition, a massive campaign of civil disobedience pledged by pro-hunters would be another headache for the Government should the Bill become law.

Following the vote to ban hunting, Mike Baker, spokesman for the International Fund for Animal Welfare, said:"Hunting is cruel and that is the thing that has persuaded the British public and the overwhelming majority in the House of Commons to vote against it.

"We are talking about a fox that has been chased for up to an hour and half, is under extreme stress, being caught and ripped to pieces - eaten alive."

But pro-hunter, the Earl of Onslow, said:"This Bill is nothing short of the most cynical thing I have seen in 30 years of politics."

It was plainly wrong for a society that had come to accept homosexuality and divorce to now criminalise hunters, he added.

MUTE SWANS ARE to be the subject of a national census this spring with volunteers welcome to help track all the birds down.

The Wildfowl and Wetlands Trust will co-ordinate the study which is an update of research carried out a decade ago.

"Mute swans are a common sight during the breeding season on all manner of wetlands, including small lakes and particularly on rivers - those habitats which are not often visited by waterbird surveys," said a WWT spokesman.

"The aim is to cover completely the most densely populated regions, with less intensive coverage of other areas.

"This will involve locating and counting all non-breeding flocks in March and April and locating all breeding pairs by the end of May.

"Although mute swans are large and conspicuous, the survey may involve a fair deal of footwork in areas with networks of small rivers and ponds, particularly given the spread of the population since the late 1980s."

Anyone willing to help should contact Peter Cranswick, head of waterbird monitoring, at WWT Slimbridge.

THE ALARM HAS been raised about unusual numbers of garden birds dying or falling sick across the country after feeding at bird tables.

The RSPB believes an infectious disease is to blame and revealed "unprecedented numbers" of telephone calls had flooded in from the public.

An initial probe by itself and the Zoological Society of London suggested that salmonellosis was responsible with species such as the greenfinch, siskin and house sparrow badly hit and the western half of England worst affected.

Dr Andrew Cunningham, veterinary pathologist at ZSL, said:"Disease outbreaks appear to be associated with large numbers of birds collecting at feeders, but further work is required before such a link can be proved."

Dr Andy Evans, head of terrestrial research for the RSPB, said:"We do not want to discourage anyone from feeding birds, but we do urge people to ensure that feeders are cleaned regularly with diluted disinfectant to reduce the risk of any infection being spread to healthy birds.

"We also recommend that feeders are moved regularly to different locations in the garden and that drinking water is changed daily to avoid a build up of infected droppings."

The RSPB would continue to monitor the situation and to work with ZSL to determine the cause of the outbreak, he added.

Anyone finding sick or dead birds in their garden is urged to phone the RSPB Wildlife Enquiries Unit.

OVER-SIZED, OVERBEARING and over here - Canada geese are being blamed for pushing out native species on the Exe estuary in Devon.

Over 800 Canada geese have flown in to feed at the Exminster Marshes, more than double the usual number from previous years.

Wildlife experts fear that the aggressive geese - introduced here in the 17th Century - will drive away other species such as widgeon, lapwing and redshank.

Although the geese normally leave the Exe come winter, they have stayed put this year and their numbers have been constantly swelled by new arrivals.

Now the RSPB fears its attempts to attract more native species to nest at the site will suffer as other birds feel too intimidated by the Canada geese.

SOME 5,000 YOUNG barbel have been introduced into the cleaned-up River Erewash as part of an Environment Agency scheme.

The fish will help bring life back to a river which was once so polluted that no fish at all were thought to survive there.

"Along with vast improvements in water quality, fish numbers are being enhanced by stocking, improvements to bankside and in-stream habitats, and the creation of fish passes on several mill weirs," said a spokesman.

"The Erewash is an important Trent tributary, flowing along the Nottinghamshire/Derbyshire border. It has traditionally suffered from having the coal and steel industry along its catchment.

"Due to the closure of the mines and heavy investment by Severn Trent Water in upgrading water reclamation works, the river - fishless 15 years ago - is becoming a thriving fishery throughout much of its length."

THE RSPB IS calling for an inquiry into a military blunder by British forces which wiped out hundreds of breeding albatrosses and penguins.

Troops moving ordnance on the Falklands started a blaze in man-high tussac grass which raged out of control and engulfed the helpless birds.

The inferno continued for five days on South Jason Island, a nature reserve owned by the Falklands Government which was being visited by British soldiers on January 12 to explode ammunition left over from the Falklands War.

Helicopters scrambled after the alarm was raised dropped water on the area and teams of beaters on the ground fought to control the blaze which killed ranks of almost fully grown chicks as well as adult birds.

Fire crews from Stanley reported the upsetting sight of burnt penguins and other seabirds crawling away through tussac grass, unlikely to escape flames fanned by ferocious South Atlantic winds.

Conservationists now fear that if the fire spreads to the underlying peat layer, the tussac grass may never return, destroying the island's status as an internationally important seabird site.

RSPB spokesman Jim Stevenson said:"We are totally astounded. In addition to albatrosses and penguins, the island was also important for sealions. No-one dreamt that such a colony was at risk from fire as no-one normally goes to the island.

"This incident raises questions about the validity of this military exercise when, in dry weather and at the height of the breeding season, troops attempted to clear ordnance which posed little or no threat to people.

"The RSPB, which is actively involved in the seabird census work on the Falklands, is seeking an absolute assurance from the Ministry of Defence that there will be an inquiry into this incident and that appropriate steps will be taken to ensure that it can never happen again."

AMBITIOUS PLANS TO transform the 40-square mile Thames Chase landscape into a rich mosaic of woods, farms, nature areas and open spaces are already bearing fruit.

Two new Forestry Commission woodlands are currently being created, on the edge of East London just next to the M25.

"This is the latest exciting project in the Thames Chase area, bringing the countryside to people's doorsteps and delivering a green vision in a quality environment," said a Commission spokesman.

FARMERS WILL NOW be able to offset losses against tax following lobbying of the Inland Revenue by the Country Land and Business Association.

Since the 1960s, farmers making losses for more than five consecutive years have been prevented from setting those losses against other income or capital gains under the Income and Corporation Taxes Act.

Now, following representations from the CLA, the Inland Revenue has announced that it is relaxing the restriction - which is peculiar to the farming industry - for the years 2000-01 and 2001-02.

According to the CLA, the concession means that farmers who have been making losses since the present recession began to bite in the mid-1990s will be able to offset them against tax payable - provided the farm business made a profit for at least one year immediately before the start of the five-year period.

Anthony Bosanquet, CLA president, explained:"The five-year rule was originally intended as a way of preventing high-earners using hobby farms to reduce their income tax bills. However, in the present farming recession, there was a real danger that genuine farming families would be caught out."

PHOTOGRAPHS OF PAW prints are being examined by a zoo to see if they belong to a big cat prowling in Cornwall.

The prints were photographed by Ken Lewis after he noticed them close to his home in Gunnislake.

Mr Lewis had been out walking his pet dog at the time and now wonders if the land near his home is safe.

The prints seemed much wider than normal dog prints, he revealed, and more like a cat's.

The photographs have been sent to Mike Thomas, managing director of Newquay Zoo, to take a look at.

ANIMAL RIGHTS PROTESTERS are claiming victory in their fight to kill off a department store's shooting club.

Animal Aid claims the John Lewis store group closed down the club following sustained pressure from its members.

A spokesman for AA said:"The John Lewis store group has ended the rearing and shooting of pheasants on its Hampshire estate.

"The move comes just 16 weeks into a high profile campaign by Animal Aid, which involved protests inside and outside the group's stores across the UK, and at the estate itself. Some 70,000 hard-hitting leaflets were distributed.

"The company also admitted trapping and killing foxes, stoats and weasels - animals attracted to unnaturally large numbers of birds in one area.

"The Partnership's Shooting Club had just 27 members, 22 of whom were department managers or more senior.

"The campaign - which came on the back of long-running protests by grassroots activists - prompted a rebellion within the ranks of the group's 37,000 employees."

Animal Aid has long opposed game bird shooting and says it is wrong for so many birds to be bred just to be blasted from the sky.

SALMON ARE AT the heart of a new intitiative by the Environment Agency to revitalise a river in North Devon which was once a national favourite with anglers.

The Agency wants to create an action plan to bring back salmon in the kind of numbers that made the River Torridge famous.

"Salmon have been dwindling in the river since the 1960s and the Environment Agency is currently inviting local people to contribute to plans being drawn up to help conserve this precious fish," said a spokesman.

"The 'River Torridge Salmon Action Plan' covers an area that includes Okehampton, Hatherleigh, Great Torrington and Bideford."

Copies of the consultation draft are currently available and anyone interested in contributing has until the end of February to offer ideas.

The early 1990s saw a slight recovery in numbers of salmon caught in the river but this was not sustained and stocks have now reached "dangerously low" levels.

The consultation draft sets out how the Agency proposes to reverse the ongoing decline of salmon in the Torridge.

Initial ideas include tackling agricultural pollution, monitoring signs of recovery in juvenile fish, and improving degraded nursery and spawning areas.

Steve Douglas, Devon fisheries manager for the Agency, explained: "Whatever work we do has to have the full support of all the people who live and work on the River Torridge.

"Getting involved now gives people a real chance to help the Agency and play a vital part in seeing a good run of salmon return to the Torridge."

HERE'S TO YOU, Mrs Robinson - a surprise cash gift from music maker Sir Paul McCartney for looking after animals.

Kate Robinson was astonished to receive a £5,000 cheque from the maestro himself to boost her work at the Willows Animal Sanctuary near Gardenstown, north east Scotland.

Ducks, horses, sheep and donkeys make up some of the 300 creatures cared for at the sanctuary.

However, it had been going through a testing time financially of late.

With dwindling money, the work undertaken at the centre was increasingly coming under threat.

Before the cash arrived, it was feared that the sanctuary might have to rein in its activities.

Mrs Robinson received the money as part of the Animal Angels project originally set up by Sir Paul's late wife Linda.

The scheme distributes cash to animal aid organisations and a plaque has now been erected at the Willows in memory of the former Beatle's ex-partner.

THE COUNTRYSIDE ALLIANCE has demanded that Home Secretary Jack Straw gets tough on anti-hunt protesters.

Chairman John Jackson wrote urging the Government to crack down hard on "the escalating violence being perpetrated against hunting people and rural communities."

He also says the Government itself may be partly to blame for the upsurge in animal rights violence.

Mr Jackson, who reveals he had alerted Mr Straw some time ago to the alarming rise of violent attacks on hunt members and supporters, warned of the outrage felt among law-abiding rural communities that they should have had to endure "not only a prejudiced parliamentary attack but an increasing wave of intimidation and extremist thuggery."

He added:"It is now believed by many that the observable increase in activity by animal rights groups - nail bombings of farmers and fish and chip shops, intimidation of stakeholders in companies conducting lawful and necessary business, attacks on hunt staff and buildings, arson, kidnapping of animals, etc - is in part due to the impressions and atmosphere created by the Government itself in its handling of the hunting matter."

MYSTERY SURROUNDS THE discovery of a mouse-eared bat in West Sussex - a decade after the species was declared extinct in Britain.

The bat, which boasts a 16-inch wingspan, was our largest native species of bat before experts consigned it to the history books.

Bat fans were therefore delighted when a single surviving specimen was discovered at a secret spot in the Bognor Regis area.

Unfortunately, the elderly female died soon after, sparking a debate as to whether it really was part of a surviving native colony.

Mouse-eared bats are still found on the Continent and it is not known if the lone creature made its way here before its demise.

So the discovery has left experts with more questions than answers.

WALKING IS A perfect way youngsters can combat a rising tide of obesity among their ranks, says the Ramblers Association.

A lifetime of ill-health due to being overweight could easily be avoided if parents learned to encourage their offspring to step out.

The Association was responding to research published in the British Medical Journal showing that the number of overweight British children is soaring.

"Walking is an easy and accessible exercise that burns calories and protects against the risk of heart disease," said a spokesman.

"It can be readily introduced into children's lives as a form of environmentally-friendly transport and an alternative to jumping in the car for short journeys.

"Walking in the countryside can be a powerful learning tool - not just for discovering and identifying wildlife, but also for understanding rural life.

"If the health prospects of our youngsters are to be improved it is vital that walking is encouraged in as many ways as possible."

KESTREL: predator dines royally at a town car park

GRACEFUL and deadly, the kestrel can hover like a sophisticated military helicopter above its prey before choosing the right moment to swoop down and make a kill.

Death comes swiftly for any vole or mouse unfortunate enough to have caught this elegant predator's attention, courtesy of its needle-sharp talons.

The kestrel is the commonest of our birds of prey and can often be spotted above a motorway verge or open field, its wingtips quivering in mute support as it gazes down in readiness to pounce on another luckless victim.

Only 33-36cms in length, with a wingspan of up to 80cms, the male boasts especially handsome plumage. His chestnut back and wings are complemented by a bluish grey head which sports a distinctive dark 'moustache'.

Although rural kestrels feed on voles, mice, insects and worms, their townie cousins make the most of small birds that come their way, such as sparrows and blue tits.

I've watched kestrels hunting many times in the wild but one of my more unusual sightings was in the middle of a town.

There, as I worked in a hot, airless office one afternoon, I happened to glance out of the window and noticed a kestrel hunting sparrows over the grey concrete car park opposite.

Dipping and rising in the breeze 30ft above the top floor, the kestrel nevertheless maintained a rigid gaze on potential victims fluttering about among the cars. While its wings remained constantly on the move, the head was stock-still, thereby allowing the eyes to pinpoint the juiciest target.

The kill, when it was made, happened out of sight but I later saw the kestrel flying away holding a pathetic bundle in its claws, testimony to its hunting success.

A spokesman at RSPB headquarters in Bedfordshire told me that a national survey into kestrel numbers was still ongoing and no final conclusions had been reached at the time.

"But there were believed to be about 50,000 nesting pairs in this country at the last survey some years ago," he said. "It appears that we have lost 25 per cent of our kestrel population over the past 25 years with the steady decline probably down to habitat changes. There is less space for kestrels to breed now and less prey as a result of how we manage the countryside."

Crop fields were more barren of potential prey than ever before and subsidies were needed for those farmers who were prepared to make fields more accessible to wildlife, he added.

Anyone who was captivated by the film 'Kes', released in the 1970s, will already appreciate the beauty of this bird.

Unfortunately, as well as being enthralling, the story about a working class boy who takes a kestrel chick from the wild and trains it, was also an incentive for other youngsters to follow suit.

Many kestrel chicks and other birds of prey were believed to have been taken from nests in abortive attempts to train them along the lines of author Barry Hines' gritty novel.

Sadly, most chicks are believed to have perished and it's worth pointing out that the taking of eggs or young birds of prey from the wild remains a criminal offence.

Kestrels lay four to five white eggs with red-brown markings but there is some suspicion that hatching success has been affected by pesticides seeping into the food chain in recent decades.

It would be a terrible shame if the kestrel was to disappear at some point from the British countryside.

Nevertheless, my own favourite image of this impressive predator remains clear - its hovering form silhouetted against a perfect blue sky as I played cricket one summer years ago.

In fact, it was difficult to concentrate on the match when not 50 metres away a more ancient game of life and death was being played out.

DOMESTIC CATS MAY be killing as many as 275 million wild creatures each year across Britain, The Mammal Society has revealed in a shock new report.

The full spectrum of carnage is thought to include 200 million small mammals, nearly 60 million birds, and 10 million reptiles such as frogs and lizards.

Previous estimates of bird killings have been as high as 75 million so the report may give some comfort to bird lovers but the whole picture still adds up to a devastating indictment of Tiddles.

Michael Woods, Mammal Society vice-chairman and survey co-ordinator, said the list of cat victims included rare and declining species such as water voles, dormice and house sparrows.

"The potential effect of cats gives considerable cause for concern," he said,"especially as cats will not bring home all the animals they kill.

"Cats can roam up to a kilometre each night and have a home range of up to 28 hectares. Many owners think that when their cat brings home a mouse it is suppressing the local rodent population but this is clearly not the case. Cats are killing animals on a much wider scale."

Nor are domestic cats as successful at keeping rats down as once thought, the report reveals, because rats put up fierce resistance when cornered and other prey is easier to kill.

Mammal Society chairman, Professor Stephen Harris, added:"This survey has given a clear indication of the threats cats pose to Britain's animal populations.

"As there are 26 times more cats than foxes and six times more cats that all wild terrestrial predators combined, no-one can doubt that cats can be a very serious problem for British wildlife.

"However no-one wishes to downplay the joy and comfort that cats can bring to their owners and our survey has also provided some clear techniques to reduce the threat posed by cats."

These included fitting cats with bells and not letting them out of the house at night.

TWO STAGS WHOSE antlers became entangled during a fight were finally released unharmed by firemen called to the scene.

The animals were believed to have been struggling to free themselves for some time before a passer-by raised the alarm at Covehithe, Suffolk.

Death from starvation is the normal fate of stags that become locked together in the wild.

THE COUNTRYSIDE ALLIANCE has seized on an apparent admission by the League Against Cruel Sports that it will target shooting next if hunting with dogs goes.

The League's Graham Sirl was quoted in a newspaper saying:"If you look at the cruelty involved in pheasant shooting, the way the animals are reared, the way wildlife is systematically destroyed, and the actual killing and wounding of the birds, it is clear that this is another so called sport which has to be abolished."

Nigel Henson, director of communications for the Alliance, said:"Graham Sirl's comments end years of the League ducking the issue about shooting.

"We now know for sure that animal rights activists, and their unnamed financial backers, will turn their attention to other country sports.

"Now the truth is out. The intentions of the League, in addition to those already declared by the Hunt Saboteurs Association, will send a shiver down the spine of the Government.

"Politicians who voted for a hunting ban will now have to face an even bigger problem than they thought.

"They will need to explain their own illogical position with greater care.

"Having been tricked into supporting a hunting ban they may now have to take a position on shooting. What next?"

THOUSANDS OF ROOSTING starlings are in for a rude awakening after council officials hit on a fiendish way to scare them off - with fireworks.

Gloucester City Council has amassed an arsenal of fireworks in a bid to get the birds to fly away for good.

Desperate residents appealed for help before Christmas after a huge starling flock chose their part of the city to roost.

Droppings had since rained daily from the sky, covering pedestrians, cars, and anything else in the area.

Previous attempts to disperse the birds have failed, including the use of automatic crow scarers.

Now officials are hoping that a nightly barrage of noise from fireworks will finally do the trick.

MECHANICAL FLAILING OF hedgerows could be a major cause of the steep decline in dormice numbers, says English Nature.

Research by Dr Paul Bright, of the University of London, shows that dormice have now vanished from 68 per cent of hedgerows where they were known to have been present as recently as the early 1980s.

"Traditionally, hedgerows were managed by hand which had a less dramatic effect on the size and growth of a hedge," explained a spokesman for English Nature.

"Hedges need at least two to three years growth to provide suitable food sources and habitats for dormice.

"Mechanical flailing cuts hedges back hard in the early autumn and reduces the amount of berries available.

"Dormice need to feed on berries, fruits and nuts in the autumn to fatten up before hibernating underground below the hedgerow amongst the leaf litter."

FARMERS' LEADERS HAVE reacted with alarm to a decisive switch by supermarkets away from meat reared on GM animal feed.

Supermarkets, under growing pressure from consumers, are seeking to stock up on GM-free meat but the NFU says this threatens to increase the present hardship for farmers struggling to survive.

NFU president Ben Gill said:"It is one thing for retailers to offer consumers choice by developing lines produced from animals fed on non-GM feed, but it is quite another for them to require the same for ALL meat products."

The NFU fears the danger of disruption to British meat supplies is so great that it has called for Agriculture Minister Nick Brown to immediately call a food chain meeting and asked retailers to suspend their proposals.

The NFU is now conducting a joint study with Sainsbury's to establish the true costs and ramifications of securing non-GM animal feed.

"We believe that the results of this study will be of benefit and interest to the whole food industry," said Mr Gill.

Concern from the farmers' union follows an announcement by Marks and Spencer that it will be increasing its range of meat products reared on non-GM animal feed to include fresh beef, lamb and chicken.

Tesco has already written to suppliers outlining its own programme with a new announcement along similar lines also made by Asda.

"Research shows that GM material is broken down naturally when eaten by animals into its component parts," asserted Mr Gill.

"Supplies of guaranteed GM-free feed ingredients are limited and a sudden increase in demand can only lead to higher costs for farmers."

A DORSET BEAUTY spot was the scene of a heart-stopping accident when a dog fell 200ft down a cliff - and lived.

South London terrier Bruiser was walking with owner Pat Hendrick at Lulworth Cove when the pair suddenly reached the cliff edge.

Instead of pausing like his master, the 15 year-old pet popped straight over and clattered all the way down to the beach.

Screams of anguish from onlookers below convinced tourist Mr Hendrick that his dog had died - but he was wrong.

The lucky dog's fall had been broken by piles of shingle and he escaped with cuts and new bruises to reinforce his name.

According to local residents, several other dogs have fallen off the cliff at the same point but all died.

THOUSANDS OF PEOPLE across Britain took part in the RSPB's Big Garden Birdwatch, the biggest and longest running national survey of its type.

The two-day survey, run by the Society's junior section, aims to identify the most commonly seen garden birds and find where species like the house sparrow are suffering worst declines.

Among those taking part was TV gardener Charlie Dimmock who emphasised the importance of data gathered during the event.

She said:"Gardens are becoming increasingly important as havens for birds and other wildlife due to a lack of natural food in the wild.

"This survey gives us valuable information on those birds most in need of help, and it is a good way to do your bit for wildlife."

Carole McCormick, project co-ordinator for the RSPB, added:"The Big Garden Birdwatch is a lot of fun for young people, their families and friends, but there is also a serious side to it. Numbers of many familiar garden birds are declining rapidly. If we are to turn these declines around, we must gather as much information about these birds as possible."

A FOX DELIVERED a painful reminder of its less than cuddly nature when a rescuer picked it up to save it from pursuing hounds.

The man, a hunt saboteur, received a deep bite to his thumb which required hospital treatment following the drama near Cullompton, Devon.

The day had already been marked by violence after the East Devon Hunt turned out in defiance of the recent anti-hunt vote in the House of Commons.

The saboteur snatched up the exhausted fox and held it above the hounds while running to a nearby hedge to drop it in.

It was then the ungrateful fox sank its needle-sharp teeth into him but the terrified animal still managed to escape.

About 10 protesters and hunters were arrested by police following heated clashes during the event.

A LEGAL RIGHT to roam in England and Wales is a step closer to implementation as key provisions of the new Countryside and Rights of Way Act now come into effect, says the Ramblers Association.

But the Association has also reminded walkers that the promised access over open, uncultivated country may still not be available for several years.

The process of mapping areas of mountain, moor, heath, down and common land to which new freedoms apply is set to begin in March under the direction of the Countryside Agency and the Countryside Council for Wales.

Kate Ashbrook, chairman of the RA's freedom to roam campaign committee, said:"This is a vital first step. The law has been passed but until we have the maps there is no freedom to roam.

"We shall be doing all we can to help with the mapping process."

ANIMAL RIGHTS PROTESTERS are being blamed for a parcel bomb which exploded in the hands of a British Heart Foundation charity shop worker in Penrith, Cumbria. The shocked woman escaped serious injury.

BRITISH SONGBIRDS ARE being illegally trapped in large numbers by crooks aiming to sell them on for cash, the RSPCA has revealed.

Hundreds of our best-loved birds are regularly being taken from the wild to feed an underground racket both here and on the Continent.

So far, the RSPCA says, 200 people have been convicted of offences relating to trapping birds but more resources are required if the practice is to be beaten.

Investigators have discovered that criminals are using a variety of heartless methods to snatch the birds from the wild, including spreading glue on branches and using large nets.

RSPCA spokesman Alistair Keen said: "Wild birds will often show signs of stress if they are kept in captivity. They appear unsteady and can end up in an appalling state."

Wings, beaks, and legs were routinely damaged in the trapping process and the birds often suffered in agony before dying.

A hawfinch died within days of the RSPCA rescuing it and was found to be almost blind, with bones protruding from its body.

Some wild birds were even found in cages in a child's bedroom when investigators moved in to rescue them and one victim, a goldfinch, had been seriously injured.

The RSPCA has called the illegal trade "disgusting" and said it has been amazed that people could inflict such cruelty just to make a little cash.

FARMERS' LEADERS HAVE issued a cross-party challenge to politicians to make farming a key part of their General Election campaigns.

NFU president Ben Gill has also called on tens of thousands of union members to ensure that prospective parliamentary candidates do not ignore farming and rural concerns.

Mr Gill said:"While there are encouraging signs that the agricultural recession may have bottomed out, the industry remains in an extremely fragile state. There has never been a more crucial time to influence politicians.

"For many farmers and growers, this will be the most important General Election of their lives."

A new document titled 'The General Election Challenge' sets out 14 key areas which prospective candidates will be asked to support.

It will be distributed to farmers across the country to enable them to challenge their local candidates.

"Over the coming months, farmers and growers have the opportunity to press home their concerns to both sitting MPs and the candidates who are standing against them," added Mr Gill.

OPPONENTS OF THE Government's Hunting Bill have underlined the real danger of innocent dog walkers being maliciously prosecuted if it becomes law.

Speaking in the Standing Committee debate, Lib Dem MP Alan Beith asked how a prosecutor would view a dog owner whose dog pursued a rat (legal) but then a rabbit (illegal unless it is shot).

While he "knowingly permitted" the former, could the same be said of the latter ?

Furthermore, Mr Beith added, innocence might only be proved after a lengthy, expensive and traumatic police investigation and court case.

Tory MP John Gummer suggested that the legislation sought to outlaw the natural instinct of animals.

Thus, he said, if a terrier mistook a rat for a rabbit it was up to the dog owner to prove that the action was an error of judgement on the part of the dog - as opposed to a deliberate intent to hunt on the part of the owner.

But Labour MP Jackie Lawrence, who supports the Bill, suggested that it was the responsibility of private dog owners to train their animals to know the difference between the species involved.

Simon Hart, director of the Countryside Alliance Campaign for Hunting, said:"Despite attempts to claim that innocent parties will not be affected by this Bill, it is now clearer than ever that they will.

"Anybody with a dog that they like to walk in the country could come under suspicion - either as a result of misunderstanding, malice, or both.

"Furthermore, pest controllers and game-keepers whose jobs depend on use of dogs will be hard pressed to ensure that both they and their dogs can walk the blurred line between innocence and guilt."

SEAGULLS LIVING INLAND at Gloucester should be given artificial cliffs for nest sites, according to a local woman.

Carole Vaughan came up with the idea after more and more seabirds began flying inland to scavenge at a local landfill tip.

The birds also nest locally, causing a mess to high-rise buildings and a health hazard to people below.

Mrs Vaughan's brainwave is being taken seriously in an area where many residents are sick of cleaning up after nesting gulls.

The ex-councillor unveiled her idea after noticing fake 50ft concrete cliffs erected among skyscrapers on a recent visit to Hong Kong.

The bogus cliffs, she says, could actually become part of an attractive, landscaped area which would remove many of the problems caused by gulls in one fell swoop.

A JOB AS a goatherd which involves wandering the hills in a Northumberland wildlife park looking after more than 70 goats has attracted 200 applications from people confident they would not feel lonely.

AGRICULTURE MINISTER NICK Brown has revealed that animal rights "nutcases" have been bombarding him with abusive letters over Government-backed badger culling trials.

SUPPORTERS OF HARE coursing are expected to turn out in force again at this year's Waterloo Cup in defiance of demonstrators and the Government Bill on hunting with dogs.

The event, which critics repeatedly condemn as "barbaric" and "outdated" is being held from February 27 to March 1 at Altcar in Lancashire.

During the competition, pairs of greyhounds are marked for their speed and agility as they pursue a hare across open ground.

Most hares escape into nearby burrows but some are caught and killed, an eventuality which rouses the fury of anti-bloodsport campaigners.

"This year the Waterloo Cup, the Blue Riband of greyhound coursing, enters its 155th running strengthened by the Government-commissioned Burns Report," said a spokesman for the Countryside Alliance.

"The Waterloo Cup is the ultimate test of a coursing greyhound - 64 dogs from all over Britain and Ireland will compete and the champion will be the one who can win six courses over three days.

"Last December, the popularity of 'Greyhound 2000 - A Millennium Celebration' confirmed that more people each year support one of the world's most ancient sports and recognise the importance of greyhound coursing in the conservation of the brown hare.

"The Burns Report, published in June 2000, recognised that a ban on hunting with dogs - which would include greyhound coursing - might lead farmers and landowners to pay less attention to encouraging hare numbers and said the loss of habitat suitable for hares could have serious consequences for a number of birds and other animals."

Richard Burge, chief executive of the Alliance, added:"With the recently appointed Independent Supervisory Authority for Hunting, the publication of the Burns Report, and the sway in public opinion against a total ban on hunting with dogs, this Waterloo Cup promises to be even more popular and well attended. I would urge all country sports enthusiasts to join me at Altcar to witness coursing at its very best."

SHOOTERS HAVE BLASTED the Government and police with both barrels after their sport was hit by firearm licensing chaos.

Gun licensing in Britain is now a shambles, according to the British Association for Shooting and Conservation and the Country Land and Business Association.

A LANDOWNER has dropped his claim for £1.25million compensation over a public footpath opened through a privately-owned forest, reports the Ramblers Association.

"The so-called Golden Path across Wychwood Forest in West Oxfordshire has been at the centre of a legal tussle for more than a decade," said an Association spokesman.

"But, in a major victory for the walking public, Lord Rotherwick has decided not to pursue his appeal for compensation against Oxfordshire County Council.

"The case was originally brought by Lord Rotherwick's late father who claimed money for interference to his land.

"The case was considered by the Lands Tribunal which decided that the maximum period during which debts of this kind are legally enforceable had expired. But Lord Rotherwick said he would take the case to the Court of Appeal and a date for the hearing was set for May."

However, the county council had now been told that the appeal was being discontinued and it has been paid costs plus interest.

Ramblers Association vice-president Chris Hall added:"The Association warmly congratulates Oxfordshire County Council for sticking to its guns and winning. If this claim had been successful, it would have effectively deterred local councils from creating new paths for the public to enjoy."

BIRD LOVERS ACROSS the country are being urged to build and put up nestboxes again during National Nest Box Week.

The event, launched each year on St Valentine's Day, "aims to get as many people as possible to put up nestboxes in order to help our breeding birds," explained a spokesman for the British Trust for Ornithology.

"Each year thousands of people become involved over the week in some kind of nestbox activity. There are hundreds of wildlife groups, bird clubs and schools across the country that organise working parties in order to make nestboxes.

"Individuals contribute, too, by putting up nest boxes in their gardens or nearby woodlands. The week also acts as a reminder to those who already have nestboxes to go out and remove old nests from the box.

"By putting up a nestbox during National Nest Box Week you will be providing our wildlife with an invalu - able and safe nesting site, a resource that is disappearing at an alarming rate in the countryside."

THE SOIL ASSOCIATION has published a packed list of planned events and campaigns involving organic food during 2001.

These include tours of Waltham Place Farm, Maidenhead, Berkshire, on the first Wednesday of each month.

"Visit the 40 acres of formal and landscaped gardens, some of which dates back to the 17th Century," urged a spokesman.

On February 16 a seminar will be held at Sheepdrove Farm, Lambourn, Berkshire, looking at direct organic meat marketing. This would examine "the opportunities for selling meat direct to consumers through box schemes, home delivery, farmers' markets and farm shops."

ONCE COMMON BRITISH birds are now declining at a faster rate than ever before, according to worried conservationists.

Alarming findings reveal that there are 22 species whose numbers show a decline of 50 per cent or more over the past 25 years and a further 10 species whose numbers have dropped by more than 25 per cent.

"The two worst declines are reported for the lesser redpoll and tree sparrow, both down an appalling 94 per cent in 25 years," said a spokesman for the British Trust for Ornithology.

Yellow wagtails were also down by 81 per cent, starlings by 61 per cent, linnets by 55 per cent, marsh tits by 52 per cent, little grebes by 51 per cent, and cuckoos by 29 per cent.

The Trust recently published a report entitled 'Breeding Birds in the Wider Countryside' which covers the slump regarding once commonplace birds.

Report authors Humphrey Crick, John Marchant, David Noble and Stephen Baillie said the most worrying aspect of the analysis was that there were eight species which had declined at monitoring sites by more than 25 per cent in the last five years.

Some species, such as the grey partridge, lesser spotted woodpecker, tree pipit, yellow wagtail, willow tit, starling, tree sparrow and lesser redpoll were becoming so rare that it was difficult to keep track of them.

The findings are said to be vital for conservation planning and several of the declining species now have biodiversity action plans devoted to them while others are in urgent need of their own schemes.

The report was funded by a partnership between the BTO and the Joint Nature Conservation Committee.

CUPID'S ARROW NEEDED to be extra sharp after a Valentine's Day stunt by wildlife lovers targeted a group of water voles.

The peaceful rodents, made famous by Ratty in 'The Wind in The Willows', have seen their numbers decimated in recent years by voracious mink and environmental pressures.

So the Mammals Trust UK brought together about 30 of the furry creatures to mate on what is supposedly the most romantic day of the year.

Cosy living quarters were provided to help the day go with a swing and pregnant females are later expected to produce as many as eight young apiece.

When ready, these offspring will then be taken from their secret love nest in Herne Bay, Kent, and released into the wild to help build up local water vole populations.

NIGHTINGALES ARE HOLDING on in Britain thanks to a woodland management technique, says The Woodland Trust.

Numbers of the sweet voiced migrant have plummeted by almost 30 per cent in recent years but 17 nightingales were found in one Kent wood mainly comprising coppiced hornbeam - thought to provide ideal nesting sites.

"There are only about 4,400 male nightingales present in the UK, all of these in the southern part of the country," revealed a Trust spokesman.

"The practice of coppicing is carried out for several reasons. It allows more light onto the woodland floor, encouraging a greater variety of plants to survive.

"It can also benefit many other species, including butterflies and dormice. The cutting does not harm the tree which is rejuvenated and sprouts a greater number of branches. Coppicing once had commercial benefits as the timber had many potential uses, including charcoal production.

"Once coppicing is started, it is important that it continues in order to maintain the health of the tree."

A MUTE SWAN is believed to have mistaken the M25 around London for an open stretch of water when it crash landed into the central reservation.

The bird, thought to be female, fell to earth in a heap causing a traffic tailback for some minutes.

A quick-thinking motorist - later named as top designer Anthony Price - went to its aid and bundled it into his car.

Mr Price, more famous for dressing swan-necked denizens of high society in expensive gowns, later released the bird on a river.

Mute swans are to be the subject of a national census this spring with volunteers welcome to help track all the birds down. The Wildfowl and Wetlands Trust will co-ordinate the study which is an update of research carried out a decade ago.

A WELSH ORGANIC farmer is the winner of a £3,000 cash prize for encouraging wildlife while producing pesticide free food.

Cliff Carnell, from Carmarthen, has been named by the Soil Association as the winner of the Loraine Award 2000 from more than 40 entries.

The award for nature conservation is given annually by the Loraine Trust to an organically managed farm, where "profitable husbandry, the production of healthy food and the conservation of native wild life work together."

The Soil Association added:"Cliff Carnell has been farming at Llystyn Farm since 1991 and the farm consists of beef cattle, sheep, cereals and vegetables.

"Nature conservation has been an integral part of the farm's workings, for example taking part in the Hedgerow Renovation Scheme which involved banking, laying and replanting miles of hedgerow on the farm, and the preservation of wetland which has at least 60 species of flower."

THE COUNTRYSIDE ALLIANCE has attacked Government ministers for wringing their hands over the recent loss of 6,000 steel jobs but "rubbing their hands with glee" over the prospect of at least 8,000 hunting jobs going.

A QUESTION MARK now hangs over arrangements for the Countryside Alliance demonstration in London after the first major outbreak of foot-and-mouth disease here in 20 years.

Despite threats that hunt saboteurs would torch the farms of those taking part, nearly 200,000 marchers had already registered for the protest demo on March 18 before the disease hit the headlines.

Restrictions on movement in rural areas are now being imposed with hunting suspended for a week and ramblers curtailing their own activities.

Speaking before news of the disease leaked out, Richard Burge, chief executive of the Alliance, said of the 'Liberty and Livelihood March':"The momentum of support and pace of registration is now huge. There is little doubt that the numbers of people taking part will exceed even those for our 1998 Countryside March.

"But this one has a different focus - civil liberty. We could be seeing the largest single civil liberties demonstration in this country's modern history. What an irony in a country famed for its commitment to tolerance and social justice."

Well over 300,000 people were expected to march on the day with counter demonstrations likely to be organised by anti-hunt groups along the route.

Alliance officials said they would be mobilising support using most of the UK's available road and rail capacity, as well as bringing in walkers by air and sea.

Over 1,000 organisations had expressed their intention to join or support the event with more than 3,000 coaches pre-booked - already 900 more than in 1998.

A block booking of 250 seats had even been made on Eurostar to bring over a contingent of supporters from France while a North Sea ferry would transport another 800 marchers from Newcastle direct to the assembly area near Tower Bridge.

Arrangements had been made so that the famous bridge would be opened specifically to allow the ferry through on the day.

THE FIRST SWALLOW of the year has been recorded at Slapton Ley, Devon, by ornithologists - a sign of an early, hot summer, some think.

HUNT SABOTEURS HAVE pledged to disrupt a series of comeback concerts by rock band Roxy Music because lead singer Bryan Ferry supports fox-hunting and his son Otis, 17, is a whipper-in for a Yorkshire hunt.

THE RSPB HAS called on New Labour to help wild birds by banning housing development on countryside flood plains.

The Society spoke out as the Government was preparing to publish its advice to developers and planners about building in flood risk areas.

It believes the restoration of flood plains is essential to bring back valuable wildlife habitats such as wet grasslands which are important for wintering and breeding birds.

Mark Southgate, head of planning for the RSPB, said:"We cannot continue to solve flooding problems by building higher flood defences.

"Government, planners and developers must not site damaging new developments in those remaining natural flood plains.

"Where possible, they should also restore former flood plains to a natural state so that these important landscape features can once again hold back floodwaters to prevent towns and cities from suffering further devastation."

THE SHEER POWER of an average bull was brought home in stark fashion after a man was accidentally butted by one and sustained serious injuries.

The victim, later named as Roy Dart, in his 50s, suffered broken ribs, spinal and head injuries in the incident at his brother's beef farm near Cullompton, Devon.

Mr Dart had to be airlifted to hospital for emergency treatment after something startled the bull while he was leading it and it swung its massive head into him.

The mighty blow knocked him unconscious and he was initially treated at the scene by a Devon Air Ambulance team before being whisked away.

There are no plans to destroy the bull.

PROPOSALS PUT FORWARD by the European Commission in response to the collapse of the beef market in mainland Europe have been slammed by British farmers' leaders as ill-conceived, unnecessary and damaging.

The NFU has pledged to fight "tooth and nail" to overturn the restrictive measures, unveiled at a meeting of the College of Commissioners in Strasbourg.

NFU president Ben Gill said:"It would be a tragedy if UK beef farmers were to be sacrificed at a time when confidence is beginning to return to our markets after all the traumas of BSE."

FARMERS ARE CAUSING serious environmental damage by letting standards slip, it has been claimed.

Research into the problem has been conducted by the Institute for European Environmental Policy on behalf of English Nature.

"Overgrazing, loss of habitat and pollution are continuing to cause problems for wildlife," explained David Arnold-Forster, English Nature's chief executive."Collaboration between the farming industry and Government is needed to raise standards, without creating any major bureaucratic or financial burdens for our already beleaguered farming community.

"We know that many farmers want to increase the wildlife benefit of their farms but find it difficult in the current framework. Our research has identified a package of measures which if applied at policy level will help improve the biodiversity in our countryside."

THE FINGER OF blame for Britain's foot-and-mouth crisis has been pointed at international trade links which may have delivered a devastating timebomb to the farming industry.

The entire country should now play a part in making sure the threat does not turn into a national disaster for rural communities, say farmers' leaders.

NFU president Ben Gill warned:"We must not panic. What we must do is be vigilant."

However, the scale of the threat began sinking in as it was revealed that foot-and-mouth disease can travel as far as 150 miles by airborne transmission alone.

Mr Gill called on the public to steer clear of farms in their local communities until the source and extent of the disease had been identified and eradicated.

A 10-mile exclusion zone has been thrown around a farm in Essex where an especially virulent strain of the disease was first spotted while other farms as far apart as Yorkshire, Buckinghamshire, and Gloucestershire are also subject to restrictions as tests are carried out.

The whole farming industry had to start asking tough questions about how the disease could have been sparked in Britain, said Mr Gill.

"Is it a coincidence that we had classical swine fever in East Anglia last year of an Asian origin and now we have foot-and-mouth in East Anglia again of an Asian origin ? Why is that happening?" he asked.

"We are all exposed to food by directly formal imports or indirectly from people coming in and bringing food with them - without the checks that there used to be and in quantities we have not experienced.

"We have to consider whether this is wise and whether we ought to be looking much more to our home production for the security that we need."

Mr Gill warned the situation would sound "the death knell " for those farmers already at the end of their tether.

THE WISDOM OF Scotsmen wearing kilts has been called into question by alarming reports of a new threat to their vitals - rats "as big as badgers."

Huge rats have apparently been sighted several times across Scotland with the rodents bearing more resemblance to bigger, tougher badgers than their own species.

Whether the reports are anything more than wild exaggeration is debatable but across the UK there has been increasing evidence of so-called "super rats" which are resistant to traditional poisons.

AN ANGLER WAS fined a total of £220 after admitting illegally introducing live fish to Lake Windermere in Cumbria as bait for pike.

The man, from Southport, also pleaded guilty before South Lakeland Magistrates to fishing with more rods than he was permitted and taking undersized fish from the Leeds-Liverpool Canal to use as bait.

An Environment Agency water bailiff who investigated after seeing the defendant and another man fishing in a boat - where seven rods were employed - had discovered bait used included live roach and live Crucian carp, the court heard.

After the case, Agency spokeswoman Liz Black said:"Enforcing laws to prevent the introduction of fish is important to ensure disease does not spread from one water to another.

"Introduction can upset the ecological balance of a watercourse, especially if the new species of fish competes with the resident species for food or territory.

"Problems can arise, for example, if the new species alters the quantity or distribution of available fish food because of what they eat.

"The fish species found in Windermere include brown trout, pike, perch, roach and Arctic char.

"Arctic char are relatively common in the Lake District but are very rare in the rest of England and it is therefore particularly important to protect them from any possible detrimental impact."

CROPS SOWN TO benefit Scottish game birds are also providing a haven for declining songbirds, researchers have found.

A survey carried out by the Game Conservancy Trust focused on farms in eastern Scotland where numbers of songbirds have plummeted.

As a result of the findings, the Trust is now joining forces with the British Trust for Ornithology to expand its research into designing a crop even more suited to beleaguered songbirds.

Dr Dave Parish, research leader for the Game Conservancy Trust, said:"Some of our familiar songbirds are really up against it at the moment and we need to take action.

"If we can show that something as simple as a strip of cropping, designed to fulfil the needs of these species, can support large numbers of birds through - out the year, then I believe we could encourage more farmers outside the shooting community to plant such crops and go a long way to reversing the fortunes of our songbirds."

ANIMAL RIGHTS CAMPAIGNERS have attacked the culling of large numbers of non-native species living in the British countryside.

Animal Aid, the UK's largest campaign group, claims "top table conservationists" often scape-goat alien species such as the mink and grey squirrel because they threaten commercial interests.

A GIANT CATFISH dubbed 'Hannibal the Cannibal' has finally been caught after terrorising Shillinglee Lake in Sussex.

The 5ft fish regurgitated almost 60 other fish after its detention and anglers revealed it had been the scourge of native species.

MOUSE: great white hunter sets out to bag the interloper

MY wife spotted it, a tiny flash of fur darting to a patch of peanut crumbs beneath the patio bird feeder in our back garden.

Then it rocketed across the flagstones into the bushes. It was a mouse all right, but what kind ?

After learning of her observation, your correspondent - the Great White Hunter - immediately vowed to set out and catch the mouse.

But more about my scaled-down safari later. In truth, there are probably dozens of mice and voles living secretly in our back gardens, feasting royally each day on the nuts and seeds we put out for birds.

If they have any sense, they normally restrict their suburban activities to pitch darkness when they are less likely to be spotted by someone half-heartedly gazing out at their neglected flower tubs, wondering what blooms to plant this year.

It must be hard living in a world where virtually every other creature wants to kill or eat you.

And yet mice, and their diminutive cousins voles and shrews, collectively enjoy a number of advantages to give them a fighting chance of survival.

Speed and agility are two of the most obvious, as well as sharp hearing and a powerful sense of smell.

Yet even these are usually insufficient to deter a determined weasel intent on a kill or a cat prepared to sit for hours until a bite-sized snack emerges from its hole.

The beastie in our garden was unlikely to be a shrew, which prefers thicker cover and feeds mainly on worms and insects.

Nor from my wife's description was it a vole, which has a much blunter face and smaller ears than a mouse.

No, it seemed it was definitely a mouse that took a chance and ventured out before darkness had properly fallen.

So the safari began.

First of all, just as any seasoned huntsman would, I winkled out every last scrap of information from the only eyewitness available - my wife - as to the exact route the mouse had taken in his daring sortie across the flagstones.

Following this, I cunningly laid an old-fashioned, glass milk bottle on the route.

This was cleverly propped up on one side so that our mouse could get in at the peanuts provided but would then find it devilishly difficult to get out again owing to the slipperiness of the glass.

It's a well-known device used by we mouse hunters, you know.

Next day, no mouse. Some peanuts gone.

Ah, it was obviously the angle of the bottle that was wrong. It was insufficiently steep to imprison the mouse. I corrected this.

Next day, no mouse. More peanuts gone.

Feeling slightly miffed at being outwitted thus far by a mouse, I painstakingly propped up the bottle at a sheer 90 degree angle using a circle of bricks.

Next day, still no mouse. All peanuts gone.

What was this, a damn Houdini mouse ?

"Have you caught that mouse yet?," my wife asked. No!

What I needed was some professional kit so, on my way home from the office, I bought a top-of-the range, highly sophisticated, state-of-the-art mouse trap from a local hardware store. Cost: £2.50.

The beauty of this simple humane mouse trapper is that it's constructed of transparent plastic so you can look your mouse in its beady little eye after catching it.

Instructions to set the trap-door were duly read, fresh peanuts inserted, and the trap itself laid.

At about 11pm, a faint and unfamiliar scrabbling noise from the patio drew my attention away from Newsnight.

I grabbed a torch and shone it out of the patio window at the trap.

Ah-ha! There, struggling vainly against a device constructed by the finest minds of mouse trap science, was indeed a mouse. But what kind of mouse ?

Closer inspection revealed it to be a wood mouse, about the most common mouse there is in this country.

Because it had given me such a runaround, I thought about knocking it on the head and selling its pelt to one of those ladies who lunch in London.

However, since its pelt would barely cover a single, perfectly manicured finger, I let it go.

Naturally, I did give it a very stern talking to beforehand, just to let it know the type of guy it was messing with.

106

OUTRAGE HAS BEEN sparked among Britain's rural media as France and other European countries put the boot in over the foot-and-mouth crisis.

One rural website, Country Reflections, commented:"The hysterical reaction of Continental Europe to the crisis in the British countryside has only brought into sharper focus the grim fortitude of those UK farmers facing financial oblivion.

"As funeral pyres of burning carcasses are etched into the memory, the sight of British tourists being frisked abroad for hidden ham sandwiches would be darkly comic were it not so tragic.

"The fact that British farmers and rural communities are probably the victims of an imported disease appears to have been lost on some parts of Europe where anti-British sentiment has been reaching fever pitch.

"To hear Continental farmers baying for yet tougher EC sanctions against our own beleaguered farmers now facing the abyss is to realise that the notion of European brotherhood - certainly in the agricultural sector - is little more than a sad mirage.

"With the crisis virtually closing down the countryside and hitting everything from racing to rambling, we might have expected a smidgen of sympathy from our neighbours across the water.

"Not a bit of it. As usual, the disaster is seen as just another opportunity to vilify the British farmer who had almost sacrificed his business on the red-taped altar of EU bureaucracy even before this latest debacle.

"The French Farmers Union, that bastion of blockade diplomacy, issues a statement blaming Britain for threatening its stock with BSE and now foot-and-mouth.

"Shoppers are 'fast losing all confidence in British produce,' it crows. And would that not suit it very well if it were true.

"But why should the French not kick our farmers when they are down ? After all, some among New Labour appear to want to do just that with their fatuous eight-hour debate about banning foxhunting while the countryside goes up in flames.

"Tory Home Affairs spokesman David Lidington said the move showed 'a warped sense of priorities'. Indeed it did. But can anyone say they are truly surprised ?"

A NEW FORESTRY Commission booklet explains the complex regulations now governing the creation or removal of woodland following recent changes in the law.

JOGGERS ARE BEING warned to watch out for a slow moving hazard beneath their pounding feet - amorous toads.

Avon Wildlife Trust has put out an alert to runners, motorists, and cyclists to take extra care during the creatures' breeding season.

Scores of the amphibians are regularly crushed to death as they move across woodland tracks and roads on their journey to traditional mating ponds.

The Trust has been trying to recruit volunteers to scoop up toads into buckets so they can be safely transported to their destinations.

Local authorities in Bristol and Bath have also been encouraged to erect roadside warning signs in a bid to reduce the death toll this year.

THE SEARCH IS on again for the best bottle of vino produced from a vineyard in England or Wales.

Vineyard owners taking part in the Country Land and Business Association's Wine of the Year 2001 competition are being invited to dispatch samples of their best dry white or sparkling wines to the CLA's London office, arriving before March 9.

CLA president Anthony Bosanquet will join an experienced judging panel which aims to highlight the high standard of wine achieved on our own shores.

Winners from each category will see their produce selected as official CLA house wines to be served throughout the year at high-profile national and international functions.

"This year we hope to continue our successful wine offers to members and run tasting sessions for the winning wines during our Game Fair at Woburn Abbey," added a CLA spokesman.

RACING PIGEONS HAVE been donning shiny sequins to save them from the fatal attentions of sparrowhawks and peregrine falcons.

The move comes after boffins at Lancaster University won a contract from the Confederation of Long Distance Racing Pigeon Unions to look into the killing of their pets by birds of prey.

Before field trials commenced, Dr Ian Hartley, from the university, explained:"Pigeons will be fitted with small devices such as reflective discs or wing transfers which look like large eyes from the point of view of an attacking falcon.

"The idea is that the attacking bird of prey will be put off by the glinting of light on the discs or the appearance of large, frightening eyes on its prey.

"The same sort of defence systems have evolved naturally in many insects - for example peacock butterflies - so they may well work for pigeons, too."

Initial tests have shown that the idea does indeed work with some swooping predators either too alarmed or confused to make a kill.

SECTIONS OF THE North Sea are now off-limits to British cod fishermen until April 30.

This is due to 'emergency powers' unveiled by the European Commission in a bid to revive vanishing cod stocks.

GAMEKEEPERS MAY BE allowed to use their dogs for flushing out deer in a proposed amendment to the Government Hunting Bill - a move only scorned by pro-hunters as showing the muddled nature of the entire Bill.

A WATCHING BRIEF is being kept by officials of the Countryside Alliance following the axing of its high profile London demonstration this month because of the shattering effects of foot-and-mouth.

Postponed from March 18, plans for the event have been put in cold storage until fears about spreading the disease have abated.

Despite threats that hunt saboteurs would torch the farms of those taking part, nearly 200,000 marchers had already registered for the protest demo before the disease hit the headlines.

But following talks with with leaders of the farming community, the Alliance has decided to defer the march until May at the earliest.

The resulting dismay among rural communities looking forward to the event has only been matched by rising fears about the long-term consequences of foot-and-mouth.

Alliance chief executive Richard Burge said:"Our prime concern in taking this decision has been to act properly and responsibly, especially in the interests of Britain's farmers as well as our own members and supporters.

"Therefore, as a precautionary move and in solidarity with the farming community, we have with regret decided to postpone our march.

"This decision has been taken in direct consultation with and with the support of the leading farming bodies, including the NFU, FUW and the Ulster Farmers Association.

"A decision on a precise date will be made following a review of the outbreak and our assessment of the Government response to the wider crisis in the British countryside."

THE RARE stone-curlew has been given a boost by English Nature in a bid to pull it back from the brink of extinction in this country.

Cash payments are being made available to farmers who help to conserve the remaining birds - now down to just 250 pairs mainly in the Brecklands area of East Anglia.

Gareth Dalglish, a senior conservation officer for English Nature, said:"Our main aim is to build on the good work carried out so far.

"The Breckland Farmland Wildlife Enhancement Scheme will pay for management which is beneficial to the birds. They like areas of sparse and low vegetation so the scheme will encourage farmers to provide these amongst the growing crops and on areas of set-aside."

Breckland is characterised by the lowest rainfall in the British Isles with very light, free-draining, sandy and chalky soils. This makes it suitable for growing crops sown in the spring when so many fields are open and stony - perfect surroundings for any stone-curlews wanting to establish nests.

CANNIBALISM HAS BEEN uncovered in the depths of the British countryside - but it happened 2000 years ago.

Archaeologists have found the remains of six human victims thought to have been sacrificed for their meat in a pit at Alveston, Gloucestershire.

The macabre slaughter is believed to have occurred sometime between 30BC and 130AD and now puts a question mark over what was believed to have been a relatively civilised rural society.

Marks made on bones with axes and knives makes evidence of what was going on incontrovertible, according to researchers involved in the dig.

But whether the cannibalism was carried out in secret by a feared cult or was part of a wider, less palatable aspect of our forefathers' dining habits is less clear.

A SPILL OF farm slurry has been blamed for wiping out over 80,000 trout at a Devon fish farm.

The slurry escaped into a small river near Barnstaple and seeped into Plaistow Mills fish farm downstream.

A three-mile stretch of Bradiford Water was affected with another 1,000 fish thought to have been killed in the river itself.

Fish farm owner Jan Wirtz has been devastated by the spill which has ruined years of work at a stroke.

It is thought that the area, formerly a wildlife haven for rare species such as otters and kingfishers, will take years to recover from the incident.

The Environment Agency says the spill is extremely serious and investigating officers will be compiling a full report on the extent of the damage.

CLIMATE CHANGE SLEUTHS are being sought by The Woodland Trust this spring to help with a national survey.

The Trust has joined forces with the Centre for Ecology and Hydrology to assist its work in monitoring and evaluating changes to nature's calendar.

Between them, the pair have launched a new web site - phenology.org.uk - which lets the public examine local trends and make online recordings of key events in their area.

Richard Smithers, UK conservation advisor for the Woodland Trust, said:"We believe that climate change is the biggest single threat to what little remains of our ancient woodland heritage.

"Variations in nature's calendar are a useful way of monitoring how climate change is affecting woodland habitats.

"Where changes are synchronous, for example a caterpillar and its food plant, impacts may be negligible. However, if the animal appears before its food source, this could have significant and potentially disastrous implications for the survival of that species.

"The more we know, the more success we will have in finding long-term solutions, which is why we urgently need to enlist more recorders."

WEBSITE Deer UK has compiled what it says is a comprehensive guide for deer managers and landowners to help them spot foot-and-mouth disease in their animals.

CHANCELLOR GORDON BROWN has been accused of allowing rural businesses to burn while being hosed down with praise for his electioneering budget.

The Country Land and Business Association, which represents 50,000 rural businesses in England and Wales, has demanded to know "what use is his £23 billion surplus when rural businesses are going down the pan?"

The CLA says the foot-and-mouth crisis ravaging the countryside has caused devastation far beyond the farm gate.

"Those who serve the farming community have also seen their businesses devastated," said CLA president Anthony Bosanquet.

"Livestock markets and abattoirs have been closed, hauliers forced to a standstill, small food processors dependent on local produce have shut down production lines, and independent butchers have not been able to source the British meat on which their businesses depend.

"Farmers' markets have also been constrained from selling meat products while export contracts are cancelled.

"Further down the chain, bed-and-breakfast premises and holiday cottages have had bookings cancelled by holidaymakers who can no longer walk in the countryside, while country hotels, restaurants and pubs have also lost trade.

"Some of these businesses may well find their viability threatened by a prolonged interruption in trade. What is needed is a disaster relief programme to help those businesses hit directly by measures to control and eradicate foot-and-mouth.

"Without help, they may not recover. At a time when the rural economy must diversify to survive, the Government must not abandon businesses trying to do just that.

"We find it inconceivable that the 'Iron Chancellor' should have made a virtue out of his savings while letting these businesses, which are at the heart of the rural economy, go to the wall."

BIG CAT EXPERT Nigel Brierley, from Devon, aims to use state-of-the-art camera equipment to track down a big cat reportedly haunting the county.

Mr Brierley wants to lure the so-called Beast of Devon onto film by using a sophisticated automatic camera baited with meat.

Sightings of the mystery animal have apparently increased of late and Mr Brierley feels confident the predator - thought by some to be a panther or puma - will soon be identified.

A HUNGRY SPARROWHAWK left a pigeon racer shocked and angry when he went into his back garden to see a favourite bird being eaten alive.

Brian Smith, who lives near Stoke Canon, Devon, frightened the predator away but his champion bird was so badly injured he could only put it out of its misery.

Mr Smith, 52, an avid pigeon fan, had just allowed his birds out to exercise when the sparrowhawk swooped.

The drama left him so appalled that he is now calling for more controls on sparrowhawks which are currently protected under wildlife laws.

He claims that sparrowhawk numbers in Devon are on the rise and attacks on racing pigeons are increasing as a result.

This was the first time that he had ever seen a sparrowhawk attack a pigeon in his garden and he had been keeping pigeons since he was a teenager.

SALMON FISHERMEN IN the North East have been helping to preserve the River Tyne as one of the best salmon rivers in the country.

A conservation scheme launched last year by the Environment Agency involves anglers fastening numbered tags to any spring salmon they catch for identification purposes.

Almost 70 spring salmon were tagged and released in 2000 with a further 250 tags issued to local salmon anglers this year and the scheme extended to include another river.

Jon Shelley, fisheries science officer for the Agency, said:"Since the 1980s the Tyne has grown to become one of the best salmon rivers for anglers in England and Wales.

"However those fish returning to the river during the early part of the year, known as spring salmon, require special protection. Nationally their numbers appear to be in decline and in the North East we are eager to do something to counter this and conserve their stocks.

"Last year this scheme received a very positive response from anglers on the Tyne. Now we are hoping to take it a step further by making more tags available and extending it to the River Coquet."

THE RISE IN popularity of organic produce continues with more people than ever before snapping it up, according to The Soil Association.

In a new report, the Association says that in 1999 the average weekly expenditure on organic food among regular buyers was just £12 compared to £20 last year.

In addition, the percentage of households choosing some form of organic produce leapt from 43 per cent to 57 per cent.

The Association says that five years ago in the UK just 50,000 hectares of land were given over to producing organic food.

That figure is expected to rocket to 500,000 by the end of this year.

An independent survey by MORI found that a third of the public now regularly buys organic food.

Some 53 per cent consider it to be healthier than traditionally grown food, 43 per cent say it tastes better, 30 per cent believe it to be GM-free, and 25 per cent consider it more animal welfare friendly.

COUNTRY SPORTS ENTHUSIASTS face fines of £5,000 if they contravene emergency guidelines issued by the Government to combat the spread of foot-and-mouth disease.

But with no-one in any doubt about the seriousness of the crisis facing the countryside, the fine threat seems largely irrelevant.

Self-regulation is believed to have been practised by the vast majority of shooters and hunters since the disease took hold.

However, following an appeal by the Countryside Alliance for clear guidelines, MAFF issued notes under the 'Foot-and-Mouth Disease Declaratory (Controlled Area) Order 2001 England and Wales'.

A MAFF spokesman said that "the voluntary suspension of all forms of hunting (including pest control) by the Hunting Associations on February 22, 2001, is now a statutory requirement in place until March 16, 2001 at the earliest.

"The definition under this order is the 'use of hounds, beagles or other dogs for the purpose of hunting or coursing any deer, fox, hare, mink or rabbit, or for hunting any drag trail'.

"This also includes all 'unregulated' hunting, not under the jurisdiction of the Hunting Associations.

"The order extends to stalking, which is not defined, and shooting. The ban does not extend to fishing although anglers are expected to observe all the usual movement restrictions.

"It is understood that even people who are walking their dog in a private capacity, which then hunts an animal, may be caught by this order.

"Where shooting, trapping and snaring are carried out for the purpose of pest/disease control or welfare only, then they are permitted. Contravention of this order could lead to a £5,000 fine."

SURVEYS ABOUT SWANS, peregrine falcons, and waders have all been abandoned - probably until next year - as part of the fight against foot-and-mouth.

A joint statement from the British Trust for Ornithology, Joint Nature Conservation Committee, RSPB and the Wildfowl and Wetlands Trust revealed virtually all field work regarding birds had stopped.

A mute swan census, meant to take place this spring, has now been axed and will probably only go ahead in spring next year.

The same goes for surveys into breeding waders on wet meadows and peregrine falcon numbers.

The RSPB, which closed all its nature reserves and visitor centres, will review the situation later.

HOUSING SPRAWL IS continuing to blight the countryside despite assurances from the Government that it would put a stop to it, says the Council for the Protection of Rural England in a damning new report.

CPRE assistant director Tony Burton revealed:"Government flagship planning policies are being thwarted by a combination of inertia and weak delivery by local authorities and its own Regional Offices."

Among report findings is the news that greenfield land has been earmarked to take another 658,000 houses - enough to accommodate the demands of the top 80 housebuilders for six years.

Government Regional Offices have also "waved through" the development of over 15,000 houses on 671 hectares of rural land while the fate of a further 4,750 houses hangs in the balance.

"The conflict over new housing in the countryside cannot be allowed to continue when the Government has already put the planning policies in place which will prevent it," added Mr Burton.

"After one year of operating the radical new planning policies, it is clear that we are only at the end of the beginning of the changes that are needed."

TAKING AN ISOLATED short cut to the pub almost cost a Shropshire man an eye when he was mugged by a tawny owl.

The owl struck Kirk Hall so hard on the head that he fell over and it was only when he glimpsed the bird flying off that he realised what had hit him.

The full extent of his injuries was revealed when he finally made it to the pub in Oswestry where staff helped to clean up blood pouring from wounds.

The owl's needle-sharp talons had slashed him across the face with one deep puncture mark barely an inch from an eye.

Mr Hall, 45, has since called on other local people to be wary of taking the same short cut through trees at night.

Wildlife experts say the tawny owl probably made the attack because its territorial instincts are at their height just now and it saw Mr Hall as an invader.

FARMERS' LEADERS HAVE blasted German meat exporters for sending potentially hazardous beef cuts into Britain during the foot-and-mouth crisis.

So angry is the NFU that it has even demanded that the European Commission "stops ALL German beef exports in light of a catalogue of incidents involving meat containing banned material."

Spine and brain material are now routinely removed in Britain as part of the ongoing fight against BSE - but the same stringent measures are apparently not being applied in some parts of the Continent.

NFU president Ben Gill said:"It is only thanks to the vigilance of the British Food Standards Agency that these problems have even been uncovered.We cannot continue accepting beef simply on trust when the track record of certain countries has proved so appalling.

"It is unfair on this country's beef farmers who have met every requirement to ensure the safety of British beef and it is unfair to expose the British consumer to risk."

THE RSPCA HAS been blasted by the Countryside Alliance for "betraying real animal interests" by taking out a raft of expensive full-page newspaper adverts against foxhunting.

The adverts, this time urging the House of Lords to ban hunting, were the latest in a series employed by the staunchly anti-hunt charity.

Nigel Henson, Alliance director of communications, said:"The RSPCA has tried to mislead peers by citing majority support for a ban which it knows full well no longer exists.

"But for it even to try to argue for a ban on this basis is a spectacular own goal. It highlights the very issue many peers are so concerned about - that fundamental matters of civil liberty and minority rights should not be decided on the results of superficial opinion polls.

"Our laws have never been made on this basis in the past and it would drag our parliamentary democracy into disrepute if this were to start now.

"The RSPCA has roped in out-of-date, one-sided figures for its advert and then pretended that these are still valid. This will not wash.

"Peers know full well that there has been a profound swing away from support for a ban in the last few years and that the most recent major independent polls suggest that such 'support' is now in the minority."

The Alliance also accused the RSPCA of acting more out of 'thought police' motives rather than from a real interest in animal welfare.

"The money wasted on this - probably as much as £250,000 - could have been put to proper animal welfare use, such as kennelling thousands of homeless animals or financing a national neutering campaign for all domestic animals," added Mr Henson.

"This would prevent the proliferation of unwanted animals and better tackle the stray cat crisis which, the RSPCA admits, is rife across the country."

A £500 CASH prize awarded to Forest Enterprise for its national butterfly conservation work has been earmarked to help one of our most endangered butterflies - the high brown fritillary.

"We will be spending the money with the conservation charity Butterfly Conservation in the Lake District," said environment manager Rod Leslie."It will be used for surveys to see how high brown fritillary are responding to a huge EU funded project that is restoring over 80 hectares of their habitat at Whitbarrow."

VILLAGE BAKERY WORKERS thought a woman was taking the rise when she told them a "panther" was patrolling countryside nearby in broad daylight.

But they soon realised she was not joking when they spotted the huge black cat themselves close to the Forest of Dean in Gloucestershire.

Baker Andrew Barnett and a colleague were alerted to the predator after the shocked woman rushed into their premises near Newnham-on-Severn and told them what she had seen.

When they peered from a window the muscular animal was still prowling along until it stopped and effortlessly leapt a hedge before disappearing back into the forest.

The drama was just the latest in a series recently involving sightings of a panther-like creature in and around the forest.

Mr Barnett says he was in no doubt about what he saw and now keeps a video camera handy to capture the big cat on film should it reappear.

WILDLIFE EXPERTS ARE celebrating the return of salmon to a North Yorkshire waterway for the first time in living memory.

Cod Beck, near Thirsk, had been presumed unfit for salmon due to the acidic nature of the water in the River Swale, into which the beck flows.

Then a salmon was spotted in the beck by anglers taking part in a fishing match. The fish, which had recently died, was retrieved and sent to York for examination by the Environment Agency.

Scientists discovered that the salmon - a female weighing over four pounds - had originally lived in freshwater for two years before entering the sea, spending the winter there before returning to freshwater to spawn.

Unfortunately it had been unable to find a mate and had perished before laying its eggs.

Environment Agency scientist Paul Frear said:"This is a clear indication that the river water quality in the area is reaching levels not experienced for many years. It is a shame that the fish was unable to spawn but at least we have been able to gather plenty of information from it.

"Last summer we also found a couple of young salmon while carrying out surveys on the Swale. This shows that at least some salmon are finding their way up river and successfully spawning."

THE SOIL ASSOCIATION has revealed that five organic farms lie within a six kilometre radius of the Government's spring GM trial sites.

The farms therefore run the risk of having their organic status for crops and land removed if GM contamination occurs.

"A risk assessment will be undertaken based on exact distances, the type of crops grown both on the organic farm and at the trial site, predominant wind direction and topography," said a spokesman.

"Baroness Hayman stated that the recommended Government separation distances of 80-100 metres should ensure that any contamination should not exceed one per cent and would generally be well below this level.

"However, the Soil Association says that separation distances of three to six kilometres are required, depending on the crop. We believe that the trial sites could lead to widespread GM contamination of the countryside which will be impossible to recall."

LABOUR MPs HAVE begun pressuring their own Government to abandon plans for a May General Election as the foot-and-mouth crisis moves closer to catastrophe.

With rural communities under the cosh and farmers isolated by emergency regulations, Labour MPs such as Tam Dalyell have joined the growing chorus of protests about continuing with election preparations.

Premier Tony Blair is expected to cave in and cancel the May 3 vote - or face a cross-party backlash which will only strengthen accusations of New Labour cynicism towards the countryside.

The Government is still planning to go ahead with local elections all over the country despite a barrage of criticism over that.

Cornwall County Council leader Pippa Englefield summed up the mounting anger as she commented:"An election in these conditions will cause huge offence."

At least 10 of 25 county councils worst hit by the crisis say there should be no election until June at the earliest.

Meanwhile, despite constant claims from Agriculture Minister Nick Brown that the disease is under control, the mounting number of cases - especially here but also in Europe - has led to a growing international ban on EU meat products and livestock.

During a debate in the Commons, Tory leader William Hague said the country remained in the grip of a national crisis.

Anyone in any doubt about that need look no further than Bryn Coch Farm, in Llanfechain, North Wales, close to the border with Shropshire.

There, sheep farmer Brian Oakley, 54, became the first human casualty of foot-and-mouth after hanging himself in despair in a barn.

Other farmers in badly affected areas are now being relieved of their shotguns by police to prevent further tragedies as hopes for the future of British farming evaporate.

A WISE OLD owl may need to go back to school after ending up trapped for two days in a chimney.

The bird, thought to be a tawny owl, was finally rescued by firefighters called to the scene at Burnham Market, Norfolk.

After the crew freed the bird, it was taken for a check-up at a local animal sanctuary.

CAPTIVE OWLS have been boosted by two unexpected bequests left to their cash-strapped Cotswold Owl Rescue Trust.

The Trust's barn and tawny owls can continue educational visits to schools after money was handed to sisters Bryony and Erin Holden who run it.

THE ELUSIVE CAPERCAILLIE is the subject of a dispute between the Government and a panel set up by Parliament to advise on the Scottish bird's future.

Environment Minister Sam Galbraith has announced his intention to offer fuller protection to the turkey-sized capercaillie under Schedule 1 Part 1 of the Wildlife and Countryside Act 1981.

However, this runs contrary to the recommendations of the Capercaillie Biodiversity Action Plan Working Group.

The group says a voluntary ban on shooting the grouse-like capercaillie remains in place and is the best option for its long-term protection.

"We think it would be inappropriate at present to move capercaillie to Schedule 1 Part 1 on the grounds that it would be a disincentive for landowners who want to be able to shoot capercaillie in the future when the population has recovered," said a spokesman.

"We propose therefore that Schedule 1 Part II is most appropriate because it retains an incentive for landowners to manage their forests on behalf of the capercaillie."

A Game Conservancy Trust submission to Sam Galbraith has also pointed out that most core capercaillie woods are in private hands with landowners encouraged through BAP workshops to manage woodland for the benefit of the birds.

THE DEATHS OF five people from the human form of mad cow disease have been put down to old-fashioned butchery techniques with the same knives used on cattle brain as other cuts.

All five CJD 'cluster' victims connected to the village of Queniborough in Leicestershire had eaten contaminated meat, according to a report by public health experts.

THE RSPB HAS welcomed a raft of new proposals from the Scottish Parliament aimed at safeguarding the country's wildlife.

Stuart Housden, director of RSPB Scotland, said:"This is a good day for Scottish wildlife. These proposals, if enacted, will ensure the proper protection of our wildlife for future generations and help make natural heritage an invaluable part of our economy.

"In particular, we are very supportive of the tough approach to wildlife crime. For too long, levels of wildlife crime have been unacceptably high.

"These proposals will empower the police and courts to better enforce and deter such criminal acts as poisoning birds of prey and egg collecting. I call on all MSPs to support this proposed legislation.

"However, our most special wildlife sites must also be properly protected. Rare plants, birds and animals must have the right habitats in which to live and thrive.

"At present, many of our most precious sites are deteriorating from neglect."

A NEW THREAT to British trees has been revealed with the arrival of a voracious Chinese immigrant - the Asian longhorn beetle.

The beetle, thought to have arrived in goods imported from China, is now established at 50 different locations across England and Wales.

The insect, almost three inches long, eats trees from the inside and is capable of decimating hardwood forests when numbers rise.

A CATALOGUE OF Government failure over the foot-and-mouth crisis has been attacked in a protest letter from the Country Land and Business Association.

Anger and frustration at MAFF's handling of the situation is underlined in CLA president Anthony Bosanquet's missive to Baroness Hayman, Junior Agriculture Minister, on behalf of the association's 50,000 members.

Key complaints include delays in diagnosis, slaughter and removal of infected stock; penny-pinching attitudes slowing down the process; lack of information from MAFF; permanently engaged MAFF helpline numbers; and confusion over whether and where people can go in the countryside.

"The issue that is being raised most is that of delays. In particular, it is the delays between diagnosis and cull, and cull and disposal, which cause most distress," said Mr Bosanquet.

"Farmers do not want to be in the position of watching their stock get ill, or knowing that they pose a risk to their neighbours. One of our members has been told that it will be five to seven days after confirmation before the slaughter team arrive.

"Another had the disease diagnosed on March 8 but the sheep concerned were not slaughtered until March 17, during which time they were kept beside a main road breathing the virus on to all who passed.

"Allied to this is the lack of slaughtermen. Although the CLA welcome the introduction of the army in some areas, it appears to be in a supervisory role only. Why is the army not being used to help with slaughtering, as well as assisting with the disposal of carcasses?

"Members have also raised concerns about logistical failure, notably in disposing of culled livestock. It has been rumoured that materials and local contractors are purchased and hired subject to tender. Surely if the Government is serious about stamping out this disease, haggling or offering desultory sums to contractors is not the way to do it.

"In one case it appears a contractor was offered £6.50 per hour to provide a JCB and man to help dispose of stock. Foot-and-mouth disease requires instant action. Penny-pinching is slowing the whole process down."

THE WILLOW WARBLER is the latest bird to show a worrying slump in numbers, according to researchers for the British Trust for Ornithology.

The shy summer migrant now shows a long-term decline of 32 per cent over the last 20 years.

ATTEMPTS TO TRAIN two dogs for hare coursing caused outrage when two men used a local common in Cambridge and left a rabbit dead at the feet of a passer-by.

The shocked woman complained to police who are now investigating the incident which apparently left the luckless rabbit in pieces.

In a statement to police the woman claimed the men had kept the rabbit in a sack and only released it when their dogs were ready to pounce on Stourbridge Common.

She revealed her disgust to the two coursers but they replied that what they were doing was legal - a claim disputed by police who say such activity is illegal on a local common.

In genuine coursing, the much faster hare is chased by pairs of dogs which are marked for their speed and agility in pursuit.

Most hares escape but some are killed, a fact which angers anti-hunt groups such as the League Against Cruel Sports.

ONE OF THE most spectacularly scenic walks ever devised in the Welsh countryside is to be reconstructed.

The route through the historic Hafod Estate near Aberystwyth will be reproduced in its former glory by Forest Enterprise Wales and its partner the Hafod Trust.

The 200-year-old 'Gentleman's Walk' was originally built into the picturesque hills of Plynlimmon by Thomas Johnes in the 18th Century.

But 100 years of neglect has made the six kilometre pathway - which passes some of the most dramatic scenery and spectacular waterfalls in Wales - virtually impassable.

Now the team managing the estate is taking on two full-time forestry workers whose first task will be to rebuild the walk as part of a £330,000 project.

"Hafod was created by Thomas Johnes between 1783 and 1815," said a Forestry Commission spokesman."He planted a romantic paradise using five to six million trees, creating walks and altering the landscape to enhance the natural beauty of the woodland."

LONG-TAILED TITS are continuing to do well despite tough conditions, according to new research, with numbers up 23 per cent on previous years, followed by whitethroats, up 21 per cent.

THE BATTLE OF Hastings is being fought afresh but this time the enemy are developers who want to build two bypasses around the Sussex coastal town at the expense of wildlife.

Opposing the plans is the Hastings Alliance - an army of allies including Friends of the Earth, the Council for the Protection of Rural England, the RSPB, and The Wildlife Trusts.

Tony Bosworth, transport campaigner for Friends of the Earth, said:"Labour promised it would be the greenest Government ever. So far it has failed to live up to this pledge.The Hastings bypasses are another test of this commitment.

"Will Mr Prescott protect our best landscapes and wildlife sites from road building, as he promised, or cave in to the road builders?"

Steve Gilbert, the RSPB senior conservation officer for south east England, said:"The bypasses will cause damage and disturbance to nationally important wildlife sites."

ANIMAL RIGHTS ACTIVISTS are using the foot-and-mouth crisis to launch an attack on dairy farmers - with Mothering Sunday as its launch pad.

Animal Aid, the UK's largest animal rights group, aims to "dish the dirt on dairy" and hopes the campaign will help turn more people into vegetarians.

Whether it will succeed is debatable but the move is certain to outrage farmers currently at their wits' end as they see their businesses going to the wall.

"With the country reeling under the foot-and-mouth crisis, Animal Aid is launching a campaign to expose the suffering inflicted on cows and calves by the dairy industry - the farming sector that is probably least understood by the general public," said an Animal Aid spokesman.

"The industry itself has admitted to being reliant on a consumer image of cows grazing in green pastures, freely offering a healthy product for human consumption.

"Industry spokespeople, furthermore, have acknowledged their need to maintain this consumer trust and ignorance.

"Our hard-hitting new leaflet, 'The Milk of Human Kindness?' reveals the truth behind that peaceful image. Campaigners throughout the UK will be distributing the leaflet outside churches and supermarkets.

"In order to produce commercial quantities of milk, dairy cows are forced to endure a constant cycle of pregnancies. Calves are usually removed from their mothers within 24 hours of birth.

"Separation of mother and infant causes acute anxiety and suffering for both animals. Most dairy calves are considered a waste by-product and are killed within a week or two for baby food or pie ingredients.

"In modern dairy farming, cows can be expected to produce between 6,000 and 12,000 litres of milk during their 10 month lactation. This means she may be carrying in excess of 20 litres at any one time - 10 times as much as would be required for her calf."

THE WILDLIFE TRUSTS are putting their trust in the foot-and-mouth crisis being under control by June after revealing plans for their Wildlife Week.

"Choose from venturing down a wilderness trail, joining a mini-beast safari or rambling round rock pools," said a spokesman.

"Or if you are seeking something more relaxing, get creative in a marine mosaic workshop, listen to a tale from the riverbank, or wander through a wild-flower meadow."

This year's Wildlife Week (June 2-10) is being dedicated to 'Children and Wildlife'.

A SCOTTISH FARMER who corralled 200 pigs into mobile pens to beat foot-and-mouth disease was devastated when fire broke out and killed them all.

It was a cruel irony that farmer Sandy Howie had been trying to protect his pigs from the same fate that has left thousands of farm animals dumped on blazing funeral pyres.

Mr Howie, who farms land near Mintlaw in north east Scotland, had put his pigs into temporary accommodation before a planned move to another farm five miles away.

Foot-and-mouth movement restrictions stopped the transportation going ahead and the pigs had only been kept in the units for two days when fire broke out.

Mr Howie said the disaster would never have happened if foot-and-mouth had not led to the pigs being put in the mobile pens in the first place.

An initial investigation has shown that the pigs probably died of smoke inhalation before the flames took hold.

Firemen spent more than two hours at the scene tackling the blaze.

A RABBIT HOLE was the unlikely starting point for a tale of danger and devotion involving two spaniels.

The drama began when the black and white bitch became wedged in the hole after pursuing a rabbit underground.

Instead of drifting off, her male partner loyally stood guard at the entrance to the burrow for two whole days.

Luckily, passing bus driver Alec Woodmass realised something was wrong and alerted police at Chester-le-Street, Tyne and Wear.

With the trapped dog facing certain death, officers called in the RSPCA but the two groups were still unable to reach the frightened animal.

Only when the fire brigade arrived to help was the exhausted spaniel bitch finally released then both dogs were checked for injuries and treated to a slap-up meal.

Later, efforts were made to trace the owner of the spaniels which were not thought to be strays.

A PLAN TO save the natural assets and rural character of the South West has been dubbed "visionary" by the Environment Agency.

Launched by the Regional Assembly and Sustainability South West, the proposals aim to secure the region's economic, social and environmental future.

An accompanying report 'A Sustainable Future for the South West' sets out how the region can develop in a way that brings a better quality of life for everyone.

Richard Cresswell, regional director for the Environment Agency, said:"The environment is one of the South West's best assets and is a foundation for social and economic progress in the region. This framework will help keep that progress on track.

"As the most rural region of England, farmers have helped shaped South West landscapes and habitats. The coastline is a valued natural, cultural and economic asset. This brings with it many challenges, particularly maintaining high quality bathing water and estuaries so important for our tourism industry and quality of life."

OFFICIALS WITHIN THE Ministry of Agriculture could be the next to be culled following widespread complaints of the department's poor performance during the foot-and-mouth crisis.

Prime Minister Tony Blair is said to be secretly furious at MAFF's slow reaction to a disaster which now appears firmly on the road to being a catastrophe.

MAFF officials have even been supplying Downing Street with incorrect figures for the spread of the disease, according to some reports.

Meanwhile, widespread confusion still reigns regarding the Government's advice to tourists to head for the countryside - but stay away from farms and farmland.

Anthony Bosanquet, president of the Country Land and Business Association which represents 50,000 landowners, said:"Advice must be crystal clear. People need to be told they must observe no-entry signs."

Hopes of bringing the disease under control quickly have now faded and researchers at Edinburgh University and the Veterinary Laboratories Agency are predicting the toll of outbreaks will have increased significantly by July.

Farmers leaders' are now holding detailed talks with the Government looking at how vaccination could help to stem the tide of the disease.

NFU president Ben Gill said:"I have continued to stress that the views and feelings of local farmers are absolutely critical in this. It is they who will have to live with the results of any further action, including any limited use of vaccination."

He said it was absolutely crucial everyone remained focused on the twin objectives of reducing identification-to-slaughter time to 24 hours, and culling all animals in neighbouring farms within a further 24 hours.

FIVE POT-BELLIED pigs went on the rampage at a Sussex animal sanctuary and reduced the cash-strapped manager to tears.

The errant pigs - quaintly named Rasher, Snuffles, Crackling, Porkchop and Porkpie - made a real pig's ear of the place, landing devastated manager Sue Algar with a £10,000 damage bill.

During their wrecking spree, the pigs ripped apart a wooden duck house, gobbled the lining to the duck pond leaving ducks stranded without water, and dug up the donkey enclosure.

But though Ms Algar has admitted breaking down in tears when she saw the destruction, she is still reluctant to let the pigs go.

However, as a result of the mayhem, the entire sanctuary at Warnham now faces closure.

WILD BIRDS DO not spread foot-and-mouth disease despite widespread fears to the contrary, claims the RSPB.

Research has revealed no foundation for concerns that birds may be responsible for spreading the devastating disease ever further.

"We understand the fears of some farmers and crofters that wild birds might spread foot-and-mouth disease," said a spokesman for the RSPB.

"In order to assist farmers and crofters to combat such worries the RSPB commissioned a survey of all the available scientific data from Professor Chris Feare, an eminent independent agricultural scientist.

"This survey confirms that there is no scientific evidence linking wild birds to the spread of foot-and-mouth. While there remains a minimal and theoretical risk of birds spreading the virus, close analysis of earlier outbreaks suggests that wild birds are not a vector in its transmission.

"Professor Feare's report has now been circulated to farmer's unions and government environment departments and agencies."

FOXES PREYING ON rare capercaillie have sparked biting criticism between the two groups managing a Scottish nature reserve.

The Scottish Gamekeepers Association has accused the RSPB of a softly-softly approach to controlling scores of marauding foxes on the Abernethy Reserve Estate in Speyside.

With numbers of the turkey-size, grouse-like capercaille down to about 100 on the estate, the SGA wants to see an all-year cull on foxes with terriers used to flush out and kill them.

But RSPB officers refuse to employ dogs as they humanely net fox cubs over five weeks each year.

The Society also claims that the reserve's caper-caille population has risen in recent years, compared to dramatic declines on other estates where more aggressive predator control methods are still used

It blames habitat destruction and poor weather at breeding times as two main causes of a slump in overall Scottish capercaille numbers from 20,000 birds in the 1960s to less than 1,000 today.

PREMIER TONY BLAIR is under growing pressure from anti-hunt groups to force the defeated Bill to ban hunting onto the statute book using the Parliament Act.

Opponents of foxhunting were infuriated by peers in the House of Lords who roundly rejected the Bill which had passed through the Commons with overwhelming support.

The peers' rejection of the Bill was equally emphatic with lords not even choosing the expected middle-way option of allowing hunting to continue under Government regulation.

Better self-regulation was the way ahead, they decided, and in doing so put the ball firmly back in the Government's court while heaping more pressure on the embattled Prime Minister.

Mr Blair, who let it be known he thought fox-hunting cruel but dodged the crucial Commons vote itself, is now in the difficult position of wanting to spare the lives of a few thousand foxes while presiding over the slaughter of hundreds of thousands of farm animals in the foot-and-mouth crisis.

The Countryside Alliance has welcomed the House of Lords' rejection of a ban.

SHEEP: golden labrador loses his lustre off the leash

SHEEP worrying by dogs has been a problem in this country for decades but it came as a shock to me recently to learn that 22,000 sheep died one year as a result of such attacks in the UK.

The figures, for 1998, were the worst ever recorded at the time and marked a startling 20 per cent increase on the previous year's bloody tally.

The death of so many sheep must be a stark warning to those who feel it's fine to let dogs off leads in fields full of vulnerable, unprotected livestock, especially as new 'right to roam' laws open up yet more of the countryside to visitors.

From my own experience, I know that sheep worrying dogs come in many guises and even the most placid animals can turn into rabid beasts at the sight of a helpless flock, usually without a ram to protect it.

My golden labrador Duke, now long dead, was a devil for chasing sheep and his weakness in that direction ruined many days out - not to mention the peace of mind of some happily grazing sheep.

Not matter how much I yelled and threatened him, no matter how tightly I kept him on his lead near sheep, he would still be up and at 'em if he got a glimmer of a chance.

He was lucky not to be shot, especially as the farmer who owned some of the fields where he ran amok was known to have blasted quite a few dogs with his shotgun. And who could blame him ?

Sheep worrying costs the industry millions each year, besides the waste of so much effort needed to raise good stock.

Only someone else whose pet has also disgraced itself will appreciate the anger and panic I felt as I tried to catch Duke whenever he slipped his lead.

Scattering sheep to all corners of the field, he would tear after them barking furiously.

It happened on too many occasions and, each time, I'd half-expect a shotgun blast to ring out, leaving my errant dog a twitching heap in the grass.

It never occurred but the very real possibility was enough to concentrate the mind.

To be fair to Duke, he was never a biter of sheep. In fact, as soon as he managed to corner an individual animal, he would become instantly bewildered and back off. Other dogs in the same situation would go for the throat.

As a journalist, I've covered enough sheep worrying stories over the years to see first hand the terrible carnage a really vicious dog can leave behind.

Even dogs like Duke cause damage as pregnant ewes are delicate creatures and can easily abort foetuses through shock.

Fortunately, not all farmers have horror stories to tell.

One, who keeps between 1,000-1,500 sheep in open fields, told me:*"I can honestly say it's only happened once to my sheep and that was about 20 years ago. I think I lost three ewes and nine lambs and we never found the dog that did it.*

"It seems to me that people with dogs are generally quite responsible. I have public footpaths going through my fields and when ewes are out with lambs I do find people take proper care of their dogs, which is good."

Elsewhere, however, the picture is not so rosy.

A spokesman for NFU Mutual, which insures the vast majority of UK sheep farmers, revealed:*"We have identified particular problems on the urban fringe where dogs are let out all day and form packs which roam the countryside terrorising sheep.*

"Most attacks result in the death or injury of one or two sheep but there have been large losses. In one of the worst cases, 41 out of a flock of 45 in-lamb pedigree Texel ewes were killed by a bull mastiff and its puppy."

Sounds appalling and few can complain if such dogs are put down.

But I wonder if a sheep aversion training scheme might be the answer for lesser villains, something I could have enrolled Duke on if it had been available.

I'm no expert but introducing dogs to sheep in a controlled environment might help - even if a bullying ram has to drive home the message.

What's the alternative ? More carnage in the countryside, I fear.

ANTI-HUNT LABOUR MPs are pledging to highlight their hatred of foxhunting in their General Election manifestos, it has been revealed.

Almost 170 have indicated that fighting foxhunting may be among promises to the electorate as they bid to regain their seats in the Commons on June 7.

Among the group is vociferous Labour MP Tony Banks who is determined that the Bill to ban hunting with dogs will not be swept under the carpet despite its rebuttal in the House of Lords.

Mr Banks, who represents an East London ward where he was recently mugged, has underlined the strength of feeling which remains in support of a ban among fellow MPs.

He said:"This issue will not just go away. No-one in the Labour leadership should deceive themselves."

The former minister, now a high-profile backbench MP, is a fierce opponent of the Countryside Alliance and recently attacked its criticism that New Labour was out of touch with rural concerns.

"The fact is that we have more Labour MPs representing rural constituencies than the Conservatives have got MPs," he said.

"So the idea that the people who got elected have no idea what is going on in their constituencies is an insult to all those MPs. It is about time the Countryside Alliance came up with a few better and different arguments than that particular one. It is inaccurate, totally insulting, but very typical."

During the Lords debate on the Bill, Labour peer Lord Stoddart of Swindon said he was once an opponent of foxhunting - but no longer.

He said:"Many years ago, I was in favour of a ban. I have now become a 'non-banner'. The reason for that change is because, if we are not careful, no-one will be able to do anything because one person's pleasure will become another person's ban.

"Next on the list will be shooting and, after that, will be fishing. In terms of cruelty, they are all cruel in one way or another. So we have to be careful about what we are doing."

MORE THAN 500 acres of new native woodland will be created in England's national parks, thanks to nearly £410,000 of special Government grants.

Forestry Minister Elliot Morley said the Forestry Commission had earmarked the cash to help fund the creation of new woods in some of the most beautiful parts of the country.

A RARE BREED of British heavy horse has won the backing of a famous rock star in its battle to beat extinction.

Strummer Chris Rea has joined more than 10,000 people aiming to haul the Suffolk Punch back from the abyss after a campaign to save it was launched by a local newspaper.

The Suffolk Punch is slightly shorter than the Shire at 16 hands high but is equally powerful and noted for its bright chestnut colouring and smooth, 'featherless' fetlocks.

Despite once being a common sight in the countryside, numbers have crashed and there are believed to be only about 200 left - making them rarer than the giant panda, say campaigners.

A prison-based stud farm in East Anglia could be the breed's last hope of survival but this is currently threatened with closure by the Home Office.

OSPREYS, BITTERNS AND marsh harriers are just three rare bird species the public will be able to spot again after the RSPB decided to re-open some of its most popular reserves.

All 160 reserves were initially closed to help in the fight against foot-and-mouth by minimising the risk of accidentally spreading the disease.

RSPB director of operations, Mike Clarke said:"We plan to offer at least limited access to sites where there is no practical risk of spreading the disease and have taken this decision following careful consideration of local circumstances.

"The RSPB has an important role in the rural economy as our reserves attract more than a million visitors a year, and the relatively small number of sites we plan to open are among our most popular.

"Nonetheless, the majority of sites will remain closed for the foreseeable future to help the farmers during this crisis. We will continue to keep all our sites under active review."

The decision means that visitors can once again enjoy spotting ospreys at Loch Garten, bitterns at Leighton Moss and marsh harriers at Minsmere.

BADGER FANS HAVE welcomed the prosecution of two Birmingham men who allowed their dog to plunge into a badger sett in Warwickshire.

At Nuneaton Magistrates Court, the pair were found guilty of interfering with a badger sett by entering a dog into it.

Both were ordered to pay a fine of £150 each plus £50 costs.

Dr Elaine King, conservation officer for the National Federation of Badger Groups, said:"This is a good result and sends out the clear message that the persecution of badgers is illegal and unacceptable."

She praised the people who made the case possible and said it showed what could be achieved when different groups worked together for the sake of badgers.

"The success of this case demonstrates the importance of teamwork and is a real tribute to the dedication and expertise shown by both police wildlife officers and the local badger group," she said.

"Entering dogs into badger setts is extremely cruel because both badgers and dogs can be seriously injured.

"Badger persecution is widespread in Britain and this incident is likely to be just the tip of the iceberg."

FOREIGN MEAT IMPORTS are continuing to deepen Britain's livestock crisis as the fight against foot-and-mouth scales new heights.

Farmers' leaders say patience with Germany in particular has run out after the seventh consignment of German beef containing banned spinal cord entered the UK.

NFU president Ben Gill blasted:"We have well and truly reached the end of our tether. The European Commission must ban exports of German beef now. The time for words has gone - we need action."

The spinal column - classified as Specified Risk Material under BSE regulations - was detected in a load of beef in Sussex.

With foot-and-mouth itself believed to have come from infected foreign meat illegally brought into the country, the idea of foreign BSE-risk beef replacing healthier British cuts is more than most farmers can stomach.

"The European Commission had no compunction in placing a ban on British beef all those years ago - it should show the same vigour now," added Mr Gill.

Meanwhile, the Country Land and Business Association has urged Government veterinary advisers to speed up gene pool plans to protect bloodlines of rare livestock from being wiped out by foot-and-mouth.

"We have already lost Welsh Black cattle herds with bloodlines recorded for 400 years as part of the policy to cull livestock contiguous to the infection," revealed CLA president Anthony Bosanquet.

"The risk to traditional Herdwick sheep which graze the Lake District uplands and the Dartmoor Grey-face - now reduced to 1,500 animals in just 120 flocks - is very great.

"Britain's native sheep and cattle breeds are a very precious part of the farming and rural tourism industries. Ways must be found to ensure that they do not disappear for ever."

A TOAD HATING thief is being blamed for the loss of roadside warning signs meant to protect the creatures from traffic as they hop to a mating pond.

Five of the triangular red signs were erected by Potten End parish council near Hemel Hempstead, Herts, but three have now been stolen.

The signs warn motorists to slow down as they approach the pond area, giving hundreds of toads more chance of surviving. In past years, many were killed outright.

A man was seen by an eyewitness ripping up one of the signs before throwing it into the back of a blue Ford Sierra and driving off at speed.

Similar toad warning signs have also vanished from the east of the county.

DESPERATE DAIRY FARMERS have been boosted by widespread public backing of milk price hikes to help them stave off bankrupcy during the foot-and-mouth crisis.

Farmers' leaders have been besieged by callers double checking that higher prices will in reality ease some of the pressure on the farming community.

Many consumers woke to an overnight increase of up to 2p per pint on the price of their doorstep milk deliveries.

According to the NFU, its offices have been inundated with telephone calls from the public seeking assurances that the price rises will mean more money for dairy farmers.

Terrig Morgan, NFU Milk Committee chairman, said:"I am heartened that members of the public are taking the time and trouble to contact us and to offer their support for Britain's dairy farmers, particularly during the current foot-and-mouth crisis.

"Each and every caller has made it clear that they have no problem with paying extra for their milk as long as they know the extra money is going back to dairy farmers."

ALMOST SEVEN IN 10 people in Britain want their council to follow scientific advice and reopen local footpaths, according to an ICM Research poll.

The poll, commissioned by the Ramblers Association, found 65 per cent of those questioned believed their council should reopen its public paths in line with veterinary guidance.

Yet a Ramblers Association survey found that the majority of councils in England and Wales were ignoring scientific advice and refusing to reopen local paths.

Another poll by the NFU revealed that nearly two thirds of people planning Easter countryside breaks had cancelled their trips due to foot-and-mouth - a shattering blow for rural businesses.

THE AREAS WORST hit by foot-and-mouth were the ones already most vulnerable to economic setbacks, says the Countryside Agency in a new report.

The 'State of the Countryside' is the Government agency's third annual analysis and highlights what it says is the "widespread dependence of the rural economy on tourism and the over dependence of the remoter rural areas on a narrow economic base of agriculture and tourism."

It says Cumbria, Northumberland and the South West consistently rank as the most deprived rural areas in England.

Ewen Cameron, chairman of the Countryside Agency, said:"This year we paint a detailed picture of the changing rural economic, social and environmental conditions.

"For many people in rural England the picture is relatively happy - in general they enjoy slightly better levels of income, health and education and suffer less from crime. But this is not the whole picture.

"The remoter parts of rural England, the South West, the coastal area stretching from Norfolk through Lincolnshire, and north Cumbria, and Northumberland, consistently suffer real and enduring deprivation.Their economies and communities are already fragile and now in many of these areas foot-and-mouth has devastated farming and tourism with little other business to cushion the blow."

THE COUNTRYSIDE ALLIANCE has attacked "biased material" in a new education pack from a foreign animal rights group - People for the Ethical Treatment of Animals (PETA).

The Alliance says the pack is being offered to GCSE English teachers and includes slanted newspaper articles and a "discussion" sheet which compares modern fieldsports to outlawed bear-baiting and cock-fighting.

Charles Jardine, director of the Alliance's Gone Fishing Campaign, said:"Once again, PETA - a well-funded foreign animal rights lobby - is interfering with British education.

"It has again shown that it has no intention of letting the facts get in the way of its animal rights agenda.

"This outfit helped distribute an anti-angling pack to British schools last year which showed the very same propaganda hallmarks evident here.

"It is deeply worrying that young minds are being subjected to this sort of biased material. In particular, 'factsheet 11', entitled 'Is fishing a bloodsport?', gives what at first glance seems to be both sides of the argument but turns out to be an intellectual con-trick."

Close inspection reveals the way the 'facts' have been slanted to suit the anti-fishing message, he asserted.

"Everything said by the fisherman is dismissed by the 'anti-angler', who is photographed smiling, whilst the angler is looking suspicious and unsympathetic in sunglasses.

"This is really police state-style black propaganda."

LONDON MAYOR KEN Livingstone took time out from being henpecked by animal rights protesters to praise a Woodland Trust tree planting scheme.

Mr Livingstone, whose nature loving credentials were questioned after he tried to rid Trafalgar Square of pigeons, helped to highlight the massive recycling of discarded yellow pages.

In London alone, 38 per cent of people now recycle their old yellow pages instead of throwing them away, according to Yell, the new name of the Yellow Pages Group.

This is a rise of 10 per cent in two years.

Mr Livingstone said:"It is really encouraging that there has been such a significant improvement in recycling across the capital.

"Recycling helps the environment by reducing waste going to landfill and incineration. I am also very encouraged to see that Yell has decided to support the Woodland Trust to help create much needed woodland."

Yell will back the Trust as it plants and cares for thousands of new trees across the UK.

SONG THRUSHES ARE being radio tagged at a Game Conservancy Trust showpiece farm in a bid to help them flourish.

The site at Loddington in Leicestershire integrates profitable farming with game and wildlife management.

A Trust spokesman said:"The enterprise is an oasis for wildlife where brown hares, harvest mice and declining farmland birds are plentiful.

"The farm is currently home to an ambitious project which involves radio tagging song thrushes so scientists can learn more about their habitat and foraging needs.

"Researchers can then advise farmers on how to attract and look after this favourite songbird which has declined dramatically in recent years."

Farming expert Alastair Leake has just been appointed head of the 820-acre farm and takes up his post in June.

Countryside Minister Elliot Morley MP launched the national Countryside Stewardship guide at the venue back in January.

A RACING PIGEON called Flash was a bit slow off the mark when it came to flying home to its Cumbrian loft from France - it took nine months.

Hopes of the bird ever returning had faded when Flash suddenly fluttered into view above the Cleator Moor garden of delighted owner Brian Fitzsimmons.

Mr Fitzsimmons had released his bird for a race home across the Channel last year but Flash hurtled off in the wrong direction - finally landed exhausted in Germany weeks later.

Mr Fitzsimmons was initially contacted with the good news by Flash's rescuer but when the revived bird was re-released in Holland it only went missing a second time.

Finally, Flash turned up back home looking fatigued and bedraggled after a 36-week mystery tour of Europe.

RISING TRAFFIC LEVELS are continuing to put the countryside and any remaining pockets of tranquillity under threat, warns the Council for the Protection of Rural England.

New investment in rural buses and solutions offered by the Rural White Paper should help, it says, but these risk being undermined by a continuing Government commitment to build new roads and allow cheaper motoring.

In its report, the CPRE says:"Tranquillity has been shattered in the countryside. In the last 30 years an area of once tranquil countryside the size of Wales has been lost in England, with new roads and rising traffic a prime factor.

"Traffic is growing faster in rural than urban areas and is forecast to double in the next 30 years without action.

"People are now travelling around a third further to reach work, school and shops than they did a decade ago.

"Over 50 road schemes planned by national and local government threaten important areas of countryside."

THE RSPB HAS welcomed a £150,000 New Labour gift to conserve wildlife - vultures in India.

The Government handout, which has angered some British bird lovers who have seen native species slump, will fund a three-year project to help save threatened vultures in a country where their presence often has human health benefits.

GOVERNMENT MOVES TO recruit untrained people for vaccination work at the height of the foot-and-mouth crisis have been slammed as folly.

The Countryside Alliance has raised serious concerns about MAFF contingency plans for vaccination after it emerged that regional officials were recruiting untrained people from job centres to vaccinate animals.

At the same time, it claims, the Ministry has been ignoring offers of help from trained vets and humane slaughter professionals.

The Alliance says MAFF officials in the West Country have been recruiting unemployed people from local job centres and 'training' them to vaccinate by injecting oranges and to tag ears by using pieces of carpet.

But for over three weeks MAFF has stubbornly turned a blind eye to offers of help from a large group of available vets.

Alliance chief executive Richard Burge said:"Surely MAFF is putting the cart before the horse. Any recruitment for vaccination should start by utilising all those best trained for the task already.

"The Alliance recently launched its own search through our website and Grass-Route network to locate trained professionals available to help with the crisis.

"We forwarded to MAFF on March 22 the contact details of over 50 vets and qualified humane slaughter professionals who had come forward offering assistance, but we know that to date many have not even been contacted by officials.

"Yet MAFF are resorting to recruiting untrained people with no previous experience of animal husbandry.

"MAFF should also look at ways of making greater use of hunt staff, especially in the South West and Wales, who are highly skilled in all aspects of animal husbandry and who have already offered assistance."

RSPCA ADVERTS AGAINST foxhunting have been attacked as misleading by advertising watchdogs.

The newspaper adverts, condemned at the time by the Countryside Alliance, claimed that the majority of the public supported a ban.

But recent surveys have shown that public support for a ban has dropped significantly.

An NOP poll conducted shortly before the adverts appeared said only 48 per cent of people still wanted a total ban.

The Advertising Standards Authority said the RSPCA was therefore wrong to suggest such a strong backing for a ban and ordered it not to repeat the mistake.

ENGLISH NATURE HAS taken the tough decision to reopen a raft of its national nature reserves while the foot-and-mouth crisis continues to wreak havoc.

Andrew Brown, director of operations, said:"Although most reserves remain closed, we have started to identify those wildlife sites that the public can visit where the risks of spreading foot-and-mouth are absolutely minimal.

"These sites will be constantly monitored and if the current situation should deteriorate then we will take immediate action to close the reserves.

"We want to provide the public with some controlled and safe access to the countryside without creating further risks for the farming community."

English Nature has stressed it is still working closely with all groups associated with the foot-and-mouth outbreak and its first priority is to do everything it can to help control and eradicate the disease.

It recognised, however, that the current restrictions were imposing heavy costs on many businesses as well as reducing the quality of life for many people.

Reserves currently open are: Castle Eden Dene, Northumbria (part - see signs on site); Lindisfarne, Northumbria (part - north shore only, see signs on site); Dungeness, Kent (part - excluding RSPB area); Swanscombe Hill, Kent; Humberhead Peatlands, Yorkshire (part - Thorne Moor only); Wren's Nest, West Midlands; Walberswick, Suffolk (part - see signs on site); Hartland Moor, Dorset; Studland Heath, Dorset (managed by the National Trust, part open); Thursley, Surrey; Bedford Purlieus, Cambridgeshire (contact Forestry Commission for details); Ruislip Woods, London; Ainsdale, Lancashire (footpath only open, see signs on site); Richmond Park, London; Palmerston Wood, Over Haddon, Derbyshire (part of Derbyshire Dales NNR. Footpath open only - see signs on site);Scolt Head Island, Norfolk; Holkham, Norfolk (part - see signs on site); Chippenham Fen, Suffolk; Cavenham Heath, Suffolk; Weeting Heath, Norfolk; Holt Heath, Dorset (part, see signs on site); Wicken Fen (part, see signs on site, National Trust).

THE EMPIRE BUILDING ambitions of Britain's only known termite colony have been quashed by a successful eradication programme.

A Government inspired crackdown begun three years ago appears to have wiped out the hungry wood-munching pests at Saunton on the north Devon coast.

The termites, thought to have been accidentally introduced in soil from abroad, had been found happily chewing their way through a holiday home.

Because their voraciousness can actually bring down buildings, the risk to other homes in the region and beyond was quickly assessed.

Experts started wiping out the million-strong colony and recent surveys on the area are said to show the colony has now been totally devastated - possibly even down to the last defiant termite.

THE RAMBLERS ASSOCIATION is continuing with the build-up to its rights of way day of action.

Thousands of people are expected to join in Footpaths Day on Sunday, July 8, set to be the biggest event ever about public rights of way.

THE RSPCA WAR on foxhunting has moved up a gear with news that the charity wants to dump respected former Olympian Richard Meade from its ranks because of his support for hunting.

The proposal has outraged hunt supporters, some of whom see the charity as riddled with so-called 'bunny huggers' whose undoubted love of animals often flies in the face of common sense.

Recently, the RSPCA was blasted by the Countryside Alliance for "betraying real animal interests" by taking out a raft of expensive full-page newspaper adverts against foxhunting.

The adverts, this time urging the House of Lords to ban hunting, were part of a series employed by the charity which considers hunting "barbaric" and makes no apologies for trying to get it banned.

According to reports, a raft of legal options was drawn up for an RSPCA council meeting which looked at ways in which Mr Meade could be ejected.

Showjumper Mr Meade, who took gold at the 1968 and 1972 Olympics, has been one of the RSPCA's staunchest members and supporters. He was made an OBE in 1974.

However, he caused fury at the charity when he established the Countryside Animal Welfare Group to try to soften the RSPCA's stance against hunting.

Informed by a reporter that his membership was to be discussed at the RSPCA council meeting, Mr Meade said:"This is news to me. If it is so, it is extraordinary to try to eject someone simply because they hold a different view to the one adopted by the Society. It is heavy-handed and plain wrong.

"This is a very sad day in the long history of the RSPCA. I will need time to consider my options. I am just astonished."

A CHICKEN LOVER in Shropshire was left feeling rather empty when he grabbed an egg from his birds for breakfast - and found it totally hollow.

The bizarre find by smallholder Harry Sherwin came just in time for Easter after he popped into his plot near Market Drayton where he keeps four dozen hens.

Although perfectly sealed and shaped in the normal way, the lightweight egg contained nothing at all - something Mr Sherwin has never encountered before in a lifetime of keeping hens.

The find has amazed him - especially as all his birds enjoy a healthy diet and have the run of his one acre plot where they scratch around for additional titbits.

Although the yolk-less egg is thought to be a one-off, Mr Sherwin has been taking a closer interest in his hens' produce ever since.

THE RSPB IS calling on gardeners to help save one of the country's most precious and scarce habitats - bogs - by snubbing peat compost.

The move comes after it was revealed that the UK has now lost 94 per cent of its lowland raised peat bogs.

Peat extraction work is actually thought to have started during the beginning of the 19th Century.

But modern compost alternatives are now available which reduce the need for peat.

RSPB peatland policy officer, Dr Olly Watts, said:"Gardeners can make a positive difference to the conservation of one of our most important wildlife habitats by buying peat-free products this spring.

"We know that the majority of gardeners are keen to stop using peat provided that suitable alternatives are made more readily available by retailers."

A recent survey found that three-quarters of gardeners would now support a total ban on the use of peat with new products available believed to be just as good or even better than peat-based products.

Research by the RSPB also revealed that 90 per cent of its members would like peat-free composts to be made more available in all garden centres.

FERRET FANS ARE fuming after their pets were denied the same rights as dogs, cats and even guinea pigs after being locked out of the 'passports for pets' scheme.

The European Union verdict has infuriated many ferret owners who wanted to compete in international shows without having to put their pets in quarantine.

To add insult to injury, Britain backed the move after ministers heard ferrets could harbour rabies because no accurate blood test was available to check them.

During the debate British ferret owners were mocked by one MEP who said they liked to put the animals down their trousers for fun.

However, the EU decision has been backed by the National Ferret Welfare Society which says it is wrong to take a ferret all the way abroad just to get a rosette.

THE COUNTRY LAND and Business Association has challenged other rural groups to dig deep into their pockets during the foot-and-mouth crisis.

It has just put £50,000 into a new account backing work by the Royal Agricultural Benevolent Institution and the Arthur Rank Centre Addington Fund which aims to alleviate rural poverty during the crisis.

CLA president Anthony Bosanquet said:"We have seen millions of pounds donated by members of the public - among them many of our 50,000 members not afflicted by foot-and-mouth - - and by the banks and other corporations.

"But we believe that the membership organisations for rural communities, and companies which supply this client base, should also show their thanks for the good times by helping out when times get tough."

The CLA has used its initial deposit to set up the Rural Help Account.

Additional payments can be made over the counter at any branch of Barclays Bank.

121

GOVERNMENT FAILURE OVER the foot-and-mouth crisis highlights a desperate need for Britain's countryside to have its own ministry, it has been claimed.

Chaos, confusion and duplication in Labour's handling of the epidemic could be avoided in future by the introduction of a Department for the Countryside and Agriculture, says the Country Land and Business Association.

Too many Government departments and agencies had been involved in making policy decisions, it claims, while a single department headed by a Countryside Minister could co-ordinate the rural actions of MAFF, DETR, DTI, the Treasury and Number 10.

With Tony Blair reportedly already preparing to abolish the Ministry of Agriculture in its present form, CLA deputy policy director Dr Alan Woods outlined a catalogue of problems encountered over efforts to reopen areas of the countryside during the present crisis.

Conflicting advice from various Government departments and agencies had led to confusion among rural businesses and countryside users, he asserted.

"There was chaos in the messages, an obvious lack of understanding and a failure to deliver," he said. "This has been a shocking example of what happens without a single focused department."

Launching the CLA election manifesto 'For the Good of the Country', president Anthony Bosanquet added: "Whitehall cannot go on having three different views on what agriculture and the countryside are for.

"The countryside is for successful rural business, tourism, farming and forestry - all pursued in a way that respects the environment and provides rural jobs and incomes. Without a coherent approach in Whitehall, no Government can succeed in the countryside.

"We need to look ahead, beyond foot-and-mouth. We need to give the next Government a map by which to steer farming to firmer ground."

COCKY LOCKY, THE pet cockerel has been threatened with death unless he curbs his natural instincts to crow at daybreak.

A time ban has been slapped on the luckless bird by environmental health chiefs at Leven, near Hull.

Neighbours complained about the bird's early morning crowing and now owners Ellen and Stephen Northgraves have been ordered to keep him quiet until 7.30am.

If Cocky Locky fails to keep his beak shut before then, he might be destroyed.

THE CURSE OF a stuffed pike has struck again with no-one wanting to buy the deadly fish after it came up for auction.

The voracious predator was caught in 1935 and had since rested near the dartboard on a wall at a club in Warrington, Lancashire.

But when a picture of the club bowls squad was hung beside it, each member of the team died.

Members of the club dominoes team, who used to sit beneath the 20-pound pike, also died.

Rumours of a curse appear to have spread because, though the fish was expected to fetch £1,000 in a local sale, not one buyer came forward to snap it up.

The pike resides in a glass case and would normally have made an excellent decorative addition to a variety of properties.

However, auctioneers have been forced to hang onto it for the time being - at their own risk.

FOXHUNTERS ARE APPLYING for Government cash to help them cope with massive losses during the foot-and-mouth crisis.

Hunt groups imposed a voluntary ban on their activities as soon as the seriousness of the situation was revealed.

But the continuing need to stay away from open ground has imposed huge financial strain on hunts - thought to have lost up to £50million since the start of the crisis.

The Countryside Alliance has been encouraging masters of foxhounds to apply for all the financial help they can get.

Despite Labour MPs recently pressing for a ban on foxhunting, the groups are actually eligible for loans under the terms of a Government scheme to support rural businesses during the crisis.

Anti-hunt groups, meanwhile, are reported to be urging the Government to withold the loans in a bid to speed up the extinction of the sport.

ANIMAL RIGHTS CAMPAIGNERS want the RSPCA to prosecute Grand National race officials after only four horses out of a field of 40 finished this year's waterlogged course at Aintree.

No rider or horse suffered serious injury but Animal Aid, the UK's biggest animal rights group, wants the RSPCA to instigate a prosecution under the 1911 Protection of Animals Act.

"The whole spectacle was a disgrace and anything but 'sporting'. It brought shame on Britain as a nation of so-called animal lovers," said a spokesman for the protesters.

"The Grand National horses were clearly exhausted, falling heavily and careering into each other.

"The organisers have announced that there were no fatalities on the day. But in the weeks and months to come, experience tells us some of the fallen animals will be disposed of once it is clear that their money-making days are over."

BATHING WATER SAMPLES are being taken off South West coast beaches again with the Environment Agency hoping standards will reach as high as last year.

Between them, Cornwall, Devon, Dorset and Somerset have 187 bathing waters identified under the European Commission bathing water directive.

"Last year bathing water quality in the South West was the best ever," said a spokesman.

WEASEL: predator a blur as it closes in on its victim

L IKE a tiny tiger in its ferocity, the weasel strikes terror into the shy inhabitants of hedgerows or fields when it sets out to hunt them.

Savage in its pursuit of prey, the bigger male still measures just eight inches long without its stubby tail and weighs about four ounces.

Whether shooting across the road like an elongated mouse, or bounding excitedly after its quarry, the weasel is usually moving too fast for close study. Described memorably by one observer as looking like an 'animated cigar', the weasel boasts a beautiful chestnut coat which gives way to a milky white underside.

Still widespread across the country, it nests in any available crevice, giving birth to five or six young at a time. Smaller than its equally vicious cousin, the stoat, the weasel's dexterity and acrobatics are legendary.

Mice and voles are its main prey but weasels will also take rabbits and rats when they can overpower them.

Nesting songbirds are another favourite target and its ultra thin body means the weasel has no difficulty slipping inside most garden nestboxes.

Even boxes whose entrance holes measure less than an inch and a quarter in diameter are not safe.

Because of this talent, weasels rarely endear themselves to bird-loving householders, especially any who have been following the progress of a mother bird and chicks only to find them slaughtered and eaten.

S trong jaws and sharp teeth help the weasel to kill most of its prey instantly with a crushing bite to the back of the head or neck - just like a tiger.

Moreover, again like a big jungle cat, the weasel is courageous and fearsome in defence of its young.

I once read of a fox spotted with a furious female weasel clamped to its throat after disturbing her nest.

Unwilling to let go, the weasel dangled from the fox's throat while the disconcerted bigger animal tried everything to shake it off.

Eventually, the weasel dropped to the ground and the fox retreated.

I have never seen anything so bizarre myself but I did once spot a weasel pursuing a mouse in and out of a dry stone wall.

The hunt was over in seconds with pursued and pursuer mostly a blur of movement.

But it was possible to make out the smaller, grey shape of the mouse desperate to get away and the longer, brown shape of the weasel determined to make a kill.

A s my eyes struggled to follow the drama, the pair disappeared for the last time into the wall.

A shrill squeak of pain rang out and that was that.

I hung around for a few minutes hoping to spot the weasel emerge with its prize but it never did.

Probably scenting me for the first time, it no doubt preferred to eat its grisly meal in private.

Pampered household cats have been known to limp home in shock after coming off worse in a fight with a weasel, their belief that they had stumbled on a harmless mouse being sadly misplaced.

Yet weasels don't have it all their own way and many are killed on the roads or by larger predators willing to take them on in a fierce battle.

It has always struck me as unfair that sly and treacherous human beings should be named after this bold little animal, or that other humans should be said to use 'weasel words' when they try to mislead.

Weasels are pitiless assassins. Of that there is no doubt.

But slyness and treachery do not figure in the mindset of this teeny killer.

ANGLERS HAVE ATTACKED a bid by TV Pet Rescue presenter Wendy Turner-Webster to get Scouts to give up "the violent pastime" of fishing.

The presenter wrote to the Duke of Kent in his capacity as president of the Scout Association, asking him to "retire the Scouts' angling proficiency badge" on the grounds of cruelty.

Speaking on behalf of PETA - People for the Ethical Treatment of Animals - she tells the Duke that "setting out to attack animals is not in keeping with the image of Scouting."

Urging him to "put the violent pastime of fishing behind us and teach children to respect rather than kill wildlife," she proposes Scouts earn a waterways clean-up badge instead.

But the views of the presenter, sister to more famous celebrity Anthea Turner, have met with widespread condemnation from the angling community.

Jill Grieve, from the Countryside Alliance's Gone Fishing campaign, said:"We have been monitoring PETA recently as they are really taking hold over here. We are doing all we can to warn anglers that they are a serious threat.

"Wendy Turner is a vegan and has always adopted an anti-fieldsports stance but, having said that, I think condemning Scouts for fishing is beyond the pale.

"Clearly, Scouts have always been encouraged to learn about the world around them and angling is an intrinsic part of that. I don't think anyone will take Ms Turner's comments seriously - and calling Boy Scouts 'blood-thirsty murderers', as another PETA spokesperson has, is laughable."

Fishing campaign leader Charles Jardine had already staged one young persons' sports day this year, she added, and there were many more to come.

"Kids up to the age of 14 were introduced to hounds, clay shooting, ferreting and angling, and the response was massively positive. Any notion that the vegan fraternity can drive the traditional enthusiasm for the outdoors out of the younger generation is badly misplaced."

THE WILDLIFE TRUSTS have highlighted the need for greater protection of marine species around Britain's coasts.

"Whilst our shores are home to an amazing variety of animals, including dolphins, turtles, seals and sharks, there are urgent problems facing the UK's marine environment," said a spokesman.

POLITICAL CORRECTNESS APPEARS not to have penetrated parts of Glasgow where residents have been trapping and killing magpies by the hundred.

Fears that the voracious predators are wiping out the area's songbirds have prompted some local people to take matters into their own hands.

As many as 400 magpies are thought to have been trapped and killed already this year with some Glasgow ladies apparently not too squeamish to join in.

When the city's starling population was found to have dropped from 50,000 to 6,000 birds, residents were in no doubt about the culprits - magpies.

However, the city council - alarmed at the magpie carnage - says a variety of predators are probably to blame and has asked avid magpie hunters to leave the birds alone.

BADGER LOVERS HAVE welcomed the prosecution of a foxhunter after a badger sett was illegally blocked up.

At Epping Magistrates Court, the master of a hunt group was found guilty of aiding, abetting, counselling and procuring interference with a badger sett at Bradwell-on-Sea, Essex, in March last year.

Magistrates issued a £250 fine plus a demand for £500 costs.

"The illegal blocking of badger setts by fox hunts is widespread, despite having serious welfare implications for badgers," said Dr Elaine King, conservation officer for the National Federation of Badger Groups.

"This conviction is an excellent result and should send a clear message to hunts that illegal blocking of badger setts is wholly unacceptable.

"It reflects the commitment and expertise shown by the North East Essex Badger Group, the RSPCA, the police and the Essex Crown Prosecution Service, who worked tirelessly to ensure a successful result."

THE HUMBLE BUMBLEBEE could be facing extinction because numbers are dropping so fast, say wildlife experts.

Intensive farming is believed to be one of the causes of the decline with traditional pollen sources harder to find.

Some 19 species existed in the UK until recently but three of these are now gone and eight others are endangered.

The best-loved large garden bumblebee is facing the toughest test of all to survive.

The British Ecological Society is currently funding a study aimed at finding ways to reverse the decline of an insect crucial to farmers for pollinating crops.

SCOTTISH WOODS ARE being reopened after many were shut down over foot-and-mouth.

The Forestry Commission said woodland trails were available once more for walkers.

Scottish Forestry Minister Rhona Brankin has urged the public to start returning to the wilds after more than 500 trails were given the all-clear.

"The woodlands of Scotland are great places to visit," said Ms Brankin.

"From the wilds of Sutherland to the spectacular scenery of the Trossachs, the majestic giant trees of Perthshire to the ancient Caledonian pinewoods, the variety is breathtaking."

LEAKED DOCUMENTS PROVE that the League Against Cruel Sports is aiming to outlaw shooting, claims the Countryside Alliance.

The documents, revealed in a newspaper, apparently show the League readying itself for a campaign to make shooting illegal.

"The disclosure of the League's hidden agenda confirms the fears of many in the countryside: that the League's assault on hunting is just the start of a 'piece meal' process of abolition," warned a spokesman for the Alliance.

"The leak will cause alarm and embarrassment amongst League supporters and staff who have tried to play down the shooting issue, fearful of the strength of the two million-strong shooting community.

"On December 27, 2000, in an interview in the Daily Telegraph, League press officer Dave Ward said his members had no plans against fishing and shooting.

"As recently as February, League member Tony Banks MP also claimed in the House of Commons that 'as far as I am aware the League Against Cruel Sports has no intention of moving onto fishing or shooting'."

The Alliance claims the League's objective will put it on collision course with Prime Minister Tony Blair who says he supports shooting.

Simon Hart, director of the Countryside Alliance Campaign for Hunting, added:"This leaked document proves not only that the League intend to campaign for the abolition of all country sports one by one, but that they have tried to conceal it.

"They have tried to hoodwink Parliament and the public into believing they have no coercive intent when it comes to shooting. They have been caught out.

"Shooting and fishing enthusiasts, as well as politicians, who have trusted the League, now know what they are dealing with."

THE QUEEN HAS been revealed as the next target of militant RSPCA bosses determined to root out members who support foxhunting and expel them.

The Queen is the patron of the 'royal' Society and her expulsion is likely to bring RSPCA members not only into conflict with foxhunt supporters but also with ardent royalists.

Former Olympian Richard Meade has already been thrown out of the RSPCA after his hunting beliefs were said to clash with official RSPCA anti-foxhunting views.

He said he was amazed and dismayed by the action following his moves to moderate the Society's anti-hunt stance.

CUMBRIAN FARMERS DRIVEN to despair by the foot-and-mouth crisis are to get free holidays to help them recover, the Countryside Agency has announced.

About 250 farming families will be able to take a free three-day midweek break at certain hotels and guest houses in the county under a 'Rest and Recuperation Scheme' run by the Hadfield Trust and funded by public and Government donations.

Margaret Clark, a Countryside Agency director, said:"People living in those parts of the country which have been worst hit by foot-and-mouth desperately need some kind of respite from their daily worries.

"This is an innovative scheme which will not only benefit the Cumbrian farming community but, as the funds are being spent within the county, will also help the wider local economy.

"Voluntary organisations around the country are rising to the challenge of helping to relieve the distress of rural families and communities."

WHISPER IT SOFTLY - plans are afoot for the third National Moth Night to trap and record Britain's myriad night flutterers.

This year's event will be held on Saturday, August 11, with the same aims as previously - to encourage widespread moth recording and gather useful data; to stimulate wider interest in moths; and to raise funds for moth conservation projects.

According to the Amateur Entomologists' Society, the event has grown in strength over the last two years and it is hoped that more money than ever before will be raised this year for moth conservation.

"We would like as many people as possible to run light-traps in as many different areas as possible," said a spokesman.

"Participants may choose to record the moths in their garden or their local patch, but we would encourage people to visit new areas that they have not looked at previously or for a number of years."

FORESTRY MINISTER ELLIOT Morley MP has announced a major review of management techniques involving English woods.

In answer to a parliamentary question, Mr Morley said:"Woodland makes an important contribution to the rural economy and is essential to the character of the English countryside. However, many of our woods are under-managed and are not delivering the potential range of benefits to their owners or to society as a whole.

"The Forestry Commission plays a key role in ensuring the sustainable management of our woodland. I have therefore asked the Commission to review management of existing woodland.

"The review will help focus the Commission's work on finding ways to engage woodland owners effectively in implementing the England Forestry Strategy.

"This will help owners sustain their own plans while supporting the rural economy and improving the environment for the benefit of all."

A LONE GANNET has been sighted sitting on the roof of a house in Brighton - fending off attacks from local herring gulls.

The Sussex coast is thought to be just a staging post for the roaming birds whose nearest colony is at Alderney in the Channel Islands.

POLITICIANS ON THE hustings should be forced to answer key countryside questions to determine exactly where they stand on rural concerns, says the Country Land and Business Association.

Country voters will then be able to judge their replies before making their minds up on polling day.

"With the General Election now set for June 7, politicians will be campaigning in their own constituencies and the three main party 'big hitters' will be boarding battle buses to electoral hotspots for press briefings and photocalls," said a CLA spokesman.

"We believe that the future of the countryside is going to play a major role during the campaign. The people who live and work in rural areas will make their minds up to vote for the politicians and the party which gives the best answer to the top issues in rural Britain today."

The key questions should include:

-Communications - how do they propose to provide the infrastructure to enable people who work in rural areas to compete on equal terms with their urban counterparts ?

-Rural entrepreneurs - these can create jobs and livelihoods for their local communities but how would they ensure that the planning system positively encourages business development ?

-How do they rate farming as a future contributor to Britain's GDP ?

-European 'standards' - these are targeted at large-scale businesses and often 'gold-plated' with UK regulations so how would they ensure that smaller rural producers had the chance to develop their businesses ?

-How would they support local schemes for affordable housing ?

-The inter-dependence of livestock farming, environment and tourism had been demonstrated unequivocally in recent weeks - so how would they ensure that our grazed landscape could be maintained ?

-Crime and drug abuse - these are spreading into the countryside, so how would they improve the security of towns and villages ?

-Foot-and-mouth disease appears to have come from imported meat - so how would they ensure that this cannot happen again ?

A COLONY OF rare wasp spiders will be captured and transferred elsewhere before workmen start building homes on land at Exminster, Devon.

The spiders, which sport wasp-like black and yellow stripes, are to be introduced to suitable new habitat not far away from the site being developed.

QUICK-THINKING RAF men scrambled into action when 10 mallard ducklings became trapped down a drain on the main runway at RAF Kinloss in Scotland.

The ducklings had been spotted earlier with their mother crossing the runway - used by some of the biggest planes in the air force.

But somehow the tiny chicks managed to fall into a 50-metre drain running beneath the runway, sending the mother into a flap and sparking worries about possible danger to aircraft taking off.

Initial attempts to lift the heavy drain cover failed so a crew of RAF firemen was brought in to help and the runway temporarily closed.

With the ducklings facing certain death in the drain, a jet of water was gently employed to drive them into a position where they could be rescued.

The birds were then released unharmed onto nearby marshland with their mother.

A RARE OSPREY caused a stir in Brighton after suddenly coming to rest on a local rooftop.

The spectacular bird of prey, which feeds on fish, appeared to have stopped short on its usual West Africa to Scotland migratory route.

Appearing exhausted and distressed it was finally rescued by bird expert Giles Talbot with the help of a local fire crew.

Falconer Mr Talbot took the white, black and grey-coloured predator into protective custody where it received medical treatment and was fed fish.

Less than 40 breeding ospreys are thought to be at large in Britain at any one time, the vast majority travelling from West Africa to Scotland in March, April and early May.

A RECORD 50,000 people took part in this year's RSPB Big Garden Birdwatch - double the previous number last year.

The survey, which compiled data from around 30,000 gardens across the UK, recorded an average 4.2 starlings per garden - just ahead of the house sparrow at four per garden.

Other birds in the 'top 10' were (in descending order): blue tit, blackbird, chaffinch, greenfinch, great tit, robin, collared dove and wood pigeon.

More than 37,000 adults and 13,000 children were involved in the counts last January with 90 per cent of surveys carried out in England.

Peter Holden, RSPB head of youth and volunteers, said:"We would like to thank all those people who took part in the survey this year. Big Garden Birdwatch is important because it provides a great snapshot of the birds visiting our gardens each January, as well as highlighting long-term population trends."

A SIX-FOOT conger eel is to be released into the open sea from a Scottish aquarium after his friskiness showed he was ready to find a mate.

The eel, known as Chippie, weighs about 80 pounds and will be released from the Aberdeenshire aquarium as soon as staff can catch and transport him.

A BLACK-BROWED albatross - twice the size of the largest British gull and normally found as far south as the Falkland Isles - has been spotted here for the first time cruising off the Kent coast.

A DIRTY TRICKS campaign was waged by the Government against farmers' leader Ben Gill during the foot-and-mouth crisis, he claims.

NFU president Mr Gill says he fell victim to smear tactics allegedly emanating from the heart of Whitehall as he struggled to put farmers first.

Prime Minister Tony Blair had suddenly decided to vaccinate stock against foot-and-mouth but the co-operation of farmers was needed - and Mr Gill remained resolutely opposed to the option.

As he fought officials, the Yorkshire farmer says he lost weight and his hair turned grey.

In an interview with a newspaper, Mr Gill said he became the target of a concerted effort by hidden conspiritors to reduce his standing.

"There was an attempt to portray me as a bully," he said.

Mr Gill claimed that he had also been attacked in a co-ordinated campaign by a raft of wealthy landowners who wanted a programme of vaccination instead of continuing mass slaughter.

Leader of this group was reportedly Lady Emma Tennant, mother of the model Stella Tennant and daughter of the Duke of Devonshire, who wrote to 100 friends asking them to lobby the NFU and the Government in a bid to get vaccination introduced.

Meanwhile, in a separate development, the NFU has branded yet another finding of banned spinal cord in beef imported into the UK "deplorable and intolerable."

Mr Gill called for the immediate closure of the abattoir in Denmark from which meat containing spinal column - outlawed under BSE rules - was imported.

ANGLING, SHOOTING, AND even hunting could be subsidised by the Government if proposals to pay stewardship fees to landowners go ahead.

A scheme being investigated by Agriculture Minister Nick Brown could change current rural emphasis from supporting food production to improving the countryside.

The move is seen as putting more importance on preserving the environment and wide open spaces for more of the population to enjoy rather than keeping land just for narrow agricultural purposes.

The proposals were handed to the Government weeks ago by English Nature.

If backed, they could add up to a new future for the beleaguered countryside after foot-and-mouth is finally defeated.

However, some feel the plans are too controversial and politically dangerous for New Labour to air them fully ahead of the approaching General Election.

BEAVERS ARE BEING used in an experiment to see if they can help restore a fragile wetland site, The Wildlife Trusts have revealed.

After a six-month quarantine, 10 of the aquatic mammals will be introduced to a secret location in Kent after being extinct in this country for almost 1,000 years.

The European beaver, once native throughout the British Isles, was wiped out in England in the 12th Century but hung on in parts of Scotland into the 16th Century.

Dr Simon Lyster, of The Wildlife Trusts, said:"It is tremendously exciting that beavers will once again be back in England playing their natural ecological role, albeit on a tiny scale. We hope they will enhance the quality of this particular site as a wildlife habitat and, if successful, that we will be able to replicate the project elsewhere in the country."

Unlike their North American cousins, European beavers rarely build dams and often nest in burrows, though family groups construct a lodge with tree branches.

Their diet comprises grass, leaves, twigs and bark, with the otter's favourite food - fish - off their vegetarian menu.

OUCH! MIND THOSE nettles - especially now that everyone seems to be waxing lyrical about the stinging weeds.

You may have thought nettles were unlovely hazards liable to spoil a good day out but organisers of 'National Be Nice to Nettles Week' insist otherwise.

Besides having medicinal and nutritional value for humans, nettles are said to be beneficial for a variety of insects.

Wildlife expert Chris Baines, a supporter of the current drive to put nettles in a better light, said:"Stingers are a vital part of growing up, giving us one of the most painful early memories of close contact with nature.

"It is much later in life that most of us realise just how valuable they are, especially for some of our most beautiful wild creatures.

"Without stinging nettles, peacock butterflies, small tortoiseshells and red admirals would have nowhere to lay their eggs, so do please find a space for nettles somewhere in your neighbourhood."

BOOZY HEDGEHOGS ARE in danger of being run down after helping themselves to beer in slug traps, it has been claimed.

Shropshire-based charity the British Hedgehog Preservation Society has issued a warning to gardeners that traditional beer traps could prove fatal for hedgehogs.

The prickly creatures love beer and will thirstily lap it up - especially in hot weather - but then the resulting effects make them more likely to be killed.

The Society's new Slug Pub is specially designed with a roof under which slugs can crawl to get at the beer but hedgehogs are safely excluded.

FALLING NUMBERS MEAN Britain's oysters are having a tough time finding mates, scientists have revealed.

A study being conducted by Hull University boffins aims to find ways oysters can get it together and boost their population.

BRITISH FARMERS' LEADER Ben Gill sparked outrage among environmentalists when he claimed eco-terrorism could lie behind the devastating outbreak of foot-and-mouth disease.

Mr Gill, president of the NFU, made his controversial statement while attending the International Federation of Agricultural Producers in the Australian capital Canberra where he has been promoting UK farming and tourism.

During a question and answer session, he said:"There is no doubt foot-and-mouth spread to the UK illegally and, unfortunately, we cannot rule out eco-terrorism. The pressures of green groups are intense in Europe, and I understand, building here in Australia."

It was the most public airing yet of widespread suspicions within the farming community about the speed and scale of a disease which wreaked such havoc.

However, Friends of the Earth has been quick to condemn the claims which it says are totally without foundation.

The Ministry of Agriculture, too, has moved to reassure farmers that it investigated the possibility of eco-terrorism at the start of the epidemic and found nothing of concern.

It says that the mass movement of sheep around the country has emerged as the far more likely reason that the disease spread so far so quickly.

Speaking later, Mr Gill added:"The interest in the impact of foot-and-mouth from farming organisations across the world is understandably massive. They have seen the news coverage of the issue and are keen to learn what it has actually been like for us.

"We have discussed Australia's stringent import control measures of which the country is rightly proud. There are certainly many useful lessons for me to take back home, not least of which are the strict precautions taken at all entry points into the country."

THE DREADED COLORADO beetle is said to pose the next big threat to British farming after foot-and-mouth and classical swine fever.

Farmers, gardeners, and vegetable importers have been put on alert for the black and yellow striped beetle notorious for causing devastation in America.

Anyone who finds a Colorado beetle, which can lay waste to potato crops, is being asked to contact MAFF or even their local police station.

Researchers say that changes in climate and lax border controls could make Britain an easy target for invasion - an event that has proved costly for countries which did not heed warnings.

EXCITEMENT HAS BEEN mounting that an English osprey nest seems poised to produce offspring - the first time this will have happened for 200 years.

No ospreys have successfully bred in England since the 18th Century, wildlife experts revealed after a pair began incubating eggs at a secret location in the north.

Dr Mark Avery, RSPB conservation director, said:"We are delighted that these wonderful fish-eating birds of prey are now breeding again outside Scotland in England.

"This is largely a result of the increasing Scottish population spreading naturally over the border.

"There are now more than 100 breeding pairs in Scotland, thanks to the ongoing conservation work that followed their successful return to the UK at the Loch Garten nature reserve in 1954."

Widespread persecution by egg and specimen collectors originally wiped out the UK population.

The last pair of ospreys were said to have bred in Scotland in 1916.

The RSPB and Forest Enterprise are currently keeping the English nest site secret to protect the birds and their eggs from disturbance and egg thieves.

A FARM contractor has been ordered to pay £3,000 in fines and costs after pleading guilty to causing pollution that killed 10,000 fish almost two years ago.

Exeter Crown Court heard how Environment Agency workers found dead fish littering the River Tamar near Whitstone, Cornwall, on July 7, 1999.

A massive three-day emergency clean-up operation was launched with pumps used to recirculate the river and hydrogen peroxide added to help lift oxygen levels.

Hundreds of fish were rescued by fisheries staff, including prime salmon and sea trout.

However, an estimated 10,000 fish still perished along a 13 kilometre stretch of water polluted by farm waste.

The defendant was fined £1,000 with £2,000 costs for causing the pollution under the Water Resources Act 1991.

The Environment Agency will also be seeking to recover £18,000 clean-up costs from him.

Environment Agency spokesman Bruce Newport said after the case:"We have been working in partnership with the farming community in the Tamar area for years and a big improvement had been achieved.

"That made this serious pollution even more disappointing to everyone involved."

WAS THAT OKAY, luvs? Badgers have been digging their new image as earthy celebrities after a permanent webcam was installed outside a man-made sett in Devon.

Kevin and Anne Atkinson spent thousands of pounds constructing the sett, complete with underground viewing chamber, at their farm near Tiverton.

The couple, keen wildlife lovers, have created an oasis for wild creatures which is also easily accessed by human visitors.

Now their badgers are on the internet after the Atkinsons joined forces with the BBC's Natural History Unit which provided the equipment.

FOXHUNTING WILL GO straight back to the top of the political agenda if Labour is re-elected, the party has confirmed in its General Election manifesto.

Bowing to pressure from Labour MPs and anti-hunt groups, Premier Tony Blair has pledged to keep the hunting debate alive and hold out the prospect of a total ban.

As expected, he has promised a free vote in the next Parliament but there is also the possibility he may invoke the Parliament Act to finally end hunting in England and Wales.

Labour also proposes setting up a Department for Rural Affairs as well as an independent commission to advise on farming.

The Conservatives, meanwhile, assert that rural communities have never been more desperate for a change of government.

Shadow Agriculture spokesman James Taice said the countryside was in dire straights even before Labour's woeful handling of the foot-and-mouth epidemic.

Labour did not care about or understand the countryside, he told a meeting of farmers in Cowbridge, South Wales.

Elsewhere, the fledgling Countryside Party has been urging its members and supporters to make their votes count and try to keep hunting alive by backing the Tories.

Addressing visitors to its website, a spokesman explained:"The Countryside Party are not strong enough as yet to make a large impact at the election, and many of you will not be able to cast a vote for us. Therefore, we would ask you - for Countryside and Country Sports - vote Conservative.

"We would not ask you to use your vote in this way if we were stronger but time is running out for our friends who hunt, and this is the only way. Please vote and make your vote count."

PROTESTS OVER RURAL foot-and-mouth burial sites have been escalating as fears about possible health risks increase.

In one of the latest incidents, 11 women and a man were arrested at a County Durham burial site after launching their own protest.

The group were charged with a number of public order offences and will appear in court later after complaining about a site at Tow Law.

Widespread protests about air pollution caused by burning pyres, and possible groundwater pollution from hundreds of thousands of buried carcasses, have dogged the Government's fight against foot-and-mouth.

In Powys, Wales, officials recently suspended the disposal of carcasses at a military range after serious concerns were raised about the pollution risk.

NESTING CROWS MOBBED a falcon showing off its skills at a school falconry display and put it to flight.

The native British birds did not take kindly to show-off Saker falcon Aziz when the winged killer invaded their territory during the display at Shrewsbury, Shropshire.

Owner Bryan Paterson was dismayed when his terrified prize bird failed to return to its aviary at Bridgnorth and put out an appeal through local newspapers for details of its whereabouts.

Days later, Aziz was found exhausted and hungry sitting on a hedge in North Wales 50 miles away - and even further removed from a Saker falcon's natural environment in Eastern Europe and Central Asia.

With Aziz safely rescued, a Cambridge centre which keeps national records on ringed birds of prey was contacted, ownership traced to Mr Paterson, and the bird returned.

A RARE JEWEL beetle topped a range of "spectacular" invertebrates uncovered during a bug hunt in an Essex wood, it has been revealed.

Hainault Forest has been found to contain vast numbers of beetles, bugs and insects of which 149 are, at the very least, uncommon.

In all, some 940 species have been identified at the wood which is proving a magnet for creepy crawlies because it harbours so many elderly and dead trees.

The vivid, iridescent jewel beetle is well named because in some parts of the world its foreign cousins are indeed worn as jewellery.

The survey was undertaken by Dr Peter Kirby, one of the UK's leading invertebrate specialists, as part of a commission from The Woodland Trust.

Geoff Sinclair, spokesman for the Trust, said:"This survey confirms that Hainault Forest is an extremely valuable site for wildlife and our manage- ment work is helping to ensure that invertebrate numbers are maintained and increased."

A MAN SELLING his house in Norfolk has turned away a raft of prospective buyers who balk at sharing the property with his sitting tenant - a goose called Lucy.

Frank Aspey says he cannot contemplate letting the £190,000 home go to anyone unwilling to share it with the favourite pet of his late father.

COMPENSATION PAYMENT DELAYS in the wake of foot-and-mouth slaughter are pushing farmers to the wall, claims the Countryside Alliance.

The Alliance says farmers are being forced to wait up to 14 weeks before being paid for the compulsory purchase of their livestock despite MAFF promises to get payments to them in less than 16 DAYS.

MAFF has apparently blamed problems with its computer system for the delay but is thought to have seriously underestimated the task ahead.

Alliance chief executive Richard Burge said:"We have had contact with many farmers who are in serious financial trouble. They have had their livestock slaughtered and have no money coming in.

"They are utterly dependent upon the compul- sory purchase funds and are being pushed to the wall by this unjustifiable delay."

ROCKETING LEVELS OF countryside crime have led to pioneering moves by a county council to set up its very own rural police squad.

In a bid to get tough on rural crooks, Kent County Council is recruiting "crime wardens" to patrol the countryside following a barrage of complaints about normal policing.

The Tory-controlled authority wants the force to have its own red and black uniform to distinguish wardens from conventional police and will be paying tempting salaries of up to £35,000.

A dozen rural wardens will be taken on initially within the next six months - a force which will complement more than 60 new officers currently being drafted in by Kent Police to combat rising crime.

With so many rural communities in Britain feeling under siege from thieves and thugs, the formation of private country police squads could happen elsewhere if this one proves a success.

Kent is one of the worst parts of the country for rural crime and local police have been accused of incompetence for allowing crooks to escape.

In March, an outraged posse of residents tracked thieves to a house after a horse-box was stolen but police allegedly took so long to react that the community's best efforts were wasted.

Last November, Britain's first conference on rural crime and policing heard that the idyllic country image of yesteryear was fast vanishing under an onslaught from professional criminals.

Mark Hudson, of the Country Land and Business Association, told delegates:"The image of idyllic life is a superficial one. There are figures which suggest vehicle crime and crimes against people are increasing. The countryside is being used as a sponge to soak up problems elsewhere."

The Lincolnshire conference was organised by the Association of Chief Police Officers of England and Wales amid an upsurge of public anger about rural crime after farmer Tony Martin was jailed for life for killing a burglar.

GOLFERS TEEING OFF at a course in High Wycombe, Buckinghamshire, were amazed to spot a puma watching them from undergrowth.

And their fears were confirmed when plaster casts were taken of the big cat's prints.

Police and animal experts later combed the area but the beast had vanished.

POLICE HAVE RECOVERED the remains of a mallard duck and her eggs which appear to have been mown down by an Environment Agency workman on a tractor mower.

The remains of the sitting duck and her smashed eggs were found in freshly cut grass on a riverbank at Swaffham Lode near Cambridge by a shocked passer-by.

Ironically, it appears that the grass cutting was only carried out after the Agency had consulted the RSPB about the work.

Resident Lorley Moxon raised the alarm after making the gruesome discovery while out for a stroll with her husband.

Two police officers subsequently visited the riverbank to collect the shattered corpse and eggs as part of an ongoing inquiry into the incident.

The Environment Agency has pledged to give them all necessary assistance.

AN ALIEN SPECIES threatening to overrun parts of Devon and Cornwall is the target of a concerted Environment Agency attack.

But there is nothing out-of-this-world about Japanese knotweed - an invasive plant whose unremitting progress across the country is alarming environmentalists.

Conservation groups are joining district and county councils alongside the Environment Agency to repel the weed which reaches three metres high and is so strong it can grow through concrete and tarmac.

Agency spokesman Trevor Renals revealed: "Controlling Japanese knotweed is one of the most important challenges facing our environment, particularly in the South West.

"It grows relentlessly and excludes native species. It is vital that we bring its spread under control."

In Cornwall, great strides have already been made to tackle the 19th Century invader and success at one local site is said to show how careful use of herbicide can halt knotweed in its tracks.

The extent of its march in Devon is less clear and residents there are being urged to report sightings to the Devon Biological Record Centre.

A NEW NATIONWIDE poll aims to find which birds are the top of the hit parade when it comes to charming us with their songs.

The RSPB's Wake Up To Birds Week runs until June 1 with visitors to its website able to listen to top-rated songsters such as the blackbird and thrush - then vote.

"What is the birdsong you most like to wake up to?," said a spokesman.

"We want you to tell us by joining in on a UK-wide poll to discover the favourite bird songs across England, Scotland, Wales and Northern Ireland.

"Is it a song thrush or a blackbird, a wren or a robin? Listen to each of six familiar bird songs and choose which you like best. The results will be made public afterwards.

"Early morning is the best time to hear birds singing and spring is the best season.

"Birds are a delightful manifestation of the natural world that we live in. As they get on with their lives we are privileged to be able to enjoy them and that is what Wake Up To Birds Week is all about."

THE SPECTRE OF a second devastating wave of foot-and-mouth sweeping across Britain has loomed large despite Labour election campaign hopes that the disease was all but beaten.

A major new outbreak affecting about 20 farms in North Yorkshire and Lancashire emerged amid claims that Ministry of Agriculture figures showing an apparent decline in cases had been falsified to conceal the truth.

Fears were raised that the new outbreak, which centres on the Settle and Clitheroe areas, could mark the beginning of a localised disaster on a scale of that which hit neighbouring Cumbria where more than 700 of the UK's 1625 cases were eventually identified.

Sixty vets were reported to be converging on the region in a bid to quickly identify the full extent of the new outbreak and 1,000 farms were put in quarantine.

Worryingly, some of the infected animals appear to have been suffering from the disease for weeks, leading to heightened concerns that it may have spread outside the region into previously unaffected areas.

Meanwhile, the scale of the initial wave of the disaster continues to shock with MAFF reporting that more than three million animals have now been slaughtered or identified for slaughter.

NFU vice-president Michael Paske said:"There was much excitement last week about the fact that we had our first 24 hours with no cases since February. But the crop of new cases shows that we were right to be cautious about this news.

"Thankfully, the general trend in the disease is still downwards, confirming that the stringent control measures are working.

"But we are only too aware that there are going to be many more cases before we are finally clear. And this could still be months away. We are not out of the woods yet, by any stretch of the imagination.

"We would urge farmers and those connected with farming in both Settle and elsewhere to continue to observe the strictest disease control measures."

WOODLARKS ARE ON the up with numbers of breeding pairs rising significantly following careful conservation, reports the British Trust for Ornithology.

The birds, similar in size and shape to skylarks, have been mainly confined to southern British areas such as East Anglia with an overall total population now put at more than 1,500 pairs after a slump to less than 250 pairs in the mid-1980s.

FARMERS ARE BEING wrongly blamed for spreading foot-and-mouth disease to deflect attention from Labour's woeful handling of the crisis, claim Conservatives.

With Labour riding high in pre-election polls and boasting an apparently unassailable lead, Shadow Agriculture Minister Tim Yeo has gone on the warpath over the way farmers themselves are being targeted.

He believes it is more than coincidence that Labour is privately attacking farmers at a time when Government handling of the crisis is being increasingly questioned.

According to Mr Yeo, there had been a growing suspicion that the true scale of the disaster has been masked with hundreds of cases going unrecorded.

He has now written to Agriculture Minister Nick Brown telling him to put a stop to off-the-record briefings against farmers unless he has evidence of widespread malpractice.

He said:"When Britain's Chinese community was the victim of similar attacks, the Minister quite rightly condemned these attacks. He must now mount a similar defence of our farmers.

"So far, Mr Brown is more interested in defending the Government against allegations that foot-and-mouth statistics are being manipulated.

"There is a straightforward way of allaying suspicion and that is to allow an independent audit of all published and unpublished foot-and-mouth statistics."

He described Labour's refusal to hold a proper inquiry into the crisis as "contemptible".

SWANS HAVE BEEN fighting back against jet-ski joyriders disturbing their peace on the River Severn in Shropshire.

According to police, several clashes have occurred with one jet-skier knocked off his high-powered machine by a swan after disturbing its nest.

Jet-ski and motorboat owners have been warned by officers to reduce their speed recently or face being taken to court.

The river speed limit is 3mph but this is regularly flouted and it is not just swans and other waterbirds which have been suffering.

Riverside residents are also furious that the wash from speeding craft bursts into their gardens and threatens their blooms.

PARTY POLITICS ARE alienating the countryside and its communities, claimed the Countryside Alliance after the launch of its 32-page election policy guide 'The Real Rural Agenda'.

Alliance chairman John Jackson said:"There is something deeply wrong with the way our country is governed when individuals feel so remote from the democratic process that they join campaigning groups just to get politicians to listen.

"Our form of Parliamentary democracy is in trouble. That is why the membership of campaigning organisations such as the Alliance continues to rise. We alone have a growth rate of 25 per cent a year.

"Britain should have learned its lesson from the suffering of the mining communities following the decline of the mining industry.

"Mainly because of the crisis in farming, rural communities across the country are in deep trouble and face the same disintegration mining communities have undergone."

THE RSPCA HAS been blasted by hunt supporters for "misleading" the public with claims it could help rehouse thousands of hunting dogs if a hunt ban is enforced.

Foxhounds, lurchers, and terriers would all need new homes if they are not put down first following such a ban, says the Countryside Alliance.

The Alliance's attack came through its Campaign for Hunting arm following publication of the RSPCA's annual report in which it admitted destroying 500 healthy dogs in the last year because it could not find homes for them.

"In evidence to the Government Inquiry into Hunting with Dogs and elsewhere, the RSPCA has consistently claimed that it could assist in the rehoming of more than 20,000 hunting dogs which would be made redundant in the event of a ban," said a spokesman.

"This has already been contradicted by the National Canine Defence League and the Association of British Dogs and Cats Homes.

"The NCDL told Lord Burns that 'rehoming hounds can only be successfully arranged in a very few cases'. Likewise, the Association stated that it 'considers that the hounds and dogs currently employed with hunts would be almost impossible to rehome and that euthanasia would be an unacceptable alternative'.

"Also, only last month, Britain's leading dog organisation, the Kennel Club, concluded that a hunt ban would be damaging to dog ownership and welfare.

"The Club decided to oppose the Hunting Bill because 'it became increasingly aware that the direction in which the Bill and its supporters appeared to be moving was becoming more and more dangerous to the future of dogs generally'."

A HUNGRY SQUIRREL has been blamed for the disappearance of a church's communion wafers in Suffolk.

The peckish creature is believed to have broken into the belfry at St Peter's Church, Spexhall, before helping itself to the sacred crusts.

COUNCIL STAFF IN Exeter, Devon, were quick to react when two peregrine falcons began nesting in a local church tower.

After the predators produced chicks at St Michael's, the authority set up a raft of high-powered telescopes at a nearby car park so people could watch the action for free.

So far, the dramatic high-speed killers of prey such as grouse and pigeons have reportedly been settling for mice and voles as their snacks of choice.

A WARNING MESSAGE has gone out to country gamekeepers after the first conviction in Britain for shooting a hen harrier - probably our most persecuted bird of prey.

The keeper was convicted at Elgin Sheriff Court of illegally shooting a hen harrier in Morayshire, Scotland, last July.

According to the RSPB, he admitted killing the hen harrier, contrary to the Wildlife and Countryside Act 1981, and was fined £2,000.

Later, Duncan Orr-Ewing, RSPB Scotland's head of policy, said:"It is a horrible irony that this is the first successful prosecution for the crime of killing a hen harrier, because this is probably Scotland and Britain's most persecuted bird.

"They are a beautiful ground-nesting bird of prey, usually found on remote moorland, but they are also reviled by some gamekeepers because they compete with the guns by taking young grouse, and are systematically killed as a result.

"This has proved fatal for hundreds of hen harriers over the last decade, as adults are shot or poisoned and their nests and young trampled to death. Such crimes have proved virtually impossible to bring before the courts."

The RSPB says there are now only 520 pairs of hen harriers left in the UK, of which less than a dozen remain in England and these risk becoming extinct because of illegal killing.

A WHOLE RANGE of wild birds now depend on Britain's graveyards to help them survive, says the British Trust for Ornithology.

A 27-year survey of 15 cemeteries revealed they provide nest sites and food stops for more than 40 species, including some endangered birds.

Spotted flycatchers, bullfinches, and linnets were among declining species found to be hanging on thanks in part to their local graveyards.

Owls, woodcocks, hobbies and firecrests were among other feathered visitors shown to make special use of areas where humans are laid to rest.

The survey found that there are presently 20,000 acres of graveyard across England alone - a vital resource for wild birds and other creatures.

However, the Trust warned that wildlife was threatened by attempts to clean up cemeteries with a drive for neatness just the thing to drive birds away.

NATIVE CRAYFISH SHOULD benefit from scientific research aimed at warding off the threat posed to them by immigrant crayfish.

English Nature and the Environment Agency joined forces to look at ways of controlling or killing aggressive American signal crayfish which carry a virulent fungal disease and can introduce crayfish plague to our native species.

"Outbreaks of crayfish plague have wiped out entire sub-populations of native crayfish, displacing them from whole river catchments," said a spokesman for the Environment Agency.

BADGER FANS HAVE welcomed the prosecution of Rentokil after a badger was poisoned during pest control work.

At Aldershot Magistrates Court, the firm was fined £2,000 and ordered to pay costs of £350 following the death of the badger.

The company admitted causing another (its employees) to use a pesticide to kill a badger, contrary to the Food and Environment Protection Act 1986 and the Control of Pesticides Regulations 1986.

132

WREN: noisy mother staunch in defence of her young

TINY and furtive, there is something almost mouse-like about the wren as it goes about its daily hunt for food in bushes or hedgerows.

Still one of our commonest birds, it is no less charming for that.

Not as small or colourful as a goldcrest, its perky demeanour and stubby tail nevertheless endears the wren to most observers.

Weighing in at a mere 10 grammes, the wren punches well above its weight when singing or chattering in anger at an intruder.

Unlike the soft, almost imperceptible *'tseee tseee'* of the goldcrest, the harsh, rattling *'chitit'* of the wren often comes as a surprise when you realise the bird that made it is only 9cms long.

I was out birdwatching recently and happened to pass a wren's nest just as the fledglings emerged en masse to try their luck in the big bad world.

The scolding the mother wren gave me was impressive.

My presence obviously could not have come at a worse time.

But as her fledglings scattered into the surrounding undergrowth, the mother stayed close to the nest site, trying to divert my attention away from her vulnerable brood.

It was a brave action by what, despite its size, is one of the pluckiest of birds.

Shakespeare himself alluded to this fact when he wrote:"*The poor wren, the most diminutive of birds, will fight - her young ones in her nest - against the owl.*"

Even so, the mother wren I encountered was probably relieved when the towering human scrutinising her family finally moved on.

Feeding mostly on insects and some seeds, wrens often have a bigger battle than most birds to survive harsh winters. The fact that they always manage to come back after numbers are decimated by heavy frosts stands as a tribute to the innate toughness of the species.

Wrens lay five or six white, slightly speckled eggs, in deep, beautifully crafted nests at the base of trees or in any available crevice.

When I was too young and daft to know any better, I used to examine the eggs of bird species and remember the sheer snugness of the wren's nest above all others.

On a cold day, the warmth generated within its soft, domed construction was amazing.

Incidentally, daft as I was, I was never an egg stealer.

Even today, some people will nab eggs, put pinprick holes in them, remove the contents, then add the lifeless, empty shell to their illegal 'collection'.

Of course, they say they can admire the eggs far longer in this state but I've never understood the logic of that kind of admiration.

Any eggs I examined were safely returned.

However, in retrospect, it is always better to leave both eggs and nest untouched.

That way, there is much less danger of rejection by the mother bird.

ON another recent walk a large, perfectly black butterfly flew right across my path.

After some thought, it was probably a 'white admiral' which is mostly black on top with white bars and a rich brown beneath.

But the absence of any obvious markings made me wonder if this was a new strain.

Just as a panther is really a black leopard, could this have been a 'panther version' of a white admiral?

BRITISH ARABLE FARMERS are facing another cash nightmare thanks to the weakness of the slumping euro, it has been revealed.

Farmers' leaders say that if the currency fails to rise this month or - worse - continues to fall in value against the pound, farmers and growers could be left without a financial safety net.

NFU president Ben Gill said:"The continued slump of the euro against the pound is a grave cause for concern for the whole of the industry but particularly arable farmers at this critical time of year.

"After all the problems of the weather, the general disastrous state of incomes and the knock-on impact of foot-and-mouth, the last thing the industry needs is a slump in the euro to hit support payments.

"If the agri-money aid package is triggered - as seems likely - we will fight for it all the way."

Arable support payments are set in euros and then converted into sterling based on the average exchange rate in June of the preceding year, meaning every 1 per cent change in the exchange rate below last June's level is equivalent to a £16 million loss in farm income.

Last June, said the union, the average exchange rate was 62.87p per euro with the current rate around 60p per euro, amounting to a support reduction of more than £40 million.

If the euro does not strengthen by the end of this month, it will hit support payments so hard, warns the NFU, that a new agri-money package for UK arable producers could be made available from July.

Then ministers would need to act fast and not dither - farmers' payments of £22million compensation are still unclaimed by the UK.

A GRANNY HEN is baffling poultry experts by still laying eggs at the grand old age of 21 - 16 years beyond the normal life span for chickens.

The bird, named Grandma by owner Maria Bedford, has been making headlines in the poultry world and beyond with its amazing longevity.

Maria, who grabs a breakfast egg each day from beneath the Red Sett hen at Basingstoke, Hampshire, hopes to get Grandma mentioned in the Guinness Book of Records alongside other record breakers.

Vets are astonished by the age and egg-laying ability of the hen, said to be almost 550 years old in our terms.

Meanwhile, reports that human grannies have been caught scratching and pecking at the earth in Basingstoke since news of Grandma's exploits broke are thought to be false.

THE SECRET BEHIND the breeding success of a pair of nature reserve kingfishers has been revealed - drainpipe.

The birds, which bred again this year at Slimbridge Wildfowl and Wetlands Centre in Gloucestershire, have reserve manager Dave Paynter to thank following his brainwave of inserting pieces of drainpipe into a bank.

"Few birds are shyer than the kingfisher and the chances of seeing one of these magnificent birds in the wild are still very low," explained a spokesman.

"Dave Paynter specifically manages the river bank at South Finger to encourage the kingfishers to breed. Using short sections of drainpipe to line the tunnel to the nest site is an idea which has now been used around the country.

"With a purpose-built hide looking out over the area used by the kingfishers, excellent views of these stunning creatures can be had whilst they raise their offspring."

A FALCONER SWOOPED to the rescue when he saw a parrot being hawked around local streets by homeless people who wanted to sell it for £50.

Bird of prey expert John Pitson knew instinctively something was amiss and paid the £50 himself at Abingdon, Oxfordshire, to take the bird into care.

His misgivings proved correct when it was revealed that the parrot had gone missing almost a month ago from rightful owner Des Smith who lives on a boat on the Oxford Canal.

Frantic Mr Smith originally spent hours trying to track down his pet, Holly, and might never have seen it again had Mr Pitson not intervened following a tip-off from a friend.

The exotic pet was soon back with its owner who then reimbursed the sharp-eyed falconer.

RSPB NATURE RESERVES are now a vital lifeline to many threatened or declining bird species, the Society has revealed.

Its network of 168 nature reserves provide protection for more than one in 20 breeding pairs of the 40 species most at risk, while more than a third of all the UK's breeding bitterns, roseate terns and black-tailed godwits nest on RSPB land specially managed to benefit them.

Gareth Thomas, RSPB head of conservation management, said:"Most species on our reserves are either stable or are significantly increasing their populations.

"For example, more lapwings and redshanks are nesting on our land every year, which is in stark contrast to the dramatic national decline of these two species.

"Without the protection of RSPB nature reserves, many species of bird and other wildlife would be even more endangered.

"Our nature reserve network contains some of the UK's most threatened and precious habitats. The Society holds nine per cent of the nation's reed beds, Caledonian pine forests, saltmarshes and seasonally-flooded grasslands."

FARMERS' LEADERS HAVE attacked an anti-milk campaign aimed at British children but launched by American-based pressure group PETA.

The group, People for the Ethical Treatment of Animals, is distributing cartoon leaflets outside schools which claim cows' milk will make youngsters spotty and fat - a move the NFU called "scandalous".

HEALTH FEARS HAVE been raised over mass-produced chicken meat and eggs - sparking exasperation at what IS safe to eat after record numbers began deserting red meat.

In a week when it was revealed that more people than ever are choosing fish as their main source of protein following widespread anger over BSE and foot-and-mouth, the Soil Association issued its alarming report on poultry and eggs.

The Association asserts that 20 per cent of chicken meat and 10 per cent of eggs contain unacceptable levels of anti-microbial drugs, harmful to human health.

In a new report, it claims that Government regulators have seriously misled the public about the high incidence of dangerous drug residues found in chicken and eggs.

Richard Young, co-ordinator of the Soil Association campaign against overuse of antibiotics in intensive farming, said:"Despite repeated assertions by regulators that nearly all poultry products are free from detectable residues, figures show clearly that about 20 per cent of chicken meat and 10 per cent of the eggs tested contain residues of drugs deemed too dangerous for use in human medicine."

Of most concern are drugs used to control intestinal parasites in poultry and game birds such as nicarbazin, lascalocid and dimetrida-zole, all of which pose potential risks to animal or human health.

However, the Poultry Meat Federation has blasted the report as "deliberate scaremongering", calling it "blatant propaganda."

Drugs highlighted in the report had all been tested for safety within production, it asserted.

The British Egg Industry Council admitted that some eggs had become contaminated accidentally with small-scale residue introduced to feed.

Yet levels were apparently so miniscule that someone would have to eat 2000 eggs per day to face even a small risk to health.

BONKERS OVER CONKERS - councillors in Norwich have sparked outrage after planning to axe seven stately horse chestnut trees in a street amid fears that falling conkers are a danger to pedestrians and motorists.

TEN PINK GRASSHOPPERS have been discovered at the Jupiter Urban Wildfe Centre in Grangemouth, Scotland, where experts are examining a variety of theories for the normally green insects' change of colour.

AN INVESTIGATION HAS been launched into the mystery death of hundreds of young fish during repair work on flood defences at West Bay, Dorset.

The bay is defended against flooding by a sea wall and a set of gates between the harbour and the River Brit.

A spokesman for the Environment Agency said:"These gates are in urgent need of repair and contractors and Agency teams opened hatches on the defences to allow the river to drop enough to get access to the bottom of the gates.

"This procedure has been carried out on numerous occasions by both the Agency and the West Bay Harbourmaster.

"This time, the introduction of the river water into the harbour caused a dramatic reaction and hundreds of fish fry died.

"The Agency's pollution experts have been investigating and early suggestions are that compounds within the silts at the bottom of the harbour had been stirred up."

A BAT FOUND living in a disused mine in North Wales has been judged a record breaker by wildlife experts.

The two-year-old animal discovered in the Conwy Valley mine at Parc Mawr is thought to be the most northerly living greater horseshoe bat in Europe.

It had also travelled a record breaking distance of around 110 miles to its new home.

The male bat had been ringed as a baby, making it simple to trace its origins back to the Forest of Dean in Gloucestershire.

Bat expert David Priddis, who originally ringed the bat, confirmed:"The Conwy find is a new record for distance as well as the furthest North ever recorded. This particular bat has broken several records.

It was also the first baby born in 1999 - on June 19 - the earliest birth record ever for a greater horse-shoe bat."

The mine where the bat was found is home to lesser horseshoe bats, too, and conservationists are pressing for a grill to be placed across the entrance to protect them.

THE COUNTRYSIDE ALLIANCE has called on MAFF to respond "unequivocally" to rumours that it is planning a mass cull of livestock after the General Election.

Fears in rural communities across the country have been fuelled by reports that, in Mid-Wales, MAFF had allegedly been stockpiling a thousand tonnes of coal, railway sleepers, timber and straw for giant pyres, says the Alliance.

Huge burial pits were also allegedly being dug while hotels in Mid-Wales are reported to have been block booked by the Ministry for its staff.

Other reports concerned lorries massing in the Devon town of Hatherly, ready to transport animals to mass cull sites.

Alliance chairman John Jackson said people were becoming worried about what might lie ahead, especially as they had suffered so much.

He said:"This could just be a precautionary measure or the advance stages of a mass culling programme. However, these preparations are causing yet more worry and concern to rural people already on the edge of despair."

MAFF later denied planning a post-election mass cull.

THE GOVERNMENT HAS been accused of blundering into new problems over the foot-and-mouth crisis with its plan for a 20-day freeze on livestock movement.

Farmers' leaders view the proposal as another ill-judged knee-jerk reaction to a disease which refuses to lie down.

NFU president Ben Gill said:"The proposal has not been thought through properly. It would put the industry in a straitjacket.

"We agree that we cannot go back to where we were before foot-and-mouth but we need a well thought out package of measures to improve biosecurity.

"In addition, we must remember that the virus was brought into the UK from abroad and more attention also needs to be given to improving controls on meat and live imports."

Meanwhile, the disease has continued to dodge the best efforts of eradication teams to stamp it out.

Fresh cases have been reported in the Settle area of the Yorkshire Dales and others in the North York moors national park.

Every sheep from one of the country's rarest breeds could be culled as a result of the latest outbreak, which has now hit about 70 farms around Settle.

Officials from the Heritage Gene Bank travelled to a farm near Clitheroe in a bid to retrieve samples from Lonk rams, a breed of mountain sheep found only in Lancashire and now facing the abyss.

Elsewhere, over 1,500 sheep are reported slaughtered at five farms in Westerdale, near Whitby.

The crisis has devastated local farmers and the tourist trade.

BIRDWATCHERS HAVE been celebrating the first hatching of an osprey chick in England in 150 years.

The event, at Rutland Water in Leicestershire, increases hopes that ospreys will soon nest more regularly south of the Scottish border.

The RSPB says that more than 100 pairs of migrant ospreys currently nest in Scotland and the hatching of the first Rutland chick marks a milestone in the bird's return to England.

Wildlife experts reacted fast when osprey eggs were first sighted, throwing a security cordon round the nest to protect it from egg thieves.

Few clues were also initially given as to its location, except that it was somewhere in the northern part of England.

Before 1954, when a pair returned from Africa to breed at Loch Garten in Scotland and were given RSPB protection, ospreys had been extinct in Britain for over 50 years as a result of persecution by man.

ANIMAL RIGHTS PROTESTERS have attacked Oxford City Council for considering a scheme to allow horse-drawn tourist carriages onto the city streets.

Animal Aid, the UK's biggest animal rights group, has been co-ordinating a campaign to get councillors to drop the idea.

A spokesman said:"Whether pounding the streets in busy traffic or operating in pedestrianised areas, experience in other cities shows that horses pay a heavy price for this tourist gimmick.

"Studies conducted in the United States reveal that carriage horses suffer enormous lung damage as a consequence of living a 'nose to tailpipe' existence. Tracheal washes and samples from the respiratory secretions of these horses show the same signs of damage you would expect in a heavy smoker.

"There are also numerous documented cases of both animal and human injuries, sometimes fatal, after carriage horses have become 'spooked'.

"A survey of carriage horse accidents in the US revealed that 85 per cent of accidents were the result of an animal 'spooking'; in 70 per cent of accidents there was a human injury; in 22 per cent of cases there was a human death.

"Injuries and fatalities resulting from collisions between cars and carriage horses have occurred in almost every city in the US which allows carriage rides."

THE DANGER OF high-voltage cables was brought home in stark fashion to a squirrel and pigeon when both perished in dramatic accidents in different parts of the country.

In Telford, Shropshire, nearly 4,000 homes were blacked out when the luckless squirrel scaled an electicity pylon and brushed against the cable.

Homes and businesses were thrown into chaos for hours before the fault was traced to the scorched remains of the squirrel and the problem rectified.

Meanwhile, the driver of a Bedford to Streatham train suffered temporary blindness after the pigeon careered into an overhead cable and exploded in a fireball.

The driver had to be replaced for safety reasons because the intensity of the flash had left him with blurred vision.

The train itself was delayed for 25 minutes to allow repair work to be carried out.

THE COUNTRYSIDE ALLIANCE has pledged to work with the re-elected Labour Government for the good of rural communities.

Alliance chief executive Richard Burge said:"There is great fear and anxiety in the countryside. Rural people have concerns over many of the same issues as urban people such as health and education.

"But they also have the specific problem of how we rebuild and sustain our rural communities after many years of neglect by all Governments.

"It is our job to work with the Labour Government to implement the good things it promised in its manifesto - especially a Department of Rural Affairs - but to oppose any measure that threatens the liberty and livelihood of rural people.

"We need to ensure that rural people are of paramount importance in the radical reform that our countryside needs."

COUNTRYSIDE CAMPAIGNERS HAVE reacted cautiously to news that the head of the new rural affairs department is to be staunch anti-hunt MP Margaret Beckett.

Mrs Beckett, 58, will lead the Labour Government's newly formed Department for Environment, Food and Rural Affairs after voting for an outright ban on foxhunting recently.

Reading, caravanning and cooking are said to be her chief hobbies - not an overly inspiring combination for rural folk hoping someone more sympathetic to their needs would be appointed.

However, Countryside Alliance chief executive Richard Burge was generous in his praise.

"The Alliance has been promoting the idea of a department of rural affairs for over two years," he said.

"We are very pleased that the Government has finally created the department, and impressed that a politician with the seniority of Margaret Beckett has been put at its helm.

"But now the real work begins. We need to create genuine livelihood in the countryside. We need to make it a place where a person's right to choose their way of life is respected - where we have confidence that the future of rural communities will be of paramount importance during the period of tough decisions and radical change that we now face."

Mrs Beckett has been brought in to replace Nick Brown, widely criticised over his handling of the foot-and-mouth crisis and now demoted to a lesser role.

As well as overseeing the thorny hunting issue, she has been told to look at animal rights issues and environmental concerns.

Not surprisingly, her political instincts are leftward leaning and she is said to be a keen member of the Fabian Society, as well as a past supporter of CND, Amnesty International and the Anti-Apartheid Movement.

A LUCKY PIG lived to tell the tale after rooting out a live grenade left by troops during exercises on Salisbury Plain.

The fortunate porker apparently thought the grenade might be good to eat since it had already dug it free of mud before the alarm was raised.

The animal had found the grenade while going about its normal routine on farmland at Everleigh in Wiltshire.

Bomb disposal experts were brought in to salvage and then detonate the grenade after the area was cordoned off.

"The pig saved its own bacon because it did not do anything rash," quipped a local resident.

A MASSIVE BOOST of 100,000 fish has been given to the River Dee on the Clwyd/Cheshire border in a bid to help decimated stocks.

The one-year-old chub, dace, roach, bream and barbel were put into the Dee between Wrexham and Chester after being reared at an Environment Agency fish farm near Nottingham.

The new arrivals joined 50,000 other fish introduced earlier to help replace an estimated 100,000 fish wiped out in a devastating pollution incident on the river last July.

Eric Humphries, spokesman for the Welsh Federation of Coarse Anglers and a member of the Steering Group set up to oversee the recovery of the river, said:"This latest stocking is tremendous news for anglers on the River Dee whose sport has been so badly affected after the fish kill last summer.

"It will also help angling clubs and various local businesses, such as tackle shops, which rely on the money spent by both local and visiting anglers.

"Before the pollution, the River Dee was providing excellent fishing and I am sure that, if we all work in partnership with the Agency, we can provide a quality fishing experience again."

THE LEAGUE AGAINST CRUEL SPORTS has attacked the Countryside Alliance for allegedly exaggerating the cost of foot-and-mouth to hunt groups.

Although the Alliance says it has lost 20 per cent of a £250 million annual turnover, the League claims total income as revealed by the Burns Inquiry is only £15 million - or £235 million less.

League chairman John Cooper said:"There is a clear discrepancy in the figures here."

RAT AND CHICKEN killing contestants in TV show 'Survivor' could face retribution from animal rights protesters after a contestant from the American version of the series was attacked.

Michael Skupin was badly pepper-sprayed by an activist in Missouri after being featured killing a pig to stave off starvation.

American animal welfare groups, such as People for the Ethical Treatment of Animals (PETA) - now increasingly active in Britain - had criticised Mr Skupin for killing the pig.

Back home the threat posed by animal rights activists was highlighted when over 300 members of the Masters of Foxhounds Association gathered earlier this month for their AGM.

Chairman Lord Daresbury paid a particular tribute to the Old Surrey, Burstow and West Kent Hunt and listed a number of incidents involving abuse and intimidation.

He said:"We cannot overestimate the fortitude of people who face death threats in pursuit of the right to hunt lawfully and peacefully in their communities."

A WILDLIFE OASIS designed by landscape gardener Alan Sargent has won a major prize at this year's BBC Gardeners' World Live Show.

Judges were so impressed with the countryside-inspired garden that they awarded it the Royal Horticultural Society's Silver Floral Medal in the Show Gardens category.

Mr Sargent had been commissioned to design a country scene illustrating how landowners can help wildlife thrive.

A COLONY OF huge red spiders sparked a safety alert after being discovered by workmen beneath the Queen Mother's weekend home in Berkshire.

The mystery spiders are said to be three and a half inches long, venomous, and with jaws strong enough to pierce human skin.

Shocked BT engineers retreated when they came across the unusual spiders while working beneath the Royal Lodge in Windsor.

Despite concerns about a possible threat to the elderly Queen Mother, entomologists have been delighted by the find.

Some believe the spiders may be a new species or a new strain of an established one such as the woodlice eating Dysderid Spider.

Expert Graham Smith explained:"It is an extremely exciting find because they are probably a new species or a species we thought had been extinct in this country for thousands of years.

"Who knows how long they have been in the royal park because they live underground. There could be thousands of them. It would be no surprise if they are underneath Windsor Castle itself."

Not being bitten by the spiders was one of the main aims at the moment, he said.

The rusty red spiders had an aggressive nature and were willing to attack at the slightest provocation.

"The species is certainly venomous and the jaws are strong enough to penetrate human skin. It will take a few days before we can work out how dangerous they are," added Mr Smith.

A two-year operation is anticipated before all the spiders lurking beneath the Lodge can be tracked down and captured.

MORE THAN 150,000 young salmon will help Old Father Thames teem with new life.

Environment Agency fisheries officers introduced the mass of fish fry to the River Lambourn and River Kennet, tributaries of the River Thames, to give them the best possible start in life.

Both waterways were chosen as they rate among the highest quality chalk streams in the country and offer excellent natural habitat for salmon to spawn.

Salmon project manager Darryl Clifton-Dey said:"Stocking the Thames with these juvenile fish is extremely important because it will encourage adult salmon to colonise areas of the river where they are most likely to spawn successfully.

"Salmon are creatures of habit and always return from the sea to where they originated to start the life cycle off once again."

The 10-week old fry were reared from eggs at Starsholt College near Winchester, Hampshire, and are part of a 20-year effort to revitalise the Thames.

THE RSPCA HAS urged new rural affairs minister Margaret Beckett MP to back measures which could make life better for millions of pigs across Europe.

Many of the 120 million pigs reared in EU countries each year are kept in appalling conditions that cause them severe distress and suffering, claims the Society.

It says many breeding sows outside the UK suffer bone weakness and muscle wastage because they spend most of their lives in narrow, individual stalls that are so small they are unable to turn around.

The Commission had proposed that sows should be kept in stalls for the first four weeks of their pregnancy - but the European Parliament insisted this should be reduced to just the first seven days and that the stalls should be large enough for the animals to turn around.

Dr Julia Wrathall, deputy head of the RSPCA's farm animals department, said:"We are delighted by the welfare improvements that the European Parliament has put forward. If implemented, these measures would make a significant difference to the lives of millions of pigs across the EU.

"We are now urging our Secretary of State to listen to the views of this democratically elected body."

A PIED WAGTAIL became the butt of mechanics' jokes after making a nest from cigarette ends under the axle of a disused truck.

But the kind-hearted New Forest workers came to the mother bird's aid when her nest was threatened by the truck's impending removal.

Plans had been made for the ancient vehicle to be sold at auction but these were abandoned and the nest site closed off to protect the mother bird and her brood.

According to the mechanics, the wagtail seems oblivious to the racket their tools make as it concentrates on its own job in hand.

HUNT SUPPORTERS HAVE attacked what they claim is a bogus interpretation of a MORI poll on hunting published in a magazine.

The Countryside Alliance has challenged an animal welfare group to explain its calculations of figures of those opposing hunting.

The International Fund for Animal Welfare claimed that the poll showed that 65 per cent of the population wanted a hunting ban but the Alliance says the true results showed that only 57 per cent of those actually questioned preferred a ban, 31per cent opposed a ban and 11 per cent answered 'don't know'.

The Alliance claimed IFAW had deleted the 'don't knows' and recalculated the remainder to increase the figure from 57 to 65 per cent.

Simon Hart, director of the Countryside Alliance's Campaign for Hunting, said:"This is a dishonest approach. The findings of the MORI poll are nearly 20 per cent down on their 1997 figure, indicating as other polls have, a considerable decline in support for a ban.

"IFAW have been caught fiddling the figures to prop up their flagging campaign. In a recent NOP poll for the Countryside Alliance, where the public were given the same choice as Parliament (the options to ban, regulate or supervise), only 37 per cent voted for a ban, the remainder preferring some system of regulation or supervision."

HUNT GROUPS ARE pressing for a resolution to the hunting impasse as Labour MPs angrily resume demands for the sport to be outlawed - outraged at Tony Blair's last minute decision to drop a second anti-hunting Bill from the Queen's Speech.

With Labour MPs threatening open revolt, the UK's nine hunting Associations told the Middle Way Development Committee that any solution must be "affordable, enforceable and truly independent."

Speaking on behalf of the Associations - which include the Masters of Foxhounds Association, the National Coursing Club, and the Masters of Deerhounds Association - Alastair Jackson said:"What is needed is an authority which gives the public confidence in what we do, which focuses on animal welfare issues and which is not vulnerable to political interference.

"We recognise that we have a duty to take account of concerns raised by the Burns Inquiry and by the public. We have addressed these issues.

"The original Middle Way Group proposals could have led to impractical regulations. These would have caused unnecessary bureaucracy and presented enormous difficulties not only to those involved in hunting, but sections of the public too."

THE COUNTRYSIDE AGENCY is giving the chance for 200 communities across England to create 'greens' on their own doorsteps in a new £13million initiative.

But what a green should be is open to wide interpretation, according to the Agency.

The greens could be anything from derelict pieces of land regenerated for community events, wildlife gardens, small orchards, or just places to sit and chat.

Countryside Agency board member Luna Frank-Riley said:"It is undoubtedly the case that having a green area where people can relax and play is good for the body and soul.

"The Countryside Agency's Millennium Greens initiative, which worked with 250 communities to create permanent greens to mark the millennium, has shown that projects of this nature unite a community, giving people a common sense of purpose and achievement.

"The beauty of this scheme is that it is up to a community what their green space looks like and how it is used.

"It will be tailor-made to meet the leisure needs of local people.

"We are now inviting applications from those communities who would like to improve their local environment by creating a Doorstep Green.

"Applications need to have strong local support, the green must be safely accessible for everyone and be open during the day, as well as involving the wider community in its design, creation and long-term care."

JUST LIKE BUSES, none come along for 150 years and then in the space of a month English osprey chicks appear at two different sites.

Following the celebration of osprey young hatching at Rutland Water, Leicestershire, birdwatchers were delighted by new offspring at Thornthwaite Forest near Keswick in the Lake District.

Forestry Minister Elliot Morley, a keen birdwatcher himself, visited the Cumbrian site to open a special Osprey Viewpoint for the public.

He said:"This is fantastic news. It is more than 150 years since ospreys last nested in England and now this is the second pair to hatch out chicks this month!

"These magnificent birds are bound to attract attention both locally and nationally and are likely to give a substantial boost to the economy of the Lake District, attracting people from far and wide.

"The Forestry Commission, the Lake District National Park authority and the RSPB have all done a tremendous job in watching over this delicate venture. I know that it represents the culmination of several years work."

RSPB North of England regional director Andy Bunten added:"We are especially grateful to the local police for providing so much support and back-up during a lengthy operation to protect the nest from disturbance and egg theft."

NEW BALLS PLEASE - so that harvest mice can use them as homes after this year's Wimbledon is over.

Officials have agreed to donate all the balls from the tournament to a scheme being run by The Wildlife Trusts.

Harvest mice's woven homes are similar in size and shape to tennis balls and previous schemes have found the hollow balls to be very effective as replacements.

With a small hole drilled in one side, harvest mice are able to build a snug new home and steer clear of their many enemies such as owls and foxes.

Intensive farming has gradually put pressure on the once common mice which are now under threat as never before.

It is hoped that balls donated by the All England Lawn Tennis Club will help the tiny creatures to flourish again.

THE RSPCA HAS unveiled its latest report into animal abuse with the startling claim that "cruelty to animals is inherent in society."

A spokesman said:"During 2000, the RSPCA responded to nearly 1.6 millions calls for help, witnessed appalling cases of animal cruelty and saw a nine per cent rise in the number of people prosecuted for harming animals."

In one rural case, a two-month-old female piglet was "chased and savagely beaten to death by a gang of teenagers on a farm in Wiltshire.

"The terrified creature was let out of her pen, chased around a field and repeatedly struck with rocks, a four-foot metal bar and a wooden pointed stake, during the incident at Tisbury last April.

"The attack lasted half an hour and ended when one of the gang threw a heavy rock on the dying animal's head. A post mortem revealed multiple skull fractures."

Four boys aged 14 to 16 were later caught and prosecuted.

QUARRYING FIRMS WHICH wreck the countryside should take a tip from two firms which have reined in their operations, says the Ramblers Association.

Environmental concerns prompted Imerys and Watts Blake Bearne to abandon china clay quarrying rights which would have hit Dartmoor National Park, revealed the Association.

Both firms now intend to relinquish planning permission that would have extended their current operations to within the park following an environmental assessment backed by archaeological and ecological evidence.

The Ramblers Association and other groups have long campaigned for an end to clay quarrying on Dartmoor due to the "extreme visual and environmental damage" it causes.

The announcement means the threat of large-scale damage to an area in the south west of the cherished national park is now lifted.

RA countryside protection campaigner Emily Richmond said:"We are delighted with the news, and congratulate Imerys and Watts Blake Bearne on taking this responsible course of action.

"Quarrying has posed a threat to Dartmoor for years and we are thrilled that these permissions have been given up.

"National park status is granted to protect those landscapes of Britain which are of outstanding natural quality. This protection should ensure that such beautiful areas are preserved for all to enjoy, and yet quarrying continues to destroy parts of our most valued countryside.

"We therefore urge the quarrying industry as a whole to follow the good example set by Imerys and Watts Blake Bearne, and reduce the extensive damage done by quarrying in all national parks."

A DISORIENTATED DOLPHIN has been dodging boats in the River Thames at the height of London's tourist season.

Police and the RSPCA monitored the creature which was seen as far up the river as Blackfriars Bridge and beyond.

Experts believe the bottlenose dolphin may be ill and came into the river from the sea looking for a place to beach itself.

A rescue attempt may be made if the animal comes to rest at an accessible spot.

Dolphins have been sighted several times close to UK beaches during the hot spell, including a group of about eight off Brighton beach in Sussex.

BEAUTY IS ONLY skin deep to an orphaned foal which was dressed in the skin of a dead foal in order to be accepted by the dead foal's mother.

The orphaned foal Hope lost her mother to colic when she was just a week old while mare Dibbley lost her own foal during a tragic birth accident.

The pining pair were brought together at Blackpool, Lancashire, with the skin of the dead foal wrapped around Hope to avoid a vicious response.

After Dibbley had suckled her new charge for two days without protest, Hope's second skin was taken off and the pair now act like any normal mother and foal.

SEVEN ANCIENT BROADLEAF woods in Wales are to be restored to their former glory in a £650,000 project undertaken by The Woodland Trust.

Most of the woods were planted with conifers in the last century or became choked with rhododendrons, destroying natural habitat for wildlife.

A Trust spokesman explained:"Ancient woodland sites are those which have been continuously wooded since the Ice Age. They represent one of our most valuable and threatened wildlife habitats.

"Yet between the 1930s and the 1960s it was forestry policy to plant them with alien conifers, creating a dense canopy which smothers the native forest flora.

"On many sites, this coniferisation has never produced economic benefits and by reversing the process we can reclaim our native woodland heritage and prepare the way for the sustainable production of hardwood in the future."

The woods that will be restored are at Parc Mawr, Rowen, Conwy; Marl Hall Woods, Llandudno, Conwy; Coed y Gopa, Abergele, Conwy; Coed Nant Gwernol, Abergynolwyn, Gwynedd; Coed Ystrad, Carmarthen; Dyffryn Woods, Bryncoch, Neath; and Graig Fawr, Margam, Port Talbot.

A SHETLAND PONY astonished its new owners at a farm near Penrith, Cumbria, by giving birth to a half-zebra foal.

The pony, named Tilly, had previously been kept in a field with a male zebra at a wildlife park.

OTTERS ARE TAKING a bite of city life after being spotted for the first time swimming through Newcastle, Glasgow, and Birmingham.

REBELLION IS GROWING among Labour MPs left outraged after Prime Minister Tony Blair dropped the promised Bill to ban foxhunting from his second term in Government.

Despite all expectations, the Queen's Speech failed to pledge the return of the controversial Bill which ran out of time before the General Election after being defeated in the Lords.

Instead, a free vote on the issue is being scheduled which might be on a Commons motion bearing no legal weight.

As usual, the rebels are being galvanised by arch anti-hunt London MP Tony Banks.

More than 150 Labour MPs are reported to have demanded a ban on foxhunting within 12 months or they will stage a revolt against Mr Blair.

However, leaks by Government insiders have apparently shown the Prime Minister is desperate to put foxhunting on the back burner as it creates so much uproar for such small political gain.

PIGEON: cruelty of wig wearer ended many lives

IF a foreign tourist was asked to name a typical British bird after visiting London they would in all likelihood plump for the pigeon.

I doubt if British people themselves would make such a choice but pigeons have become so synonymous with London that for many tourists a trip to the capital would seem incomplete without a "*me-with-pigeons-in-Trafalgar-Square*" snapshot.

I suppose the pigeons themselves are happy with this arrangement.

I haven't been to Trafalgar Square to see how many remain following recent attempts to scale down their numbers.

But I would imagine there are still a fair few around.

Even when I was there last time, dishing out my own pot of tourist bird seed, I couldn't help feeling a little depressed. Several birds looked diseased or, at least, distinctly ill.

Urban pigeons have an impressive background and are descended from the rock dove, one of the hardiest of birds, whose offspring have also evolved into the modern racing pigeon.

Wild rock doves still eek out a precarious existence on remote coastal cliffs where the biggest danger is not being stepped on by a fat foreign tourist but being gobbled up by a hawk.

We've become so used to seeing pigeons flapping round our rail stations and town centres that we often overlook how handsome they are.

Although mostly grey, black and white, a pigeon's neck boasts a startlingly attractive multi-coloured sheen.

Urban pigeons generally lay two white eggs in a rough nest high up on a building.

But compare this to the habits of their bigger, more colourful cousin, the woodpigeon.

This builds its nest in woodland and is a little warier of man - a wise move as thousands are shot each year as game.

Other birds which are wilder than urban pigeons but part of the same family are the turtle dove, stock dove, and my own favourite, the collared dove - slimmer, pinker, and more delicate looking than the rest.

I was lucky enough to see a couple of these in the garden the other day and it's little wonder doves are associated with peace. Just observing them made me feel, well, strangely peaceful.

As a student, I used to work in factories during the summer months to earn some cash and one of these ghastly places will forever be associated with pigeons in my mind - although hardly for peaceful reasons.

At this particular hell-hole, I came across one of the cruellest people I have ever known, a lumbering lunatic sporting an ill-fitting wig.

This was in a section of the factory where various pieces of machinery were lowered on chains into a huge vat of industrial acid for cleaning.

So deadly was this stuff that jets of air were arranged around the lip of the vat to blow back fumes.

A small flight of steps brought you to the edge of this bubbling cauldron and I was tentatively gazing down on my first day when someone whacked me between the shoulder blades.

"*You wouldn't last long in there, mate,*" chortled Mr Wig-head, leering.

Most people with a bad reputation rarely live up to it.

This character did. He'd done time for a sex crime involving an old lady and had various unpleasant habits.

More than anything, however, he hated the pigeons that fluttered harmlessly around the factory and conducted a private, bloody war against them.

His favourite trick was to switch off the big extractor fan high up on the wall at night. Come morning, he would quietly check to see if any pigeons had flown between its blades to roost in the chamber behind.

If they had, he would immediately switch the fan on again without giving them prior warning.

Some pigeons made it out through the blades before they picked up speed. Others were horribly killed.

Of course, Mr Wig-head always claimed it was an accident and this was well before today's better vigilance against such cruelty. So he got away with it.

By the end of that summer I could have tipped him wig-first into the acid and skipped out of the factory with a song in my heart. The pigeons would have cheered.

A SUMMER CAMPAIGN against hunting has been launched - just as animal welfare chiefs come under a barrage of criticism about their own organisations.

The RSPCA and League Against Cruel Sports, both fiercely opposed to hunting, have been attacked by former members for the way they manage their affairs.

Olympic champion and hunt supporter Richard Meade, ousted from the RSPCA recently for trying to modify its vehement anti-hunt stance, has led a protest against what he sees as its increasingly extremist views.

Mr Meade, who was accused of trying to recruit thousands of hunt supporters to the Society's ranks, said:"The RSPCA council is dominated by the views and personalities of the animal rights movement. Militant vegetarianism has overtaken reason."

He also warned that the Society's position could become even more extreme in future with livestock farmers likely to face open condemnation.

Meanwhile, the League Against Cruel Sports has just unveiled a new campaign film dubbed 'Chaos in the Countryside - the Secret Face of Hunting Exposed.'

A spokesman said:"The video, an unprecedented collection of footage taken by League investigators and others, powerfully exposes the secret face of hunting with dogs which supporters of the pastime would prefer left unreported - from covert film of badger and fox baiting to the shocking realities of deer and foxhunting, hare coursing and hunt violence.

"The film is very different from the glossy facade of hunting so often championed by its chief proponents."

However, the League was recently plunged into controversy itself when its former chief executive Graham Sirl said he now accepted that hunting stags on Exmoor was part of deer management.

Mr Sirl, who went on to set up the alternative National Animal Welfare Society, has since been challenging the League to modify its views.

His new organisation has also mounted an attack over the League's decision to employ a former hunt saboteur, previously jailed for demo activities, as a press spokesman.

POLICE AND VILLAGERS joined forces at Cheriton Bishop, Devon, when a herd of buffalo went walkabout after escaping from their field. All the animals were collected and returned unharmed.

BRITISH HOUNDS AND country produce captured the eye at a game show attended by 80,000 people in France.

The Countryside Alliance says members enjoyed a successful weekend on their stand at the 20th French Game Fair, held in the park of Francois I's Loire chateau of Chambord.

"The main themes this year were the hounds and the French Hunt ceremony," said a spokesman."Visitors were greeted with a breathtaking exhibition of over 4,000 hounds and terriers in more than 300 purpose built kennels that demonstrated nearly every breed and type of working hound in France today.

"The majority of main ring displays involved the judging and parading of hounds from both mounted and foot packs. In addition, a considerable amount of horn blowing took place. It is an important and popular part of the French hunting culture.

"Sunday morning started with a Mass of St Hubert in the Grand Ring, attended by hunt staff in uniform each parading a single hound. Watched by thousands of people, the Bishop gave an address highlighting the veneration in which hunting and hounds are held.

"The Alliance stand included otterhounds from Wales, beagles from the Brittania beagles, a duckpunt and wildfowling display, sporting art by Daniel Crane and Ann Seward, fly-tying with Charles Jardine, a selection of preserves and bottled goods, and a wealth of display literature that covered all of the Alliance's broad range of campaigns and interests.

"Richard Burge, chief executive of the Alliance, attended and spent his time touring the show, meeting members of French associations and welcoming visitors to the Alliance's stand."

TWO OTTERS USED their intelligence and playfulness to 'jail' their keeper at a wildlife centre in the Lake District.

The pair snatched keys belonging to keeper Warren Crutchley after he had just locked himself in their enclosure at the Aquarium of the Lakes attraction.

Despite his pleas and offers of food, otters Smudge and Filly disappeared with the keys into their pool.

Colleagues were eventually alerted and Mr Crutchley was freed after half an hour of captivity.

To prevent any more jailings, the otters have now been given their own keys to play with.

RED KITE CHICKS can be studied for the first time in their nest via an internet webcam, English Nature has revealed.

"The red kite is one of our most stunning birds of prey with a wonderfully graceful and effortless flight," said a spokesman."Once a familiar sight across much of England, it was wiped out by the end of the 1800s after enduring centuries of persecution.

"English Nature, together with partner organisations including Forest Enterprise and the RSPB, has worked hard to restore the species.

"Now, after more than 10 years of releasing young red kites in England, breeding populations are well established in the Chilterns in southern England and in the East Midlands.

"The webcam, broadcasting from a secret location in Rockingham Forest, reveals the two chicks' life in the nest."

A DIRE WARNING has been given on the state of British farming with farmers said to be desperate for financial aid as thousands face the abyss.

With 51,000 jobs already lost to the industry in the last two years, NFU president Ben Gill says the result of foot-and-mouth may be thousands of new redundancies.

Latest available statistics showed average earnings of just £5,200 per farmer, he said, with total borrowings rising to a new high of more than £10 billion.

The income from the whole of farming was also £3 billion less than it was five years ago at £1.88 billion.

Cereal producers had fared just as badly as livestock farmers, he revealed, since last year's floods meant that the harvest this year could be down by four million tonnes, hitting incomes further.

Mr Gill said:"We are halfway through the year and what a disaster it has been so far. At the Royal Show last year we thought things were bad - but foot-and-mouth has taken us out of the frying pan and into the blast furnace.

"If we are to get through the next six months and into 2002 we will need a clear recovery programme. We are working on this with the new Department of Environment, Food and Rural Affairs.

"But we also know that, at the end of the day, the only way we will ever really recover is to focus even more on the marketplace. Only then can we put the profit back into farming and turn today's depressing statistics into something to be proud of."

The NFU is pressing for a recovery programme that will include prompt payment by the Government of the £34million 'agri-money' package currently triggered for arable farmers.

The union also wants to see dramatic improvements in import controls to stop foot-and-mouth ever happening again.

And it believes emergency measures are necessary to help sheep farmers cope with the disappearance of their export market, includ-ing a swift addressing of the desperate need for sheep movements.

SUPERSTORE GIANT TESCO is to buy addi-tional British lamb this year to help prevent the sheep industry going into meltdown, it revealed.

The company has pledged to take some of the two million "light" lambs reared for an export market which currently does not exist due to foot-and-mouth.

UP TO 250,000 fish are feared dead following a major pollution incident near Uttoxeter in Staffordshire.

Environment Agency investigators rushed to the scene after being alerted that a substantial amount of pollutant - possibly farm slurry - had contaminated Picknall Brook running into the River Dove.

Up to six kilometres of the fish rich brook is believed to be affected and the incident is thought to be a disaster which could take months to put right.

Rare water voles which live in the area are also at risk.

Meanwhile, in a similar crisis, mature sea trout and salmon were among hundreds of fish thought to have died in a pollution incident in Wales.

Environment Agency officers have been probing a section of the River Aeron, upstream of Aberearon in Ceredigion, after it was hit.

River water and fish samples have been taken to laboratories in Llanelli for analysis with full scale fisheries and biological surveys started to measure the full impact of the incident.

Environment protection officer Hannah Wilkinson said:"It is crucial that anyone storing, handling or treating polluting materials takes extra care at this time of the year. Even minor spillages of polluting liquids can have a major impact when there is so little water in the rivers for dilution and when fish are restricted to deeper pools and cannot escape pollutants."

SCOTTISH BIRDWATCHERS FLOCKED to a remote spot when news broke of the arrival of a feathered visitor not seen in their country for a century - a whiskered tern.

Huge excitement greeted the arrival of the elegant seabird, which is greyer than other terns, after it touched down at a loch near Collieston in Aberdeenshire.

Normally inhabiting southern Europe, the whiskered tern has been spotted several times in England but Scottish birdwatchers had been denied a sighting for 100 years.

The bird is thought to have arrived within a flock of other terns which had flown all the way from Africa as part of normal migration.

THE SOIL ASSOCIATION has joined forces with hundreds of other organisations to promote the Organic Food and Farming Targets Bill.

The Bill calls for the Government to pledge that 30 per cent of agricultural land in England and Wales would be given over to organic produce by 2010; 20 per cent of the food we consume would be organic by 2010; and organic food would be accessible to many more people.

"Getting the Bill adopted would make the Govern-ment take the organic farming industry seriously," said a spokesman.

"At present, Government spending on organic farming schemes comprises only 0.6 per cent of its total agricultural budget.

"We are importing over 70 per cent of our organic food but much of it can be produced here, helping local communities.

"The farming industry is in crisis but organic farming, being a profitable industry, could reverse the economic decline."

THE BATTLE FOR the hearts and minds of Britain's schoolchildren has intensified with the launch of two classroom education packs by the Countryside Alliance.

Titled 'Waters Matters', the Gone Fishing campaign pack is in direct contrast to recent drives by animal rights groups such as PETA which have tried to steer youngsters away from "cruel" angling.

This pack, made available to primary school teachers, focuses on issues such as wildlife, life cycles of fish, and angling itself. A separate Alliance pack, 'Our Countryside Matters', is aimed at older students.

Charles Jardine, director of Gone Fishing, said they wanted "to give primary school children an introduction to Britain's waterways - to teach them that some of Britain's most beautiful landscapes would not exist if not for the angling community.

"The health of hundreds of species of wildlife is dependent on a clean environment which is nurtured and protected by angling clubs, water bailiffs and conservationists.

"It is important that the younger generation understands this. I learned to fish as a child and have loved it all my life. It is saddening to think that the average age of a fisherman is now 48.

"Hopefully, the pack will play a positive role and encourage children to take an interest in angling and conservation - and get out there and fish."

Recently, TV pet show presenter Wendy Turner-Webster - sister of more famous Anthea - appealed to the Duke of Kent in his capacity as president of the Scout Association to retire the Scouts' angling proficiency badge on the grounds of cruelty.

Writing on behalf of PETA - People for the Ethical Treatment of Animals - vegan Wendy asserted that killing fish was inconsistent with the Scouts' wholesome reputation.

The letter appealed to the Duke to "put the violent pastime of fishing behind us and teach children to respect rather than kill wildlife."

A NATIONAL CENSUS has been organised to look at the prickly problem of hedgehog decline.

Numbers of the popular mammal are thought to be falling because of various factors such as loss of habitat and growing scarcity of their favourite foods.

Thousands of volunteers are being recruited to take part in an extensive survey during the summer.

The Mammal Trust, which is behind the census, has admitted that regional population numbers are a mystery.

TV wildlife expert Chris Packham said:"Hedgehogs are unique among mammals and this survey will be vital in ensuring we can conserve them."

FEARS HAVE BEEN raised that dangerous mako sharks may be breeding in British waters after a 33-inch juvenile was reeled in off the Cornish coast.

Rising sea temperatures are thought to be behind angler John Lock's catch off Looe while taking part in a specialist shark fishing event.

Mako sharks, which can reach 12ft, are thought to be the fastest fish in the seas and have a reputation for attacking and sometimes eating humans stranded miles offshore.

Like their larger cousin, the great white, they are aggressive and have been known to launch furious assaults on fishermen's boats after being hooked.

SEAGULLS ARE FAST becoming Public Enemy no.1 on the South Coast this summer after a spate of incidents - the latest involving almost 100 ducklings.

The ducklings were hacked to death and eaten in a series of attacks by voracious herring gulls at a park in Truro, Cornwall, despite efforts to protect them.

Earlier, the death of a Yorkshire terrier in Brixham, Devon, made national headlines after the dog was found to have suffered a fatal peck.

But several humans have also been attacked with a Devon grandmother needing treatment for a head wound.

Apart from the ducklings taken as food, most other attacks have been blamed on gulls' ferocious protective instincts regarding their young chicks, especially when they fall from nearby nests.

However, locals are baffled by one incident in Llandudo, North Wales.

There a seagull pounced and flew off with an elderly man's false teeth left to dry on a window ledge!

A BOTTLENOSE dolphin spotting dodging boats in the Thames recently has been found dead after beaching itself on a bank at Wapping.

Dolphins are known to do this when illness or advanced age mean they can no longer support their own body weight in the water.

A TWO-YEAR extension has been announced to the Forestry Commission's special grant scheme which promotes new native woodland in England's national parks.

Forestry Minister Elliot Morley said:"This scheme has been a great success.

"More than 1,000 hectares of new native woods have already been created.

"These new woodlands will form important networks of habitats for our wildlife and further enhance these unique landscapes.

"They will increase woodland cover and, at the same time, encourage community support, public access and recreation.

"The Commission has worked very closely with the National Parks and English Nature.

"This is an excellent example of partnership working at its best."

The New Native Woodlands in England's National Parks Challenge Fund has been running for four years.

It has a total investment of more than £3million of Government grant aid from the Forestry Commission.

The sheer enthusiasm of park staff is said to have played a key role in helping make the scheme a success.

FATIGUE IS THOUGHT to have played a role in a horrific accident which saw a farmer killed as crippling work pressure continues to undermine the entire industry.

Jim Combellack, in his 40s, slipped into the revolving blades of a huge mechanical plough as his young son looked on at their farm in Victoria, Cornwall.

But with an investigation launched into exact events surrounding the accident, farmers' leaders have revealed many farmers are now working 80-hour weeks in a desperate bid to make ends meet.

Farm suicides were also recently shown to be on the rise as some farmers give up trying to overcome a massive workload for little or no return.

The prospects for many UK hill farmers now appear so bleak that a special NFU delegation recently met EC officials in Brussels to raise concerns.

The delegation led by William Jenkins, chairman of the NFU's Less Favoured Areas Committee, highlighted issues such as the impact of foot-and-mouth movement restrictions on hill producers.

Mr Jenkins said:"Hill farmers are desperately concerned about their prospects this autumn. We usually export most of our smaller hill lambs but our export market is closed. We also sell our store lambs and breeding stock through the network of auction markets, but these cannot operate currently. It is clear that we will need help from the UK Government and the European Commission to overcome these marketing problems."

A RISE IN the number of ponies being abandoned may be due to many being sold at ultra-cheap prices, says the RSPCA.

A group of 12 New Forest-type ponies were recently rescued by the Society after being discarded in a field in Surrey.

The ponies, which the RSPCA set about rehousing after lengthy treatment, had been found in an emaciated state and suffering from a variety of health problems following their abandonment in a field at Leatherhead.

Surrey's RSPCA chief inspector Martin O'Sullivan said:"Unscrupulous dealers are able to buy foals for as little as £5 in the hope of making a huge profit by selling them on as children's ponies.

"Sadly, in order to achieve these profits, they are often prepared to skimp on paying for feed, veterinary costs and suitable grazing and shelter, and will simply walk away if things get too expensive.

"There appears to be overbreeding which has created oversupply and this, coupled with falling demand for these ponies, has forced the price down. This is a picture being mirrored at horse sales across the country."

MAGISTRATES IMPOSED THE maximum possible fine on a firm responsible for a blocked path crossing the Uckfield estate of millionaire Nicholas van Hoogstraten.

The court at Lewes, Sussex, found that Rarebargain Ltd - the company registered as owning the land over which the 140-year-old path runs - was guilty of three offences of failing to comply with a previous order to clear the path by April 17.

The company was fined a total of £15,000 - the largest possible amount for these offences - and given 21 days to pay.

In March, the same magistrates instructed Rarebargain to remove the barbed wire, locked gates and refrigeration unit blocking the ancient footpath within 28 days.

After learning the obstructions were still in place, the magistrates asserted that the company had "wilfully disregarded" the court order.

The protection and maintenance of the path is the legal responsibility of East Sussex County Council, says the Ramblers Association which claims the council has failed to respond to repeated pleas from the public to clear the route.

Ramblers Association executive committee spokesman Kate Ashbrook, who brought the case to court, said:"This is an excellent result. It's a clear message to all landowners that if they obstruct a path then they are in for a hefty fine.

"We now expect East Sussex County Council to act. The court has given a strong signal to the council to get rid of the obstructions once and for all."

ONE OF THE last bastions of threatened red squirrels in England has been analysed by boffins to ward off the threat posed by bigger, tougher grey squirrels.

The American immigrants have already forced native red squirrels out of most parts of England but a few hundred still remain in a woody enclave in Northumberland.

Newcastle University scientists believe a woodland management plan they devised will protect Kidland Forest red squirrels from being driven off by aggressive greys to face an uncertain fate.

The project includes planting far more conifers - red squirrels' main food source - instead of trees more likely to attract grey squirrels, such as oak.

Without measures to help them, researchers felt it was only a matter of time before the local red squirrels vanished for good as so many others have done elsewhere.

THE SHEER STRENGTH of a swan's wing was brought home in stark fashion when a blow from one left a man dazed and bloodied.

Ironically, Lee Collins was there to help swans on the River Thames as one of the Queen's Swan Uppers.

Mr Collins and the rest of the group had been compiling the annual survey of the birds when the accident happened.

After losing his grip on a swan, he was smashed on the side of his face with considerable force.

Blood streamed from the resulting gash which, fortunately, turned out to be not quite as bad as it looked.

Stitches were not required and the 30 year-old worker later returned to the fray following his recovery.

MORE THAN 50 people were killed in British farm accidents in the last year, according to the Health and Safety Executive's annual report.

The tragic tally has prompted farmers' leaders to call for greater attention to safety and does not even include the horrific recent death of farmer Jim Combellack in Cornwall.

Of the 53 farmers and farm workers who died in the 12 months to April, more than half were aged over 50 while 22 per cent were over retirement age.

NFU president Ben Gill said he feared the figures not only reflected the ageing farming population but also the danger posed to those battling on with a drastically reduced workforce.

He urged farmers not to struggle on without taking account of the risks that might be involved.

He said:"I fear that the huge job losses from the industry, falling profitability, under-investment, and the stress that goes with this, all have a part in the story behind these headline figures.

"Every death is a desperate tragedy. That is why the NFU's work to raise awareness among farmers of the many dangers remains a priority."

The NFU is currently throwing its weight behind the HSE's cross-industry 'Revitalising Health and Safety' initiative.

The scheme sets out to raise awareness of the risks to farmers and aims to reduce farm accidents over the next four years.

THE SECOND BATTLE Of Hastings appears to have been won with barely a shot fired in anger as conservationists cheer a victory for commonsense.

With a collection of environmental armies lining up to take on the Government over plans to construct wildlife-threatening bypasses around Hastings, ministers seem to have backed down.

Secretary of State Stephen Byers announced that the scheme involving regeneration and transport improvements for Hastings and its rural hinterland would not, after all, involve the construction of two controversial bypass sections.

"This is good news for this special part of the countryside," said Duncan Mackay, Countryside Agency regional director for the South East and London.

"It was a difficult decision weighing up economic and social concerns, as well as environmental.

"We agree with Mr Byers that the balance of arguments in favour of the bypasses is not sufficient to outweigh the very strong environmental requirements.

"In particular, we had been concerned about the likely impact of the bypass schemes on the High Weald Area of Outstanding Natural Beauty. I am pleased to see that the Government has taken full account of those concerns."

THE COUNTRYSIDE ALLIANCE has attacked Britain's recently toughened firearms laws which it says have done little to stop the rise in gun use by hardened crooks.

Criminal use of handguns increased by almost 40 per cent in the three years up to 2000, despite legislation introduced in 1997 banning such firearms following the tragedy of Dunblane, revealed the Alliance.

Last year, handguns were also used in a far greater proportion of offences involving firearms - 54 per cent compared to just over 10 per cent for shotguns.

The claims by the Alliance's Campaign for Shooting group are based on a new report titled 'Illegal Firearms in the UK'.

This was compiled by the Centre for Defence Studies at King's College, London.

The study, commissioned by the group, took a year to complete.

It was written by former Detective Constable John Bryan, ex-head of the firearms intelligence unit at New Scotland Yard.

David Bredin, director of the Campaign for Shooting, said:"Looking at the research, it is crystal clear that the existing gun laws do not lead to crime reduction and a safer place.

"Policy-makers have targeted the legitimate sporting and farming communities with ever-tighter laws.

"But the research clearly demonstrates that illegal guns are the real threat to public safety.

"Furthermore, Home Office statistics are unreliable and measures to identify and counter the threat to public safety seem haphazard and ineffective."

SYDNEY THE vulture gave his handlers the runaround for days after escaping from a falconry school near Biggleswade, Bedfordshire.

The African white-backed vulture, which boasts a 10ft wingspan, was a spectacular sight as he struck out on his own to follow in the celebrity footsteps of Foster, a Ruppells vulture.

He hit the headlines after fleeing a Norfolk zoo last month.

NEW COUNTRYSIDE SUPREMO Margaret Beckett MP has launched a scheme aimed at helping to revitalise rural life.

Mrs Beckett unveiled the Countryside Agency's new 'Vital Villages' initiative by awarding its first grant for a Parish Plan to Dymock parish council in Gloucestershire.

Agency spokesman Ewen Cameron said:"Smaller communities in rural areas are a vital part of the fabric of our countryside - indeed one in 10 people in England lives in a village.

"But village communities need help to ensure they prosper and to maintain diversity in the age groups and social backgrounds of people who live in them.

"The work of our Vital Villages programme will focus on helping communities to solve a variety of the challenges which villages face in the 21st Century.

"We will help communities to take stock of their position and the problems they face and create an action plan to address their own needs.

"We will also provide advice and funding for villages which wish to improve local transport and essential services."

A WARNING MESSAGE has gone out to anglers and fisheries' bosses after the first conviction in England for the illegal shooting of a cormorant.

The RSPB has used the prosecution as a chance to highlight its aim to stamp out unlawful slaughter of the fish-eating birds.

Luton magistrates fined a man from Letchworth in Hertfordshire £250 following the illegal shooting of a cormorant at a fishery in Bedfordshire.

Commenting on the case, Julian Hughes, head of the RSPB Species Policy section, said: "Three years of Government-commissioned research have found no evidence that cormorants damage fish stocks at a national level.

"In those exceptional cases, at a local level, where cormorants have been proved to cause problems, we want to work with fishery managers and anglers to seek lasting solutions.

"We have no desire to be in court seeing people being convicted for committing these needless crimes."

Terry Mansbridge, of the National Anglers Alliance, added: "The country's biggest angling and fisheries' organisations absolutely reject the illegal killing of birds in the name of fishing.

"Our members are concerned about fish-eating birds but breaking the law is not a solution.

"Actions of individuals will have little effect on overall predation of fish stocks."

Under the new Countryside and Rights of Way Act, the maximum penalty for wildlife crime has been increased to £5,000 for each offence, with the threat of a jail sentence reserved for the most serious offenders.

GIANT RODENTS HAVE been unsettling villagers in deepest Worcestershire after popping up unannounced.

At first, Brotheridge Green residents feared they had been invaded by rats as big as dogs but the newcomers were later revealed to be South American capybaras.

Wildlife experts have warned locals to steer clear of the rodents as they can be dangerous if cornered and have a savage bite.

Several capybaras have been sighted, raising concerns that they may have escaped from a public zoo or wildlife park.

In the wild capybaras are preyed on by jaguars, anacondas, and pirhana fish - so leafy Brotheridge Green might well be paradise in comparison.

However, the creatures are said to be vulnerable to freezing weather and might be doomed in the event of a cold snap.

A SURPRISE BOOM in bird numbers has been hailed a success for the conservation efforts of Britain's beleaguered farmers.

The Common Birds Census, conducted by the British Trust for Ornithology, revealed large increases for 14 species of bird with significant improvements recorded on overall figures kept for the last 25 years.

The census, covering farmland and woodland birds, even showed welcome signs of population increases among some threatened species on the list of Conservation Concern.

Song thrush numbers leapt by 17 per cent after declining by 55 per cent since 1974 while blackbirds went up by six per cent after falling by 23 per cent over 25 years.

Tawny owls rocketed by 33 per cent, up from a 15 per cent decline, while dunnock numbers jumped by 10 per cent, up from a 44 per cent slump.

The census also showed an increase for the robin (up 13 per cent), the wren (up eight per cent) and the chaffinch (up seven per cent).

According to the NFU, environmental schemes such as Countryside Stewardship have helped farmers invest in environmental initiatives at a time of desperately low farm incomes.

More than 25,000 farmers entered a million hectares of farmland into conservation schemes during the 1990s, the union revealed.

The DETR Countryside Survey 2000 also showed there were now more hedges and ponds in better management than there were 10 years ago.

NFU president Ben Gill said:"In the last few years we have started to see bird numbers steady or begin to creep up.

"Given all the doom and gloom of recent months, these latest figures will be seen as a very welcome signal for farmers that their efforts are having a positive and important influence on wildlife.

"There is still work to be done to increase habitats for seed-eating birds but we hope proposals to extend the Countryside Stewardship Scheme will go a long way to help farmers achieve this."

A RACING PIGEON travelled first class but went seriously off course after landing on the US-bound QE2 luxury liner.

Released in Plymouth, the pigeon was supposed to race back to owner Ron Horrocks in Cleethorpes - but ended up perched on the ship as it powered away from Southampton.

Taking pity on their bewildered guest, the crew put it in an area reserved for travellers' pets and kept it fed and watered all the way to New York - and back.

As the ship docked again at Southampton, a UK pigeon group was contacted for help and managed to trace Mr Horrocks from a number on the bird's leg ring.

The pampered pigeon was released a second time but this time its instincts were spot on and it made it back home without problem.

ANGLERS ARE HUNTING a huge 40-pound catfish currently snacking on native fish in the River Darent, Kent.

If caught, the giant is destined for an aquarium where it will be powerless to devour any more young trout.

147

FINGERS ARE TIGHTLY crossed that the reopening of about 85 per cent of English public footpaths will not lead to a devastating summer resurgence of foot-and-mouth.

Putting tourism and country businesses first is the risky strategy now adopted by a Government convinced that the threat of foot-and-mouth is subsiding in most areas.

In line with this gamble, around 80 local authorities now have all their countryside paths open - the highest number since last February when the crisis first unfolded.

A spokesman for the Countryside Agency said:"Major changes contributing to this success have occurred in Somerset. There, large areas were reopened bringing the figure for the county to 91 per cent open.

"In the Forest of Dean in Gloucestershire, the Forestry Commission has reopened all its land. Also, the full length of the South West Coast Path - the longest National Trail at 614 miles - is again open. This increase is part of an ongoing trend."

However, to combat what it calls the "minute risk" of foot-and-mouth, the Agency has issued some guidelines for countryside visitors to follow:

-DON'T go on farmland if you have handled farm animals in the last seven days.

-AVOID contact with farm animals and keep dogs on a lead where they are present.

-IF you step in dung, remove it from your boots before you leave the field.

-DON'T go on paths still marked with a local authority 'closed' notice.

PIPE DREAMS CAN come true for fish set to benefit from new artificial shelters placed underwater at secret locations on the River Ouse in Yorkshire.

The shelters, made from concrete pipes, were introduced after sonar studies by the Environment Agency revealed a lack of natural refuges for local fish at key locations.

The pipes, strapped together and secured to the river bed, were initially loaded onto a British Waterways barge at Naburn Lock near York before being transported upstream to their mystery destinations.

Anglers will not be told where the shelters are located in a bid to help fish flourish undisturbed while using them.

Simon Cranmer Gordon, fisheries officer for the Environment Agency, said:"These shelters will provide havens for fish away from fast river flows and predators such as cormorants, as well as attracting invertebrates that will act as food."

THE FIRST OSPREY chick hatched in England for more than 150 years has been testing its wings at Rutland Water nature reserve in Leicestershire.

The bird, produced last month after a single egg was laid, is expected to fly to Africa - ospreys' normal wintering location - within weeks.

THOUSANDS OF BRITISH piglets, lambs and calves are being culled by a method too cruel for vets in the US, claims Animal Aid.

It says young animals have been slaughtered under foot-and-mouth emergency measures using a technique outlawed by the American Veterinary Medical Association because members consider it too barbaric.

A spokesman alleged:"The method involves injecting a drug directly into the heart and has the backing of Roger Eddy, the president of the Royal College of Veterinary Surgeons - the body in charge of setting and monitoring standards throughout the profession.

"Mr Eddy has even admitted in correspondence with Animal Aid that he has used what is known as intracardiac injection himself on dogs, cats, lambs, piglets, and 'on one or two occasions, calves'.

"The 2000 Report of the American Veterinary Medical Association Panel on Euthanasia was unequivocal. It stated:'Intracardiac injection must only be used if the animal is heavily sedated, unconscious or anaesthetised.'"

Animal Aid, the UK's leading animal rights group, has now called on the Department for Environment, Food and Rural Affairs to order an immediate ban on intracardiac injection by foot-and-mouth killing gangs.

It has also demanded the resignation of RCVS president Mr Eddy.

Animal Aid claims it was contacted by a distressed member of a killing gang in Dumfries and Galloway who had seen injected lambs writhing on the ground and taking a long time to die.

The group says a kinder way of killing the young would be to administer presedation to the point of coma.

"This could easily and painlessly be done with drugs such as xylazine. Then the animals could be shot or injected with a lethal drug."

Animal Aid director Andrew Tyler added: "It seems that, for the convenience of the killing gangs, very young animals are being put through totally unnecessary additional pain and trauma.

"The American veterinary authorities recognise that this is wrong but the president of the leading UK professional body defends it. We demand an immediate end to this brutal activity and that Mr Eddy resigns his post."

QUAIL EGGS BOUGHT at a local superstore were placed beneath a hen for a joke - and hatched.

Four of the six eggs purchased at a Sainsbury's store in East Sussex produced chicks after being slipped beneath a chicken called Speckly.

Lesley Lake had laughed with boyfriend Mick Remmer about the eggs but never thought they would crack open.

The bizarre entrance into the world of the four chicks happened after Speckly got to work at Sedlescombe.

Sainsbury's later blamed the difficulty in separat-ing male and female quails for the eggs on sale having been fertilised.

BASKING SHARK SPOTTING is the thrilling prize offered to youngsters taking part in a competition organised by The Wildlife Trusts.

The lucky winner will be given a rare opportunity to look for basking sharks off the Cornish coast on a special research yacht.

148

STARLING: lucky escape from depths of a kitchen wall

STARLINGS have always struck me as the bird-table equivalent of human muggers - brash, noisy, bullying, and usually descending in a gang.

On countless occasions I have watched them muscle in en masse to establish their own pecking order when food is laid out.

Most garden birds take fright and give way to them immediately, although I've seen the odd brave blackbird fight back and drive them off.

Not the prettiest of birds, the starling nevertheless boasts glossy feathers which can look quite stunning when they catch the light.

Drab grey-browns are then suddenly suffused by rich blues, purples, and greens.

Quite a large bird at 22cms length, the starling is omniverous, feeding on worms, caterpillars, and insects, as well as fruit, seeds and household scraps.

Lacking a distinct song itself, it still produces an amazing variety of rattles and whistles, even mimicking other birds when the mood takes it.

Common throughout the country, starlings sometimes gather in huge flocks during winter.

On a few occasions, up to a million birds have been estimated at giant roosts that have left local trees and buildings devastated.

A few summers ago, weeks apart, I had two encounters with starlings at my home, one happy and one rather sad.

Both incidents involved holes located beneath the guttering on opposite sides of the house.

Birds have roosted and nested in these ever since we came to live here.

The first incident occurred after starlings made a nest as usual in the larger of these holes.

This year, however, they somehow broke through to the recess between the house's outer and inner walls with tragic results.

A luckless fledgling tumbled down into the darkness despite its other siblings safely leaving the nest.

For two days, the mother starling frantically tracked its doomed offspring with an unremitting series of heartbreaking cries, all weakly returned by the terrified younger bird.

There was little I could do except hope that it found its way back up to the spot where it had slipped through.

At one point, the fledgling briefly appeared behind an ivy-covered stone air vent set mid-way up the outside wall.

But before I could work out how to break or prise this off, it was gone again.

Short of smashing down the entire wall, nothing could be done.

Eventually, by the third day, its pathetic calls had petered out altogether.

So upsetting was all this that I asked a builder working on a neighbour's house to seal up the hole so nothing similar could happen again.

Bizarrely, two weeks later, an almost exact repeat occurred, this time involving an adult starling and the smaller hole on the opposite side of the house, by now probably enlarged to make a decent sized nest site.

This time, the victim had managed to get itself caught between the inner and outer kitchen walls, a fact I only discovered when I was alone in the house one morning and about to go to work.

Putting down my case, I finally traced its scuffling progress to a patch of wall inside a large kitchen cupboard.

I grabbed a hammer and screwdriver then tried to knock a hole through to it.

No success. But just as I was contemplating the dismal death of a second starling, I discovered a plastic air vent set into the wall behind the metal central heating box.

Tearing this off in a moment, I stood back and kept as quiet as possible.

Light had obviously flooded into the trapped bird's position because, after only a few seconds, a beak, then a dusty little head, popped out of the cupboard wall.

At this, I gingerly opened the kitchen window and stepped further away.

As I did, a filthy starling shot out of the cupboard like a rocket, did a slight mid-air flight correction over the sink, then clattered out through the window.

It settled on the nearest garden bush where I watched it shaking and cleaning its feathers for the next two minutes.

After that, with a triumphant chatter and whistle, it flew off.

Job well done, I thought.

THE SIMMERING HOSTILITY between anglers and animal rights protesters could explode into open warfare later this summer with the launch of another controversial PETA campaign.

Anglers have been outraged by the planned high-profile assault on their sport using a faked picture of a dog hooked through its muzzle.

The image, part of an attack by American-based animal rights group PETA (People for the Ethical Treatment of Animals), aims to highlight the apparent suffering of hooked fish.

It will be used in poster form with the campaign itself expected to leap from newspaper adverts onto TV screens to reach the majority of the population.

Poised to launch the drive against angling and fish-eating is American Dawn Carr, a 32 year-old vegan newly arrived in Britain to spread the word and backed by a multi-million dollar publicity budget.

In an interview with a UK newspaper, Ms Carr claimed that angling was barbaric, fish fingers were as cruelly attained as foie gras, and fish and chip shops were worse than pornography.

"Playing a fish on a line, just for the thrill of it, is horrible, like bear baiting," she said."Nearly half of these fish will die - lactic acid builds up in their bodies; they lose scales; the hook mutilates them. It's still murder."

The campaign will also make a direct appeal to the British population - most of whom eat fish at some time - to turn away from the high protein fayre.

"My family and friends don't order fish with me," revealed Ms Carr."They know that every time they stab its flesh, I want to scream. I can't stop thinking of how it was killed. Fish are dragged along the ocean bed. They suffer excruciating decompression, their swim-bladders rupture, their eyes pop out, the oesophagus and stomach get pushed through their mouths. Then they're tossed on board, while still alive, and their bellies and throats are cut open."

Angling organisations have condemned the planned campaign with the Countryside Alliance's angling leader Charles Jardine dubbing it "ridiculous" and "alarmist."

A SEAL PUP is recovering at a wildlife sanctuary after being attacked by a dog when it was washed up on a beach at Gourock in Strathclyde, Scotland, with no sign of its mother.

SECRET HOMES ARE being built for otters to help them flourish again on Teesside.

Artificial otter holts, made from concrete blocks and plastic pipes, are being provided by the Environment Agency but the locations will not be revealed to protect parents and cubs.

Otters are among Britain's rarest mammals and have come under increasing pressure in recent years as natural habitat is reduced by development.

Katy Dickson, a conservation officer with the Agency, said:"This is a great opportunity to help these wonderful creatures and we are very grateful to the landowners who have been very pleased to co-operate with us in our aims.

"During flood defence works we have identified sites where we know otters can be found but where natural cover is limited and these are ideal locations for our artificial holts.

"There will be a number of other flood defence schemes happening in the Agency's Dales area in the future and we shall continue to look for further opportunities to help local wildlife in the process. We would also love to hear from any other landowners who would be willing to help."

A LAKE AT the centre of a 'crocodile' scare two years ago has finally given up its mystery predator - a 20 pound American snapping turtle.

Searchers drew a blank after the so-called croc was apparently sighted menacing the Swan Pool in West Bromwich and the story eventually faded.

But young angler Harry Billingham, aged 14, appears to have got to the bottom of the mystery after hauling in the giant turtle with the help of an adult relative.

The vicious predator, which feasts on fish and water plants, put up a violent struggle before its capture and the pair had to take care as snapping turtles can easily chomp off fingers.

The RSPCA, who later took the turtle into custody, believe it was dumped in the lake after becoming too large and dangerous for its owner.

TREE LOVERS ARE trying to kick into touch plans to build a new national soccer complex that threaten ancient trees.

The Woodland Trust, the UK's top woodland conservation charity, and the Ancient Tree Forum, have formally objected to the Football Association's planning application for a new National Football Centre, west of Burton upon Trent, Staffordshire.

The Trust warns the proposed development could destroy some of Europe's most spectacular ancient trees.

Although it welcomes the development of a centre of football excellence, it says the process is being rushed and with better research, layout and design, many of the threatened trees at Byrkley Park could be saved.

Jill Butler, the Trust's ancient tree expert, said:"Byrkley Park is the best parkland in the county and is one of the top sites in the UK for ancient trees. It therefore has great significance in mainland Europe because northern Europe has very few ancient trees or wood pasture left.

"The park retains at least 77 ancient trees, of which 58 are ancient oaks. The planning application does not reflect the importance of the site and the potential to restore this already damaged parkland. The environmental survey work the Football Association has had done is simply inadequate."

THE DEVASTATION WREAKED on sheep farmers by foot-and-mouth is highlighted in the latest appraisal of the disease's impact.

According to the NFU, 3.9 million sheep have now been culled because of the crisis - a large chunk of the national flock.

"The size of the national flock varies throughout the year, " explained a union spokesman."In December 2000, there were 27.6 million sheep in the UK. But during the spring and early summer the national flock would have expanded as the lambing season progressed. It was expected to reach around 39 million animals in June before foot-and-mouth struck.

"The latest figures available show 3.9 million sheep have been slaughtered because of foot-and-mouth - 2.9 million for disease control reasons and one million for welfare reasons.

"This represents between 10-14 per cent of the national flock, leaving approximately 30 to 35 million sheep.

"Because of the culling of breeding ewes and lambs and the retention of many ewe lambs for restocking, lamb production is likely to fall next year by between 25-30 per cent."

The financial vulnerability of sheep farmers was now acute with most struggling against bleak reality.

"The crisis has come at a time when live stock farmers are already experiencing one of the most pronounced agricultural recessions since the Great Depression of the 1930s. The typical upland livestock farmer made an income of only £3,500 in the year 2000-1 - a drop of 83 per cent from 1996-7.

"At the same time lowland livestock farmers have been struggling just to break even."

PIGEON PROBLEMS WERE dealt with in two very different ways in London - the first solution was to use a hawk to frighten them off, the second was to let sharp-eyed lawyers get to work.

A Harris hawk has been employed twice weekly to scare away pigeons fouling a new £230 million office block built for MPs in Westminster.

Although the birds are not killed, it is hoped the fierce hawk will terrorise them enough to drive them elsewhere.

Meanwhile, Railtrack is faced with a bill for £70,000 after the Court of Appeal ruled it was responsible for keeping a bridge in Wadsworth free of pigeons and their mess.

The rail company must foot a cleaning bill and put up netting to stop pigeons nesting after an action was brought by Wadsworth Borough Council on behalf of angry pedestrians.

The successful action could now open the floogates for similar claims against Railtrack.

A MAN SPOTTED knocking down a house martin's nest and putting the contents in a skip has become probably the first person convicted of destroying a house martin's nest at their own home.

The defendant, from Lincolnshire, was fined £250 for destroying the nest after being seen dislodging it with a pole then dumping its contents.

Commenting on the case at Stamford Magistrates Court, RSPB spokesman Mark Thomas said:"Each year the RSPB deals with a number of reported incidents involving the alleged destruction of house martin nests.

"The RSPB believes that many people are unaware that house martins are a protected species and that the destruction of their nests constitutes an offence for which the maximum penalty, in England and Wales, has recently been increased to £5,000 or a six-month prison sentence.

"Obviously the RSPB does not want to see members of the public being convicted of such crimes through ignorance of the law so we have launched a public awareness drive reminding people of the severity of these offences."

House martins, swallows, and swifts, which regularly nest on properties, have become familiar symbols of British summer but winter in Africa.

THE SHINBONE OF a newly born calf was all that remained of the animal after a puma-like creature was spotted prowling near a Shropshire farm.

Several sightings of a huge black cat were reported throughout the county before the calf went missing from the farm at Ellesmere.

Farmer Don Stokes later revealed he himself also witnessed the mystery predator crossing one of his fields - close to the area where a cow had just given birth.

When the calf vanished, a search was made of surrounding fields but all that could be found was a single bone - subsequently identified as a calf shinbone.

Mr Stokes said it now seemed certain that the puma, or whatever it was, had killed and eaten the calf after dragging it away.

OPPOSING INTERESTS sparked by the controversial Countryside and Rights of Way Act 2000 are to be aired at a national one-day conference, now being organised.

The event, on September 12 at the University of Nottingham, will be opened by Sir Martin Doughty, chairman of English Nature.

"Is the Countryside and Rights of Way Act 2000 all good news?," asked a spokesman."Do conflicts arise between access and wildlife in relation to land, inland waterways, coastal habitats or inshore waters?

"If conflicts arise, will careful management solve them? The conference aims to illuminate the issues surrounding these questions and to seek some answers."

Speakers will be taking part from The Countryside Agency, the CLA, British Waterways, The Ramblers Association and The Wildlife Trusts.

The conference is aimed at local authority officials, recreational and facility managers, land managers and agents, professional ecologists and owners of land and water.

BRITAIN'S NATIONAL WHEAT harvest could be down by four million tonnes after the devastating twin impacts of flooding and foot-and-mouth.

The destruction of thousands of acres of cereal crops last autumn seems certain to make this year's harvest one of the lowest for years.

According to the NFU, farmers will need to strike the best deal possible for their grain after the wettest autumn and spring on record coupled with the knock-on effects of foot-and-mouth.

Vice-president Michael Paske said: "Farmers have battled to plant and in some cases re-plant crops. It is now even more important that they have information that will help them negotiate a realistic price for their products in an increasingly complex trading environment.

"We also continue to encourage farmers to work together to help reduce their input costs and to achieve a better price from the grain chain."

In recent years producers have sold around 17 million tonnes of grain direct from their farms so the loss of four million would be a substantial blow.

Meanwhile, the NFU has said it will have little sympathy for anyone caught ignoring measures to fight foot-and-mouth in one of the worst hit regions.

The union was responding to claims that almost 50 farmers have been found breaking regulations aimed at stamping out the disease in North Yorkshire.

Disinfectant footbaths were often not properly provided and many vehicles were not being disinfected as they travelled from farm to farm, according to police and trading standards officers who launched a crackdown.

Police have apparently been shocked by the extent of the problem and have vowed to take a tougher line with transgressors.

AN UNBORN CALF was found to be unharmed after its pregnant mother plunged 70ft off a sea cliff in the Outer Hebrides.

The cow is believed to have toppled over when the tide was in, the sea water helping it to survive the fall as well as protecting the calf in its womb.

Following its impromptu dive, the cow was later spotted trapped at the foot of the cliff in North Uist.

Emergency services were alerted and a helicopter scrambled to stop the animal being swept to its death when the tide came back in.

The cow was airlifted to safety and both she and her unborn offspring were pronounced fine after a series of checks.

WORK HAS BEGUN on the final link in a chain of 'fish passes' which should help salmon thrive in the River Thames once more.

The Environment Agency is rebuilding a weir at Greenham Mill, Newbury, to allow salmon to reach ideal spawning grounds west of the Berkshire town.

Experts have identified the River Kennet, one of the cleanest chalk streams in the country, as a great area for salmon to lay eggs and breed successfully.

But without the groundbreaking chain of fish passes now in place, the salmon's path from the Thames would be forever blocked by man-made locks and weirs.

A spokesman for the Environment Agency said:"The completion of the final pass will mean that for the first time there is a real chance of a self-sustaining salmon population in the Thames for over a century.

"Salmon are creatures of habit and always return to the place they were spawned in order to start the life cycle off once again.

"Young fish swim out to sea to feed for a year off the coast of Greenland and the Faeroe Islands before returning to the River Thames.

"Once in the Thames, they have to negotiate 20 locks and weirs before reaching the Kennet. To reach the best spawning sites a further 17 obstacles have to be overcome.This made it almost impossible for salmon to breed success-fully until the series of passes were constructed."

A CAMPAIGN HAS been launched to get the BBC to drop plans to axe its only fishing programme - the much-loved radio show 'Dirty Tackle'.

In a note to the Countryside Alliance's Gone Fishing group, series producer Helen Stiles confirmed the blow.

She said:"We have enjoyed making the programmes and are very sorry to see it go. Programme schedules must change but it is a pity that there will no longer be a fishing programme on the radio.

"The decision to bring Dirty Tackle to an end was made by Five Live's commissioning editor Moz Dee who feels it is time to move on and use the transmis - sion slot for something else. We had hoped that the situation might change and that 'Dirty Tackle' could continue but that seems unlikely."

Gone Fishing spokeswoman Jill Grieve said:"This will come as a huge disappointment to Dirty Tackle's many fans within the angling community and we must try to save it."

She urged people to write in to protest.

"There are more than three million anglers in Britain. Before we know it, there won't be any rural interest programmes on offer at all."

FARMERS IN CUMBRIA are claiming that animal parts contaminated with foot-and-mouth have been deliberately dumped on their land in a covert bid to continue the spread of the disease.

Infected animal bones, cow tails, and sheep body parts have reportedly been found at various locations in the last month.

FOUR WATER BUFFALO have been released at Chippenham Fen nature reserve in Cambridgeshire. Conservationists hope they will maintain the site without the need for mechanical cutting equipment.

152

BADGERS FANS HAVE welcomed a Government rethink on bovine TB which appears to move away from heaping blame on the popular mammals for the disease's spread.

The National Federation of Badger Groups has been delighted with the latest report published by the Government's Independent Scientific Group.

"This report represents a massive shift away from blaming badgers and endorses our proposals for solving the problem," said Dr Elaine King, NFBG conservation officer.

"There is no doubt that the lessons of foot-and-mouth disease have helped swing this debate our way. It is no longer possible for the farming industry to ignore the central role that it must play in controlling this disease."

However, the NFBG attacked the "scientific arrogance" of the Ministry of Agriculture, Fisheries and Food, which, it claimed, had hindered research.

"For over two years, we have criticised the Government's TB99 questionnaire. This critical piece of research was supposed to identify the differences between farms with bovine TB and farms without.

"That information is essential if farmers are to understand how they can prevent bovine TB. But MAFF failed to undertake enough studies of farms without the disease.

"The scientific arrogance of MAFF meant that our warnings were ignored. The Agriculture Select Committee also warned that not all necessary data was being collected. Even the Independent Scientific Group warned that TB99 was not being properly implemented.

"Over two years after it started, the study is useless because former ministers refused to give TB99 adequate resources. It is an absolute disgrace."

CRAB FISHING TACKLE used by naive tourists has been blamed for a spate of injuries to young swans in Devon.

Despite advice that crabs can be caught easily on lines without the use of hooks, tourists have still been using the deadly tackle.

One swan eventually died after being rescued from a pond near Paignton where it was seen struggling to release a crab hook from its throat.

Wildlife experts from the RSPCA and Torbay Wildlife Rescue have been called out repeatedly over the summer to help swans choking on crab lines.

The RSPCA has revealed its workers were called out three times in a single day to help victims.

Young holidaymakers and their parents throw out baited hooks to catch crabs but swans think it is food for them, the Society explains.

With a panicking bird on their line, the tourist quickly abandons it but the swan is then left in agony with a hook stuck in its mouth, throat, or stomach.

OUTRAGE OVER 37 farmers made millionaires from foot-and-mouth compensation was branded absurd and unfair by the Countryside Alliance.

Chairman John Jackson said:"The furore being whipped up over this issue is unhelpful and misleading. Not only is it unfair to farmers - who clearly suspect that the details of the larger payouts may have been leaked mischievously - but shows a complete misconception of the rationale for compensation.

"Farmers have lost their livestock not through any fault or responsibility of their own but due to public policy. It would be absurd to suggest that their whole means of sustainable, perennial livelihood, built up in some cases through generations of hard work, should be taken from them without adequate compensation.

"Comment and media coverage have put the levels of compensation in a quite misleading context. Farmers hit either by foot-and-mouth itself or by the draconian contiguous cull policy have lost all their capital merely as a direct result of public policy, not as a result of ordinary market forces.

"It is not only their income but their whole perennial income-generating source which has gone. The compensation levels reported are not excessive when set against the fact that these payments need to compensate farmers for the destruction of their businesses' prime assets - which may have taken them a lifetime to build up and which could take them another to rebuild."

RARE STONE CURLEWS have made themselves at home to such an extent in East Anglia that English Nature has given part of the region special status.

Breckland Farmland Site of Special Scientific Interest covers an area twice the size of Guernsey in the Brecklands of Norfolk and Suffolk and supports over 40 per cent of the national stone-curlew population.

With only 254 breeding pairs of stone-curlews recorded in the UK, the special status is seen as vital to protect one of our scarcest breeding birds.

As their names suggest, stone-curlews need open, stony ground for their nests and such conditions are easily found in the unique landscape of the Brecks - much of which is still intensively farmed for arable crops.

English Nature has praised local farmers and land managers.

ANIMAL RIGHTS PROTESTERS have claimed victory after Oxford City Council scrapped plans for a horse-drawn omnibus following their campaign.

Under controversial proposals to increase tourism, two shire horses would have pulled a 25ft omnibus filled with tourists around Oxford's busy city centre.

"No doubt those in favour thought that the trade would appeal to the romantic and nostalgic nature of potential visitors," said a spokesman for Animal Aid.

"But the reality - based on evidence from other countries with similar operations - is very different.

"If the Oxford scheme was given the green light, this thankfully-rare form of exploitative entertainment in the UK could take off in other urban areas. Our victory, therefore, has wide-ranging and positive implications. Councillors were left in no doubt about the strength of public opposition. An online petition generated in excess of 1,200 e-mails in seven days."

153

PRESSURE IS MOUNTING on the Government to reverse its controversial decision not to investigate the foot-and-mouth crisis with an open public inquiry.

Allegations of a cover-up were bitterly made as soon as new rural affairs minister Margaret Beckett MP smilingly revealed there would not be an "all singing, all dancing" public inquiry into one of the biggest national disasters in living memory.

The Countryside Alliance has now backed a petition calling for a full public inquiry into the crisis which is being organised by Farmers Weekly and several other major publications.

Chief executive Richard Burge said:"We are supporting Farmers Weekly's initiative because the Government owes it to the country to ensure that any foot-and-mouth inquiry is comprehensive, publicly transparent and truly independent.

"It is particularly important that the various inquiries should all be able to take evidence in public and have the power to summon ministers and their officials to give evidence. Unfortunately, the Government's recent pronouncements on the proposed format for the inquiries suggest they do not fit this bill at all. The Government must demonstrate it is prepared to be fully accountable to the rural community."

Earlier, NFU president Ben Gill said it was absolutely crucial for any probe to be seen as open and transparent by the farming industry and for reports to be published in full.

However, he welcomed the Royal Society inquiry into the transmission, prevention and control of all epidemic outbreaks of infectious diseases in livestock, which will be led by Sir Brian Follett.

Mr Gill said:"Fundamental questions like where the disease came from and how the Government can prevent further outbreaks of diseases from abroad need to be answered."

A GOLDEN EAGLE was found dead on a Scottish estate popular with celebrities.

Tests have been carried out on the protected creature which was discovered near an area where game birds are reared on the Cawdor Estate close to Nairn.

Celebrities such as David Beckham and Eric Clapton are known to favour the estate, famous for its stunning views and game.

Police recently launched an investigation following allegations that foxes had been illegally snared in the area.

The dead eagle was taken to the Scottish Agricultural Science Agency in Edinburgh for analysis.

GROUSE SHOOTERS BLASTED off the new season with hopes high that foot-and-mouth would not hit profits from the multi-million pound industry.

The sport, disliked by animal rights groups, kicked off this year on August 13 as the Glorious Twelfth fell on a Sunday.

While grouse shooting and its associated tourism is thought to be worth over £90 million annually to the Scottish economy, the new season is said to have brought an immediate £12.5million boost to the struggling English rural upland economy.

"This is a vital shot in the arm," said Oliver Harwood, head of rural economy for the Country Land and Business Association.

"Income from grouse shooting-related tourism is crucial to the prosperity of thousands of local businesses."

According to the CLA, figures released by the Moorland Association revealed grouse shooting in England and Wales supported 279 full-time equivalent keepering jobs as well as an estimated 32,500 additional casual labour days.

This meant that vital employment would be provided in some of Britain's most isolated areas during the season which runs to December 10.

Following representations by the CLA, The Moorland Association, NFU and other organisations, DEFRA's Animal Health Division announced it had put in place a licensing provision to allow grouse shooting to go ahead in foot-and-mouth restricted areas.

With at least 60 per cent of heather moorland in England and Wales falling within infected areas, shooting would have been prohibited on the vast majority of grouse moors in the north of England and the Scottish Borders, said the CLA.

The licensing provision now allows shooting to take place outside a 3km radius from infected premises provided 30 days have elapsed since the place was cleansed and disinfected.

A SNAIL LESS than two millimetres wide that thrived at the time of the woolly mammoth is being given extra elbow room by the Forestry Commission in North Yorkshire.

Known only by its Latin name Vertigo Geyeri, the mini-mollusc is at the centre of a conservation effort which has already resulted in 1,000 trees being felled at 8,600 acre Dalby Forest near Pickering.

"The creature is a relic of the last Ice Age 20,000 years ago when tundra-like flora and fauna colonised the land as glaciers retreated. But as the weather warmed, it declined and now clings on to existence at only one other English location," said a spokesman.

"As part of a survival blueprint the Forestry Commission, in partnership with English Nature, has felled two acres of conifers adjoining the snail's limestone rich pasture habitat to encourage it to branch out and occupy the newly cleared ground."

ENGLISH LONGHORN CATTLE are the stars of a painting helping to raise cash for farmers hit by foot-and-mouth.

Devon artist Michael Lees originally captured the rescued breed on canvas as a tribute to Robert Wales, a farmer who played a major part in saving it from extinction in the 1950s.

Now prints of the "gorgeous rural scene" are on sale in a bid to raise £45,000 for the Royal Agricultural Benevolent Institution.

RECONNECTING PEOPLE WITH the farm on which their food is grown is the only way forward for devastated British farming, claims the Soil Association.

Its new report 'A Share in the Harvest' was launched as furious farmers prepared to protest at Gatwick airport over illegal food imports in the wake of foot-and-mouth.

The report focuses on how 'Community Supported Agriculture' could help farmers and their customers develop a relationship based on mutual support and trust.

Rupert Aker, project co-ordinator for the Soil Association, said:"Making local food more widely available is fundamental to CSA. We need to encourage the public to participate in supporting local food, thereby taking direct responsibility for how their food is grown and the conservation of the country-side they value. Then buying local food can become the norm rather than the exception.

"This report provides practical solutions to the problems facing British farming and is a model for change. It presents a guide for farming that meets both the needs of farmers - who receive a guaranteed income - and consumers, who know where their food comes from."

The report is based on two years research by the Soil Association and was funded by the Department of Environment, Food and Rural Affairs (DEFRA).

Meanwhile, farmers and countryside campaigners have been continuing to press for a transparent, open public inquiry into foot-and-mouth instead of the series of smaller inquiries promised by Labour.

NFU president Ben Gill said the crisis, now six months old, had changed the lives of every livestock farmer in the country forever.

The event had been a disaster which had landed an unprecedented body blow on Britain's battling agriculture industry - with much of the bruising still to come out.

HORSE SHOES PROVED lucky for a horse struck by lightning - not having any on, that is.

Eight year-old mare Sadie is thought to have survived a direct hit because she was not wearing metal horse shoes - helping the giant charge to earth itself more easily.

Although knocked cold by the bolt which struck the mare in its field at Lawford, Essex, death or serious injury were avoided.

Thelma Scrutton, the horse's owner, came upon the animal seconds after seeing lightning strike its field.

Despite being badly bruised and suffering a burnt tail, her pet is expected to make a full recovery following the drama.

CORNISH BADGER FANS are celebrating victory in their fight to prevent development next to one of the county's badger setts.

Following a site visit by an inquiry inspector in July, planning permission for proposed building work at Clodgy View, St Ives, has been refused on appeal.

Roger Driver, co-ordinator of the West Cornwall Badger Group, said:"We would like to thank everyone that has helped in the fight to protect this large and active badger sett, and particularly Mr Dickinson, the planning inspector, for his understanding of the consequences to the badgers had this proposal been allowed to go ahead."

In his summary, inspector Mr J. L. Dickinson said:"Although some neighbours strongly object to the presence of badgers within a built-up residential area, there is no dispute that badgers are a protected species under either the 1992 Protection of Badgers Act or the 1981 Wildlife and Countryside Act.

"This last Act effectively states that badgers may not be killed or taken by certain methods and is therefore of less significance than the PBA in the determination of this appeal.

"Amongst other things, the PBA makes it an offence to damage a sett or to disturb badgers when they are occupying it. Additionally paragraph 47 of the 1994 PPG9 states that the presence of a protected species is a material consideration when planning permission is being determined."

BASKING SHARKS AND dolphins have been at the centre of a book blunder involving a Scottish loch.

Residents near the loch could be forgiven for scratching their heads if they pick up a new guide saying the impressive creatures can be found in the murky waters.

For Loch Muick is miles from the sea without any connecting river and all creatures found within it are of the freshwater variety.

However, a new Reader's Digest guide on wild creatures found in the UK announces that basking sharks and dolphins can be spotted at the loch.

The editor of the guide has reportedly apologised for the mistake which will be corrected in later editions.

BAT FANS ARE in for a treat with a host of events being held during UK International Bat Week running until September 2.

Organised by the Bat Conservation Trust, the week is supported by The Woodland Trust which provides havens for a large part of Britain's native bat population.

Bat walks, illustrated talks, children's workshops, barbeques and demonstrations on how to make bat boxes are all part of a nationwide schedule of events.

Actress Prunella Scales, TV wife of Britain's battiest hotelier Basil Fawlty, is one of the more high profile supporters of the twilight flutterers.

She said:"Bats are marvellous creatures and there are many surprising myths about them. Bat Week is designed to help people understand and appreciate bats.

"By conserving older trees, keeping as much deadwood as possible and by limiting human intervention, the Woodland Trust is able to encourage bats, along with a host of other woodland flora and fauna."

A WARNING MESSAGE has gone out to egg collectors after a suspended prison sentence was given to a man who raided eggs from some of the country's most spectacular birds of prey.

The man was charged with three offences contrary to the Control of Trade in Endangered Species Regulations 1985 involving scores of eggs taken from species such as peregrine falcons, golden eagles, Montague harriers, merlins, and barn owls.

The RSPB says it is delighted at the three-month suspended sentence handed down to the defendant at Durham Crown Court. He was also ordered to pay court costs of £1,150.

A spokesman said:"The case represented a number of 'firsts' in the battle by conservationists and police against this senseless crime. It was the first case involving the sale of eggs under endangered species regulations, and the first time that a custodial sentence has been handed out to an egg collector.

"It was also the first time that an egg collector has been convicted largely on evidence from computer records as well as diaries."

In his summing up Judge Foster said that the man was one of a group of people who knew that stealing wild bird eggs was illegal but who had become obsessed with it.

He added that birds were part of our natural heritage to be enjoyed by all, but the defendant had seen their eggs as trophies.

AN ENDANGERED BEETLE affectionately dubbed 'ET' is the subject of a survey involving 10 lime wood regions in England and Wales.

The Forestry Commision has enlisted the help of Britain's top lime bark beetle expert Tony Drane to carry out the £5,000 study into the threatened beetle's distribution and status.

Recently, the survey uncovered evidence of its existence in several woods in Essex.

Mr Drane said:"The small-leaved lime woods of Essex are mainly concentrated in an area between Braintree and Colchester. Many are being actively managed by re-introducing coppicing. It was exciting to find a totally new stronghold for ET there.

"Of the six woods surveyed, four showed extensive colonisation. The next step is to make sure that both beetle and woods survive, and we'll do this by making sure that woodland management plans take their needs into account.

"Continuation of coppicing regimes and retention of dead and cut lime wood on site should safeguard ET's future."

He explained that the fate of ET (Ernoporus Tiliae) is inextricably bound up with the conservation of our native lime woods, where it breeds in moribund branches in the treetops or in dying coppice poles.

It is not a pest species and does no harm to the trees, only taking up occupancy once timber is cut or dying.

THE GLOVES ARE off in the fight over fishing between anglers and animal activists following the recent unveiling of PETA's negative publicity weapon - a hooked dog.

The Countryside Alliance has now drawn up its battle tanks alongside the National Angling Alliance in a combined effort to counteract the actions of the American pressure group which wants to see UK angling banned.

Angling groups were outraged when it was revealed that a planned high-profile assault on their sport would involve a faked picture of a dog hooked through its muzzle.

The image, controversially concocted by PETA (People for the Ethical Treatment of Animals), aims to highlight the apparent suffering of hooked fish and help to get angling outlawed by turning British public opinion against it.

Launching the drive against angling and fish-eating here is American Dawn Carr, a 32 year-old vegan newly arrived in Britain to spread the word backed by a multi-million dollar fighting fund.

Alliance chief executive Richard Burge, a keen angler himself, said:"We are pleased to be working alongside the National Angling Alliance to help defeat this unwarranted attack on angling, which is a vital part of the rural economy.

"Its demise would have a serious impact on the lives of those who enjoy it as a pastime and those who derive their livelihood from it.

"The Countryside Alliance will continue its robust, comprehensive and detailed protection of angling against all unwarranted and dishonest attacks. In particular, we are hoping to bring our considerable experience in counteracting the misinformation of the animal rights industry to the campaign."

Charles Jardine, director of the Alliance's Gone Fishing campaign, added:"I want to remind all animal rights activists that anglers are the heartbeat of rivers and lakes throughout the British Isles. Over generations, they have cared for and loved the worlds in which they fish.

"We are conservationists and countrymen first and foremost and will not bow to an American organisation prepared to inject millions of dollars into an arrogant and inaccurate campaign designed to criminalise three million decent people."

A CORNISH LOBSTER could be set for a life of crustacean celebrity after being deemed too huge to cook by a London chef.

The lobster, almost a metre long, was found to be too large to fit into a pot at a Mayfair restaurant and was handed to the London Aquarium.

Experts there think it may well be nearly 70 years old and could be the biggest specimen ever caught in Britain or the rest of Europe.

The lucky lobster's fame is spreading far and wide but it might not be allowed to get too comfy in its new abode - staff at the aquarium may release it back into the sea.

WETLAND SPECIES ARE being given a boost with the publication of a new manual on how to conserve their threatened habitat.

The Wetland Restoration Manual, published by The Wildlife Trusts, boasts expertise drawn from a cross section of sources.

It provides case study examples to help land managers achieve Biodiversity Action Plan targets.

THE WAITING GAME has begun for farmers nationwide not yet touched by foot-and-mouth who want to see whether their own futures will be dragged down by an autumn resurgence of the crippling disease.

The Government's controversial decision to reopen the countryside to tourists over the summer months may yet come back to haunt livestock businesses if infected animals return from the hills.

Already, some farmers are desperate for ministers to close down the countryside again in a bid to limit potential damage to their flocks and herds.

So far, 1,987 cases of foot-and-mouth have resulted in the slaughter of 3,768,000 animals - a nightmarish scenario to anyone confidently contemplating the future of British farming before the outbreak.

Despite a rash of new cases in Northumberland, the Government announced a relaxation of regulations governing the movement of animals.

The change means farmers who have been unable to move livestock will now be able to do so, although they will come under more stringent scrutiny.

Meanwhile, according to a new report published by the Countryside Agency, the impact of foot-and-mouth has spread far beyond farming and the areas immediately affected by the disease.

Ewen Cameron, chairman of the Agency, said:"Foot-and-mouth disease has had a profound impact on rural areas, created distress and difficulty for many, threatening livelihoods and the very fabric of rural life."

Speaking at the launch of 'Foot-and-Mouth Disease: the State of the Countryside' report, he called for robust regeneration measures in the worst affected areas.

"The full effect of the way the disease has impacted will not be known for some time. There will be more bankruptcies, fewer jobs and rural communities will suffer for years to come," he added."In the areas hardest hit, agriculture was already in recession and many households depended on rural tourism."

ORANGE FLOATS WERE deployed in the Bristol Channel in a bid to better understand how pollution affects the West Somerset coast.

Using tracking devices attached to the fluorescent floats, the Environment Agency aimed to get a better picture of how the tides and currents move between Watchet and Minehead.

Made from recycled bottles, the floats - called drogues - were released at strategic points to establish how pollution is carried along.

RED SQUIRRELS ARE being backed by woodland experts to ensure the Highlands of Scotland remain a stronghold.

A new group of volunteers has come together to protect the squirrels from encroachment by grey squirrels, introduced here from North America in the 19th Century.

"Fortunately, as far as we know, the grey squirrel has not moved into the Highlands yet," said group member Ian Collier, a woodland officer with the Forestry Commission in Dingwall."However, their spread is relentless so there is no room for complacency.

"Latest research shows that many of the region's big conifer forests could be key places to conserve healthy numbers of red squirrels. This is because grey squirrels don't like conifer forests but reds seems quite happy in them, especially if they have plenty of Scots pine and Norway spruce trees.

"The smaller, more delicate red squirrel is better adapted to getting the seeds out of pine and spruce cones, whereas the bigger grey squirrel prefers larger foods found on broadleaf trees, such as hazelnuts and acorns.

"Research suggests that conifer forests of at least 5000 acres stand the best chance of supporting viable numbers of red squirrels and keeping grey squirrels out.

"In some areas it might also be possible to support smaller populations in woodlands as small as 500 acres if we manage them the right way and create buffer zones that deter grey squirrels from entering.

"We also have a golden opportunity in the Highlands to gather information on red squirrels that are not affected by greys."

HORSES ARE MAKING a comeback in Welsh forestry work - just to show how it used to be done.

Today, heavy lifting equipment is king and the days of horses dragging timber through commercial woodland appear long gone.

But the Horse Logging Specialist Group aims to highlight the advantages of horses as an effective woodland management tool, causing little or no damage to standing timber, soil structures, or sensitive ground flora and fauna.

Together with The Woodland Trust, the group has arranged a public display of horses moving timber at Silia Wood near Presteigne, on the Powys/Herefordshire border.

"Silia Wood was given to the Trust by the Presteigne and Norton Town Council in 1994," said a spokesman."It is an unusual wood, an ancient woodland site on which an arboretum was created in the 1860s.

"Some of the weaker trees need to be felled for reasons of good woodland management but the wood does not have suitable tracks to remove the timber. Rather than spending money on building an intrusive roadway though the wood, the Trust decided to step back in time and use a more traditional method of moving the timber - the heavy horse."

WHITE-BEAKED DOLPHINS, a minke whale, and porpoises have all been sighted offshore in the Shetland Isles during a busy period for wildlife watchers. Recently, a ringed seal - more at home in the High Arctic - was spotted for only the second time there while, less happily, a 40ft sperm whale was found dead on Haroldswick beach.

157

WILD SALMON AND sea trout are under growing pressure from illegal poaching but the law is hitting back hard, the Environment Agency has revealed.

The Agency spoke out after the latest apprehension of a suspected poacher, this time spotted by a passer-by handling a net stretched across a West Sussex river.

Police and fisheries officers seized the net on the River Ems as evidence and the man was questioned and could now face charges.

"Challenging individuals is thanks in no small part to the help we receive from members of the public who report suspicious behaviour on rivers across the country," said Stuart Taylor, the Agency's fisheries and ecology manager for Sussex.

Poaching now posed a serious threat to the already declined stocks of salmon and sea trout that populate UK rivers.

"It is difficult to understand why, when the cost of commercially farmed salmon and trout is relatively cheap, that people are still prepared to risk a criminal conviction to poach these fish," added Mr Taylor.

"If the case against this suspect is proven then he risks a substantial fine and a criminal record from the courts.

"With modern technology, professional expertise and support from the public and police, our fisheries officers are well equipped to combat this threat and so preserve the future of fish stocks for future generations to enjoy.

"So poachers, beware - the balance is now tipped in the fish's favour."

A POLLUTION INCIDENT was nipped in the bud by an alert member of the public.

The Environment Agency has praised the unnamed person who contacted its hotline to report a pollution spill affecting a stream at Nutley, East Sussex - part of a Site of Special Scientific Interest.

The stream is home to rare freshwater crayfish as well as other species and the prompt call allowed the Agency's emergency team to swing into action to battle the worst effects of a sewage spill.

Environment protection officer Jamie Barker said:"When we arrived, we could see fish gasping for breath. The sewage, which was partially treated, had caused the dissolved oxygen levels to fall very low making the fish suffocate.

"We deployed aeration equipment to raise oxygen levels in the stream from 15 per cent to over 60 per cent but unfortunately about 100 trout had already died.

"Rain that followed will help dilute the effects of the sewage and will raise the river's oxygen levels further. But it is fortunate we were able to get to the incident as quickly as we did, thanks to person who contacted us, otherwise the situation could have been a lot worse."

BETTER RURAL TRANSPORT is the target of a £50 million scheme unveiled by the Countryside Agency.

But local groups applying for cash need to come up with imaginative rural transport plans which meet the needs of those working in villages and market towns, as well as helping visitors to the countryside.

Pam Warhurst, the Agency's deputy chairman, said:"Access to affordable, reliable, and safe public transport is a key issue for rural people and visitors alike.

"Most people living in rural areas have to rely on a car to get to work, to the shops, or to other services, whether in their local market town or further away.

"This is because of the lack of suitable alternatives. As a result, those without a car are isolated and excluded from participating fully in rural life.

"At the same time, many visitors to the countryside would use public transport if it were available and more welcoming.

"We want to encourage more people to do so, to reduce congestion, promote more sustainable forms of tourism, and increase visitors' enjoyment of the countryside.

"Conventional transport won't always work. We have to think of different ways of meeting needs with solutions tailored to local circumstances and involving local people in their planning.

"Rural Transport Partnerships bring together local groups of operators, transport planners and users to devise an integrated approach to local transport schemes.

"And Parish Transport Grants get money right down to community level to support small, locally-generated projects."

TENS OF THOUSANDS of farmed salmon are feared to have escaped from a site in Northern Ireland, sparking concern about the risk to wild salmon stocks.

The fish broke out of their underwater pen at a fish farm north of Belfast and angling groups are worried they may now breed with wild salmon and compromise their quality.

However, Government investigators are monitoring the situation and have tried to calm fears.

They also claim that inter-breeding of the two salmon types is unlikely.

A NUMBER OF sheep have been found savagely slaughtered by a mystery predator close to an area where a 'lioness' has been reportedly sighted.

Discovery of the latest victim takes the grim tally of North Somerset farmer Robert Harding's sheep to four.

Now he is thinking of setting a trap to catch the killer.

Mr Harding believes a big cat is to blame since he has never before come across the type of wounds inflicted - all the victims were ripped open with claws, one even had its face skinned.

A lioness was apparently sighted by several people recently, stalking fields around Churchill on the fringes of the Mendips.

Experts later said the animal was more likely to be a puma or mountain lion, which could look like a lioness at a glance.

MAGPIE: a neighbour's pet killed by DIY wizardry

HIGHLY visible in his black and white plumage, the magpie sparks terror in the hedgerow among vulnerable nesting birds.

Equipped with a pickaxe beak and keen intelligence, this voracious predator has been blamed in part for the steady decline of many of our songbird species whose chicks are snatched from their nests.

I have watched a magpie return again and again to a sparrow's nest until every last helpless chick is either devoured on the spot or carried away struggling in that deadly beak.

It's grisly stuff but magpies have a right to eat like the rest of us and are, in fact, omnivorous, choosing seeds, berries, and fruit when meat is in short supply.

There are definitely more magpies about these days and it is frequently possible to make inroads into that magpie-counting rhyme:*"One for sorrow, two for joy, three for a girl, four for a boy, five for silver, six for gold, seven for a secret never to be told..."*

I'm not sure what comes next, or if anything does, but I've certainly seen five magpies together at once recently.

Unluckily for smaller birds, magpies tend to stay rooted in the same general territory and will comb local trees and hedgerows remorselessly for chicks and eggs during the breeding season.

Magpie nests are constructed of twigs arranged in a large dome shape and lined with soft grass and soil.

When the boot is on the other foot and their own young are threatened, magpies can be very brave in defence.

I myself have watched a lone female driving away two menacing crows. Magpies are actually part of the crow family but at just 250 grammes full grown are much leaner and smaller than, say, the rook or carrion crow. Yet they are still bigger than their more colourful cousin, the jay.

There doesn't seem to be much love lost between any of these 'relatives' but I've observed the natural animosity between magpies and jays at closer range.

When I was a child, we used to live next door to an accident-prone family, one of whose sons tried to raise a young magpie as a pet.

Not to be outdone, my older brother acquired a jay and these two birds would threaten and insult each other all day over the garden fence.

In the wild, the weaker jay would be driven off with a nasty peck for its impudence.

The jay didn't live long, proving the folly of taking birds from the wild. But the magpie's death wasn't far behind either.

Nor was it a surprise.

An attempt by its owner to build a complex home for his pet mice failed when they suffocated. (He'd forgotten air holes.)

In fact, the death of his magpie involved more DIY wizardry.

It had probably seemed a good idea at the time to nail a razor-sharp piece of metal vertically down a back door to keep out draughts.

That was until the wind blew the door shut on the magpie, almost cutting it in half.

Some time later, the boy's own mother fell foul of the same device when it sliced off a finger.

However, she grimly carried the severed digit to hospital in a plastic bag where it was successfully reattached.

I often think of her when anyone uses the phrase: *"the fickle finger of fate."*

THE MILK WAR between animal rights activists and the dairy industry seems set to intensify despite producers celebrating an Advertising Standards Authority judgement against their opponents.

American-based group People for the Ethical Treatment of Animals (PETA) has pledged to continue its campaign aimed at schoolchildren despite the judgement.

Meanwhile, in a precursor of how the campaign might develop here, American students are currently being urged by PETA to drink beer instead of milk - because it's "healthier".

"PETA is urging college students to wipe off those milk moustaches and replace them with foam," said a spokesman on their US website."The largest animal rights group in the world is releasing the results of research showing that beer is actually better for you than milk. PETA is giving away bottle openers that say 'Drinking Responsibly Means Not Drinking Milk - Save a Cow's Life' to college students."

Among advantages of choosing beer over milk, it says, are that: beer has zero fat while milk is loaded with fat; beer has zero cholesterol while milk contains 20 mg of cholesterol in every 8 oz serving; beer does not contain hormones or antibiotics while milk contains an ever-increasing variety of pesticides and antibiotics fed to cows, including a "notorious growth hormone that can give guys breasts."

In the UK, PETA cards bearing the headline 'Milk Suckers' were handed out to youngsters across the country - to the disgust of the Dairy Council, NFU, and Royal Agricultural Society.

The cards blame milk for causing a variety of problems such as acne, wind, and obesity.

In its judgement, the Advertising Standards Authority attacked PETA for playing on children's anxieties and ordered it to stop distributing the cards.

However, the group says it will just reword them more in line with ASA guidelines and continue to target children.

A DEPRESSED PIG was put on a herbal version of Prozac to try to lift her mood after her sister died.

The Peruvian pygmy porker, named Poddington, suffered a severe slump in spirits at an animal centre in Kentchurch, Herefordshire.

The body of her sister was left with the mourning pig for a whole day to help her come to terms with her loss - but she stopped eating and began fighting with other animals.

GAME MEAT COULD soon be much more widely available under an initiative launched by the Countryside Alliance's Campaign for Shooting.

Campaign director David Bredin said:"For some time now we have been concerned about the imbalance between supply and demand for this product on the home market and the risk that this will be exacerbated by the additional surplus of venison following the ban on export due to foot-and-mouth disease.

"What is urgently needed is a programme of co-ordinated activities to help shoots market game, to make it more attractive to consumers, and to increase demand both here and in Europe."

Working with the National Game Dealers Association and the National Gamekeepers' Organisation, campaign organisers have introduced a raft of projects to increase the domestic market and revitalise the UK's existing export market for game meat.

Among these is a bid to help more shoots help themselves since a number of shoots have already found effective ways of marketing game meat to local consumers.

Guidance on how to deal with shot game has been provided for shoot organisers and keepers in a booklet entitled 'Making the Most of Your Game'.

Mr Bredin added:"Over the coming weeks, months and years, the Campaign for Shooting will ensure that much of its resources are given over to the task of establishing the proper status that British game meat deserves as one of the most nutritious and flavoursome foods we produce."

A YOUNG COW sparked a race against time after plunging 300 feet off a cliff in Devon.

The heifer, named Neptune by her rescuers, had been grazing at the top of the cliff at Shoe Ledge Cove, near Start Point, when she fell to the beach below - somehow escaping major injury.

Exeter regional control centre received an emergency call from a fisherman who had spotted the stranded animal, prompting a team of four RSPCA men to scramble their rescue boat.

With the tide coming in fast, the cow was sedated by a vet then carried into the boat before being transported to safety.

Inspector Len Rankin said:"We were in a race against time as the tide was coming in, and it was a precarious rescue because of where the animal had fallen. Owing to the overhang of the cliff, there was no way a helicopter could have been used so we sedated the heifer and got her into the boat as soon as possible. Because of the professionalism of the team, the rescue went like clockwork."

A SEAL PUP has abandoned the sea for a life sunning itself on the banks of a Dorset river.

The pup, dubbed Sammy by locals, has settled in the River Stour at Bournemouth where it has been observed catching fish and lazing on the banks.

The RSPCA has asked people not to feed the pup in case this compromises its wild instincts and makes it more vulnerable.

Some believe the pup, which is aged about six months, may have become disorientated and separated from a colony in Cornwall.

But why it chose to set up home inland remains a mystery.

160

FARMERS BATTERED BY the worst outbreak of foot-and-mouth anywhere in the world greeted the UK's 'black landmark' 2,000th case with grim resignation - and tried to look on the bright side.

NFU deputy president Tim Bennett admitted:"In our worst nightmares we could never have imagined just how significant an epidemic this would be when we heard about that first case. But, despite the bleak headlines, the huge efforts being made mean the situation is improving every day."

To back up his claim, he pointed to four key findings:

-AN average of just three fresh cases a day were reported for the seven-day period ending August 26 - compared with 40 per day at the height of the epidemic.

-OUT of 137,523 holdings that have had infected area restrictions imposed since the start of the outbreak, 100,720 have now had restrictions lifted - a reduction of 73 per cent.

-OF 9,126 farms which have had their animals slaughtered, 6,433 have begun cleansing and disinfection - with more than a third starting to look at re-stocking.

-UP to 100,000 blood samples each week are being taken from 'at risk' sheep - but less than one per cent are proving positive.

Mr Bennett added:"We are under no illusion about the amount of work left to do. We know that as the autumn approaches the cooler weather will not help us in our efforts to stamp out the disease.

"There must be no repeat of the worrying sparks like those in Northumberland in recent days and everyone who goes anywhere near a farm must keep up the vital biosecurity measures.

"When this disaster is finally over we need to have some answers about how this could have happened. It is still a matter of disgust for farmers that while they are battling foot-and-mouth, the door is still open to illegal imports."

THE AMOROUS ANTICS of two hedgehogs put the wind up staff at a Yorkshire nursing home and sparked an emergency alert.

Jane Bailey and Pam Ratcliffe became so alarmed by the odd sound in the early hours that they dialled 999.

Police raced to investigate the noise at the Hoyland home but came upon the prickly mammals still in the throes of passion.

Officers left them to it, beat a retreat, and told the red-faced nursing pair of their discovery.

A recent burglary attempt at the home was blamed for making staff extra cautious about unfamiliar noises emanating from outside during the night.

AN APPEAL HAS been launched to raise £250,000 aimed at making life safer for whales, dolphins and other marine life around Britain's coasts.

The Wildlife Trusts says their Marine Appeal, if successful, will help them increase their efforts regarding vital conservation work.

"Every year, thousands of whales, dolphins and porpoises die needlessly in UK waters," said a spokesman."These waters are increasingly under threat from pollution, oil spillage, excessive fishing and 'incidental bycatch', where dolphins and harbour porpoises are caught accidentally in fishing nets.

"Even with the existing conservation work the death toll of some of our amazing and majestic marine wildlife continues to rise. For example, during seasonal fishing of sea bass in the English Channel, which lasts six weeks, the dolphin death toll is estimated to be several thousand.

"Our coastline has suffered from more oil slicks than any other in Europe and in the Celtic sea gill nets for hake kill an estimated 2,200 harbour porpoises a year."

Joan Edwards, marine conservation manager, added:"Porpoises can go close to nets in safety provided they know they are there. We are developing a number of devices and conducting research and surveys aimed at directly helping dolphins and porpoises survive fishing nets."

A NORTHUMBERLAND BOG has gone up in the world and received the UK's highest conservation ranking - National Nature Reserve status - in a bid to safeguard rare birds.

"Whitelee's blanket bog and lower moorland slopes are important for a number of rare bird species, such as hen harrier, peregrine falcon, merlin, golden plover, black grouse and skylark," revealed a spokesman for The Wildlife Trusts.

"Other notable birds include dunlin, curlew, snipe, redshank and red grouse. Heather, hare's tail cotton grass, sphagnum moss, and purple moor-grass typically dominate the area and the reserve supports badgers, otters and a herd of feral goats, dating back to medieval times.

"The 1,500 hectare reserve is owned by Northumberland Wildlife Trust who are now actively managing it to conserve its prized species and habitats. Whitelee moor adjoins Kielderhead National Nature Reserve - the two sites together constituting an internationally recognised wildlife resource."

THREE KENT MEN have been prosecuted by the Environment Agency for fishing without rod licences.

Following the case at Folkestone Magistrates Court, Jim Roden, from the Agency's legal team, warned:"Fishing without a rod licence really is a false economy.You will get caught - it's that simple."

The first defendant, aged 21, from Sandwich, pleaded guilty by post to fishing without a licence on May 27 at Friends Lake, Betteshanger. He was fined £33 and had costs of £80 awarded against him.

The second man, aged 33, from Deal, pleaded guilty by post to fishing without a licence on May 13 at Cottington Court Lakes, Deal. He was fined £33 and had costs of £80 awarded against him.

The third man, aged 26, also from Sandwich, was found guilty in his absence to fishing without a licence on May 7 at Cottington Court Lakes, Deal. He was fined £110 and had costs of £80 awarded against him.

LIVESTOCK FARMERS ARE facing the bleakest of winters as gloom over foot-and-mouth deepens.

NFU president Ben Gill said:"Farmers face the daunting prospect of winter approaching, with depleted feed supplies, increased stock numbers, and a severe lack of cash-flow because they have had no income for many months.

"Our prime objective is to restore farmers' access to commercial markets but where this is not possible farmers need support from Government."

The NFU had been making the case strongly for enhanced payments under the Livestock Welfare Disposal Scheme and he himself is holding urgent talks with ministers to ensure the plight of farmers is not ignored.

Mr Gill voiced his concerns for livestock farmers in England and Wales following DEFRA's clarification of livestock movements that will be permitted this autumn.

Rural affairs minister Margaret Beckett announced that under new rules counties around the country would be divided into three categories - 'high risk', 'at risk' and 'disease-free'.

Counties labled 'high risk' would be subjected to tighter controls than those free of the disease, where restrictions on animal movements will be reduced.

Generally, there will be more movement of livestock, but under more stringent controls.

"Farmers' first priority is to rid this country of the foot-and-mouth virus once and for all," admitted Mr Gill.

"In producing these changes to livestock movements, it has been necessary to negoti-ate a course that recognises the need to stamp out the disease and allows, where possible, the industry to move stock and prepare for the months ahead."

MIRROR, MIRROR ON the stable wall - which horse-faced nag is the fairest of all ?

Researchers at the Lincolnshire School of Agriculture have discovered that stressed horses are calmer and happier when a mirror is placed in their stable.

Typical stress behaviour, such as swaying the head from side to side, is substantially reduced after a plastic mirror is sited nearby.

Horses which had exhibited stress symptoms for as much as six years were soon 'cured' and appeared far more relaxed.

Scientists think the animals may be comforted by the apparent appearance of a companion to help them while away long hours spent alone.

THE JAILING OF a man described as a serial egg collector has been widely supported by conservationists.

The man, from Northumberland, was sentenced to four months imprisonment at Bedlington Magistrates Court - the first person in the UK to be jailed for illegally collecting wild birds' eggs.

Welcoming the sentence, Keith Morton, an investigations officer with the RSPB, said:"Regrettably, prison sentences may be the only way to deter eco-vandals who have persisted in collecting the eggs of some of the country's rarest birds such as goshawk, osprey, and golden eagle, placing even more pressure on these already rare birds."

The defendant had four previous convictions for egg collecting, the most recent being May 2001, when he was fined £1,000 for possessing over 1,200 wild birds' eggs.

The magistrates indicated they would have considered a custodial sentence had that option been available to them at that time.

The Countryside and Rights of Way Act has strengthened the Wildlife and Countryside Act, in England and Wales.

Under the Act, courts were given a wider range of sentencing options, including jail terms for those persistent criminals for whom fines were not a sufficient deterrent.

After the case, the RSPB thanked PC Paul Henery, wildlife liaison officer for Northumbria Police, "whose diligence has ensured a successful outcome".

NEW MEASURES HAVE been announced to help conserve the endangered turkey-sized capercaillie bird in northern Scotland.

These include a ban on shooting plus a Forestry Commission fund to help woodland owners remove hazardous fences.

THE LEAGUE AGAINST Cruel Sports has warned members that they are "at a crucial time in the campaign to ban hunting" and must remain active and vigilant.

Chief executive Douglas Batchelor said:"The hunters are pushing DEFRA hard to be allowed to resume hunting.

"Despite the obvious risks associated with any resumption of charging about the ountryside, amongst the sheep, the hunters are raring to go - foot in mouth!

"Cub hunting has been delayed by the foot-and-mouth restrictions but, nonetheless, the hunters are doing what they can to prepare for a new season's cruel and barbaric sport.

"Any evidence you have/can find of artificial earths, packs out on agricultural land and hunters failing to carry out proper biosecurity measures will be helpful to our campaign.

"While Backbench MPs seem as keen as ever to ban hunting, Downing Street seems reluctant to listen to its Backbenchers and get on with the job.

"The business agenda for the new parliamentary session will provide early evidence of the Government's intentions.

"Current thinking is that any resumption of hunting as foot-and-mouth restrictions are eased will be accompanied by the Hunting Bill being re-introduced to Parliament."

AIRGUN TOTING YOUTHS are becoming the scourge of Britain's wildlife as they use their weapons to maim and kill indiscriminately, claims the RSPCA.

The Society formally investigated over 700 airgun attacks on birds and animals in England and Wales during the last year, although many more incidents are believed to have occurred.

Swans and ducks are often targeted with a broken wing or deep wound ensuring the shot bird dies a lingering death.

Pets, especially cats, are also in the firing line and this has added to the Society's determination to back a private member's Bill pressing for the legal age for unsupervised use of low powered airguns to be raised from 14 to 18.

RSPCA chief superintendent Kevin Degenhard had no doubt that the 779 cases of airgun maimings and killings investigated lately did not show the full picture.

"Worryingly, this is likely to be the tip of the iceberg," he said. "Many animals, including wildlife, will simply crawl away and suffer an agonising death."

Last year, the RSPCA condemned the Government for failing to crack down on airguns, saying a clampdown could help relieve the suffering of thousands of creatures injured or killed in airgun attacks annually.

Chief superintendent Degenhard gave evidence to a Home Affairs select committee, urging the Government to introduce licensing for low-powered airguns and raise the legal age for unsupervised use of such guns.

However, to the Society's dismay, both measures were subsequently missing from a Government announcement on firearms.

Following that, Chief superintendent Degenhard said: "We will continue to call for all airgun owners to have a certificate outlining their reasons for possession and their competency in using the weapon.

"Hopefully this would take away the possibility of malicious attacks on animals and also make it easier to trace gun owners."

THE BIGGEST NATIONAL celebration of British food is drawing nearer as organisers put the final touches to this year's Host A Roast event.

On October 27, people across the country will show their support for local producers by hosting dinner parties, barbecues, or spit roasts using local meat, vegetables, cheese and other produce.

The Countryside Alliance's 2001 event promises to be bigger than last year when over 500 dinners were held across the country by various groups which included a Host A Roast wedding reception.

THE HUMBLE COCKLE could get legal protection in Cornwall as stocks of the sand-burrowing molluscs continue to dwindle despite efforts to protect them.

The Environment Agency says it is seriously considering the move because the average size and number of the traditional seaside snacks have fallen sharply.

Fishermen and representatives from fishing associations and conservation groups have been invited by the Agency to a meeting to consider byelaws proposed to safeguard remaining stocks.

Discussions will focus on the need to preserve the cockles in Cornish estuaries while the setting of a minimum size limit for collection has also been suggested.

It is hoped a fresh approach will leave smaller cockles to breed and so help preserve a small but important part of Cornish seaside heritage.

"While we consult on the proposed byelaws we are appealing to everyone who picks cockles to leave behind any that are smaller than a 20p coin to help the species continue to breed," said James Burke for the Agency.

"Protecting the biodiversity of our rivers and estuaries is of prime importance if we want to preserve the environment.

"Hopefully, we can all help reverse the fortunes of the humble Cornish cockle."

A SINGLE DAFFODIL is the annual lease 'fee' for 100 islands and islets of the Isles of Scilly to be taken over by The Wildife Trusts.

Under the bizarre lease agreement, landlord the Duchy of Cornwall will transfer about 2,500 acres of land, 26 SSSIs, and 906 archaeological sites from the Isle of Scilly Environmental Trust into the care of The Wildlife Trusts.

The islands are famous for their rich variety of bird and marine life, particularly exotic species. Notable wildlife includes roseate terns, oystercatch - ers, golden orioles, hoopoes, ringed plovers, puffins, basking sharks, dolphins, and seals.

The territory also boasts a variety of corals, sponges and jewel-anemones as well as outstanding rocky shores, underwater cliffs, sheltered lagoons, sandy flats, sand bars and a wealth of native and exotic flora.

Dr Simon Lyster, director general of The Wildlife Trusts, said:"I am sure this new arrangement will help protect and enhance this wildlife jewel."

A THREE-LEGGED CAT with a broken leg had a change of luck when it was finally found weeks after going missing from a holiday camp site in rural Cornwall.

Unlucky tabby Spice lost a leg as a kitten then broke one of its remaining three legs shortly before owner Carol Oliver took it on vacation with her to the New Perran site.

But Ms Oliver's efforts to bring a little joy into her pet's life backfired when the vulnerable animal vanished at the site.

Despite all efforts to trace the injured cat, it had seemingly gone forever.

However, searching RSPCA officers stumbled upon it cowering in a hedge - three weeks after it was last seen.

The moggy had somehow escaped further harm and was quickly returned to an overjoyed Ms Oliver in Plymouth.

ONE-STOP SHOPS could be the key that unlocks the door to new vibrancy for rural communities, says the Countryside Agency.

Chairman Ewen Cameron called on all those involved in providing vital rural services to consider the possibilities and benefits of providing more than one service from a single location.

Speaking at the Countryside Agency's 'Joining Up Rural Services' conference, he said:"The accessibility of a wide variety of services in our countryside has been in decline for some time now.

"On top of this we are seeing more rural services threatened by the impact of foot-and-mouth, particularly in those areas which are heavily dependent on tourism.

"Accessing basic services in rural areas can be difficult and causes serious problems, especially for the low paid and unemployed, those without transport, young people and the elderly.

"Providing services jointly through one outlet is one of the most promising ways of retaining and enhancing rural services.

"The economies of scale and synergies created by combining one service with another means there can be services provided where they would otherwise be uneconomic, as well as benefiting the customer who only has to visit one location.

"Today's conference is encouraging service providers to think about all the ways they can work together to provide services to rural areas, for example partnership working and pooled budgets, and new ways of delivering key services perhaps by using new technologies.

"The case for joint provision is definitely there.

"We hope that this conference will encourage more people to come up with innovative ways of providing services to benefit rural communities."

A RARE BARBASTELLE bat has been found on the Isle of Wight for the first time in a century.

Only a few thousand squat-faced barbastelles are thought to exist in the whole of the UK so the find has delighted local conservationists.

The male bat was discovered in Briddlesford Wood, a nature reserve on the island, raising hopes that it may be part of a new undiscovered colony.

Barbastelles have been badly hit by changes to the modern landscape as they need large tracts of ancient woodland to thrive.

The find was made by the People's Trust for Endangered Species which owns the site where the threatened creature sparked excitement.

TREES SHOULD BE more seriously considered as a potential energy source for the nation, claims The Woodland Trust.

The UK's leading woodland conservation charity has contributed to the Cabinet Office's current energy review by asking for full recognition of the importance of using wood as fuel.

Currently, less than a third of one per cent of total national fuel supply comes from wood fuel but the Trust believes this could be much higher.

"The Government says that by 2010, 10 per cent of the country's energy must come from renewable sources," said a spokesman.

"The Trust believes this target is unattainable unless there is a significant increase in funding to encourage people to use wood fuel.

"The benefit to the environment is enormous since burning wood is better for the environment than using fossil fuels like coal and oil.

"If there is an increased demand for wood, the Trust says this will benefit rare and precious ancient woodland because it will encourage the return of traditional woodland management techniques such as coppicing.

"This provides a 'crop' of timber, encourages re-growth and benefits woodland species of plants and butterflies."

SEVEN PEOPLE ARRESTED while "monitoring" a foxhunt have been awarded £3,000 compensation each.

Police took the group into custody after they were spotted watching the hunt from a minibus near Brecon in mid-Wales.

Officers suspected the seven were planning to disrupt the Sennybridge Farmers Foxhunt in November 1998 and acted to prevent a breach of the peace.

The four men and three women were held in custody for 10 hours, despite telling police that they had not intended to disrupt the hunt's activities.

They complained they had been eating their lunch when officers intervened and had never aimed to sabotage the event.

In an out of court settlement, Dyfed Powys Police have now paid £21,000 compensation to the group after their lawyer alleged the police had gone too far.

THE COUNTRYSIDE ALLIANCE says it will point the way to rural recovery with its new GreenFinger Route campaign.

The grass-route driven programme will involve both short-term and long-term policy ideas and initiatives, starting with explicit recommendations for a 10-point plan of immediate Government action to kick-start rural revival.

Alliance chief executive Richard Burge said:"We will be calling this programme the GreenFinger Route for two reasons.

"Firstly, green symbolises the countryside and the finger will be used as a symbolic visual device for pointing out to policy makers the route to rural recovery.

"Secondly, the term 'green finger' has another relevant well-known metaphorical meaning: that of coaxing new plant life from the land.

"In this context, we are using the term also to symbolise our initiative's aim of nurturing new livelihoods from the land, as well as to ensure that as many of these jobs as possible are derived from the sustainable use of the living land itself."

BRITISH POTATO GROWERS are celebrating a move by the world's top chip producer to set up another giant state-of-the-art plant here.

McCain announced its intention to build the £70 million factory with hopes for the future of farming at their lowest ebb in the wake of recent blows such as torrential flooding and foot-and-mouth.

The new factory at Rugeley in the West Midlands will be an addition to the Canadian company's existing UK operations in Scarborough and Peterborough.

An extra 380,000 tonnes of potatoes will be needed from British growers - more than six per cent of the total UK crop and taking the company's requirements in the UK to well over a million tonnes.

NFU vice-president Michael Paske said:"This is extremely good news. We are delighted that McCain has shown so much confidence in British farmers.

"This investment shows that the company has faith in the long-term production capability of our producers and will provide them with much-needed security.

"We look forward to working with McCain on future initiatives for producers."

AN ESCAPED PET falcon tried to make a meal of a tiny Yorkshire terrier out walking with its owner in Devon.

Pensioner Philip Stone needed help from nearby community hall members to free his screaming pet from the claws of the predator in Exeter.

The bird, an unidentified species, fell silently out of the sky onto terrier Monty and used its hooked bill and claws to attack.

Mr Stone, 72, suffered cuts to a hand in the drama while his pet sustained injuries to its neck and back requiring treatment by a vet.

As the bird finally flew off, a leather strap on a leg betrayed the fact that it was a pet that had escaped back into the wild and reverted to its natural killer instincts.

CHUB, DACE AND other fish are being given a helping hand to reach their spawning grounds in the River Kyle near York.

Low flows have made it increasingly difficult for coarse fish to breed so the Environment Agency, in consultation with North Yorkshire County Council and the local Internal Drainage Board, has started a project to install fish passes.

A CRUSHING ANALYSIS of the Government's attempt to deal with foot-and-mouth has been delivered by the Council for the Protection of Rural England. It claims ministers' response to controlling the disease has potentially been more economically damaging than the disease itself and revealed a failure to understand the modern economy of the countryside.

RED SQUIRRELS ARE going down the tubes as conservationists battle to save them from long-term extinction.

Pieces of PVC drain pipe are being employed to track our native British squirrels and build up a complete picture of their whereabouts.

The Forestry Commission has come up with a variety of reliable assessment methods - one of which involves the collection of squirrel hairs on sticky tape attached to the inside of 65mm diameter drainpipe.

"Sunflower seeds, peanuts or maize are placed in the middle of the pipe so that the hungry squirrel must move through the tube to get the food," explained a spokesman."The sticky tape picks off hairs which can be analysed later and referenced against the hairs from other animals such as mice, voles, weasels, and stoats.

"The small diameter of the tube means that larger animals such as polecats and pine martens cannot enter. Although colour alone is not enough to distinguish between red and grey squirrels, the difference can be spotted by staining the hairs with ink and viewing them under a microscope."

Forestry Commission researcher Brenda Mayle added:"The red's survival is threatened by loss of habitat and by the spread of the non-native grey squirrel. To focus efforts on the best sites for red squirrel conservation we need good information."

ONE HEN WAS not enough for Rocky the cockerel who drove suburban residents mad with his frustrated crowing.

Despite having one female companion, Rocky wanted more and let rip every day from 5am onwards at Ellesmere Port in Cheshire.

Now the rooster is off to live on a farm after locals complained to council officials about their noisy neighbour.

But no-one was more surprised by Rocky's antics than the family who own him.

Originally, they bought two fluffy chicks which they expected to become nice quiet hens clucking round the garden. Unfortunately, one turned out to be Rocky.

THE RARE MARSH fritillary butterfly could vanish completely from some areas of the country as a result of foot-and-mouth, claims English Nature.

The conservation group's new foot-and-mouth assessment report provides a mixed picture of how wildlife is faring in the face of culling and movement restrictions.

But the threat to the marsh fritillary butterfly has been balanced by the effects of reduced grazing which has allowed some rare species, sych as the marsh saxifrage, to flourish.

Chief executive David Arnold-Forster said:"The countryside and rural economy are still seriously suffering the effects of the continuing foot-and-mouth crisis.

"Our report confirms that the disease also affects the management of internationally important wildlife and Sites of Special Scientific Interest.

"We must continue to do all we can to eradicate this disease but now is the time to look to the future. We need plans to provide appropriate grazing levels to prevent already scarce species from disappearing altogether and we need to capitalise on those that have benefited from less grazing."

PHEASANT: tasty meat spoiled by teeth-jarring shot

PLUMP, handsome and good to eat, the pheasant has become a stalwart of the British country-side - quite an achievement for a bird whose origins lie in Asia.

Now common because of their popularity as game birds, thousands are reared and released each year to run the gauntlet of the hunters' guns. The noisy, strutting male pheasant is the most colourful with a striking, bright red face, lustrous green head, and white collar prominent on his speckled, long-tailed body

Quite heavy at up to 1.5 kilo-grammes, it is perhaps not surprising the male will often try to flee danger on foot.

However, a line of beaters usually puts paid to his efforts to disappear into undergrowth during a shoot.

In such circumstances, he is forced to take to the air

18th Century poet Alexander Pope captured the moment of death when he wrote:*"See! From the brake the whirring pheasant springs, And mounts exulting on triumphant wings. Short is his joy. He feels the fiery wound, flutters in blood, and panting, beats the ground."*

Smaller and drabber in colouring, the female is cleverly designed to sit unnoticed on her nest during the breeding season, hopefully escaping the attentions of marauding foxes and stoats.

A ground-nesting bird, she will lay up to 15 olive-coloured eggs in a quiet spot, concealed from view.

Seeds, grain, insects and fruit make up most of a pheasant's diet but they will also kill and eat lizards and mice if they can catch them.

The males can be quite aggressive during the mating season and I have seen them square up to each other, almost oblivious to any potential hazards nearby.

Despite their physical attractiveness, pheasants have never struck me as the brightest of birds.

While driving, I have sometimes been forced to slow down and creep round big males standing in the middle of the road.

This has denied me some good meals while reinforcing the pheasants' bird-brained belief in their own invincibility.

A friend of my father used to shoot and we occasionally enjoyed a brace of pheasant to eat as children.

Once tasted, that rich dark meat is never forgotten and was only spoiled by the frequent teeth-jarring discovery of hidden lead shot.

I've never shot anything myself but can see the attraction of a pheasant's quick, clean death as opposed to that which follows the lingering half-life of a battery reared chicken.

Incidentally, as a young reporter, I was once sent to interview an ancient couple celebrating their platinum wedding in the same residential home.

After 70 years' marriage, you might think they would have something nice to say about each other

But it took all my best efforts to turn each ill-humoured grunt and growl into a sort of misty-eyed tenderness.

Both wheelchair-bound, each was a picture of abject misery.

I seem to remember that the husband had been a hunter as a younger man.

If he could have chosen his own death right then, I suspect being knocked out of a perfect blue sky on a crisp, bright day might have held some appeal.

Then again, if he could only get hold of a shotgun, I'm sure he would have settled for potting his wife instead.

THE APPOINTMENT OF Margaret Beckett MP as the Government's new rural supremo looks even less popular following her controversial Labour Party conference speech.

The Countryside Alliance accused DEFRA Secretary of State Mrs Beckett of "missing the point" about the main reasons for British agriculture's problems.

Chief executive Richard Burge said:"Mrs Beckett talks about the need for farmers to be 'market-led' and 'consumer-driven' but she must realise that it is the CAP itself which denies farmers proper exposure to and access to free markets.

"Moreover, it is British consumers' unsustainable expectations of ever-cheaper food - comparatively now amongst the cheapest in Europe - which drive so much of the trend towards unsustainable intensive farming practices.

"The Government could already have done much to encourage a switch to more sustainable farming methods, for example by making full use under the CAP of its powers of modulation.

"This would enhance the prospects for our small-scale farmers and promote sustainable environment and employment aims into the bargain. The French government has done this already with their Land Management Contracts.

"For Mrs Beckett to cite farmers' intransigence and resistance to change is, frankly, itself an 'unsustainable' excuse!"

BADGERS COULD BE finally cleared or found guilty of passing tuberculosis to cattle within four years, it has been revealed.

According to the Independent Scientific Group, results from the Government's badger culling trials should be available by 2004/5.

The trials, which have seen thousands of badgers killed and outraged conservationists, have been disrupted to some extent by the impact of foot-and-mouth.

A COLONY OF water voles prompted British Waterways to change its canal improvement plans in the West Midlands.

Workmen had descended on the Titford Canal as part of a £300,000 project involving installation of new moorings when the threatened voles were discovered.

The rodents, which have faced being wiped out in recent years by predatory mink and loss of habitat, appear to be thriving in the area.

They were initially spotted during work to restore an ancient pumphouse which was burnt down by arsonists a few years ago.

Docking points for boats will now be moved further away so the vessels will not disturb the shy mammals.

MILLIONS OF PHEASANTS are going uneaten as factory farm production methods produce a gross excess of birds, it has been claimed.

Animal Aid launched a new report into the sport to coincide with the start of the pheasant shooting season which financially supports many rural communities and businesses across the UK.

"So many pheasants are being factory-reared in order to satisfy the base instincts of a new breed of vain and boastful gunman that millions of birds are going uneaten," claims Animal Aid, the UK's leading animal rights group.

"Many are even being buried in specially dug holes in order to dispose of the embarrassing evidence of excess. Huge numbers also end up mown down by traffic.

"This is the wretched picture of modern 'sport shooting' in Britain, as described by several of the industry's own leading lobbyists, writing recently in magazines for fellow gun enthusiasts.

"One wrote despairingly of 'Britain's game mountain'. In fact, greed, macho posturing and a callous disregard for the lives of their quarry and for the wider environment are jeopardising the future of the commercial pheasant rearing and shooting industry, according to these shooting advocates.

"Unlike grouse, which are born and killed in the wild, pheasants are 'mass produced' in industrial hatcheries and fattened in sheds like commercial chickens, before being beaten up into the sky to be shot down for pleasure.

"It is now acknowledged that millions of these birds go uneaten - there is no market for them."

Supporting Animal Aid's protest, Liberal Democrat MP Norman Baker added:"Most people believe that shooting is about killing a bird for the pot. This is no longer the case.

"Today it is about blasting birds out of the sky for some kind of twisted pleasure. This gluttony of firepower is killing huge numbers of birds and causing environmental damage.

"Even shooters themselves are now expressing concern about these bloated and unsustainable practices. Moreover, these practices are bringing shooting into disrepute. Traditional shooters are being swamped by the new style of braggarts who feel that more birds killed means the more there is to brag about."

QUACKERS - THE SIGHT of sheepdogs round-ing up ducks instead of sheep in a bizarre new competition.

But there is method in the madness of officials who launched The National Dog and Duck Championships at Aberfoyle in Scotland.

Foot-and-mouth restrictions have put more traditional sheepdog trials on ice so the dogs were allowed to display their prowess by other means.

And the duck herding championships have proved so popular they may become an annual fixture even when life returns to normal.

THE HUNT IS on to find the Young Environment Champion of the Year - and give him or her a cash prize of £2,500.

Budding David Bellamys who have helped wildlife or made a positive contribution to their local environment can all enter. The Wildlife Trusts have teamed up with Severn Trent Water and BBC Wildlife Magazine to launch the UK-wide competition.

CONSERVATIONISTS ARE celebrating an apparent climbdown by developers who spent 14 years pressing to build a sprawling housing estate next to one of Britain's most precious wildlife habitats.

The decision by three developers to withdraw their joint applications to build a new settlement of 1,350 homes adjacent to internationally important heathland at Holton Heath in Dorset, has been described as "stunning " by the RSPB.

After a 14-year struggle by English Nature, the Dorset Wildlife Trust, and the Society itself, the tide had turned against a damaging development and in favour of nature conservation, said the RSPB.

However, concern remained that local councils were continuing to support the development of the Wareham area site in the Purbeck local plan.

Conservation bodies were therefore still faced with opposing the local authorities at a forthcoming public inquiry.

But Gwyn Williams, the RSPB's head of site conservation, said:"The developers' last-minute change of heart gives Dorset County Council and Purbeck District Council a great opportunity to reverse their own positions and safeguard the future of some of the nation's rarest wildlife, including Dartford warblers, nightjars, and sand lizards, for which Dorset is so important.

"The decision by the developers to withdraw their damaging applications should encourage the local authorities to reverse their long-term commitment to support a new settlement at Holton Heath.

"We call on the councils to work with us to identify a new way forward for south-east Dorset, one that truly values its rich natural heritage and provides a sustainable future for both its wildlife and its people."

Over the past 200 years Dorset has lost nearly 90 per cent of its heathlands and those that remain are said to be highly vulnerable to neglect and to the effects of development, disturbance and predation by cats and dogs.

A TAWNY OWL called Sweet Pea has become a fixture on Shropshire cyclist Cliff Yapp's handlebars.

The brazen bird has taken to riding on the bars of his mountain bike as he pedals around the village of Wistanstow, where he runs an owl rescue centre.

The owl fluttered onto the handlebars one day by chance as falconer Cliff was taking a ride and now sits there comfortably each time he goes out.

Friends and neighbours were startled at first but have now got used to seeing an owl which prefers to travel by pedal power.

THE ARRIVAL OF fieldfares, leaf changes, and fruit ripening are three things The Woodland Trust wants people to record as part of its sweeping investigation into autumn.

The Trust says urgent public help is needed to build a definitive national database for the world's largest season change survey.

On a previous, smaller scale, recorders noted leaf colour, leaf fall, the departure of swifts and swallows and the arrival of fieldfares and redwings.

This showed that the timing of these naturally occurring events in the year 2000 happened several days later than they did in autumn 1999 - beech leaf colouring on average three days later; field maple five days later; departure of swifts seven days later.

"Traditionally, people have recorded spring events but not what happens in autumn," explained a Trust spokesman."It is important to fill this gap with more recorders, in order to get a good geographical spread to develop a full picture of what happens across the UK."

BBC weather presenter Isobel Lang added:"The 20th Century saw a steady increase in temperature, with the 1990s being the warmest on record. This is already having an impact on trees, plants and insects in woods.

"For example, higher temperatures now mean that trees are coming into leaf sooner and staying on trees for longer. This will undoubtedly affect the whole woodland habitat and the plants and animals that live there."

CHASING A SEAGULL off a 140ft cliff in Sussex ended in a lucky break for a dog called Henry.

When the potty pet flew straight off Seven Sisters cliff near Eastbourne, no-one expected it to live.

But the crazy canine survived with a broken leg after the sea broke its terrifying fall onto the beach below.

Distraught owner Louise Chavannes discovered her injured pet still alive and paddling back to shore after she raced down steps and along the beach, expecting to find its body.

Vets inserted a metal plate in the broken front leg, as well as treating the dog for cuts and bruises.

THE RAMBLERS ASSOCIATION has vowed to press home its legal fight involving a multi-millionaire currently facing a murder rap.

Officials say the company responsible for a blocked path running across the estate of millionaire Nicholas van Hoogstraten has failed to clear the route.

This is despite a court order demanding removal of obstructions which include a locked gate, barbed wire, refrigeration units and a barn.

"In March the Ramblers Association persuaded magistrates to order the removal of the obstructions on the High Cross Estate at Uckfield, East Sussex," said a spokesman.

"We are now returning to Lewes Magistrates Court to apply for daily fines to be imposed against Rarebargain Ltd, the company to whom the land is officially registered, because of the failure to deal with the obstructions."

Mr van Hoogstraten has been charged with murder and conspiracy to murder following a probe into the death of Mohammed Raja, a wealthy businessman who was shot and stabbed at his Surrey home in July 1999.

FARMERS' LEADERS HAVE welcomed news that an extra £52 million will be ploughed into a healthy eating scheme for children.

The cash will further boost the National School Fruit Scheme which began as a pilot last November in 33 schools in London and Leicester and is part of a drive to prevent cancer and heart disease by increasing consumption of fruit and vegetables.

According to the NFU, the extra funding means that over a million children aged four to six will receive a free piece of fruit a day from 2002 to 2004.

The union is now calling on the Government to expand the amount of home-grown produce it uses and include vegetables.

NFU vice-president Michael Paske said:"The Government, by providing increased funds, is demonstrating its commitment to encouraging children to eat healthily.

"There is, however, a need to provide children with variety and we would like to see vegetables such as carrots, celery and tomatoes included in this scheme."

Meanwhile, NFU president Ben Gill called on food chiefs to ensure equality for farmers in the food chain during the Institute of Grocery Distribution's annual convention in London.

Mr Gill told of the huge efforts made by UK agriculture and horticulture to meet the challenge of producing safe, traceable quality food while maintaining high regard for animal welfare and the environment.

But he added that farmers needed a sufficient share of overall profits to sustain investment and development.

"Farmers must be treated as equal partners in the food chain, not the poor cousin," he said."British agriculture and horticulture make a massive contribution and are capable of so much more. But profitability and progress go hand-in-hand."

AN OLD BRUSH discovered on a doorstep turned out to be rare white hedgehog, it has been revealed.

The female hedgehog, since named Blondie by rescuers, was actually at death's door after falling victim to sunstroke and dehydration.

Sudden movement by the 'brush' startled Blondie's finder at Washington near Newcastle but a hedgehog rescue centre was soon alerted.

The bizarre looking mammal has since made a good recovery although it is probable Blondie will never return to the open countryside.

Such obvious colouring is normally a death sentence for a wild animal which, in addition, would be shunned by other hedgehogs.

A PROBE INTO young salmon and sea trout stocks has been launched by the Environment Agency at the River Esk in North Yorkshire.

The two-week survey aims to find out whether recent improvements such as provision of fish passes and better enforcement of laws against illegal angling have borne fruit.

Ian Dolben, Agency fisheries scientist, said:"Data from previous surveys clearly show that the Esk has an excellent population of sea trout, which is steadily improving. In fact, some say that the Esk is possibly the best sea trout river in the country.

"However, there is still concern over salmon stocks which were in decline until 1987 when new byelaws were introduced to reduce illegal exploitation in the tideway. This decline has now halted but salmon stocks appear to be a lot slower to recover than the sea trout.

"We hope that the results of this survey will show that both salmon and sea trout numbers are once again on the increase. We shall continue to do all we can to bring the fish stocks in the Esk back to their former glory."

Part of the survey involves passing an electric current through the water, temporarily stunning fish, enabling scientists to easily net them and take measurements before returning them to the water.

THE RAMBLERS ASSOCIATION is coming down from the country to campaign for more walking in towns and cities across the UK.

President Andrew Bennett MP is due to outline the benefits of forsaking the car at an open meeting in Manchester.

Mr Bennett, chairman of the House of Commons Urban Affairs Select Committee, said:"Walking needs to be re-established as an important mode of transport as well as a means of improving our health. To encourage people to get out of their cars in towns and cities, facilities for pedestrians need to be greatly improved.

"The emphasis should be on keeping cars out of the way of pedestrians, rather than herding pedestrians out of the way of cars."

ENGLISH NATURE has become a major sponsor of the 'In Praise of Trees' project which will culminate with the Salisbury Festival 2002.

The project aims to draw together a number of woodland issues ranging from the aesthetic to the practical.

"Man's association with trees and woodlands spans thousands of years," said a spokesman. "Historically, they were a truly sustainable and renewable resource providing building materials, tools, fuel, furniture and food for the local community.

"This historical management is written into the landscape and structure of woodlands and even into the shapes of the trees.

"Some of Britain's rarest species live in woodland. Many have experienced dramatic declines in the last 50 years. These include dormouse, five species of fritillary butterfly, woodlark, and bats.

"English Nature supports a number of initiatives, providing grants to landowners to help them manage their woodlands. While supporting wildlife this also helps landowners maintain a healthy and productive woodland. 'In Praise of Trees' aims to raise awareness and understanding of our rich woodland heritage."

HUNT SUPPORTERS HAVE welcomed controversial findings of a survey which appear to reveal UK vets overwhelmingly back foxhunting.

Simon Hart, spokesman for the Countryside Alliance's Campaign for Hunting, said:"This is a significant survey as it takes account of nearly five per cent of members of the Royal College of Veterinary Surgeons.

"The overwhelming finding is that the veterinary profession opposes a ban on hunting on the basis that it is likely to increase animal suffering.

"In rural areas, the emphasis on opposition is even greater than anywhere else. However, it is interesting to note that opposition to a ban is still significant, even taking into account urban vets, too.

"Also, it was significant to see that the huge majority of vets, particularly vets in rural areas, agreed that there is a need for culling foxes in their areas.

"We are therefore not talking about if foxes need controlling, but how. It is therefore the responsibility of politicians to promote best practice and the findings of this report suggest that, more often than not, the use of dogs is a legitimate method."

The survey, said to be the largest and most detailed of its kind, was published in a national newspaper on October 14, and its main findings were that:

Some **63 per cent** of rural vets oppose a ban on hunting on welfare grounds while only **30 per cent** support a ban.

On the subject of the Government's last Hunting Options Bill, **66 per cent** of rural vets supported hunting with dogs in general, subject to statutory regulation (**32 per cent**), or self-regulation subject to independent supervision (**34 per cent**). Only **24 per cent** of those questioned supported the 'total ban' option.

Meanwhile, **79 per cent** of rural vets considered that fox control was necessary in rural areas, only **15 per cent** saying that it wasn't.

Over half (**52 per cent**) described their practice as serving a predominantly rural area, **38 per cent** described theirs as 'urban', while **10 per cent** said they did not know what their area was.

BARNEY THE GIANT lobster has been returned to the deep off Plymouth after becoming a crustacean celebrity when a London chef took pity on him.

The metre-long lobster, thought to be the biggest ever caught in European waters, was too large for the pot at a Mayfair restaurant which saved his life by donating him to the London Aquarium.

Staff there helped him recover from his traumatic time almost ending up as lunch and decided he should be returned to the sea.

Care was taken to choose an isloated spot where Barney, thought to be about 60 years old, could spend the remainder of his days without being fished out again.

BADGERS HAVE AS much reason to fear fox hunts as foxes because their setts are often fatally blocked up, it has been claimed.

"Before a hunt takes place, earth stoppers visit all the badger setts in the vicinity and block them up," said the National Federation of Badger Groups.

"In theory, this work is done in accordance with the Protection of Badgers Act 1992. The Act lays down strict conditions for the blocking of sett entrances, and stoppers are only permitted to use materials which are easy for the badgers to remove.

"However, we have received many reports of setts being blocked with materials such as rocks, tree trunks and heavy soil. Often, badgers cannot dig their way out and die underground.

"Hunting also causes problems for badgers in other ways. For example, over the years a number of hunt terriermen and other people with strong connections to their local hunts have been convicted of badger offences.

"When the Burns Inquiry into hunting with hounds was set up, the NFBG decided to submit a report giving details of the impact of hunting on badgers. With a Government-sponsored Bill to ban hunting with hounds on the way, the NFBG's report is still very topical."

A GATHERING OF up to 40,000 overwintering pink-footed geese was a magnificent spectacle for visitors to the Scottish Wildlife Trust's reserve at Montrose Basin.

On one occasion hot breakfast was followed by a guided tour given by Trust rangers around the tidal basin of saltmarsh, reedbeds and grassland.

"As the weather grows inclement, the geese fly to Scotland from Iceland and Greenland - where they spend the summer months - and set-up home until April," explained a Trust spokesman.

"The pink-footed goose is a rare species of bird with a world population of 230,000 and the congre - gation of up to 40,000 of them at the reserve forms one of the world's largest clusters. Watching them take off en masse is a rare and wonderful sight.

"The estuary provides a rich feeding ground for thousands of resident and migrant birds.

"In addition to the pink-footed geese, the basin is also home to curlew, oystercatcher, knot, dunlin, wigeon, mallard, cormorant, sedge warblers and greylag geese."

HUNDREDS OF BROWN trout have been released by Environment Agency officers into the River Blyth in Northumberland.

It is hoped the new arrivals will help revitalise the river which was hit by a major pollution incident last year.

Trout, minnows, stoneloach and lamprey were wiped out in the incident which led to the prosecution of Northumberland College.

The college admitted a pollution offence and was fined £7,000.

Agency officers released about 700 three to eight-inch brown trout from a North Yorkshire trout hatchery to replenish the stocks that were lost.

Jeremy Westgarth, Agency fisheries science officer, said:"This is a popular area with the angling community so we are pleased to be restocking the river following last year's incident."

RSPCA EFFORTS TO ease the animal welfare crisis caused by foot-and-mouth were hampered by red tape early in the outbreak, a public inquiry heard.

John Tresidder, RSPCA south west regional superintendent, told the Exeter hearing that initial reluctance by MAFF to involve the RSPCA limited help the Society was able to offer in the early stages.

A report submitted to the inquiry outlines serious welfare problems caused by delays in issuing movement licenses, inadequate supervision of slaughter, and delays in issuing guidelines to slaughter teams.

At the height of the outbreak, the RSPCA set up a brokerage scheme as there was no official aid for sourcing or supplying feed and bedding.

The same scheme is still in operation and is believed to be vital in coming months for farms that are overstocked and have already used up all winter supplies.

Superintendent Tresidder said:"In the West Country, particularly in Devon, the RSPCA had to deal with daunting welfare problems. Livestock was stranded away from home on barren and waterlogged fields. At the height of the crisis we were dealing with livestock suffering in a way that ought to lead to prosecution.

"However, DEFRA and RSPCA liaison is now working well. We must build on this to develop effective contingency plans for the future, with safeguards for animal welfare at the forefront. The coming winter will be a severe test."

One third of RSPCA staff in Devon worked full time dealing with the welfare problems at the height of the crisis.

More than 750 farmers in the county were helped with licence applications and supplies of feed and bedding.

The operation in Devon has so far helped over 103,000 animals.

The Exeter inquiry, called by Devon county councillors, is independent of the three proposed by the Government.

FARMERS ARE BEING encouraged to cash in on funding available if they restore native woodlands to their land.

A two-year extension has been given to the Forestry Commission's New Native Woodland Challenge funding scheme.

National Parks say valuable new woodland could be created at no cost to farmers or landowners taking part in the project.

But since Challenge funding is based on competition with other applicants - and now only has two years to run - it is vital that they act quickly.

NEW SHOOTERS FLOCKED to clubs around the country as part of a joint initiative by the Countryside Alliance and Leadshot.com to introduce people to the delights of clay pigeon shooting.

Events were organised at the North of England Clay Target Centre in York, the Doveridge Clay Sports Club in Uttoxeter, and at the Mid Norfolk Shooting School in Norwich.

Olympic shooters Richard Faulds and Ian Peel supported the scheme by attending and providing expert guidance with all tuition, guns, cartridges and clays provided free of charge.

David Bredin, director of the Countryside Alliance's Campaign for Shooting, said:"There is no doubt that the success of our two Olympic champions has aroused much public interest in the sport.

"However, it is crucial to maintain and nurture this interest by welcoming more newcomers to the fold.

"Our initiative has not only given people the opportunity of trying the sport but also helped to boost the membership and lessons of the participating clubs. The results speak for themselves."

Wesley Stanton, managing director of Leadshot.com Limited, added:"This new scheme has hit exactly the right target market - people who have never shot before.

"Shooting sports stand to benefit greatly from the tremendous personal successes of our Olympic champions.

"On-going projects such as this are what's needed to capitalise on their achievements."

HUNDREDS OF MINK are being hunted in the Hampshire countryside after they were released from a fur farm in the New Forest.

Animal rights campaigners are believed to be behind the incident which police and conservationists say threatens local pets as well as wildlife.

Up to 500 mink are thought to have escaped from Crow Hill farm near Ringwood, which was previously targeted by activists in the late 1990s when thousands of mink were released.

Hampshire Police warned local residents not to approach or try to catch mink they find.

THOUSANDS OF BIRCH, oak, alder and ash trees are being planted with the help of local people to create The Woodland Trust's third largest Scottish wood.

The Trust says the site, near Dollar, will change the landscape and play host to a wide variety of wildlife for hundreds of years to come.

It acquired the 950-acre site under its work with the Scottish Forest Alliance, one of the largest native woodland regeneration programmes in Scotland's history.

"This is a fantastic opportunity for people to create a new native wood which can be enjoyed by their children and grandchildren, and to be part of a revival for native woods in Scotland," explained Angela Douglas, operations director for the Trust in Scotland.

"We are beginning to create an ancient woodland of the future."

Three guided walks were also taking place, enabling people to "put their foot down" in support of the Trust's wider campaign to raise awareness of the loss of ancient woods across the UK.

HUNT SUPPORTERS HAVE accused the League Against Cruel Sports of "blatant hypocrisy" over its public stance against violence.

The Countryside Alliance's Campaign for Hunting arm has called upon League chairman John Cooper to make clear exactly where he stands with regard to animal rights violence following his letter to a national newspaper.

The letter responded to an article which suggested that animal rights violence was commonplace in hunting in the UK.

But Mr Cooper said there was no place for such activity on the hunting field and that the proper place for debate on the hunting issue was in Parliament.

"However, the Countryside Alliance can reveal that last year the League Against Cruel Sports knowingly employed Andy Wasley in their press office only months after his release from jail for attacking a policeman at a demonstration at Hillgrove Cat Farm in Oxfordshire," claimed a spokesman.

"Also, that a member of the Executive Committee of the League, Peter Anderson, took part in a raid on the Unilever soap factory in Bedford.

"The Alliance can also reveal that the League have regularly made use of, or relied on information supplied by Michael Huskisson, a well known animal rights extremist noted for the desecration of a huntsman's grave and involved with the theft of beagles."

Campaign for Hunting director, Simon Hart, added:"On the one hand, John Cooper paints a cosy picture of opposition to violence and intimidation.

"On the other, he either employs or does business with those with records of violence and intimidation against law abiding citizens."

HERRING GULLS PLAGUING a Sussex village could be in for a shock as residents prepare to bamboozle them with bird distress calls.

So sick of the gulls are locals in Rustington that they came up with the idea as a way of fighting back.

Being a coastal area, some gull noise has always been present.

However, residents say it now regularly exceeds acceptable levels.

Many people report being woken up as early as 3am by gull cries.

They are then irritated because the noise makes it impossible to get back to sleep.

The birds also seem to be becoming more aggressive and think nothing of swooping down in attack if they feel their young are threatened.

ORCHARDS ARE VITAL habitats for a host of birds, mammals, and insects, according to The Wildlife Trusts which led celebrations of national Apple Day.

The Trusts had organised a number of activities for people up and down the land to get their teeth into, including orchard visits, tastings, and the chance to buy local produce at one of several Apple Day fairs.

"Not only do orchards provide us with harvests of fabulous fruits, such as apples, pears, cherries and plums," said a spokesman,"they are also wonderful habitats for wildlife, providing refuge for many birds, insects and small mammals.

"Orchards frequently reflect the uniqueness of their local areas. You can taste freshly pressed cider apples in Somerset, buy some locally grown Darcy Spice in Essex, or visit some of the oldest bramley apple trees in the world in Nottinghamshire.

"Sadly, orchards are rapidly disappearing throughout Britain. Increased road and housing development has led to almost a 65 per cent decline in these special places in the past 30 years.

"The Wildlife Trusts aim to protect vulnerable old orchards, plant new ones and encourage everyone to help save and enjoy these tranquil habitats for the benefit of both people and wildlife."

A PEACEFUL WALK ended in pain and terror for a pet dog after it disturbed a wasps' nest on Dartmoor.

Vets say Bruno, a miniature Schnauzer, was lucky to survive after being stung about 200 times by the furious insects.

The unfortunate animal was said to have fallen into the low-lying nest as it trotted about near its owner.

A team of four vets was later required to extract stings from all over Bruno's body and the animal was given adrenalin and antihistamines.

The pet is now expected to make a full recovery despite its frightening ordeal.

THE FUTURE OF Margaret Beckett MP as the Government's rural supremo looks even shakier after she was ridiculed for her performance in the House of Commons when she gave more details of how the BSE sheep/cow brain mix-up happened.

Earlier, she had admitted it was "perhaps in error" that she ordered the late night publication of a massive research blunder which had seen cows' brains analysed as sheep brains for four years.

On BBC Radio 4's Today programme, she asserted:"I gave instructions, perhaps in error, that the statement that had been drafted to explain what we knew should be put into the public domain as soon as possible.

"Yes, we didn't have time to brief specialist correspondents, we hadn't known for long enough, yes, we didn't wait and have a press conference in the morning.

"We immediately put in hand a scientific audit to find out what happened, what went wrong, whether there's still anything to learn from the experiment."

Rural Affairs Secretary Mrs Beckett, a surprise appointment to the post in the first place, was also widely criticised following her controversial Labour Party conference speech recently.

FARMERS' LEADERS HAVE attacked a report by the Food Standards Agency for not spotlighting the need to crack down on illegal food imports - widely believed to lie behind the devastating outbreak of foot-and-mouth.

Although the NFU welcomes many of the findings about general controls on food imports, it says better policing of illegal imports is needed.

NFU Food Standards Committee chairman Michael Seals said:"A great deal of practical ground was covered by the report, much of which we agree with.

"However, the FSA should look more closely at the problem of illegal imports, how these should be controlled and how to prevent them from entering the country in the first place.

"The FSA must ensure that sufficient resources are made available - both in finance and personnel - to implement controls.

"As well as looking at how current resources can be utilised more effectively, the FSA must also consider whether more manpower is needed to improve controls and look at ways of funding these controls."

The report issued at the FSA's open board meeting included 10 proposals to ensure that loopholes in the existing system are tied up.

They include bringing imports of animal products under the control of the FSA, increased powers for port health officers over personal imports, and the establishment of an electronic information database for port health authorities.

But farmers remain concerned that lax import controls could bring a repeat of the crippling foot-and-mouth disease outbreak.

The NFU has run an on-going campaign to tighten up controls of illegal food and plant imports, including a petition signed by more than 30,000 people which was handed to the Government.

FOXES ARE ON the rampage in Gloucestershire because of the hunting ban imposed by foot-and-mouth, it has been claimed.

Numbers of foxes have been rising fast as a direct result of being left alone, according to local farmers.

Fears have been raised that the increasing number of foxes will impact on the lambing season next February unless something is done now.

Colin Pearce, of Home Farm at Berkeley, believes there are now so many foxes around at night that they are knocking things over and damaging his buildings and equipment.

The local Berkeley Vale Hunt also claims to have received many calls from farmers desperate for hunting to resume and says the Government appears to be dragging its feet on the issue.

THE FIRST SALMON in 70 years has been seen jumping a weir on the River Dove in Derbyshire on its way to spawning grounds upstream.

The sighting marks the culmination of a three-year programme by the Environment Agency aimed at re-introducing the fish to one of its traditional nursery rivers.

"For centuries, the Dove was recognised for its value as a spawning ground for salmon," said a spokesman. "Rapid, stony rivers such as this are favourite places for salmon to breed.

"In a report to Parliament on salmon fishing back in 1864 Lord Devonshire said 'With respect to the Dove, I have examined it carefully and there is not a finer breeding river in the kingdom, nay, more than that, many persons enjoy good salmon fishing there'.

"But by the end of the 1800s the Industrial Revolution had taken its toll on water quality. Pollution and obstructions in the river prevented the salmon from returning. The last salmon seen returning to the Dove was reputed to be in the 1930s and the Atlantic Salmon is now recognised as a globally threatened species."

Agency fisheries officer Gary Cyster, who spotted the salmon, added:"I hoped that we would see the first fish return this year and I was elated when I saw it jumping the weir. I have been working towards this for the last 20 years."

WITH BEEF BACK on the menu for exporters, a warning note has sounded for the Government not to forget the plight of arable farmers.

The slow resumption of beef exports is seen as a sign the rural economy is on the road to recovery.

But the Country Land and Business Association has used the moment to renew its call on the Government not to miss the deadline for claiming agri-monetary support from the EU.

CLA president Anthony Bosanquet said:"It is particularly exciting that such an important sector of the rural economy is receiving such a timely opportunity to get back on its feet.

"However, in a season which has seen harvests 25 per cent down, the arable sector is at risk of being set back if the Government don't claim the available agri-money from the EU."

'GOLDEN RULES' booklets are being handed to farmers to help them safely restock after their flocks and herds were decimated by foot-and-mouth.

The two documents -'Golden rules for a healthy herd' and 'Golden rules for a healthy flock' - have been produced by DEFRA.

Both underline the importance of co-operation between farmers and vets which is considered vital if herds and flocks are to be kept free of major infections in future.

There are also tips for stock buyers and sellers to ensure proper preparation is carried out prior to any sale, plus a list of endemic and notifiable diseases with a preventive strategy to combat each one.

Farmers' leaders have generally welcomed the guidelines, with some criticisms.

Jan Rowe, vice-chairman of the NFU's Animal Health and Welfare Committee, said:"The golden rules will act as a sensible reminder for all farmers thinking of restocking but the Government should give the process of cleansing and disinfection a higher priority.

"This will help ensure British farmers can fully rebuild their businesses and start earning income."

FANS OF HARE coursing claim they are being kept in the dark over whether or not their controversial sport will ever resume.

A decision by DEFRA had been expected recently but no clue was given to make the overall picture any clearer to supporters.

Hare coursing has long been attacked as 'cruel and barbaric' by detractors but remains as popular as ever among supporters who say the objective is to test the speed and agility of dogs - not to kill hares.

"DEFRA has completed its Veterinary Scientific Risk Assessment of coursing," reported a spokesman for the National Coursing Club."This report is now with ministers and it is their sole responsibility to make a decision on it in due course.

"There is no timetable for this decision, and we have no knowledge of when and if coursing might resume. A meeting of DEFRA ministers and their scientific advisers on October 25 passed without a decision being announced.

"If a decision is taken by ministers to permit coursing to proceed, it will be under strict regulation. Coursing would only be allowed in risk free areas, and then on ground where there is no danger of dogs and participants coming into contact with livestock. Strict disinfectant procedures would all be necessary.

"When a decision by DEFRA is known, the Standing Committee of the National Coursing Club will meet and inform as soon as possible the affiliated clubs of its procedures for coursing."

Officials behind The Waterloo Cup - the sport's top event - have issued a badge for the 2001 meeting which was cancelled due to foot-and-mouth.

The £5 badge has a green surround with 'Waterloo Cup 2001' inscribed plus the hat and crown insignia engraved in the centre.

Proceeds from selling the badge will go towards the losses made this year after the event was cancelled.

GREATER PROTECTION FOR the marine environment around England and Wales has come a step closer after the Marine Wildlife Conservation Bill, supported by Uxbridge MP John Randall, completed its second reading in Parliament.

A delighted Mark Avery, RSPB director of conservation, said:"John Randall has striven tirelessly to ensure this vital Bill continues its passage through the stormy waters of Parliament.

"Thanks to his dedication and the support of backbench MPs, the future of our marine wildlife is at least a little more secure."

The Bill had received full cross-party support.

MISTAKES WERE MADE by the Government in its handling of the foot-and-mouth outbreak, admits Food and Farming Minister Lord Whitty.

Responding to a preliminary report from a Devon public inquiry into the crisis, he denied that the Government was badly prepared for the epidemic but said its contingency plan should have been better publicised.

A plan was continually updated but it was not sufficiently shared with stakeholders, he conceded.

In future, plans should be shared around more and be better tested to make sure they were effective, he believed.

However, he still defended the policy of trying to cull stock on infected farms within 24 hours and animals on farms nearby within 48 hours.

Lord Whitty said he understood concern about having huge burning pyres in the countryside which were obviously not the best method to deal with the disease.

He also acknowledged that illegal meat imports, blamed by many for introducing foot-and-mouth this time round, were a serious problem.

A STAFFORDSHIRE BULL terrier went berserk and broke into a family's house through the cat flap after being terrified by fireworks.

The Lufflum family, equally shocked, barricaded themselves in a room as the powerful, bleeding animal ran amok at their Hednesford home - in Staffordshire.

The dog had first broken into their garden by crunching and wrenching off woodwork at the bottom of their gate.

At first, the Lufflums tried to keep the distressed animal at bay with a metal stool but it even began to chomp on that, so they fled.

Police called to the scene managed to get the crazed dog out of the house and it was later returned to its owner after calming down.

THE LEAGUE AGAINST Cruel Sports is pressing the Government not to allow hunting to resume despite the financial hardship imposed on hunt groups during the national foot-and-mouth crisis.

The League claims the sport should remain banned because "it is cruel and unacceptable to the majority of the public and to MPs, the last few months have shown that there is no ill-effect from there being no hunting, and hunting is an unnecessary risk while Britain is still under the shadow of foot-and-mouth disease."

More controversially, the League also claims that some hunt groups have been quietly flouting the ban.

"Even though hunting is illegal, the hunts are still out," said a spokesman.

"We are compiling video evidence of hunting during the ban and would be grateful if our supporters could keep their eyes and ears open over this.

"Hunting is illegal, drag hunting is illegal, 'mock hunting' is illegal, and hare coursing is illegal.

"Any filmed or picture evidence of the law being broken will add to our arguments that Ministers should not permit hunting to resume now that hunters cannot be trusted to abide by the terms of any 'licence'."

SWALLOW: snatching insects near a jagged roof

QUICKER and sleeker than the vast majority of birds, swallows are a harder target than most for a hungry hawk to try to bring down.

Breathtaking in their high-speed pursuit of insects, swallows are perfectly adapted to life in the fast lane and outflying a marauding raptor is more of a possibility than for less athletic species.

In addition, swallows boast incredible stamina and will trek thousands of miles each year on migrations back and forth to Africa. They can be spotted arriving in this country anytime between March and May and will generally stick around until October, sometimes even as late as November.

It seems amazing that year after year they can still find their way back to the same nest site in a disused British barn or outbuilding, some having set off from the southernmost regions of Africa and triumphing over a host of hazards en route.

The nest itself is a concoction of mud, grass, and anything else that can be moulded into a small cup shape and stuck beneath a roof or ledge.

Up to five white, speckled eggs are laid with the fledglings needing to learn their parents' flight skills promptly.

Sitting on an open branch or telephone wire, waiting to be fed, swallow youngsters are as vulnerable as any others to passing predators.

Once on the wing, however, it's a very different matter and most native birds of prey can be out-jinked and out-paced.

However, another African visitor to our shores, the hobby, preys with great success on young swallows. In fact, this small, ferocious falcon specialises in feeding on them and their cousins, the house martins and swifts.

Adult birds are, of course, a tougher proposition.

From the tip of his small, streamlined head to the end of his long V-shaped tail feathers, the bigger male swallow measures about 20cm.

He's also the more handsome of the sexes with a vivid red forehead and red throat complementing the glossy blue feathers above and pinky white feathers below.

I've watched swallows closely twice in recent months and marvelled at their sheer manoeuvreability as well as their speed.

The first time I took special note was in a large field close to a local river. There, a solitary male was ignoring a group of slightly dumpier house martins, picking off the choicest insects for himself as he powered from one end of the field to the other like a SAM missile.

Later, during a visit to a farm, I noticed another male swallow tearing in and out of the courtyard, snatching insects perilously close to a jagged barn roof.

A few starlings nearby seemed positively clumsy in comparison.

So mercurial and silky are the swallow's flight skills that it is perhaps not surprising some mention of them has crept into poetry down the ages.

Alfred, Lord Tennyson was keen on using swallows in his work, with one love poem including the line:

"O Swallow, Swallow, flying, flying South, Fly to her and fall upon her gilded eaves, And tell her, tell her, what I tell to thee."

I'm sure a duck carrying such a message would not have produced the desired romantic effect.

Then again, I suppose it depends on the woman.

SONGBIRDS ARE STILL being decimated en route to Britain by illegal trapping in Cyprus, it has been revealed.

A joint operation by the RSPB and the BBC's Countryfile programme found illegal trapping still accounts for the annual slaughter of millions of migratory birds, including many familiar species such as robins and blackcaps.

"Birds are still illegally caught on limesticks, a centuries old practice," says the RSPB."But the most serious problem lies with modern mist nets in conjunction with electronic bird calling devices, allowing trappers to catch hundreds of birds during a single morning.

"After having their throats slit, the birds are prepared to supply island restaurateurs and shopkeepers with the principle ingredient of the local delicacy ambelopoulia, which despite contravening Cypriot law is widely sold on the island.

"Each bird is worth around £1.50 and during spring and autumn migrations trappers can bag in excess of £1,000 a week."

Graham Elliott, the RSPB's head of investigations, added:"Following protests from the RSPB and other conservation groups, the island authorities have increased the number of arrests of trappers. But with little action being taken against retailers and restaurateurs fuelling this black and lucrative trade, many millions of birds will surely continue to perish."

MOST HEDGEHOGS HAVE little to fear of being trapped in Bonfire Night fires if the results of a survey are to be believed.

Over three quarters of people questioned between October 31 and November 5 claimed they would always check their bonfire for hedgehogs before lighting it.

Market research company My Voice approached nearly 1,000 adults with a variety of questions about Bonfire Night, including the one about hedgehogs.

Whether or not the vast majority of people really do bother to check their bonfires for hedgehogs might be debatable.

It seems possible that repeated warnings from such organisations as The Hedgehog Preservation Society are at last having an effect.

However, cynics believe the truth might be much simpler - no-one wants to be seen as a thoughtless killer of one of the country's favourite mammals.

A THREE-FEET long barracuda weighing 12 pounds has been netted six miles off the Cornish coast.

It is the first time the vicious predator has been caught in British waters.

Normally found in tropical seas, the barracuda is to be offered to the Natural History Museum for preservation.

FOXHUNTERS ARE becoming increasingly desperate to get their sport resumed following the devastating ban imposed by foot-and-mouth.

Lord Daresbury, chairman of the Masters of Fox Hounds Association, told members:"Every possible pressure is being brought to bear on ministers at DEFRA to publish the Veterinary Risk Assessment for Hunting, completed some six weeks ago.

"Representatives from the MFHA, the Campaign for Hunting and Countryside Alliance have visited ministers several times.

"Parliamentary questions have been asked, legal opinion sought, ministers have been spoken to individually and support has been given by the NFU, Jockey Club and others. Media coverage has also added to the pressure."

Although publication of the risk assessment appeared imminent, matters could not progress until it had been made public, he added.

Meanwhile, The League Against Cruel Sports has condemned the Countryside Alliance for shedding "crocodile tears" over foot-and-mouth restrictions at the start of the hunt season.

Chief executive Douglas Batchelor, said:"The hunts aren't normally out from the beginning of April to November anyway, so this is just crocodile tears, unless they are suffering a drastic reduction in support and therefore their funds are dwindling.

"At a time when Britain is still reeling from the foot-and-mouth epidemic, and before the disease has been entirely eradicated, the hunters are putting self-interest ahead of the needs of country people.

"To start hunting again now would be unnecessarily risky, given the movement of people between rural areas which it often entails.

"The Countryside Alliance cannot have it both ways - arguing on the one hand that foot-and-mouth is a continuing problem, and on the other, that they want their supporters to be able to resume hunting with dogs.

"The foot-and-mouth outbreak has put hunting with dogs in its proper context. There are clearly far more pressing issues facing the countryside than campaigning to save an unpopular, unnecessary and cruel minority leisure pursuit."

WATER VOLES ARE to benefit from flood control work being undertaken by the Environment Agency at Gosforth near Newcastle.

Ouse Burn will be desilted and re-profiled at a cost of £50,000 with natural river features such as backwaters and bends restored to boost the voles.

Anne Lewis, an ecology officer with the Agency, said:"As we work on the river bank there will be a lot of disruption to wildlife but we are using this as an opportunity to improve habitat.

"The first step is to create a large refuge area for the water voles.

"This has been made possible by the generosity of City of Newcastle Golf Club which has allowed us to create a wildlife area on their land.

"We are also creating new wetlands and other environmental enhancements that will improve conditions for other wildlife in the area.

"And we are reusing the clay we extract to repair the flood bank at Blackhill Mill in the Derwent Valley, thus saving money and resources by recycling material."

FARMERS' LEADERS HAVE blasted the Government's handling of a new code of practice between supermarkets and their suppliers as "disastrous".

NFU president Ben Gill has written to the Secretary of State for Trade and Industry about the fact that the industry was kept in the dark about the issuing of the code.

He was angry at the DTI's decision to publish the code without any prior dialogue with the NFU and other organisations representing suppliers.

In the letter to Patricia Hewitt, he stressed the sudden announcement was particularly galling as the industry had been waiting seven months for it.

Mr Gill wrote:"The handling of the code's publication could not have been worse. During the seven months in which your department had the code you consulted with the major supermarkets but virtually excluded ourselves and other suppliers' organisations.

"Despite this delay, we had hoped in vain that you would prescribe a code that would protect farmers' and growers' trading relationships with the supermarkets. To then also publish it without any prior notification has added insult to injury.

"We need to find a way ahead which is far more even handed. The retailers are here to stay. We need an agreed proper trading relationship and I fear that your decision will make progress much harder.

"It is critical that every avenue is explored to find a fair set of trading relationships between buyers and sellers within the food chain.

"The NFU will continue to meet retailers to press for proper implementation of the code, poor though it is, and for voluntary agreements on sectors which have been excluded, such as plants and flowers."

The NFU initiated the need for a code after complaints that farmers and growers felt threatened by the unreasonable demands of supermarket contracts.

SEVEN DUCKLINGS HAVE hatched out six months too early in Cornwall after the warmest October on record.

The ducklings, all mallards, appeared on a lake at Newquay Zoo which their mother and other mallards use as their home.

Zoo staff have been amazed by the their arrival and would not normally expect to see them until at least April. Workers have pledged to protect the youngsters by bringing them indoors if the weather turns nasty.

TWO RIVERS MILES apart have been restocked with fish by the Environment Agency in a bid to revitalise them.

In all, 1,000 roach and 4,000 bream were released into the River Anker at Ratcliffe Bridge near Atherstone, Warwickshire.

"The fish are being stocked in the river to enhance the population and to introduce a younger generation," said an Agency spokesman."Once they have been restocked at this point, they will be able to migrate up and down stream."

Meanwhile, 1,800 young unspecified fish bred at the Environment Agency's fish farm in Calverton, Nottingham, were released into Picknall Brook near Uttoxeter racecourse.

"The fish are being stocked in the river to restore the population after a severe pollution incident which occurred in the brook last summer," said the spokesman.

"At the end of June 2001, the Environment Agency received reports of fish dying in the brook. Officers visited the site and investigated the scene. The source was found and work was carried out to stop the pollution entering the brook.

"Surveys later showed that the pollution was organic in nature. An investigation was carried out into how and why the pollution occurred and a report was drafted and is now being considered to see whether any further action can be taken."

YEW TREES IN a cemetery face the chop after a fungal disease turned them bright orange.

Previously dark green, the ancient trees at Newport Cemetery in Shropshire have become infected by a condition known as phypoptahera.

As many as 16 trees could be felled by town council workmen unless someone comes up with a plan to beat the disease.

Many of the trees are 150 years-old and locals are upset by the thought that they might have to be cut down for safety's sake.

Specimens from the trees have been sent to the Central Science Laboratory in York for a second opinion before felling work can be given the go-ahead.

POLICE FEAR A backlash from animal rights protesters following the death of fanatical campaigner Barry Horne.

Horne, 49, considered a legend by many in the Animal Liberation Front movement, died in prison after being on hunger strike since the summer.

He had been serving an 18-year sentence for plotting a ruthless campaign of firebomb attacks on a variety of targets.

Formerly an inmate at Long Lartin high security prison in Worcestershire, he had recently been admitted to hospital with liver problems brought on by his fast.

Horne died at Ronkswood Hospital in Worcester from liver failure, according to the Prison Service.

A FLOCK OF Scottish starlings has been playing host to a rare cousin which went seriously off course.

The rose-coloured starling normally migrates from Iran to India but this time ended up sampling the chillier delights of an area near Aberdeen.

Twitchers flocked to see the bird after the RSPB declared its presence in the UK to be extremely rare.

The bird is thought to be a juvenile.

BRITISH BEEF FARMERS have been given another slap in the face by the French who have taken new action to underline illegal beef import restrictions.

Farmers' leaders are furious and have sent angry letters to officials in France, to the European Commission, and to our own Government.

In a stunning move, French farming organisations - supported by the French Government - have joined forces with other meat sector groups to ban foreign beef during the month of November in response to poor consumption and low prices.

NFU president Ben Gill has written to the president of the French farmers' union, Jean-Michel Lemetayer, as well as to Agriculture Commissioner Franz Fischler, Food Safety Commissioner David Byrne, and DEFRA Secretary of State Margaret Beckett.

He said:"We are amazed and appalled at this action. After everything that British beef farmers have been through in recent years from foot-and-mouth to the strength of sterling, they will be flabbergasted at this deplorable move.

"It strikes at the very core of the principles of the single market. No-one has had a worse time than Britain but we have never sought to undermine the common market in this way."

The physical impact on Britain will be limited because of the effect of continuing foot-and-mouth export restrictions but the French action completely undermines the principle of community solidarity, said Mr Gill.

It is the latest in a string of controversial actions by the French including the continuing illegal ban on British beef and proposed unilateral action to remove the spinal column from British sheep meat imports.

Mr Gill added:"The UK Government and the European Commission cannot overlook this. They must bring every possible pressure to bear on the French Government, forcing them to resume free trade in beef immediately. The French must decide whether they want to be in or out of the European community. They cannot have their cake and eat it."

A FEATHERY SUPERSTAR thrilled pupils at a school when it popped in with its real-life owner.

Hedwig, the snowy owl, has become world famous as the pet of Harry Potter but was brought in to meet surprised youngsters at Oswestry School, Shropshire, by animal expert Roger Pearson.

PLANS TO REFOREST large parts of Scotland have been given a boost with a woodland conference attracting more than 100 delegates from local communities.

The delegates came together in Dalbeattie for the two-day Community Woodland Conference to share experiences and receive help and advice from forestry experts.

"The rapidly growing community woodland movement, spearheaded by such communities as Laggan, Assynt and Eigg, is attracting world-wide interest," said a Forestry Commission spokesman."The experiences of Scottish groups are also being used as templates for community participation in land ownership in Europe.

"Over 100 community groups now own or manage about 50,000 acres of land across Scotland. From a five acre plot at Darnick in the Borders to almost 3,500 acres of conifer forest at Cairnhead in Dumfriesshire, Scotland's community woods are the result of the vision, action and dedication of local volunteers. They also bring social, environmental and economic benefits to communities."

Scottish delegates were joined by others from elsewhere in Europe, such as Sweden and Estonia, he added.

The conference, organised by Reforesting Scotland and the Community Woodland Network, was co-hosted by the Dalbeattie Forest Community Partnership.

SUPERMARKETS ARE FACING claims that English apples are being downgraded in favour of foreign imports.

English Apples and Pears, the group which represents the vast majority of the country's 400 growers, accuses supermarkets of not displaying native types prominently.

Adrian Barlow, chief executive of EAP, told a newspaper:"Last year we had a light crop due to the very wet weather. But this year, the weather has helped the crop, producing an abundant harvest with the best skin appearance for 25 years.

"It is therefore particularly frustrating for both growers and consumers that supermarkets are not devoting the necessary shelf space."

A BADGER FOUND badly injured by a snare has been released back into the wild by the North East Essex Badger Group.

'Judy', as the female badger was named, had been found on September 23 in the St Lawrence area near Dengie.

She was spotted by a passer-by who initially believed her to be the victim of a traffic accident.

However, when badger group members attended, it soon became clear that the animal had been hurt by a snare.

"Although the snare was no longer attached, it had left serious wounds which had become septic," said a spokesman."As a result, Judy's condition had deteriorated - probably over the course of several weeks - before she was found in a weak and very poorly state.

"She had also lost the use of her left foreleg. The vet believed that this was because she had been keeping off the leg due to pain. This had led to muscle wastage."

Despite her injuries, Judy responded so well to treatment that she was released and her case is now being used to warn of snares.

THE COUNTRYSIDE ALLIANCE has accused MORI of "seriously misrepresenting" findings of the Government Inquiry into hunting with dogs in relation to a recent poll.

So angry are members of the Alliance that they have sent a letter to Lord Burns, chairman of the Inquiry, to bring the situation to his attention.

A spokesman said:"In a set of questions shown to the Countryside Alliance, MORI's preamble to the issues upon which they seek public opinion claimed that the Burns Inquiry, set up by the Government last year, dismisses the significance of hunting.

"The question uses expressions from the report out of context and which would lead the casual reader to believe that the Burns Report found 'against hunting'.

"Furthermore, MORI offer the public eight single words to describe hunting designed in such a way as to lean heavily in favour of criticism."

Simon Hart, director of the Countryside Alliance's Campaign for Hunting, added:"MORI chairman Bob Worcester has never made any attempt to conceal his personal sympathies for the animal rights movement.

"However, in his capacity as chairman of MORI and indeed, the Market Research Society, he has a duty to ensure that poll questions can be easily understood and do not lead potential respondents into providing answers that, had they been in full possession of the facts, might have been different."

OWLS COULD FALL victim to Harry Potter mania as youngsters pester their parents to buy them as pets not knowing how difficult they are to keep, conservationists claim.

The Raptor Foundation fears many owls would be abandoned after their novelty value wore off and would then face an uncertain future.

Scores of kestrels were thought to have been taken from the wild and later abandoned following the release of the film 'Kes', about a boy who trains a kestrel, three decades ago.

Today, snowy owls - like the one in the Harry Potter movie - can be bought for as little as £400 with barn owls a snip at just £25.

The RSPB has warned parents that owls need special handling and are not suitable as pets.

ORGANIC GOOSE AND turkey are among a huge variety of Christmas fayre currently being promoted by the Soil Association.

"Our Christmas list provides a brief outline of where to buy organic produce for this year's festivities," said a spokesman."As well as enjoying a delicious organic Christmas meal, you can also help the organic movement by joining the Soil Association or by giving one of our original Christmas gifts."

CONTROVERSIAL DRAFT maps of fresh places to walk under new right to roam laws have been published for the first time by the Countryside Agency.

Ramblers are celebrating the move which will eventually see them able to walk across more open country and all registered common land under the Countryside and Rights of Way Act - despite furious objections from some landowners.

Speaking at the launch of initial drafts covering the South East and lower North West of England, Pam Warhust, deputy chairman of the Agency, said:"Today marks an important step in turning the Act into action.

"The Countryside Agency has taken forward a complex piece of legislation and is putting the groundwork in place so that people will feel confident about using their new rights.

"We've taken a great deal of care to produce these maps, using a wide range of existing data. We've delivered on time.

"Now we want people to look at them, see what land has been included and tell us if we've got it right or not.

"During the next three months we will be out and about, running road shows so that people can come and look at the maps, hear about how they were created and how they can comment on them, and talk to our staff direct.

"People can also look at the draft maps on our website or in local council offices, some libraries, national park visitor centres and in the Country-side Agency offices.

"This year's foot-and-mouth outbreak has made clear how important it is that adequate safeguards are in place to protect the business that sustains the countryside.

"When the current crisis is over, the more that people can find a warm welcome and experience the English countryside, the more they will understand the importance of the systems that support it.

"Every effort is being made to ensure that all means of access to England's countryside link up and that everyone, whether landowners or users, are clear on their rights and responsibilities, before full access rights come into force."

However, a backlash is already underway with John Lees, secretary of the Peak Park Moorland Owners and Tenants Association, telling BBC Radio 4's Today programme that the draft maps contained mistakes.

He also said that farmers without internet access would find it hard to see them, and the three-month consultation period was too short.

RARE SHEEP AND hens are to benefit to the tune of £10million left to them in the will of a country loving multi-millionaire.

Miles Blackwell was fascinated by rare breeds so left a huge chunk of his £65million fortune to The Rare Breeds Survival Trust when he died.

The Trust has been staggered but delighted by the gift - especially since foot-and-mouth has wreaked havoc with its finances lately.

Mr Blackwell, heir to the Blackwells bookshop fortune, died aged 56 less than a month after his wife Briony, 46.

They devoted pair are reported to have kept spiral horned Manx Loghtan sheep and rare Scots Dumpy hens.

ONE OF THE most important public inquiries for wildlife conservation in the UK over the last decade has got underway at Wareham, Dorset.

The RSPB, English Nature and the Dorset Wildlife Trust will all be giving evidence against Purbeck District Council's plan to allow 1,350 houses to be built at Holton Heath in south-east Dorset.

The conservation bodies are the main objectors to the proposal which, they say, poses a serious threat to wildlife and claim that Dorset has a responsibility to look after its heathland - one of the most important remaining areas of heathland in Europe.

RSPB conservation officer, Richard Archer, said:"Holton Heath is home to some of our rarest and most vulnerable wildlife such as nightjars, woodlarks, Dartford warblers and silver-studded blue butterflies.

"If this proposed allocation is approved, these species are at serious risk, simply through having thousands of people living so close to such sensitive heathland area.

"Urbanisation brings the increased danger of illegal fires, disturbance to nesting sites, damage to vegetation, predation by cats and dogs and, obviously, a huge increase of road traffic in the area. This combination inevitably causes serious damage to wildlife and the environment."

The RSPB, English Nature and the Dorset Wildlife Trust have contested this and other development schemes at Holton Heath for the last 14 years.

TWO AMOROUS BADGERS had to be plucked to safety from a private swimming pool after plunging in while mating.

RSPCA officers were called to the scene near Newport in Shropshire and rescued the pair after being alerted by the pool's owners.

Fortunately, the pool had been virtually drained recently and the badgers were found splashing about in just a few inches of water.

However, while they escaped the threat of drowning, they could easily have starved to death if no-one had noticed their predicament.

Luckily for them, the noise of their passionate encounter had reached the ears of residents before they fell into the pool.

TURKEY FARMERS ARE being warned to watch out for fowl play by rustlers in the run-up to Christmas.

With thousands of birds stolen annually, the Country Land and Business Association is urging small-scale producers in particular to beware of crooks eager to cash in on the seasonal demand for turkey, goose, chicken and duck.

Poor security measures could result in disaster for farmers unlucky enough to attract the attention of criminals, warns the CLA.

RACING FANS HAVE been boosted by the Countryside Alliance's pledge to stand shoulder to shoulder with their sport against looming threats.

The Alliance unveiled plans to work more closely with racing's various organisations to support the industry and the livelihoods of the 60,000-plus people involved.

In particular, it wants to use its experience of countering animal rights "propaganda" to neutralise the escalating anti-racing activities of well-funded groups such as People for the Ethical Treatment of Animals (PETA) and Animal Aid.

The Alliance says its commitment will also include political monitoring, early warning and pre-emptive lobbying action, as well as public relations efforts to help safeguard racing against legislative threats and the activities of anti-racing pressure groups.

Commenting on the Alliance's plans Christopher Spence, senior steward of the Jockey Club, said: "We welcome the support of the Countryside Alliance to counter the threat to racing."

Alliance chief executive Richard Burge said:"The people of the countryside both support and benefit significantly from racing, so it is a natural step for the Alliance to be campaigning more specifically for racing itself.

"Through stepping up our own efforts, we hope to complement and add to the sterling work from the racing organisations to date.

"This is an industry which employs 60,000 people with a further 40,000 employed in the betting industry - which relies on horse racing for some 70 per cent of its business.

"It is essential that an industry of this scale has the strongest possible campaigning voice. We have publicity and lobbying expertise which I hope and believe will 'bring something to the party'.

"One of our priorities must be to help remove racing altogether from the animal rights industry's agenda. The Alliance will do everything it can within its resources to defend racing and racing people - whether owners, trainers, jockeys, grooms, thoroughbred breeders, farriers, racecourse groundsmen and many others - in Parliament, in the media and in public opinion."

THE LEAGUE AGAINST Cruel Sports claims the post foot-and-mouth resumption of hunting with dogs will further convince people of the need for a permanent ban.

Although it made strong submissions to Government ministers against a comeback of "the so-called sport" it believes resumption will ultimately backfire on hunts.

League chairman John Cooper said:"We are resolutely against the resumption of hunting but it is nonetheless the case that we will now see further evidence of the need for a ban.

"This hunting season will again witness the wanton cruelty of hunting and occurrences of 'hunt havoc' - where hunts cause chaos by crossing railway lines, invading people's gardens and, unfor-tunately, more gruesome deaths of family pets.

"The public and MPs have long accepted the clear evidence for a ban. We deeply regret that hunting is still taking place and that innocent people will have to endure the problems caused by hunting for another season."

A SYMBOLIC WOOD was created in the middle of London in a bid to send out a national alert over Britain's disappearing ancient woodlands.

The Woodland Trust, one of the country's leading conservation charities, set the wood in Trafalgar Square to highlight the threat to ancient woodland.

Until the late 1600s, much of the area around Trafalgar Square was wooded but now it mostly comprises a man-made landscape of concrete and granite.

"How would you feel if the National Gallery, St. Martin-in-the-Fields and Nelson's Column were ripped down?," asks the Trust."This outrageous desecration of history, heritage and culture would lead to public fury and Government action.

"Such devastation is unlikely since these monuments are legally protected. But did you know that the country's 'natural cathedrals', its ancient woods, face daily threats of destruction?

"Currently, a shocking 85 per cent of ancient woodland has no national protective designation. Ancient trees and woods can be damaged or destroyed."

THE LIFTING OF foot-and-mouth restrictions at farms across Cumbria has given a huge boost to local morale.

The decision to drop the so-called Penrith Spur restrictions follows an intensive programme of blood testing to detect undisclosed disease.

The removal of restrictions has ended severe limitations on movement of animals inside an area including Melmerby Fell, Dufton Fell, Kirkby Thore, Shap Fells, Martindale Common and Penrith.

Cumbria's regional operations director Ray Anderson said:"This is a landmark in the efforts to restore Cumbria to normality following the outbreak of foot-and-mouth disease."

OYSTERCATCHERS AND RINGED plovers are among many bird species threatened by proposed port development plans at Dibden Bay, Southampton, claims English Nature.

The Government's nature conservation advisers believe work will badly affect the internationally important wildlife area if the port expansion scheme goes ahead, a public inquiry heard.

ENGLISH FORESTS ARE fighting back against human encroachment with a significant increase in tree cover during the second half of the last century, it has been revealed.

According to the Forestry Commission's National Inventory of Woodland and Trees in England - a definitive record of the nation's trees completed in 2000 - broadleaved woodland is now the dominant forest type and oak is the most common tree.

Forestry Minister Elliot Morley said:"There are now around 1.3 billion trees in the English countryside which makes about 25 trees for every person living in England."

THE COUNTRYSIDE ALLIANCE has painted a lurid picture of what it says Scotland's anti-hunt Bill is really about - prejudice.

"The cat of bigotry has leapt spitting and snarling from the bag of parliamentary democracy in Scotland," claims chief executive Richard Burge."With a single bound it has freed itself from the fetters of democratic constraint and moral tolerance and is now unfettered, a creature with the prerogative of the harlot - all power and no responsibility - at the throat of a minority whose only error is to be different.

"Are we talking about illiberal attitudes to someone's colour, or their religion, or even their views on the use of force to overthrow the state? No, we are talking about what Scots men and women are allowed to think, and the manner in which they are allowed to enjoy themselves.

"The 'Watson' Bill has now discarded its pretence of claiming that hunting with dogs is cruel. The debate on second reading in the Scottish Parliament has exposed the mendacity of the claim that the principle of the Bill is to improve animal welfare.

"To have people saying 'English hunters are the very redcoats who will flood over the border..' makes it clear that the motivation of those parliamentarians is hatred of a minority, and their hatred is matched by their determination to use the power of law to suppress human rights.

"If we substituted 'red coat' with the colour of a person's skin or 'English hunters' with their religion, we would all be appalled and would demand the police acted. We would take to the streets if such bigotry and hatred exercised by powerful people were not constrained by the criminal courts.

"And that is why we should all be worried, especially those of us who - like me - do not hunt with dogs but belong to other equally vulnerable field sport minorities who are engaged in activities whose defence will make the battle for hunting look like a picnic.

"The only thing that stands between us and a similar fate is electoral convenience. It is a thin veneer - very pretty but to shelter behind it is crass stupidity.

"It is not lightly that the Countryside Alliance uses the slogan 'the countryside fighting for liberty' or that we called our postponed march 'Liberty and Livelihood'. Without livelihood, liberty is a meaningless drudge - it is the shell of existence without the vibrancy of life.

"But livelihood without liberty is the false promise of the Fascist, and it is the descent into the society of the Gulag."

A GREY SQUIRREL has been blamed for causing neck injuries to an inventor who was testing out a bizarre bird-feeding hat.

The squirrel pounced from a tree to get at nuts carried on the hat by Mike Madden while he was assessing his invention.

The 48 year-old nature lover was knocked to the floor by the force of the blow and suffered whiplash injuries requiring a neck brace.

He only came up with the nutty idea for the hat so that he could feed birds as he strolled near his home at Honley in West Yorkshire.

But now it's back to the drawing board after the welder decided to destroy the hat to save himself further injury from low-flying squirrels.

MOLE: preposterous digger that inspired a morbid poet

ONLY someone with their head in the sand could have missed Britain's wild celebrations of the eclipse - which is probably what got me thinking of the mole back then and his happy ignorance of galactic matters.

Weather conditions prior to the eclipse must have made life difficult for the mole.

Soaring temperatures baked some areas of soil as hard as concrete while the downpours that followed could easily have turned the finest mole 'des res' into sludge.

Fortunately, moles can swim and their velvety fur is water resistant so most will have escaped being drowned in their intricate underground burrows.

There is no mistaking the mole for any other small mammal because he looks so, well, preposterous with his short fat body, large snout, pinprick half-blind eyes, and colossal, clawed front feet.

Yet there is no doubt he is superbly adapted to his subterranean domain.

A mole uses his whiskers and sensitive nose to guide himself daily through his tunnel network, hunting down worms or slugs that have fallen in through the walls.

Weighing in at about 4oz, an adult mole can shift twice his own weight in soil in a minute, which is a tribute to the sheer power of those front claws.

At one time, catching and killing moles was a common country pastime with the dark pelts used to make a variety of clothes.

Even as recently as four decades ago, up to a million moles were being caught in Britain each year.

Man-made furs have now largely replaced moleskin, which some may think is a good thing.

But the manufacturers of my weather-proof jacket claim the 'muffler' pockets are lined with genuine moleskin and it certainly feels as if they are.

Soft and silky, they keep my bare hands warm in the coldest of weathers.

I interviewed one of the country's few remaining professional mole-hunters some years ago and was struck by his affection for this busy little creature. Like a lot of hunters, he actually admired his quarry above all other animals - so much so that I came away wondering if he had actually made the wrong career choice.

The mole's work rate is relentless and even caught the eye of 17th Century poet George Herbert who morbidly observed:"*Death is still working like a mole, And digs my grave at each remove.*"

Perhaps his comment was fairly understandable. He died aged 40.

As for the eclipse, I was out in the countryside at the time and felt, more than saw, its unsettling effect.

During a fairly torrid domestic week, with my wife away, I'd found myself in a barley field with our two young children as the witching hour approached.

One thing I noticed beforehand was a large flock of woodpigeons flying in a frantic manner around an adjoining field, then heading for the horizon.

Birdsong ceased and the whole landscape seemed charged with foreboding, as if a terrible storm was about to strike.

Yet nothing major happened during the eclipse period itself and, with no protective gear, I didn't look too closely at the sun. Shortly after, driving slowly home through a weird, ethereal light, I noticed two wild rabbits in the road and stopped the car to watch them.

Both just sat there dazed until I drove away. Further on, a mouse or young rat briefly scurried alongside the car. All tame stuff, I know, but there was a genuine air of disturbance and unease.

However, the most curious report came from my wife.

Seconds before the eclipse started, a bumble bee had flown into her sister's high-rise flat in Torquay and was ignored as the group there tried to get into position for the best view.

When the eclipse ended, the bee was spotted again on the floor. Stone dead.

BRITISH MEAT EATERS are still being threatened by consignments of BSE-risk beef from abroad.

Despite stringent measures implemented within our own farming community to stamp out home-grown hazards, foreign exporters are continuing to put UK consumers at risk.

The NFU has expressed its outrage that a second consignment of Belgian beef containing banned spinal cord has been intercepted entering the country within weeks.

Spinal column - banned under the EU's BSE regulations - was found in the latest load at Eastbourne.

Earlier, on November 15, also at Eastbourne, another consignment from a different Belgian plant had been found to contain illegal material.

NFU president Ben Gill said:"It is bad enough that this should happen. But the fact that this beef has come from Belgium - the heart of the European Union and the place from which the rules originate - makes it worse still. The Belgians should be ashamed of themselves.

"The Belgian meat plant should be shut down immediately and investigated until it can be proven that it is up to the job.

"Once again, the Food Standards Agency has been left to defend us against these abuses of the rules - rules which British farmers have been working to for years. As ever, we continue to encourage shoppers to buy British every time."

Holland, Spain, Italy, and Denmark have all exported beef with spinal cord still attached to the UK in the past.

However, Germany had sent an "appalling" eight consignments.

This has sparked calls by the NFU for exports from that country to be completely banned by the Commission.

PUFFINS, RAZORBILLS AND shags are among bird species getting the Big Brother treatment under the gaze of a camera monitoring system identical to that used in the controversial Channel 4 series.

Big Brother contestant Elizabeth Woodcock even launched the scheme at a seabird colony on the Isle of May off the coast near Edinburgh.

More than £100,000 has been poured into the project by the Scottish Seabird Centre which hopes to make a much bigger sum from tourists viewing the cameras from the centre.

Hidden cameras can be remote controlled to give excellent views of day-to-day life - hopefully more interesting than the tedious goings-on in the human Big Brother house.

WITH 2001 SET to be the worst year for recorded strandings of sea life on British shores since 1913, The Wildlife Trusts have appealed for help with a survey.

The Trusts want volunteers to help discover the causes of marine strandings by reporting all stranded creatures and thereby enabling conservationists to build up a comprehensive picture.

Each year, whales, dolphins and porpoises are stranded on our coasts with 421 marine animals reported last year, including 45 whales, 120 dolphins and 197 porpoises.

But by August this year the number of recorded strandings had already exceeded this figure with a significant rise in strandings partly attributed to severe weather conditions and strong on-shore winds.

Joan Edwards, marine policy director of The Wildlife Trusts, said:"The death of even one animal matters greatly. Winter is a critical time for strandings and we would like people visiting, working or living near the coast to be extra vigilant and report any sea life in trouble.

"The more strandings that are reported and analysed the greater our understanding becomes and the sooner we can lobby for changes to fishing practices and marine legislation."

A FOX NOW thinks it's a dog with bizarre food tastes after being adopted as a cub by a nature loving couple.

Found abandoned and afraid next to a road, 'Foxy' was taken in by Miles and Gie Baddeley until it grew strong.

Today the adult animal wolfs down curry and cake and rolls on its back like a dog to let the couple tickle its tummy.

Despite being released back into the wild, Foxy still discreetly returns to the couple's home for treats and pats after the pair saved his life.

THE GOVERNMENT MUST improve support for British organic farmers, the Soil Association has told the Policy Commission on the Future of Farming and Food.

The UK's leading organic campaign body said organic farming provided a "win-win" solution to many of the crises facing agriculture and should be used to spearhead the move towards more sustainable food production.

But increased financial support was needed for farmers who went organic and on-going 'stewardship' payments should be given in recognition of environmental benefits afforded by organic farming.

"Organic farming is the most developed form of sustainable agriculture and delivers environmental and health benefits, with high standards of animal welfare," says Gundula Meziani, policy manager for the Soil Association.

"However, improved financial support for domestic farmers is vital to help develop the UK organic sector.

"Although sales of organic food are increasing year-by-year, imports account for the majority of purchases and are putting many UK farmers - particularly those producing milk and meat - at a severe disadvantage.

"Our reliance on food from abroad also means that the environmental benefits of organic farming systems are being reaped in Europe, and not at home."

WITH THE QUEEN under fire recently for breaking the neck of a wounded pheasant during a royal shoot, Animal Aid has attacked the 'blooding' of children in the sport.

"Every year in Britain millions of shed-reared pheasants are beaten up into the sky and shot down for pleasure," says the UK's leading animal rights group.

"Many of the shooters are mere children, aged seven years or even younger - there being no legal restriction on the age at which a child can use a shotgun to kill animals.

"Depressed by the downturn in the number of shotgun owners and users in the wake of the 1987 Hungerford shooting and the Dunblane massacre of 1996, the shooting lobby is engaging in a hard-sell strategy.

"Free bird-shooting days are on offer. There are 'uplifting' tales of young children being smeared with the blood of animals they have helped to slaughter.

"Parents write enthusiastically of their young children's interest in shotguns. And there is no shortage of photos showing children - in one instance, aged five - posing with guns amidst neatly arranged dead birds.

"Dr Peter Squires, a Reader in Criminal Justice at the University of Brighton and member of the Gun Control Network steering group that was set up in the wake of the Dunblane massacre, laments the lack of serious consideration given to the consequences of encouraging young children to kill for pleasure."

THE RAMBLERS ASSOCIATION launches its Festival of Winter Walks from December 22 with a host of gentle treks planned all over the country.

The walks, sponsored by Regatta, go on until January 1 which will be a longer period than normal for the annual event.

"We are hoping that lots of people will be encouraged to get out and about during this time," said a spokesman.

"As Christmas Eve falls on a Monday, many workplaces will close for Christmas on Friday the 21st. The extra four days will mean more people have the opportunity to try out walking with a Ramblers Group.

"The walks take place throughout England, Scotland and Wales. Many of them are themed and all take place in interesting locations.

"All Festival walks are free and open to everyone. You don't need to be a Ramblers member to take part and if, after going on a Festival walk, you want to join, you will receive 20 per cent off the price of membership."

Some of the more unusual walks this year include:Fife - a night walk to the top of West Lomond to celebrate New Year; Devon - a visit to ancient settlements;London - a walk through haunted Hampstead; and Sussex - visiting three sites of Second World War interest.

HARE COURSING GETS underway again from December 17 following a series of "constructive discussions" between the National Coursing Club and DEFRA.

Meets will be able to proceed under permit in "risk free" areas where there is no livestock in surrounding fields.

"Clubs will be able to seek the necessary permits from their divisional DEFRA offices," said the National Coursing Club.

"DEFRA's intention is that a single permit will cover all the meetings which a club may wish to run in a particular divisional area.

"If a club runs a meeting outside the divisional area in which the permit was granted, it will be obliged to inform the divisional area office concerned. DEFRA hopes to avoid the bureacracy of clubs running in different areas being obliged to seek more than one permit.

"Clubs will be obliged to follow regulations meticulously. Although the provisions concerning biosecurity - and those concerning livestock on the land in the 28 days previous to a coursing meeting - may seem burdensome to some, it should be remembered that coursing has not been forced to observe many of the constraints placed on hunting.

"Coursing clubs will not be obliged to issue attendance certificates to all participants, and there are no restrictions on who might attend a coursing meeting."

AN ARCTIC SEAL pup has finally made it back to the North Sea after a saga which saw it stranded thousands of miles away.

The female pup, dubbed Cleo by rescuers, was released off Orkney after hitting the headlines last August by being found in Spain - 3,000 miles from its natural habitat.

Transported back to Britain, the eight-month-old pup was fed and looked after by helpers at a wildlife centre in Wick, Caithness.

From there the pampered animal was taken to Orkney by boat and is now expected to swim the last 400 miles to meet up with other Arctic seals in Iceland.

How it came to be sunning itself in Spain remains a mystery.

FARMERS' LEADERS HAVE called for a raft of tough new measures to combat the threat of foot-and-mouth returning in the future.

Clear shortcomings and uncertainties in the handling of the present crisis must be addressed if the UK is to avoid a repeat of the disaster, union bosses say.

More investment is needed in research into animal diseases to find new and better diagnostic and epidemiological methods, the NFU claimed in its response to the Royal Society's Inquiry into Infectious Disease in Livestock.

Inadequate contingency plans and ineffective controls of UK and European borders against illegal imports were also highlighted.

NFU president Ben Gill said:"We simply cannot go on with the current situation where spending on these areas is being continually pared down. If anything comes out of this disastrous episode it must be to convince the authorities that they cannot scrimp on spending money in the area of animal diseases. Foot-and-mouth has shown this to have been a catastrophic false economy."

TRADITIONAL CHRISTMAS hostilities have broken out between turkey producers and the animal rights lobby.

As a new NFU Turkey Hotline informs consumers where they can buy local, fresh turkey direct from the farm, Animal Aid is trying to make 2001's Christmas "cruelty free".

The UK's leading animal rights group says:"It is the great irony of the 'festival of peace' that it is celebrated by feasting off the bodies of slaughtered animals.

"Roughly 10 million turkeys are killed for the Christmas market in this country alone and many other creatures are killed and feasted on as part of the holiday ritual.

"Like most areas of retail trade, Christmas is a boom time for the slaughter industry. Most turkeys are intensively reared in crowded windowless sheds. The birds are genetically selected for high meat yields and to put on weight as quickly as possible.

"This often causes their legs to buckle under them, as they can barely carry their own heavy weight. Turkeys have a natural life span of approximately 10 years, yet they are slaughtered for the dinner table at the tender age of 12-26 weeks.

"Apart from replacing the dead animal with a favourite vegetarian dish, the compassionate Christmas scoffer has also to look out for animal ingredients in products such as cakes, chocolates, wines, biscuits and other luxury foods.

"Numerous animal-free mince pies and Christmas puddings are now available and there are also a few Christmas cakes completely free from animal ingredients on the market."

TV WEATHERMAN IAN McCaskill is leading a Christmas campaign by The Woodland Trust to get people to record seasonal changes.

Researchers claim that the traditional chilly Christmas is no more with winter being squeezed out by longer autumns and earlier springs.

Song thrushes can now be heard at Christmas, they say, whilst chiffchaffs and blackcaps are increasingly over wintering here.

Dressing up as a redundant Santa is the way Mr McCaskill aims to drive home the news and underline the importance of helping the Trust monitor changes.

The former BBC weather forecaster said:"Changes in temperature are affecting our wildlife. Many migratory birds are remaining in the country much later than we'd expect and some animals are hibernating later in the year.

"To get a better picture of what's happening to the environment, please help The Woodland Trust by recording natural events that you see around you in woods, parks and gardens."

COUNTRY FOOTPATHS ARE being allowed to fall into disrepair by neglect and lack of cash, it has been claimed.

Following the Countryside Agency's latest rights of way condition survey, the Ramblers Association has called on local authorities to get their path networks in good condition.

The survey - the only independent overview of England's paths - shows there has been no significant improvement in the last six years.

A quarter of all paths are still not easy to use, and only two-thirds are signposted at a time when rural communities desperately need people back in the countryside to help aid financial recovery.

The Agency's Rights of Way Condition Survey concluded that £69million was needed to get paths into top condition - a small slice of the estimated £2.7billion income walkers and other path users generate each year in the countryside.

Jacquetta Fewster, the RA's head of footpath campaigns, said:"We fully endorse the Countryside Agency's call for local authorities to spend more on their path networks.

"As well as being important for recreation and sustainable transport, paths mean profits for rural businesses.

"But profits are lost if the paths are shut off because of obstructions and other serious problems.

"Local authorities throughout England must wake up to this fact, and invest now to get all their paths in good condition."

The survey reveals that the West Midlands and Surrey have shown the greatest improvement to their networks.

Areas with the most unsatisfactory and unusable paths were judged to be Cornwall, Lincolnshire, North Yorkshire, Shropshire and Bedfordshire.

TERENCE THE TURKEY has been revelling in his new-found fame after making a great escape from turkey farm to bird sanctuary.

The story of how the bird destined for the table made a three-mile trek to the Hampshire sanctuary has amazed the nation and delighted vegetarians.

Some even suspect the bird has mystical powers after it homed in on the New Forest Owl Sanctuary run by one of the few local people who never eats turkey for Christmas - Bruce Berry.

Several local farms raise turkeys for the Christmas market and none could initially tell if one was missing from the thousands they stock.

But that didn't bother Terence who has been happily tucking into sweetcorn and other snacks at his new abode.

THREE BABY SEALS are to be 'treated' to Christmas TV in their enclosure to make up for the loss of human contact.

Common seal pups Starburst, Edgeley and Web are used to being cared for by staff at the Sea Life Centre in Weymouth, Dorset.

But the captive-bred trio will have to make do with the telly on Christmas Day as staff take a well-earned break and will not be around to provide fun.

What the seals think of the usual festive fayre endured by the rest of the nation is anyone's guess - flippin' lousy might be the response.

HARD-PRESSED FARMERS have been given some Christmas cheer with news that livestock markets are poised to restart in England and Wales.

Easing the tough regime regulating animal movements following foot-and-mouth will also loosen the strait-jacket constricting farmers, says the NFU.

The changes - likely to come into force in February - will make a huge practical difference to farmers and have followed long and complex talks between the Government and union leaders.

NFU president Ben Gill said the changes were a recognition that the battle against foot-and-mouth had been all but won - there have been no new cases for nearly three months.

Mr Gill said:"This is a massive step forward from the current situation where farmers need a licence for every single movement. Farmers will be nothing short of delighted to see the reopening of livestock markets.

"Farmers have understood the fact that they have had to comply with restrictions to stop the spread of the disease.

"But the complexity and bureaucracy of the system - not to mention the physical impact on how farmers operate their businesses - has been very hard. They will be extremely relieved at this news.

"It is important to point out that this is an interim regime. It can be further relaxed next year as we gain experience in the operation of the system and the threat of foot-and-mouth recedes further.

"We will then be better placed to determine the long-term management of animal movements in the UK. A key element of future discussions will be the issue of the 20-day movement standstill and the impact this will have on farmers.

"We are pleased to see Lord Whitty has made it clear to producers that DEFRA will be looking at other elements of fighting exotic diseases, including the operation of import controls on meat and animal products.

"Strengthening our defences has been one of the NFU's key priorities."

A TURKEY HAS escaped becoming Christmas lunch by learning to walk a tightrope and jump through a flaming hoop.

Yorkshire farmer Colin Newlove taught Trevor the turkey tricks so he could make something of himself, apart from dinner.

Mr Newlove, who lives near Malton, says Trevor loves to perform - and given the alternative perhaps that's not surprising.

SHEEPDOGS ARE BEING shot or abandoned by the hundred after foot-and-mouth wreaked financial havoc on their owners, it has been revealed.

Animal rescue shelters around the country are recording unusually high numbers of border collies in need of new homes after being thrown out by their hard-pressed masters.

Shropshire-based Animal Samaritans has confirmed it has been rescuing almost 40 dogs per week which would otherwise have been put down.

However, the centre has advised people against buying the dogs as Christmas presents for young children.

Many border collies are used to roughing it by living in barns, may not even be house trained, and need long walks with a lot of stimulation.

Carol James, spokeswoman for Animal Samaritans, told a newspaper:"A half-hour walk, two or three times a day, can be enough as long as the dog is given tasks such as 'retrieve' and 'come back'.

"If they do not get this employment and stimulation they will come home and find their own employment - like tearing down the curtains. Young children are no good but a home with active teenagers, especially a few footballers, is ideal."

PEAT BOG EXPERT Dr Hugh Ingram has been honoured for his ecology work by the Royal Society for Nature Conservation - parent charity of The Wildlife Trusts.

Dr Ingram, a renowned plant ecologist, has been awarded the 2001 Christopher Cadbury Medal for "outstanding services to the advancement of nature conservation in the British Isles."

He developed the "ground water mound hypothesis" - an application of soil physics that accounts for the shape and stability of raised mires.

WITH 10,000 PEOPLE expected to take part in the Ramblers Association's 'Festival of Winter Walks', a new poll has found that most people believe walking is best for losing weight.

The survey, commissioned by the Association, revealed that 53 per cent of respondents would put losing weight top of their New Year resolutions list, with 51 per cent preferring walking to weight training, yoga, or aerobics.

Walking is not only effective for burning calories but also for protecting against heart disease and reducing the risk of osteoporosis, says the group.

RA member Jane Kiely even used last year's winter walking festival as a fitness target after breaking her ankle in a nasty fall.

"I set my sights on my first long walk being the one we were leading in the Festival of Winter Walks," she said."It was a 12-mile local walk and I worked hard beforehand, exhausting the dog, walking just a bit further every day. What I hadn't bargained for was snow. However, we set out on the most wonderful day with a clear blue sky and the sun shining, the weather cold and crisp with pure white snow underfoot. It was one of the best walks ever, and we even managed a picnic, in the sun, sheltered by a hedge.

"My physiotherapist was walking with us and didn't really believe I could do it.

"My doctor couldn't believe that I had actually walked 12 miles in those conditions four months after breaking my ankle."

FOXHUNTING RESTARTED with plans already underway for a raft of co-ordinated Boxing Day protests against it by anti-hunt campaigners.

As the League Against Cruel Sports finalised its arrangements, the Campaign for Hunting celebrated resumption nearly 300 days after hunting's suspension, saying it marked an important step towards the countryside's return to normality.

Campaign chairman Sam Butler said:"The resumption of hunting will be seen by many thousands of people as a clear signal that their lives can now begin to get back to normal. The farming community and hunting are one and the same, and the way in which hunting can now resume reflects this."

However, only a small number of hunts were expected to ride out initially - with probably 30 or so of Britain's 300 hunts granted the necessary licences.

Hunts are still banned in 'infected' or 'at-risk' areas, including large regions such as Cumbria, North Yorkshire and Northumberland.

These areas were among the worst affected by foot-and-mouth with dozens of villages almost cut off at the height of the crisis.

Simon Hart, the campaign's director, called resumption a huge boost both economically and in terms of morale for rural communities.

Meanwhile, farmers across the UK are said to have recorded a noticeable increase in fox numbers since the ban on hunting started.

In a recent letter to the Federation of Welsh Packs, the Farmers Union of Wales confirmed:"All counties in Wales have reported an increase in fox numbers and predation since the hunting authorities commenced their voluntary ban on February 22.

"The union's county branches are receiving an increasing number of calls from farmers concerned at the effects of a protracted ban on fox control."

ABOUT 2,000 HOMING pigeons have been given new homes to make way for an Environment Agency flood defence scheme.

But the racing birds have been relocated to lofts only a short distance away so as not to confuse their homing instincts.

The Manchester pigeons had been blocking a project which involves giving better protection to Salford from the River Irwell. Hundreds of human homes will now be guarded against potential flooding with the construction of an 80-acre basin and earth barriers where the pigeons used to live.

FRIENDS OF THE Earth has called for the prosecution of bio-tech firm Aventis following the discovery of GM oilseed rape 'weeds' on a Lincolnshire farm trial site.

The weeds, which were flowering, were destroyed a week after FoE reported their presence to the authorities.

FoE says it wrote to Margaret Beckett, the Secretary of State at DEFRA, on November 30 informing her of the presence of the weeds at the Witham-on-the-Hill site.

It claims the Government's GM Inspectorate delayed visiting the site until December 3 then reported back to DEFRA who ordered Aventis to destroy the weeds on December 5.

Pete Riley, real food and farming campaigner for FoE, said:"It's extraordinary that it took the Government and the GM company seven days to make this field safe.

"Quite obviously, these sites have not been properly monitored by Aventis, even though it is legally responsible. If it hadn't been for the alert behaviour of a local farmer and Friends of the Earth these GM weeds would still be polluting the local environment. The Government must now show how seriously it views this incident by prosecuting Aventis."

DORSET WILDLIFE HAS been given a boost after a consortium of conservationists and local authorities won funding to restore heathland habitat.

The 13-strong group, led by English Nature, secured cash from the Heritage Lottery Fund for a large-scale project involving restoration work on lowland heathland across the Dorset Heaths Natural Area.

The 'Hardy's Egdon Heath' scheme will see contractors with the necessary expertise and skills undertake tree and scrub clearance, gorse control, bracken control, and fencing work.

Locations for the £2million project range from large rural sites next to agricultural land to smaller sites on the fringe of urban areas.

Most locations lie within national and international nature conservation sites. Some are on military land and many have open public access.

LANDOWNERS ARE DEMANDING that the Government makes public all findings from the final foot-and-mouth inquiry, dubbed 'Lessons to be Learnt'.

Failure to do so would diminish the entire exercise, claims the Country Land and Business Association.

President Sir Edward Greenwell said:"The CLA asserted from the outset that the inquiries announced by the Government must be held in public. Dr Iain Anderson has promised to hold some of the sessions in public and this is entirely the right way to build confidence in this inquiry.

"However, it is essential that all the findings of the inquiry are made public also. The outbreak affected millions of people in all sorts of ways, many of which were wholly unexpected and highly damaging. People need to be reassured that this inquiry, in particular, asked the right questions and got the right answers.

"The CLA is gathering evidence from our members. We will present our evidence to the inquiry in March 2002 and will most definitely be publishing it on our website."

SWAN: a sad story of beauty and the beasts

BEAUTIFUL and majestic, swans have the power to charm us like few other birds as they glide elegantly by in the water.

A group of swans on my local pond reminded me of this fact the other day as they drew admiring comments from onlookers.

Bigger and more regal than geese, it is not hard to see why swans enjoy special historical links to the Crown - despite the fact that swans were once more likely to be seen on platters at a giant royal feast than taking titbits from passers-by.

With their snow-white feathers and long graceful necks, swans could be birds created in a fairytale, which is probably why they captured the hearts of poets down the ages.

Strangely, a lot of the poems I've read link them with death or dying, which seems a tad unfair on such a vivacious creature.

This, by Alfred Lord Tennyson, is a fairly typical reference: *"The woods decay, the woods decay and fall, The vapours weep their burthen to the ground, Man comes and tills the field and lies beneath, And after many a summer dies the swan."*

Thanks for that, Alf. Not the cheeriest way to think of a bird which, more often than not, actually cheers you up.

We are lucky in this country to have three main species of swan to enjoy; the mute swan, Bewick's swan, and whooper swan. (The Australian black swan is more of an ornamental import.)

The smallest of this white trio at only eight kilogrammes, the Bewick's swan has an impressive flight record, making a perilous migration back to our shores from Siberia each year.

The whooper, too, makes it over here from Iceland every winter when temperatures there plunge too low for comfort - quite an achievement for a bird weighing up to 14 kilogrammes.

The mute swan, similarly large, could probably be classed as our most 'native' swan though it has declined in many areas due to a combination of factors, including being poisoned by eating anglers' lead shot.

Despite their physical beauty, swans can be aggressive and there are many tales of them killing or badly injuring other water birds that come too close to their nests at breeding time.

Even so, from childhood, I can still remember the outrage that was sparked in my village when louts attacked two swans which had nested beside a local stretch of water year after year.

The female always settled in a patch of wild rhubarb close to some trees and the sight of her leading her downy chicks to water was an annual treat for we toddlers.

However, these yobs - who were never caught, I believe - decided to put paid to all that.

Not content with killing the male with bricks, they smashed all the eggs and drove the female away.

She returned briefly a day or so later, pining for her dead partner.

It was a small tragedy in the general scheme of things but it still left a mark on me when I was told about it.

Long after the wild rhubarb was cleared and the area surrounding the lake flattened and landscaped into a kind of barren green desert, I still remembered what had happened there.

Perhaps those poets had it right after all. Perhaps it takes the death of a swan to make you realise what you've lost.

RARE CAPERCAILLE ARE being given a boost in Scotland with the removal of 87 kilometres of deer fences across their favourite areas this winter.

Following the move by the Scottish Executive to help save the birds from extinction, Deputy Environment and Rural Development Minister Allan Wilson said:"This is good news for the capercaillie, which is a symbol of Scotland's woodland heritage.

"I am delighted that so many woodland owners have come forward to take up our offer to help them protect the capercaillie in their woods.

"Research has shown that the serious decline in the capercaillie population is due to a number of causes, including loss of habitat, predation by crows and foxes, and climate change - in particular a string of wet, cold breeding seasons that have caused high numbers of chick deaths.

"Some of these reasons, such as climate change and bad weather, we cannot do anything about, while we have made good progress on others, such as reversing habitat loss.

"However, collisions with deer fences have also been identified as a significant cause of capercaillie deaths, and the Executive was pleased to make special funding available to help with the costs of removing and marking fences that pose a risk to existing populations of the birds."

AN INJURED FOX almost threw travellers into chaos when it was spotted on Tube train tracks leading to Terminal 4 at Heathrow Airport.

The Tube station at the airport had to be closed so that RSPCA officers could try to reach the animal and take it away for treatment.

The morning drama dragged on for over an hour until the fox was eventually cornered and caught.

Despite closure of the station, anxious passengers were still able to reach Terminal 4 on the Heathrow Express link.

A PET DOG called Otto is recovering after spending five days trapped on the cliff face of a quarry over the Christmas holiday.

Owner Tom Oliver believes the two-year-old Bernese Mountain dog only survived sub-zero temperatures because of the hardiness of its breed.

Otto vanished while out for a walk in Somerset's Quantock Hills and Mr Oliver, his wife and two children spent hours fruitlessly combing the area as temperatures plummeted.

Other local people joined in the search and Otto was eventually spotted stuck in a bramble patch on the cliff face, half a mile from home.

A fire crew had to winch the exhausted, starving animal to safety before it could be taken home to recover from its ordeal.

HARE COURSING FANS celebrated resumption of their controversial sport after the first meeting of the season took place at the Isle of Ely course over the festive season.

Government go-ahead after foot-and-mouth has buoyed up supporters who are now looking forward to a whole series of meets following that first event.

Biggest among these will be the Waterloo Cup held near Liverpool, scene of several clashes between supporters and animal rights groups over the years.

London Mayor Ken Livingstone is among protesters who have branded the event "cruel" and vowed to get it stopped, alongside hunting with dogs in general.

The National Coursing Club said:"At last ! Owners, trainers, and greyhounds can get back on the field, even if they do have to dip their boots and paws in disinfectant before they do so.

"Schedules are already beginning to come into the NCC office for a bright start to the New Year. Cotswold and Kimberley will hold one-day meetings, and North Lincs will stage its big Benroy Cup for 32 runners.

"The question everyone is asking is: 'Will there be a Waterloo Cup?' The Waterloo Cup Committee announced just before Christmas that the coursing classic will go ahead on its scheduled dates of February 26, 27 and 28.

"The DEFRA requirement most obvious to all will be the disinfecting procedures. We shouldn't whinge too much about this. It's been going on all summer at horse shows and pony clubs, and we'll have to get used to it for the time being.

"Coursing has far fewer restrictions to put up with compared with hunting. Coursing meetings are still open to everyone, no matter which part of the country they come from, and participants are not required to sign the attendance forms which all hunt followers are obliged to complete."

Critics of hare coursing, such as the League Against Cruel Sports, say it is barbaric and degrades spectators who watch hares being torn to pieces.

But supporters point out that hare coursing is a country tradition which is about testing the speed and stamina of pursuing greyhounds.

Few hares, they say, are actually killed in comparison with numbers chased and their deaths are incidental to the main drama.

SWANS, DOLPHINS, OTTERS and other wild creatures have helped veterinary pathologist Vic Simpson win a top honour.

Vic received the Veterinary Award at the inaugural BBC Animal Awards for advancing the care and treatment of wildlife.

Investigative work by the Cornwall Wildlife Trust member is said to have resulted in breakthroughs in areas such as lead poisoning of swans, dolphins dying in fishing nets, and monitoring otter populations.

Vic, who recently retired from MAFF, has now set up the Wildlife Veterinary Investigation Centre where it will be possible to post mortem every creature submitted.

He said."This award has given a real boost to the centre.The future of our wildlife depends on our understanding the threats they face and, provided sponsorship is forthcoming, the centre should be ideally placed to do this."

POPPING CHAMPAGNE CORKS over New Year helped to keep alive one of Europe's most important wildlife habitats, says the RSPB.

The cork oak forests of southern European countries such as Portugal and Spain are vital for some of the continent's most charismatic wildlife, such as the lynx, and migrating birds.

But the greatest threat to these forests is the increasing use of plastic wine bottle stoppers.

So bad is the situation that, if the use of plastic wine bottle stoppers continues to increase at the current rate, the cork industry could crash in less than 15 years, resulting in the disappearance of one of Europe's most valuable habitats.

The RSPB believes that plastic stoppers have already grabbed an estimated 5-7 per cent of the £500-800 million global bottle-stopper market - far higher than the industry's own estimate of only one per cent.

Britain is the world's largest importer of wines and now has up to 20 per cent of its wine bottles sealed with plastic 'corks', three times the global average.

The RSPB says this is largely due to the influence of supermarkets which demand plastic stoppers from wine suppliers, claiming that cork can cause some wines to taste 'musty'.

Hannah Bartram, the Society's agriculture policy officer, said:"The RSPB is urging peopler to boycott wine bottles with plastic 'corks'."

SALMON AND SEA trout will no longer have a hell of a time negotiating Devil's Water in Northumberland thanks to a new scheme involving the Environment Agency.

Migrating fish in the River Tyne tributary at Corbridge used to hit a diabolical obstacle in the form of a weir - the remains of the power supply for a 19th Century mill.

So the Agency joined forces with the Northumbria Rivers Project and raised £51,000 to build a pass.

The project has already been hailed a success after recently spawned fish, including a 12 pound salmon, were spotted upstream.

The pass, constructed by a local firm, comprises a series of stepped pools to allow fish to leap up the weir in stages.

LONDONERS ARE CELEBRATING the return of the bittern - one of Britain's rarest birds.

Three of the shy booming-voiced birds were spotted by staff at the Wetland Centre in Barnes, creeping among reeds.

Less than two dozen males are thought to remain in the whole of the UK following widespread destruction of their habitat.

GARDENERS ARE BEING urged to take part in a new survey which could save wild animals from being made homeless when new houses are built.

The survey, 'Mammals in your Garden?' is being undertaken by The Mammal Society in association with BBC wildlife and gardening magazines and aims to assess the impact of the housing boom which is expected to cover an area equal to the size of Hertfordshire in the next 15 years.

January readers of the magazines are being asked to complete a form detailing the mice, hedgehogs, foxes, badgers and other mammals they see in their gardens during 2002. Forms are also available from The Mammal Society itself.

The information will be used to build a comprehensive picture of the role urban and rural gardens play in wildlife conservation, and provide guidance to planners when they look at house development proposals.

The assessment is needed because of fears that the current housing boom will damage British mammal populations as new houses and gardens replace their favoured rural habitat.

Chairman of The Mammal Society, Professor Stephen Harris, said:"The aim of the survey is to help us plan urban developments to minimise their impact on wild mammal populations.

"It will mean we can advise local authorities on how far different mammals will travel into urban areas and whether they should be retaining brownfield sites or restricting the size of new housing developments so that they are always close to corridors of semi-natural vegetation."

Rosamund Kidman Cox, editor of BBC Wildlife Magazine, added:"We know that household gardens are vital to wildlife conservation. They provide shelter and food all year round for a wide variety of mammals and they take on special importance in severe weather, when the food and water they offer, or which gardeners put out, can mean the difference between life and death.

"This survey will help us assess the real importance of gardens to wildlife, and to learn how to harness it."

As part of the survey The Mammal Society has also produced three factsheets on garden mammals: 'Encouraging mammals in your garden'; 'Studying mammals in the garden'; and 'Dealing with problems mammals can cause in the garden'.

PLANS TO REINTRODUCE wild beavers to Scotland have moved up a gear with a bid to import a whole colony from Norway.

Scottish Natural Heritage is pressing the Scottish Executive to approve introduction of 12 European beavers next month.

The animals would make up the UK's first wild beaver colony for 400 years after previous populations were hunted to extinction.

If the colony gets the go-ahead and proves a success, it could result in an even bigger reintroduc - tion scheme later.

The first beavers would be closely monitored at Knapdale Forest in Argyll after being radio-tagged and allowed to breed.

Although some landowners and farmers fear beavers will wreak havoc if reintroduced, conserva - tionists say they are confident this would not be the case.

190

LOCAL COUNCILS ARE being urged to change the way they prepare road and housing schemes to avoid more costly head-to-head battles with conservation groups.

As a public inquiry over heathland protection in the county wound up, the RSPB, English Nature and the Dorset Wildlife Trust jointly called for a sea change in the way local authorities act.

All three organisations have opposed Purbeck District Council's allocation of 1,350 houses at Holton Heath, near Wareham, next to internationally-important wildlife-rich heathland.

They gave "compelling evidence" to the inquiry that fire, disturbance and other urban pressures would cause irreparable damage to some of Britain's rarest wildlife.

The groups argued that Dorset's rural heaths must not be put under the same intolerable pressures as urban heaths at Poole and Bournemouth, and that future new housing development must be sited well away from sensitive heathlands.

RSPB chief executive Graham Wynne said:"We have made an overwhelming case to the inquiry that the Holton Heath scheme should never have come forward and should be thrown out.

"The damage it would cause to internationally-important heathland sites is unacceptable at the beginning of the 21st Century. We must find a new way to meet the genuine housing needs of the people of Dorset while continuing to enjoy the county's rich heathland heritage."

The groups called on Dorset councils to develop a more environmentally-friendly approach to planning new houses and roads that avoids conflict with nature conservation.

THE WOODLAND TRUST hopes to make a big impression on the public after its 2002 Christmas card recycling scheme was launched by TV impressionist Alistair McGowan.

The celebrated impersonator said:"Recycling cards is fun and easy. By simply taking cards to your nearest WHSmith or Tesco for recycling you can help improve the environment.

"The scheme reduces waste going to landfill and funds raised will be given to the Trust to support the creation of much needed native woodland throughout the UK.

"Last year over 800 tonnes of card were recycled. Would you believe it that for every tonne of card recycled 17 trees are saved! So think of it as the biggest Christmas present you could give to nature."

With the introduction this year of recycling bins at all WHSmith's High Street stores and all Tesco stores, it was now easier than ever for people to recycle cards, he added.

ANIMAL AID IS claiming a campaign victory after local council pigeon culls were suspended in West Norfolk.

"Pigeons in Kings Lynn use the town centre to roost and are sustained by the grain spillages at many grain merchants' facilities, and also by deliberate public feeding in the town itself," said a spokesman for the animal rights group.

"The availability of food has artificially boosted pigeon numbers and, in response to this, the council trapped and shot pigeons over a number of years with no real success.

"Animal Aid mailed out to all Kings Lynn councillors twice and West Norfolk Animal Rights lobbied hard with petitions and demonstrations.

"The cost-effectiveness and success of the pigeon cull were questioned as they were an ongoing burden on the local taxpayer.

"Scientific research has proved conclusively that all lethal methods of pigeon control are totally ineffective in the medium and long-term.

"In areas where lethal control operations have been carried out it has been noted that, within a matter of weeks, pigeon numbers will have increased to pre-cull figures and, in most cases, will have exceeded them."

WAXWINGS, KINGFISHERS AND hawfinches were among the rarer visitors last time round - now the RSPB hopes for similar success with this year's Big Garden Birdwatch on January 26-27.

"Last year over 50,000 garden birdwatchers took part in nearly 30,000 gardens, making it the biggest survey of its kind," said a spokesman.

"Its simplicity is the key to its success. All participants need do is spend one hour watching the birds in their garden, park or school grounds, count the maximum number of each species seen at one time and send in the results. You can take part individually or as part of a group - it's up to you.

"Last year more than 90 species were recorded. The most unusual garden visitors were waxwings, kingfishers, lesser spotted woodpeckers, hawfinches, mandarin ducks and ring-necked parakeets. An amazing four per cent of gardens recorded wintering blackcaps."

RURAL AFFAIRS MINISTER Margaret Beckett has now been attacked by the Countryside Alliance for making "misplaced and unproductive" comments on farming.

The DEFRA Secretary of State risked needlessly antagonising an already demoralised sector and could set back the cause of diversification into more sustainable farming, claimed Alliance chief executive Richard Burge.

Mrs Beckett had criticised farmers for failing to take up free business advice available through DEFRA and had said they needed to "get real" if they wanted to make their businesses more viable.

But Mr Burge challenged Mrs Beckett to set out how her own department was planning to drive the transition.

"It is fine to talk of creating co-operatives or switching from food production into environmental products," he said. "We welcome Mrs Beckett's conversion to such ideas - not least since we have been urging DEFRA to consider them for some time. But these won't come about by magic. DEFRA has so far failed to lay out a clear route map for helping to ensure that radical diversification can, in fact, be commercially viable."

CASH-STRAPPED FARMERS are suffering further financial hardship because of Government incompetence over cattle scheme payments, it has been claimed.

The NFU has expressed its anger and frustration at long-term delays in Suckler Cow Premium Scheme payments, which should have started arriving last November.

President Ben Gill has written a strongly-worded letter to the Minister for Food and Farming, Lord Whitty, hitting out at the delays and calling for interest to be paid on late payments.

He criticised DEFRA officials for a list of excuses, including software problems due to modulation on heifer percentages being incorporated, continuing DEFRA strike action, and foot-and-mouth.

Mr Gill said:"None of these excuses are valid. For example DEFRA staff have been aware of the software problems since 1999.

"The other reason given is the foot-and-mouth outbreak. However, everyone else in rural organisations - and indeed the entire farming community - has had to cope with this and keep their businesses running.

"DEFRA is well aware of the extremely difficult times farmers are facing at the moment and these continuing delays are making a dire situation even worse.

"If the delays had been the other way round, we would not be allowed to use these excuses, and the fact that your officials have made these statements has further angered farmers who are currently suffering severe financial hardship.

"I hope you will now act on your promises made last autumn on payments and ensure payments are made swiftly."

THE SOIL ASSOCIATION has attacked a survey which disputes that organic food is healthier and safer than conventional food.

Responding to the Mintel survey, a spokesman said:"Two new studies published last year have shown that organic crops contain higher levels of vitamin C and essential minerals such as magnesium, iron and calcium. Higher levels of nutrients were particularly evident in spinach, lettuce, cabbage and potatoes.

"Organic processed food also delivers health benefits. Health problems as diverse as heart disease, osteoporosis, migraines and hyperactivity have been linked to food additives whose use is banned under organic standards.

"Hydrogenated fat, which should be avoided in order to help maintain a healthy heart, is not allowed in any organic food. Consumers should also be assured that organic food reaches the highest standards as all organic farms and food processors are inspected and licensed annually."

THE WILDLIFE TRUSTS are urging country lovers to celebrate World Book Day this coming March by visiting woods and meadows which actually inspired some of our favourite authors.

"Acres of sweeping valleys, enchanted forests, and babbling brooks have inspired writers and poets to put pen to paper and create some of our best loved stories, poems and characters," said a spokesman.

"Wordsworth fell for the Falls of Clyde, an area of ancient woodland and spectacular waterfalls near Lanark, cared for by the Scottish Wildlife Trust.

"Wayland Wood, a magical forest protected by Norfolk Wildlife Trust, is thought to have been the inspiration behind the classic fairytale 'Babes in the Wood'.

"And if you want to find the home of Winnie the Pooh and Piglet, take a trip to Sussex Wildlife Trust's Old Lodge reserve in Ashdown Forest, the setting for A.A. Milne's popular tales.

"Who would have thought that a patch of tranquil gardens in Oxford could be the birthplace of the fantastical worlds of Narnia and 'hobbit territory' Middle Earth ?

"Follow in the footsteps of J.R.R. Tolkein and C.S. Lewis who were known to stroll together through this reserve while dreaming up the magical realms of 'The Lord Of The Rings' and 'The Lion, the Witch, and the Wardrobe'."

Other sites lay behind such tales as 'The Wind In The Willows', 'Squirrel Nutkin', and 'Tarka the Otter', the spokesman added.

A FRIGHTENED COW leapt from its pen and charged passers-by before it was shot dead by a police marksman.

The animal had already been marked for slaughter before it made its bid for freedom at Lancaster Auction Mart.

After jumping out of its 6ft pen, the cow first fled into a warehouse where it became confused and ran at shocked workers.

Police were called in to help amid fears that the cow would eventually find its way onto a nearby motorway - the M6 - where carnage could result.

An hour after the drama started, the cow was cornered in a nearby car park and shot dead.

HELPING SALMON THRIVE in Cumbria's River Derwent will be the subject of talks between local residents and the Environment Agency.

A consultation document has been produced by the Agency with views now sought from anglers, landowners, conservation bodies and anyone else with an interest in salmon or the river.

Spokeswoman Jane Atkins said:"It is very important that we hear the views of as many interested people as possible so that work can be done to help the salmon."

At a forthcoming meeting, the Agency will set out its proposed plan of action, highlighting the present status of the river and its current salmon stocks.

But the Derwent will not be the only river to benefit from what is an ongoing initiative.

Salmon Action Plans are currently being written for all major salmon rivers in England and Wales in accordance with the Environment Agency's strategy to boost fish.

ANTI-HUNT MPs have increased pressure on Premier Tony Blair to bring a new hunting Bill before Parliament.

They relaunched their fight to ban the sport on the first anniversary of the House of Lords vote which defeated the Government's last Bill on hunting with dogs.

Meanwhile, the Campaign for Hunting has described the latest attempt by animal rights groups to 'reinvent' themselves as the final gasp of a dying movement.

It says the desperation of the new group - which has changed its name from 'Deadline 2000' to 'Countdown to a Ban' - is compounded by the fact that recent evidence has shown 63 per cent of rural vets are opposed to a hunting ban on welfare grounds; public support for a ban has slipped below 50 per cent; and farmers across Britain have revealed a sharp increase in the fox population during the period of suspension due to foot-and-mouth.

Simon Hart, director of the Countryside Alliance's Campaign for Hunting, said:"I am surprised that these organisations haven't rid themselves of the rather embarrassing title of Deadline 2000 before now.

"We were all assured that hunting would be banned in the millennium year but as usual these animal rights groups can only talk a good game. They can change their name as often as they like but that won't hide the fact that they have nothing new to say.

"Their latest re-branding means they have been re-launched more times than the Space Shuttle.

"But it is no more likely to be successful than any of the others in their history."

A LONG, DARK shadow has been lifted from the British countryside after it was formally declared free of foot-and-mouth, says NFU president Ben Gill.

With the last county affected by foot-and-mouth declared clear of the disease, a dreadful blight had been lifted from the country almost a year after it first struck, he said.

He was speaking as Northumberland - the sole area still designated 'at risk' - was finally also granted 'free' status by DEFRA.

Mr Gill said the move would help draw a line under eleven months of hell, although it could still be some weeks before the country was officially recognised as clear of the disease by the rest of the world.

"This is the news that farmers across the UK have been waiting for,"he said.

"We all hope that this is truly the beginning of the end of this appalling chapter.

"But we must now go to European and world authorities as soon as possible to get our disease-free status back."

A MAJOR INVESTIGATION has been sparked by undercover filming which appeared to show the illegal dumping of deer carcasses around fox holes on the Duke of Beaufort's estate.

The film, taken by the International Fund for Animal Welfare, was aired on Channel 4 News and apparently revealed a series of foxes feeding on rotting carcasses at the Gloucestershire estate.

Animal welfare organisations claim the carcasses are being dumped on purpose to encourage more foxes for hunting.

This has been denied by the Beaufort Hunt and estate managers have told Channel 4 that they are urgently looking into the allegations.

The Beaufort is perhaps the best known hunt in the country, attracting the cream of society along with high-profile members of the Royal Family.

But secret filming by the International Fund for Animal Welfare in woods on the Beaufort estate recorded graphic scenes of deer - apparently from the Duke's own herd - left dumped near man-made foxes' dens.

As well as being illegal on health grounds, the dumping of carcasses is said to break the hunt's own rules of only pursuing foxes in their natural wild state.

RSPCA vet Bill Swann told Channel 4:"I'm concerned about deer. You've got potentially a disease risk because in moving deer you may be moving them to areas where there are other domestic animals.

"Dogs, for example, can scavenge off the carcasses and you may also have contact with other domestic animals so I just don't think this is good practice."

The Beaufort Hunt says it categorically denies any involvement in the allegations and asserts that all members of hunt staff are fully briefed to comply with legislation.

A spokesman for the Duke of Beaufort told Channel 4:"The Duke was not aware of any of the matters which you have raised but he has asked us to look into them as a matter of urgency.

"As you would expect, we always seek to ensure that the estate and the deer park are managed to the highest standards."

MORE THAN 60 greyhounds are scheduled to contest this year's Blue Riband hare coursing event - the Waterloo Cup.

The controversial event, run at Altcar in Lancashire since 1836, is said to be the ultimate test of a greyhound, although it is regularly attacked as cruel.

The National Coursing Club says:"Sixty-four of the best coursing greyhounds in Britain and Eire will contest the historic prize on February 26, 27 and 28."

A PAIR OF hand-crafted Purdey shotguns worth £95,000 is the prize in a fund-raising competition organised by the Game Conservancy Trust.

Entrants are being asked to put a cross where they think a pheasant is flying overhead, as well as fill in a speech bubble coming out of the mouth of a gundog.

Each entry costs £50 in a competition organised by the trading arm of the Trust charity.

"It's just a bit of fun," said spokeswoman Liz Scott.

The two 12-bore side-by-side hammerless ejector guns will be custom made for the lucky winner.

ILLEGAL HARE COURSING is to be the target of an intensified campaign by the League Against Cruel Sports.

The move comes amid claims that illegal coursing is on the increase with speculation that organised crime is involved.

Douglas Batchelor, chief executive of the League, said:"We have long campaigned for tougher laws against this cruel activity. The only difference between legal and illegal coursing is that, in one case, the landowner has given permission for the activity. Both are equally cruel and inflict equal levels of suffering on the hares that are killed.

"The Universities Federation for Animal Welfare carried out 53 post mortems on coursed hares. The evidence, published in the Government's Burns Inquiry report, showed that none of them had been killed by 'a bite to the neck' and a number had to be killed by handlers after they were retrieved from the dogs.

"League undercover investigators are monitoring illegal coursers and passing details to the police for prosecution.

"But we will also be campaigning politically for tougher laws. At the moment, police powers and court fines are restricted by 19th Century legislation.

"The Hunting Bill, which the League Against Cruel Sports wants to see returned to Parliament, will address the issue of illegal coursing by: increasing the fine from £200 to £5,000; removing the excuse of allegedly having landowners' permission; and giving police new powers, including the right to arrest coursers and to seize their dogs.

"We deeply regret that hunting interests, such as the Countryside Alliance, have been so quiet on this important area of countryside crime. We hope that this is not because of the close connections between legal and illegal coursing, which are suspected to involve numbers of the same individuals."

SWANS ARE BEING targeted by an air rifle thug in Shropshire where two of the majestic birds have been found badly injured.

Furious locals have banded together to offer a cash reward for information which leads to the arrest of the shooter.

Leading the hunt is local RSPB member Alan Rutter, from Wellington, who says people across the county have been outraged by the attacks.

One swan was hit in the head at a pond and had to be rescued by firemen who used a boat to reach it.

But even as the bird was being treated, another swan was shot in the neck in a separate incident elsewhere.

Police are said to have the name of a suspect.

THE RSPB IS calling for tougher laws to protect wildlife after two men were jailed for smuggling birds of prey into the UK from Thailand.

At Isleworth Crown Court, the first man, from Norfolk, was sentenced to six and a half years while a second defendant, from Birmingham, received a 22 month sentence, 11 of which were suspended.

RSPB investigations officer Duncan McNiven said:"This was a blatant attempt to avoid the controls of the Convention on International Trade in Endangered Species which are in place to protect wildlife from unregulated trade.

"It is important that these controls are not weakened and that they are vigorously enforced. The RSPB is concerned that recent changes to the EU's CITES regulations will result in offences becoming more difficult to detect.

"Proposals to weaken domestic wildlife legislation being considered by the Department of the Environment, Food and Rural Affairs will also seriously undermine the good work done by HM Customs and the police in tracking down wildlife criminals."

A RARE BLOND hedgehog - not an albino - has been living in the lap of luxury after being found by a Cambridge schoolgirl.

Alfie, who still has dark skin and eyes, was found by Bryony Hall who first mistook the white-spiked creature for a stone.

The British Hedgehog Preservation Society has revealed that few blond hedgehogs are ever found alive on mainland Britain because their colouring makes them a target for predators.

But blond hedgehogs are a recognised genetic strain commonly found on the island of Alderney in the English Channel, where two were introduced four decades ago.

Thin and scrawny when found last November, Alfie has put on considerable weight after being hand fed treats like cat food and roast chicken.

Soon, the lucky mammal will be handed over to a wildlife centre where he will live out the rest of his days.

TRADITIONAL GRAZING WILL be restored to Wiltshire's flower-rich meadows and downland thanks to a grant of £50,000 from the Heritage Lottery Fund.

The cash will be used to find the best animals to graze the herb-rich pastures following the slaughter of cattle during the foot-and-mouth outbreak.

Sir Martin Doughty, chairman of English Nature, welcomed the award and said:"The very special herb-rich pastures of Wiltshire are a result of the labour of generations of livestock farming communities.

"Farmers own and manage many of these special sites. So much of our wildlife is in their hands and helping local people find long-term solutions following this dreadful disease and the general downturn in farming, is important."

Caroline Dudley, chairman of the Heritage Lottery Fund's Committee for the South West, added:"The rural economy of the South West has been particularly badly affected as a result of foot-and-mouth.

"We are delighted to be able to use Lottery money to help re-establish traditional and local farm practices where the culling of livestock has had the worst effects on the landscape and environment."

194

THE BATTLE BY British farmers to win back foreign meat markets after foot-and-mouth has taken a giant leap forward following a decision in France.

The UK has regained its status as a foot-and-mouth disease free country at an international meeting of vets in Paris.

This clears the way for farmers to resume the export trade in animals and animal products internationally.

At a meeting of the Office International des Epizooties, a panel of experts agreed to restore the UK's status for the purposes of international trade.

Food and Farming Minister, Lord Whitty, said: "This is a very encouraging step and extremely good news for farmers. But we must not lower our guard.

"There is a great deal of work still to do with more testing, careful re-stocking and implementation of a new movement regime for livestock."

NFU president Ben Gill said: "This decision means we are recognised on the world-wide stage as having beaten this dreadful disease.

"It's great news that this has happened so quickly and is a testament to everyone who has worked hard to achieve this, including Government, vets and scientists.

"We must now get international exports moving again quickly so that this global stamp of approval is translated into positive economic benefits for British farmers."

Exports of British beef, sheep and pig meat, along with live pigs, have already re-started within Europe but all require a special animal health certificate.

Following the Paris decision, the European Commission's Standing Veterinary Committee will further consider restrictions still in place on British exports.

COWBOY TREE SURGEONS are leaving a trail of havoc in their wake across the country, warns the Environment Agency.

The public is being urged to think twice about employing anyone who calls at their door looking for tree pruning work.

The warning comes after a series of complaints to the Agency about workers who are paid cash-in-hand to prune trees but scarper without clearing up.

Residents in one area complained that tree 'litter' was left strewn across gardens, roads and pavements after workmen vanished.

Trading Standards' advice is to choose a tree surgeon who regularly advertises in Yellow Pages or another business directory, or try someone personally recommended by family and friends.

THE SPOTTING OF an ultra-rare bird has sparked a hi-tech research project to pinpoint its mystery breeding grounds.

Only 50 slender-billed curlews were thought to exist in the whole world before one of the wading birds was spotted among a flock of ordinary curlews in Northumberland four years ago by Tim Cleeves, a Yorkshire-based RSPB conservation officer.

The slender-billed curlew, the rarest bird to be seen in Britain since the extinction of the great auk two centuries ago, has just been accepted onto the official British list by the British Ornithologists' Union Records Committee.

Now the RSPB is aiming to to hunt down its breeding grounds and find out more about this enigmatic bird.

Mr Cleeves said:"It is every birdwatcher's dream to see rare birds, but to spot the ornithological highlight of the last two centuries is beyond anyone's wildest hopes.

"Although there have been claimed sightings of other slender-billed curlews since 1998, none of these have been officially accepted. I could have the dubious honour of being the first birdwatcher in Britain to see a slender-billed curlew in Britain and one of the last in the world to see one alive."

The slender-billed curlew is so rare that only one nest has ever been discovered - more than a century ago.

Despite many expeditions, its main breeding grounds, thought to lie in the wildernesses of western Siberia or northern Kazakhstan, have so far eluded detection.

BLACKBIRDS AND ROBINS are driving residents near an Essex car park crazy by singing all night after floodlights fooled them into thinking it was daytime.

Bosses at BT in Colchester say the lights were left on all night for security reasons but they may now have to reconsider.

Mark Griggs, one of the sleepless residents, said the lights used to go off at about 10pm before the firm decided to keep them on all night.

Essex Bird Society believes the birds are singing to establish territory, just as they would during the day at this time of year.

A MAJOR CONFERENCE has been organised to look at the climate change implications for 'England's Green And Pleasant Land'.

Delegates from all over Britain will attend the Country Land and Business Association event which aims to examine the threats and opportunities of climate change for the rural economy.

"Flooding, coastal erosion, smog, storm damage - all have been blamed on one of the most worrying phenomena of recent decades - climate change," said a CLA spokesman.

"Whilst a few still debate its very existence, an increasing body of evidence is building up in support of the notion that this is one of the most serious challenges facing the world in the 21st Century.

"Professionals from the environmental industry, local authority and Government agencies will join rural business leaders and landowners on February 26 for a tightly focused conference. The venue, the National Motorcycle Museum at the M42/A45 junction near Solihull, has been chosen to make the conference easily accessible to delegates."

DOLPHINS AND PORPOISES are regularly being washed up dead after storm force winds battered South West coasts, it has been revealed.

Between the New Year and January 29, scores of the aquatic mammals have been discovered lying lifeless in England and Wales, say The Wildlife Trusts.

So far, 80 have been found - double the figure recorded at the same time last year - with 65 reported since the start of gales on January 14.

"Year on year, hundreds of carcasses of common dolphins and porpoises are washed ashore in the South West," said Joan Edwards, marine policy director for the Trusts."These are unacceptable levels of deaths within UK waters and current Government legislation is simply not doing enough to address the problem."

Marine 'strandings' are said to occur for a number of reasons, such as sickness, disorientation, natural death, extreme weather or injury.

But the main cause of dolphin and porpoise deaths recently is thought to be from their accidentally being caught in fishing nets - known as bycatch.

The accidental capture of creatures in nets is now considered to be one of the greatest threats to the world's whale, dolphin and porpoise populations.

The Wildlife Trusts say they are pressing the Government to reduce such deaths by a variety of means which include:-

-Establishing an independent observer scheme to obtain reliable estimates of total marine mammal bycatch in a fishery.

-Proposing that the Common Fisheries Policy contains clear and measurable commitments to reduce bycatch significantly in the next five years.

-Calling for Government action to improve the way we manage the demands we make on the environment.

DESIGNING FORESTS FOR public enjoyment has led to glowing praise for the Forestry Commission.

After being commended in the 2001 Business Commitment to the Environment Awards, the Commission was described as 'exemplary' for its efforts in creating environmentally acceptable and sustainable woodland.

Now Geoff Hatfield, Forest Enterprise's territorial director for England, will receive an award from DEFRA minister Margaret Beckett MP at a ceremony in London.

He said:"Modern forestry is about people and the environment, not just about trees."

THE COUNTRYSIDE ALLIANCE has backed a new public information campaign aimed at drawing tourists back into the countryside.

The 'Your Countryside - You're Welcome' campaign, launched by ministers, is being co-ordinated by the Countryside Agency in partnership with leading rural 'stakeholder' organisations such as the Alliance.

The Alliance will be running a programme of rural activities beginning in March to tie in with the start of the campaign.

Among these are a North West Food Lovers' Festival; a series of young anglers' demonstration and tuition days; private garden openings, countryside educational tours, open days at hunt kennels; and a 'Local to Locals' campaign promoting country pubs which have won the Alliance's 'Honest Food' award for locally produced food.

Unveiling the Alliance's programme, its chief executive Richard Burge said:"Our countryside is a national asset. But in turn, it must be the responsibility of the whole nation to ensure it survives and prospers.

"Just visiting and spending time in the country is not enough.

"The countryside needs its visitors to spend some money there as well - especially at this time, when the rural economy has been so long under the cosh.

"And whilst many of the forthcoming activities we have helped lay on are in themselves free of charge, we are urging people to give custom to the local amenities."

MOLE-CATCHING HAS been raised to a higher level after the Queen granted her personal mole-catchers a Royal Warrant.

Bert Hewitt, 80, and Victor Williamson, 62, have spent 10 years catching the burrowing mammals on the Queen's Sandringham estate in Norfolk.

So effective have they been that the Queen has now allowed them to put her Royal Warrant insignia on their trusty mole-catchers' van.

Wherever they drive, bystanders can now read 'By Appointment to Her Majesty Queen Elizabeth II Mole Controller'.

"It's good for business," Mr Hewitt said."People will think if we're good enough to catch the Royals' moles, we're good enough to catch theirs."

THE WILDLIFE TRUSTS are urging flower lovers to shake off the winter blues at one of their wildflower meadows in the next few weeks.

"After the bleakness of winter, the cacophony of colour is one of the pure joys of the natural world," said a spokesman."Treat yourself to the stunning spectacle of a wood filled with vibrant yellow wild daffodils or blankets of beautiful bluebells.

"Wood anemone, snowdrop, primrose and orchid can all be seen - join a local Trust expert on a guided walk to help you identify the myriad of wildflowers in bloom.

"The beauty of wildflowers makes them attractive to birds, insects, and people but please resist the temptation to pick any when out on a walk."

Not only was this discouraged, it was illegal.

"All wild plants are protected against intentional uprooting by the Wildlife and Countryside Act," added the spokesman.

LIZARD: facing roaring motorbikes and killer cats

IT IS nice to know that sensitive wildlife areas are to get better protection, as confirmed in a Queen's Speech not too long ago. Nice, because when I lived beside one, you could barely hear yourself think for idiots on scrambler motorbikes churning it up.

There was no doubt they knew it was a so-called SSSI (Site of Special Scientific Interest) but, basically, they didn't give a toss.

As far as they were concerned, that nice piece of Dorset heathland was the perfect place to perfect their 'wheelies' and burn rubber

Beneath their wheels, however, rare sand lizards, smooth snakes and adders were trying to eke out a precarious existence.

I have no doubt some were killed or driven off as a result - which is why I felt like cheering every time one of the idiots toppled off his motorbike.

Unfortunately, as often occurs in these cases, police attempts to get the vandals to go elsewhere only resulted in the problem escalating.

Riding a motorbike down those dirt tracks just made each little twerp in the saddle appear more daring and heroic to his mates.

I must confess, dark thoughts about stretching bungee rope across the motorcyclists' favourite routes did cross my mind.

But common sense prevailed. After all, those heathland creatures had suffered enough without having a great lump of crumpled twit on top of them.

Even so, the idea of seeing one of these masked Darth Vaders being 'twanged' backwards through a gorse bush held huge appeal.

I never actually saw an adder on the heath in the six months or so I lived beside it, though there was plenty of evidence they were about.

I did spot a smooth snake which is thinner than an adder and even rarer I also had the opportunity to study slow-worms which, despite the name, are really legless lizards.

Like lizards, but unlike snakes, their eyes boast eyelids.

My favourite creatures were the perky sand lizards, the males in particular beautifully marked with bright green flanks and striped backs.

Occasionally, my partner's cat would bring one of these into the house and present it to her the way cat's do - something she never appreciated properly in my view, especially if she was in bed at the time!

The cat never ate these lizards or their cousins, the common lizard, which it also hunted.

Instead, it would just bring them in and play with them till they were exhausted, dead, or had escaped by leaving their still wriggling tails behind.

A neat trick, that.

These days, my local wildlife Trust looks after 88 nature reserves - half of them SSSIs - across Berkshire, Buckinghamshire and Oxfordshire.

"The Trust has listed 100 key threatened species within each of the three counties, which it is trying to protect," explained a spokesman.

"Each one is in danger. It either used to be common in the Chilterns or Thames Valley region and has suffered recent dramatic population decline, or is already a rare species in need of special protection."

If my own experience is anything to go by, achieving that special protection is never going to be easy.

Not until some threatened species learn to deploy bungee rope themselves.

Or even Semtex.

NEW FEARS HAVE been raised over GM crops following a study commissioned by English Nature.

So called 'gene stacking' of genes from cross-pollinating GM plants in Canada have produced plants super resistant to normal herbicides.

The Canadian system of voluntary guidelines advising farmers to leave a distance of 175 metres between different GM varieties also seems to have broken down, says English Nature, and 'gene stacking' is now widespread there.

A code of practice for farmers growing GM crops in the UK has already been developed by the industry body SCIMAC.

However, Dr Brian Johnson, English Nature's biotechnology advisor said:"Our report shows that the SCIMAC code is probably inadequate to prevent gene stacking happening in Britain, if these crops were commercialised.

"The consequences for farmers could be that volunteer crops would be harder to control and they might have to use different, and more environmentally damaging, herbicides to control them.

"We do not yet know how 'stacked gene' plants would behave either in farmers' fields or in the wild. The European regulatory system has not yet approved GM herbicide tolerant oilseeds for general release.

"English Nature will be working with DEFRA and ACRE to ensure that risks from possible gene stacking are properly addressed, and that we avoid the mistakes that have been made in Canada."

A PANTHER HAS apparently been seen stalking two goats in the Welsh countryside by their 15 year-old owner.

Laura Jones says she spotted the dangerous black cat peering intently at her goats Thistle and Willow when she went to bring them in at dusk.

Both goats had seemed unnerved for some reason, she said, then she saw the huge cat ready to spring from the shadows near Llangorse, mid-Wales.

She and the goats froze and, after a minute, the panther seemed to lose its nerve and sank back into the gathering gloom, she claimed.

A SEAL WAS spotted trying to clamber over a weir on a Yorkshire river by the startled landlord of a village pub.

Ian Fuller contacted wildlife experts to pass on the sighting and they began following the bizarre inland progress of the seal around Linton-on-Ouse, north of York.

Miles from the sea, the seal is thought to have clambered over locks along the River Ouse to reach its present position.

ANIMAL RIGHTS CAMPAIGNERS are planning their "biggest ever" demo to disrupt this year's Grand National at Aintree.

The protest on April 6 is being co-ordinated by Animal Aid and campaigners claim they intend it to be peaceful.

However, their message that "this event brings shame on Britain as a nation of animal lovers" is unlikely to go down well with thousands of race-goers drawn to the much-loved event or the millions watching at home.

Urging protesters to attend in force, a spokesman for Animal Aid said:"If you find that you can't bear to watch the horrors of the race unfold from your living-room, be there on the day instead to make a stand against it.

"The three-day Grand National meet is designed to push horses to their limits - and beyond. It is run over an extreme distance of 4.5 miles and confronts horses with a bewildering combination of 30 punishing jumps. Deaths are routine. The death toll in recent years is as follows - 2000, five deaths; 1999, four; 1998, five; 1997, eight.

"Every year, around 300 horses are raced to death in Britain. During the 1999/2000 National Hunt season (the Grand National is raced to National Hunt rules), 247 horses died. That's one in 31 of all those that raced.

"Very few horses make it to events like the Grand National - half the 8,000 foals bred each year never even see the starter's flag before they are put down. These include the 'hot-headed', the weak, the accident-prone and the deformed.

"Racehorses are stabled for up to 20 hours a day, causing frustration and stress. Horses are social animals which are meant to be continuously grazing and moving.

"During a race such as the Grand National, the heartbeat of a horse can increase tenfold - leading to potential collapse and heart attack.

"The majority of horses suffer stress-related lung haemorrhages during a race. And a veterinary study found that ulcerated stomachs were universal amongst racing horses.

"Five thousand racehorses end their careers every year. Few enjoy a decent retirement. Many go into a wretched downward spiral, passed from owner to owner. Some end up as pet food, or go into the human food chain."

THE PLANNED REVOLUTION in British agriculture has already met with strong opposition from farmers' leaders who fear proposals to slash support payments will leave members even poorer.

Union bosses spoke out following the publication of the Food and Farming Commission's controversial report.

NFU president Ben Gill said that farmers would be angered about one of the report's core proposals - that of taking away 10 per cent of farmers' support payments from 2004 to fund rural development and environmental measures.

He said:"With the industry in its current dire state, it is hardly surprising that we oppose suggestions of taking money from farmers in this way. It equates to taking away cash that farmers simply do not have.

"I must stress that we are not opposed to rural development and environmental spending - quite the reverse. But we have always been against this way of paying for it and the report has not changed our minds."

LEARNING TO SHOOT is good for children, the Countryside Alliance claims.

In addition, the Alliance says 77 per cent of the public believes that learning to shoot is better for youngsters than playing violent computer games or watching adult films.

It bases its conclusions on a new consumer survey conducted by the Consumer Analysis Group and commissioned by the Alliance itself.

Chris Jackson, the Countryside Alliance's English national director, said:"Responsible youth organisations, such as the army cadets and sea cadets, as well as countless rural and farming families, have long known that learning how to use legal firearms early in their development and under proper supervision is beneficial for children.

"It demystifies any unhealthy glamour or allure of firearms and encourages a prudent attitude that stays with children throughout adult life.

"Learning about shooting encourages children to be safety-conscious and to exhibit a mature, responsible attitude towards firearms.

"This is an especially needed counterbalance to the worrying trend amongst many young people - who have never been properly exposed to firearm use under supervision - towards viewing firearms as some kind of fashion accessory or symbol of power. The survey strongly suggests that many people's concerns are based on false assumptions or misunderstandings."

A GREYHOUND BOUGHT and trained by a 13 year-old schoolboy has won two of its first three races.

Sammy Supple, from Sevenoaks, Kent, took on the job of training Goodbye Tessa himself after buying the bitch as a pup.

He built the dog up to a competitive standard by hours of racing it in the garden, coupled with careful attention to diet.

Already, Sammy has pocketed £100 in winnings and is hoping for even greater success.

The dog was named after the teenager said farewell to a Tessa savings account set up for him by his father, using the cash for his greyhound instead.

TREE LOVERS ARE being urged to donate their St Valentine's Day cards to a Woodland Trust recycling scheme.

Karl Mitchell, director of fundraising for the Trust, said:"Should you have been lucky enough to receive a Valentine's card, this is a brilliant way of doing your bit for the environment.

"Last year Valentine's Day cards made a significant contribution to our card recycling scheme, which collected over 800 tonnes of cards. This year you can help us smash this target."

ANCIENT WOODLAND IN Wales has been betrayed by planning policy with a raft of the Principality's most important forests now under threat, warns the Woodland Trust.

Sites are most under threat from infrastructure and transport developments such as new roads, according to a joint report by the Trust and the WWF global environment network.

Increased housing, sport facilities and even leisure activities such as paint balling are also causing concern for conservationists.

Ancient woodland is land that has been continuously wooded for at least 400 years, says the Trust, and it now covers barely two per cent of Wales.

What remains is irreplaceable and is so rich in flora and fauna that it is sometimes known as 'Wales' rainforest'.

Sites under threat include Blackwood in Gwent where nearly five acres of ancient semi-natural woodland is to be destroyed when the Sirhowy Enterprise Way is built to provide a new access road to industrial development.

Elsewhere, two miles east of Dolgellau, in the Snowdonia National Park, an acre of ancient woodland is threatened by plans to realign part of the A470.

And two miles north of Bridgend, a 10 acre site containing ancient wood Coed Cae Helyg, is threatened with destruction as a result of a new link road.

Jerry Langford, the Trust's operations director in Wales, said:"Local development plans vary widely in their policies regarding ancient woods, from unequivocal protection at one end of the scale, to no mention at the other.

"Even where local plans specify ancient woods should be protected, planning permission has sometimes been granted in direct contradiction of the policy."

Nevertheless, the tide was turning in Wales with new measures being introduced to protect ancient woods, ideas which could also benefit England.

Morgan Parry, head of WWF Cymru, said:"Our ancient woodlands face destruction by stealth because of the planning authorities' failure to recognise them as an important resource to be monitored and protected.

"A proper and easily accessible inventory of these woods must be compiled urgently to prevent this essential part of our natural heritage slipping quietly away under a tide of concrete and tarmac."

HORSE RIDING TESTS are being upgraded by officials terrified of a new phenomenon - saddle rage.

Failed students and their parents are increasingly launching vicious attacks on examiners who give them negative verdicts, according to the British Horse Society.

Because of a rising number of incidents, examiners will no longer tell students face-to-face whether or not they have failed.

Day-long tests will in future be followed by letters sent to students' homes giving them good or bad news more safely.

With most parents spending thousands of pounds on training, plus the £300 test fee itself, and top jobs in the equestrian world often at stake, parents and their offspring can explode at a 'failed' verdict, explained the Society.

CONFUSION REIGNS AFTER Scottish MPs voted to ban hunting with hounds and hunt supporters pledged to exploit "loopholes" in the controversial new Bill.

The Bill to ban hunting with dogs in Scotland was finally passed after a heated debate lasting more than six hours.

But with anti-hunt campaigners overjoyed that the country will now be the first part of the UK to outlaw foxhunting and hare coursing, hunt supporters have pledged to challenge the Bill in the courts and even cross over the border with England to continue traditions stretching back centuries.

Sam Butler, chairman of the Campaign for Hunting, said:"The result merely confirms what we already knew - that the Bill is a disreputable shambles.

"It is not clear what the Bill does. But what is clear is that it is a vindictive and shoddy piece of legislation which needlessly declares war on decent, hard-working people and seeks to put many of them out of work without a penny of compensation.

"This attempted infringement of human freedoms will be challenged in the Scottish courts as incompatible with the European Convention of Human Rights."

He called on all in the UK who care about civil liberty and tolerance to raise their voices in protest to help safeguard the freedoms of the Scottish people.

Alliance chief executive Richard Burge, echoing his criticisms, said the Bill proved the folly of trying to create legislation based on personal moral judgments.

"This Bill's sponsors long ago abandoned any pretence that it was about animal welfare," he said. "The Bill is now revealed as a blatant attempt to seek to interfere with human thought and behaviour.

"Competent politicians should know better than to try to frame legislation that merely seeks to impose their own personal opinion on the community - and especially on cultural minorities.

"That is why this Bill was destined from the first to be an unworkable mess - and the lesson should not be lost on politicians beyond Scotland."

A RECORD NUMBER of bird fans took part in the RSPB's Big Garden Birdwatch this year with the starling currently edging ahead of the house sparrow in prevalence as results are compiled.

Over 57,000 people participated via the RSPB's website - spotting a million birds.

This ended up beating last year's total web participation figure of 52,000.

ANGLERS HAVE AGREED closer ties with the Countryside Alliance in a new move to defend their sport.

"The National Angling Alliance and the Countryside Alliance have signed a 'Memorandum of Understanding' providing a framework within which the two organisations will collaborate closely on angling issues," said a spokesman.

"That framework is based on the concept that the National Angling Alliance is the principal organisation representing and promoting angling and the interests of anglers and that the Countryside Alliance is the principal organisation defending all country sports in the context of rural livelihood and liberty.

"Tony Bird, chairman of the National Angling Alliance, will join the board of the Countryside Alliance immediately and Richard Burge, chief executive of the Countryside Alliance, will attend the meetings of the National Angling Alliance."

The NAA comprises six organisations representing about a million members while the Alliance has 95,000 individual members plus 250,000 affiliate members from a wide range of country sports clubs and societies.

SCOTTISH RED SQUIRRELS have been given a road safety boost with the construction of specially designed rope bridges to help them cross the road.

A series of ropes are being strung high in the tree tops in Glenmore Forest Park, Strathspey, to help the popular mammals beat traffic.

Forestry Commission staff are installing the 15-metre bridges at the spot because it is becoming a recognised feeding area.

Forester Neil McInnes explained:"Of the 160,000 red squirrels in Britain, 120,000 live in Scotland. Sadly, many deaths are caused by traffic and the concept of these rope bridges has been developed to reduce these.

"We know that given the choice, red squirrels prefer staying in the tree canopy rather than coming to the ground. The rope bridges take advantage of this behaviour and so should prove to be a safer and more successful option than coming to the ground.

"We're confident that the bridges will help sustain the population of the red squirrel, by reducing deaths caused by traffic. Sometimes the simplest ideas prove to be the best ones."

HOW TO BOOST wildlife is the subject of a two-day course organised by the Game Conservancy Trust.

The course, aimed at wildlife wardens, rangers, foresters and farmers, was dreamt up to help countryside workers improve their environment.

Titled 'Wise Ways with Conservation', it comes hard on the heels of the Curry report about greener farming and covers subjects such as: ensuring field margins are valuable habitats; the best use of set-aside; making the most of grassland, moorland and woodland; improving wetlands, rivers and streams; and controlling predators.

The course will run at the Game Conservancy Trust's Fordingbridge headquarters in Hampshire on February 28 and March 1.

"The Trust has extensive experience of research into habitat management for game and its associated wildlife," said a spokesman."The course focuses on how to integrate wildlife conservation and land management."

200

FRESH THINKING ON flood defences is needed by the Government to benefit people and wildlife, says the RSPB.

Phil Rothwell, the RSPB's head of countryside policy, said:"The Government spends £380 million a year on flood defence - 90 per cent of that comes out of taxpayers' pockets.

"Surely, the time has come to invest that money in a way which is good for the environment and people. We cannot prevent heavy rainfall and flooding, but ministers could address the issues which are affecting the same areas again and again.

"The current system of hard defences, such as embankments along stretches of rivers, protects certain areas but the water has to go somewhere. All too often it ends up flooding homes, businesses or farms further downstream which are not protected.

"It is not practical, or economically viable, to defend every yard of every river by building higher and higher embankments. What is needed is a catchment-wide approach. In addition to walls through our towns and villages, the Government also needs to look at how the land is managed to reduce the quantity and speed of the rainfall that ends up in our rivers.

"But primarily, the Government needs to create flood storage areas to hold water at times of high rainfall and act as natural reservoirs, keeping water away from homes and businesses."

HARE COURSING WILL be fought over again as animal rights protesters make their views known at the sport's top event, the Waterloo Cup 2002.

The League Against Cruel Sports is planning a protest at the Altcar course in Lancashire on February 26 "to demonstrate the level of public opposition to hare coursing," according to a spokesman.

"It is hard to believe that this barbaric activity remains legal in modern Britain. Hare coursing is pure 'sport' - with a lot of gambling thrown in - for a tiny minority of people who enjoy watching animals suffer.

"There is immense suffering. In hare coursing, two dogs compete in a test of speed and agility in pursuit of a live hare.

"The terrified hares are made to run for their lives to provide 'entertainment'. When caught, they can end up in a brutal tug-of-war between the jaws of the dogs. The hare will often scream in terror as it is fought over.

"Of 53 coursed hares post-mortemed by the Universities Federation for Animal Welfare, none had been killed by a bite to the neck. A number had to be killed by the handlers after they were removed from the dogs."

However, supporters of hare coursing say the ancient sport is about testing the speed and agility of pursuing dogs, not killing hares.

OUTWARDLY PEACEFUL SHEEP could have a hidden side as voracious flesh-eating predators, according to evidence from a top ornithology expert.

Dr Niall Burton was horrified to see a sheep attack and gulp down a grouse chick on Muggleswick Common, near Stanhope, Durham.

He told a national magazine he had been watching a mother grouse and her eight chicks when suddenly a sheep "ran forward, picked up a chick, and ate it whole.

"The alarmed female grouse quickly removed her remaining chicks but the sheep was only prevented from taking a second chick by my intervention."

Sheep elsewhere are also reported to have engaged in similar predation on ground-nesting birds and scientists believe they may be just desperate to replace nutrients missing in their diet.

WATER VOLES LIVING near Hull will soon be on their way to new homes thanks to the Environment Agency.

The Agency is working at Thorngumbald to improve existing tidal flood defences but needs to build an embankment across the natural habitat of the popular creatures.

To solve the dilemma, ecology experts have created a new home for the animals by dredging out a nearby drainage ditch to increase water levels.

Helen Richardson, Agency ecologist, said:"The food the voles needed was already in place in the new home - it's just that the conditions were not ideal, so we had to create them.

"We hope to coax them into the new habitat first by removing the vegetation in their current home but we'll be setting humane traps for them later to ensure we have moved them all. We expect the whole process to take around three to four weeks."

Water voles have undergone a significant decline in recent decades and their habitat is protected under the Wildlife and Countryside Act 1981.

The Agency had to get permission from English Nature before the work could proceed.

The £6million flood defence scheme will involve building a new flood bank between 250 and 500 metres inland of the Humber Estuary to protect east Hull and nearby industry.

At the same time, the work will create over 70 hectares of inter-tidal habitat, which is likely to support internationally important species of waders and wildfowl.

ANGLERS HAVE BEEN given a boost with the launch of a comprehensive new guide to fishing in the Anglian region.

The Angle Directory gives a full range of fishery locations that should suit anglers of all types, from beginners to experts, pure pleasure anglers to specimen hunters or match regulars.

Dr Nigel Tomlinson, Environment Agency regional fisheries development officer, said:"Whilst our previous guides have been successful and well-received, the Angle Directory is the most detailed version ever, updated and printed in an entirely new format. Such a massive collation of angling detail could not have been completed without the help of fishery owners and clubs. We are very grateful to all who submitted information for the Directory, and hope this will encourage even more people to sample the joys of fishing in the Anglian region."

MOST FARMERS WHOSE livestock was culled during the foot-and-mouth outbreak are determined to restock, according to a Government survey of more than 1,000 farmers.

Only six per cent have been so devastated that they want to move out of farming.

Many farmers are now looking at diversification, entering 'green' schemes or turning organic, claims the Government.

Findings show that:78 per cent of infected premises intend to restock and continue farming as soon as possible; 25 per cent of holdings surveyed are 'definitely' or 'possibly' planning to diversify into non-farming activities; there is interest among a small percentage of farmers in running an organic enterprise.

Lord Whitty, Minister for Food and Farming, said:"All of these farmers suffered terribly over foot-and-mouth and it is very encouraging that they are thinking positively about the future.

"It is particularly pleasing that many are seriously considering new diversified and environmental options for their farms so that restocking takes place in an environmentally sustainable context.

"The Curry Policy Commission on the future of food and farming has indicated that it sees this as the future and the Government is in full agreement with this."

Meanwhile, farmers and rural businesses are to receive an extra £2million to help them recover from the effects of foot-and-mouth.

THE RAMBLERS ASSOCIATION has urged walkers to return en masse to the Yorkshire Dales and nearby areas - but they will need to check their routes first.

Ninety-five per cent of all rights of way are now open although some walkers may still be confronted by closed paths unless they check in advance.

Several footpaths will remain closed for some time, due to delays in procedures to disinfect farms and land affected by foot-and-mouth disease.

RA officials have pressed for a co-ordinated, well-advertised hotline to give accurate up-to-date information to walkers about paths in affected areas throughout Yorkshire.

The Yorkshire Dales National Park is now offering an information service on 01969 667450 and for paths outside the National Park, North Yorkshire County Council is providing a five day service on 01609 532245.

Keith Wadd, area secretary for the RA's West Riding Area, said:"After campaigning for this much needed service for walkers, we are delighted that now there is somewhere for walkers to access up-to-date information on footpaths.

"This is particularly important as the Easter holidays approach and a flood of visitors is expected in the countryside."

ENGLAND'S HEATHLANDS COULD be restored with expert help from Down Under as part of a long-term research project.

Ian Davies is project manager for English Nature's 'Tomorrow's Heathland Heritage' scheme, a partnership with the china clay industry that is re-creating the lowland heathland landscape of mid-Cornwall.

Now he is off to Australia and New Zealand to learn from the "best in the world" how to restore landscapes following mineral extraction.

Having been awarded a Winston Churchill Travelling Fellowship and with support from English Nature, Mr Davies is going to look at landscape restoration in Western Australia, Queensland and New Zealand over the next two months.

Tips on best practice will be brought back to the UK for use in Cornwall and beyond.

"We've been learning to do things differently in Cornwall and the result can be seen in the large-scale heathland we have been re-creating here in partnership with our colleagues in the clay industry," he said.

"I do feel there is still more we can learn from Australia and New Zealand where they have been doing this sort of thing on a much bigger scale and for a lot longer, and I'm sure there are techniques that we can benefit from.

"I've been very encouraged by the support and interest I've received from experts in Australia and New Zealand and am looking forward to seeing how they do things.

"I've no doubt it's going to be hard work with a schedule that takes me right across the two countries, but I'm sure this is going to help us to restore our landscapes better and put us in a world-leading position."

A FALLOW DEER appears to have been 'adopted' by a flock of sheep in Wroxham, West Norfolk.

The animal, a male thought to be about two years old, has been eating and sleeping alongside the sheep for almost two months now.

Local opinion is divided as to whether the behaviour is a freak of nature or the deer is actually someone's pet that has got free and become lonely.

Fallow deer are rare in the area and some believe the animal was released to escape being culled under foot-and-mouth regulations.

FARMERS' LEADERS HAVE welcomed Government moves that could ease a desperate shortage of casual farm labour.

The new immigration and asylum White Paper takes into account concerns about the pressing need for more seasonal workers to boost farms and horticultural units, says the NFU.

A spokesman revealed the paper "recognises the clear need for short-term casual labour for farmers and growers who often need extra help during busy periods.

"The NFU has been pressing Government for some time to get an increase in the number of permits for seasonal workers from abroad as it is often difficult to get British casual workers because of the country's low unemployment.The White Paper proposes to look again at the operation of the long-standing Seasonal Agricultural Workers Scheme and build on its principles to see how the needs of the agricultural sector might be better met."

FOXHUNTING COULD BE outlawed within 18 months in England and Wales as the Government prepares a ban on hunting with dogs.

Prime Minister Tony Blair has promised MPs another chance to end hunting on the heels of the Scottish Parliament imposing its own ban.

A vote is expected before Easter and could see all hunting with dogs in England and Wales made illegal before the end of 2003 - throwing thousands of country workers out of work.

Most Labour MPs support an outright ban but pro-hunters are hopeful that a middle way compromise might be reached in which hunting continues under licence.

In the Commons, Mr Blair had been questioned by Labour MP Colin Pickthall - whose West Lancashire seat covers Altcar, the venue for controversial hare coursing event The Waterloo Cup.

He asked:"Do you share the disgust of the 81 per cent of people surveyed in the most recent poll with this activity, who want to see hare coursing banned?

"When will the will of the House, which has been expressed by overwhelming majorities in recent years, be implemented?"

Mr Blair's surprise pledge was seen by many as a reward to backbench Labour MPs who had turned out in force the day before to support Stephen Byers, the embattled Transport Secretary.

Hunt supporters, meanwhile, have promised to do all they can to keep the sport legal in England and Wales.

CLOSURE OF A Dutch abattoir is being demanded after its latest failure to comply with BSE regulations when exporting beef to Britain.

A consignment of Dutch beef containing banned spinal cord was intercepted after entering the UK - the third time the abattoir in question has breached the rules.

Condemning the latest failure, NFU president Ben Gill said:"This abattoir has persistently failed to stick within the rules. It must be closed down until it can be proved that it is up to the job.

"The Dutch authorities must look seriously at how the BSE rules are being enforced there. All too often, breaches of the regulations emanate from this country. We cannot continue to rely on our own Food Standards Agency to pick up on their mistakes."

Banned spinal cord material was found during unloading of 148 quarters of beef at Eastbourne.

Just a month or so ago, a consignment of beef from animals over 30 months old was also intercepted after arriving from Holland.

Mr Gill added:"Once more, we would urge shoppers everywhere to buy British."

A PRIME FRIESIAN bull slaughtered during the foot-and-mouth outbreak could earn as much as £244,000 for its owner from Government compensation coffers, it has been revealed.

The valuation of Marshside Rocket 3 - the highest for a single animal - has already prompted a probe by rural affairs Secretary of State Margaret Beckett who thinks it too high.

However, the bull had sired 2,000 offspring before its untimely death and could have sired many more, probably generating almost £3million in stud fees.

Experts think it unlikely that Rocket 3, bred on a farm near Carlisle by farmer William Bell, is worth less than the figure put on him by a Government approved valuer.

However, DEFRA officials will be looking at the figure again to see if a 'compromise' sum can be agreed with the animal's owner.

FARMERS ARE STILL holding their breath as they await final results of tests involving two sheep suspected of contracting foot-and-mouth.

Initial tests on the sheep, from a farm in North Yorkshire, proved negative and many think this will be the final conclusion.

Even so, the devastation wreaked by the original outbreak was so severe that the merest hint of foot-and-mouth starting up again is a terrifying threat to farms and country businesses nationwide.

As a precaution, the two suspect sheep were slaughtered and livestock movements in a five-mile radius around their Hawnby farm banned.

THE WILDLIFE TRUSTS are encouraging young and old alike to come out of their shells this Easter with a host of attractions on offer at reserves up and down the country.

"Choose from hundreds of activities, including egg trails, nest building, rubber-duck racing and lots more family fun," said a spokesman.

"All ages can join in with birdwatching trips, illustrated talks, hillside walks and fetes. And for younger nature nuts, the event list is bursting with rockpool rambles, mini-beast hunts and themed tea parties.

"Every Easter the natural world is bursting with new additions. Visit a Trust reserve and see if you can catch a glimpse of some of the new-born birds and animals.

"There's something to appeal to everyone. We care for almost 2,500 nature reserves, from remote Scottish islands to inner city wildlife gardens."

FOREST MANAGERS ARE being urged by the Government to think ahead and start planning for the effects of global warming.

At the publication of a Forestry Commission report on climate change and its impact on forests in London, Forestry Minister Elliot Morley said forestry practice would need to adapt.

"Climate change will have a variety of impacts on our forests," he said."Our trees and woodlands play a role in locking up carbon, are a source of renewable energy and a very sustainable construction material. But they are themselves also vulnerable to environ-mental change. Our forestry practices are based on our current state of knowledge of the most likely effects of climate change. They will have to be reviewed and revised as we gain in our overall understanding of the impacts and the consequences of climate change."

203

A LONE DRUMMER led 150 'peaceful protesters' in a demonstration organised by The League Against Cruel Sports at top hare coursing event The Waterloo Cup.

Animal rights protesters carried placards and banners to the entrance of the Lancashire field where the three-day event was being staged.

"Inside, greyhounds were being set to chase and kill hares for the pleasure of spectators," said a League spokesman.

"Coursers claim that the object of coursing is to test the dogs' speed, agility and stamina. But the rules of the National Coursing Club still award a point to a dog that kills a hare 'through superior dash and skill'."

Once again, he repeated that in evidence submitted to the Government's Burns Inquiry, the Universities Federation for Animal Welfare had post-mortemed 53 hares killed at hare coursing events. None of them had been killed by 'a bite to the neck' and a number had to be killed by the handlers when they were retrieved from the dogs.

However, the National Coursing Club, which champions the historic sport, maintains that the killing of hares remains incidental to the main purpose of the event - testing one dog against another.

Meanwhile, 'celebrity couple' Jamie and Louise Redknapp are also reported to have joined the campaign to ban coursing.

Jamie Redknapp said:"The Waterloo Cup should be consigned to history. Hares should not be chased and torn apart for amusement in this day and age. This cruelty must be banned."

His wife added:"I cannot understand how anyone could be entertained by watching dogs savage hares. Other so-called sports where animals are set on other animals for human amusement were banned long ago.

"The Waterloo Cup is cruel, outdated and unnecessary and I hope to see it banned in the very near future."

A MUD-COVERED lamb which became a symbol of foot-and-mouth devastation is now preparing to become a mother itself.

Pictures of the distressed young sheep stranded in mud had flashed round the world and its fate had seemed sealed, along with millions of other animals.

However, Lucky the lamb was rescued from slaughter and became a pet at its owner's farm in Norfolk.

Now farmer Peter Key has revealed that the animal is expecting its own offspring in April.

In addition, Lucky will always remain a pet and will not go to market, he stressed.

THE NEW FOREST is being designated a national park after the Countryside Agency submitted proposals to Government rural affairs supremo Margaret Beckett.

Commenting on the plan, Forestry Commission chairman Lord Clark said he was delighted by the move.

"I am particularly pleased that the unique features of the Forest - including its high nature conservation value, the statutory roles of the Verderers and the Forestry Commission, and the importance of commoning - have all been recognised in advice put forward on the administrative arrangements for the New Forest National Park.

"The new national park would be unusual in having a large tract of land owned by the Crown at its heart. These lands, managed by the Forestry Commission since 1923, have given the public privilege of access on horse and foot and have been used as a recreational resource by locals and visitors for many years."

Donald Thompson, Forestry Commission deputy surveyor in the New Forest, added:"Whilst no changes are proposed to the Forestry Commission's statutory powers or its mangement of the Crown lands, it is clearly essential that we work closely with others to help make these proposals work.

"I envisage that the National Park Authority will provide a strategic overview for the Commission's activities in managing this jewel."

BEEF CAN NOW be delivered direct to your door from a wildlife-friendly farm which uses an RSPB-endorsed wildlife management plan.

Family-run Sunderland Farm on the idyllic Hebridean island of Islay - which borders the RSPB Loch Gruinart Nature Reserve - has the distinction of being the first farm in the UK to receive such approval for its wildlife-friendly farming methods.

Stuart Housden, an RSPB director in Scotland, said:"The right type of farming is vital for the future of many species of wild birds. We are pleased to endorse the wildlife management plan at Sunderland Farm which will benefit the important wildlife of Islay and bring benefits to the local community."

The island plays host to many threatened bird species such as the hen harrier and is grazed by rare Silver Dun Galloway cattle, a hardy breed said to thrive in non-intensive, natural farming environments.

And the verdict on the meat itself ?

"Outstanding! Tender and full of flavour - this is what meat should taste like," said RSPB member Peter Roberts.

SIX MEN HAVE been acquitted of charges relating to digging for badgers and being cruel to a dog.

The offences were alleged to have taken place at a badger sett in Llanfrothen, Gwynedd, North Wales.

At Dolgellau Magistrates Court, the six had been charged with interfering with a badger sett by causing a dog to enter a sett, damaging a part of a sett and disturbing a badger while occupying a sett.The men were also charged with digging for a badger.

In addition, one defendant was charged with causing unnecessary suffering to an animal by allowing a dog to go to ground and receive injuries.

The magistrates said the prosecution had failed to prove that it was an active badger sett and agreed the defendants were actually foxhunting.

CHICKENS: jolted awake by a noisy newcomer

KEEPING chickens is apparently the latest craze among metropolitan couples who swap their luxury city pads for country homes at the weekend.

So popular have humble hens become as the new 'in' hobby that a stack of books have recently been written on how best to look after them.

Most chickens in this country are descended from the Old English Game Fowl, a bird kept as much for its fighting prowess as its meat. Cock-fighting dates back over 2,000 years and continued here long after it was outlawed in the middle of the 19th Century.

Even the Roman conquerers commented on the obsession of native Britons for their sporting birds, although cock-fighting probably paled in comparison with the bloody combat at the Coliseum.

Few people today look at chickens the same way and the vast majority are kept for their meat, their eggs, or simply as an attractive diversion.

It has to be said that there is something deeply relaxing about watching a few hens unhurriedly scratching around a patch of dry earth looking for insects and worms. I learnt this first-hand when one of my brothers acquired a magnificent white cockerel and five sandy brown hens.

These newcomers were swiftly penned behind some wire in our back garden, with an old rabbit hutch employed as their dormitory I can still remember the beaming smile on my brother's face as he proudly introduced his new charges. We, all still kids, beamed back. The neighbours beamed over the fence.

Everyone beamed.

But at about 4am the following morning, no-one felt like beaming anymore.

A blood-curdling, ear-splitting noise shook the house, and all the other houses in our row.

Everyone woke with a start. "What was that ?," we gasped. There it was again. Even worse this time. The cock was crowing.

Somehow, in all the fuss and excitement, the possibility of a cockerel doing what cockerels do naturally had been overlooked. Outside, it was still dark.

Why the cockerel crowed so early no-one could understand. Perhaps it was an early bird.

After a week of being jolted from our sleep, everyone - especially the neighbours - agreed the cockerel had to go.

My brother tried to overturn the verdict, desperately trying to shut the bird up using a variety of methods. None worked.

It was a sad day when we chased the cockerel round the garden until we finally managed to get it into a large cardboard box.

Then it was taken back to the farm it came from.

Unfortunately, greater sadness was to follow.

A vital function of a cockerel is to protect the hens.

Without the protection of a cock's hawk-like beak and sharp claws, hens are vulnerable.

Sure enough, within a few weeks, a terrier got into the pen and killed every one of the hens.

I doubt it would have happened with the cock still there.

All casualties were dutifully buried - a terrible waste of protein in retrospect.

THE COUNTRYSIDE ALLIANCE has pledged to organise a "massive" protest march to show the depth of country disgust if hunting with dogs in England and Wales faces the end.

Chief executive Richard Burge said:"If the Government does bring forward legislation to ban hunting, a massive new Liberty and Livelihood march in London is a racing certainty.

"The tone of our strategy will be set by the announcement, which the Government has said it will make on the way forward, before Easter.

"We are constantly reviewing the logistics for possible events in London or elsewhere in the UK. The march team is on standby and we are in touch with London authorities to keep an eye on dates so that we are ready.

"The Alliance will continue to review whether any event is appropriate to coincide with the votes in Westminster on March 18 and 19 in the Commons and Lords respectively.

"Whatever is decided will be designed to show that those who support hunting are reasonable, decent and law abiding people. The object will be to strengthen the resolve of our supporters in Westminster, to convince the undecided of the rightfulness of our cause, and to expose opponents' lies.

"The essential thing now is for everyone to write to their MPs and to peers reminding them, now that Lord Burns has resolved the issue of cruelty in favour of hunting, the vote is simply a question of whether the MP or peer supports civil liberty or not.

"No MP, particularly those with rural parts to their constituency, and no peer, should be able to say they have received no letters from those who support hunting."

A DEAF BORDER collie faced a bleak future until it was adopted by a couple who used to teach deaf children.

Now Sam is being taught sign language by Peter and Margaret Jones at their home in Condover, Shropshire.

Today, the outlook seems sunny for the two-year-old dog which may have faced a death sentence when its disability was first discovered.

Fortunately, Sam was given to a pet rescue centre when his farmer owner realised he was useless at rounding up sheep because he could not hear commands.

The centre publicised his plight and was swamped with replies.

However, because of their background, retired teachers Mr and Mrs Jones were chosen as Sam's new owners, especially as they were also looking for a pal for their labrador Liza.

NEW AIRPORT PROPOSALS which threaten more than 155,000 wintering birds have been branded "absurd" by the RSPB.

The Society says it is ridiculous to think that marshland on the banks of the Thames at Cliffe in North Kent could ever be identified as a site for a new airport.

Chris Corrigan, RSPB South East regional manager, said:"This is not something that is just unacceptable - it is unthinkable. The Thames is the fourth most important site for waterbirds in the UK, supporting an average of over 155,000 wintering birds.

"In environmental terms, it is hard to think of a worse site for an airport in the South East, and we look forward to hearing that this proposal has been immediately consigned to the wastebasket where it belongs.

"What is most astonishing about this proposal is that it is barely a year since the Government strengthened laws protecting wildlife. There is no place that could be chosen for an airport in the vicinity of the South Thames Marshes that would not have a disastrous impact on the wildlife there, and we will fight it all the way. "

EIGHTEEN COWS ARE helping to turn the clock back for one of England's ancient woodlands.

The bullocks have been let loose to graze Penn Wood in Buckinghamshire - the first time cattle have returned to the wood in 150 years.

Experts from The Woodland Trust, which owns the wood, hope that the bullocks will make the envi - ronment even more welcoming to wildlife by turning it back into a once traditional woodland pasture.

Releasing cattle into woodland is an ancient practice thought to date to medieval times and ultimately makes life easier for a range of wildlife such as butterflies, beetles, and even ground-nesting birds.

Because small mammals are likely to increase, visitors to the wood may also be treated more frequently to the sight of birds of prey scouring the area.

RARE SAND LIZARDS are to be reintroduced to Berkshire under a national release programme organised by The Wildlife Trusts.

The lizards were once widespread in the country but are now mostly reduced to small populations hanging on in Dorset, Surrey and Merseyside.

To help boost numbers nationwide, about 50 captive-bred sand lizards will be freed on sandy heathland habitat at the Wildmoor Heath Nature Reserve in Berkshire.

First, however, crucial preparation work will be undertaken at the site before their autumn release.

"Lizard-loving volunteers will be felling trees, clearing scrub and making sandy tracks to work as fire breaks to create suitable conditions for the lizards," said a Trusts spokesman.

"The 100-hectare site offers space and a good level of protection for the vulnerable lizards."

Sarah Ruff, senior biodiversity officer for the Berkshire, Buckinghamshire, and Oxfordshire Wildlife Trust, added:"The future for the sand lizard is far from secure in the UK and they haven't been seen in Berkshire since 1965.There are few natural sites suitable for their survival and we must ensure a growing population by undertaking strategic reintroduction schemes such as this."

CUCKOOS ARE DECLINING so fast that their traditional spring calls may be silenced in parts of the country, it has been revealed.

Over the last 30 years, the cuckoo population has fallen by 20 per cent in farmland areas and by a staggering 60 per cent in woods, according to The Woodland Trust.

This spring, the Trust has joined forces with the British Trust for Ornithology in asking people to listen out for the cuckoo, as part of a survey monitoring the impact of climate change on the environment.

"Everyone is needed to listen out for the first cuckoo they hear. Even if you usually hear the cuckoo but don't hear one this year, please let the Trust know by taking part in the survey," said a spokesman.

"The cuckoo, which resembles a sparrowhawk or a kestrel in flight, can be difficult to identify. However, it would be very hard to mistake the distinctive song of the male and the unmistakable bubbling noise of the female, as they exchange calls during courtship.

"The bird occupies a wide variety of habitats throughout the UK, generally close to suitable species that act as surrogate parents, and near supplies of its favourite food - hairy caterpillars.

"The Woodland Trust believes trees and woods are extremely susceptible to global warming. The UK's ancient woodland is becoming increasingly fragmented and isolated, often due to intensive land use and development, and is a much more hostile environment for many bird species.

"The cuckoo - famous for its parasitic practice of laying eggs in other birds' nests - may be suffering from a reduction in host nests, loss of suitable habitat, and fluctuating food supply in the UK or in its African wintering grounds."

WORKING WITH WILDLIFE is the subject of a one-day careers fair organised by The Mammal Society's youth group Mammalaction on March 16.

Spokesman James Packer said:"Many young people want to work with wildlife whether as a wildlife photographer or as a nature reserve warden but don't know how to get these jobs or where to start looking.

"Mammalaction has invited 15 of its experts to explain what their job entails, how they got it, and provide advice on how young people can get into their field."

Aimed at 13-17 year-olds, the day will cover the different types of jobs that are available with animals, the qualifications needed, the best courses to do and the voluntary work that may be needed.

The event takes place at Bristol Zoo Gardens between 10am and 5pm.

POLICE HAVE SWOOPED to recover a haul of 300 eggs from some of the rarest birds in Britain - including osprey, avocet, and peregrine falcon - from an address in Liverpool.

Working with the RSPB, officers also used a search warrant issued under the Wildlife and Countryside Act to seize other items, including climbing equipment, a computer, a mountain bike, and over 30 stuffed birds.

A large number of documents have been taken away for further examination.

Following the seizures a 40-year old man was arrested and interviewed then released on police bail, without charge, pending further enquiries.

Among the haul were six clutches of osprey eggs, eleven clutches of little tern eggs and three clutches of avocet eggs, as well as eggs from marsh harrier, peregrine falcon and roseate tern.

The stuffed birds included Montagu's and marsh harriers - both rare in the UK.

PC Andy McWilliam, wildlife liaison officer for Merseyside Police, said:"This is one of the most important seizures of wild birds' eggs and information in recent years."

RSPB investigations officer Guy Shorrock added:"Ospreys have been plagued by egg collectors since they recolonised Scotland in the 1950s with over 100 clutches stolen. To find six clutches at a single address is very disturbing."

A CHICKEN HAS been named 'Lucky' after surviving a lorry crash, going on the run, then being rescued by animal rights campaigners.

The fortunate hen was among more than 4,000 left stranded when a lorry taking them for slaughter crashed at Winchester in Hampshire.

But while the other chickens were finally rounded up and sent to meet their fate , Lucky fled into undergrowth and went on the run for eight days.

Even then, her luck didn't desert her because she was eventually found by Compassion in World Farming campaigners Angie Greenaway and Rob Hill.

Now, instead of ending up on someone's dinner plate, a life of pampering lies ahead for the happy bird.

SCOTTISH TREES ARE being celebrated in a new scheme launched at the Royal Botanic Gardens in Edinburgh.

The project to toast the country's "rich legacy of 'heritage' trees - trees that are notable or remarkable for any reason" - was launched by Scottish Forestry Minister Allan Wilson.

The scheme is part of 'Treefest Scotland 2002', a year-long festival of events to celebrate Scotland's trees, woods and forests.

"One of Scotland's greatest claims to fame is its rich and diverse legacy of heritage trees," Mr Wilson said."Heritage trees might be trees of great age or size. They might have historical significance or botanical interest or they might simply be unique or exceptional in some way.

"Some of Scotland's most ancient trees are already well known, such as the Fortingall Yew in Fortingall, Perthshire, and the veteran oaks at Cadzow, Hamilton.

"Others trees will have heritage value by virtue of their association with people and events in Scotland's history, acting as living links with our past. Examples are the Wallace Yew in Elderslie, Renfrewshire, and the Covenanters' Oak in Motherwell."

THE END OF the hare coursing season has coincided with fears among supporters that the ancient sport may soon be consigned to oblivion for good.

Coursing traditionally stops between March 11 and September 14 but recent moves to ban hunting with dogs in England and Wales have made the lengthy stoppage more symbolic this year.

The National Coursing Club says MPs and Lords should be reminded of the many arguments in favour of allowing coursing to continue.

According to a spokesman, the sport "conserves enormous numbers of hares - and kills very few. No-one can run a successful meeting on his land without taking active measures to conserve hares.

"It is the only field sport where the objective is not to kill the quarry - the better the hares run, the better the dogs are tested.

"Can you imagine a fisherman saying what a wonderful day he'd had when the river was black with fish, but they were so clever he didn't catch one all day? With coursing, that's the kind of day you want!

"Seven out of eight hares escape. The only hare that is killed is ill, slow, clumsy or old. As nature has decreed for millions of years, it is killed by natural selection. Shooting, of course, is indiscriminate.

"The hare is the only mammal in creation with complete vision behind and a blind arc in front. It was designed by evolution to evade pursuit - not to be shot by guns or run over by cars it cannot see.

"In no coursing season since the War have more than 350 hares been killed, as opposed, for instance, to the 600 in a day shot on one East Anglian estate in February, and that is not to mention the wounded that probably hopped about for a few days subsequently.

"Finally, if a hare is killed, its death is quick. No death is pleasant, but there is not a man on the planet who wouldn't settle now if he knew his end would be as swift."

RURAL AFFAIRS SUPREMO Margaret Beckett took a leaf out of Tony Blair's globe-trotting book by flying all the way to South Africa to learn more about 'helping the environment'.

The DEFRA Secretary of State was said to be probing "the issue of building a sustainable future by visiting a coastal management project and environmental centre in Cape Town."

At the same time, she was aiming to learn more about bird life conservation and how schoolchildren's knowledge of their environment can be improved.

Critics claim staying at home would have been more helpful for the environment.

A REIGN OF terror against ramblers has ended with the capture of an eagle owl on Ilkley Moor in Yorkshire.

For two years, the owl swooped down and threatened anyone unlucky enough to wander too close to its territory on the desolate moor.

But the bird, which boasts a 5ft wingspan, has now been caught after one incident too many when it terrorised schoolgirl Holly Minnikin, aged six.

Only the presence of her parents, who scared the owl off, is thought to have saved the youngster from serious injury as the bird menaced her with razor-sharp talons.

Council rangers set a baited box trap near its lair and the bird, a male believed to have escaped from captivity, was soon imprisoned.

Eagle owls are native to Scandinavia and are the world's biggest owls - powerful enough to kill small deer and foxes, though they normally feed on smaller mammals and birds.

A PIKE CALLED 'Isaac' has been helping scientists build up a picture of the homing skills of its species.

Researchers at the Centre for Ecology and Hydrology in Dorchester have spent two years monitoring Isaac as part of a study into pike at the River Frome in Dorset.

What they found amazed them - Isaac would spend eight months hunting up and down the river before returning to the same spot.

Pike appear to migrate into different areas during autumn and summer but the fact that they can then remember where they started from has prompted speculation that they are much brainer than first thought.

Then again, perhaps the scientists' own mothers could have told them that eating fish was said to be good for brain power - and pike are voracious eaters of other fish.

GOVERNMENT SPIN DOCTORS are being backed by a multi-million pound budget to 'rebrand' the countryside in the wake of foot-and-mouth devastation.

The move, supported by celebrities such as Anthea Turner and Joan Collins, is aimed at burying forever the depressing images pumped out worldwide of Britain's countryside in crisis.

Instead of mass funeral pyres and weeping farmers, the Government aims to fill potential tourists' heads with positive pictures of a green and pleasant land.

At stake is billions of pounds in takings for rural businesses if country tourism returns to its previous high levels.

Rural Affairs Minister Alun Michael said there was a need to remind people that the countryside was open again for business.

He said:"The rural economy took a terrible knock last year.

"Few people, including many farmers, had realised how important tourism was to the rural economy."

Surprisingly for many, Mr Michael chose to launch the scheme in Leicester Square in the heart of London.

Actor Trevor Harrison - Eddie Grundy in The Archers - was brought in to kick off a display of country activities while the benefits of fresh air and rural fun were outlined.

208

YET MORE TALKS are planned before legislation is finally issued by the Government on hunting with dogs in England and Wales.

The political hot potato was effectively dropped for now by Rural Affairs Minister Alun Michael who told MPs he wanted to find common ground between pro and anti-hunters.

Conflict should be tempered by tolerance, he said, with six months of fresh consultation aimed at delivering a Bill which would settle the issue once and for all.

Many MPs are furious that their huge majority in favour of an outright ban has been blocked again after peers voted overwhelmingly in favour of the so-called Middle Way approach.

Richard Burge, chief executive of the Countryside Alliance, said:"The old Bill has gone for good. The Alliance will participate in this new process and we will seek - with vigour and determination - to ensure the outcome is one which safeguards individual liberty, and enables public confidence to be placed fairly in the accountability of hunting, and in the conduct of hunting people.

"Any changes, or even discussion of those changes, will be developed and approved by the Council of Hunting Associations as the leaders of the hunting world.

"No-one should read this moment as either one of success or failure. It is neither. It is simply a staging post on a long road, the outcome of which we are all resolved must be a lasting and secure peace for hunting as part of a diverse and tolerant countryside.

"We still have a dangerous and perilous path to tread and our level of alert remains at its highest. No-one should doubt that the 'march' is still available and will be used. But it will be deployed at the moment when it will have a decisive impact on the battle."

GOLDEN EAGLES ARE being boosted in Scotland as Forestry Commission rangers join forces with a variety of groups in the Trossachs area to protect the birds from ruthless egg collectors.

Scottish police, the RSPB, and the Loch Lomond Interim Park Committee are among groups teaming up with rangers and local volunteers to keep a 24-hour watch on vulnerable nest sites.

A spokesman for the Forestry Commission said Eagle Watch 2002 was supported by three initiatives: the Partnership for Action against Wildlife Crime; Stirling Council's Safer Central Rural Initiative; and the National Park Crime and Disorder Partnership.

All the parties involved gathered for the first time deep in the would-be National Park at Strathyre village where the task ahead was discussed.

TOAD PATROLS ARE being organised nationwide by The Wildlife Trusts in a bid to protect the creatures from traffic as they return to breeding areas.

Volunteers are being recruited to save thousands of toads from a violent end on busy roads as they make their way to ponds and lakes.

"From March to May, toads will be moving from hibernation sites to breeding ponds, instinctively following centuries-old routes, many of which are now crossed with busy highways," said a Trusts spokesman.

"Under cover of darkness, their dangerous journey can take several nights to complete with many never reaching their destination.

"Volunteers will be helping to either erect signs to warn passing motorists, encouraging toads to use specially constructed underpasses or physically carrying them across in buckets.

"Toad populations in the UK are in decline and face a number of threats in addition to heavy traffic. Each year, wild ponds are lost due to road building development, pollution, intensive farming, and drought.

"Information on the location of spawning ponds, hibernation places, and migration routes gathered from toad patrols is vital in continuing the conservation of the species."

OVER 23,000 YOUNG salmon are being released across Lancashire and Cumbria after the Environment Agency joined forces with hatchery workers.

About 10,000 'pre-smolts', each about 12 months-old and five inches long, were first released into the River Lune and four of its tributaries - the rivers Rawthey, Greta, Wenning and Hindburn.

The fish were reared at a hatchery at Garsdale, near Sedbergh, from eggs taken from Lune salmon and were stocked in a joint operation by the Agency and the Middleton Hatchery Group.

After being added to the River Lune at Broadraine near Killington and once acclimatised in a purpose-built holding area, the fish will head downstream and out to sea.

The remaining pre-smolts will be released at 11 further locations across south Cumbria and north Lancashire.

GROUSE AND PROBLEMS caused in Scotland by their winged predators have been put under the spotlight again by the Game Conservancy Trust.

Chairman Andrew Christie-Miller said:"We need little convincing about the importance of game to the Scottish countryside and Scottish economy.

"The 'Economic Study of Scottish Grouse Moors: an update 2001' confirmed the important impact of grouse shooting both in terms of employment - 940 full time equivalent jobs across Scotland - and also, in economic terms, in supporting £17million worth of GDP in Scotland.

"The contribution that grouse shooting makes through countryside conservation measures and green tourism is impressive."

However, solutions were still being sought to "the difficult and perennial subject of raptors".

"We are the only organisation in my view that can offer a practical way forward based on sound science that benefits both grouse and raptors. We are currently engaged in dialogue with a range of interested parties - both governmental and non-governmental on both sides of the Border," he added.

FARMERS' LEADERS HAVE attacked France's continuing, illegal ban on British beef as a "farce".

NFU president Ben Gill said farmers were exasperated and in despair at the fact that France is continuing to get away scot-free with its ban.

His attack came as the European Commission agreed to launch 'infraction procedures' against France for disobeying a court ruling last year that it must lift its ban.

This will send a formal notice to the French, paving the way for potentially heavy fines to be levied on the country - though there is no evidence it will make the slightest bit of difference.

The slowness of the system also means that there could be years of correspondence between France and the Commission and yet another round of hearings in the European Court before any concrete action is taken.

Mr Gill said:"The situation can only be described as an intolerable farce.

"We have already had a ruling from the European Court of Justice - France is breaking the law.

"That we now have to go through many more months of legal argument and procrastination before any further action can be taken is ridiculous.

"If the system is to blame then it needs to be changed. At the moment, it is making a mockery of the European Union."

The European Commission first lifted the ban on British beef in August 1999.

When France refused to accept British beef imports, the Commission began legal proceedings resulting in a ruling in the European Court of Justice in December 2001 that it was breaking the law.

The NFU started its own legal action against France in 2000 with the European Court of Justice's final ruling expected by the end of the summer or early autumn.

WILD SALMON ARE being helped by a new scheme aimed at rivers in the West Highlands.

Stocks of wild salmon have plummeted in recent years from almost 2,000 tonnes per year 30 years ago to less than a quarter of that now.

The project, which centres on Strathcarron, in north west Scotland, involves the capture of wild salmon which are relieved of their eggs and then returned to the water.

Being protected and monitored means their eggs stand a much better chance of becoming young fish than they would in the wild.

The young salmon are then returned to six different rivers in the region where, it is hoped, they will help numbers of wild salmon thrive.

THE COUNTRYSIDE ALLIANCE says it is "bitterly disappointed" by the failure of a legal challenge to the Government's decision not to hold a full public inquiry into the foot-and-mouth crisis.

Chief executive Richard Burge said:"We have long called for a transparent and independent public inquiry into what happened last year. I believe that it is the only way to learn fully the lessons for the future - identify where any incompetence lay and restore confidence among members of the rural community.

"The case has raised issues of constitutional significance far beyond foot-and-mouth disease, which have attracted the interest and support of a number of liberal and reforming organisations. We do, however, welcome the fact that this case will now be actively pursued through the appeal process.

"This decision was made public on the day final submissions were due to the Government's own 'Lessons Learned' Inquiry. Our submission shows that the incompetent handling of foot-and-mouth by the Government was exacerbated by the distinct lack of contingency planning.

"The resultant poor communications systems, inadequate organisation and poor management left rural people feeling bewildered and confused. These issues need to be urgently addressed by the Government."

A PET TIGER has been causing a stir in the Welsh farming community after its owner applied to keep it at a local farm.

Ex-zookeeper Elizabeth Hamer had her application turned down by Carmarthenshire County Council and now year-old Siberian tiger Torrick faces an uncertain future.

Ms Hamer has handled the fearsome predator since his birth at Dartmoor Wildlife Park and wanted to move him to her farm at Crymych.

However, farmers' leaders and police had objected to Torrick staying there because of the danger to humans if he escaped.

Fully grown Siberian tigers can crush the skull of a bear and are among the world's most ferocious hunters.

BLUEBELL WOODS ARE the star attraction currently being promoted for The Woodland Trust by beefy actor Brian Blessed.

The Trust has compiled a list of woods ready to bloom and is asking people to get in touch if they want to learn where the spectacle nearest to them will be located.

Mr Blessed said:"When I walk in woods I am always amazed by the great variety of wildlife that exists within these magnificent places. There is nothing I like better than wandering through bluebell woods during late spring and experiencing the magic of being so close to nature."

A Trust spokesman added:"The location of woods and the weather determine when is the best time to see bluebells. Depending on the amount of sunlight reaching the woodland floor and region of the country, these spectacular flowers can be seen from early to mid-April until mid-May, and sometimes later.

"Visitors are urged to stay on footpaths and are asked not to damage or pick the plants. The UK's bluebell woods are of international importance. The British bluebell represents 20 per cent of the world population of the flower so it is important to take care while enjoying bluebell woods."

BADGER ABUSE BY hunt groups is set to continue because of the Government delay in implementing a ban on hunting with dogs in England and Wales, it has been claimed.

The National Federation of Badger Groups has attacked the planned six-month consultation period between pro and anti-hunt groups as a waste of time.

Dr Elaine King, chief executive of the NFBG, said:"The Government should respect the views of the majority of people in this country and introduce a ban on hunting with dogs without further delay.

"Foxes, deer and hares are not the only animals which suffer at the hands of those who hunt with dogs.

"Badgers also suffer when their setts are blocked up or dug into as part of foxhunting. Legal hunting of foxes with terriers and lurchers also provides many unscrupulous people with a cover for illegal hunting of badgers."

The NFBG recently published a report alleging badgers are sometimes buried alive when setts are blocked by fox hunts.

The report also listed examples of huntsmen and terriermen who had been prosecuted for offences against badgers.

In addition, it detailed cases of illegal interference with badger setts that had taken place in the months since hunting resumed after the foot-and-mouth outbreak.

"Badger baiting with dogs is illegal, but it continues to be carried out, often by the same people who carry out legal control of foxes," claimed Dr King.

"When caught digging into a badger sett or entering dogs into a sett, many offenders claim that they are digging lawfully for foxes or rabbits, or that they are digging into the sett to rescue their dog.

"A ban on hunting with dogs would remove this excuse."

A FOX SPARKED a high-rise rescue mission when it became trapped on scaffolding high above Brighton city centre.

The animal, thought to have been hunting seagulls, was stuck three floors up but was saved by RSPCA officers supported by firemen.

Two fire crews were needed in the hazardous chase, using a turntable ladder to get them closer to the panicking creature.

RSPCA inspector Marie Stevens netted the fox at one point but it chewed through the mesh and almost fell off the scaffolding to its death.

Finally, after two hours, the fox was captured in front of a large cheering crowd and treated by a local vet before being released at a more rural location.

GM CROPS USED at UK trial sites pose a high risk of contaminating neighbouring crops, according to a new European Commission report.

The Soil Association says European experts have identified the three crops being planted in Government-sponsored trials - oil seed rape, sugar beet and maize - as having a high risk of contaminating conventional and organic crops.

In addition, scientists believe that wild plants are at risk of being contaminated while research also shows that UK separation distances between GM and other crops are completely inadequate.

Peter Melchett, the Soil Association's policy director, said:"This confirms what organic farmers have been saying about the threat that GM crops pose to the integrity of organic farming.The Government and GM industry seemed to have picked three of the most contaminating crops to test in the UK. This new report confirms that commercial growing of these crops threatens the future of British organic food and farming."

GANGS OF ILLEGAL bait diggers on the River Adur in West Sussex could be putting homes and farmland at risk from flooding, warns the Environment Agency.

"Gangs have been observed recently bait digging on the tidal reaches of the River Adur between Shoreham-by-Sea and Bramber," said a spokesman.

"Not only is this activity illegal, it also threatens to seriously damage the tidal flood defences with possible high risk consequences for surrounding homes and farmland.

"Most of the River Adur is a specially protected wildlife area and the activities of these unscrupulous gangs will also damage the delicate ecological balance of the area which includes some important species of birds.We are asking anglers in Sussex to ensure that they obtain their bait from reputable sources and to report any suspicious activity."

EU RED TAPE threatens to drive some of Britain's smaller game shoots out of business, it has been revealed.

New rules being drawn up in Brussels could result in a welter of fresh restrictions being placed on shooters.

Under stringent health and hygiene rules planned by the EU, vets could be required to be present at every single pheasant and grouse shoot to check game hygiene.

FARMERS' LEADERS SAY recent action to stop illegal meat and plant imports is beginning to take effect.

But NFU Food Standards chairman Michael Seals pledged his union would continue to pressure the Government over the issue.

He said:"We are now determined not to lose the momentum we have gained. We are extremely pleased with the progress made but the proof of the pudding is in the eating."

THE RAMBLERS ASSOCIATION has called on the Government to establish a protocol on access to the countryside should a foot-and-mouth outbreak ever occur again.

In its submission to the Lessons Learned Inquiry, the charity said that the blanket closure of country footpaths during the recent outbreak was wrong.

RABBIT: how two pets were driven to an early grave

WATCHING that darkly entertaining rabbit saga 'Watership Down' for the umpteenth time recently reminded me how much we take this likeable little creature for granted.

Sociable and attractive, rabbits enliven our countryside and provide a steady source of food for many predators.

Unfortunately, they also cause many problems for Man.

Farmers often regard rabbits as pests, not only because they eat crops but also because they undermine fields by building warrens.

Spotted scurrying around in local fields, rabbits seem perfectly at home but it's worth remembering they were only introduced to this country in the 12th Century from Europe.

Back then, they were prized for their meat and fur and became a major factor in the rural economy.

Today, rabbit meat has fallen way behind other meats in popularity despite remaining a lean and tasty addition to the table.

The population explosion of rabbits was initially curtailed in the 1950s with the introduction of the killer virus myxomatosis.

This not only wiped out the vast majority of rabbits but also led to the decline of many wild predators that fed on them such as buzzards and stoats.

Since then, rabbits have fought back to their original high numbers and have developed a resistance to the virus which once decimated their ranks.

Breeding success is at the heart of the rabbit's survival with the mother rabbit able to produce up to 20 young each year.

Even these offspring can then breed themselves when they are only four to five months old.

No wonder farmers often become exasperated by the sheer numbers of rabbits devastating their crops.

However, Mother Nature tries to even things out.

Most rabbits die before reaching their first birthday, either taken by predators or from more mundane killers such as cold and wet.

Although highly exaggerated in 'Watership Down', rabbits do have a complex social structure within the colony.

Females can be dominant, as well as males, and will drive off subordinate rabbits which trespass on their private patch of warren.

Domesticated rabbits can make great pets, and I should know.

One of my brothers and I used to keep two and spent many happy hours cleaning out their cages, introducing fresh straw, water, and feed when we came back from school.

It gave us a fascinating insight into the animal world.

Sadly, this idyll was soon ended when we also got a dog.

One fateful day, I'd tied the dog up while I let the rabbits 'stretch their legs' on the lawn.

Within seconds, the dog was free and chasing the rabbits round and round the garden in crazy fashion.

I managed to catch the dog eventually and recovered both rabbits from neighbouring gardens.

But by then they were severely traumatised and soon died of shock.

After a fitting ceremony, we buried them under a large brick to stop the malicious mutt digging them up again.

RIP Honey and Bubbles.

COUNTRY DWELLERS ARE being let down by Labour ministers who made great play of promising to help them, claims the Government's own top rural adviser.

Countryside Agency chairman Ewen Cameron said the Government had already broken its pledge to assist rural people.

In the first report on Labour's commitment in the Rural White Paper to 'think rural', Mr Cameron said:"It was a bold move by the Government to commit itself to 'rural proof' its own policy making.

"In our first annual report on how well it is doing in putting the needs of the countryside at the heart of Whitehall, most Departments have put the basic building blocks in place for rural proofing, and half are doing more.

"But I am convinced that policy makers generally need to do more to give sufficient thought to the impact on the countryside, and the people who live there. This does not mean they need to develop specific policies for rural areas.

"It means ensuring that mainstream policies for health, education, crime, transport and the rest are designed to meet the needs of rural people as much as those of urban dwellers.

"More than one in five people live in rural England. On my visits around the country, people tell me they are worried about the lack of affordable housing, continuing post office closures, problems accessing the doctor or dentist, difficulties with public transport, bureaucratic red tape faced by rural entrepreneurs and communities, and magistrates' courts closures.

"Dealing with the impact of foot-and-mouth was, understandably, a top priority during the last year. If real results are to be achieved in future, rural proofing must become automatic. Only then we shall start to see outcomes in the shape of service delivery that meet the needs of rural people."

FERRETS ARE GROWING in popularity among young, single women, new research has shown.

Once the favourite pets of country boys, the furry mammals are being sold to growing numbers of urban women who also want them as pets.

Researchers at the University of Warwick discovered that the sometimes malodorous animals are usually snapped up in pairs to keep each other company.

Despite being feared for their painful bites, working women apparently find ferrets less trouble to look after than dogs or cats.

Playfulness and intelligence were two character-istics which attacted buyers to ferrets which were also content to live in cages till their owners got home from work, researchers found.

ANIMAL AID HAS been quick to attack the Grand National following the reported deaths of two more horses in the famous steeplechase.

A spokesman for the animal rights group said:"Animal Aid condemns the grotesque spectacle of the 2002 Grand National, in which only 11 out of 40 runners finished.

"The Last Fling was shot after breaking his back while Manx Magic perished from a broken neck.

"The news of these fatalities - coming on top of earlier Thursday deaths at Aintree of Desert Mountain and Anubis Quercus - was held back by the Aintree authorities and the BBC, thereby limiting wider media coverage.

"Hundreds of protesters were at Aintree to register their opposition to the sick spectacle."

Some 27 horses had now died in six years at the course, the spokesman added.

A DOG WHICH plunged off a 40ft cliff in Scotland was discovered alive 11 days later.

Distressed owner Jenny Mair, 61, had virtually given up hope of seeing her terrier Calach again.

The pair had been out walking in Moray when the animal suddenly vanished and a search party failed to locate it.

Then, 11 days later, some teenagers found Calach at the bottom of the cliff and alerted the authorities.

It appeared the dog had only been stunned by the fall but could not climb back up the cliff to safety.

THE WOODLAND TRUST says 28 million Christmas cards were donated for recycling this year following the festive season.

Thanks to the public's "fantastic efforts", new woodland will now be created and enhanced by the woodland conservation charity.

Actress Prunella Scales, a Woodland Trust supporter, said:"It is really encouraging that the public have supported the recycling scheme in such a big way.

"Each year we send millions of cards over the festive season so it seems logical that we should recycle this paper.

"It is also staggering to think that we have lost over 50 per cent of our precious ancient woodland heritage since the 1930s. Everyone who has generously supported this scheme will have helped to create much needed woodland throughout the UK."

Since its launch, The Christmas Card Recycling Scheme has been run by the Trust in partnership with WHSmith and Tesco.

UP TO 2,000 fish are feared dead after pollution hit the River Tame near Stockport.

Officers from the Environment Agency have been investigating the deaths and trying to trace the pollution source.

Fish, including gudgeon, minnow and roach, were found dead along a stretch of the river from Tiviot Way, Stockport, to Haughton Green, Hyde.

The incident was reported to the Agency by a ranger at the Reddish Vale Country Park who had been alerted by a member of the public.

Samples from the riverbed have been taken which will be analysed in a bid to help investigators.

Agency protection manager Keith Ashcroft said:"This is a very serious incident and an extensive investigation is underway."

A NEW REPORT which highlights France's failure to meet key BSE safeguards underlines the "blatant hypocrisy" of its own illegal ban on British beef, it has been claimed.

The damning report by the European Commission's Food and Veterinary Office shows that the French ban on British beef is in place for political reasons, said NFU president Ben Gill.

An angry Mr Gill stormed:"The French Government has used the pretext of public protection as the basis for its illegal ban on our beef since it was imposed in August 1999.

"Yet as this report shows, they need to get their own house in order. Their ban is merely a cynical attempt to unjustifiably prevent British farmers from re-establishing their important meat markets in that country.

"This study only serves to underline the untenability of the French Government's position. They should now lift this ban immediately."

The FVO study took place to verify the implementation of European rules on protective measures against BSE.

Its recently published report concludes that the measures designed to prevent potentially infected material getting into animal feed were not being effectively implemented.

Last month the European Commission launched legal procedures to pave the way towards the imposition of heavy fines on the French Government.

This followed the December 2001 European Court of Justice ruling that the French beef ban was unlawful.

The NFU is also pursuing its own legal action against the French Government.

RARE NEWTS HAVE put a stop to renovation work being carried out at Stansted Airport in Essex.

Electricians stumbled on a colony of great crested newts while they were replacing high-voltage gear.

Because the newts are a protected species, bosses at London Electricity Services have had to apply to DEFRA for a special permit allowing them to be moved elsewhere.

Fortunately, the newts live in a remote part of the airfield so disruption is being kept to a minimum.

PEAT BOGS ARE now so precious The Wildlife Trusts are renewing calls for gardeners to choose peat-free products to help protect them.

"Far from simply being soggy patches of land they support some fascinating wildlife, such as carnivorous plants, beautiful dragon and damselflies and a wide variety of birds," said a spokesman.

ENGLISH NATURE HAS joined forces with English Heritage to publish the first ever guidance on the conservation and management of cemeteries.

'Paradise Preserved' is primarily aimed at local authority cemetery managers, conservation officers, and local people interested in caring for their own cemeteries.

English Nature said cemeteries had long been recognised as places of quiet and peaceful contemplation, valued by the families and friends of people buried there.

But they are also used by the wider local community as an escape from the pressures of urban life, for the study of local history, and for conservation of wildlife.

"Cemeteries can provide a range of habitats that can support a diversity of wildlife," said a spokesman."The common toad, hedgehog, woodmouse, deer, badger, and a chorus of birds such as woodpecker, wren, and blackcap, are found in cemeteries, as well as a surprising variety of wildflowers, fungi and lichens.

"Some cemeteries are sanctuaries for uncommon or protected species, such as bats, spotted flycatcher, slow worm, stag beetle, and orchids, that are otherwise rare in our towns and cities."

Mathew Frith, English Nature's urban adviser, said the recent sighting of three handsome green woodpeckers perched on a headstone in one cemetery summed up their value for both people and wildlife.

A COW BECAME stuck on the roof of a factory in West Yorkshire when its feet crashed through tiles.

The animal had burst out of its field at Todmorden and run onto the factory roof which is set into the hillside.

Firemen called to the scene used a forklift truck to rescue the panicking creature, tying hoses round its body before hoisting it clear.

THE COUNTRYSIDE ALLIANCE has warned the Government that a 'summer of discontent' over its anti-hunting stance will culminate in another mass march.

Accusing the Government of failing to heed rural pleas for fairness, Alliance chief executive Richard Burge said its pronouncements had provoked a level of anger which must be brought to its attention.

Mr Burge warned that DEFRA ministers and "prejudiced MPs" would be subject to consistent law-abiding protests at official engagements, as part of a sustained campaign by rural people which was now highly likely to include a reinstated London March.

He added:"There is a clear attempt to use hunting as a sacrificial lamb on the altar of political convenience. Quite simply, we will not allow anyone to get away with it."

WILDLIFE COULD BENEFIT from a new levy on quarrying which came into effect on April 1.

The levy will act as an incentive to cut quarrying in the countryside and increase recycling and the use of alternative materials for construction.

According to critics, the current low price of quarried material means that companies use it wastefully and the environment suffers.

The new levy has been welcomed by a raft of conservation organisations concerned about damage to the countryside caused by quarrying.

FARMERS AND THE rural community have been failed by Chancellor Gordon Brown's Budget, it has been claimed.

NFU president Ben Gill said Mr Brown's statement conspicuously omitted any mention of the continued suffering in the countryside following foot-and-mouth and years of financial trouble.

He said:"There was little for farmers and growers in the Budget. Opportunities to help them rebuild their businesses following last year's disaster were not taken."

While the Chancellor did not raise fuel duty, Mr Gill pointed out that British hauliers still pay on average around £10,000 a year more in tax than their European counterparts.

This adds a massive cost to rural-based industries that are heavily dependent on road transport.

The Chancellor's failure to give larger tax breaks for bio diesel - produced from crops grown on farms - will also hold up the development of a potentially important industry.

Mr Gill said:"To be competitive, bio fuel needs to have an extremely low level of duty. This is an industry that needs to be encouraged, both for the sake of the environment and for farmers and growers to boost their businesses. The Chancellor failed to do this."

However, Mr Gill welcomed the introduction of working tax credits which will assist farmers with little or no profits and the fact that there was no increase in inheritance tax and stamp duty.

Moves to give tax breaks to small businesses were also of some comfort to farmers and growers, he added.

MARAUDING SEAGULLS HAVE met their match after terrorising a primary school in Strathclyde, Scotland.

Two Harris hawks are being used to scare the gulls away each day from Barassie Primary after they became increasingly aggressive.

Pupils had become afraid of eating snacks outside because the gulls had begun trying to snatch their food away.

With Barassie on the Clyde coast, hungry seagulls have been a growing problem in recent years. However, the hawks' daily appearance is having the desired effect and pupils can now eat outside again without risk of being pecked.

A PILOT SCHEME has been launched with green-top milk going on sale for customers who want to pay more to help farmers help wildlife.

Selected Sainsbury's stores are taking part in the experiment where more expensive milk will help farmers look after creatures such as brown hares, pipistrelle bats, and curlews. If successful, the scheme will be expanded to take in more outlets.

MANY OF BRITAIN'S favourite birds have been hit by a slump in breeding success with vast numbers of chicks not surviving to adulthood, it has been revealed.

Recent research shows that more than half of 24 species monitored have sustained serious declines in the percentage of chicks leaving the nest.

Of these, the blue tit was the worst hit, showing a downturn of 43 per cent, followed by the long-tailed tit (39 per cent down), greenfinch (34 per cent), reed bunting (33 per cent), blackbird (32 per cent), sedge warbler (32 per cent), blackcap (30 per cent), chiffchaff (24 per cent), dunnock (24 per cent), reed warbler (23 per cent), and robin (15 per cent).

Chris Mead, spokesman for the British Trust for Ornithology, said the results were worrying and highlighted a depressing lack of breeding success.

"It may represent a simple glitch for some species as conditions in the summer of 2001 were not good for them," he admitted."But one has to wonder about some species such as the blue tit, which seems to have got out of synch with the caterpillars needed to feed their young."

Other recent findings relate to starlings and sparrows, at one time both easily the most common garden birds.

Starlings have now dropped out of the top 10 places for common birds for the first time ever while even house sparrows have fallen to seventh position.

THE BIGGEST SURVEY of garden butterflies and moths ever undertaken in the UK has been launched by Butterfly Conservation and its vice-president - celebrity gardener Alan Titchmarsh.

The 'Garden Butterflies Count' is aimed at everyone with a garden or even just a window box.

"Over the last 50 years, many species of butterfly and moth have declined dramatically in both abundance and range," say organisers."More than half our native butterfly species are now under serious threat and five are already extinct in the UK.

"We would like to know which butterflies and moths are visiting gardens so that we can monitor their progress and act to halt their decline. At the same time, people can discover more about these beautiful creatures and how to turn their garden into a butterfly paradise."

GAME BIRDS WILL have the chance to feed on patriotic red, white and blue cover crops as part of celebrations for the Queen's Golden Jubilee Year.

Pheasants and partridges will also be able to hide in the crop, a unique blend of seeds giving fields a blaze of colour from the national flag.

"The Beaters Organisation, in association with the NGO, has made available from its web site a unique cover crop to celebrate the Queen's Golden Jubilee," said a beaters' spokesman.

"Beaters have asked Pearce Seeds to blend a cover that will give a dramatic touch of red, white and blue - with golden medallions of yellow - to a shoot. All shoots that take part in this celebration will receive a Golden Jubilee certificate for their participation in a once in a life time occasion.

"Each pack ordered will cover a one-acre area that is suitable for pheasant and partridge, providing cover and feed into the New Year."

ENGLISH NATURE IS to give key evidence to a public inquiry about the threat to thousands of waterbirds by proposed development near Southampton.

The conservation group will outline to the Dibden Terminal Public Inquiry "the wealth of precious nature at risk if the port development goes ahead.

"The Solent and Southampton Water SPA is used by 50,000 waterbirds every winter making it one of the most important places in the country for wintering wildfowl," said a spokesman."Some 15,000 of these feed in Southampton Water and Dibden Bay is the jewel in the crown.

"Twice the number of birds feed on the Dibden foreshore, compared with other areas of similar size. It is especially popular with oystercatchers.

"Up to a fifth of the local population gather on the foreshore at feeding time along with grey plover, wigeon, curlew and lapwing - all attracted to Dibden's rich feeding grounds. The Bay also supports internationally important numbers of dark bellied Brent geese.

"The salt marshes of Southampton Water are important, too, containing specialist plants and flowers that thrive in salt water, such as cord grass, marsh samphire and sea purslane."

English Nature chairman, Sir Martin Doughty, added:"The conservation of our natural resources is vital to our future well-being and prosperity because a healthy environment supports a long-term sustainable economy and contributes to a healthy and balanced social framework. English Nature is determined to safeguard this essential facet of our lives."

FRESHWATER CRAYFISH HAVE a devastating weapon which they use in fights with each other - urine.

Researchers in Hull discovered battles are often settled when one crayfish succeeds in urinating on the other.

Although the crustaceans can tear limbs off each other in violent disputes, the study found that a jet of urine was the most effective attack.

Scientists believe it may be because the other crayfish can immediately pick up telling details from the urine such as the health and strength of its opponent - then backs down.

A RESCUE MISSION involving the RAF and RSPCA was launched to save six Charolais cattle stranded on an island in a river close to Goole on Humberside.

The cattle were reported to have panicked and run into the river after apparently fleeing a big cat said to haunt the area.

FARMING UNIONS WILL wreck tourism in the countryside for a second year running if they continue to demand a cull of badgers, conservationists claim.

According to the National Federation of Badger Groups, the NFU and other unions have launched an aggressive media campaign claiming that badgers are spreading bovine TB to cattle in Wales and the west of England.

"These claims are grossly irresponsible," said Dr Elaine King, chief executive of the NFBG."The rise in bovine TB can be firmly attributed to last year's foot-and-mouth disease restrictions, not badgers.

"When cattle were cooped up for long periods, low levels of the disease were amplified in herds. Now cattle are being traded, spreading the disease to new places.

"Farming will have to change if bovine TB is to be brought under control and the unions are clearly opposed to modernisation.

"Tighter movement restrictions will have to be placed on infected cattle and the TB testing regime will need a radical overhaul.

"We want the Government to provide grant aid to farmers to help them through this difficult time. But the unions are destroying the last vestiges of public sympathy for farmers by calling for an unjustified extermination policy.

"The ridiculous campaign has no basis in science or logic. Calling for badger culling is no better than calling for witch burning. But the tragedy is that the public is starting to worry that the countryside will become a no-go area again. If this harms tourism, the unions will be cutting off their members' noses to spite their faces.

"The NFBG has asked the farming unions for the science backing their claims that badger culling will be effective. But there is none. The unions have confirmed that they do not know how many or what proportion of badgers should be culled; they do not know how the badgers should be culled; they do not know who should do the killing or how it should be financed.

"Following their disastrous policies during the foot-and-mouth crisis, the farming unions are attempting to show that they still have a purpose. Instead, they are likely to wreck tourism in the countryside all over again."

A CRACKDOWN ON illegal fishing for elvers has been launched in a joint operation by police and the Environment Agency in Gloucestershire.

The annual springtime migration of elvers up the Severn Estuary is reported to be attracting many fishermen.

Although most have the required licences and use legal means to catch elvers, a "significant minority" do not.

Only traditional hand held elver nets can be used and it is illegal to fish for elvers from a boat, says the Agency.

"During the period of high spring tides the Agency and police are patrolling the river banks by foot and the river itself by boat to check that people are fishing legally," said a spokesman.

"Enforcement action will be taken against those elver fishermen who are found to be fishing without a licence, using illegal nets or fishing from a boat. This may involve seizure of any illegal nets and prosecution that could result in a sentence of up to two years imprisonment and/or a fine of up to £2,500."

THE MYSTERY CULPRITS who killed 100,000 fish by polluting the River Dee in Cheshire may never be identified, the Environment Agency has admitted.

Despite a thorough investigation, the Agency has been unable to find those responsible - but promises the case will remain open.

David Gatehouse, the Agency's North Area manager, said:"While we are all frustrated at not having yet been able to bring this matter to a satisfactory conclusion, the investigation has enabled us to learn a number of important lessons.

"The enhanced scientific and hydrological understanding of the complex mechanisms within the Dee and the implementation of the recommendations from our internal review will ensure we will be in a stronger position to investigate and mitigate against any such catastrophes in the future.

"I would like to thank the organisations, groups and individuals who have assisted us during the investigation and my own Agency colleagues for their enormous commitment throughout."

The Agency has now produced a 'Dee Pollution Incident' briefing paper which outlines the steps taken and the lessons learned following the incident in the middle reaches of the Dee on July 29, 2000.

The pollution resulted in a catastrophic reduction of oxygen in the water leading to the deaths of 100,000 fish by suffocation.

Emergency measures were also taken to protect the drinking water supply to three million people.

These were located in parts of North Wales and the North West.

Lessons learned relate to both technical and procedural aspects of its work, says the Agency, along with more general issues about communication.

However, its report also notes that nothing could be done at the time of the incident to prevent such large scale fish deaths.

WALES' ANCIENT WOODLANDS are being given special protection for the first time ever.

From April 16, new guidelines came into force under the Welsh Assembly which help local authorities deal with planning applications which affect woods.

TV birdwatcher Iolo Williams, who featured in a recent BBC wildlife series, joined The Woodland Trust in urging local authorities to back the changes.

Mr Williams, Wales' best-known bird watcher, has written to all 25 Welsh local planning authorities.

NEW LAWS ARE being introduced which will make it illegal for salmon farmers to try to cover up escapes of farmed fish.

The move comes amid claims that Scotland's wild salmon are being driven to the edge by more than a million farmed salmon escapees.

Weaker farmed salmon which breed with the wild variety are endangering the quality of wild stock, a study found.

Two years ago, more than a quarter of a million farmed salmon escaped from cages off Shapinsay in what is thought to be the biggest ever single release.

But with no legal requirement to report escapes, many ecologists believe that far more than a million salmon have actually escaped into the wild.

Laws being introduced within weeks will mean that any salmon farmer not reporting escapes could face fines of up to £2,500.

A FLOCK OF 14 sheep are being held to ransom on the Isle of Sky after they wandered onto a neighbouring estate.

The animals are being held by George Kozikows-ki who has told police he is fed up with the sheep coming onto his land and damaging property.

Now he wants £50 each to release them and police say he is within his rights to detain the flock under the Detention of Straying Animals section of the Roads (Scotland) Act 1984 until there is a settlement.

The sheep have ruined a garden, gobbled food meant for his hens, and damaged young trees, says Mr Kozikowski.

The sheep belong to the Highlands and Islands Enterprise which owns the neighbouring estate and has pledged to stop the animal wandering in future.

But Mr Kozikowsk says he will hang onto the flock until he gets the money.

CONFUSION REIGNS OVER whether sparrows and starlings are becoming more or less common following publication of a new survey.

In a snapshot survey of 200,000 gardens, the RSPB found that starlings came out on top with an average 4.5 per garden with house sparrows close behind on 4 per garden.

However, this flatly contradicts findings of an earlier survey by the British Trust for Ornithology which revealed that starlings and sparrows had fallen out of the Top 10 most common garden birds and were fast declining.

Commenting on the RSPB survey, a BTO spokesman said at the time it was undertaken the research would have included winter migrants - something their own, year-long survey did not do.

So sparrows and starlings were actually declining overall, despite the RSPB results.

Other findings in the RSPB 'Big Garden Birdwatch' were that robin numbers were falling, putting the popular birds in joint ninth place with wood pigeons.

RAMBLERS ARE TO get lifetime access to Forestry Commission forests following a landmark decision by the authority.

Commission chairman Lord Clark announced that all freehold forests in England and Wales will guar-antee access for walkers. The move means access will be safeguarded to all Forestry Commission woodland, even if the land were ever to be sold.

UP TO 150,000 young salmon are feared dead after pollution hit an Environment Agency hatchery on the River Dee in Clwyd.

Investigators have learned that the pollution originated in a tributary upstream of the hatchery near Corwen and contaminated its water supply.

The Agency team has conducted a detailed probe and is said to be satisfied it has already identified the source and cause of the pollution, subject to confirmation by laboratory analysis.

A spokesman said:"Once we have confirmation of the cause of the pollution we will consider pursuing formal enforcement action, including the recovery of costs, against those responsible.

"It is essential that all those who keep potentially polluting materials in this catchment do so in such a way that they cannot cause pollution.

"The Dee and its tributaries are an extremely sensitive and important environment and we will not hesitate to take action against those whose actions or inaction result in its pollution."

The incident comes shortly after the Agency admitted that the mystery culprits who killed 100,000 adult fish in an earlier incident on the Dee may never be identified.

Salmon are reared in tanks at the Clwyd hatchery to replenish stocks in the Dee and it had been possible to save some fish, the spokesman revealed.

However, it had been confirmed that up to 150,000 young salmon had been wiped out.

The incident is expected to have a big impact on stocks of juvenile fish and has also depleted adult stock fish which provide future fish populations for the rivers Alwen and Tryweryn, as well as the Dee.

THE WILDLIFE TRUSTS are on the hunt for new volunteers to take part in their Wildlife Week event this coming June.

"The time and skills offered by volunteers are vital to the success of nature conservation," said a spokesman."This year, the Trusts are celebrating the tireless dedication of their 23,800 volunteers who put a staggering total of one million work hours a year into helping UK wildlife.

"Being a wild volunteer can be great fun and gives you the chance to meet like-minded people in your area, with many Trusts running social events for you to join in with.

"People of all backgrounds, ages and abilities can get involved and you don't have to be a wildlife expert to volunteer for us. There are heaps of opportunities available from nature reserve management and survey work, to helping at events and working in Wildlife Trust gift shops."

A MALE OSPREY which travelled more than 3,000 miles from West Africa has landed in Olive the osprey's nest at Loch Garten near Aviemore.

He has already gallantly confirmed his intentions by bringing fresh fish to what reserve staff hope is now a mother-to-be.

Despite several other ospreys hanging around the nest during the last few days, none had managed to win Olive's affections until now.

"It's not the latest we've had a pair at the reserve settle in for mating but there certainly was growing concern that for the first time since 1959, the nest could have been without a breeding pair of osprey. So this new male is really a positive sign and we're quite excited about it," admitted reserve warden Richard Thaxton.

There were also concerns that, had Olive failed to attract a new mate, a younger pair of ospreys may have kicked her out of the nest to use it themselves.

A YOUNG ROE deer stag sparked a major rescue operation after plunging off a 180ft cliff into the sea.

A team of 20 people took five hours to save the deer after it toppled over the cliff at Port Isaac, Cornwall.

First the animal needed guiding back to shore by a lifeboat crew before it could be swept out to sea.

Then, after the deer became trapped in a cove, it was tranquillised by a vet before being winched up a sheer cliff face to safety.

Apart from cuts and scratches, the deer seemed to be unhurt and will be released at a spot further inland.

BATS AND ANIMAL TRACKS should both be easier to identify following publication of two new field guides.

'A Guide to British Bats' and 'A Guide to British Mammal Tracks and Signs' have been published in laminated form by The Mammal Society and the Field Studies Council and are ideal to take out and about.

The bats guide, which costs £2.50 (including post and packaging), was penned by bat experts Kate Jones and Allyson Walsh, covers identification of all British bats, and is illustrated with colour photos by Frank Greenaway.

The tracks guide, which costs £3.25 (also including post and packaging), was written by Simone Bullion, author of the popular 'Key to British Land Mammals' that was published in the same series in 1998.

This covers identification of all the field signs that mammals leave behind - footprints, droppings, nests, burrows and feeding remains.

There is also a useful table that shows how to distinguish between different species of animals such as deer, whose droppings are all very similar, while hedgehog droppings remain highly distinctive.

A PET LABRADOR dog leapt at a squirrel in a tree - and fell 40ft from the window of a Brighton flat.

Leo plunged onto the pavement below after pushing open the window and attacking the temptingly close squirrel.

Owner Colin Rowland feared the worst when he ran to Leo's aid and discovered him lying almost motionless.The dog appeared to have suffered fatal internal injuries but Mr Rowland took him to a local vet where the animal staged an astonishing fightback and is expected to make a full recovery.

RARE HEN HARRIERS appear to be staging a revival just as conservationists move to offer them better protection.

With the launch of a project to save the most endangered bird of prey in England came news that 35 hen harriers had been spotted on northern English moors in a single fortnight.

Sir Martin Doughty, chairman of English Nature, said:"This is very encouraging news as we launch our hen harrier project, and we hope that these birds will be able to breed and produce chicks in safety.

"The hen harrier is one of England's most spectacular birds of prey and nothing can be more memorable than seeing males 'sky dancing' in front of prospective mates in their annual courtship displays."

English Nature has become increasingly concerned about the hen harrier.

Following a prolonged decline, the English population now comprises just a handful of breeding pairs and there is still a danger that the species will become extinct here within a few years.

English Nature says it is committed to restoring the English hen harrier population and will run its project for three years to monitor and help increase current numbers.

A DUCK CALLED Helen was 'arrested' by police who found it waddling in an uncertain manner down a main street.

Officers were especially concerned for the mallard because its impromptu walkabout happened in the early hours.

The duck had also suffered a gashed foot so police took it from Market Drayton town centre to a place of safety - a police cell.

It was held there while the local paper publicised its plight, alerting owner Tracy Topham.

She rushed happy Helen back to her farm - none the worse for its jailbird ordeal.

GM CROPS HAVE been attacked three times in a week by protesters in Scotland.

Police were repeatedly called to the controversial trial site at Munlochy in the Highlands following a series of disturbances.

A number of anti-GM campaigners have been arrested and could face vandalism and breach of the peace charges, police reported.

However, protesters said more than half the GM oilseed rape crop at Roskill Farm had now been destroyed.

Following the latest attack, the protesters released a statement saying:"We have been forced to take responsibility for protecting the health and environment of our own community by the only course of action now open to us.

"Our action was peaceful and nobody was injured. That people are more afraid of GM crops than of being arrested by police speaks for itself."

NEW POTATOES ARE being backed by a concerted 'Buy British' campaign aimed at encouraging more shoppers to sample the harvest this year.

The campaign will be launched next month in Cornwall where the first 'new arrivals' are collected, followed by new potatoes in Pembrokeshire.

At the beginning of June, a crop in Kent will be lifted while other new potatoes are set to be collected in Shropshire at the end of the month.

Gloucestershire grower and NFU Potatoes chairman Graham Nichols said:"The start of the new potato season is always keenly awaited, but many shoppers don't know when to expect the new arrivals. We hope this promotion will ensure no-one misses out on this year's harvest."

According to the union, the new 'stars' of the seasonal calendar - which also include early potatoes from Scotland - will be publicised through in-store promotions and by the roaming British Potato Council bus.

The BPC bus will be touring the country from May 6 to July 27, along with representatives on quad bikes who will be handing out leaflets.

A new recipe book, education packs and in-store competitions offering weekend breaks on a farm are included in the campaign.

The sheer versatility and nutritional value of new potatoes will be underlined, adds the NFU.

DORMICE ARE going down the tubes - thanks to a new scheme to boost their numbers launched by The Mammal Society.

The nest tubes are being used as indicators of dormice presence, especially in areas of 'non-traditional' dormouse habitat such as hedgerows and scrub.

Each tube comprises two parts - a small wooden 'tray' and a plastic nest tube with the tray used to seal one end.

Professor Stephen Harris, chairman of the Society, said:"Nest tubes provide a cheap and easy method of determining dormouse presence within a habitat. They can be an effective alternative to more expensive wooden nestboxes."

A minimum or 20 tubes should be used at one time, he said, and they should be set out 20 metres apart or in a 20-metre grid.

A DAY OF music was how the Ramblers Association celebrated the 70th anniversary of a mass trespass on Kinder Scout in the Peak District.

The celebration was held at Bowden Bridge Quarry, Hayfield - the original starting point of the trespass in 1932 which was said to be an important catalyst in the long-running campaign for the freedom to roam.

Chief speaker in a packed schedule was Minister of State for the Environment, Michael Meacher MP, while broadcaster, comedian and former Ramblers president Mike Harding led the celebrations.

Other speakers included Kate Ashbrook, chief executive of the Open Spaces Society and chairman of the Ramblers Access Committee.

The leader of the original mass trespass was Benny Rothman who died in January but his son Harry led one of the day's guided walks laid on for ramblers of all levels of experience.

One of the walks followed the actual route of the trespassers into William Clough towards the once-forbidden mountain of Kinder Scout.

219

BLACKBIRD: one-eyed victim takes its chances

WITH its distinctive fluty song and familiar appearance, the blackbird remains one of the most popular birds of town or country.

Males, of course, are the black sex whereas females are brown.

Males also tend to be territorial, especially during the nesting season, and most people will have seen one blackbird ejecting another from their garden at some time.

From its size and shape, it is easy to see that the blackbird actually comes from the same bird family as the thrush.

Even the way a blackbird moves is similar and brown female blackbirds can look a lot like thrushes from behind.

Worms are a staple part of their diet with berries, insects and fruit also taken wherever they are found.

During nesting, up to five bluish-green speckled eggs are laid in a suitable spot, usually halfway up a tree or high in a bush away from predators.

As with black cats, the blackbird's colouring has probably helped to get it mentioned in folklore and nursery rhymes more often than paler bird species.

And, for me at least, one of the Beatles' most haunting ballads remains 'Blackbird' (*Blackbird singing in the dead of night, take these broken wings and learn to fly...*').

I'm not sure how often I've heard a blackbird singing in the dead of night but they frequently throw out a note or two at dusk in my garden.

In the 17th Century, poet Joseph Addison wrote: "*I value my garden more for being full of blackbirds than of cherries and, very frankly,*
give them fruit for their songs."

I lived on a rather grim estate on the East London/Essex border for a year and was surprised to see several blackbirds there.

Unfortunately, the area was also dominated by aggressive, low-flying crows that terrorised the other birds in the neighbourhood, including blackbirds.

One morning I awoke to some commotion in the back yard and, when I peered out, saw one of these crows attacking something in the corner.

I quickly discovered a young male blackbird, badly injured with one of its eyes gone.

Myself and my wife took it in and tried to look after it.

For a while, it seemed to rally

Using its remaining eye, it even pecked half-heartedly at some baked potato we offered it.

In the end, though, it grew frantic to get out of the house.

I phoned a wildlife helpline number but, to my frustration, constantly got the engaged tone.

So there was a simple choice to make - put the blackbird out of its misery or let it go.

In my time I've knocked a few birds on the head that have been badly mauled by cats.

It is the kindest thing in the end. So I let the blackbird out into the yard again and looked for a stick.

Unfortunately, before I could find one, the blackbird had fluttered away on a crazy one-eyed flight path.

I had no option now but to let Nature take its course.

How long a wounded, one-eyed blackbird would last with the crows and stray cats of that awful estate on its trail is anyone's guess.

Not long, I would imagine.

But I often wonder.

THOUSANDS OF SEABIRDS are at risk after the discovery of a two-mile oil spill floating close to an RSPB sanctuary in Scotland.

The slick is believed to have seeped out of a disued pipe from an old oil refinery off Ayrshire and has been steadily increasing in size.

Horse Island, the RSPB reserve, lies only half a mile away and is home to a variety of vulnerable seabirds.

The Scottish Environment Protection Agency has launched an urgent probe to establish the possible effects of the spill on the picturesque coastline and its wildlife.

Meanwhile, local conservationists are keeping their fingers crossed that the spill does not turn out to be an environmental disaster for the area.

Various groups, including RSPB Scotland, are actively monitoring the slick which was first spotted by a passing ship close to Ardrossan Harbour.

A coastguard spokesman said:"Right now, there are no reports of birds having been affected but we are keeping in touch with the reserve over the situation."

A RABBIT AND a dog called Arthur met with very different fates when Arthur chased the rabbit over a sheer 80ft cliff in North Devon.

The rabbit plummeted onto rocks and died instantly while Arthur, a golden retriever, landed on a ledge 30ft down and survived.

Arthur's horrified owner alerted coastguards who dispatched a lifeboat and cliff rescue team to save the stranded pet near Combe Martin.

The lucky animal was eventually winched to safety after suffering only cuts and bruises.

SALMON ARE BEING given a boost on two of Devon's best known rivers thanks to a "historic decision" to phase out salmon netting in the joint estuary of the Taw and Torridge.

The rivers were made famous by Henry Williamson in his novels 'Tarka the Otter' and 'Salar the Salmon' but salmon numbers there today are a fraction of what existed in the writer's day.

Back then, annual rod catch for the two rivers regularly exceeded 900 salmon compared to a catch last year of just 133.

Net fishing has also seen a dramatic decline with net fishermen now taking a quarter of the 3,000 or so fish taken annually in the 1960s.

As a result, DEFRA has approved a Net Limitation Order proposed by the Environment Agency which will see the phasing out of salmon netting until stocks recover - the first time such an order has been approved in England and Wales on purely conservation grounds.

"These measures should allow hundreds of additional salmon into the Taw and Torridge to spawn. It is a major conservation initiative and should boost salmon stocks in both rivers," said Steve Douglas for the Agency.

HORSES ARE AT the centre of a new road safety campaign which aims to make motorists more careful around them.

The 'horse sense' campaign is part of the Government's wider pledge to make roads safer for all.

The British Horse Society believes that there are over 3,000 road accidents a year involving horses with recent figures showing that during the year 2000 there were 147 rider casualties and two fatalities.

A new TV advert and supporting leaflet was launched at the Badminton Horse Trials and urged motorists to take more care when driving near riders and their horses.

The leaflet says drivers who comes across horses on the road should slow down, give plenty of room and be ready to stop; never sound their horn or rev the engine; never try to pass unless they can give the horses a wide berth; treat horses as a potential hazard and expect the unexpected.

Transport Minister David Jamieson said:"Horse riders are particularly vulnerable on the road and it is important that anyone who drives should be considerate to their needs.

"Riders have as much right to use the roads as anyone else and should be able to enjoy riding without fear of dangerous behaviour by other road users."

The Minister added that horse riders also had a duty to themselves, their horse, and motorists to use the road safely.

Riders should never use roads without first taking the Horse Society's road proficiency test and should also make sure they wear fluorescent reflective clothing so they are more visible.

RED SQUIRRELS are just one species made easier to observe in Scotland thanks to a new guide which pinpoints wildlife sites.

'Watching Woodland Wildlife' was launched at a conference in Aviemore by Professor Roger Wheate, chairman of the Tourism and Environment Forum.

The guide was published as part of Treefest Scotland 2002, a year-long festival of more than 750 events which celebrate the country's trees, woods and forests.

From red squirrels at Glentrool to red kites at Kessock, the leaflet highlights 21 places where birds and animals can be observed, sometimes with the aid of closed-circuit television or camouflaged hides.

Forestry Minister Allan Wilson said:"Scotland's expanding woods and forests - and the wild plants and animals that live in them - are being recognised more and more as tourist attractions in their own right, alongside our more traditional visitor attractions.

"Of course, it is important that when we go into the woods to watch wild animals, we do so in a way that does not disturb or harm them. Therefore, I am delighted that the leaflet highlights the best places to observe birds and animals without doing either."

HUNT STAFF FROM the Beaufort, Bicester with Whaddon Chase, Vale of Aylesbury, Hampshire, West Somerset and Quantock Staghounds gathered with horses and hounds in Horseguards Parade, close to 10 Downing Street, and blew their horns at 6.30am to deliver a 'wake-up' call to Tony Blair.

The Prime Minister's reaction is not recorded.

FORGET BECKHAM'S FOOT, England soccer fans travelling to the World Cup should take extra care not to bring foot-and-mouth disease back with them when they return, say farmers' leaders.

The NFU is calling on England fans to take precautions to ensure they don't reintroduce the devastating disease to the UK after visiting South Korea.

The union says it needs the support of fans who travel to Jeju for the England v South Korea World Cup warm-up match on May 21.

The match is the only game England will be playing in South Korea - currently fighting its own foot-and-mouth epidemic - and it poses a very real threat to UK farmers.

NFU president Ben Gill said:"Farmers wish our England football team the very best of luck but it would be an absolute tragedy if we let down our guard and let foot-and-mouth back into the country.

"I would implore those fans who attend the South Korean friendly to stay away from infected areas and avoid coming into contact with livestock during their travels.

"We would also urge them not to risk bringing South Korean food or meat back with them to the UK."

Mr Gill said he was also writing to DEFRA Secretary of State Margaret Beckett to call for enhanced vigilance and decontamination efforts at border crossings and airports to ensure a "real team effort" against the disease.

BIGGER WOODS MEAN better protection for wildlife, says The Woodland Trust in a new campaign.

Backing its move to extend woods wherever possible, novelist Jilly Cooper said: "Buying even relatively small areas of neighbouring land and planting it with trees will really improve the quality of existing woodland."

The famous Trust supporter is currently helping to lead a campaign to extend a wood at Bridport, Dorset.

"By extending the wood at Allington Hill, which lies in an area of outstanding natural beauty, both wildlife and the people of Bridport will benefit, " explained Jilly.

Allington Hill is part of the Dorset Heritage Coast.

The hill comprises open land and mixed woodland, providing stunning views across the Dorset landscape.

The Trust hopes to increase the size of the wood by acquiring a further eleven acres on its northern edge.

"But the Trust still needs to raise one-third of the appeal target - so please make a pledge and help secure the future of this special place, " added Jilly.

WHALES AND DOLPHINS will continue to die needlessly after the Government fudged a chance to help them, claim The Wildlife Trusts.

All the Marine Stewardship Report does is promote yet further discussion, debate and research while UK seas are dying, said Dr Simon Lyster, director general of the Trusts.

The Trusts have challenged the Government report and called for immediate action and legislation in the form of a Marine Act to secure the future of our marine environment.

"Every year, thousands of whales, dolphins and porpoises die in UK waters," said Dr Lyster.

"These deaths represent the tip of the iceberg in terms of the crisis in our marine environment. This report falls far short in terms of actions and financial commitment."

Colleague Joan Edwards, marine policy director for the Trusts, added:"The system of marine conservation in the UK is woefully deficient. The Government is dithering in its recommendations."

A BEWILDERED LAMB faced a watery end when it plunged into the River Severn in Shropshire and became stranded on an island in the middle.

The lamb was joined by its mother and another sheep which also became stranded on the little patch of land at Buildwas near Telford.

Fortunately, the fire service was soon alerted and a water rescue team set out to save all three animals before they could drown.

Using a boat, firemen took two hours to ferry the animals back to the safety of the bank where they appeared none the worse for their chilly adventure.

THE HATCHING OF red kite chicks has delighted conservationists following the death of their mother in a suspected poisoning.

The dead kite was found in a garden near Oundle, Northamptonshire, and sparked an urgent search for her nest by Forestry Commission officials and local people.

"They were in a race against time to locate it before the eggs became too cold to hatch," explained a Commission spokesman.

"Three eggs were found by ranger Karl Ivens and local raptor expert Derek Holman.

"The Duke of Buccleugh's head gamekeeper volunteered to incubate the eggs alongside hundreds of pheasant eggs.

"When the first kite chick hatched it was promptly named Gremlin by its surrogate human parents."

Mr Ivens added:"We were thrilled when Gremlin made his appearance.

"It's the first time in the Midlands that red kite eggs have been successfully recovered and hatched.

"Another chick has now emerged and tapping sounds can be heard from the last of the clutch. We hope this egg will also hatch successfully."

It is hoped that the chicks will soon be 'adopted' and reared naturally by other red kites.

EGG THIEVES HAVE managed to snatch the eggs from two osprey nests in Scotland - despite both Tayside sites being heavily protected and monitored by conservationists.

Police and wildlife officials are now investigating the incident.

They hope to track down the culprits.

CONIFER TREES IN the Lake District are under attack from a voracious beetle which has managed to break out of areas where it was previously contained.

The great spruce bark beetle is a listed pest which was first discovered in Britain near Ludlow, Shropshire, in 1982 after apparently being imported in logs brought over from continental Europe.

Although established in Wales and a few southern English counties, it had previously been contained by biological controls and statutory restrictions on the movements of conifer wood.

Roddie Burgess, head of the Forestry Commission's Plant Health Service, said:"It is not possible to state categorically how the spread has occurred.

"It might have been by natural means, such as beetle flight, or it might have occurred through the illegal movement of infested timber or wood debris such as branches or bark residues on timber wagons or harvesting machinery travelling from long-infested areas to the Lake District."

Mr Burgess said 23 affected woodland sites have already been found in the Lake District, adding "once the scale of this new outbreak has been determined the Forestry Commission will be consulting woodland owners and wood processors about changes to the current statutory controls."

In Britain, the beetle attacks and breeds in all species of spruce, but particularly Norway and Sitka spruce.

It lays its eggs under the bark, where the developing insects feed on the inner bark layer, eventually encircling the tree and killing it.

Damage to individual trees is variable and it can take several years before a tree is completely girdled and dies.

However, long before individual trees are killed a large breeding population can build up, risking a bigger spread and more damage to nearby timber crops.

A NESTING CARRION crow has been blamed for vandalising cars during services at a church in Worcestershire.

The crow has been swooping down while parishioners at St Andrew's in Poolbrook are busy with their hymns and prayers.

Rubber from windscreen wipers has proven particularly popular for lining the bird's nest in a nearby tree and locals are furious.

Mabs Allbright-Web, 71, has had her car windscreen wipers damaged four times by the bird. Patrols have now been organised to keep the vandal at bay during services.

THE COUNTRYSIDE ALLIANCE says it is stepping up its defence of hunting after becoming disillusioned by the Government 'consultation' process.

"It is now seven weeks since the Government announced that it was going to hold a six-month consultation period on hunting," said a spokesman."So far, interested parties have received a four paragraph letter from Alun Michael which did little to enhance confidence or move the process forward.

"Whilst the Government makes up its mind what to do, we cannot afford to wait any longer for an opportunity that might be presented to us.

"The Countryside Alliance is therefore going to hold its own public forum at which the issues of 'cruelty' and 'utility' can be explained and debated in the presence of the media, experts on those two issues, and politicians.

"This forum will be timed to coincide with the end of the consultation process and will show the public the quality of evidence that has been submitted from a wide range of organisations across the board. The evidence will, we believe, show that there is no justification or need for banning hunting on any grounds."

A MAN WAS arrested and cautioned by police after staging a bizarre sit-down protest in front of oncoming horses at a country point-to-point race.

The 35 year-old racegoer stunned spectators at the event near Wroxeter, Shropshire, by clambering onto a fence then sitting in front of it as competitors thundered towards him.

Officials were shocked that the man had put himself, the horses and their riders in such danger while mounting a protest apparently about personal freedom.

Fortunately, no-one was hurt but the Jockey Club is studying video footage of the incident and the man faces a lifetime ban from UK racecourses.

GARDEN NESTS ARE the subject of a new RSPB survey which aims to find out which birds are using our gardens most to raise their young.

The RSPB hopes that 25,000 people will participate in Nestwatch UK during the Society's Wake Up To Birds Week, which starts on May 25.

One in every four pairs of song thrushes nest in gardens, says the RSPB, but gardens form a "hugely important" haven for other birds which are rapidly declining in numbers such as the house sparrow, starling and spotted flycatcher.

Britain's gardens cover an area more than three times the size of Greater London so gardeners can make a huge difference to the most rapidly declining birds.

Dr Andre Farrar, organiser of the Nestwatch UK project, said:"As vitally important for birds as the RSPB network of nature reserves are, we will only ever have a tiny fraction of song thrushes and other garden birds within our care.

"By telling us about their gardens and which birds are nesting in them, Nestwatch UK participants can greatly increase the understanding of what these birds need and how we can help to protect them in future.

"We know many people are deeply interested in birds in their garden and want to help us understand more about them."

Anyone wishing to take part should contact the RSPB for more details.

CONSERVATIONISTS ARE celebrating successful breeding by a pair of wild choughs - the first time these increasingly rare birds have bred in England for 50 years.

The choughs, red-billed members of the crow family, produced a brood of four chicks which hatched in Cornwall.

The birds nested in a cliff cave owned by the National Trust on the west coast of Cornwall and have been protected in a round-the-clock watch by RSPB staff and local volunteers.

"This is a cause for great celebration for the Cornwall Chough Project, a partnership between the RSPB, National Trust, English Nature and DEFRA, and for Cornish people everywhere," said a spokesman for the RSPB.

"The choughs' gradual decline in numbers throughout the last century has been attributed to loss of grazing along Cornwall's coasts, the use of more intensive methods of agriculture, and persecution thanks to their rarity value.

"Their return vindicates nearly 10 years' hard work by the partnership to provide suitable nesting and feeding habitats.

"This has been achieved through agreements with local landowners and farmers managing their land for nature conservation, supported in some areas by DEFRA's Countryside Stewardship Schemes.

"Choughs forage on grassy cliff tops grazed by cattle and ponies for their food, which is mainly insects and other small invertebrates.

"The chicks' future is still uncertain as they reach the critical fledging stage but there is an air of cautious optimism that this is the start of a slow but steady re-colonisation by choughs of their traditional breeding ground.

"The RSPB, National Trust, English Nature and DEFRA wish to acknowledge the considerable help provided from local people and volunteers who watched over the nesting location to prevent disturbance and to ward off egg collectors."

AN ANGLER HAD an unusual catch while fishing at a lake near Telford, Shropshire - a box of kittens.

The kittens and two adult cats had been dumped beside the lake, as if someone had balked at the thought of drowning them at the last minute.

According to the RSPCA, the box had been strongly sealed with black tape so the cats could not escape and they were in great distress by the time the fisherman found them.

But all were recovering well and will be rehomed.

The Society has pointed out it is an offence to abandon an animal in a situation likely to cause it suffering and culprits face a fine of up to £5,000.

SALMON AND SEA trout are to benefit from a £250,000 Environment Agency scheme to build a fish pass on the River Taff at Trefforest Weir near Pontypridd.

The pass will allow fish migrating through Cardiff Bay to gain access to their historical spawning grounds for the first time in more than 200 years.

Work begins shortly and the scheme is expected to be completed by late autumn in time for the spawning period.

The weir was originally constructed to assist the abstraction of water for industrial use but this ended decades ago, says the Agency.

However, the weir could not simply be removed because of the possibility of damage being caused to structures such as bridges and river banks upstream.

Peter Gough, Agency team leader, said:"The restoration of the fishery should send a very positive message to local residents and to potential investors in the area about the much improved quality of the environment.

"It will also enhance a valuable recreation resource for residents of the valleys in years to come."

BIRD LOVERS ARE being asked 'Who's having sex in your garden ?' as the normally staid RSPB moves to raise the temperature of its latest survey.

Carole McCormick, organiser of the RSPB-led Nestwatch UK survey, explained:"If people think there's too much sex on TV, they may blush at the thought of what's happening just outside their kitchen windows.

"In spring, birds have a few things on their minds but the key one is reproduction. In fact, most of their waking lives will be spent attracting a mate, fending off rivals, building a nest, and rearing and defending their young. Of course, much of this behaviour will be on view to many people as millions of pairs of birds continue the cycle of life in our gardens.

"By telling us about their gardens and what birds are nesting in them, Nestwatch UK participants can greatly increase the understanding of what these birds need and how we can help to protect them in future."

INNER CITY LONDON youngsters will get a deeper insight into rural life by seeing the 'Countryside Live', say organisers.

Over 3,500 schoolchildren are expected to descend on the Syon Park site in Brentford, Middlesex, this year as the annual event gets even bigger.

Organised jointly by the Countryside Foundation for Education, the Game Conservancy Trust, Hounslow Education Business Partnership, and Syon Park, 'Countryside Live' is said to be a vital link in helping city children get a better understanding of the countryside as a living, working environment.

James Crowley, of the Game Conservancy Trust, believes it is essential city kids are 'reconnected' to the countryside.

He said:"Some of the messages coming from the countryside are not always positive. 'Countryside Live' helps to redress the balance by showing the countryside in a very positive light. The children will be able to see eggs hatching, to milk cows, shear sheep, feel encouraged to take up a new hobby such as fishing or learn about the rewarding countryside job opportunities that are available. There will certainly be lots for everyone to do and see."

DELAYS IN IMPLEMENTING new, tighter controls on food and plant imports could lead to another foot-and-mouth epidemic, MPs have been warned.

In a submission to the Environment, Food and Rural Affairs Select Committee inquiry into Illegal Meat Imports, the NFU says Government proposals are not only overdue - tabled over 12 months after the UK's foot-and-mouth outbreak began - but may also be insufficiently watertight and workable.

NFU Food Standards chairman Michael Seals said:"A recent report by European inspectors highlights the fact that UK import controls are still woefully inadequate.

"Swift implementation of the Government Action Plan and other measures we have been calling for are crucial to securing our first line of defence against disease."

Many of the NFU's suggestions have been written into the Government's proposals.

However, the union insists there is still no effective means of co-ordinating the efforts of numerous enforcement agencies at ports and airports - such as Customs and Excise, local authorities and Port Health Authorities.

NFU president Ben Gill added:"The proposals fail to take account of an important potential route of infection - the personal traveller's allowances for food and agricultural produce. The UK Government should be pro-active in Europe and pressing for a review of the present legislation on personal allowances which is complex, confusing and insufficiently policed.

"The clearest solution would be to abolish the allowances altogether, with some exceptions, for example milk for babies or items essential for medical purposes."

THE COUNTRYSIDE ALLIANCE is continuing its pressure on the Government to keep hunting legal by organising a raft of protests and demonstrations all over the country.

June 9 has now been chosen as the date for a new mass march in London to show the extent of rural anger at New Labour.

Latest campaign events included the Union of Country Sports Workers holding a protest 'meet' in Smith Square, London, for all its members and supporters.

During preparations, a spokesman said:"For this particular event, having considered the public relations aspect, we request all mounted followers come dressed in their everyday working clothes.

"Although this may seem to be an unusual request, what we are trying to illustrate is that all sorts of ordinary working people also enjoy the occasional day out following hounds, and in reality we are no different to anyone else."

Hunts are also being urged to get more actively involved in their local communities.

FRIENDS OF THE Earth has blasted proposals to build massive new toll roads across swathes of open countryside.

Instead, the environmental campaigns organisation wants congestion charging on existing roads and more research on alternatives to the car.

Roger Higman, transport campaigner for FoE, said:"At long last the motoring lobby is beginning to realise that urgent steps are needed to curb car use. We support the RAC's call for congestion-charging - but not its demand for more roads.

"New roads are part of the problem, not the solution. They wreck the countryside and encourage more cars, more pollution and eventually, more congestion. The Government must ensure that alternatives to the car are attractive, affordable and available.

"Cleaner vehicles are urgently needed and the RAC is right to call for them. But new technology won't prevent pollution unless the energy comes from renewable sources like the wind, waves and sun.

"The Government must urgently review its targets for renewable energy to make sure clean power sources are available for new vehicles."

RED KITES ARE the stars of the show again in a new webcam facility set up by English Nature.

"Following the success of last year's red kite webcam, we have again managed to catch a red kite family on the nest and are broadcasting images from a new, secret location in Rockingham Forest," said a spokesman.

"The red kite is one of our most stunning birds of prey with a wonderfully graceful and effortless flight. Once a familiar sight across much of England, it was wiped out by the end of the 1800s after enduring centuries of persecution.

"English Nature, together with Forest Enterprise and the RSPB, has worked hard to restore the species. Now, after more than 10 years of releasing young red kites in England, breeding populations are well established in parts of the Chilterns in southern England and in the East Midlands."

RURAL HOUSING IS rocketing beyond what country people can afford and pricing them out of their own communities, it has been claimed.

The Countryside Agency's latest 'State of the Countryside 2002' report paints a picture of relative stability for rural England but the biggest problem is said to be the pressure on housing as rural homes become less affordable.

Agency chairman and rural advocate Ewen Cameron said:"We have been highlighting for some time the lack of affordable homes in rural England. The figures confirm that a significantly higher proportion of rural people (57 per cent) would have to commit more than half their income to mortgage costs - nearly double that of urban residents (32 per cent).This is a major hurdle for new households and those on less than average wages. Taken alongside the much lower availability of rural social housing, with only 14 per cent public or social rented housing compared to 23 per cent in urban areas, the countryside could become the preserve of the wealthy, threatening the whole nature of rural communities and viability of services."

Crimes of violence, low wages, and rural post office decline were other concerns, he added.

THE WILDLIFE CARNAGE on Britain's roads has been highlighted in a new report which claims many deaths could actually be prevented.

Each year, an estimated 100,000 foxes, 100,000 hedgehogs, 50,000 badgers and 50,000 deer are killed.

But The Mammal Society, which carried out the survey, says better thinking by humans could save many of these lives.

Professor Stephen Harris, chairman of the Society, said:"The survey provides us with the information we need to reduce mammal deaths on roads. It shows that the number of deaths is directly related to the landscape as much as to the numbers of mammals and that improved road design will reduce the numbers of dead mammals on our roads."

The National Road Death Survey was carried out over a year with volunteers across Britain recording mammal deaths on roads as well as details of the road itself and the surrounding habitat.

The survey found that the location of fatalities was associated with several features.

These included 'wildlife corridors' which connect with or cross roads, funnelling animals towards their doom.

Creatures often forage for food along linear features as well as using them for territorial boundaries, explains the report, so deaths are commonly recorded where these meet roads.

This was true for hedgehogs, badgers, foxes, mink, otters, deer, stoats and weasels.

Road boundary features such as ditches and lines of trees were also often used as temporary cover before animals attempted fatal road crossings.

In addition, badger numbers are highest in areas of pasture, says the report, so a lot of badger deaths occur next to this habitat while hedgehog road deaths are more associated with urban areas.

Such findings can be used to identify where most deaths occur, adds the report, so changes can then be made by planners.

A FARMING COUPLE were stunned by a strange animal wandering casually onto their land.

At first Malcolm and Julie Cox could only stare at the llama - an animal more at home in South America than rural Hough, Cheshire.

But they took the long-necked stranger in and cared for it before handing it over to the RSPCA.

Officials later checked with zoos and private llama owners but could find no-one who had lost one of the distinctive animals. Now the British Llama and Alpaca Association is looking after the stray until a new home is found.

THE IMPACT OF predators on threatened ground-nesting birds such as lapwing, golden plover and curlew is the subject of Britain's biggest ever heather moorland experiment.

Concentrating on 48 square kilometres of heather moorland at Otterburn, Northumberland, the eight-year Otterburn Wader Experiment is being undertaken by a team of scientists from the Game Conservancy Trust.

"Appropriate grazing and heather burning is thought to have a beneficial effect in conserving heather uplands but active control of common predators such as foxes, crows and stoats for similar benefit is more contentious,"explained a Trust spokesman.

"For the first time, researchers plan to isolate the effects of predation control by gamekeepers from other factors, such as variations in habitat, in order to measure the effect on some of Britain's best-loved birds.

"The Trust hopes the results from the experiment will help in the conservation of Britain's unique heather moorlands."

EGG THIEVES MAY face a sharper enemy in future after kukri-wielding Gurkhas were enlisted to train RSPB wardens in anti-poaching measures.

But bird lovers infuriated by recent egg thefts might be disappointed to learn there is no chance the deadly kukri knives will be used against intruders.

The Gurkhas will be teaching RSPB recruits the finer points of field craft, such as lying low and secretly observing their adversary's movements.

Wardens will be taught at the Gurkha's base in Kent before using their skills to protect threatened birds such as Montagu's harriers.

A LIVERY YARD which turns away business from hunt riders has been praised by the League Against Cruel Sports.

Farmer Chris Skinner, of High Ash Farm, Caistor St Edmund, near Norwich, asks potential clients if they hunt when they first inquire about stabling their horses with him.

However, despite his stance, he claims never to have sent a customer packing.

"The fact is, the issue has never actually arisen," he said."Hunting is not as popular as it is made out to be. The majority of horse riders do so purely for leisure and pleasure. They have no interest in hunting and do not want to be involved in killing things.

"Most horse owners are working, professional people who want to spend their leisure time in a relaxing way, and all this talk of blacksmiths losing their jobs if hunting is banned is nonsense. The large majority of their work is leisure horses."

John Cooper, chairman of the League Against Cruel Sports, said:"It is refreshing to see a farmer taking such a strong stand against hunting. Livery yards like Mr Skinner's are bound to be a success story. Only seven per cent of horses in England and Wales are used for hunting so it is not surprising that a yard run purely for leisure riders has gone down so well. There is a large proportion of horse owners and riders who would like to see hunting banned."

THE SOIL ASSOCIATION is urging families to visit an organic farm over the Bank Holiday to give children a better insight into healthy food production.

Patrick Holden, director of the Association, said:"There's plenty to do and learn."

226

CATS: ruthless enemies of our garden birds

MOST cat lovers like garden birds and are horrified when Tiddles reverts to type and snuffs out the lives of a nest of young robins or blue tits.

With so many cats around, such bloody massacres are now common but the facts on cat predation still shock.

Worldwide, the rise of the cat has been linked to the decimation of many rare species of birds and mammals.

In Britain our cat population has now topped 7.2 million pets which are estimated to kill over 75 million birds each year.

No wonder birdsong is almost extinct in some areas.

But even this pales in comparison with the USA where cats are believed to kill 1.4 BILLION birds annually.

I like cats. I also like birds. However, the difficulty of enjoying both was brought home to me again the other day when my wife spotted a normally placid cat in our garden gleefully torturing a thrush.

After she hammered on the window to distract the cat, the badly injured thrush managed to struggle free and hide in undergrowth.

But a scattering of torn feathers the next morning betrayed its fate.

Cats are born killers. Even more than dogs, they seem to have retained many of their natural instincts which is part of their attraction.

Cats fitted with bells are, of course, less likely to surprise a bird.

However, some cunning pets learn to muffle these as they close in on their victim.

A new electronic collar now on the market is said to be far more successful at saving garden birds. This lightweight device emits a sharp sonic warning signal at the cat's approach and has won praise from the British Trust for Ornithology. But domestic cats are not the only feline threat to birds.

Feral cats are now part of the landscape in this country and assorted colonies or loners survive on their wits in most towns and cities.

Cats that go wild in rural areas probably have the toughest lives. Without human handouts to fall back on, their in-built hunting skills come to the fore.

Voles, mice, rats, and rabbits are among a range of creatures which regularly feel the cutting edge of cats' needle-sharp teeth and claws.

At one time, a friend of mine had a huge male cat which specialised in hunting rabbits near her home.

So powerful was this pet that it was capable of dragging an adult rabbit into the house through its cat flap.

My friend would often be appalled to find a terrified live rabbit awaiting her when she came downstairs at dawn.

Usually, she managed to fend off her cat long enough to save these quivering bunnies.

She returned them to their field - much to her pet's dismay.

But cats being cats, this one discovered an effective way to stop all that irritating bunny hugging.

Unfortunately, biting the rabbits' heads off did not go down too well either.

In the end, the cat went completely feral and never came home.

This was probably a relief to both of them.

It can't be easy to watch your hard-earned meal being thrown into a rubbish bin.

Nor is it pleasant to have your pristine living-room turned into an execution chamber.

THE WAR OVER badgers and bovine TB rumbles on with farmers' leaders giving a cautious welcome to a Government bid to introduce an improved test for TB in cattle.

However, the NFU has also stressed that the underlying problem still needs urgent action.

Conservationists recently warned that farming unions could wreck tourism in the countryside for a second year running if they continue to demand a cull of badgers.

According to the National Federation of Badger Groups, the NFU and other unions have launched an aggressive media campaign claiming that badgers are spreading bovine TB to cattle in Wales and the west of England.

"These claims are grossly irresponsible," said Dr Elaine King, chief executive of the NFBG. "The rise in bovine TB can be firmly attributed to last year's foot-and-mouth disease restrictions, not badgers.

"When cattle were cooped up for long periods, low levels of the disease were amplified in herds. Now cattle are being traded, spreading the disease to new places."

Jan Rowe, vice-chairman of the NFU's Animal Health and Welfare unit, said the new 'gamma interferon' blood test would be useful in giving a clearer picture of the scale of the problem in the British herd.

But he said that the core issue of how cattle are getting the disease in the first place and why it is accelerating at such an alarming rate needs to be tackled.

Mr Rowe said:"This new test is good news. Anything that increases the battery of measures to help stop the disease must be welcomed, although we need clarification of what exactly enhanced testing entails.

"We desperately need hard facts on this disease and only the Krebs trials can give us those. There is simply no doubt that wildlife is a significant reservoir of bovine TB."

OTTERS ARE BEING given a boost in the Lake District with plans to stop them being killed in traffic.

So hazardous is their favourite land route that officials propose to build an underpass beneath a busy road.

More than £3,000 will be spent at the spot between Derwentwater and Bassenthwaite Lake, near Keswick.

Although similar passes have been built for other creatures, this is thought to be the first one for otters.

Otter loving bosses from the Highways Agency have revealed they may build 250 such underpasses over the next decade.

NEW TECHNOLOGY FROM Canada is being used to learn more about salmon and sea trout numbers in the north of England.

According to the Environment Agency, scientists based in York have taken delivery of a 'rotary screw trap' designed and built in Canada.

"The traps are made up of a rotating drum, which is covered in mesh and sits between two pontoons," explained a spokesman."Baffles inside use the movement of the river to turn the drum and fish are guided into a holding area at the back of the trap.

"Made from lightweight aluminium, they are relatively portable which means that scientists can place them on any river, exactly where they want. The design also means that they work in almost any flow conditions.

"The new trap is currently being put through its paces on the River Tees and will hopefully be used throughout Yorkshire to monitor the numbers of juvenile salmon and sea trout, known as smolts, going out to sea.

"The results will show how fast the numbers of salmon and sea trout in rivers such as the Tees, Esk and Ure are increasing and so will help in drawing up management plans for their future."

IT HAD SEEMED so friendly but experts believe a dolphin haunting Weymouth harbour in Dorset could soon drown someone with its 'sexual aggression'.

Swimmers have been warned to stay away from George the dolphin which has been showing increasingly amorous behaviour towards them, be they male or female.

American expert Ric O'Barry, who worked as a trainer on the Flipper TV show, believes the powerful animal is exhibiting growing signs of sexual frustration and is easily capable of accidentally drowning a would-be chum.

So far, Mr O'Barry has failed in his attempts to draw the dolphin back to French coastal waters after it became dangerously attracted to the propellers of local boats.

However, his main fears now centre on the many swimmers who are trying to befriend the dolphin rather than on the dolphin itself.

NESTING SKYLARKS HAVE more to fear from grazing cows than prowling badgers or foxes, according to new research.

An investigation has found that cattle are responsible for 60 per cent of all nest destruction with badgers and foxes causing just 15 per cent.

In a briefing to the Government TB Forum, Dr Chris Cheeseman from DEFRA's Ecological Research Unit, confirmed the team's findings.

He also claimed that no evidence had been found to link an increase in the badger population to the increase in bovine TB in cattle.

Conservationists have welcomed the report as well as Dr Cheeseman's attack on farming unions for claiming badger numbers were "exploding".

"Farming unions have been blaming badgers for the decline in skylarks for years," said Dr Elaine King, chief executive of the National Federation of Badger Groups. "We are delighted that sound scientific research has confirmed that the unions should look to their own stocking practices as the primary cause of nest destruction. In addition to skylarks, lapwing and golden plover are also affected."

A CRACKDOWN ON illegal fishing led the Environment Agency to net over 500 licence dodgers in a massive blitz on waters across England and Wales.

The culprits were caught during a clampdown over a single weekend when 740 waterways were targeted and 7,971 anglers checked.

Dodgers comprised 6.5 per cent of those quizzed - a drop of almost two per cent on a similar blitz last year - and now each faces fines of up to £2,500, says the Agency.

Dr Dave Clarke, head of fisheries, said: "It gives us no pleasure prosecuting offenders. It means we've failed to make them realise that when they fish without a licence they aren't just cheating the Agency, they're cheating their fellow anglers out of money that would have been ploughed back into the sport.

"However, the drop in the latest evasion rate is very encouraging and shows that, through extensive campaigns, we are getting through to increasing numbers of people."

The Agency recently launched a high profile national and local media advertising campaign urging anglers to buy a licence.

Soccer legend Jack Charlton is also fronting a series of radio adverts encouraging anglers to keep within the law.

Jack, a member of England's 1966 winning World Cup team and a keen angler, also stresses how easy it is to get a licence.

There are around 17,000 post offices and other outlets which sell them direct and, for a small additional charge, they can be purchased over the phone.

Dr Clarke added:"We'd rather people learned this way than through enforcement. But for those who are hearing our message and choosing to ignore it, we've arranged further national and regional blitzes throughout the summer."

MORE THAN 1,000 people representing rural and farming interests took part in a series of meetings looking at the future of food and farming in England.

According to the Government, the events brought DEFRA ministers and officials together with representatives from a wide range of groups with food, farming, rural, and environmental interests.

DEFRA Minister Lord Whitty said:"There has been a real determination demonstrated to take forward the recommendations of the Curry report and turn them into a cohesive reality."

Sir Donald Curry chaired the Policy Commission on the Future of Farming and Food with the Commission making recommendations in a report which said "sweeping changes" were needed.

The meetings were held in each region of the country and covered a variety of subjects.

AN ANCIENT TRAIL dating back 6,000 years is under threat from trailbikes and four-wheel drive vehicles, warns the Ramblers Association.

The Ridgeway Trail, thought to be the oldest surviving road in England, needs urgent protection if it not to be badly damaged.

Recently, the Ramblers' Association, along with the Friends of the Ridgeway and the Country Land and Business Association, withdrew its support for a voluntary code of respect among drivers and riders originally designed to protect the Ridgeway.

Now Swindon Borough Council has announced a plan to impose a temporary traffic regulation order on two sections of the trail - banning non-essential vehicles for six months.

A spokesman for the Ramblers Association explained:"After two month's research, the council became so concerned at the deteriorating condition of the trail caused by vehicles, it was decided measures were needed.

"The Ridgeway is an ancient trail dating back some 6,000 years. It is said to be the oldest road in England. Along its length can be found Iron Age hill forts, ancient burial grounds and important wildlife habitats."

A COW CAUSED motorway mayhem after escaping from a lorry and going on the run down a slip road between the M1 and M18.

The animal got loose after the lorry transporting it was involved in a collision with a number of vehicles near Rotherham, South Yorkshire.

Hundreds of drivers were forced to a halt as police and vets tried to corner the cow which was reported to be injured.

Motorists were told to stay in their cars for their own safety as the animal rampaged around in panic.

Vets eventually subdued the runaway and restrictions on traffic were lifted.

DOGS NOT KEPT under proper control could be the scourge of ground-nesting birds in the Scottish Uplands if new laws are passed, it has been claimed.

So concerned is the Game Conservancy Trust by the threat that it is urgently drafting amendments to the Land Reform (Scotland) Bill.

These include dogs being kept on a short leash on the open hill during the grouse shooting season or when waders and other moorland birds are nesting.

The Trust says it regards most walkers as responsible users of the countryside but wildlife has to be protected.

"Some bird species are pretty hardy," said a spokesman."The red grouse, for instance, will sit tight when nesting unless walkers stumble straight onto the nest.

"However, if they have dogs, the grouse can be seriously disturbed and then eggs or chicks are lost.

"But many birds are far more sensitive and some will not return to their chicks if approached to within 200 metres.

"Disturbance, especially repeated disturbance, will cause them to abandon their clutch or chicks."

Twite, golden plover, merlin, dotterel and ptarmigan were among many species under threat if dogs were allowed to roam under the legislation in its current form.

WILDLIFE GROUPS ARE being offered a share of a £10million bonanza aimed at boosting conservation in and around quarries.

English Nature says it is bracing itself for an "avalanche of applications" for a slice of the massive cake over the next two years - its biggest ever grant scheme.

"The cash comes from the Aggregates Levy Sustainability Fund, announced by Chancellor Gordon Brown and Michael Meacher in April's Budget," explained a spokesman.

"The money, raised from a tax placed on every tonne of rock taken from quarries, will benefit local communities by increasing bio diversity, conserving geological features and could even be used to buy out long-standing mineral extraction rights threatening the existing countryside.

"The first of many grants, up to £350,000 could be awarded as soon as July by a panel of geologists, biodiversity specialists, the Fieldfare Trust and an English Nature council member together with representatives from the Quarry Producers Association and Mineral Planning Authorities.

"An English Nature Grant Management Team will provide guidance and will be able to award grants up to £50,000 between Grant Panel meetings."

Sir Martin Doughty, chairman of English Nature, added: "This is the biggest spending programme that we have been asked to manage. This scheme could help to improve quarried landscapes in England by replanting woodland, creating great swathes of reed beds and habitat for birds, recreating heathland as home for a myriad of species, and improving access and interpretation of geological sites.

"Using the funds to buy out extraction rights can also halt further environmental damage. This money is only available until March 2004, so we'd like to encourage local groups, big or small, to get in contact with English Nature straightaway."

POLICE WERE LEFT scratching their heads after a dead wallaby was discovered on the M40 in Buckinghamshire in the early hours.

The animal, normally more at home Down Under, had apparently been living wild in nearby countryside.

Checks with zoos and wildlife parks have revealed no missing stock so investigators are in the dark over how long the animal had been running free before meeting its end.

Reports of a wallaby hopping across local fields had been circulating in the High Wycombe area for more than a year.

THE THREAT OF foreign diseases like foot-and-mouth breaching British border defences again is "just a click away" on the internet, it has been claimed.

NFU Food Standards chairman Michael Seals explained:"The internet allows us to window shop around the world. In navigating a handful of sites myself, I was just one click away from buying meat products from anywhere on the globe whilst sitting at home in Derbyshire.

"Imported disease is a real and perhaps an increasing threat. Alongside improvements in global biosecurity and world-wide efforts to control diseases, effective import controls and surveillance have a crucial role to play.

"We must recognise that unless our front line - our first line of defence - is working properly and effectively, then more problems will follow."

Foot-and-mouth plus classical swine fever had both been imported in recent times with disastrous results, he said.

But other huge losses continued to be suffered by British agriculture and the countryside at the hands of imported diseases like rhizomania - which affects sugar beet - and Dutch elm disease.

Mr Seals added:"The Government says it is serious about biosecurity and border controls but reform is long overdue.

"Failure to act will only expose us unnecessarily to diseases that will once again decimate our animals, our trees and, one day, even our population."

ESSEX BIRDS ARE tougher than anywhere else in the country - or so it seems if latest research is to be believed.

"While new results from over 400 Essex gardens show just how rapidly some of our familiar bird species are declining, they also highlight the fact that some species are doing better in Essex than they are nationally," explained a spokesman for the British Trust for Ornithology.

"The pattern of house sparrow decline we are seeing in Essex is similar to that seen in other parts of the country - although it seems that more Essex gardens have house sparrows than gardens elsewhere."

However, the national decline in sparrows continues and could be due to changes in the way houses are built, adds the Trust.

Older properties often have nesting birds in their roof spaces but more modern properties, with their plastic bargeboards and close-fitting roof tiles, restrict access.

SCOTTISH WILDLIFE WILL get better protection under new proposals to crack down on countryside criminals.

Custodial sentences and greater powers of arrest are proposed as the Scottish Executive commits itself to addressing the issue of wildlife law reform.

RSPB Scotland director Stuart Housden said:"It is excellent news that action to combat wildlife crime will be in the legislative programme.

"Scotland has seen an upsurge in the persecution of protected raptors like hen harriers, and has suffered the barbarities of egg collectors. Osprey, chough and black-throated divers, some of our rarest species, have suffered. We look forward to working with the Executive on wildlife crime.This is a good day for Scottish wildlife."

230

EIGHTY MASKED SABOTEURS wielding hammers and clubs are said to have launched a vicious attack on a hunt.

One member of the Three Counties Mink Hounds was taken to hospital with facial injuries following the attack which took place shortly after the hunt had met in Bidford, Warwickshire.

According to the Countryside Alliance, the injured man, aged 19, had a chemical substance sprayed in his face and two other members of the hunt, a man and a woman, were also attacked, thrown to the ground and kicked.

Mark Allen, spokesman for Three Counties Mink Hounds, said:"This latest attack by anti-hunting thugs shows clearly that they are not animal lovers but people haters. What excuse is there for going out into the countryside armed with hammers and pick-axe handles, assaulting a woman and spraying a young man in the face with chemicals?

"Hunting is a legal activity and those who take part in it should be able to do so without fear of violence or intimidation. This is anarchy at its worst."

Simon Hart, director of the Countryside Alliance Campaign for Hunting, said:"We will be making urgent representations to the Home Office to assess how this kind of violence can occur in Britain's countryside, and finding out what proposals the Home Secretary has to address it.

"This mindless attack comes at a time when people on both sides of the hunting debate have been invited by the Government to take part in a consultation process on the future of the activity.

"This incident illustrates that the animal rights movement has nothing to contribute to this process other than violence and intimidation. This is yet more proof that the animal rights movement is driven by spite, hatred and vindictiveness, rather than a desire to improve animal welfare. It comes as no surprise that anti-hunt MPs are deafeningly silent at moments like this."

A GOVERNMENT BID to educate and train young people in the countryside has been welcomed by the Country Land and Business Association.

President Sir Edward Greenwell said:"Creating opportunities for young people in the countryside is something which we have been advocating for some time. We want young people to see the countryside as a place where they can build a future. Young people in the countryside need a vibrant and profitable rural economy."

AN INCREASE IN deaths and horrific injuries caused by snares has led to a 60,000-signature petition being handed to Downing Street.

Campaigners want to ban snares which are being blamed for "torturing to death" badgers and other wildlife, as well as domestic pets such as cats.

"These barbaric devices are indiscriminate and often result in gruesome and protracted strangulation for a strong, heavy animal such as the badger," said Dr Elaine King, chief executive of the National Federation of Badger Groups.

"In many cases, the snare cuts deep into the neck or abdomen as the animal struggles to break free, causing terrible injuries and a lingering death."

Illegal 'self-locking' snares are still being used to inflict terrible suffering on badgers - often intentionally, she said, while legal 'free-running' snares can leave badgers almost cut in half or decapitated.

"All snares present an unacceptable risk to wildlife and other animals. The only way to stop the indiscriminate cruelty they cause is a total ban on all snares," she added.

A SEAL IS being hailed a hero after apparently coming to the rescue of a drowning dog in the River Tees.

The dog had fallen into the fast-flowing river and quickly became too exhausted to haul itself out.

But witnesses report that, as it began to sink beneath the surface, a seal appeared from nowhere and nudged it to safety on the bank.

The drama happened near Newport Bridge, Middlesbrough, and emergency services were alerted.

Firemen later captured the bemused mongrel which was found to have suffered only minor injuries during its watery ordeal.

CARP, ROACH AND gudgeon were among 5,000 fish killed by a mystery pollutant which hit a canal in Middlewich, Cheshire.

Environment Agency staff have been trying to discover how the fish died in a half-mile stretch of the canal between Town Bridge and Big Lock.

First reports were of a much smaller incident but later the full extent of the fish kill became apparent and a full-scale clean-up was organised by British Waterways.

No obvious cause of the fish deaths has been found but an Agency probe is continuing with water samples being analysed and post-mortems carried out on some of the fish.

Agency spokesman John Ellaby urged anyone who knew what killed the fish to get in touch.

"Whatever killed these fish has left no obvious trace," he said.

"It is a tragedy that this canal, so popular with anglers, has been affected in this way.

"There was a major boat festival on the canal at the weekend, and if anyone has any information that could help solve the mystery they should contact the Environment Agency."

A STAFFORDSHIRE bull terrier survived after plunging 50ft into the sea off cliffs at Llandudno, North Wales.

It was feared that the powerful pet would drown. However, coastguards used a lifeboat to rescue it unharmed.

FOXHUNT GROUPS HAVE pledged to redouble their efforts to preserve the sport despite efforts by anti-hunt campaigners to crush them.

Addressing 300 members of the Masters of Foxhounds Association, chairman Lord Daresbury said the battle could only be won if they all remained united.

"The Association also stands shoulder to shoulder with the Countryside Alliance," he stressed. "Furthermore, we all - inside and beyond hunting - need a solution for the future which is politically achievable, legally secure, continues to be supported by the media and is underpinned by favourable public opinion.

"Our position is not a defence of cruelty, which is indefensible. It is a straightforward explanation of the positive role that hunting plays in the countryside, and how it is properly and effectively regulated.

"Hunting provides selective and area-sensitive fox management; the creation of habitats which promote wildlife and bio-diversity; a fallen stock service to farmers; valuable local jobs in rural communities; and a focus for social life, especially in isolated areas.

"Properly conducted, hunting has nothing to hide. The more open and accountable we are, the more we welcome public scrutiny, the easier it will be for us to engage in dialogue with those in positions of public responsibility."

At the same meeting, Sam Butler, the chairman of the Countryside Alliance's Campaign for Hunting, also explained the rationale behind the Alliance's 'Summer of Discontent' campaign.

"The thinking behind the campaign is entirely focused on devising and carrying out the sorts of activities which generate sympathy and understanding from the general public," he said.

"I cannot overemphasise the importance of this point.

"We must understand that belligerence, aggressiveness and causing major inconvenience to the public will quickly erode sympathy and support."

SECOND HOMES IN the countryside could help provide the money for more affordable rural housing, it has been claimed.

The Country Land and Business Association says raising the full council tax levy on second homes could fund the provision of affordable housing in the countryside and bring an end to rural social exclusion.

FRANCE'S NEW GOVERNMENT must lift its predecessor's illegal ban on British beef and drop its scientifically unjustified proposals to extend controls on sheep, say farmers' leaders.

In a letter to DEFRA Secretary of State Margaret Beckett, NFU president Ben Gill said the UK Government and European Commission must press for early action by the new French administration to meet its legal obligations.

"The illegal French ban on British beef imports has already deprived UK producers of millions of pounds of sorely-needed income from its previously important export market," said Mr Gill.

"The very existence of the ban continues to cast a scandalous and unjustified slur on our product throughout Europe.

"But the previous French administration's proposals to extend its Specified Risk Material list to include spinal cord in sheep over six months old now threatens to hit our sheep industry as well by putting extra costs and impossible demands on our sheep meat exports."

In his letter, Mr Gill reminded Mrs Beckett that EU Health and Consumer Protection Commissioner David Byrne had questioned the French SRM proposal - due to come into force on July 1 - at the EC Agriculture Council meeting in April.

At that meeting he said there was no scientific justification for the measure - a view which echoed the findings of the EU's own Scientific Steering Committee.

A ONE-TONNE British bull that sleeps on a water bed has been hailed as the cattle world's top superstud.

Cogent Courier, a Holstein bull, can earn £1million annually from stud fees and lives a life of pampered luxury.

Owned by Britain's richest man, the Duke of Westminster, the bull lives at a Chester stud farm where it enjoys the perfect bachelor's life.

Sex is constantly available and the best food and drink are supplied each day to keep the precious animal in prime condition.

Weighing a mighty 168 stones and 12ft long from nose to tail, Cogent Courier was judged the leading stud in the world after experts researched the milk yield and strength of hundreds of offspring.

HORDES OF RAMBLERS have been helping to stamp out complacency over the state of the nation's footpaths.

Many paths are in a poor condition, says the Ramblers Association, and local authorities need to recognise this.

During Footpaths Week 2002, the biggest event of its type ever held, ramblers roamed far and wide in a bid to spotlight the issue.

While putting pressure on highway authorities to improve their rights of way networks, the week raised the profile of all footpath issues and stressed the value of rights of way to the entire community, said an RA spokesman.

Walkers had lobbied for improvements to paths in their areas and various events which highlighted pathway issues were held across England and Wales.

Walkers who contacted their local councillors had stressed how important a usable path network was to them.

FARMERS' LEADERS HAVE welcomed the ultimatum issued by the European Commission to France over its illegal ban on British beef.

Any refusal by the country to act would now be sheer arrogance, says the NFU.

NFU deputy president Tim Bennett said:"We hope this ultimatum will leave France in no doubt about the seriousness with which its illegal action is viewed by the entire European Union.

"The very existence of the ban continues to cast a scandalous and unjustified slur on our product throughout Europe.

"France must take heed and meet its legal obligations as soon as possible."

Earlier this month the NFU called on the UK Government and the Commission to put pressure on the new French administration to lift its predecessor's illegal ban.

France now has a short time to put measures in place to lift its embargo.

If it fails to act, the Commission can take the matter back to the European Court of Justice and apply for fines to be imposed on France.

Mr Bennett said that if France refused to act, the Commission must seek to impose substantial fines at the earliest opportunity.

He said the illegal activity by France had already spanned more than two-and-a-half years.

THEY CALLED IT the eighth wonder of the world but now the £90million Eden project in Cornwall is under attack - from seagulls.

The seabirds have been pecking their reflections in delicate plastic panels covering the giant domes and damaging them.

A number of the hexagonal panels have needed replacing since seagulls became bold enough to attack.

Buzzards which live around the project site often scare the marauding gulls off but now bigger efforts are being made to resolve the problem.

Plans have been drawn up to play recorded seagull distress calls outside the complex to drive the birds away for good.

THREE DONKEYS HAVE been targeted by a mystery knifeman who slashed off their tails as they stood in a Shropshire field.

The animals were left shaken but otherwise unhurt in the sinister attack at Knockin.

The donkeys are part of the Stonehill Donkeys racing team from Ellesmere and two had starred in the county's West Mid Show.

Owner David Mills was left horrified by the bizarre attack, although he is grateful none of the animals was injured.

Police are investigating and other donkey and horse owners in the area have been warned to be vigilant.

NEW ALLEGATIONS HAVE been made about covert fox-feeding activities by hunt groups said to want more foxes for better sport.

According to the League Against Cruel Sports, a fierce critic of foxhunting, the pest control claims of England's 'upland' fell hunting packs have been exposed as fantasy.

During what it calls "a major undercover investigation" the League claims to have established that foxes are being bred and fed for hunting in Cumbria.

Chief executive Douglas Batchelor said:"The findings of this investigation blow apart claims that upland fell hunting is concerned with pest control.

"The breeding and feeding of foxes for hunting is hypocritical and immoral anywhere, but the fact that we've uncovered that it is taking place in upland areas where hunts have claimed to be different exposes a grave deception by the pro-hunt lobby in Cumbria.

He called on the Central Committee of Fell Packs to immediately suspend any hunt under suspicion of being involved in activities against their own rules of hunting or in breach of the law.

Mr Batchelor also challenged the upland farming community to end practices that encourage a healthy fox population for hunting.

"We believe that animal carcasses are being deliberately dumped as food for foxes in Cumbria by people connected to foxhunting. But we also believe that the careless practices of dozens of farmers are contributing to this situation," he said. "The shoddy - and often illegal - discarding of carcasses in open pits, in fields, woodland and on mountain crags is tantamount to laying on a fast food meal for foxes and not conducive to keeping fox numbers low.

"It is hypocritical and immoral that upland farmers carelessly dispose of their dead animals then claim that supposedly spiralling fox numbers require the 'essential' services of fox hunts. What we're seeing in Cumbria is at best a farcical cycle of countryside mismanagement on the part of farmers and hunters and, at worst, a racket designed to ensure good hunting."

BITTERNS COULD BE the main beneficiaries of a new initiative to create the UK's largest man-made wetland.

The Hanson-RSPB wetland project is said to be "a visionary partnership" between industry and nature conservation aimed at creating a 700-hectare reserve at Hanson's Needingworth quarry, near Cambridge.

Graham Wynne, chief executive of the RSPB, said:"This exciting and far-sighted project will create Britain's biggest reedbed and will become one of the most important wetlands for wildlife in southern Britain, with the potential to double the current UK population of bittern from 30 to 60 pairs.

"We also anticipate attracting significant numbers of other nationally-scarce species such as marsh harrier, bearded tit and otter."

RURAL GROUPS HAVE urged the Government to use the July Comprehensive Spending Review to invest in the future of the countryside.

The Country Land and Business Association, RSPB, Countryside Agency, Food and Drink Federa-tion, National Consumer Council, and the National Trust came together to send a joint message on how the countryside can be best helped.

233

SKYLARK: when a perfect summer's day goes wrong

FOR such a small bird, it seems amazing that the skylark features in so many people's memories of perfect summer days. From its lofty vantage point way up high in a clear blue sky, the skylark's continuous warbling used to be as familiar during summer as the feel of hot sun on skin.

So I must admit I was shocked to learn that 75 per cent of our skylarks have been lost as a result of yet more bureaucratic bungling.

The drastic decline in skylark numbers has been traced to an EU initiative for UK farmers to move from spring-sown to autumn-sown cereals, according to research by the RSPB.

It seems that sowing cereals in spring was a great help to this little brown and white bird because it meant that stubble left over until then provided food and cover through the harsh winter months. With the area of spring-sown cereals now reduced from 73 per cent to just 16 per cent of available UK land, it is little wonder skylarks have virtually gone to the wall.

Urgent attempts are now being made to address the loss.

Even so, the long-term fate of this shy, crested bird remains in the balance.

Apart from having that piercing voice and an ability to remain a tiny dot in the sky for minutes on end, the skylark seems quite plain when it falls back to earth.

Weighing about 45 grammes, it lays up to five brown and white eggs in a nest among grass; eats seeds, insects and worms; and prefers to walk around rather than hop.

Personally, I will always associate skylarks with getting my first real watch the summer after I passed my 11-plus.

Lying on my back in the grass, a procession of skylarks singing high above me, I must have examined that watch's glorious gold and silver face for hours.

Life seemed rosy until I was irritated by some kids from my old primary school messing about next to a nearby pond.

A commotion started and I sat up to look.

It seemed that one of them had dropped his bicycle into the pond and could not fish it out.

Tut-tutting at this interruption, I strode over.

Within seconds, I was in full command of the situation, lying on my stomach and reaching down into the pond to grab the bike's front wheel, just visible underwater

"Hey, Dave," one of the miserable wretches suddenly chirped.*"Is your watch waterproof?"*

"It's new," I said.*"Of course, it's...."*

I glanced at my watch from which a line of tiny bubbles was now escaping, making its way towards the surface.

"...waterproof."

Abruptly, I dropped the bike back in the pond and, peering intently at my beloved watch, set off running back home.

Before I got there, the watch's face had misted over and it had stopped. Never to go again.

It wasn't waterproof at all.

Even the perfect summer's day can hit the buffers, skylarks or not.

Let's hope these beguiling birds enjoy a better fate than my watch - and time does not run out for them.

A THREE DECADE decline in songbirds has been totally reversed within three years at an experimental farm site.

The details are contained within a "ground-breaking " report produced by the Game Conservancy Trust that promises to bring a new approach to farming and wildlife conservation in this country.

Titled 'Where The Birds Sing', the report is based on research carried out by the Trust on the 333 hectare Allerton Project's demonstration farm in Loddington, Leicestershire.

It shows, by practical example, how farmers and conservationists can effectively increase biodiversity and improve habitats for wildlife through the introduction of beetle banks, conservation headlands and set-aside strips.

The report has been warmly welcomed by conservationists and country campaigners.

Environmentalist Jonathon Porritt said: "At a time when Government wants substantive change and public expectations of farmers rise even as their income falls, this booklet provides clear, scientifically and economically validated lessons.

"The Game Conservancy Trust has shown that it is perfectly possible for commercially viable farming and wildlife to coexist on the same land.

"The achievements of the Allerton Project should encourage all those concerned with conservation. It represents an exciting and feasible way forward for many British farmers."

Topics covered in the report include woodland management; wild bird cover crops; predator control; beetle banks and set-aside strips of land.

BUTTERFLIES ARE APPEARING weeks earlier than they did in the 1940s because of climate change, research has shown.

Some species can now been seen as early as mid-January with one red admiral spotted on January 19 - still winter - when it was rarely seen before the end of May in the '40s.

Scientists believe this is because the red admiral, normally a summer migrant, is overwintering in this country as our weather increasingly remains mild.

Five species which overwinter in their adult state - the red admiral, peacock, comma, brimstone and small tortoiseshell - show up here an average of 74 days earlier than 60 years ago.

The researchers, whose work has been published in British Wildlife magazine, discovered that all butterfly species appeared earlier in the 1990s than they did in the 1940s or even the 1970s.

WOLVES AND LYNX should be reintroduced to Scotland to boost tourism and help keep rising deer numbers under control, according to a local landowner.

Paul van Vlissingen, owner of an estate in the Highlands, explained to a Scottish newspaper:"Scotland could be divided into zones, with some areas where the deer have practically been eliminated - areas where you specifically want to encourage the natural regeneration of forests.

"In other areas, deer would be managed as part of a concept of wild land and in that concept wolves and lynx would fit very well.

"The current culling of deer under the official policy is not effective if you want to regulate the size of the herd. It's grim but you simply have to eliminate the deer. It cannot be done half and half."

Wolves and lynx were badly needed back in Scotland to boost tourism, he said.

"Scotland is losing in the tourist industry. There are so many other places in the world that are so much more exciting. Scotland has to create more excitement than the Loch Ness Monster because that monster is rather old and tired. You have to create in Scotland more excitement about your rural areas. You have to do something exciting in the international tourist business.

"I think it would create tremendous excitement where people can come and stalk and have a good chance of seeing wolves hunt. I think there is a market for that and it needs to be exploited."

CHICKEN DROPPINGS SHOWERING on residents have caused a stink in a quiet Shropshire market town.

Locals are furious with a farmer in Wem whose uncovered lorries travel through the town up to seven times a day - all loaded with chicken droppings which scatter over the sides.

Veteran councillor Peggy Carson was among the latest victims, drenched from head to foot in foul-smelling muck as she cycled beside one truck.

Shoppers and children have also complained of having clothes and hair covered in filth.

Now Wem Town Council is calling for police to crack down on the lorries.

By law, all such loads should be properly covered to offset the health risk to residents.

WOODLAND BIRDS HAVE slumped by 20 per cent across 33 species over the last 25 years, it has been revealed.

Some species, such as the lesser spotted woodpecker, spotted flycatcher and willow tit have declined by more than 50 per cent since the late 1960s.

Launching major new research into the problem, Forestry Minister Elliot Morley said:"We don't know yet which factors are driving the change in woodland bird populations but this important survey will help us to determine what is going on.

"Whilst many species are falling in numbers there are some which are actually increasing and there are marked regional differences.

"We have already made significant progress in determining the factors involved in the decline of farmland birds. It is now time to focus more attention on woodland birds."

THE FOX WHICH attacked a baby in its home may have been too weak from illness to capture its natural prey, it has been revealed.

Fourteen-week-old Louis Day was left covered in blood as the fox tried to drag him outside at Dartford, Kent.

But parents Sue Eastwood and Peter Day have told how the animal slumped on the carpet before fleeing - an unnatural reaction to danger.

The intruder also appeared to be suffering from mange and was carrying an injured back leg.

The horrifying incident has all the hallmarks of similar attacks on humans by wild animals around the world, when sickness or injury makes them too slow to catch normal prey.

Although both urban and country fox numbers are said to be rising in Britain, such attacks are virtually unknown here.

Trevor Williams, of the Kent-based fox rescue organisation Fox Project, said:"This is not just rare, it's unheard of. There's been no evidence of this sort of thing happening before."

Nevertheless, six years ago, another baby was said to have been attacked by a fox in Croydon, Surrey, although those claims were never proven.

BUTTERFLIES COULD BECOME a regular feature of any garden with just a few changes, say The Wildlife Trusts in a summer campaign.

"Choosing the right plants is essential to attract both the butterfly and the caterpillar," explained a spokesman."Butterflies require nectar for energy whilst caterpillars love the leaves or sometimes the flowers or leaf buds.

"Providing nectar rich flowers for butterflies and buds for caterpillars will secure your place as a butterfly's best buddy. You can better your buds for butterflies all year round. Spring flowering plants attractive to butterflies include primrose, forget-me-not, snowdrop and crocus.

"The bird cherry, crab apple or wild pear trees can also bring on the butterflies with their blossom in spring. In the summer, a buddleia will be bursting with butterflies as will sweet william, hyssop and thyme.

"As autumn draws in, the ice plant, hemp agrimony and michaelmas daisy will keep their wings in a flutter. Growing vegetables such as cabbage, runner beans or brussel sprouts will also not go amiss.

"Why not place a rock or pile of bricks in a sunny spot for them to warm up on and bask in the sunshine? If you can leave a sunny corner of long grass and nettles in your garden, the caterpillars of the small tortoiseshell, red admiral and peacock butterfly will thrive there.

"Growing your plants in sunny yet sheltered spots in close proximity to one another will also increase your butterfly hits. For more tips, The Wildlife Trusts also run a variety of courses and talks on butterfly gardening."

DENSE CONIFERS PLANTED in Britain's ancient woods are threatening the survival of some of our rarest plants, animals and fungi, The Woodland Trust has claimed.

Unless urgent action is taken, precious woodland species will vanish forever, the Trust warns in a report titled 'Reclaiming Our Forgotten Inheritance'.

Between the 1930s and the 1980s, hundreds of thousands of hectares of ancient woodland were felled and replanted - mostly with conifers, or a mixture of conifers and broadleaved trees.

But the report says that this well-intentioned commercial strategy has been a disaster with dire consequences for wildlife.

Richard Smithers, UK conservation adviser for the Trust, said:"These sites are as valuable as ancient monuments yet many are in the last chance saloon.

"We need the Government to act now to enable the Forestry Commission to restore all ancient woods planted with conifers on its own estate and to stimulate comprehensive action by other landowners.

"It might seem a mammoth task but it is a unique opportunity and one of the most significant actions we can take to help woodland wildlife in Britain to survive in the face of accelerating climate change."

To prevent the potential permanent loss of wildlife in a third of Britain's ancient woods the Trust is calling for a raft of measures to be implemented.

These include the Government enabling Forest Enterprise "to commit itself to restoring all its ancient woodland sites planted with conifers - and in doing so act as a catalyst by setting an example to other landowners."

The Trust also wants the Forestry Commission "in its current reviews of incentives for woodland management in England, Scotland and Wales to give high priority to restoration of conifer planted ancient woodland sites and to target incentives for restoration to give maximum benefit to biodiversity."

A DEER KEPT in an all-female enclosure inside a 6ft fence has given birth to a fawn - its second surprise birth in two years.

Staff at Prinknash Bird and Deer Park in Cranham, near Gloucester, believe the deer leapt the fence to have a twilight tryst with a stag called Boris.

Last year, Boris himself was blamed for leaping into the enclosure when no-one was looking.

However, this year the stag had so many females to contend with, it is believed the frustrated doe herself went in seach of his affections.

Park owner Philip Meigh, 76, said her actions were understandable as Boris is a particularly handsome stag.

FARMERS' LEADERS HAVE welcomed the launch of public information leaflets about import restrictions for holidaymakers.

NFU Food Standards chairman Michael Seals described the DEFRA leaflet's core message 'If in doubt, keep it out' launched by Antony Worrall-Thompson, as a useful reminder for holidaymakers that restrictions are in place.

However, he said food and plant allowances still remained too complex and an EU-wide ban on personal imports would be simpler and better.

BLACK GROUSE AND golden plover are just two rare bird species set to benefit from the RSPB's purchase of an upland farm in Cumbria in a move aimed at boosting wildlife.

The acquisition of Tarn House Farm, near Brampton, was made possible thanks to cash support from a number of groups.

RSPB reserves manager Dave Barrett said that Tarn House Farm is expected to be an outstanding area for moorland birds such as the black grouse, golden plover and hen harrier.

He said:"We are thrilled to have acquired this very special part of the North Pennines, which gives us the opportunity to actively manage this area to enhance its potential for wildlife. In a few years time, the area around Tarn House Farm will be an oasis for wildlife as a range of important habitats are restored here.

"Although already part of our Geltsdale nature reserve, until now we have not owned the freehold of the land and so our hands have been tied over doing any significant wildlife habitat improvement work.

"From today we can begin to make a real difference to the wildlife value of this superb site, although it will take many years of work and continued investment to achieve our ultimate vision."

Tarn House Farm has existed for centuries and will continue to be farmed, he said, but running alongside its traditional upland sheep-farm role will be new conservation initiatives.

The Society paid in excess of £750,000 to buy the land with the purchase made possible thanks to grant aid from the Heritage Lottery Fund (£263,000), the Countryside Agency (£221,000) and English Nature (£9,000).

SALMON RETURNING TO the River Avon in Dorset will be more accurately recorded with the installation of two new 'fish counters'.

A similar underwater counting system already exists elsewhere but under certain river conditions it can be bypassed by salmon.

Having two automatic counters positioned at the Christchurch site will enable the Environment Agency to monitor salmon with greater accuracy.

"Accurate information on the number of salmon returning to the River Avon is a fundamental requirement of effective stock management and the new counters will take us a step closer to achieving this," explained Agency spokesman Andy Stevens.

Construction work starts shortly when contractors move on site and the new system should be up and running by the autumn.

A nearby public footpath, part of the Avon Valley trail, will remain open during the work.

THE WAR BETWEEN hunt groups and anti-hunt campaigners has been intensifying in London with hapless hounds now the focus of fresh animosity.

According to the League Against Cruel Sports, a fierce critic of hunting, plans by the Union of Country Sports Workers to bring hounds into the capital again were ditched after the League and others complained to police.

Met officers had apparently promised to investigate the League's claims that the dogs were causing a serious hazard on the capital's busy roads.

"The decision on hounds by the Union of Country Sports Workers follows complaints of traffic chaos caused by their last protest on May 22," claimed a spokesman for the League.

"At the time protesters implied they would bring hounds again, telling the Shooting Times that the hounds 'enjoyed it a lot, they might want to come back again'.

"But the League has since discovered the Union of Country Sports Workers won't be bringing hounds onto the streets again unless hunting is banned.

"Meanwhile, the League is waiting for the Metropolitan Police to clarify the law, which makes it an offence to 'suffer to be at large any unmuzzled ferocious dog.' The matter has been referred to their legal services department."

Douglas Batchelor, chief executive of the League, added:"The hunters have made it very clear on several occasions that they consider hounds to be ferocious dogs that would be impossible to re-home in the event of any hunt ban. If this is the case then surely they have broken the law by bringing these ferocious animals, unmuzzled, into the centre of London.

"The hunters will now probably try and deny that the hounds are ferocious, in which case we would be proved right all along that these animals could, in fact, be happily re-homed."

THE 'SPIRIT OF Trees' is the haunting theme of a conference now being organised where nature lovers will explore the "symbolic powers and mystical connections" of trees.

The conference, from October 5 to 12 at the Findhorn Foundation in Morayshire, Scotland , is part of Treefest Scotland 2002, a festival of events throughout the year which celebrate the country's trees, woods and forests.

Organised jointly by the Findhorn Foundation and the Forestry Commission, a spokesman said:"Writers and speakers from many parts of the world will be at the conference, which is believed to be the first of its kind in the world , and will give people the opportuni -ty to learn about how other cultures live with trees.

"The line-up includes a healer who uses tree imagery for inner healing and a native North American with special connections with the black ash tree. There will be workshops, concerts, sacred tree dancing, multimedia shows, a tree-planting ritual, basket-making, and a woodcrafts market ."

RURAL COMMUNITIES ARE being held back in the slow lane of internet communication by BT, claims the Countryside Alliance.

Chief executive Richard Burge said:"If broadband is the future of communication then it must be available across the board. It is not. Rural areas have been sidelined from broadband."

CONTROVERSIAL PLANS FOR new GM crop trial sites have been revealed by the Government despite mounting opposition from many farmers and conservationists.

"Depending on weather and soil conditions, sowing of GM oilseed rape is expected from August 19 onwards," said a Downing Street spokesman.

"This is the last year of the three-year programme of Farm-Scale Evaluations.

"The Independent Scientific Steering Committee, which oversees the evaluation programme, has approved the selection of 18 oilseed rape sites to be included in the autumn 2002 sowing round.

"The total number of sites over the three-year programme is unchanged at 60-75 for each crop. The list of autumn locations was agreed between the steering committee, the research consortium, SCIMAC (the farming and biotechnology industry body) and farmers.

"The Government believes that it is important for people to know as soon as possible what is happening in their neighbourhoods. The announcement comes six weeks before the first seeds are to be sown in order to give people time to find out about evaluations in their area.

"Detailed information on the FSE programme is being sent by DEFRA to parish councils and local authorities in host areas."

DOLPHIN FANS ARE being given the chance to study the popular creatures as part of new research undertaken by marine scientists.

The Mammal Society and Sea Watch Foundation will be running three training courses involving dolphins at Cardigan Bay Marine Wildlife Centre in New Quay, West Wales.

"Cardigan Bay has the UK's only truly resident population of bottlenose dolphins that are accessible and can be seen from the land," said a spokesman.

"Participants can expect to see bottlenose dolphins and harbour porpoise as well as seals and seabirds. Courses consist of illustrated lectures and video presentations as well as headland watches and boat surveys aboard the MV Sulaire."

Two types of course are on offer.

These are the Beginners' Weekends which cost £89 and give an introduction to UK whales and dolphins and the problems they face, and a three-day Advanced Course.

This costs £135 and covers surveying and monitoring techniques.

"These courses are part of a three-year project organised by The Mammal Society and Sea Watch Foundation to train cetacean surveyors and contribute monitoring information to the National Cetacean Sightings Network," added the spokesman.

THE TURKEY-SIZED great bustard could be about to stage a remarkable comeback in Britain after dying out here nearly 200 years ago.

The bird was once common in Suffolk and Norfolk before hunters drove it to extinction around the 1830s.

Conservationists are currently seeking a licence from DEFRA to transport great bustard chicks from the Russian steppes next spring.

The Great Bustard Steering Group aims to introduce about 20 chicks a year for the next five to 10 years to build numbers up.

The birds can weigh up to 35 pounds with cocks reaching 40 inches in height and, although not the fastest of fliers, have sturdy legs to flee at speed from predators.

Dr Patrick Osborne, a scientific adviser backing the steering group, said:"Bringing the great bustard back is the last big challenge to conservationists. We aim to put back what we had 200 years ago."

GREEDY HEDGEHOGS UNDER threat of death have now had their plight raised in the House of Lords.

All 5,000 hedgehogs on the Scottish island of Uist have been given a stay of execution for the time being after conservationists decided to rethink plans to slaughter them.

The prickly creatures - threatening the survival of wild birds on the island by feasting on their eggs - have rocketed in numbers from just a handful introduced in the 1920s.

But in the House of Lords, some members praised the errant hedgehogs and called for them to be transferred to England to help gardeners.

Liberal Democrat environment spokesman Baroness Miller said:"English gardeners are crying out for hedgehogs to predate on slugs, which are an enormous problem in a wet summer like this."

GREY PARTRIDGES HAVE been recorded in Britain as far back as the Iron Age, reveals the Game Conservancy Trust which uses the birds to help preview a new exhibition.

Under the theme 'Farming and Wildlife - Past, Present and Future', the Trust's stand at this year's CLA Game Fair "graphically explains the fascinating interaction between man, beast, flora and fauna, since farming methods were first developed," according to a spokesman.

"Designed to entertain, educate and inspire both younger and older visitors, The Trust has delved deep into our historical past - from Neolithic up to the present day - to accurately depict farming methods through the ages and explain how the countryside has dramatically changed, often to the detriment of the wildlife that it supports.

"The grey partridge, which has been recorded as far back as the Iron Age, is one of our truly native farmland gamebirds but due to modern farming methods its numbers have dwindled so much that it is now a Biodiversity Action Plan Species.

"The Game Conservancy Trust is the lead partner for the plan which aims to improve stocks to some 150,000 pairs by 2010.

"The exhibition display area will depict different farming eras and a wide range of historical farming implements, fencing and even an Iron Age round house. The overriding message of the exhibition is to learn from our past in order to make a positive contribution to the health of our wildlife in the future."

COUNTRY CAMPAIGNERS face a fresh round of bitter battles with planners as new housing developments threaten more pressure on Britain's precious Green Belt areas.

Even before John Prescott gave the go-ahead for an explosion of new building work, conservation groups had condemned the notion that sprawling estates could fit snugly into new areas with little impact on existing rural communities and wildlife.

And although Chancellor Gordon Brown has pledged to concentrate fresh social housing on brownfield sites, the Council for the Protection of Rural England warns of the dangers in any massive development scheme.

Neil Sinden, CPRE's assistant director, said:"A boost to social housing offers the potential to increase investment in deprived urban areas, make better use of previously used land and buildings, and deliver high quality, higher density housing which better meets the nation's housing needs.

"We welcome the Chancellor's commitment to making good use of our urban areas and protecting the countryside. But this will not be achieved by side-stepping the planning system or ignoring the views of local communities in town and country."

The Government, he said, should ensure that new housing development resulted from a long term planning strategy which local communities had helped develop, based on maximising opportunities for urban renewal and minimising any countryside loss.

The plans should form part of a national strategy to take pressure off the over-heated South East and tackle areas of low housing demand in other regions.

Mr Sinden added:"For too long Governments have relied on private housebuilders to meet the bulk of the nation's need for affordable housing. This has manifestly failed to deliver the right type of housing in the right location. It has fuelled the exodus from urban areas, deprived towns and cities of much needed investment, and resulted in an unsustainable, car-based urban sprawl."

FARMERS' LEADERS HAVE welcomed the call by the European Commission for France to be fined the equivalent of £100,000 a day for its cynical ban on British beef.

NFU president Ben Gill said:"We can only hope that the threat of this financial penalty will finally bring the French Government to its senses. This debacle has dragged on for far too long."

The news follows an NFU letter to European Commission president Romano Prodi demanding action after France failed to respond to the latest request by the Commission to lift its illegal embargo.

THE CAPERCAILLE HAS been boosted by a £5million conservation project aimed at ensuring it never becomes extinct in Scotland again.

A funding package, put together over 18 months by the Caledonian Partnership, involves cash from the Forestry Commission, Scottish Natural Heritage, the RSPB, the Cairngorms Partnership, the Scottish Executive, and the EU.

The scheme also involves more than 25 private forest owners.

A Forestry Commission spokesman said:"The capercaillie is the biggest grouse in the world and in Scotland depends mainly on Scots pine forests for successful breeding and for its main winter food of pine needles.

"It became extinct in Scotland in the late 18th Century due to a combination of habitat loss and hunting, which coincided with a period when summers were cold and wet.

"It was successfully reintroduced from Sweden in the early 19th Century. However, since the late 1970s it has declined from an estimated 20,000 birds to fewer than a thousand today.

"The project will form the core of a wider strategy to try to reverse the decline in numbers. It will work in partnership with private and public forest owners to establish and monitor new management techniques and restore forest habitat.

"The aim is to improve breeding success and increase the overall capercaillie population."

HUNGRY COWS BROKE down a fence and munched through rows of pampered cabbages days before the impressive vegetables were to be judged in a gardening competition.

Gardeners who tend the allotment site in Newport, Shropshire, were left distraught when the disaster was revealed.

As well as eating the cabbages, the 16 cows also chomped through carrots and runner beans and trampled the carefully maintained site underfoot.

Months of work were destroyed in minutes with the gardeners left so upset that Newport Town Council is thinking of compensating them.

A RECORD 500 dolphins were discovered fatally stranded on Britain's shores in the last year, research by The Wildlife Trusts has revealed.

Post mortems proved that the vast majority had been injured or drowned in fishing nets.

A report by the Trusts has also warned that bottlenose dolphins could become extinct in our waters within 10 years if nothing is done to help them.

Dr Simon Lyster, director general of the Trusts, said:"Our marine environment is in much more trouble than people realise.

"We are still fishing in ways that result in the deaths of hundreds of dolphins and porpoises each year, and in the destruction of rare marine habitats."

A JACK RUSSELL terrier survived tumbling 50ft down a disused mineshaft and being trapped for three days.

The pet, named Tiny, was finally rescued when its yelps were heard and the emergency services were called to the former tin mine near Truro in Cornwall.

A fireman was lowered into the shaft and found the dog hungry and thirsty but otherwise unhurt at the bottom.Tiny's owner, Jeanette Evans, had scoured the area before realising her missing pet had plunged down the shaft located in a field close to her house.

THE WOODLAND TRUST is appealing for more people to take part in research aimed at building a vital picture of the effects of climate change on our trees.

"Down the ages the oak and ash tree have been used as living barometers to test whether the summer weather will be rainy or dry," said a spokesman."If the 'oak (leafs) before the ash, then we're in for just a splash'. If the 'ash before the oak, then we're in for a soak'.

"Now this folklore is being both reinforced and challenged by an award-winning project called Nature's Calendar, a collaboration between the Trust and the Centre for Ecology and Hydrology.

"Volunteer phenologists are taking part in the project to record the timings of natural events such as arrival of birds or the first flowering of plants, and are reporting a marked increase in oak leafing before ash.

"Their observations reinforce trends discovered by earlier phenologists showing the oak responding far faster to warmer temperatures due to climate change than ash. Oak is leafing up to 10 days earlier than it did 20 years ago."

Nick Collinson, conservation policy adviser at the Trust, added:"This new data has serious implications for woodland. If some trees such as oak, sycamore and horse chestnut are coming into leaf earlier than others they will gain a competitive advantage. Their early leafing will cast shade over their slower neighbours. It will mean many winners and losers as species of animals and plants fight for survival."

MORE THAN 500 fish died in a quiet brook when a dairy farmer allowed slurry to seep into it, Worcester magistrates heard.

The farmer, from Evesham, pleaded guilty to a charge of polluting Battleton Brook before he was fined £2,000 and ordered to pay £1,066 costs.

The court was told that on January 16 last year, the Environment Agency was alerted to a pollution incident at the brook.

When an officer visited the site, he found 546 dead fish from five different species with signs indicating that the pollution had been caused by slurry.

A probe revealed that it had seeped into the brook due to a faulty slurry pump having been replaced by an inadequate one.

In mitigation, Richard Wilkes told the court that the incident was an unforeseeable, unintentional pump failure over Christmas and that bad weather had contributed to the situation.

However, speaking after the case, John Kelly, an Agency environment protection officer, said:"People handling potentially polluting substances have a responsibility to ensure that they make every effort to keep them under control at all times."

BIRDWATCHERS ARE CELEBRATING after a pair of bee-eaters hatched chicks in this country for the first time in nearly 50 years.

With their 'kaleidoscopic plumage', bee-eaters are said to be one of the most beautiful species in Europe and news of their successful breeding is expected to draw thousands of visitors to the Durham village of Bishop Middleham.

The birds arrived there on strong southerly winds at the start of June and had soon exchanged their normal nesting area in southern Europe for a disused local quarry.

Mark Thomas, of the RSPB, said:"Bee-eaters are stunning birds and to have a pair nesting again in the UK after nearly half a century is an amazing event. They have brought a brilliant splash of unexpected continental colour to northern England this year."

Kevin Spindloe, wildlife warden at the quarry, added:"Now that the eggs have hatched, we expect that many people, and not just keen birdwatchers, will want to come and be part of this event.

"A larger, third viewing area has now been set aside for visitors, with telescopes available for visitors to use. We hope that over the coming weeks many visitors will enjoy watching these beautiful birds.

"The Durham Wildlife Trust and the RSPB wish to acknowledge the invaluable support provided by local people, volunteers and police, who have helped watch over the nesting location to prevent disturbance to the bee-eaters."

The rarity of the birds has made the bee-eaters a potential target for wildlife thieves and a military-style operation with 24-hour surveillance will continue at the site.

Bee-eaters were last recorded breeding in the UK in 1955 when two pairs nested in a sand-pit in Sussex and raised seven young.

Before that, their only other known nesting attempt was in Scotland in 1920 but normally they nest no nearer to the UK than Paris.

The behaviour of the adults first alerted observers that the eggs had hatched with both parents now delivering food to the chicks.

Bee-eaters lay their eggs at the end of a burrow which can be up to three metres long, dug into vertical cliff-faces.

The chicks will not leave their underground nest site until next month so the number of chicks hatched is still not known.

BLUE TITS LIKE to raise chicks in nests decked out with a variety of pungent plants such as lavender and mint to help ward off parasites, fungi, and harmful insects, according to research published in Nature magazine.

A LLAMA CALLED 'Spot' is proving a blot on the landscape for foxes and other predators which it furiously chases away from sheep on a West Sussex farm.

Owner Sue Booth says dozens of newborn lambs were being lost before she invested in the South American guard animal at her Henfield property.

But she and her husband Peter are not alone in taking on llamas to protect sheep in their fields.

The animals are said to be gaining popularity fast among sheep farmers because they have an affinity with their woolly charges and are not afraid to come to their aid.

CONSERVATIONISTS ARE gearing up for one of their toughest ever battles aimed at stopping Government airport expansion plans decimating wildlife.

Controversial proposals outlined by Transport Secretary Alistair Darling include a third runway at Heathrow airport and a new four-runway airport at Cliffe near the River Thames in north Kent.

The RSPB said:"Following speculation early in the year, the RSPB's chief executive Graham Wynne wrote to John Spellar in March 2002 and made it clear that we would oppose vigorously any proposal for an international airport at Cliffe as it threatened internationally important wildlife wetlands and our own reserves in north Kent.

"The RSPB will do everything in its power to prevent an airport at Cliffe becoming a reality and will welcome the full support of others to ensure success. We have already appointed Perry Haines to co-ordinate the 'No Airport at Cliffe' campaign."

However, while pledging to defend wildlife equally fiercely, English Nature has struck a more conciliatory pose.

It says it "welcomes the strategic approach to this issue taken by the Government and will engage positively in the consultation process."

A BLACK LABRADOR which plunged overboard off its owner's yacht near the Isle of Wight managed to swim 10 miles to safety.

Peter Loizou feared the worst when a four-hour search for his pet dog Todd ended in failure.

But as he was trying to come to terms with the apparent loss of his beloved pet, the dog was still struggling for life at sea.

The two-year-old labrador never gave up until it reached the shore near the New Forest in Hampshire where it was found exhausted a few hours later - just eight miles from home in Cadnam.

Police traced Todd's owner from a microchip buried in the animal's skin.

BIRDS ARE DECLINING even faster in urban areas as useful man-made spaces disappear under the bulldozer, it has been claimed.

Leading birdwatcher Andy Horton says wildlife is suffering as more playing fields and allotments are built over, remaining wasteland is developed, and housing becomes more densely packed.

"Loss of playing fields is much more common than the loss of allotments, and the birds displaced are mainly kestrels and oystercatchers," he said.

But loss of allotments was bad news for song thrushes, greenfinches, blackbirds, and robins, as well as snakes and lizards, he explained.

"Town cramming is even more serious and build - ing on these last refuges results in the disappearace of jays, woodpeckers, titmice, thrushes, and spar - rowhawks," added Sussex-based Andy, who also highlighted urban cat numbers as another problem.

THE COUNTRYSIDE ALLIANCE is urging its members to seize a golden opportunity to promote its views on saving hunting.

Chairman John Jackson explained:"Between now and the end of September there is a huge opportunity for us all. It is now certain that the process of consultation which the Government is running will include three days of hearings in September, in public and within the precincts of Parliament.

"These three days, which will be chaired by Alun Michael, the Minister responsible, will be centred on evidence to be given by experts on questions put to them.

"The starting point will be the Burns Inquiry. The questions to be addressed by those experts will relate to the areas of utility, cruelty and the practical aspects of any legislation based on utility and the need to avoid cruelty.

"The experts will be examined by us and others on their evidence. The proceedings will be available to the television channels, including BBC Parliament.

"These public proceedings will take place on September 9, 10 and 11 - i.e. two working weeks before the March on September 22. For this reason it is now even more important that the March is the largest that London has ever seen.

"It is also important that it is demonstrably a march by peaceful but determined people pressing for hunting and all rural matters to be dealt with fairly, without prejudice and on the evidence.

"It is not possible to over emphasise the significance of the coming two months. We owe it to our countryside and each other to make the most of it and to do so in ways which attract warm public sympathy and support."

DARTMOOR PONIES WILL be boosted by a new website being set up by the Friends of the Dartmoor Hill Pony aimed at raising the animals' profile and making them more valuable in the market place. At the moment, many are sold for small change or shot as worthless.

RAMBLERS HAVE PLEDGED to continue their battle with controversial landowner Nicholas van Hoogstraten, even though he has just been found guilty of manslaughter.

The multi-millionaire, convicted of hiring two men to attack business rival Mohammed Raja, is still involved in a 12-year dispute with walkers over a public footpath which crosses his Sussex estate.

A Ramblers Association spokesman said:"Mr van Hoogstraten caused widespread outrage when he described anyone who wished to use the footpath as 'scum of the earth' and 'the great unwashed'. Walkers who attempted to use the path were frequently subjected to intimidation and threats.

"As a result of four court actions brought by the Association, Lewes Magistrates Court ordered the obstructions removed as well as imposing substantial fines on the landowner.

"But the fines totalling over £85,000 remain unpaid and the Highway Authority at East Sussex County Council has failed to carry out the court order.

"Kate Ashbrook, chair of the Association's Access Committee, who brought the original case, is currently taking East Sussex County Council to court for failing to clear the obstructions. The case goes to appeal in October."

241

ANTS: savage fire game almost ended in disaster

RUTHLESSLY efficient, ants would probably be ruling the Earth by now if only they were not so tiny.

Black and red ants - our two most common species - measure only about four millimetres in length but their awesome energy and strength help them construct comparatively huge nests.

By living in colonies, they also achieve far greater protection than they ever could themselves and are a force to be reckoned with if attacked.

Each colony comprises three distinct kinds of individual - a single, all powerful queen which lays the eggs; subordinate males which mate with the queen; and undeveloped females called workers which specialise in tasks such as guarding the nest or looking after the eggs.

Each summer, when the weather is humid, young winged ants burst out of the nest and take to the skies.

After mating, the males die but the females become individual queens ready to start their own colonies.

When she has bitten off her own wings, a solitary queen burrows into the soil to lay an initial batch of eggs.

These develop into worker ants which begin the enormous task of building another nest.

The pampered queen then concentrates on the only job left to her - laying more and more eggs until the nest becomes a teeming mass of life.

Ancient civilizations often revered ants and even in the Bible (Proverbs) the idle can read:*"Go to the ant, thou sluggard. Consider her ways and be wise."*

Children, too, are often enthralled by ants.

When I was a child, our gang used to spend hours tramping around local woods and moors specifically looking for ants' nests.

Every likely stone was flipped over to reveal either nothing at all or an impressive, seething ant city.

Unfortunately, we were not very politically correct.

One of our worst tricks was to take a platoon of red ants and introduce them forcibly into a nest of black ants.

The ensuing battle made the violent movie 'Gladiator' look like a picnic.

Next, a cohort of black ants would be introduced into a red ants' nest and so on, until our cruel fascination was sated.

Among our number was an older boy, the only smoker.

He delighted in squirting lighter fuel into the nests.

That done, he would toss in a match to bring down a holocaust on the ants.

This worked well enough until one fateful day when he let me have a go.

But instead of concentrating the fuel on the nest I spilt some onto a surrounding mass of tinder dry gorse bushes.

Within a minute, the bushes had exploded into flames shooting 15ft into the air.

I was lucky not to be incinerated along with the ants.

It was only after staring, open mouthed, at my terrifying handiwork that I noticed everyone else had scarpered.

For days afterwards, I walked around with one side of my face painfully scorched red.

Served me right, too.

I steered clear of ants' nests for a while after that.

GLOW WORMS HAVE been found in the new Loch Lomond and Trossachs National Park - the first recorded Scottish sighting of the phosphorescent beetles in years.

And in a double triumph for wildlife enthusiasts, within hours of that find, the rare and elusive nightjar was also confirmed as being present in the area.

The twin discoveries have been hailed as "a major milestone" in the drive to boost the variety of Scotland's plants, insects, animals and birds.

Stirling biodiversity officer Jonathan Willet, who discovered the glow worms during a night search, said:"The fact rare species like this are being sighted in the National Park shows what an important area it is for all kinds of wildlife.

"Glow worms are incredible creatures and finding them for the first time in the Aberfoyle area was an extremely exciting and rewarding moment."

His find had been prompted by local forest district manager Hugh Clayden who briefly spotted what he thought could be glow worms while out searching for nightjars.

Within hours of their glow worm success foresters were celebrating again when the first nightjar sighting in eight years was also confirmed.

Hugh explained:"Following up Jonathan's confirmation of the glow worms we decided to include that general area in our search for the elusive nightjar. Shortly before midnight a small group of us, including Jonathan, were fortunate enough to see and hear this remarkable visitor from Africa."

A RECORD NUMBER of visitors flocked to this year's CLA Game Fair at Broadlands, Hampshire, organisers have revealed.

The three-day countryside extravaganza attracted 126,000 people.

"As the crowds poured in, thermometers went up and visitor and sales records were broken on many areas of the showground," said a spokesman.

"The international flavour of the Game Fair was underlined when American Steve Choate won the Musto International Spey Casting Championship with an amazing 50-yard cast on Hampshire's premier chalk stream river - the River Test. The salmon even played their part as one rose to a fly during the finals."

Philip Weatherliegh-Davies, of the Salmon and Trout Association, added:"Things don't get much more exciting than the final of that championship.

"We had two Americans come over from Washington State especially to compete. We then had a tie for first place and had to stage a cast off. There were some amazing skills on show."

Game Fair director David Hough, added:"This has been a fantastic show. To have beaten our all-time attendance record is really quite amazing."

A PREMIER PIKE and bream lake has been saved from destruction following a bizarre pollution incident involving a milk tanker.

Almost 20,000 litres of milk are estimated to have threatened Staffordshire's Rudyard Reservoir after the tanker was involved in an accident nearby.

Environment Agency protection officers worked late into the night to arrest the flow of milk after the tanker crashed into a bridge over a brook which runs directly into the reservoir.

Staffordshire Fire and Rescue Service, Severn Trent Water, Staffordshire Moorlands District Council, and a local builders' merchant also joined in the emergency clean-up.

"Milk has a devastating affect on aquatic environments, stripping the water of oxygen and, depending on the nature of the watercourse and the amount of milk spilt, killing many types of wildlife present, including fish," explained a spokesman.

"Agency officers attended the scene and worked with firemen to retain the spilt milk in the brook. Booms were deployed on the drainage channel which feeds the reservoir and dams were built using sandbags."

Agency team leader Susan Bowen added:"Although there is some discoloration in the feeder channel and the final impact is yet to be clarified, it appears that by working together, the various organisations involved in this incident have prevented a massive fish kill."

RARE GREAT CRESTED newts are being gobbled up by an alien intruder called Crusty at a lake in Wigan.

The terrapin, which has only three legs, earned his nickname because his shell is said to resemble a meat pie in both shape and colour.

As has happened elsewhere, it seems Crusty is a former pet that was dumped in the lake to fend for himself but is coping remarkably well.

However, the lake is home to the newts and a variety of bird life - both on the menu for the 3ft red eared terrapin.

The hungry predator has even been observed launching an assault on a grebe's nest.

THOUSANDS OF GIANT bonfires will light up the countryside on September 16 in a blaze of publicity for the London March six days later, the Countryside Alliance has revealed.

Other beacons will be lit abroad and there will also be "a synchronised launching of Livelihood rockets spreading the message across the country," according a spokesman.

"Europe, USA, Hong Kong and Australia have pledged support so far - this is a tangible way that our far-flung supporters can support the British countryside.

"The Liberty Beacons aim to involve every village or town in the UK to encourage the widest possible attendance, last stage registrations, and reinforce local community marching spirit."

In another move, meant to coincide with the launch of a national anti-hunt roadshow, the Alliance's Campaign for Hunting has released a new report about hunting with dogs.

This is said to examine the views of several significant leaders and members of the animal rights movement over the last 30 years.

BATS ARE GETTING a boost after former England cricketer David Gower agreed to 'open the batting' for European Bat Night on August 24.

Bats are said to be under threat as never before but with David's help The Woodland Trust and the Bat Conservation Trust hope to improve awareness of the animals.

By taking part in European Bat Night and other related events around the country, young and old alike are being invited to discover more about the twilight creatures.

David said:"As you might imagine, I'm all in favour of batting averages rising for cricketers but I am also very keen to see that things improve for the bat - not the one made out of willow, the other one.

"Although bats and their roosts are legally protected, they are often persecuted because what little people know about these wonderful creatures is based on falsehood and myth. Many bat habitats, such as trees and woods, are not fully protected, which adds to the pressures faced by bats. To learn more about these wonderful flying mammals, contact your local bat group for information about European Bat Night and other activities near you."

David's five favourite bats are:-

Pipistrelles:"loved by children because they are so tiny. On average, a pipistrelle weighs about five grams - less than a £1 coin. At only 4cm long, if it folded its wings it could fit into a matchbox."

Brown long-eared bat:"adored by many because of its big, long ears, big eyes and 'smiley' mouth".

Horseshoe bat:"cherished for its rarity. It is estimated that in Britain the number of greater horseshoe bats has declined by over 90 per cent".

Noctule bat:"big and beautiful, these can be quite a handful."

Leisler's bat:"king of bats because of its 'lion's mane-look' created by the fur around its shoulders and upper back".

CRABS WERE THE target in an annual summer competition at a Suffolk coastal village.

Almost 600 children and adults fished for the clawed crustaceans at Walberswick where the winning crab weighed just 3oz - far short of the 1981 record of 7.25oz.

Actress Caroline Quentin, who lives locally, presented the crab hunt champion's trophy to Suffolk schoolboy Ashley Welsh, aged 11.

Hot weather may have driven the bigger crabs out of reach of their pursuers during the British Crabbing Championship event, according to officials.

All crabs were later returned to the sea.

SCOTTISH HUNT GROUPS have suffered a bitter blow after their bid to overturn a ban on hunting in Scotland failed.

The Court of Session in Edinburgh rejected a challenge by the Scottish Countryside Alliance against a new law banning hunting with hounds.

Pro-hunt campaigners had been hoping to stop the Protection of Wild Mammals (Scotland) Act coming into force.

Allan Murray, director of the Scottish Countryside Alliance, pledged to keep fighting to protect the individual from unacceptable political dogma.

"This legislation will shatter livelihoods and businesses in rural Scotland," he warned."Yet the court appears to have merely rubber-stamped the Act passed by the Scottish Parliament."

However, the same decision left anti-hunt campaigners overjoyed.

Les Ward, leader of the Scottish Campaign Against Hunting with Dogs, said:"We are all delighted that the judge has confirmed hunting will end.

"At long last this barbaric sport will no longer be practised on Scottish soil and foxes, hares and mink will be spared the unbearable suffering of being chased and killed by a pack of dogs.

"We believe that hunting is cruel and unnecessary and MSPs were fully justified in following their constituents' wish to ban it.

"The will of the Scottish Parliament was always clear on this issue, and this has been reflected by the judge's decision today."

Meanwhile, the fledgling Countryside Party has launched a recruitment drive to raise cash for the Scottish elections in May 2003.

Leader Jim Crawford is looking for 300 new members to help the party capitalise on "voter apathy".

HONEY BEES ARE getting a boost in their battle against a deadly parasite which has already wiped out up to 70 per cent of colonies - from fungi.

Tests have revealed that the fungi is successful at killing Varroa, the parasitic mite that fatally weakens bees and has had a devastating effect on the British honey industry.

Research has shown that the tiny mites are becoming increasingly resistant to chemical curbs which, in addition, may do more long-term harm than good.

However, investigations at the Horticulture Research International Association in Warwickshire have revealed that special fungi could soon take over the task of killing the mites before they can kill bees.

Now the only problem involves producing a saleable version of the fungi fast for beekeepers before the mites wreak more havoc.

A PIG MADE a bid to save its bacon by fleeing an abattoir in Scotland and taking to nearby woods.

Police and slaughterhouse workers tried to track down the 100kg black boar and return it to meet its fate.

However, their initial efforts were foiled following the incident at Dunblane, Stirlingshire, and the animal remained at large.

Police decided to leave the pig in the wood overnight as visibility deteriorated.

They warned the animal could be dangerous if cornered.

THE PROSPECT OF hundreds of seals being washed up dead on UK shores could become a reality, scientists fear.

A devastating virus that has been wiping out seals across Europe has now spread to UK waters with the first few corpses already discovered.

Five seals washed up on beaches around East Anglia and Lincolnshire all died from the phocine distemper virus.

Their discovery was an ominous reminder of what occurred across Europe in 1988 when almost 20,000 dead or dying seals were left scattered on beaches and in coastal waters after contracting PDV.

Paul Jepson, of the UK Institute of Zoology, said:"In 1988, some 50-60 per cent of common seals in Europe died. This could be a major threat to their long-term viability."

Initially, the virus returned to Denmark back in May and is estimated to have killed 2,000 seals since then, not only in Denmark but also in Norway and Sweden.

Scientists fear PDV will rapidly spread down the UK east coast, leaving seals dying on a variety of English and Scottish beaches, before spreading to the west coast and Ireland.

According to the RSPCA, the virus is a particularly frustrating enemy because there is no treatment available and no way of preventing seals in the wild contracting it.

PVD is similar to distemper among dogs causing the same onset of flu-like symptoms and death.

RABBITS TURNED ACCIDENTAL archaeologists to uncover the remnants of a precious glass window centuries old.

The furry burrowers unwittingly unearthed pieces of the window thought to come from a 14th Century manor house.

As they excavated a Warwickshire mound, the rodents brought to light several pieces of hand-painted medieval glass.

Now the exact location of the site is being kept secret by English Nature until it can ensure its security against further disturbance.

Meanwhile, glass experts are working to preserve the materials which are thought to be in danger of deterioration after being exposed.

A WILDLIFE CENTRE has taken receipt of an angler's angry catch - a huge snapping turtle.

Paul Backhouse heaved the 23-pound creature in after hooking it at Ashby Ville Lake in Scunthorpe, using mussels as bait.

The animal thrashed and growled as it emerged from the water, startling the angler who initially believed it to be a large fish.

Taking care not to lose a finger in its powerful jaws, Mr Backhouse freed the hook from the turtle's mouth and later handed it to the sanctuary.

BADGER FANS HAVE reacted with fury to what they say are plans by some conservation groups to paint the powerful creatures in an excessively negative light.

To back up its claims, the National Federation of Badger Groups said it had "obtained documents from a meeting organised by the British Association for Shooting and Conservation, in partnership with organisations including the Game Conservancy Trust, the National Farmers' Union, the Countryside Alliance, the Union of Country Sports Workers and the National Gamekeepers' Organisation.

"The so-called 'Snares Liaison Group', under planned 'future work', agreed 'that, with care, the excessive popularity of badgers needs to be reversed and the problematic image of the fox maintained!'

"The meeting was held on April 23, 2002, to address concern amongst farming and country sports organisations that further restrictions may be placed on the use of snares.

"The NFBG has recently published a report outlining how snares are cruel and indiscriminate. The report demonstrates that many badgers and other animals die painful and protracted deaths because illegal 'self-locking' snares are still being widely used.

"The illegal 'self-locking' snare has a ratchet action, getting tighter and tighter as an animal pulls to get free. Permitted 'free-running' snares should not tighten in this way, but often produce the same result by twisting or tangling."

Dr Elaine King, chief executive of the NFBG, added:"These countryside organisations claim to support nature conservation. In reality, their sole objective appears to be the ruthless exploitation of the countryside at any cost to wildlife. By planning to vilify badgers through exploiting the media, these organisations seemingly reveal their true colours.

"Until recently, for example, some of these organisations have claimed that badgers harm other wildlife by destroying the eggs of rare ground nesting birds. Now, scientists have shown that badgers and even foxes have relatively little impact on ground nesting birds, compared to cattle, which cause four times as much damage.

"Real conservation organisations like the NFBG base their claims on robust scientific research. In contrast, these countryside bodies apparently prefer to rely on myth and spin to argue their case."

ORGANIC FARMERS HAVE hailed the Government's new organic action plan as a huge boost to their ambitions.

The objective of the scheme is to more than double UK-grown organic food and ensure that British farmers supply at least 70 per cent of the domestic organic market.

Patrick Holden, director of the Soil Association, said:"This is a major breakthrough for organic farmers. Immediate on-going payments will start to put our farmers on a level playing field with those in Europe and will help increase the amount of organic food produced here.

"The Government now recognises the significant benefits to society delivered by organic farming and has stated that it is better for wildlife, has high animal welfare standards, and causes lower pollution."

COCKLE FISHERMEN HAVE had their hearts warmed with news that they should be able to harvest cockles again on the Dee estuary from September 16 until the end of October.

The Environment Agency, which is responsible for the regulation and management of the estuary, is now consulting with fishermen and conservation bodies on the proposals.

This follows a survey of cockle numbers which showed that they have recovered to allow more harvesting without threatening stock levels.

Cockling on the estuary is a traditional activity which is carried out by hand at low tide with cockles checked to ensure only the largest are removed.

However, the cockle industry has declined over the past 20 years, partly because of 'over-cropping'.

Since the estuary is also internationally important for its wildfowl and waders, the recent improvement in cockle stocks is also considered good news for those birds which feed on them.

Nigel Kendrick, the Agency's area fisheries manager, said:"There are still lessons to be learnt about factors affecting cockle stocks in the Dee estuary and how best to manage them.

"We need to address this issue in partnership with others but we believe that allowing more harvesting of large cockles that would otherwise die off naturally is in everyone's best interest."

A GIANT FISH which reportedly dragged a swan underwater is being hunted at Martin Mere wildlife centre in Lancashire.

The fish, dubbed the 'Monster of the Mere', has apparently been sighted several times and is thought to be responsible for various alarming incidents besides the swan being pulled down.

Experts believe the fish may be a huge Russian wels catfish and recently a four-man team from the Centre for Fortean Zoology spent five days at Martin Mere trying to catch it.

A spokesman for The Wildfowl Trust, which owns the lake, said of the team:"During their investigation they are said to have had three sightings of a large fish with oily black skin. They also state that their fish finder registered a large sonar blip. But it is yet to be confirmed whether there is a large fish in the lake and indeed what it might be."

The incident involving the swan had been properly recorded, he added.

"We will be keeping a close eye on the lake and should there be any cause for concern this coming winter, then further investigation will take place next summer. This is likely to involve a netting exercise, " added the spokesman.

A GUIDE ON hare conservation has sparked a row about cruelty.

The guide, published by the Game Conservancy Trust and produced with the support of English Nature, provoked criticism from Stroud MP David Drew and the League Against Cruel Sports.

Mr Drew, chairman of the Labour Rural Group of MPs, attacked English Nature for backing the booklet 'Conserving the Brown Hare'.

He said:"This biased and misleading booklet puts forward an entirely uncritical view of the bloodsports of hunting, shooting and coursing hares.

"Hares have special status as a Biodiversity Action Plan Species yet this booklet seems to suggest they are simply a pest. This is absolutely not the case.

"It is totally inappropriate that English Nature should lend its respected name to a publication which glosses over the inherent cruelty that these sports involve."

The League's Head of Public Affairs, Mike Hobday, has also written to Sir Martin Doughty, chairman of English Nature, asking him to justify the decision to support the guide.

In a section that would not alarm hunters but has infuriated 'antis', the guide comments:"The brown hare has long been a favourite quarry for a number of field sports. Its substantial size, fast speed and good eating make it an important game animal."

A HUGE RALLY of horses and riders aims to underline the threat posed to equestrian traditions by the move to ban hunting in England and Wales.

The Countryside Alliance said:"Over 500 horses are expected to parade through Leicester city to highlight the links between hunting and the equestrian industry and to raise awareness of the real threat to equine welfare in the event of a ban."

The day after, in a similarly high-profile event, 1,000 hounds will parade down Newmarket race-course as the Alliance intensifies its ongoing campaign to prevent a ban.

LAWS ON KEEPING birds of prey could be relaxed after a Government consultation was launched into the Bird Registration System.

A Downing Street spokesman said:"The options seek to ease regulations on those who keep birds, particularly birds of prey, whilst ensuring that populations of the UK's wild birds are sustained and endangered species protected.

"At present, any regulated bird of a species must be registered with the Department for Environment, Food and Rural Affairs (DEFRA) and fitted with a ring supplied by the department.

"During the last two decades, some species that were classed as being under threat in the Wildlife and Countryside Act 1981 have recovered. The legislation now needs to be reviewed to take into account current environmental circumstances.

"This consultation looks for views on whether the current system is the most effective way to protect our birds now and in the future."

About 6,500 birds are registered with DEFRA and issues under consideration include: whether a registration scheme should include non-indigenous species, whether hybrid specimens should still be included, and other possible alternatives to the current system.

SIX HEN HARRIER chicks have been reared in the Yorkshire Dales National park this year, English Nature has announced.

Conservationists are jubilant at the success of their Hen Harrier Recovery Project, set up to help one of England's rarest breeding birds.

It was the first time the threatened harrier had bred in the Dales for nine years while only three pairs were recorded nesting across the entire north of England in 2001.

The six Dales chicks were reared by a single pair of harriers over the summer and all were wing-tagged to help researchers collect as much information on them as possible.

In addition, a few were also radio-tagged to allow field workers to follow their progress more closely.

This would provide detailed information on feeding areas and general movements.

Richard Saunders, English Nature's Hen Harrier Recovery Project co-ordinator, said:"The hen harrier is close to extinction in England and our project is vital to its survival.

"We are absolutely delighted that this pair of birds has managed to raise six healthy chicks.

"They are a credit to everyone involved in the project, including the Yorkshire Dales National Park Authority, the Yorkshire Dales Upland Bird Study Group and the Moorland Association.

"We are also particularly grateful to the local landowner for allowing us access."

BEES WERE TO blame for a pollution scare involving a quiet Somerset town, the Environment Agency has revealed.

Agency staff flew into action after receiving a complaint of small dots of yellow liquid falling on cars and garden furniture in Watchet.

With the finger pointed at local industry, and concerns by local residents that the substance could be sulphur, samples were quickly taken and examined.

But when biologists peered into their microscopes, they came up with a surprising discovery.

The strange yellow dots were bee droppings containing mainly pollen grains.

"We had a similar case in Bridgwater a couple of years ago so we already had our suspicions that the bees might be the cause," explained Alan Trevelyan, for the Environment Agency.

"Apparently, it is really quite a common phenomenon and natural behaviour for bees leaving the hive on 'cleansing flights' after they've digested pollen.

"We do see some unusual things in this job but this is one of the most interesting and we are glad to be able to reassure the residents of Watchet that their strange yellow dots are, in fact, harmless bee poo!"

DRAGONFLIES AND WATER voles are among wildlife being given better protection from thirsty cattle after the installation of Britain's first solar-powered drinking trough.

The trough, whose water is regulated by a pump system controlled by the sun, has been set up at Bathampton, Somerset, to stop cows trampling the edge of the Kennet and Avon Canal.

Conservationists had been looking for a way to keep the cattle away from the canal but the nearest power source to automatically top up their trough was too far away.

After some deliberation, the new solar-powered trough was put in place by the Kennet and Avon Canal's Heritage Lottery Fund Project with help from WinSund, experts in providing solar energy schemes.

Already, the trough, similar to others in use abroad, has been so successful that additional schemes are being planned.

MORE THAN 80 per cent of shoppers say they would be willing to pay up to 5p more for their daily pinta if they knew the money was going directly to dairy farmers, it has been claimed.

According to a survey of 1,000 shoppers, 60 per cent of city dwellers do not realise most dairy farmers get less for a pint of milk than it costs to produce, 40 per cent of people can't recall how much they pay for a pinta, and 84 per cent of people would pay 5p more if it genuinely went to help farmers.

NFU deputy president Tim Bennett welcomed the survey data, which he claimed highlighted the injustice of the farm gate price of milk.

He said:"These findings show that while retail price wars and promotions 'de-sensitise' many shoppers to the costs of food production, they do care and they don't want to see farmers ripped off.

"Farmers will be heartened by this clear show of support for Britain's dairy industry."

A LEADING ANGLER went fishing for more understanding of country life when he took over the Countryside Alliance's vigil on Parliament Square.

Charles Jardine, director of the Alliance's Campaign for Angling, spent the night in the square which, since May 15, has had a different hunt in attendance each day.

It was the first time the vigil was not manned by a hunt in protest at plans to outlaw hunting in England and Wales.

Mr Jardine explained:"Even leaving aside the political threat to hunting, angling and shooting are now clearly next on the list for the antis and also for many politicians.

"I will do everything in my power to protect my own sport, and the hunting community has already been immensely supportive.

"We must show a united front and do all we can to ensure the continuance of country sports, not just for ourselves, but for future generations."

MANAGING WOODLANDS AND their mammals will be the subject of a two-day conference at London Zoo in November.

The event is being organised by The Mammal Society and the Forestry Commission.

Professor Stephen Harris, chairman of The Mammal Society, said the symposium would bring together scientists, conservationists and woodland managers to discuss helping woodland mammals while solving the problems they can cause.

THE BBC HAS been forced to admit one of its reports wrongly implied that badgers routinely transmit TB to cattle when scientists still dispute the facts.

The National Federation of Badger Groups says it welcomes the Corporation's admission that it had 'implicitly accepted that badgers transmit TB to cattle', when this was not scientifically proven.

Lord Dholakia of Waltham Brooks had made a complaint regarding a BBC news report broadcast on Radio 4 at 7am on June 27.

The report was in response to a paper published by the Royal Society showing that badgers can enter farm buildings to consume cattle feed, urinating on the feed as they do so.

"The BBC report claimed 'scientists believe they have discovered how cattle catch tuberculosis from badgers'. In fact, the scientists had found that if you leave food lying around in open barns, wild animals will come in and eat it," said Dr Elaine King, chief executive of the NFBG.

"We welcome the acknowledgement that the BBC inaccurately reported this research. The mistake was made despite the NFBG specifically advising the BBC's journalist and the producer of the Today programme, the night before, about what the research did and did not reveal.

"We were also critical of some of the claims made in the study, in the absence of statistical data to support them.

"We trust that the BBC's correspondents will treat research associated with badgers with more caution in future. The NFBG always backs its claims with sound scientific evidence and it is essential that the BBC recognises that small organisations, such as ours, have an important voice in these complex scientific debates."

A MALE AND female swan attacked by an airgun yob on Christmas Day have both been shot at again in the same pond, it has been revealed.

Firemen helped RSPCA staff to rescue the traumatised birds following their latest ordeal at the pond in Telford, Shropshire.

Both birds have now been taken to a wildlife centre to recover with the female treated for an airgun pellet wound close to an eye.

In the Christmas Day attack, it was the male of the mating pair which was shot.

Other swans have also been shot in the same pond but efforts to catch the lout responsible have failed.

Police are investigating the latest incident.

A RED TAPE threat to traditional rural events such as village fetes and farmers' markets has been removed following pressure from the NFU.

It had been feared that the Government would in future insist that organisers of occasional events like gymkhanas or food fairs would have to get planning permission following recent consultation on the issue by the DTLR.

However, the Deputy Prime Minster's Office has now issued a statement saying that there will be NO change to the temporary use provision in current planning legislation.

NFU Planning chairman John Seymour said:"We are extremely pleased that the case presented by the NFU has been acted on.

"The Department has recognised that these events have operated successfully for decades under the current system without problem and that they have a huge social and economic value to rural communities and farmers."

OTTERS ARE THE subject of a special event being held at the National Film Theatre in London.

Organised in association with The Wildlife Trusts, young wildlife enthusiasts will have the chance to discover 'otterly' fascinating facts from an ottery expert and then see the animal in action in 'Tarka the Otter'.

"The otter faced extinction across much of Britain 20 years ago, but this shy, sinuous fish eater is now returning to places where it has not been seen for decades," revealed a spokesman for the Trusts.

"A workshop will introduce youngsters to the life of an otter, what they eat, where they live and some of the games they play."

The August 31 event starts at 12.20pm and the film at 1.30pm. Tickets cost £3.50 per child and £4 per adult for the film and the workshop.

The film is being shown as part of the National Film Theatre's children's movie programme 'Movie Magic'.

LAPWING AND REDSHANK are just two bird species set to benefit from a new scheme to create havens for wetland wildlife across the UK.

The project, launched at RSPB Otmoor Nature Reserve in Oxfordshire, involves state-of-the-art machinery shipped from Ohio to Beckley to speed up the creation of habitats for wetland birds.

The £40,000 laser-guided rotary ditching machine is the first of its kind in Europe and has been funded with support from the Heritage Lottery Fund.

The aim is to create 170km of wildlife-rich ditches and shallow scrapes on wet grassland reserves over the next couple of years.

WELSH MOUNTAIN LAMB is at the centre of a new commitment to the environment.

The RSPB and Severn Trent Water have joined forces to help launch the organic meat in a bid to promote 'wildlife-friendly' food.

The range is launched in partnership with Graig Farm Organics, an award-winning agri-food business that operates a producer group network across the heart of Wales with a UK-wide home delivery service.

The lamb is reared on Lake Vyrnwy farm in the Berwyn Hills.

This incorporates part of the largest remaining heather moorland in Wales.

The farm itself completed organic conversion in 2001 and has a flock of 3,500 sheep.

FARMERS' LEADERS HAVE welcomed a 10 per cent increase in Government support for farmers battling to make a living in some of England's most unforgiving regions.

The move comes after DEFRA announced that the Hill Farm Allowance budget for England in 2003 will increase from a total of £37.4 million to £41.1 million.

NFU deputy president Tim Bennett said:"This rise in payments is very good news. Farming in the uplands is unquestionably important for both the landscape and the rural economy and we are pleased that the Government has recognised this."

The NFU has run a long campaign for more Government support to enable farmers to continue caring for upland areas, said to be among the most difficult and least productive land to farm.

NFU Less Favoured Areas chairman William Jenkins added:"Hill farmers will welcome this increase in payment rates. It means that the support they will get in 2003 will be much higher than anyone expected."

However, the NFU remains concerned that the 'safety net' payment - intended to compensate for loss of income following changes to the way hill farmers are supported - will fall from 80 per cent to 50 per cent, before disappearing for good in 2004.

EEL FISHING WITH unlicensed nets resulted in a 51 year-old Kent man being taken to court, fined £150 with £80 costs, and losing his £1,000 nets into the bargain.

Chatham magistrates heard how on April 15 this year at Cliffe Pools in Cliffe, an Environment Agency fisheries officer saw the defendant leaving the area in a van and noted down the registration number.

The officer found two single nets and two double nets pegged out to catch eels.

These were subsequently removed and retained by the officer.

Confronted later, the man, from Allhallows, admitted the offence.

Environment Agency fisheries officer Chris Conroy said after the case:"Licensed nets-men should produce returns of eels caught so that we know the current state of eel stocks. Clearly if people are not properly licensed then there is a danger that we will not have an accurate picture of what is really happening."

BRITAIN'S BEST-loved apple - Cox's Orange Pippin - is expected to be in the shops two weeks early this year.

This is said to be due to a heavy burst of sunshine in July when temperatures soared across the country.

The first apples of this year's harvest are expected to be picked in the key growing areas of Kent, Herefordshire and Worcestershire on September 20 with other regions following.

HIS PICTORIAL GUIDES of the Lake District are world famous and now the late Alfred Wainwright looks set to get his own official fan club.

Some 50 years after he penned the first of his guides to the Lakeland Fells, a meeting is being held to discuss the formation of a Wainwright Society.

A Ramblers Association spokesman said:"His guides went on to capture the imagination of millions of Lakeland fell walkers.

"The gathering on Saturday, November 9, at Ambleside Youth Hostel will be preceded by a climb to Dove Crag in the footsteps of a walk that inspired Wainwright's first entry in 'Book 1 - The Eastern Fells'.

"The walk will leave at 9.30am from outside the Salutation Hotel in Ambleside and is expected to take around four and a half hours to complete.

"The meeting will commence at 3pm and should last no more than one hour. For anyone wishing to stay overnight in Ambleside on either the Friday or Saturday nights, special rates have been agreed with the hostel."

THREE MEN DESCRIBED by a judge as "cruel and savage", have been sentenced to six weeks in jail for digging for a badger, and six weeks jail for interfering with a badger sett.

Both sentences will run concurrently.

The trio were also banned from keeping dogs for three years following a prosecution involving Merseyside Police.

RED GROUSE NEED good management if their decline in parts of the country is not to become more widespread, according to the Game Conservancy Trust.

Speaking after red grouse moved from conservationists' green list to amber, Dr Nicholas Aebischer, deputy director of research for the Trust, said:"Red grouse are not rare or endangered and in many parts of upland Britain they still remain plentiful, especially on managed grouse moors.

"However, in south west England, Wales and Northern Ireland, in areas of unmanaged moorland, we have seen declines of about 50 per cent.

"It is this decline that has triggered the amber listing of red grouse, which is based on a moderate decline in the overall UK breeding population over the last 25 years."

He said the amber listing of red grouse underlined the Trust's commitment to conservation.

A MOTH WHICH can devastate horse chestnut trees has been discovered in the UK for the first time after a London woman raised the alarm.

Minister for Forestry Elliot Morley is said to have written to Wimbledon resident Marian Comfort thanking her for her swift action after discovering what has proved to be the first-ever occurrence of the horse chestnut leaf miner in this country.

"The moth's larvae feed on the leaves of horse chestnut trees and have already caused devastation to horse chestnuts in mainland Europe," said a Government spokesman."Although they do not cause the trees to die, the leaves they inhabit turn brown and fall prematurely, and conkers will not be produced. There is no threat to human health."

Mrs Comfort had noticed the effects of the pest in her garden and sent a leaf to the Royal Horticultural Society.

CROW: last laugh for a bird of ill-omen

CRAFTY and resourceful, the carrion crow continues to flourish in this country despite the gradual decline of more popular bird species.

Best known for its scavenging nature and opportunistic eye, the crow also harbours a predator's instinct to home in on any vulnerable creature too weak or feeble to resist.

This formidable bird comes from the same family group as the jay, jackdaw, magpie, rook, raven and chough - all known for their intelligence.

While the chough is now the rarest of these, the crow is among the leaders in terms of its rocketing population, with magpies and jackdaws also faring remarkably well.

Hated and feared the world over as a bird of ill-omen, the crow has nevertheless managed to thrive in the face of Man's often cruel attempts to suppress it.

According to research by the British Trust for Ornithology, crow numbers here have increased constantly over the last 30 years.

In one year alone, national numbers were thought to have leapt by as much as 12 per cent as the crow continues to gorge on road kill flesh and game bird eggs - both blithely provided by humans.

With its strong, knife-like beak designed for tearing flesh, the crow is even a match for birds of prey such as the buzzard which it often mobs and drives away.

Other, smaller birds are more easily terrorised and I've written before about a young blackbird losing an eye in a savage assault by a crow.

The black carrion crow is now widespread throughout England, Wales and most of Scotland.

It gives way to a sub-species, the hooded crow, in north west Scotland and Ireland.

The hooded crow is similar to the carrion crow in every respect apart from its distinct piebald colouring, its 'hooded' black head being starkly contrasted by a light grey back and underside.

But wing and tail feathers are still black.

Both types will eat virtually anything, attacking lambs and even sheep that have become too sick to defend themselves.

It is probably for this reason that farmers have had a traditional dislike of crows.

Years ago, it was not uncommon to see rows of shot crows strung up outside a farm as a warning to their chums.

The human-like 'scarecrow' was also obviously devised with the express intention of keeping this unpopular bird away. But both measures have clearly failed.

Today, in any town or open stretch of country it is usually not too long before those great black wings flap into view.

Shakespeare was well aware of the morbid atmosphere conjured up by the brooding presence of crows.

In 'Macbeth', he wrote:*"Light thickens and the crow makes wing to the rooky wood; Good things of day begin to droop and drowse, whiles night's black agents to their preys do rouse."*

In spite of such negative imagery and continued persecution, crows, it seems, have every reason to crow.

BEE-EATERS WHICH bred successfully in Durham this year are now thought to have left the country after the two adults and two youngsters began flying south.

It was the first time in nearly 50 years that the birds, one of Europe's most colourful species, had successfully hatched chicks in the UK.

Following the announcement of their presence by the RSPB and Durham Wildlife Trust in July, thousands of people flocked to see the insect feeders at the village of Bishop Middleham.

The exotic visitors, which arrived in County Durham following southerly winds at the start of June, had exchanged their normal nesting area in southern Europe for a disused local quarry.

The birds, which lay their eggs in burrows, were lucky that the quarry was part of a local nature reserve and received round-the-clock protection by RSPB staff and Wildlife Trust volunteers.

Bee-eaters were last recorded breeding in the UK in 1955 when two pairs nested in a sand-pit in Sussex and raised seven young.

Before that, their only other known nesting attempt was in Scotland in 1920 but normally they nest no closer to the UK than northern France.

POLICE CALLED TO investigate a big cat sighting in South Wales were amazed not only to spot a puma-like animal but also what appeared to be a cub beside it.

Two officers had been sent to probe the sighting near Newport after worried local people reported a huge cat stalking the area.

Following the officers' report, two police helicopters were brought in to try to track the cats but no trace of the sleek, black animals was found.

Only recently, officials from the British Big Cat Society, an organisation which monitors such sightings, said there was growing evidence that big cats were breeding in the countryside.

The latest incident is only 15 miles from the spot where a schoolboy claimed to have been slashed by a big cat two years ago.

HEBRIDEAN SHEEP, HIGHLAND cattle and Exmoor ponies are among grazing animals getting busy in a scheme to benefit wildflowers, butterflies and birds.

The Wildlife Trusts have been awarded a three-year contract by English Nature to run the Grazing Animals Project.

This will see the Trusts managing a project membership of about 800 conservation 'graziers' covering grasslands, heathlands and wetlands for the benefit of wildlife.

An assortment of advice will be given to managers and their teams working with farmers or landowners currently grazing, or wanting to graze, wildlife rich sites.

A NEW STUDY claims the ban on foxhunting during the foot-and-mouth outbreak had NO effect on fox numbers - despite a barrage of complaints by some farmers and landowners that their land was almost overwhelmed by foxes.

The controversial findings of The Mammal Society survey, funded by the anti-hunt International Fund for Animal Welfare and anti-hunt RSPCA, are published in science magazine Nature.

The results of the study are sharply at odds with reports given to the Countryside Alliance during the hunting ban which apparently revealed many farmers were desperate for hunting to resume.

Professor Stephen Harris, chairman of The Mammal Society, said:"This is the first scientific study into the impact of hunting on fox numbers and it shows quite clearly that hunting plays no role in regulating fox numbers.

"In fact these results add weight to the argument that foxes regulate their own numbers and that all forms of fox culling are less important than hitherto believed.

"During the foot-and-mouth epidemic, hunting was banned and other forms of fox control were curtailed to varying extents. Yet despite the ban on hunting and restrictions on a variety of rural activities for nearly a year, fox numbers did not increase or decrease.

"In fact actual numbers declined slightly, although not in a statistically significant way."

The study is said to provide the only quantified data on the impact of the hunting ban on fox numbers and "refutes claims from a number of lobby groups that fox numbers increased significantly during foot-and-mouth."

The Mammal Society claims it also lends support to Lord Burns, chairman of the Committee of Inquiry into Hunting with Dogs in England and Wales, "who concluded that a permanent ban on hunting is unlikely to result in an increase in fox numbers."

During the study 160 randomly selected 1-kilometre squares of land throughout Britain were surveyed by volunteers and paid staff between February 1 and March 17 in the two winters immediately preceding foot-and-mouth - 1999 and 2000.

The outbreak started in February 2001 and hunting was banned for 10 months and severely curtailed for another two months.

Each square was resurveyed between February 1 and March 17, 2002, as soon as foot-and-mouth was officially declared over.

Counts of fresh scats (faeces) were used to compare fox densities immediately before and immediately after the ban on hunting with volunteers and staff visiting each square twice during the six-week survey period.

BADGER LOVERS WERE left outraged at claims that road workers painted a white line over the corpse of a badger.

An investigation has been launched by Somerset County Council after photographs were taken of the paint-striped badger on the A361 near Frome.

The county council says its own staff were not responsible for doing the road markings but they had contracted out the work to a private firm.

Salesman Chris Crabtree, from Bristol, stopped to take photographs after being saddened by the sight.

251

ENGLAND IS NOW bottom of the European 'tree league' in numbers of forests for people to enjoy, it has been revealed.

The Woodland Trust says English people have less woodland to escape to than any other European country - apart from Northern Ireland.

The Trust is calling for urgent help from the Government to reverse the situation by making big investments in tree planting schemes.

James Cooper, spokesman for the Trust, said:"We want the Government to recognise that woods can increase the health, happiness and well-being of people in England.

"The Government needs to look at the whole of England's landscape and social needs when discussing woodland creation.

"There is a need for natural green space close to where people live, as well as the need for a more sustainable and wildlife friendly countryside. New woods have a major role to play in the future of both urban and rural areas."

Trees now cover a mere eight per cent of England's landscape compared to a European average of 30 per cent.

The Trust says it sees the Government's current review of woodland creation as a unique opportunity to increase tree cover, bringing us closer to our European neighbours.

Future investment should not simply be focused on the management of existing woods, it says, because tree planting enhances nature and can actually improve communities' quality of life.

The charity believes new trees bring a wide range of public benefits.

It says trees increase people's sense of well-being; help hospital patients recover faster; provide more opportunities for recreation; create better air quality; and increase wildlife.

HOLLY THE SPANIEL is recovering after plummeting down an almost vertical 300ft cliff at Capel Le Ferne, near Folkestone.

Luckily, her plunge was interrupted two thirds of the way up the cliff face when she somehow managed to scramble onto a ledge.

Her elderly owner raised the alarm and she was plucked to safety, barely the worse for her ordeal.

Just as remarkable was the number of people involved in the 90 minute rescue - 19 - a figure made up of firefighters, rock climbers, police and others.

The dog was finally hoisted free by firefighters Paul Garrity and Mark Seal who were lowered down to her using a thermal imaging camera to see better in the gathering gloom.

THE WILDFOWL AND Wetlands Trust is celebrating reaching its milestone target of 100,000 members.

The charity, dedicated to wetlands conservation, was founded by the late Sir Peter Scott in 1946 and now operates nine visitor centres in the UK, including award-winning developments in London and Slimbridge, Gloucestershire.

WWT's membership has grown by about a third in just over two years, a period which has seen big developments by the charity.

The London Wetland Centre, which opened in May 2000, won the British Airways Tourism for Tomorrow Global Award 2001, and just recently received a commendation in the London Tourism Awards.

Meanwhile, Slimbridge, WWT's national centre and HQ, is now one of Gloucestershire's leading attractions.

This year it received two accolades - 'Bird Centre of the Year' and 'Best Family Attraction in Gloucestershire', in the Good Britain Guide 2002.

Tony Richardson, managing director of the WWT, said:"Reaching 100,000 members is a crucial milestone in our history which will help raise our profile as the largest UK charity dedicated to international wetlands conservation.

"The impact of the decline of wetlands and its effect on wetland birds is a key driver for our growing membership. The loyalty from our members is vital to our continued success in saving these wetland habitats and the wildlife they support."

BROWN TROUT HAVE been the main victims of a "major fish kill" caused by pollution at a river in South Wales.

Environment Agency investigators are still probing the cause of the incident on the River Clyne in Swansea.

After being alerted by a member of the public, Agency officers discovered large numbers of dead fish, mainly brown trout, in a stretch of the river between Blackpill and Killay.

Samples are being taken both of the river water and the fish.

A spokesman for the Agency said:"Investigations are continuing to identify the exact source of the pollution and to more accurately learn the numbers and types of fish that have been killed.

"The environmental health department of the city of Swansea has also been notified in case any actions are required to safeguard amenity interests."

FARMERS' MARKETS ARE now earning cash-strapped producers £166 million a year - two and a half times that of just two years ago, NFU research has revealed.

"It shows that the phenomenon - which started in 1997 with a single fledgling market - is today a thriving industry in its own right in virtually every area of the country," said a union spokesman.

"The massive increase is due to large numbers of farmers wanting to supplement their income during the farming crisis and the growing interest amongst consumers for fresh, locally produced food.

"The stall-holders at farmers' markets farm in the local area and have grown, reared, cooked, brewed or baked the goods themselves."

NFU deputy president Tim Bennett added: "Farmers' markets are becoming more and more a part of people's shopping habits."

BRITISH FARMERS AND growers get little more than a quarter of what shoppers pay at the checkout for food, their union claims.

On average, a basket of farmed produce - including beef, eggs, milk, bread, tomatoes and apples - typically costs £37 in the shops.

But a farmer only gets £11 for it at the farm gate - just 30 per cent, says the NFU.

The huge discrepancy was revealed by NFU president Ben Gill during the union's nationwide public information blitz.

In some sectors, farmers do not even get a quarter of the final price, he said.

Cereal farmers receive a "paltry eight per cent" of the price of a loaf of bread, even though wheat is the main ingredient.

Pig farmers also receive just "a shocking 14 per cent" of the final sale value of bacon.

To make his point, Mr Gill set up shop in the centre of London selling fresh produce to passers-by at farm gate prices.

He added:"It is shocking that farmers get so little of the final price of food. Crops and livestock are tended and nurtured by farmers for many months or even years. That investment and care justifies more reward. This price discrepancy shows why farmers are having such a difficult time."

ROCKY THE ROOSTER has been causing a bit of a hullabaloo in Hullavington, Wiltshire.

Sleepless residents mounted a campaign to give him the bird because his early morning crowing was driving them crazy.

His owner Alison Ayliffe, in her 60s, only moved to the village in the last two years from the south coast and brought Rocky with her to save him from slaughter.

She even bought him three hens as company but neighbours lost patience with the cockerel's 4.30am wake-up calls and were backed by the local council.

Now Rocky has been given to a friend's farm where he can crow as loud as he likes.

A SERIES OF crucial hearings have been held to decide the fate of thousands of countryside jobs and scores of hunts.

Evidence for and against hunting with dogs was presented to the hearings as part of a much heralded consultation event.

A Downing Street spokesman said:"Both the content and the experts invited to give evidence to the hearings had been agreed with the three main interest groups - the Campaign for the Protection of Hunted Animals; the Countryside Alliance; and the Middle Way Group. These were the three groups that proposed alternative forms of legislation on hunting with dogs during the previous Parliamentary process."

Rural Affairs Minister Alun Michael chaired the hearings that took place in the Boothroyd room at Portcullis House, Victoria Embankment.

Mr Michael will publish a report summarising key findings later in the year.

BRITAIN'S SEASONS ARE getting so muddled up that many of our favourite animals, insects, and trees may go into sharp decline, researchers fear.

A spokesman for The Woodland Trust said:"By measuring the start and finish of the seasons, via the observation of natural events, almost 17,000 volunteer phenologists have gathered information showing that the arrival of spring is no longer constrained to its traditional March slot and the end of autumn now continues well beyond late October.

"Higher than average temperatures from January to April led to almost every characteristic of this year's spring occurring up to three weeks earlier than in 2001.

"On average, insects such as bumble bees and butterflies were three weeks early while plants flowered two weeks ahead and many birds, including the turtle dove, arrived a week earlier than usual.

"Other notable early spring signs included the unmistakable call of the cuckoo five days earlier; hazel flowering 23 days earlier; emergence of snowdrops seven days earlier;the first bluebell carpets 16 days earlier; alder leafing 13 days earlier; and hawthorn leafing 17 days earlier.

"Interconnected and complex relationships between trees, insects and animals in woods are also affected by early spring arrivals.

"For example, results from this spring show that some synchronous relationships between birds, insects and plants could become disturbed.

"Crucially, for many species, this could have serious implications for their future survival. As ancient woods become even more fragmented and isolated, some characteristic plants and animals may face further threats as the climate changes."

Former Tomorrow's World presenter and science broadcaster Judith Hann is supporting research carried out jointly by the Trust and the Centre for Ecology and Hydrology.

She added:"There's nothing I like better than spending time in my garden, observing wildlife and keeping and eye on changes over the seasons.

"Recently, I have noticed that changes in the weather have delayed autumn. During 2001, oak leaves were still on trees in mid-November because of the warmest October on record."

A GIANT EAGLE with a 12-metre wingspan is helping the RSPB drive home its message to wine lovers - choose bottles with cork stoppers and save wildlife.

The eagle sculpture, made entirely from cork, has been sited at the celebrated ecological Eden Project in Cornwall and represents an imperial eagle, just one of the birds under threat if cork forests are undermined by modern plastic bottle stoppers.

Created by Cornwall-based artist Robert Bradford from some of the 350,000 wine corks collected by RSPB supporters during 2001, the sculpture aims to raise awareness of the growing threat to cork oak forests in Portugal and Spain.

"Cork is a wonderful example of a sustainable industry that benefits people and wildlife," said RSPB conservation director, Dr Mark Avery."Cork bark can be harvested many times over a long period, ensur - ing the survival of the trees and the cork industry, as well as the people and wildlife that depend on it."

253

THREATENED RED SQUIRRELS are being boosted by an event aimed at raising their shy profiles from under the shadow of bigger, tougher greys.

The Wildlife Trusts' 'Red Squirrel Week' starts on September 14 with a host of activities planned to help the creatures fight back against the march of immigrant American grey squirrels.

"Our native Nutkin is possibly one of the most loved animals in the UK," said a spokesman. "With its distinctive russet fur, tufted ears and twitching tail, a red squirrel is always a captivating sight in the forests of the UK. Yet these flashes of red are becoming more and more scarce.

"Red squirrels were once widespread in the UK but are now largely confined to Scotland, with small pockets in Wales, Northern Ireland and parts of England.

"Battling against the loss and fragmentation of their natural forest habitat, our reds are also under increasing pressure from non-native grey squirrels that now out-number reds by 15 to one.

"During Red Squirrel Week, you could be 'seeing red' at heaps of squirreling events, walks, talks and activities across the UK.

"By joining The Wildlife Trusts in celebrating our ravishing reds you can learn all about the current plight of the red squirrel and help raise funds to continue our vital conservation work.

"If you can't make it to an event, you can always squirrel spot.

"Join in with a local Trust species survey for Red Squirrel Week. If you 'see red' out on a woodland walk, make a note of when and where you saw it and report it to your local Wildlife Trust.

"Monitoring numbers is an important part of conservation work and you will be directly helping red squirrels with the information you supply."

PUFFINS HAVE BRED on an island for the first time in 50 years after conservationists wiped out rats there.

Tonnes of rat poison had been deployed on Ailsa Craig, off Ayrshire, Scotland, because rats continually preyed on puffin young and eggs.

Rats were thought to have invaded the island during the late 19th Century and went on to devastate several bird species.

But puffins live in burrows so are particularly at risk from attacks by voracious rats.

Pest control company Rentokil gave help and advice to conservationists in their long fight to eradicate rats.

The campaign had started back in 1991.

HUNDREDS OF FISH, including eels and brown trout, were killed when a local firm polluted their Lancashire stream, a court heard.

Magistrates have now fined an animal feed manufacturer £10,000 following the incident.

The company pleaded guilty to polluting Worston Brook with vegetable matter in August last year. More than 600 fish were counted dead at the scene.

As well as being fined, the company was ordered to pay £1,527 costs to the Environment Agency, which brought the prosecution.

Estelle Palin, prosecuting for the Agency, told Blackburn magistrates that investigating officer Carol Holt had gone to Worston Brook following a complaint about pollution.

She found the brook to be foul-smelling, heavily discoloured and foaming, containing dead fish and large deposits of animal feed.

She traced the pollution to an outfall serving the defendant company, although the polluting discharge had by then stopped.

The court heard that the firm's boss later wrote to the Environment Agency explaining how he believed the pollution occurred.

He said a blockage in the foul sewer system had caused excess water to flow into the surface water drains, which in turn overflowed into the brook.

ABOUT 50 SAND lizards have been released at a nature reserve as part of a national reintroduction programme.

The lizards were once widespread in the UK but have now been mostly reduced to a few colonies in Dorset, Surrey, and Merseyside.

The captive-bred sand lizards were released at Wildmoor Heath Nature Reserve in Berkshire - a county where such lizards have been extinct for 30 years.

Sarah Ruff, a senior biodiversity officer with the Berkshire, Buckinghamshire and Oxfordshire Wildlife Trust, said: "Existing sand lizard populations are isolated, making it impossible for them to recolonise naturally.

"There are few sites remaining which provide suitable habitat for the vulnerable sand lizard and therefore strategic reintroductions such as this are necessary to ensure a growing population. "

The main threat to sand lizards remains the destruction of their favourite habitats.

The reptiles live among lowland dry heath and coastal sand dunes - both places increasingly at risk from urban development.

BOYCE THE SPANIEL is making a good recovery after having a lucky escape between the blades of a combine harvester.

The pet slipped between the deadly blades when owner Rodney Belbin was harvesting a wheat field at Blandford Forum, Dorset.

Fortunately, the animal was so tubby that his rolls of fat prevented him being sucked into the 15ft blades too quickly.

This gave farmer Mr Belbin a chance to switch off the machine before Boyce sustained fatal injuries.

Horror quickly turned to delight when Mr Belbin realised his pet would live.

After a vet inserted 70 stitches in his torso, the chastened dog is expected to completely recover.

A NEW ATLAS which charts the distribution of every flowering plant and fern species across Britain and Ireland has been launched at Kew Gardens in London.

According to Downing Street, the giant book is expected to be "a huge asset to anyone involved in framing national, regional and local policies affecting wildlife and the countryside, as well as to botanists, conservation agencies, academics and amateur naturalists.

"It will assist the Government's review of policy on non-native species and the implementation of the UK Biodiversity Action Plan, research into the impacts of atmospheric pollution and climate change, and the development of biodiversity indicators.

"The 910-page volume, produced from nine million records, features 2,412 maps. The Atlas builds on research carried out in the 1950s which was documented in the 'Atlas of the British Flora,' published in 1962. The new book contains 750 species not listed in the previous volume."

Secretary of State for the Environment, Food and Rural Affairs, Margaret Beckett added:"This atlas will be a tremendous resource as we consider how we can respond to major strategic challenges such as atmospheric pollution, climate change and the decline of biodiversity and as we begin to chart the progress of our network of Sites of Special Scientific Interest and agri-environment schemes."

TWO PIGLETS WHICH wandered off from the school which reared them have returned from a nearby forest safe and well.

'Wolver' and 'Hampton' - named after a soccer team - emerged from woods together after they had disappeared 10 days earlier.

Staff and pupils at Dean Hall School in the Forest of Dean were worried about the animals' safety when they vanished and are delighted by their return.

The porky wanderers, originally rejected by their mother, now seem even smaller and thinner than before their ordeal.

However, they are being pampered and fed back to fitness again at their old abode, a special school for children with learning difficulties.

SEAL SPOTTING IS normally fun but English Nature is hoping to recruit volunteers for a grimmer task - reporting on seals killed by virulent distemper virus PDV.

"In order to assess accurately the impact of PDV on seals, scientists need to recruit a network of volunteers around the UK (especially around seal colonies) to help with the reporting of dead seals," said a spokesman."This will enable accurate information on seal mortality rates in local areas to be assessed on a regular basis."

DOZENS OF CELEBRITIES are expected to stand shoulder to shoulder with a vast army of more than 330,000 people on the Countryside March in London.

Stars of the sporting world such as jockey Frankie Dettori, Stirling Moss, and Jimmy Hill will be joined at the event by actors Jeremy Irons, Diana Rigg, Edward Fox and keen shooter Vinnie Jones.

Chefs Antony Worrall Thompson and Marco Pierre White will set out on the route with broadcasters Janet Street-Porter and Melvyn Bragg, comedian Jim Davidson, lyricist Tim Rice, explorer Sir Ranulph Fiennes, and writers Joanna Trollope and Frederick Forsyth.

The mass protest will swamp large parts of the capital as rural Britain descends in force to show the extent of its anger and frustration with New Labour.

Meanwhile, rebellion against an expected ban on hunting with dogs is deepening, with several landowners claiming they will defy any ban.

Philosopher Roger Scruton, who supports foxhunting and rides with two hunts, believes such civil disobedience is inevitable.

"There will be protests if governments pass laws that take away freedoms on which communities have built their identities," he said.

"You need a strong reason for doing this, such as an over-riding public interest but the case against foxhunting has not been made."

Recently, a meet of staghounds and foxhounds took place on Exmoor as part of a relentless campaign to keep hunting legal.

The Devon and Somerset Staghounds, the Quantock Staghounds, the Exmoor Foxhounds and the Dulverton West Foxhounds all came together at Simonsbath.

The colourful event was described by the Countryside Alliance as "a unique occasion, as never before have the staghounds and foxhounds met together on Exmoor."

Over 300 riders and in excess of a thousand hunt supporters took part in the event to show their support and "reinforce the united spirit of hunting on Exmoor" with the occasion reckoned to be the largest joint meet of hounds ever held in the West Country.

Baroness Ann Mallalieu, president of the Countryside Alliance, John Jackson, chairman, and Richard Burge, chief executive, all attended what was the highest profile event in the south west before the Alliance's Liberty and Livelihood March.

A BABY SQUIRREL called Sammy is bouncing back to health after being found abandoned beside a road in Shropshire.

The tiny animal, hairless and still blind, was discovered helpless in Ellesmere and taken to a local veterinary centre where it initially seemed kinder to put it down.

However, Pat Arrowsmith, who works in an office at the centre, decided Sammy should be given a chance and painstakingly nursed him to health on a diet of cow's milk.

The grey squirrel, only two or three days old when first discovered, has gaining considerably in strength and size some six weeks later.

Now Sammy eats solid food, sleeps in a hamster cage, and enjoys playing with Pat's family in her garden.

255

FRANCE'S BELATED MOVE to back UK beef has been hailed a "hollow victory" for British farmers.

After years of cynical gamesmanship, the country's food experts said they now acknowledged the high quality of British beef and believed it to be safe.

NFU president Ben Gill stormed:"This whole lamentable situation should never have happened. The French Government must now listen to its food safety agency and lift the ban. Unilateral illegal action like this must never be allowed to happen again.

"This is a victory for British farmers - but a hollow one. Who knows how much desperately-needed cash our industry has been deprived of in the last three years because of this ban?

"Who knows what damage has been done to the credibility of the European Commission and the single market?

"Our farmers were left in limbo for three years by the arrogant prevarication and shameless protectionism of the French."

MORE THAN 1,000 seals are now thought to have died from phocine distemper virus down Britain's east coast - a third of the region's seal population.

Animal rescue workers are reported to be taking four seals to the RSPCA Norfolk Wildlife Hospital every day where staff battle to save their lives.

However, out of the 100 seals already admitted there, only 40 or so have survived.

The last mass PDV outbreak hit northern Europe in 1988 and killed 18,000 animals - 1,500 in the Wash alone. In the present outbreak, over 4,000 seals have so far died around the Scandanavian coasts, hundreds off the Netherlands and now the UK is being badly hit.

Alison Charles, deputy manager at the Norfolk hospital, said:"What we find hard is we can't say which ones are going to survive. Some come in very sick, having convulsions, because PDV has already affected their nervous systems, and we give them Valium and they battle on to survive.

"Others seem to have minor symptoms on admission but, because they are in the very early stages of the viral attack, rapidly worsen and die."

THE RSPB HAS called for assurances that Maltese bird hunters and bird trappers will not be given concessions on Europe-wide bird protection laws as a 'sweetener' to aid Malta's entry into the European Union.

The Society says it believes that a behind-the-scenes deal between the European Commission and the Maltese Government could allow the island's bird hunters and trappers to continue their trade.

Many targeted birds migrate northwards to Britain and elsewhere through the island and include quail, turtle dove, goldfinch, chaffinch, and greenfinch.

RSPB international director Alistair Gammell said:"It is outrageous that the European Union and the Maltese Government should be attempting to broker a deal that would undermine bird protection."

WITH PRINCE CHARLES still embroiled in a row with New Labour over leaked letters and his support for foxhunting, the sheer size of the Countryside March in London appears to have shaken anti-hunt groups.

The League Against Cruel Sports has called on its members to treat the claimed marchers' figure of 407,000 with scepticism.

"Observers placed by animal welfare groups near the Alliance counting machines reported a myriad of irregularities," said a spokesman."One said:'It looks like they just decided what they wanted the final number to be and set the clock ticking towards it.'

"Rather than counting individual heads, the Alliance estimated the flow rate - the number of marchers passing per minute - before setting the counter ticking accordingly.

"Observers from animal welfare coalition CPHA noted that the speed at which the counter ticked 'bore no relation to reality. It started going up by 101 every few seconds but, even when marchers dwindled, the counter kept increasing at a similar rate.'"

Meanwhile, following the high-profile event, the Movement for a Socialist Future announced:"The size of the Countryside Alliance march is a warning that a populist right-wing movement is well underway in Britain.

"Landowners, Tory leaders and the fox-hunters appeal directly to the rural population over the heads of Parliament.

"They call for 'livelihood and liberty', invoking the Tolpuddle Martyrs and the Chartists. This makes a mockery of the historic struggle for rights by the dispossessed and early trade unionists. These movements were, of course, directed against the predecessors of the very people who organise the Countryside Alliance.

"The Countryside Alliance leaders are cynically exploiting the real hardship and suffering experienced by the rural poor and lower middle classes, pretending they share the same interests as big landowners and the interests of corporate agribusiness."

A CURIOUS PILOT almost wrecked the first World Sheepdog Trials by buzzing the event at Bala in North Wales.

Now a Ministry of Defence probe is underway to find out how a low-flying military jet came to be in the area.

Furious organisers of the event, which attracted competitors from 13 countries, say they had been promised an MoD no-fly zone overhead while the competition was in progress.

But the military blunder occurred on the opening day of the trials when a French contestant and her dog were forced to abandon their routine.

However, following talks with International Sheep Dog Society officials, the woman was allowed to repeat the routine later when the jet had moved off.

THOUSANDS OF FISH, including salmon and trout, were put at risk after the River Dee was hit by a new pollution drama - the latest in a long line.

Environment Agency investigators are probing the North Wales river after nearly a quarter of a million gallons of industrial effluent seeped into it.

A Cefn Mawr company has reportedly admitted waste liquid from a storage tank poured from the site into the river via a local brook.

CUCKOO: treacherous visitor on a deadly mission

DESPITE their welcome calls each spring, cuckoos would soon be given short shrift if their ruthless trickery was translated to the human world.

Their cycle of treachery begins with the mother cuckoo sneakily laying her own egg in the nest of another bird and abandoning it to its fate. This egg is a timebomb which is primed to explode into life as quickly as possible, something often achieved before the eggs of the host bird hatch.

From then on the ferocious cuckoo chick concentrates on expelling from the nest all other eggs or chicks it finds around it - and it will not rest until this is accomplished. Genuine offspring unfortunate enough to be pushed from the safety of the nest are, of course, doomed.

In the grotesque charade that follows, the cuckoo chick somehow manages to dupe its new parents - often tiny meadow pipits or reed warblers - into treating it as their own.

The conned parents exhaust themselves rearing a fledgling that becomes so large it eventually fills the entire nest.

Yet they continue slipping more insects into its gaping mouth until it chooses to leave.

Oddly, perhaps, the parasitic behaviour of cuckoos was first observed and recorded in the 18th Century by Dr Edward Jenner, the same man who went on to discover a vaccination for smallpox.

How cuckoos came to perfect their technique for leeching off other birds remains a mystery but perfect it they have with lethal success.

Even their appearance is a sort of con-trick because adult cuckoos actually look like sparrowhawks in flight and, as such, are given a wide berth by large birds which might otherwise attack them.

This particular trick can sometimes backfire, however, when smaller birds gang up to mob cuckoos, as they might an owl or hawk.

Although their distinctive call carries far, cuckoos are surprisingly difficult to spot and I have enjoyed good views of them on only a few occasions.

The male cuckoo actually makes the 'cu-coo' call while the female emits an unusual bubbling sound.

Cuckoos are migratory and normally make it to our shores at the end of April after spending the winter in Africa.

By September, most will have left again.

The diet of adult cuckoos consists of hairy caterpillars which are avoided by other birds because their cumulative effect is poisonous.

Yet cuckoos boast another modification to help them survive even this - an especially thick stomach lining which can be shed and renewed.

Some years ago, an opinion poll was conducted by Mori which asked which bird had the most beautiful song or call.

The winner was the song thrush but the cuckoo also made it into theTop 10.

This seemed to prove that, despite its nasty habits, we still love the cuckoo's haunting call.

FRANCE HAS ENDED "years of evasion and prevarication" by finally agreeing to lift its illegal ban on British beef.

NFU president Ben Gill said that even though the French have now lifted the ban, they must not go unpunished.

He said:"France's decision must mark the end of a sad and sorry episode in the history of the European Union. The French have cynically exploited false consumer protection issues in a shameless attempt to protect their own beef producers.

"The European Commission must not let the matter drop now that the French have lifted the ban. The EC must be able to take rapid punitive action in the future.

"It is unacceptable that such a clearly illegal ban has been able to be imposed for this length of time. It is equally unacceptable that the French can walk away from this disgraceful situation at the last possible moment before fines are imposed."

France was the only country that continued to block imports of British beef following the lifting of the European Commission BSE ban in August 1999.

The illegal embargo has resulted in the NFU taking action in the French courts for damages.

The case was referred to the European Court of Justice where a ruling is due shortly.

Mr Gill added:"We must now focus on getting French shoppers to buy our product again. We intend to show them what they have been missing all these years.

"Our beef was always regarded as the best in the world. Now the door has been opened again to one of our biggest export markets, we intend to fully restore that reputation.

"This sends a clear message to the rest of the world about the safety of British beef."

A NEW RURAL council will be set up to represent the whole of the countryside, the Countryside Alliance has announced following the huge success of its Liberty and Livelihood March.

All rural organisations are to be invited to a major conference in the next few weeks with a view to setting up the council.

After more than 407,000 people marched in the capital, Alliance chairman John Jackson explained:"The unions have their TUC. Business has the CBI. The countryside needs a Rural Council. Such a unified representation is long overdue.

"The Government responded 18 months ago to the countryside's calls for a Department of Rural Affairs with the creation of DEFRA. It is clear that DEFRA needs a partner which speaks for all rural stakeholders."

He would also be contacting Tony Blair with a 10-point action plan to help the countryside.

A HONEY BUZZARD reared in Scotland is feared drowned after going hundreds of miles off course on its first migration to Africa.

Wildlife experts tracking the young bird by satellite fear it may have ditched in the Atlantic from exhaustion after flying for days on end out at sea.

The buzzard, fitted with a radio transmitter, failed to follow its father's more sensible route to Africa - over France, then Spain, and across the Mediterranean Sea into Morocco.

Instead, the youngster crossed Britain from Inverness to launch itself off Land's End in Cornwall.

From there it began a tortuous odyssey over the open sea, reaching a spot 150 miles north east of Madeira two days later.

Worryingly, it has now disappeared from the tracking system and conservationists fear it may simply have dropped into the Atlantic and drowned following a week of continuous flying.

However, some still hope that the bird has found land or a passing boat to rest on before resuming its haphazard journey to Africa.

A NEW FIELD guide published by the Forestry Commission is designed to help foresters identify different types of soil.

Launching the guide - 'The Identification of Soils for Forest Management' - Commission chairman Lord David Clark said that, thanks to its long and complex geological history, Britain's soils were very varied.

In the 1960s, he explained, the Forestry Commission developed a classification for British forest soils that has since become standard throughout Britain's forestry industry.

Commission staff have identified and mapped soils on about half the 800,000 hectares of forests and woodlands they manage - and soils in many private forests have also been identified and mapped.

"However, there remains a significant proportion which still needs mapping,"Lord Clark added. "Knowledge of the type of soil in a forest is vital for a range of management options in modern forestry, including tree species choice, drainage and cultivation planning, remedial fertiliser applications, planning harvesting operations, and predicting windthrow."

ANGLERS CAN NOW use a different kind of net to check the movements of fish in three north east England rivers - the internet.

Figures from fish passes on the rivers Tyne, Wear and Coquet are now available by logging onto the Environment Agency's website.

"When a fish passes over a weir or fish pass, electrodes send a signal to the fish counter," said an Agency spokesman."The counters can distinguish between upstream and downstream movements of fish and eliminate counts caused by debris.

"Results are checked by Agency scientists to ensure the counters are working properly and the figures are accurate."

Agency Fisheries scientist Jon Shelley added:"Fisheries officers were being approached by anglers for this kind of information so we decided to make it available on the internet.

"Information from the fish counters is used to assist us in managing salmon and sea trout stocks in the area and also helps us understand how the stocks are performing."

SALMON FARMING IS in the dock again after scientists found evidence that wild fish are being infected by farmed salmon.

Sea lice were apparently discovered in huge numbers close to the mouth of Scotland's River Shieldaig, an area where juvenile trout swim on their way out to sea.

The parasites, which can devastate fish by draining their strength, are believed to have come from underwater cages being used to farm salmon.

Wildlife experts believe the discovery is part of a wider danger to natural fish stocks caused by intensive fish farming.

Wild salmon are reported to have slumped by more than 66 per cent in the last three decades and are said to be vulnerable to further advancement by the salmon farming industry.

A catalogue of findings has now been presented to a scientific debate on the issue which has been convened in Denmark.

Salmon farmers, who supply thousands of outlets worldwide, deny that their industry is threatening wild stocks and say new techniques they employ cut the risk to other fish substantially.

Salmon farmers across the whole North Atlantic are said to have produced just 4,783 tonnes in 1980 compared to a massive 658,735 tonnes two years ago.

Greenpeace, the Atlantic Salmon Federation, and the WWF, want to see the introduction of zones free of fish farms to help protect wild stocks.

They also seek closure of commercial wild salmon fisheries sited on migratory feeding grounds.

THE WOODLAND TRUST is campaigning to protect ancient woods and wildlife from expansion plans at dozens of provincial airports.

"Government proposals to develop airports could rip the heart out of vital ancient woods that are home to birds, animals and plants," said a spokesman.

"The Trust is calling on nature lovers to sign our petition to try and prevent this from happening.

"Ancient woodland is land continuously wooded for at least 400 years - often much longer - and is one of the great glories of our natural heritage.

"Ancient woods are our richest habitat for wildlife, including more threatened species than any other UK habitat.

"They are places of inordinate beauty, reservoirs of evidence for environmental change, archaeology and economic history, and a source of inspiration for local culture and folklore. Our resource of ancient woodland is finite and cannot increase, so what remains is precious and irreplaceable."

Ancient woods close to airports are currently under threat from Stansted in Essex to Inverness in Scotland, warns the Trust.

A HERD OF cattle trampled a farmer and left him fighting for his life in hospital.

Victim David Jones, 48, suffered multiple injuries in the incident which saw him lying in a field undiscovered for 11 hours.

The drama started when Mr Jones, of Dolfrwynog, Llanerfyl, near Welshpool, went into a neighbour's fields to retrieve one of his heifers.

As he tried to catch the animal, cattle already in the field became disturbed and charged him.

He was left stranded on the ground after the attack, suffering a range of injuries which included broken ribs, collapsed lungs and facial wounds.

With Mr Jones still unable to walk, the alarm was only raised when night fell.

A search was organised and all the likeliest places visited.

Eventually, after being found by his family, Mr Jones was taken to hospital where his condition was later said to be stable.

KINGFISHERS, BUZZARDS AND even an escaped zoo snow goose are among hundreds of bird species spotted at a former disused gravel pit which has been turned into a nature reserve.

Over 3,000 children have visited the Wood Lane Nature Reserve near Ellesmere in Shropshire since its transformation.

But Shropshire Wildlife Trust wants more people to see for themselves the sheer variety of birdlife lured to the area.

Cups of tea and guided tours are currently being offered at the reserve, just off the A528, to tempt more people along.

MISTAKES AND SLOW progress are dogging the introduction of new 'right to roam' routes across the country, it has been claimed.

Following legislation introduced under the Countryside and Rights of Way Act, provisional maps showing new areas to walk in were unveiled by the Countryside Agency.

However, according to the Ramblers Association, "the provisional map showing open country in the South East was published on July 29 but has since been withdrawn by the Agency because of inaccuracies found after publication.

"There have been problems and delays in producing the maps as well as in publishing detailed regulations covering how the legislation introduced under the Act will work.

"The publication of one set of regulations covering local access forums was put back no fewer than seven times."

Walkers were standing by waiting for the opportunity to assist in the giant project.

"Our volunteers are keen to help check maps of new access land but we would like to see the freedom to roam introduced region by region as the mapping process is completed around the country," explained the spokesman.

"This would give walkers the chance to enjoy new rights of access as soon as possible - on land that has been off-limits for generations.

"A recent opinion poll conducted for the Ramblers Association showed seven out of 10 people want this to happen.

"Minister for Rural Affairs Alun Michael has expressed his sympathy for region by region implementation although he has given no firm commitments."

HARE COURSING IS at the centre of a new spat between supporters and those who want the ancient sport banned.

Countryside Alliance comments regarding a recent Advertising Standards Authority adjudication have been branded 'self-satisfied' by League Against Cruel Sports chairman John Cooper.

Commenting on a ruling by the ASA stating that over 250 hares are killed each year at organised coursing meets, Mr Cooper has called on 'Campaign for Hunting' director Simon Hart to clarify why any deaths in the name of sport are acceptable.

He said:"At coursing meets hares are killed purely in the name of sport, in some cases with onlookers cheering the death of the innocent quarry.

"Mr Hart's self satisfied comments clearly condone this barbaric practice with his willingness to admit that 'only' 252 are killed at organised coursing events.

"His readiness to do so shows just how out of touch the Alliance is with the strength of public feeling against the bloodsports it seeks to promote."

Mr Cooper claimed that recent ASA rulings had already shown bloodsports were cruel and did not have the public support the Alliance said they did.

GEORGE THE DOLPHIN has been hailed a crime-busting hero after helping police nab a jewellery thief.

The bottlenose dolphin, which has repeatedly hit the headlines for getting frisky with swimmers, helped Dorset officers stop the fugitive.

By swimming in front of a ferry at Swanage, George delayed its departure just long enough for police to board the vessel and arrest the fleeing suspect.

"George saved the day and helped us put a thief in jail, " confirmed a spokesman for Dorset police.

A man has now admitted stealing jewellery from a local shop and been jailed for 10 months by local magistrates.

REDSHANK AND OTHER wading birds are set to flourish in newly created saltmarsh which is part of an innovative flood defence scheme.

The project, on the banks of the Wash, works by harnessing nature to protect 80,000 hectares of low-lying prime agricultural land and thousands of homes in Lincolnshire.

Three 50 metre breaches have been cut into the outer sea bank at Freiston Shore to the east of Boston, allowing salt water from the Wash to gently encroach on 78 hectares of farmland owned by the RSPB.

Project manager Chris Allwork said:"This is a great flood defence project. We are creating saltmarsh and are also providing a habitat for birds such as the redshank and a range of plants and insects."

A FAMILY OF badgers evicted from their sett by development in the 1970s may be exterminated after they made a new home in neighbouring gardens, it has been revealed.

The National Federation of Badger Groups has attacked Elliot Morley, Animal Welfare Minister, for ignoring its advice that remedial action could deal with the badgers' excavations in Saltdean, East Sussex.

A licence for the slaughter of the badgers is to be issued in spite of efforts made by the NFBG to persuade the Ministry to explore other options.

"This is a deadly precedent," said Dr Elaine King, chief executive of the NFBG."It is the first time that a minister has licensed extermination of a large badger family, apparently in order to increase the value of private property and to prevent seemingly minor damage. It is entirely against the spirit of the Protection of Badgers Act 1992."

The badgers established a new sett when their existing home was bulldozed to make way for a new block of flats in 1970, says the NFBG.

The sett now extends to four adjacent gardens with the badgers even able to climb walls to move between properties where they forage for earthworms.

"These badgers have not invaded private property," fumed Dr King."Instead, relentless new development has swamped prime badger habitat. Other badgers have territories in the surrounding countryside. These badgers have nowhere else to go."

The NFBG criticised Mr Morley for licensing the slaughter of the badgers even though the only threat to buildings appears to be from excavations beneath one corner of an integral garage and beneath a garden shed.

Dr King says further upheaval caused by the badgers could be prevented by installing underground fencing.

DEFRA, she claimed, had failed to seek local knowledge of the status of badgers and their setts; had closed other badger setts in the area - without considering the effect that excluded badgers might have on neighbouring properties; and appeared to have no methodology for issuing badger licences so that the spirit of the Protection of Badgers Act 1992 could be upheld.

"The Government's approach to nature conservation seems to be people first, wildlife last," added Dr King."Every year DEFRA issues numerous licences to exclude badger families from their setts. This is usually because development has encroached on badger habitat, forcing them into conflict with people. Now, Mr Morley has gone one step further. Rather than making badgers homeless, he has approved their extermination."

NEW WAYS TO protect woods are being mooted following publication of the 'Sustaining England's Woodlands' report.

Key areas for Forestry Commission action include building better partnerships with woodland owners and increasing income from the woods themselves.

Paul Hill-Tout, the Forestry Commission's chief conservator for England, said:"Over the years, the relationship between the Forestry Commission and woodland owners has become focused on the payment and receipt of grants but grants alone will not implement the England Forestry Strategy."

HEN HARRIERS BROUGHT in to kill and scare off pigeons in London have led to new hypocrisy charges being levelled at the Government.

The birds of prey have been employed to combat mess being caused over Treasury offices where Chancellor Gordon Brown works.

Lord Mancroft, director of the Countryside Alliance, has accused ministers of double standards in trying to ban hunting on animal welfare grounds while allowing pigeons to be terrorised and killed.

During a meeting in Bournemouth, he said:"The Government held these extraordinary hearings in Portcullis House over their claim that hunting is cruel in the same week that Gordon Brown hired hen harriers to stop birds doing poo poo on his office roof.

"Those of you familiar with falconry will understand that hen harriers are not clean killers."

Meanwhile, in Scotland, Lord Watson, the Labour MSP responsible for outlawing foxhunting there, reportedly now wishes he had never sought a ban in the first place.

Two of his constituents claim he informed them at a surgery that he regretted steering anti-hunt legislation through the Scottish Parliament.

According to newspaper reports, Billy Shaw and Jacqueline Prosser, both from Lord Watson's Glasgow constituency, revealed he wished he had never started the process because it caused so much upset - a charge Lord Watson denies.

Allan Murray, director of the Scottish Countryside Alliance, later said:"We all wish he had never started this process. He wanted the glory of creating legislation but chose a subject which he knew nothing about. The result of his action is destroying a way of life in the countryside, threatening many people's livelihoods and doing absolutely nothing for animal welfare."

A DEAD STAG is at the centre of a health alert in Shropshire after thieves hoping to make a profit snatched it from a roadside.

For the animal had been injected with a powerful drug which could harm or even kill humans if ingested.

Hungry gourmets will be in for a shock if they tuck into its flesh after vets injected the dying stag with the sedative pentobarbitone.

The deer had been left beside the A4117 near Ludlow after it was involved in a road accident.

But by the time its collection had been arranged, the carcass had vanished.

SHOOTING MAKES A vital contribution to Britain's rural economy and remains highly popular, according to enthusiasts.

Nearly one per cent of the population will take part in game shooting during the coming weeks, says the Countryside Alliance, and their recreation will bring hundreds of millions of pounds to hard-pressed rural businesses.

Speaking at the start of the pheasant shooting season, campaign director Nigel Davenport underlined the popularity of shooting in the British countryside.

"It's easy to characterise shooting as a sport of the privileged few but with around 500,000 participants the sport has never been more popular or more accessible," he said.

"There are more women than ever before going shooting, and the promotion of game and other sporting shooting opportunities on the internet has brought the sport in front of a whole new and enthusiastic clientele.

"Shooting has always paid its way in the countryside. Unlike most other recreational activities, it pays valuable rent to farmers and landowners for the use of their land, and at a time when farming is in the worst depression that has been seen in a generation, income from shooting is a very welcome addition."

He added that shooters also spend large amounts of cash on everything from cartridges and clothing to tuition and hotel accommodation.

RABBITS HAVE BEEN driving ground staff crazy at a Scottish football club - days before a vital cup final match is played on their pitch.

The animals have been merrily digging holes and eating turf at Clyde Football Club which is sited in countryside near Cumbernauld.

Unfortunately, the Bell's Scottish League Challenge Cup final between Brechin and Queen of the South is due to be played there.

Barriers and other measures are now being used by worried groundsmen to try to bring the problem under control.

THE MAMMAL SOCIETY is hunting for volunteers to help it keep track of wild animal numbers during the winter.

Chairman, Professor Stephen Harris, explained:"The Winter Mammal Monitoring project provides an excellent opportunity for everybody who is interested in wildlife to contribute to our understanding of Britain's mammals.

"Volunteers will be asked to visit an area near their home looking for any mammals that they see and any signs of mammals such as footprints or droppings that they can find."

One person signed up already is Vicky Harrison, 26, who said:"I went out with my Dad to an area near where we live which had a canal, a bit of scrubland, part of the local park and a school playing field in it.

"Although it wasn't very rural we had a really nice walk and saw three feral cats, two grey squirrels and a red fox. I am looking forward to going back again and seeing whether we can find any sign of water voles by the canal."

Dr Jeremy Greenwood, director of the British Trust for Ornithology, is also taking part.

He said:"Information collected by volunteers over the course of the project not only tells us about mammal populations but may also provide vital information about the state of Britain's countryside."

261

RARE WATER VOLES are being wiped out accidentally by people who mistake them for rats, it has been revealed.

The blunt-faced mammals, confusingly also known as water 'rats', are much cleaner and less vicious than the brown rats they are often taken for.

According to The Wildlife Trusts, many people - including pest controllers, builders and developers - poison endangered water voles or disturb their homes thinking they are brown rats.

In one instance, an entire group of water voles was exterminated because of mistaken identity.

Water voles have vanished from almost 90 per cent of the sites they once occupied in the UK in the last 60 years because of loss of riverbank habitat and falling prey to voracious non-native American mink.

The discovery of a significant number of deaths because of mistaken identity is thought to have serious implications for an already vulnerable and declining mammal.

However, a new initiative launched by The Wildlife Trusts - 'Know Your Vole' - is aimed at halting further decline of the animals.

It involves providing identification guidelines for the general public and more technical information for pest control professionals and developers to avoid further cases of accidental poisoning.

Dr Simon Lyster, director general of the Trusts, said:"To small and vulnerable water vole populations, the death of any water vole is a significant setback.

"The Wildlife Trusts are working tirelessly to restore water vole homes along riverbanks and to combat the serious issue of indiscriminate poisoning.

"The key to overcoming the problem is to build awareness of the characteristics of a water vole and for people to take an active part in reporting any water vole discoveries to the Trusts."

THE FORESTRY COMMISSION is leading a "ground-breaking" project to estimate the amount of wood fuel available in British forests.

A spokesman explained:"The study will examine the potential wood fuel resource from forests in each of the Commission's Forest Districts and apply harvesting and environmental constraints to give an actual wood fuel availability.These constraints will then be applied to private sector forests.

"The study will also assess the wood fuel resource available from short rotation coppice, primary processors of timber and arboricultural operations."

THE AMOUNT OF organic land in the UK has almost doubled in the last year with sales of organic food here now the second highest in Europe, it has been claimed.

The area of fully organic land is said to be equivalent to three times the size of Greater London - having rapidly increased from 240,000 hectares to 458,600 hectares.

Almost 80 per cent of households are reported to buy organic food, spending around £920 million, more than any other European country apart from Germany.

The data is revealed in the Soil Association's 'Organic Food and Farming Report 2002' - believed to be the most comprehensive UK survey of the organic market ever compiled which draws on information from organic businesses, retailers, 15,000 shoppers and the Government.

"This is an exciting time for the organic movement - the organic market is one of the fastest-growing areas of the UK food and drink sector," said Patrick Holden, director of the Soil Association.

"The majority of households now buy organic food, all the leading supermarkets see organic food as a major growth area and, in the last year, organic farming has been given crucial financial backing from the Government.

"The challenge ahead is to encourage consumers and retailers to increase their support for UK farmers by choosing home-produced organic food wherever possible."

PETS TERRIFIED OF fireworks could be helped by playing them a CD of explosions, according to a Cheshire vet.

With Bonfire Night looming large - the worst time of the year for nervous cats and dogs - Peter Coleshaw says the CD could help animals learn how to cope in advance.

Mr Coleshaw dreamt up the idea after being dismayed that his own Jack Russell terrier shivered with fear each November 5.

He believes the CD, played slightly louder each day in the run-up to Bonfire Night, really helps pets come to term with bangs and whizzes.

However, the RSPCA has urged caution for anyone thinking of using the idea and says it is not yet proven.

SALMON AND SEA trout are to get better protection from poachers in North Yorkshire.

A clampdown on poaching in the region has been announced by the Environment Agency as numbers of the fish returning to local rivers increase.

Agency officers are to carry out extra enforcement checks along the Ouse, Ure, Esk and Tees in the next two months in a bid to protect fish returning from the sea to spawn.

Surveillance cameras have also been set up at key locations.

John Shannon, fisheries team leader, said:"It's important to stop the illegal capture of these wonderful fish so they can go on to produce the next generation.

"Numbers are finally increasing, but only slowly, and if we want this rosy picture to continue then these fish must be allowed to reach their spawning grounds. We're keeping a close eye on the waters and taking a strong line against anyone caught poaching."

GREY PARTRIDGES ARE staging a solid revival at an experimental farm site after years of decline, according to the Game Conservancy Trust.

Figures just released by the Trust confirm that for the first time in decades wild grey partridges are making a comeback after receiving special help.

The research site, on farmland at Royston, Hertfordshire, was set up specifically to restore grey partridge numbers and the species has responded well to the Trust's intensive recovery programme.

A recent count of partridges revealed that young partridge numbers have soared from just 19 to 216 in 12 months at the site.

Dr Nick Sotherton, director of research, said:"This is a fantastic outcome for our first year. We now have a good stock to work with and we hope that with continuing protection from predators, good habitat management, and a specially designed feeding regime, our 216 young partridges will have another successful breeding season next year."

The grey partridge has suffered a massive 83 per cent decline over the last 30 years due to a number of factors, virtually disappearing in many areas, says the Trust.

As lead partner in the Government's Bio-diversity Action Plan, the Trust is charged with halting the decline of the grey partridge through a sympathetic management regime, which will eventually be rolled out nationwide.

A RAM SOLD at auction for an amazing £101,000 has prompted speculation that some farmers are throwing money around from huge foot-and-mouth compensation packages.

The Swaledale ram - the UK's first six-figure sheep - was sold in the Cumbrian town of Kirkby and immediately sparked concerns that many farmers may have been over-compensated for foot-and-mouth.

NFU spokesman John Kinnaird said:"It's absolute madness, because no sheep is worth that sort of money. Neither the general public nor the Government will be amused by this farce."

Other rams are said to have been sold for sums nearer £50,000 but the latest figure is a huge leap and shows the determination of farmers to build up quality flocks after stock was decimated.

Two Cumbrian farmers are reported to have bought the £101,000 ram together after their region was the worst hit by foot-and-mouth.

PINK-FOOTED GEESE have been the stars of the show recently at Wildfowl and Wetlands Trust reserves with 13,000 recorded on one day.

Swans have also been returning to WWT reserves from their breeding grounds, adding to the spectacle. Some 745 whooper swans have so far been recorded - but only eight Bewick's swans.

ANTI-SNARE CAMPAIGNERS are claiming victory in their efforts to get a major landowner in West Sussex to outlaw snares on his land.

According to the League Against Cruel Sports, Viscount Cowdray has revealed he wants to ban snares.

"The move follows intensive lobbying by the National Anti-Snare Campaign and comes after a tenant gamekeeper was questioned and formally cautioned by police investigating an incident where a badger was discovered attached to an illegally set snare on the Cowdray estate," claimed a League spokesman.

"A recent investigation by the League Against Cruel Sports and the National Anti-Snare Campaign discovered dozens of illegally set snares on some of the UK's most prestigious country estates used for game bird shooting.

"Snares are designed to catch wild animals that are deemed to pose a threat to expensive game bird stocks and typically set within the immediate radius of intensive game bird breeding facilities or pheasant release pens, where young birds are managed prior to the shooting season.

"Although advocates of snaring maintain the practice is a humane form of pest control, footage obtained by the League / NASC and released in a comprehensive Video News Release suggests many victims suffer horrific injuries during the process.

"Earlier this year, investigators found a female badger with its abdomen torn open by a snare in South Yorkshire, and a cub found dead at a nearby sett.

"Police are also continuing to investigate after around a dozen snares attached to dragpoles 4ft long were discovered near pheasant release pens on the prestigious Polesdon shooting estate in Wiltshire."

Douglas Batchelor, League chief executive, added: "All snaring is cruel and unnecessary and a menace to wildlife and domestic pets, but the illegal setting of snares on unanchored dragpoles is particularly disturbing. It is just another cruel by-product of the pointless bloodsport that is game bird shooting."

WITH THE NATION'S clocks about to go back, the RSPB is urging people to 'take the time' to feed hungry birds in their garden and help prop up more vulnerable species.

Some 24 million people are already believed to feed the birds in their garden at least once a week during the winter - but the Society now wants even more to join in.

Its 'Time for Birds Weekend', from October 25 to 28, coincides with the end of British Summer Time and the onset of winter.

RSPB spokeswoman Caroline Osborne said:"Many people are already working hard for birds but we would like every household to take on the challenge of feeding our feathered friends - not just during Time for Birds, but all year round.

"Providing feeders, bird tables and a clean water supply not only helps birds through the winter, but can also provide hours of entertainment."

Time for Birds also aims to raise the profile of birds such as the house sparrow, which have declined severely in the last few years for reasons not fully understood.

Once sparrows disappear from an area, says the RSPB, they can be very difficult to encourage back.

AN AMBITIOUS BID has been launched to save the wildlife of England's internationally important lakes and waterways from growing environmental threats.

English Nature is investing £1.3 million over the next two years in a flagship scheme aimed at ensuring that many of the country's 400 water-based Sites of Special Scientific Interest retain their full range of native plants and animals.

Wildlife at the sites is under threat for various reasons, including effluent discharge and agricultural run-off; introduced invasive aquatic plants; changes in land management; changes in fish populations and disturbance of sediments.

Areas targeted include the Norfolk Broads where major restoration of lakeshore habitats is now underway.

Elsewhere, at West Midland Meres, lakeshore habitats are also being restored on several meres by removing heavy shading from tree and shrub cover to encourage growth of aquatic plants.

Meanwhile, at sites in the West Midlands and Lincolnshire, efforts are being made to control New Zealand pygmyweed, an introduced invasive aquatic plant.

Project manager Allan Stewart said:"Healthy lakes not only provide for good wildlife but also support human needs such as recreation. The importance of maintaining or restoring the biodiversity of lakes is now recognised and throughout the country efforts are being made to address this.

"Water companies are installing treatment processes to reduce the amount of nutrients discharging into watercourses from sewage effluent, resulting in clear water and plant-rich lakes which can only be good news. Despite this, there still remains a great deal to do if we are to protect lake SSSIs and English Nature is rising to the challenge."

AN ANONYMOUS DONATION of over 500 acres of farmland at Fordham, Essex will be used to create a massive new woodland and wetland habitat, says The Woodland Trust.

Announcing the acquisition Mike Townsend, Trust chief executive, said:"This gift is truly magnificent and we are determined to use this opportunity to show what woodland creation can do for wildlife and people.

"Essex has lost many thousands of acres of woodland over the centuries and now is the time to let children and adults start to shape their future landscapes."

Creating the new wood will require additional funds and the Trust has set a £500,000 fundraising target for public donations to the project.

GREY SQUIRRELS CAN rest easy - a probe into using contraception to control them is being abandoned after trials proved inconclusive.

But the north American immigrants, which have ousted native red squirrels from most of their ancient territories, may actually suffer more in the long-run since lethal controls will still exist.

The dumping of the contraception control plan was revealed in a joint announcement by the Forestry Commission and Joint Nature Conservation Committee.

However, the Commission and its research partners still believe 'immuno-contraception' could one day prove a useful method of controlling grey squirrels' impact on native red squirrels and timber crops.

"Although a great deal has been learned from the research, the attempt to repeat under field conditions the good results that were achieved under laboratory conditions has proved unsuccessful," the Commission's scientific adviser, Dr Steve Gregory, admitted.

GRAYLING NUMBERS ARE to be recorded across a variety of waterways in England and Wales.

The aim of the Environment Agency project - run in conjunction with the Grayling Society - is to 'monitor the performance of local grayling fisheries'.

Spokesman Richard Cove explained:"Such information, collected over a number of years, will inform and direct management of this important species and advance scientific knowledge."

Anglers who take part will be asked to record simple details in a logbook supplied by the Agency and will then get a summary of the results.

Grayling are believed to be present in all Agency regions although they only inhabit a few rivers in Anglia.

In southern England, grayling are said to be most densely populated in chalk streams, particularly the Test, Itchen and Avon.

FOXES HAVE BEEN blamed for putting motorists' lives at risk in Surrey after chewing through brake cables.

More than 20 cars were attacked at Epsom and police first feared they were hunting a maniac intent on causing a fatal accident.

But an investigation revealed the true culprits - young foxes which have become addicted to the taste of brake fluid.

Driver Maggie Haywood was just one victim left terrified for her life when the brakes on her Mitsubishi car jammed.

After her narrow escape in busy traffic, police staked out an area of just a few streets to catch the madman responsible.

But the truth was soon uncovered - Epsom has a high number of hungry young foxes trying to find food and the sweet taste of glycol in brake fluid proved irresistible.

TASTEBUDS ARE IN for a treat during British Food Fortnight, a national celebration of British food and drink starting on October 26.

The two-week celebration is a joint project run by the Countryside Alliance, the Guild of Fine Food Retailers and the Campaign for Real Food.

Thousands of producers are taking part in a bid to make the freshest, tastiest ingredients available to hungry participants.

CONSERVATIONISTS WERE horrified by news that the leaders of France and Germany have stitched up a deal on farm spending to facilitate EU enlargement.

Phil Rothwell, head of countryside policy for the RSPB, said:"This is nothing short of disastrous for the environment, farmers and consumers. It seems extraordinary that Jacques Chirac and Gerhard Schroeder can dictate the actions of the EU-15, soon to become the EU-25, and apparently fail to see the problems caused by the out-dated Common Agricultural Policy."

In a recent letter to the RSPB, Secretary of State Margaret Beckett underlined the UK Government's commitment to CAP reform - now undermined by the Franco-German deal.

The new deal is said to threaten a death blow to EU Agriculture Commissioner Franz Fischler's proposals which would make agriculture more environmentally friendly.

Mr Rothwell added:"Chirac and Schroeder have shown their true colours as politicians who care more about the bottom line than about citizens and the environment.

"Margaret Beckett and Tony Blair must lead a reform process that will protect the countryside in the UK, EU-15, and the accession countries alike.

"Otherwise we will continue to face declining wildlife, landscape losses, bankrupt farmers and challenges from a population tired of paying three times for the CAP: once in taxes, once at the till and once more for environmental damage."

BLACK GROUSE AND capercaillie are now being closely monitored by Forestry Commission staff in Scotland in a move to boost numbers.

Workers are said to be playing a key role in helping conservationists figure out ways to preserve fragile populations of the rare birds.

Without help, black grouse face imminent extinction while capercaillie numbers have dwindled to a mere thousand.

Over the spring and summer, Commission staff carried out a count of both species during 'lekking' time, when male birds gather to display and fight for the attention of females.

Kevin Peace, Kincardine forest district manager, said:"Capercaillie tend to lek deep in the woods to keep away from prying eyes, and the leks can trigger fierce fighting between the turkey-sized males.

"Black grouse leks are altogether more civilised affairs and are usually held on open grassy fields or clearings in the forest. The males produce a strong soporific bubbling call and jump about with their lyre-shaped tails fanned out.

"Specially trained dogs, usually German short-haired pointers, helped with the count, sniffing out and locating the hens and their broods, enabling the dog handlers and helpers to count the chicks."

CASH-STRAPPED ARABLE farmers denied compensation over late payments have now had their case taken up by union leaders.

The NFU is planning to take the Rural Payments Agency to the Parliamentary Ombudsman over its failure to pay arable farmers interest on late 2001 Arable Area payments.

The decision follows a victory for the NFU in achieving interest payments on late 2001 beef payments.

The Rural Payments Agency has agreed to provide compensation for delays in making the 20 per cent of beef scheme payments outstanding - where it believes farmers were not to blame for inconsistencies in their claims.

The interest payments relate to the balance of payments for 2001 Suckler Cow Premium, Slaughter Premium and Beef Special Premium.

NFU president Ben Gill said some farmers were still waiting for payments, despite the deadline having passed at the end of June.

He said:"We are extremely pleased that after prolonged pressure from the NFU, the RPA has agreed to compensate farmers who have been forced, through no fault of their own, to wait for this desperately needed income.

"However, I am horrified that arable farmers who were also paid late have not had a similar offer.

"This decision on beef payments only strengthens our determination to get justice for arable farmers.

"Producers' entitlement to interest on late payments has already been considered on one occasion by the Parliamentary Ombudsman.

"We will now be taking the arable case there. I see the beef case as a precedent - arable interest payments must follow."

BIRDWATCHERS IN BLACKPOOL were astonished to learn one of the world's rarest birds had been spotted ambling along their promenade.

The northern bald ibis - an odd looking species 18inches high with a 3ft wingspan and a 7in bill - was photographed by a couple out for a stroll.

Experts have been left scratching their heads as to how the bird reached the resort since only 220 remain in the wild on a north African reserve.

Most captive birds are here in Britain although no zoos have reported any missing.

Some people believe the ibis may have flown all the way from Morocco.

But others think it is either the product of a smuggling operation gone wrong or has escaped from a private collection.

A DEER TERRIFIED by stormy weather took refuge in the bedroom of a local property - startling a man from his slumber.

Gale force winds and thrashing debris had prompted the deer - named Rain - to flee a wildlife park near Looe in Cornwall and sneak into neighbour Phil Strathen's flat.

Its presence soon caused a shock.

Mr Strathen could barely believe his eyes when he awoke to find the animal in his ground-floor bedroom.

But he calmed down when the truth emerged.

Rain is a hand-reared pet belonging to his landlady Joy Palmer who also owns Porfell Animal Land wildlife park.

RAM: fancy footwork needed to avoid being flattened

WHEN you consider that, before foot-and-mouth struck, there were an estimated 40 million sheep in this country, it comes as a shock that the Government still wants to tattoo or tag every single one.

Many farmers were dismayed by this EU-inspired directive.

The national bill to ensure that no individual animal remains anonymous in the system is likely to top £6million.

Under proposals first announced by former Agriculture Minister Nick Brown, each sheep could either be tattooed on its head or have a tag attached to its ear.

Critics say the scheme is a waste of time, amounting to yet more bureaucratic interference which will further shackle farmers.

But supporters of the plan say it will help trace outbreaks of disease back to the farm where affected sheep originate from.

Whatever your views, there is no doubt that a lot of work will be needed on farms before millions of sheep are individually dealt with.

Britain is host to many different types of sheep and they are all hardy animals capable of withstanding appalling weather conditions.

One of the toughest and most common breeds is the Scottish Blackface sheep, found not just in the Scottish Highlands but on Dartmoor and other windswept territories.

The blackface is, not surprisingly, so named because it has a black face which contrasts markedly with its long, shaggy white coat.

Rams of the breed are quite striking with a prominent, high bridged nose and big horns.

They also enjoy a fight with each other during the October breeding season when the clash of horns can be heard for miles across open country.

Rams can be pretty impressive animals at close quarters.

Years ago, I was walking home one day when I suddenly heard a thundering noise ahead of me on the country track I was following.

Within seconds, I was confronted by a huge ram racing at full pelt towards me.

It had obviously just escaped from some farm hands, now in hot pursuit.

If I hadn't stepped smartly aside I would have been flattened by its enormous spiralled horns.

I watched in awe as this mighty animal then leapt a 5ft gate behind me like a cat and carried on going with the breathless farm hands struggling to catch up.

I must admit I felt distinctly grateful that they were the ones trying to tackle this enraged, snorting beast.

That ram was not a black faced sheep.

Its face was actually white like its coat and, from looking at sheep pictures since, I think it was possibly a Whitefaced Woodland ram.

Coincidentally, rams of this type are sometimes used to breed with the ewes of black faced species to pass on their greater size and weight.

In fact, many species are cross-bred to take on board the finer points of others. Sheep seem very adaptable.

Much of the traditional land where they graze would be too inhospitable for cattle or horses.

This makes them an invaluable, practical resource - at least until foot-and-mouth rears its head again.

I fear even tattoos and tags would make little difference then.

DORMICE, BATS, BADGERS and more than 60 species of birds are threatened by plans to bulldoze an ancient Welsh wood.

The move has angered conservationists who have formed a coalition of nine groups opposing proposals to fell 117 acres of Hendre Wood near Monmouth so a golf course and leisure complex can be built.

The application would involve destroying land which has been wooded for at least 400 years, according to The Woodland Trust.

Mike Townsend, chief executive of the Trust, said:"If this development were to go ahead, it would lead to one of the greatest losses of ancient woodland in the UK since the building of the Channel Tunnel.

"Hendre Wood is one of the largest blocks of ancient woodland remaining in Wales so this application will be a hugely important test case for the new protection for ancient woodland in Planning Policy Wales."

Dr Stephanie Tyler, one of the region's most respected wildlife experts, added:"Over two thirds of the ancient woodland which existed in the old county of Monmouthshire in the 1930s has already been lost. We simply cannot afford to lose any more. We know that the woods contain a range of rare and threatened species."

Dormice, lesser horseshoe bats, badgers, great crested newts, spotted flycatchers, turtle doves, and wood white butterflies were among inhabitants now facing an uncertain future, she added.

ONE IN 10 British rams could be gay, according to researchers who have been studying the sexual inclinations of sheep.

Although the epitomy of masculinity, certain rams are only turned on by their own gender, scientists found.

After analysing the brains of nine gay rams, the study discovered marked differences when compared to the brains of 'straight' rams.

The study, carried out in America, showed that a specialised area of the brain could be responsible for influencing sexual preferences in all mammals - not just sheep.

DOLLY THE SHEEP is being offered as an optional extra in the sale of a £500,000 house in Kent.

The ewe is an efficient grass trimmer and keeps the lawns in top shape at the property in Wrotham.

Owner Ray Turnell realised Dolly would probably like to stay when he put the house on the market and thought she might also be an asset to buyers.

Local estate agents made a note of his comments and have been advertising "a three-bed detached house with separate annexe, triple garage - and optional sheep!" Hay fever-sufferer Ray originally bought Dolly to munch down his grass so he would not be made ill by constant lawn mowing.

FEARS HAVE BEEN raised for the future of Britain's peregrine falcons following evidence of increasingly poor breeding success.

The spectacular birds were the subject of a Scottish study this year organised by the British Trust for Ornithology and supported by Scottish Raptor Study Groups and Scottish Natural Heritage.

"Returns for some areas indicate low chick survival rates," revealed a spokesman for the Trust.

"In Central Scotland and Western Perth and Kinross, for example, the overall number of successful nests was only half that recorded a decade ago.

"The peregrine falcon is a key barometer of the state of the environment and, historically, declines in numbers and breeding success of peregrines heralded the adverse impacts of pesticides in the countryside.

"Much of the failure is likely to have been due to severe weather in spring and early summer. Other trends reported by fieldworkers include reduced occupancy of a number of traditional breeding sites in upland areas, notably on some areas with grouse moors.

"There are also some reports of suspected persecution of the birds, for instance in parts of south east and north east Scotland. These factors will be examined in more detail once all the data have been returned.

"The picture emerging in 2002 is different from 1991, when the results indicated that peregrines had recovered from a population crash in the 1960s caused by the use of organochlorine pesticides.

"This was heralded as a success for wildlife conservation and proof that the environmental threat posed by these chemicals had been overcome in most areas of the UK."

Professor Des Thompson, chairman of the Scottish Raptor Monitoring Group, said:"These early signs are worrying, not least because the peregrine is known to be such a good indicator of the health of the environment."

Patrick Stirling-Aird, of the Scottish Raptor Study Groups, added:"There is evidence from some upland locations that peregrine territories are unoccupied as a result of persistent criminal persecution in the supposed interests of red grouse management.

"In other cases, however, the underlying cause of territory desertion may be reduced numbers of prey species, something that touches on fundamental land management practices."

PUFFINS HAVE BEEN boosted on Lundy Island in the Bristol Channel after an operation began to wipe out 40,000 rats which prey on chicks and eggs there.

The tubby, colourful ground-nesting birds have been driven to the point of extinction with less than 10 breeding pairs now existing on the three-mile long island.

Extermination teams have been brought in by English Nature from New Zealand to kill all the rats on the island with poisoned bait, hopefully by next Easter.

After the rats are gone, conservationists will try to build up puffin numbers again, along with similarly threatened Manx shearwaters and other species.

HEDGEHOGS ARE approaching their most hazardous time of year as places where they snuggle down to rest turn into real hot spots - blazing bonfires.

Once again, The Wildlife Trusts are urging people to take care no prickly guests get toasted.

"The beginning of November is when our hedgehogs settle down for a seasonal snooze," said a spokesman."Bonfires are just an added risk for the sleeping hedgehog and can be fatal. Whether you are the organiser of a community bonfire night, or holding it with friends in your own back garden, by following just a few guidelines you can save a hedgehog from a fate like Guy Fawkes.

"Before you build the bonfire, place some hedgehog boxes in the surrounding area a safe distance from the fire. Hopefully the hedgehogs will occupy the boxes.

"Build your bonfire as close to the night as possible to minimise the chance of a hedgehog moving in. When collecting material to burn in the days up to bonfire night, pile it in one place, but build the bonfire in another.

"If you burn the pile of collected material it is more likely that a hedgehog will have moved in. And finally, always check the bonfire thoroughly using a torch before it is lit. Any hedgehogs that are found should be carefully placed in nearby hedgehog boxes or in a safe dry spot away from the fire."

A GREY SQUIRREL which viciously attacked six people in Cheshire was shot dead by the grandfather of its youngest victim.

The squirrel had become notorious in Knutsford for scratching and biting anyone close to its territory in local woods.

Grandad Geoff Horth was left outraged after the squirrel turned on Kelsi Morley, aged two, when she was out with her mother Karen.

The little girl suffered a deep bite to the head and other wounds before her terrified mum managed to drag the animal off.

After hearing the tale, grandad Mr Horth grabbed an air rifle and went in search of the errant squirrel - shooting it dead when he found it.

CONSERVATIONISTS ARE celebrating the largest coastal realignment project ever undertaken in Europe with the breaching of the sea wall at Abbotts Hall Farm, Essex.

"This will convert 200 acres of arable farmland into saltmarsh and grassland as part of a nationwide initiative to restore the UK's rapidly declining coastal wetlands," explained a spokesman for English Nature."At this morning's high tide, the sea swept through the man-made breaches created in the 3.5km sea wall. The flooded area should gradually regenerate as natural saltmarsh and saline lagoons, both internationally important wildlife habitats."

FINE WORDS AND good intent are not enough to prevent another foot-and-mouth disaster - the Government must deliver on its promises, say farmers' leaders.

NFU president Ben Gill said:"The Government's response is full of good intent, work in progress and resolve. What is important is that all the strategy developments, cultural shift and structural changes that are described are implemented and then tested, reviewed and updated on a continuing basis.

"Many would feel it should never have taken so long to introduce what to many are common sense measures."

Mr Gill spoke out after DEFRA Secretary of State Margaret Beckett gave the Government's official response to both the Lessons to be Learned and Royal Society's inquiries on foot-and-mouth.

The NFU remains opposed to any suggestion that the costs of Government disease control programmes should be borne by producers.

Mr Gill said:"Any move in this direction would be a complete abrogation of the Government's responsibilities in dealing with an outbreak of exotic animal disease, which has arisen from the Government's failure to properly protect our borders."

Some 400 days on from the end of the outbreak, and after half a dozen inquiries, farmers would be pleased that the Government had at long last acknowledged the importance of disease prevention rather than cure, he added.

The NFU welcomed the Government's recognition that more money must be spent on research, surveillance and monitoring of animal diseases, plus effective action and better co-ordination of control agencies in the fight against illegal imports.

The NFU also recognised the need to establish on-going measures to prevent the spread of disease.

Mr Gill said that the Government's stated commitment to electronic tagging of animals was to be welcomed but Government itself must take a clear lead.

The union was also keen to work with the Government to improve biosecurity awareness on farms.

THE FALCONRY BUSINESS is booming in London where hawks are increasingly being employed to scare off pigeons, it has been revealed.

Experienced falconers are now vying for business around some of the capital's most famous buildings.

Contracts worth as much as £40,000 per year are being handed out to falconry firms.

In turn, they promise to keep messy pigeons away - and save companies vast sums on cleaning bills.

Each day at 4am, one hawk is even allowed to fly from the roof of the Treasury Department.

It swoops around the area - terrifying roosting pigeons into taking flight.

Some pigeons are killed by this and other 'scare' hawks - prompting complaints from animal rights groups that the activity is cruel.

However, the falconers themselves say the aim is only to scare birds away.

There is no intention to kill any of the pigeons that are brought down.

THE PLIGHT OF badgers living under a death sentence at Saltdean in Sussex is going national with supporters launching a nationwide petition to save them.

The badgers were recently granted a stay of execution while more consultations were carried out with local residents.

But the National Federation of Badger Groups believes the lives of the badgers are still at risk because of burrowing activities said to be undermining local properties.

Launching its petition, the NFBG called on as many people as possible to sign - before it is too late.

The Saltdean Badger Coalition, which includes the NFBG, has also accused DEFRA of ignoring its own advice when confronted with the badgers v residents problem.

The Coalition, which worked with local residents to halt the culling of badgers in October, says it has unearthed a document by the same DEFRA official who has been advising Minister Elliot Morley.

In the document, the official describes how badger licences should be assessed, implemented and monitored.

"It's incredible," said Dr Elaine King, NFBG chief executive."He spelt out what should be done but has failed to do it. DEFRA made its decision with little of the essential information to hand. It doesn't even know how many badgers are living in the sett.

"In separate statements, it has said there are 'six to eight' and 'eight to 10' badgers, while the licence says 15 badgers. It's a complete shambles."

SUPPORT FOR A hunting ban is waning fast among the public, claims the Countryside Alliance.

An NOP poll carried out for the Alliance asked 1000 adults which of the possible outcomes for hunting legislation they would personally support.

Some 28 per cent thought that hunting with dogs should be controlled by a Government licensing scheme with 26 per cent saying that hunting should remain as it is - subject to self-regulation.

"Only 43 per cent thought it should be made a criminal offence. In an earlier poll carried out in March of this year, 48 per cent opted for hunting with dogs to be made a criminal offence, suggesting declining public support for a ban," said a spokesman for the Alliance.

"Following the publication of the Government Inquiry into Hunting with Dogs in 2000 and the recent Government consultation process, support for a ban has slipped from a maximum 76 per cent to a 10-year low, flying in the face of claims made by animal rights organisations that a majority of the public demand the activity to be made a criminal offence."

Simon Hart, director of the Campaign for Hunting, added:"The more the facts about hunting emerge, the more obvious it is that there is no case for a ban."

ALIEN CRAYFISH ARE being caught by 'sex traps' laid in British waters.

Scientists are using the pulling power of the traps to lure the invasive crustaceans from native waterways.

In a project sponsored by the Environment Agency and English Nature, North American signal crayfish are being tricked by 'pheromone baits' into thinking they'll be shown a good time if they enter the underwater baskets.

Environment Agency spokesman Peter Sibley said:"Although pheromones have been used in pest management for a number of years on land, this is one of the first attempts to use them to improve trapping success in water.

"Signals really are the bullies of the crayfish world and the trouble they cause isn't confined to crayfish. In large numbers they can be a threat to spawning salmon by taking fish eggs. They have been known to wipe out whole areas of aquatic plants and, by burrowing into banks, they can damage the habitat of endangered species like water voles.

"The problem is, they like it here. The largest signal in the world was pulled from waters in Nottinghamshire in 2000. It weighed more than 200 grammes. This species is thriving well at the expense of our own species and we need to find effective ways to control them."

MADONNA IS A cow and so are Posh and Kylie, say farmers who are increasingly naming their animals after celebrities.

According to an NFU survey, more and more dairy farmers are dropping traditional names such as Buttercup and Daisy in favour of celebrity tags.

NFU deputy president Tim Bennett said:"The influence of celebrities is just as likely to be felt in a farmer's field as in cities and towns. These days Marigold, Bluebell and Buttercup have to compete with Kylie and Posh.

"More importantly, our study shows that dairy cows are very much part of the family on a farm and are cared for accordingly. Giving them names strengthens the emotional bond that farmers have with them."

RED SQUIRRELS CAN be 'adopted' as Christmas presents this year under a wildlife friendly gift-giving scheme organised by The Wildlife Trusts.

"Dorset Wildlife Trust runs an adoption scheme to help protect this struggling UK species," explained a spokesman. "Participants receive a photograph and certificate, a red squirrel tie pin and a CD Rom.

"If you pay by direct debit you will also receive a fluffy red squirrel toy. Perfect for both children and adults."

Adopting a squirrel costs £15 and anyone interested should call Dorset Wildlife Trust.

Similar schemes are being run by Trusts elsewhere.

"The Wildlife Trust of South and West Wales protects one of the largest colonies of puffins in southern Britain. There are 100,000 pretty puffins on Skomer Island and you can become a puffin pal for £10 a year. You will receive an adoption certificate, picture and newsletter."

Meanwhile, Cheshire Wildlife Trust provides hibernation boxes for dormice and gift givers can help by adopting a dormouse for just £10 a year.

FEARS WERE RAISED that rabies could be spreading throughout Britain's bat population after a bat conservation worker was bitten and left fighting for his life.

However, health officials now say that initial tests for rabies on victim David McRae have proved negative - though he is still critically ill.

Mr McRae, who is being treated at Ninewells Hospital, Dundee, is suffering from suspected infection with European bat lyssavirus.

The 55 year-old licensed bat consultant regularly handles a variety of bats during the course of his work.

If rabies is eventually found, Mr McRae, from a village north of Dundee in Scotland, will become the first person in a century to catch the disease while in Britain.

Scottish Natural Heritage, for whom Mr McRae works as a bat handler, said his fellow workers would be issued with guidelines to reduce the risk of anyone else falling ill.

A TREE SAPLING in a coffin formed the centre - piece of a mock funeral held outside the Department of Transport in London.

The event, organised by The Woodland Trust, was meant to underline the death facing thousands of such saplings if Government airport expansion plans get the go-ahead.

Rare animals, plants and insects also face a similar fate if the ill-thought out schemes to increase air traffic are allowed, warns the Trust.

"An area of irreplaceable ancient woodland equivalent in size to the combined city centres of Durham, Chester, Bath and Canterbury will be wiped out if the Government's plans get the green light," said a spokesman."Some of our richest terrestrial habitats will be destroyed."

The sapling, representing 60 ancient woods under threat from the proposals, was 'buried' in con - crete as it lay in a coffin, watched by the 'grim reaper'.

Conservationists were highlighting the potential desecration of 2,450 acres of ancient woodland.

SPECTACULAR BIRDS OF prey such as the golden eagle, peregrine falcon, goshawk and merlin could be under threat from proposed Government 'penny-pinching' cutbacks, warns the RSPB.

"Currently, anyone wanting to keep certain rare birds in captivity has to have the birds ringed and listed under a Government-run registration scheme, similar to the vehicle licensing scheme," said a spokesman.

"However, under Government proposals, certain species would be removed from the scheme or the registration scheme could even be completely scrapped. The RSPB believes this would lead to an increase in nest robberies and a decrease in the detection of these crimes.

"The Registration Scheme allows the birds and their offspring to be located for DNA testing. DNA testing in the mid-1990s showed that over 10 per cent of peregrine falcons and goshawks declared as captive bred were illegally taken from the wild."

HUNT GROUPS HAVE been left none the wiser about the probable fate of their sport following the latest Queen's Speech.

The Countryside Alliance said the content of the Speech regarding the future of hunting was broadly as expected - namely that a Bill will be introduced to enable Parliament to reach a conclusion on hunting with dogs.

There was no mention of a proposed ban or partial ban.

The Alliance added that it expects the Government to keep its word and propose fair hunting legislation based on principle and evidence.

Chairman John Jackson said:"The Alliance looks forward to seeing the actual shape of the forthcoming legislation, which this announcement leaves unclear.

"We expect the Government to keep its word and make proposals which are fair and based on principle and evidence.

"Any departure from this would result in resistance - not only by rural people but by all who value social justice."

The Alliance now awaits either a statement from Alun Michael, as promised following the consultation process, or to hear more of the timing of draft legislation.

In the meantime, the Alliance's Campaign for Hunting has reiterated the contents of its Declaration of Cohesion signed by the Council of Hunting Associations, noting that "an attack on any form of properly conducted legal hunting will be treated as an attack on all."

Everyone is committed to unity and success, asserts the Alliance, with meticulous contingency plans prepared should a hostile announcement eventually be made.

Sam Butler, chairman of the Campaign for Hunting, said:"We should be aware that the real fight could be about to start and, although we should not underestimate the real dangers, we are well positioned through our joint efforts to meet the challenges.

"In doing so we need to be very careful not to lose our hard won public support whilst ensuring that we continue to make ourselves heard."

BRITAIN'S BASKING SHARKS have been boosted by getting better international protection from shark hunters.

The gentle giants were added to a list of protected creatures at a meeting of the Convention on Trade in Endangered Species in Chile.

Basking sharks - the largest sharks found in our waters - are harmless plankton feeders.

However, they are treated the same as other sharks by fishermen who hunt them for their 6ft fins to make expensive soup.

Following pressure from the UK Government, products from the shark can now be sold only with special permits.

Minister Elliot Morley revealed he was delighted that Britain had finally got the support needed to protect the sharks.

He explained:"Taking action now is vital. Basking sharks have a slow growth rate and a low birth rate which makes them particularly vulnerable to over exploitation.

"This is all about sustainable use of the world's natural resources and that is exactly what we have achieved with the success of this proposal."

270

SALMON ARE THRIVING in what was once one of the country's dirtiest waterways - the River Mersey on Merseyside.

According to the Environment Agency, the fish have often been seen leaping a weir at Woolston, near Warrington.

Since October, the Agency has employed a fish trap to catch salmon at the weir so their condition can be examined.

So far 25 have been trapped, as well as two brown trout, one sea trout, three lamprey and two dace.

Roger Lamming, the Agency's environment manager, said:"The results so far suggest we have had a substantial run of fish, especially in the river's high flows following recent rain. Salmon have been pushing in for some time, with regular sightings.

"It is very exciting news and just reward for the efforts of so many Environment Agency staff to secure improvements in the quality of rivers in the Mersey catchment area.

"Now we must all build on this and ensure the Mersey continues to improve and that it can once again be known for its salmon rather than its pollution."

THE CATTLE RING of London's Royal Smithfield Show was milked for dramatic effect by cattleman Neil Lloyd after he wed sweetheart Sally Burnett.

The happy couple, from Herefordshire, had their wedding vows blessed in the show ring after tying the knot at Hammersmith and Fulham Register Office.

The event unfolded during the annual carol service at the show and the lovebirds were helped to celebrate by hundreds of guests.

The pair had looked for a novel way to start married life before deciding to use the popular agricultural show.

Mr Lloyd has shown his cattle there for years and even had four of his animals entered in this year's competitions.

THE RSPB SAYS it is becoming increasingly concerned about an oil pollution incident off the East Anglian coast which could be affecting large numbers of seabirds.

The birds - mainly guillemots and gulls but also including red-throated divers - are being washed ashore along the coast and taken into care by the RSPCA.

Sharon Thompson, of the RSPB, said:"With the sinking of the Prestige, everybody's minds are focused on the environmental damage caused by major oil pollution incidents.

"However, around the UK coastline, far more oiled birds are reported every year with incidents like this, which undoubtedly are caused by unscrupulous tanker captains washing out their vessels' tanks at sea."

In recent years, she added, the RSPB had helped bring about major improvements to reduce these risks to seabirds and other marine life.

THE BATTLE FOR the gay vote on hunting has been won by the anti-hunt camp, claims the League Against Cruel Sports.

A move by the Countryside Alliance to attract minority groups - including gay men - to its pro-hunt stance had flopped, claims the League, while its own full-page advert in Gay Times had proved a roaring success.

The advert, showing a young disembowelled fox, prompted nearly 200 hits on the League's website within a day of appearing, according to a spokesman.

He explained:"The League took out the full-page ad titled 'Victim of Tolerance?' in the same edition as the hunters featured an advertisement showing two gay hunters and calling for a 'free country'.

"But the hunters' campaign to try and attract ethnic minorities and homosexual men appears to have backfired. Within hours of the December magazine hitting the shops, 188 people had logged on to the Gay Times page on the League's website to read the ad and find out more about our work."

League chief executive Douglas Batchelor added:"It is clear that the Alliance's six-figure advertising campaign is a flop. The majority of people - gay or straight, of all races - believe hunting to be cruel and unnecessary.

"The point is, it does not matter what colour people are, or what their sexual preferences are, no-one should have the freedom to inflict suffering on a wild creature in the name of 'sport'."

Earlier, the Countryside Alliance had welcomed the introduction by Lord Donoughue of a Bill to amend the Wild Mammals (Protection) Act 1996 to make it an offence to intentionally cause undue suffering to any wild mammal.

Alliance chairman John Jackson said:"We endorse the thinking behind this Bill. During DEFRA's recently held hunting hearings, consensus clearly emerged that legislation should deal with cruelty to all wild mammals equally. Any measure designed to promote higher standards of welfare coupled with greater openness is to be welcomed.

"Properly conducted, hunting has nothing to fear from legislation of this nature. This Bill provides an opportunity to build on common ground established during the hearings and to increase public confidence in the circumstances and manner in which hunting is conducted."

ENGLAND'S SEAS AND coastline are damaged and declining, according to a disturbing English Nature report.

"Despite important initiatives to protect our marine environment, it is showing signs of significant stress and low resilience to continuing pressure," said a spokesman.

"All this adds up to an alarm call for those who use and manage our coasts and seas and care about their future."

The report says the seaside remains an important cultural and economic asset and in one year (1998) 51 per cent of people in England were thought to have visited it, supporting the local economy.

Half of the UK's total biodiversity (around 40,000 species including corals, sea horses, fish and mammals such as dolphins and whales) is found in the sea.

AN ANTI-CRUELTY group has been accused of allowing a herd of deer on its own land to suffer unnecessarily.

The League Against Cruel Sports faces allegations that dozens of deer at its Baronsdown sanctuary near Dulverton, in Somerset, are being left to die of starvation and disease.

The claims come not from traditional critics within the Countryside Alliance but have been made by one of the League's own workers, an elderly man who has managed deer for decades.

According to a Sunday newspaper, Gordon Pearce, 72, has worked for the League for more than 30 years and it was his job to put down injured or diseased red deer.

However, he claims that the League has ignored several warnings that old or diseased animals must be culled to prevent others in the 350-strong herd from dying of starvation or disease.

Too much sentimentality about killing animals has also made matters worse, he said, with one deer trailing around a broken leg in agony for two weeks because he had not been allowed to dispatch it at once.

League chief executive Douglas Batchelor told the paper:"Gordon Pearce brought his views to our attention. We have listened to what he's said, looked at our land and its carrying capacity, looked at the number of deer on it and the health of them and come to the conclusion we do not need to cull deer.

"Therefore we have not taken his advice. We have listened to his views but we disagree with him. Nature is the biggest controller of deer populations due to the weather, basically. If it's cold and wet you will get losses due to hypothermia."

PROPOSALS TO BUILD an airport over Cliffe Marshes in Kent are a major threat to the UK's wetland wildlife, warn conservationists.

"As well as being an important area for wintering wildfowl and waders, the North Kent Marshes are important breeding areas for many duck species such as shoveler, shelduck, gadwall, garganey and teal," explained a spokesman for the Wildfowl and Wetlands Trust."In addition, some of the best wader breeding habitat in the country is to be found in the area."

WILDLIFE WHICH DEPENDS on hedges to survive has been given a boost with the publication of a new handbook.

The book, available free from DEFRA, will "help identify hedges that are in good shape, as well as those in need of management and restoration. It will also help pinpoint the best places to fill gaps in the hedgerow network with new planting", according to a spokesman.

OTTERS HAVE BEEN recorded in many of the UK's towns and cities for the first time in up to 30 years, The Wildlife Trusts have revealed.

Delighted conservationists have discovered the aquatic mammals in over 100 urban environments throughout the country.

"Whilst otters have been recovering in some areas, they had only been recorded until recently on city margins or within a 10 or 20-mile radius of major urban areas," said a spokesman for the Trusts.

"But recent survey work undertaken by the Trusts' 'Water for Wildlife' project now identifies otters as regular users of major town and city waterways.

"Of over 100 towns and cities, otters are now present in Edinburgh, Glasgow, Newcastle, Carlisle, Leeds, Doncaster, Norwich, Bristol, Canterbury and Cardiff.

"Thirteen urban areas, including Newcastle, have resident otters, whereby otters live and breed in the urban water courses.

"The movement of otters into urban areas generally reflects improvements in water quality, increases in available food, and otters extending their travelling range."

Dr Simon Lyster, director general of The Wildlife Trusts, added:"The recovery of the otter is the most exciting success story of the last decade and is a tribute to volunteers and professionals that have worked so hard to make this recovery possible.

"Watching otters at play has largely been restricted to remote areas of countryside but now otters seem set to become a part of urban wildlife too.

"Important wildlife habitat can exist in urban areas and people are now more likely than ever to be able to catch a glimpse of one of the UK's most charismatic creatures."

However, the Trusts warned of the danger of complacency.

Most riverside construction and development does not make any allowance for the possible presence of otters so the Trusts are now calling for local planning authorities, developers and builders to consider the needs of otters along urban waterways.

Otters require suitable breeding habitat and resting sites, say the Trusts, and this often involves sheltered vegetation and gently sloping riverbanks.

The introduction of a number of helpful features could also be considered, including ledges within bridge arches for otters to travel across, floating rest platforms, otter fencing alongside road edges, and a drop weir scheme whereby rocks or steps guide otters safely down weirs.

SHELLFISH PLUCKED FROM the sea ended up in a freshwater stream following a bizarre road accident in Shropshire.

A lorry loaded with 40 tonnes of mussels collided with a wall on the A41 near Whitchurch and overturned.

Tonnes of mussels were spilled into a nearby field and stream where many of the molluscs drifted away.

The driver of the lorry was taken to hospital suffering from an injured arm during the drama which occurred just before 5am.

ROBIN: friendly garden bird is a violent foe

OF all our native garden birds, it is undoubtedly the robin that takes the prize for popularity at Christmas.

Go into any card shop in the country at this time and the robin's red breast will be blazing forth from a variety of cards, often with a snow or holly-decked background to maximise the effect.

For such a pretty little bird, it comes as a surprise to some that the robin can actually be a violent thug in defence of its territory.

Male robins, despite being just 14cms long, will battle ferociously to cling onto an area they regard as theirs.

Such fights sometimes end in death, the result of a savage pecking from that tiny beak.

Even a piece of red or orange cloth can become a target for a robin maddened by its territorial instincts during the nesting season.

Robins have been associated with Christmas since the middle of the 19th Century when the idea of sending greeting cards first took off.

At the time, postmen were nicknamed 'robins' because they wore bright red work jackets.

Thus, the link was made between this distinctive bird and the idea of it bringing glad tidings during the festive season.

Our own native robins are supplemented each year by an influx of robins from abroad.

These are slightly paler in colour and some say they are also quieter and shyer than native robins.

There is probably some truth in this because huntsmen on the Continent have no compunction about killing small birds for the pot, though the amount of meat on a robin is negligible and it would take several to make a feast.

It must therefore have been a native robin that I encountered earlier this year cheekily hopping along a fence at my elbow at a watermill site in Somerset.

So bold was this particular bird that I was sure that if I stretched out my hand, it would hop aboard.

It didn't in the end. However, gardeners and others who slowly build up a rapport with robins are often rewarded in this way.

Despite their savagery with each other, 75 per cent of young robins never make it to adulthood and are picked off by a host of predators, the domestic cat being the most prolific killer.

Robins feed on a wide variety of insects, as well as worms, berries, and garden titbits.

Up to seven eggs are laid in the nesting season and these are typically white in colour with red spots.

Unlike many bird species, the male and female robin look the same so it's often difficult to tell which is which - until it comes to the mating season.

During this period, it is the female robin that pursues the male until he decides he wants her after all.

Then he courts her by stuffing her with food.

As well as a sharp "tic-tic-tic" alarm call, the robin has a fine singing voice which it exercises throughout the year, sometimes even at night.

In past centuries, having such an attractive voice could have seen the robin captured and imprisoned in a cage, something which prompted 18th Century poet William Blake to write:"*A Robin Redbreast in a Cage, Puts all Heaven in a Rage.*"

Today, a robin in a cage would put PC Plod in a rage because it's illegal.

MOUSETRAPS ARE AS cruel as foxhunting but are unlikely to be banned in our muddled society, says the Game Conservancy Trust.

"We are incredibly inconsistent in our attitude towards wildlife," said a spokesman. "The common mousetrap is known to fail international standards of humaneness.

"The poisons approved for use against rats, mice, and moles are also of doubtful humaneness and environmental safety. But we use them, accepting that their utility outweighs these problems.

"In the Queen's Speech it was mentioned that the Hunting Bill would be 'based on evidence and principle'. It would seek common ground between the opposing factions and would be soundly based on 'the principles of cruelty and utility'.

"Is this so sound? The debate over hunting with dogs has thrown up many inconsistencies and ethical dilemmas for which, as a society, we have yet to develop coherent solutions.

"In a thought-provoking submission to Minister Alun Michael, the Trust questions whether the 'principles' invoked can be applied consistently across all our dealings with wildlife. If not - if they have only limited relevance - what is their value as principles?

"The submission - now published as 'Cruelty and Utility: Comments on Principles and Acceptability' - was drafted by the Trust's expert on predation control studies, Dr Jonathan Reynolds.

"Dr Reynolds argues in the submission that existing animal welfare legislation was framed for domesticated animals, which rely on man and for which there is a clear duty of care. The extension to broader wildlife issues, including hunting with dogs, is problematic. He says: 'Wild animals, by definition, are not reliant in this way and indeed are severely stressed by human interference. All the same, many of us feel we do have a parallel duty of care for wild animal populations. We call it conservation.'"

TURKEYS HAVE EVERY reason to want to trot off at Christmas - but some in South London might be even less amused by approaching festivities.

A dozen birds are being raced at Catford on December 20 - with the winner being spared the chop. The so-called Gobble Cup will even be shown on the internet by the Blue Square betting service after all the birds are dressed in greyhound-type racing jackets. Losers will end up as dinner while the winner is promised a life of pampered luxury.

AN ARMY OF up to 250,000 starlings has descended on a Gloucestershire wildlife centre voraciously looking for food.

The massive flock started building in October at the Slimbridge headquarters of the Wildfowl and Wetland Trust and just got bigger and bigger.

"These starlings are putting on an amazing display every day now in the skies over Slimbridge," said a Trust spokesman.

"Every afternoon around 4pm they can be seen swooping, swarming and swaying in huge numbers across the dusky sky as they group together in preparation for an evening's roost in dense bushes and trees.

"They began to increase in number from October onwards and, with their preference for low lying areas where the temperature is slightly warmer, Slimbridge is one of the best places to see them.

"Trying to count them appears to be a tricky task - the wardens challenge any visitor to have a go.

"They are roosting in large numbers for warmth and for protection from local predators.

"During spring and summer breeding, starlings resident in the UK are more likely to be found in the countryside adjacent to urban conurbations.

"However, as the weather turns cooler they move into towns, cities and low-lying areas to roost because of the temperatures being higher.

"As winter approaches, starlings tend to migrate south and west. Some winter in southern Europe and north Africa. Scandinavian populations winter in the British Isles, increasing the UK population to many millions."

'I WANDERED LONELY as a sheep' might not have a great poetic ring to it but sheep really are to help write poetry.

In a scheme many see as simply dotty, poet Valerie Laws will spray words from one of her works on the back of 15 sheep.

She will then study the animals moving around from a platform to watch new poems being randomly 'created'.

The so-called 'Quantum Sheep' scheme is funded by £2,000 from Northern Arts, a charity set up to encourage community 'artworks'.

This 'artwork' will be staged at the Whitehouse Farm Centre, in Morpeth, Northumberland.

DRAG HUNTERS ARE being warned to tone down their public enthusiasm for the sport by pro-hunt groups fighting the proposed ban on hunting live quarry, claims the League Against Cruel Sports.

According to the League, drag hunters find their sport faster, more exciting and more challenging.

In addition, it says a recent MORI poll showed 72 per cent of people back drag hunting.

"In Scotland, where live quarry hunting is now illegal, one hunt has already switched to bloodhound hunting, allowing jobs, tradition and hound packs to survive," said a spokesman.

Douglas Batchelor, League chief executive, added:"It is blindingly obvious that drag hunting could easily replace foxhunting and that most riders and other followers enjoy it more than chasing and torturing wild animals. It is despicable that the hunting fraternity are effectively trying to gag these people and prevent them from publicly saying that drag hunting is the ideal alternative."

BRITAIN'S COUNTRYSIDE IS threatened more by commonly sold exotic plants than from potential new GM 'superweeds', it has been claimed.

Lord May, a leading voice among the UK's scientific elite, believes genetically modified crops are a smaller threat to biodiversity than some imported plants.

He attacked lobby groups opposed to GM crops for dismissing scientific facts.

In an address to the Royal Society, Lord May called for an open public debate about the effects of GM crops on other species and about the larger role of scientists in society.

He said the risks posed by GM plants had been exaggerated.

"Pollen from 'conventional' crops, many of which have been produced by very hi-tech methods in recent years and which could easily be seen as Frankensteinian if you so chose, blows around, and does create hybrids," he said. "But, far from being super-weeds, these are typically wimps. There are, however, real problems with invasive species in the UK. But they come from plants you can buy at garden centres.

"Among several current examples are the invasive aquatic weeds, especially Australian swamp stonecrop, Crassula helmsii, which now infests over 2,000 sites nationwide."

A QUIET COUNTRY walk almost ended with a lethal bang when a pet dog brought back a live grenade to its owner.

Shadow the collie was out with owner Gordon Husband when she came across the deadly device beside the River Wye in Hereford.

Mr Husband, who recognised the grenade from his National Service army training days, freed it from his pet's mouth and took it home.

Army bomb disposal experts were called and confirmed the grenade was still live before blowing it up nearby.

The area where Shadow found the device later proved to be just a few miles from an old SAS training camp.

TURKEY AND ALL the trimmings could soon be a thing of the past for Christmas dinner as beef tells it to moo-ve over in the popularity stakes.

Newly released figures show more people than ever are growing tired of gobbling turkey and are returning to traditional cuts of meat with beef leading the way.

Beef outsold turkey by more than £3million last Christmas - the second time in three years that beef has beaten turkey on Yuletide dining tables.

Chris Lamb, spokesman for British Meat, said:"I think people have just got bored with having the same old thing every year. Beef is a traditional winter meal and one that popularity tops polls as people's favourite meal - so it's not surprising that more people are choosing to serve it as the centrepiece to their Christmas meal."

STAG HUNTING AND hare coursing should not be banned under any proposed hunting Bill, the Countryside Alliance has warned.

Following the Government's 'fudged' solution to the thorny hunting debate, which managed to infuriate both sides, Alliance chairman John Jackson responded angrily.

"The Alliance rejects entirely the Bill's proposed ban on stag hunting and coursing, especially given that the Government has provided no rational grounds for singling out these activities," he said.

"However, regarding the Bill's central principle of a registration and licensing scheme, we have long made clear that we would consider such a concept constructively, provided that it is seen to be based on the Government's own criteria of 'principle' and 'evidence'.

"It is not yet clear whether the proposed scheme meets these criteria and to this end we will study the Bill's details closely before responding to the Government."

Meanwhile, Labour MPs who pressed for an outright ban on all hunting have also reacted with fury.

They were stunned when it was revealed that Alun Michael, the Rural Affairs Minister, will publish legislation that bans hunting with hounds in all areas of England and Wales but sets up tribunals to which local hunts can apply for licences to continue.

Those hunts which apply must pass 'utility and cruelty' tests, showing that there is a real need for the sport in their area regarding pest control and that the activity will be 'humane'.

Hunters will only be prosecuted if they sink into cruelty or if they continually breach conditions of their hunting licence.

Labour backbenchers, spearheaded by Gerald Kaufman MP, are said to be outraged that the Bill will fall short of a complete ban.

An unnamed senior Labour MP told one newspaper: "This is a silly attempt to have it both ways. As far as we are concerned it is a ban, a total ban and nothing but a ban.

"If Alun Michael thinks we are going to accept this then he is more mistaken than we feared. He can forget it."

PIGS' CHEEKS HELPED a farmer in Oxfordshire trot off with first prize in a national competition about 'long forgotten' foods.

Mick Eadle, from Beckley, used the cheeks in a recipe called 'Baths Chaps' which delighted British Food Fortnight judges aiming to find great recipes which have been lost over time.

Cheeks for the dish were taken from Mr Eadle's own outdoor reared Landrace/Duroc pigs, making his competition entry all the more traditional.

Countryside Alliance chief executive Richard Burge said:"This competition has unearthed some timeless recipes.

"This had to be the winning entry because it embodies what British Food Fortnight was all about - namely, to use hand-made, locally produced ingredients from a small producer.

"We are delighted with how well the competition has gone and hope we can put some of the recipes back onto the national menu.

"We are encouraging the public to be a bit more adventurous in what they eat and to enjoy our culinary heritage."

275

WALKERS IN THE south of England have been celebrating news that new access under the Countryside and Rights of Way Act 2000 will be introduced to their region by the summer of 2004.

Following an announcement by Alun Michael MP, Minister for Rural Affairs, a spokesman for the Ramblers Association said:"This means that people in this area will have access for the first time ever to some of our most beautiful countryside.

"It covers the South East and Central Southern regions of England. These areas combined stretch from Bristol down to the Dorset/Devon border and then across to Kent.

"We view this as a vital step forward and a much-needed boost to rural economies. Allowing people the right to walk over open, uncultivated country will encourage more visitors to the English countryside and help the recovery of rural businesses affected by foot-and-mouth disease."

Nicky Warden, leader of the RA's Freedom to Roam Team, added:"Walkers have been waiting for better rights of access for hundreds of years and there is still a long way to go. We welcome this commitment by the Government to provide new rights as quickly as possible but we would urge them to also grant access in the lower North West during this time frame.

"The lower North West, which includes Kinder Scout, is a historically important area for walkers. It was severely affected by foot - and-mouth disease and would benefit from the increased number of rural visitors that freedom to roam will bring.

"Granting access regionally, before the 2005 deadline when all access land has been mapped, is an important step for walkers and rural economies and it is something the Ramblers Association has argued for since the CRoW Act became law."

A ROBIN SINGING in the depths of winter shows just how healthy it is, according to new research.

Robins that chirp through the chill reveal that they have built up enough fat stores to last them, say scientists.

A Bristol University team studied both wild and captive robins with captive birds trained to weigh themselves on special electronic balances.

It became apparent that the birds stored extra fat when food started to get scarce and the nights became colder.

When it was warmer at night, they had more fat left at dawn so were able to sing and defend their territories.

But freezing nights could deplete their fat stores, leaving them weak and unable to expend energy by singing.

RED ADMIRAL BUTTERFLIES have been used in pioneering research to create mini-machines that fly like insects.

The butterflies were closely monitored by scientists at Oxford University after being put in wind tunnels so that their complex wing movements could be replicated.

As a result, researchers hope they have gained enough knowledge to boost ongoing efforts to create 'micro air vehicles'.

Dr AdrianThomas, part of a two-man team, told the BBC:"There is a lot of interest in this sort of thing from toy manufacturers and, of course, the military.

"We are now moving in the direction where we will soon be able to build 10cm wingspan aircraft, either radio controlled or autonomous.

"They would make an entertaining toy but if you put a camera on them then the security agencies could send them into small spaces such as caves to see what was going on."

During the project, red admirals were taught to fly to and from artificial flowers located in the tunnel while smoke was blown over their wings to help with observation.

"The fluttering of butterflies is not a random, erratic wandering, but results from the mastery of a wide array of aerodynamic mechanisms," Dr Thomas and his partner Dr Robert Srygley reveal in Nature magazine.

Six different ways the butterflies flapped and circled their wings to stay airborne were identified during the research.

The insects switched easily from one method to another "much like a horse might switch between walking, trotting and galloping depending on what it wanted to do," Dr Thomas added.

For their size, butterfly wings produce 10 times the lift achieved by the wings of aircraft.

Researchers have learnt that mini-planes - just scaled-down versions of the full-size machines - never get airborne.

Only by copying butterflies and other insects will scientists be able to launch micro air vehicles into the air.

A TALL DARK stranger left a Shropshire teacher terrified when it wandered around the back of her village home - and she realised it was an ostrich.

Beverley Wilkinson thought she was dreaming for a moment when the giant bird began nosing about near her home in rural Little Ness.

But after telephoning a friend who warned her it could be dangerous, she barricaded herself inside - worried that the ostrich might attack her or her two cats.

Police were alerted and raced to her house but by the time they arrived the stranger had fled into nearby fields.

Initial attempts to discover where the ostrich came from unearthed no clues.

HORSE RACING PUNDIT and former jockey champ Willie Carson is the latest in a group of celebrities backing a Woodland Trust bid to buy a threatened ancient wood.

The Trust, which hopes to acquire over 222 acres of ancient Credenhill Park Wood in rural Hereford-shire, recently launched an appeal to raise over £70,000 to buy the site and secure its future.

Willie said:"The Trust's commitment to retaining ancient woodland is imperative for our heritage."

THE BATTLE TO save stag hunting and hare coursing has begun after the ancient sports were revealed to be facing an immediate ban in new hunting legislation.

Protesters are to hold a march in the heart of London in a bid to help them overturn the proposed ban.

"The Government has thrown down the gauntlet in proposing to ban coursing and stag hunting out of hand and without the opportunity to prove their case to the proposed regulator," said the Countryside Alliance.

"We have marched in record-breaking numbers. Now join the launch of the historic protest campaign at the heart of Westminster. We will be united in publicly condemning the discrimination against coursing and stag hunting and ensuring, with a wall of light and sound, that politicians listen to the real world outside Parliament.

"This lawful, determined, Mass Lobby of Parliament will be preceded by a protest rally nearby and end with a sight and sound finale that will leave parliamentarians in no doubt that we will never be divided or deterred from securing a fair deal for all hunting, and that it is they who are out of step with a freedom loving and tolerant countryside."

The rally will start at 2.30pm on the appointed day near the House of Commons and is expected to finish by 5.30pm.

"Turn up to support the freedom of all forms of modern hunting, dressed warmly and with a torch to help shine a light on prejudice and something to make as much noise as possible to ensure we are heard.

"We have a massive campaign to mount over the coming months to defend freedom, tolerance and justice for all. This is the start, but a start you will never forget.

"The messages we are looking to convey are: a fair deal for all hunting; we will never accept unjust law; and we are angry and ready to protest till we win."

THE WOODLAND TRUST says it is dismayed that planned expansion of Gatwick airport could be back on the Government's agenda.

Development of Gatwick would spell even more destruction for Britain's dwindling ancient woodland, warns the conservation charity.

The airport is surrounded by ancient woods which could be cleared if expansion were to go ahead.

Mike Townsend, spokesman for the Trust, said:"The last thing we need is for yet another needless expansion proposal to be on the agenda. Ancient woods are irreplaceable natural habitats and we cannot afford to lose any more."

A LANCASHIRE FIRM was fined a total of £11,000 after magistrates heard how it polluted a local river, killing thousands of fish.

Pollution spread along more than three kilometres of the River Yarrow after highly acidic waste was washed from a sink by the Chorley company, Leyland magistrates heard.

Fish killed in the incident last May included nearly 3,000 chub, dace, gudgeon, roach, brown trout, eels, pike, perch, bream, barbel and flounders.

But many more smaller fish were also killed, including stoneloach, bullheads, minnows and sticklebacks.

The company pleaded guilty to an offence under the Water Resources Act 1991, of causing polluting matter to enter the Yarrow, and four offences under the Environmental Protection Act 1990, of failing to comply with Waste Management Licence conditions.

As well as being fined, the firm was ordered to pay £6,000 costs to the Environment Agency, which brought the prosecution, with money going towards restocking the river with fish.

The court heard that a director of the firm had told Environment Agency officers that the sink had been used for the first time on the day of the pollution incident, as a laboratory was still being built.

Following the incident the company arranged for the sink to be connected correctly to the foul sewer.

THE WILDLIFE TRUSTS are urging people to lay on a festive feast for birds and other creatures hunting for food this winter.

"A bird table is a must-have for your winter wildlife garden," said a spokesman."Birdseed mix, slices of apple, scraps of bacon fat and soaked brown bread will attract blue tits, robins and, hopefully, the elusive sparrow to the dinner table.

"Bird feeders containing nuts will attract birds and squirrels alike, whilst the badger's favourite nibble is peanuts. Although hedgehogs and dormice are in hibernation, foxes, badgers and squirrels still forage for food. If you have mammals regularly visiting your garden, a saucer of tinned cat or dog food will be appreciated by a hungry fox, or even by a hedgehog as he moves to another hibernation nest.

"If you have fruit trees, leave fallen fruit on the ground as this is a particular favourite of winter thrushes. Water is also as important for winter wildlife. A birdbath or a simple tray of water kept fresh and free of ice will quench their thirst."

A HERD OF cows in Somerset was spooked by a traffic calming scheme - yellow lines newly painted on a road.

Farmer Gordan Brinson, of Compton Bishop, near Axminster, says they refused to cross the lines - probably because they feared they were a cattle grid and their hooves would get stuck.

Unfortunately, Mr Brinson needed to bring the cattle down the road to their winter quarters and was left scratching his head about what to do.

Several attempts to get the animals to cross the lines ended in failure.

In the end, the frustrated farmer was forced to divert some cows across fields to his farm and carry others in a cattle truck. Horses have also been baffled by the lines with at least one choosing to jump them, Mr Brinson revealed.

CONSERVATIONISTS HAVE reacted with horror to news that Deputy Prime Minister John Prescott wants to allow almost three million new homes to be built across England.

The massive development programme, which would destroy parts of England's remaining countryside forever, is likely to be opposed at every step.

Wildlife and places of natural beauty are put under threat by the plans which would allow greenfield sites to be breached by a party which came to power promising to protect them.

Worst hit will be 'picturesque' counties like Cornwall - which must build more than 30,000 homes by 2016 with about half on greenfield sites - Devon, which must build 65,000 homes by 2016 with about half on green sites - and Derbyshire, which must build 50,000 homes between 2001 and 2021.

Mr Prescott, widely lampooned for his apparent lack of success in every area of government he has handled, seems determined to put his stamp on something before leaving power - and rural England appears to have been given the dubious honour.

Kate Parminter, chief executive of the Council for the Protection of Rural England, said:"Our figures show that an area the size of John Prescott's home city of Hull will be concreted over each year. We want at least 75 per cent of new homes on derelict brownfield land."

WATER VOLES MAY now get stronger legal protection after their slump towards extinction was judged to be accelerating.

The Wildlife Trusts have welcomed a recommen - dation by the Joint Nature Conservation Committee to increase protection of the UK's fastest declining mammal.

Water voles have now disappeared from more than 89 per cent of the sites they occupied just 60 years ago and Dr Simon Lyster, director general of the Trusts, warned:"The plight of the water vole has never been more urgent."

BIRD LOVERS APPEAR to have triumphed over hedgehog fans after thousands of the prickly mammals were finally condemned to death.

A cull of hedgehogs in the Outer Hebrides has been given the go-ahead to offset the threat the animals pose to birds.

Scottish Natural Heritage and the RSPB say the hedgehogs feast on eggs and are endangering the future of birds such as oystercatchers and lapwings.

But animal rights groups attacked proposals to give hedgehogs lethal injections in North Uist, South Uist and Benbecula so that the hedgehog population can be greatly reduced from its present level of about 5,000 animals.

THE VIOLENT CLASHES between hunt supporters and police as Parliament debated introduction of an 'unfair' law could become a turning point in Britain's history of democracy, claims the Countryside Alliance.

Hundreds of hunt supporters were involved in running battles during a noisy demonstration outside the Commons in London.

Several arrests were made and many people suffered minor injuries as police, aiming to stop two pro-hunt groups totalling 4,000 protesters linking up, came under intense pressure.

Some demonstrators climbed traffic lights, lamp posts and even scaled the gates of the Parliament building during the fracas.

Others set off fireworks and sounded horns or klaxons as police struggled to keep order.

Later, Richard Burge, chief executive of the Alliance, said:"Thousands of people came to London with the intention of protesting peacefully against the Hunting Bill. What actually happened may be a watershed in the history of our democracy.

"No-one in the countryside really wanted this to happen this way. But these events will have left Government in no doubt about the pitch of anxiety and anger many rural communities have reached. These people are facing injustice and prejudice in Parliament. It is Parliament which must ask itself what has driven decent people to such uncharacteristic excess.

"We cannot condone lawlessness, neither will we condemn the emotion, fear, and anger that gave rise to these events."

Simon Hart, director of the Alliance's Campaign for Hunting, added:"Smoke, fireworks, sweat and a few tears. No, this was not Ulster in the Seventies or the Gaza Strip. This was our friends and our communities once more in Parliament Square. And why?

"For some time now we have warned the Government that if it chose to pursue a solution to the hunting debate that was unjust, that was not supported by evidence and without principle, then fury would erupt. We were right.

"Most of our friends think twice before parking on a double yellow line. They believe fervently in law and order. I have always hoped, perhaps naively, that we would never see scenes like this and that the Government would be robust enough to resist backbench pressure and to concentrate on evidence rather than expediency. As I stood in Parliament Square my main reaction was one of sadness.Yet again the good honest pillars of our rural communities had been forced to beat on the gates of democracy."

SIGHTINGS OF A big cat on the loose in Scotland were proved true when a starving lynx was captured in a trap.

However, the animal had only recently escaped from Kirkcudbright Wildlife Park in Dumfries and Galloway. Thin and disorientated after three weeks on the run, the Alsation-sized cat was caught in a trap specificially set for it back in Kirkcudbright.

THE RSPB SAYS the Government's new Strate-gy for Sustainable Farming and Food needs to be implemented urgently if it is to have any worthwhile effect. The general principles of using public money to buy public goods and supporting a sustainable food chain were timely and needed, it added.

FOXES: killed by the milk of human kindness

FOXHUNTING has been back on the national political agenda in a big way in recent years with 'pro' and 'anti' hunt groups tearing each other to pieces. There can be few rural issues which rouse people to fury as quickly as foxhunting - whether you support it or are implacably opposed

As I've said before, I have never hunted.

But I have been an angler, which to some people is equally cruel.

Before the ban, I supported foxhunting and still do, although it is not an activity I choose to pursue myself.

However, I don't feel morally outraged by it, as many others undoubtedly do.

It seems to me there are limitless aspects of life people can feel morally outraged about.

Even in the current Government, there are individuals whose personal tastes would probably have seen them imprisoned or even executed in past centuries.

Yet these same individuals too often claim the high moral ground in lecturing country groups on how they should be conducting themselves.

Times change but our need to demonise minority groups in our midst appears to stay the same.

Critics of foxhunting like to compare it with bear-baiting which is misleading as tethered bears stood absolutely no chance of escaping, unlike foxes. Even so, I felt alarmed by revelations at the time that certain foxes were being fed and pampered in artificial earths, specifically so that they could be caught more easily by hounds.

This is a genuine perversion of hunting and I was relieved to see the Countryside Alliance unreservedly condemning the practice.

Whatever happens in the battle over the current foxhunting ban, it is unlikely to affect the fortunes of our urban foxes.

Most towns and cities now have their own thriving populations, well away from any threat posed by hounds. For these foxes, the chief killer is the car but human sentimentality can prove just as deadly.

In Bristol, foxes were once so plentiful that they were regularly spotted scavenging for food in daylight.

Delighted residents fed them by hand and, of course, numbers multiplied yet further.

At its peak, Bristol's fox population boasted 33 adult animals per square kilometre, an amazing number.

Hundreds roamed the city at night, to the surprise of twilight onlookers.

But eventually this unnaturally high concentration proved the foxes' downfall.

When disease struck, they were powerless to escape each other and the population crashed.

Less than three per cent of the Bristol population survived the ravages of a virulent form of mange. The rest died in agony.

What happened in Bristol should be a lesson to us all to rein in our rose-tinted view of the natural world. It is different from ours.

And sometimes, the milk of human kindness can turn out to be a poison for animals.

SEA EAGLES FACE extinction again in Britain because of persecution by poisoners, the RSPB has revealed.

Two mature adults were found poisoned in the last year and conservationists believe others may have been killed but not found.

The spectacular white-tailed hunters became extinct here 100 years ago but have been the subject of a reintroduction programme in Scotland since 1975.

Even so, this saw emergence of just 25 mature breeding pairs, a number still vulnerable to human interference.

Alison MacLennan, of RSPB Scotland, said:"It is an uphill struggle increasing the sea eagle population in Scotland with only small numbers of young produced each year.

"Although the adult birds are long-lived, it takes them four or five years to reach maturity and enter the breeding population.

"With only 25 breeding pairs at present, the loss of any individuals is significant and worrying but the loss of breeding birds is tragic."

SALMON AND SEA trout have benefited from one of the wettest autumns on record in Wales, according to the Environment Agency.

High water levels have allowed fish to swim far upstream and make full use of spawning areas on the upper tributaries of many rivers.

In some west Wales rivers, says the Agency, large numbers of fish have been spotted returning from the North Atlantic to spawn.

During 2002 the Agency worked with project partners on tributaries of the Tywi, Cleddau and Teifi, restoring and enhancing spawning and nursery habitats for migratory fish.

"One initiative is on the River Cerdin, a tributary of the Teifi near Llandysul," said a spokesman."Agency staff, contractors and volunteers from Llandysul Angling Association recently completed a habitat restoration scheme, clearing large amounts of wood from the lower reaches of the river.

"Over the years fallen trees and branches had formed dams across the river, obstructing salmon and sea trout attempting to return to their native spawning grounds.The dams were also choking water plants."

BOXING DAY PROTESTS against foxhunting were even more widespread as the last year neared its end, claimed the League Against Cruel Sports.

League members, supporters, and other 'anti' organisations were out in force, protesting at the hunt 'celebrations' which took place, according to the group.

Placards were made available for all those who wanted them but protesters representing the League were asked to make every effort to ensure that the protests were peaceful and orderly.

"Abusive language, violence or the threat of violence should not be tolerated and should be discouraged in others," said a spokesman.

HARE COURSING FANS remain defiant in the face of Government moves to end their controversial sport once and for all.

Three January meets across southern England have been cancelled but this is said to be because of flooding problems rather than enthusiasts giving ground to animal rights campaigners.

In a bullish message to its members, the National Coursing Club says:"No-one should be rushing to write a premature obituary of the sport of coursing in this country.

"The Government's Hunting Bill may wither and die first. One estimate is that it might not become law until December 2004 at the earliest, if at all.

"Events inside and outside the Houses Of Parliament in the week before Christmas have made a successful passage for the Bill, drawn up by Rural Affairs Minister Alun Michael, look extremely unlikely.

"Michael's bid to find a 'Third Way' between the political pro's and anti's is floundering knee deep in its own fudge.

"Firstly, the unexpectedly vigorous protest outside the House Of Commons on the afternoon of the Second Reading of the Bill must have surprised the Government.

"The Government could have hoped that, by offering limited opportunities for foxhunting to continue, the level of support for coursing and stag hunting from the rest of the hunting community might be negligible.

"The 5-6,000 protesters who, with only a week's notice, advanced angrily on Parliament on December 16 must have come as a nasty shock. All shades of hunting opinion were represented, and the Government must expect more of the same on key dates in the diary of the Bill's progress.

"Secondly, the Bill looks set for a rocky ride through Parliament despite receiving its Second Reading by a huge majority.

"The Bill pleased no-one on either side of the argument.

"Use of the Parliament Act remains untested in law. It is accepted, however, that, if it is to be used, in two successive Parliamentary sessions, a Bill, identical in the second session to that proposed in the first, must be refused by the Lords. Parliamentary tacticians could have a field day with this.

"It may not come to this. The Government will need considerable political will to carry the Bill that far, particularly if in a time of national crisis."

SWANS HAVE SPARKED a flap in a Cambridgeshire village by causing power cuts at the same time every day.

At first, villagers in Aldreth were baffled by their power going off each afternoon - until they realised swans coming in to land were brushing past local power lines.

The mystery went on for two weeks, with a regular power loss between 4.30pm and 4.45pm, until it was solved.

An investigation revealed this was the time the birds were coming down to roost on local land.

Electricity firm 24Seven says it plans to replace the old power lines with new ones.

These will carry bright reflectors to deter swans from getting too close.

HEN HARRIERS ARE struggling to hold on in the Orkney Islands.

Loss of hunting habitat has been identified as the most likely cause of decline, the Game Conservancy Trust says.

Trust researcher Dr Arjun Amar said:"Despite the fact that there is no human persecution of this population, hen harriers on the Orkney Islands have declined by over 70 per cent in the last 25 years.

"Recent research has shown that there is a shortage of food for birds on Orkney and that this decline is most likely due to changes in land use causing a reduction in the amount of rough grassland, which is their preferred hunting habitat."

Using a Geographical Information System with digitised maps created from satellite images, the research team examined whether the proportion of rough grass habitat had an influence on breeding success.

If such a relationship existed, this would provide support for creation of the same type of habitat as a conservation measure.

"We found that such a relationship did indeed exist. Birds which nested in areas with more of this habitat had better breeding success - they were more likely to hatch their eggs and more likely to fledge their young compared to birds which had less rough grass around them," Dr Amar added.

A DOG HAS died despite being plucked to safety from a freezing river in Shropshire.

The black poodle was originally saved from drowning by police and firemen as it struggled in the River Severn near Shrewsbury.

The animal's frantic barks had alerted a passer-by who raised the alarm and prompted concerns that the dog's owner might be in difficulty.

But no-one was found and the drenched, exhausted dog seemed the only casualty.

Later, the rescue team's joy turned to sadness when the poodle died as a result of its ordeal.

POLICE MARKSMEN ARE hunting two 'pumas' in the Black Mountains of mid-Wales after a man was apparently confronted by the snarling animals.

Shocked Mike Sheppard alerted officers after being warned off by the big cats which he found when he went looking for a missing pet whippet at Llangadog.

He finally discovered the dog dead in a garden - killed by one of two huge black cats which immediately began to menace him.

Backing off, Mr Sheppard, 62, fled indoors and raised the alarm..

Police who rushed to the scene spotted one of the cats slinking away and marksmen were called in to shoot them.

Dyfed-Powys Police say the incident was worrying because, unlike other events involving big cats, this happened in a residential area.

THE WINTER SPECTACLE of thousands of pink-footed geese arriving in Britain from Iceland could be under threat, according to the RSPB.

The Society has accused the Icelandic Government of putting British wildlife at risk by sanctioning two hydro-electric schemes that will affect thousands of pairs of nesting pink-footed geese.

Iceland plays host to almost 90 per cent of the world's pink-footed geese and almost all of them winter in the UK, mainly in the coastal areas of East Anglia, Lancashire, and in eastern and south western Scotland.

RSPB spokeswoman Nicola Crockford said:"We estimate that as many as one in seven pink-footed geese visiting the UK in winter could be affected or displaced by these hydro-electric schemes.

"The two sites are globally recognised for their importance for birds and other wildlife but Iceland seems determined to renege on its international conservation commitments and damage and destroy substantial portions of these sites."

Work has already began on the Karahnjukar hydroelectric scheme, in Iceland's central highlands, and once completed the scheme will damage the breeding, feeding and moulting areas for 3,800 pairs of pink-footed geese - an eighth of the birds visiting the UK in winter.

The scheme, which will flood up to 56 square kilometres of wilderness, was initially rejected by the Icelandic planning agency, following an environmental impact assessment which showed unacceptable levels of damage.

However, the agency's decision was reversed by the Environment Minister, Siv Fridliefsdottir.

A second proposed dam at Thjorsarver will, if built, stand 578 metres high and will destroy a further 42 square kilometres of habitat used by more pink-footed geese.

The area is thought to be the most wildlife-rich site in central Iceland.

Both schemes will be created to provide power for proposed North American-owned aluminium smelting plants based in Iceland.

Johann Oli Hilmarsson, of the Icelandic Society for the Protection of Birds, said:"Our Society has campaigned vigorously to persuade the Icelandic Government to refuse permission for these dams to be built and is asking for our Government to protect the Karahnjukar and Thjorsarver areas for future generations. If these projects go ahead it will be a loss not only to Iceland but also to the world."

THE PINE MARTEN is the subject of a new booklet written by expert Johnny Birks and published by The Mammal Society.

"The booklet contains all the latest information about this elusive mustelid, including consideration of whether reintroductions would help conserve populations outside the main strongholds of Scotland and the west of Ireland," said a spokesman.

"Lavishly illustrated, it covers both the biology and ecology of the species and makes required reading for enthusiast and expert alike.

"Subject sections include social organisation and behaviour, field signs and watching pine martens."

'The Pine Marten' costs £3.50. Other books in the series on British mammals include 'The Otter', 'The Water Vole', and 'The Hedgehog'.

TORRENTIAL DOWNPOURS AND the big freeze have wreaked havoc with farmers' set aside fields.

The NFU says it will be asking DEFRA to compensate farmers who cannot harvest crops because of recent bad weather.

Under the Arable Area Payments Scheme, land required for set aside must have in place a suitable cover crop by January 15 or a late harvested crop removed.

But poor conditions could make this difficult for farmers who have yet to remove traditionally late harvested root crops such as sugar beet.

NFU Cereal Committee chairman Richard Butler said:"Farmers would be hoping that those administering the Arable Area Payments Scheme would acknowledge that this situation is beyond their control.

"Through no fault of their own, farmers could have their plans to use set aside as a part of a crop rotation strategy thrown into chaos because of the weather.

"Farmers hope DEFRA will agree to extend the January 15 deadline to allow farmers the chance to get onto the soaked fields in question and remove existing crops and establish appropriate cover crops."

The NFU's regional offices are now assessing how much land may be affected.

Mr Butler added that the NFU would be requesting that our Government ask the EC to extend the set aside deadline.

A BULLOCK WEIGHING over 90 stones went berserk and trampled a mother-of-three on a farm in Shropshire.

Farmer's wife Tracey Jones, 33, was airlifted to hospital suffering broken ribs and other internal injuries following the drama near Bridgnorth.

Later, with his wife out of danger, husband Simon revealed that the accident happened after a number of cows were packed together in a cattle crush so he could conduct tuberculosis tests.

The bullock suddenly panicked and battered its way out, trampling over his wife who was helping.

FARMLAND BIRDS MAY still be at risk from GM crops despite GM supporters praising its 'wildlife benefits' in a new report, it has been claimed.

Friends of the Earth says fresh research on GM sugar beet, partly funded by Monsanto, will provide the Government with little new information on which to base crucial decisions on any commercialisation of GM crops.

The research team reported that GM sugar beet yield was potentially higher than under a conventional system and potentially produced more weeds, providing more insects beneficial to wildlife.

But FoE campaigner Pete Riley said:"This research tells us nothing about the impact of GM sugar beet on farmland birds but shows that Monsanto is desperate to find a case for promoting GM seed."

BADGERS COULD BE saved from extermination at a site in East Sussex because of findings in a new report, claims the National Federation of Badger Groups.

The burrowing mammals are in conflict with Saltdean residents amid fears that they are undermining local properties with their sett.

Government inspectors say they might have to be killed or moved elsewhere but the NFBG believes leading badger ecologist Professor Stephen Harris has raised vital issues in a new study.

His survey of archaeological records found that the sett is constructed in a ridge of soil formed by prehistoric farmers who ploughed the hillside above where the houses now stand.

This overspill of soil provided the badgers with easy ground for digging when a development of flats destroyed their ancestral sett in 1970.

"This discovery is important for two reasons," said Dr Elaine King, chief executive of the NFBG."First, it shows that the sett is large because of the underlying soil - not because there is a large number of badgers as DEFRA first believed. Second, the badgers cannot easily establish similar setts in other gardens because the underlying soil is not suitable.

"We are sure that Professor Harris' report will provide the viable alternative solution to the problem sett that Mr Morley has been looking for.

"Many details have yet to be finalised in partnership with local residents and with the assistance of DEFRA, and we look forward to revealing the detailed scheme for the badgers in coming weeks.

"We are also delighted that an experimental excavation by DEFRA has revealed that the badgers have not burrowed beneath the gable end of a house, as was previously alleged.

"This confirms our original assessment that the badgers do not pose a risk to human health or property. This also means that we have time to implement a more carefully considered solution to the Saltdean sett."

THE GOVERNMENT'S FAILURE to get to grips with gun crime has been blasted by the Countryside Alliance.

It criticised as "pointless and unfair" Labour's intention to tighten restrictions on airgun ownership as part of a new crackdown on armed crime.

The Alliance called on Home Secretary David Blunkett to "address the real issues on gun crime and misuse rather than place further restrictions on responsible and legal firearm owners."

Director of the Campaign for Shooting, Nigel Davenport, said:"Victimising law-abiding people who own and use air weapons properly does nothing to reduce gun misuse by the criminal fraternity.

"UK restrictions on legitimate airgun ownership and use are already amongst the toughest in the world and have been continuously tightened - yet armed crime has steadily proliferated.

"Tightening the screw still further on the law-abiding use of air weapons will do nothing to reduce the criminal misuse of such weapons.

"The problems we are facing here are three-fold: the huge recent increase in armed crime and the growing number of illegally held guns being one, with the misuse of airguns and replicas being the other two."

AN OSPREY FEARED drowned after going off course on its first migration to Africa from Scotland has finally turned up - exhausted but unharmed.

The ringed predator was found on a Cape Verde island in the North Atlantic after haphazardly covering over 3,000 miles in seven weeks.

The bird, ringed in July last year at a monitored nest in Stirling, had been tracked by satellite until it disappeared from signals on monitoring equipment.

Conservationists at first believed it may have simply plunged into the sea, unable to go on over vast stretches of open water.

But its great soaring skills saved its life, carrying it on rising winds safely to land.

RSPB Scotland says the osprey, which is still 400 miles away from its likely destination, is the furthest travelling bird on its records.

Other ospreys simply fly to Africa from Spain, over the Strait of Gibraltar, so they face only the narrowest stretch of water.

A TINY WORM no longer than a thumb nail has put the brakes on a £150million bridge building programme in Kent.

Discovery of the mud living lagoon worm in the River Medway has seen work on an M2 bridge delayed by months.

The worm is protected under conservation laws and workmen are unable to join up both ends of the new bridge until a colony of the little creatures is relocated.

The Environment Agency, which has been involved in the wriggly drama, explained that the particular habitat in which the lagoon worm lives is now rare.

Finding or creating an alternative habitat will not be easy but all efforts are being made to accomplish the task.

MORE FRUIT AND veg growers are being urged to consider supplying a programme providing fresh food for schoolchildren.

The National School Fruit Scheme is seeking 'expressions of interest' to supply about a million pieces of fruit and/or vegetables per week to schools in the East and West Midlands from April next year.

The programme already supplies children aged between four and six with one whole piece of fruit or vegetable each school day.

NFU Horticulture chairman Michael Holmes said:"The scheme can provide an important market for growers, supplementing the more traditional methods of selling produce.

"The contract to supply the Midlands' 1,600 schools runs for 12 months, providing a steady market for a significant amount of produce and a guaranteed and predictable income.

"I would encourage growers to consider if the Fruit for Schools programme offers a useful market for their produce."

DOLPHINS COULD VANISH off Britain's coasts if nothing is done to stem an alarming rise in fishing net casualties, it has been claimed.

The Wildlife Trusts welcomed a parliamentary debate about dolphins dying in fishing nets in UK waters.

The debate had been prompted by the concerns of Matthew Taylor, Liberal Democrat MP for Truro and St Austell.

Joan Edwards, marine policy director of The Wildlife Trusts, said:"Hundreds of dolphin and porpoise carcasses are being washed upon our shores with evidence of death due to being caught in fishing nets. This is not a regional problem. The dramatic increase in numbers of dead dolphins represents a significant proportion of the UK's total dolphin population.

"If we don't act now, dolphins could disappear from our coasts altogether. Matthew Taylor's debate is well timed to highlight the escalating evidence of a shocking UK environment problem."

Despite growing evidence of dolphin deaths caused by fishing nets, the Trusts say the type of fishing responsible - bass fishing - continues unabated and the European Commission will do nothing without further scientific evidence.

The Wildlife Trusts, along with the WWF-UK, are calling for the Commission to take immediate action to reduce the number of dolphin and porpoise deaths by establishing an independent observation scheme.

The scheme would obtain reliable estimates of total marine mammal catch in a fishery.

Conservationists also want urgent efforts from the UK Government to work with the Commission to curb further deaths among marine wildlife.

Since the start of 2003, over 50 dolphins have already been washed up dead on the shores of Devon and Cornwall.

Dr Simon Lyster, director general of The Wildlife Trusts, added:"We strongly support Matthew Taylor's efforts to get a pelagic bass fishery closed. It is unsustainable, it is bad news for inshore bass fisheries and coastal economies because it is destroying fish stocks, and it is resulting in the deaths of hundreds of dolphins. This fishery is a scandal and should be closed immediately."

AN ARMY OF birdwatchers will go into action this month in a bid to set a record, says the RSPB.

"Hundreds of thousands of people will be watching their gardens and flocking into local parks on January 25-26 in an attempt to set a new world record in the RSPB's Big Garden Birdwatch," said a spokesman.

"The Big Garden Birdwatch, now in its 24th year, is the UK's biggest garden bird survey. Last year's event saw an astounding quarter of a million people take part.

"This year the RSPB is hoping to increase that number and set a new world record for the highest participation for any worldwide bird event.

"The record for the biggest bird event currently stands at 300,000 participants, held by BirdLife International's 2001 World Bird Festival.

"This month-long event spanned 88 countries and involved more than 175 organisations but the RSPB hopes to exceed this level of participation during its two-day UK only event."

283

FARMHOUSE BREAKFAST WEEK has been highlighting the benefits of breakfast for youngsters with schools all over the UK urged to take part by serving up traditional British breakfasts.

According to a survey by the NFU, nearly a third of British schoolchildren do not eat breakfast - with some even admitting they skip it to lose weight.

Disturbing numbers of children aged between four and 14 are missing out on the meal, says the union.

NFU member and Farmhouse Breakfast Week organiser Maggie Berry said:" Breakfast is the most important meal of the day but it's rapidly becoming a thing of the past for some schoolchildren.

"Eating breakfast provides energy to start off the day and increases concentration and mental performance, which are vital for school lessons. We were shocked by how many children skip it - and some for very worrying reasons indeed.

"Farmhouse Breakfast Week aims to remind us all how crucial breakfast is to everyone's health and wellbeing, but particularly to our children's."

A BULL WAS shot dead by a police marksman after going on the rampage in Oswestry, Shropshire.

The enraged animal had escaped from a local livestock market and began charging staff and customers who were forced to flee.

Police closed the A483 Wrexham to Welshpool road to minimise danger to motorists as firearms officers travelled to the scene from Worcester.

Despite trying to escape the town, the bull was finally cornered in part of a timber firm's premises.

There, an officer was able to dispatch it.

A FISH PASS which allows salmon and sea trout better access to a northern Welsh river has received a ministerial visit.

Environment Agency Wales organised a special visit for Welsh Assembly Deputy First Minister Mike German to the Conwy Falls pass near Betws y Coed.

"The fish pass was opened in 1994 and allows salmon and sea trout access to an additional 40 per cent of the River Conwy catchment upstream of the 10 metre high Conwy Falls, which form a barrier to migration," explained an Agency spokesman.

"The pass itself was constructed in a tunnel excavated from solid rock adjacent to the waterfall. The falls are a well-known beauty spot and the concealed pass does not spoil the scenic nature of the site in any way. By swimming and jumping through a series of 25 large pools within the pass, the fish are able to bypass the waterfall.

"When the fish pass opened, 60 salmon and sea trout were electronically counted using it. This figure had more than quadrupled to 257 in 2001, the best run yet. After a slow start in 2002, a total of 210 fish migrated through the pass with 102 fish in August alone, the highest monthly total on record. Numbers of fish using it are still rising."

OWNERS OF SMALL woodlands are being given a boost in their efforts to make the most of their plots - for their own pockets as well as for the environment.

A pilot project to investigate barriers they face seeking forest certification to the UK Woodland Assurance Standard has been launched at a handful of English sites by Forestry Commission chairman Lord Clark.

Lord Clark said:"We have a good story to tell on sustainable forestry and forest certification. Certification has been widely embraced by the owners of large woodlands but we would like to see greater uptake by the owners of smaller woodlands.

"These woodlands are a significant and valuable resource and pose a particular challenge as they often receive little or no management. As a result they are not realising their economic, environmental or social potential.

"Small woodlands are a precious commodity in England. As more wood users demand certified forest products, there is a risk that products from small woodlands will be excluded from the market.

"Linking producers to users by developing local chains of custody will be an integral part of breaking down the barriers to certification. Woodland owners will be offered the support, advice and training that they need."

Over the next three years the project will examine a range of actions to encourage owners of small woodlands to achieve certification.

The scheme is being launched in separate regional pilot areas: Yorkshire - Yorwoods, the English Marches; West Midlands - Heartwoods; and Greater Manchester/Merseyside - Red Rose and Mersey Community Forests.

The four main aims of the project will be to identify and evaluate appropriate incentive and support mechanisms; to increase the uptake of certification, bringing woodland into sustainable management; to evaluate what certification delivers in terms of economic, social and environmental outputs; and to evaluate how any benefits achieved can be maintained.

WILD GREY PARTRIDGES should be spared by shooters in the final days of the season, the Game Conservancy Trust says.

"This is the time of year when birds begin to pair up. Shooting them now damages next year's stock," explained a Trust spokesman.

"The grey partridge has suffered a massive 83 per cent decline over the last 30 years due to a number of factors, including lack of chick food insects, predation and weather. As the lead partner in the Government's Biodiversity Action Plan, the Trust is responsible for restoring grey partridge numbers and in the past year this rapidly declining species has responded well to our intensive recovery programme in Hertfordshire.

"Research unequivocally shows that shooting game does give landowners a tremendous incentive for retaining and enhancing habitats.

"However, the Trust recommends that grey partridges in particular should not be shot unless there is a careful management regime in place that has produced a sustainable surplus. The wild grey partridge is a ground-nesting bird that responds positively to management regimes such as feeding, habitat management and protection from predators."

FARMERS HAVE REACTED with a mixture of fury and bemusement to news that they face three months jail if they fail to put toys in with their pigs.

Failure to follow the "barmy" Brussels law could also see them fined £1,000 for each offence.

Technically, farmers are ordered to give pigs 'environmental enrichment' by making 'manipulable material' available to their animals.

Later, DEFRA - apparently happy to go along with Brussels - said:"We mean footballs and basketballs. Farmers may also need to change the balls so the pigs don't get tired with the same one.

"These rules are based on good welfare. We don't want to come across as the Nanny State but the important thing is to see pigs happy in their environment and they like to forage with their noses."

Worried farmer Neville Meeker revealed he had already given the 1,200 pigs at his farm in Warminster, Wilts, a plastic plane and a teddy bear to play with - just to be safe from prosecution.

"But these toys won't last two minutes," he admitted."I suppose I will just have to buy some balls.

"The day of the toy inspector has arrived and it is not a TV spoof. It is the dictators of Europe who have thought this up. Good job the January sales are on. Hamleys here we come!"

A DOG AND cat both needed rescuing from the River Teign in Devon after the dog chased its quarry into the water.

Firemen from Newton Abbot raced to the scene after being alerted to the animals' distress and plucked them to safety.

Devon Fire and Rescue Service later said animals often fell in the river but it was rare to get two in together.

It appeared that the dog had chased the cat which had jumped into the river to escape and the dog had simply gone in after it.

While the dog seemed fine after its ordeal, the cat required treatment for shock.

A PIG'S SNOUT was used in a bizarre protest in a rural community by a man who posted it through his neighbour's letterbox, magistrates heard.

The snout had been taken from a local village roast event in Farlow, Shropshire, and posted through the letterbox of a local pub - in protest at plans to transform the property into a house by its owner.

Following the incident, which happened after a campaign to save the pub had failed, the snout poster admitted using threatening behaviour at Bridgnorth Magistrates Court. He was bound over to keep the peace for a year in the sum of £500.

THE WOODLAND TRUST is going into battle to save a Dorset wood after being outraged by planning proposals put forward by a local council.

A decision favouring a new bypass for Weymouth - taken by Dorset County Council's Cabinet on January 23 - has enraged the Trust, the UK's top woodland conservation charity.

The Trust, which owns Two Mile Coppice in Weymouth, has thanked worried local residents who have already contributed over £1,000 to a fighting fund.

To defend the wood at an expected public inquiry will probably cost about £30,000 so the Trust is now calling for more help from the public.

Initial residents' contributions have been used to help pay for a special report sponsored by the Trust, the Campaign for the Protection of Rural England, and Friends of the Earth, aimed at saving the wood.

"However, the implications of the report's findings were completely ignored by the Cabinet," said Graham Bradley, spokesman for the Trust.

"I believe that the Cabinet was trying to avoid any contentious issues, as proven by the lack of debate on our Economic Impact Critique that had been circulated to the members before the meeting."

The Trust's current fund-raising appeal follows one that enabled the charity to buy the wood in 1998.

Both Dorset County Council and Weymouth and Portland Borough Council contributed to the appeal, as did hundreds of residents who now regularly enjoy walking and picnicking there.

Two Mile Coppice is Weymouth and Portland District's only remaining fragment of rare ancient woodland, says the Trust.

The wood, it adds, is one of the few to have so-called protective designation as well as protected bluebells. Nationally, barely two per cent of Britain contains ancient woodland, and Weymouth has even less.

Mr Bradley went on:"We are absolutely appalled at the council's decision. We're going to fight it all the way.

"All the road will do, once it has damaged a much-loved wood, is shove the traffic problems a bit further down. Not only that, but significantly more houses will now be even closer to the revised east-west route along Littlemoor Road when it is upgraded under the proposed plans."

BIG CAT SIGHTINGS seem to be on the increase - especially in Wales - with more people left shocked after apparently coming face to face with large predators in the countryside.

In the latest case, a police helicopter was called in to investigate after a woman reported seeing a 'panther-like' animal.

The woman alerted Dyfed Powys Police after spotting the mystery cat ambling away from the A40 through fields at Dryslwyn, between Llandeilo and Carmarthen.

Police said a thorough search was conducted in the area but nothing else was seen.

Just recently, armed officers searched the Llangadog area, near Llandovery, after a man saw a puma-like cat which killed a dog.

Another animal was later seen twice within days at Llangadog Creamery and Fairfach.

285

ANGLING AND SHOOTING will be next to go if the Government succeeds in banning hunting, claims a leading Labour MP.

According to the Countryside Alliance, Kate Hoey, the most prominent pro-hunting Labour MP, has penned an article for the next issue of The Field magazine in which she alleges that the Government is deliberately misleading the public over the future of shooting and fishing.

She says that Minister Alun Michael's so-called utility test, which determines whether various forms of hunting are necessary for pest control, is a precursor to future bans on shooting and fishing.

"If the utility test were to become law, then game shooting and coarse fishing would be drawn in by the same criteria," she writes."The zealots who want to ban hunting will waste no time, if they are successful, in turning their campaign to ban other sports."

Meanwhile, Alliance chairman John Jackson has reacted with anger to apparent manipulation by the anti-hunting dominated Commons Committee - with Alun Michael's co-operation - of the criteria for judging whether or not hunting should be licensed.

"Amongst many unjustified amendments the Committee has stacked the cards against licence applicants by requiring them to prove hunting 'causes the least suffering'," fumed Mr Jackson."Most seriously, the Committee has now manipulated the central premise of the Bill to ensure the only criteria for registration for hunting would be pest control. As it stands this Bill now makes a sad mockery of the Minister's pledge to base any hunting legislation clearly on 'principle and evidence'.

"The Minister's stated intention to find an honourable and fair solution appears now to have been surrendered to party political expediency. The Alliance has done everything in its power to co-operate with the Minister on this issue. Sadly, it has become apparent he is prepared to betray that trust."

WOODS AND FORESTS in the south west of England are now worth a "staggering" £575 million to the region's economy - in timber and woodland recreation - according to a report published by the Forestry Commission and the South West Regional Development Agency.

LOCAL AUTHORITY inspectors, working with DEFRA, have identified two farmers suspected of exposing cattle to pet food containing bovine material, in breach of BSE-related feed controls, says the Government.

FOXES ARE BEING killed at a fantastic rate by hunt groups in a bid to keep the sport alive, claims the League Against Cruel Sports.

The League has accused hunts of trying to "fiddle their killing records" to try to prove to MPs that they are a legitimate form of pest control.

Anti-hunt campaigners have apparently reported "a sharp rise in the number of foxes being killed by hunters at all costs as they try desperately to fill pages in their log books.

"Monitors have reported hunts in Kent, Surrey, West Sussex and Hampshire doing more holding up of foxes to ensure a kill, as time runs out for them to enjoy their bloodsport," said a League spokesman.

"Holding up - a practice used for autumn cub hunting where riders surround a wood to stop a fox escaping - is not allowed during the full season under the Master of Foxhounds' own Code of Conduct. It's also claimed more badger setts are being disturbed in the process.

"Police have been called to investigate three separate claims of the illegal use and disturbance of badger setts by protesters who monitor the Chiddingfold, Leconfield and Cowdray Hunt. Their huntsman has admitted to anti-hunt campaigners that they are killing six times as many foxes as they used to.

"But despite this, a League informant has found that one hunt in the West Country is struggling to find any foxes at all, proving what we've said all along - that fox numbers do not need to be controlled.

"The informant was told that despite having several 'blank days' because they were 'short of foxes' they would not give up hunting because it was 'something we've always done and we enjoy the riding and the social side'."

League chief executive Douglas Batchelor added:"An animal is either a pest or it isn't. There is no excuse to go killing for the sake of it to try and prove some futile point to MPs. The whole thing is a desperate con."

BROWN HARES, BUTTERFLIES and bumble bees are just three species which could benefit from a new wildlife friendly training scheme for farmers.

Launched by Prince Charles, the Game Conservancy Trust scheme is aimed at helping 'small and medium sized farmers' access wildlife friendly farming grants.

The Trust is running a three-year pilot project, funded by DEFRA and The Crop Protection Association, on its 333-hectare Allerton Project demonstration farm at Loddington in Leicestershire.

In a report published last year, the Trust showed how a 30-year decline in songbird numbers was reversed in just three years and a huge increase in brown hares, butterflies and bumble bees was recorded through the introduction of beetle banks, conservation headlands and field margins.

These are now nationally recognised prescriptions, adopted by the Countryside Steward - ship Scheme that were originally invented by the Trust to encourage wildlife.

Alastair Leake, the Trust's project manager at Loddington, said:"We are pleased that The Prince of Wales is showing such interest in our work and delighted that he agreed to launch the new Pathfind - ers Vocational Training scheme, which will help smaller farmers access grant aid for wildlife conser - vation on farmland."

DEER: dawn vision after a hellish night in car

ELUSIVE and fleet of foot, deer can move like shadows through the densest forest or bound effortlessly away across the most treacherous moor.

But from the mighty red deer to the tiny muntjac, each of our six wild species still needs natural, unspoilt land to flourish.

Red deer stags boast a shoulder height of about 48 inches, making them the biggest of Britain's remaining wild mainland creatures.

The vast Scottish Highlands provide a stronghold for red deer with an estimated population there of over 200,000.

Others can also be found scattered throughout England and Ireland.

Roe deer, meanwhile, are far daintier in appearance.

Compared to the red, the roe male has flimsy antlers and stands almost two feet shorter.

With their prominent black noses and pretty eyes, roe probably bear the closest resemblance to Walt Disney's famous 'Bambi' character.

Red and roe are classed as Britain's two truly indigenous species.

But this seems a bit unfair on fallow deer which have been around for centuries and only miss out on this classification due to a historic blip.

Fossil evidence has revealed that fallow deer were actually native to this country before the last Ice Age, died out during it, but were then reintroduced from abroad.

Spotted and white-rumped, fallow are not quite as large as red deer but the antlers of their stags are broader, heavier and possibly even more impressive.

Sika deer, meanwhile, were introduced to this country from Japan about 140 years ago.

Looking like a smaller, more mottled version of the red, the first sika were actually held at London Zoo.

From there, offspring were sent to parks all over the country.

However, several animals escaped into the wild and bred, sometimes with native red deer.

Muntjac deer are said to be the world's oldest species of deer, perhaps even prehistoric.

Introduced here from China about 100 years ago, they are also our smallest deer with a shoulder height of around 19 inches.

Despite their tiny size, their resilience has been remarkable.

So much so that muntjac are now widespread.

Finally, also imported from China, are Chinese water deer.

These were once native to the banks of the Yangtze River but again were first kept here at London Zoo.

Nowhere near as successful in the wild as the muntjac, less than 1,000 are said to roam free.

As with muntjac, however, the males have curious tusk-like teeth which they use to defend themselves.

My own favourite image of a deer owes much to my late father's dubious sense of direction.

With five children and my mother crammed into the car, he managed to get us all lost in the Welsh mountains en route to our summer holiday resort.

When darkness fell, we stopped at a remote spot to try to get some sleep.

It was a hellish night but there was to be some compensation later.

As dawn broke, I peered out of the car to see a magnificent fallow stag emerging through mist just 20 feet away.

He watched me.

I watched him.

Then he slunk off.

It was probably the most exciting moment of the whole trip.

CLAIMS THAT BADGERS can be as dangerous as big cats have been dismissed as "irresponsible nonsense" by the National Federation of Badger Groups.

The NFBG reacted with anger after a pet dog was savaged and its lady owner, a Farmers Union of Wales member, blamed a badger in a newspaper report and said badgers were as dangerous as the bigger predators said to roam the countryside.

According to the NFBG, Gwent woman Jill Bowen-Bravery admits she never even saw the attack on her collie whose non-fatal wounds were probably caused in a fight with her other dog, a labrador.

"She also suggested that if her grand-daughter had been outside instead of her dog, the child would have been killed," said a NFBG spokesman. "She went on to draw parallels between the alleged threat of attacks from badgers and recent stories of predation by big cats in Wales.

"The Farmers Union of Wales' Gwent county executive officer Neil Smith was quick to grab this opportunity to have a go at badgers - and foxes too.

"The newspaper quotes him as asking:'How many more children and old people have to be maimed by badgers or foxes?' Our question is:'Do you know anybody who has been maimed by a badger or a fox?'

"You would think that the Farmers Union of Wales would want to encourage rural tourism. Stories of marauding wildlife maiming children and old folk would seem more likely to have the opposite effect."

A PREGNANT COW went walkabout for 10 miles and ended up plunging 40ft down a cliff at the seaside.

But the rare Irish Moiled cow was plucked to safety at Barton-on-Sea, Hampshire.

Despite its delicate state, the cow had managed to escape from farm premises in the New Forest before tramping to a coastal caravan park.

After tumbling over the cliff in darkness, it remained stranded in mud the whole night before a 30-strong rescue team could save it the following day. Now safely back home after its near fatal adventure, the fugitive is said to be recovering well.

A SNOW-COVERED field in Shropshire has been playing host to an unlikely guest from hotter climes - a zebra.

But passers-by who do a double take at remote Edgton really can believe their eyes because the zebra is no fake.

His name is Zulu and he belongs to circus owner Peter Jolly who has been grazing the animal outside at his 10-acre farm site. And so far, Zulu appears to be taking the wintry weather in his stride.

HARE COURSING FANS are planning to meet as normal this month for the biggest event in their calendar - The Waterloo Cup.

Despite the death knell having apparently sounded for the controversial sport, defiant supporters will be gathering in force again at their historic northern course.

A spokesman for the National Coursing Club said:"The Waterloo Cup is the Blue Riband of coursing.

"Run at Altcar in Lancashire since 1836, it is the ultimate test of a greyhound. Sixty four of the best coursing greyhounds in Britain and Eire will contest the historic prize.

"This year's meeting will be held on February 25, 26 and 27. The first brace of runners will be put into slips at 9.30am each day. Spectators are advised to arrive by 8.30am to be in good time for the start.

"Coursing meetings last for as long as necessary to run out each day's programme. As a rough guide, expect the first day to be the longest - until about 4pm, and the third day to be the shortest - until about 2pm.

"Refreshments are available. Winner's prize-money is £5,000, kindly sponsored by Mr Oliver Coughlan. Entry from £15 each day, children free, car park free."

Large numbers of protesters are also expected at what could be the last year of the event following Government moves for an outright ban on both coursing and stag hunting.

Anti-coursing campaigners claim the sport is barbaric and it is wrong for hares to be ripped to pieces in front of a cheering audience.

However, supporters claim the intention of coursing is to test the skill and determination of dogs, hare deaths are incidental and most get away anyway.

BASS ARE GETTING a boost in the South West after the Environment Agency made moves to protect the fish from over-enthusiastic anglers.

Fishermen in Cornwall are being reminded of a new Agency byelaw aimed at conserving bass in the county's estuaries.

The byelaw, approved by DEFRA, increases the minimum landing size for bass caught in Cornish estuaries from 36cm to 37.5 cm.

This means that the bass size limit is now the same for catches made off the coast or in estuaries, ending years of confusion caused by differing sizes in both Agency and Cornwall Sea Fisheries byelaws.

The anomaly also made it difficult to prove cases against those taking undersize fish.

It is now illegal to retain any bass caught anywhere in Cornwall, out to a six mile sea limit, if it is below 37.5 cm in length.

Special weatherproof signs depicting life-size bass have been commissioned by the Agency to remind local anglers of the new law and will be placed in ports, harbours and coves.

"Now the law has been simplified and there is no ambiguity on the minimum landing size for bass in Cornwall we will be increasing our checks on anglers and commercial fishermen to make sure undersized fish are not being taken," warned Agency spokesman Mark Pilcher.

Bass are slow growing, long lived fish and a 37.5cm long specimen will be about six years old, he added, though the fish can actually live up to 30 years.

288

AN EEL FISHERMAN in Dorset has been prosecuted for endangering the lives of otters with his nets.

The man was ordered to pay £500 in fines and costs for using the nets in Poole Harbour during a case brought by the Environment Agency.

Appearing before East Dorset magistrates, the Poole fisherman pleaded guilty to using prohibited instruments, namely 48 fyke nets without otter guards, for the period between April 22-23, 2002.

The court heard a water bailiff had discovered the nets near the entrance to Poole Yacht Club during routine patrols.

On inspection, he saw that none of the nets were fitted with otter guards or Agency licence tags.

After removing fish, eels and crabs, the bailiff seized the nets and took them to the Agency's boathouse at Wareham.

Following the case, the Agency revealed that some months ago a mother otter and her two cubs were killed by an illegal net spread in the River Stour, drowning as they failed to disentangle themselves after going in to feed on eels.

"Poole Harbour is one of the most important areas for otters in the country with a healthy population," said a spokesman for the Agency. "Surrounding rivers including the Frome, Piddle and Shoford are also showing signs of growing otter numbers.

"The recent death of a mother otter and her two cubs in a fyke net shows how dangerous unguarded nets can be.

"This also illustrates how important it is for the Environment Agency to remain vigilant and enforce the law."

PUTTING GREY SQUIRRELS on the pill to control numbers has proved a flop, according to a Government minister.

Lord Whitty told fellow peers that tests involving a special vaccine had been dropped despite early signs that the scheme would work and stop the march of immigrant American greys.

However, while laboratory tests had gone well, the scheme had proved too difficult to implement in the wild and so it was back to the drawing board.

A EUROPEAN EAGLE owl caused a flap in Shropshire when it escaped from its cage.

Almost 100 people called a local 'owl hootline' when the hand-reared bird took to the skies near owner John Chadwick's home in Bridgnorth.

Some calls were believed to come from too far away to be postive and so it proved - Jess the owl was eventually discovered just 200 yards from home.

Hungry but unscathed after a week on the run, the runaway was soon back in its cage.

'PRESCOTT-TOPIA', the Deputy Prime Minister's £22 billion housing vision for more affordable housing in England, has sparked growing concerns among conservationists about the threat to wildlife and green spaces.

Honor Gay, head of people and wildlife for The Wildlife Trusts, said:"Biodiversity has been given short shrift in this plan. The Trusts believe urban green spaces should be safe and welcoming environments for people and wildlife.

"Green spaces are more fulfilling if they are wildlife-rich, not sterile deserts. This plan does not go far enough in setting real targets for improving urban wildlife and making it relevant to people's everyday lives."

Kate Parminter, chief executive of the Council for the Protection of Rural England, said:"As they stand, the Government's proposals could actually undermine progress towards urban renaissance, sharpen the regional economic divide, and severely curtail opportunities for public involvement in the big planning decisions on issues like housing.

"In the last few years the Deputy Prime Minister has been instrumental in driving forward positive new policies on urban renaissance and planning for housing.

"CPRE has campaigned hard to ensure early implementation of those changes.The fear now is that we are seeing a return to the discredited predict-and-provide approach to housing and greenfield developments."

However, a Downing Street spokesman said:"Housing in England has received a massive multi-billion pound boost as a major part of the Government's drive to tackle deprivation and shortage of affordable housing.

"The package announced by the Deputy Prime Minister marks a critical change in delivering the supply of high quality, affordable housing; reforming the planning system; reversing the causes of decades of low demand and abandonment; and ensuring all social housing reaches a decent standard by 2010.

"During the next three years £5 billion will be invested in new affordable housing, including £1billion provision for key workers."

FEARS FOR THE welfare of British sheep being exported for slaughter during a Muslim festival in France have prompted a statement from the Government.

Animal Welfare Minister Elliot Morley said:"The Department enforces animal health and welfare rules rigorously. All consignments of sheep for slaughter or further fattening are subject to strict scrutiny.

"Since the resumption of live sheep exports this includes pre-export veterinary inspection for health and fitness to travel and tighter animal health controls over the pre-export mixing of animals.

"DEFRA would prefer a trade in meat rather than live animals for slaughter. However, the law is clear that we may not prevent exports on the grounds that the animals might be subject to poor welfare in the country of destination.

"For this reason we welcome the steps taken by the French authorities to stop the horrendous practices seen in past years.

"We understand that this year special arrange - ments will be made to ensure that all animals must be slaughtered in approved abattoirs in accordance with welfare and hygiene rules."

DOLPHINS, PORPOISES AND other marine creatures are to get better protection from noisy boats filled with sightseers which get too close.

The country's first 'wildlife-friendly accreditation scheme' aims to reduce numbers of incidents involving disturbance and harassment of creatures in UK waters while promoting safe observation.

The scheme is designed to work with commercial pleasure craft owners to encourage marine ecotourism to operate in a more wildlife-friendly way.

The project is supported by The Wildlife Trusts, WWF-UK, The Shark Trust, and funded by English Nature, Marine Southwest and the South West Regional Development Agency.

"Year on year the number of incidents of marine wildlife harassment have increased," said a spokesman for the scheme.

"Marine conservationists throughout the UK are aware that marine wildlife, such as dolphins, porpoises and basking sharks, may be physically harmed and can show serious signs of stress when approached in an insensitive manner by leisure or commercial pleasure craft, who may be unaware of the sensitivity of marine wildlife."

Colin Speedie, a marine conservationist, added:"Marine ecotourism holds many potential benefits for boat operators, visitors and residents alike. We want people to enjoy our marine wildlife whilst ensuring it comes to no harm."

The new scheme would help, he added.

GLOBAL WARMING IS causing hayfever hell for more and more sufferers, according to The Woodland Trust.

"This is because, in response to global warming, many flowers (which includes tree and grass flowers) are flowering earlier and for longer, therefore releasing pollen for longer periods than before," said a spokesman."Some 95 per cent of hayfever is triggered by grass pollen. It is compounded by the fact that, in some parts of the country, mowing the lawn has become a constant year-long chore.

"Although cut grass is usually too short to flower, sap allergens released by cut grass add to our woes. This spring, the Trust and the National Pollen Research Unit are asking people to record the early flowering grasses such as Yorkshire fog, cocksfoot, meadow foxtail and Timothy grass, as part of the UK Phenology Network's survey."

TV weatherman and Trust supporter Michael Fish, said:"Higher temperatures are extending the grass flowering season. Like me, many more people will be condemned to longer bouts of sneezing, itchy eyes, headaches and a throbbing nose.

"Information collected by amateur phenologists will help to forecast the start of the pollen season."

SECRETLY FILMED VIDEO footage of emaciated hounds has prompted the RSPCA to raid a hunt kennels in Cumbria, according to the League Against Cruel Sports.

The anti-hunt League says it had long suspected hunts of mistreating their dogs but this was the first time such compelling evidence had been obtained.

However, despite the League obtaining the footage of hounds "in a shocking condition", RSPCA inspectors were apparently unable to locate the dogs in question.

This had prompted speculation from anti-hunt campaigners that hunters had taken drastic action to avoid prosecution.

"Hunts regularly shoot hounds that are unable to hunt," claimed a League spokesman, adding:"The suffering of hounds belonging to the Melbreak Hunt is documented in a special report called 'The Futility of Upland Hunting' published after a 10-month long undercover investigation into Britain's mountain fox hunts.

"Documents obtained by League investigators confirm the horrific allegations made by a lifelong fell hunting supporter who approached the League with information.

"Mr X, forced to remain anonymous for fear of retribution, claimed the hounds were not being fed properly because there wasn't room for all the dogs to reach the trough at feeding times.

"Another concerned supporter bought an extra feeding trough, but the huntsman reportedly turned it upside down and refused to use it. The dossier of evidence has now been passed to RSPCA inspectors for investigation."

A GOAT WAS at the centre of a health scare when it went to visit the Welsh Assembly HQ in Cardiff, South Wales.

The animal, an army mascot, was given its marching orders after relieving itself on the floor of the building - the new focus of power in the land.

The goat had been brought by soldiers from the Royal Regiment of Wales on an official trip to the site but Mother Nature somewhat undermined the solemnity of the occasion.

Assembly staff feared the goat's action had produced a health hazard and refused to serve food until it was removed from the building and its mess cleaned up.

BULLYING COCK GROUSE are responsible for restricting the size of red grouse populations, according to a report in Nature magazine.

A cock bird which likes to fight will take over more territory than it actually needs and so restrict normal breeding activity.

Researchers at the Centre for Ecology and Hydrology at Banchory, Aberdeenshire, focused on red grouse in various parts of Scotland and England.

They found that in crowded conditions, testosterone levels in males went up and so did subsequent aggression.

However, fights were often prolonged longer than the crowded conditions existed and the result could actually be a population fall.

Yet there may be a simple solution.

Grouse managers can reduce the declines, scientists believe, by preventing local grouse populations from becoming too crowded and aggressive in the first place.

BADGER LOVERS HAVE attacked the Princess Royal after she alleged that the mammals infected cattle with bovine TB.

The National Federation of Badger Groups says it understands that Princess Anne, speaking at a farming conference, asserted:"If anyone tells me there is no proven link between bovine TB and badgers I will see them outside later..."

Dr Elaine King, chief executive of the NFBG, said:"In the wake of foot-and-mouth disease, there was a rapid increase in bovine TB when farmers in previously unaffected areas unwittingly restocked with infected cattle. This confirmed that cattle infect one another.

"The Environment, Food and Rural Affairs Select Committee has just heard from Dr Chris Cheeseman - a leading Government badger ecologist - who said that badger culling might have no effect on TB in cattle or could make the situation worse. In short, nobody knows for sure the extent to which badgers are involved, if at all.

"The Princess Royal, by purporting to have access to privileged knowledge that contradicts current scientific thinking, has done a great disservice to the countryside.

"The Princess Royal should have consulted Prince Charles first. In 1994, 15 badgers were trapped and killed on Prince Charles' Highgrove Estate, for allegedly giving TB to his cattle. All were subsequently found not to have the disease.

"We know that farmers have been lobbying Prince Charles to call for badger culling for more than a year. This latest outburst from Princess Anne suggests to us that the Royals are being unduly influenced by the farming unions."

A KENT FISHING lake has fallen victim to an unusual type of pollution - hundreds of used nappies.

Environment Agency officers are trying to get to the bottom of the bizarre situation which has seen over 300 nappies turn up in recent weeks.

The disposable nappies have been regularly appearing in Broomwood Lake, Orpington, via the River Cray.

Due to the persistence of the problem, a full survey is being carried out by investigators.

As well as being unsightly, the nappies threaten wildlife and increase the risk of flooding by blocking sluices, pumps and grilles.

"We are keen to track down the person or people responsible for this unusual and distasteful environmental crime," said probe leader Paul Bennett."The brand is quite unusual - German-made Moltex-Eco - and this has to narrow down where they could have come from."

RAMBLERS ARE CELEBRATING the reopening of "the country's most notorious blocked footpath".

The so-called 'van Hoogstraten path' at Framfield in East Sussex, is being cleared of barriers and debris for public use.

The Ramblers Association said:"In a stunning victory for walkers, demolition squads moved in on Monday, February 10, to remove obstacles that have blocked the right of way for 13 years.

"The Association was there to cut the wire and the padlock on locked gates while heavy machines removed concrete pillars and old fridges illegally placed on the path.

"The path runs across land owned by Rarebargain Ltd., a company associated with disgraced property tycoon Nicholas van Hoogstraten, currently serving a 10-year sentence for manslaughter.

"Barbed wire, padlocked gates, refrigeration units and a barn have illegally obstructed the path. The local authority, East Sussex County Council, has a duty to keep the route clear of obstructions.

"Instead of forcing the landowner to clear the obstructions, and contrary to their stated policy, East Sussex County Council attempted to divert the path.

"But last year Kate Ashbrook, chairman of the Ramblers Association Access Committee, won a case in the Appeal Court against East Sussex County Council that led to the council abandoning the diversion and issuing a legal notice to clear the obstructions."

TWO NEWBORN LAMBS have been plucked to safety from a 12ft deep hole in Devon.

The stranded animals would undoubtedly have died if they had been left to fend for themselves after tumbling into the disused badger sett.

Farmer Eric Palmer lowered himself head first into the sett on his land near Kingsbridge in the south of the county.

As friends kept hold of his feet, he used a walking stick to pull the lambs towards him before hauling them free.

Both lambs were soon suckling happily on their mothers again following their ordeal.

It was thought fortunate the sett was empty at the time as badgers are not known for showing much kindness to intruders.

TOAD PATROL VOLUNTEERS are being signed up again to stop thousands of the ambling amphibians dying on roads over the breeding season.

The Wildlife Trusts' scheme has proved popular in recent years among young and old alike who gather up toads - and frogs - in buckets to prevent them being crushed.

"From March to May our frisky frogs and toads risk life and limb to reach their breeding ponds," said a spokesman."But with many of these ancient routes now crossed by roads with heavy traffic, many toads never reach their final destination.

"Luckily, the Trusts' annual toad patrols save thousands of amphibians every year. Toad patrol volunteers carry frogs and toads across roads in buckets, erect warning signs asking drivers to slow down and encourage toads to use specially constructed underpasses. As well as making sure the toads can get to their mates in safety, volunteers also track migration routes and monitor numbers - vital information for the future of amphibian populations."

THE COUNTRYSIDE ALLIANCE says it wants Rural Affairs Minister Alun Michael to consider his position "as his Hunting Bill degenerates into farce".

A spokesman explained:"The call follows the Minister's refusal to vote for his own Bill over a committee amendment to ban all hare hunting.

"Pro-hunting and 'middle way' MPs were astounded by the Minister's failure to support his own Bill and by the decision of his parliamentary private secretary, Peter Bradley, to support the amendment.

"Former Tory Environment Secretary John Gummer, said:'In 25 years in Parliament, I have never before seen a minister not vote for his own Bill'.

"Hare hunting with beagles, basset hounds, and harriers is carried out by over 90 registered packs of hounds and supported by over 30,000 people.

"All hare coursing would also be banned by the amendment, which would affect an estimated 100,000 lurcher owners who use their dogs for hunting, as well as the 24 registered coursing clubs already prohibited in the Bill."

Simon Hart, director of the Campaign for Hunting, added:"The Minister's position is disappointing and completely indefensible. Rural people put their trust in his pledge to base the Bill honestly on 'principle and evidence'.

"His behaviour is incomprehensible unless, as has been claimed, it was for him never a question of 'if' hunting should be banned but 'how' it should be banned. The process in the House of Commons is now degenerating into farce and the Minister should consider his position."

BADGERS ARE AT the centre of a row in rural Scotland over delays to reopening a vital local road which has already been closed to the public for over 100 days.

Furious residents of the Moray hamlets of Boharm, Mulben and Maggieknockater have been informed that the discovery of badger setts will further hamper any reopening of the road, currently undergoing repairs.

Local people have been enduring diversions of up to 40 miles a day to get to work after part of the main A95 Keith to Craigellachie road subsided, leaving an 80ft crack along one half of the carriageway.

Almost 100 of them staged an angry protest after being told that subsequent discovery of the setts would see their travel problems prolonged.

Under the Protection of Badgers Act 1992, it is an offence to kill or injure a badger, damage its sett or disturb it when in residence.

SALMON AND SEA trout caught illegally are the subject of a sweeping probe by the Environment Agency in Devon.

The Agency says a number of special checks are being carried out at hotels and restaurants, especially in the Plymouth area.

Buyers of wild salmon and sea trout must be able to prove to the Agency that they have obtained them legally.

Special measures to protect spring salmon and encourage wild stocks to increase mean that salmon caught by rod before June 16 must be returned to the water alive - and licensed netsmen must not catch salmon before June 1.

"We are checking hoteliers, caterers, pubs and restaurants in the area to make sure the salmon they have is bona fide and has come from either a fish farm or was legally caught in the open season and subsequently frozen," said Agency spokesman Bruce Newport.

"Anyone buying wild salmon or sea trout must get a receipt including the name and address of the seller and details of where and when the fish was caught with the name and licence number of the angler or netsmen. It is up to the person buying, selling or possessing the fish to prove it was caught legally."

If someone suspected that illegally caught salmon or sea trout were being offered for sale they could contact the Agency in confidence.

"The illegal taking of these migratory fish can have devastating effects on future fish stocks in our local rivers," added Mr Newport.

GREAT CRESTED NEWTS are the secret weapon in a battle by residents in Shropshire to stop new housing development on a local flood plain.

Campaigners fighting the construction of 26 new homes in rural Wem say the rare creatures live on the plain and are threatened by the scheme.

The newts are protected under wildlife laws and the developers may have to redraw or scale down plans to save them.

However, proof of their existence is required so campaigners are combing the land to track down the amphibians on the eve of their breeding season.

HUNT SUPPORTERS USED the country's top hare coursing event to rally support for all types of hunting.

The 155th Waterloo Cup at Altcar in Lancashire provided a focus for defiance, with several breeds of hunting dogs displaying unity against any ban.

Foxhounds, staghounds, beagles, terriers, hare hounds and lurchers took part in an opening parade for the premier event in the coursing calendar as a Bill seeking to ban coursing outright makes its way through Parliament.

Before the three-day event got underway, Liz Mort, the Countryside Alliance's coursing spokesman, said:"The entire hunting community is standing strong against any ban on hunting but there will certainly be a shadow over Altcar this year. Alun Michael, the Minister for Rural Affairs, originally promised that his Hunting Bill would be fair and would be based on principle and evidence. Instead, he has chosen to ban competitive coursing and deer hunting out of hand and has steadfastly refused to explain why.

"The Bill that is about to leave the Commons is a banning Bill in all but name. Representatives from all areas of the hunting world will be at Altcar to tell the world that this is not acceptable."

BIRDS OF PREY have been boosted by a move which underlines the threat they face from agricultural poisons.

Advice contained in a new leaflet from English Nature and the RSPB draws on the knowledge and experience of pest control and conservation experts.

It sets out to offer sensible and practical ways to minimise rodent infestations while reducing the threat to vulnerable birds of prey.

English Nature said:"The type of rat poison and methods landowners, farmers and pest controllers use to control rodents can make the difference between life and death for some of the UK's most spectacular birds of prey. Today, leading conservationists are asking for help to save birds from accidental poisoning.

"English Nature and the RSPB are concerned about poisoning and widespread contamination of birds of prey by chemicals used to control rats and mice.

"Post-mortem surveys show that birds can be killed by eating animals poisoned by certain rodenticides.

"Red kites, barn owls, kestrels and buzzards sit at the top of the food chain and are an important and highly valued part of our countryside's wildlife.

"But they are at risk of building up a fatal dose of toxins from eating poisoned rats and mice. Red kites are particularly vulnerable as they mainly scavenge on dead animals, increasing their risk of being poisoned.

"Controlling and preventing infestations of rats and mice are important jobs on farms and other businesses in our countryside. The leaflet offers ways to minimise rodent infestations and guidance on how to use rodenticides more safely."

Between 1998-2001 around 30 incidents were reported involving birds of prey, especially red kites and buzzards, where rodenticides were thought to be the cause of death.

Other surveys have found 70 per cent of red kites and kestrels, and 40 per cent of barn owls, with detectable levels of rodenticide residues in their bodies.

BADGER FANS HOPE new ideas of dealing with bovine TB will save the underground burrowers from being culled.
"Proposals discussed at a meeting of the Government's TB Forum mark a significant step forward in DEFRA's approach to dealing with TB in cattle," claimed a spokesman for the National Federation of Badger Groups.

WORKING TERRIERS COULD soon become jobless after MPs voted to stop them flushing out foxes to guns or killing them underground.
An amendment to the Hunting Bill has been supported by MPs which means that gamekeepers will find their jobs much harder to do, according to the Countryside Alliance.

"Terrier work is a crucial method of fox control especially for gamekeepers and in upland areas," said a spokesman."In mid-Wales, the Burns Report found that over a third of the annual cull of foxes was as a result of terrier work. Terrier work is also a crucial animal welfare tool to ensure that orphaned fox cubs are culled rapidly when vixens have been shot."

The future of game shooting in its present form is also thought to be threatened by the move, as foxes will be left to hide in cover.

The Alliance called the situation an extraordinary display of political cynicism by Rural Affairs Minister Alun Michael who voted against his own Bill, supporting the amendment banning all terrier work.

Simon Hart, director of the Countryside Alliance's Campaign for Hunting said:"Alun Michael has caved in to pressure from backbench and DEFRA colleagues to such an absurd degree that he has ended up voting against his own Bill. This is a betrayal of evidence and a betrayal of principle from a minister who claimed to be wedded to both.

"It is also a betrayal of the Government's 2001 election manifesto since the impact of this amendment on gamekeepers will clearly breach the claim that they had no intention whatsoever of placing restrictions on shooting.

"Since the Minister appears to have been impotent in protecting his Bill from his own backbenchers in committee, his vague assurances that he will move amendments on the floor of the house to protect shooting would seem to be worthless. Such a move would anyway be grossly and transparently discriminatory.

"Alun Michael personally presided over a process of consultation and hearings and then ignored all the evidence brought before him. His shambolic handling of the committee stages suggest that the Hunting Bill is nothing but a deceitful attempt to ban hunting under the guise of a regulatory system and has brought the parliamentary process into contempt."

However, Douglas Batchelor, chief executive of the League Against Cruel Sports, asserted:"Terrier work is an extremely barbaric aspect of the hunting scene."

WALK TO BEAT London's controversial congestion charge, says the Ramblers Association.
Most of central London is easily and quickly navigated on foot and walking just one day per week will save £260 per year, it adds.

THE WOODLAND TRUST says Tony Blair's pledges on reducing pollution are "fine words" but action is needed.

The Trust has welcomed the Prime Minister's stance on climate change - especially his target of a 60 per cent reduction in carbon emissions by 2050.

But spokesman Ed Pomfret said:"An ambition is meaningless without clear targets and action to back it up. We support the words but we must see action to ensure that such a step change is implemented."

GRASS: wild type a world away from garden chore

MOWING the lawn must be one of the most tedious chores Man ever invented for himself, especially if - like me - you have a deep aversion to it.
Nor am I much good.
I must be the only person I know whose garden looks *worse* after I have been at it with the mower.
This is why my wife often insists on doing the smaller garden at the front of our house herself (i.e. the one everyone sees).
The commercially developed grass in most of our gardens seems a world way from the native wild grasses still found in our woodlands and meadows.
Neatness and colour regularity provided by commercial grass may look appealing to humans, but insects and other wildlife get far more benefit from wild grasses allowed to run rampant.
Wild grasses can be startlingly pretty when viewed close up and some of their names are intriguing.
Woodland grasses include Creeping Soft, Wood Melick, Wood False-Brome, Giant Fescue and Hairy Brome.
That last one, Hairy Brome, is a typical woodland grass, the tall sort whose feathery spikes are probably plucked by your fingers during a leisurely stroll.

Tiny hairs project from the lower leaves giving it its name and it prefers shady, moist areas where it can grow in abundance.
Meadow grasses, meanwhile, range from Tufted Hair and Crested Dog's Tail to False Oat and Meadow Foxtail.
Of this group, the final one - so named because its head resembles a tiny fox's brush - is very common in low lying meadows, particularly valleys.
Wetland grasses have equally appealing names with Common Cotton, Black Bog Rush and White Beaked Sedge among the more notable.
Another well-known variety, Reedsweet, is a pinker, more slender grass found on the banks beside running water and even growing in still water.
The 'sweet' part of its name may derive from the fact that farmers once found it a good fodder grass for their animals.

Elsewhere, grasses growing on exposed limestone cliffs and scrub areas include Quaking, Creeping Bent, Sheep's Fescue and Blue Moor.
Blue Moor gets its name from an attractive blue tinge which sets it apart from other grasses.
Smaller than most wild grasses, it has quite a delicate appearance but looks are deceptive.
Like all wild grasses, it is tough and survives on northern rock ledges and cliffs against the worst the weather can throw at it.
Modern garden grass seems bland in comparison and provides little consolation as you labour behind your mower.
I doubt that the poet Rupert Brooke would have felt so inspired by it to pen the line:"*Breathless, we flung us on the windy hill, laughed in the sun, and kissed the lovely grass.*"

A NATIONAL BID to promote angling - and eating fish - is due to reach its climax in the food hall of a top London store despite being scorned by anti-angling campaigners.

The Countryside Alliance's Campaign for Angling director Charles Jardine intends to complete a week-long national 'Fishing 4 Food' tour by "cooking up a fishy-storm" in Selfridges, Oxford Street.

Fishing 4 Food is an Alliance initiative run in conjunction with Selfridges and Fuller's Brewery with the aim of promoting fishing and teaching people new and different ways to cook what they catch.

During the tour Mr Jardine and sous chef Gary Champion fished for as many British fish as possible while giving cooking demonstrations at different Fuller's pubs across the South East.

Hundreds turned out to see the events and there was said to have been an enthusiastic response to recipes such as trout in oatmeal and trout tagliatelle.

Mr Jardine said:"Saturday will be a grand finale to this successful initiative and we hope that Londoners will be inspired to go and fish for their dinner once they have seen a demonstration. Our message to everyone during Fishing 4 Food has simply been 'get out there and catch your own dinner'. Fish is delicious, nutritious, fun to catch and even more fun to cook."

In stark contrast, British members of anti-angling group PETA were in Oslo recently holding a sign reading 'For Cod's Sake, Go Vegetarian!' and brandishing a 7ft tall model fish mascot as part of the organisation's global campaign against commercial fishing.

"PETA's giant fish wishes to remind residents that fish - whose sinking numbers have caused a sea of controversy - are individuals who experience fear, feel pain and suffer an agonising death when they are hauled from their ocean homes," said a spokesman.

A COW NEEDED rescuing after a bizarre accident on a Shropshire farm saw it slip backwards into a drain.
The animal was jammed solid in the 3ft by 3ft drain at Highley, with only its head and upper body left sticking out.
Firemen took almost two hours to free the cow, dragging it clear inch by inch.
But the operation could only be completed when a JCB was brought in to dig round the 8ft-deep drain.
Its walls were also demolished.
The distressed cow was treated by a vet and soon seemed well on the way to recovery.

CIRL BUNTINGS HAVE been boosted in Devon after 80 farmers got involved in a pioneering project to save the little birds.
Once widespread across southern Britain, the buntings are now mainly restricted to the West Country.
The RSPB,recognising that agri-environment schemes in the early 1990s did not cater for the needs of the bird, came up with a special project under the umbrella of the Countryside Stewardship Scheme.
"Farmers in the area, covering 3,600 acres, have embraced this to provide over-winter stubble fields and insect-rich grass margins for these birds," said a spokesman for the Society.
"Now approximately nine out of 10 of the national cirl bunting population live within one kilometre of a Stewardship agreement.
"This is important because the birds are known not to travel very far. Farmers managing their land in this way have thrown these birds a lifeline which has seen their numbers rise from only 130 pairs in 1989 to around 450 pairs today.
"Farmer John Andrews' family have farmed a 300 acre site in south west Devon for 99 years. He operates a mixed farming system with suckler cattle, sheep and cereals.
"This mix of grazing and cereals has helped cirl buntings to survive. John entered Countryside Stewardship in 1999. The agreement was tailored to fit his needs and improve the habitat for cirl buntings."
Mr Andrews himself added:"The initial interest was sparked by the fall in cereal prices but I also had a general feeling that it was what I wanted to do. Originally, I was including work on hedges etc to score more points, but I enjoy being in the scheme and I am always looking for more things to do around the farm.
"I have increased all my arable margins to six metres - they make sense economically, gives a good edge to the field and can make them easier to work, even in smaller fields.
"It is especially in these margins and the stubble fields that I notice the change in wildlife. There are lots of birds in the stubbles, including 60-70 linnets the other day.
"I would definitely recommend Stewardship to others but with a little warning. Do not cram too many capital works into the first five years. Spread them out, otherwise it can become too expensive and time consuming."

HUNDREDS OF HEDGEHOGS and scores of badgers are killed each day on Britain's roads, researchers say.
Motorists crush an average of 273 hedgehogs per day while commuting to and fro, according to Auto Express magazine.
And some 137 badgers die daily as the country's drivers travel to their destinations.
Other wildlife is also caught up in the massacre with 110 deer killed per day and 14 birds of prey.

'DEEP SNIFFING' BY great crested newts has been the subject of Swedish research.
A scientist found that the rare newts shunned ponds too full of fish as fish are major predators of newt larvae. Newts holding their heads high in the air and taking deep breaths beside a pond could be finding out if it smells too 'fishy' and is not worth the trouble of laying eggs in.

FROG SPAWN HAS been the subject of a wide ranging study, according to English Nature.

"Each year, those of us with garden ponds await the influx of common frogs and the subsequent frenzy of spawning," said a spokesman.

"The more assiduous backyard naturalists keep notes of when the frogs turn up and spawn, and for years it has been understood that frogs work to more or less fixed regional timetables. So South West frogs, for example, always have an ETA far in advance of their cousins elsewhere in country.

"But until very recently, no one fully understood exactly what causes the difference in spawning dates.

"However, Liz Chadwick, of the University of Wales, has painstakingly sifted through spawning dates collected over the years.

"The key factor seems to be the cumulative number of warm days from December to February, with the precise spawning date being influenced by a last-minute rise in maximum temperature.

"Rainfall is not nearly so influential. So if you've not had to wrap up warmly for the last few weeks the chances are there'll be spawn soon. What is certain is that if you live around the Wash, your frogs will be the last in the country to spawn."

SHEEP WERE CHASED and 'arrested' by police after escaping from a field in Lancashire.

Some 30 woolly fugitives went on the run from Hutton, near Preston, after contractors left a gate open, sparking comic scenes.

First, the animals charged half a mile over fields and through the grounds of a local school.

Then they descended on a quiet cul-de-sac among homes, munching their way through residents' prized plants and shrubs.

Finally, police were helped by a farmer to round the animals up and bring the chaos to an end.

THE RSPB HAS expressed its astonishment that Labour is continuing to consider Cliffe in Kent ripe for airport development.

"For the Government to continue to propose Cliffe as a viable option is a nonsense," said RSPB spokesman Paul Lewis. "It's the most expensive option, it's the most environmentally damaging and it could pose a serious threat to passenger safety.

"It would also face a lengthy battle in the courts due to the strong protection this area enjoys under national and international wildlife laws. What's more, the airlines don't want it and the City isn't prepared to pay for it. Government should acknowledge it's a hopeless non-starter and kick it into touch ahead of the White Paper.

"The mudflats and marshes around Cliffe support up to 200,000 wading birds and wildfowl in winter."

VORACIOUS WILLOW EATING beetles could soon be outsmarted by new traps which will stop them wrecking a scheme to reduce dependence on fossil fuels.

The Game Conservancy Trust says that since the Earth Summit in Rio in 1992, the Government has tried to encourage the use of renewable resources.

"Farmers have been encouraged to grow crops that could be burnt in specially adapted power stations," said a spokesman. "The main crop on which many hopes have been pinned is the willow tree. This can be sown densely and within three to five years the four-metre high crop can be cut, ready for processing. Unfortunately, when such a dense crop of willow is created it becomes a haven for the blue willow beetle.

"This beetle usually eats the leaves of wild willows but in the biomass crops it can become superabundant with thousands of animals per square metre, simply because there is so much food available.

"With so many bugs eating the trees it's not surprising to find that tree growth can be limited and the harvest disappointing, which has proved to be one of the factors inhibiting the wider use of such crops.

"However research carried out in Scotland by the Trust and the University of Dundee may help save the beleaguered biomass industry.

"Detailed studies of the beetles over three years by Dr Peter Marshall suggest that they may have a weakness. During the autumn, the adult beetles start to move out of the willow crop and look for places where they can spend the winter.

"These are usually small cracks and crevices that they can crawl into and remain out of sight of predators and away from the elements.

"This was exploited by designing small traps made of corrugated cardboard that were very attractive to the beetles. They crawl into these traps and can then be removed from the crop and so prevented from moving back into the willows again during the spring when they start to eat the crop.

"The preliminary studies suggest this can reduce beetle numbers significantly, but further experimental trials are planned for the near future to fully test this. It is hoped that in due course a trap will be available for use across the country in willow plantations that will prevent beetles from becoming a problem and thus make the willow crop more viable."

PEAT BOG WILDLIFE has been given a boost by a new leaflet urging gardeners to buy alternatives to peat.

The new 'Where to Buy Peat-free Products 2003' guide, published by The Wildlife Trusts, provides information on where to find everything to make a garden flourish without harming precious peat bogs.

"Gardeners and indoor-plant lovers can do an enormous amount to improve the diversity of plants and animals, whilst ensuring that they do not damage some of our finest natural habitats - peat bogs, " said a spokesman.

"Gardeners currently account for around 70 per cent of peat use. Peat extraction from bogs can lead to irreparable damage and habitat loss, not to mention affecting the fascinating wildlife it supports, such as beautiful dragonflies and damselflies, carnivorous sundew and bladderwort plants."

BIRDWATCHERS ARE celebrating arrival of the UK's largest ever single flock of avocets after 1,150 of the waders were counted at a Dorset nature reserve.

The Dorset Wildlife Trust reserve on Brownsea Island is one of the most important wintering sites for avocets in the UK with numbers steadily increasing over recent years.

Chris Thain, the Trust's reserve manager on Brownsea, said:"We feel very lucky to have these unusual and impressive birds in such large numbers on the island during the winter.

"As the tide rises in nearby Poole Harbour, the feeding avocets seek a quiet roosting spot on the reserve's lagoon, and it's at the high-tide point that we can count the birds. We believe that the avocets originate from both continental and UK breeding populations."

Avocets are among the most distinctive of waders, being large, black and white, with unmistakable upcurved bills - very different from the straight or downturned bills of other species.

Brownsea Island is the largest of the islands in Poole Harbour with the increase in avocet numbers made possible by repair work undertaken on the sea wall by the National Trust in the early 1990s.

The sea wall is said to protect the lagoon from Poole Harbour and create ideal, undisturbed conditions for avocets to roost.

BROWN TROUT IN Kent are being trained to be more 'streetwise' to beat poachers, according to the Environment Agency.

Local anglers are also involved in the scheme to train trout in the art of self-defence to combat poaching in the River Darent.

"In the past the trout have been stocked as adult fish," said an Agency spokesman."However, because they are usually bred in tanks and are used to being fed on a daily basis they are quite 'tame' and therefore vulnerable to poachers.

"In a pioneering experiment for Kent, at a secret location on the River Darent, Agency officers have been working with the angling club to trial a new incubation box to breed more resilient fish.

"The box, which contains trout eggs, is placed in the flow of the river and allows the fish to develop in their natural environment. Once they have hatched, they can either disperse from the exit pipe of the incubator, or can be collected and stocked at points along the river."

Chris Conroy, from the Agency's Kent Fisheries Team added:"So far the results are very promising. The fish seem to be thriving, although it's a little early to say how they are faring in comparison to the farmed fish.

"But it's thought that they will be wilder and therefore hardier than those that have been reared on a farm."

RED SQUIRRELS ARE under threat from a deadly virus carried by grey squirrels which could wipe out hundreds of the smaller native mammals.

The virus, usually fatal when contracted, has been discovered in Sefton, Merseyside, which hosts the most southerly mainland population of reds.

According to The Wildlife Trusts, red squirrels in this area form a significant proportion of the UK's declining red squirrel population.

One red is already confirmed as having died from the 'parapox virus' which is borne by greys without causing them harm.

Once infected, reds normally die within weeks, or even days, and treatment is rarely successful.

Conservationists are working to bring the disease under control and stop it spreading to other red squirrel strongholds.

Recent outbreaks of the virus across the Rufford and Ormskirk areas, north of Liverpool, have almost wiped-out red squirrel populations there.

Fiona Robertson, an assistant conservation officer for The Wildlife Trusts, said:"The public can provide vital help by reporting sightings of any grey squirrels or of sick or dead red squirrels. With this information, we can try to limit the spread of this devastating disease."

Meanwhile, residents are also strongly advised not to touch or pick-up sick or dead squirrels as it is not yet known whether the virus can be passed to humans.

A COLONY OF "rare" dragonflies has been devastated by pollution in West Sussex.

Investigators have not yet revealed the species of dragonfly affected by the incident beside the upper reaches of the River Arun but say a pesticide was the cause.

"The pesticide has killed fish and wiped out invertebrates on a small tributary and along a 10 kilometre stretch of the main river near Horsham," said a spokesman.

"The section of river affected is designated a Site of Special Scientific Interest because of the rare dragonflies that live in this area. It is thought signifi - cant damage has been caused to the colony."

'SEASONS IN THE Sun' songwriter Terry Jacks has joined The Woodland Trust's campaign to protect England's remaining pockets of ancient woodland.

"Hundreds of hectares of precious woods are destroyed every year," said a Trust spokesman."But a new initiative by the Trust aims to help reverse this decline, offering free and uncomplicated information on how people can take action to save local woods.

"By simply going to http://www.woodland-trust. org.uk/policy everyone can access guidance on how to secure the future of threatened woodland.

"The online guide gives useful details of felling licences, tree preservation orders and conservation areas. A straightforward and practical checklist explains how to oppose planning applications and lists other sympathetic organisations that may be willing to assist you.

"The campaign has received a boost from musician and songwriter Mr Jacks. Sending a message of support from his Canadian home, he says:'Ancient woodland is one of England's most precious habitats - home to thousands of rare species'."

297

FARMERS ARE SEEING red over yet more red tape imposed by the authorities, warn union chiefs.

In future, says the NFU, a farmer who hires out a tractor to his neighbour will have to gain approval as a 'fuel dealer' from HM Customs and Excise if the vehicle has any fuel in its tank, according to new rules starting on April 1.

The legislation - originally intended to license bulk suppliers of red diesel and kerosene in an effort to cut fraud - initially received broad approval from the union.

But guidelines issued by HM Customs and Excise on how it intends to apply and implement the registration scheme have been attacked as "ludicrous" by the NFU.

The rules will also affect equipment hire companies who supply equipment or vehicles containing kerosene or red diesel.

Registration will require these fuel 'dealers' to complete yet more paperwork every month listing who the fuel was supplied to and how much.

NFU spokesman Marcus Themanssaid that the union would be appealing against the "over zealous" interpretation of the law.

He said:"Of course we understand the need to stop any widespread abuse of the system but this interpretation of the law beggars belief. It is entirely disproportionate to the level of fraud risk.

"This interpretation is so ridiculous one could be forgiven for thinking that the introduction of this on April 1 is some sort of April Fool's joke.

"These regulations need to include a sensible minimum level of fuel to ensure that simply lending a tractor to a neighbour doesn't require a ridiculous paper chase."

STARLINGS HAVE BEEN flocking en masse to Shrewsbury in Shropshire, sparking a flap among residents.

Up to 50,000 birds are thought to collect daily on trees and local buildings, creating spectacular displays as they land and take off.

However, while enjoying the spectacle, locals are not so keen on the resulting noise and mess.

But county wildlife experts have advised them to do nothing as the starlings will soon disperse when the weather warms up.

THE WILDLIFE TRUSTS have welcomed the launch of the new entry-level agri-environment scheme which aims to help create a 'greener' farming industry.

The new scheme, a result of negotiations between conservationists and the Policy Commission on the Future of Farming, was launched by Michael Meacher MP, Minister for the Environment.

BUTTERFLIES ARE FACING their toughest ever fight for survival as development encroaches onto their territories, according to a leading butterfly charity.

Richard Fox, surveys manager for Butterfly Conservation, said:"In Britain, butterflies are like fine summer days - glorious but fleeting, and they always seemed more common in the old days. Indeed they were.

"Fossils show that butterflies have been around for 40 million years. However, in a few short decades, human activity has brought some species to the brink of extinction and plunged others into steep declines from which they may not recover. Unless, that is, we have the will to do something about it.

"During the last five years of the 20th Century, 10,000 people took part in a massive survey organised by Butterfly Conservation and designed to map the distribution of each butterfly species.

"The results make depressing reading. Since 1800, over half of our 59 resident butterfly species have undergone substantial declines. This includes five that have become extinct in Britain and 15 that have declined by more than 50 per cent. Worryingly, declines have continued during the past two decades, despite increased emphasis on nature conservation.

"Most of the declining species are ones that ecologists would term 'habitat specialists'. They are the butterflies of unimproved meadows, heaths, chalk downs and ancient woodlands.

"A new landscape-scale approach to conservation is needed to prevent the extinction of many more species. Large habitat networks must be maintained and restored."

KIND-HEARTED RESIDENTS who try to help 'overcrowded' frogs by removing them from ponds should think again, warns the Environment Agency.

Frogs and their spawn should not be taken from apparently overpopulated ponds and pools this spring, it says.

"When the weather is warming up and still fairly wet, frogs and other amphibians come out of hibernation and head for their breeding ponds," said a spokesman."It is at this time that garden ponds can seem to be overcrowded with clumps of spawn, tadpoles, and adult frogs. But this is perfectly normal.

"Amphibians can experience huge fluctuations in their numbers and laying large amounts of eggs ensures that at least some offspring will survive.

"Moving adults and spawn is unlikely to significantly reduce future frog populations as numbers will quickly build up in subsequent seasons, replacing those removed.

"Moving spawn and frogs can also increase the risk of spreading diseases, parasites, unwanted predatory fish or invasive plants.

"There is also the danger that the animals may be introduced to an unsuitable area. Even if a pond looks good for frogs to breed in, it may be useless unless there is suitable cover in the vicinity to permit foraging and safe over-wintering.

"If the movement of amphibians is unavoidable, then they should be released as close as possible to the collection site, in a garden location, and preferably to a new pond.

"The new home should ideally be within half a kilometre of the original pond. This is the distance that individual frogs, toads and newts may disperse."

BROWN HARE NUMBERS have fallen by 75 per cent in the last 60 years, according to the Game Conservancy Trust.

"There are at least two important factors that have caused this reduction. Firstly, many predators are now more abundant than they were a century ago and, secondly, modern agriculture is less suited to hares than was traditional farming," said a spokesman.

"A recent survey suggested that wintering numbers in Britain may be around 800,000. However, the Biodiversity Action Plan proposed that measures should be taken to improve numbers so that by 2010 our countryside should support at least two million animals in winter.

"A companion of Aphrodite, representing love, fertility and growth, the hare is also traditionally associated with the moon, dawn and Easter and a symbol of increase.

"It is therefore poignant that the brown hare was one of the first animals to be considered in the Biodiversity Action Plan programme.

"Although this lowland-dwelling mammal is not rare, endangered or under any kind of threat, it was once very common, was widespread and has declined significantly.

"It has been estimated that numbers have dropped by about 75 per cent since the War, a pattern that is also typical of many other European countries.

"The Allerton Project in Leicestershire, a 333-hectare farm run by ourselves and the Allerton Research and Educational Trust, has pioneered new farming methods that have reversed the fortunes of many wildlife species, including the brown hare.

"Brown hares have responded well to these wildlife-friendly special management techniques. In 1992 there were less than a dozen hares on this farm whereas now it supports a population of around 200."

Other species to benefit from the project include songbirds, gamebirds, harvest mice, a number of butterfly species and bumblebees.

SEAGULLS HAVE TREATED with disdain an attempt in Scotland to frighten them off using 'robot' falcons.

The gulls have long been a nuisance at Fraserburgh on the Aberdeenshire coast and when earlier efforts to scare them away failed, the 'robot' peregrines were introduced.

Each fibreglass falcon is programmed to run through a threatening assortment of wing flaps, head movements, and cries.

But the resort's council officers found that rather than being terrified, the gulls simply massed together to scare off the intruders.

FOXES ARE BEING encouraged to breed in several man-made earths by a top hunt, it has been claimed.

A leading supporter of the historic Heythrop Hunt, which covers Oxfordshire, Gloucestershire, and Warwickshire, was watched at the brick-built underground chambers by secret video, says the League Against Cruel Sports.

"Covert pictures show the prominent Heythrop Hunt supporter entering a disused building housing one artificial fox earth and encouraging two terrier dogs to enter the plastic pipe entrances in an apparent attempt to seek out foxes that may be resident," said a spokesman."Secret video footage also shows a fox entering a second artificial earth near Chipping Norton."

League campaigners claim they also located animal carcasses illegally dumped as food for foxes on land north of Eyford Park, Gloucestershire, where the Heythrop Hunt held its final meet of the foxhunting season.

Douglas Batchelor, League chief executive, added:"Fox hunters invariably deny allegations of fox breeding, blaming gamekeepers, farmers, the army or just about anybody other than themselves, but our secret footage for the first time proves a direct link between a person connected to a prominent hunt and artificial earths.

"The hunt in question has artificial earths in its territory, is cruel, hypocritical and spectacularly fails to convince that it has anything to do with pest control."

BADGERS SNACKING ON birds is the subject of a PhD study in Gloucestershire by researcher Tim Hounsome.

"I am investigating the effect of badgers on bird populations, either through direct predation of adult birds or through the eating of eggs or chicks," explained Tim, based at the Central Science Laboratory in Nympsfield.

"Recorded incidents of badger predation on birds seem to be few and far between but, the more I investigate the subject, the more it seems to me that many observations are simply not published.

"I would therefore be very pleased to hear from anyone who has actually seen cases of badger predation on birds, or has compelling evidence of such an occurrence. It is my aim to collate both published and un-published reports."

SALMON ARE POURING into the River Tweed on the border between Scotland and England, it has been revealed.

For its size, the river is now said to be the most productive for salmon anglers across the whole of the North Atlantic with 10,300 salmon landed by rod there in 2002 - the biggest tally for a decade.

Sea trout are also finding the river to their liking with 1,740 taken there last year - the largest catch since records began over 50 years ago.

The details, just published by the River Tweed Commissioners, are a boost not just for anglers but for conservationists.

Removal of dams and weirs, plus other barriers to fish migration, has raised the productive capability of the river by a third.

John Lovett, the RTC's chairman, said:"It is impressive to see how rapidly these newly opened up areas have been naturally recolonised without any expensive and artificial human intervention."

A HUGE CULL of urban deer is being planned to offset the problems the animals cause to motorists and precious plants.

Tens of thousands face being shot by marksmen in a move initiated by English Nature to curb the destructive activities of wild fallow, roe, and muntjac deer, it has been revealed.

Because of their secretive nature, no exact national figures can be compiled for the animals but estimates point to an explosion in numbers - possibly tenfold - in recent years.

According to one Sunday newspaper, the Highways Agency now believes that deer straying onto roads cause up to 40,000 accidents annually, resulting in the deaths of about 12 people.

With traffic levels rising, that toll is expected to get worse unless deer numbers are substantially reduced in the years ahead.

Deer are also threatening rare flowers such as oxlips and bluebells and destroying cover for other animals such as the dormouse, say critics.

HARRY THE HARRIS hawk has been retired after a number of embarrassing mistakes at his public displays.

Worst among these was the one where the hawk, based at Thorp Perrow Arboretum in North Yorkshire, snatched off a man's toupee and tried to devour it.

But the mischevious bird has also punctured a children's bouncy castle and spoiled ice cream by flying into an ice cream van and trampling the tub.

Owner Tom Graham says this will be Harry's first season out of the limelight but he should still enjoy himself - he is being given the chance to breed.

GARDENERS ARE BEING urged to encourage more wildlife into their gardens as more and more open spaces vanish beneath development.

The Wildlife Trusts have initiated a programme whereby gardeners can learn to garden not just for themselves for also to provide a boost for a variety of species.

"Work with worms, frolic with frogs and read up on your birds and bees. The Trusts offer a recipe of gardening activity to entice wildlife into your garden," said a spokesman."Beginners' workshops, 'open garden' days, weekend courses and general advice on a variety of wildlife gardening subjects are now available throughout the UK.

"Every garden, no matter how big or small, formal or informal, can provide a home for the UK's vanishing wildlife. If you've ever wanted a garden flourishing with brilliant blue cornflowers, opulent poppies, hedgehogs, woodpeckers and delicate butterflies turn to the Trusts for inspiration and practical guidance on what to do.

"Wildlife gardening experts run courses to inspire garden designs and offer practical wildlife gardening skills. In addition you can hone your pot planting and hanging baskets skills, not to mention composting, pond building and advice on choosing trees, shrubs and plants that will delight you, whilst providing your garden wildlife with food and shelter."

THE STARLING HAS emerged as the UK's garden bird champion, taking top spot in the RSPB's record breaking Big Garden Birdwatch.

But the survey also revealed that the number of starlings has plummeted to an average of just 4.9 birds seen per garden compared to an average of 15 in 1979, the first year of the event.

Overall, the number of starlings recorded by the Big Garden Birdwatch has declined by 67 per cent since 1979.

House sparrows came in as the second most common with an average of 4.8 birds seen per garden, a decline of 52 per cent since 1979 when an average of 10 birds were seen per garden.

This year's event saw 303,000 people taking part, including 44,000 children - beating last year's figure of 262,000 and even the previous world record for the biggest bird event held by BirdLife International's 2001 World Bird Festival.

Richard Bashford, Big Garden Birdwatch co-ordinator, said:"The RSPB is delighted with the level of participation for this year's event. This demonstrates the interest and concern people have for the birds around them.

"It is essential that surveys like this continue to gather important scientific information if we are to reverse the decline of our best loved garden birds, such as the starling and house sparrow."

Big Garden Birdwatch had asked participants to spend one hour counting the birds in their garden, school grounds or local park and to record the highest number of each species seen at any one time.

The 'top ten' most common garden birds in this year's Birdwatch were (in descending order): starling, house sparrow, blue tit, blackbird, chaffinch, greenfinch, collared dove, great tit, robin and wood pigeon.

While the house sparrow remains one of our more familiar birds, studies over the last 25 years have shown that their population has more than halved but the reason for their decline is still not known.

EIGHT OF ENGLAND'S most beautiful private gardens will be opened to the public this summer - seven for the first time, it has been revealed.

Leading garden experts will give private tours of the gardens and then join visitors for lunch, says the Countryside Alliance.

The summer openings are timed to show the gardens off at their best but ticket numbers are strictly limited so enthusiasts are advised to book early.

All profits from the openings will be donated to the Alliance and speakers have apparently given their expertise free.

Alliance chief executive Richard Burge said:"This is the second annual garden openings series. Last year was a sell-out and we hope to repeat that success this year as lovers of the countryside are guided from folly to sunken garden by experts from the world of horticulture.

"As ever, we are immensely grateful to the owners of these gardens, both for throwing open their garden gates to the public and for donating money to the Alliance's coffers at a time when we need it most.

"We are also grateful to the garden experts who will be speaking at each opening, as they will be able to provide vital insight into the history and colour of some of the most beautiful corners of England."

BADGERS UNDER THREAT of being culled at Saltdean in East Sussex could be moved to an artificial sett instead, it has been claimed.

The underground burrowers have been at the centre of a row because their activities were said to be undermining local properties.

Government investigators initially planned to kill the animals but suspended the killings after a vigorous campaign to protect the badgers was launched.

The National Federation of Badgers Groups, which has backed the protest, said recently that the Government's public gloom towards finding a solution did not reflect the reality of recent private talks.

"Although a DEFRA news release gave the impression that a satisfactory solution to the problems caused by the urban badgers had not been found, in fact a detailed report outlining such a solution had already been discussed," claimed an NFBG spokesman.

"The report in question was compiled on behalf of the NFBG by Professor Stephen Harris of Bristol University, a leading authority on urban badgers, and Paul Skinner of the Mid Sussex Badger Protection Group.

"This was submitted to DEFRA at the beginning of January. NFBG chief exective Dr Elaine King and Professor Stephen Harris then met DEFRA officials to discuss the report and agree a way forward.

"Dr King and Professor Harris told DEFRA at the meeting that two sites for an artificial sett had been identified, and that the owners of the properties were very keen to help.

"It was a constructive meeting and it was agreed that the NFBG and DEFRA would draft a detailed schedule for carrying out the work. It was also agreed that local residents and other interested parties would be consulted on the plans."

WILLOW WARBLERS AND swallows are among birds recorded entering Britain in a spring migration watch.

"Willow warblers have arrived in small numbers over the last couple of days with records coming from Bristol, Cambridgeshire, Newport, Northants, Somerset, Wokingham and Worcestershire," said a spokesman for the British Trust for Ornithology.

"Swallows have been seen in Dorset, Durham and North Yorks - still very thinly spread.

"A tree pipit was at Southend on March 25 and sandwich terns have been seen in Kent and Cumbria.

"House martins have also been seen in a few places, including Bedfordshire, Greater Manchester, Merseyside and Northants."

ORGANISERS OF THE Glastonbury Festival have been ordered to pay £13,500 in fines and costs for polluting the River Whitelake which runs through the festival site in a case brought by the Environment Agency.

Agency officers detected high concentrations of ammonia in the river as far as two miles downstream of the Pilton site, a court heard.

Through detailed investigations the problems were traced back to toilet facilities at the festival which were found to be leaking and allowing large volumes of sewage to enter the river.

During last year's festival weekend around 120 fish were found dead in the river, Wells magistrates were told.

"The case is particularly disappointing as we had previously warned festival organisers that any reoccurrence of the problems caused last time may result in us taking legal action," said Andrew Leach, of the Environment Agency.

Magistrates fined Glastonbury Festival 2002 Limited of Worthy Farm, Pilton £10,000 with £3,500 costs after the firm pleaded guilty to polluting controlled waters contrary to the Water Resouces Act 1991.

AN INCREASE IN the National Minimum Wage will add £34 million to the wages bill paid by hard-pressed farmers, the NFU has warned.

The Government announced the minimum wage for adults will rise to £4.50 in October, up from the rate of £4.30 set by the Agricultural Wages Board.

NFU Employment and Education chairman Bob Fiddaman said farmers and growers fully accepted the need for permanent staff to be well skilled, trained and paid.

"However, for unskilled casuals, which are an essential element for some businesses, this rise represents a major increase in costs for no increase in efficiency," he said.

"An increased cost burden of this magnitude makes its more difficult for UK farmers to compete against their European counterparts who pay much lower wage rates. We could see jobs exported to other European countries."

THE FIRST 'ONE-stop' rural shop in England has been opened at Waters Upton in Shropshire.

The Government says the Waters Upton Parish Centre will bring public services to the rural community instead of expecting people to travel to the nearest town.

It includes a post office, village shop, ATM cash machine, ICT access centre, community office, and 'regular police surgeries'.

The project, part of the Vital Villages programme and the Countryside Agency's first National Demonstration Project, was supported by a Government grant of £250,000.

Sir Ewen Cameron, Countryside Agency chairman, said the Agency had "for some time been researching and testing the opportunities for bringing those who provide services for rural communities together, so that they can enjoy the benefits of joint working. These benefits, for example sharing overheads, make providing a wider range of services more viable for rural communities.

"Through the Countryside Agency's programme of National Demonstration Projects we supported the development of this excellent centre in Waters Upton, so are delighted to see it opening its doors for residents to use."

BAT: revenge of the affronted council tenants

MANY people are squeamish about bats and I must confess to finding some of the Central and South American species pretty hard to stomach myself.

In particular, I'm thinking of blood-drinking vampire bats and giant bird-eating bats whose gruesome nocturnal activites have been featured in gory close-up on TV.

Our own bats, however, are quite attractive in comparison and enjoy feeding on insects, doing us all a favour in the process by keeping numbers down.

At present, we have 16 species of bats in this country, 11 of which are already scarce or rare.

We used to have 17 species but in 1991 the mouse-eared bat was formally declared extinct after years of teetering on the edge of the abyss.

Our commonest bat, the pipistrelle, weighs about five grammes, which is less than a pound coin and miniscule in comparison to the huge fruit bat found in tropical forests.

Shakespeare was fond of using bats to help create an atmosphere of foreboding, as in 'Macbeth':*"Ere the bat has flown His cloister'd flight, ere, to black Hecate's summons The shard-borne beetle with his drowsy hums Hath rung night's yawning peal, there shall be done A deed of dreadful note."*

Despite their sinister reputation, bats are actually quite fascinating creatures and the more you learn about them, the more fascinating they become.

They are not blind but prefer to hunt at night when more insects are on the wing, using sophisticated echolocation to track down their prey.

Although they have been compared to mice, they are not related to mice at all.

In fact, unlike mice, they can live for up to 30 years which is amazing for such a small mammal.

Equally incredible is the fact that even the tiniest pipistrelle bat can munch its way through 3,000 insects in a single night.

But such an appetite is necessary to provide fuel for yet more frenetic flight.

The biggest threat to bats remains Man and his ceaseless destruction of their roosts, whether located in old buildings or within ancient trees.

But bat fans cheered one small victory in recent times when bats hit back courtesy of the law courts.

In what was said to be a landmark case, Leicestershire County Council was fined £2,500, with £400 costs, after being found guilty of damaging a bat roost at one of its properties.

A local company which carried out the roof work for the authority was also fined £1,000 with £225 costs.

It was apparently the first time a prosecution had been brought under the Conservation Regulations 1994 for the protection of bats.

Following the case, a spokesman for the Bat Conservation Trust said:*"The result has massive implications. It is now clear that the onus is on local authorities to ensure that surveys for bats and other protected wildlife are conducted before proceeding with any work on buildings owned by them. They cannot leave the responsibility to their contractors."*

Local councils, be warned. Bats are on the march.

ANOTHER OTTER HAS been found drowned in an illegal eel net sparking fresh concern among Environment Agency officers.

The adult male otter trapped in a fyke net was dredged up near the Poole Harbour Yacht Club in Dorset.

It is the second fatal incident within a year.

Last year a mother otter and her two cubs were killed in an illegal eel net placed in the River Stour in Dorset.

The Environment Agency warns that all fyke nets must be licensed and are illegal unless fitted with otter guards.

Enforcement officers are now stepping up their monitoring of eel fishing to ensure that nets meet the required standard.

Recently, a Dorset man was ordered to pay £500 in fines and costs for using illegal eel nets in Poole Harbour.

The harbour is one of the most intensive eel fisheries in the country and is also one of the most important areas for otters.

"Fyke net licences are issued by the Environment Agency and all licencees are told of their responsibility to fit otter guards," said Andy Strevens, spokesman for the Agency."We keep a stock of guards and issue them free to eel fishermen on request. There is no excuse for an unguarded net."

KILLER WHALES ARE thought to have been terrorising seals in recent months off the northern tip of Scotland following the discovery of scores of corpses.

Some 40 dead seals were found last January alone, washed up on beaches in Orkney - all bearing serrated teeth marks, the hallmark of a killer whale attack.

Although more intermittent now, the attacks appear to have continued.

As well as a plentiful supply of seals, killer whales are believed to be increasingly drawn to the area by escaped farmed salmon.

Half a million salmon are said to have escaped into waters around Orkney in the last three years.

A TRAINED GUNDOG blasted away problems facing workmen by swimming across a river with a cable in its mouth.

Joss the springer spaniel came to the rescue of contractors puzzled as to how they could get the cable across the River Nidd in Knaresborough, North Yorkshire, at a point too deep to wade.

Joss's owner Trevor Green, 72, a former engineer, had been out walking with his pet when the pair came across the workmen wondering how to stretch the winch cable across the 40ft wide river.

The cable was vital for dragging piping across the river before it could be rested on the river bottom.

After learning of the problem, Mr Green dispatched Joss to swim over and pick up the cable in his mouth from the opposite bank, which he did - returning to a round of applause.

BADGER FANS HAVE been cleared of misleading the public in an advertising campaign which raised hackles among the farming community.

The Advertising Standards Authority has dismissed nine complaints made against a TB campaign leaflet issued by the National Federation of Badger Groups.

"The NFBG's 'Scapegoat' leaflet was issued as an insert inside a number of magazines during 2001 and 2002 and has successfully recruited many hundreds of supporters for the NFBG," explained a spokesman for the wildlife group.

"However, a cattle farmer's wife from Cumbria raised an objection to the leaflet with the ASA. Her objection included nine specific complaints. The ASA has ruled that none of the complaints be upheld.

"The ASA made their adjudication after careful consideration of the issues raised, over a period of several months.

"During this time, in response to the initial objection and several further letters from the complainant, the NFBG made a number of detailed submissions to the ASA.

"The evidence provided by the NFBG included references to, extracts from and summaries of numerous scientific reports and articles in specialist publications, plus leaflets, press releases, reports and other materials issued by DEFRA and its predecessor MAFF.

"The ASA found that the statements made by the NFBG in the Scapegoat leaflet were supported by the evidence provided and were unlikely to mislead people."

Badger group chairman Steve Jackson added:"The NFBG undertakes meticulous research in order to ensure that our campaign materials are factual and honest and we are widely respected for the quality of the information we produce.

"Our Scapegoat leaflet, which pointed out the threats posed to Britain's badgers by badger 'culling', and highlighted the need for reform of modern farming practices, has been subjected to the closest scrutiny by the ASA.

"The complaints made against our leaflet questioned the truthfulness of the information we present and the integrity of the NFBG as an organisation. I am very pleased, but not surprised, that the ASA's adjudication shows that neither are in doubt."

OSPREYS ARE EXPECTED back at their usual Scottish nesting spot any day now, the RSPB has reminded members.

"The Loch Garten ospreys usually arrive at this superb Highland nest site by April 1 so these fantastic birds are due any day," said a spokesman.

"We will have our webcam ready for their arrival and we'll post regular updates on how things are going.

"We warmly welcome visitors to our Loch Garten Osprey Centre but it is crucial that the birds settle before visitors arrive to see them at the centre.

"To give them the best start, we will keep the Osprey Centre closed until the birds have settled. We can then give you breathtaking views of the birds first-hand - via our live CCTV link to the nest or right from the centre. We'll bring you great webcam images again this year. We have already received reports of four sightings in Strathspey - so we expect to see an osprey pair at Loch Garten any day now."

PRO-HUNT EXTREMISTS have been blamed for a chainsaw attack on a memorial wood set aside to honour ex-Beatle Paul McCartney's late wife Linda.

Mrs McCartney, a vegetarian and staunch animal rights supporter, was reviled by some hunting fanatics during her lifetime for her anti-hunt stance.

The League Against Cruel Sports, which owns the southern English land on which the wood is sited, branded the attackers "sad and sick."

A spokesman said:"Gateposts, gates and fencing were discovered hacked down with a chainsaw. Similar damage had also been inflicted at Paul McCartney's St John's Wood, which is in trust to the League.

"Two gateposts into the League's Heming-way sanctuary were also sawn through.

"Linda's Wood was planted as a memorial to Linda McCartney and the enclosure within it contains some of her favourite trees. About three years ago someone drove a quad bike through it, flattening some of the trees.

"It's thought the latest damage was inflicted by an extremist fringe of the region's pro-hunt community."

The League's sanctuaries manager Paul Tillsley added:"Whoever did this is both sad and sick. They obviously have no respect for other people's property or the countryside in general."

Recently, the League claimed it had compiled a report detailing incidents of violence and intimidation by members of prestigious hunts in the South West during the last hunt season.

The report is being sent to Rural Affairs Minister Alun Michael "as further evidence of the damage hunting is inflicting on the countryside."

Although the phrase 'Thugs, Wreckers and Bullies' was used by former Home Secretary Michael Howard to describe anti-hunt campaigners, the League claims it actually applies more to the hunting community.

BRITISH FOXES ARE being painted as unlikely victims of the war in Iraq after it was disclosed that a Hunting Bill designed to give them better protection might be shelved.

According to reports, a vital debate has been blocked by Labour business managers who believe hunting too trivial a matter to discuss while troops and civilians are dying.

A senior ministerial source told one paper:"Everyone accepts that whilst we want a ban it would not be appropriate to do it now. This is not the most pressing legislation at the best of times and at the worst of times should not be on the radar."

THE COUNTRYSIDE ALLIANCE has called for more jobs, not fewer, to be based in the country to safeguard our rural landscape.

New jobs and new businesses must not replace, but add to, a rural economy still centred on the economic use of the land itself, the Alliance warned in response to the Countryside Agency's report 'Rural Economies'.

The report revealed that nearly all new jobs in the countryside were being created from non-traditional businesses started by urban 'incomers', whilst traditional rural employment was still fast contracting.

Alliance chief executive Richard Burge said this trend could destroy the character of the countryside irrevocably unless special efforts were made to find new ways of expanding the sustainable use of the land.

The best future for rural communities, in his view, would be through reform of agricultural subsidy to maximise the sustainable use of the land whilst removing barriers to enterprise and investment in non-traditional sectors.

"New jobs, from any source, are badly needed by indigenous rural communities and are to be welcomed," Mr Burge said, "but not if these jobs reduce the productive and cultural value of the land.

"This would merely suburbanise the rural landscape and the attitudes of its communities, which would be a disaster."

DORMICE AND DOLPHINS are two very different species covered in a new programme of courses organised by The Mammal Society.

The courses start this month, run until October, and are being held in Cornwall, Perthshire, Wales and Northern Ireland.

Development officer Georgette Shearer said:"The Mammal Society is well known for the quality of training it delivers in all aspects of mammal work. So far over 3,000 people have attended our courses and last year 95 per cent of people rated their course as good or very good."

Besides courses on whales and dolphins, others include: 'Small Mammals: Ecology, Survey and Man - agement' which looks at how to trap and survey animals, and 'Dormouse Ecology and Conservation' which shows how to check dormice nest boxes and become a dormouse handler.

A DAMNING STUDY which underlines the risks of collision between birds and aircraft at a possible new airport in Kent has now been published.

Creating the airport at Cliffe is one of the options set out in a consultation paper on the future of air travel in the south east of England - but it has met with fierce opposition from conservationists.

The report was produced by the Central Science Laboratory and the British Trust for Ornithology.

It provides a detailed assessment of the populations, movements and behaviour of birds at and around the site, along with the risks of birdstrike.

The study's key conclusion is that "without a comprehensive and aggressive bird management programme in place, an airport could not operate safely in this location. But even with such world class management and mitigation measures in place, the hazard posed by birds is severe and would probably be higher than at any other major UK airport."

Transport Secretary Alistair Darling said he would study the report before reaching any conclusions.

RURAL AFFAIRS MINISTER Alun Michael has been attacked for branding himself 'Minister for the Horse'.

It was also wrong for him to claim that he was committed to the equine industry, said the Countryside Alliance.

"Evidence submitted to the Government's own consultation on hunting makes it clear that the Minister's Hunting Bill would have a devastating effect on the equine industry and on horse welfare," asserted a spokesman.

"Submissions to Alun Michael's consultation on hunting by the British Equestrian Trade Association, the International League for the Protection of Horses, and the British Horse Society all agree that a ban would have a huge impact on the equine industry.

"BETA said:'Hunting provides our membership with £72.1 million turnover representing 3,134 jobs' while both the BHS and the ILPH agreed that a ban on hunting would lead to a collapse in the market for horses and serious consequences for equine welfare."

Simon Hart, director of the Campaign for Hunting, added:"Alun Michael certainly has a nerve. To claim that he is committed to the long-term future of the equine industry, while promoting a Bill which would lead to the destruction of equine businesses, a collapse in market values and the death of thousands of horses is extreme hypocrisy, even by his standards.

"Once again the Minister seems blind to the devastating consequences of his Bill."

WAKEY,WAKEY AND listen out for International Dawn Chorus Day, say The Wildlife Trusts.

The event on May 4 is an annual celebration of the world's oldest wake-up call - the dawn chorus - originally conceived by The Wildlife Trust for Birmingham and the Black Country.

"Throughout the UK, people with gardens that attract birds are encouraged to wake up early, just after 4am, and hear the dawn chorus from their bedroom window," explained a spokesman.

"For those who want to experience the dawn chorus in the wild, the Trusts have organised early morning bird walks and dawn chorus breakfasts at a selection of their 2,500 reserves.

"This 'early bird' wake-up call is a celebration of the beauty of bird song. In the last three decades our songbirds have been in decline due to loss of habitat and intensive farming.

"The skylark has rapidly fallen in number by 52 per cent, the corn bunting by 84 per cent, and the tree sparrow by a staggering 87 per cent.

"Why do we have a dawn chorus? A little bird tells us that the male birds sing to protect their territory and to warn off other males. However, after hours of darkness, the birds are hungry and as soon as it is light enough to look for food, the dawn chorus comes to a close."

THE BATTLE TO save thousands of Hebridean hedgehogs from sudden death has intensified after the culling of the animals began.

The first few hedgehogs from a population of over 5,000 were killed by lethal injection on North Uist by a team from Scottish Natural Heritage.

However, more than 30 hedgehogs were saved by Uist Hedgehog Rescue, an alliance of animal welfare groups pledged to do what it can to limit the cull.

Almost two thirds of the rescued animals were handed in by islanders but it is not known if residents were motivated by compassion or the £5 offered by UHR for each hedgehog.

Snipe, redshank and lapwing have been decimated on the isles of North Uist, South Uist and Benbecula because hedgehogs feast on their eggs and chicks.

Conservationists said this was unacceptable and the hedgehogs had to go before the bird populations were completely wiped out.

Hunters used spotlamps to locate and kill the first hedgehogs while checking 60 acres of croftland during the second night of the cull.

Ross Minett, of Advocates for Animals, said rescued hedgehogs would be relocated to new homes on the mainland.

"Scottish Natural Heritage has been intent on pushing ahead with this unnecessary killing spree and now they have blood on their hands," he said."We are continuing to rescue as many hedgehogs as possible."

Scores of baited cage traps have been laid down in a bid to catch the hedgehogs, which are more densely populated on South Uist and Benbecula.

Sniffer dogs will also be brought in to find hidden hedgehogs although Scottish Natural Heritage has stressed they would not be allowed to harm their quarry.

SOME 5,000 COMMON bream have been released into the River Dee in Cheshire to help offset the problems caused by devastating pollution incidents.

The move is part of an ongoing programme to replenish fish stocks following the last major crisis, in July 2000, when over 100,000 fish were killed.

The Lower Dee was worst affected by that incident and, as bream are only to be found there and not in the river's tributaries, the targeted restocking should provide a real boost.

About 4,000 fish were released at Eccleston Ferry outside Chester .

Another 1,000 were let go at Farndon.

THREE DAYS OF "tough" agricultural wage negotiations resulted in a settlement that the NFU has described as a fair outcome for all parties.

The union, which represented employers in the Agricultural Wages Board talks, secured a 15-month package starting in July 2003.

The talks saw the abolition of the Starter Rate and a new Harvest Worker category available for 30 weeks a year - a key victory for the NFU, it believes.

The cost of the deal is estimated at £88 million over 15 months or £70 million over 12 months.

Under the agreement, there will also be an extra day's holiday.

NFU Employment and Education chairman Bob Fiddaman said:"We think the deal takes the industry forward and is a fair outcome for all parties."

PEREGRINE FALCONS IN South Wales are to play a a high-tech role in catching egg and chick thieves thanks to a new DNA solution.

The liquid, which is being painted on the eggs and legs of falcons, is invisible when dry and will provide investigators with evidence of crime.

Peregrine nests in Dare Valley Country Park will also be protected by cameras, with pictures relayed to a visitors' centre.

Sergeant Ian Guildford, of South Wales Police, explained:"Peregrines across South Wales are still heavily persecuted. Egg collectors have raided the site at Dare Valley and there have been many incidences of poisoning."

Ruth Billingham, spokeswoman for the RSPB Wales, added:"This is a great opportunity for the people of South Wales to meet the fastest flying predator on earth. Cameras will watch the site until the chicks are old enough to leave at the end of June."

An estimated 1,285 pairs are now all that remains of the UK peregrine population.

FERRETS ARE ON the march after a Europe-wide travel ban was finally lifted.

The Countryside Alliance says its campaign for ferret freedom has proved successful with the European Parliament giving ferrets the same rights to roam the EU as cats, dogs, hamsters, rabbits and guinea pigs.

Alliance head of political research, Sarah Godderidge, said:"We never understood why ferrets were discriminated against and called for them to be included in the Pets Travel Scheme in our 2001 election briefing.

"This is a victory for the UK's ferrets which gives them equality with other domestic and working animals. There are 25,000 working ferrets contribut - ing towards the social and economic fabric of the countryside. Downing Street thought that our recommendation was a joke but it's good to see that Brussels is taking the issue more seriously."

HUNDREDS OF FRESHWATER fish have been returned home to a Newcastle park after a year-long 'holiday'.

Carp, roach, bream, tench and perch were moved from Leazes Park lake back in April 2002 before the lake was drained as part of a refurbishment project.

Now Environment Agency officers have used a specially adapted trailer to transport the fish back to the park, which is overlooked by Newcastle United's football ground.

The fish, including a massive 20-pound carp, were first netted from their temporary home at nearby Exhibition Park.

They were then placed in tanks on the trailer, which also contained piped oxygen to keep them relaxed during their short road journey home.

Fisheries officer Phil Rippon said:"We were more than happy to get involved in this project as part of our continued support for angling."

SALMON AND SEA trout were taken illegally by a man using an outlawed fishing net, Carlisle Crown Court heard.

The man, from Flookburgh, was fined £1,000 and ordered to pay £500 in costs to the Environment Agency after being jointly charged with another man, also of Flookburgh, who was found not guilty by a jury after a four-day trial.

Daniel Frieze, prosecuting for the Agency, told the court how in August 2001, a fisheries officer saw a boat from the River Kent near Allithwaite being loaded onto a trailer behind a tractor parked on the bank.

The officer saw one man take a sack, from which a salmon's tail protruded, and put it into a fish box in the back of the tractor.

When the officer approached both men and looked into the fish box, he found several salmon with marks on them suggesting that they had been caught in a mono-filament gill net.

Following the case, an Agency spokesman explained:"Fishing for salmon with gill nets is tightly controlled by legislation, as putting a net in a river or an estuary traps fish that may be migrating to or from spawning grounds.

"Mono-filament gill nets are totally prohibited for the use of catching salmon as they are extremely harmful to fish, causing them serious injuries. Once a fish is enmeshed in a gill net it becomes trapped and is highly unlikely to escape.

"The two men told the officer that the fish had been caught in a lave net - a small hand-held triangular net used to scoop fish out of the water - which they were both licensed by the Agency to use. However, fish caught in a lave net would not usually be marked like the ones found in the fish box.

"The officer was sure the injuries present on the fish - 10 salmon and one sea trout - had not been caused by a lave net, and he also found a large quantity of gill netting in the boat."

HOUSE MARTINS NOW back in Britain and Ireland badly need help from human homeowners to nest, it has been revealed.

"Following their long migration from south of the Sahara, one of their first jobs will be to find a house for the summer," said a spokesman for the British Trust for Ornithology.

"Homeowners across the country can help house martins by letting them build on their houses or by providing artificial nests.

"House martins are messy birds. They carefully construct nests made from rolled up balls of mud - a real architectural feat - but their droppings whitewash walls and garden paths and make them unpopular with some tidy homeowners.

"A tray on the patio under a nest makes clearing up easier. Following a journey of in excess of 3,000 miles we should do all we can to help house martins nest successfully.

"Providing a good source of mud is one of the easiest ways of helping. Regularly topping up muddy puddles in periods of dry weather will ensure there is a ready source of mud for nest building.

"The house martin still remains a great bird of mystery - where do they winter and how do they roost?

"Although 290,000 house martins have been ringed in Britain and Ireland, only one has been found south of the Sahara, in Nigeria."

ENGLISH HEN HARRIERS are being put at risk by intentional heather burning on moors, it has been claimed.

According to English Nature, the future of England's few hen harriers now hangs in the balance following the torching of key areas of heather moorland around hen harrier breeding sites.

In 2002, England had seven breeding females which successfully raised 22 chicks but in 2003 the future of this majestic predator looks doubtful.

Mature heather was burnt at Bowland Fells Special Protection Area and at both known nesting sites in the North Pennine Moors Special Protection Area.

These are said to be internationally important wildlife areas known for breeding hen harriers.

At Bowland Fells, an uncontrolled fire of around 250 hectares burnt out the most important moorland nesting area for hen harriers in the country.

The fire even destroyed two active hen harrier nests and possibly a third nest of a female that appeared to be settling in the area.

At least one of the fires in the North Pennines was intentionally targeted at last year's nest site, said English Nature, to prevent the birds settling again in 2003.

"This is dreadful news," said English Nature chairman Sir Martin Doughty."Hen harriers use mature heather as cover and protection when building their nests and raising their young. They return each year to traditional nest sites.

"It is unlikely that they will settle and nest in these newly burnt areas without this deep heather cover. The sites where the harriers nested last year were well known to many people so it is extremely disappointing that heather has been burned in these areas."

A MAJOR SCHEME is underway to breathe life back into what was once one of England's best trout rivers.

According to the Game Conservancy Trust, The River Monnow Project is one of the largest UK trout habitat restoration projects ever undertaken.

As a reflection of the importance placed on the river, DEFRA has awarded a grant of £1.1m to restore it to its former glory.

"The River Monnow in Herefordshire was once one of the most productive trout rivers in England," said a Trust spokesman."However, over the last 30 years, and in common with many other rivers, substantial declines have been recorded of its wild trout and grayling populations. This is also echoed in the reduction in abundance of several other important species such as otters, water voles and our native crayfish."

FLORA, PRIMROSE, hyacinth and violet are just a few of the spring wildflowers that can currently be discovered in England's ancient woods.

To help find them, two handy pocket-sized 'Exploring Woodland' guides have been produced by The Woodland Trust, charting 101 carefully selected woods for flower and wildlife spotters.

"Harrocks Wood near Chandler's Cross, Rickmansworth, is a good example of ancient woodland with a fantastic display of bluebells, dog's mercury, celandine and primrose," said a Trust spokesman.

"Later you can see speedwell and campion plus the more unusual coralroot bitter-cress. Harrocks Wood offers five woods for the price of one as it is linked by footpaths to four other sites - Whipendell Wood, Merlin's Wood, Dell Wood and Newland's Spring.

"There are lots of butterflies including the red admiral and it's not uncommon to spot muntjac and fallow deer.

"Ancient woodland is particularly special, not only is it breathtakingly beautiful, it is home to more species of conservation concern than any other UK terrestrial habitat - as irreplaceable and precious as the rainforests.

"Ancient woodland has been around for over 400 years or more and you can hunt for clues to its age in the species of trees, flora and fungi that live there.

"Wildflowers that live in ancient woodland include ramsons (wild garlic), yellow pimpernel, early purple orchid, sweet woodruff, sanicle and bluebells - sometimes called wild hyacinths.

"Trees include small-leaved lime, oaks, hornbeam, the wild pear and wild service tree. Some of these pockets of woodland are virtual time capsules of landscape and habitats which have mostly been swept away over the last 1,000 years."

A SALMON POACHING seal has been leading divers a merry dance as they try to capture him in Scotland.

The grey seal, dubbed Andre, managed to evade capture several times on the River Leven, at Balloch, West Dunbartonshire.

The divers are part of a team from the SSPCA brought in to save Andre from being shot by irate fishermen.

They want to return the seal to a wild colony out at sea but Andre has other ideas.

A WEEKEND BLITZ by the Environment Agency reeled in nearly 50 anglers caught fishing without a current valid rod licence in the North East.

Fisheries enforcement officers from the Agency's Newcastle office toured selected rivers, streams and still waters in Northumberland and County Durham to check that anglers were fishing legally.

They checked 383 valid licences but also discovered 46 anglers not in possession of a current licence or unable to produce one.

Those anglers who were unable to produce a valid licence were given seven days to come up with one or face being hauled before the courts.

Agency spokesman Kevin Summerson said:"I can't understand why anglers still take the risk and fish without a licence because they could be fined up to £2,500 and also have all their fishing tackle confiscated by the court."

ANGLERS HAVE REACTED with fury to scientific research claiming to show that fish feel pain which has given a huge boost to anti-angling campaigners.

Scientists from the Roslin Institute and the University of Edinburgh claimed to have demonstrated that fish could perceive pain by injecting poison into the lips of rainbow trout, after which their physiology and behaviour were monitored.

But anglers' misgivings about this now also have scientific backing, according to the National Angling Alliance.

Dr Bruno Broughton, a fish biologist and scientific advisor to the NAA, is unconvinced by the claims that fish can feel pain.

He said:"I doubt that it will come as much of a shock to anglers to learn that fish have an elaborate system of sensory cells around their mouths. Nor is it a surprise that, when their lips are injected with poisons, fish respond and behave abnormally.

"However, it is an entirely different matter to draw conclusions about the ability of fish to feel pain, a psychological experience for which they literally do not have the brains."

The NAA asserted that all known evidence points towards the fact that fish are not capable of feeling pain as it is perceived within mammals.

Apart from scientific arguments, common sense dictated that a fish with a hook in its mouth would not fight against such pain, nor would it feed on diets which included spiny-finned fish, molluscs and the like.

Speaking on behalf of the NAA, Paul Knight - also the director of the Salmon and Trout Association - added:"We do not accept that fish feel pain, but the wider issue of fish welfare is a subject that good anglers take seriously.

"That is why the sport is governed by national legislation, fisheries byelaws, fishery rules and codes of conduct, all designed to assure the fish's well-being."

A MAJOR CAMPAIGN to highlight the link between our countryside and our stomachs is being launched over coming months by farmers and growers.

The NFU says:"The countryside we all love just wouldn't be the same without British farming. Farmers produce some of the highest quality food anywhere in the world - think of a tasty bacon butty using prime British bacon and freshly-baked bread.

"But intimate knowledge of food production and the countryside is no longer handed down through the generations so too often this contribution goes unrecognised."

FOXHUNTERS IN Scotland may already have fallen foul of the controversial new law there banning hunting with dogs.

To the fury of hunt groups, two of the country's top huntsmen have been reported to the procurator-fiscal under the new legislation.

Rory Innes, the Master of the Jedforest Hunt, and Trevor Adams, Master of the Buccleuch Hunt, have both been accused of deliberately hunting a fox with dogs.

Scotland's 10 main hunts, including the Jedforest and Buccleuch have continued to meet since the Protection of Wild Mammals (Scotland) Act became law last year.

They are allowed under the terms of the Act to shoot foxes so long as it purely part of a pest control service.

However, animal rights protesters claim a loophole in the Act permits foxes to be killed by hounds if they are injured or if they remain concealed in woods.

Alan Murray, of the Scottish Countryside Alliance, explained:"These two men have looked after hounds for quite a few years and they know the law. We are absolutely amazed that this has happened.

"The police have attended about 90 per cent of hunts and if there was anything untoward, they would have known."

WOOD MICE PLACE little signposts around them in the wild to make sure they can find their way about, say researchers.

Dr Pavel Stopka and Dr David McDonald conducted a series of tests on wood mice as part of a study at Oxford University.

Their report reveals:"During their movements in the wild, wood mice distribute small objects, such as leaves or twigs, which are often visually conspicuous. Our experiments demonstrate that these marks serve as points of reference during exploration.

"Way-marking, as we call it, may diminish the likelihood of losing an 'interesting' location, perhaps following disturbance by, for example, a predator."

A MANX SHEARWATER is believed to be Britain's oldest bird at 52.

The bird, found on Bardsey Island off North Wales, is estimated to have flown an incredible five million miles during its lifetime during lengthy feeding trips and migrations to South America.

It was first ringed in 1957 when already aged about six, caught for the second time in 1961 and again in 1978.

The black and white bird, which is nocturnal on land and nests in abandoned rabbit burrows, was taken again last year and researchers thought that would be the last they saw of it. But it has now turned up again - caught this time by Steve Stansfield, warden of Bardsey Bird Observatory - and given a new ring before release.

WATER VOLES ARE being fitted with radio tracking collars in a scheme to rentroduce them to the wild.

So far, 15 have been fitted with the tiny collars and released at a secret site near Bristol.

All the animals are captive bred and it is hoped the collars will help conservationists keep track of their progress. At one time, the UK was believed to have supported millions of water voles but now less than 900,000 may remain.

KITE: hard-won triumph for conservationists

WHEN the red kite soars high in the sky, it is easy to see why admirers on the threshold of the new Millennium dubbed it *"the success story of the century"* among British birds.

With a wingspan almost as large as the golden eagle's, the red kite offers a thrilling spectacle to anyone watching it ride soft country breezes.

Human intervention was needed to bring this fork-tailed predator back from the brink of extinction with the Chilterns region of southern England - where I live - playing a leading role in the conservation project.

Although still not a common sight everywhere in the UK, the vision of that great rust-coloured body scything through the sky is something more and more people can now enjoy while out walking.

It seems a little ironic that one of the chief causes of the bird's decline in the first place was Man's stupidity

Countless numbers of the birds were killed by farmers, landowners, and gamekeepers, afraid that they would prey on newborn lambs or decimate game bird stocks.

Even today, with more people recognising that kites are mainly scavengers of carrion and killers of rabbits, they can fall victim to the mindlessly wielded shotgun.

Some are also poisoned or die from eating other creatures which have themselves been poisoned.

In addition, red kite eggs are highly prized by illegal egg collectors and a constant vigil is needed at the birds' secret nest sites by teams of wildlife minders.

Taking all this into account, the resurgence of the red kite marks a remarkable achievement for the joint efforts of the RSPB and English Nature who originally brought in new red kites from Spain.

From the start, the Chilterns was at the forefront of the project with those first 'foreigners' released locally to recolonise the area.

Since then, during one particularly successful year, breeding pairs of red kite reared 153 young at various sites all over the country.

The Chilterns' own population is now so well established that its young are regularly transported to recolonise suitable new areas.

Birds from the Chilterns were originally released into the East Midlands back in 1997 and 1998 with other young starting new lives in Yorkshire and elsewhere after that.

But there have also been setbacks.

At one point, concerns increased about red kites scavenging dead rats on farmland.

In one short period, eight kites perished and, when examined, their bodies all revealed the same cause: rat poison.

Even so, the RSPB remains quite confident that the birds will continue to go from strength to strength.

"Red kites have now become a familiar sight in several different parts of the country," said a spokesman. *"They are very much at home in areas where they have been missing for over a century. This is a real conservation success story."*

And a pat on the back for the Chilterns too.

CASH-STRAPPED RURAL communities and their fight for survival are highlighted in a worrying new study.

The Countryside Alliance warns that the latest 'State of the Countryside Report' by the Countryside Agency profiles a countryside whose communities could soon be under threat from economic dysfunction.

Richard Burge, chief executive of the Alliance, said:"The report paints a picture of a 'curate's egg' countryside, one which is only good in parts - and increasingly mainly for the better-off.

"It is becoming ever more difficult for the less well-off to live and work in the countryside, and this in particular could be very bad news for the upkeep of the land itself. However, the Agency's report also confirms that one of the great strengths of rural communities is that they still think and act as communities.

"The Government must ensure that its rural policies recognise and respect rural communities' own sense of values and identity.

"The report paints a bizarre and paradoxical picture of the pressures on our countryside. It claims that nearly 30 per cent of the UK's population now live in the countryside -- an increase of 1.5 million people in the last two decades alone.

"Yet over the same period a whole panoply of rural services and amenities in the countryside - such as village shops, post offices, banks, pubs - has been disappearing at a rate of knots.

"This is wholly unsustainable. The spectre emerges of a countryside increasingly crowded residentially but largely denuded of the commercial and social amenities that its communities will need.

"Unless something is done to reverse this decline, our countryside faces a massive destructive volume of constant road traffic ferrying country dwellers to scarce rural services or into the towns."

TROUT FISHERMEN AND conservationists have been snapping at each other in a row over a river.

Bad feeling first arose two years ago when the Hampshire and Isle of Wight Wildlife Trust banned fishing on a 1,300-yard stretch of the Itchen, north of Winchester.

The Trust said over-zealous anglers were creating a desert for wildlife and wanted the banks returned to their natural state.

However, anglers have now hit back, saying the area is so badly overgrown that wildlife has dwindled and the river's status as a Site of Special Scientific Interest is in the balance.

BADGERS ARE IN the dog house in Essex after digging up scores of human bones at a local church yard.

Mourners are dismayed that the animals, protected by law, have accidentally exhumed more than 100 bones at St Peter's Church in Thundersley.

In a horrific twist, a number of skulls have even been found above ground as the powerful burrowers undermine ancient graves around the 13th Century church.

Problems caused by badgers at the site have been getting worse for some time and a few years ago a proposal was mooted that would involve transporting all the animals to a new sett elsewhere.

However, the sticking point was money - the church would have been saddled with a bill for almost £200,000, though the same project today would probably cost twice that.

Conservation laws, and a genuine affection among locals for badgers, have resulted in numbers of the hardy mammals living at the site swelling to more than 100.

But with more and more human remains popping up, the local community is expected to take steps to sort out the problem once and for all in the near future.

OVER 2,000 BROWN trout were rescued "almost at their last gasp" after their stream dried up in East Sussex.

Members of the public alerted the Environment Agency to the trouts' plight and an emergency operation was launched to pluck the fish to safety.

"Agency officers acted immediately and began a rescue operation in which juvenile and parent trout were saved from the rapidly diminishing Winter-bourne in Lewes," said a spokesman.

"Because the Winterbourne is dry for much of the year, the young fish can find themselves in a near perfect environment with little competition from other fish, few predators, and ideal water quality.

"Unfortunately, this habitat literally disappears as the stream dries up again, leaving the juvenile fish and any remaining parent fish stranded in pools on the stream bed gasping for air.

"The rescued fish were transported in oxygenated polythene bags to several locations on the upper Bevern Stream, a tributary of the River Ouse.

"These trout now have a second chance to survive. Some will remain within the Bevern and mature while others will choose to migrate to sea."

ANIMAL RIGHTS CAMPAIGNERS held a demo at Bideford, Devon, to save the black rat currently facing extermination by conservationists on the island of Lundy off the coast.

"An undercover investigation has put the notorious Lundy foursome to shame over their conduct of the rat eradication programme on Lundy Island," claimed a spokesman for Animal Aid.

"The so-called 'Lundy Seabird Recovery Project' consists of English Nature, the Landmark Trust, the National Trust and the RSPB, and their aim was to make the island rat-free by Easter.

"So far only four rat carcasses have been found - this by the foursome's own admission. This means that either the rest of the rats have not been killed, or they are dying underground.The latter is highly unlikely as it is a rat's instinct to die in the open. There may still be time to save the Lundy ship rat!"

A BADGER WHICH went berserk and attacked five people shows the danger of domesticating wild animals, say experts.

Boris, a one-year-old male badger, is believed to have been stolen or intentionally released from Vale Wildlife Visitor Centre at Evesham Country Park, Worcestershire, on May 7.

"Boris had been hand reared and was hand-fed by staff at the centre on a daily basis, and had never shown any sign of aggression," revealed the National Federation of Badger Groups.

"But on finding himself alone, hungry and frightened in a strange environment, he bit five people on May 8 and 9 and even chased police officers onto the bonnet of their patrol car.

"Boris was captured by members of the Worcestershire Badger Society on the evening of May 9 and was euthanased by a vet. It was only on May 10, following reports of the incident, that staff at the Vale Wildlife Centre discovered that he had been taken from his familiar environment."

Dr Elaine King, chief executive of the NFBG, added:"Badgers are powerful animals and we strongly advise against their domestication. Boris's behaviour was quite unlike that of a wild badger which would have an instinctive fear of humans.

"He arrived at Vale Wildlife Centre having already been domesticated. It was therefore necessary to care for him in perpetuity in a managed zoo environment under a zoo licence. It appears that someone hoped to take him for a pet and he was probably released when hunger made him aggressive.

"Organisations that rescue and release orphaned cubs and injured badgers take great care not to domesticate them.

"Boris's tragic encounter with strangers in an unfamiliar environment illustrates how important it is to allow animals intended for release into the wild to develop and maintain their natural fear of people."

DORMICE ARE BEING helped to cross the road with the construction of a special high-rise bridge in West Sussex.

The bridge at Haywards Heath is 18ft above ground and made from woven steel ropes providing both durablity and good grip.

When a new relief road was built, local conservationists feared their dormice would quickly fall victim to cars. But Graham Roberts, senior ecologist for West Sussex County Council, came up with the idea of an aerial walkway like those already used by red squirrels on the Isle of Wight.

MAGPIES HAVE BEEN back in the news after a housewife hit the headlines for systematically culling the birds to protect the eggs and chicks of local songbirds.

Following that controversy, the Game Conservancy Trust says the truth of whether magpies decimate songbird offspring is complex.

"Ecological studies of magpies show that they are largely omnivorous and only a small fraction of their diet comprises the eggs and nestlings of other birds," said a Trust spokesman.

"However, this can be misleading for two reasons. Firstly, it reflects diet over the whole year and obviously bird eggs and nestlings are only available to the magpies in spring and early summer.

"Second, beetles and grubs are more common than birds' eggs, so the relative effect of magpie predation is likely to be more significant on songbirds than on insects.

"What one needs are not studies of magpie diet but of the effect of magpie predation. Attempts to do this have come mainly from the British Trust for Ornithology.

"One of these showed that breeding numbers and nesting success of songbirds could not be associated with increasing magpie numbers - the scientists concluded that magpies were not affecting songbird numbers.

"A more recent study did, however, show that losses of eggs and nestlings of blackbirds and song thrushes are higher, on average, in parts of the country where magpies are common."

A WILDLIFE GARDEN is one of the main attractions at this year's Chelsea Flower Show.

The entry, from Chris Caligari, has won the backing of the RSPB for the way it supports bird life.

"The 'Stonemarket Room for Wildlife' is a true garden for people who may not have the greenest of fingers, but who have green hearts," said the RSPB.

"Chris Caligari is a renowned ecologist and garden designer, who puts wildlife and the environment into the core of his garden designs."

NIGHTJARS ARE AMONG the latest birds recorded in the British Trust for Ornithology's ongoing migration study.

A number of the strange, secretive birds - occasionally seen at dusk hunting moths - were spotted in Norfolk after making a long perilous journey from Africa.

"A late fieldfare was also still in North Yorkshire on May 4 but generally most redwing and fieldfare have now departed," added a BTO spokesman.

"Spotted flycatchers are arriving in good numbers and were recorded as far north as Tyne and Wear and the Isle of Man, and as far west as Waterford in Ireland.

"Lesser whitethroat and hobby are still largely confined to southern England. May is an interesting time for waders and almost anything can turn up anywhere. A temminck's stint was seen in North Yorkshire on May 4 and a wood sandpiper was in South Yorkshire on the 5th.

"Two dotterel stopped off on their migration in South Yorkshire on the 4th.

"Seawatching was quite good with a few pomarine and Arctic skuas recorded. Common terns were recorded in superb numbers in Kent (335) and Hampshire (174)."

OTTERS ARE SLOWLY returning to English land they were driven from nearly 50 years ago, a new report has revealed.

The National Otter Survey for England, published jointly by the Environment Agency and Wildlife Trusts, says areas supporting otters have increased five-fold in the last 25 years.

Of the 3,327 riverbank and wetland sites surveyed, almost 35 per cent showed evidence of otters (footprints and spraints), rising from just 5.8 per cent in 1977-79.

The animal, one of the UK's most charismatic and popular mammals, has suffered serious decline throughout Europe, primarily due to widespread use of pesticides.

By the 1950s-60s the UK's once-thriving population had been reduced to remnant populations in the south west of England, East Anglia, parts of Wales and Scotland.

Andrew Crawford, the survey's author, from the Environment Agency, said:"The otter - one of our best-loved mammals - is now on the road to recovery. Overall, the survey suggests a real and continued increase in otter range, which in turn reflects a considerable increase in population."

Alastair Driver, the Agency's national conservation manager, added: "Despite the good news, we can't become complacent. Otters are not increasing as fast as we would like in some areas and we will need to concentrate on ways to protect them from the motor car which continues to be one of their biggest threats."

The otter's resurgence is thought to be based upon a combination of factors, including enhanced water quality, local improvements in fish stocks, and changes in riverbank management.

RARE BITTERNS HAVE been given a boost by a project aimed at improving the reedbeds they need to survive.

The secretive heron-like birds - whose males are famous for their strange 'boom' calls - have been in decline since the 19th Century because of persecution and drainage of wetlands.

Fears were raised in recent years that they were heading for extinction but enlarging reedbeds is thought to be the best way to prevent this.

Eight conservation groups, including the RSPB, have joined forces to launch the project with 60 per cent of £4million funding coming from the EU.

A network of 19 improved sites will stretch from Kent and Suffolk to Cornwall and Lancashire.

Project manager Sarah Alsbury explained:"When nesting, bitterns need large reedbeds with areas of open shallow water. By 1997, conservationists feared they were on the edge in Britain, when only 11 calling males were noted in just four counties."

THE WOODLAND TRUST reacted with fury to news that BAA is backing controversial plans for airport development which threaten ancient woods.

BAA's move flies in the face of its earlier statements about the importance of ancient woodland, says the Trust which warns that expansion of Stansted and Gatwick airports will destroy swathes of this irreplaceable natural habitat.

Trust spokesman Ed Pomfret said: "What BAA has said in response to the Government's consultation on airport growth is a recipe for disaster. It is laughable that BAA's response is entitled 'Responsible Growth'. These are the most destructive options for airport expansion.

"Ancient woodland contains more threatened species than any other UK habitat. In the past BAA has claimed ancient woodland is important and that the company 'aims to enhance wildlife' at each site. Given what they've just said, this now appears to be just green-wash."

Mr Pomfret said the proposals to build a second runway at Gatwick and two new runways at Stansted would directly destroy over 247 acres of ancient woodland and seriously affect hundreds more acres in the surrounding area due to increased pollution.

Additionally, forecasts show that aviation will be one of the biggest single contributors to climate change - the biggest threat to nature.

And once airports expand, associated transport and housing will further encroach on green spaces.

Mr Pomfret pledged that the Trust would continue to fight any proposals that threaten ancient woodland, a rare habitat that now covers only two per cent of the country.

A GIANT WHITE horse carved into a hillside at one of the country's top wildlife sites is illegal, it has been claimed.

The UK Government has reportedly been sent a letter of 'formal notice' by the European Commission which says that the UK acted against EU laws in giving the go-ahead to the carving of the horse.

The horse, still being created near Folkestone in Kent, now looks set to be the subject of legal action in the European Court where the Government could face massive fines and even be ordered to restore the damaged habitat.

According to Friends of the Earth, the row over the horse could just be a forerunner of future European challenges over proposed roads, ports and airports on or near our best wildlife sites.

A RARE DEER rejected by his own mother is being brought up in a Scottish caravan.

Colin, a Pere David's deer, is being hand-reared by Carolyn Morrison, a worker at the Blair Drummond Safari Park in Stirlingshire.

The tiny deer - which took the name of vet Colin Scott who delivered him a month ago - is being bottle-fed by Ms Morrison.

Pere David's deer originate from China and are named after a French missionary and naturalist called Father David who observed them in the wild.

After being driven almost to extinction in China, a number of the deer were brought to Europe and introduced to wildlife parks in the 1800s.

A COUNTRY WALK is more hazardous today because of aggressive maternal beef cows, it has been claimed.

Speaking after a Cumbrian woman walking her Jack Russell was attacked by 20 beef cows and left in a coma, a spokesman for the NFU said:"Unlike dairy cows, which are milked twice a day and are used to human contact, beef cattle will probably only see their farmer once a day and are not handled in the same way.

"A cow will still see a dog, no matter how small, as a predator and can get very aggressive if one comes near."

In the last decade, more and more farmers had changed from dairy to beef cattle, he said.

Businesswoman Shirley McKaskie, 45, was left in a coma and underwent brain surgery at Newcastle General Hospital after she and her dog Tina were attacked near their home at Greystoke Ghyll.

Mrs McKaskie is believed to have picked up her pet when the cows, many with calves, became alarmed by its barking.

When the cattle attacked, she was trampled underfoot and was only saved when farmer John Cameron went to investigate the commotion.

He spotted the furious cows throwing an object around in the field and at first thought it must be a dead calf.

But he was horrified when he realised the bellowing cattle were hurling a badly injured woman around and rushed into the field to stop them.

The cattle immediately backed off and he managed to get Mrs McKaskie back to the farm out of harm's way before calling for an ambulance.

However, doctors treating her at the hospital are not certain that she will make a complete recovery from her injuries.

Her pet Tina, the cause of the attack, is thought to have escaped serious harm.

AN ATTEMPT BY discount retailer Lidl to drive down the farm gate price of milk runs against prevailing market forces, warns the NFU.

Farmers have been campaigning for a significant increase in milk prices on the back of the slump in the value of the pound and stronger world commodity markets, says the union.

NFU Milk Committee chairman Terrig Morgan said:"Lidl's actions are completely unjustified and may result in producers having to sell below the cost of production. At a time when the market indicators support the push for a price rise, it is appalling to have a retailer attempting to drive the price in the opposite direction for their own ends. Our campaign will be continuing."

OWLS HAVE BEGUN breeding through the winter months as Britain's weather warms up, say ornithologists.

Increasingly mild winter conditions have encouraged owls to breed right through the Christmas and New Year period.

"Perhaps barn owls and tawny owls should replace robins on our Christmas cards in recognition of their year-round breeding performance," said a spokesman for the British Trust for Ornithology."Kind weather and high mouse and vole populations have contributed to a bumper crop of baby owls.

"The BTO Barn Owl Monitoring Programme showed that, having started their 2002 breeding season two weeks early, 10 per cent of birds managed to produce late clutches too. Second brood successes were recorded in Lincolnshire, Sussex and Nottinghamshire in November and December."

David Glue, Trust research biologist, added:"When BTO nest recorders Bryan Perkins and Colin Lythgoe undertook the annual spring-clean of their Cheshire nestboxes on February 27, they were surprised to be confronted by a large fledgling tawny owl.

"Three youngsters, out of five, successfully left the nest.The clutch of eggs must have been laid during the mild Christmas to New Year period. Other early clutches were laid in January, two months earlier than expected.Tawny owls adjust their breeding season around an often fickle food supply but such exceptionally early clutches are rare.

"In autumn 2002, a huge crop of beech mast and other woodland fruits fuelled locally high populations of rodent prey, enabling tawny owls to start nesting very early."

CATCHING EELS, TROUT and coarse fish without £22 rod licences left four anglers facing a total of £840 in fines and costs in cases heard at Hereford Magistrates Court.

Following the cases an Environment Agency spokesman said:"Those who choose to fish without first buying a licence are depriving the Agency and licensed fishermen of income that would be re-invested in improving fishing. Buy a rod licence - it's cheaper than getting a fine."

THE SPECTRE OF unrestricted GM crop growing seems a step nearer reality after the Government appeared to surrender to Brussels over the issue.

Conservationists were horrified when Minister Michael Meacher revealed the Government 'may be forced' to let UK farmers grow GM crops even if the public does not want them.

Mr Meacher told BBC Radio 4's Farming Today programme:"We have to act in accordance with the law. The law at the present moment is set down in an EU directive and the key and sole criteria for taking action with regard to GM crops is: Are they a harm or risk to the environment?"

Friends of the Earth, which has long campaigned against gene-modified crops as a potential hazard to our environment, attacked Mr Meacher.

What he said showed New Labour just ignored mass public opinion whenever it felt like it, said a spokesman.

Meanwhile, the public fight against GM crops goes on with campaigners recently attacking a field in Fife, Scotland.

FARMERS AND GROWERS want all 'gangmasters' to be licensed to prevent harvest-time headaches being created by unscrupulous operators, says the NFU.

The union has told the Commons' EFRA Select Committee that while labour supply agencies, or gangmasters, play a valuable role in providing the industry with sufficient short-term staff at peak production times, a statutory register is now essential to curb abuses.

Vice president Michael Paske said: "Whilst hard evidence is, understandably, difficult to come by, experience and information received suggests that problems surrounding some gangmasters are getting worse.

"The industry has recognised this and has worked hard to introduce codes of practice and initiatives to hamper any illegal activity. However, it has consistently called for the introduction of statutory guidance and licensing of gangmasters.

"Successive governments have, however, not acted on this request, primarily due to an apparent lack of Parliamentary time."

NFU Employment and Education chairman Bob Fiddaman added:"Gangmasters provide an important supply of short-term staff at key times in the farming year. The last thing a farmer or grower needs is for his crop to go rotten in the field or for contracts to be lost because his workforce, supplied through a gangmaster, turns out to be working illegally and has been removed by enforcement officers.

"Farmers and growers and those in the supply chain would feel happier that illegal practices are being prevented if gangmasters were forced to register. The majority of gangmasters should have nothing to fear from a national register. It is important to grade out the rotten apples for both the industry and workers."

THE HUMBLE hedgehog is top of the pops in a vote to find Britain's most welcome garden visitor.

In a poll organised by The Mammal Society and the BBC, the prickly creatures collected the highest number of votes.

Cats and rats were householders' least favourites.

A STARLING CAME up with a first class place to raise a family - the same post box it has now nested in for the third year running.

Sympathetic postal bosses once again ordered the box at Frinton-on-Sea, Essex, to be taped shut - apart from the letter slot - so the starling could come and go in peace.

DOLPHINS WHICH SWIM off Britain's coasts have been given a boost with moves to deploy safer fishing nets stepped up.

The Wildlife Trusts have welcomed DEFRA's announcement that trials of special grid nets to reduce dolphin deaths had proved successful.

"However, the threat to dolphin survival is now so severe that in order to save the UK's dolphins we are calling for a temporary ban on bass pelagic trawlers across the whole of Europe," said a spokesman for the Trusts.

"The fishery, which operates in the south west of England, should not be reopened until the grid net trials have been completed.

"Almost all the trawlers involved in the bass fishing fleet are French. The UK Government can only make UK boats use the grid nets and any European fleet operating in UK waters would not be subject to using dolphin-friendly fishing nets.

"Since the beginning of 2003, 265 dolphins have been washed ashore in Cornwall and Devon representing an estimated five per cent of the total number of dolphin deaths through entanglement in fishing nets.

"The Wildlife Trusts are calling for the fishery to be temporarily closed until further research is conducted, grid nets become mandatory, and until an independent observer scheme is put in place."

Joan Edwards, head of marine conservation for The Wildlife Trusts, added:"We have to be cautious until the whole trial and report is completed. We are still very concerned about the impact of the grids on the escaping dolphins. Research into similar nets in New Zealand has shown that the grids have caused severe trauma to the escaping animals. However, if initial indications are correct we must ensure that these nets are deployed now across Europe."

AN OSPREY WHICH arrived in Leicestershire has had birdwatchers there scratching their heads over its ancestry.

"At the end of April, the osprey was seen for the first time at Rutland Water with a red ring on its right leg," said a spokesman for the Anglian Water Osprey Project."Initially the ring number could not be read so we set about working out what the possibilities were. Our first thought was that red rings were used on the right leg of the English juvenile ospreys in 2001. Scottish juveniles were ringed on the left leg that year. Could this be a two-year old male bird returning already? Usually when two-year old birds have reappeared it has been much later in the summer. Another thought was that this could have been a bird ringed as a juvenile in Scotland in 1996.

"The possibilities were soon reduced when the bird was identified as a female. Only three female birds had been translocated in 2001 and all three were satellite tracked.

"U03 probably perished in central Sahara where it arrived less than 18 days after leaving Rutland Water. U04's body was recovered from a beach on Fuerteventura, Canary Islands, and U06 spent the winter and following spring near Lisbon, Portugal - most unusual - then moved north through the UK in June 2002 until transmissions ceased.

"Other possibilities involve the 2001 Rutland-bred chick, which may have been female, or a Lake District chick or, of course, a much older Scottish female from 1996. So which of these birds could the Rutland Water bird be?"

THE SHY CORNCRAKE is fighting back from the verge of extinction.

The elusive bird, which has become one of the most rarely spotted in recent years, had seemed to be in terminal decline.

However, in Scotland at least, the efforts of farmers and conservationists are finally paying off.

Last year, according to RSPB Scotland, there were more than 670 calling male corncrakes recorded, the highest number since survey work started in 1978.

Now a countrywide survey is trying to establish whether this record has already been broken and if the species really is back on the road to recovery.

The survey, which began on May 20 and will end in July, wants people who hear a corncrake's distinctive call to contact the Society.

RSPB Scotland's Mark O'Brien, co-ordinating the survey, said:"The corncrake was once a common species in rural Britain but with changes in agricultural practices, numbers suffered heavily.

"Up until the mid-1980s, its population plummeted. Through the combined efforts of farmers, crofters and conservationists, we believe this threatened bird is now staging a comeback. Last year saw more than 670 calling males recorded. This year we hope to see more than 700.

"To count corncrakes is a very difficult task. They skulk in tall vegetation and are hard to see. The best method for recording them is to monitor their calls.

"They make a rasping 'crek crek' noise and at this time of year are getting quite vocal so, hopefully, if people know what they are listening for, we can get a very accurate picture of how this species is doing."

DANGEROUS BULLS WERE at the centre of two separate dramas in Staffordshire and Lancashire.

First, hikers were warned to be on their guard after a huge, aggressive bull - weighing one-and-a-half tonnes - escaped its farm and took to the hills near Calton, on the Staffordshire moors.

Then another bull hit the headlines when it rampaged through an antiques shop in Lancaster after fleeing a local market.

This bull, which injured a woman after knocking her aside, was later shot by police - but not before its fury was captured on the shop's CCTV cameras and later aired on national TV.

THE POTENTIAL DANGER of GM crops to Britain's countryside has once again been underlined by scientists. Genetically modified crops will need close study for years before their effects can be truly known, warns the Royal Society.

MINK COULD SOON be brought under control by a new floating raft trap which will benefit native wildlife such as water voles and seabirds.

The voracious predators, originally introduced here in the 1920s for their fur, have become a scourge of the countryside since they escaped or were released into the wild from UK fur farms.

"It is well known that feral mink are seriously implicated in the dramatic decline of water vole populations," said a spokesman for the Game Conservancy Trust."It is perhaps less well known that nesting seabird colonies in some parts of the British Isles are endangered by this predator.

"But mink can be elusive creatures, to the extent that even population estimates vary enormously. In the early 1990s, the breeding mink population of England and Wales was estimated to be 56,000, though a more recent estimate suggests only 18,000.

"Interaction with the recovering otter populations, and disease, are putative reasons for an apparent decline in mink numbers but the process is still very unclear.

"Jonathan Reynolds and Mike Short from the Trust's Predation Control Studies team have designed a small floating raft to act as a mink detector. The raft incorporates a wooden tunnel housing a clay tracking pan which is kept permanently moist to record visiting wildlife. In the event of mink being recorded, the wooden tunnel is big enough to house a mink trap.

"To test the device Rhian Leigh, an MSc student from Reading University, working with the Trust's team, deployed 72 rafts on 36 sections of the Upper Avon catchment. The rafts were then checked at intervals for signs of visiting mink."

Rhian himself commented:"It turned out that mink loved these rafts and left very clear prints in the clay, making it easy to identify their presence.

"Although we are currently using this method just to survey mink populations and as a tool to research specific questions about mink control, it could easily be used as a cost effective method to trap them as well."

SWIFTS SEEM TO be soaring over British towns and cities in larger numbers this year.

"The latest results from our Migration Watch project shows that more birdwatchers are recording swifts during their birdwatching visits compared to the same time last year," confirmed the British Trust for Ornithology.

"The sound of swifts screaming above our historic towns is one of the most evocative things of summer. They are one of the latest summer migrants to arrive in Britain and Ireland from their wintering grounds in Africa, south of the Sahara. They spend virtually all their time on the wing, only landing to nest and raise their young. They almost certainly spend all winter on the wing, at a height of 600 metres or more."

A DEADLY DISEASE that kills carp and other coarse fish has been detected at a fishery and fish farm in Worcestershire.

The Environment Agency has alerted Midlands fishermen and given local angling clubs advice on how to minimise the risk of spreading spring viraemia of carp (SVC). The disease, which is always fatal when contracted and can decimate fish stocks, was detected at the Woodland View Fishery and Woodland View Fish Farm at Hadley, near Droitwich.

PEREGRINE: predator puts on a powerful display

FAST and ferocious, the peregrine falcon is in a class of its own when it comes to hunting other birds.

During a stoop, when it folds its scythe-like wings and plummets out of the sky, it can reach speeds of up to 200mph.

If it hits its prey cleanly the outcome is usually instant death, courtesy of its rapier talons.

Peregrines inhabit secluded areas and can be found in hilly ranges, quiet moorland, or along sea cliffs. Prey usually comprises large birds such as pigeons, grouse, or crows but small mammals are also taken.

I watched a captive peregrine being worked by a falconer at a falconry display recently and its power and grace were awesome.

It was also interesting to observe other birds fleeing from nearby trees as this killer took to the air.

The threat it posed was obviously very real to them.

Short, rapid wingbeats were first employed as the display peregrine drove itself high into the sky.

Then it turned and dropped like a stone, shooting across a field to hit the lure wheeled on a string by the falconer.

The force of impact was impressive.

For such a magnificent bird, the peregrine has suffered a particularly rough time over the last 60 years.

It was even shot on sight during the Second World War in case it brought down carrier pigeons.

Many have since been killed by gamekeepers while pesticides absorbed in the food chain were also blamed for making peregrine egg shells too thin for the young inside to survive.

But conservation efforts have paid off and the UK population of peregrine falcons is now thought to number about 1,400 pairs.

Lately, however, the RSPB has been sounding the alarm over another traditional enemy of the peregrine - the pigeon fancier.

A poisoning campaign has apparently been waged by some disgruntled fanciers who mistakenly blame the predators for high mortality rates among their birds.

The RSPB says it has taken more than three decades for peregrines to recover from the worst effects of accidental poisoning by pesticides.

It would therefore be "*tragic*" if conservation success was now to be reversed by malicious, deliberate poisoning.

"*We have received at least nine reports of peregrine falcons being poisoned or suspected poisoned bait being laid,*" revealed Graham Elliott, head of the RSPB's investigations unit.

"*At half a dozen locations, we think pigeon fanciers have left tethered pigeons doused in poison close to peregrine nests in the hope that the adults are attracted by their distress and prey on them.*"

You can't help feeling sorry for the pigeons themselves - sacrificed in such a shoddy way by people who profess to admire them.

Humans, it seems, can still stoop faster and lower than a peregrine.

FOUR SPECIES OF wetland birds have suffered worrying declines across England and Wales as their traditional habitats disappear, it has been revealed.

The Breeding Waders of Wet Meadows survey, funded by the RSPB, DEFRA and English Nature, found that several species were under threat but worst hit were the lapwing, curlew, snipe, and redshank.

In the last 20 years, numbers of these four birds have slumped dramatically, say researchers who undertook the survey for the British Trust for Ornithology.

According to the report, land drainage for housing development has left the countryside increasingly dry with wetland habitats vanishing so completely that birds are driven away.

Some 60 per cent of snipe, 40 per cent of lapwing and curlew, and 20 per cent of redshank had been lost compared to numbers recorded before the early 1980s.

RSPB spokesman Phil Rothwell said: "Seeing lapwing, snipe and redshank in the spring should be a familiar part of the countryside. It is a tragedy that once widespread birds are now largely confined to the oases of nature reserves within the desert of the wider countryside.

"To halt further declines, we need urgent action through a range of Government-backed measures, such as more funding for wildlife-friendly farming, and new measures to restore wetland areas to our thirsty countryside."

Andy Wilson, for the BTO, added:"Half the sites visited during the survey contained no breeding waders at all. The contrast with those sites that are carefully managed was stark.

"In parts of England and Wales, snipe are now approaching local extinction - in the West Midlands, for example, only four were recorded from a total of 106 sites."

WILDLIFE ON A remote Scottish island is being given the Big Brother treatment with the installation of CCTV cameras.

Birds and other creatures on St Kilda will be observed going about their daily routines after the £120,000 scheme was given the go-ahead.

Similar technology to that being used on Channel 4's controversial human Big Brother show is to be deployed to make sure none of the drama is missed.

Pictures will be beamed back to the mainland from the National Trust-owned island and could show anything from the UK's biggest seabird colonies, to the whales and dolphins that patrol offshore.

THOUSANDS OF FISH have been killed following three pollution incidents on Yorkshire waterways.

At two of the sites, raw sewage had been discharged while at the third a detergent caused the river to foam, says the Environment Agency.

The worst incident was reported after a member of the public spotted a large number of dead fish in Pocklington Beck at Pocklington, near York.

Sewage had flowed into Pocklington Canal, a well stocked coarse fishery, wiping out many of the inhabitants.

Agency spokesman Pete Stevenson said:"The dead fish included trout and a variety of coarse fish such as roach, bream and perch. This is a tragic and unnecessary loss of life and it will take years for the river to recover.

"There is a picnic spot at the head of Pocklington Canal and we would urge families to avoid playing near the water until the problem has been rectified.

"Yorkshire Water has confirmed that raw sewage has been discharging into the beck. Raw sewage uses up oxygen in the river which can cause fish to die."

Agency officers were also called to a near-identical sewage incident at the River Worth, near Keighley, while a detergent spill was blamed for the deaths of dozens more fish along a two-mile stretch of the River Holme, near Holmfirth - famed as the setting for the BBC's Last of the Summer Wine series.

A PEACEFUL WALK almost ended in disaster for a deaf woman who was saved by her dog when a 20ft tree crashed to the ground beside her.

Pensioner Valerie Smith was startled when her collie Tommy suddenly barred her way and began barking during a walk near Plymouth, Devon.

As Mrs Smith stopped in her tracks, the age-rotted tree crashed down, scratching her arm with a branch.

Creaking timber is thought to have alerted her pet as the tree came loose and began to topple.

BUTTERFLIES IN SCOTLAND have been given a boost with the opening of a new nature reserve especially for them.

Wildlife charity Butterfly Conservation has unveiled its first Scottish nature reserve at the site near Fort William.

"The Allt Mhuic Nature Reserve is home to two of Scotland's rarest butterfly species, the chequered skipper and the pearl-bordered fritillary," said a Forestry Commission spokesman.

"The chequered skipper's entire UK population is centred within a 20-mile radius of Fort William, while the pearl-bordered fritillary is one of Britain's fastest declining butterflies.

"The reserve is 200 acres of ancient, semi-natural broadleaf woodland and open heathland in the Forestry Commission's North Loch Arkaig Forest.

"It will be managed in partnership by Butterfly Conservation Scotland - which works to conserve Scotland's native butterflies and moths - and the Forestry Commission.

"It will be helped by cattle grazing to encourage good butterfly habitat, and butterfly populations will be monitored to determine the effectiveness of this management. The public will be encouraged to enjoy the reserve."

HUNTING FOXES AND shooting game both help to conserve the countryside, according to new research.

Landowners whose land is used for field sports take far more trouble to maintain natural habitats, says the study.

And those whose land is used for both hunting and shooting conserve the most woodland, a vital resource for wild creatures.

The study was undertaken by Nigel Leader-Williams and a research team at the University of Kent in Canterbury.

The group reported:"We found that landowners participating in field sports maintained the most established woodland and planted more new woodland and hedgerows than those who did not, despite the equal availability of subsidies.

"Therefore, voluntary habitat management appears to be important for biodiversity conservation in Britain."

Simon Hart, director of the Campaign for Hunting, said:"This research supports what land managers have always argued - that country sports are beneficial to landscapes, wildlife and biodiversity."

The Campaign has just launched a concise leaflet version of its booklet 'Hunting the Truth' which covers each different form of hunting with dogs.

Spokesman Darren Hughes said:"We have produced the 'Hunting the Truth' leaflet following the huge success of the original booklet - so far nearly 15,000 copies have been produced and distributed. The leaflet will satisfy the huge number of enquiries we receive by post, e-mail, telephone and at show stands.

"It is ideal for people curious about hunting but anyone who would like more in-depth information can also order the original booklet or can contact the Campaign for Hunting office."

WILD SALMON ARE increasingly being threatened by farmed salmon in Scotland, it has been claimed.

Conservation groups, including the Worldwide Fund for Nature, say the Scottish Executive is doing too little to save wild salmon from ongoing contamination.

Salmon farming has always been big business but with many sea lochs around Scotland now employed in this way, the impact on wild stocks is said to be getting worse.

Decline in wild salmon numbers has been linked to an explosion of sea lice at farmed salmon sites and interbreeding between escaped fish and those in the wild. Across the North Atlantic, there are now thought to be almost 50 farmed salmon produced for each salmon born in the wild.

ENGLAND'S SHINGLE BEACHES face a serious threat from developers, claim conservationists.

English Nature warns prompt action is needed to counter the risk to the beaches' long-term survival.

Although they can appear like stony deserts, the beaches actually support a rich mosaic of wildlife on our coastal fringes.

Tim Collins, English Nature's head of coastal conservation, said:"Time and tide wait for no man, and time is running out for shingle on our coastline. We need to take action now to conserve this unique resource before we damage it beyond recovery."

It is hoped that new guidelines published by the organisation will be used by both developers and conservationists to help preserve and restore shingle beaches.

Co-author Dr Roland Randall, Fellow of Girton College, Cambridge University, said:"We are lucky in England to still have some of the most extensive shingle banks in Europe because our coastline reveals chalk cliffs yielding flint shingle. It is very rarely found outside Europe, New Zealand and Japan. This new guidance manual provides the very latest thinking on the best way to conserve these special areas."

As well as providing a home for rare bees, insects, seabird colonies, and tiny plants, shingle beaches act as natural flood defences.

WATER VOLES ARE the lively subject of a student's final year ecology project at the University of East Anglia.

Sally Firth said:"I am doing work experience with the North York Moors National Park Authority, helping them carry out a water vole survey over the summer which I am hoping to include as part of the analysis for my project.

"I live in Knaresborough and I am also hoping to do water vole research around my local area.

"As part of my project I have to scientifically analyse raw data - either that I have collected or has been collected by others - to try to investigate several hypotheses."

She invited anyone with knowledge of water voles in their area, or who has already collected data on the furry creatures, to contact her.

BIRDWATCHERS ARE BEING urged to look out for late arrivals of swallows, house martins and other migrant birds.

Mark Grantham, leading the British Trust for Ornithology's Migration Watch scheme, has received reports that birds are still arriving from Africa.

"The first swallow was reported back on March 5 in West Sussex three months ago and it is tempting to assume that all our 16 million migrant birds have arrived by now," he said.

"However, according to recent reports from home and abroad, there are still birds on the move. Reports of new arrivals include house martins, which immediately started nest building, and extra pairs of farmyard swallows.

"Possibly, these are birds which have got caught up in bad weather somewhere between southern Africa and here. We have certainly seen reports of unprecedented numbers of swallows south of the Sahara as late as mid-May.

"For migrant birds, arriving back in Britain late is bad news. There can be fierce squabbles as new arrivals try to claim territories."

318

FISH AND WATERBIRDS were killed at an Essex beauty spot after a local pond was polluted by oil.

Hundreds of fish and several birds were found dead when Environment Agency investigators raced to the pond at Great Notley, near Braintree, following a tip-off.

A clean-up operation was launched to contain the damage and a probe began into who was responsible.

John Parish, the Agency officer leading the investigation, said:"Although this was a relatively small incident, it has ruined a beauty spot much enjoyed by local people.

"Irresponsible disposal of any amount of oil can cause a great deal of damage. It will take a couple of days to clear up the oil and, unless the polluter can be traced, will cost taxpayers several thousand pounds."

Oil stops normal oxygenation of water, causing the fish and other pond life to suffocate, he added.

Oil on feathers quickly reduces their normal function so they become saturated with water and their owners are left unable to fly or move about to find food.

OUTDATED GRAIN TRADING practices are preventing Britain's cereal industry from achieving its full potential, warns the NFU.

In a series of meetings with traders and millers at the industry's Cereals 2003 event, union president Ben Gill called for modern thinking and a new alliance across the grain industry for the common good.

Mr Gill said:"There is no room for practices that seek to keep half of the supply chain in the dark. Changing consumer demands, environmental regulation, challenging criteria on quality, and the commercial reality of an extremely competitive global market, mean we must all be pulling together.

"We need to be working towards a modern, responsive and transparent trading partnership."

The NFU also believes there needs to be increased sharing of crop intelligence.

NESTING TERNS ARE in the spotlight thanks to the latest webcam operation set up by the RSPB.

The common terns are making themselves at home on a special raft at Rye Meads in Hertfordshire.

"Contrary to their name, common terns are not really that common," said an RSPB spokesman."The nesting raft is designed to create a safe nesting area away from predators but with just the conditions that these beautiful birds need to raise a family.

"The fluffy chicks are already hatched and performing well to our camera, which can change views to bring the best shots and allow us to follow the chicks' movements around the raft.

"Our webcam console means you can keep the images updating on your computer without you having to do a thing. So keep up with these long-distance migrants as they raise a family ready for the great return journey to Africa in autumn."

Peregrines, ospreys, and great tits are other species already observed by RSPB webcam.

CONSERVATIONISTS ARE stepping up their battle against Labour's "mad and destructive" drive to build new airport runways in the South East.

While the RSPB demands that the Government commits itself to a sustainable aviation policy, The Woodland Trust has pledged that opposition will not be simply bulldozed away.

The RSPB is opposing calls for a new airport to be built on internationally important wetlands at Cliffe in north Kent.

It warns that development there would be an unprecedented act of environmental vandalism.

Graham Wynne, RSPB chief executive, said:"A wildlife refuge of internationally recognised importance is threatened by these development plans. An airport here would be a disaster for birds and make a laughing stock of wildlife protection mechanisms.

"It's a dangerous place even to think of putting an airport. And it will destroy one major RSPB nature reserve and devastate several others which members' subscriptions have helped to buy and maintain."

He called on supporters to help the RSPB stop "this madness" before it is too late.

In the RSPB's formal response to the Department for Transport's consultation on the future of air travel it outlined how future demand for air travel in south east England could be met without building new runways - and without increasing air fares.

Aviation is now the world's fastest growing source of greenhouse gas emissions, says the Society, and creates serious noise and air pollution problems.

Continued airport expansion would pose a major threat to the UK's countryside and wildlife.

Meanwhile, The Woodland Trust has been intensifying its own publicity campaign to halt further development at Gatwick Airport.

Anti-runway protesters are preparing to symbolically hold a bulldozer at bay at the entrance to an "irreplaceable" ancient wood near the airport.

The bulldozer would represent the destruction of the natural and residential environments that would be caused by new runways, explained the Trust.

Speeches at the event will also be made by local MP Sir Paul Beresford, representatives from the Trust itself, and from the Gatwick Area Conservation Campaign.

"This is the last chance for a major public protest against the proposed expansion of Gatwick Airport before the close of the Government's airport consultation process,"said a spokesman.

"A Trust-owned ancient wood would be destroyed if one of the proposed runways is built. The ancient village of Charlwood would also be devastated.

"GACC and the Trust are calling for everyone who cares to join in."

A BIRD-BRAINED pigeon caused a flap in Shropshire after building its nest in a car wash machine - getting soaked dozens of times a day.

But staff at Sutton Farm Service Station in Shrewsbury think the bird is not as daft as it seems - it comes and goes when it likes and the spray has kept it cool during recent soaring temperatures.

A DEER SHOT near the boundary of the League Against Cruel Sport's Baronsdown sanctuary has tested positive for TB, claims the Countryside Alliance.

The discovery has prompted the Alliance to renew its calls for a full scale review of the welfare status of deer at the Exmoor site.

The Alliance claims Government vets carried out post mortems on two deer on behalf of the British Deer Society and found both to be "in very poor bodily condition with a total absence of fat."

One was confirmed as carrying TB while the other was undergoing further tests.

Although the League has strongly denied deer at the site are suffering, Simon Hart, director of the Campaign for Hunting, said:"The evidence that LACS management policies are seriously compromising the welfare of the deer at Baronsdown is growing by the week.

"First, we had reports from LACS' own stalker reporting that he found over 100 deer dead or dying in a 12 month period, then the State Veterinary Service found a deer with a foot missing on Baronsdown and advised LACS to consult a specialist in deer management and feeding.

"Now we have evidence that Baronsdown deer are infected with TB and in appalling condition. We have seen these deer suffering for long enough - LACS must immediately make available the results of post mortems, blood tests and faecal tests on the deer.

"If they are unable to counter the clear accusations of mismanagement, DEFRA must act to enforce the implementation of a sustainable wildlife management plan in conjunction with the other joint keepers of the deer. In the interests of other animals, neighbouring farmers and the deer themselves, this situation cannot continue."

HORSES FOR COURSES goes the saying and once again horse power *reined* supreme over man when it came to a gruelling country trek.

The 'Man Versus Horse' race at Llanwrtyd Wells, mid-Wales, saw 300 runners aiming to complete the 22-mile course before 30 horses and riders.

Many may wonder why the runners bother as not once in the race's 24-year history has a man managed to outrun all the horses - and this year was no exception.

Superfit Mark Croasland was the first runner home in a time of two hours and 19 minutes.

But that was still 17 minutes behind Robyn Petrie-Ritchie and her mount Bruimgig Shemil.

However, Mark is not giving up yet - two years ago he finished just a tantalising minute behind the lead horse and a win that would have netted him £20,000.

BADGER FANS HAVE been buoyed up by recent developments which have boosted their favourite mammal.

Steve Jackson, chairman of the National Federation of Badger Groups, told members:"The last few months have seen some important - and very welcome - developments in DEFRA's approach to bovine tuberculosis in Britain.

"After years of campaigning by the NFBG, the Department is now seriously considering many of the cattle-focused control measures that we have proposed.

"DEFRA's Parliamentary watchdog, the Environment, Food and Rural Affairs Select Committee, has also backed many of the NFBG's recommendations in its report on bovine TB.

"Killing of badgers outside the areas covered by the culling trial has been firmly ruled out both by DEFRA and the EFRA Committee. The culling trial itself is also under review."

Meanwhile, a satisfactory solution to problems caused by the headline hitting badgers of Saltdean, East Sussex, now looks certain to go ahead as a result of funding from DEFRA, added Mr Jackson.

The solution, which involves relocating the badgers to artificial setts, had been put forward in a report by Professor Stephen Harris, working on behalf of the NFBG.

A RARE OSPREY chick has died after hatching out in the Lake District, it has been revealed.

The tiny bird is thought to have succumbed to recent wet weather.

However, observers of the nest site at Bassenth - waite Lake, near Cockermouth, believe a second chick is still alive.

Members of the Lake District Osprey Project were dismayed by the first chick's death, especially as they hoped two young ospreys might fledge at the spot for the second year running.

GREY SQUIRRELS COULD have their destructive tendencies curbed thanks to new advice for woodland owners and managers.

Damage limitation strategies and population control methods have been made available on the Forestry Commission's website.

Early summer is when the non-native squirrel's most destructive habit of stripping bark comes to the fore, says the Commission, so now is the time for action to control numbers and prevent damage occurring.

Researcher Brenda Mayle of Forest Research, the Forestry Commission's scientific agency, said up to five per cent of trees under attack by grey squirrels would die, with many more losing value and becoming susceptible to disease.

"As well as displacing Britain's native red squirrels, grey squirrels frequently cause damage to woodlands by stripping bark from the main stems and branches of trees," she said.

"This not only reduces the value of broadleaved and conifer trees planted for timber but also impacts on woodland conservation, biodiversity and sustainability.

"In time, susceptible species such as beech and oak may be lost from the mature woodland canopy, with loss of associated fungi, invertebrates and their predators. Grey squirrels may also compete with other woodland animals such as the dormouse and the red squirrel for food, and predate wild birds."

320

CUMBRIAN SALMON WILL benefit from fresh rules introduced by the Environment Agency.

New byelaws mean netting on the Leven Estuary is now banned during June, with the netting season reduced to July and August only.

Also, a 'catch and release' byelaw means rod-caught salmon in the Leven and Crake catchment, upstream of the Leven viaduct near Ulverston, must be returned to the water unharmed.

The Leven and Crake catchment includes waters inland of the Leven viaduct, including the Rivers Leven and Crake, Coniston Water, Windermere, Esthwaite Water, Rydal Water, Grasmere, Elterwater, and any associated tributaries.

The byelaws will be in force for at least the next 10 years, after which they will be reviewed.

In the meantime, the Agency will monitor fish stocks and carry out various habitat improvements, working closely with anglers and landowners.

Spokesman Jeremy Westgarth said:"We are very concerned about the salmon stocks in that catchment. These new legal measures are vital to the conservation of these stocks. All anglers need to be aware of the changes and make sure they comply with the law.

"By using 'catch and release', anglers can continue to enjoy their sport and fish can safely continue to their spawning grounds. Anglers can support us by doing all they can to help increase the survival of healthy fish."

GRASS SNAKES MAY be an occasional sight on some allotments but in South Yorkshire allotment holders have been warned to keep their eyes peeled for something bigger - an 11ft Burmese python.

The huge, powerful snake escaped from a house in Sheffield and appears to have made a break for freedom among local residents' cabbages and carrots. Although many locals have laughed off the danger, the python's owner Paul Tomlinson, 34, warns that his hungry pet may pose a genuine threat to pets and small children.

POPPIES ARE SURGING back to prominence in a nationwide blaze of colour, according to English Nature.

More farmers are leaving fields unsown to receive EU grants and thereby providing ideal conditions for the welcome return of poppies.

As a result, the stunning sight of a field of poppies in full bloom is becoming more common.

Dr Jill Sutcliffe, botanical manager for English Nature, revealed that during the First World War poppies were as common in England as they were later to become in Flanders. Golden corn marigolds and common blue cornflowers might also be seen more often in future, she added.

FURIOUS POLITICAL DEBATE on hunting leaves most of the country cold, it has been claimed.

An NOP poll commissioned by the Countryside Alliance shows that just two per cent of people believe hunting should be a political priority.

The research has been published as the Hunting Bill awaits its report and third reading in the House of Commons.

Respondents who were asked which issues they considered most important for the Government to tackle put the NHS top of their list - at 35 per cent - while sorting out the asylum seeker crisis came next at 31 per cent.

Education got 17 per cent of the vote, anti-social behaviour another 14 per cent, and the hunting with dogs issue - which has had many Labour MPs in a lather - just two per cent.

Simon Hart, director of the Campaign for Hunting, said:"Hunting is not a priority but out of touch dissident MPs remain obsessed by it. Because of them, Parliament continues to waste time and resources on a discredited Bill which could be spent on more important issues.

"Politicians keep asking how they can re-engage with the electorate, encourage people to participate in political debate and use their votes. They could start by dropping this sort of discrimination against a decent, responsible minority and instead concentrate on something that voters are actually interested in."

Earlier, the Hunting Bill was dragged into further controversy following revelations that the Government had been in secret negotiation with the RSPCA and had given a number of earlier undertakings to animal welfare groups.

The details emerged in a leaked letter from Rural Affairs Minister Alun Michael to Deputy Prime Minister John Prescott.

Mr Hart said:"Alun Michael is publicly trying to claim that his Bill is reasonable while privately admitting that to try and rescue what's left of it he has capitulated to every demand of the anti-hunt lobby. This letter reveals that he is engaged in an act of collusion with animal rights groups and that the Government's Hunting Bill is in deep trouble."

MORE FARMERS ARE boosting wildlife by taking part in a project to care for the countryside.

An excellent take-up of the Government's pilot 'green farming scheme' shows farmers' growing commitment to protecting the environment, claims the NFU.

More than 250 farmers have so far applied to join the new Entry Level Scheme which supports farmers in their efforts to look after the landscape.

The NFU helped design the scheme and has been instrumental in encouraging farmers to sign up to it in the four areas where it is on offer - Durham, Lincolnshire, Berkshire and Devon.

However, the project will be rolled out across the whole of England in 2005.

NFU spokesman John Seymour said:"The high level of uptake of the pilot scheme is excellent news.

"It is important that we test the pilot on many different types of farms to ensure that the final scheme is designed to be attractive and accessible to as many farmers as possible."

The union backed the project as many farmers who already helped wildlife were frustrated at being unable to get support from other schemes.

GREYHOUND RACING IS now in the sights of vociferous anti-cruelty campaigners.

The popular sport has been attacked by the League Against Cruel Sports for allegedly causing unnecessary suffering.

"While banning hunting will continue to be the League's absolute priority, there are many other sports where animals suffer for the sake of human entertainment," said a spokesman.

"One of the worst of these is greyhound racing. It is not inherently cruel but the current lack of regulation causes greyhounds to suffer before, during and after their racing careers.

"Such suffering is unnecessary. It is cruel. And it is preventable. Not least because this is a £1.6billion industry. The League seeks changes to the forthcoming Animal Welfare Bill to protect greyhounds. We want to force the industry to give a penny in the pound from gambling turnover directly to greyhound welfare."

DEVON'S GLORIOUS countryside is facing disaster from plans for two sprawling tracts of new urban development, it has been claimed.

Proposals for the new settlements are now being challenged by the Council for the Protection of Rural England at a public inquiry.

The proposals could mean 3,500 new dwellings at Sherford, South Hams, and 2,900 houses - as well as business development - at Broadclyst, near Exeter.

If approved, the new settlements would result in the needless destruction of Devon countryside by urban sprawl, says the CPRE.

THE WOODLAND TRUST has enlisted the moral authority of former hostage Terry Waite in its fight against Essex airport expansion.

"If proposals to expand Stansted Airport are accepted, countryside that has inspired poets, painters and visitors for centuries will be destroyed," warned a Trust spokesman.

Mr Waite had agreed to lead campaigners at a Stop Stansted Expansion event on Sunday, June 29, he added.

THOUSANDS OF WILD geese are the spur to urgent work to upgrade a birdwatching tower owned by the Wildfowl and Wetlands Trust.

The race is on to complete refurbishment and redesign of Saltcot Tower at WWT Caerlaverock in Scotland before the geese return this winter.

"The merses - traditionally managed salt marshes - are the most important part of the reserve at Caerlaverock, itself the largest area under WWT's management and protection," said a spokesman.

"This rare habitat provides some of the most exciting birdwatching, especially on wild winter days when the sea rushes over the merses and the air is full of wheeling flocks of wildfowl and waders.

"Only one of the hides overlooks the merses. Saltcot Tower was built over 40 years ago and it has aged, of course, during that time."

WOMEN ARE ON the march to save foxhunting after the Countryside Alliance switched tactics to show its softer side.

With the Hunting Bill now returning to the Commons for its report and third reading stage, women supporters of the sport have come to the fore.

In a surprising move, NHS nurse Sarah Bell, from Warwickshire, has been launched as the new face of the pro-hunting lobby.

Miss Bell is featured on an Alliance poster in opposing pictures - one dressed in full hunting uniform and the other in her nurse's outfit.

The photographs are accompanied by the questions 'Now they hate her?' - as a huntswoman, 'Now they don't?' - as a nurse.

Miss Bell, who is a children's nurse, is said to have ridden to hounds since she was 12 and now rides with the Worcestershire hunt.

She said:"I just see the other side of what I feel should be Government priorities - the NHS, education and so on. I cannot understand why the Government should spend so much time on hunting when there are so many more important areas.

"Some think we (hunters) are all Lord of the Manor but we are not. We are just a group of people in the countryside, managing the number of foxes. I am a nurse at the end of the day. We are just a normal group of people."

Meanwhile, a two-day Women's Vigil in Parliament Square was organised by the Families 4 Hunting group to coincide with debate on the Bill.

A spokesman said:"It is a women's vigil to emphasise the fact that there is no contradiction between being a caring wife and mother and supporting hunting with dogs."

MORE THAN 30,000 acres of new woodlands were planted in Britain last year to bring forest cover to its highest level in over 300 years, says the Forestry Commission.

The estimated woodland area of Great Britain is now 2.7 million hectares - or 11.9 per cent of the country's entire surface - with 1.9 million hectares owned by private woodland owners and non-Commission public sector bodies.

Most recent planting is of broadleaf species - almost 9,000 hectares, compared to 3,000 hectares of coniferous species. Almost 14,000 hectares of land was restocked after being felled all over the country.

A BAKERY POLLUTED a local river with savoury egg glaze which turned the water white and threatened wildlife, a court heard.

The glaze affected three kilometres of the Ouse Burn near Newcastle, Gosforth magistrates were told.

The bakery admitted knowingly causing polluting matter to enter the river on or about April 23 last year and was fined £4,000 and ordered to pay £2,513 costs.

Alerted by the public when the river turned white, Environment Agency officers worked with Northumbrian Water to trace the pollution back to the bakery, which claimed there had been a "small" spill of egg glaze.

However, Agency officers thought a small spill was unlikely to have such an effect on the river and analysis showed a biological oxygen reduction worse than that caused by raw sewage.

WASPS: luckless fly falls foul of a striped killer

WASPS are best known for their painful stings but if you ever see one dismember a fly you quickly realise their jaws are equally formidable.

I watched closely as this became the fate of an irritating bluebottle which had buzzed around the house for hours.

I had finally cornered this pest myself and, after a few mad flicks with a tea towel, managed to stun it and render it flightless.

For some reason I did not kill it outright while it was at my mercy. Instead, I picked it up and lobbed it out onto the patio where it began tottering around on the sun-baked flagstones.

By sheer chance, I glanced out at my former tormentor some minutes later and saw the 'coup de grâce' had actually been delivered by a wasp.

Not only that, but the wasp was now slicing the bluebottle into pieces using its mighty mandibles.

For the next few minutes I observed the wasp flying away with carefully packaged pieces of bluebottle meat and then returning.

It repeated the process until the whole corpse was gone.

It was not hard to imagine where the bluebottle ended up.

Wasps feed their larvae on insects so the grounded bluebottle's fate was sealed as soon as it attracted the attention of its executioner.

Our common and German wasps are so alike as to be almost one species. Both are widespread, about 18 millimetres long, with the distinctive black and yellow markings of typical wasps.

Both build grey, papery nests for their young and both sting. (I've written here before about being badly stung by wasps as a child after my brother wilfully enraged a nest).

Despite their similarities, there is a quick way to tell which wasp is which.

If you can get close enough to see, the German wasp's face carries three distinct black dots while the common wasp's sports a kind of anchor shape.

Hornets, of course, are also wasps but are more easily identified.

They are much bigger than either of the above pair at 30 millimetres in length, with distinctive tawny brown and dull yellow colouring.

Wasps have a reputation for being among the most powerful species in the insect world.

This was even alluded to in 18th Century poet Jonathan Swift's attack on legal injustice:*"Laws are like cobwebs, which may catch small flies, but let wasps and hornets break through."*

I much prefer to leave nature alone when I can.

However, when our two young children were stung recently, I knew action was needed regarding a growing wasps' nest in our front garden.

A neighbour kindly lent me an anti-wasp spray and this was duly used to douse the nest at night.

However, torrential rain seemed to wash the poisonous white dust away and many wasps survived.

It was only after the same neighbour emptied the entire spray into the nest and blocked off the exit that these tough insects finally succumbed.

Nervous bluebottles in the garden must have cheered.

NATIONAL MAMMAL WEEK is launched soon with the aim of helping humans get closer to their 'warm blooded relatives'.

Event organisers hope to raise awareness of all British mammals, many of which - the red squirrel, dormouse and water vole in particular - face extinction.

"The Mammal Society is keen to encourage people to make records of their local mammals so that it can build accurate distribution maps of mammals in Britain and monitor their status," explained a spokesman."Mammals are seriously under recorded. In fact, they account for only 0.5 per cent of all biological records in the UK.

"Whereas creatures like butterflies and birds are active by day, mammals are nocturnal and elusive. Sadly, this means people are far less familiar with many British mammals and far fewer records are collected.

"We cannot protect vulnerable species effectively if we don't even know where they occur or whether their status is changing.

"Mammal records, of common as well as rare species, could make an important contribution. An example of where long-term mammal recording can directly aid mammal conservation involves the water vole.

"Until recently the water vole was relatively common. However, the species underwent a massive population crash during the 1980s and 1990s before the decline in numbers was fully realised.

"Historical records, gathered over 60 years, were used to establish decline rate."

KINGFISHERS AND SKYLARKS have helped farmer Charles Bransden pick up a prestigious new wildlife award.

The birds are among a host of species which have made their homes on Mr Bransden's farm, a restored gravel pit producing vegetables and other crops.

The farmer was named as the first recipient of English Nature's Farming for Wildlife Award when it was launched at the Royal Show as part of the NFU's Farming Excellence Awards.

Open to all NFU members, the award recognises achievements in nature conservation.

A RARE FLY is the quarry of a former banker being backed by the Forestry Commission to learn more about it.

Roy Crossley has been given funding to shadow the elusive insect known as 'the colonel' because its distinctive markings look like an army uniform.

Although once believed extinct in England, Mr Crossley's research first located the fly during the 1980s in Dalby forest on the North York moors. Discovery of the creature is one of the reasons the wood has now been given special protection from development.

THE OUTRAGE FELT by hunt groups at Labour's shock move towards a total hunting ban shows no sign of abating with many hunters privately pledging to break any new law.

With thousands of full and part-time jobs connected to hunting reportedly at risk - as well as the lives of thousands of hounds and horses - the issue appears to rest on whether the Government will force through its anti-hunt Bill using the Parliament Act if, as expected, it is rejected by the House of Lords.

However, a new ICM poll commissioned by the Countryside Alliance found that the majority of those asked felt the Government should not make use of the Parliament Act in such a controversial way.

During a snap survey of over 1,000 voters, 52 per cent thought the views of the House of Lords should definitely be taken into account.

Simon Hart, director of the Campaign for Hunting, said:"The message of this poll could not be clearer. The Government must not facilitate the use of the Parliament Act on the Hunting Bill.

"The Commons has voted to ban hunting on the basis of prejudice and discrimination. We remain confident that the Lords will amend the Bill to reflect principle and evidence, acting in the best interests of animal welfare and rural communities. Their voices shouldn't be ignored."

Almost 18,000 hounds may have to be destroyed if a ban on hunting comes into effect, hunt supporters fear.

The trade in horses, which is often dependent on the supply of animals for hunting, would also dwindle with many animals put down to save costs.

Hunt groups have attacked those MPs who presented themselves as caring about animals while knowing their decision on foxhunting could mean death for so many dogs and horses.

The idea that hounds in particular could be domesticated as family pets has been scorned by pro-hunters who say the animals are bred to be hardy and operate in a pack.

Meanwhile, the League Against Cruel Sports has led celebrations by anti-hunt groups of the move towards a total ban.

Chairman of the League, John Cooper, said:"The Government tried to frustrate the will of Parliament and MPs in the run up to this vote by invoking procedural tactics and by making veiled threats to backbenchers, suggesting it was 'take it or leave it' with the Government's muddled compromise on hunting.

"In the end, MPs proved they were not willing to be thwarted in their desire to vote for a total ban. As a result, the Government was forced to withdraw its compromise and return the Bill to the standing committee.

"The Government is now committed to removing the licensed hunting provisions from the Bill and to quickly return a 'total hunt ban' Bill to the House for a third reading to ensure it reaches the House of Lords in time for the Parliament Act to apply in 2004, if necessary."

HUNDREDS OF BROWN trout and other fish were killed in a pollution spill on the isle of Anglesey in North Wales.

A probe by Environment Agency Wales found over 400 dead trout on the Afon Lligwy, near Moelfre, following a tip-off.

THE BATTLE OVER hunting with dogs reached a noisy crescendo as legislation to ban it finally cleared the House of Commons while hunt supporters protested outside.

Hundreds of hounds - most reportedly facing death if the anti-hunt Bill becomes law - had been brought by campaigners to their 'Democracy Going to The Dogs' demo in Parliament Square.

One protester, Jane Bayley, of the Royal Artillery Hunt in Wiltshire, fumed:"The Government has no feeling for dogs or the countryside or people's way of life.

"We all have to conform to their views. They have got no idea of the depth of feeling in the countryside."

Already passed by a vote of 317 to 145, the Hunting Bill is now being sent on to the House of Lords where pro-hunting peers are expected to reject it.

During a late-night Commons debate, Rural Affairs Minister Alun Michael said he believed the Government had made a genuine effort to produce a workable piece of legislation.

He denied that police think the Bill would be unenforceable and asked Opposition Tories to encourage respect for the law.

However, Conservative MP James Gray labled creation of the Bill "the most dreary, despicable, unfair, illiberal and undemocratic parliamentary process" for a long time.

He said he believed it would just make criminals of thousands of decent, law-abiding members of the public.

TROUT RIVERS WERE given a boost by a range of experts explaining how to make them thrive.

River restoration techniques that improve habitat for trout and other wildlife were all demonstrated during the Wild Trout Trust's open day at Bourton-on-the-Water, Gloucestershire.

A variety of bank restoration skills and invertebrate monitoring techniques at the event were sponsored by English Nature.

The grand finale of the day involved the installation of a 'riffle' in the River Windrush.

David Fraser, English Nature's freshwater fisheries adviser, explained:"Many rivers have been dredged and straightened in the past making them less suitable for wild trout and other river wildlife.

"By putting the bends back, re-installing spawning gravels and keeping silt out of the rivers, these can again become diverse wildlife corridors.

"This is not only for wild populations of brown trout but also for species such as water voles and the white-clawed crayfish.

"These demonstrations showed how this can be achieved."

BASKING SHARKS ARE the subject of a UK-wide survey which has just been launched by The Wildlife Trusts.

It is hoped the study will help scientists uncover the secret life of the largest shark to be found in our waters.

"The survey, undertaken on a 39ft sailing yacht, will journey around the coast, including Devon, Cornwall, South Wales, North Wales, Ireland, and the Western Isles of Scotland," said a spokesman.

"The project aims to build and develop our knowledge and understanding of the basking shark in order to ensure its future safety by monitoring populations, identifying its favoured locations, examining behaviour and recording movement.

"Little is known about the basking shark's activities, which makes effective conservation very difficult. Without accurate population numbers and an awareness of their behaviour it is difficult to help this internationally endangered species and to ensure that it is safe from harm during its time in UK waters.

"Basking shark populations in the UK have been decimated in the past century by over-hunting, from which they have still not recovered.

"It is believed that basking shark numbers are now only a fraction of what they used to be. The creature's main attraction now lies in its highly valued, gigantic dorsal fin, which is a delicacy in the Far East.

"Whilst hunting is now banned, the basking shark is still at risk from hunting and a variety of other threats, including collisions with boats, entanglement in fishing nets and changes in sea temperature due to climate change."

Measuring up to 12 metres long, and weighing up to seven tonnes, an adult basking shark is bigger than a double-decker bus.

However, it feeds only on plankton, filtering the equivalent of two swimming pools of seawater through its gills per hour.

A SPARROW CHICK took its life in its hands when it leapt onto the back of a pet Harris hawk in a suburban garden.

But the hawk, named Maximus, just grabbed the wild, young interloper in its formidable beak and set it down unharmed - to the astonishment of the hawk's Buckinghamshire owner Roy Rossow.

Mr Rossow, who captured the drama on camera, said the befuddled chick tried to befriend the hawk five times in his High Wycombe garden and was lucky to survive.

BRITAIN'S BIRDS WILL benefit from the long-awaited agreement on Common Agriculture Policy reform reached in Luxembourg, says the RSPB.

The UK can now sever the link between farm production and payment enabling more money to be diverted into rural farming schemes that benefit birds and other wildlife.

The production-subsidy link, which led to the intensive and environmentally damaging management of land, was central to CAP, over which agriculture ministers have haggled for months.

Phil Rothwell, head of Countryside Policy at the RSPB, said:"This landmark agreement could help reverse the devastating declines in some of our most popular species of birds."

FLYING INSECTS MAY be becoming scarcer - and that is bad news for the birds which feed on them, says the RSPB.

The Society revealed its fears as it unveiled a controversial scheme to help it calculate insect numbers using a 'splat-ometer'.

RSPB researchers "hope to measure the abundance of flying insects with a clear piece of sticky plastic, a bit bigger than a postcard, which would fit to the front of a car or lorry," said a spokesman.

"These could then be peeled off - without damaging the car's paintwork - and sent to the RSPB for analysis.

"Having already raised a lot of interest, the idea is still being tested and checked with various authorities but the splat-ometers would be initially analysed to show the relative amounts of flying insects in different parts of the UK.

"If the splat-ometer gets the go ahead, it could give the RSPB huge amounts of information about the relative quantities of insects in different areas and help to build a picture of how this relates to birds.

"We have already started to receive requests for splat-ometers even though, for practical reasons, we can't yet start the trials. However, we will make sure that RSPB members and supporters get the opportunity to help when the project gets off the ground, which we hope will be in summer 2004.

"But have the birds we're working to protect already taken note of the 'splat' factor? According to an observation from a Mr Dennis Clements in the West Midlands, it's a distinct possibility. He said:'At Sandbach Services on the M6 we witnessed birds diving into lorry front grills and pecking away for a time, presumably eating dead insects. They then flew onto the mud flaps behind the front wheels. Maybe they have already recognised the number of insects being splattered there'."

MANURE-STUFFED ENVELOPES may soon be the weapon of choice among British country people enraged by New Labour meddling.

The idea comes from New Zealand where farmers are showing their anger at a so-called 'flatulence tax' on livestock by sending smelly letters to the Government.

The Countryside Alliance, which represents scores of UK hunting and farm groups, flagged up the idea by carrying a direct link to the story on its website.

However, anyone thinking of adapting the scheme for Britain needs to remember that here - as in New Zealand - it is an offence to send noxious material throught the post.

DELICATE DAMSELFLIES ARE back in Dorset for the first time in almost 30 years thanks to the efforts of conservationists.

One bright blue damselfly found on heathland has confirmed that the attractive insects are apparently recolonising the area.

Similar to dragonflies in shape and colour but smaller and less robust, damselflies have vanished from several areas in England and Wales where they were once common.

In a recent joint operation involving National Trust land, the Environment Agency and Dorset Wildlife Trust, a welcoming stream habitat was created to tempt them back into the county.

Now the National Trust's Purbeck Estate is believed to be the first place in the country to have lost its damselfly population then retrieved it through targeted human effort.

Emma Rothero, of the Environment Agency, commented:"It's amazing that we've seen almost instant results. On our very first visit to the finished site we spotted a male specimen on the water's edge. If others follow, it'll be a real success story that we hope we can replicate at other sites across the country."

Andrew Pollard, spokesman for Dorset Wildlife Trust, added:"We set up the partnership to promote joint projects like this and it shows that by working together we can turn around years of decline and help threatened species to survive."

MAGPIES MAY BE considered a pest by some but they now have a new champion in the unlikely form of a High Court judge.

Mr Justice Leveson asserted that magpies do have rights, although they are often blamed for decimating songbird populations by eating chicks and eggs.

At the London hearing, Mr Leveson quashed a decision by Shropshire magistrates to clear a local man who caged one magpie as a decoy so he could snare and kill other magpies.

The ruling has been applauded by the RSPCA which has pledged to prosecute anyone else who uses 'cruel' bird traps.

It comes after the controversial trial of Telford resident Norman Shinton, 58, who was cleared of causing unnecessary suffering by district judge Mr Philip Browning at Telford Magistrates Court last year.

However, the London case was a legal test and Mr Shinton will not now be sentenced.

A NOISY COCKEREL has landed its owners in court facing legal fees of over £3,000.

Parsley the cockerel caused a flap with its early morning crowing at a farm in Botany Bay, a small village in North London.

Its owners, a couple who keep a variety of animals at the farm including five cockerels, were taken to court by a local council following complaints.

At Enfield Magistrates Court, the pair received a 12-month conditional discharge, were bound over to keep the peace, and ordered to pay costs of £100 each for failing to comply with a noise abatement notice.

They will also have to pay their own legal fees, estimated at about £3,500.

As a result of the case, Parsley will now be locked up each day and let out when his crowing is less likely to cause offence.

SEA TROUT WERE saved by prompt action when pollution threatened an area where they gather in numbers.

The fast reaction of Environment Agency officers is being praised for saving the trout in an estuary of the River Beaulieu, Hampshire.

The team had been warned by Southern Water that a main sewer had failed at Lyndurst and that sewage had entered the river.

Officers from the Agency raced to the site to investigate the incident and its impact on the river.

Environment officer John Elliott said:"The team worked very hard into the early hours of the morning, monitoring the river and ensuring that Southern Water had carried out the necessary work to prevent further sewage escaping.

"Undoubtedly, the actions of the team prevented further damage, saved the greater majority of sea trout in the estuary and helped bring the river back to its normal state."

TAIL DOCKING FOR dogs is another bone of contention among country groups as Labour moves to ban it.

"The Government is proposing to introduce an Animal Welfare Bill which would prohibit the docking of dogs' tails," explained a spokesman for the Countryside Alliance.

"At present, docking is legal provided that it is carried out by a veterinary surgeon. It is particularly important in working breeds such as spaniels, hunt-point-retrieve breeds and terriers, which are expected to hunt through heavy cover and are at risk of tail damage.

"The Council of Docked Breeds campaigns to retain the docking option and is currently running an online petition which will be sent to DEFRA."

Anyone who supports tail docking can now visit the campaign's website and register their protest.

ABOUT ONE MILLION house sparrows were individually recorded during the UK's first national 'Sparrowatch' survey, reveals the RSPB.

"An incredible quarter of a million people actually looked for sparrows from May 1 to May 8," said a spokesman."This colossal effort has collected very useful information, allowing us to map the distribution and abundance of house sparrows in gardens. Despite being a familiar sight around our homes, their presence has been largely taken for granted.

"Although long-running countryside surveys have shown a steady decrease in their numbers (down 62 per cent over the last 25 years), it was not until the early 1990s that we noticed that their numbers in our towns and cities were also falling dramatically.

"People recorded around a million house sparrows. We also asked people to send in their results even if they did not see house sparrows, as this is equally valuable information. We received around 15,000 forms where people did not record any sparrows at all.

"We now have a huge amount of information that we are continuing to analyse."

FARMLAND BIRDS ARE still suffering the consequences of the switch from traditional stubble fields by farmers, say researchers.

Today, winter sowing of cereal crops and the consequent lack of normal stubble fields are highlighted as a major cause of farmland bird declines.

Research by the British Trust for Ornithology, involving 1,000 volunteers, shows that most stubble fields now support NO birds at all.

Between them, the volunteers spent over 500,000 hours counting farmland birds to see which habitats were most important.

Their observations showed just how hard it was at present for birds like the skylark, yellowhammer and linnet to find food in winter.

BTO spokesman Simon Gillings, organiser of the Winter Farmland Bird Survey, said:"This was a really depressing survey for many of our volunteers, with so few birds to see.

"Some were fortunate to find game cover crops or other habitat specially provided by farmers to support birds like tree sparrows but in most areas newly-sown crops, sterile stubble fields and improved grassland provided little in the way of food for birds."

The results of the survey, funded by the Joint Nature Conservation Committee, provide the first available figures on the amount of stubble field available for birds to feed in during the winter.

One key finding showed that by managing their harvesting and weed-spraying regimes - so that there is seed available for birds to eat in winter - some farmers are creating vital feeding stations for skylarks, finches and buntings.

Other findings were that: stubble is only useful if there are weed seeds and spilt grain upon which birds can feed; traditional cereal stubble fields are good because they provide a resource throughout the winter; harvested oil-seed rape fields are sought out by birds in the late autumn while harvested sugar-beet fields are also good for short periods; and barley stubble fields are better than wheat stubble fields.

THE SHY CORNCRAKE has been given a boost by conservationists trying to return it to England.

The first brood of chicks, bred in captivity at Whipsnade Zoo, is almost ready for release in a quiet English field.

In recent years, the birds - whose males are known for their distinctive croaking calls - have been restricted to parts of Scotland because of intensive farming methods south of the border.

Now the Corncrake Project aims to re-establish the bird, which migrates to Africa each winter, as a species nesting regularly in England.

RSPB spokesman Grahame Madge explained:"About 150 years ago, you'd have found corncrakes in just about every parish with suitable habitat across the British Isles. They'd certainly have been in every county.

"They like to live and breed in thick grassland vegetation.

"When farmers cut that just once a year, they left time for the corncrakes to rear a brood. But with up to three cuts a year nowadays for silage, the birds don't have a chance.

"So you mainly find them in places like Orkney and the Hebrides where crofting, which is less intensive than most farming methods, means the grass is there long enough for them to breed."

BLOOD-SUCKING TICKS are currently the subject of an intensive study by the Game Conservancy Trust.

"Ticks are small, spider-like beasties that gorge themselves on blood and they're here in their millions," said a spokesman."Despite their diminutive size, this is one species of wildlife you don't want to meet when out enjoying the countryside this summer.

"The tick, or castor bean tick, lives off the blood of mammals and birds and can kill either by transmitting a variety of diseases or by blood loss and 'tick worry' caused by their sheer numbers upon one host.

"At this time of year, ticks are 'rising', climbing up vegetation and waiting for a mammalian host to brush past before grasping onto it and feeding.

"A tick needs to feed thrice in its life cycle but this cycle can span as much as seven years with the tick remaining safe in a damp layer of dead leaves and moss that occurs under vegetation until conditions are right for it to 'rise' again.

"The Trust is currently seeking ways of controlling tick numbers and reducing the burden of ticks on host species which live in upland areas of Scotland.

"Heading our research is Dr Alison Taylor, responsible for the large amount of monitoring needed to develop ways of identifying and implementing safe and effective methods of reducing tick numbers."

Humans were just as much at risk as animals, warned the Trust.

"Removing these parasites, once they've buried their heads into your skin, can be tricky and if they are not removed entirely they may cause infection at the source of the bite."

A SNAKE WHICH slithered out of countryside to interrupt a game of golf in Lancashire was identified as a boa constrictor.

The 4ft snake startled the golfers half-way through their match at Baxenden and District Golf Club, near Accrington.

RSPCA investigators who took the snake away believe it had been abandoned and would have died if recent weather had not been so hot.

A YOUNG SWAN suffered an agonising end when fishing line sliced through its beak and jaw like cheese wire.

The distressed bird was rescued from a lake in Shropshire by the RSPCA and taken to a wildlife hospital for removal of the tangled line.

However, only on close inspection was the full horror of the wound discovered and the swan was put down. Anglers in the county have now been urged to take more care with discarded tackle.

THE DISCOVERY OF two rare bumblebees on a South Warwickshire farm shows just how well conservation work can succeed, say scientists.

Ecologists stumbled on the bumblebees in wildflower field margins specially planted under DEFRA's Countryside Stewardship Scheme.

Bumblebees need flower-rich landscapes to flourish and today only six of the UK's 19 native species are easily found in lowland Britain, with five listed as 'priority species' on the UK Biodiversity Action Plan.

The Countryside Stewardship Scheme offers payments to farmers and land managers to improve the natural beauty and diversity of the countryside.

At Ditchford Farm, near Shipston-on-Stour in Warwickshire, wide margins were planted around fields with a variety of grass and wildflowers providing a mix of nectar sources beneficial to bees and other wildlife.

The large garden bumblebee, one of the two bees found there, is one of the biggest bees in Britain and boasts queen bees more than an inch long.

Once common across lowland Britain, the species has declined by 95 per cent in the last 100 years, mainly because the deep flowered plants they prefer, such as comfrey and trefoils, have become increasingly scarce.

The other bee discovered, the all-black bombus harrisellus, is an even rarer species that has suffered even worse declines.

Steve Falk, senior keeper of natural history at Warwickshire Museum, said:"It has been the most delightful discovery to see these bees back in Warwickshire, and I really hope we can secure their long-term future here."

Sam Somers, of DEFRA's Rural Development Service, added:"Bumblebees are a very good indicator of a healthy environment. Being larger and heavier than other types of bee they need to feed more so their presence is tied in to a readily available supply of food.

"This also means they can stay in flight for longer and cover greater distances, which makes them excellent pollinators of crops and a real boon to farmers.

"Research carried out for DEFRA by the Centre for Ecology and Hydrology has identified the particular plant species bumble bees prefer, so we can tailor options to suit those preferences and support bees. It's tremendously encouraging to get evidence of this sort that the Countryside Stewardship Scheme is making a difference."

RURAL CRIME HAS shot up under Labour despite its electoral pledge to be tough on crime, it has been revealed.

According to figures released by the Home Office, burglaries, robberies and assaults have rocketed by more than 25 per cent in many rural parts of England and Wales.

Violent crime in North Yorkshire is said to have risen by 30 per cent, burglaries in Northamptonshire by 27 per cent, and car crime in Devon and Cornwall by 10 per cent.

Police believe the countryside is now feeling the effects of a crime crackdown in urban areas, with crooks forced to try their luck elsewhere.

But that will bring little comfort to vulnerable residents in rural communities where police are already often criticised for doing too little too late.

BIRDS OF PREY are still being persecuted by landowners determined to protect narrow commercial interests at all costs, it has been revealed.

The RSPB's 'Birdcrime 2002' report shows that more than half of almost 600 incidents involving wild birds reported across the UK were crimes against birds of prey.

Graham Elliott, head of the RSPB's investigations unit, said:"Birds of prey such as the red kite and peregrine falcon are among the best-loved birds in Britain but the persecution of these protected species ranks as some of the most serious of wildlife crimes.

"These crimes belong more to the late Victorian era than today's supposedly more enlightened times."

The report also revealed that there were 102 reported incidents involving the illegal use of poison which resulted in the deaths of at least 32 birds of prey.

Last year, over 30 people were prosecuted for crimes against birds, six of whom received jail sentences.

BUZZARDS HAVE BEEN bringing terror to walkers in a quiet part of Worcestershire.

Ramblers there are being urged to avoid an area near Kerswell Green after several were attacked by two parent birds thought to be protecting their young.

Police and the local council have even become involved in an operation to safeguard the public.

The worst attack involved Dick Bridges, an RAF veteran, who was whacked by the two adult buzzards together, leaving him with blood pouring from three slashes to his head.

It is hoped the over-zealous parents will vacate the area as soon as their young mature.

FORESTRY BRINGS SOCIAL and environmental benefits worth over £1billion a year to people in Britain, according to a report from the Forestry Commission.

The study, carried out by a team of economists led by Newcastle University, is the first to provide a comprehensive picture of the economic benefits provided by forestry in this country.

The research found recreation and biodiversity were the most highly valued benefits of woods.

The average value of recreational visits to woodlands in the study was calculated at £1.66 per visit.

Forestry Minister Ben Bradshaw said:"Well managed forests are a vital resource in providing wide-ranging benefits.

"The findings of this study confirm that society places a huge value on these benefits."

Professor Ken Willis, who led the research team, added:"The study examined a wide range of services and benefits provided by forests and woodland, including wildlife, recreation, landscape, carbon sequestration and air quality.

"This is the first time that this broad range of benefits has been analysed in one study and the results have given us a clearer picture of the full economic value of forestry."

FOXHUNTERS STILL believe they can save their sport despite the determination of Labour MPs to ban it.

In a morale-boosting note to members, Countryside Alliance leader John Jackson explained:"I have said many times that the fight to save hunting is winnable, and it is.

"From now until the next General Election the vigorous and varied campaigning of the Alliance, in which we will all be involved, will underpin our attack.

"We will seek to persuade the House of Lords that the Hunting Bill should be based on regulation and a registrar whose remit will cover all forms of hunting and coursing with dogs and whose decisions will reflect evidence and proper definitions of utility and least suffering.

"In anticipation of the Labour Party's backbenchers continuing to reject this approach for reasons which are 'totemic' to them, we will, at a time of our choosing and armed with the advice of leading counsel, mount a challenge in the courts under the Human Rights Act.

"Totemic is the word used by Tony Banks. What does it mean? Visualise savages dancing mindlessly round their tribal totem pole inscribed with the words 'ban hunting' while they roast alive captives they have already scalped. That is what it means - we will not let it happen."

Use of the Parliament Act will also be challenged in court and the wildlife benefits of hunting promoted.

HOW TO QUICKLY tell a moving water vole from a brown rat is one of the topics in an updated book.

The new version of 'How to Find and Identify Mammals' is the latest publication from The Mammal Society.

Sections covered include identification from sighting - especially of similar looking species such as brown rats and water voles or grey squirrels and edible dormice.

Identification from signs such as droppings, footprints, and burrows is also included as well as the best time of year to find and survey different mammals.

The book is already used as a teaching aid on the Society's training courses but is also said to provide an invaluable guide for anyone interested in mammals.

How to Find and Identify Mammals costs £7.50 and is available from the Society.

SPARROW CHICKS MAY be dying in their thousands before ever leaving the nest, new research has found.

The national slump in the UK's formerly huge population of sparrows has prompted several studies.

But Kate Vincent, 25, a PhD student from Leicester's De Montfort University, believes her own lengthy research into sparrow breeding may shed some light.

After studying more than 600 nestboxes across Leicestershire, she found that second or third brood chicks in urban areas often died before leaving the nest.

If replicated on a national scale, this loss would be catastrophic and might explain why sparrows are vanishing at an alarming rate.

Disease and lack of available insects as the year progresses are two reasons why sparrow chicks born later in the year may be especially vulnerable, Ms Vincent says.

FEARS THAT BIRDS could suffer worse declines through genetically-modified crops have been underlined by new research.

Independent scientists have endorsed concerns that GM crops could accelerate the population slump of some of our most popular songbirds.

The report by the GM Science Review Panel backs warnings from the RSPB that the cultivation of GM crops, and particularly their management via weed killers, will deprive farmland birds of essential food.

Powerful weed killers used with some GM crops kill non-crop plants before they produce seeds on which many birds depend during winter, warns the Society.

They also kill foliage that attracts insects - and insects are the main food source for most nestling birds in spring and summer.

The report's researchers say in their conclusions:"We do not yet have sufficient evidence to predict what the long-term impact would be on weed populations and the wildlife that depends on them for food.

"Above all other concerns, this poses perhaps the most serious potential harm arising from these particular crops."

Dr Mark Avery, director of conservation at the RSPB and a member of the panel, said:"The RSPB has been warning for five years that the commercial release of GM crops could make a bad situation for farmland wildlife even worse.

"This report shows that eminent scientists, as well as environmental organisations, fear GM cultivation will adversely affect wildlife."

Birds at risk include the skylark, yellowhammer, tree sparrow and corn bunting, whose numbers have declined by up to 95 per cent in the past 25 years.

The RSPB says that the Government must await the results of trials on four GM crops - maize, oilseed rape, sugar beet and fodder beet - before deciding whether to allow them to be grown commercially.

A GIANT LOBSTER has died after finding the celebrity life too stressful.

Lucky the lobster shot to local fame after being caught off the Gower Peninsula coastline in Wales.

He was handed to a Welsh aquarium instead of a restaurant.

But the crustacean, two feet long and thought to be 40 years old, was found dead the next day in his new tank at the Silent Night Aquarium in Tenby.

Stress of being in the spotlight was blamed for his untimely demise.

BRITAIN'S COASTLINE NOW supports an estimated 2.1 million wintering wading birds - hundreds of thousands more than previously thought.

Better methods of calculating bird numbers have seen the estimated total number leap by 11 per cent compared to earlier figures, says the British Trust for Ornithology.

"Great Britain is of considerable international importance for waders," stressed a spokesman.

"It holds more than 50 per cent of the East Atlantic Flyway populations of four species of wader - knot, bar-tailed godwit, redshank and turnstone - and more than 25 per cent of the East Atlantic Flyway population of a further nine species."

However, some birds are definitely doing better than others, admits the Trust.

"Seven of the 14 species that have shown population changes of more than five per cent since the last set of population estimates have declined in numbers.

"It is thought that climate change may be a factor in explaining some of these fluctuations."

Revised estimates of wader numbers include: dunlin - still a massive 555,800; oystercatcher - 315,200; knot - 283,600; curlew -147,100;redshank -116,100; bar-tailed godwit -61,590; grey plover - 52,750; turnstone -49,550; ringed plover -32,450; sanderling-20,540;purple sandpiper - 17,530; black-tailed godwit - 15,390; avocet -3,395; green-shank -597; and spotted redshank - 136.

GREEDY GREY SQUIRRELS are piling on the pounds at a Shropshire beauty spot with a diet of nuts, crisps and Dairylea sandwiches.

Like squirrels elsewhere with access to easy pickings, the animals at Hawkstone Park, near Wem, are rocketing in weight.

Now park wardens are trying to work out how to stop the squirrels munching through food put out for birds before devouring fatty titbits supplied by well-meaning visitors.

A LIVE SALMON full of eggs was found on two Cumbrian men after a poaching trip to the River Ehen at Ennerdale Bridge.

The pair, aged 43 and 22, admitted two offences when they appeared at Whitehaven Magistrates Court and were fined £500 each.

They were also ordered to pay £125 costs each.

Neil Pilling, prosecuting for the Environment Agency, told magistrates that the pair were spotted by bailiffs near Ennerdale Bridge on December 14 last year.

When stopped and searched, the bailiffs found a salmon - still alive - weighing about five pounds in a plastic bag in one of the men's jackets.

The fish had two hookmarks in its stomach and the jacket also concealed an extendable 'gaff hook' - an illegal pole with a hook attached, used for landing large fish.

Both the gaff hook and the dying salmon were confiscated.

After the hearing, the Agency's fisheries team leader Jeremy Westgarth said:"Poaching is a serious crime and this case shows the Agency is determined to stamp it out.

"The fish these men had was spawning and contained about 4,000 eggs which have now been lost from the Ehen river system. We will take action against anyone we catch poaching."

ENGLAND'S LAKES AND rivers have been boosted with the signing of a binding agreement by anglers and conservationists, it has been claimed.

English Nature and the National Angling Alliance say they will jointly aim to promote a healthier future for England's freshwater environment.

The two bodies have agreed to work together to tackle threats such as pollution, siltation and the spread of aggressive alien plants.

It is also hoped that closer contact will help forge better understanding between anglers and conservationists on the ground.

Sir Martin Doughty, chairman of English Nature, welcomed the agreement, saying:"We want to work together with all those who use the countryside and value wildlife.

"Anglers are in regular contact with nature and are aware of the pressures on our rivers, lakes and other freshwater habitats.

"We have a common interest in promoting policies that will reduce pollution from agriculture and industry and facilitate the physical restoration of rivers, to achieve better conditions for aquatic habitats and the fish and wildlife that depend on them."

Paul Knight, secretary of the National Angling Alliance, added:"Anglers and fishery managers have done fantastic work over the last century in protecting and enhancing our aquatic environment and it makes perfect sense for the Angling Alliance and English Nature to be in partnership to continue this work."

TROUT, SALMON AND stoneloach were among hundreds of fish killed by a spill of farm effluent into their river.

The fish died along a six kilometre stretch of the River Ive near Carlisle in Cumbria.

An investigation has been launched into how the pollutant, a mixture of silage and slurry waste, managed to seep into the water.

The liquid waste stripped oxygen from the river, suffocating fish in its path, and a huge drive was launched to prevent more fish dying by increasing oxygen levels.

Environment Agency staff deployed aerators, which pump oxygen into the river, as well as pumps to pump water onto the riverbank before allowing it to drain back containing higher levels of oxygen.

Agency spokesman Simon Barron said:"This is a serious incident and we are doing all we can to protect as many fish as possible as the pollutant flows downstream. We are grateful to the people who called us and allowed us to respond quickly. Without them, it could have been a lot worse."

PHEASANT SHOOTING AND conservation are highlighted in a new guide.

'Woodland Conservation and Pheasants' is aimed at anyone involved in game management or woodland conservation and is produced by the Game Conservancy Trust.

Historically, says the Trust, pheasant shooting has been an important motivation for the planting of new woods and the management of existing ones.

Much of this management, including habitat improvement, not only benefits pheasants but other wildlife, too.

However, concerns have arisen that releasing pheasants in large numbers can damage sensitive woodlands.

The new eight-page guide explains potential areas of conflict and offers advice to landowners, farmers and conservationists in how to address any negative impact caused by releasing birds.

Dr Rufus Sage, the Trust's head of gamebird research and author of the guide said:"The guide has been designed as a useful reference offering recommendations to encourage integrated nature conservation and pheasant management in woodlands.

"Planting and managing woods for pheasants can be beneficial to other species if undertaken sympathetically."

Many woods in the UK that have pheasants, particularly ancient woodlands, are also important habitats for rare or declining wildlife species, he added.

A FORMER POLICE horse seems set for the record books following a dramatic working life.

Dartagnan, a 34 year-old Irish Draught chestnut gelding, could soon be in the Guinness Book of Records as the oldest police horse still alive.

During its working life with Merseyside Police, the retired thoroughbred battled through the Toxteth riots and led in Red Rum four times for the Grand National.

BRITISH BIRDS ARE increasingly carrying the potentially fatal West Nile virus, scientists have found.

The virus, transmitted by mosquitoes, was discovered in more than 20 species, including magpies, swallows, crows, ducks, chickens and turkeys.

Although the birds themselves were healthy, the virus can kill humans by causing a fatal inflammation of the brain.

So far, there have been no recorded deaths in the UK but the virus is believed responsible for killing almost 300 people in the United States alone last year.

Researchers at the Centre for Ecology and Hydrology in Oxford tested birds in Cambridgeshire, Dorset and South Wales.

WELSH LAMB HAS joined Cornish clotted cream, West Country farmhouse cheddar cheese and Stilton cheese on a list of 34 UK products recognised by the European Union for their quality and regional identity, says the Government.

The lamb has been awarded the designation of 'Protected Geographical Indication', meaning that only lamb born and reared in Wales can be marketed as 'Welsh Lamb' within the EU.

"This is excellent news," said Lord Whitty.

THRUSH: wind-blown disaster in the garden

IF you've ever watched a thrush extricating a snail from its shell, you've got some idea of the determination of this clever, busy bird.

Time and time again, it will crack the shell against a stone until it finally gains access to the juicy prize inside.

Even an especially tough-shelled snail will usually be snatched out and eaten in the end, such is the thrush's single-mindedness as it toils for its food.

The thrush's vividly speckled breast and light brown feathers easily distinguish it from the similar sized, brown female blackbird which feeds at the same locations.

The thrush's determination in pursuit of snails also extends to finding worms, insects, fruit and berries to see it through the harshest of winters.

We have two resident species of thrush in this country, the song thrush and slightly larger mistle thrush.

Neither seems anywhere near as common to me as I remember them being as a child, but then the same goes for most birds.

Mistle thrushes, in particular, can be reckless in defence of their nests and will even drive away a cat or human with a few well-aimed pecks.

It must therefore have been a song thrush that I remember as a child nesting in a flower pot thrown randomly into a privet hedge in our garden.

I can still recall the thrill of peering into that privet, gazing at the mother sitting tight on her nest while she grimly stared back at me, less than an arm's length away.

I have no idea how long the pot had previously been stuck in the privet hedge but it seemed to make a perfect nest site for this mother. However, it was not quite as perfect as I thought.

Days later, high winds struck the area and I woke the next morning to find the mother bird fled, the pot upturned, and the blue speckled eggs broken and wasted on the ground.

That, unfortunately, was that.

However, in later years, other thrushes returned and built their nests in the garden with more solid foundations.

As well as our own two resident species of thrush, the UK plays host to two 'foreign' species that visit us each winter in large flocks.

Of these, the fieldfare is the most elegantly coloured with a grey head, red-brown back, and brightly speckled breast.

Its cousin, the redwing, meanwhile, is the smallest of all four species and boasts a distinct reddish tinge beneath its wings, hence the name.

Despite their smaller size, redwings travel from as far away as Iceland to get here each year, although many are believed to perish en route.

Poet Robert Browning seems to have been quite taken by one native thrush's singing voice.

"*That's the wise thrush,*" he wrote."*He sings each song twice over, Lest you should think he never could recapture, The first fine careless rapture.*"

Reminds me of someone I know, after he's had a drink or three.

CITY SLICKERS ARE tearing the heart out of Britain's countryside by snapping up farms and farmland at an alarming rate, it has been claimed.

Once thriving rural communities are being turned into the prettified playgrounds of business executives filling the void as more and more farmers go to the wall.

Worrying, almost two-thirds of farms bought between April and June this year went to non-farmers, new research has found.

Foot-and-mouth only accelerated the decline for most farmers who have given up, many with land farmed for generations by their families.

Plummeting returns for produce and devastating foreign competition have also played major roles in decisions by increasing numbers of farmers who turn their backs on their land and sell up.

With the average income for a farmer put at about £8,000, thousands have been driven to the edge by mounting bills and debt.

Developers have not been slow to exploit the sea change and, together with the Government's determination to build thousands of new homes, have created the perfect opportunity for wealthy urban families to live a cherished rural dream.

However, a survey by the Royal Institution of Chartered Surveyors has discovered that most now snapping up small and medium farms have no desire to farm, just to live in an attractive location.

Simon Hart, 24, from Cornwall, is typical of the army of young farmers giving up - even though he had always wanted to farm with his father Michael.

Simon, who had attended agricultural college in preparation, now works in the building trade while his father continues his battle to make money.

Mr Hart senior said:"I would have loved my son to work with me until I retired and handed the farm over to him. But I don't blame him for leaving farming - most of us are struggling to break even."

PIERRE THE FRENCH racing pigeon is making a good recovery after being found stuck in the grille of an English couple's car.

The bird, which had suffered a damaged wing and broken leg, was only spotted two days after George and Irene Cowie returned from a weekend jaunt across the Channel.

Mechanics freed the pigeon at a local garage following the couple's return home to Warwickshire.

An identity tag found on Pierre was used to trace its owner to Calais.

FOX NUMBERS APPEAR to be rocketing in Scotland with many farmers saying their businesses are suffering as a result of the ban on hunting with dogs.

In the year since the Scottish Parliament enforced its Protection of Wild Mammals (Scotland) Act, lambs and other farm animals have been killed at a worrying rate, it has been claimed.

The claims have been supported by the Countryside Alliance which recently revealed several farmers had been in contact to report "significantly higher than normal fox predation" since the ban was enforced.

One angry farmer from the Borders area said:"In the spring I lost more than 30 lambs in a fortnight - which is far higher than anything I have ever seen. I cannot carry on losing animals at that sort of rate."

Scottish Countryside Alliance director Allan Murray said:"We have consistently said that any ban on hunting would have an adverse impact on animal welfare, and it gives us no pleasure whatsoever to find that we were right.

"This ban was based on prejudice and intolerance. It was not based on concerns for animal welfare. But now, one year on from the Watson Act, both people and animals are suffering.

"This huge number of foxes will mean an increase in disease and malnutrition within the population, resulting in more and more farm animals being taken.

"We are currently pursuing a case to overturn the ban through the Scottish courts but, while we are in this state of limbo, farmers, hunt staff, the equestrian industry, the animals themselves, all will continue to suffer from a piece of legislation that has done something to them rather than for them."

MUSIC-LOVING PIGS have hit the wrong note with Hampshire residents who say their slumbers are being disturbed.

Farmer Ray Collier, 63, plays classical music to his porkers to keep them relaxed and help them nod off.

But neighbours at Locks Heath want the volume lowered or the music stopped and have complained to Fareham Borough Council.

Mr Collier has denied playing his classical favourites too loud, says he has played them over 30 years to his animals, and blames developers for building new houses too close to a working farm.

BLACK GROUSE AND lapwing are among seven farmland birds targeted in a new £1million scheme in Wales.

The project -'Aren't Welsh Birds Brilliant!' - also aims to help chough, grey partridge, bullfinch, tree sparrow and yellowhammer.

Dr David Trotman, one of the people behind the move, said:"This is an extremely important and exciting project that promises much for the people and environment of Wales.

"'Aren't Welsh Birds Brilliant! will bring a total of 15 new jobs, and promises to boost local economies by enhancing opportunities for community involvement and engaging with tourists and visitors to Wales."

Bob Farmer, from Forestry Commission Wales, added:"We look forward to working in partnership with the RSPB over the next three years."

RARE WHITE-TAILED sea eagles appear to be flourishing in Scotland.

The breeding success of the majestic birds has doubled this year with the recording of the highest number of chicks to fledge since the species was reintroduced in 1975.

The previous record for the young eagles fledging in a year was 13 but this year, says the RSPB, that record was smashed with 26 chicks successfully flying the nest.

There are now more than 30 territorial pairs in Scotland.

RSPB spokeswoman Dr Alison MacLennan said:"To double the number of young produced in one year is a huge success and very rewarding.

"Each year the number of territorial pairs has gradually increased but, for the last five years, the number of young fledged annually has remained between 11 and 13 birds.

"Their success this year may be due to the adult birds being in particularly good condition for breeding after unusually settled weather in the west of Scotland last winter.

"A number of young territorial pairs have now also come of an age to breed for the first time and boosted the productive population.

"One of the spin-offs from this success is that people will have an increased chance of seeing our largest bird of prey in future.

"That leads to huge eco-tourism benefits, particularly in Mull and Skye, where opportunities for seeing the birds are greatest."

FARMERS IN CUMBRIA are being urged to take extra care with sheep dip this year to avoid accidental pollution on top of the ravages of foot-and-mouth.

Gerry McLaughlin, area environment manager for the Environment Agency, explained:"Sheep dip contains chemicals called organo phosphates and synthetic pyrethroid compounds.

"When these chemicals get into rivers and streams, they kill invertebrats such as insects and other small water creatures, and so deprive fish of their main food source.

"Sheep dip spills can also get into groundwater and pollute our drinking supplies."

To help farmers reduce the risk of pollution, the Agency has been offering advice which includes:

ONLY use sheep dip when really necessary.

EMPLOY good flock management to avoid the spread of parasites.

DISPOSAL of used sheep dip must be carried out in accordance with a Groundwater Authorisation, issued by the Agency.

MAKE sure the dip bath is free from leaks and in good condition, and all drain holes are permanently sealed.

USE appropriate splash control around the tub and check that draining pens are in good repair and drain back into the tub.

CORNISH SEA ANGLERS have been scanning the waves around their boats for the dreaded triangular fin of a great white shark.

Teenager Chaynee Hodgetts, 15, has stuck to her story that she watched through binoculars as a 14ft great white fed on fish off the north Cornwall coast.

She told a local TV programme that she noted the distinctive conical snout of the shark and even saw its awesome teeth.

The claims of Chaynee, a marine biology student, might normally be dismissed as fanciful but have been backed by experts who believe rogue great whites do sometimes visit our shores.

Now an expedition has been organised to try to track down the dangerous visitor.

PEREGRINE FALCONS HAVE attracted over a million visitors to their Gloucestershire breeding site in the last 20 years.

During that time, more than 50 young have been reared at Symonds Yat Rock, say conservationists.

Telescopes set up at the site on the edge of the Forest of Dean have enabled visitors to follow some dramatic hunts by the spectacular predators.

Warden Susan Taylor said:"Projects like this are a great way of getting people interested in birds and other wildlife. It's brilliant to hear people say 'Wow' when they look through the telescopes for the first time and see the peregrines.

"With a million visitors, and the peregrines at the site successfully rearing 55 fledglings over the last 20 years, this has to be one of the RSPB's most successful and well known projects."

The scheme began in the early 1980s as a 24-hour nest-watch after peregrine eggs were stolen but has now become a way to celebrate the birds in their natural setting.

SALMON AND SEA trout are being given a boost with a second release of water from the Kielder reservoir into the River Tyne near Newcastle.

It is hoped the action will help the fish move up river after Environment Agency officers collected 497 dead salmon and 33 sea trout from the upper estuary.

The deaths are being blamed on a combination of low concentrations of dissolved oxygen in the estuary and high freshwater temperatures.

Agency spokesman Roger Inverarity said:"We arranged for a similar release from Kielder for two days back in July. This coincided with a small amount of rainfall and apparently encouraged some fish to move upstream.

"Over a three-day period, the number of fish counted through the Agency's fish counter at Riding Mill near Corbridge was about 400 higher than the preceding three days.But the total number counted throughout July was 6,000 so while the release appears to have resulted in extra fish movement it was not a spectacular result.

"With the current hot weather, we think that there is a risk of further fish deaths so arranged a further release of water from Kielder for two days. We hope that this will encourage more fish to move out of the estuary before conditions deteriorate too far."

THE NESTING ANTICS of a small brown finch are creating a flap among Scottish scientists.

Large numbers of twite, normally a heather nesting bird, are being found in trees.

GIN AND CHOCOLATE are providing a tasty boost to a North Yorkshire farming couple's fortunes.

During tough times for farmers nationwide, Richard and Julia Brown are being held up as a shining example of enterprise by the Country Land and Business Association - even though the couple's most succcesful crop this year did not actually grow in their fields.

The sloe berries they harvested for a promising new business venture grew wild in the 12 miles of hedgerows around their land in Malton.

According to the CLA "Richard and Julia were not slow to realise that the abundant sloe fruit in their hedges could be harvested and turned into traditional sloe gin and sloe liqueur chocolates.

"After marketing advice from the CLA, and after meeting the requirements of HM Customs and Excise and Trading Standards, they are now busily bottling the sloe gin into flasks and packing the handmade after-dinner sloe chocolates 12 to a box."

The traditional Yorkshire recipe is a family secret.

"It is sloe gin as it should be," said Julia, whose three-year-old daughter Georgia lent a hand with the harvest. "The family alone picked more than half a tonne of fruit, and a very prickly job it was too."

The bumper sloe harvest was the result of cutting the hedges only once in three years.

"We worked out that the yield was 20 times greater than that from hedges cut annually," explained Julia.

A SHEEPDOG SAVED the life of a Scottish hermit after retrieving his message in a bottle.

Following a collapse, Robert Sinclair, 55, scribbled a note, put it in a bottle, and threw it out of a window at the derelict farmhouse near Falkirk where he lives.

Days later, sheepdog Ben, owned by local farmer Brian Bisler, came across the bottle and took it home - prompting his master to alert the emergency services who rushed to the hermit's aid.

Mr Sinclair was later said to be recovering in the intensive care unit of Falkirk Royal Infirmary.

A FEMALE SEAL has been nicknamed Marilyn Monroe after sunning itself daily on the banks of the River Thames near Chiswick in West London.

The animal, miles from the sea, is thought to have swum up river in search of fish and become attached to its sedate surroundings.

During recent high temperatures, Marilyn has often been spotted lounging and lazing about, as if reluctant to plunge back into the chilly Thames.

However, experts believe the 20-stone common seal will soon follow the river back out to sea.

ONCE TRANQUIL COUNTRY lanes are being increasingly turned into dangerous rat runs by motorists, campaigners warn.

"The pleasure of walking, cycling or riding along a country lane without fear from speeding traffic is fast disappearing," says the Council for the Protection of Rural England.

"Speeding vehicles, rising traffic levels, and heavy lorries are making many country lanes unpleasant, unsafe and intimidating for other users - stripping them of their character and shattering their tranquillity.

"In 2002 alone, 2,061 people lost their lives on rural roads, a shocking 60 per cent of all fatalities."

In a bid to tackle the problem the CPRE has now issued guidelines aimed at making country lanes safer and more attractive for all.

Its 'Guide to Quiet Lanes' encourages drivers to slow down and drive more considerately.

The guide also explains what Quiet Lanes are and their benefits, and includes a step-by-step process for encouraging local authorities to designate country lanes as Quiet Lanes.

Kent and Norfolk County Councils were the first to designate Quiet Lanes with the help of the Countryside Agency.

But CPRE campaigners across the whole of England are now working to get their own local authorities to implement Quiet Lanes.

Already, 31 authorities have expressed interest in working with communities to provide Quiet Lanes in their area.

However, while more communities are interested in the prospect of protecting their country lanes, CPRE revealed that, despite all its promises on helping the country's rural population, New Labour is still dragging its feet on Quiet Lanes.

Three years after supporting legislation for Quiet Lanes in the Transport Act 2000, the Government still hasn't published regulations required to help local authorities designate them.

Paul Hamblin, CPRE's head of transport, added:"CPRE's new pack will provide people with the resource to help protect their country lanes and preserve an integral and beautiful part of the English countryside.

"It is time to regain our lanes as Quiet Lanes for the benefit of all."

JUICY BRITISH PLUMS are flooding into the shops on the back of a heritage drive by the NFU.

"You might not believe it but the humble plum has been a part of Britain's heritage for many thousands of years," said a spokesman.

"The earliest recorded cultivation of the fruit was during the Roman age. When the Tudor ship the 'Mary Rose' sank in 1545, it was found to be carrying over 5,000 of them.

"Plums have entered the language too. 'Speaking with a plum in your mouth' means to speak with a posh or upper-class accent.

"Plum is a corruption of the original word which was probably 'plumb' (lead), referring to the awkward speech of someone wearing false teeth, which were made from bone hinged with lead.

"The British climate is one of the world's best for growing plums.

"They thrive on our mild and moist seasons - making great British plums unique in flavour, their flesh tender, and their juice enriched with vitamins."

SIGHTINGS OF SUNBATHING snakes could rocket as temperatures hit record highs, according to English Nature.

"Some of this country's shyest creatures are more active in sunny weather and the chances of seeing one dramatically increase after heavy rain follows a prolonged dry spell," said a spokesman.

"But around 95 per cent of calls to the English Nature inquiry service turn out to be a case of mistaken identity, with most callers believing they have spotted an adder when it is much more likely to be a grass snake or slow worm.

"A new leaflet published by English Nature has clear photographs to help people tell them apart and gives advice on what to do if you find one."

English Nature's reptile specialist Jim Foster added:"We appreciate that some people are terrified when they first see a snake in the garden but there is rarely anything to be truly worried about. Snakes and lizards get a bad press. The hot weather doesn't mean there will be more snakes but sightings are more common because people are outdoors."

OVER A THOUSAND fish, mostly brown trout, were plucked to safety in a rescue operation near Worcester.

The Environment Agency said:"Fisheries officers rescued the fish in the River Teme after it began to look likely they would have been left stranded if the current hot weather continued.

"During prolonged dry weather, parts of the river dry up as water levels fall, leaving the fish trapped in small pools with insufficient oxygen.

"The limited quantity of water remaining in the river starts flowing instead through the gravel of the river bed. The upper reaches of the Teme are home to a very special community of brown trout. In most rivers, there is considerable inter-breeding as different families of brown trout are introduced.

"In this part of the Teme, however, research on the DNA of the trout has shown that they are unusual in that they have not inter-bred and belong to the same blood-line. The Agency rescued the fish using a mild electric shock which is harmless but stuns the fish so that they can be caught. They were then transported to a safe location down river."

A GIANT CONGER eel has been blamed for causing the death of an angler in a sea fishing competition.

Albert Marhsall, 43, was swept away by waves as he battled the huge fish at Kirkcudbright Bay, Dumfries and Galloway, Scotland.

Conger eels can grow to 10ft long, weigh over 200 pounds, and are known to be vicious and aggressive when hooked.

Labourer Mr Marshall was wearing chest high rubber waders which are thought to have become waterlogged as he struggled with the eel at the end of his line. Searchers later found the waders.

BADGERS HAVE BEEN clashing with gardeners as prolonged hot weather makes finding food harder than usual.

According to conservationists, hundreds of well-kept lawns have been dug up as badgers search for their favourite food - worms.

Dr Elaine King, chief executive of the National Federation of Badger Groups, explained:"The cause of the problem is not a rise in badger numbers. On the contrary, the dry weather has deprived badgers of earthworms - their staple diet - and they are being forced to dig for their dinner wherever they can find it. They are upsetting gardeners in the process.

"The extremely dry conditions in 2002 and 2003 have meant that almost no badger cubs have been raised for the last two years.

"The most convincing evidence comes from 50 setts in Wytham Woods, Oxfordshire. Badgers there only produced 12 cubs in 2003 - the lowest number for 28 years. In 2002, the badgers only managed to produce 15 cubs."

The NFBG says it has also gathered a large amount of anecdotal evidence from around the country which appears to support scientific data that badgers have suffered a substantial decline.

Most badger groups have reported few or no cubs at regularly monitored setts.

They have also reported large numbers of badgers suffering from dehydration and starvation.

"Gardeners can help badgers through this difficult period by changing their gardening strategy. For example, we are encouraging gardeners who water their lawns to do so last thing at night," added Dr King.

"As well as conserving water, this also encourages worms to the surface at exactly the time that badgers want to eat them.

"This simple strategy should discourage badgers from digging up lawns and gardeners will have the added bonus of watching badgers forage on their doorstep."

BIRDS, BATS AND other creatures could be helped by a Government pledge to support wildlife on its own land.

Ministers have drawn up targets involving more than 200 Sites of Special Scientific Interest on the Government Estate.

Treasury Green, connected to the Cabinet Office in London, already hosts a small pond, home to frogs, newts, dragonflies and plant life.

It also boasts bat and bird boxes as well as wild grasses that attract a variety of insects.

Elsewhere, bird surveys at Richmond in Surrey, have already discovered a 28 per cent rise in farm - land birds and a 21 per cent rise in woodland birds.

The Government land is also home to the double-line moth, a rare species found at few other places, as well as rare spiders.

RARE BIRDS SUCH as the Dartford warbler and nightjar would benefit from a doubling of lowland heathland in England, says the RSPB.

The Society is pressing the Government to introduce doubling as a target, especially as localised heath improvement in Dorset had proved such a conservation success.

Graham Wynne, chief executive of the RSPB, said:"The RSPB is seeking commitment to double the area of heathland to 64,000 hectares by 2020."

GROUSE SHOOTERS ARE hoping for a better season this year, says the Game Conservancy Trust.

"Following weeks of early starts and bracing walks on the heather moors to conduct grouse counts, the Trust's advisers and researchers suggest reasonably good prospects for some areas," revealed a spokesman.

"Our advisors count red grouse in the immediate weeks prior to the shooting season to establish breeding success and overall numbers.

"From these samples the optimum harvesting strategy - the shootable surplus - can be estimated, thus ensuring the right level of stock to leave to overwinter and provide breeding stock for the following spring.

"Pointing dogs are used to locate pairs and coveys of grouse and hold them, allowing the team to count the individual birds, identify young and old, and monitor their state of growth. The latter is important when deciding the ideal time to shoot.

"The information gathered from counts is crucial for moor owners and grouse keepers to plan their season and to calculate the right time for shooting. Ideally, it is best to take out the older birds and leave the younger members of a covey because they are less liable to have disease and therefore make better stock for the following year."

Ian McCall, the Trust's director in Scotland, confirmed many of his clients were looking forward with cautious optimism to a better grouse season.

"Most of Scotland enjoyed a great early spring. Despite some cold April nights we had warm weather during the grouse nesting season and the birds looked to be in good condition," he said."Clutch size of nests found were often at or above average in several regions. During May, hillkeepers whom we advise, have rung in reporting good hatches across much of Scotland."

BRITISH BIRD EXPERTS are behind the resurgence of a bizarre looking African bird once revered by the Pharaohs.

According to the RSPB, the extremely rare northern bald ibis is now staging a spectacular comeback in its Moroccan heartlands.

The ibis, a distant relative of storks and herons, was once widespread across northern Africa and even had its own hieroglyphic symbol in Egypt.

Now, thanks to an on-going emergency conservation programme launched by the RSPB, the bird's population has increased by almost 60 per cent to 85 pairs.

ANGLERS COULD BE given a cash boost if the Tories return to power - fishing licences would be abolished.

The surprising - and some might say desperate - bid to to win votes would affect a vast army of anglers who dutifully shell out for rod licences each year.

Under instructions from leader Iain Duncan Smith, Conservative central command is said to be drawing up plans to bring the idea to fruition after the next election.

Mr Duncan Smith, a keen angler himself, apparently believes that it is unfair to make anglers buy a licence when they already have to cough up a separate charge to fish in many lakes or rivers.

At present, the Environment Agency dishes out about a million rod licences a year with coarse fishing licences costing up to £22.25 and game fishing licences up to £61.25.

Anyone caught fishing without a rod licence faces being fined up to £2,500 and having their fishing equipment confiscated.

Money collected from licences is meant to go towards helping the environment but Mr Duncan Smith thinks, under the system today, much is actually wasted on bureaucracy by Labour.

He feels bailiffs should be urged to concentrate on other, practical duties instead of acting as angling tax collectors.

The licence is also supposed to help ward off irresponsible fishermen but the Tories think the majority of anglers take proper care of lakes and rivers.

TWO PIGS THAT escaped from a Wiltshire slaughterhouse and went on the run are set to become film stars.

The BBC is making a £2million comedy drama about the so-called Tamworth Two who evaded capture long enough to make national headlines and win freedom permanently at an animal sanctuary.

'The Legend Of The Tamworth Two' will tell the story of the two Tamworth Gingers, Butch and Sundance, who managed to save their own bacon five years ago.

WHALES AND DOLPHINS off Britain's coasts are to be the focus of a huge national survey again.

The Sea Watch Foundation is asking people to look out for the spectacular marine creatures over the weekend of August 30-31.

Viewing points will be placed at more than 200 sites around the UK's coastline with RSPB nature reserves and staff also involved in the event.

Organisers say that this is the project's second year - and anyone can take part.

Nature lovers can easily combine a visit to an RSPB nature reserve with time spent looking out for whales and dolphins.

Among a list of selected RSPB sites already well-known for whale and dolphin watching are: Mousa, Shetland (harbour porpoise, minke whale, killer whale); Sumburgh Head, Shetland (harbour porpoise, minke whale, white-beaked dolphin, Atlantic white-sided dolphin, humpback whale, killer whale); Campfield Marsh, Solway Firth (harbour porpoise, bottlenose dolphin); Rathlin Island, Co. Antrim, (harbour porpoise, bottlenose dolphin);Ramsey Island, Pembrokeshire (harbour porpoise); and Dungeness, Kent (bottlenose dolphin, harbour porpoise).

337

BATS ARE UNDER a growing threat from people who illegally disturb their roosts, it has been claimed.

A joint study by the Bat Conservation Trust and the RSPB urges building firms to carry out proper surveys into local wildlife before starting renovation work.

Researchers found that residents and even church staff were also guilty of destroying bat roosts without consulting specialists first.

Amy Coyte, chief executive of the Bat Conservation Trust, said:"This report provides concrete evidence for the first time that bat crime is rife in the UK and that the major perpetrators are developers.

"We are aware of the need for development but this must be done sustainably, taking bats into account before building work starts and ensuring that the appropriate legal procedure is followed."

Of the 16 bat species remaining in the UK, six are now endangered or rare while six others are vulnerable.

Joan Childs, author of the report, added:"There is so much destruction of bats and their roosts that it must be having an effect on bat conservation. This seems to be a good reason for the decline of bat species.

"But we suspect this is just the tip of the iceberg and there's a lot more crime out there."

However, on a brighter note, some bats whose roost was ruined by the biggest earthquake to hit Britain in 10 years are being given a new one.

The creatures' former home was destroyed by the so-called Dudley Earthquake.

Dudley Council is now moving the bats to a secret location, an old mine, where they are expected to flourish.

The quake, which shook Britain in September last year, registered 5 on the Richter scale.

BOOMING BITTERNS OWE their resurgence to the sheer skill of conservationists at building new reedbeds.

Numbers of the rare heron-like bird have reached at least 42 'booming' males - four times that recorded six years ago, says the RSPB.

The Society believes the rise is due to measures such as painstakingly rebuilding the type of reedbeds bitterns enjoy.

Gillian Gilbert, RSPB bittern expert, said:"The bittern is still so rare that we know each of these birds individually. But these results are extremely encouraging and point to the achievements of recent conservation work."

A £4m bittern rescue scheme was launched recently involving eight conservation groups and three county wildlife trusts.

STOCKING DISEASED FISH in a pool near Far Forest, Worcestershire, proved costly for two Kidderminster men.

The pair pleaded guilty before local magistrates to two offences relating to stocking fish without obtaining the necessary consent.

The charges, brought by the Environment Agency under the Salmon and Freshwater Fisheries Act 1975, saw one of the men fined £500 and ordered to pay costs of £1,398, the other fined £150 and also ordered to pay costs of £1,398.

Prosecutor Helen Kidd told the court that Environment Agency officers mounted a surveillance operation at Yewtree Caravan Park in June after receiving a tip-off.

During the night, Agency officers spotted the men arrive at the site, remove a dustbin from a van and empty the carp it contained into the pool.

The men returned to the van to collect another dustbin and at this point an Agency officer approached them and asked if they had the necessary consent for stocking the pool.

Neither man could provide evidence of having such a permit.

Tests on the fish found in the second dustbin later showed that they were infected with a parasite that could infect other fish stocks.

Agency spokesman Andy Roberts said later:"The illegal movement of fish without consent increases the risk of introducing foreign parasites and diseases to our waters. As native fish do not have immunity to these infections there is a risk of damaging fish stocks."

A LARGE PUMA-type animal was hunted by armed police following an alert at Shrewsbury, Shropshire.

Police said the mystery cat had been spotted prowling around in countryside outside the town.

Animal experts including Bob Lawrence, head warden of a West Midlands safari park, joined the hunt which was also backed up by a police helicopter.

However, the 6ft-long beast apparently managed to slink away and evade being killed or captured.

TOTAL TREE COVER in Britain more than doubled during the last century, according to the Forestry Commission.

A new report, the 'National Inventory of Woodlands and Trees' has brought together all available data published earlier for Scotland, England and Wales to summarise the picture at the start of the 21st Century.

The report found 11.6 per cent of Britain is covered by woodland totalling over 2.6million hectares.

"This represents a 26 per cent increase in woodland cover since the previous inventory of woodland in 1980," said a spokesman,"and a more than doubling of woodland area in Britain over the course of the 20th Century.

"Scotland has the most woodland with 16.4 per cent cover, a high proportion of which is coniferous, followed by Wales with 13.8 per cent and a more even balance between coniferous and broadleaved trees.

"England has 8.4 per cent woodland cover, with broadleaved woodland now the most dominant type and oak the most common tree."

The survey was carried out by the Woodland Surveys branch of Forest Research.

PINE MARTEN: tough hunter on its way back

PINE martens could soon be a common sight again in southern English woodlands - which is bad news for a certain American upstart.

The grey squirrel, which has driven our native red squirrel almost to extinction, would certainly be on the menu for these ferocious predators. Nimble and agile, pine martens can climb trees as fast as squirrels and will pursue them into the topmost branches - unlike foxes and stoats, which are often left floundering below.

According to English Nature, it should now be possible to reintroduce pine martens back to their historic haunts throughout the country.

"About 150 years ago, pine martens were widespread throughout Britain," a spokesman explained. *"However, in a few short decades they were almost completely exterminated to protect game birds on large shooting estates.*

"Today they are one of our rarest mammals with good populations restricted to Galloway and north west Scotland."

Fully grown, pine martens are about the size of a cat and have rich reddish-brown fur with a creamy yellow throat. Comparatively long legs, fur-padded paws and large bushy tails deployed for balance all contribute to their climbing skill.

They can live for up to 12 years, preferring a wooded habitat surrounded by rough grassland. Besides squirrels, pine martens will eat rabbits, voles, mice, small birds, frogs and even supplement their diet in the autumn with berries.

Recent findings concluded that there was no practical reason why pine martens should not be reintroduced to their old stamping grounds - provided people want them.

A research team has already surveyed woods in Devon, Somerset, Dorset, Avon, East Sussex and Cumbria for suitable habitats.

The team also asked local people about their attitudes to pine martens and an average 64 per cent of farmers, 65 per cent of gamekeepers and 90 per cent of local residents were in favour of reintroduction.

As a result, a broader national public consultation was launched to assess the acceptability of a general pine marten reintroduction programme. Despite their ferocity, pine martens remain shy of Man and are mostly nocturnal, glimpsed occasionally at dawn or dusk.

They nest quietly in crevices or underground lairs and are virtually silent hunters, only making cat-like calls during the breeding season. Females produce a litter of young between April and May each year, usually a trio of offspring.

The grey squirrel, meanwhile, was introduced to this country in the 19th Century from hardwood forests in the United States.

Bigger and more aggressive than the British red, it gradually drove out our native squirrel which now only exists in remote parts of its old national territories.

It will be interesting to see how this American tough guy reacts when it learns the pine marten is back in town.

KINGFISHERS ARE staging a remarkable comeback on Britain's lakes and rivers with efforts to clean up waterways really starting to pay off.

Numbers of the exotic blue and orange fish-eaters are on the rise with a huge 76 per cent increase recorded in latest research.

But the so-called 'jewel of the riverbank' is not the only bird bouncing back, according to the annual breeding bird survey by the British Trust for Ornithology and the RSPB.

Some 52 species are now said to be thriving, including the great spotted woodpecker, up 72 per cent, and the goldcrest, up 65 per cent.

Even blackbird, robin, crow and song thrush are all up on previous years by more than 13 per cent.

Predictably, however, it is not all good news and a British bird made famous by Gilbert and Sullivan in The Mikado has suffered a steep slump.

Sightings of the willow tit, whose favourite damp woodland habitat is under pressure, fell by 72 per cent between 1994 and 2002.

RSPB spokesman Grahame Madge said:"The willow tit is hugely important because, being a bird of woodland, it is arguably more native to Britain than others.

"There was a time when Britain was cloaked in woodland - largely oak with ash. To have woodland birds suffering is a real cause for concern because, above all others, they should be more adapted to the British environment than any other breed."

The willow tit is one of two birds apparently undergoing a population reduction of more than 50 per cent.

The other is the wood warbler which has now slumped in number by 58 per cent, according to the survey.

RARE ORCHIDS AND wildlife have been given a boost by former MP Lord Biffen who is leading a £20,000 appeal to protect their Shropshire hill.

Crickheath Hill, near Oswestry, is said to be home to over 300 plant species - including 12 types of orchid - as well as a variety of birds and butterflies.

Lord Biffen, formerly the MP for North Shropshire, has launched a Shropshire Wildlife Trust campaign to purchase 30 acres of woods and meadows at the site.

Conservationists say the appeal represents the best chance to save what is a much-loved local resource.

Besides the orchids, among the most significant plants are fairy flax, eyebright, and various strains of St John's Wort.

The rare pearl-bordered fritillary is just one of several threatened butterflies at the site.

HUMMINGBIRDS ARE being reported across Britain by confused gardeners who fail to spot the hovering 'birds' are actually moths.

"Hummingbird sightings are coming in thick and fast," reports the RSPB,"but as the birds are only native to the Americas, how can it be? The answer lies in a medium-sized, day-flying moth, known as the hummingbird hawkmoth.

"Every year in late summer, the arrival of these moths from Europe causes a stir among gardeners and wildlife-watchers.

"These moths are every bit the hummingbird mimic, down to the way they fly from flower to flower. Add that to their very similar shape, and you have an amazing - and confusing - conundrum.

"These migrating moths start to move up from Mediterranean areas during late summer and many are blown across the English Channel to the UK.

"However, even though they are known to breed in the UK, they can't survive the chill of winter and their presence here is only able to continue because of the appearance of their European cousins each year.

"Preferring bright sunlit days for flying, this is a great time of year to be on the look-out for these amazing mimics.

"They are particularly fond of red valerian, honeysuckle, jasmine, buddleia, lilac, escallonia, petunia and phlox. So if you're outside over the coming weeks, keep your eyes peeled for these amazing visitors."

A BEMUSED SWAN caused a 12-mile tailback after mistaking a glistening motorway for an open stretch of water.

The bird touched down during the rush hour and sauntered across all three lanes on the eastbound carriageway of the M4 in Berkshire.

Irate motorists were forced to wait in line for their turn to pass the bird, obviously puzzled as to why the welcoming water had vanished.

Recent heavy rain is believed to have played a role in confusing the swan, the latest bird in a long line to have been fooled by motorway mirages.

BASKING SHARKS SPOTTED off Scotland have rocketed in number this year, according to scientists.

Last year, there was only a single confirmed sighting compared to almost 40 basking sharks seen during 2003 so far.

Across the UK, some 255 individual basking sharks have now been identified this year with their details carefully logged by The Wildlife Trusts.

Steve Sankey, chief executive of the Scottish Wildlife Trust, said:"Last year's survey was distinguished, if that is the word, by the lack of sightings in Scottish waters. This year has been much more encouraging but we cannot afford to be at all complacent.

"The basking shark population is still recovering from the over-hunting that devastated populations last century. There are huge financial interests at stake too. Each year, the coastal economy generates £1.7billion worth of revenue for Scotland.

"It's vital we protect this unique resource from exploitation and pollution by managing it sustainably and for the long-term future."

RECENT RAIN HAS been welcomed by the Environment Agency which says that continued dry weather was proving disastrous for fish and other aquatic life.

High temperatures and a heavy demand on water supplies dried out ponds and reduced flow levels in rivers, especially throughout Kent, Sussex, Hampshire and the Isle of Wight.

The Agency's Hampshire and Isle of Wight area manager, Peter Quarmby, said:"The prolonged warm spell and lack of rain means that some juvenile species will not survive, causing damage to both current and future fish stocks.

"This is particularly devastating in sites where fish populations, such as salmon and trout, are already in decline.

"The upper reaches of rivers fed by surface water, like those in the New Forest, have been particularly affected by the hot weather and low rainfall.

"Unfortunately, there is no quick fix. Simply pouring more water into dry ponds doesn't work - the damage has already been done. The bed of the pond or river has hardened, destroying the habitat of invertebrates and killing plant life that the fish need to live on.

"Although we have had some successful fish rescues this summer, moving them to a new location is not always possible and, in any case, it can put fish under more physical stress and kill them.

"Re-oxygenating the water using chemicals and machinery can provide short-term relief but unless water levels are restored, it can just postpone the problem. It is not a permanent answer. The only real solution is for it to rain and for time to allow natural recovery."

BUZZARDS ARE STARTING to seriously threaten game birds due to their resurgence in numbers, gamekeepers claim.

Scotland, in particular, has seen a sharp rise in buzzard numbers to 61,000 pairs - four times the number 20 years ago.

Although conservationists say the birds of prey mainly scavenge carrion, gamekeepers claim they now predate more regularly on young game birds such as pheasants and partridges.

Buzzards have been blamed for killing more than 500 pheasants on one Aberdeenshire estate alone since the start of 2003.

The Scottish Gamekeepers Association has now lodged a petition with the Scottish Parliament seeking an urgent review of the impact of the soaring birds.

Gamekeepers want permission to cull buzzards while conservationists remain vehemently opposed to the idea.

TERRITORIAL SEALS ARE proving increasingly dangerous to swimmers off England's east coast after a second attack left another man with a shattered leg.

Window cleaner Wesley Cook, 32, was the latest to fall victim as a common seal broke his right leg in three places near Great Yarmouth, Norfolk.

Mr Cook claims he could easily have drowned if his brother-in-law had not heard his screams and come to his aid.

His right foot was left twisted horrifically in the wrong direction after the ramming attack which occurred when he was floating on a body board near a seal colony.

"Seals are supposed to be nice, friendly things but this one could have killed me," he said later.

Weeks ago, teacher Levi Clarke, 21, also had a leg broken in three places in a seal attack at Leigh-on-Sea, Essex.

Experts believe the animals may be becoming more territorial and anxious to protect their young.

ANIMAL RIGHTS FANATICS have been blamed for a blaze at the Dorset home of a man accused of breaking new laws against foxhunting in Scotland.

Rory Innes, 26, was recently summonsed to appear before a Scottish court to answer a charge of hunting a fox with dogs while a member of the Jed Forest Foxhounds.

But shortly after Mr Innes moved south to become master and huntsman of the South Dorset Hunt, his property was attacked by arsonists.

Hunting trousers and other clothes were snatched from a washing line and set alight against the back door of his home at the South Dorset Hunt kennels in Bere Regis.

Fortunately, Mr Innes woke up before serious damage was caused to the premises but was shocked at the recklessness of the act.

He denies any offence in Scotland where new laws mean that dogs can still be used to flush out foxes but the fleeing animals must then be shot, not killed by hounds.

THE USEFULNESS OF national forests to the social, economic and environmental life of Scottish people is being explored in a new review.

Undertaken by Forestry Commission Scotland, the Scottish Executive and Scottish Natural Heritage, together with an external assessor from the forest industries, the review aims to assess any future role of the nation's forests.

Announcing the scheme, Scottish Forestry Minister Allan Wilson said:"Our national forest estate covers nearly one tenth of Scotland's land area and provides direct employment to some 1,000 people as well as jobs for contractors, hauliers and other parts of the forest industries.

"Couple this with the fact that our forests contribute so much to recreation and tourism in many rural areas and it is easy to see just how important these woodlands are.

"A recent survey also suggested that Scotland's forests bring social and environmental benefits worth £104 million each year to the country.The purpose of this review is to take stock of our national forest estate and to ask whether its current size, nature and geographic distribution are appropriate for the 21st Century."

BADGER LOVERS HAVE attacked the authorities in Northamptonshire after the first badger was killed on the new A6 Rothwell and Desborough bypass - despite tunnels being dug to save the creatures' lives.

The National Federation of Badger Groups says that when the road was opened by Transport Minister David Jamieson on August 14 the Highways Agency bragged that thousands had been spent on installing tunnels to protect badgers and other wildlife.

"But Richard Turner from the North Northants Badger Group has discovered that more than 3,000 metres of fencing, required to ensure that the badgers use the tunnels, has not been installed," blasted a spokesman.

"As a result, the first badger has been killed on the road, within weeks of it opening. The body was removed by a contractor just hours before it could be filmed by local news crews."

Mr Turner himself added:"I am appalled. From the moment David Jamieson opened this road, badgers have been at risk and a serious road traffic accident could occur as a result.

"It is a disgrace for the Highways Agency to state that nature conservation work has been carried out when these essential measures are not in place.

"We have been working with the Agency and its contractors for 12 years to ensure that the badgers would have their safety guaranteed. The Minister's decision to open this bypass before it is complete has left us incensed."

WILDLIFE COULD ACTUALLY benefit from further development of new housing estates, English Nature has controversially claimed.

Agricultural land is often so poor as habitat that carefully managed, low population estates might provide a better alternative, the Government's wildlife advisory body explained.

Dr Keith Porter, an environmental spokesman for English Nature, told a three-day national science conference that intensive agriculture had driven many plants and animals away but sensible property growth might be the best way to encourage them back.

Low-density developments with gardens and public open spaces would provide better habitats than the huge pesticide-drenched cereal fields that dominate much of the countryside now, he said.

"By placing housing in these areas with innovative designs you can build in the corridors and the linkage the wildlife need to come back in. You would be certain to increase biodiversity," he said.

He was not calling for unrestrained development, he explained, but English Nature wanted to work with planners to see what they could do to improve the prospects for wildlife.

A THIRD OF English footpaths are now virtually impassable despite new right to roam laws opening up the countryside, say ramblers.

Overgrown routes, barbed wire, and broken stiles are just some of the problems walkers face, according to the Ramblers Association.

Billions of pounds and hundreds of thousands of jobs connected to rural tourism could be jeopardised unless the problem is tackled, the Association warns following publication of a new report.

Local councils are attacked for years of under investment and neglect in the report which urges them to spend millions rectifying the situation before tourist cash is lost forever.

Research for the report was conducted by Dr Mike Christie, of the University of Aberystwyth, who revealed that almost 180,000 obstacles were found on the rights of way network while 105,000 signposts had vanished.

Ramblers run into a serious obstruction every mile and a quarter on average while 1,000 routes cross busy roads unsafe for pedestrians.

BRITAIN'S 40 MILLION sheep are under threat from a deadly virus dubbed 'blue tongue'.

The virus, carried by midges and one of the most feared livestock diseases in the world, can decimate flocks.

According to researchers at the Institute for Animal Health, the disease is moving north after a series of hot summers but was once found only in Asia and Africa.

It began to ravage Europe during the last decade and has already killed more than half a million sheep on the Continent.

Sheep farmers, still recovering from the impact of foot-and-mouth, are being warned to brace themselves for its expected arrival here within five years.

WELSH SALMON AND sea trout are no longer required to go for the 'high jump' on the River Twrch, a tributary of the Tywi near Pumpsaint.

Thanks to work being carried out by Carmarthenshire County Council and Environment Agency Wales, two barriers to migrating fish can now be negotiated en route to spawning grounds upstream.

"For years fish migrating to spawn in the upper reaches of the Twrch were faced with two serious obstructions. One was the existing road bridge on the A482 and the other the remains of the redundant Irish Bridge," said a spokesman for the scheme."Now Carmarthenshire County Council's highways department has built a fish-friendly bridge on the A482 which incorporates a series of low weirs and pools which act as a fish pass.

"The complete removal of the second obstruction, the remains of the Irish Bridge, has also been carried out. The total cost of the whole project, including the fish pass, was £1.7 million."

Agency technical officer Ida Tavner added:" Removing these obstructions has improved access to over 10 kilometres of additional habitat.

"It is not often we get the chance to improve access on such a scale.

"In the past, poor access, especially during low flows has restricted reproduction of salmon and sea trout in the upper reaches. The quality of the habitat is very good but if the fish can't get there it is of limited value."

CRICKET FANS HAVE been celebrating of late but their interest is less bat and ball, more gryllus campestris - the British field cricket.

In recent weeks, the Zoological Society of London and English Nature have released over 1,000 captive-bred British field crickets into the wild.

The project has taken place as part of an ongoing recovery programme to re-introduce endangered species into suitable habitat.

The crickets, captive bred at London Zoo, were released at two sites - Arundel Castle Cricket Ground, and a secret location elsewhere in West Sussex.

The move follows a previous release of another 1,000 crickets on the Isle of Wight.

Arundel Castle Cricket Ground already had a small population of captive-bred British field crickets that could be heard singing in the summer following release into the wild in past years.

But it is hoped this year's scheme will boost local numbers and help preserve a healthy population for the future.

Dave Clarke, head keeper at London Zoo, said:"The British field cricket release programme has proved to be a great and ongoing success story, highlighting the important role captive breeding programmes play in helping to maintain the wildlife of the British countryside.

"The species is extinct in surrounding areas, so to ensure that the cricket population is secure and expanding we have to bring in captive-bred crickets, mimicking natural recruitment from surrounding populations.

"Re-introduction to the wild is the ultimate aim of all captive-breeding projects so it is fantastic to be achieving these results."

WADING BIRDS AND wildfowl will benefit from Environment Agency work to improve their habitat on the Severn Estuary at Slimbridge in Gloucestershire.

The Agency's 24-tonne hydraulic excavator has been used to create a new channel at the site and raise 'bunds' - low dams.

"These dams hold water in lagoons at the Wildfowl and Wetlands Trust's reserve for longer, creating better breeding and wintering habitat for birds such as lapwing, redshank, rare black-tailed godwit and teal," explained a spokesman.

"Black-tailed godwit have been present at the Slimbridge centre for the first time this year and it is hoped that the work done by the Agency to provide a suitable habitat will encourage them to stay and breed."

Martin McGill, spokesman for the Trust, added:"The Agency's work is a godsend for us. It would take years to get the funds together to create these areas of specialist habitat that provide a niche for special birds. We are hoping this work will encourage more birds to breed here."

RARE BATS ARE the latest weapon employed by The Woodland Trust to beat off a bid to build a huge new road in Dorset.

Evidence has been collected that two rare types - barbastelle and Bechstein's - may be among several bat species roosting in woods threatened by the Weymouth relief road development.

"The Trust has been fighting proposals that would cause irreparable damage to a Trust-owned wood known as Two Mile Coppice," said a spokesman."The wood is Weymouth and Portland District's only remaining fragment of rare ancient woodland.

"A survey, just published, reveals the presence of several species of bat, some of which roost in trees along the edge of the wood.

"In the UK, all wild bats are protected by the 1981 Wildlife and Countryside Act. Further protection is also afforded to all bat species under the 1992 European Habitats and Species Directive.

"At the moment, proposals for the Weymouth road involve damaging and destroying trees and woodland. So far, bat species found in the wood include the rare barbastelle and possibly Bechstein's, the vulnerable noctule and the common pipistrelle.

"The barbastelle and pipistrelle bats found at Two Mile Coppice are listed as UK Biodiversity Action Plan species.

"Clearly, Two Mile Coppice woodland is important for bats and must not be damaged. Any activity that might disturb the bat habitat must gain prior approval from DEFRA. Granting of a licence will delay approval of the road and could lead to a legal challenge."

It is hoped that efforts to accommodate the tiny bats might ultimately make the entire project financially unworkable and therefore sink it.

BRITAIN'S RABBITS COULD be turned into a cash cow if country entrepreneurs follow the example of a Russian man - who milks them.

Long regarded more as pests than a source of food here, boffin Yuri Shmakov has nevertheless revealed his first experiments produced a high-fat milk which tasted like cream.

Each female produces about a third of a pint of milk per day but Mr Shmakov believes a couple of dozen rabbits would yield as much as a cow.

Now he intends to use a miniature version of a dairy milking machine to set up a rabbit milk business in his home town of Ulyanovsk.

With British farmers constantly looking for new ways to diversify, the urge to hop to it and start producing rabbit milk might soon prove irresistible.

A NEW BOOKLET aims to help woodland owners get to know their woods better and care for them more successfully.

Launching the Forestry Commission publication 'So, You Own a Woodland?', Minister Ben Bradshaw said:"This practical guide to understanding your woodlands is really aimed at those new to woodland ownership and management but there is something in it for everyone. It has a refreshing, straightforward approach to getting the best out of your woodland and, most importantly, it explains how owners benefit when a woodland is managed. Small, privately owned woodlands make a significant contribution to the landscape and play a vital conservation role."

RURAL ROADS WHICH are badly designed have been posing a huge risk to motorists, the AA has warned.

The organisation has just published a new league table showing the most lethal rural roads in Britain.

The top 10 worst country roads, listed in order of the greatest hazard, are: the A537 Macclesfield to Buxton road; A534 Welsh boundary to Nantwich road; A682 via M65 (J13) to A65 Long Preston; A54 Congleton to Buxton road; A631 Gainsborough to A1103 road; A683/A6 to Kirkby Lonsdale road; A61 Barnsley to Wakefield road; A1101 Outwell (A1122) to Long Sutton (A17) road; A44 Leominster to Worcester road; and the A53 Leek to Buxton road.

John Dawson, director of the AA Motoring Trust, said:"It's easy to forget the true death toll on the roads because the accidents are scattered and usually involve only one or two people. Yet there are many people alive today thanks to the relatively inexpensive changes made on (improved) roads we have identified.

"It's right that billions of pounds are being spent on railway safety, which works out at around £10 million for every life saved.

"But we can save hundreds more people every year on the roads for just a fraction of that, and deliver massive savings to the NHS into the bargain."

A CARELESS COW has been blamed for wrecking a holiday caravan after it stumbled over the edge of a quarry and plunged 30ft onto the vehicle.

The cow had been grazing at the edge of the quarry near Combe Martin, Devon, seconds before tumbling onto Derrick and Patricia Cogan's caravan.

The elderly Bristol couple normally keep the caravan in storage at the location - believing it safe there - and only learnt of the disaster when they turned up to collect it, ready for a relaxing week's break.

When the site owner told them their caravan had been flattened by a low-flying cow, they first thought he was joking - sadly, he wasn't.

However, despite one side of the caravan being smashed, the determined pair still used it for their holiday.

Repairs will cost thousands of pounds.

The cow survived with an injured leg.

PEREGRINE FALCONS ARE continuing their resurgence in many parts of the UK , according to the British Trust for Ornithology.

"There were 1,402 breeding pairs in 2002, compared with 1,283 in 1991 and 874 in the 1930s before the population crash," said a spokesman."Thus the population has increased by 10 per cent since 1991 and is now 61 per cent higher than in the 1930s."

Since 1991, says the Trust, the number of 'known potential peregrine territories' in the UK and Isle of Man had risen by 26 per cent to 2,032 sites.

ANTI-FOXHUNTING laws might not be enforced by rural magistrates if they are passed in England and Wales, a Labour peer has claimed.

Lady Mallalieu, one of the leaders of the campaign against the Government's Hunting Bill, said she already knows some rural magistrates who would refuse to deal with cases against people ignoring a ban.

She also claims the Government's entire legislative programme could be shattered in the run-up to the General Election if Tony Blair pushes through a ban on hunting using the Parliament Act.

Lady Mallalieu, president of the Countryside Alliance, said employing the Act in such controversial circumstances might lead to serious political fallout for the Government.

The Alliance recently announced that it will issue a legal challenge to the Hunting Bill, possibly even by the end of this year.

In its lawyers' view, the Bill goes directly against the Human Rights Act.

Meanwhile, Alliance chairman John Jackson has tried to put a positive slant on the second reading of the Bill in the House of Lords.

In a note to members, he said:"The debate showed massive support on all sides of the House for the Alliance's call for a workable regulatory solution for all hunting and a strong move towards restoring the original architecture to the Government's Bill.

"To pick out individuals from such a long list of those who spoke vociferously against a ban is difficult but Lord Carlile, Lord Bragg and Lord Hurd, enormously respected figures from the three main parties, all provided clear cut cases for a regulatory solution and our own Baroness Mallalieu and Lord Mancroft highlighted the prejudice that had driven Labour MPs to amend the Bill to ban all hunting.

"The newspapers have picked up on remarks made by DEFRA Minister Lord Whitty, winding up the debate, which suggest that the Government could still consider using the Parliament Act to force a ban onto the statute books.

"Given the massive Labour majority in the House of Commons and their obsession with banning hunting this has always been a possibility.

"The only way that we can ensure that the Government is less likely to force through this illiberal legislation is by making it clear that the political cost of banning hunting in the run-up to a General Election will be far greater than the short-term pain of disappointing Banks, Kaufman and the Parliamentary Labour Party."

WOLVES COULD BE the answer to the problem of massive deer herds devastating the Scottish countryside.

With red deer in Scotland now at record numbers, supporters of a scheme to reintroduce wolves seem likely to win over previous sceptics.

The Wolf Trust is a charity set up to educate the public about wolves and actively promotes a wolf reintroduction and recovery programme for the Scottish Highlands.

"Wolf research began some decades ago. Yet most people still know only the traditional mythical wolf," said a spokesman."The Wolf Trust replaces the traditional wolf with the real wolf based on scientific knowledge and rational understanding."

NEW LABOUR WOULD be foolish in the extreme to ignore the staunch public rejection of GM crops, warn campaigners.

Following publication of a report on the Government-sponsored national GM debate, Friends of the Earth's GM spokesman Pete Riley said:"The Government will ignore this report at its peril.

"The public has made it clear that it doesn't want GM food and it doesn't want GM crops. There must not be any more weasel words from the Government on this issue.

"It must stand up to US and corporate lobbying, honour the findings of its own consultation, and rule out commercialisation of GM crops."

The report's key findings were that: people are generally uneasy about GM; the more people engage in GM issues, the harder their attitudes and more intense their concerns; there is little support for early commercialisation; there is widespread mistrust of Government and multi-national companies; there is broad desire to know more and for more research to be done; developing countries have special interests; the debate was welcomed and valued.

The research project 'GM Nation' had encouraged people to fill in a questionnaire with 36,557 forms returned.

More than half of respondents said they NEVER want to see GM crops grown in the UK. A further 18 per cent would find GM crops acceptable ONLY if there was no risk of cross-contamination while 13 per cent wanted more research before any decision was made.

Only two per cent said that GM crops were acceptable 'in any circumstances' and only eight per cent were happy to eat GM food while 86 per cent were not.

RED DEER ON a remote island have horrified birdwatchers by turning their attentions to live seabird chicks - and eating them.

The pathetic corpses of Manx shearwater chicks have been found strewn across the Isle of Rum, south west of Skye, with heads and legs grazed off.

The odd behaviour of mostly vegetarian animals has previously been observed in sheep and is thought to be a desperate measure to overcome dietary deficiences on the sparse island.

WILDLIFE COULD BE helped by a new booklet aimed at boosting Britain's rarest indigenous conifer tree - the juniper.

Author Alice Broome, of Forest Research, said:"Juniper is a crucial conservation species. It is a rich source of food for many insects and the berries are eaten by a number of birds, including thrushes, fieldfares and waxwings."

HUNT SUPPORTERS HAVE attacked Liberal Democrat leader Charles Kennedy and anti-hunting Lib Dem MPs for backing a move to ban all hunting.

Rural campaigners descended on the party's conference in Brighton to make their displeasure known.

Leaflets distributed and banners unfurled posed the question - 'A Hunting Ban. Liberal? Democratic?'.

The demonstrators were joined by supportive Lib Dem MPs Lembit Opik and Roger Williams.

Simon Hart, chief executive designate of the Countryside Alliance, said:"The Lib Dems have an opportunity to show they can make a positive difference to rural Britain - and many of their policies have been welcomed by rural communities.

"But the party's image in the countryside and their electoral success will always be limited because of the support of their leader, and many of their MPs, for the criminalisation of hunting.

"Why aren't they willing to even discuss a regulatory solution which would do more good for animal welfare than a ban, as well as respecting civil liberties? "What is 'Liberal' about banning things when there is no rational case for doing so? And what is 'Democratic' about a measure that would unjustly criminalise a minority's way of life when fewer than half our MPs, half our parliamentarians and half the electorate even support a ban?"

OVER 500 LITTLE tern chicks were raised this summer in East Norfolk - easily the best year ever, according to the RSPB.

English Nature's Rick Southwood added:"We are delighted with this year's successful nesting season and would like to thank residents and volunteers for their support and help."

RARE LAMPREYS ARE among species set to benefit from improvements to the fish pass at Boroughbridge on the River Ure in North Yorkshire.

The Environment Agency and British Waterways have put the finishing touches to a £76,000 joint scheme to improve fish passage over Boroughbridge Weir which will help lampreys, an internationally protected species, to migrate and breed.

"Lampreys are one of only two surviving remnants of the most primitive invertebrates, the Agnatha or 'jawless fish'," said a spokesman."Today, only three species of this eel-like creature remain in Britain and their habitats are protected by an EC directive."

GREY PARTRIDGES APPEAR to be flourishing in parts of the country thanks to recent warm weather, says the Game Conservancy Trust.

"Early brood counts from landowners participating in the Grey Partridge Count Scheme confirm the general feeling of a very good breeding year for the wild grey partridge, especially in the east and north of the country," said a spokesman.

"This increase is attributed mainly to the hot and dry weather conditions across the country with the exception of isolated storms at the end of July that hit some stocks severely.

"The increases have been particularly encouraging where there have been brood-rearing covers that have produced high numbers of insects and predators have been controlled."

345

BARN OWL: saved by help from Malaysian rats

BARN owls have long been on the list of our most threatened species but there are signs, at last, that they may have turned the corner away from extinction.

This majestic owl, slightly smaller than the tawny owl but with longer legs and more dramatic colouring, has been a living barometer of the countryside's health.

Numbers plummeted over recent decades as agricultural pesticides laid waste to wildlife, making barn owls' traditional prey more scarce. Widespread destruction of green spaces accelerated the decline, especially since barn owls appeared unable to adapt to an alternative urban lifestyle, unlike tawny owls. Isolated barns favoured for nesting - hence the name - also vanished by the thousand as developers turned them into desirable homes for humans.

As a result, only a few thousand barn owls remain in the wild, scattered in pockets of countryside not yet badly disturbed by traffic or people.

However, the continual fall in their numbers appears to have been halted - and, strangely, the bird owes a debt of thanks to rats at the other side of the world.

Voracious Malaysian plantation rats were finally brought under control after local owls were encouraged to breed among them in special nest boxes erected on tall poles.

This simple scheme was so successful that it was later adapted to help our own barn owls with the Hawk and Owl Trust putting up 1,000 pole nest boxes around the country.

Now the Trust has announced: *"The decline has been stopped. The population has stabilised and we currently have about 4,000 pairs."*

Good news then for barn owls, although a population of only 4,000 pairs means they are still in danger of extinction should their fortunes take a new downturn.

Usually nocturnal, barn owls use their phenomenally strong hearing to first detect rodents rustling through the grass.

Then their powerful eyesight takes over.

Yet even in periods of impenetrable darkness, hearing ability alone is often sufficient to guide them to a foraging vole or rat.

Barn owls routinely fly with their 'undercarriage' lowered, so their murderous talons are instantly ready for action.

These are the tools of their trade with the outer toe on each foot reversible to cut the chances of a struggling victim managing to escape.

Eerily silent in flight with distinctive white and pale brown plumage, barn owls can appear almost ghostly creatures if spotted at dawn or dusk. The overall effect can be bewitching, as recorded by 19th Century poet George Meredith who wrote: *"Lovely are the curves of the white owl sweeping wavy in the dusk, lit by one large star."*

Thanks, in part, to the rats of Malaysia, such visions might not become a thing of the past here after all.

HUNT GROUPS ARE opening up their sport as never before in a determined bid to show the public what goes on despite a total ban looming across England and Wales.

According to the Countryside Alliance, more than 60 hunts have issued open invitations to the public to come and see for themselves what hunting is all about as part of its so-called 'National Newcomers' Week'.

Up until October 11, the hunts will be holding special introductory days for newcomers who wish to learn more about the controversial sport.

The Alliance says hunts will advertise in local papers as well as delivering leaflets inviting members of the public to come and enjoy a day's hunting absolutely free of charge.

Spokeswoman Nicky Driver said:"Hunts up and down the country are enjoying increased support. Now 59 per cent of the public say 'Keep hunting' and more and more people have expressed interest in coming and trying hunting themselves.

"Newcomers' Week will make it easier for people to find out more and, by making hunting more accessible, we hope to improve understanding of our activities.

"Hunting in the 21st Century has nothing to hide. Everyone is welcome and we look forward to meeting people who would like to learn the reality, rather than the propaganda, about hunting."

Predictably, however, the move has left anti-hunt campaigners unimpressed.

Recently, the League Against Cruel Sports told members to redouble their efforts to win a total ban.

"I urge you to recognise that there is still a great deal of work to be done before the Hunting Bill is passed and becomes law," said an official,"and it is important that the general public are made aware of this. We still need your help and support in the weeks and months ahead until the cruel and barbaric practice of hunting with dogs is finished once and for all."

SONGBIRDS FIND IT just as easy to warble a complex mating tune as they do to utter a simple 'cheep', say researchers.

Scientists at the University of St Andrews in Scotland, expected to find that more sophisticated songs took much more effort but this was not the case.

Dr Sally Ward, one of the research leaders, said:"We studied whether singing is energetically costly for songbirds because it intuitively appears to be hard work. But this was not the case. Singing didn't take much energy."

A DRAMATIC LOSS of wading birds and aquatic life is the real picture behind the Government's trumpeted view that England's waterways are cleaner than ever, says the RSPB.

"The Environment Minister, Elliot Morley, has said that current water quality figures indicate 'rivers and estuaries in England are cleaner than at any other time on record'," said a Society spokesman.

"However, the RSPB is deeply concerned about continuing nitrate and phosphate pollution from agriculture and the water industry.

"In the light of the imminent OFWAT pricing review and water company investment plans, there is a perfect opportunity for setting improvement measures in place. The RSPB is calling on Mr Morley to direct water companies to make improvements part of their new plans.

"The water quality figures show that over 50 per cent of our rivers suffer from too many phosphates and a third from too many nitrates.

"These high levels of 'nutrients' are choking rivers and lakes with growths of algae and weed smothering the spawning grounds of fish and pushing out plants and invertebrates that can only survive under specific nutrient conditions.

"Whilst it is true that we no longer have raw sewage on our beaches, or dead fish in our major rivers, this masks a chronic, long-term decline in the ecological quality of our waters. The facts speak for themselves.

"Dramatic declines in wetland breeding birds include a 47 per cent loss of lapwings, 31 per cent of curlews, 40 per cent of redshanks and 65 per cent of snipe in lowland river valleys in the last 20 years."

EELS, PIKE AND trout were among fish rescued from a tributary of the River Wye in Herefordshire after water levels reached a low point.

Environment Agency spokesman Bill Purvis said of the Yazor Brook operation: "Members of the public alerted us to the plight of the fish. We received a substantial number of reports.

"Following these, a visit was made to the worst affected reaches. This assessment coupled with the forecast of more dry weather left the Agency with little option but to rescue the fish.

"The operation was a great success and about 50 brown trout, 10 pike, 20 chub and 30 eels, as well as bullhead and stone loach were transported to a nearby section of the main River Wye. In addition, several hundred sticklebacks were also rescued from the worst affected areas."

COUNTRY CAMPAIGNERS are gearing up to fight massive new housing development along the M11 corridor through three English counties.

The Campaign to Protect Rural England has pledged to resist Government proposals for between 157,000 and 194,000 new homes in largely rural parts of Essex, Cambridgeshire, and Hertfordshire.

Sean Traverse-Healy, vice chairman of CPRE's East of England region, said:"Growth on this scale is far, far beyond what is currently planned by local councils.

"It would swallow up a great area of greenfield and have an enormous impact on the quality of life and the environment across an area which is rich in valued countryside and historic, attractive towns and villages."

RARE BLACK GROUSE have been given a boost with a new initiative aimed at restoring numbers.

The project, supported by the Game Conservancy Trust, is striving to restore the bird to the south east of Scotland with the help of local landowners.

Spearheaded by the Duke of Northumberland, the 'Lammermuir Black Grouse Recovery Initiative' aims to create the habitats and conditions in which black grouse thrive.

"Black grouse lekking on a spring morning is one of the marvels of Britain's wildlife," said the Duke. "I have been lucky enough to witness this amazing display not far from my home in the Lammermuir Hills on many occasions and it has given me the determination to do what I can to bring them back from a dangerously low ebb.

"Once, black grouse could be seen throughout the British Isles but management practices have eradicated them almost everywhere. It is now up to landowners, farmers and managers to reverse this trend by habitat improvement and predator control, and I am delighted to be involved in this scheme to increase their spread throughout south east Scotland."

The Duke himself is creating a 'feathering' of sitka spruce over a 500 hectare block with Forestry Commission approval in a bid to encourage the birds back onto his land.

Hugo Straker, the Conservancy Trust's adviser in the area, has also been working with landowners to enhance habitat and control predation to benefit the birds.

He said:"I began counting the leks in 1993 when I saw 80 cocks. Now, 10 years later, I have only counted 39. This 50 per cent decline is a clear illustration of how serious the plight of the black grouse is within south east Scotland.

"The Lammermuir initiative aims to incorporate all the landowners in the area - from the large estates to the farmers on the hill fringe. All provide a piece of the fine mosaic of habitat which makes up the bird's territory."

THE LURE OF the wild proved irresistible for a rare owl bred in captivity which escaped from its aviary in mid-Wales.

Horatio, a young European eagle owl, fled his home at Bacheldre, near Churchstoke, prompting fears he would not survive.

But the six-month-old bird returned after just two nights of freedom and allowed owner Arthur Williams to collect him from a tree.

PINE TREES INSIDE one of the country's most popular forest parks have been ravaged by a disease which attacks their needles.

Red band needle blight has caused widespread damage to Corsican pine trees in Thetford forest in south east England, reports the Forestry Commission.

Last year the disease was also identified for the first time in forests along the Scottish Borders.

Experts from Forest Research, the investigations arm of the Commission, have reported unusually high levels of the disease for the last five years.

Fortunately, new information providing advice for woodland owners and managers faced with the disease has now been published.

'Red Band Needle Blight of Pine' assesses the scale of the infection in Britain and describes a number of methods which can be successfully used to halt its advance.

"Red band needle blight is a fungal disease which can affect many species of conifer," explained Anna Brown, one of the authors of the report. "However, pines are the most common hosts of the disease and, in Britain, Corsican pine appears to be particularly susceptible.

"In 2003 we have seen the most significant occurrence of red band needle blight in the UK over the past 40 years. The reasons for this are unclear. However, increased spring rainfall in recent years coupled with warmer springs may have created optimum conditions for infection."

A DROWNING LAMB was saved by a cat with no tail in one of the more bizarre rescue stories of recent times.

The struggling lamb faced certain death in a private swimming pool at Cheltenham, Gloucester - shire, until the frantic miaowing of tailess Puss Puss brought help.

Garden workers Karen Lewis and Adrian Bunton had realised their pet was trying to tell them something.

They left the site they were working on, followed Puss Puss, found the lamb and plucked it to safety.

The lucky animal had become separated from a flock of sheep in a local field.

HEN HARRIERS ARE fighting back against a host of setbacks which threatened to wipe them out in England.

Illegal persecution and moorland fires are among problems said to have driven the winged predators further to the edge of extinction this year.

However, eight nesting attempts were successful, producing 26 young.

Richard Saunders, an English Nature hen harrier recovery project officer, said:"Despite its extreme rarity in England, conserving the hen harrier remains unpopular with some people and it is unfortunately still a target for persecution.

"However, on behalf of English Nature, I would like to extend our thanks to the owners and gamekeepers of grouse moors where we have received support and to the Moorland Association, Game Conservancy Trust and RSPB for their continued co-operation and assistance."

Sir Martin Doughty, chairman of English Nature, added:"Given the adversities this magnificent bird has to contend with, both natural and man-made, it is truly remarkable that it survives at all."

THOUSANDS OF RAINBOW trout in a Scottish loch have been left blinded by a horrific parasitic infestation, it has been revealed.

The disaster at Loch Leven is not only a crisis for the fish themselves but also a blow to hundreds of anglers who have each paid £30 for a day's fishing at the loch.

With the fish unable to see brightly coloured lures or bait, anglers have been wasting their time as the trout grope to feed themselves.

The trout are believed to have fallen victim to the parasitic 'eye fluke' which is borne by a species of water snail.

The loch is stocked by up to 30,000 rainbow trout each year from ponds where the snail flourishes.

Jamie Montgomery, director of Kinross Estates which owns the loch, told a Scottish newspaper:"Brown trout are immune to the parasite because they are also indigenous but the rainbow trout, from North America, are not.

"The parasite does not pose the same problem to the fish which are in the loch, as the concentration of both fish and parasite is much less than in the rearing ponds.

"By trying to save money by rearing our own trout instead of buying them in, we have, in effect, shot ourselves in the foot."

The fluke attaches itself to the eyes of its victims with affected fish incurable.

The problem is thought to occur more during warm summers when the water's temperature reaches 16 degrees C.

Cataracts slowly form on victims' eyes, eventually causing total blindness.

SALMON AND SEA trout were helped to migrate across shallow stretches of a Welsh river by the release of water from a local reservoir.

The Environment Agency came to the fish's aid following an extended period of low flows in August and September.

The controlled release took place over five days, encouraging fish to enter the river at Carmarthen.

According to the Agency, the reservoir Llyn Brianne is situated in the headwaters of the River Tywi and, when created in the late 1960s, a 'water bank' was provided to help fish migrate at critical times of the year.

This is the third release this year - the first came in the spring to encourage juvenile salmon and sea trout to leave the river, followed by a release earlier this month to encourage mature salmon and sea trout to enter the river.

"The River Tywi is a highly important salmon and sea trout fishery attracting large numbers of visitors from around the country to fish," said a spokesman.

MORE THAN 12,300 animals are killed by gamekeepers on British game bird shooting estates each day, according to the League Against Cruel Sports.

The figures form part of a new investigative report which, says the League, "details a largely unreported and frequently illegal programme of predator control by gamekeepers who snare, trap and poison wildlife to protect the millions of game birds shot every year by wealthy businessmen, tourists, and amateur shooters keen to experience a day or weekend of country shooting.

"The report reveals that animals, including protected badgers, foxes, hares, stags, owls, kestrels, and domestic livestock and pets, often die excruciating deaths because they were in the wrong place at the wrong time.

"In just one example, a 'vermin return form' sent to Sir Jocelyn Stevens by gamekeepers on his Millden estate in Scotland records that in just one month, gamekeepers killed 698 rabbits, 37 hares, 19 stoats, 23 crows, three magpies, three jackdaws, one rook, three foxes, two 'feral' cats, six gulls and one stag.

"Millden is just one of the 2,000 estates and farms currently involved in this industry. Amongst those willing to pay £400 to £2,000 per day for a day of shooting are celebrity enthusiasts including Madonna, Guy Ritchie, Vinnie Jones, Jamie Oliver, Bryan Ferry and Marco Pierre White."

THE HORSE WORLD is still buzzing over the odd case of the prize-winning stallion found to be missing two vital components - its testicles.

Black Prince , a Clydesdale, has been stripped of the many awards he won in Scotland after it emerged that he had been castrated as a youngster.

The animal even picked up more prizes at this year's Doune and Dunblane Show as well as a prize at the National Stallion Show.

Now plans to sell him as a star stud have been scrapped after shocked owner Kevin Cargill discovered the truth when a vet closely inspected his pet.

Judges at show events are thought to have missed the problem as stallions often retract their testicles on parade.

CRUCIAN CARP ARE under serious threat from a surprise enemy - the humble goldfish.

Environment Agency scientists fear the popular household pets could soon force crucian carp out of existence.

Goldfish get into the wild by escaping from ponds during floods, are released illegally, or accidentally stocked by fishery managers.

Now, in-depth research commissioned by the Agency has revealed that the ornamental fish are not only competing for food and living space but are mating with crucian carp causing hybrid offspring.

Environment Agency spokesman Phil Bolton said:"The crucian carp is a fish that should have no problem thriving in the British Isles. It is hardy and adaptable.But interference has tipped the balance in favour of goldfish. Crucian carp are already suffering from habitat loss and introduced disease.

"This research has revealed that the presence of introduced goldfish and common carp has led to interbreeding and hybridisation in wild populations. Native crucian carp could be wiped-out as a result."

BRITISH APPLES HAVE been filling up supermarket shelves this year in a glorious retort to increasing foreign imports.

More than 150,000 tonnes of apples were harvested from British orchards in 2003 after one of the sunniest summers on record.

Now, varieties such as Discovery, Bramley, Cox and Gala will be celebrated in Trafalgar Square, London, at a special event on October 12.

"Attendees will be able to sample their favourite English varieties, brought straight to the event by the grower, as well as some of the more unusual ones such as Howgate Wonder or Pineapple Pippin and even the Devonian cider apple Slack Ma Girdle," said a spokesman for the NFU.

"Apples first originated in the Middle East over 4,000 years ago and their organised cultivation is thought to have been brought to Britain by the Romans who gifted land to army veterans to encourage them to settle.

"The creation and cultivation of different species of apple has taken place for at least 1,000 years, with specific varieties arriving in Britain with the Normans in 1066.

"After the decimation of rural areas in the 13th Century through the Plague and War of the Roses, fruiterer Richard Harris set up the first large-scale orchards, on the instructions of Henry VIII.

"Harris searched the known world for the best varieties and created his orchards in Teynham, Kent.

"Over the next few hundred years, apples were sold as a luxury in London with the Old English variety being the main dessert apple. The cooking equivalent was the Costard, which gave rise to the term costermonger, first applied to apple salesmen.

"The number of varieties exploded in the Victorian era as explorers scoured the world for new varieties and brought them back to Brogdale in Kent, expanding its orchards and forming the basis for the National Fruit Collection which now contains over 2,000 varieties."

GARDEN BIRDS ARE being helped to beat winter starvation by four celebrity chefs.

Ainsley Harriott, Antony Worrall Thompson, Jane Asher and Rick Stein have cooked up a range of recipes as part of the RSPB's 'Feed the Birds Day' on October 25 aimed at keeping garden birds well fed during the cold months ahead.

The RSPB says:"Everyone can help by getting out in the fresh autumn air, cleaning their bird tables, filling their feeders and putting out water to help birds through the winter ahead."

FEARS ABOUT SOARING numbers of wild boar in south east England were raised long before current calls for a cull.

Farmers estimate up to 1,000 animals now roam woodland, posing a potential hazard to livestock and ramblers.

However, as far back as 1998, an unpublished report from the Central Science Laboratory stated:"Computer modelling suggests that the wild boar population in East Sussex and Kent is viable and will increase and spread.

"This risk assessment has shown that wild boar are a particular concern to the agricultural industry regarding crop damage and animal health. Wild boar are also an important concern in relation to public safety, road traffic accidents and conservation issues.

"It is recommended that the Government formulate a policy with regard to wild boar and their management in the UK. The policy would need to resolve whether, for example, they should be regarded as an undesirable invasive species or a reintroduced native species.

"Three broad control and management options could be considered for the wild boar - total eradication, selective control or no control, although actual control methods may need further research.

"However, wild boar have a high reproductive rate and no natural predators in the UK.

"Their numbers are therefore likely to continue to increase and some management will be required in the future."

A STRANDED SWAN caused a flap when workers at a Welsh factory discovered it clinging precariously to their roof.

Firemen were brought in to rescue the bird which was stuck on the roof of Texplan in Newtown, Powys.

After efforts to scare it off using their siren failed, the firefighters managed to coax the bird down using long poles.

The swan, which was unhurt, was later released on a local river.

The RSPCA, who assisted in the rescue, explained the bird had simply touched down in an awkward spot too difficult to take off from again.

ONE OF THE best examples of ancient woodland in Britain has celebrated its 10th birthday as a National Nature Reserve.

Burnham Beeches, near Slough, has one of the largest collections of beech trees in the world, one of which is thought to be more than 800 years old.

"The forests are virtually irreplaceable and are steeped in history," said a spokesman for English Nature."In 1880 the Corporation of London acquired Burnham Beeches to save it from threatened development and over the years it has been popular among artists, poets and country lovers.

"Thomas Gray, Sheridan and Mendelssohn are known to have visited the forest frequently and been inspired by the wild woodland and the character of the old trees.

"Burnham Beeches is celebrated for its pollarded beech trees, the largest collection of old beech trees in the world, and for being one of the best preserved examples of early woodland management.

"The average age of the pollarded beeches is known to be more than 400 years. The largest tree, known as the Druids' Oak, is probably over 800 years old."

BIRD EXPERTS ARE begging gardeners not to give up on their sun-scorched lawns and cover them with decking or patios.

The British Trust for Ornithology is alarmed that after one of the hottest summers on record many gardeners are considering doing away with their frazzled lawns completely.

"Your lawn may look dead but it is a 'living carpet' supporting an amazing variety of wildlife, from invertebrates to our favourite garden birds," said a Trust spokesman.

"Birds such as song thrushes and blackbirds find much of their food on lawns so a so-called make-over would be really bad news for garden biodiversity.

"Blackbirds play life or death tug-of-war with unwilling worms. On damp nights, hedgehogs will snuffle their way across the grass to eat the exposed worms and, while in your garden, will also devour slugs.

"Robins will feast on insects too small for us to see and if you are really lucky, in the drier areas, green woodpeckers will discover an ants' nest, giving you hours of entertainment.

"The best wildlife lawn will be a little bit wild so let some weeds flourish. There is no finer sight than goldfinches wrestling with the dandelion seed-heads.

"Clover attracts bees, which in turn pollinate your vegetables and fruits. In the dampest parts, moss will flourish, beautiful to look at, maintenance free and essential for many nesting birds."

BIG CAT SIGHTINGS are on the increase with 15 recorded in one week across Britain recently.

Danny Bamping, founder of the British Big Cats Society, believes sightings are becoming more common as people no longer feel foolish reporting them.

Ernie Carey, from Ickenham, near Uxbridge, is among the latest spotters left shocked after confronting what appeared to be a black panther in rural Cookham, Berkshire.

Wife Barbara had been driving their car in a quiet lane when the cat suddenly loped across the road in front of them, prompting Mr Carey to hurriedly close his open passenger window.

"It was huge, with paws like a tiger's," he said.

DAI THE RAM will be the star of a charity fund-raising 'sheep wedding' at a farm in mid-Wales.

Bets of £1 are being placed on which ewe out of a flock of 200 dashing Dai will choose first.

The lucky sheep will win its sponsor £50 in the event at Ty Nant farm, in Penybontfawr next month.

Montgomeryshire Young Farmers Club has organised the fun to raise cash for a memorial shield to honour farmer Ifan Evans, 19, tragically killed in a car crash.

THE NEW LEADER of the Countryside Alliance has signalled his resolve to fight even harder to protect hunting in England and Wales.

Chief executive Simon Hart has previously revealed that a campaign of civil disobedience may be the result if Labour MPs win a total ban.

In an article for a Welsh newspaper, he wrote:"It has become increasingly obvious that a large majority of Labour MPs are determined to try to force through a total ban on hunting with dogs.

"This could trigger the emergence of a civil resistance movement the like of which the UK has not seen before.

"Several thousand people from one of the most law-abiding sectors of the community - including many from across Wales - have already signed a formal declaration that in the event of a ban on hunting they would, as a responsible means of protest, openly disobey such a law.

"And they would do so not in the hope of evading punishment, but willingly accepting the personal consequences of their unlawful but peaceful actions.

"How has it come to this? Parliament should only limit the rights of a minority if there is conclusive evidence that such action would be in the clear public interest.

"No such case for a hunting ban has been made. Indeed most anti-hunting MPs have consistently paraded their ignorance and prejudice on this subject even to the detriment of the farming and rural communities in Wales.

"First, they ignored the evidence of the Government's independent Burns Inquiry into hunting, commissioned expressly 'to inform the parliamentary debate' and which had found no grounds for a blanket ban on hunting.

"Yet hardly any of the anti-hunting MPs bothered to read the inquiry's report or even turn up for the debate on its publication.

"They also ignored the evidence emerging from the Government's subsequent consultation process and torpedoed the 'licensing' Bill the Government then brought forward.

"And national polls show that these MPs are totally and consistently out of step with public opinion which no longer favours a ban.

"Indeed recent polls show the majority do not believe that Parliament should even be wasting scarce time on this issue."

SALMON AND TROUT were among hundreds of fish killed in a mystery pollution spill on the River Ebbw near Newbridge, South Wales.

"An initial report was received of a discharge into the river and dead fish being seen and officers immediately started investigations," said a spokesman for the Environment Agency.

"At present, the pollutant is unidentified but it is believed to be some form of detergent discharged via a culverted watercourse.

"Two industrial sites, each with a large number of units, have drainage systems linking to the water-course. Companies based at the Croespenmaen and Pen y Fan Industrial Estates should check their drainage systems for blockages or anything that may have caused this discharge and contact us for advice if a problem is found.

"Samples of fish, including trout and juvenile salmon, have been sent for analysis and the investigations are continuing."

EFFORTS HAVE BEEN stepped up to save one of Britain's most famous heavy horse breeds, now more threatened than the giant panda.

The Suffolk Punch was once a common sight, especially in England, and was even mentioned in a Charles Dickens novel, 'David Copperfield'.

Slightly shorter than the Shire horse but equally powerful, only 300 Suffolk Punches now survive in the UK.

Bright chestnut in colour, Suffolk Punches also differ from other heavy horses in that their hooves are unfeathered, a distinction which some think makes them seem more elegant.

The Rare Breeds Survival Trust lists the animal as 'critical' and is campaigning for cash to preserve the DNA of remaining horses at its newly opened genetic archive in Devon.

Conservationists believe it would be tragic for the breed to vanish but there are currently only 18 Suffolk Punch stallions registered nationwide.

The scheme to preserve DNA costs over £2,000 per horse and to date just six stallions have had material collected.

Also pushing the project is the Suffolk Horse Society, of Woodbridge, Suffolk.

Spokeswoman Amanda Hillier says the Society aims to encourage breeding by promoting the horses.

"It's sad to let this source of power disappear because we never know when we might need it again," Ms Hillier said. "It's an insurance policy for the future."

AN ESCAPED PELICAN caused a ripple of amusement among birdwatchers when it settled among native birds on a Leicestershire lake.

The large, long-beaked white bird - more suited to scooping up fish in tropical climes - was identified as a pink-backed pelican by Leicestershire and Rutland Ornithological Society.

It has been making itself at home on the local Eyebrook Reservoir alongside the usual swans and grebes.

The bird is believed to have escaped from a wildlife park or private collection.

BRITAIN'S BATS ARE the subject of a new booklet from The Mammal Society just in time for Halloween.

"Bats are often associated with the supernatural or gothic. However, in 'Bats' the authors show just how fascinating these maligned and misunderstood creatures are," said a Society spokesman.

Written by Dean Waters and Ruth Warren, 'Bats' costs £3.50, is lavishly illustrated with colour photographs of bats and their habitats, and covers all 16 types of bat resident in Britain.

THE MYSTERY OF why Premier Tony Blair persists in flag-waving for GM crops against fierce public opposition has deepened.

Following hard on the heels of a recent poll showing the public resolutely against GM crops, the results of a three-year scientific experiment on the environmental impact of the crops largely showed more dubious 'benefits'.

Wildlife actually suffered in field trials of GM oilseed rape and sugar beet which were the biggest scientific tests of their kind on GM crops anywhere in the world.

Three different crops were selected for the experiment: oilseed rape, sugar beet and maize, with the genetically modified versions planted alongside their conventional counterparts for comparison.

Despite a public outcry in 1999, Mr Blair had given the go-ahead for the controversial tests to take place to assess the impact of GM crops on wildlife, plants, and other crops.

Even Michael Meacher MP, Tony Blair's former Minister for the Environment, admitted:"I cannot see that the Government could now logically, consistently, or morally go ahead with allowing GM crops to be grown (commercially)."

Before publication of the results of the tests, hundreds of anti-GM protesters had gathered in London to underline public opposition.

"Welsh pianos played all the way from St Davids, coffins were towed from Inverness, and cow-shaped trolleys spearheaded a festive parade," said a spokesman for the event.

"Many others travelled by foot, bike or tractor to join over 1,000 consumers demanding their right to a GM-free Britain. The rally was organised by Friends of the Earth, GM-free Cymru, Genetic Engineering Network and the Five Year Freeze campaign.

"Bedford Square, in the heart of Bloomsbury, was the starting point for the final push in a pilgrimage of well over 600 miles for some."

Clare Oxborrow, Friends of the Earth's GM spokeswoman, added:"Tony Blair must listen and refuse to allow GM crops to be grown in the UK."

AVOCETS HAVE HAD a train line named after them after 500 of the distinctive waders took up residence on a southern English estuary.

The busy railway between Exeter Central and Exmouth has changed its name to the 'Avocet Line' in celebration of the wildlife of the Exe Estuary, revealed the RSPB.

"A specially repainted train, decorated with images of birds including the avocet - symbol of the RSPB - made the 'maiden' journey to Exmouth," said a spokesman.

"Staff from the RSPB and East Devon District Council Countryside Service provided commentary for passengers on the bird life to be seen from carriage windows.

"The project is a joint venture between the RSPB, various local authorities in East Devon, Wessex Trains and the Exe Estuary Partnership, which balances the needs of wildlife with other activities on the river.

"The Exe estuary is an important wintering site for more than 40 different species of wildfowl and wading birds, including internationally important numbers of black-tailed godwits and up to 500 avocets."

352

WILD SALMON OFF northern Britain remain at grave risk from the shoals of farmed salmon escaping into their midst, according to new research.

Interbreeding between weaker farmed salmon and stronger wild salmon may degrade and even eventually wipe out Atlantic salmon stocks altogether, warn scientists.

A 10-year study by Irish scientists from Queen's University, Belfast, and the Marine Institute, Galway, found that the genes of wild salmon are changed by interbreeding with escaped fish, potentially lowering their natural survival rates.

Each year, about two million salmon are thought to escape from fish farms across the north Atlantic, equal to about half the total number of wild adult salmon at sea.

Last year there were apparently 450,000 escapes from Scottish fish farms alone and latest figures show that another 96,000 have broken free off Scotland in 2003.

Dr Paulo Prodohl, one of the scheme's researchers, said farmed salmon have both genetic and competitive impacts on wild populations.

"The results of this project have provided a convincing and clear warning to the people involved," he said."The farm industry is now starting to address the problem and work to avoid such high numbers of escapes and we hope that it will become more controlled."

ODD CIRCLING BEHAVIOUR by two short-eared owls has had birdwatchers scratching their heads.

Birder James Walsh observed the antics at Burton Marsh beside the Dee Estuary on the Wirral.

"I spotted one short-eared owl," he said."Minutes later it was joined by another and they began flying round and round in tight circles about 20 yards above the ground for about two minutes or maybe more.

"They were gaining very little height in the process, only about 10 yards, and it certainly worked up some of the local carrion crows. I couldn't think of any real explanation for this behaviour."

Fellow members of Cheshire and Wirral Ornithological Society have been equally baffled .

FEMALE WOLF SPIDERS are less likely to devour males who remind them of their first 'love', say scientists.

The spiders, which hunt prey on foot instead of building webs, are common in the UK.

But the finer details of their courtship rituals have remained obscure until now.

Males are known to sexually mature faster than females and, though unable to mate with immature females, still seem to leave a good impression on youngsters they try to woo.

Mature females are later more accommodating to similar looking males - and much less likely to snub and eat them.

THE WAR OVER hunting has intensified after the House of Lords threw out efforts by Labour MPs to totally ban it.

Ministers and Tory peers hurled insults at each other during a bad-tempered debate as the Upper House inflicted a number of defeats on the controversial Hunting Bill.

Simon Hart, chief executive of the Countryside Alliance, said later:"Rural Affairs Minister Alun Michael admitted that the Hunting Bill was 'wrecked' when the House of Commons passed amendments to ban all hunting. The Lords have now started to 'un-wreck' it.

"The Lords are attempting to produce a more workable version of the Government's original Bill based on the evidence brought forward in the Burns Report, Alun Michael's consultation process, and the public hearings in Portcullis House.

"The vote shows that the Hunting Bill, in the form it left the Commons, is almost unique in having no respect from any quarter of the House of Lords. Opposition to the Bill is overwhelming and cross party.

"By producing an improved version of the original Bill, the House of Lords will create an opportunity for the Government to honour its commitment to allow Parliament to reach a conclusion based on principle and evidence."

During the heated debate, Labour peer Lord Alli, who supports hunting, said:"Freedom in my view is a precious thing. You have to want freedom, very, very badly.

"You have to want freedom badly enough to allow two men to walk down a road, holding hands and kissing. You have to want freedom badly enough to watch British Muslims burn a Union flag and you have to want freedom badly enough to allow people to get on to horses and hunt."

CORNCRAKES ARE BATTLING back from the verge of extinction in Britain, according to latest figures from the RSPB.

"Across the UK, 820 calling corncrakes have been recorded, a massive increase of more than 140 birds compared with 2002," said a Society spokesman.

"This includes two in England, down from 11 recorded during the last full survey in 1998. But this is the highest overall number of corncrakes since detailed surveys began in 1977."

RSPB Scotland director Stuart Housden added:"This is great news for a globally threatened species. In years gone by, the corncrake's range reduced drastically in the UK, their numbers were in freefall, and they became red listed as a bird of high conservation concern.

"Conservationists working alongside farmers and crofters have now reversed this decline. We believe that support from the Scottish Executive's agri-environment schemes as well as the RSPB, Scottish Natural Heritage, and the Scottish Crofting Foundation corncrake initiative, has been a key part to this success. It's a major achievement for all concerned."

Helen Riley, an ornithologist with Scottish Natural Heritage, said:"We are delighted to hear of this year's large increase in the corncrake population.

"There is, however, no room for complacency as the corncrake remains a species with the potential to decline quickly in the absence of sympathetic management."

353

HARE COURSING FANS have been boosted after their controversial sport was given support by the House of Lords.

Despite many expecting an outright ban to be upheld by peers, a Lords decision to reject such a ban - coming a week after a similar vote on hunting with dogs - has stunned anti-cruelty campaigners and further angered Labour MPs.

Mike Hobday, spokesman for the League Against Cruel Sports, believes any compromise on the embattled Hunting Bill is now dead and use of the Parliament Act to force through legislation more likely.

Following a debate, the Upper House voted by 129 to 59 against removing part of the Bill that would make hare coursing illegal.

Labour peer Lady Mallalieu, president of the Countryside Alliance, said any ban on hare coursing would lead to further unlawful poaching.

She claimed:"The amendment is neither pro- or anti-coursing. It does not water down this Bill."

But Labour peer Lord Faulkner said:"Hare coursing is an activity whose purport is to give pleasure to bystanders by giving them the opportunity to watch a beautiful animal being subjected to a gruesome and agonising death."

In a recent defiant message, the National Coursing Club insisted:"Our supporters will seek to bring coursing and stag hunting within the regulatory process and the importance of the role of hunting sports in encouraging conservation of a species will be recognised as a qualification for their continuance."

WOOD FUEL WILL heat a Nottinghamshire school this winter in the first modern scheme of its type.

Forestry Minister Ben Bradshaw was shown how the new 'green' heating system being installed by Nottinghamshire County Council is going to provide warmth for children and staff at the school in Forest Town, near Mansfield.

The wood fuelled boiler is the largest single site installation of its kind in the UK, according to the Forestry Commission.

Mr Bradshaw said:"This project, and others like it, constitutes a giant step forward in the modern use of wood as a fuel.

"As an energy resource, wood fuel has so much potential, whether in schools, leisure centres, factories or in our homes. It is a competitive, and very exciting, alternative to fossil fuels.

"It also takes forward the Government's commitment to using renewable energy, and can provide a real contribution to stabilising carbon dioxide concentrations in the atmosphere."

DOLPHINS AND DORMICE are among target mammals for a new range of natural history training courses next year.

Opportunities to meet some of Britain's more elusive mammals were unveiled by The Mammal Society as it launched its new programme for 2004.

The Society's training officer, Angela Gall, said:"There are lots of opportunities to meet the mammals in question, whether it's out on a boat looking for dolphins off the coast of Wales or checking dormouse nestboxes in Somerset."

The Mammal Society will be running six different mammal courses all over the country, from Devon to Perthshire and from Wales to Northern Ireland.

Angela added:"The courses are very practical and range from introductory courses on identifying land mammals to more detailed ones on small mammals and whales and dolphins.

"There are also opportunities to learn about conserving one of our most threatened mammals, the dormouse."

Last year over 95 per cent of participants rated the courses as good or very good, says the Society.

One popular two-day course is 'Mammal Identification', an "excellent introduction to British mammals", which provides the knowledge and skills needed to recognise land mammals and their signs.

The course includes practical sessions in live mammal trapping and owl pellet analysis.

FARMERS FEAR NEXT year's harvest could be a disaster following one of the driest autumns on record.

Massive areas of arable farmland are said to be verging on dustbowl conditions because of the lowest rainfall count in 30 years.

In a huge belt of prime land stretching from Oxfordshire to Lincolnshire, seeds planted by farmers over two months ago have still not germinated.

Farmer Paul Warburton, 61, who owns 500 acres near Wallingford in the Thames Valley, said:"All the farmers I know attended harvest festival. We all sank to our knees and prayed.

"Oilseed rape sown in August should have come up in five days but still there is no sign. What little wheat is showing is very vulnerable to pigeons because it is so small.

"There is a big chance of the crops failing altogether, forcing me to reseed in spring. It's looking frightful and if we have another dry spring like this year, we could get totally clobbered."

WILDLIFE SHOULD BE boosted by getting more EU funds chanelled into green farming schemes, says English Nature.

Referring to the end of consultation on implementing the recently reformed Common Agricultural Policy, English Nature's agricultural expert Alastair Rutherford said:"The big disappointment of the recent reforms is that farmers are not encouraged to manage their land for environmental benefit.

"If we want our finest wildlife sites to be in pristine condition or if we want to see a recovery in the massive declines of once common farmland birds, then we need to ensure that a much greater portion of farm support is paid through 'green farming schemes' such as Countryside Stewardship or the Entry Level Scheme."

KINGFISHER: shy jewel of the riverbank

AS dazzling and beautiful as a precious stone, the kingfisher gladdens the eye like few other birds as it goes about its hunt. In overcast conditions, its distinctive blue and orange plumage seems to glow with a strange kind of light as it darts around a stream or river.

This voracious fish eater is one of our most visually stunning birds with its unusual, almost exotic, appearance enhanced by a beak which makes up a quarter of its 16cms length.

British kingfishers are actually only one strain of what is generally a tropical species, with other kingfishers located from Africa to New Guinea.

For such a glamorous bird, the kingfisher's nesting arrangements are surprisingly un-glamorous. Like a supermodel with disgusting habits, it is without doubt one of the messiest home-makers of the bird world.

In a deep hole, hollowed out of a steep bank, the female will lay up to seven white, roundish eggs.

When the eggs hatch, the nest quickly becomes littered with stinking fish remains and droppings.

The smell carries, which is probably why the kingfisher is wise enough to make the nest site as inaccessible to predators as possible.

So filthy can the nest become that kingfishers often have to start the day with a refreshing dip to clean feathers that have become soiled.

Fish are the only food on its menu, any that can be speared by that beak and quickly subdued long enough to be eaten.

Kingfishers fly into water at speed, closing their eyes before they hit the surface and hoping their initial calculations about the fish's position were correct.

If they are, they will quickly regain their perch and batter their unfortunate prey into submission before swallowing it head-first.

I last glimpsed a kingfisher about a year ago, hunting along a quiet stretch of a local disused canal.

It was quite a dark, drizzly day but the kingfisher's appearance was electrifying, like seeing a small blue lamp fluttering above the water

Because kingfishers have such a restricted diet, they are especially vulnerable to starvation during harsh winter months when lakes and streams ice over.

Pollution is another threat as it kills off their food source and they constantly have to fly elsewhere to survive.

A few years ago, a study of 100 wetland wildlife sites found that the majority were suffering from 'eutrophication' - an over enriched state where all water life is slowly suffocated due to pollution.

An English Nature spokesman concluded that if nothing was done *"we may have to forgo our favourite lakeside walks with kingfishers, dragonflies, and water lilies. Instead, we shall be faced with an unattractive algal soup, devoid of any wildlife."*

Not an appetising scenario - especially for the hungry kingfisher trying to find a meal.

A WIDESPREAD CULL of Ruddy ducks by amateur shooters is a cruel and backward step for the countryside, say protesters.

DEFRA's decision to issue a general licence to cull the ducks, supported by the RSPB, has been branded a declaration of war on Britain's birdlife by the League Against Cruel Sports.

The League has attacked the move to permit amateur sports shooters to shoot the ducks as part of a strategy to protect native duck species.

Chairman John Cooper said:"It is horrific that the planned killing is seen as acceptable by the RSPB and DEFRA. Both organisations should be protecting Britain's wildlife - not seeking to eradicate it.

"The culture of countryside 'management' by shooting to kill is totally unacceptable. To embark on such a programme with respect to the Ruddy duck is simply taking a backwards step.

"Given that non-target species were killed as part of the 'controlled' trial, we should not be surprised if this 'licence to kill' for amateur shooters gives rise to an uncontrolled slaughter of both Ruddy ducks and non-target species.

"It is bad enough to seek to eradicate a whole species but to do so using licensed amateur shooters makes it much more likely that birds will be wounded, or that the wrong birds altogether are targeted."

FROGS AND VOLES might not be among those celebrating the planned reintroduction of the great bustard to Britain - the giant bird eats them.

Weighing nearly three stone and with an eight-foot wingspan, the great bustard is omniverous and will pack away anything it can, including a variety of small creatures.

Conservationists aim to release 40 chicks each year for the next 10-15 years around Salisbury Plain, Wiltshire.

Great bustards died out here 170 years ago after being hunted for their considerable meat and the imported birds will all come from Russia.

Although frogs and voles won't like them, hungry foxes would relish the chance to snap one up and are thought to be the biggest hazard to the scheme.

Stoats and even mink are also believed to be possible dangers to the success of the project.

GREY SQUIRRELS HAVE been beating the battle of the bulge at a Shropshire beauty spot.

The chubby animals caused alarm by piling on weight at Hawkstone Park, Weston-under-Redcastle, after maniacally munching through food put out for birds and scraps left in bins.

However, following introduction of squirrel-proof bird feeders and other guards, park staff report the furry mammals have now become noticeably slimmer.

BADGER LOVERS HAVE hailed a Government decision to suspend badger culling as a huge blow to farming unions.

Supporters of the popular mammal made their views known after Minister Ben Bradshaw revealed that reactive badger culling had actually increased the rate of bovine TB in cattle by 27 per cent.

Mr Bradshaw announced an immediate suspension of reactive culling in the 'Krebs experiment' because there was now enough data to show that it increased the disease in cattle, rather than reducing it.

"We congratulate the Minister for acting decisively on the information currently available," said Dr Elaine King, chief executive of the National Federation of Badger Groups.

"These extraordinary results confirm the warnings that I and other scientists have been giving for years. It also means that farmers who have been illegally killing badgers have actually made their situation worse rather than better.

"This announcement is a massive blow to the credibility of the farming unions. They have consistently called for reactive badger culling outside the existing experimental areas.

"It is imperative that the farming unions stop making ill-advised calls for badger culling and work with us and the veterinary profession to implement effective schemes to control the problem of TB transmission between cattle.

"There is already clear evidence that cattle are infectious with bovine TB long before the skin test identifies the problem. This serious infection route must be addressed as a matter of urgency."

The Krebs experiment began in 1998 to test whether culling badgers reduces bovine TB in cattle.

"The reactive culling data confirms that there is a bovine TB link between badgers and cattle - that comes as no surprise. But the data shows you cannot break the link by killing badgers," added Dr King.

"Instead, reactive culling makes the situation far worse and even suggests that cattle are giving the disease to previously uninfected badgers. We therefore have to look elsewhere for a solution."

SUGAR BEET FARMERS are toasting the sweet advance of the buy British 'Little Red Tractor' scheme.

The distinctive food logo will be rolled out on 1kg packs of Silver Spoon sugar in supermarkets across the country from mid-November.

The move follows the launch of a farm assurance scheme for sugar beet devised jointly by the NFU, British Sugar - which owns Silver Spoon - and Red Tractor-operator Assured Food Standards.

NFU president Ben Gill said:"This is a positive development for British sugar beet growers.

"It has taken a lot of hard work by all partners in the industry to put together a sugar beet assurance scheme.

"It will benefit everyone in the chain, from growers to shoppers."

NFU Sugar Beet Board chairman Mike Blacker added:"It is a big achievement that this everyday product will be added to the list of British farm produce able to sport the Little Red Tractor.

"It will help shoppers identify home-grown sugar produced to independently checked standards."

ILLEGAL EEL NETS containing over 300 pounds of eels were seized by Environment Agency officials on the River Thames in London.

Returning to their boat moorings after a routine survey at Greenwich, the officers spotted something suspicious attached to one of the river structures in the Barking Reach area of the river.

"The patrol boat edged closer to investigate," said a spokesman."On doing so, they found a weighted line descending into the water that was clearly in place to allow the retrieval of something from the riverbed.

"Suspecting that this may well be a set of fyke nets, the officers retrieved the line, pulling in two anchors and a string of five unlicensed fyke nets. These had captured a large number of eels, later estimated to be in excess of 300 pounds in weight.

"As there were no Agency tags on the nets they were seized and taken back to the patrol boat mooring. A quick assessment of the quantity of eels was made and photographs taken. All the fish were then released alive back into the tideway.

"Commercial eel netsmen are required to purchase a licence from the Agency and on doing do, are issued with numbered tags. These must then be fitted to the nets whenever they are in use. If the nets are found not to be tagged, they will be seized by Agency enforcement staff during regular fisheries enforcement patrols."

Phil Bolton, the Agency's principal fisheries officer for the Thames Region, added:"The investigation and successful capture of these illegal nets sends a strong message to unlicensed eel fishermen on the tidal River Thames.

"If people fish with untagged nets they run the risk of losing their fishing gear and facing possible prosecution."

A BRITISH INITIATIVE to introduce the common crow to East Africa has gone badly wrong with the aggressive birds killing or driving out many native birds, it has been claimed.

Up to 500,000 crows now dominate Tanzania's capital Dar es Salaam alone and moves to control them have come to nothing.

Conservationists say the crow was introduced to East Africa in 1891 by the British governor of Zanzibar.

He had wanted to use their scavenging habits to help clean up Zanzibar's streets.

However, he had badly underestimated crows' ability to thrive.

Now numbers of the robust birds have rocketed and spread like a plague across the continent.

FEARS HAVE BEEN raised that the planned abolition of English Nature is yet another move by New Labour to silence any inconvenient opposition.

The Government wants to axe its own independent scientific body which has shown itself to be an effective watchdog on countryside issues and not afraid to use its teeth.

Ministers claim they want work to be taken over by a new group which will protect the land and deliver better services in rural areas.

But the move has outraged conservationists who fear it is yet another cynical attempt by the present Government to quell complaints and allow it to better manage its spin on contentious issues such as GM crops.

The proposal comes amid a number of new rural policies drawn up by Lord Haskins.

He believes that English Nature, the Government's official wildlife monitor, is too old after 50 years' service and needs replacing.

Tom Burke, on the board of English Nature, told the BBC:"It's potentially an act of barbarism. As far as I can see, what's proposed will amount to selling the biodiversity police to the agricultural mafia, and that's a completely outrageous proposition."

Shadow Environment Secretary David Lidington added:"My fear is that the Government just wants to get rid of an uncomfortable and inconvenient critic."

RARE BIRDS CONTINUE to flit in and out of Britain on their travels around the globe.

In recent weeks, rare species have included a yellow-rumped warbler spotted on Orkney, a pine bunting and dusky warbler on Shetland, pied wheatear in Norfolk, Radde's warbler on the Isle of Man, and olive-backed pipit in East Sussex.

Elsewhere, unusual feathered visitors to the Midlands have included a slavonian grebe and four caspian gulls.

BITTERNS AND BLACK-tailed godwits are among birds that should benefit from an ambitious RSPB wetland scheme.

Plans to create 5,000 hectares of new wetlands are at the heart of the Society's vision for the East Anglian Fens.

The new wetland, equivalent in size to Loch Ness, will prove a lifeline for England's vanishing wetland wildlife.

Launching the project at the recently recreated Lakenheath Fen, the RSPB's chief executive, Graham Wynne, said he saw the future of the Fens as a challenge that must be met head on if once widespread wildlife is to return.

The East Anglian Fens once stretched from Lincoln to Cambridge, he said, covering 5,000 square kilometres.

They were home to a spectacular array of wetland wildlife, some now lost from the UK entirely, such as the large copper butterfly and nesting black terns.

Mr Wynne added:"We have already made a start - lost fens have been recreated promising early benefits for rare nesting birds such as bitterns.

"This is just the beginning. By creating the right habitat, small and vulnerable populations of black-tailed godwits can also be given a secure future and, in time, long lost birds of the Fens such as cranes and spoonbills may find a home once more."

SHOOTING FANS HAVE blasted the "astonishing ignorance" of journalists and animal rights campaigners who have launched an attack on wildfowling.

A probe into wildfowling on conservation sites in a national Sunday newspaper was backed up by the League Against Cruel Sports.

According to the newspaper, an unnamed senior conservationist admitted:"It's clearly bonkers to have shooting going on at a nature reserve."

But Simon Hart, chief executive of the Countryside Alliance, fired back:"The report shows an astonishing level of ignorance about the work and practice of wildfowling clubs and stands as a warning that no country sport is safe from attack by animal rights organisations.

"Wetland conservation as we know it simply would not exist without wildfowlers and their continuing work is of massive benefit to the quarry species and the wider environment.

"In return they take an ecologically sustainable harvest of wildfowl.

"For animal rights groups to criticise wildfowling when their own record on wildlife management is so risible is pure hypocrisy.

"Their agenda has nothing to do with conservation or animal welfare - it's about hatred of all country sports and those people involved in them."

OTTERS HAVE RETURNED to Surrey for the first time in 40 years.

The popular aquatic mammals were once found in waterways across the county but disappeared during the 1960s due to environmental changes.

Now, after years of working on habitat improvements in an attempt to encourage otters back, Surrey Wildlife Trust members have announced their return.

Evidence found this year indicates that otters have been present in the Farnham area.

Chris Matcham, Surrey's Otters and Rivers project officer, said:"We have had a great number of false alarms over the years.

"Perhaps this time the otters will not be mere tourists but will be the first of a resident population in the county."

The Surrey Wildlife Trust's otters project has been running since 1997.

It has involved extensive habitat work as well as raising public awareness of the benefits of otters.

Earlier this year, a survey sponsored by the Environment Agency highlighted a dramatic improvements in the otter population as a whole over the country with otter numbers increasing sharply at many sites.

A PIG FARMER was ordered to pay over £12,000 by Oxfordshire magistrates after polluting a river with farm slurry, killing thousands of fish.

The man pleaded guilty to polluting the River Evenlode and Sars Brook with pig slurry following an equipment failure at his farm in October last year.

Environment Agency officers were alerted to the incident after members of the public reported the River Evenlode had turned black and many fish had been killed.

Officers attending the scene quickly established the source of the pollutant to be the farm.

During the investigation, officers discovered the incident had been caused when irrigation equipment spreading pig slurry had run out of fuel after being left unattended.

The Banbury court heard the irrigator failed to shut down automatically as a farm employee had over-ridden the fail-safe mechanisms because the machine kept on cutting-out.

The slurry seeped through cracks in the ground into the land drainage system which discharged the pollutant into Sars Brook, a tributary of the Evenlode.

The court noted that the irrigation equipment should not have been in use as the field was very dry and badly cracked.

Farming codes state that irrigation equipment should not be used when the land is in such a condition, said the Agency.

The defendant was fined £10,000 under the Water Resources Act 1991 and ordered to pay the Agency £2,310 in costs.

CIRL BUNTINGS ARE fighting back from the edge of extinction at their Devon stronghold.

The pretty little birds, similar to more common yellowhammers, have slowly increased their population from 118 pairs to almost 700, according to an RSPB survey.

However, only direct action by local farmers - paid to maintain their land in a way the birds liked - was enough to save them.

Once common across the whole country, cirl buntings are now restricted to pockets of southern Devon.

Farmers who took part in the project maintained tracts of land which supplied large numbers of insects in summer to feed cirl bunting chicks while, in winter, also providing abundant seeds.

Cath Jeffs, the RSPB's cirl bunting project officer, said:"The cirl bunting is one of our most attractive birds but it's also one of our fussiest. To thrive, it needs insects in the summer and seeds in the winter but because cirl buntings don't migrate these feeding sites need to be in the same place."

AN ESCAPED PELICAN is settling back into captivity after going on the run among native British birds.

Lucy the pelican has now had her wings clipped to ensure she does not flee again from Birdland in Bourton-on-the-Water, Gloucestershire.

The long-beaked bird, more suited to tropical climes, has now swapped the new friends she made on the outside - swans, ducks, and the like - for her old chums back inside, three other pelicans.

Lucy went missing for about a week and was starving hungry on her return - wolfing down a pile of herrings and sprats offered by keepers.

WATER VOLES ARE battling back from the brink in Sussex where habitat improvement work has tripled their numbers within three years.

Conservationists are delighted by the success of the scheme - which bodes well for similar projects nationwide - especially as water voles were expected to become extinct in the county by 2003.

Loss of habitat and predation, especially by mink, have seen national numbers of water vole decimated in recent years.

But in Sussex at least, the secretive animal immortalised as 'Ratty' in Wind in the Willows because of its other name, 'water rat', appears to be thriving.

Some 342 water voles have now been counted across the region compared to barely 100 when the scheme began.

Sussex Wildlife Trust, local farmers, West Sussex County Council, and other bodies, had joined forces to reverse the slump in numbers.

The group created over 60 kilometres of 18ft wide grass margins along waterways so that voles could shelter and live undisturbed.

Paul Smith, spokesman for the Environment Agency which also played an important role, said:"Due to the plight of water voles facing extinction we had to take conservation action in the Sussex area.

"The main problems were as a result of intensive farming. Watercourses where the voles make their habitats had suffered from heavy engineering work for flood defence and land drainage purposes.

"Predators such as mink were also a major factor in their decline."

He hoped the future of water voles in Sussex was now secure.

WILDLIFE AND RAMBLERS seem set to benefit from a new zero-tolerance policy towards illegal off-road vehicles in a picturesque part of Wales.

Already, the Brecon Beacons National Park Authority's adoption of the policy seems to be proving successful.

A spokesman for the Ramblers Association said:"The Park Authority has been working closely with the police to clamp down on the number of illegal 4x4 vehicles and off-road motorbikes tearing up the park.

"Since the zero tolerance policy was adopted, 17 scrambler bikes and two 4x4 vehicles have been caught by police. On-the-spot fines have been issued or, in some instances, court cases are to follow.

"The Park Authority was increasingly aware of damage that off-road vehicles were causing to areas of the park not designated for vehicular access. Their main concern was the illegal use of the open hills, forcing them to adopt the policy."

POTATO FARMERS COULD be facing disaster after the world's most damaging potato disease was found in Britain.

It is the first time that ring rot has been unearthed here and the outbreak is being put down to imported Dutch seed.

Growers have pledged to totally eradicate the disease - discovered at a farm in mid-Wales - and their efforts will need to be thorough as ring rot can devastate crops.

A DEFRA statement said:"Action is being taken to prevent any spread of the disease from the infected farm and to trace any related potato stocks."

Officials in Holland are being asked to reveal other UK locations to which infected seed may have gone.

It is hoped that all potatoes from the infected Welsh farm will be located and destroyed.

Since the disease favours cooler climates, as we have in Britain, it could become established here if not wiped out, the statement added.

SALMON IN TWO Cumbrian rivers have been given a boost after officials decided to draw up a plan to protect them.

The public are being consulted over proposals to ensure salmon continue to thrive in the rivers Esk and Irt.

According to the Environment Agency, the scheme will assess the status of the rivers' salmon stocks, identify factors which could be adversely affecting the fish, and propose remedial measure to tackle problems.

Jeremy Westgarth, the Agency's local fisheries team leader, said:"This is an opportunity for anyone interested in the Irt and the Esk to influence the future management and conservation of salmon in these catchments.

"We want input from as many individuals and interested groups as possible so we can ensure all the issues are raised and actions identified.

"The final action plan will be vital for managing the fisheries and delivering the actions in it will be a high priority for us."

HUNT GROUPS CLAIM a new animal protection Bill would do more to safeguard foxes and other wildlife than the controversial anti-hunt Bill launched by Labour MPs.

The Countryside Alliance says that the Wild Mammal Protection Bill - also known as the Donoughue Bill - seeks to address real animal welfare concerns rather than some MPs' prejudices.

What is more, it has successfully completed its passage through the Lords.

Simon Hart, chief executive of the Countryside Alliance, said:"The Government has a clear choice - 'wrecked' hunting legislation based on back bench bigotry or a sensible approach to animal welfare legislation.

"The Donoughue Bill, which addresses the question of cruelty, is concerned with all aspects of wild mammal management.

"The Donoughue Bill should attract the support of all who have a true interest in animal welfare and I hope that the Government is able to give it support in the next parliamentary session.

"The Alliance, like all the organisations backing the Bill, is ready to address any reasonable concerns the Government might have in the drafting of the legislation."

BRITISH BIRDS ARE being put at risk by meddling Brussels bureaucrats, claims the RSPB.

A European Commission decision now threatens more than 300,000 hectares of wildlife-friendly farmland, says the Society.

The Commission wants to halve the area of set-aside land - land taken out of production but which benefits wildlife - by 50 per cent next year because of this summer's poor harvest.

Yet farmland birds such as skylarks and yellowhammers have already declined dramatically and need sympathetically managed 'set-aside' land for nest sites and food.

Reversal of farmland bird declines was previously trumpeted as a major Government target.

Dr Darren Moorcroft, the RSPB's agriculture policy officer, said:"Long-term protection of farmland birds can only be achieved by schemes designed to benefit them, not ones which provide benefits by chance.

"Agri-environment projects, like the Countryside Stewardship Scheme, provide farmers with the opportunity to help wildlife in a much more targeted way. If more than 300,000 hectares are seized back for production, only greater funding for such schemes will safeguard the UK's wildlife from the adverse effects of this decision."

NATIVE CRAYFISH ARE under threat from foreign invaders at two of their strongholds in the north east of England.

British crayfish in the rivers Wansbeck and Aln, near Newcastle, face danger from the spread of the aggressive North American signal crayfish, Environ - ment Agency officers have warned.

Angling clubs, conservation groups and other organisations have all been informed that signal crayfish have already been discovered in the River Derwent, a few miles south.

As a result, measures have been put in place to try to halt their spread.

Agency conservation officer Anne Lewis, said:"The American species of crayfish is bigger, more aggressive and out-competes our native crayfish. Most importantly, it also carries a fungal disease known as crayfish plague that has already wiped out our native crayfish from most rivers in the south of England."

A DEAD HORSE has sparked a bizarre police investigation in Shropshire.

Officers are investigating the mystery of how the brown stallion came to be dumped in a ditch.

The animal was found lying in the ditch near Shifnal, covered by two sheets. One theory is that the horse was struck by a car in the country lane but no-one has reported any such incident.

HUNT GROUPS BELIEVE the tide may be turning in their favour after a Bill outlawing hunting with hounds was left out of the latest Queen's Speech.

Labour MPs were furious that the Government appeared to have gone back on its promise to make the Bill law and are now clinging to the hope that legislation can still be introduced via a private member's Bill.

However, the absence of the Bill in the Queen's Speech came after MPs and peers were warned that a ban on hunting with hounds could breach European human rights laws.

The Joint Committee on Human Rights announced that depriving individuals of income received from hunting would go against European legislation.

Simon Hart, chief executive of the Countryside Alliance, has pledged that any attempts to force through the controversial anti-hunt Bill would be met with fierce legal challenges.

He said:"The Government should not even be considering encouraging Parliament to spend further time on a Bill which infringes human rights. MPs are considering ignoring the needs and interests of local people and introducing a Hunting Bill as a private member's Bill have been warned that they will be challenged in their constituencies.

"Nowhere in the country do voters put a ban on hunting anywhere near the top of their priorities and the Alliance is ready to help deliver that message.

"The Government promised legislation based on principle and evidence and we will hold them to that. Anything less and they can be sure that their actions will be met with implacable resistance - especially if the Government shows more interest in supporting payback politics than addressing issues of animal welfare.

"Our supporters have brought the Alliance this far. A huge amount has been achieved in winning political, public and media support for our cause.

"The road ahead is still a dangerous one and any weakening of our resolve will be seized on by our opponents. We must keep up the pressure to ensure that there is no possibility of the return of legislation to ban hunting."

NEW MINK TRAPS are benefiting Britain's threatened water vole population, says the Game Conservancy Trust.

Elusive mink are being more easily caught using cleverly designed rafts which act both as mink detectors and trap sites.

Already, the project has been described as "revolutionary" for mink control and water vole conservation by the Environment Agency.

In a pilot project on the River Itchen, co-funded by the Agency and Hampshire Wildlife Trust, mink rafts were laid over nine miles of river corridor.

Initially the rafts, which measure 4ft x 2ft, were used in monitoring mode to determine where mink were present.

But when mink were shown to be present, traps were added to the rafts to catch the animals.

Dr Jonathan Reynolds - who heads the project - said:"In a very short time we caught every breeding female mink in the area and, importantly, we could demonstrate that none were left. Satisfyingly, the water vole population has then been very productive and successfully colonised suitable habitats."

TURKEY WARS ARE already breaking out between farmers and cruelty campaigners for the hearts and wallets of Christmas shoppers.

As the NFU reveals that it is handing out soothing CDs to keep turkeys calm before the mass festive chop, pro-veggie Animal Aid is calling on people to give meat a miss this year.

The farmers' CD initiative was dreamt up to keep birds relaxed and help them grow faster with discs which included whale sounds and wind chime noises.

NFU spokesman Simon Rayner said:"We hope to begin a serious study. Wind chime CDs are proving most popular, though the birds seem to like listening to radio as well."

Meanwhile, Animal Aid says:"Each year, around 10 million turkeys are slaughtered for the Christmas table, and millions of pigs, ducks and geese will get the chop, too.

"Give animals the gift of life by leaving meat off your menu. There are so many delicious veggie options available. Nut roast needn't get a look in."

A YOUNG SWAN trampled during a fireworks display at a Gloucestershire bird sanctuary may have to be put down.

The cygnet was apparently stepped on by an excited visitor to the event at the Cotswold Swan and Wild Bird Rescue Centre.

Although the five-month-old bird has received treatment since the night, it can only drag itself around now using its wings.

A second swan, pheasant, and tufted duck all died from shock after the November 1 display in Cirencester.

Staff at the centre have been involved in a row with organisers of the event which also saw much louder fireworks than anticipated used.

LINNETS, TURTLE DOVES and reed buntings are among birds feared to be facing starvation after failure of the winter oilseed rape crop.

Bees, too, are likely to suffer after a dry autumn devastated crops this year, leaving hundreds of fields all but dead.

Although many people find oilseed rape unpleasant, several creatures have come to rely on it, say conservationists.

Rape seeds are similar to various kinds of seeds that birds used to feed on before the introduction of widespread changes in agricultural practices.

Following record temperatures in the summer and autumn, many fields are still brown and dormant at a time when new green rape plants would normally be springing up.

It appears that hundreds of thousands of oilseed rape seeds have simply failed to germinate, leaving a ticking hunger timebomb in store for birds next year.

Meanwhile, various bees - but particularly bumble bees - will badly miss the plants' pollen which they have come to rely on.

WILD BOAR MAY have alarmed many with their population surge in the South East but one couple are delighted with the hairy pigs.

Livestock farmers Neil and Susan Adams believe they may be on the road to farming success after setting up Brampton Wild Boar farm near Beccles in Suffolk.

According to the NFU, the couple now produce a wide range of tasty boar products, from roasting joints to bacon, Parma-style ham to six different flavours of sausages.

These they sell at farmers' markets and to restaurants, butchers and farm shops.

"Having experience with cows, horses, sheep, dogs and children doesn't really prepare you for rearing wild boar," admitted Neil, who said the philosophy behind the business is keeping the animals content.

"The one thing you must do with these animals is have patience and not force anything because they can easily turn if stressed and you can get hurt."

Wild boar are classed as dangerous wild animals in Britain and require special fencing and an annual licence.

Some farmers believe the classification should be relaxed but not Neil and Susan.

"Most of the time the animals are fine but at the end of the day, although these are four generations or more from being out in the woods, they are still wild animals," added Neil.

ANGLERS IN THE north east of England have been given a boost with the introduction of 15,000 fish to two local rivers.

The rivers Tyne and Wear had their fish stocks rejuvenated as part of an Environment Agency scheme.

About 8,000 roach and 7,000 chub were introduced at locations on both rivers as the Agency underlined its commitment to regenerate urban fisheries.

FISH ARE THRIVING in what was once one of Britain's dirtiest waterways, it has been revealed.

After a three-year clean-up operation, water quality is now so good in the Manchester Ship Canal that the number and size of fish have rocketed.

Before the scheme got underway, the water was so polluted with chemicals that critics said it was even in danger of bursting into flames.

However, after hundreds of tonnes of liquid oxygen were pumped into the canal, life is returning to the murky waters.

For the first time in years, fish such as roach and perch are spawning, with all adult fish growing at a rate equal to anywhere else in the country.

"This is a minor miracle in environmental terms," said a spokesman.

CULPRITS WHO CAUSED a pollution crisis on a Leicestershire river will probably never be traced, investigators have admitted.

More than 400 gallons of waste oil was dumped in the River Soar back in May, killing ducks and moorhens, and prompting the rescue of 50 badly affected swans.

Dozens of the worst hit swans, ducks and coots spent weeks recovering at Leicestershire Wildlife Hospital, Kibworth, after being found struggling in the oil. But a full-scale investigation has drawn a blank and locals are furious the culprits have escaped.

STOAT: predator that caused a national outcry

SLEEK and deadly, the stoat has a particularly fiendish trick up its sleeve when it wants to catch a rabbit - hypnotism.

At least, that is what it often seems to use when it creeps closer to any young, inexperienced animal and grabs its attention.

Gazing into its victim's eyes, sometimes almost nose to nose, it will weave and bob its head until the prey forgets about fleeing and is somehow lulled into dropping its defences.

The stoat then pounces and a crushing bite to the neck is delivered with lightning speed.

Birds, rats and mice are also on the menu of this voracious hunter but it can survive on insects when times are hard and other prey is scarce.

Larger than its equally ferocious cousin, the weasel, a stoat first tracks its quarry by scent before pursuing it by sight.

Despite its short, stubby legs, a stoat can race along at 20mph, its distinctive chesnut and white body constantly thrown forward in a series of leaps and bounds.

Few animals manage to outrun it in a straight sprint.

Death is almost inevitable for any creature too slow to climb, fly away or scurry down a tinier hole than the slim stoat itself can squeeze into.

Stoats are so savage they can easily overwhelm animals more than twice their own size.

The male stoat is just 13 inches long from the tip of his inquisitive nose to the end of his black-tipped tail. Females are smaller and thinner but equally feared as hunters and sporting the same colouring.

The two sexes come together briefly to breed, after which six or so fierce youngsters emerge.

These can often only be told apart from weasels by their black tail-tips.

The voraciousness of stoats was underlined some years ago by a desperate move to control them - not here, but in New Zealand.

Stoats and weasels were introduced there from Europe in the 19th Century to control burgeoning rabbit numbers.

However, so successful have they become that they are now threatening the survival of many indigenous species.

Among these is New Zealand's national bird, the flightless long-beaked kiwi.

As he unveiled a multi-million dollar fightback fund, New Zealand's Conservation Minister Nick Smith admitted at the time:*"Stoats are public enemy number one for our bird life. They are decimating kiwi populations.*

"Every year, 15,000 kiwi chicks - 60 per cent of those born - are killed by stoats. Kiwi will not survive on the North and South Islands unless we find an effective way to stop this.

"New Zealand must save the unique species that help give us our sense of national identity. A stoat research budget is our best hope for saving our kiwi."

Fearsome as they are, it still seems bizarre that one of Britain's less celebrated exports - stoats - could come close to causing a national identity crisis overseas.

SALMON AND SEA trout struggling to reach spawning grounds on several Welsh rivers have been saved by torrential rain.

"The recent rains came just in time for fish on many rivers, including the River Neath and the River Teifi," said a spokesman for the Environment Agency.

"The low river flows in summer and early autumn meant that fish migrating up the rivers and into the tributaries had been delayed in reaching the spawning areas in the upper reaches.

"Now they are taking full advantage of the increased flows but are also benefiting from improvements introduced to promote local fisheries.

"A new fish pass on the Nant Gwrelych, a tributary of the River Neath, has already proved a success with salmon and sea trout being seen upstream and on the Cerdin, a tributary of the River Teifi.

"A survey carried out recently shows that the number of 'redds' - gravel scrapes migratory fish create for spawning - has nearly doubled this year as a result of habitat improvements.

"On the Nant Gwrelych, indications show that the fish pass is allowing increasing numbers of fish to pass safely through a culvert which formerly proved a barrier."

Agency fisheries project officer Gareth Davies added:"This will be the first year for a long time that salmon and sea trout will be able to gain access to the upper reaches of the Nant Gwrelych. This year the run of salmon and sea trout will hopefully pave the way for future generations returning to the river.

"The increase in spawning success will ultimately lead to an increase in the number of adults returning to the system. The contribution made by the Nant Gwrelych to the system will add to the total production of the Neath catchment, increasing its potential as a sustainable fishery."

EXPERTS ARE STUDYING the droppings of one of the UK's rarest birds in a bid to help it survive.

Scotland's capercaillie - a turkey-sized bird related to the grouse - has faced extinction in recent years as more wild areas are lost.

Now researchers aim to find the ideal capercaillie habitat by studying numbers of parasite eggs in its droppings.

Boffins at Dundee University believe too many parasites show the bird is suffering from stress or illness, making it less likely to breed.

Fewer parasites will show the type of environment where it feels most comfortable and more likely to flourish.

BLACKCAPS ARE CHOOSING to spend winters more in chilly Britain than the Mediterranean, researchers have found.

Parts of southern England, the Midlands, and Wales are now favoured wintering locations for the warbler which sports a distinctive black 'cap'.

The British Trust for Ornithology has highlighted the importance of gardens in attracting the small migrant bird here.

"This species of warbler is found breeding across much of Europe, including Britain and Ireland, and normally winters in southern Europe around the Mediterranean and North Africa," said a spokesman.

"As such, the blackcap is regarded as being a summer visitor to Britain, where it nests in thick scrub, bramble patches and woodland.

"However, increasing numbers of blackcaps have started spending the winter here, surviving on the food put out on bird tables and typically arriving in gardens from late December and remaining through into March.

"What is particularly interesting is that these wintering blackcaps are not British birds that have decided to remain here but instead are birds from breeding populations in Central Europe that have migrated north west during the autumn."

TREE SPARROWS ARE the subject of a joint monitoring project between farmers and conservationists.

Like their urban cousins, tree sparrows are one of the fastest declining breeding birds in the country.

But sharp-eyed farmers are already proving their worth with the discovery of a previously unrecorded colony in Kent.

RSPB survey organiser Andy Cotton said:"We are delighted to find out about this colony. Tree sparrows are birds of the farmed landscape, which is why we turned to the very people who know farmland best to find them - farmers. The more tree sparrow sites we know about, the more we can do to try and save them."

So far, however, the RSPB had been saddened that the survey has only turned up three new breeding sites throughout the whole of south east England.

"It all goes to reflect the perilous state that tree sparrows are in," added Mr Cotton."It is astonishing to think that in 1981 tree sparrows were still considered common birds in Kent."

NEW FACTS ABOUT forests have been published by the Forestry Commission in its latest booklet, 'Forestry Statistics 2003'.

The £15 publication reveals that the total woodland area in the United Kingdom is now 2.8 million hectares with 13.5 thousand hectares of new woods created over 2002-03.

A total of 7.2 million green tonnes of British timber (roundwood) was delivered to primary wood processors and others in 2002, a slight decrease from the previous year.

The UK was the fourth largest net importer of forest products in 2002, behind China, Japan and the USA. while the largest net exporters were Canada, Finland and Sweden.

Wood products imported into the UK in 2002 were valued at £5.7 billion and were equivalent to 49 million cubic metres of timber.

About two thirds of adults in the UK have visited woodlands in the last few years.

DEER SPOTTING IS one of the Yuletide treats being lined up for visitors to reserves owned by The Wildlife Trusts.

"Flying reindeer, the pattering of tiny hooves on your roof, Rudolph with a glowing red nose - deer are steeped in magic over the Christmas period," explained a spokesman. "To bring these magical creatures to life this winter The Wildlife Trusts offer some stunning reserves with ideal walks for deer spotting.

"The UK has seven species of deer roaming the countryside. The roe and red deer are our only native species whilst we are also home to many muntjac, Chinese water deer, fallow, sika and some reindeer.

"As the UK's largest wild land mammals - the majestic red deer stag can measure up to 120cm at his shoulder - they are easy to discover and provide a truly magnificent sight.

"Deer are often active during the day and, with practice, you can learn their habits and anticipate their whereabouts.

"Discover sika deer at Higher Hyde Heath, Tadnoll reserve or Winfrith reserve, all managed by Dorset Wildlife Trust.

"At the Warburg reserve, managed by the Berks, Bucks and Oxon Wildlife Trust, you can see fallow, muntjac and roe deer in the woodland.

"The Scottish Wildlife Trust's Pass of Ryvoan boasts stunning red deer whilst at Rushy Mead, reserve of Essex Wildlife Trust, Chinese water deer can be enjoyed."

ONE OF BRITAIN'S top salmon fishing rivers is facing threats from two foreign invaders - one natural, the other a man-made hazard.

The Tweed Foundation, which manages the famous river dividing England from Scotland, is aiming to combat American import the signal crayfish as well as driving off a Norwegian fish farming company.

Signal crayfish, daily getting closer to the Tweed, carry a fatal disease for native crayfish while also being voracious feeders on the eggs and young of salmon and trout.

Meanwhile, Norwegian firm Pan Fish is planning to create the first salmon farm on the Tweed at a time when escaped farmed fish have been blamed for weakening wild fish stocks.

Members of the Foundation have declared war on both invaders.

HERONS HAVE BEEN distracting motorists near a busy road in Gloucestershire.

Up to seven of the large, distinctive wading birds have been settling together on a grass verge beside Cirencester's ring road.

Often the birds move away, only to collect again later in a nearby field. Experts believe the birds may be feeding together or are trying to pair off.

RED KITES ARE set to soar over the north east of England for the first time in 150 years after a project to reintroduce them there won £300,000 lottery funding.

The RSPB says that the North East Red Kite Project is a world first in proposing to introduce the birds of prey into a semi-urban environment in Gateshead's Derwent Valley.

Kites were once widespread throughout the north of England but have been absent from the region for around 150 years.

However, reintroduction schemes in southern England and the Midlands have already seen the spectacular birds soaring again over local fields.

The latest project, jointly managed by the RSPB and English Nature, also has the financial backing of Gateshead Council, which has pledged £250,000 over five years, while Northumbrian Water is donating £15,000 for each of the first two years.

RSPB regional director Andy Bunten said:"We are thrilled that the Heritage Lottery Fund has chosen to award such a significant sum to this exciting project.

"Red kites have been absent from the skies of northern England for far too long and we are all looking forward to helping bring them back home."

Tony Laws, area manager for English Nature, added:"Without the lottery money it wouldn't have been possible to bring back this stunning bird of prey.

"We're confident that the red kites, with their five-foot wingspan, rust-red plumage and forked tail, will be a major benefit to Gateshead.

"The return of the ospreys to the Lake District has been a huge boost to the local economy there and we're hoping that northern kites will achieve similar gains for the North East."

In the summer of 2004, up to 30 young kites - from an established population in southern England - will be released into the wild from a secret site in Derwent Valley.

Further releases are planned for 2005 and 2006 and it is hoped that the population will soon become self-sustaining.

THE NFU SAYS it has finally won its hard-fought legal action against the French ban on British beef.

According to the union, the highest civil court in France has now ruled that the country was wrong to continue to block imports of British beef once the European Commission lifted its BSE ban in August 1999.

NFU president Ben Gill praised the judgement in the Conseil d'Etat that ends nearly four years of legal wrangling.

France was the only major country to continue to stop the import of British beef after the Commission ban was lifted and did so until October 2002.

Mr Gill said:"France's unlawful ban tarnished the image of British beef in the eyes of French and European consumers. The purpose of challenging the French Government in its own courts was to show the world that not only was the French action illegal in a technical sense, it was also plain wrong.

"This is a significant victory for British farmers. The safety of British beef has been vindicated once and for all."

France was the biggest market for British beef before the ban with 106,000 tonnes sent there in 1995.

WATER BUFFALO HAVE been making a splash with conservationists in Wales.

For the past three years the Wildlife Trust of South and West Wales has employed Asian water buffalo to graze its Teifi Marshes reserve in Cilgerran, Cardigan.

Now the North Wales Wildlife Trust has followed suit - to help a rare plant re-establish itself.

"Three Cornered Meadow is a species-rich hay meadow on the Wrexham-Chester border and a valuable island of semi natural habitat within a sea of intensively managed farmland," said a spokesman.

"Hay meadows have declined by over 95 per cent since 1945 so this site is particularly important for wildlife. It supports hare, water vole, and a variety of wildflowers including mousetail, which is not found anywhere else in Wales.

"Recent years have seen the wildlife on the site threatened, however. For years the land was managed as a hay meadow and grazed with cattle in the autumn.

"This form of management was ideal, and the 'poaching' of the ground by the cattle produced the conditions for mousetail to flourish.

"Unfortunately, it is not a particularly economical form of management. When the long-term grazier retired in 1999, finding a replacement grazier was very difficult - as was finding a buyer for the flower-rich hay.

"The outbreak of foot-and-mouth disease in 2001 added to the problems and cattle movement restrictions contributed to a lack of grazing in 2002. Last year, no mousetail was seen on the site.

"This summer, however, things got back on track. Contractors cut and baled the hay, which was removed by the landowners, Grosvenor Estates.

"In return, the Trust has agreed to manage the entire site using 20 buffalo and is now confident that mousetail will reappear by next year."

A PET CAT needed to have a leg amputated after falling victim to a trapper operating in countryside around the Shropshire-Powys border.

Otters, foxes, badgers and other domestic pets have been killed in recent years by the mystery lawbreaker who uses outlawed gin traps.

The cat was saved when an elderly woman heard its frantic cries near her house at Llanfyllin and went to investigate.

She found the tabby in agony, dragging the trap and its shattered leg behind it.

Police and the RSPCA are investigating.

WADING BIRDS AND aquatic wildlife have been put at risk from a new Harbours Bill which makes a mockery of official efforts to protect them, it has been claimed.

The RSPB has attacked ports authorities for starting to give evidence on how to improve marine conservation - just a day after backing a Bill that seriously threatens habitats around English and Welsh shores.

"The Environment, Food and Rural Affairs Committee, currently investigating the conservation status of the marine environment, will be hearing evidence from the United Kingdom Major Ports Group and the British Ports Association," said a spokesman.

"Yet the Harbours Bill - re-submitted on December 2 by Lord Berkeley in the House of Lords, with the backing of the ports industry - could pave the way for quicker port development, threatening sites protected by UK and EU laws.

"The Bill would eliminate the right to a public inquiry from any objector to new applications for deep-sea container ports, of which there are four currently under consideration. All four would damage protected wildlife areas."

Duncan Huggett, senior policy officer at the RSPB, added:"The Bill could make a mockery of both UK and EU environment laws and do untold damage to our seas and the wildlife - including thousands of birds - that depend on them.

"The right to give evidence at public inquiries on developments at sea is crucial to wildlife protection because proposals invariably affect highly sensitive areas."

The RSPB fears that if the Harbours Bill becomes law, stringent checks on port and other marine developments would be weakened while protected sites could be lost forever.

SHEEP AT A Scottish farm have been sprayed with bright paint in a bid to frighten off a prowling big cat.

Farmer Charlotte Brayley hit on the bizarre idea after a panther-like animal was spotted stalking sheep at Dalry in Ayrshire.

Red, green and purple paint has now been sprayed on six of her animals with the hope that it will confuse any predator.

Ms Brayley, 21, said:"I read about the recent sightings of a black leopard or panther in the area. These cats prey on sheep and there was no way I was going to allow any of mine to fall victim.

"It only took about 15 minutes to paint each one and they were quite content to have it done. It doesn't matter that the colours are bright. It is the patterns that are important because cats only see in black and white."

NATIVE BRITISH TREES may be at serious risk from a disease which has destroyed thousands of Californian oaks.

Up to now, 'sudden oak death' fungus has only been found in UK shrubs and a tree species native to the US.

But the Forestry Commission says the disease has now attacked beech, horse chestnut, and holm oaks in Cornwall.

There is no known cure for the fungus which destroys trees' bark leaving the trees themselves to die.

The fungus is believed to have wiped out 80 per cent of one type of oak in the western US.

CHRISTMAS TREES ARE a sweet-smelling link with Britain's past, says the NFU as it encourages more people to ditch the popular plastic alternatives.

"No British Christmas is complete without the fresh scent of pine needles that a newly chosen Christmas tree brings to your home," said a spokesman.

"Traditionally, the Christmas tree came direct from the forest as families would harvest their preferred tree and carry it home. Nowadays, most Christmas trees are grown on a plantation, tended to, and then harvested like any other sustainable crop.

"Although Christmas trees were not entirely unknown to Britain, it was Prince Albert of Saxony, the Prince Consort of Queen Victoria during the 19th Century, who encouraged this trend of having a decorated tree at Christmas time. The idea was adopted enthusiastically.

"Depending on the desired size, it can take from six to 13 years to grow the beautiful, fragrant trees that symbolise the festive season. Each year young trees are shaped, pruned and fertilised. Correct pruning of the tree prevents rapid upward growth and encourages the tree to branch more quickly and achieve the full bushy appearance of a traditional Christmas tree."

A BOUNTY OF £1,000 has been offered to any shooter who can bring down one of Britain's fabled big cats.

However, the offer by Sporting Shooter magazine has sparked anger among animal rights campaigners and big cat fans.

The magazine says it is offering the money to determine once and for all whether the mystery panther-like creatures reported for decades really do exist.

"They are encouraging their readers to go out and shoot these cats dead," fumed British Big Cats Society founder Danny Bamping:"We have had reports of farmers shooting and injuring what may have been big cats, even before this bounty was offered. There is no need for these animals to be shot. We believe we already have 14 carcasses collected over the past 40 years, and there is also the risk of other animals being shot by over-zealous shooters spurred on by the reward."

ANGLERS HAVE BEEN given a boost in North Wales and Cheshire with 12,000 new coarse fish introduced to the River Dee.

The one year-old fish were introduced at Farndon, Almere Ferry and Eccleston Ferry.

The fish comprised 6,250 chub, 3,750 bream and 2,000 barbel, supplied from the Environment Agency's National Coarse Fish Hatchery at Calverton in Nottinghamshire.

It is hoped the young fish will quickly adapt and contribute to improving the quality of the river.

BATTLE IS SET to intensify for woods and wildlife after the Government published new runway plans to widespread anger and alarm.

The Woodland Trust said the new airport White Paper flies in the face of good sense and warned its proposals would damage some of the UK's richest wildlife habitats.

The Trust has been campaigning to protect 86 hectares of ancient woodland and trees at Stansted, 22 hectares at Birmingham, 75 hectares at Gatwick and 45 hectares at Manchester which will be destroyed if expansion schemes go ahead.

Trees have grown in these woods for at least 400 years, says the Trust, and they are our best habitats for wildlife, containing more rare and threatened species than any other habitats while covering just two per cent of the country.

Trust spokesman Ed Pomfret said:"The Government is ignoring its own conservation policies and is conveniently forgetting its commitments to protect ancient woodlands.

"If we really are to have a sustainable aviation policy we must manage demand to ensure that we don't damage this irreplaceable habitat.

"The proposals in the White Paper reveal fundamental flaws in Government thinking about sustainable development and climate change. Ancient woodland must be protected from these destructive plans."

Meanwhile, while welcoming news that there would be no new airport at Cliffe in Kent, the RSPB says it is hugely disappointed that the wider environmental impacts of unconstrained air travel had not been addressed.

"At last the Government has accepted the blindingly obvious about Cliffe," said the RSPB's chief executive Graham Wynne."To include it in the first place was downright ludicrous.

"It is disappointing that we have been forced to fight to save a site that is already protected by Europe's toughest wildlife laws.

"Cliffe was not even a runner from an aviation perspective - the risk of birdstrike meant that it would have been the UK's most dangerous airport by far.

"But the Government has, after all, given in to a 'predict and provide' approach to air travel under pressure from the aviation industry.

"We don't need the two new runways proposed in the White Paper for south east England - at Stansted, Heathrow or Gatwick - and extraordinarily, Government has failed to include any measures to manage demand for air travel at all. This is a far cry from the sustainable aviation policy the Government promised at the outset."

GOAT RUSTLERS HAVE struck at a Somerset farm for the second time in a year.

This time the raiders snatched 21 milking goats from Alan and Lesley Mowlem's Stogursey farm.

The crime came as the Mowlems were still trying to get back to normal after thieves broke into their farm the first time back in March.

That time the gang escaped with nine adult goats and 25 kids.

The two raids are thought to have cost the Mowlems over £7,000 in total.

Mr Mowlem, who has commercially farmed milking goats for over a decade to make cheese, said:"This second raid has all the hallmarks of being done by the same people."

THE GREY PARTRIDGE, immortalised in traditional Christmas carol 'The Twelve Days Of Christmas', is fighting back from possible extinction.

Although the bird has suffered a massive 85 per cent decline over the past 30 years, new research shows it may at last be turning the corner with a five per cent upsurge recorded.

The Game Conservancy Trust said:"This quintessentially English species has been recorded as far back as the Iron Age but in the past three decades numbers have plummeted to such an alarming extent that it has become a Government biodiversity action plan species with the Trust appointed lead partner for the plan."

Dr Nicholas Aebischer, deputy director of research with the Trust, added:"It is estimated that in Edwardian Britain there were about one million pairs of grey partridges but, even with the latest increase, the partridge population is currently very low, standing at just 80,000 pairs.

"The last two warm summers, and a big increase in the number of landowners and farmers implementing a range of measures recommended by the Trust, are beginning to make a difference. It can only get better for the grey partridge."

The Trust is spearheading a massive campaign to halt any further decline and has raised in excess of £450,000 to fund a £2million research programme.

In addition, the body is enlisting the support of 1,350 farmers and landowners across the country to join in an annual count scheme.

THE RAMBLERS Association says it is asking the Government to take immediate action to prevent a loophole in the law from destroying some of Britain's most beautiful countryside.

Alun Michael MP, Minister for Rural Affairs, has just published a consultation paper on recreational motor vehicles such as 4x4s, trail and quad bikes using the countryside.

Due to a legal anomaly, however, any right of way established as a carriageway in the days of the horse and cart can still be legally claimed as having full vehicular rights.

The Association, along with a coalition of environmental, wildlife, farming and land owning groups, believes that this is not only wrong but that byways of great importance are being irrevocably damaged by off-roading.

Many of the routes are of ancient origin, such as Roman roads or even Neolithic trackways.

Their use by recreational motor vehicles not only shatters the peaceful enjoyment of the countryside, says the Association, but brings increased danger to walkers, horse riders and cyclists.

HUNT GROUPS ARE aiming to make this year's Boxing Day hunts the best ever after sensing the tide may be turning in their favour.

Labour MPs and animal rights groups were furious when a Bill to ban hunting with dogs in England and Wales was left out of the Queen's Speech.

Now, while anti-hunt campaigners hope a private member's Bill can rescue the legislation, pro-hunt supporters are planning to celebrate the continuing survival of their sport.

The Countryside Alliance says it wants to make December 26 the biggest day's hunting in history.

Every hunt is advertising details of its meet and extending an open invitation for anyone to join them in a celebration which has remained unchanged for centuries, says the Alliance.

People are invited to watch the work of both hounds and huntsman while working off the excesses of Christmas Day.

Chief executive Simon Hart said:"Hunts are proud of their way of life and the good they do for our countryside, wildlife, communities and the rural economy. That is why they encourage people to join them, not just on Boxing Day but throughout the year, and why more people are hunting now than ever before."

BARELY HALF OF England's wildlife and conservation sites are now in a good condition, according to English Nature.

An exhaustive survey by the Government's independent wildlife advisers found more than 40 per cent of sites in urgent need of improvement.

The study, 'England's Best Wildlife And Geological Sites: The Condition Of SSSIs In England In 2003', marks the first total national assessment of sites of special scientific interest.

There are currently 4,112 English SSSIs, which cover about seven per cent of England.

English Nature's chief executive, Dr Andy Brown, said:"The Government has made a commitment to ensure 95 per cent of all SSSIs are in favourable condition by 2010.

"Meeting this challenge will be a huge effort for everyone. We must recognise that improving and maintaining England's natural assets needs ongoing investment, alongside changes to legislation and the reform of environmentally-damaging policies."

CHRISTMAS CAME EARLY this year for Lancashire anglers with 130,000 coarse fish released into the county's rivers.

The massive influx of new roach, dace and chub into the rivers Alt, Lune, Douglas, Ribble, Darwen and Wyre was part of the Environment Agency's fish stocking programme.

The fish, all bred at the Agency's fish culture unit in Leyland, were released at several different locations on the rivers and their tributaries.

In the case of the River Lune, a long-absent species - dace - was reintroduced.

The Agency, together with the Lune Habitat Group and the Lune and Wyre Fisheries Assocation, released 10,000 dace into the river.

Although the Lune was once known for its shoals of dace, damage to their spawning beds caused them to die out.

Now that the spawning areas have been cleared, it is hoped that dace will start to breed in the Lune for the first time in many years.

A SCOTTISH RED kite has set an amazing long distance flight record, according to the RSPB.

"The young bird was found in northern Portugal, more than 2,000 kilometres away from its home in central Scotland," said a spokesman.

"It has flapped its way into the record books with the longest distance flight of any UK red kite.

"Workers at a small quarry near Airao, just north of Portugal's second largest city of Porto, recovered the bird. It was identified by its unique metal leg ring and by red wing tags.

"Suffering from a fractured wing, it has been taken into care at a raptor recovery centre at the nearby Alvao National Park. The kite has since undergone veterinary treatment and is expected to make a full recovery.

"The lucky adventurer will be released in Portugal and then RSPB staff will be keeping an eye out to see if it returns home.

"This is an amazing record, although the circumstances in which the bird was found are unfortunate.

"In spring 2004, we will be watching the bird's home area near Stirling to see if he comes back as is usual for this species."

A BRITISH ANGLER can spend the rest of his life regaling pals about the one that didn't get away - a 955lb, 13ft long tiger shark.

Don Metcalfe, 72, from Weston-Super-Mare, reeled in the maneater after a three-hour fight while fishing off the coast of Kenya, Africa.

The gaping jaws of the monster were awesome, as Don later recounted.

"When the shark was hanging up, the jaws could have dropped over me, without touching me," he said.

The shark, one of the biggest ever caught by rod, was later cut up and eaten by villagers at Watamu near Malindi.

Don, founder of the Bristol Channel Federation of Sea Anglers, had used yellow tuna as bait to hook the monster fish and was "absolutely shattered" when he first saw the size of it.

RED SQUIRRELS LIVING by a Scottish river have been given a boost with the construction of a rope bridge to span the hazardous water.

Squirrels living in Gight Woods alongside the River Ythan at Methlick were thrown a lifeline by conservationists and forestry workers.

Forestry Commission Scotland and the Scottish Wildlife Trust have strung two parallel heavy ropes between treetops on opposite banks of the river, allowing squirrels to pass back and forth more easily.

This will enable some of the UK's last remaining native squirrels to reach a supply of tasty hazelnuts previously only reached via a daunting footbridge much used by humans.

The rope bridge is thought to be the first in Britain erected to enable red squirrels to cross a river since all the others erected traverse busy roads.

ANTI-HUNT GROUPS were reported to be unimpressed by record crowds of over 275,000 people said to have attended 350 Boxing Day meets across the country.

And while the Countryside Alliance stresses that an NOP survey found just two per cent of people now think hunting should be a Government priority, anti-hunt campaigners point to their own recent survey.

According to the League Against Cruel Sports, the MORI poll signalled "strong and continued public support for a hunting ban, with 76 per cent of those surveyed saying hunting with dogs should not be legal."

However, following his group's massive festive turnout, Simon Hart, chief executive of the Countryside Alliance, said:"The unprecedented crowds at the Boxing Day fixtures are a clear indication that hunting has a place in the hearts of hundreds of thousands of ordinary people, from town and country alike.

"It is a proper reflection of solidarity and resolve, not only from the hunting community but also from the many thousands of people who support the freedom to hunt."

FREEZING WEATHER SAVED fish from suffocating to death when a tanker lorry overturned and dumped thousands of litres of milk into their Shropshire brook.

Milk spills are usually deadly for fish but Environment Agency experts said that the icy cold saved fish swimming in Cound Brook, near the A49 at Dorrington, by inhibiting its oxygen-sapping effects.

An estimated 13,000 litres of milk had seeped into the brook before fire crews and environmental workers could begin their clean-up.

The road was closed for eight hours while the job was completed.

The tanker driver, who sustained head injuries in the accident, was taken to hospital for treatment.

SEAGULLS ROOSTING INLAND or on storm lashed cliffs are the subject of new research.

The 6th Winter Gull Roost Survey aims to provide latest estimates of the numbers of gulls wintering in the UK.

According to the British Trust for Ornithology, the last survey took place in January 1993, during which over 2.5 million gulls were counted across mainland Britain.

A further 19,000 gulls were also found in Northern Ireland, 3,850 on the Isle of Man and 8,500 in the Channel Islands.

OFFSHORE WINDFARMS could be a menace to birds and other wildlife, say conservationists.

A Crown Estate announcement on December 18 outlined the locations of successful bids for the second round of offshore windfarms.

However, serious concerns have been raised about their potential impact on birds and important marine wildlife habitats.

The RSPB's conservation director, Dr Mark Avery said:"An initial analysis of the proposed sites suggests there could be serious problems for birds. We already know that large numbers of red-throated divers congregate in the Greater Thames and off the north Norfolk coast in late winter.

"It is vital that the Government collects more detailed data about bird numbers and movements this winter to inform any final decisions."

368

WATER VOLE: on the run from savage invader

SHY, secretive, and facing extinction in recent years, the water vole is yet another native creature driven to the edge thanks largely to an American immigrant. Just as the American grey squirrel evicted our own red squirrel from most of its old stamping grounds, the mink has been driving out the water vole.

However, unlike the grey squirrel, the ferocious mink actually preys on its victim and has developed quite a taste for water voles (traditionally also known as 'water rats').

Countless numbers of these small, peaceful rodents - made famous by 'Ratty' in The Wind in the Willows - have been killed and devoured by mink after the intruders were first introduced here from North American fur farms in the 1920s. Feeding solely on vegetation, water voles are easily distinguished from real rats thanks to their blunter faces and rounder, shorter bodies.

Unmolested, they live in a system of burrows dug into banks beside rivers and lakes, the male often spending his entire life within a 150-metre territory.

The female water vole needs even less territory but is more likely to up sticks and move. Even without the explosion of the mink population, water voles already faced a host of deadly predators, from herons and owls to pike and stoats.

It's been a long time since I heard the distinctive 'plop' of a water vole fleeing into water at my approach. Years ago, at a small Lancashire lake I frequented, not only would you hear the noise but, if you stood still long enough, you might even catch a glimpse of the water vole that made it.

This is far less likely now.

Indeed, I haven't spotted one in the wild for years.

Water voles have disappeared from almost 90 per cent of the UK sites they once occupied.

Without efforts to protect them, it is estimated that these timid, harmless creatures would soon be extinct.

Unlike true rats, which can also swim, water voles thrive only in quiet stretches of clean water - which brings us to the second major cause of their decline: loss of habitat.

Fortunately, Wildlife Trusts around the country have made it a priority to try to save 'Ratty' from a terminal slump and protect his remaining territories. As well as controlling mink predation, their efforts involve managing the kind of habitats that water voles require.

Simon Lyster, director general of The Wildlife Trusts, explained:*"The peaceful riverbank that was the scene of Ratty's adventures has changed out of all recognition in many areas over the last 50 years. "Riverside building, changes in farming practices and changes to rivers themselves have all contributed to the destruction of the water vole's haunts.*

"As a result, water voles are hanging on in the few refuges where conditions are suitable. It is our duty to 'Ratty' to involve everyone in water vole conservation and we are determined to do all we can."

For poor Ratty's sake, I hope it's enough.

SIGNS OF PROWLING big cats will be recorded by farmers nationwide during 2004 as part of a scheme to get a fuller picture of their presence.

The NFU has asked members to pass on details to the British Big Cats Society which is already involved in conducting research.

NFU deputy president Tim Bennett said:"There is anecdotal evidence amongst farmers and society at large that there are big cats wild within our countryside. But while there are many local legends, such as the Beast of Bodmin Moor, we have no firm evidence of how many instances of unidentifiable creatures there are.

"By helping the British Big Cats Society with its study, we aim to reach a clearer picture.

"This is a serious issue for farmers who need to be aware of threats to their animals from worrying and attacks."

BBCS founder Danny Bamping said:"We are delighted by the NFU announcement and hope that this will be the start of a long-term productive working relationship.

"The farmers represent a large key group of people whom the BBCS can rely upon for valuable and credible information.

"Over the years I have 'listened harder' when talking about big cats or evidence of them with farmers - they know their business and they know what they have seen."

DEEP BELCHING GROANS are the sound of true love for fallow deer, according to a new £3.50 booklet from The Mammal Society.

"Fallow deer are well known for their 'rut' where males compete for the amorous attentions of the females through ritualised displays and fighting, accompanied by deep belching groans. Once heard this is unlikely to be forgotten," said spokeswoman Georgette Shearer.

The Mammal Society has published 'Fallow Deer', the latest booklet in its British Deer series, with help from the British Deer Society.

Fallow deer were reintroduced to Britain by the Normans in the 11th Century after dying out here.

Today there are well over 100,000 of them living wild in Britain and a further 20,000 in parks and farms.

ZEBRA STEAKS WILL be the highlight of a Burns Night supper in a controversial move by a Scottish restaurant.

Thick chunks of the striped African animal will be served with traditional haggis, neeps and tatties by the Zanzibar restaurant in Inverness.

Zanzibar chef Stuart Walker, who has previously served up kangaroo, ostrich, alligator and crocodile, said zebra would be popular because of its light flavour.

But animal rights campaigners Advocates for Animals have been outraged by the event, saying it was exploitative.

SCOTTISH BIRDS OF prey may get greater protection after gamekeepers emerged as chief culprits in their decline.

Pesticides used to poison them could soon be outlawed in a Scottish Executive move aimed at boosting raptor conservation.

According to the RSPB, illegal poisoning on sporting estates has ended the lives of almost 100 red kites north of the border.

Red kites were originally released as part of a concerted effort to reintroduce the spectacular species to the country.

Although over 300 red kites have been brought in to breed and settle across three sites in Scotland since the late 1980s, the rate of illegal poisoning has shot up.

The fork-tailed birds are thought to feed on game bird chicks which makes them a pest to gamekeepers charged with providing birds for the multi-million pound shooting industry.

RSPB Scotland spokesman Duncan Orr-Ewing revealed that Scotland was now one of the worst places in Europe for illegal raptor persecution.

"Our aim was to re-establish a breeding population of a bird which was exterminated during Victorian times. The red kite was once part of our native fauna," he said.

"The intention was for all three sites to eventually join up and re-establish a population. But we have a problem with illegal poisoning which is mostly associated with sporting estates.

"Poisoning is the most serious problem affecting kites. We calculate that 31 per cent of the birds released have been poisoned."

He welcomed the decision by the Scottish Executive to urgently address the issue.

Poisons commonly found in dead kites are carbofuran, a pesticide used for vegetables; phoserin, which protects fruit; and alphachlorolose, used to kill rats.

"Sadly, there is still a significant minority engaged in laying out poison bait and, predominantly, we suspect gamekeepers are involved," added Mr Orr-Ewing.

"Blackspots seem to be around grouse moors near the Black Isle, Perthshire and Dumfries and Galloway."

SALMON AND SEA trout are being boosted by a scheme to help them thrive in a South Wales river.

Ideas on how to protect the fish in the River Afan, Port Talbot, are also being invited from the local community as Environment Agency Wales launches a new action plan.

According to the Agency, salmon and sea trout stocks in the Afan have already improved thanks to conservation measures despite virtual elimination by the early 1800s.

However, sea trout currently constitute the majority of local catches.

The most recent rod catch survey showed six salmon and 96 sea trout caught.

Agency spokesman Niall Reynolds said the action plan "is the latest in a series of plans put forward to develop salmon and sea trout in the area and will be a framework for the management of stocks in future.

"It is particularly important in view of the general global decline of salmon identified in recent years and the major contribution that fishing makes to the local economy."

DUMPING CHRISTMAS TREES after the festivities can cause flood problems in local countryside, the Environment Agency has warned.

"As this year's festivities draw to a close with decorations soon to be packed away for another year, the Agency is urging the public to help reduce the risk of localised flooding by recycling Christmas trees," said a spokesman.

"Every year following Twelfth Night, hundreds of old Christmas trees are dumped in rivers and streams which not only look unsightly but can block river flows and increase the risk of flooding.

"Dumped trees have to be fished out at public expense by flood defence officers who patrol the river banks to ensure the rivers flow as freely as possible and so are better able to cope with extra winter rainfall.

"If the trees are not removed they can quickly cause localised flooding as debris builds up behind them and vital flood channels and drains become blocked.

"Over five million Christmas trees are bought every year. If they were all thrown away they would create an additional 9,000 tonnes of waste - enough to fill the Albert Hall three times over.

"But with local authorities offering Christmas tree recycling facilities it is now easier than ever to dispose of your old tree responsibly so it can be put to good use and help keep flood risk to a minimum."

A BLAZE OF rural yellow in the New Year might be due to Britain's flourishing daffodil industry.

According to the NFU, Britain is now one of the world's leading growers and exporters of daffodils, boasting an export value of more than £4.2 million.

Lincolnshire and Cornwall are the two most prominent daffodil growing regions but daffodils are also grown in Scotland and Hampshire.

The union says the daffodil season is separated into two different periods, the bulb season and the flower season.

The harvesting of daffodil bulbs begins during July but the harvest period for the flowers peaks after Christmas and the New Year.

Britain's soil is good and the climate very favourable for daffodils, says Richard Barlow, managing director of F. Dring and Sons Ltd producers in Lincolnshire.

"That's why we're one of the largest daffodil producing countries in the world," he explained.

Brian Taylor, head of the British Horticultural Association, said British daffodil bulbs are generally larger than those from other nations.

Larger bulbs produce more and higher quality daffodils than smaller bulbs, he said.

Mr Taylor added:"It is not uncommon for people to purchase bulbs in the Netherlands, only to find that they have been exported from Britain to begin with."

OTTERS ARE AMONG wild creatures boosted by a successful bid to protect a 500-acre wildlife site beside the River Thames.

Members of the Berkshire, Buckinghamshire and Oxfordshire Wildlife Trust are celebrating news that their emergency appeal to safeguard the site near Bampton has now topped £243,000.

And among several projects already planned is one aimed at encouraging otters to breed there by building holts.

The Trust had secured pledges of £1.1 million from national and local charitable organisations but still needed to raise at least £100,000 itself in order to release the funds to purchase land at Chimney Farm.

BBOWT spokeswoman Philippa Lyons said:"We had a deadline to raise the funds before the land went back onto the open market and we are thrilled that people in our region have responded so generously.

"Some £100,000 was desperately needed to purchase the site in the first instance but we also had to find at least a further £100,000 to restore the land to its former glory. This amazing response will allow us to do both and the Trust would like to say a huge thank you to everyone who has supported our appeal."

A RARE NORWEGIAN robin flew all the way to Britain only to end up as dinner for a birdwatcher's cat.

The bedraggled, exhausted bird is thought to have flown over 400 miles before landing at Eccles, Manchester.

A local woman birdwatcher was shocked to find the robin - one of just eight to arrive here in recent years - dangling from her pet's mouth.

After retrieving a ring from its leg attached in Norway, she confessed what had happened to the British Trust for Ornithology.

Officials there were appalled at the gruesome end for a robin which made such a gruelling flight.

Norwegian robins are similar to our own but have darker breasts and some believe them to be even prettier.

THE MYSTERY OF why some nestboxes are more successful than others in attracting birds is addressed in the British Trust for Ornithology's 8th National Nest Box Week scheme.

Originally launched in 1997 by Chris Mead, the scheme continues to highlight the need for the British public to put up suitable nestboxes for birds.

However, many people are disappointed when nestboxes have not been used.

Chris du Feu, the author of a new book and a leading nestbox expert, has spent years gathering together information on different box designs.

He said:"Sadly, you often see boxes which are damaging to birds' breeding prospects. But in the book - 'The BTO Nestbox Guide' - I have attempted to show what makes a good nestbox.These can often be made from very cheap or recycled wood."

Nestboxes are not a new phenomenon.

"When schoolboy David Warden built a nestbox in 1947, little did he realise that the same box would still be in use over 50 years later," reveals the Trust.

"A very conservative estimate is that this box could have produced as many as 250 young tits since it was first put up - and David is now one of over 500 people monitoring 30,000 nests each year for the BTO Nest Record Scheme."

A GRANDMOTHER HAS told how a rampaging wild boar broke her leg in two places in Gloucestershire.

Jean Kirton, 72, is thought to be the first person injured by one of the animals in modern times following their resurgence in the UK.

After escaping from an abattoir, the 600-pound boar charged around Cinderford in the Forest of Dean, scattering shoppers as it looked for an exit.

But before fleeing to local woods - where genuine wild boar are thought to lurk - it thudded into Mrs Kirton on a zebra crossing.

She said:"I waved to acknowledge the lorry driver who had stopped for me at the zebra crossing and the next thing I knew there was this enormous crash.

"My trolley just went and I crashed to the floor. I think I must have been knocked out for a bit because the next thing I knew, the girl from the hairdressers was helping me up and telling me to come in for a cup of tea.

"I was really shocked when people told me I'd been knocked over by a wild boar. At first someone said it was a large labrador but the drivers who had stopped saw it was a pig. It must have been travelling like the clappers because I didn't see a thing. I certainly felt its snout but I didn't see it at all."

However, it was only the next day when Mrs Kirton hobbled to hospital in agony that doctors discovered her leg was broken in two places.

SWANS HAVE BEEN causing a flap in different parts of Britain for very different reasons.

Over 3,000 families in Telford, Shropshire, were left without power for three hours during the day after a swan flew into an electricity cable there.

That bird is thought to have been killed.

But elsewhere, in chilly Aberdeen, Scotland, locals were delighted when a rare black swan took up residence on the River Dee - the first time most had seen one.

The swan, native to Australia, is thought to have escaped from a wildlife park, like another unexpected visitor to the Dee in recent years - a white pelican.

GARDENERS ARE BEING urged to buy a CD Rom this year which shows them how to attract more wild creatures into their gardens.

'Gardening with Wildlife in Mind' - published by the Plant Press at £9.99 and available through English Nature - reveals how gardeners can avoid creating an unkempt wilderness while providing an attractive environment for wild visitors.

The disc has photographs of more than 500 plants and 300 creatures from bats to bumble bees, hoverflies to hedgehogs.

Chris Baines, broadcaster and author, said:"Wildlife in the garden benefits people. Contact with nature can reduce stress."

FURY IS GROWING after the Government decided to ignore protests and open the countryside to possible growing of commercial GM crops - perhaps within weeks.

Although 90 per cent of people surveyed are opposed to so-called 'Frankenstein Foods', Premier Tony Blair has ignored charges of being anti-democratic and even anti-British to support the cultivation of foreign sourced genetically modified maize.

The lifting of restrictions was formally backed by the Government's Advisory Committee on Releases to the Environment and few doubted Blair himself - an advocate of GM science - would object.

ACRE has also refused to rule out the commercial development of GM beet and oil seed rape despite acknowledging that GM crop trials showed they would cause 'adverse environmental effects'.

But it gave strongest support to GM fodder maize, claiming it 'did not demonstrate evidence of adverse environmental impacts'.

However, Friends of the Earth said that maize GM crop trials could not be used to justify their commercial development as they were flawed.

FoE campaigner Pete Riley said:"ACRE refuses to rule out the commercial development of GM beet and oil seed rape despite overwhelming evidence of the damage this would cause.

"It also appears to support the commercial development of GM maize even though trials of this particular crop were fatally flawed.

"GM crops are unpopular, unnecessary and a threat to neighbouring crops and the environment. The Government must not allow them to be commercially grown in the UK."

A WINTER CRACKDOWN on illegal movements of fish from one watercourse to another has been launched by the Environment Agency.

"With a decrease in water temperature due to the onset of winter comes an increase in numbers of fish being removed and stocked into waters across England and Wales," said a spokesman.

"During this period, the focus of the Agency turns to the auditing of these movements. This auditing is not only focused on countering illegal movements but also checking compliance with movement consents.

"Unauthorised fish movements could endanger otherwise healthy populations through the spread of fatal diseases. They can also upset the natural ecology of the watercourse through predation and direct competition for food and space.

"The focal point for these audits are high risk fish movements, such as those taking place at Sites of Special Scientific Interest, waters that may contain 'unusual' species, and those with which there is a risk of diseases being introduced into the water environment.

"In Kent four high-risk fish introductions have been audited, three high-risk removals audited, and four Import of Live Fish Act compliance checks carried out.

"These checks have led to the issuing of three warning letters and the launching of an investigation into illegal fish removals.

"The Agency's Kent Area team, in conjunction with the National Fish Movement Enforcement Team, has also been busy advising fishery owners on how to comply with any consents and licences they are issued."

COASTAL BIRDS SHOULD get better protection from developers thanks to a truce on a new ports Bill.

Plans that could scupper conservationists' right to demand public inquiries into new port developments may now be altered.

Lord Berkeley has promised to introduce an amendment to his Harbours Bill to allow English Nature and the Countryside Council for Wales to demand a public inquiry if they object to schemes.

The RSPB and British Ports Association both back his proposed amendment.

Duncan Huggett, a policy officer for the RSPB, said:"The amendment is a sensible compromise that ensures the protection of important wildlife sites. It is about getting the balance between nature conservation and development right."

There are four deep-sea container port proposals currently being considered and all could seriously damage wildlife sites protected by UK and EU laws.

Lord Berkeley will introduce the amendment at committee stage, probably within the next two weeks, according to the RSPB.

However, several peers have claimed it will oblige conservation bodies to object to all harbour development plans.

AFRICAN HEDGEHOGS HAVE sparked a prickly row involving the British Hedgehog Preserva - tion Society.

The Shropshire-based Society has attacked a local pet shop after it began stocking and selling tiny African pygmy hedgehogs.

BHPS chief executive Fay Vass said:"Our first and main concern is for the welfare of the animals themselves.

"Very little is known about African pygmy hedgehogs. Veterinary care, as with a lot of exotic species, is not as easy to obtain.

"Another fear is that, as so often happens with pets, the novelty will wear off and the owners will set the hedgehogs free. Due to the huge climate differences, an African pygmy would have no chance of survival at all in this country in the wild."

However, the pet shop has hit back, saying it acts responsibly in a heavily regulated industry and that special books and equipment are supplied with all exotic pets.

OSPREYS ARE TO have their resurgence in Scotland marked by 'golden jubilee' celebrations.

It is now 50 years since the majestic fish-eaters made a comeback at Loch Garten in Strathspey after being wiped out by Victorian hunters.

'Osprey 50th' scheme spokesman Duncan Orr-Ewing said:"Although this bird recolonised Scotland naturally at first, its population increase has been achieved largely as a result of hard work by conservationists and land managers.

"We can all be proud that this magnificent bird is now doing so well."

DEAD DOLPHINS AND porpoises are again being washed up in large numbers on beaches across England and Wales.

Storm force winds may have brought the corpses ashore but the culprits are fishermen using outdated practices, according to The Wildlife Trusts.

In the first two weeks of 2004 almost 50 corpses were reported.

"Year on year, hundreds of carcasses of common dolphins and porpoises are washed ashore in the south west of England," said Joan Edwards, marine policy director for the Trusts.

"These are unacceptable levels of dolphin deaths within UK waters and current UK and European legislation is simply not doing enough to address the problem.

"Dead dolphins on the UK's beaches are just one sign that we need radical changes in the way we look after the marine environment on which we all depend. Government needs to act now before our marine wildlife is totally destroyed."

Some 33,000 people have signed The Wildlife Trusts' dolphin petition, pledging support for a campaign to ban the pelagic trawl sea bass fishery in the English Channel.

This form of fishing has killed an estimated 67,500 common dolphins in the last 15 years.

Dolphins and porpoises are trapped and killed in nets dragged at high speed through the English Channel and the Bay of Biscay during December, January, February and March.

SKYLARK, YELLOWHAMMER and other farmland bird species have crashed across Europe in recent decades because of modern farming practices, it has been claimed.

Most of the Continent has seen bird populations affected by intensive agricultural methods, according to a new report.

The international study of the population trends of wild birds was undertaken jointly by the RSPB, BirdLife International and the European Bird Census Council.

In all, modern farming across Britain and Europe has seen numbers of 24 common bird species slump by a third in a quarter of a century.

The report includes information for species of farmland bird from 11 present members of the EU, five others which will join this May, and Norway and Switzerland.

The RSPB said:"Declines have been severest in countries in north west Europe. In the UK, for example, between 1970 and 1999, the skylark declined by 52 per cent, the yellowhammer by 53 per cent and the corn bunting by 88 per cent."

A RED KITE created a stir when it circled low above rooftops in Chesham, Buckinghamshire.

The majestic, fork-tailed bird was first spotted by a local woman before a small crowd of onlookers gathered to watch its surprising antics above Darvell Drive.

Ignoring the efforts of smaller birds to drive it away, the predator circled above one particular garden for several minutes.

Two years ago, the woman resident of the house had complained that a huge unidentified bird had swooped down and carried off the carcass of her Christmas turkey.

A buzzard was blamed but it now appears that the true culprit may have been revisiting the scene.

373

A SHOCK REPORT on Britain's hill farmers claims they are battling to survive on less than the minimum wage for a 58-hour week.

Research by the Peak District Rural Deprivation Forum was funded by Oxfam and studied income levels among a snapshot of hill farmers in Derbyshire.

Farmers in the area were among the poorest in the country with incomes dependent on subsidies, according to the 'Hard Times' study.

Without subsidies, they would be in debt by as much as £2,300 a year.

The report revealed the only farmers to make a profit without subsidies were dairy farmers estimated to earn a tiny £4,622 each.

Overall, farm incomes were said to have dropped by 75 per cent over the last 10 years, with hill farmers especially hard hit by the slump in agriculture.

However, the NFU has been quick to attack the report for what it leaves out.

NFU president Ben Gill said:"Nowhere within this report is there any recognition of the benefits of CAP Reform - the most radical changes ever - and the benefits it will bring to farmers, society as a whole, and the third world. The reforms will bring us a more market-focused agriculture industry, vast environmental benefits, a fairer trading system that will break down trade barriers, and potentially less bureaucracy."

BROWN TROUT AND salmon are being boosted in separate schemes involving two different English counties.

Native brown trout are being helped by a move to increase their numbers in Oxfordshire's rivers, a project which is already showing signs of success.

Eggs are said to be currently hatching in special incubation boxes placed in six river locations in the Lechlade and Coln-St-Aldwyns areas last December.

Meanwhile, in Devon, efforts are being stepped up to encourage more wild salmon back.

The Environment Agency, which is co-ordinating both projects, said of the salmon initiative:"Devon is rightly famous for its wild salmon with fish returning each year from as far afield as the Faroes and Greenland to spawn in the county's rivers.

"Recently, however, there has been a huge decline in the numbers of salmon returning. There are many different causes, including pollution, over fishing, silting up of streams and poaching."

Now individual plans had been formulated for each Devon river.

BRITAIN'S FINEST COUNTRY foods are set to stalk the corridors of power as part of a new initiative at the Houses of Parliament.

Members of 'Heart of England Fine Foods' kicked off the regional food promotion with Shropshire venison, Staffordshire oatcakes and Warwickshire truckle cheese just some of the tasty titbits on offer.

The project will last for two years.

EFFORTS TO BAN game bird shooting appear to be increasing in the light of recent negative publicity about the multi-million pound industry.

With foxhunters still fighting a rearguard action to defend their sport, shooters are now finding the same level of animosity directed against them by protesters.

According to the Countryside Alliance, the RSPCA has confirmed that it now has a policy of opposing game shooting for sport despite claiming only a month ago it was not targeting shooting at all.

Following publication of photographs of the Queen dispatching an injured pheasant, an RSPCA spokesman was quoted saying: "We believe game shooting does not justify the causing of suffering to birds and other animals."

Simon Hart, chief executive of the Alliance, said:"This statement comes as no surprise to us but will cause the Society embarrassment since they wrote to me only a month ago stating the exact opposite.

"It might be embarrassing for the RSPCA to admit that their real agenda is so far removed from the core animal welfare work on which we and many of their members believe they should be concentrating, but in all honesty they can no longer continue to deny their opposition to shooting."

Animal Aid, a leading animal rights group, is particularly scathing about pheasant shooting.

"Every year in Britain, 35 million pheasants are mass produced inside hatcheries and rearing sheds," it says.

"From the sheds, they are moved to fattening pens before being released to serve as feathered targets for shooters. Only about one quarter of the total produced are actually eaten."

HARE COURSING FANS are pressing ahead with plans for the biggest event of their year - the Waterloo Cup 2004.

In the continuing absence of an expected legal ban and despite ongoing threats of disruption from animal rights groups, the controversial sport is carrying on as normal.

The National Coursing Club said:"Some 64 of the best coursing greyhounds in Britain and Eire will contest the historic prize. This year's meeting will be held on February 24, 25 and 26.

"The event is generously sponsored for the second time by Oliver Coughlan. The winner's prize money will be £5,000. The first brace of runners will be put into slips at 9.30am each day."

THE WOODLAND TRUST is investigating the tricky problem of how to dispose of plastic tree tube guards after they have served their purpose.

"For the first 10 years of their lives many new trees have been aided by the use of tree shelters which protect them from the weather, voles, deer and rabbits to increase survival rates and encourage growth," said a spokesman.

"The shelters, tubes, sleeves and spirals are made from plastics and polypropylene, most of which are not degradable.

"Until now they have been disposed of by burning, chipping or landfill waste, none of which are environmentally friendly so alternative methods are being sought."

The Trust planted 300,000 trees last year using the guards.

WOODLAND MAY SOON spring up in abundance on Scotland's storm lashed Western Isles following a double boost for islanders.

As the Western Isles Council launched a strategy for woodland development, the Scottish Executive announced a new grant to help islanders themselves plant new trees.

Forestry Minister Allan Wilson said:"The Western Isles, with their strong winds and rugged, maritime climate, are a part of Scotland where even quite small areas of well sited new woodlands can make a real difference to the environment and improve people's lives.

"I therefore congratulate the Council on this excellent new local strategy which identifies where different types of woodlands will provide the benefits that we want local people to enjoy from trees, woods and forests.

"It captures the considerable enthusiasm shown by the people of the isles for trees and woodlands.

"I am also delighted that the Executive can support the strategy with a locational supplement. These grants have proved popular in other high-priority regions where we have made them available in support of local woodland strategies, notably Shetland and Orkney, where the challenges facing woodland managers are very similar to those in the Western Isles.

"Indeed, I am pleased to hear that links between woodland interests in the three island groups are developing to share experience and expertise."

POLICE ARE INVESTIGATING after foxhounds ran amok in a family home while in pursuit of a fox.

Chris Owens, 48, his wife, and two teenage daughters were terrified by the sudden invasion of their home in Clotton, Cheshire.

Mr Owens was twice bitten and knocked over when several of the hounds burst into his home and he tried to get them out.

"They were going berserk," he said later."They were so powerful that I soon found myself flat on the ground."

The Joint Master of Cheshire Hunt, Thomas Randle Cooke, has apologised but explained that a fox had dashed into the family's garden.

ESTUARY BIRDS ARE the subject of a new book which comprises information from seven years of observations by 600 volunteer birdwatchers.

Elliot Morley MP, Minister for the Environment, launched 'Estuarine Waterbirds at Low Tide' after contributing to the tome himself.

Mr Morley, a keen birdwatcher, took part in the book's research by counting birds on the Humber Estuary and, like all volunteers, earned himself a free copy.

Andy Musgrove is the book's main author.

FOXHUNTERS AND animal rights campaigners are being involved in new clashes as frustration among anti-hunt groups grows.

In Kent, according to the Countryside Alliance, a 38-year-old hunt follower was dragged from his horse and brutally beaten by three balaclava-clad anti-hunt protesters in front of his wife and two children.

Graeme Worsley, one of the Masters of the Old Surrey, Burstow and West Kent Hunt, feared for his life during the attack at West Peckham near Tonbridge.

He received hospital treatment for injuries to his face, jaw and throat.

Later, he said:"Three hunt saboteurs were verbally abusing and threatening my children so I asked them to stop. The next thing I knew I had been grabbed from behind and me and my horse were pulled to the ground.

"I really feared for my life as last year a hunt saboteur had threatened to kill me - at one point one of the attackers had his foot on my throat while the others were hitting me. My wife tried to help but was also pushed to the ground and my children fled the scene. It took me over an hour to find them.

"Both mine and my wife's horses became loose and bolted. We found them 10 miles away on the busy A20 an hour and a half later. Thankfully, this did not cause an accident and neither of the horses was injured but it could have been a very different story."

A Bill to ban hunting with dogs was left out of the last Queen's Speech despite having the overwhelming support of Labour MPs.

Campaigners still hope to kick-start the legislative process via a private member's Bill.

HOMING PIGEONS ARE being knocked off track in their thousands because of the increasing number of mobile phone masts, it has been claimed.

Birds of prey and poor weather are also thought to have played a role in almost 60,000 pigeons going missing last year, according to the Royal Pigeon Racing Association.

But phone masts are causing most concern as the radio waves they emit are thought to be sending the pigeons' homing instincts haywire.

RPRA spokesman Peter Bryant said their Stray Birds Committee was currently investigating whether GPS tracking devices could be strapped to pigeons' backs to shed light on the problem.

HEDGEHOG FANS FIGHTING to save the prickly mammals from being killed in the Outer Hebrides hope a planned scientific study will show relocation to be a better option.

Uist Hedgehog Rescue group has been looking at ways to stop a second Scottish Natural Heritage cull on the islands.

UHR hopes that a £160,000 independent scientific study proposed by the People's Trust for Endangered Species will go ahead soon and settle the issue.

Research would centre on the survival chances of removed hedgehogs after they were relocated to mainland villages.

Last year 66 hedgehogs were killed by lethal injection at a cost of £100,000.

The project was thought necessary because hedgehogs eat the eggs of ground-nesting birds which are now threatened.

TROUT: caught more easily with a playful tickle

STRONG, fast, and spirited, the brown trout seems to hold a special place in the hearts of many anglers.

Smaller than the salmon but also prized for its flesh, this wily fish can soak up hours of a fisherman's time as he tries to entice it onto an expertly tossed barbed fly.

A native of British waters - unlike the flashier rainbow trout of North American origins - the brown trout has been powerfully designed to shoot up and down streams or run against the flow of the heaviest river.

When hooked, it is a fighter which is a big part of its attraction to those anglers who dislike gently reeling in more placid species.

Growing up to 80cms long on occasion, the brown trout boasts a pattern of striking red-rimmed spots down its flanks.

A close cousin is the sea trout but the pair can be told apart by the sea trout's more silvery colouring when it deserts the sea to spawn.

Feeding on smaller fish as well as insects, the brown trout is vulnerable to the angler using a spinner as bait.

When I used to fish for trout, I always used the spinner.

But this was because I never possessed the greater skill of the fly-fisherman.

Nor, having had a few basic lessons from my father in how to use a fly rod, was I ever likely to.

My father was actually the Inspector Clouseau of fly-fishing, with ambition that far outweighed his ability.

Accompanying him one day to a local lake where he wanted to try out a brand new rod, I was ordered to stand well back.

I stood well back.

I was told to stand further back.

I stood further back.

After a few tentative movements, the master finally cast a fly onto the still water.

So far so good.

Next, he flicked the line backwards over his head and, more confident this time, cast out a second time with more force.

I don't know who was the more surprised, him or me, when the top of his new rod came off and flew into the lake.

He had forgotten the first rule of fly-fishing...make sure your rod is properly screwed together.

I stood even further back as he ranted and raved about his *"hopeless"* new equipment and tried to reel in the lost piece.

Unfortunately, he failed again and was forced to wade out to retrieve it.

How I kept a straight face I'll never know.

I probably enjoyed greatest success catching brown trout using the technique Shakespeare mentioned in Twelfth Night when he wrote:*'Here comes the trout that must be caught with tickling."*

Tickling trout could be highly entertaining, though it usually involved more snatching and grabbing when I did it.

Basically, myself and a friend would just walk upstream at a shallow brook, dipping our hands beneath any likely looking rocks.

If we felt a slippery trout, we would first gently work out its position, then try to grasp it.

We were quite successful, although the trout we caught were way too small to be worth eating so we released them. Great fun, though.

HERONS HAVE BECOME the subject of the longest breeding season monitoring scheme for any bird anywhere in the world.

The British Trust for Ornithology's 'Heronries Census' - the organisation's longest running survey - recently celebrated its 75th year.

To mark the success of the scheme first begun in 1928, Thames Water has donated £18,000, a sum which will help the tireless work go on.

According to the Trust, the company's reservoirs in Walthamstow are home to London's oldest and largest heronry.

Established in 1916, the reservoirs were host to a staggering 110 nests at the last count.

But plans are also under way for the construction of an artificial heronry on the Thames Water nature reserve at Crossness Sewage Treatment Works, which will be built in time for the beginning of the next breeding season.

Dr Peter Spillett, Thames Water's head of environment, quality and sustainability, said:"Many of our sites are on or near habitats such as streams, rivers and reservoirs and we try, wherever possible, to make them more attractive to encourage a wide range of wildlife."

A top freshwater predator, herons are said to be excellent indicators of environmental health in wetland ecosystems.

Breeding colonies are traditional and some areas have been used for centuries.

In Britain and Ireland, says the Trust, herons use a variety of freshwater wetlands with standing fresh waters heavily used in summer and autumn, while lowland streams, river margins, and estuaries provide year-round habitats.

RED SQUIRRELS HAVE been boosted with the opening of a forest refuge in Cumbria to block the onward march of greys.

With native reds now outnumbered by as much as 66-1 by bigger, more aggressive American greys, drastic action was thought needed to prevent 'natives' being wiped out.

Whinfell Forest in Cumbria comprises mostly conifer trees disliked by greys and has been made a protected spot for its 150 red inhabitants.

A chain of other refuges is proposed across England's North West, one of the reds' last remaining strongholds.

Naturalist David Bellamy, who unveiled the haven, said:"If there's the right mixture, with lots of conifers rather than too many bald leaf trees, then the red seems to win out over the grey."

The forest area is equivalent to about 650 football pitches in size.

'ANGLERS IN THE North East are being urged by the Environment Agency to adopt a softly, softly approach to handling caught salmon.

That's because the Agency wants to ensure that fish are kept safe to return to their spawning grounds the following year.

On the River Tees and northwards to the Scottish borders the salmon fishing season opened on February 1 but on Yorkshire's rivers it is still illegal to fish for salmon until April 6.

In both cases, however, all salmon caught must be returned to the water until after June 15.

A number of kelts - salmon returning to the sea after spawning - have recently been caught in the Yorkshire Ouse system, reports the Agency.

This has prompted it to remind anglers that all salmon taken at this time of year must be returned to the water as quickly as possible without harm.

Spokesman David Morley said:"Unlike the Pacific salmon, which only spawns once, the Atlantic salmon can return to the sea to ascend the rivers to spawn again.

"After spawning the fish are weak and, if they are to survive to spawn again, must be handled very carefully so that they do not become damaged or stressed.

"The number of salmon in the River Ouse system is increasing year on year and these fish are vital if salmon stocks are to return to the numbers last seen in the 1930s."

TWO WHALES HAVE beached on western Scottish shores within days of each other, sparking a riddle for scientists.

First, a beaked whale was found washed ashore on the isle of Mull then a 50ft sei whale was found dead on the isle of Coll.

Commenting on the second whale, Coll conservationist Sarah Money said:"This is extremely saddening to see.

"It is such a beautiful creature and, as far as we can tell, there is no reason for it to have been washed ashore. We have alerted the experts who plan to positively identify it as soon as possible and try to determine why this has happened."

GAME SHOOTERS HAVE suffered another blow with the loss of a national firearms committee which protected their interests.

The Countryside Alliance warns that the Home Office must provide assurances to the shooting community in the wake of the decision not to renew the Firearms Consultative Committee.

According to the Alliance, after its establishment in 1988 the Committee had provided sensible, considered and balanced advice to successive Home Secretaries on matters related to firearms legislation.

It had provided a statutory forum in which firearms experts could offer opinion alongside the police and other regulatory groups.

Simon Hart, chief executive of the Alliance, said:"We are disappointed and concerned that representations made by the Alliance and the British Association for Shooting and Conservation on behalf of shooting have been rejected.

"This is a negative step for the shooting community which now needs urgent assurances from the Government. The Home Office must put in place measures that ensure that their legitimate interests are treated fairly and that they are properly represented."

ANTI-HUNT MPs have been accused of trying to wreck new legislation aimed at giving better protection to wild animals such as foxes.

Lembit Opik MP's private member's Bill to amend the Wild Mammals (Protection) Act 1996 was talked out in the House of Commons by anti-hunting MPs, jeopardising its chances of success.

The Bill would create a new offence of 'intentionally causing undue suffering' to all wild mammals and removes exceptions in the 1996 Act for lawful hunting, shooting, coursing and pest control.

Countryside Alliance chief executive Simon Hart said:"This piece of legislation would be an important step towards rationalising the current piecemeal and incoherent animal welfare laws relating to wild mammals and, as such, is supported by the Alliance because of the improvements in animal welfare which it would undoubtedly bring.

"Unfortunately, the short debate was hijacked by a handful of MPs who have once again highlighted their obsessive desire to get hunting with dogs banned at the expense of improvements to animal welfare.

"It is this disgraceful attitude which exposes the fact that anti-hunting MPs have no interest in animal welfare whatsoever. By jeopardising this wide-ranging animal welfare measure purely to satisfy their own prejudiced agenda, they are denying wild mammals improved legislative protection."

NEW NFU PRESIDENT Tim Bennett has called on farmers to redouble their efforts to ensure customers continue to buy British.

Mr Bennett, a 50-year-old livestock farmer from Carmarthenshire in Wales, spoke out after being elected.

He said:"We are proud of our industry, our safe food, and the wonderful countryside that we manage.

"But key to this, we must ensure that our passion for what we do as farmers is really understood by our consumers so that British farmers remain their preferred supplier of food.

"If we succeed in this, retailers and government will have to listen to us. There are many things to be done, and the NFU is the only organisation that can really make a difference."

Mr Bennett was born and brought up in the West Midlands and, on leaving school in Worcestershire, studied agriculture at Seale Hayne Agricultural College.

He then worked in France and Herefordshire before moving to South Wales in 1978 to farm in partnership with wife Susan and children, James, 26, and Victoria, 24.

The family runs a 200-acre grassland farm in a Less Favoured Area, 12 miles from Carmarthen, and is currently establishing a beef suckler herd.

BRITAIN'S TOPSY TURVY weather is having a crazy effect on birds which are already nesting and producing chicks.

According to the British Trust for Ornithology, some birdwatchers planning to help birds nest by cleaning out boxes had been caught out.

"Hot on the heels of recent blizzards and sub-zero temperatures, the 2004 breeding season is underway with birds in boxes already," said a spokesman."Birdwatchers at Sandwich Bay Bird Observatory in Kent recently heard from a local resident who was going to clean out nestboxes when he heard a load of noise from one box.

"On opening it, he found it full of half-naked blue tits - several months early. He wrapped the box in bubble wrap to protect it against any ensuing winter weather and hoped for the best.

"Amazingly, the half-grown chicks did survive the cold spell and by the end of January, four of them were sat in the lucky birdwatcher's conservatory being fed by their parents.

"But it's not only blue tits that are starting early. A nest recorder from the BTO opened a nestbox in Spalding, Lincolnshire to find a couple of new great tit eggs.

"However, it's still not too late to get a box up for the birds. These oddities are just the brave birds trying their luck breeding in winter.

"Most of our birds will be looking for a nest-box in the next month or two and need our help. BTO staff have been encouraging people to put up nestboxes during National Nest Box Week which starts on February 14."

A MASSIVE FLOCK of starlings up to 250,000-strong has been delighting visitors to a Gloucester - shire wildlife centre.

The birds have been gathering at the Wildfowl and Wetlands Trust headquarters in Slimbridge with staff laying on special 'starling watch' events at dusk.

Starlings are known to collect in large numbers each winter but the annual flock at Slimbridge appears to be getting bigger and bigger.

The spectacular sight as the birds begin to roost is only matched by the huge noise emitted.

HEDGEHOGS ON THE Western Isles off Scotland must face up to their prickly fate following abandonment of plans to stop them being culled.

The People's Trust for Endangered Species axed a plan to relocate them to the mainland after Scottish Natural Heritage decided that funding a £160,000 independent scientific study would be a waste of taxpayers' cash.

A cull of hedgehogs on Benbecula and North and South Uist began last spring and will continue for three more years to save rare ground-nesting birds.

Despite their popular image, hedgehogs introduced to the remote islands 30 years ago commonly snack on birds' eggs and chicks.

THE CHEVIOTS AREA of outstanding natural beauty in Northumberland is being given better protection from motorbike mayhem.

Northumberland National Park Authority has become the latest authority to take action to prevent irresponsible off-roading.

A special action group has been formed to tackle the growing problem of illegal use of pathways.

Police have been carrying out patrols in the Coquet and Rede Valleys and have prosecuted a number of motorcyclists.

BASS, MULLET AND flounder were among fish taken illegally by two poachers, a court heard.

The pair claimed they only wanted some fish for a barbecue after they were caught red-handed in Poole Harbour with an illegal fixed net.

Environment Agency officers pounced on the duo after they returned to their gill net to recover their catch.

The net was discovered during a routine boat patrol on July 23, 2003, and was found to contain a variety of fish.

The net was held in position by an anchor and attached to two floats and a rope near a catamaran but was not visible from the surface, Bournemouth magistrates heard.

The two local men were apprehended after they returned in a small dinghy to retrieve the net and remove any fish.

One was fined £220 and ordered to pay £280 costs after being found guilty in his absence to placing an unauthorised gill net in tidal waters in contravention of the Salmon and Freshwater Fisheries Act 1975 and the Salmon Act 1986.

His fishing companion, who owned the boat, was dealt with at an earlier hearing where he was ordered to pay £100 costs and given a one year conditional discharge.

"The defendants were fishing illegally. The law clearly states the use of fixed nets is not permitted in Poole Harbour between April 1 and September 30," said Clive Tyler for the Environment Agency.

The pair's catch of six fish was forfeited and the Environment Agency is set to destroy their £100 fishing net.

A MALE BITTERN spent the most romantic time of the year 'booming' repeatedly in hope of finding a mate at a Lancashire nature reserve.

The rare bird arrived at the Leighton Moss reserve three days before Valentine's Day and set about finding a female.

Despite the odds against success being high, the bird impressed reserve workers with his determination.

"A bittern's boom - which has been likened to the sound made when blowing across the neck of a milk bottle - can be heard up to four miles away as he calls to attract a mate," said a spokesman.

"In 2003, a single male at the same site did find a mate and bred successfully but staff are holding their breath to see if the same will happen this year.

"Back in 1997, Leighton Moss supported five booming male bitterns but numbers have been falling at this small and isolated place.

"There is good cause for hope, however. Expansion work and improvements to the bird's reedbed habitat started last autumn."

MUCH OF THE wildlife in England's lowlands is still battling to survive despite great efforts by conservationists, say experts.

The loss of creatures and plants continues apace, warns English Nature, which has called for lowland areas to get special management.

The Government advisory body believes lowlands must be managed as entire landscapes rather than just pockets of landscape within a bigger picture.

However, it also claims people would benefit as much as wildlife from long-term improvements a new approach would bring.

In 'State Of Nature: Lowlands - Future Landscapes For Wildlife', the organisation sets out key steps required to achieve environmentally sustainable countryside management.

Dr Keith Duff, English Nature's chief scientist, said:"England is internationally renowned for its lowland landscapes, such as the chalk downs and Dorset heathlands.

"However, its wildlife suffered dramatically in the 20th Century from the impact of human activities.

"This landscape-scale approach will also help the natural processes on which we all depend, for example reducing flooding and securing clean water.

"We now know that taking care of our natural resources is also good for our mental and physical health, and is essential economically, for example through tourism.

"We don't have some romantic notion about recreating the past, but believe we must move forward to sustainable land management in a modern context."

A SNOW GOOSE, a red-breasted goose, and some genuine Canada geese all the way from Canada have delighted birdwatchers on the Isle of Islay in the Hebrides.

All three species are rare visitors to Britain, although British-bred Canada geese are a common sight.

The snow goose was said to have arrived amid a flock of regular visitors, some Greenland white-fronted geese.

The red-breasted goose, meanwhile, ended up at the same Loch Gruinart reserve after flying from Siberia.

And six genuine Canada geese touched down at the reserve after apparently travelling all the way from their namesake homeland.

WILD BOAR HAVE gone on the run after escaping from a farm in Dorset.

Up to 30 of the animals - said to be dangerous if cornered - have taken to the woods and hills around the Bridport farm.

Their owner estimates their joint worth to be £20,000 and has warned the public not to approach them.

Although mostly nocturnal, wild boar are said to present a potential hazard to walkers and livestock - especially the adults which can be armed with sharp 'tusks'.

Hundreds of boar are now thought to be living wild across southern England.

It is thought the escapees may try and join up with one of these herds.

However, efforts are being stepped up to shepherd them back to the farm.

THE FIGHT OVER hunting with dogs is being reignited with Government plans to introduce a new Bill seeking a total ban, it has been revealed.

Despite the Countryside Alliance warning of massive opposition, Labour is poised to bring out plans for new legislation within weeks.

A previous Bill won overwhelming support in the House of Commons last summer but ran out of time in the Lords where it met a hostile reception.

The move to unveil fresh legislation will see the Government again taking on the Countryside Alliance and hundreds of thousands of its supporters who feel a ban would be an outrageous breach of their civil liberties.

The Alliance has said before that it would mount a legal challenge to any legislation, possibly on the grounds that it infringed the human rights of hunt groups.

The Government is believed to have drawn back from using the Parliament Act to force the previous, beaten Bill through the Lords.

Thousands of hunt supporters have pledged to go to jail in support of hunting - a prospect which could see courts clogged for years with a backlog of cases involving families never before in trouble with police.

STONE-CURLEWS ARE being given a boost to try to increase numbers.

The haunting cries of the bird may ring out more often thanks to a unique project funded by Thames Water and the RSPB.

At present, there are estimated to be just 260 stone-curlew pairs breeding across the whole of the UK.

The rescue project involves working with farmers to increase remaining numbers of the bird on the Wessex Downs before encouraging it to return to historic breeding areas such as the Chilterns.

Leading the scheme is the RSPB's Mike Shurmer who explains stone-curlews need safe, open, bare ground to nest as well as a good supply of large insects.

"We have a wonderful opportunity to work alongside farmers to protect birds that are spectacular, fascinating and an important part of our natural heritage," he said.

SWALLOWS HAVE AMAZED birdwatchers in Shropshire after arriving there a month earlier than usual.

More than 20 of the fork-tailed birds swooped into the south of the county from Africa.

Normally, the birds only arrive back in Britain in mid-March when temperatures are generally on the rise. But members of Shropshire Ornithological Society were shocked to observe the swallows in the Diddlebury area on a chilly February 11.

BADGERS ARE AT the centre of a new row with conservationists outraged by fresh calls from farmers to gas them.

The National Federation of Badger Groups says it has been contacted by many people alarmed to read strong suggestions that the Government is seriously considering gassing badgers to control bovine TB in cattle.

However, it moved to reassure callers that the primary focus of the Government's proposed TB strategy was still on dealing with transmission of the disease between cattle.

"The Government strategy does consider the possibility of badger culling but we anticipate that the practical, economic and political implications of such a measure are not likely to make that justifiable," said a spokesman.

"In addition, the so called Krebs Trial has not yet yielded any data suggesting that badger culling will effectively control bovine TB in cattle. "The call for the gassing of badgers has been initiated by the NFU's outgoing president, Sir Ben Gill. In what the NFU described as a 'major scientific report', Sir Ben suggests that gassing badgers is an effective and humane means of controlling bovine TB.

"No evidence is presented to support this hypothesis. And a review of previous gassing strategies by the Government's Independent Scientific Group found no evidence that they were effective."

In Gloucestershire, however, NFU dairy farmer Andrew Cozens said the matter was not so clear cut.

"We are not against badgers. We want to see healthy wildlife and cattle. But we have to look at the wider picture and not be blinkered," he said.

"The Government tests are flawed. We know badgers are helping spread the disease and we have to get it under control. We can't do nothing as the Government did in the first week of foot-and-mouth.

"We have let the problem fester but now we have to do something about it. Gassing is an effective way to kill an animal cleanly and swiftly."

FIVE BARN OWLS, a tawny owl, two buzzards and a kestrel have reportedly been found dead on a shooting estate in the Borders, Scotland.

Police and conservation officials who launched a raid on the unnamed estate are also said to have found banned poisons and pesticides.

The probe came after members of the public complained of six dead buzzards in the area, four of which were later found to have been illegally poisoned.

Only recently it was revealed that a scheme to reintroduce the red kite to Scotland had been jeopardised with 100 of the majestic fork-tailed birds being illegally killed.

Gamekeepers protecting the multi-million pound shooting industry were thought to be to blame.

THE DELICATE ART of bird ringing is being thrown open to the public at a Forestry Commission depot in Mosstodloch, Scotland.

Bird lovers are being given the chance to see at close quarters how birds are ringed by wildlife rangers. Details of caught birds that come to the depot to feed on nuts and seeds will also be noted down during the two-hour event.

PEREGRINE FALCONS ARE now being actively encouraged to nest in the heart of East London after signs were found that the spectacular predators had previously tried to breed at a precarious site there.

The birds are being helped to nest on the Barking Barrier via installation of a nestbox close to the top of the 60-metre high flood defence structure.

The Environment Agency granted English Nature permission to site the nestbox at the lofty spot after signs were found that peregrines had tried to nest there last year.

Peter Massini, spokesman for English Nature, explained:"The prospect of these magnificent birds of prey breeding atop a major piece of flood defence infrastructure demonstrates that even in the urban environment a little bit of lateral thinking and partnership work can yield small but significant enhancements for biodiversity.

"If successful, the site will provide an opportunity for local people to see and enjoy these birds at relatively close quarters.

"A future option may also be to install a webcam to beam live pictures of breeding peregrines to local schools and libraries."

David Webb, for the Environment Agency, added:"We are hopeful about the success of the scheme and look forward to seeing the results."

Peregrine falcons are one of the fastest predators in the world, capable of reaching speeds of about 200 miles per hour when swooping on prey.

The overall process of organising and planning the installation of the nesting box took five months.

Plans have been laid for the box itself to be installed shortly, in time for the start of the nesting season.

A MYSTERY BEAST left a walker terrified when the pair came face to face in Scottish countryside.

The jet black 'big cat' confronted the man, an accountant, while he was out rambling with his dog in an Aberdeen wood.

"I just looked up and about 75 yards ahead there was a big black cat standing in front of me," he told local press.

"It was jet black. It was too small to be a deer and too big to be a dog. It just stood there, stock still, looking at us.

"Then it about-turned and went back the way it came. When I got to the spot where it had been standing, I saw it running across a field.

"It was terrifying - the hairs on the back of my neck were standing up."

The rambler, a local father-of-two, asked not to be named following the drama.

HARE COURSING HAS come under attack from pop star Mel C.

The singer, formerly one of the Spice Girls, has spoken out against the 'Waterloo Cup', Britain's biggest hare coursing event.

The three-day championship, which sees greyhounds controversially tested against live hares, is held every year in late February at Altcar close to the star's home city of Liverpool.

As usual, this year's event was attended by thousands of supporters who ignored noisy protests from about 200 determined anti-cruelty campaigners.

Hare coursing fans say the aim is not to kill the hares but to test the running skill and stamina of pairs of dogs against each other.

In addition, the vast majority of hares always escape.

However, that cuts no ice with Mel who said:"The Waterloo Cup is an horrific 'sporting' event where harmless creatures are cruelly used by Man for a sick form of entertainment.

"I don't understand why human beings cannot enjoy a sport that tests their own physical abilities rather than inflicting pain on animals and having the nerve to call it 'sport'.

"You can't blame the poor dogs that are encouraged to hunt and kill. The dog owners are to blame, along with anyone else who participates in any of these cruel sports."

THE COUNTRYSIDE ALLIANCE has pledged to support the appeal of a Derbyshire gamekeeper following his prosecution over a goshawk's nest.

The man was given a three-month suspended jail sentence by Buxton magistrates over charges relating to the predator's nest.

Kay Chapman, Alliance regional director, said:"The Countryside Alliance is opposed to any illegal persecution of raptors and supports the police in bringing anyone who has carried out such acts to court.

"We do, however, have considerable concern about the safety of this conviction. The gamekeeper was cleared of 16 charges, including several which, in our view, should never have been brought.

"He has had a long and distinguished career at Ronksley and has worked with local raptor groups while the goshawk population on the estate has grown. We believe that his case deserves review and will be supporting his appeal."

WATER VOLES HAVE severely declined or become extinct in parts of Berkshire, Buckinghamshire and Oxfordshire, despite the best efforts of conservationists to preserve them.

The Berks, Bucks and Oxon Wildlife Trust says that several water voles populations that were recorded in 2001 are now believed to be either extinct or dangerously near to extinction.

Sites hit by the slump include the River Cherwell and the lower area of the River Windrush in Oxfordshire, the Wendover Arm of the Grand Union Canal in Buckinghamshire, and the California Country Park in Berkshire.

BBOWT's water vole project officer, Catharine Shellswell, said:"It is very disturbing that water vole numbers have declined so dramatically in our region. Our Water Vole Recovery Project offers free advice to landowners to help them create the right conditions for water voles. We would love to hear from people who would like to help water voles."

'FOX DROPPINGS FOR Families' is the pungent title The Mammal Society is using to headline a celebratory raft of new courses.

"Introduce your children to fox, badger and deer droppings," explained a spokesman,"or let them fondle seal, squirrel or rabbit skulls this year at a hands-on introduction to mammals run by the Society as part of its 50th anniversary celebrations.

"These free, one-hour, interactive work-shops will be held across the country in school holidays throughout the year and during the Society's National Mammal Week in July to inspire children of eight and above to learn more about our country's mammals.

"British mammals are hugely diverse, ranging in weight from the pygmy shrew, at less than 10 grammes, to the 10 tonne minke whale. We also have 16 species of bats, 25 species of whale and dolphin, and interna-tionally important populations of fallow deer, badgers and otters.

"There are 18 'Unearthing Mammals' sessions to choose from around the country starting at the Edinburgh Museum on April 17 and finishing at the Wildfowl and Wetlands Trust in Llanelli on October 29.

"Subjects covered at the sessions could include 'What's For Dinner? - nibbling, gnashing or gnawing. A look at teeth adaptations, skulls, teeth and feeding. Identify nuts nibbled by dormice.

"'It's All In The Nose' involves identifying droppings from carnivores and herbivores. How do scientists use droppings to identify species and study them? 'Furs And Skins' looks at how mammals adapt. Can you identify a badger from a single hair?"

CHAFFINCHES HAVE BEEN sparking concern in Wiltshire after many were spotted with severe disabilities.

Some birds appear to have no feet at all, just stumps, while others have toes gathered together in clumps.

Birdwatchers have been scratching their heads over whether the birds are carrying injuries caused by predators or if they hatched that way.

For the time being, no-one seems able to get to the bottom of the mystery.

Chaffinches are the commonest British finches and one of the most popular spring songsters.

HALF A MILLION deer may be shot in Britain as part of plans by the Government to crack down on the animals.

Ministers believe that deer are out of control and causing extensive damage to crops and trees.

Encouraging the public to eat more venison and relaxing shooting limits are two ideas being discussed to reduce the country's estimated 1.5 million deer population by about a third.

HOUSE SPARROWS ARE being boosted with a new advice leaflet telling people how to produce suitable habitats for the little birds.

In the last 30 years sparrow numbers have fallen from about 12 million pairs to fewer than seven million pairs, according to the RSPB which adds that suburban and urban gardens have seen the most marked declines.

It is hoped that the leaflet 'House Sparrows in Great Britain', funded by DEFRA and produced in partnership with the Society, will help to reverse the slump.

Minister for Nature Conservation, Ben Bradshaw, said:"The friendly chatter of sparrows is a much loved part of British life. This is a very dramatic decline but it is not irreversible. If we all play our part the population of this treasured bird can be increased.

"The leaflet we are launching provides some effective proactive advice on how individuals and communities can improve the habitat in their local area by making it house sparrow friendly.

"Through these actions I hope we can begin to redress the balance and allow these birds, which we all know and love, to thrive once again."

ANYONE HARRYING HEN harriers could be harried themselves in future - by the police.

Only a few dozen nesting pairs of the winged predators remain in the UK because their taste for grouse chicks has made them a sworn enemy of gamekeepers.

However, the Association of Chief Police Officers of England, Wales and Northern Ireland has now pledged to join conservationists in a last ditch effort to stop the surviving harriers being wiped out.

In recent years, hen harrier nests have been destroyed and their eggs smashed by gamekeepers determined to protect the multi-million pound grouse shooting industry.

Even isolated tracts of moorland favoured as nesting spots have been torched to drive the harriers away.

However, police have now warned that surveillance operations could be mounted to catch the culprits responsible who face heavy fines and jail sentences.

PLANS TO PUSH ahead with GM maize in the face of overwhelming criticism could land the Government in the dock, warns Friends of the Earth.

The environmental group says it will consider mounting a legal challenge if Labour insists on forcing through the controversial crop for commercial growing.

Friends of the Earth's GM campaigner Clare Oxborrow said:"The British Government must listen to the concerns of the Welsh Assembly, the Scottish Parliament, and the British people. This maize has not been shown to be safe and it should not be grown commercially."

According to FoE, the controversial maize - technically labled T25 Chardon LL - gained its approval for food use through a fast track route for which Aventis/Bayer relied on a report produced by the UK's Advisory Committee on Novel Foods and Processes in 1996.

However, claims FoE, the committee did not even see the relevant study.

Had T25 maize been submitted to the current regulatory system, it was unlikely to have been granted approval.

382

SPARROWHAWK: fierce mother keeps an eye on chicks

DASHING through woods in pursuit of its prey, the sparrowhawk is a relentless hunter of small birds such as blue tits and chaffinches.

With shorter, more rounded wings than those of other raptors, it can pursue its quarry deeper into undergrowth to make a kill.

The sparrowhawk also has long legs and a long central toe on each claw to make it easier to hold a frantically struggling bird when captured.

Now our second most common bird of prey behind the kestrel, it declined drastically in the late '50s and early '60s because of the careless use of pesticides.

Tough regulations imposed on the use of pesticides have since allowed sparrowhawk numbers to recover and the national population was recently estimated to be around 34,500 pairs.

Not too long ago, I drove up North to visit a sick relative and set out at 5am to beat the traffic.

Within an hour I had spotted two sparrowhawks hunting beside the deserted motorway, which seemed to bear out their resurgence.

Kestrel numbers have been falling of late but still stand at about 50,000 pairs so the sparrowhawk has some way to go yet before taking top spot.

Nevertheless, it is interesting to compare these two similar sized predators and the different ways they attack their prey.

Kestrels are falcons and use their pointed wings to hover in the sky above ground-based targets before stooping on them with lightning speed.

Voles and mice are the main victims but small birds, worms and insects are also taken.

Sparrowhawks, on the other hand, feed almost exclusively on birds which they chase and catch on the wing.

As a result, their growing population has been blamed for the loss of many of our songbirds.

But this is nonsense, according to the RSPB, which says that scientists have found no genuine link between vanishing songbirds and the rising number of sparrowhawks.

Overall numbers of studied songbirds hardly changed in years when sparrowhawks were present compared to those years when they were not, it said.

Meanwhile, findings by the Institute of Terrestrial Ecology have shown an increase in the percentage of sparrowhawk deaths caused by starvation.

This is thought to be due to their traditional prey birds becoming scarce, owing to changes in agricultural practices.

As a teenager, I once climbed a tall tree and examined two sullen sparrowhawk fledglings at close quarters - perhaps not a wise thing to do, as mother sparrowhawks are the bigger of the two sexes and their talons are razor sharp.

Nothing untoward happened, though the mother did fly around the tree once or twice as I gingerly inspected her young.

No doubt, the outcome would have been more gruesome had I been a cheeky blue tit.

HIGH PROFILE COUNTRY sports enthusiasts are said to be urgently reviewing their security arrangements after animal rights activists posted their personal details on the internet.

More than 100 celebrities involved in country activities have had their names, home addresses and telephone numbers published by the mystery group 'Badgers Unknown'.

Fears that some of the more isolated people named may now be targeted in twilight firebomb attacks are reported to have prompted anti-terrorist Special Branch police to offer advice.

The celebrities, which include DJ Chris Tarrant, actor Jeremy Irons, and comedian Billy Connolly, were apparently selected because they support or are involved with hunting, shooting, or fishing.

The protest group, which calls those named 'Celebrity Bloodsports Scum', has itself been labled 'vicious and dangerous' by the Countryside Alliance.

Billy Connolly, whose 15-acre Highland estate in Strathdon, Aberdeenshire, has its own trout lake, seems a particular hate figure.

Two years ago, he reportedly angered animal rights protesters when he turned up at his local Highland Games dangling a badger's head on his sporran.

Grampian Police are said to be monitoring Mr Connolly's situation but are keeping secret any security plans.

'Watership Down' author Richard Adams is also on the list because he is known to be an avid angler, as is actor Bernard Cribbins.

Other famous names include Sting, Roger Daltrey, Andrew Lloyd Webber, Sir Jackie Stewart, Ian Botham, Jeremy Clarkson, and Raymond Blanc.

BIRD LOVERS ARE pledging to fight Labour plans to build more windfarms around Britain that might threaten flocks.

Conservationists fear carnage could be the result if the windfarms - which feature massive rotating blades - are sited near large bird populations.

The RSPB has promised to launch legal action if sensitive sites are targeted.

At the moment, virtually all sites licensed for a second round of windfarms are in areas considered by English Nature as potentially of international importance for birds.

Dr Mark Avery, RSPB director of conservation, said:"We will object to any windfarms that seriously threaten important populations of birds and their habitats.

"Urgent research is needed into the locations, numbers and movements of birds around our coasts to help us understand potential impacts."

GREY SQUIRRELS HAVE again been blamed as culprits for the decline of woodland birds.

A new study, 'Possible Impacts of Grey Squirrels on Birds and Other Wildlife', says the furry animals devour eggs and young chicks, take over nest sites, and eat seeds and nuts which would otherwise be eaten by birds.

Speaking about the report, Dr Rob Fuller said:"Grey squirrels live at considerably higher densities and are larger animals than the native red squirrel.

"The species is already blamed for much commercial damage to forestry and linked to the demise of the red squirrel.

"In this paper we look at how the grey squirrel may also be affecting woodland bird species, several of which are red-listed as birds of conservation concern."

Researchers found that when grey squirrels were controlled at one Norfolk farm, the predation rate of open nests fell from 85 per cent to less than 10 per cent.

Meanwhile, the arrival of grey squirrels in Durham coincided with a marked decline in abundance of open-nesting species such as thrushes and finches.

MOLES HAVE CAUSED mayhem on a school sports field in Cornwall.

Youngsters at Sandy Hill Primary School, in St Austell, have to tread carefully while playing football as their pitch is covered in hundreds of mole hills.

Not only do the piles of earth interfere with play, the young footballers risk injury if they stumble into a hole.

The problem has become so bad that all the school's soccer fixtures are now played away while experts are sought for help.

OTTERS WERE PUT at risk by a fisherman who set dozens of illegal nets in Poole Harbour, a court heard.

The Dorset man was found guilty in his absence by Bournemouth magistrates who fined him £1,500 and ordered him to pay £1,500 costs for placing and using unauthorised fyke nets in tidal waters on or about July 23, 2003.

Eel fishing is strictly controlled by the Environment Agency to protect stocks, magistrates heard, and each fyke net must be licensed.

Fishermen must also fit their nets with otter guards to prevent otters from drowning.

Magistrates heard that officers were patrolling Poole Harbour when they found 182 fyke nets set in three separate areas within the harbour.

A third of the nets were not displaying Agency licence tags while there were no otter guards fitted to 37 of the 62 nets seized.

Otters are attracted to eels caught in fyke nets and can drown if they get trapped inside a net, the court was told.

Following the case, Environment Agency spokesman Julian Wardlaw said:"Otters are a protected species and we are fortunate in Dorset to have seen an increase in otter numbers on local rivers in recent years.

"Sadly, there have also been fatalities. Two years ago an adult otter and two cubs were found dead in an illegal fyke net in the River Stour and another otter drowned in a net in Poole Harbour.

"It is therefore very important that eel fishermen ensure their nets are fitted with otter guards."

SHEEP FARMERS WHO help wildlife have been given a boost with renewal of a scheme which pays them for their efforts.

The farmers, many of whom manage some of the country's toughest tracts of land for a pittance, have been told the scheme will receive a further £3million.

The Sheep and Wildlife Enhancement Scheme was only launched last year with £2.5million which directly benefited wildlife and sheep farmers.

SWES project manager Dan Hunt said:"This scheme is about finding practical solutions for balancing sheep farming and wildlife on the farm.

"We are helping farmers deliver real change for wildlife and improve the viability of their farm business as well. The response from farmers has been excellent."

The scheme supports sheep farming at Sites of Special Scientific Interest by providing financial support to those who manage the land.

Many important wildlife habitats need sustainable grazing to keep them healthy but experts realise this often requires the skill of sheep farmers.

English Nature, which backs the initiative along with DEFRA and the Rural Payments Agency, said:"The scheme tackles both overgrazing and undergrazing, and has proved that with the right incentives and the skill of sheep farmers, changes in grazing can be introduced which really transform the landscape.

"By improving grazing regimes on habitats in unfavourable condition, the scheme is making a positive and significant contribution to meeting the target that 95 per cent of habitats should be in a favourable condition by 2010.

"Currently, 42 per cent of the land area in England's SSSIs is in an unfavourable condition. English Nature is addressing this in partnership with farmers and a wide variety of organisations and individuals."

RED-BLOODED RED squirrels are being given help to cross busy roads during the mating season.

Rope bridges are being constructed at Formby, Merseyside, after a number of the amorous animals from a rare English colony were killed by traffic.

Five bridges are being built across the A565 since the former Tufty road safety icon has shown itself to be hopeless at following its own guidelines.

At one time, the animals used to cross the road by leaping from tree to tree but recent branch trimming work means they can no longer reach.

So the Highways Agency came up with the life-saving idea to stop Tufty being wiped out by cars.

BROWN TROUT AND other fish were killed by pollution of their brook following a breakdown at a water treatment centre, magistrates heard.

Yorkshire Water Services Ltd were charged with causing polluting, toxic or noxious matter to enter a controlled watercourse, namely Cod Beck, contrary to the Water Resources Act 1991.

The company pleaded guilty and was fined £4,000 and ordered to pay costs of £857 to the Environment Agency which brought the case.

Northallerton Magistrates Court heard that in September 2002 the Agency received a call from Yorkshire Water to report a problem with their Osmotherley Water Treatment Works and an officer attended the site to investigate.

On arrival he discovered a number of dead fish in Cod Beck, the nearby watercourse to which all water from the site drains.

Agency fisheries officers later collected dead brown trout and bullheads from downstream of the site's outfall into the beck.

During the investigation Yorkshire Water admitted to the Agency that there had been a problem with the treatment system and the sodium hyperchlorite tanks on site had been drained so staff could deal with it.

However, staff mistakenly thought that there would be enough water in the lagoons into which the chemical was drained to dilute it to an acceptable level.

Although Yorkshire Water took immediate action to rectify the problem, there was still a big impact on the beck.

In mitigation Yorkshire Water said that it has now spent £135,000 on modifications to the plant including containment and upgraded telemetry systems.

INSECT EATING BIRDS from warmer climates were probably the worst affected by the recent cold snap, say experts.

House martins, swallows, and wheatears were attracted to Britain earlier than normal by mild weather - then the big freeze hit.

Dawn Balmer, organiser of the British Trust for Ornithology's 'Migration Watch' said:"Swallows and house martins are aerial feeders and need a good supply of insects if they are to survive."

One swallow had been seen desperately hunting for insects over a reedbed in Cornwall for an entire week.

"The first wheatears usually arrive in the first week of March when the weather is generally milder and more food is available so we were really surprised to see them here so early," added Ms Balmer.

"Wheatears pick up insects from the ground so a covering of snow or ice makes it extremely difficult for them to get enough food."

STARLINGS ARE BEING credited with promoting a better community spirit on a Somerset estate.

Neighbours have begun coming out together to watch the birds' spectacular aerial display each night at the estate near Taunton.

Fans of the feathered invaders say the sight and sound has become a major talking point among residents.

Wheeling and crying in huge balls, the birds descend at dusk almost as one to roost in trees.

It is thought to be the first year that starlings have massed in such numbers at the spot.

TRAGEDY IS LOOMING for England's countryside if "unnecessary" mass house building goes ahead, warn campaigners.

Nor will the Government's plans to concrete over much of what remains of some of the most beautiful parts of the country reduce house prices, says the Council for the Protection of Rural England.

Neil Sinden, CPRE's policy director, said:"Boosting housebuilding at the levels proposed would result in an unnecessary environmental disaster, placing huge areas of countryside at risk and undermining urban regeneration - without bringing significantly more housing in reach of those people who are least able to afford it.

"England is the most built up country in Europe, yet the quality of our big cities and urban living lag behind the rest of the continent. We need to make best use of land.

"Our economic analysis of the research underpinning Kate Barker's proposals demonstrates that there is no solid evidence of an under supply of new homes in the UK, and no evidence that a massive increase in housebuilding would solve the problem of the lack of homes people on lower incomes can afford.

"Boosting housebuilding by relaxing greenfield constraints in the South East and increasing urban sprawl across countryside would be environmentally devastating and ultimately fruitless.

"It would be in direct contradiction to the Government's objectives for urban renewal and reducing disparities between the regions.

"We need to use the planning system to redouble our efforts to re-use previously developed land, to get away from wastefully low densities and to secure a higher proportion of affordable housing as part of planned housing provision."

A HUNGRY SPARROWHAWK spoiled the show when dozens of birdwatchers focused on a rare American robin - by eating it.

The thrush-sized robin had somehow gone thousands of miles off course before ending up on an industrial estate in Grimsby.

Only 10 or so of the robins had ever made it to Britain before, a fact which saw hundreds of birdwatchers head to Grimsby in recent weeks to catch a glimpse.

Unfortunately, however, the sparrowhawk spied the grey feathered robin just as the latest batch of birdwatchers were enjoying its presence.

In a second, as the horrified throng looked on, the hawk had killed the robin and proceeded to devour it.

Graham Appleton, from the British Trust for Ornithology, said later:"It was a terrible moment."

SWALLOWS' FORAGING HABITS are the subject of a forthcoming survey by bird experts.

"The swallow is our quintessential summer migrant, always anticipated, common and widespread," said a spokesman for the British Trust for Ornithology.

"Unfortunately, there is evidence of regional declines of swallows that have identified gaps in our knowledge of their use of habitats.

"Compared with most common species, we know relatively little about the importance of different crops, hedgerows, tree lines, field margins or even different livestock types for their foraging needs.

"To obtain a national picture, a small amount of information is needed from many different locations across the UK.

"To get this information, the Swallow Feeding Survey requires observers to make two visits, between May and August, to four points within a 2km square area, spending 10 minutes at each point.

"You can also count martins, swifts and their potential predators such as kestrel, hobby and sparrowhawk. The total survey time amounts to less than 2.5 hours per visit."

More details on the survey are available direct from the Trust.

CURBS ON RECKLESS rural gangmasters have been welcomed by the NFU.

The union says it wholeheartedly supports the Government's decision to accept the principles of a private member's Bill to introduce a licensing system for gangmasters.

NFU president Tim Bennett said:"We are very pleased that the Government has recognised the extent of the problem and thrown its support behind this laudable private member's Bill. We urge ministers to put effective legislation in place."

OTTERS AND WATER voles are among wild creatures set to benefit from water companies' improvements to local environments across England and Wales.

New guidelines from DEFRA are aimed at reducing water abstraction and improving sewage treatment to give a significant boost to wildlife.

Fresh investment by water companies should improve the condition of more than 100 Sites of Special Scientific Interest, around 5,000 kilometres of river and up to 2,200 square kilometres of wetlands.

Among birds whose habitats will benefit are lapwing, twite, snipe and curlew.

Dr Mark Avery, director of conservation for the RSPB, said:"Birds, mammals and plants are all now going to be better off. This is an excellent deal for wildlife and the water environment.

"The Government has shown both courage and good sense in resisting pressure to reduce investment in nature conservation. It shows that ministers are living up to their environmental promises.

"Many wetland birds, such as the lapwing, are now nearly extinct from areas where they were once common.

"This investment will help to reverse that trend and ensure they remain part of our landscape for many years to come."

ELVER FISHING HAS sparked a rash of criminal activity in Gloucestershire.

But the authorities are fighting back with a new joint initiative involving Gloucestershire Police, Gloucester City Council, British Waterways and the Environment Agency.

With elvers fetching up to £300 per kilo on the open market, the lucrative trade is said to be attracting people who display little regard for either their fellow citizens or their more responsible colleagues.

Gloucester City Council says it is concerned about damage caused to stiles and fences, often by chainsaws, close to elver fishing spots.

The wood is believed to be used by the fishermen for fires to keep warm during long cold nights spent fishing.

In one incident, a herd of rare breed cows was allowed to wander onto a road.

Derek Brown, city council countryside manager, said:"There has to be mutual respect. We respect the long-standing tradition of elver fishing but there needs to be respect by the fishermen towards the city council's land and our use of it as a nature reserve. Actions which put our visitors and animals at potential risk are unacceptable."

Inspector Emma Davies, from the Gloucestershire Police force, said:"The Constabulary welcomes the opportunity to work in partnership with all of the other agencies and we will be working closely with them to enforce the legislation surrounding elver fishing."

BASKING SHARKS ARE to be tracked around Britain's coasts again in a new survey starting in May, it has been revealed.

The gentle giants of the deep, which feed on plankton, are one of the most thrilling marine sights still available in this country.

According to The Wildlife Trusts, the survey yacht will depart from Falmouth and travel around Devon, Cornwall, South Wales, North Wales, and Ireland, reaching the Western Isles of Scotland by mid-September.

The survey will be led by Colin Speedie who skippers the 39ft yacht accompanied by a small group of marine conservationists and volunteers from around the UK.

"The survey monitors shark populations and activities, " said a spokesman."Basking sharks are already known to travel considerable distances in search of food.

"One of the main aims of the survey is to find out which areas are important feeding and breeding grounds for the sharks and if they return to the same places each year.

"Photo-identification and video recording carried out in previous surveys allows the team to track the movements and behaviour of individual sharks over long periods."

SNARES IN THE Scottish countryside should be banned, say three celebrities.

Actresses Jenny Seagrove and Annette Crosbie have joined scriptwriter Carla Lane in demanding that snares be outlawed north of the border.

The group have contacted the Scottish Executive in an effort to get the "barbaric" traps made illegal.

They hope MSPs will reject a section of the new Nature Conservation (Scotland) Bill which would permit such trapping to remain legal.

Only recently, the environment and rural development committee refused to outlaw snaring after studying the Bill.

In a statement, Ms Seagrove said:"I am horrified that snares are still widely used in Scotland. I strongly urge Scottish politicians to seize this opportunity to rid the beautiful Scottish countryside of these cruel and indiscriminate devices that cause animals so much suffering."

Meanwhile, Ms Crosbie, who starred in 'One Foot In The Grave', added:"It is unbelievable and disgraceful that in a so-called civilised country these barbaric devices are still being used to torture and kill animals."

A VICIOUS COCK pheasant has hit the headlines after waging war on a local postman in Devon.

The postie, 59-year-old Jeffrey Patton, has been injured on his hand and leg following repeated attacks at Swimbridge.

"I think it is the van's red colour which triggers the aggression," he admitted." Pheasants have sharp spurs on their legs and it tries to get me with them or peck me.

"It seems to see me as a giant pheasant which it has got to ward off. It is totally obsessed. I have been attacked by dogs before but never by a pheasant."

WILD BOAR COULD become a new big game species for shooters if numbers continue to rise.

"After an absence of 400 years this re-introduction of a once native beast and potentially a new big game species is seen by some as a welcome addition to the British countryside," said the Game Conservancy Trust.

"Conversely, wild boar are fast-breeding mammals that rapidly rotivate pasture, damage valuable crops, and potentially carry swine fever and foot-and-mouth disease.

"The inclusion of wild boar in the Trust's National Gamebag Census, which has been analysing game records for over a century, is a reflection of the interest being shown in their return to this country.

"Wild boars roaming the countryside can be traced back to the storm of 1987 when many escaped from farms.

"A subsequent report by the Central Science Laboratory suggested that this was not a case of a few big animals on the loose, but that a substantial population had developed.

"Scientists from The Trust have in the past given their expert opinion to Government on whether action should be taken to control wild boar.

"At that time, the Trust recommended that boar numbers should be controlled before the situation got out of hand, particularly as other countries such as France and Germany have seen their wild boar populations spiralling out of control. It is estimated that in Germany alone over 500,000 beasts are shot annually."

ANGLERS ARE FACING a nationwide probe on 'cruelty' to fish in a controversial move by the RSPCA.

The Countryside Alliance has attacked the animal help organisation's priorities amid reports that it intends to investigate anglers and fish farmers.

The move comes at a time when angling has never been so important for the national economy.

In Scotland alone, a new study shows that it contributes £113 million a year and supports nearly 3,000 jobs.

North of the border, the sport also generates £50 million a year in wages, salaries and self-employed income.

However, the RSPCA and SSPCA believe that controversial research published last year by the Roslin Institute shows that fish can feel pain.

The SSPCA says:"We believe that fish do have the capacity to suffer and the thinking of government, the fishing industry and sports fishermen should take this into account."

But Charles Jardine, director of the Alliance's Campaign for Angling, said:"There remain huge questions about the conclusions drawn from last year's study yet groups like the RSPCA seem to be determined to accept that fish feel pain despite inconclusive and conflicting research.

"The real question is why an organisation which is closing regional centres and laying off staff in response to financial constraints should choose to waste scarce resources on such a pointless campaign. Britain's 3.5 million anglers know that their sport is entirely legitimate and that it has massive benefits for river and still water habitats. Anglers certainly do far more for fish than the RSPCA ever has."

APPLE ORCHARDS COULD become a thing of the past in southern England because of climate change, it has been claimed.

Dr Simon Thornton-Wood, of the Royal Horticultural Society, said that in coming decades orchards might vanish while other native fruit may also dwindle.

However, peaches and similar fruit from southern Europe may become easier to grow in England.

Increasingly mild winters would fail to offer the drop in temperature that many plants need to produce flowers and fruit, Dr Thornton-Wood said.

He added:"We've lost a lot of orchards in the UK but apples are still an important crop. I think the climate will mean it becomes harder to get a decent crop in the south of England so apples may head north to find a cooler place to grow.

"But I imagine it will be easier to grow crops like peaches instead. It's swings and roundabouts."

THE GOVERNMENT HAS shown "two-fingers" to the British public by allowing GM maize to be commercially grown, claims Friends of the Earth.

The environmental pressure group attacked the Government after it gave qualified approval for the development of GM maize, saying it ignored the House of Commons Environmental Audit Committee, public opinion and many scientific uncertainties.

FoE Director Tony Juniper said:"The Government has given the thumbs-up to GM maize and shown two fingers to the British public.

"In demonstrating its pro-GM credentials, the Government has ignored considerable scientific uncertainties, shown contempt to Parliament and utterly disregarded public opinion.

"Moreover, this crop will be fed to cows to make milk not labelled as GM."

FOXES ARE IN for a kicking if they threaten lambs in a North Wales park - from a llama.

Laurence the Llama has been hired to protect lambs at Ty Mawr park, near Wrexham.

Head ranger Liz Carding explained:"During the foot-and-mouth outbreak we were closed for months and the park became inundated with foxes.

"We are involved with conservation and wanted to find an environmentally friendly way of dealing with them.

"We hope Laurence will do a good job. He has already seen off a couple of pheasants."

SWIFTS ARE EVEN higher high-flyers than first thought and soar to 10,000ft at night-time - about 4,000ft further than previously known.

When night falls, other birds descend to roost in a tree or on a building but swifts soar straight up into the sky in pitch darkness, where they remain until morning.

Working with Lund University, in Sweden, BBC film-makers found that swifts - one of our most familiar annual visitors - also routinely navigate while asleep on the wing, using a kind of automatic pilot.

Every summer, like swallows, the birds migrate thousands of miles here from Africa and can be seen soaring above most towns and cities.

PIGS AND SHEEP could go under the knife as part of controversial new moves to train up budding surgeons.

The Royal College of Surgeons is pressing for a relaxation of laws which currently limit trainees' practise operations to rodents.

If the Royal College gets its way, pigs and sheep would be routinely terminally anaesthetised so that young surgeons could make their mistakes on them - rather than on humans.

However, the British Union for the Abolition of Vivisection has blasted the idea, calling it unethical.

SAMMY THE SEAL faces being shot for raiding fish from nets off the Essex coast.

The popular bull seal, well-known to residents and holidaymakers at Mersea Island, near Colchester, has angered a local fisherman so much he has applied for a firearms licence to shoot him.

The unnamed complainant may not get his wish but any firearms licence holder could carry out the killing for him if Sammy is proved to be ruining his business.

However, the RSPCA and conservationists are outraged and have pledged to save Sammy.

BADGERS HAVE BEEN threatened at a man-made, well protected sett in Yorkshire by suspected badger baiters.

The mystery attackers broke into the sett to get at any animals they could find.

However, the artificial sett was only recently used by badgers for the first time so it is not known if any were taken in the attack.

"One of the greatest threats facing badgers in many parts of Yorkshire is badger digging and baiting," said a spokesman for the National Federation of Badger Groups.

"The Wakefield Badger Group has therefore built numerous artificial setts to protect local badgers against such attacks.

"Various materials have been used to construct the setts, including heavy duty plastic pipes for the tunnels and breeze blocks and paving slabs for the chambers.

"These setts are usually impenetrable but in mid-March the Group found a severely damaged sett in one of the district's favourite countryside spots.

"The group's field officer said:'The diggers had gone to great lengths to break into the sett. An attempt to penetrate the pipe was abandoned but they eventually smashed their way right into the chamber. The sett is now wide open. We will be repairing it as soon as possible because we know from experience that they will be back to have another dig.'"

ENGLISH BULLHEAD FISH are causing dismay among Scottish conservationists after they began infesting local waters.

Tens of thousands of the tough, carniverous fish have appeared in Brox Burn in West Lothian, Gogar Burn near Edinburgh's airport, the River Almond in Cramond, the River Esk in Musselburgh and the Water of Leith.

The 18cm-long predators, normally found in southern English waters, devour fry, fish eggs and compete for food with native Scottish fish.

Dr Colin Bull, Forth Fisheries Foundation's executive manager at Stirling University, said that bullheads were a worry.

"The bullhead is the most abundant fish now in the Water of Leith, the Brox Burn and the Gogar Burn," he said. "We are concerned because while they are increasing, trout and salmon are decreasing. There seem to be no salmon now in the Almond and the trout density is very low there."

ASIAN WATER BUFFALO have been making a splash to help wildlife in Cheshire.

The RSPB has recruited nine buffalo for its Gayton Sands nature reserve on the Dee estuary to create ideal conditions for nesting lapwings.

The mighty animals, which can each weigh over 1,600 pounds, should prove a particular boost for lapwing chicks by grazing down dense rush growth and creating numerous shallow pools which attract tasty insects.

A STAGGERING 100 million birds collide with windows across Britain each year, experts estimate.

Millions die or are badly hurt and now the British Trust for Ornithology wants help in investigating the problem.

"Many birdwatchers are aware that birds occasionally collide with windows," said a spokesman."In order to find out how accurate this estimate (of 100 million) is, and to establish why birds collide with windows, we will be carrying out research during the summer.

"Some gardens are more prone to window strikes than others. By looking at things like how close bird feeders and nestboxes are to windows, and working out whether reflections are the problem, we should be able to suggest ways to minimise collisions and deaths.

"Figures suggest that up to a third of the birds colliding with windows die as a result. Others fly away unharmed or are only dazed.

"Sometimes, the only evidence that a window strike has occurred is the pattern of feather dust left on the window. Some birds produce more feather dust than others and leave a clearer imprint.

"The only information we have at the moment about the potential effects of windows strikes on birds comes from the National Ringing Scheme, co-ordinated by the BTO.

"Some 11,000 ringed birds are reported to the BTO each year, half of which are found dead. Where the cause of death is known, seven per cent of song thrushes and three per cent of house sparrows had collided with windows.

"Some 34 per cent of sparrowhawks, for which a cause of death was reported, had flown into windows. Corresponding figures for other species include: blackbird, seven per cent; chaffinch, 20 per cent; greenfinch, nine per cent; and robin, four per cent."

COLLARED DOVE AND woodpigeon are now five times more common in our gardens than in 1979, according to the results of the RSPB's 25th Big Garden Birdwatch survey.

Collared doves, seen in 62 per cent of gardens, have increased by 525 per cent while woodpigeons, recorded in 54 per cent of gardens, were up by 594 per cent.

The birds, which do not feature in 1979's top 10 birds, now hold 7th and 9th place respectively.

A record breaking 409,000 people watched their gardens and local parks during the RSPB's Big Garden Birdwatch in January.

Some 8.6 million birds were recorded and 247,000 gardens surveyed.

FARMERS ARE DELIGHTED by 'eggscellent' news about British eggs.

A report by the Food Standards Agency has confirmed the effective eradication of salmonella in UK eggs.

An FSA survey of British produced eggs showed no traces of salmonella within any of the eggs, says the NFU.

It also found a significant fall in shell contamination with only nine shells testing positive out of a total of 28,518 eggs.

The NFU has now called on the Government to insist that all eggs imported into the home market are produced to the same high standards.

389

HORSE: three disasters in the saddle and a telling off

HORSES have been a central feature of the countryside since records began with our distant ancestors quickly learning how to domesticate them.

Today's biggest breed, the Shire horse, was originally developed to carry armoured knights into battle during the 13th Century and can weigh up to a tonne.

From the 18th Century onwards this powerful creature even replaced the ox as our main cart-pulling beast, hence its old English name, 'cart horse'.

A typical Shire horse stallion stands a lofty 17 hands high with a single 'hand' being 10cms and the measurement taken from its shoulder or withers.

In addition, a Shire horse's fetlocks are always 'feathered' with long hairs spreading around the hooves.

These days, the Shire horse is more likely to be found in the show ring than the farm yard but some are still used by breweries to pull drays loaded with beer.

Slightly shorter than the Shire at 16 hands but reputedly just as strong is the Suffolk Punch, another massive breed designed to drag enormous loads.

Unlike the Shire, which is usually a mixture of brown, black and white, the Suffolk Punch is always bright chestnut in colour.

Another difference involves its fetlocks which are smooth and not 'feathered' like those of the Shire or other heavy breeds such as the Clydesdale.

I remember seeing a Suffolk Punch at a country show as a child and was stunned by its awesome physique.

I was equally shocked to learn recently that only about 200 of these marvellous animals now survive worldwide, making them even rarer than the giant panda.

Thankfully, a campaign has been launched to save them from extinction.

Horses for riding are based on a vast range of breeds, anything from the tall, Yorkshire-bred Cleveland Bay horse to the shorter Shetland or Exmoor ponies.

Riding is great if you're any good at it. Unfortunately, I'm not, although I've pony-trekked in the Lake District, galloped down Moroccan beaches, and trotted through the Welsh hills.

All three experiences were pretty disastrous.

In the Lake District I was aged about nine and dragooned into taking part with my family.

My mount - a headstrong black Dales pony - kept turning round and sloping off back to its stable.

One of our guides had to constantly chase after us.

In Morocco, I hurtled scarily fast down various beaches trying to keep up with my then girlfriend, an expert rider who fell in love with our two mangy, flea-bitten Arab mares.

The country was baking in a heatwave at the time, though I was too terrified of falling off to care.

Under the blazing sun, I eventually noticed an odd tickling sensation on my bare shoulder.

When I glanced down, the skin had started to bubble.

Yet only later did I feel the full, excruciating effects of sunstroke.... helpfully twinned with food poisoning.

The last time I rode a horse was years later in Wales.

Saddling up on two Welsh cobs, myself and a friend were waved off from the courtyard of the picturesque stables by the charming lady owner.

Immediately my horse began to walk, I was embarrassingly unseated.

However, I somehow managed to grab my mount's right ear to stop myself hitting the deck.

I hung there, awkwardly suspended, for a few long seconds before the stable owner levered me back into the saddle. She was fine about it.

The horse wasn't.

It shook its painfully yanked ear and neighed at me in disgust.

JNTING WITH HOUNDS is back on the itical agenda after ministers agreed to)port another anti-hunt Bill.

The move will mean a new clash with intry campaigners and the House of Lords, :h previously determined to resist a nplete ban across England and Wales.

London Labour MP Tony Banks, leader of anti-hunt movement, claims that Tony iir has promised to force through a ban this ie if - as before - legislation stalls.

Meanwhile, the Countryside Alliance has idemned the activities of anti-hunt estigators and the allegations made against Plas Machynlleth Hunt in Wales.

A Federation of Welsh Packs committee inquiry, held at Builth Wells, found that malpractice allegations were unfounded.

"Representatives of the Countryside iance and the Federation of Welsh Packs l earlier viewed un-edited video footage on ich the allegations were based with a igue Against Cruel Sports official and a rnalist," said an Alliance spokesman.

"The League representative was unable to nt to evidence supporting the specific :gations of malpractice made against the it."

Alliance Welsh director Adrian Simpson led:"The Plas Machynlleth Hunt has been illy cleared of all allegations by the inquiry iel. Whilst the hunt was suspended, over lambs were killed or wounded by foxes in area within which the hunt operates.

"The unedited video footage showed quite arly that the foxes that were given to inds were humanely destroyed with a :nsed firearm."

A GENDER BENDING fish is one of the stars of iew online tour through a top British wildlife :rve.

Lundy Marine Nature Reserve is a small rocky nd in the middle of the Bristol Channel and is ie to a range of marine life including the sex- nging cuckoo wrasse.

Now, for the first time, visitors to English Nature's isite can see the fish and other wonders of dy's underwater world through an on-line virtual .

The bizarre cuckoo wrasse is expected to stand - when the male dies the dominant female nges sex, colour and patterning to become the t male.

Other attractions include the cotton spinner sea umber and the barrel-shaped baked bean sea- irt - which draws water into its body through one ion and expels it again through another.

English Nature spokesman Ian Reach l:"Lundy is an incredible place. The virtual tour is you a feel for the magnificent landscape, res and unique wildlife of this island."

THE DECISION TO drop controversial plans to grow commercial GM crops in the countryside has been welcomed by environmentalists.

Despite getting the go-ahead from the Government in the face of mass opposition from country groups, bio-tech firm Bayer has decided not to commercialise its GM maize Chardon LL in the UK after all.

The company said this was because the Government wanted to impose too many conditions which would make Chardon LL economically unviable.

Withdrawal means that GM crops are now unlikely to be grown in the UK until 2008 at the earliest.

Friends of the Earth's GM campaigner Pete Riley said:"This is very welcome news. This GM maize had serious question marks about its safety and performance and should never have been given UK approval. But this was ignored by Bayer and the Government in their blind rush to push GM on the public.

"This episode will be acutely embarrassing to ministers and of deep concern to Bayer's shareholders.

"The Government must now abandon this dangerous and unpopular technology and concentrate on protecting our food, farming and environment from GM contamination and put real effort into genuinely sustainable agriculture."

However, Environment Minister Elliot Morley has defended the Government's stance over the controversy.

He asserted:"We always said it would be for the market to decide the viability of growing and selling GM once the Government assessed safety and risk.

"Number 10's Strategy Unit report on the costs and benefits of GM last year did say there would be limited short-term commercial benefits in the UK for growing GM."

BARN OWLS ARE almost always dead owls when they encounter busy roads, a new report reveals.

The silent twilight predators appear virtually helpless at protecting themselves near heavy traffic, according to research by the Barn Owl Trust.

It is estimated that 72 per cent of barn owls that fly above major roads are killed.

With only a few thousand pairs left scattered across Britain, the birds remain under serious threat.

"Road deaths have more impact on barn owls than any other creature," said a Trust spokesman.

"On major roads, barn owls are three times more likely to be found dead than seen alive."

Increased traffic in once tranquil, rural areas has proved a disaster for the birds, researchers found.

THREE HORSES BROUGHT terror to one of the most remote towns in the Scottish Highlands after bolting through the high street.

Shoppers dived for cover in Thurso on the northern coast when the runaways clattered past pursued by vets, police, an animal welfare officer, and members of the public.

After tearing around busy town centre roads for 40 minutes, the horses were finally caught.

Pranksters were blamed for letting the animals free from a local field.

Fortunately, neither the horses nor any passers-by were injured.

391

GREAT CRESTED NEWTS, dragonflies, otters and water voles are among threatened English wildlife set to benefit from a £1million cash injection.

Some £400,000 of the funding came from an Environment Agency offer to DEFRA but that money is more than matched by further funding from a variety of external partners, taking the figure to over £1million.

More than 50 separate projects will receive cash.

In just one example, money will go towards helping to protect a Yorkshire chalk stream recognised for its national importance - West Beck in the River Hull headwaters.

"The River Hull headwaters are nationally important as the country's most northerly chalk streams and as an excellent trout fishery," said a project spokesman.

"The Environment Agency has already been working closely with English Nature, the Yorkshire Wildlife Trusts, landowners and fishing clubs to bring about many improvements to West Beck.

"A major section of the beck has been fenced to prevent the banks and margins of the river being damaged by grazing cattle.

"Cattle can cause riverbanks to erode which then leads to silt problems in the water. All this has implications for wildlife, including water voles, fish and invertebrates such as dragonflies and mayflies.

"Work to narrow sections of the river to aid 'self-cleaning' has also taken place using 'green engineering' - hazel faggots staked to the riverbank and back-filled with silt to improve river flows and bankside cover."

Further schemes were now being planned to improve the area.

TWO HUGE WHALE jawbones are being hunted by scientists after vanishing on the Scottish island of Coll.

The 12ft jawbones disappeared from a 56ft, 25-tonne female fin whale that was washed up on the island weeks ago.

However, while scientists from the National Museums of Scotland managed to slowly collect and transport the rest of the skeleton to their Edinburgh research base, the jawbones appear to have been confiscated.

Museums curator Andrew Kitchener said:"The disappearance of these jawbones is a most unusual zoological phenomenon. We would be very grateful to anybody on Coll who might happen to stumble across them.

"We don't have a complete fin whale skeleton so finding these jawbones would help fill a massive gap in our collection."

Rumours abound on the island - population 100 - that the jawbones have been hidden but will reappear soon as garden ornaments.

A KENT FARMER was fined £750 and ordered to pay costs of £1,650 for running an illegal landfill operation at a nature conservation site which is home to rare water voles.

At Dartford Magistrates Court, the farmer pleaded guilty to the offence which took place on his own farmland.

The court heard that in April last year, Environment Agency officers observed a queue of lorries waiting to deposit waste on the land and witnessed a number of lorries actually tipping.

Under Section 33 of the Environmental Protection Act, landowners cannot allow waste to be tipped on their land without a permit.

Although the farmer was warned an offence was being committed, the tipping continued for three more days.

In court, he apologised for his actions.

He said as soon as he was aware that an offence was being committed he had tried to stop the tipping but had been unable to do so.

A BUTTERFLY WHICH became extinct here is now making a powerful comeback thanks to conservation work.

The large blue is thought to have died out at the end of the 1970s but numbers have now rocketed to over 6,000.

This is thought to be the biggest number of large blues ever found in the UK in the last 60 years.

However, the population leap was only made possible by bringing in large blues from Sweden and reintroducing them to the British countryside.

Of 25 sites where the butterflies have been settled, nine already host thriving colonies.

Although there are six large blue species in the world, only one is native to Britain.

Despite its resurgence, all six species remain under threat .

TROUT FACE A busy Easter Saturday at the hands of a Lancashire schoolgirl who has pledged to hunt them down.

Lisa Isles, 15, is aiming to raise cash with a sponsored 'fishathon' for the England Youth fly-fishing team, of which she is a member.

The Poulton teenager wants to catch trout at eight different spots across Lancashire and south Cumbria to meet her challenge.

Chauffeured by her grandad, she hopes the event will raise the profile of junior fly-fishing while also boosting the national youth team.

"Once I've caught a fish at a specific fishery, I can then move on to the next venue, where I will stay for a maximum of two hours before moving on again," she said."I've no intention of killing any fish, and anything I do catch will be returned to the water."

TWO BATS PUT organisers of a Scottish model car race in a flap by making themselves at home in the command centre.

The Stonehaven and District Radio Car Club were forced to call off an event at the Mineralwell Park track when the bats and heavy rain conspired against them.

Club chairman Dan Rowlands discovered the bats hanging upside down from the shutters of the command centre where computers record lap speeds and public announcements are made.

However, after the animals were put in a box and the SSPCA informed, organisers were still forced to abandon the meet when it began to pour.

WILDCATS MAY HAVE been wiped out thanks to cross-breeding with domestic cats gone wild, scientists believe.

A decade of research in some of Scotland's remotest areas has led scientists to conclude that none of the animals may now exist in their original, truly wild form.

Professor David Macdonald, head of Oxford University's Wildlife Conservation Research Unit, explained:"The wildcat was once found throughout Britain but our data suggest it may no longer exist in its original form, having inbred extensively with domestic cats. It is now possible that no genetically pure wildcats remain."

His study, sketched out in the yearly report of The Mammals Trust, will be the precursor to a more detailed 200-page report released soon.

Although similar in size and shape to domestic cats, the wildcat is a much fiercer, more powerful animal altogether in its pure form.

Professor Macdonald hopes that if pockets of real wildcats do still exist, these can be found and protected from mating with feral cats.

Colleague Andrew Kitchener, mammals curator at the National Museums of Scotland, who co-authored the report, believes a few pure wildcats could remain.

"Ten years ago we surveyed 300 wildcats, mostly killed on the roads, and around 12 per cent seemed to be pure-breds," he said."There ought to be some left but there is an urgent need for more research and a plan to save them."

HEDGEHOGS ARE NIGHT shift workers that really get busy in April but need our help, say The Wildlife Trusts.

"Make sure your garden has secret places where a hedgehog can make a nest," said Trust education development officer Mary Porter.

"Hedge bottoms full of old leaves, long grass or other vegetation, twigs etc, will provide just the sort of thing a hedgehog needs.

"Don't tidy under hedges - a pointless exercise if you want wildlife in your garden. Hedge bottoms provide a safe refuge for all kinds of wildlife, not just hedgehogs.

"You can provide a hedgehog hibernation box (either bought or made) but unkempt corners such as under sheds or compost heaps will naturally do the trick.

"Gardening organically will provide plenty of invertebrates for your hedgehog to hoover up for you - they will consume vast quantities of slugs and snails for instance.

"You can provide extra food artificially. Dog food and water are good or specially prepared food, available from many pet shops."

LABOUR MPs HAVE been threatened with the wrath of pro-hunt voters if a total ban on hunting across England and Wales becomes law before the next election.

Prime Minister Tony Blair is said to be considering forcing through a ban if a new Bill meets implacable opposition in the House of Lords once more.

As many as 50 Labour MPs are thought to be vulnerable to moves to unseat them because of their support for a total ban.

"They will not know what hit them," said Yorkshire Countryside Alliance member James Craven, referring to a particular group of local MPs.

Mr Craven, who hunts with the Middleton Hunt, said that protesters would support any candidate best placed to unseat a sitting Labour MP.

However, at least one local MP has laughed off the threat.

Constitutional Affairs Minister Chris Leslie said:"I am pleased that they will draw attention to my determination to ban foxhunting."

BROWN TROUT TAKEN from waterways on the Queen's Balmoral Estate are unlikely to catch fire - after shocked scientists found they were riddled with flame-retardant chemicals.

The bizarre discovery was made in a survey by Spanish and Norwegian researchers who found trout in Scotland's Lochnagar region contained high concentrations of so-called PBDEs.

The chemicals, commonly used as flame-retardants in a variety of plastic materials and foam, are thought to have arrived in dust or rain.

Of a number of European lochs and lakes studied in the survey, the Lochnagar region was found to contain the highest levels.

Scientists are concerned about the long-term health effects on creatures that feed on the fish such as otters, herons - and even humans.

THE RSPB IS urging local authorities to halt all hedge cutting between now and September because of the threat to nesting birds.

More than 40 species use hedgerows to raise young but many birds will be scared off and nests destroyed if hedges are trimmed during spring and summer, says the Society.

Common birds, such as the blackbird and robin and more elusive species, like the bullfinch and spotted flycatcher, often seek nesting sites in hedgerows and hedgerow trees.

Dr Mark Avery, RSPB director of conservation, said:"Hedgerows are bristling with life and alive with the song of wild birds at this time of year. They are one of our most important wildlife habitats, hosting a huge variety of species in a relatively small area.

"We are urging councils not to trim hedges until the autumn and let their residents enjoy the wildlife that will quickly take advantage."

In its new leaflet, Protecting Hedgerows for Birds, the RSPB has drawn up a set of best practice guidelines to help landowners keep their land wildlife-friendly.

In addition to birds, more than 70 rare invertebrates find sanctuary in hedgerows, including Lesne's earwig and the Chobham comb-foot spider while peacock, gatekeeper and brown hairstreak butterflies feed on hedgerow nectar. Hedgerows also give cover to the dormouse and other tiny mammals.

ORGANIC FARMERS HAVE been given a cash boost for their efforts to help conserve Britain's wildlife.

Following five years work by the Soil Association, the RSPB, English Nature and others, the Government has announced that a new scheme to encourage wildlife on farms will have a special Organic Strand, worth £60 per hectare per year.

Non-organic farmers who want to help wildlife will get half that - or £30 per hectare.

Peter Melchett, the Soil Association's policy director, said:"The announcement of an additional £30 per hectare for organic farmers shows that organic farming will be a major part of the future of British agriculture. The Soil Association is delighted at this clear signal of support for organic farming.

"It also represents a brilliant deal for the public. DEFRA's business case for organic farming showed that organic farms deliver a minimum of £130 per hectare of public goods and benefits.

"So for £60 per hectare, the public are certainly getting more than their money's worth.

"And to be eligible for the scheme, all farmers will have to undertake conservation work on their farms.

"Detailed research shows that organic farms have much higher numbers of farmland birds, wildflowers, bats and butterflies, and this new scheme will help organic farmers do even more to bring back wildlife to the English countryside."

BRITAIN AND IRELAND support some of the world's most important populations of seabirds, according to 'Seabird 2000', the latest review of seabird numbers around the British Isles.

The survey, which took four years to compile, is the latest assessment of the seabird populations of the United Kingdom, the Republic of Ireland, the Isle of Man and the Channel Islands.

Its results show that, overall, numbers have risen steadily over the last 30 years to around eight million birds today.

However, the survey also reveals that some species, particularly several species of tern, are suffering sharp population declines.

Other findings include:

-In Scotland, breeding seabirds (5.2 million) now outnumber people (5.1 million).

-Sand eel shortages have been a major factor in the population decline of Arctic skuas (down 37 per cent), black-legged kittiwakes (down 23 per cent) and European shags (down 25 per cent).

-Aberdeen may now hold the world's largest urban-nesting gull population.

-Island refuges of many seabird species are under serious threat from introduced predators such as rats, cats and mink.

OSPREYS HAVE BEEN spotted migrating in numbers back to Britain which bodes well for the future of the spectacular fish eaters here.

The birds, once driven to extinction, are now firmly re-established in Scotland and are even resurgent in a few isolated parts of England.

According to the British Trust for Ornithology, ospreys migrate here through Morocco, Spain, Portugal, and north west France before arriving in late March and early April.

Sometimes, the birds gather at 'bottlenecks' such as Gibraltar - the narrowest sea crossing between Africa and Europe - and it was here that an impressive total of 32 ospreys were recorded in less than two hours recently

Trust spokeswoman Dawn Balmer said:"Keep an eye on the sky over the next few weeks for migrating ospreys. They are often mobbed by crows so if you hear a commotion in the sky, look up and you might be lucky."

A COW'S DEATH is being blamed on moped joyriders who are thought to have chased it into a ditch in Oxfordshire.

A group of youths was regularly spotted playing on a moped in the Kennington field before the animal was discovered.

It is thought the cow became stranded in the ditch and was unable to drag itself out.

Three youths, aged in their mid-teens, were spotted chasing sheep and cattle before the cow was found.

Days earlier, a sheep was also discovered dead in the same field but was thought to have been savaged by someone's pet dog.

UP TO 40 great bustard chicks are due to be relocated from Russia to their new home on Salisbury Plain any day now - almost 200 years after the species died out here.

The choice of location seems especially apt as conservationists aim to launch a military-type operation to protect the youngsters from predators such as foxes and stoats.

The birds will be under 24-hour surveillance for months but it is hoped that they will leave their holding pen by September.

Some will be radio tracked and all will be able to return to the pen if they feel under threat.

When fully grown, the bustards will be Europe's largest land birds and, at more than 40lb, the heaviest flying birds in the world.

HUNGRY CORMORANTS HAVE been outwitted with the creation of underwater hiding spots for thousands of fish.

The Environment Agency helped to create refuges for threatened fish at a Carnforth fishery in Lancashire.

The hiding places were built at the bottom of Borwick Waters to protect fish from predatory cormorants circling the lakes.

The £7,500 initiative, run in conjunction with British Waterways, was launched after an influx of the predatory seabirds saw flocks of up to 40 arriving.

Agency spokesman Steve Whittam said:"Such is the scale of this problem that it is already threatening to have a significant effect on the fish population there. Cormorants have become increasingly trouble - some recently as they move further and further inland looking for food, and by doing this we hope to give greater protection to the fish."

OTTER, MINK AND heron are chief suspects after the horrific discovery of more than 100 mutilated toads in Scotland.

Police at first feared human sadists had pulled the legs off 115 carcasses found on the Monymusk Estate in Aberdeenshire.

But SSPCA spokeswoman Doreen Graham said:"From the information we have now, the feeling is that it may be otters because when they eat toads they only eat the legs since the rest of the skin is poisonous."

Meanwhile, local vet Peter McCormack believes herons may be the cause of the horror after hearing stories of the birds eating the legs of toads in Ireland.

He said:"When I was over there years ago there was a similar incident. It was fully investigated and herons were found to be the cause.

"The circumstances may be different in this case. But it is possible and should not be ruled out. Things like this do happen in nature and we should keep an open mind."

A BAN ON hunting with hounds across England and Wales would spark a huge revolt among normally law-abiding people, it has been claimed.

Countryside Alliance spokesman Tim Bonner warned:"There will be a very serious campaign of civil disobedience on this."

Mr Bonner was speaking after 216 MPs signed a Commons motion calling for the early re-introduction of a new Hunting Bill.

The motion was tabled by Labour's Gerald Kaufman and Tony Banks, Ann Widdecombe, a former Tory minister, and Norman Baker, Liberal Democrat MP for Lewes.

However, the Alliance says those MPs who signed risk bringing ridicule on the Government since a recent NOP poll found that 98 per cent of the public think that there are more important issues for the Government to tackle instead of hunting.

Alliance chief executive Simon Hart said:"What the constituents of these MPs will make of their ongoing obsession with this issue will be revealed at the next election when their votes will be decided not by hunting, but by delivery on health, education, immigration and crime. The Government should also remember that it was elected, and re-elected, because it was viewed as moderate and reasonable, not vindictive and obsessive."

SHARK AND TUNA are among subtropical marine fish which scientists claim could soon replace traditional British coldwater species like cod because of climate change.

Both are being increasingly found in our waters chasing fish with even a great white shark spotted off the Devon coast.

Scientists at the Southampton Oceanography Centre say more leatherback turtles are also being attracted to our seas because they feed on jellyfish which thrive in warmer water.

And in another development, a squid fishery is springing up off the Aberdeen coast in Scotland as squid numbers continue to rise.

FARMERS HOPE A surge of patriotism will send sales of British beef soaring on St George's Day.

"St George is most famously known as the slayer of the dragon and heroic saviour of the maiden, although little is actually known about him," says the NFU.

"He is thought to have been a brave Roman soldier and early Christian martyr with much myth and legend surrounding the stories of his days.

"He became the official patron saint of England in 1425 after Henry V's victory at the battle of Agincourt. The cross of St George is flown as England's national flag, and also forms part of the Union flag.

"By tucking into some beef on St George's Day (April 23), you'll be doing your health a favour. Red meat can play a valuable role in a balanced diet.

"Beef is an excellent source of iron and zinc. A lack of iron can cause deficiency diseases such as anaemia while zinc is vital to help wound healing and increase fertility. Red meat is also a good source of protein, B vitamins, vitamin D and magnesium."

A DAREDEVIL BIRD has been surprising motorists in Leicestershire after nesting in traffic lights.

The bird, thought to be a thrush or blackbird, began making its nest weeks ago but no-one thought it would stay at the precarious spot in Oadby.

However, it perservered and is now believed to be hatching a clutch of eggs on the lip of the flashing amber light.

MORE THAN HALF Britain's 30 species of ancient underwater stonewort plants are now rare or extinct, according to Plantlife International.

Pollution is to blame for a catastrophic decline of the plants which are unusual in that they build an external skeleton made of calcium carbonate instead of using cellulose.

Spending their entire lives underwater, stoneworts can form dense forests when conditions are favourable.

However, says Plantlife International, 76 per cent of their favourite UK sites are now suffering under a variety of different pollutants, from agricultural fertilisers to detergents.

SALMON AND SEA trout will now find it easier to spawn in several South Wales rivers following dogged conservation work.

Environment Agency Wales has restored more than 100km of river by clearing various obstructions and improving overall accessibility for fish.

"Spawning areas and habitat for young fish have been made accessible through the removal of blockages such as fallen trees and other accumulated debris,"said a spokesman.

"As a result, migratory fish such as salmon and sea trout will now find it easier to reach the upper stretches of rivers.

"And once they make it to the spawning grounds, they are now more likely to find a habitat to their liking and more suitable for their offspring.

"These habitat developments will also benefit fishing tourism. Today, angling makes a major contribution to the Welsh economy."

A HIGHLAND COW protecting its calf killed a pensioner on a walking holiday in Scotland.

Victim Brian Williams, 74, was tossed into the air by the furious mother during a leisurely walk at the Inverinate Estate in Wester Ross, a fatal accident inquiry heard.

Mr Williams, from Hertfordshire, suffered a brain haemorrhage and died in a Glasgow hospital the following day.

His son, Mark Williams, 45, also from Hertfordshire, told the Dingall inquiry that his father had been walking in front of him, his mother, wife, and two children when the cow attacked last summer.

He said:"We just saw a cow with a calf and then it all happened so quickly. The cow ran across and butted my father and tossed him in the air.

"It was almost like slow motion. It was like a cartoon - he was conscious but badly shaken. He was complaining of a headache.

"He said it felt like he had gone three rounds with Cassius Clay. The children were screaming and my wife Wendy got them to a position of safety. We walked my father slowly out of that area."

Estate manager David Glover, 51, told the inquiry it was the first time anything like that had occurred and the path where the attack happened was regularly used by walkers.

However, arrangements allowing mothers and calves in the vicinity were now being reviewed following the tragedy.

NIGHTJARS ARE TO be the subject of a summer study aimed at learning more about the strange, twilight flying birds.

Organised by English Nature, the British Trust for Ornithology, RSPB, and the Forestry Commission, research will take place between late May and late July, it has been revealed.

"The nightjar is a breeding visitor to the UK, wintering in Africa," explained a spokesman for the Trust.

"In the UK, the bird's historical distribution used to extend across the whole of mainland Britain, although it was always most numerous in southern England and Wales.

"The last national survey of nightjars was in 1992 and revealed a total of 3,400 churring males at 1,194 sites, representing an increase of 50 per cent since the previous survey in 1981 and a partial recovery following a decline in breeding range between the 1930s and 1970s.

"The majority of males were found in forestry plantations and lowland heath.

"Its 1992 distribution was particularly sparse in Scotland with small numbers recorded in Dumfries and Galloway but few elsewhere. In the UK the nightjar's amber-list criteria reflects its limited breeding distribution and vulnerability to habitat change."

OYSTERCATCHERS AND other wading birds have been boosted by the rejection of plans to build a container port at Dibden Bay, near Southampton.

Transport Minister Tony McNulty said:"One important factor in making the decision was the environmental impact of the proposals on internationally protected sites."

Celebrating the news, English Nature said:"The Solent and Southampton Water SPA is used by 50,000 waterbirds every winter, making it one of the most important places in the country for wintering wildfowl.

"Some 15,000 of these feed in Southampton Water and Dibden Bay is particularly special. Twice the number of birds feed on the Dibden foreshore, compared with other areas of similar size.

"It is especially good habitat for oystercatchers. Up to a fifth of the local population gather on the foreshore at feeding time along with grey plover, wigeon, curlew and lapwing - all attracted to Dibden's rich feeding grounds. The Bay also supports internationally important numbers of dark bellied Brent geese."

LYNX SHOULD BE reintroduced to Britain to help control numbers of grazing animals such as deer, a zoologist has suggested.

The fast, deadly killer was once common here but was driven to extinction by hunters.

Now, with an estimated 50-100 big cats already on the loose in the countryside, zoologist Chris Mosier says the lynx would be an ideal cat to properly reintroduce.

Mr Mosier, an adviser to the British Big Cats Society, said:"While reintroduction of exotic felines may be a criminal offence, it is not necessarily a bad idea.

"Most biologists, including at least one professor, believe that our populations of grazing animals do not have enough predators to keep their numbers under control.

"The reintroduction of the lynx might, if handled correctly, help to balance this situation. With an increased wariness of firearms plus the increasing unacceptability of hunting with dogs, the return of one of our long-lost predators may give hope to farmers and landowners."

MINK ARE BEING increasingly killed or driven off by bigger native otters, a report reveals.

According to 'The State of Britain's Mammals 2004', compiled by the Wildlife Conservation Unit at Oxford University, ferocious immigrant mink are meeting their match as otter numbers rise.

"The otter, which was once in danger of dying out, is breeding again in many parts of north west Scotland and England," the report says.

"A by-product of this is that the American mink population has declined - reducing by about 65 per cent between 1989 and 1998 - while the otter population has increased.

"Both compete for aquatic prey, such as fish. As the density of otters increases, mink shift towards terrestrial prey such as rabbits and voles.

"But when these are scarce, mink will often be killed by otters or abandon the area. Mink are also predators of water voles so their decline helps this creature, now scarce in many parts of Britain."

A NEWBORN FOAL was killed by two children in a shocking act of cruelty that stunned the animal's owner.

Two boys are believed to have stoned the helpless animal to death in its field at Pensford near Bristol.

Heartbroken owner Sarah Clements, who keeps rescued and unwanted horses, is now campaigning for a crackdown on rural crime and vandalism in the area.

She said:"I have had to call the police every week due to theft, vandalism, criminal damage and, worst of all, a staggering amount of animal cruelty.

"My mare Whiskey gave birth to a colt, unfortunately quite close to a footpath, and I found him dead.

"I didn't realise how he had died until a group of children told me that two boys had stoned him."

Although several children had been interviewed about the incident, police could not gather enough evidence to bring anyone to court.

Other incidents included bricks being thrown at ponies, horses let out of fields, sheds being burned down and grooming equipment stolen.

BATS HAVE PUT a church congregation in a flap after invading and driving parishioners away.

Now St Hilda's in Ellerburn, North Yorkshire, may be forced to close after more than 1,000 years' service.

Natterer's bats set up home in the church after getting in through gaps in the walls but cannot be removed because of European wildlife laws.

However, Reverend Dave Clark, the vicar, said parishioners are deserting because of health fears and the church may be forced to close.

"The little beggars come flying in, fly around in the church itself, and have a fine old time during the summer," he said.

"Their droppings are a health hazard - urine and black muck up and down the walls.

"Bishop Galliford's wife was ill some time ago and she put it down to having taken a service at the church.

"When you're taking a service, of course, you take deep breaths and you're liable to inhale anything that's vaporised around you - and bat dirt can be part of it."

OVER A THOUSAND barbel have been stocked in three Kent rivers by local angling clubs.

The Medway, Stour and Brede received a total of 1,200 two-year-old fish from the Environment Agency's Calverton fish farm.

"These Kentish rivers had been stocked with barbel in the past and the fish are now a regular feature in anglers' catches," an Agency spokesman said."In fact, specimen barbel of around 17lb have been caught in the River Medway. It is also encouraging that some juvenile fish are being caught, as this indicates signs of natural breeding."

RARE WATER SHREWS face being wiped out but most people know little about the tiny creatures, it has been claimed.

The Mammal Society says that, unlike other popular animals, water shrews didn't star in 'The Wind in the Willows' or feature in Beatrix Potter books.

Chairman Michael Woods said:"The real problem is that no-one knows much about water shrews, where they are found or what they need to live.

"We are concerned that they may be disappearing from our countryside due to habitat loss, pollution and pesticide use."

The Society has just announced the start of long-term efforts to conserve the water shrew.

To gain an insight into numbers, small plastic tubes will be used as bait stations and placed near water for two weeks.

"Shrews are naturally inquisitive and will enter the tubes to eat the bait and deposit droppings," explained Mr Woods.

"We can then examine the droppings to see if they were left by a water shrew or by other shrews or rodents."

ONE RAM SURVIVED out of a flock of eight when a pack of dogs attacked.

Police are investigating the incident which saw the rare Oxford Down sheep killed in their Bucking - hamshire field.

The dogs struck at Chiltern Open Air Museum, Chalfont St Giles, in the early hours of the morning.

Three rams were killed outright while four were so badly injured they had to be destroyed by a vet.

RARE WHITE STORKS sparked fears for their safety when they decided to nest on top of an electricity pole in West Yorkshire.

The storks, whose last recorded nesting in Britain was back in 1416, flew in to Horbury Bridge, near Wakefield, from the Continent.

However, birdwatchers were shocked at their choice of nest site so bosses at Yorkshire Electricity Distribution came up with an idea - a specially-designed 4 ft by 4ft nesting platform on top of a tall pole positioned close by.

RSPB conservation manager Roy Taylor said:"It's exciting that these birds have turned up and may be showing signs of breeding. Large birds, such as storks, do not always breed in their first year but often go through a routine of nest building without laying.

"The RSPB will be monitoring the activities of these magnificent birds over the next few days and, if it appears they are indeed going to breed, we will then set up an appropriate nest protection scheme. In the meantime, the birds can be easily viewed from the Calder and Hebble navigation tow path and bridge without the risk of disturbance."

ANIMAL HEALTH Minister Ben Bradshaw has announced the publication of a report from an independent scientific panel reviewing a controversial random badger cull trial.

He said:"Bovine TB is a complex disease and a worsening problem for farmers and the Government. I welcome this report. The recommendations are complex and have potentially far reaching conse - quences for TB policy."

The scientific trial was carried out to determine what links, if any, could be found between TB in badgers and TB in cattle.

397

OTTER: fighting back to reclaim its old haunts

STRONG, streamlined, and equipped with powerful webbed feet, otters are the master fishermen of those waterways where they still hunt. Males are the larger of the sexes, measuring over 4ft from their inquisitive noses to the tips of their thick, muscular tails.

When diving, otters reduce their oxygen requirement by slowing down their heartbeats.

They can stay underwater for four minutes at a time and have been known to cover 400 metres without resurfacing.

They can also see as clearly below water as above but use stiff bristles on their snouts to search for food in murkier conditions.

All these facts only added to my surprise when it was revealed otters had actually been among the worst-hit wildlife victims of recent flooding in the UK.

Faced with the threat of rapidly rising flood water, sleek, hardy otters might have been expected to cope easily.

But in reality their swimming skills only added to their problems as they became disorientated by swollen rivers overflowing into urban areas.

Many otters were thought to have perished after being struck by cars while some young cubs simply drowned in their bankside dens or 'holts'.

In London, up to a third of the semi-aquatic creatures were feared dead after their refuges along the Thames became swamped.

Icy conditions which followed the floods can hardly have helped those that remained.

It seemed ironic to me that conservationists, who had worked so hard to re-establish this shy predator in the capital, had Mother Nature to thank for setting their efforts back. Despite this, national otter numbers have been showing a steady resurgence as various schemes bring the animal back from the edge of extinction in many regions.

The Mammal Society says:*"In the late 1950s and early 1960s otters underwent a sudden and catastrophic decline throughout much of Britain. The cause was probably the combined effects of pollution and habitat destruction, particularly the drainage of wet areas.*

"While otters completely disappeared from the rivers of most of central and southern England in just 50 years, their future now looks much brighter. There is evidence that in certain parts of the UK the otter is extending its range and may be increasing locally.

"However there is no room for complacency. Otter populations in England are very fragmented and the animals breed only slowly."

In Scotland, where most British otters are still found, females generally give birth in the safer summer months.

But in England, otter cubs can be born throughout the year - a fact which makes their young especially vulnerable to sudden winter floods. If English otters could only learn from their Scottish cousins, their fightback might become even more successful than it is now.

ANGLERS NOW SPEND an astonishing £3billion annually on Britain's favourite pastime, a report confirms.

Almost four million people, of all ages and backgrounds, love the sport despite animal activists and even the RSPCA increasingly believing it has 'cruelty' implications.

'Our Nations' Fisheries', published by the Environment Agency, is said to be the most comprehensive report ever produced on the state of freshwater and migratory fish.

And it contains a lot of good news.

Coarse and freshwater fish are generally thriving with the most 'species rich' sites said to be the River Mole in Surrey and the River Lymm in Lincolnshire - both of which play host to 14 different species - while the most abundant stocks were found on a tributary of the Warwickshire Avon.

But some news is less positive - salmon stocks are seriously depleted with 70 per cent of salmon rivers in England and Wales failing to meet conservation targets, and eel stocks have also sunk critically low.

However, sea trout have increased in the majority of rivers in the past 30 years, in many cases significantly so.

Grayling populations are also healthy and, at the majority of sites surveyed, juvenile trout numbers were above the average of a decade ago.

Dafydd Evans, head of fisheries at the Environment Agency, said:"This report marks a key milestone in our monitoring and understanding of fish stocks in England and Wales. But while it demonstrates that a lot of excellent work has been done, there is much still to do, particularly with eel and salmon."

ENGLAND'S SOLE PAIR of wild, breeding choughs have done it again with hopes high that a third clutch of eggs has hatched - making it three years in a row.

According to the RSPB, observers at the Lizard, south Cornwall, have reported a flurry of activity by the nesting choughs - rarest members of the crow family - a sure sign that there are chicks to feed.

RSPB chough project officer Claire Mucklow said:"When the choughs first came back to Cornwall of their own accord in 2001, we had our fingers crossed they would stay. We never imagined they would be so successful. This will be the third generation of Cornish choughs and with any luck there will be some females in this brood."

Ivan Nethercoat, the RSPB's 'Aren't Birds Brilliant!' project manager, added:"This scheme provides people with fantastic views of choughs, a bird which had been absent from Cornwall for many years until 2001. They are very charismatic birds and quite a spectacle to watch."

The choughs at the Lizard raised three chicks in 2002 and a further three in 2003.

GARDENERS ARE FACING fresh pleas from conservationists to turn their backs on peat to help save rare plants and wildlife.

Olly Watts, RSPB peatland policy officer, said:"The bogs from which gardeners' peat comes are one of Europe's rarest wildlife habitats.

"These are home to some amazing wildlife, from carnivorous plants, rare butterflies, dragonflies and other insects, birds like golden plovers and snipe, and the sphagnum bog mosses that form the richly coloured peatland carpet.

"It's a dreadful irony that gardeners still use peat to grow plants - thereby denying rare plants and animals their place to live."

The RSPB and the National Trust have now joined forces in an anti-peat campaign amid concerns about the continued dependence on peat despite the availability of much 'greener' alternatives.

In the 1950s, peat was considered a universal solution for gardeners' needs but is now recognised as a finite resource of environmental and historical importance.

Accelerated consumption in recent decades has been driven by demand from the amateur gardening market, with Britain's gardeners currently snapping up two thirds of all peat used in horticulture.

So high has been the demand that 94 per cent of the UK's lowland peat bog has now been lost.

Mike Calnan, the National Trust's head of gardens and parks, added:"Many people remain unaware of the remarkable natural and human history within peat bogs.

"What has taken 4,000 years to grow has taken us less than 40 years to destroy. The special wildlife and archaeological treasures preserved in peat bogs are being lost forever through peat extraction."

LIZARDS AND SNAKES are set to flourish unmolested after a former nuclear research site was decommissioned 30 years earlier than planned.

The site, at Winfrith in Dorset, will be left to nature as operations there are wound down.

Chris Barrett, a landscape manager working on the scheme, said:"We've got Dartford warblers here, common and sand lizards, grass snakes, smooth snakes and adders - you've got to watch out for them when they're basking.

"The threat of a new reactor here has gone, and there'll obviously be a gain to several species. But there won't be any restoration of the Dorset heathland, or any addition to it.

"What there will be is more heathland corridors linking some of the existing patches, and that really will be a gain."

MORE HEDGEHOGS ARE being saved than killed in the Outer Hebrides as the 'bounty' on a rescued hedgehog's head rises to £20.

So far 138 hedgehogs are reported to have been saved by Uist Hedgehog Rescue or passed to its members for a £20 fee - compared to 136 culled in a Scottish Natural Heritage campaign.

The £200,000 cull was launched amid fears that hedgehogs were wiping out native bird species by feasting on their eggs and chicks.

Dozens of the rescued hedgehogs have already been taken to mainland Scotland and released.

COUNTRY SHOOTERS ARE angry that the Government is aiming to blast them again with more red tape as urban gun crime rockets out of control.

Restrictions on ownership and use of legitimate firearms would do nothing to counter gun crime and would break the Government's manifesto commitment not to place 'restrictions on the sport of shooting', warns the Countryside Alliance.

A new Home Office 'Controls on Firearms' consultation paper proposes restrictions on shotgun licences, bringing them into line with existing firearms certificates, and restrictions on the possession and use of guns by young people.

However, The Centre for Defence Studies published research in 2001 - commissioned by the Alliance - showing that there was no link between legitimate gun ownership and incidence of gun crime.

Simon Hart, chief executive of the Alliance, said:"Tackling gun crime by funding community schemes is entirely sensible but restrictions on legitimate gun use, when research has shown that there is no link to gun crime, is not.

"The Government said in its 2001 manifesto that it had 'no intention whatsoever of placing restrictions on the sport of shooting'. If it is to keep to that commitment it should not even be considering many of the options raised in this consultation paper. Legitimate gun owners, and the wider rural electorate, would not stand for knee-jerk firearms legislation in reaction to rising gun crime."

RAMBLERS ARE CELEBRATING the unveiling of a timetable for new access to the countryside.

DEFRA has announced the likely dates for the rollout of regional access to open country under the Countryside and Rights of Way Act.

The first two regions, the South East - including parts of the proposed South Downs National Park - and Lower North West - including large parts of the Peak District and the Forest of Bowland - will be open to the public from September 19 this year.

This will be followed by Region 3 (Central Southern) in December; Region 4 (Upper North West) and Region 5 (North East) in May 2005; Region 6 (South West) in August 2005; Region 7 (West) in October 2005; and finally Region 8 (East) in November 2005.

Rural Affairs Minister Alun Michael MP said:"The Countryside and Rights of Way Act will enable people to walk on land in some of the most beautiful areas of countryside that were previously off-limits, whilst ensuring balance with conservation and land management."

OSPREYS HAVE BEEN involved in a violent drama in Scotland with two females viciously attacking each other.

Following a series of dust-ups between the birds, RSPB staff checked the Loch Garten nest at Abernethy Forest Reserve in Strathspey and found it still contained three eggs.

The nest, Scotland's best known, had been without a successful breeding pair for two years.

However, this year's success was marked by a number of clashes between two females that could have ended in tragedy.

"Last month saw weeks of ferocious fighting between the resident female and an intruding female bird," said a spokesman.

"Later, people watched in horror as the resident osprey, known as White EJ from her identification leg ring, removed a broken egg from the nest.

"Many believed the stress would be too much and no more eggs would be laid - the nest would remain empty for another year. However, the resilient White EJ has delighted RSPB staff and fans of the Loch Garten ospreys by laying a full clutch of eggs."

Loch Garten site manager Richard Thaxton added:"Only a handful of times in the last 50 years has an osprey laid a clutch of four eggs. It is almost unheard of. So to see there are still three eggs in the nest, in spite of all the suffering White EJ has been through, is a huge relief and we're all thrilled."

WILD ATLANTIC SALMON were behind a crackdown on crime launched by the Environment Agency in London.

Fisheries enforcement officers questioned retailers in the capital regarding the illegal sale of the fish.

"Wild salmon are in decline," explained an Agency spokesman.

"It is a sensitive species and when the fish is caught illegally it does set back the species recovery plan.

"Environmental legislation protects wild stocks of salmon by making it a criminal offence to sell them without accompanying receipts to verify their origin. Retailers caught with wild poached salmon can face fines of up to £2,000."

THOUSANDS OF FISH were killed by a pollution spill into a tributary of the River Blithe, Newcastle under Lyme magistrates heard.

Brown trout, bullheads, minnows and sticklebacks were among species which died and led to a £7,500 fine for a leading ceramics company.

Johnson Matthey Plc pleaded guilty to a charge of causing polluting matter - diluted caustic soda washings - to enter a tributary of the River Blithe.

The charge was brought by the Environment Agency under Section 85 of the Water Resources Act 1991 and saw the company also ordered to pay £2,583 costs.

In mitigation, Robert Temmink, for the company, told the court that the incident was an accident, that the company admitted full liability and that it had co-operated fully with the Environment Agency.

He stated that the company had done everything it could to clean up the discharge, purifying the sewage system with 5,000 litres of clean water.

He also informed the court that the site had now been decommissioned.

ANTI-FOXHUNTING MPs are increasing pressure on Tony Blair to reintroduce a new Bill to ban hunting with dogs in England and Wales.

Campaign leader Tony Banks warned the Prime Minister:"Without immediate action, the Government will continue to face a loss of public trust."

A Commons motion pressing for the reintroduction of the Hunting Bill has reportedly achieved a record 250 signatures.

And a report compiled by anti-hunters is strategically headlined 'Time To Deliver the Ban', although hundreds of thousands of pro-hunt supporters will vehemently disagree with its sentiments.

Londoner Mr Banks says:"I am amazed that in today's modern and so-called civilised society, people still congregate in parts of England and Wales to chase an animal to exhaustion before killing it with dogs.

"Furthermore, they do so in the name of sport and in the knowledge that it is perfectly legal."

Tory MP Ann Widdecombe, another anti-hunt campaigner, added:"The message to the Government is clear and simple. There can be no further delays, now is the time to get on with the job and ban hunting with dogs."

However, the Countryside Alliance has scorned the anti-hunt camp's urgency to reintroduce the Hunting Bill.

Even Labour members believed the Party was out of touch with the country on the issue, said the Alliance, with just one per cent in a recent survey thinking it should be a priority.

A MASSIVE SEARCH of British woodlands has failed to find any further cases of 'Phytophthora ramorum', a potentially lethal disease which can infect both shrubs and trees.

In the largest and swiftest survey of woods ever undertaken in response to a specific threat, more than 1,000 woodland sites across England, Scotland and Wales were checked.

Specialist teams swung into action after the first cases of the disease in British trees were recorded in Sussex and Cornwall in November and December last year.

Forestry Minister Ben Bradshaw welcomed the findings and praised the survey teams from the Forestry Commission's research agency.

But he warned that, while encouraging, the results still did not prove the disease was not present among Britain's wider woodlands.

He said:"This was an outstanding response to an urgent need to find out the scale of the problem in our woodland environment. While we cannot be sure that the disease is not present in our woodlands, the survey carried out by the Forestry Commission gives us good grounds for optimism."

PIKE ARE FEARED to be threatening stocks of trout and char in Scotland after being illegally introduced to several waterways there.

Although the Pike Anglers Club of Great Britain claims the fish has existed in Scottish waters for at least 10,000 years, conservationists believe thrill-seeking anglers are putting the voracious predators in protected waters.

The World Wide Fund for Nature says there is evidence that some pike fishermen are releasing adult pike into Scottish waterways for sport.

WWF spokesman Mike Donaghy said:"We have a group of selfish and irresponsible pike anglers who see it as their duty to move pike around and populate more rivers and lochs to suit themselves.

"My main concern is that the pike will feast on brown trout and char. But worse than that, there are many lochs where there are no fish and they have a rather unique ecosystem where the top predator is a newt. If pike end up in there, they will eat everything and it will be a complete ecological disaster.

"Pike are ferocious and very hungry. They continue feeding way past being full - they just keep eating.

"Females are often found stuffed-full because they are highly opportunistic and lay even more eggs the bigger they are."

THREE DUCKLINGS WERE rescued by builders who downed tools to pluck the fluffy balls to safety from a sewer.

The builders had been working round an adult bird and her 14 ducklings after the mother - thought to be a mallard - had decided to nest on the roof of Keynsham police station, near Bristol.

The four workmen, currently refurbishing the station, went into action when they noticed three of the ducklings had vanished.

To their dismay, they realised the birds had slipped down a drainpipe into the sewer system.

However, by taking apart the drainpipe and ripping up a heavy manhole cover, all the ducklings were saved and returned to mum.

Foreman Simon Moore said:"It was lucky it was not raining because they would have been washed away, game over."

Later, the birds were moved to a less hazardous spot and released.

MESSY NESTING BIRDS have been given a boost by police in Scotland after officers warned the public to leave them alone.

Each year, according to Tayside Police, house martins and swallows have their nests illegally interfered with because they cause a nuisance.

But this year the force has reminded the public that the birds are protected under wildlife laws and their nests should not be poked or prodded with sticks.

Alan Stewart, Tayside Police's wildlife and environment officer, said:"The Wildlife and Countryside Act protects nesting birds from the minute they start to build their nest.

"My advice to people who have nesting house martins and swallows on their premises is to enjoy them, even if a bit more cleaning up has to be done.

"The alternative - payment of a fine of up to £5,000 for every nest or egg damaged - could be extremely costly."

NEGLECT AND A lack of understanding is threatening to permanently damage one of our most important natural resources - soil - experts warn.

The Environment Agency's 'State of Soils Report', which looks at the health of soils in England and Wales, has found that our disregard and a lack of knowledge about soil is causing damage which may have serious consequences for future generations.

Resulting problems include soil erosion and contamination, homes being damaged by 'muddy floods', and water being polluted with silt and fertilizer with a knock-on effect for wildlife and fish.

Barbara Young, chief executive of the Environment Agency, said:"For too long now we have been building, working, farming and consuming without understanding its impact on the land and as a result we are now seeing growing signs of soil related problems.

"If we continue to neglect this, sooner or later the consequences will be evident and once soils are badly damaged they are almost impossible to restore to a healthy state.

"We need to understand more about soil. More specifically, we need to know more about what it does and how it does it and how we can protect it.

"This isn't just about encouraging more sustainable farming techniques, this is about understanding what effect our actions are having on the ground underfoot."

The report says that eroded silt from surrounding land can smother riverbed gravels - harming aquatic plants, invertebrates and the eggs of fish.

Trout spawning beds in 29 out of 51 river reaches surveyed in southern England contained more than 15 per cent of fine sediment, a point at which half the eggs and larvae are likely to die.

Salmon, already found to be dwindling in many rivers, are also affected in the same way.

PEREGRINE FALCONS ARE to be protected by hawk-eyed volunteers aiming to outwit poisoners in Devon.

Two peregrine chicks have hatched in a nest on a cliff face at Plymbridge Woods near Plymouth.

Now a 24-hour watch has been mounted at the site to prevent the chicks being harmed or killed.

Peregrine falcons have nested at the spot for years but attempts have been made several times in the past to poison the birds.

In one incident an adult and chick perished.

The National Trust, RSPB and Plymouth College of Further Education have united to find volunteers willing to protect the site.

POLICE ARE INVESTIGATING the shooting of an osprey - one of Britain's rarest birds of prey.

Although not killed, the fish-eating predator was brought down by gunfire and badly hurt in Lincolnshire.

Officers from the Lincolnshire force are currently trying to ascertain whether the bird was hit by shotgun or airgun to give them a clue as to who the culprit might be.

The osprey was found in the North Scarle area of the county, close to the Nottinghamshire border, and has been taken into a Lincoln-based wildlife hospital.

RSPB spokesman Grahame Madge said:"The osprey is one of our most charismatic birds of prey. This bird was heavily persecuted and was extinct in Britain for several decades until it recolonised here in 1954.

"It is ironic then that in the year bird lovers are celebrating the 50th anniversary of its return, we are again reminded of the osprey's continued vulnerability."

HEDGEHOGS ARE TO be given 'asylum' in England from Scottish cull teams as part of a scientific study.

Two dozen of the prickly mammals will be saved from death in the Western Isles and transported to Bristol University.

There, boffins will assess whether the animals can thrive in a new environment.

Professor Stephen Harris, of Bristol University, explained:"We will be assessing the animals' health and general condition as well as any impact they may have on the local hedgehog population."

Scottish National Heritage and the RSPB want to cull the 5,000 hedgehogs on the Western Isles because they eat the eggs and young of vulnerable native birds.

However, animal rights protesters have been saving the hedgehogs - even paying £20 for every one handed to them.

DETECTIVE WORK BY bird experts has traced the origins of two rare white storks currently nesting near Wakefield, in West Yorkshire.

If the pair are successful, it will be the first time white storks have bred in Britain since 1416.

"Both of these birds are ringed, and one even has a coloured leg ring to aid recognition," said a spokesman for the British Trust for Ornithology.

"The female of the pair has a French ring and the male has a Belgian ring.

"The female was originally found in poor condition in Calais in September 2002 and taken into care.

"After its recovery five months later, it was then ringed and released near Lille in northern France.

"The male also has a slightly odd history. It was originally caught as a free-flying bird at an animal park at Mechelen in Belgium in April 2002.

"When caught it was wearing a blue 'chicken ring' so was presumed to be an escaped bird, but of unknown origin.

"Bizarrely, this isn't the first we've heard of this bird, as it was seen at Alton Water in Suffolk in April 2003 with an unringed bird. Maybe it was already looking to set up home.

"So although neither of these birds are part of an official reintroduction scheme, their histories are both rather chequered."

ILLEGAL HARE COURSING is proving a major headache for farmers in East Anglia where many have been threatened and even attacked by gangs of coursers.

The NFU says it surveyed more than 100 of its members across the region to identify the scale of the problem and find possible solutions.

Some farmers feel the situation is getting out of control with aggressive groups of up to 50 men coming onto their land with dogs.

More than half of respondents said they had been threatened or attacked by illegal hare coursers.

One Suffolk farmer said:"Two hare coursers were approached by myself about a week before about 40 turned up. They offered a bottle of wine for permission to course hares. I told them to go. I think they were preparing for the big meet a week later. I received threatening phone calls for a week after this, mainly aimed at my wife."

A Cambridgeshire farmer said:"My mother was walking our dogs up a private track. The dogs noticed the coursers in a field next to it and barked at them. The coursers then came towards my mother threatening to kill her and the dogs. She was forced to run away."

Other incidents include: a farmer's son beaten up, needing hospital treatment; an air rifle fired through a farmyard while a farmer's 11-year-old daughter was fetching in their horses; an arson attack on a farm; and coursers who tried to run over a farmer in their car.

The NFU wants to see the law toughened up to make it easier for police to act against illegal hare coursers, backed by harsher penalties for transgressors.

THE PLIGHT OF seven ducklings brought part of a South Wales town to a standstill.

The birds were spotted struggling in a river at Pontarddulais near Swansea after becoming separated from their mother.

With little chance of survival by themselves, a horrified crowd gathered but no-one knew what to do. Then local man Clive Hedges plunged in and waded out to the distressed birds.

Mr Hedges, a former RSPCA worker, managed to gather up the youngsters and take them to safety.

A BLITZ ON angling licence evaders netted over 100 cheats in a crackdown across the North West.

Environment Agency enforcement officers found 126 licence evaders during initial checks at fishing spots across the region.

Rod licences were due for renewal on April 1 and to enforce the regulations the Agency has appointed extra staff specifically to catch cheats.

NESTING PEREGRINE FALCONS had a lucky escape when guards chased away a mystery man carrying a high-powered rifle near their Peak District nest.

The man, wearing camouflage gear, was spotted by off-duty policemen on a round-the-clock watch over nests in the Upper Derwent Valley.

Sgt Alan Firth, South Yorkshire Police wildlife crime officer, said:"We scrambled up the crag towards the nest of a peregrine and watched the man through binoculars for 10 minutes or more.

"We couldn't find any reason for him being there and as soon as he saw us, he ran off over the moor and we were unable to catch up with him. We can only assume he was there to shoot the nesting peregrine.

"In the Upper Derwent Valley, birds of prey such as goshawks and peregrines have been repeatedly persecuted in recent years. In the last two years alone, ravens in the same area have failed to produce chicks and we strongly suspect this was down to human interference.

"Sadly, some people still see birds of prey as a threat and others try to illegally exploit them. However, through schemes like Peak Nestwatch we are determined to beat these criminals and wipe out their illegal activities."

Following the incident, police officers are now reviewing their tactics and stepping up protection efforts.

A FAMILY OF robins was destroyed by an Avon garden centre firm in a move which has outraged the RSPCA.

Although the Wyevale Garden Centre acted legally by obtaining a proper licence, the animal charity has condemned the action.

The robins had set up home in the Milton Heath garden centre's restaurant, causing a health hazard as they fed their two chicks where food was prepared and eaten.

A Wyevale spokesman said:"The company's health and safety officer brought in a pest control firm and a licence to destroy the robins was obtained from DEFRA. The nest was taken from the site and the birds shot."

However, one adult robin is thought to have escaped.

BRITISH FOODIES ARE said to be salivating at the prospect of a fresh crop of their so-called 'arrows of desire' - asparagus.

The NFU says:"The next few weeks are very dear to the hearts of food lovers all over Britain.

"May and June are the growing season for delicious British asparagus, regarded by foodies as the very best in the world.

"The British climate provides the ideal growing conditions for cultivating the most delicious, tender and sweet asparagus, helped by the fact that it can be distributed from the field to the plate in a matter of hours, preserving all the freshness and flavour."

Some people might not know that asparagus had a long history in Europe, he added.

"Asparagus is native to the northern Mediterranean and was as prized by the Greeks and Romans as it is by food lovers today.

"Initially, the Greeks and Romans harvested wild asparagus, the Romans even sending out fleets of ships to get it."

EFFORTS ARE BEING stepped up to save one of Britain's rarest trees - the black poplar.

Conservationists need to work closely with river managers and flood engineers to give the trees a chance, according to new research.

'Conservation of Black Poplar' - the Forestry Commission's booklet on preserving this elegant tree - reveals that numbers have dwindled to less than 7,000.

Author Joan Cottrell said:"The appearance of black poplars in the background of several of Constable's paintings is testament to the fact that this was once a common tree along the natural floodplain forests which lined the riverbanks in southern Britain.

"During the 17th and 18th Centuries, poplar timber was much in demand. Its fire resistance made it popular for flooring near fireplaces, and its shock absorbing qualities made it an ideal choice for rifle butts, wagon bottoms and brake blocks.

"However, canalisation of rivers and the drainage of fields has removed the natural habitat of these trees and as a result its numbers have dropped dramatically."

Since many of the remaining black poplars had been derived from cuttings, the number of different individuals was low, she added.

Females are now particularly rare because cuttings tended to be taken from male trees, the report explains.

This is because males do not produce seed fluff which is considered unsightly by some.

Only about 600 female trees are now believed to remain.

A MALE SWAN has sparked fears among pet owners in Nottinghamshire after apparently drowning two dogs.

The bird has been reacting furiously in defence of its mate and cygnets at a pond in Warsop.

But initially, when one dog swimming at the pond drowned, most believed it to be an accident.

Then witness George Kennedy saw the second dog - a springer spaniel - being viciously attacked and drowned by the swan.

As the dog paddled towards the young birds, the adult male swan rushed at it, battered it with its wings, then dragged it under the water to its doom, leaving its owner distraught.

Mr Kennedy said:"The dog didn't stand a chance."

EELS AND BROWN trout made up the larger part of hundreds of fish killed by a pollution spill involving a Welsh river.

The Environment Agency said the incident on the River Lliedi at Llanelli was serious and mounted an emergency clean-up operation .

"An incident room was opened to co-ordinate our response and staff were sent to investigate," said a spokesman.

SNIPE DECREASED FASTER than any other species of wading bird between 1982 and 2002, according to a national survey.

The 'Breeding Waders of Wet Meadows' survey found a loss of 61 per cent of the snipe population in lowland England and Wales.

"Declines were particularly steep (more than 90 per cent) in the East Midlands, West Midlands and south east England," said a British Trust for Ornithology spokesman.

"In 1982, snipe was the third most numerous species of wader on lowland grassland but by 2002 oystercatcher and avocet outnumbered it.

"The populations that remain in the lowland are now concentrated onto a few key sites, such as the Ouse and Nene Washes and the Lower Derwent Valley. Three per cent of sites surveyed held 90 per cent of the snipe population.

"Oystercatchers have been expanding their range inland over recent decades. Overall, 973 pairs were located in 2003, representing a population increase of 52 per cent.

"One reason for the increases in oystercatcher numbers is that they are adaptable birds, able to feed in a wide range of habitats.

"Lapwings are still the most widespread wader on lowland wet grassland but are now scarce in Wales and south western England.

"Although still found on almost half of sites surveyed, there was a large drop in numbers between 1982 and 2002. The largest populations of lapwings on lowland wet grassland are on the Norfolk Broads and North Kent Marshes."

A COUNTRY MAGAZINE has identified what it believes to be the 10 most beautiful British landscapes under threat from windfarm development using dozens of 300ft turbines.

Country Life's threatened landscapes are found at: Ramsbury, Wiltshire; Bradworthy, North Devon; Saddleworth Moor, Lancashire; Romney Marsh, Kent; Whinash, Cumbria; Burton Latimer, Northampton-shire; Parham, Suffolk; Knabs Ridge, North Yorkshire; Pentre Tump, Radnor Forest, Powys; and Loch Ness, Scottish Highlands.

RARE STONE-CURLEWS will continue to enjoy maximum protection at a wildlife site after the Court of Appeal upheld the location's present status.

The 13,000 hectare Breckland Farmland SSSI lies between Bury St Edmunds in Suffolk and Swaffham in Norfolk and supports almost half the breeding stone-curlews in Britain.

The Honourable Patrick Fisher of Kilverstone Hall, near Thetford, had legally challenged English Nature's decision to confirm the site's SSSI notification.

He argued that, although he agreed the land should be recognised as internationally important for its wildlife, it did not need to be an SSSI.

He also argued that the SSSI status imposed unnecessary and disproportionate restrictions that contravened the European Convention on Human Rights.

However, the Court of Appeal has upheld an original judicial review decision which backed the legality of English Nature's view that the land is of special interest and should be notified.

Dr Andy Clements, English Nature's director for designated sites, said:"We are delighted that our scientific opinion has been upheld again following a rigorous legal test.This is good for stone-curlews."

GREAT TIT: nesting birds spark embarrassing encounter

BIGGER and tougher than the blue tit, the great tit is reputed to be the hard man of the entire tit family in this country.

Its strong beak and aggressive manner often puts other birds to flight and there is evidence of great tits killing and eating smaller birds, including the tiny goldcrest.

However, like its perky, more peaceful cousin, the great tit normally restricts its menu to caterpillars, insects, seeds and fruit.

The great tit also expends a similar amount of time and energy collecting food.

It is just as inventive, too, when it comes to exploiting human resources and can easily break into milk bottles to steal the cream.

Dramatic black and yellow colouring visibly sets it apart from the blue tit, as does its size - about 3cms longer at 14cms.

But it is generally found in the same environment and is almost as acrobatic.

Not too long ago, a survey of British birds put the great tit in seventh place out of the 20 most common garden visitors.

Unlike some species, it is not too difficult to tell the two sexes apart. The male great tit sports a bold, unbroken black band along the length of his bright yellow belly.

The female has less black there and also a less glossy black cap.

The male takes hardly any part in the nest building process, leaving the job almost completely to his partner.

But he will loyally feed her while she lays and incubates their red-spotted white eggs.

Some years back, I was lucky enough to stumble upon a sizeable colony of great tits living in woods at the back of a house myself and my wife had rented. Unfortunately, their presence led to one of the most embarrassing episodes of my life.

Two of the great tits began nesting under the eaves of a nearby house and I was naively following their progress one day with binoculars.

All at once, I found myself confronted by the angry face of the formidable spinster who lived at the property.

After glaring at me from a bedroom window, she drew the curtains shut in a very emphatic manner.

The meaning was obvious.

Oh no ! How should I smooth things over ? Go round and apologise ? (*"Sorry, madam, I was just observing those lovely...er..."*)

I half-expected PC Plod to come round and seize the binoculars as evidence of my heinous crime.

In the event, nothing happened but it was a stark lesson in the inherent risk of using binoculars near other houses.

Worse discomfort was to follow.

A few days later, I realised I was standing behind this lady in the local newsagents.

For a few seconds, I wracked my brain as to how I could jocularly explain my impertinence.

(*"Madam, how lucky you are to have those...er...nesting cosily under your...er..."*)

It was no use.

I kept my mouth shut.

Perhaps if the birds in question had been some other species I might have stood a chance.

Spotting my blushes, she sniffed haughtily before using her 15-stone bulk to bulldoze a path through me and about three other customers.

Did I imagine it or was there a half-smile playing around the red-painted lips in that lantern jaw of hers as she marched away ?

I will never know for sure.

In any case, I did not dare look at those particular great tits again.

PRO-HUNT SUPPORTERS are in hot water over "misleading" advertising claims about how many people want to keep foxhunting.

The Advertising Standards Authority accepts that a poll commissioned by the Countryside Alliance does show there is no majority of public opinion for a total ban on hunting.

However, it has also attacked the Alliance for using advertisements with the phrase '59 per cent say keep hunting', claiming that such an interpretation of the poll results on which the advert was based may be misleading.

Alliance spokesman Darren Hughes said:"The ASA, like most objective observers, has accepted that there is no majority of public opinion for a total ban on hunting. This has been shown by every poll carried out since December 2000 offering the Government's three options for resolving the hunting issue: a ban, regulation or keeping the status quo.

"The Alliance disagrees with the ASA's adjudication, which is based on the rather strange logic that someone who supports the continuation of an activity under regulation could actually want a significant 'partial ban', and has appealed against it. Angling, for instance, is regulated through closed seasons and rod licences but no-one is talking about banning it.

"We will continue to use the poll on which the advert was based to show that 59 per cent of the population don't want a ban on hunting."

The League Against Cruel Sports said:"The League, IFAW and the RSPCA commissioned a poll last November which clearly spelt out the facts - 76 per cent of the population want hunting with dogs to be made illegal."

Nevertheless, their own poll has also been criticised for its findings.

GREY PARTRIDGES APPEAR to be fighting back after numbers plummeted.

According to the Game Conservancy Trust, the bird owes much of its resurgence to careful management of its habitat.

A decade into the 20th Century, it was estimated that the country played host to a million pairs of breeding grey partridges.

But modern farming methods saw numbers slump to about 70,000 breeding pairs.

However, numbers are rising again and the Trust says a pilot conservation scheme in Hertfordshire led the way to achieving this.

Now, by leaving wild edges to cultivated fields, and creating rough patches where the birds can forage, landowners know they can provide the right conditions for partridges to thrive.

GREEDY DEVELOPERS SHOULD not be allowed to carve up the countryside because of New Labour's meddling with planning laws, campaigners say.

Nigel Kersey, spokesman for the Council for the Protection of Rural England, called for sensitivity to countryside and wildife if massive Thames Gateway development goes ahead.

"The Thames Gateway project should not be allowed to become a Trojan horse for developers greedily hoping for a greenfield feast," he said.

"That would damage or destroy fragile habitats, landscapes, and designated Green Belt land. It would also undermine the Government's principal objectives for urban regeneration in the area.

"Given the Mayor of London's welcome aspirations to accommodate 120,000 new dwellings on brownfield sites in the London part of the Gateway alone, there can be no excuse for allowing greenfield growth anywhere in the Thames Gateway for the foreseeable future.

"The Thames Gateway offers unprecedented opportunity to help meet housing needs and relieve the pressure for urban expansion on green fields across south eastern England.

"We support the Government's broad objectives, but - despite the rhetoric - the policy tools required to deliver the Government's Sustainable Communities objectives are missing."

PEREGRINE FALCONS SPOILED the party when Shropshire birdwatchers drew up plans to study them - by flying away.

A project to observe a pair of birds at Clee Hill had to be scrapped when the falcons left the area after failing to mate and raise chicks.

RSPB spokesman Daniel Farber said: "Peregrines have nested successfully at Clee Hill for 10 years. This year there was a younger male peregrine and it may not have been mature enough to mate. But the pair appear to be setting up a bond and we believe they will nest next year."

SALMON AND SEA trout will soon find it easier to navigate a Welsh river after work started on a fish pass.

The pass is being built at Bontuchel Weir on the Afon Clywedog, near Ruthin, Denbighshire with the Environment Agency saying the £250,000 project will bring major environmental improvements.

Work is due to be completed in August, if weather conditions are favourable.

At five metres high, the weir, constructed over 100 years ago, currently forms an impassable barrier to migrating salmon and sea trout, preventing them from reaching 12 miles upstream.

The new pass will consist of two separate structures - a downstream pool and weir pass, and an upstream ladder.

Julian Bray, sustainable fisheries project manager for the Agency, said:"By improving the upstream access for migratory fish we will be making real environmental improvements which should benefit not only the fish stocks but also the communities and economy of the Afon Clwyd catchment. The improvements should attract visitors to the area, to fish or just to enjoy the natural environment."

PIRANHA FISH FOUND in a pond near Manchester have prompted a stern warning from the Environment Agency.

The Agency said fines of up to £2,500 could be issued after two dead piranhas were discovered at a popular fishing spot in Middleton by a local angler.

The tropical fish were netted by Mark Ward at the Rhodes Lodges pond while he was fishing there with friends.

Fisheries enforcement officers were alerted and attended the scene shortly afterwards.

They established that the two piranhas had been introduced to the water illegally and that the fish died from exposure in an environment far too cold for them to survive.

Bernie Chappel, the Agency specialist who attended the scene, said:"Putting tropical fish into lakes and ponds is not only illegal but extremely cruel. The water would have been far too cold and the fish would have suffered a slow death.

"Introducing non-native species of fish, even goldfish, into UK waters without advance authorisation from the Environment Agency is against the law and can cause damage to our own natural fish stocks. Anyone found guilty of such activity can be fined up to £2,500."

Darren Bedworth, the Agency's regional enforcement officer, added that his team regarded the incident as an extremely serious offence.

He said:"We would ask anyone who has information concerning where the fish originated from to contact us."

BADGERS ARE BEING locked out of their sett in Somerset in a bid to force them to move elsewhere.

Gates are being fitted to badger holes as a means of forcibly evicting the creatures which are standing in the way of repairs to a vital traffic bridge.

Hutton Moor bridge was originally closed because of damage caused by a burst water main.

But motorists - already fuming at the delay in reopening the route - have been told they face further weeks of waiting until badgers have left a local sett and the work can commence.

In the meantime, gates are being fitted to badger holes one by one in the hope that the burrowers will get the message and move on voluntarily.

However, birds nesting in the area are another problem delaying the start of bridge rebuilding.

North Somerset Council spokesman Richard Turner explained:"We haven't got any choice. This has all to be done under the Wildlife and Countryside Act."

SPOTTED FLYCATCHERS, SONG thrushes and other threatened birds owe much of their survival to wildlife friendly gardens, a report reveals.

Research by the British Trust for Ornithology has found that gardeners really make a difference by giving species under pressure a chance.

Britain's gardens now spread over an area more than double the size of all the country's nature reserves.

Blue tits were found to be the top nesters in domestic settings.

Richard Bland, one of the report's authors, said:"If all of the gardens in Britain were as bird-friendly as those surveyed, the total number of pairs of birds that would be nesting nationwide could be 30 million.

"That's not bad when national surveys have shown there are only some 60 million pairs of birds in Britain."

NOISY HOUNDS LED a hunt to court and resulted in a judge's decision that could have serious implications for other hunt groups.

The Isle of Wight Hunt may now have to shut after District Judge John Willard, sitting at Isle of Wight Magistrates Court, Newport, upheld a noise abatement order on the pack.

Neighbours had claimed they were unable to sleep because of baying hounds and investigating council officers said the noise was horrendous.

Following the case, Andrew Sallis, Master of the hunt, and Ronald Holland, its chairman, said they were worried that anti-hunt protesters might now use the ruling to challenge other packs nationwide.

Judge Willard rejected claims that the two neighbours, who run guesthouses, were being malicious or over sensitive about noise from the kennels.

A GOLDEN EAGLE chick owes its existence to the appliance of science after becoming the first bred from frozen sperm.

Scottish scientists have set a new benchmark on such experiments after three-week-old Crystal was produced.

The success of the project could revolutionise conservation of threatened bird species all over the world.

Dr Graham Wishart, from the University of Abertay in Dundee, said the scheme promises to overcome many problems inherent in breeding such birds in captivity by more natural methods.

WATER VOLES AND even an otter are being increasingly attracted to a spruced up Staffordshire waterway.

Endangered water voles appear to be increasing their numbers on the Wom Brook in Wombourne while local conservationists have also discovered an otter is out and about there.

Kate Dewey, co-ordinator of the Wom Brook Water Vole Project run by Staffordshire Wildlife Trust, said that hard work is paying off.

"We have seen lots of signs of water voles, including burrows and droppings, and even spotted a young water vole," she said.

But what had really surprised volunteers was the discovery that an otter had been active right in the centre of their village.

"We knew that otters were present downstream but never thought they would venture up into the village," said Kate.

BUMBLEBEES NEED A boost so get busy in your garden, say The Wildlife Trusts.

Expert Sue Tatman said:"Bumblebees are fascinating visitors to any garden. Their gentle buzz typifies a summer afternoon. They help to pollinate garden flowers and fruit, and almost never sting.

"Bumblebees form small colonies, much smaller than those of honey bees, and will often build their nest in a garden. They will choose a sheltered site, often using old mouse nests in underground burrows.

"The most important factors for a bumblebee nest is it must be dry, in a sheltered location, and as a bonus warmed by the sun. To encourage them, make an artificial nest site by burying a medium sized clay flowerpot in the ground in a sunny border.

"Use a short piece of pipe (old hose pipe will do) to make an access tunnel. Put some nesting material inside - bits of dry grass, moss, material from an abandoned bird's nest or bedding for small rodent pets. Don't use cotton wool as this can get caught up in bees' feet. You can build more elaborate boxes from wood, which will be better insulated, but remember to put it in a warm dry site, and sheltered from prying eyes - bees like their privacy.

"Bumblebees are in decline in the wider countryside so any help we can give them is valuable. To provide them with food all summer long, grow a variety of nectar-rich flowers, preferably in sunny, sheltered spots.

"Many of the old-fashioned cottage garden flowers such as hollyhocks, rosemary and daisies are favoured by bumblebees. They also appreciate heather, fruit tree blossom, many flowering herbs and wildflowers.

"Some bumblebees have long tongues so can easily reach the nectar in deep flowers such as clover, knapweed and thistles.

"Others are strong enough to push right inside the closed flowers of snapdragons. In my own garden, foxgloves are a particular favourite, with the bees disappearing right inside each bell-shaped flower in turn."

SHEEP GET STUCK on their backs more often in summer, a Northamptonshire farmer says.

In an NFU seasonal farming article, Trevor Foss writes:"The very warm, dry weather has caused us a few problems back at Hawtoft. Sheep get cast, or stuck on their backs, at any time, but in a hot spell with all their wool on it is far more common. This has meant shepherding twice a day to tip upright any ewe that is lying on its back unable to get up."

BUZZARDS ARE PROVING hazardous to a particularly vulnerable section of human society - hang-glider enthusiasts.

Although the birds' attacks on cyclists and walkers have been well documented, the danger they pose to hang-glider and paraglider fans has just been revealed.

In a letter to The Times, Shropshire man Tim Dunn said:"As a hang-glider pilot, I frequently fly in the company of buzzards, often no more than 10ft from a wing tip.

"They provide excellent markers for thermals, the answer to the unpowered pilot's prayer. I personally have found them inquisitive in the air but never more than that.

"However, other members of our club have been attacked, notably in 2002, the year following the foot-and-mouth outbreak which prevented us from flying.

"Both hang-glider and paraglider wings were attacked while flying, with a 12in tear in one paraglider. On one occasion, a buzzard followed a paraglider pilot down to a valley field and attacked him after he had deflated his wing and removed his helmet.

"I assume the sense of territory or potential threat was strengthened by the lack of human activity on the moors the previous year.

"Perhaps cyclists could take some comfort from having less far to fall."

A SEAL COLONY in a Scottish loch is reported to be under threat from a mystery gunman.

A second common seal in the Loch Etive colony, within North Argyll, has been found killed by a clean shot to the head.

The first seal shot in the loch was discovered washed up on the shore a few months ago.

Both animals appear to have been killed by a high-velocity rifle with the point of entry behind the ear.

In neither case were there any indications that the seals had been caught up in nets before being shot.

The SSPCA is concerned as the loch seal colony is small, quite isolated from other seals, and its future could soon be put in doubt by further killings.

BLACK GROUSE ARE staging a revival in northern England after becoming one of Britain's most threatened birds.

Farmers and landowners had joined forces with conservationists in the region to try to help the bird with their joint efforts now bearing results.

Phil Warren, spokesman for the English Black Grouse Recovery Project, said:"Counts of displaying males this spring showed a 30 per cent increase in numbers since 1998.

"In 1998, the population was estimated at just 773 males, which was below the Government's Biodiversity Action Plan target of 800 lekking males in England. From our latest count figures we estimate the population is now closer to a thousand males.

"This latest increase is very encouraging and means we are meeting the first objective of our plan which is to stem the decline of black grouse. Our next objective is to increase the population and its range.

"To achieve this, we have been targeting our advisory efforts to the southern fringe of the birds' range in North Yorkshire and to the north in Northumberland. In Northumberland we are developing an application for lottery funding and hope to achieve a target of £3million to fund the project."

OVER A THOUSAND fish were wiped out when a Northumberland river was hit by pollution.

Hundreds of trout were killed after a mystery pollutant entered the River Gaunless downstream of South Church.

Investigators found that the pollution stretched for more than two kilometres to where the Gaunless meets the River Wear.

Conservative estimates indicate that at least 500 trout and 500 other coarse fish died as a result of the incident.

Environment Agency spokesman Ian Preston said:"We are investigating this serious incident with a view to prosecuting the offenders.

"We do currently have some leads and will be following these up in the next few days. Unfortunately, due to the confines of the legal process, we can't elaborate any more at this time."

Polluting a watercourse is an offence under the Water Resources Act 1991 and can result in a fine of up to £20,000 and prison sentence of three months if dealt with by magistrates.

However, the fine is unlimited in a crown court case and the sentence may be two years.

SKYLARKS COULD BE helped by farmers leaving patches of cereal fields unsown, a study has found.

The birds' breeding success rocketed by almost 50 per cent when areas were left fallow, researchers learnt.

Because the little birds have been among the worst hit by intensive agricultural methods, Government subsidies may soon be offered so that farmers don't plant crops over entire fields.

Experts believe that leaving two small patches bare per hectare could reverse a massive drop in skylark numbers over the last 30 years.

Environment Minister Elliot Morley said:"I hope farmers across the country will make the most of (unsown) patches so skylarks will once again become a common sight on British farmland."

RAMBLERS ARE GEARING up to celebrate National Parks Week in July with a series of walks.

The importance of the nation's parks will be recognised from July 1 to 9 with the Ramblers Association organising several treks across them.

"The week is intended to raise awareness of the unique qualities our national parks have to offer," said an Association spokesman.

"Our parks contain a mosaic of rich landscapes, including sweeping heather moorlands, dramatic coastlines, stunning upland and mountainous areas that are worthy of celebration.

"The Ramblers Association was hugely influential in the formation of national parks, working alongside other environmental and heritage groups to ensure legislation was passed to protect these wonderful landscapes."

TERN CHICKS HAVE proved the wisdom of floating rafts being installed at a Hertfordshire nature reserve.

Three chicks were hatched on the rafts at Wilstone Reservoir Nature Reserve near Tring.

Although terns regularly hunt fish and feed at the reservoir, they have not bred there for 10 years because of a lack of suitable nesting sites.

The birds normally nest on beaches but now the rafts fill that gap, acting as floating 'mini-beaches' and helping to keep eggs and chicks safe from hungry predators such as foxes, mink and magpies.

Judy Adams, chief executive of the Herts and Middlesex Wildlife Trust, said:"This is the Trust's 40th anniversary so it is wonderful to have little, but significant, successes like this to celebrate.

"Projects like this prove that wildlife is often quite quick to capitalise on opportunities put before it and this is always very encouraging for the people and organisations who have worked hard to make it happen. It really proves that we can all make a difference."

John Taylor, spokesman for Friends of Tring Reservoirs, added:"The work of building and launching the rafts was very much a joint effort and it is extremely rewarding for everyone involved to see their dedication transformed into new life."

BEES HAVE BEEN swarming up and down the country as the hot weather heats up the countryside.

Among human 'victims' of the activity was a schoolgirl who came back from a shopping trip to find her bicycle covered in 12,000 bees at Petersfield, Hampshire.

Alice Gilmore, aged 12, was horrified to find the bees clustering round her bike's handlebars and saddle.

Bee experts called in to remove the swarm believe it may have been caused by the insects' queen pausing to rest on the bike.

ORGANIC FOOD AND crafts will be celebrated all over the country in early September, it has been revealed.

From the 4th to the 9th of the month, 'Organic Week' aims to introduce the advantages of organic food and materials nationwide at a packed programme of events.

Highlights include: organic 'family fun' promised at Arlingham, Gloucester, where the workings of an organic dairy farm can also be explored; free entry to Sedlescombe Organic Vineyard in East Sussex; organic skin care advice from Neal's Yard Natural Remedies, Norwich; and on the isle of Mull, visitors to a local farm will be shown a weaving mill where the wool of the farm's own Hebridean sheep is woven.

"The last year saw a resurgence in sales of local organic food," said a spokesman for the Soil Association."Many members of the British public downed their supermarket basket in favour of a box of fresh seasonal produce delivered direct from the farm.

"What is great is that it seems there is still tremendous potential for future growth in local sales.

"But being local and organic is not enough. Businesses supplying local markets must be highly professional in their growing, marketing and customer service in order to be successful."

REMOVAL OF DEADLY deer fencing is one of the measures thought to be behind the resurgence of threatened capercaillie in Scotland.

The turkey-sized birds were judged the most likely British birds to become extinct before conservationists launched a series of efforts to save them.

Among these was removal or marking of 300 kilometres of hazardous deer fencing.

The fencing had proved a serious obstacle to the birds over the years with many capercaillie found dead after colliding with it.

Other helpful measures included habitat management and predator control - and the work appears to be paying off.

A survey carried out by RSPB Scotland and Scottish Natural Heritage, with support from Forestry Commission Scotland, has revealed that there are now an estimated 2,000 capercaillie, as compared to just 1,000 in a 1999 census.

Kenny Kortland, capercaillie project officer, said:"This very positive result can be attributed to the huge effort made by many public and private forest managers in recent years to save this species. The level of co-operation has been tremendous and should be a model for other projects."

John Markland, chairman of Scottish Natural Heritage, added:"Although it is too early to know if we are likely to see a longer term recovery in numbers, this survey is certainly very good news for the capercaillie and conservation in Scotland."

AN EGG THIEF is risking serious injury or even death after repeatedly targeting a Scottish ostrich farm.

For over a year, the human culprit has been launching noctural forays at Parkhead Farm, in Maryculter, Aberdeenshire, scaling a fence to get at the eggs.

Several of the huge, 7lb eggs were taken last year and five more eggs have already vanished this year.

But farmer John Skinner says the thief is riding his luck to the limit and any one of the field's nine occupants could launch a sudden, ferocious attack.

He said:"What this person doesn't know is that they are putting themselves at serious risk. An ostrich kicks forward and will aim for the stomach or ribs.

"They have a great big talon at the front of their feet which is very sharp and hard and can burst the stomach.

"There comes a stage when you have to say enough is enough. Whoever is doing this probably thinks they are being very smart but they haven't got a clue of the danger they are in. These animals have to be respected and it needs to stop before someone gets hurt."

ALBINO BIRDS MAY be more common than first thought and are the subject of the latest quest for information by bird experts.

Partial and full albinos are often seen visiting gardens and now the British Trust for Ornithology wants to build up a clearer national picture.

Mike Toms, the Trust's Garden BirdWatch organiser, said:"We sometimes get sent photographs of, or letters about, birds with unusual plumage. Many of these birds have white feathers in place of more normally coloured ones and so look very different.

"Most of the reports we receive refer to blackbirds, house sparrows, jackdaws and crows but albinism has been recorded in many other species over the years.

"We'd really like to know what sort of species are showing this type of plumage abnormality at the moment and where in the country these birds are being seen."

The Trust says that albinos probably lose out to birds showing normal colouration.

They may find it difficult to attract a mate because they look different, are more obvious to potential predators, and also tend to suffer from poor health.

A RAMPAGING BULL was shot dead by police after fleeing a livestock market in Shropshire.

The enraged animal went on the run in Shrewsbury and police were called in amid concerns it may hurt or even kill a passer-by.

Trains also had to be stopped as the bull careered near local lines during the hour-long drama.

A Shropshire police spokesman said:"It had been rampaging around and causing problems. It kept running in and out of residential areas and streets.

"A police marksman brought the bull down. It wasn't that far from a railway line and two trains had to be held back. It also buffeted several cars and was clearly in a panic."

Local residents, especially children, were thought to be at serious risk so a decision was taken to kill the animal.

PLANS TO BUILD hundreds of thousands of new homes across England will damage the environment and promote more global warming, the Government has been warned.

Philip Sellwood, chief executive of the official Energy Savings Trust, has attacked any notion that the present scheme can be environmentally friendly.

Deputy Prime Minister John Prescott horrified countryside campaigners when he unveiled highly controversial plans to concrete over much of southern England.

His £22billion programme for 'sustainable communities', includes house building in the Thames Gateway east of London; down the London-Stansted-Cambridge corridor; in Kent; and in Milton Keynes.

Mr Sellwood said:"To build this number of homes will have a serious impact on the environment, which the Government should be trying to offset by implementing and then enforcing some much higher environmental standards."

He added that Mr Prescott's project could make the Government's targets for reducing emissions of carbon dioxide "very, very difficult to achieve indeed."

410

MORE PET FISH than ever are being released into the wild with devastating results for native British fish, it has been revealed.

Ponds, lakes and rivers appear to be at increasing risk from ornamental fish owners whose pets have outgrown their tanks.

After a spate of native fish deaths in the Midlands, owners of pet fish are being warned by the Environment Agency not to release them into the wild.

"Ornamental fish from home tanks or ponds can harbour diseases that can devastate wild populations," explained an Agency spokesman.

"Domestic fish can develop a degree of resistance but once released into a pond or stream, they can infect wild fish.

"Infections such as these kill fish or leave them vulnerable to natural changes in their environment that a healthy fish might overcome.

"If too many fish are put into a pond the fish will also suffer due to the competition amongst themselves.

"The pet fish itself will have a poor chance of survival in the wild where it has to find food and avoid predators.

"In addition, it is against the law for anyone to introduce any fish into the wild without prior written consent from the Environment Agency."

The Agency's fisheries team leader Al Watson added:"People may believe that this is a kind way of dealing with fish that they can no longer provide a home for, but that isn't the case.

"It isn't kind to the fish itself, or other fish already living in the wild.

"If you have a pet fish that has outgrown its tank or pond, or that you can no longer look after, get some advice from a pet shop or a vet that specialises in fish.

"Don't just release it into the nearest pond or watercourse."

SEABIRDS OFF Britain's coasts are struggling to find enough small fish to feed their young, researchers have learnt.

Scientists believe a drop in small fish numbers could have a devastating effect on numbers of chicks which fledge this year.

Even the fish themselves are becoming smaller, something being blamed on a fall in plankton stocks as water temperature rises.

A study of bird populations on islands like the Shetlands has found that kittiwake numbers have halved in the past five years.

And with small fish such as sand eels getting scarcer, species like puffins and guillemots may also face a serious slump.

A WALLABY FOUND dead on the remote western Scottish island of Islay has sparked a mystery of how it came to be there.

The animal was discovered near the island's airport and is thought to have been killed by a car.

But how long it had been living wild in the area no-one knows.

Some believe it may have swum all the way through treacherous seas to get there - but not from its native Australia.

A colony of wallabies is based around Loch Lomond near Glasgow on the mainland but SSPCA spokeswoman Doreen Graham thinks it unlikely the animal had swum so far.

"I think wallabies can swim," she said,"but it would have been a very long way for the animal to have travelled if it had come from Loch Lomond."

A BIRD STUCK up a tree had to be rescued by Bristol firefighters.

The emergency workers were summoned to help out when local falconer Paul Hand lost one of his charges.

At first, firemen were convinced the call was a wind-up but they soon realised Harry the Harris hawk was indeed stuck, after his leash became tangled in branches.

Using a ladder to scale the 50ft tree, the crew first cut away branches to reach the bird then cut off the branch it was tangled to before lowering both bird and branch to the ground.

Mr Hand said:"They thought it would be better to let me handle him so as not to stress him out too much. But he sat on my hand like nothing had happened. He wasn't stressed at all. We were more stressed than he was."

Mr Hand, who also has five other birds of prey, said he was delighted by the firemen's work.

SEAHORSES COULD BECOME a feature of British marine life again after dying out here two centuries ago, scientists believe.

The discovery of a seahorse in the Thames has been taken as proof that conditions may be improving enough for the bizarre creatures to return long-term.

The gentle, horse-headed fish are the only species where the male becomes pregnant.

Spotted near Southend-on-Sea, the 15cm seahorse was discovered by an angler living in shallow water.

It was tranported to Southend's Sealife Centre where it now shares a fish tank with two crabs.

Curator David Knapp called the find "remarkable", adding:"It suggests the cleaner water of the Thames and the recent hot weather is at last encouraging seahorses to venture back into these waters."

THE SHOOTING OF three robins in Gloucester-shire by a pest control company brought in by a Wyevale garden centre was legal and proper procedures were followed, the Government says following an investigation of the incident.

However, a report published by DEFRA makes recommendations "to encourage Wyevale garden centres to have a more forward looking approach to wildlife management and their pest control company to have a more thorough understanding of the legislation."

MISTLETOE: happily kissing under the dung branch

KISSING under the mistletoe at Christmas has been a tradition stretching back centuries but kissers are usually too preoccupied to wonder why this poisonous, parasitic shrub should symbolise peace and love.

In fact, there are several theories, some dating back to the Celtic Druids who were said to have used mistletoe's dark green leaves and sticky white berries in their ceremonies.

Two white bulls were traditionally sacrificed during a full moon in one of these rites to bring good luck to all the participants - although the bulls might have wanted their money back.

Mistletoe was thought to possess magical powers and the ability to ward off evil, making it a great healer of animosity between warring groups or individuals.

But mistletoe itself is anything but peaceful to the trees to which it attaches itself.

Unlike most shrubs, which draw their own water and nutrition from the soil, mistletoe sucks the life from any host tree after first drilling through the bark.

Although its appearance is slight and stringy compared to the tree itself, it grows fast and can live for a decade - weakening and causing the gradual decline of its host.

Oak, poplar and apple trees are particularly susceptible to attack. Mistletoe will also attach itself to birch, beech and plane trees, though the relative smoothness of their bark can defeat it.

Mistletoe is actually only partially parasitic as its leaves contain chlorophyll enabling it to photosynthesise and produce its own energy.

The name 'mistletoe' is said to spring from an ancient belief that this distinctive evergreen only grew in trees where birds left droppings. 'Mistel' is thought to be an old Anglo-Saxon word for dung while 'toe' is derived from another word to describe a twig or branch.

'Mistletoe', therefore, came to mean 'dung on a branch'. (Not the most helpful info for any partygoer trying to lure someone under a sprig during the festive season.)

Later, the development of botany led to the discovery that mistletoe could indeed be spread by seeds passed through birds' digestive systems.

So those initiators of ancient folklore were pretty observant.

Despite having a poisonous effect on humans, various birds enjoy mistletoe berries.

Mistle thrushes were apparently so named because they find them especially delicious.

The stickiness of the seeds mean they often become stuck to foraging birds' beaks before being wiped off on another tree, spreading mistletoe in a secondary way.

As a young man, I once hovered hopefully beneath a sagging sprig of mistletoe clutching a glass of wine at a party.

Beer was my usual choice in those days but this time I had decided on a more sophisticated appearance.

My luck was in.

I was soon targeted.

Unfortunately this was not by the beautiful hostess of the party but by her ugly friend.

I almost lost my front teeth as she proceeded to tear at my face.

The shock stayed with me for weeks - and put me off mistletoe for life.

THE GAME BIRD industry has been spotlighted by anti-cruelty campaigners who say birds are being raised in unacceptable conditions.

The League Against Cruel Sports claims its investigation "has exploded the myth promulgated by the shooting industry that game birds such as pheasant and partridge are an organic, free range alternative to intensively reared livestock.

"Secret filming at game farms in Suffolk, Warwickshire, Gloucestershire and West Sussex graphically illustrates the battery-like conditions in which pheasants and partridges are raised to provide target practice for punters on commercial shooting estates and to fill the demand for gamebirds in restaurants and shops.

"From day-old chicks to fully matured birds, the animals are crammed into sheds with little access to daylight, grass or outdoor exercise.

"The experience of investigators - who secured seasonal employment at a number of pheasant farms - also belies assertions that birds 'are reared by professional animal husbandry and good management in a natural environment' and that wounded birds 'are dispatched as humanely and quickly as possible'.

"The investigators witnessed numerous incidents of cruelty, including cannibalisation of weak or wounded animals, inexperienced workers taking numerous attempts to kill birds and chicks developing foot deformities as a result of encrusted faeces on their claws."

The League's chief executive Douglas Batchelor added:"Anyone who claims these poor animals are free range is a liar. Consumers have a right to reject the product of this bloody business."

THE PLIGHT OF dormice, red squirrels and water voles will be highlighted during National Mammal Week.

The event, which runs until July 11, aims to raise awareness of all British mammals but especially those that need help.

"Throughout the week, special events and activities for all the family are taking place across the country," said a Mammal Society spokesman.

These include 'Unearthing Mammals' workshops - a hands-on introduction to British mammals for children - at six venues across the UK; walking round reedbeds looking for 'Red Deer at Dusk' in Lancashire; exploring 'Mammals of the Sand Dunes' in Ceredigion; and learning about bats in 'Go Bats' at Vane in Perth and Kinross.

To celebrate its 50th anniversary this year, the Society is also launching a sponsored mammal sightings competition.

THE GOVERNMENT IS accused of standing by as two of the UK's most important wildlife sites are destroyed by commercial peat extraction.

On the second anniversary of English Nature's recommendation to designate Solway Moss and Bolton Fell Moss in Cumbria as Special Areas of Conservation, the RSPB says it is still waiting for action.

Meanwhile, each day, more and more peat is extracted and the 7,000 year-old wildlife rich bogs continue to vanish.

Andy Bunten, the RSPB's regional director, said:"I am concerned that the Government may not be taking its responsibility seriously in this case.

"The UK Government has a target for 90 per cent of materials for horticultural growing media and soil conditioners to be peat-free by 2010.

"Yet Cumbrian peat bogs earmarked as nature conservation sites of European importance are still being worked for commercial peat extraction.

"It's not too late for the Government to step in and show its commitment to saving these sites, but the clock is ticking.

"Once the peat has gone, it's gone for good and we will have lost forever not only an important wildlife habitat but also a unique and irreplaceable 'time capsule' of thousands of years of local human history."

The RSPB is urging the Government to confirm Special Protection Status on Bolton Fell Moss and Solway Moss without further delay to safeguard both sites.

THE RED KITE faces a tug-of-war over its 'nationality' after Welsh politicians proposed to claim it for themselves.

Plaid Cymru wants the spectacular, soaring bird - brought back from the edge of extinction across both England and Wales - to become the national bird for Wales.

The party's Euro MP Jill Evans said:"With the formidable current success achieved in conservation of the red kite and the increased numbers and geographical distribution of the bird across Wales, I firmly believe now is the right time to adopt the red kite as our national bird."

But the plan is not without pitfalls - rare chough and black grouse have been at the centre of equally positive conservation stories in Wales.

And English conservationists, who have had tremendous success reintroducing red kite to places like the Chilterns, are unlikely to warm to the idea.

NEW FEARS HAVE been raised for some of Britain's most loved summer flowers.

Botanical charity Plantlife International warns that arable flowers, such as buttercups and poppies, are fast declining.

Researchers are worried that several of the plants - once thought of as weeds - have slumped to the verge of extinction.

Names of such plants can be as vivid as their appearance with 'weasel's snout' and 'dwarf spurge' among the most bizarre.

Unfortunately, survival in barren agricultural landscapes is becoming harder with many flowers susceptible to farmers' herbicides.

Plantlife International wants more deep ploughing to bring back long-buried seeds, thus encouraging the return of butterflies and other wildlife.

BRITAIN NOW PLAYS host to about 19 million sheep, according to census figures.

Although the figure seems high, numbers of sheep were calculated at 40 million before foot-and-mouth struck - but how many of those were lambs destined for slaughter is not clear.

"As most people are aware, sheep are not just used for their wool," says the NFU. "Sunday's roast lamb is one obvious product that we have to thank them for. In fact, profits from lamb sales account for 90-95 per cent of sheep rearing income.

"As well as being a valuable source of food, sheep provide us with a number of bi-products including the skin - used for clothing and furnishings - and lanolin. Lanolin is sourced from the fleeces and is commonly used in the cosmetics industry.

"Sheep are also an integral part of the natural environment. They are an excellent means of improving soil fertility and have grazed on British hills and dales for generations, assisting to preserve habitats for the wildlife and plants they live alongside.

"Sheep's ability to exist in mountainous regions, where other domestic livestock cannot, provides essential employment and income to support rural communities in remote areas.

"A century or more ago, various breeds of sheep were developed in Britain for specific purposes. Many of these breeds continue to thrive. In fact, there are very few breeds of sheep in the world that are not pure English breeds or have not descended from British stock."

A 900 YEAR-old tree with a massive 27ft girth is facing the axe to make way for a new airport runway.

The ancient chestnut, which has been a natural resource for countless generations of wild creatures, is under threat at Halfpenny Green on the Shropshire border.

The tree grows on land earmarked for runway development at Wolverhampton Airport.

However, campaigners have vowed to save the tree, which they say is almost unique.

Protester Dave Giddings said:"We think there might be one of a similar size and age down in Gloucestershire but, other than that, this is the only one in the country."

Mr Giddings, chairman of WAAG (Wolverhampton Airport Action Group), believes proposed airport expansion would be a scar on the landscape.

The huge tree could vanish forever if South Staffordshire Council give airport bosses the go-ahead to bring in as many as 500,000 new passengers each year.

Many other trees would also be felled.

ANTI-HUNT MPs appear to be gearing up for a huge last gasp effort to push a new Bill banning hunting through the House of Commons - in a single day.

Ministers are reported to have bowed to pressure from MPs who want the ban in place before the next General Election.

However, with fierce opposition expected as before, it is thought the legislation could be forced through in a single day when members return after their summer break.

Using measures normally applied with emergency laws, the Government appears set to limit time taken to debate the Bill and so cut the chances of it being 'talked out'.

The 'slippery' tactics seem certain to outrage hundreds of thousands of people who want to see hunting continue.

The Countryside Alliance, which has often threatened to invoke human rights legislation, faces the prospect of the matter being settled before it can properly launch its legal defence.

However, thousands of its members have threatened a massive national campaign of civil disobedience if the sport is consigned to history by mostly Labour MPs accused of waging misguided class warfare.

Meanwhile, in a bid to boost the public profile of hunting, the Alliance is preparing to launch 'National Countryside to Town Week' on August 7 when information stands will appear in town centres across the country.

A FEMALE MALLARD was saved from death when a vet removed a fish hook from its gullet - then its 'partner' and their nine youngsters came to visit.

The duck was rescued at Marlborough in Wiltshire after swallowing the hook and attached line.

Vet Juliette Hayward first thought it might be kinder to put the duck out of its misery then decided to try to remove the hook.

The operation at the Riverside Veterinary Practice was a success and the duck was transferred to an outside pen to recover.

But staff were later amazed to find a male mallard and nine ducklings standing outside the pen beside the recovering bird.

One said:"It was dad and their ducklings. They had squeezed under a fence to reach her."

The female is expected to make a full recovery and be released soon..

WILD HORSES ARE at risk from a mystery attacker in South Wales.

An orange stuffed with scores of nails was slipped into a bucket used to feed the roaming animals near Swansea.

The RSPCA is now trying to track down the culprit amid mounting anger from locals.

The killer orange was found by pensioner Bernard Watts in the bucket he uses.

Any horse that swallowed the fruit would have died in agony.

Mr Watts said:"The horses often come to congregate in my back garden in the hot weather. I give them water to drink.

"The other day my wife saw what she thought was a ball in the bucket.

"But when I looked I was shocked to see an orange which had been spiked with 60-odd three-quarter-inch nails. It's a wicked thing to do."

DAIRY FARMERS MAY be forced out of business because of the slump in milk prices, Rural Affairs Secretary Margaret Beckett has admitted.

Mrs Beckett says she knows farm gate milk prices are below the cost of production and that controversial reforms of the Common Agricultural Policy may drive those prices even lower.

But she also claims the reforms will benefit farmers while ruling out Government help to prop up milk prices.

"We appreciate that many dairy farmers are not making enough money to sustain their businesses," she said.

"Milk prices are likely to fall further as a result of the reforms to the CAP. We expect some dairy farmers will leave the sector, accelerating the existing long-term trend. However, the reforms to the CAP also provide opportunities for the industry."

Lib-Dem rural affairs spokesman Andrew George, MP for St Ives, said the destruction of dairy farming was "almost criminal."

"The truth is the Government is happy to stand idly by and watch our desperate dairy farmers pushed beyond the edge of viability," he added.

FOUR WATER BUFFALO are helping to boost bird life at a Hertfordshire nature reserve.

The animals have been brought in to Rye Meads Nature Reserve near Hoddesdon by Herts and Middlesex Wildlife Trust.

It is hoped the move will lead to a return of breeding lapwings, redshank and snipe.

"Water buffalo have been introduced for the summer months to graze the area and control sedges and rush," explained a Trust spokesman.

"The conditions make it extremely difficult to get mowers, machinery and people onto the reserve at certain times of the year.

"Other grazing animals - like sheep and cows - do not cope as well with the ditch areas and mud scrapes. But water buffalo thrive in wet conditions and over the summer can graze the meadow to control plants that will take over if not managed.

"As a result of their work, the vegetation next spring should be suitable for ground nesting birds like snipe, redshank and lapwing. Grazing will also encourage the return of wild plants and insects, which the birds feed on."

A HERRING GULL had a lucky escape when one of its wings became tangled on a rooftop TV aerial in Devon.

The bird was spotted flapping helplessly on the aerial at Brixham before the alarm was raised.

Firemen were called in to help by the RSPCA who were unable to reach the stricken creature.

Using a hydraulic platform and protective gear to guard against the gull's frightened pecks, the firefighters managed to release it.

The bird seemed none the worse for its ordeal.

BADGER LOVERS HAVE angrily accused the Government of burying alarming new research about bovine TB in deer.

The attack, from the National Federation of Badger Groups, coincides with the publication of the NFBG's own detailed report into bovine TB in deer.

The report says that:
-Five out of the six species of deer in Britain are infected by bovine TB, with infection detected in between one per cent and 15 per cent of sampled deer.
-Researchers concluded that deer should be considered as a potential source of infection for cattle - not just badgers.
-In fallow deer, when whole carcasses were examined, the estimated prevalence of infection could be as high as 16 per cent.
-There are between 1.25 and 2.6 million wild deer in Britain, compared to around 300,000 badgers.
-Deer are particularly vulnerable to bTB infection and exhibit symptoms which mean they can be highly infectious. They also frequently share the same pasture, feed and water troughs as cattle.
-European scientists have suspected deer of transmitting bTB to cattle - and even to badgers - since 1938.
-The Government has known for more than 10 years that deer are very susceptible to bTB, but has only just begun to examine the problem. It has spent just £750,000 on the latest study, but continues to spend much of its annual £20 million bTB research budget on research involving badgers.

Dr Elaine King, chief executive of the NFBG, said:"Our investigation has uncovered what appears to be a systematic attempt by DEFRA to conceal the existence of bTB in deer and maintain the media's attention solely on badgers as a wildlife reservoir of bTB in cattle.

"Only last Friday afternoon, DEFRA slipped out a major new study of bTB in deer and other wildlife without press releasing it. This study confirms that bTB is found in a very wide range of wild animals. The authors warn that deer 'could pose a significant risk' of bTB to cattle and recommend that 'it seems prudent to consider deer as a potential, although probably localised, source of infection for cattle'.

"We know from previous experience that had this report been about badgers, DEFRA would have broadcast its results nationwide. Yet DEFRA appears to have buried this report to avoid drawing media attention to the true complexity of the bTB problem."

AN OWL AND a puppy dog are putting a new slant on Edward Lear's famous poem 'The Owl and the Pussy Cat' at a Staffordshire wildlife centre.

Yerevan, a two-month-old eagle owl and Masie, a puppy of about the same age, have become friends at Gentleshaw Wildlife Sanctuary, in Eccleshall.

So much so that the female eagle owl has been sampling Masie's biscuits while the pup has been launching itself into the air in a bid to fly.

A sanctuary spokeswoman said:"They are quite an unusual pairing and at the moment they're just about the same height but Yerevan will get quite hefty later on. There's one week between them and they're like a little team - both cause mischief."

OSPREY CHICKS DIED in a freak accident after the parent birds nested in North Wales for the first time.

Local birdwatchers were delighted when a pair of the fish-eating predators nested near Porthmadog but their joy was not to last.

The birds' nest gave way and the chicks were thrown out.

"Ospreys have been annual visitors to Wales when they are migrating to or from Africa," explained an RSPB spokesman. "But records show they have never nested there before. A pair of birds chose to nest near Porthmadog - the first time ever.

"They were seen early in the breeding season and, in co-operation with the landowners, North Wales police, Countryside Council for Wales, and local volunteers, RSPB Cymru set up a round-the-clock watch to make sure the ospreys and their eggs were kept safe.

"The ospreys incubated eggs and two chicks successfully hatched. Unfortunately, due to harsh weather conditions, the nest collapsed and, sadly, the chicks did not survive."

However, the adult birds were still in the area and could be easily observed.

Conservationists hope that any future osprey nest at the site fares better.

SKYLARK EGGS WERE saved from being crushed by the deft footwork of Northamptonshire farmer Trevor Foss.

In an article for the NFU, he revealed:"When shepherding around the farm I very nearly stepped on a skylark that flew up from under my feet.

"On closer inspection of the spot, I found hidden in the grass a wonderfully camouflaged nest containing four skylark eggs.

"The bird was singing away directly above me trying to draw my attention away from her nest. I carefully marked the spot and moved swiftly on, the sound of the skylark's voice sounding far more relaxed as it descended back down to earth."

NIGHTJAR, WOODLARK, AND Dartford warbler are three birds set to benefit from a local tree clearance project.

Over 12 acres of pine trees are being cleared at Black Park country park in the south of Buckinghamshire to create better habitat for rare birds.

Originally planted following a blaze which hit the park in 1976, the earmarked trees have declined in recent years after being badly affected by moth larvae.

The felled pines will be turned into woodchip and burned at a power station as a natural fuel.

Although the pines are being axed, other trees such as oak and birch will remain in place.

It is hoped the area will gradually turn back to heath pasture and, in time, cattle may be brought in to graze there.

FARMERS ARE URGING ramblers and other visitors to the countryside to take note of the updated Countryside Code.

"Whether you're in the countryside for a gentle stroll, relaxing picnic or a heart pumping long distance walk, the countryside provides many opportunities for enjoyment and relaxation," says the NFU.

While farmers welcomed visitors they also asked that they respect and protect the countryside as a workplace and haven for wildlife.

The new code contains a variety of advice such as:

- Plan ahead and follow signs. Make sure you find out where you are allowed to go, as from time to time public access may change or become restricted, for example during breeding seasons.

- Leave gates and property as you find them. A farmer will normally leave a gate closed to keep livestock in, but may sometimes leave a gate open so that animals can reach food and water.

- Protect plants and animals and take your litter home. Litter and leftover food not only spoils the beauty of the countryside, it can also be dangerous to wildlife and farm animals.

- Keep your dog under control. Dogs can easily disturb and scare farm animals or wildlife and it is every owner's duty to keep their dog under control.

- Consider other people. Don't block gateways or roads. Also, keep out of the way and be patient when you come across animals being gathered or moved by the farmer.

More advice is available from the Countryside Access website.

A FARMER'S PLAN to diversify into 'pet cremations' has suffered a blow in East Sussex.

Robbie Dick spent £50,000 building a special incinerator at Ayrshire Farm in Ripe, near Lewes, before local planners rejected his scheme.

Officials think the only animals that should be cremated at the spot are fallen farm stock.

However, Mr Dick was hoping to offer a service to pet owners and was willing to cremate anything from lizards to ponies.

Bereaved animal lovers would have been welcomed at the farm and offered a chance to say goodbye to their pets with a fitting ceremony.

GENDER BENDING FISH may be a bigger problem than first thought in England's waterways.

Findings published by the Environment Agency confirm that the sex change phenomenon is now widespread in English rivers, raising concerns about the long-term threat to fish populations.

In a survey of more than 1,500 fish at 50 river sites, over a third of male fish exhibited female characteristics.

The research, which is the latest stage of a 20-year investigation, shows that the feminising effects seen in fish come from domestic sewage effluents.

The natural steroid hormones 'oestradiol' and 'oestrone', and the synthetic hormone 'ethinyloestradiol', are excreted from women naturally or as a result of taking the contraceptive pill.

The number of fish affected and the severity of the effects are said to be related to the proportion of sewage effluent in a river.

Male fish suffering changes in their sexual organs are less able to reproduce, with serious implications for fish populations.

LONDON ANGLERS ARE delighted that trout and other fish are returning to a tiny river in the middle of the capital.

"It sounds an ecological impossibility," the Independent newspaper reports,"a trout stream in the middle of London. But trout are flourishing in the River Wandle, one of the capital's largely forgotten rivers such as the Fleet, the Walbrook and the Tyburn.

"The Wandle has been reborn in one of the most remarkable environmental transformations seen in Britain. In 25 years, what was a lifeless drain through industrial estates and dense Victorian housing, entering the Thames just down from Clapham Junction, has come alive with substantial fish such as dace, roach, chub and barbel.

"Most astonishing is the population of brown trout, fish which need clear, well-oxygenated water. They are the surest sign of river health.

"Last year, a fly-fisherman caught a two-and-a-half pound trout in a section of the river next to Wandsworth council's bin lorry depot. This is believed to have been the first trout caught in London for 70 years, and the first caught on the fly for more than a century."

GOAT RACING IS the latest craze to pack in the crowds at a Shropshire country park.

The wacky races have been running at Hoo Farm Animal Kingdom in Telford.

Sheep racing was a previous event at the park but now their smoother coated cousins are being told to get ready, get set, goat...

Fluffy toys are strapped to their backs to look like jockeys with the goats given training by William Dorrell, 13, son of the park's owners Edward and Carolyn.

The teenager even offers a running commentary on the races staged daily throughout the summer holidays.

ABOUT 15,000 fish died after a five-mile stretch of the River Thame was polluted, a court heard.

Water utilities company Thames Water Ltd was fined £50,000 and ordered to pay costs of £20,005 following the devastating incident.

During a five-day long trial, it was revealed that pump failures at Thames Water's sewage treatment works in Aylesbury led to a significant discharge of untreated sewage effluent into the River Thame on July 8 and 9, 2002.

A probe by the Environment Agency, which brought the prosecution, revealed two of the plant's three pumps used to pump sewage for treatment had been out of action for a number of weeks.

As a temporary measure, Thames Water stored sewage in its storm tanks while the pumps were repaired but after a period of rainfall the stored, untreated sewage was flushed out with the storm water into the river.

Thames Water argued the discharge process was legal.

QUIETER AND SMALLER than its 'greater' namesake, the lesser spotted woodpecker also appears to be having a tougher time.

While its bigger cousin seems to be holding its own, numbers of the lesser spotted have slumped so badly it has been put onto the 'red list' of birds causing serious conservation concern.

Similarly marked with red, white and black colouring as the larger species, the lesser spotted woodpecker is the size of a sparrow and tends to stay nearer the tops of trees out of sight.

"You can sometimes locate one early in the year from its drumming - a softer sound than that made by its larger cousin," said an RSPB spokesman.

"But for every four lesser spotted woodpeckers one might have heard 30 years ago - drumming from a partly rotten oak or hornbeam branch in early spring - you'll now only hear one."

Other woodland birds are also declining so fast that the RSPB has set up an appeal to pay for urgent research into the problem.

"The gently cascading notes of the willow warbler, the rich notes of the nightingale singing in 'full-throated ease' - those magical sounds, of which treasured memories are made - have become much harder to find," warns the Society.

OSPREY EGGS FROM a nest in the Lake District are to be examined scientifically to see why they failed to hatch.

The two eggs were gathered from a tree in Wythop Forest where a single egg did hatch and its chick appears to be doing well.

It is hoped that the underlying reasons why the two other eggs failed to hatch will be revealed and can help conservationists in future.

Pete Davies, of the Lake District Osprey Project, supervised a 'health-check' for the lone chick.

He said:"It was a privilege to have an opportunity to see this amazing bird at close quarters and to see how fast she has grown in just five weeks.

"The health-check was over very quickly and the chick was returned to the nest where the adults will continue to feed it for several more weeks. We are now looking forward to the special day when this young osprey makes its first flight."

RARE GOLDEN PLOVERS and other wading birds may be at risk from escalating tick attacks, researchers fear.

"It might be small but the tiny spider-like tick packs a powerful punch and its population is on the increase," explained the Game Conservancy Trust.

"But it's not just humans that are affected by this growing problem. Many wildlife species are either succumbing to diseases transmitted by the blood sucking tick or are simply dying through the impact of 'tick worry' caused by the sheer numbers feeding upon one host.

"New research by the Trust has identified a further potential tick problem. It seems that important populations of moorland breeding wader birds, particularly the rare golden plover, might also be suffering from the impact of an increasing tick population and the pathogens they transmit."

Lapwing and curlew are two other species also thought to be suffering as a result of rising tick numbers, warns the Trust.

417

A DEAD HERON is at the centre of a pollution spill mystery which has angered environmentalists.

The bird was discovered after hundreds of litres of cooking oil - thought to be from a restaurant - seeped into the Duke of Northumberland's River in West London.

The Environment Agency says the river, which runs through Hounslow, is an important wildlife corridor and supports a good population of fish.

But the cooking oil reduces oxygen in the water and can also be deadly if it gets onto a bird's feathers, as happened to the heron.

Alex Chown, senior environment officer, said:"In recent weeks, cooking oil has severely polluted the river and the water quality has deteriorated dramatically. The oil is not only offensive to look at but is also harming the local environment.

"We will not tolerate the actions of individuals or companies that pollute our rivers and we are working hard to find the perpetrators in this case. Our aim is to ensure that the 'polluter pays' and we will prosecute where necessary."

RE-HOMING HUNTING hounds was the thorny issue discussed in a new report.

The Countryside Alliance has already attacked the report by the Associate Parliamentary Group for Animal Welfare, launched by anti-hunting MP Ian Cawsey.

According to the Alliance, it did nothing to challenge the findings of the Government's own inquiry - the Burns Report - which concluded that 'where homing had been tried, it had failed because the hounds would not settle and invariably returned to their hunt kennels...'

Alliance spokesman Darren Hughes said:"Much of the detail is confused and inaccurate but the report does confirm that large scale re-homing of hounds would be impractical without seriously compromising their welfare.

"Hounds would need to be kennelled in a pack environment and given the opportunity to hunt in order to have the 'freedom to express normal behaviour'. We've always said that the re-homing of hounds is impractical, rather than impossible, but very few people would be able to offer such facilities."

A NEW ONLINE weapon to protect dwindling ancient forest has been unveiled by The Woodland Trust.

The new site - www.woodsunderthreat.info - aims to offer the latest details of threats to almost 300 rare ancient woodlands, giving local residents more time to act to protect them.

Trust spokesman Ed Pomfret said:"Ancient woods are irreplaceable and yet we are seeing them disappear under a wave of concrete. We now have a publicly accessible map of the location of all the threats that we know about."

The Trust says the website will also help planners themselves make more woodland-friendly decisions.

ELUSIVE AND SHY, the woodcock has just been the subject of successful, wide ranging research.

The first national survey of breeding woodcock in Britain was conducted by scientists from the Game Conservancy Trust with help from the British Trust for Ornithology.

Due to its secretive nature, the ground-nesting bird has previously been hard to study but estimates point to a 74 per cent decline.

Volunteers monitored a total of 947 woodland habitats across the UK, including 10 in Ireland.

Overall, woodcock were recorded in 416 (44 per cent) of woods visited, but there was huge variation between regions.

In Wales, woodcock numbers were said to be especially disappointing with birds recorded in just 20 per cent of woods.

Figures were highest in Yorkshire and Lincolnshire, where woodcock were reported in more than 70 per cent of woods.

The highest densities, however, were found in an 'arc' lying across southern Scotland, northern England and the north Midlands down through eastern England into East Anglia, including the counties of Norfolk, Lincolnshire, Yorkshire, Northumberland, County Durham and the Scottish Borders.

A second, core population was found in central and southern England, including Dorset, Hampshire and Wiltshire.

Game Conservancy Trust spokesman Dr Andrew Hoodless said:"Initial analyses show that while 'region' has the strongest effect on woodcock numbers, various aspects of habitat are also important. Woodcock numbers were greatest in mixed woodland, lowest in coniferous, and intermediate in deciduous."

SHAG CHICKS AND eggs which faced being wiped out on a Scottish island could be saved - by rock climbers.

The seabirds' young and eggs have been under increasing attack from rats on cliffs at Canna.

However, the National Trust was looking at a whopping £180,000 bill in its plan to bring over a New Zealand group of abseiling ratcatchers to wipe out the pests.

Fortunately, a Fort William company - Thistle Rope Access - has offered to do the perilous job for a much lower price.

Thistle's staff are all rock climbers and have previously rescued animals from cliffs and crags.

Saving shags from rats should be just another day's work.

SEA FISHING NOW reels in a massive £538m each year, according to a new report.

The DEFRA-commissioned independent report also found that 1.1 million households in England and Wales contain at least one person who has been sea angling in the past year.

It also revealed that the sport's popularity seems to be on the increase.

Charles Jardine, director of the Campaign for Angling, said:"Sea angling's contribution to the economy and tourism cannot be overestimated and this report illustrates the massive benefits the sport brings to England and Wales.

"It is vital that Government policy is not dominated by commercial concerns but also reflects the importance of sea angling to the economy."

GOOSE: tough harbinger of a drop in temperature

SMALLER and less elegant than swans, wild geese are nevertheless just as hardy and have come to symbolise the approach of bitter winter. Able to thrive in freezing temperatures, geese are equipped with powerful wings, strong legs, and tough beaks to root out food. Their diet covers a wide selection of vegetarian fayre, ranging from water plants and algae to seeds, grass and crops.

About seven species of wild geese have either settled in this country or regularly migrate here.

Biggest and most recognisable with its black and white head is the Canada goose.

This can actually seem quite tame compared to the truly wild flocks still found in its native land. Introduced to Britain in the 17th Century, Canada geese are now a common sight on our lakes and ponds.

So comfortable are they with their adopted homeland that they have lost their migratory instinct and remain in this country all year round.

In contrast, wilder white-fronted geese make it over here en masse either from Greenland or the Siberian tundra each year. Pink-footed geese, too, travel from as far away as Iceland to take advantage of our milder climate during winter with thousands gathering at estuaries around the country.

The barnacle goose is perhaps the prettiest of these common immigrant species.

Its white face, small beak, and black and white feathers make it almost as distinctive as the Canada goose, though it is much smaller

Flocks of barnacle geese arrive each year from Greenland or Russia, as do brent geese, a slightly shorter, darker version of the barnacle.

Other well-known wild geese are the greylag goose and bean goose, with the beautiful snow goose and red-breasted goose being much rarer, more exotic visitors.

Because of what they eat, wild geese are often at odds with farmers and various studies have shown the extent of devastation they can wreak.

The Scottish island of Islay is a typical example with farmers there regularly losing thousands of pounds in profit because of grazing by hungry geese. Goose watching by ornithologists and organised shoots bring money back to the island - although this might not end up in aggrieved farmers' pockets.

At one time roast goose was the favourite Christmas treat in this country until it was gradually replaced by imported American turkey.

Now turkeys are bred by the million here for UK tables.

Goose, of course, is still eaten during the festive season but in nothing like the quantity that was once consumed. My wife and I tried roast goose ourselves for Christmas for the first time only recently.

Unfortunately, we rather overcooked it and what should have been a succulent treat ended up tasting like a giant piece of shoe leather. Yum!

BRITAIN'S FOX POPULATION has been estimated at 250,000 in a professor's report.

Although the number seems large, it is thought to have remained much the same for the last 25 years.

The Countryside Alliance has seized on the findings as evidence that the present system of managing foxes - including hunting - is working perfectly well.

The report, by Professor Stephen Harris of Bristol University, was funded by the anti-hunting International Fund for Animal Welfare.

Alliance spokesman Darren Hughes said:"The long-term stability of the British fox population suggests that the current system of managing foxes, using hunting, shooting and other legal methods, is working perfectly and producing a stable and sustainable population acceptable to farming interests.

"One part of that management has been the creation and conservation of natural habitats by hunts, which has been carried out for hundreds of years and is recognised by a number of reputable research establishments as having far reaching biodiversity benefits.

"The research only looked at a tiny proportion of the land area of Britain. The findings are, however, entirely consistent with the most comprehensive survey of fox numbers recorded by 200 hunts twice a week throughout the autumn and winter.

"In the absence of any evidence that hunting is any less humane than other methods of control, as confirmed by the Burns Report, it would seem that Professor Harris' work proves that the best result for foxes, wildlife and farming is achieved by enabling the current proven systems of management to continue."

MOST GULLS APPEAR to be increasing their numbers, according to latest findings.

Although not yet complete, the ongoing Winter Gull Roost Survey has found the majority of gull species are doing well.

The British Trust for Ornithology, carrying out the research, said:"Since the first Winter Gull Roost Survey in 1953, wintering and breeding populations of gulls have generally increased greatly, partly as a response to greater food availability although also through reduced human persecution."

However, initial data suggests that the UK's breeding population of herring gulls is now in decline - something that might surprise coastal communities plagued by the noisy birds.

In Aberdeen recently, cyclist Colin Davenport, 42, was taken to hospital when three gulls - thought to be herring gulls - swooped at his head, causing him to fall off on a busy city centre road.

AGGRESSIVE ALIEN INVADERS have been blamed for a marked decline in England's chalk river wildlife.

American mink and crayfish, plus Himalayan balsam and Japanese knotweed have all contributed to the loss of life, says a new report.

The study, by the Environment Agency and English Nature, found that almost a third of the country's 161 chalk rivers and streams are in a poor state.

Water extraction is another problem - it reduces flow and allows pollutants to stay in the river in a more concentrated form.

"Our chalk rivers are a valuable part of the English landscape but they are under huge pressures," said Sir John Harman, chairman of the Environment Agency.

"We need policymakers, environmental regulators and communities to take up the challenge of restoring this fragile ecosystem to ensure that generations to come are able to enjoy the unique heritage."

Numbers of chalk stream salmon, water vole and white-clawed crayfish are also low.

However, there is some good news - aquatic plants such as water crowfoot and animals such as otters are bouncing back from decline.

AN OSPREY CHICK with a broken wing was rescued before a predatory fox or stoat could nab it in Scotland.

The bird, thought to have tumbled from its nest in Perthshire, was spotted by walkers who reported it to the nearby Loch of the Lowes Wildlife Reserve.

Manager Peter Ferns soon located the chick but thought hard before taking it into captivity.

He said:"Taking a wild animal into captivity should really only be done as a last resort and in the case of ospreys there are also legal issues.

"However, in this case it was pretty obvious to me that the chick had no chance of returning to the nest, nor would it have been fed by its parents.

"It would have certainly also been easy prey for any predator. By taking this bird into our care, we now have an obligation to look after it and work towards eventually returning it to the wild."

A vet later re-set the bird's broken wing.

WILD GOATS HAVE been gunned down by council contracted marksmen in Devon because they were causing a "nuisance".

As many as 12 goats are thought to have been shot in the Valley of the Rocks, a popular tourist spot at Lynton where goats are said to have roamed for centuries.

The move has angered local supporters of the creatures despite council claims the animals were straying into gardens and frightening tourists.

Jan Hunt, a member of the Friends of Lynton Goats group, told local media that simple fencing erected by residents and the council would solve any trouble.

"There is just no need to kill these goats," she said. "In the past there have been some goats getting into gardens and we have always said it is the duty of the property owners to fence them out. We have helped some people do so.

"The goats are very much needed for grazing and as a tourist attraction. Culling will not solve the problem, the males will still have an instinct to roam."

ARABLE FARMERS ARE being urged to throw a lifeline to starving birds.

With the harvesting season underway, the RSPB is asking farmers to retain half a tonne of grain, or seed-rich tailings, to feed to sparrows, finches and buntings over the winter months.

"The declines of some of our most familiar seed-eating farmland birds have been dramatic," said a spokesman.

"For example, for every 100 tree sparrows in the UK in 1970, we now have only five.

"For three years, under its Bird Aid scheme, the RSPB has worked with 60 farmers across the UK to feed seed-eating birds over the winter.

"Using the huge numbers of birds visiting the feeding sites as a measure of success, the RSPB now wants the largest possible number of farmers across the UK to do the same.

"The combined effect of more efficient farming operations and changes in farming practices have reduced the availability of seeds over winter, causing a shortage of food for some birds, particularly sparrows and buntings.

"Seed-eating birds, such as the corn bunting, tree sparrow and yellowhammer, are suffering from a shortage of food over winter.

"More effective herbicides mean fewer weed seeds for food while weed-rich winter stubbles are disappearing because crops are now being planted in winter rather than spring.

"There is also less grain spilt during harvest because of more efficient harvesting machinery - and so less food for birds."

Richard Winspear, the RSPB's farmland advisor, added:"Many farmers are keen to help the declining birds on their land. Some of those in the scheme have been amazed at the huge flocks of birds visiting the feed sites."

SALMON AND SEA trout have been hit by a pollution spill at a Welsh stream.

Environment Agency officers were called to the Nant yr Aber stream in Caerphilly after the alarm was raised.

Within a short time, some 68 dead salmon and 78 dead trout were found scattered over a 100 metre area.

Investigations are continuing and samples of the stream water and dead fish have been sent for analysis.

Initial findings indicate a possible local source of the pollution and the Agency is concentrating investigations in that area.

Local people have been asked not to handle or remove any dead fish.

HORSE OWNERS HAVE been given more time to make their animals 'legal' with their own 'passports'.

Under a new scheme all owners must now obtain a passport for each horse they own.

The Government says that from next February, animals without a passport can't be sold, bought, exported, slaughtered for human consumption, moved for attending a competition or show, or moved to new premises for breeding.

It explains the EU-inspired aim is to prevent horses entering the food chain if they have been given medicines not intended for food-producing animals.

But so far, out of about a million horse owners in the UK, only a third have applied for the passports with many attacking the scheme.

So-called 'Minister for the Horse' Alun Michael told the BBC's 'Countryfile' programme that the cut-off date had been extended because of the 'longer than anticipated' time it was taking to process applications.

Explaining the decision to use around 70 Passport Issuing Organisations, he said:"We could have done a very bureaucratic job. We could have said 'We are putting up a Horse Passport Agency, we'll put inspectors on every corner' but we didn't.

"We said 'Let's work with the horse industry'. We did it the way that the organisations already issuing horse passports - the breed societies, the British Horse Society, all the other organisations - said was the best way to do it. Now, it has turned out to be a job that was bigger than they thought. That's why we extended the time limits. This is a common sense approach that we are adopting."

DOLPHINS, SEALS AND porpoises are the subjects of new research looking at the Thames Estuary in London.

The Zoological Society is aiming to recruit volunteers to help assess local numbers of the marine mammals.

Information collected will be pooled into a database to help future conservation of the creatures.

The UK population of grey seals is put at about 124,000 while there are 350,000 harbour porpoises and around 300 bottlenose dolphins.

BETTER CATTLE MANAGEMENT is the way to control bovine TB, according to Welsh Assembly members.

The National Federation of Badger Groups has welcomed the Assembly's report amid controversial calls for more badger culls.

The NFBG's chief executive, Dr Elaine King, said:"This report is a triumph for common sense, supporting our argument that cattle-based measures will deliver the most immediate and effective control of bovine TB.

"We welcome the fact that Assembly members have recognised that a range of effective measures can be implemented immediately, such as pre-movement testing, increased testing frequencies and improved cattle husbandry."

However, the NFBG expressed concern at the recommendation that wildlife be removed if it is found to 'carry and transmit TB'.

Dr King explained:"This recommendation goes beyond scientific knowledge. No reliable method currently exists for diagnosing bovine TB in living wildlife."

BIG CAT: dangerous hunter 'stalking our hedgerows'

IT is not too difficult to imagine pumas or panthers living unseen in our countryside today, patrolling the shadows and killing at will.

These creatures would obviously not be native species but the offspring of exotic pets released into the wild when laws on keeping dangerous animals changed.

So many incidents have been recorded that circumstantial evidence of the existence of large feline predators is almost overwhelming.

I myself even noted something which has only fuelled my own interest, but more of that later.

No-one can deny that glimpses of big cats, real or imagined, are being reported with increasing regularity. For some reason, these sightings often occur in clusters but not always in the same area.

One such cluster involved a panther-like animal seen stalking game birds on an estate in Norfolk.

Days later, police in Wiltshire began a hunt for their own big cat after a pet dog was savaged, sustaining deep bite wounds to a shoulder

In Essex, over the same period, a farmer blamed a huge puma-type animal for leaving bite marks and scratches on his car.

One of his pet cats was slaughtered and another vanished in the drama. Elsewhere, in Devon, in a different time spell, an animal also believed to be a puma leapt a 5ft high hedge with ease after being spotted by a motorist as he drove along the A396 close to Tiverton.

And during that same week, Scottish police issued an alert after a Grampian farmer found the remains of a sheep meticulously stripped of its flesh.

Experts later confirmed the work as that of a voracious cat.

All of which brings me to my own, modest experience early one morning following a heavy snowfall.

On this day, my neck had begun to ache as a result of peering up at trees, looking for birds.

So I began to amuse myself by following the tracks of deer and scavenging foxes - easy to do in the virgin snow.

After a while I noticed something odd next to a patch of snow-covered brambles - a large, fresh paw print.

It was scuffed at one edge and I suppose it could have belonged to a huge dog but its size and shape still electrified me.

It seemed far more feline than normal dog prints and there were no accompanying human tracks at all.

Other prints lay among the brambles. But these were less clear and could have belonged to any number of creatures.

I was just contemplating my next step in the six-inch deep snow when a sudden commotion behind made me jump.

I spun round to see two tiny muntjac deer uncharacteristically breaking cover in panic, darting 30 metres into another tangle of bushes.

But there was nothing obvious in pursuit.

Could they, I pondered, be fleeing the mystery big cat said to stalk local woods?

I tip-toed around for a while but failed to pinpoint any lurking predator.

I even managed to spoil the original paw print.

But the experience left me wondering if there really could be something dangerous hunting local game.

SCIENTISTS HAVE MOVED swiftly to contain a worrying fish virus outbreak at an Environment Agency fish farm.

Tench rhabdovirus, if confirmed, has only been encountered once before in England and Wales, causing a number of fish deaths in lakes and ponds in 1999.

Although the disease is thought to have affected just a small number of stock at the Agency's fish farm in Calverton, Nottinghamshire, the implications of the outbreak are huge.

"We have halted all movements of fish to and from the site, which are low during the summer anyway," said a spokesman.

"If the test results confirm the virus is present, we will take measures to contain and subsequently eradicate it and ensure that everything that can be done is done to prevent a reoccurrence."

A robust disinfection plan would be implemented with the humane destruction of infected fish and further testing until the site was shown to be clear.

"We cannot speculate at this time on the likely origin of the disease but a thorough investigation has begun to identify the possible sources.

"Unfortunately, this situation may mean that we fall short in our planned coarse fish stocking programmes for the next two years. Current and planned research projects may also be affected."

Area environment manager Jeff Dolby added:"We are extremely concerned that this virus may be present at Calverton and the implications this might have for our fish restocking work.

"Everything possible is being done to deal with this situation."

CROWS TOOK ADVANTAGE when diggers moved in to rip out a hedgerow - pouncing on a defenceless robin chick whose nest had been wrecked.

The hedgerow, formerly a haven for wildlife at Bitton, near Bristol, was destroyed by the work which has left local residents outraged.

One householder, Melissa Whitworth, said:"When the machines had left I went to have a look and saw a robin's nest on the ground with one remaining fledgling still in it.

"Because it had been ripped out of the hedge, it was left with no protection and some crows came down and snatched it away. The adult robins were distraught.

"It is simply not fair. There was a beautiful hedge with trees, blackberries and wildlife. These hedgerows are here for everybody."

District councillors have launched a probe into who authorised the destruction.

SAND MARTINS ARE among birds boosted by a competition aimed at making businesses more wildlife friendly.

Over 90 business sites around the UK have proved their commitment to the environment by competing in the BTO-Hanson Business Bird Challenge.

"Organised by the British Trust for Ornithology, the competition recognises the efforts that industries are making to provide habitats for birds, involve local communities and initiate conservation action plans," said a spokesman.

"So far this year, observers at the sites have counted an impressive total of 238 species.

"The lengths participants have gone to in order to accommodate wildlife are impressive, particularly considering that many are working sites.

"At Hanson's Horton Quarry in North Yorkshire, returning sand martins have found more nesting holes than they expected. The quarry foreman has provided 100 new starter homes and these have now been colonised.

"And at British Energy's Gale Common Ash Disposal Site in South Yorkshire, a moat has been specially created to protect nesting birds from predatory foxes."

CORN BUNTINGS ARE being helped to hang on in the Outer Hebrides after cash was offered to crofters to make old-fashioned corn stacks.

The islands - once one of the little bird's strongholds - have latterly experienced a slump in buntings because of modern farming practices.

Now RSPB Scotland is offering money to crofters in North Uist and Barra who put in the extra effort to create corn 'stooks'.

The small stacks were once common in Scottish fields and provide a bonanza of seeds for corn buntings and other threatened birds.

Corn buntings suffered a 70 per cent drop on the islands after machines were introduced two decades ago to convert corn into arable silage, rather than drying it out in stooks.

THE HATCHING OF four red kite chicks at the same nest in West Yorkshire has thrilled local conservationists.

The production of quads is a very unusual event for birds of prey and has provided fans of the red kite with more evidence of its resurgence.

Some 113 of the birds have now been bred in the region since an initial colony of 17 were introduced to the Harewood estate near Leeds five years ago.

RSPB spokesman Doug Simpson said:"The idea behind the release schemes throughout England and Scotland is to form a chain of kite colonies which will eventually link up and see the birds distributed throughout the country."

The soaring bird was driven to extinction across Britain but has gradually fought back with the help of conservation schemes.

The colony in West Yorkshire includes Lightning, who the RSPB says still makes long trips to his Chilterns birthplace.

HUNDREDS OF COUNTRY lovers are getting ready to put their best feet forward for the Ramblers Association's walking festival from September 18 to 25. The week "is designed to introduce the joys and benefits of walking to all with many of the walks short, at an easy pace, and suitable for all the family."

BRITAIN'S FARMS HAVE gone too far down the tourism and leisure route when they should be producing more food, it has been claimed.

John Cresswell, the Country Land and Business Association's north east chairman, has attacked Government attitudes to farming.

He said:"For decades we have depended on food imports and, of course, this will continue. What seems different today is this Government's attitude that it is of no consequence in terms of food security if we produce ANY food domestically.

"It may not sound like it but the consumer has actually been lucky this year. Despite the devastation to UK crops, other countries have had a successful harvest and we can rely on imports.

"If this had happened last year when other countries also suffered, it would have been much more difficult. Our farms are no longer treated as food producers but as providers of leisure facilities and visual amenity. I truly believe that we have gone too far down this route and need to return to farm for food.

"World food stocks are shrinking. As an example, while vegetable oil stocks ran at about 12 per cent of annual usage throughout the 1980s and 1990s, this has steadily declined since 2000 to less than half this level. World cereal stocks have similarly declined every year over the last five. If the trend continues, we will simply run out.

"It is time we recognised that domestic food production is crucial, not a by-product of using our land as a theme park - as DEFRA and many others seem to believe.

"We already rely on imported oil and are at the mercy of price rises and supply shortages.

"The same has been proven with our gas supplies with the latest unacceptable increase in gas prices by British Gas.

"We are still in a position to protect our food industry but we must act now, and that means taking whatever measures are necessary to keep farmers farming."

A SALMON WEIGHING almost 15 pounds pulled a canoe across a loch after being hooked by a boy.

Jamie Sullivan, aged seven, from Barvas on the Isle of Lewis in the Outer Hebrides, had been fly fishing with his father on the loch 10 miles from Stornoway when the fish pounced.

Mr Sullivan's 17-foot canoe was pulled along before the pair managed to reel in the fish.

It was thought to be the largest caught by fly at the spot for 20 years.

A BAN ON hunting with dogs in England and Wales has come a major step closer following a vote by MPs.

To the delight of anti-hunt campaigners, the House of Commons passed the new Hunting Bill with an overwhelming majority of 339-155.

"This should be the last time MPs will have to vote on hunting," said a spokesman for the League Against Cruel Sports.

"They also passed the 'suggestion' that asks the House of Lords to agree a delay in the implementation of the ban on hunting with dogs till July 31, 2006 (though hare coursing would still be banned in mid-February 2005).

"While we see no need for such a lengthy lead-in period, after many years of campaigning, we are extremely pleased that we can finally see an end to this barbaric activity.

"The Bill and the 'suggestion' will now be passed to the House of Lords in October. We expect them to reject the Bill and they will also decide on the suggested delay.

"The Parliament Act can then be used to ensure that the will of the elected House of Commons prevails.

"The Hunting Bill should receive Royal Assent in November this year and will come into effect on August 1 2006.

"Therefore, the final legal day of hunting will be July 31, 2006. Under the terms of the Bill, the hare coursing ban should come into effect in February 2005.

"While we are not quite there, we would like to take this opportunity to thank our supporters for their support over the years. We are also extremely grateful to the many MPs who have supported the campaign. Their support was absolutely vital."

Outside Parliament, as the Bill was passed, pro-hunt protesters were involved in more violent clashes with baton-wielding police.

A PEREGRINE FALCON youngster has vanished from the Forest of Dean near Gloucester and is feared dead by birdwatchers.

The bird, which hatched just months ago, was the only fledgling this year at Symonds Yat.

Peregrines have bred at the site for the last 21 years although numbers have steadily dwindled.

Every year thousands of bird lovers observe the cliff face nest from a raft of telescopes and binoculars provided by the RSPB.

Since the event started, 55 chicks have been hatched and raised there.

RSPB spokesman Steve Turner said:"The parents managed to raise only one youngster this year. It got to 18 weeks and unfortunately then went off on a hunting trip with its mum and didn't return."

A SMALL beached whale was helped back to sea by rescuers at Llangranog near Cardigan on the Welsh coast.

At first, the RSPCA, coastguard staff and other helpers, thought the stricken animal was a dolphin.

However, it turned out to be a Sowerbys beaked whale.

"It had a small amount of blood on its beak but apart from that its body condition was good. The rescuers put the whale on a stretcher and kept it steady in the surf until the tide came in," reported a spokeswoman for the British Divers Marine Life Rescue.

MINK: superb predator hated in its adopted homeland

DETESTED and feared in equal measure, the mink still possesses a number of admirable qualities despite being such an unpopular immigrant.

It swims well, climbs easily, and runs fast - making it a superb all-round predator able to take fish, fowl or other prey such as rabbits and voles.

A ruthless killer, it is perfectly adapted to survive harsh winters in the forests of North America but was introduced to our tamer countryside by fur farmers in the 1920s.

Kept in tiny cages, the first wild mink either escaped or were released when some farmers hit financial problems.

It was not too long before these American invaders were running riot in our woods and meadows, dispersing along rivers until they had colonised most parts of the country.

They quickly learnt to snack on our native wildlife, particularly the harmless water vole which has been driven to the edge of extinction as a result.

Fish farmers soon came to hate mink since their swimming skills enabled them to feast on captive trout or salmon, costing businesses thousands of pounds in devoured stock.

Most mink are a deep chocolate brown colour but some can be sandy brown or grey, a throwback to the different strains commercially bred to provide a variety of pelts.

Females produce a single litter of up to six young each year, usually in a hole in a riverbank or among rocks. The male is slightly larger than the female, about 21 inches from the tip of his nose to the end of his thin furry tail.

This is much smaller than the 4ft otter yet swimming mink are often mistaken for otter.

Although now firmly established in the British countryside, evidence has emerged that numbers of mink are falling fast and are currently well below an estimated high of about 110,000 individuals just a decade or so ago.

One of the reasons for mink decline is thought to be the steady resurgence of our native, more powerful otter.

This equally voracious predator is actually killing and eating mink, some wildlife experts believe.

More mink are also being driven away from their hard-won breeding sites by territorial otters.

Animal rights protesters have cited the mink as one example of non-native species being unfairly culled.

Animal Aid, the UK's largest campaign group, claims "top table conservationists" often scapegoat alien species such as the mink and grey squirrel because they threaten financial interests.

It may have a point.

But whatever the rights or wrongs of culling mink today, there is no doubt that human greed brought the animal to this country in the first place.

Human stupidity also created the perfect vacuum for it to flourish thanks to widespread persecution of the otter, now at last being reversed.

AN ISLE OF Wight hunt has been suspended by its governing body after animal carcasses were dumped in Brighton as a protest against anti-hunt MPs.

In its adjudication, the Masters of Foxhounds Association said its disciplinary committee had "considered and found proven a case of misconduct against the Masters of the Isle of Wight Hunt, following the dumping of animal carcasses, particularly that of a horse, in Brighton on September 28.

"The committee considered that the Masters had taken no action to ensure that specific M.F.H.A. instructions of such issues sent to Masters, hunt chairmen and hunt staff were adhered to, and in particular that initiatives and stunts should be cleared in advance with the relevant country sports authority.

"The committee regretted the ill-judged action at Brighton, particularly the dumping of the horse carcass, and considered that this could have been avoided as it was caused by the negligence of the Isle of Wight Hunt and a failure of supervision of its employees.

"The committee also regretted the assistance given to the stunt and its publicity by other outside organisations, all of which had had a harmful effect on the good name of foxhunting, and that of the Countryside Alliance.

"The committee suspended the Masters of the hunt and the hunt itself for a period of four weeks from October 6, although it was made clear that the Masters should continue to arrange for the proper welfare of hounds and horses during that time."

However, the committee did not think that the person responsible should be sacked.

"The committee did not deal with the case of the Hunt employee, as this is currently sub-judice, but it indicated that it would anyway not be recommending his dismissal."

A RABID BAT has sparked off safety fears in Surrey.

The infected female Daubenton's bat was handled by an unwary member of the public who discovered it in an alley in Staines.

Tests have shown the bat to be carrying the same strain of rabies that killed bat expert David McRae in Scotland two years ago.

It is not known if other bats in the area are infected but DEFRA has put out a statement saying that rabies, generally, remains at low levels in UK bats.

The infected bat was taken into care by the Bat Conservation Trust and later died.

The man who found it was not thought to have been bitten or scratched but was still vaccinated as a precaution.

TWO OTTERS HAVE moved into a tailor-made riverside home built for them by a Welsh farmer.

It is hoped the pair will soon produce young at the six-room, tree-trunk construction.

The holt at Rhysgog Farm, near Llanafan, Powys, was paid for by the Tir Gofal farm scheme which urges environmentally-friendly farming in Wales.

Farm owner Pip Tapping said:"I've always been interested in protecting wildlife and working on a project like this is a great way of doing that without disrupting normal work on the farm.

"It's clear that a few changes and a bit of work can have real environmental benefits."

Julia Phillips, Tir Gofal spokeswoman for the Countryside Council for Wales, added: "Building an otter holt is a quick and simple task.

"It could be one of the most beneficial wildlife projects a large commercial farm could undertake alongside a stretch of river that has sparse vegetation cover along its banks.

"It only takes a few hours, can utilise home-grown farm timber and hedgerow brash, and can be grant-aided."

A MINK CAUSED a stink when it invaded offices in Essex.

The brazen animal put staff to flight after it was found tearing around the offices of CPS International in Saffron Walden.

Quick-thinking director Andrew Streeter managed to trap the snarling creature in a stairwell before alerting the council animal warden.

"We were trapped in our office until, after a lengthy struggle, the vicious thing was overpowered and caged," said company spokeswoman Louise Gedge.

"The council's animal warden caught it but not without it releasing what can only be described as its final 'Weapon of Mass Destruction' - a pungent scent that left our stairwell unfit for human habitation for the rest of the afternoon."

The mink, thought to be hunting for food when it crept into the building, was later taken to an animal sanctuary.

BROWN HARES WILL be among topics of debate at The Mammal Society's forthcoming Annual Autumn Symposium.

Methods of boosting numbers of the fleet-footed mammal are to be discussed at the two-day event next month at London Zoo.

Revised population estimates for all British mammal species will also be presented during the conference.

"Ten years ago members of The Mammal Society published estimates of the numbers of each species of British mammal," said a spokesman.

"This was very much a collaborative exercise, with most mammalogists in Britain contributing information, ideas and unpublished data to the project.

"The figures produced in 'A Review of British Mammals' remain widely quoted to this day.

"'British Mammal Populations - 50 years of Change', which celebrates 50 years of The Mammal Society, builds on this work and brings together our current knowledge on the population status, ecology and management of wild mammals in Britain, as well as identifying key challenges for the future."

MORE THAN THREE quarters of the public support shooting - so long as it is carried out safely, legally and responsibly, according to a survey.

In an independent opinion poll conducted by the Opinion Research Business for the British Association for Shooting and Conservation, 77 per cent of respondents backed the sport.

The poll also found that 91 per cent of people thought pheasants and other game birds living in the countryside had a much better life than battery hens, and that 51 per cent considered shooting to be the most humane method of controlling pests.

BASC spokesman Simon Clarke said:"These results are very encouraging and show that there is growing understanding of the purpose of shooting sports in the UK.

"BASC insists that its members shoot safely, legally and responsibly. We always encourage the highest standards of behaviour in the field, reinforced by codes of practice covering many different aspects of shooting and pest control.

"The survey also shows that there is an appreciation that pheasant shoots produce healthy wild birds.

"Some of the more extreme animal rights campaigners attempt to portray pheasant shooting as little more than factory farming. This is utter nonsense.

"Pheasant rearing has been closely examined by ministers and civil servants at DEFRA over the last 18 months as part of work on the Animal Welfare Bill.

"DEFRA has decided to approve the National Game Farmers' Association code of practice on game bird rearing and support continuing self-regulation of the industry."

AN OSPREY BLASTED from the sky over Wiltshire is making a good recovery at a specialist hawk centre.

The bird, nicknamed Ossie by rescuers, was shot by an unknown gunman and found bloodied and terrified in a field near Alderbury.

Police have launched an investigation into who shot the bird and say a shotgun was used.

With the osprey receiving treatment for pellet wounds at the Hawk Conservancy Trust near Andover, Wiltshire Police wildlife officer PC Richard Salter, said:"This is an extremely rare and beautiful bird of prey.

"The offender could not possibly have mistaken it for any species of bird that could lawfully be shot. They are so rare they are priceless. Their nests are kept secret to protect them. To shoot this creature was a mindless act."

If caught, the gunman faces up to six months jail and a £5,000 fine.

FOXHUNTERS ARE now eyeing the next General Election as the final desperate battleground to save their sport.

Pro-hunt groups are increasingly asking their supporters and members of the public who back hunting with hounds to use their votes wisely to unseat anti-hunt Labour MPs.

A host of campaign websites have also joined the fight.

One, Votehunting.com, says:"If this vindictive and prejudiced Government is re-elected, hunting is almost certainly finished. If enough anti-hunting MPs lose their seats, hunting will most probably be saved.

"We therefore have no alternative but to seek, by democratic means, to unseat enough anti-hunting MPs to give us a House of Commons which is prepared to leave our way of life alone.

"We did not want this fight. The VoteHunting campaign took a strictly non-partisan line, targeting individual anti-hunting MPs of all parties.

"But the Government has declared war on the hunting community. Instead of individual anti-hunting MPs we now have, for the first time, an openly anti-hunting Government, and that changes everything.

"If we can pull this off, we'll change the political landscape forever. We'll make hunting a no-go area for all the political parties for years to come."

MILLIONS OF BIRDS are now deserting British shores for warmer climes as part of their annual migration.

"Thirty million birds are on their way to Africa," said a British Trust for Ornithology spokesman.

"At this time, birdwatchers' eyes are on the departure of these summer migrants and on the mass arrival of birds from nesting grounds far to the north and east.

"Most of the young birds that leave Britain and Ireland each autumn do so without their parents, relying remarkably on their inbuilt sense of direction and an urge to migrate. Many will not make it as far as Africa and others will end up in the wrong place.

"Shortly, we will see the first geese arriving from Greenland and Iceland. Young birds fly south with their parents and spend the rest of the winter in Britain and Ireland.

"For smaller birds, their on-board compasses bring them here en masse to take advantage of our relatively mild winters."

A CHARITY WHICH protects wildlife has come up with a new autumn book that celebrates game species - by eating them.

The Game Conservancy Trust says that it is committed to promoting best practice in all aspects of game management from conservation, rearing and releasing to harvesting and, ultimately, consumption.

"Now that autumn is here, our appetites should be whetted by the variety and quality of fresh, wild game now available to buy," said a spokesman.

The Trust reveals that its 'Game and Fish Cookbook' has been produced in conjunction with Farlows of Pall Mall and is now available to buy.

"Packed full of easy-to-follow classic recipes, the book also contains sections on sauces, salsas and relishes, vegetables and accompaniments, instruction on the preparation of game and a guide to shooting seasons," added the spokesman.

NIGHTINGALE: sweet voice snuffed out by developers

FAMED for its sweet song and shy manner, the nightingale has enjoyed a special place in the nation's heart for centuries.

Looking like a large robin but with a buff underside instead of a reddish orange breast, the nightingale also moves around in the same hopping, tail-flicking manner.

Two centimetres longer than the robin at 16cms, it is nevertheless much more difficult to spot.

Singing nightingales usually hole up in dense cover where the only thing betraying their presence is a distinctive stream of strong, fluty notes delivered in a variety of beguiling combinations.

They sing at night, too, especially on warm evenings between April and June when open windows mean householders are more likely to appreciate their efforts.

Nightingales are migrants and journey to the southern part of Britain from Africa each year when the heat there becomes too intense and the coldest weather here has departed.

Like robins, they feed mainly on insects which they hunt on the ground but will also take fruit and berries.

Nightingales have been among species worst hit by changes in farming practices which have seen Britain's overall bird population drop by 34 million over the last 20 years.

In one study conducted by the British Trust for Ornithology, nightingale numbers were found to be down almost 30 per cent.

I have a soft spot for nightingales as one sang each year from the depths of a small wood behind a house we used to rent.

I would often lie in bed listening, marvelling at the sound.

This ancient wood was the main reason we chose the house and our daughter spent her first three years there.

Besides a solitary nightingale, all kinds of birds, wild creatures and flowers flourished in the wood which, despite being only a few acres in size, formed a natural oasis in an otherwise urban wilderness.

Come rain or shine, a cheery old man we got to know would walk each day through the trees with his friendly Scottie terrier.

For 10 years before our arrival, he informed us, residents had fought a successful battle against property developers to hang onto 'their' wood.

However, after we moved in, a thrusting new political party took over the council and the same developers reapplied to build over the wood for the umpteenth time.

This time they got the go-ahead.

One terrible day, instead of listening to the nightingale, I heard the rumble of bulldozers and the buzz of chainsaws as an army of workmen began laying waste to the wood.

Within weeks, every stately tree and delicate bloom had vanished to make way for a new red-brick sprawl of identikit homes - all apparently needed by destitute families.

As the houses sprang up, that old man and his terrier still tentatively set out on their morning stroll.

But now when they retraced their favourite route, it ended at a dirty, anonymous spot where four wheelie bins were parked.

What became of that lonesome nightingale is anyone's guess.

We upped and left soon after.

SCOTS SALMON FARMERS are currently celebrating a leap in popularity of the food - despite dire health warnings from critics.

Consumption of farmed salmon has rocketed by 20 per cent even after fears were raised that the food can cause cancer.

A probe across UK households showed that farmed salmon was eaten during more than 86 million meals between March and May this year, compared with just 72 million during the same period last year.

Back in January researchers in the United States claimed that eating too much farmed salmon could lead to an increased risk of developing cancers.

They warned consumers to eat no more than two ounces of Scottish farmed salmon a month because of the dangers posed by chemicals in the fish.

Brian Simpson, chief executive of Scottish Quality Salmon, said:"Despite a degree of media hysteria at the time, British shoppers have shown themselves to be pretty sensible in evaluating this food scare.

"They took the American study with the pinch of salt it deserved and relied on just about every other authority in the world to confirm that not only is Scottish farmed salmon safe to eat, it is both delicious and extremely good for you."

OWLS ARE THE subject of urgent research to find out how best to conserve them.

"There are five species of British owls, most of which are usually nocturnal," says the British Trust for Ornithology, which is behind the move.

"Two are already species of conservation concern - the barn owl and short-eared owl - while two others are poorly monitored, nocturnal and also in decline - the tawny owl and long-eared owl - and the fifth is susceptible to changes in agricultural practices - the little owl.

"It is not easy to count birds in the dark so it is not surprising that we know less about owls than about other species.To conserve owls, we need to find out where they live, how many there are and which habitats are important."

Dr Humphrey Crick, senior ecologist at the Trust, added:"It is really quite scandalous how little we know about our populations of tawny and other owl species. If we are not careful, they could begin to disappear without anybody really noticing."

SICK SWANS HAVE had conservationists in a flap in Bristol.

Nine of the majestic birds were found to be seriously ill recently and four had to be put down because they were so poorly.

However, the cause of the sickness has proved a riddle for animal welfare workers.

All the birds were found on Bristol docks between Redcliffe and Bristol Bridge.

Each was listless and unable to hold its head up because it was so weak.

BRITAIN'S 200 MILLION oak trees could be at risk from a deadly new tree disease, the Forestry Commission has warned.

"Two cases of a new pathogen have been found in native oak trees in a wood near Redruth in Cornwall," said a spokesman.

It is thought to be the first time the disease has been found in oak.

"The new disease was first discovered in the wood in Cornwall earlier this year when it was found on rhododendron plants and a beech tree," revealed the spokesman.

"The disease - known informally as Phytophthora taxon C - is so new it does not yet have a formal scientific name but the tree pathologist who first discovered it, Clive Brasier, Professor Emeritus at the Forestry Commission's Forest Research agency, has now dubbed it Phytophthora kernovii – the ancient name for Cornwall.

"Professor Brasier and colleagues at the Commission's Surrey-based research centre, are monitoring two more oak trees in the area which they suspect may also be infected.

"The pathogen is related to Phytophthora ramorum - known in the USA as Sudden Oak Death - because of the widespread blight it has caused on American oak species.

"However, until now, native British oaks have proved to be resistant to both pathogens. Since the first discovery of P ramorum in Britain early in 2002, neither laboratory tests nor painstaking surveys of over 1,500 woodland and forest sites across Britain have established susceptibility to native oak trees to the deadly fungus.

"Although P ramorum is known to exist in over a dozen countries throughout Europe, the new Phytophthora is thought to be specific to Britain.

"A major concern is that laboratory tests and observations in the wild indicate that it is more aggressive, and much faster spreading, than P ramorum. Rhododendron, the main host and source of infection succumbs in just a few weeks rather than months.

"This latest discovery raises fears over the pathogen's potential impact on Britain's 200 million oak trees, as well as other native tree species that may now prove to be susceptible."

Roddie Burgess, the Forestry Commission's head of plant health, added:"The infected trees are already within an area quarantined because of the presence of P ramorum. Any infected plants are being destroyed, as are any potential hosts in the immediate area."

A SURGE OF 'big cat' sightings in Yorkshire has sparked a special investigation in the county.

The British Big Cat Research Group says there has been an increase in sightings of large cat-like animals roaming the region.

Spokesman Mark Fraser said:"Yorkshire seems to be a current hotspot so we spent some time in the area during May of this year and are returning over November to try and catch one of these elusive animals on camera.

"We shall spend several nights in the countryside with night vision equipment, including infra-red cameras, and spend the days looking for any evidence such as spoor or casts."

Three types of big feline beast have been repeatedly spotted in the county - a lynx-like cat, a tawny animal, and a black cat.

THE GREY PARTRIDGE is said to be making a remarkable fightback from slumping numbers on a patch of English land.

New figures released by the Game Conservancy Trust show that the partridge, one of Britain's most threatened birds, is making an amazing recovery on farmland in Hertfordshire.

Autumn count figures reveal that grey partridge numbers have increased sevenfold, from 7.6 birds per 100 hectares in 2001 - just before the project started - to 53.4 birds per 100 hectares in 2004.

This equates to a total of 533 birds in 2004 on the 1,000-hectare demonstration site at Royston, which is intensively managed by the Trust for grey partridge.

Dr Nick Sotherton, director of research with the Trust, said:"This is a fantastic outcome. Despite a mediocre season with very wet weather, the grey partridges on our demonstration site have thrived with breeding success high.

"We now have a good stock to work with and it is our hope that the young produced this season will survive winter and go on to breed next year.

"The next spring count in 2005 will therefore be crucial to demonstrate that we are starting to turn the corner and that we can meet our first Government BAP target.

"With the support of many enthusiastic farmers and landowners across the country we are confident that we will meet this target. However, we must not be complacent. We need more people to manage their land for grey partridges by following our successful management prescriptions, including protection from predators, creating good habitat and supplementary feeding."

BATS COULD SOON be top of the pops after the release of a CD featuring the creatures.

According to English Nature, 'Bat Beat' is "a funky composition mixed by young people from South Gloucestershire, featuring sampled sounds from bats into a unique track.

"The CD is a result of a pilot project to see how young people connect with their local environment. Using sonic bat detectors, members of the Green Hut Youth Club made sound recordings of bats.

"They recorded an array of sounds including 'sharp ticks' and 'metallic chinks' with fluttering noises which indicated that a number of different species of bat, including pipistrelles, were present."

Bat conservationist Dan Merrett added:"This innovative project shows how local people can get involved in helping raise awareness of bats.

"Species recorded included common pipistrelles and Daubenton's. A fun night out was had by all and a cracking CD has been produced."

HEDGEHOGS WERE GIVEN a boost by safety advice issued to prevent them dying in the prickly heat of a bonfire hot spot.

Helen Freeston, The Wildlife Trusts' people and wildlife manager, said:"Hedgehogs start preparing for hibernation in early November when temperatures regularly drop below 16 degrees.

"They use twigs, leaves and dry grasses to build a cosy winter nest and may move to a new site at least once during the winter months.

"To a sleepy hedgehog, a ready made nest such as a compost heap or a pile of timber seems ideal and a newly built bonfire will look like the perfect place to bed down."

Her advice includes:

-Try to build the bonfire as close to the night itself as possible to reduce the chance of a hedgehog moving in.

-Ideally, make your pile of material next to the bonfire site and re-build the stack prior to lighting.

-Before lighting, search the bonfire for any hibernating creatures using a torch and rake, to gently pull back twigs or vegetation.

-Move any hedgehogs found to a ready made hedgehog box or somewhere dry and safe away from the fire.

-If possible, before bonfire night, create an alternative hedgehog home by placing some hedgehog boxes in the surrounding area or raking up grass cuttings or autumn leaves into a pile a safe distance from the fire.

THOUSANDS OF BIRDS could die needlessly this winter because garden feeders are being left empty.

According to the RSPB, three million bird feeders are left empty each day across the UK.

In the summer this is not a problem but in winter, when temperatures plummet, birds can die as a result.

As a reminder, the RSPB urged everyone across the UK to fill a feeder to celebrate its 'Feed The Birds Day'.

Minister for Nature Conservation, Ben Bradshaw, backed the campaign.

He said:"With the right food and habitat, you can help the birds in your garden through the tougher times of winter. Having a filled bird feeder can attract a wide variety of bird species and provide you with many hours of enjoyment."

Project spokesman David Spencer added:"The RSPB is urging everyone to start feeding and its Feed The Birds Day provides the perfect opportunity. Providing a little food, water and shelter can help birds through the winter and turn your garden into a wildlife haven for you to enjoy."

NEW EU MOVES on protecting animals during transport - such as fitting satellite navigation equipment to trucks - will help provide improved animal welfare, says the NFU.

The regulations, which will come into effect in 2007, will have no impact on journey times or stocking densities but will make it easier to enforce animal transport codes, the union believes.

NFU livestock transport spokesman Marcus Themans said:"The new regulations will help tighten the noose on a small minority of operators who are flouting the rules, without punishing the rest of the industry."

PIG: merrily rooting out a live grenade for lunch

GUZZLING and arguing their way through life, pigs have often seemed the most 'human' of all farm animals to me. Medical science obviously agrees, which is why various pig body parts are so often employed to aid human health.

Even their skin is said to be similar to ours with some pigs suffering sunburn if they stay out in the hot sun too long.

Most of today's modern breeds are descended from animals which were imported from Asia and mixed with our native wild boar.

Like other cloven-hoofed species, pigs had a tough time when foot-and-mouth disease cast its shadow on the land.

But just as swine fever blows were absorbed, so has foot-and-mouth been.

Pig breeds are numerous and a surprisingly wide range of sizes, shapes and colours are available to provide diversity in any farm yard.

The UK's most common breed is probably the pale-skinned Large White with its heavy build, perkily erect ears, and strong jawline.

Males weigh up to 510 kilos, which is pretty heavy, while sows can produce two litters each year - often racking up more than 20 piglets in total.

Almost as large but more vividly marked is the black and white Saddleback.

This is a much hardier breed, more frequently kept outside, with sows said to make sweeter tempered mothers than those of the Large White.

However, all domesticated pigs can sometimes be aggressive and stories occasionally emerge somewhere in the world of people being attacked and killed.

As a child, I was once forced to take refuge in a tree after some pursuing pigs became angered by myself and a friend messing about in their field.

I can still remember peering down and realising with dismay how big their jaws were and how many teeth they had.

We managed to escape eventually after they lost interest and ambled off but I was always more wary of pigs after that.

Wild pigs and their sub-species can be exceptionally dangerous.

A few years ago, I read of some South American natives stumbling upon the severed hind legs of a jaguar still clamped to a tree trunk deep in the jungle.

The rest of this supreme killer had been ripped to shreds and eaten by a herd of wild pigs.

Apparently, it had tried to prey on one pig but been overpowered and slaughtered by its furious chums.

Must have been quite a battle.

Pigs are known for their inquisitiveness and powerful sense of smell, which makes them popular on the Continent for rooting out gastronomic treasures such as truffles. However, their noses occasionally lead them into trouble and one pig caused a safety scare after unearthing a live grenade left by soldiers on Salisbury Plain.

The wandering animal apparently thought the explosive might be good to eat since it had carefully dug it free of mud before the alarm was raised.

Bomb disposal experts were brought in to salvage and detonate the grenade while the pig was safely returned to its sty on nearby farmland.

It was lucky.

As someone quipped, it saved its own bacon because it did not do anything too rash with the mystery object.

431

RARE BLACK-TAILED godwit and water voles are at risk following a serious pollution incident in the Humber Estuary.

Conservationists are worried by an oil spill which has occurred at the Lindsey Oil Refinery on the banks of the estuary.

According to The Wildlife Trusts, the estuary is internationally important for its wildfowl and waders such as the black-tailed godwit.

But water voles and other small mammals are also in danger.

"Lincolnshire is a stronghold for water voles, the UK's fastest declining mammal," explained a spokesman for the Trusts. "The voles live in burrows in drainage ditches and these burrows are protected under the Wildlife and Countryside Act 1981.

"Oil has been leaking into drains and into the estuary, damaging habitat and threatening several species."

The local Lincolnshire Trust is said to be disappointed at the way in which the spill has been handled by the refinery.

Lionel Grooby, warden at Far Ings Nature Reserve, said: "Oil has been discharging into the drains for over 24 hours, and it was 16 hours before any action was taken to contain it. This is an extremely bad example of emergency planning. It simply should not happen in the 21st Century. All oil refineries must have good emergency plans to deal with situations like this."

Two other nearby Trust nature reserves, Killingholme Haven Pits and Rosper Road Pits, both of which have apparently been damaged by oil in the past, are also said to be threatened.

Caroline Steel, the Trusts' assistant director of conservation, added: "Now this oil spill has occurred, Lindsey Oil Refinery must take responsibility for the clean-up and for minimising the damage. A similar spill occurred a few years ago. Measures must now be taken to ensure that it never happens again."

A BULLFINCH AND a yellowhammer were among 22 wild birds allegedly netted by one man in Scotland.

Police investigators are reported to have raided a pensioner's home in East Lothian where the birds were being held captive after being trapped.

A number of siskins were also found at the address.

It is claimed the man had been taking the birds with a view to selling them abroad on the black market to collectors.

The man was later charged with offences relating to his alleged activity.

WOMEN TRYING TO get in the 'family way' should tuck into turkey this Christmas, according to a farming union.

"Turkey is good for women trying to get pregnant as 100g will provide almost 50 per cent of the recommended daily allowance of folic acid," reveals the NFU.

More than 33 million turkeys are now eaten each year across the UK with about a third of those gobbled up at Christmas.

"There are 28 different modern breeds of turkey but all originally stem from the North American wild turkey," adds the union.

"Turkeys were introduced to Europe from the Americas in the 16th Century and have become synonymous with Christmas.

"Since they were introduced into Britain the popularity of turkey meat has soared.

"Turkey is very low in fat and is also low in calories at just 140 per 100g. It's also a good source of all B vitamins, as well as potassium, phosphorus and zinc."

A GREAT TIT has shocked bird experts by completing a 1,359km jaunt overseas.

The little bird flew from Norfolk to the Baltic on its epic journey.

"Since the 1960s, great tits have been slowly getting bolder and bolder, moving further and further from home," says the British Trust for Ornithology.

"It is very rare for a great tit to travel over 100km but the BTO has been receiving an increasing number of reports of such long-distance journeys. The most recent movement was of a young female bird ringed near Fakenham, Norfolk.

"It was re-caught in Lithuania near the Baltic. This is a staggering 1,359km from Fakenham.

"Great tits really aren't built for migration but this bird broke all the rules.

"This is only the third time a ringed great tit has ventured so far east."

HARE COURSERS ARE preparing for what may be the last premier event of their year in the shadow of the new Hunting Act.

New dates have now been announced for the 2005 Waterloo Cup.

The controversial event, known as 'The Blue Riband of coursing' is normally held over three days at the end of February but this time will be run at Altcar on the 14th, 15th and 16th of the month.

Hare coursers themselves remain defiant in the face of the ban.

Many are pledging to fight on to retain the ancient pastime.

The sport sees greyhounds tested against each other in pursuit of a hare - often with fatal results for the hare itself.

It is that aspect which most upsets objectors.

With the ban poised to go live on February 18, the National Coursing Club - founded in 1858 - is rallying its members by quoting Britain's most famous wartime leader.

"Sir Winston Churchill famously said 'Now this is not the end'," said a spokesman.

"'It is not even the beginning of the end. But it is, perhaps, the end of the beginning.'

"No-one should believe that the House Of Commons forcing through the Hunting Act by means of the Parliament Act is the end of this story, or the end of coursing. "

A SCOTTISH HUNT Master has been cleared of contravening new laws in the country on hunting with hounds.

In the first case of its type to be heard under the Protection of Wild Mammals (Scotland) Act 2002, Hunt Master Trevor Adams was found not guilty of deliberately hunting a fox with 20 dogs contrary to the Act.

Anti-hunt groups were disappointed by the verdict but pleased the case had been brought as a warning to others.

Douglas Batchelor, chief executive of the League Against Cruel Sports, said:"The fact that this case came to court sends out a warning to Scottish hunts that charges will be pressed if they are thought to be acting illegally. The Sheriff confirmed that using dogs to deliberately kill a fox is an offence."

Ross Minett, director of Advocates for Animals, said:"Whilst accepting the verdict in this case, our fear is that some hunts may still be chasing foxes with dogs in the traditional manner. These hunts must remember that the chasing of foxes with dogs remains illegal."

Phyllis Campbell-McRae, UK director of the International Fund for Animal Welfare, commented:"We expect police to now keep a close eye on hunts' activities and anybody thought to be breaking the law must be prosecuted."

POACHERS ARE BEING hunted by the Environment Agency which is also asking the public to help.

Enforcement officers are urging residents to help them 'pull in a poacher' by reporting anyone acting suspiciously along Northumberland and Durham's waterways.

With the salmon and sea trout season for anglers ended, the enforcement team hopes people will keep an eye out for anyone trying to take advantage of quiet river banks to steal fish.

Team leader Kevin Summerson said:"We have already stepped up our covert surveillance operations thanks to an increase in tip-offs from the public which have helped us catch a number of poachers.

"But we want the public to remain vigilant at this important time.

"The River Tyne is regarded as the best salmon river in England and Wales and there are other rivers in the region which are following its success.

"As a result, angling is making a major contribution to the local economy so it is vital we ensure that our fish stocks are protected and poachers are prevented from stealing."

The Tees, Tyne, Wear, Coquet and Aln are all rivers used by migratory fish, says the Agency.

Each legally-caught salmon helps to boost the local economy.

GREAT CRESTED NEWTS have been given a major boost at a site in Peterborough.

A disused brick pit in the Hampton area of the city now has 'permanent legal protection' as the most important site for the rare creatures in Britain.

English Nature's ruling council has finalised declaration of the site as a nationally important Site of Special Scientific Interest.

Objections to the declaration had been made by O & H Hampton Ltd and Peterborough City Council, who own part of the land.

But English Nature's director of designated sites, Dr Andy Clements, said:"The old brick pits at Hampton provide the most amazing haven for great crested newts."

Pools created in the clay at the pit, together with ponds in nearby woodland and scrub, are said to provide perfect conditions for the newts.

Researchers estimate there are now more than 25,000 newts living there, making it possibly the most important site in Europe for the species.

JUST 400 WILDCATS are now thought to survive in the Scottish Highlands.

Numbers of all UK mammals have been revised following the Mammal Society's Autumn Symposium on British Mammal Populations.

Chairman Michael Woods said:"The 2004 figures reflect true changes in population size and also changes in our knowledge which have enabled us to revise our original estimates.

"What was very alarming was to hear that there may be as few as 400 wildcats left in the Scottish Highlands and urgent action needs to be taken now to prevent extinction.

"Dormouse populations are also declining, demonstrating the continuing importance of taking them into consideration in development proposals."

However, the good news was that otter and polecat populations were recovering.

The Society says it will continue to work with English Nature and other bodies to ensure that effective guidelines assisting wildlife remain in place.

THE VAST MAJORITY of the public believe police should not enforce the ban on hunting, according to an ICM poll.

An amazing 70 per cent of respondents said that officers should concentrate on other crimes when the legislation goes live in February.

Just 20 per cent thought that police officers should be used to enforce the ban.

The figures add up to another headache for police already contemplating the new law with dread as pro-hunt groups plan to launch mass acts of civil disobedience.

Alistair McWhirter, the Chief Constable for Suffolk and hunting spokesman for the Association of Chief Police Officers, says officers will have major problems.

In an interview with Horse and Hound magazine, he said:"If people want to exercise hounds, that's lawful. There isn't an offence until they actually hunt a mammal.

"But we wouldn't always know what constitutes hunting - and the police wouldn't want to get involved in that.

"This law will affect our relationship with rural communities. Many people who hunt are the police's greatest supporters."

NETTLE: the stinging friend of butterflies

JOLTING the unwary with its painful sting, the common nettle is one of our most unpopular weeds so it may come as a surprise that wildlife experts have been singing its praises of late.

Perhaps it passed you by, but 'National Be Nice to Nettles Week' saw plants you thought were just unlovely hazards of the garden or field become environmental heroes. You might wonder what the world is coming to when you can no longer duff up a few nettles with a clear conscience but there was a good point to be made.

Naturalist Chris Baines, a supporter of the drive to put nettles in a better light, explained: "*Stingers are a vital part of growing up, giving us one of the most painful early memories of close contact with nature.*

"*It is much later in life that most of us realise just how valuable they are, especially for some of our most beautiful wild creatures.*

"*Without stinging nettles, peacock, small tortoiseshell and red admiral butterflies would have nowhere to lay their eggs, so do please find a space for nettles somewhere in your neighbourhood.*"

Nettle fans won some prestigious backing after Buckingham Palace head gardener Mark Lane got involved in the campaign.

"*Within the Palace gardens, nettles play an important role in wildlife habitat areas as they provide a valuable food source for caterpillars,*" he said.

The common nettle (Urtica dioica) can grow up to a metre high with its jagged edged leaves and stem armed with ranks of tiny stinging hairs primed to repel any threat.

Each hair is hollow, filled with an acid-like stinging liquid and tipped with a tiny gland which reacts to touch.

In this country nettle stings remain painful for just a few minutes but the sting of an Australian species is so severe that it occasionally kills.

Like its leaves, nettle flowers are also green and dangle beside the stem with male and female flowers located on different plants.

In times past, nettles were dried and turned into hay for livestock with nettle seeds commonly mixed into horse feed to produce a sleeker coat.

But humans have benefited, too. Nettles were once routinely added to soups and stews to provide extra nutrition and still pop up in some of today's recipes.

A Northumberland company currently offers a "*gouda style, creamy and smooth*" nettle cheese which exploits the nettle's unique flavour as well as its nutritional value.

I myself tried a pint of nettle beer at a country show once - okay, but nothing to shout about.

I tried a couple more pints just to confirm my first impression and decided I quite liked it.

But by then, I quite liked everything. According to organisers of 'National Be Nice to Nettles Week', 17th Century diarist Samuel Pepys was known to eat "*nettle porridge*", which he found delicious.

Cooked nettles lose their ability to sting but some people believe there is an easy way to avoid the uncooked nettle's sting. This belief is even summarised in rhyme by 18th Century writer Aaron Hill:

"*Tender-handed stroke a nettle, and it stings you for your pains. Grasp it like a man of mettle, and it soft as silk remains.*"

I took his advice and experimented. Ouch! Ow! I am obviously not a man of mettle. Try testing his theory yourself - if you dare.

A VORACIOUS BEETLE which decimates lilies and other favourite flowers is spreading inexorably north across the whole UK, experts fear.

Latest research shows that the 8mm bright red lily beetle is now cutting a swathe through parts of the North East.

Beetle expert Andrew Duff told the British Wildlife journal:"The most worrying trend is a big increase in the number of lily beetles attacking native snake's-head fritillary, one of our most beautiful and rarest wildflowers.

"I am very concerned that this beautiful, but devastating, beetle will devastate our few remaining fritillary meadows unless steps are taken now to monitor them carefully and to eradicate any lily beetle infestations."

The Royal Horticultural Society added:"The growing number of specimens sent to us from places such as Durham, and even parts of Scotland, suggest that this beetle is still on the move.

"It reproduces rapidly and can strip a lily plant in full flower in a matter of days. "

FROZEN RABBITS WERE tossed on the fire as fuel during one of the harshest British winters ever experienced, according to a new book.

Dartmoor farmer Colin Pearse's memories of growing up on his family's farm are featured in his 400-page book, 'The Whitefaced Drift of Dartmoor's Prapper Sheep'.

The book also recalls some feezing winters when livestock were killed by the conditions and even humans struggled to survive.

In 1947, writes Colin, sheep deaths reached four million while 50,000 cattle expired and 200,000 acres of winter corn were ruined by frost.

"One farmer's wife, whose husband was ill, had no fuel for heat," he recounts."The only fuel she managed to find was frozen rabbits with which she kept a fire burning."

MINK SHOULD BE wiped out in Wales to save other native species, conservationists have warned the Welsh Assembly.

Mike Griffiths, a wildlife analyst for The Mammal Trust, believes the fierce predators - introduced in the 1920s from America - are on the verge of driving voles to extinction in the north of the country.

"Because they are short-sighted, voles are easy prey for mink," he said.

"However, mink are opportuni-predators, taking a wide range of small mammals, fish, birds and invertebrates.

"We've seen a 75 per cent decline in moorhens in the Alyn Valley and mink are now moving into pheasant-rearing areas.

"We have repeatedly called for a mink extermination programme in Wales. The Assembly is sympathetic but concerned about the reaction from animal rights groups.

"Some limited trapping is ongoing, mainly by landowners, but it needs to be done more systematically."

BADGER FANS CLAIM confusing new research in Ireland only underlines the futility of killing badgers to control bovine tuberculosis in cattle.

Commenting on a new scientific paper published about the Republic's badger culling trial, Dr Elaine King, chief executive of the National Federation of Badger Groups, said: "This trial suggests that badger culling only reduces TB in cattle if every single badger is exterminated.

"Even if you exclude the moral and political implications of such a strategy, the Irish study does not show whether the effect is large enough to warrant the massive economic cost of the slaughter."

Dr King revealed the NFBG had contacted the paper's author to establish why its researchers had concluded that widespread culling was "feasible" but "not viable".

"He said:'It would be technically possible to try and do it if it were legal or desirable or moral. But it's neither legal, nor morally justified, or anything like that, especially when there are alternatives'."

The trial had involved culling 2,360 badgers across 1,214 square kilometres in Cork, Donegal, Kilkenny and Monaghan between 1997 and 2002.

The NFBG said this was similar to the "proactive" badger culling strategy currently being implemented in the Krebs' experiment in Britain but badgers had been virtually eradicated from the study areas in Ireland.

Dr King added:"This paper fails to answer the key question that every cattle farmer in Britain will be asking - what was the reduction in bovine TB? Eighteen months ago, the Irish researchers told Radio 4 that badger culling reduced TB in cattle by an average of 80 per cent. That claim is simply not supported by this paper. In fact, it's impossible to determine the actual reduction in TB that has been achieved in Ireland by badger culling.

"We have been advised that the Republic of Ireland has slaughtered more than half its badgers over the last 10 years, reducing the population to less than 100,000 badgers. Badger densities are significantly lower in Ireland compared to Britain. Yet in 2002, the last year for which data is available, 6.5 per cent of Irish cattle herds were under TB restriction.

"In Britain, which has three times more badgers than Ireland, 3.6 per cent of herds are under movement restriction.

"Ireland's futile badger slaughter has simply confirmed that badger culling will never be a solution to the problem of bovine TB. This makes it vital that DEFRA focuses all its energies on controlling the movement of infected livestock and removing all infected cattle by implementing the more accurate gamma interferon TB test."

A GOLDEN RETRIEVER is being hunted in Shropshire following a savage attack on a rare breed sheep.

The dog, a breed normally known for its placid nature, was seen covered in blood emerging from its victim's field.

The rare Soy sheep had to be put out of its misery when its injuries were judged too serious for it to be saved.

Police are warning livestock owners to be on their guard until the culprit is caught.

GAME BIRD SHOOTING now seems the top target of 2005 for Labour MPs and animal rights groups following their victory in achieving a foxhunting ban.

On the eve of the New Year, and despite a welter of still unresolved legal arguments over hunting in England and Wales, the League Against Cruel Sports called on supporters to lobby for greater control over commercial shooting.

Meanwhile, the Labour dominated Environment, Food and Rural Affairs Committee recently launched its own attack on the rearing of game birds and suggested 'limiting the numbers of game birds that are able to be reared'.

The committee also rejected the Game Farmers Association's code of practice and was concerned that "of the game birds being reared, only 40 per cent end up being shot."

Successful moves are likely to impact on large estates such as pop star Madonna's on the Wiltshire/Dorset border where wealthy shooters are invited several times a year.

Simon Hart, chief executive of the Countryside Alliance, said:"Anyone who still believes that shooting is not now under serious threat should read this (committee) report.

"The agenda of animal rights organisations and Labour MPs is one and the same and shooting is now the top item.

"Even if DEFRA ministers do not collude with MPs, as they have in the past, they will again be powerless to control the vast majority of their colleagues."

A TURTLE WHICH survived a vicious shark attack is being cared for at a Scottish wildlife sanctuary.

The animal, nicknamed Shell by staff at the Scottish Sea Life Sanctuary in Oban, has only three flippers after one was ripped off in the assault.

"Shell swam 4,000 miles to a Scottish beach, even though she was attacked by the shark and had one of her flippers taken off, " said a spokesman for the centre.

"She was found washed up on a beach at North Uist, in the Outer Hebrides."

At first, her condition worried staff who believed she might not live much longer.

"When she arrived, she could hardly move or eat because her body was so cold," explained the spokesman.

"But over the next few days we slowly raised the temperature of the water she was in and she responded by becoming more active.

"With our help she is starting to get some much needed nourishment.

"Her eyes are also responding and are now looking much better."

FARMERS AND SMALL shop owners are being put out of business by supermarket giant Tesco, Friends of the Earth has warned.

FoE's supermarkets campaigner Sandra Bell said:"Many retailers are reeling from their worst Christmas trading for years yet Tesco is expected to announce healthy trading figures.

"The retail giant's uncontrolled growth is destroying our town centres by putting local shops out of business leaving the public with no choice but to go to Tesco, while the its thirst for profits is leading to many British farmers going out of business.

"The Government must set out more robust planning policy, introduce stronger protection for suppliers and call a moratorium on any further takeovers."

It needed to stop putting big companies first.

If it didn't, there would be fewer local shops, more farmers would go out of business and there would be little hope for a more sustainable future for UK food and farming.

FoE urged the Government to use two upcoming crucial opportunities to change policy on supermarkets.

"The Department of Trade and Industry currently has a chance to amend the supermarket Code of Practice so that it protects suppliers from the bullying behaviour of the big supermarkets," it said,"while John Prescott's office is due to issue new planning policy guidance on town centres, which could give a boost to local shops and local economies.

"According to the latest data, the Christmas period helped Tesco achieve a record share of the grocery market at 29 per cent. Yet recent polls show that people still value local shops and have greater trust in food sold by small specialist shops rather than by giant supermarkets."

TV TWITCHER BILL Oddie was whacked over the head with his own telescope by an angry landowner while birdwatching as a boy.

He's also been squirted with slurry, blasted at with firearms, and has pronged his privates on barbed wire in his eagerness to spot birds.

During a Dorset ramble to celebrate the lifting of right to roam restrictions across southern England, he said:"One sound that really conjures up the atmosphere of the countryside for me isn't the song of the skylark or the call of the lapwing - it's 'Oi! What are you doing there? Get out of it!'

"Just about everywhere was private once and birding was, frankly, a matter of just trespassing.

"It was amazing how violent and possessive some landowners could be."

AN EXPLOSION OF flytipping in pretty country areas is one throbbing New Year headache expected by the Environment Agency.

Sally Coble, an environment manager with the Agency, said:"Christmas produces waste, there's no getting away from it. But dumping the problem onto someone else is hardly in the festive spirit.

" We've been steadily building up our surveillance capability and now have good coverage of known hot spots. And whenever we get someone on camera, there's a very good chance it will lead to a prosecution, a hefty fine, and a criminal record. I can't think of many Christmas presents worse than that."

Last year, clean-up costs reached almost £150 million in England and Wales.

LAPWING: stop-go scurry caught Shakespeare's eye

ELEGANT but noisy, lapwings used to be a common sight in our countryside where they gathered in huge flocks on open fields and grasslands.

Like other farmland species, the speed of their recent decline has been startling and desperate attempts are currently being made to halt this.

Lapwings are long-legged waders but are easily distinguished from other waders thanks to their short beaks and long, thin, backward trailing crests.

From a distance, lapwings appear plain black and white but closer inspection reveals their beautiful, deep glossy green plumage, hence another name for them - 'green plovers'.

Many people also call them 'peewits', a word derived from their far-carrying 'pee-wit' cries.

But the more common name is lapwing, which is equally apt as the bird's broad, stubby wings seem to lap at the air in flight.

Such wings actually offer great manoeuvrability and enable lapwings to mob and drive off marauding crows and magpies which threaten their nests.

These are bare scrapes in the ground where up to five mottled brown eggs are laid each year between March and June.

During this period, male lapwings put on spectacular tumbling flight displays and call loudly to females.

Insects and worms are the main food items and lapwings pinpoint these during a constant stop-go scurry across open ground.

This method of moving about even caught Shakespeare's eye.

In 'Much Ado About Nothing', he wrote:"*Now begin, for look where Beatrice, like a lapwing, runs close by the ground to hear our counsel.*"

Lapwings have a chequered history. Commercial egg collectors originally started the birds' decline as far back as the 19th Century when lapwing eggs were prized as snacks.

Drainage and enclosure of land by farmers also saw flocks evicted from many of their ancient breeding grounds.

The Lapwing Act of 1926, which clamped down on egg collecting, improved their fortunes for a while. But their long-term recovery was never going to last, especially when faced with the stupidity of EU bureaucrats.

Not content with wrecking our farming and fishing industries, our would-be masters in Brussels have also ruined the prospects of many farmland birds - including those of the lapwing.

Today, EU-inspired agricultural practices - such as the switch to autumn-sown crops - have seen the lapwing join the growing ranks of threatened species.

Breeding populations may have slumped by as much as two fifths from a high of about 250,000 pairs in the 1980s.

I sometimes wonder what kind of bird-brains dreamt up the entire EU project in the first place.

Shouldn't we now be netting these individuals, ringing them, and packing them off to the Arctic tundra for a few harsh winters as payback?

437

THE PROPOSED HUNTING ban has become mired in almost comical confusion as Labour bends over backwards to avoid mass protests before the expected General Election.

Anti-hunt groups have been outraged to learn that anyone falling foul of the controversial law across England and Wales will not be given a criminal record.

Accusing Labour of yet more breathtaking political cynicism, campaigners say it is ludicrous for transgressors not to be given a criminal record for cruelty to animals when the Bill becomes law.

John Rolls, director of animal welfare promotion for the RSPCA, said:"I shall be making some very strong representations to ministers and police chiefs.

"We have not gone through this long battle, including High Court action, to have people getting off without criminal records. If people are guilty of cruelty to animals they should be prosecuted and they should have a criminal record.

"We expect police to act on hunting in the same way as any other crime."

Speaking on behalf of the Association of Chief Police Officers, Nigel Yeo, the Assistant Chief Constable of Sussex, confirmed that offences under the hunting Act still carried a fine of up to £5,000.

Yet he added:"They are not recordable or notifiable under the national crime recording standards and I am advised by Home Office lawyers that persons convicted of offences under the Hunting Act will not secure a criminal record."

The news is a boost to pro-hunt groups who failed in their first legal challenge against the ban.

The Countryside Alliance plans to continue its courts campaign until every legal avenue is exhausted.

OTTERS COULD BE scared away if a new Devon bypass gets the go-ahead, critics claim.

Many other creatures such as badgers, lesser horseshoe bats, and cirl buntings, are also said to be affected by plans for the £78million road from Penn Inn, Newton Abbot, to Hamelin Way near Torquay.

Seven wildlife sites would be disrupted by the road with construction resulting in loss of half the Edginswell Farm wetland site and most of the Aller Bridge wildlife site, say conservationists.

However, engineers claim the actual planning application contains measures to minimise the impact on wildlife.

They say special feeding areas would be created for the bats, a stream would be modified to shelter otters, and tunnels would be dug so that both badgers and otters would not be killed by traffic.

SALMON HAVE BEEN given a boost in Wales with the introduction of new byelaws closing down so-called 'mixed stock' net fisheries.

For many years, fisheries simultaneously took salmon from a number of different places in coastal areas and estuaries.

"They present significant management problems because it is very difficult to determine the level of exploitation of each of the individual river stocks involved," said the Environment Agency.

"Even if the overall level of exploitation in the fishery appears to be satisfactory, exploitation of one particular river stock could be just too high."

Mixed-stock net fisheries already closed through the new byelaws include drift nets at the mouth of the River Usk; coastal wade nets in parts of St Brides Bay and Carmarthen Bay; sling nets off the mouth of the River Clwyd; and seine or draft nets around the north coast of Anglesey, in the Menai Straits, around the coast of the Lleyn Peninsula and off the mouth of the River Dwyfawr.

"One mixed-stock salmon net fishery remains in Wales - the Black Rock lave net fishery in the Severn Estuary, near Caldicot.

"Although it operates on a mixed-stock basis it is likely that the Black Rock lave net fishery has only a minimal impact on salmon stocks and its impact is not considered to be significant in conservation terms.

"A further 11 rivers will continue to support net fisheries, each exploiting stock from single river systems. These are the Mawddach, Conwy, Dyfi, Dysynni, Glaslyn, Dee, Nevern, Tywi, Taf, Teifi and Cleddau.

"In contrast to mixed-stock salmon fisheries, these single-stock fisheries can be managed to limit the exploitation of salmon in each river to a sustainable level."

FOUR HORSES CAUSED havoc when they burst out of their field in Shropshire and charged around local roads.

Yobs were blamed for the drama at Telford after apparently startling the animals by driving a car into their field.

The frightened foursome stampeded across busy roads, their actions sparking a series of dramatic near misses among traffic.

Fortunately, none of the horses were hurt and motorists, too, escaped injury.

Later, all four horses were returned to their field.

THE GAME CONSERVANCY Trust has announced it will run a "touring roadshow" this spring, offering expert advice to farmers, game managers and landowners on new agricultural reforms.

Peter Thompson, biodiversity officer with the Trust, said:"These are the biggest changes in agriculture in the last 30 years and our objective is to make sure that farmers and game managers make the most of their land for wild game and other wildlife as well as ensuring that they claim the correct subsidies for improving the environment."

During the roadshows, experts from the Trust will explain how farmers and game managers will be able to access a share of the £1.7billion of subsidies available and how they will need to meet the cross compliance standards designed to give extra protection to the environment, soil, wildlife habitats and the landscape.

POLICE ARE INVESTIGATING after a peregrine falcon was found shot dead.

The RSPB says it is outraged at the discovery of the dead peregrine near its Bempton Cliffs nature reserve in East Yorkshire.

The body of the adult female was found in a field and a post mortem analysis has confirmed that it was shot.

RSPB Bempton Cliffs warden Trevor Charlton said: "Sadly, it seems that yet another rare bird of prey has been killed by a criminal act of destruction.

"I am shocked by news of this incident and angry that such a spectacular and exciting bird has died in this way.

"We were hopeful that peregrine falcons might once again colonise the cliffs at our Bempton reserve, giving pleasure to thousands of visitors, so the death of this female is a real setback."

A report produced by the RSPB revealed that crimes against birds of prey were still at an "unacceptably high level."

The Birdcrime 2003 report documented 560 crimes against wild birds, including 143 cases of shooting and destruction of birds of prey and 91 cases of poisoning.

Peregrine falcons are still rare breeding birds with the most recent survey in 2002 giving a total of just 1,402 pairs in the UK.

The bird is the fastest in the world and can reach speeds of about 200mph when it stoops to kill.

RSPB regional director Andy Bunten added: "Our research shows that there is still a major challenge ahead to ensure effective enforcement and suitable penalties bring to an end the needless persecution and poisoning of our spectacular birds of prey.

"I hope that anyone who has any information at all about this incident will contact the police."

Humberside Police are currently appealing for witnesses.

WILD GOATS ARE facing a mass cull after developing a taste for flowers at a cemetery.

The goats also plunder the blooms growing in residents' gardens, according to Lynton and Lynmouth Town Council in Devon.

Up to 120 goats are now thought to inhabit the Valley of the Rocks, causing various problems for local people.

But chomping on flowers left at the graves of loved ones is their worst transgression - and the final straw for many.

Under controversial proposals, three quarters of the hardy animals could be shot, leaving a more manageable number in place.

HUGE DAMAGE TO the countryside could result from Deputy Prime Minister John Prescott's dream of colossal new urban sprawl, warn rural campaigners.

Many campaigners welcome the building of affordable, subsidised homes for families unable to afford market housing.

However, there are still major concerns that the Government wants a giant increase in the output of new homes for sale on the open market.

"This would do massive damage to the environment and the countryside," says the Council for the Protection of Rural England.

"The Government has just got to be more ambitious about making better use of previously developed brownfield land.

"Its target is for 60 per cent of all new homes to come from conversions or building on brownfields.

"It hit that target eight years early and the level has now reached 66 per cent.

"The Government should raise its sights right now to 75 per cent, benefiting towns and cities by bringing in more investment whilst protecting the countryside."

Shaun Spiers, chief executive of the CPRE, added:"We need greater recycling of previously developed land and buildings, a shift to higher densities across the country, a much stronger focus on urban regeneration, and effective measures to reduce regional divide in prosperity.

"We simply cannot build our way out of our housing problems by big increases in provision of market housing which, even if this were achievable, would do nothing to reduce house prices and cause environmental damage."

OWLS IN SCOTLAND are to get their first dedicated owl centre to help the public 'wise up' about their ways.

With numbers of the twilight birds dropping, falconer Patricia Downie - an expert on owls - is planning to open the new centre at Huntly in Aberdeenshire.

Nine owls have already been trained and readied for the venture by 26 year-old Miss Downie who has worked with owls since childhood.

She said:"Women, children and disabled people, in particular, love owls. This will give them a chance to hold them and for disabled and elderly people it can be very therapeutic.

"The other good thing about this is that it will help a lot of people realise that owls are not as popular as they once were.

"It will let people see where to find them, what to do if they find one, and how many owls there are in the world, not just this country."

A JUDAS TREE growing in the garden of a Buckinghamshire woman has been found to be one of the largest ever to grow in the country.

Janet Brunswick, who lives near Aylesbury, had contacted the Tree Register after seeing an article about 'champion trees' in her newspaper.

She gave details of her own thick-trunked sprawling tree and was delighted to learn she had one of the largest Judas trees (Cercis siliquastrum) ever recorded in the UK, according to Tree Register officials.

The organisation works in partnership with The Woodland Trust to record Britain's veteran and ancient trees.

SPARROW: garden mystery leads to double blow

THE humble house sparrow has declined so sharply in recent years that fears have been raised for its long-term future, something unimaginable a few decades ago when flocks were common.

According to the RSPB, house sparrow numbers fell by a staggering 64 per cent between the 1970s and the 1990s - an estimated loss of almost 10 million birds.

While no-one seems to know what lies behind its continuing decline, everyone appears united in admiration of this perky little bird.

Even 19th Century writer Henry David Thoreau said:*"I once had a sparrow alight upon my shoulder for a moment while I was hoeing in a village garden and felt more distinguished by that circumstance than I should have been by any epaulet I could have worn."*

I've been thinking of house sparrows quite a bit lately after a pair nested in a hole high up on an outside wall at our house.

This nest sparked a little sadness and a lot of mystery when my wife noticed three waxy pink, featherless chicks close by.

All were dead and the hole itself deserted.

Surprisingly, none of the chicks were lying directly beneath the hole as casualties in previous years had been found.

Two were discovered on top of a plastic garden table 15ft away next to some fir trees, the other beneath the table.

Very odd.

None could have glided so far on their tiny, stunted wings.

In addition, all three corpses seemed unusually large and heavy for sparrow nestlings.

Two possibilities originally sprang to mind: (1) The chicks had been snatched from the hole and then dropped by one of the predatory birds that haunt our garden.

(2) They had just fallen from the hole and their frantic mother had tried vainly to retrieve them, hoisting two as far as the table top.

Neither theory was correct, as I later discovered.

I should really have taken more note when I saw an angry female blackbird driving off a magpie in our garden days earlier.

In the branches of a fir tree, just above the table, I found an empty blackbird's nest.

Of course, the dead nestlings were blackbird chicks all along.

Unknown to us, there had been TWO nests outside our kitchen door at the same time.

This was the nest which had actually been attacked.

Whatever had happened, both sites were now deserted, the sparrow's eggs in the wall apparently left unhatched.

A desperate drama had been played out involving the nearby blackbird's nest, too traumatic for the mother sparrow to remain in place.

Rather than stick around to see her own chicks massacred, she had left them to die in their shells.

Sad.

Well, there was now no handy excuse for me not to venture out into our back garden

So I could no longer put off one of my least favourite chores.

After days of nagging, I finally mowed the damn lawn.

BUTTERFLY FANS HAVE warmly greeted this month's launch of the new Environmental Stewardship Scheme as a major boost to their favourite insects.

Butterfly Conservation hopes the scheme will help reverse the rapid decline of farmland butterflies and moths.

A spokesman said:"The crisis facing butterflies and moths is very deep. Seven out of every 10 species are declining and four butterflies and 60 moths became extinct during the last century, often due to the intensification of farming practices."

The new scheme, launched by Secretary of State for the Environment, Margaret Beckett, is said to represent a big change in the way subsidies are paid to farmers.

They will now be rewarded for better environmental management rather than just production.

"Research by Butterfly Conservation has already shown that the earlier agri-environment schemes such as Countryside Stewardship have slowed or even reversed butterfly declines and we are hopeful that the new scheme will bring even greater benefits," explained the spokesman.

"Species that have already benefited include some of our most spectacular downland species, such as the chalkhill blue and dark green fritillary, and threatened species, such as the silver-spotted skipper."

Dr Martin Warren, chief executive of the charity, added:"The new scheme brings some light at the end of a dark tunnel of butterfly declines and gives us real hope that farming and biodiversity can once again thrive together.

"Butterflies and moths are especially sensitive to changing farm management and are valuable indicators of our farmland biodiversity.

"We look forward to working with DEFRA in monitoring and evaluating the new scheme and urge Government to press for even greater reform of the Common Agricultural Policy in coming years."

POLICE ARE INVESTIGATING after two ducks from a Shropshire collection which has delighted children for years were found with their throats cut.

Yobs are thought to have broken into the birds' enclosure in Clun.

The ducks were whisked away from the scene and then brutally killed.

Their pathetic carcasses were later found discarded in a field, adding to the impression that they had been killed for fun rather than food.

GOLDEN EAGLES ARE among birds threatened by a massive windfarm development proposed for the Isle of Lewis in the Hebrides, warn conservationists.

Plans would involve the construction of 234 wind turbines on "an extremely fragile and special wildlife site" on the north Lewis moor, claim campaigners.

The RSPB says it is objecting in the strongest terms because the turbines would be spread across the Lewis Peatlands Special Protection Area - home to golden eagles, merlins, black-throated divers, red-throated divers, dunlins and greenshanks.

Anne McCall, RSPB planning and development manager, said:"The Lewis Peatlands are a gem in Scotland's natural history crown.The developers are proposing to put a massive industrial complex on a very important site for wildlife. This is asking for conflict.

"We believe this windfarm proposal is not just bad for birds but bad for the development of renewables as well."

The wind turbines would each be 140 metres tall with a rotor diameter of 100 metres - longer than a jumbo jet.

The development would also include new roads, nine electrical sub-stations, a control building and 56 kilometres of overhead lines, supported by 210 pylons.

As well as the breeding birds for which the site is designated, the Lewis Peatlands are said to be a thoroughfare for migrating whooper swans, corncrakes and Scotland's vulnerable population of white-tailed sea eagles.

A CROW NAMED Russell has battled its way into top place in the affections of a Scottish grandfather.

The cheeky bird, named after Aussie 'Gladiator' star Russell Crowe, has relegated Meg the dog to second place in the eyes of Bill Glennie, from Dyce.

The crow was nursed to health by Bill and his wife El after one of their grandchildren found it almost dead beneath a tree.

Now the free flying bird knocks on the couple's window each day to be fed, follows Bill around like a pet, and even hitches a lift in his car.

"He's really very clever and very cheeky," Bill, 63, explained.

"He's a great character. If I'm working outside, he'll stay with me the whole day. Sometimes I'll be walking up the lane and he'll fly down and land on my shoulder, then sit there while I'm going in and out of the shed."

FOXHUNTING GROUPS BUOYED up by massive support are still pursuing legal moves to overturn the new law banning hunting with hounds across England and Wales.

A petition has now been lodged with the House of Lords requesting that they hear an appeal in the case challenging the validity of the 1949 Parliament Act.

According to the Countryside Alliance, the Court of Appeal recognised the constitutional significance of the challenge to the validity of the Act in its judgement and supported the argument that the Act was subordinate legislation.

The judges, however, rejected the case on the grounds that the 1949 Act was only a 'relatively modest' amendment to the 1911 Parliament Act, and added that the 1949 Act had been assumed to be valid for 55 years.

WOODLAND BIRDS ARE continuing to slump in numbers despite massive efforts to conserve them, according to researchers.

A new study, published in the March edition of the journal 'British Birds', says up to four-fifths of some species have vanished with scientists unable to give a simple explanation.

The worst hit species are less familiar than common garden birds such as blackbirds and robins which may be why their plight has gone largely unnoticed.

Numbers of spotted flycatcher, lesser spotted woodpecker, lesser whitethroat, lesser redpoll and tree pipit all fell by more than 75 per cent between 1966 and 1999.

The researchers have come up with seven possible causes for the declines:

-Pressures on migrant birds during migration, or in African wintering grounds.

-Climate change in Britain, especially changes in the timing of the emergence of insects used as food, and the drying-out of woodlands.

-Reduction in the actual numbers of insects and other invertebrates.

-Impact of changing land use on woodland edges and on habitats outside woodland.

-Reduced management of lowland woodland.

-Intensified habitat modification by deer, which eat the woodland bushes, shrubs and grasses, and stop regeneration of trees, reducing nesting areas and insect populations.

-New pressure on nests and young birds from predators, such as grey squirrels, members of the crow family, and great spotted woodpeckers.

A FARM IN Berkshire has been honoured for its water efficiency at a top awards ceremony after making annual savings of 1,600 cubic metres of water by re-using treated wastewater.

Sheepdrove Organic Farm was the winner of the Agriculture and Horticulture category of the Environment Agency's Water Efficiency Award.

The award, presented in London, rewards and celebrates farmers that help to conserve water.

The 2,000-acre farm had developed "a whole-farm approach to water conservation," judges heard.

"One important initiative was to install a sophisticated reedbed water treatment system. This treats all wastewater from the farm, staff cottages and conference centre. After the water has been cleaned in the reedbed it overflows to a willow plantation, before soaking back to the aquifer from which the farm abstracts.

"Some of the treated water is also removed from the lake for other uses, including pig wallowing and the irrigation of trees.

"The whole system supports a significant population of birds, fish and invertebrates."

BABY EELS ARE at the centre of a clampdown by the Environment Agency which fears stocks on the River Severn could be damaged by widespread illegal fishing.

"With this year's elver fishing season already underway," said a spokesman,"the Agency's enforcement teams are again patrolling the banks of the Severn alongside partners such as the police and local authorities to catch fishermen operating without a licence or acting illegally.

"The patrols aim to put an end to the irresponsible behaviour that in the past has been associated with this lucrative activity."

However, it's a tough job as the Severn flows 220 miles to the Bristol Channel.

"With elvers fetching up to £300 a kilo on the open market, the competition for fish can lead to the use of illegal equipment, damage to property and, in some cases, even violence," said the spokesman.

"The huge majority of elver fishermen who operate within the law have nothing to fear. We will not restrict the number of elvers caught, or stop elver fishing, and we are keen to preserve this historic activity along the banks of the River Severn.

"With the Europe-wide decline in eels, Severn elvers, legally caught and in good condition are becoming increasingly important for stocking programmes.

"Fishing without a licence and using illegal equipment that harms elvers gives some an unfair advantage and threatens the future of elver fishing.

"We urge fishermen to help us to stamp out the illegal activities of some of their less savoury competitors who show no regard for livelihoods and safety of fellow fishermen."

HARES ARE BEING boosted by a new conservation effort across six UK counties, the Game Conservancy Trust has revealed.

"The brown hare, or 'Lepus europaeus', has been a familiar face across the British Isles since Roman times," said a spokesman."However, a substantial decline in numbers since the 1960s has led to its classification as a 'vulnerable species'."

Several groups, including the Trust and The Mammal Society, have now come together with the aim of doubling brown hare numbers by 2010.

BADGERS MAY FACE a 'strategic cull' after more than 300 vets pressed for the move.

Although many conservation groups deny badgers are responsible for spreading TB, the vets insist the powerful burrowers are mainly responsible for passing the disease on to cattle.

All the vets signed an open letter in which they also sought a vote of no confidence in Environment Secretary Margaret Beckett.

Most vets who signed the letter are from England's South West region which is thought to be the worst hit by bovine TB.

They claim the disease has shot up every year since 1986 with almost 3,000 cases reported last year.

However, the National Federation of Badger Groups said:"The vets leading the campaign to kill more badgers are calling for a policy that some of them created in the 1970s. The Government's own Independent Scientific Group has shown that this policy failed to deliver a reduction in bovine TB."

DORMOUSE: rural encounter on a freezing day

NOCTURNAL and secretive, the dormouse has always been one of the more difficult creatures of the countryside to spot.

Whenever it does pop into view, its fluffy tail and orangey brown colouring instantly set it apart from other mice.

Nor can it be confused with the larger, grey edible dormouse or 'glis glis' - a squirrel-like creature only introduced to Britain at the turn of the century and now surviving mainly in the Chilterns.

The common dormouse has been a well-established inhabitant of this country for centuries, albeit living mostly in southern hedges and forests.

With so many birds and animals eager to snap it up for lunch, it is hardly surprising the dormouse stays well hidden during the day and only ventures out to feed at night.

Then, as it forages for insects, seeds and nuts, its three-inch body is anchored and balanced among branches by that downy tail of almost equal length.

Thorn bushes are a favourite breeding ground during the summer months when the dormouse builds a tightly domed nest and gives birth to a litter of up to seven offspring.

Winter sees it building a nest closer to the ground to hibernate alone, often among tree roots or at the foot of a hedge.

Numbers of dormice are thought to have plummeted of late with the rise of the domestic cat blamed as one cause.

However, our own technological ingenuity has also played a role.

English Nature revealed that mechanical flailing of hedgerows had caused severe problems for dormice.

"Traditionally, hedgerows were managed by hand which had a less dramatic effect on the size and growth of a hedge," explained a spokesman.

"Hedges need at least two to three years growth to provide suitable food sources and habitats for dormice.

"Mechanical flailing cuts hedges back hard in the early autumn and reduces the amount of berries available. Dormice need to feed on berries, fruits and nuts in the autumn to fatten up before hibernating."

Whatever the causes of their decline, dormice have now vanished from almost 70 per cent of the hedgerows where they were present only 20 years ago.

I once noticed a solitary dormouse on a stone beneath a hedge while out seeking casual labouring work at local farms when I was a student.

There had been a severe frost the night before and the tiny creature seemed immobilised, virtually frozen in place.

It would have made the perfect snack for any passing weasel or stoat so I carefully picked it up and slipped it into a crevice in a wall.

I hoped this would also give it shelter from the biting spring wind which was whipping across nearby fields.

When I walked past a few minutes later, it was still there.

Its beady little eyes stared at me in the same baleful, fixed way.

But now its nose was twitching more busily.

I took that as a good sign and walked on.

BARN OWLS COULD be barnstorming back to healthier numbers after the discovery of early breeding success in Wiltshire.

The Hawk and Owl Trust has reported unusually early broods of the owls in the county which are now encouraging hopes of a national resurgence of the species.

Some young barn owls have even been ringed two months earlier than normal, reveals the Trust.

One brood of four owlets was ringed near Salisbury Plain on April 9 by retired army officer Major Nigel Lewis, a Trust trustee and one of its voluntary advisers on barn owl conservation.

Major Lewis, who has put up hundreds of nestboxes for birds of prey in the area, estimates that the eggs were laid during the first week of February.

He said:"I am not supposed to be checking barn owls yet but early breeding by other species caused me to take a careful look at some of their nesting sites."

The early owlets were well fed, he found, and even had a larder of five wood mice still to be eaten.

Local tawny owls and kestrels were also on eggs early, he said, and some had above-average clutch sizes.

"Judging by the numbers of eggs in other barn owl nests, 2005 should be a good year," added Major Lewis.

"Although they are still at the mercy of late spring weather, this early success is a happy contrast to last year when breeding productivity of barn owls in and around Salisbury Plain hit an all-time low. There was a 30 per cent decline in breeding pairs in the area, compared with 2003.

"At the Hawk and Owl Trust we think this could be due to several factors, such as competition from other birds for the same food, vole population dynamics, or loss of rough grassland - vital for the barn owl's main prey of short-tailed voles. We urge farmers and landowners to safeguard field margins and conserve more rough grass habitat."

At the last count, only 4,000 breeding pairs of barn owls were found in the UK.

MOUNTAIN BIKERS ARE being challenged to have a go at one of the most gruelling country riding competitions ever held in Scotland.

'10 Under the Ben' will challenge entrants to ride as many circuits of a 10-mile loop near Ben Nevis as they can in 10 hours this June.

According to the Forestry Commission, the route takes in the famous Witch's Trail in Leanachan Forest, near Fort William.

DARTMOOR PONIES ARE dying out and could be extinct within five years, experts fear.

The link between Man and the small but sturdy ponies can be traced back over 3,000 years at the animals' West Country stronghold.

But the ponies themselves are thought to date back much further.

Elizabeth Newbolt-Young, one of the founders of the Dartmoor Pony Heritage Trust, said:"All the alarm bells are ringing.

"They will not be here in five years time if we do not do something now."

The plucky ponies were once much in demand with many bought as pit animals for coal work or used in West Country tin mines.

Now, however, they have hardly any financial value and are not even wanted as pets.

Only a few hundred are thought to remain at large, wandering to and fro on the wind-blasted moors.

Dru Butterfield, the DPHT's project officer, said:"The greatest need is cash so we can sustain the scheme we've put together and educate the public.

"If people aren't aware this breed is likely to die out, then of course they'll do nothing to help. But if someone makes a decision to buy or to support a breed of pony, then we want that pony to be a Dartmoor."

A local campaign has been launched to save the ponies.

OTTERS KILLED ON a stretch of Scottish road may not have died in vain.

The traffic deaths of almost 50 otters on the A9 between Perth and Pitlochry have been used to build a picture of the worst accident blackspots.

Russell Coope and his wife Beryl have compiled a map that shows the location of 47 otter deaths during the last decade.

It is hoped that, as a result, concerned locals will be better able to devise ways to help otters cross the road safely at their favoured crossing points.

Chris Hodkinson, treasurer of a Pitlochry wildlife group, said:"Simple reflectors on posts at black spots might make a real difference and slight alterations to the culverts could make them more otter-friendly at little cost."

SPRING 2005 HAS bamboozled nature with frogs among creatures worst hit, according to The Woodland Trust.

"Over 60,000 wildlife sightings from the general public show that many of our native species are struggling to cope with climate change," said a spokesman.

"Early reports indicate that the 'stop-start spring', with major fluctuations in temperature, resulted in widespread sightings of frozen frog spawn."

Commenting on the findings, TV birdwatcher and naturalist Bill Oddie said:"When I was a lad we had 'proper' winters and spring started in April.

"Now that seems a thing of the past. When compared to records from previous years these results show that some of our insects and plants are appearing several weeks earlier.

"Climate change is not something happening a million miles away.

"It is going on in our back gardens and parks, affecting common everyday species."

THE BATTLE OVER hunting is set to rage on despite the hunting season itself drawing to a close.

The Countryside Alliance said hunts around the country continued hunting despite the Hunting Act coming into force.

The groups took part in more than 1,000 days of hunting and about 800 foxes were killed using a variety of methods including flushing the animals to guns and employing terriers to protect gamebirds.

Alliance chief executive Simon Hart, said:"It is a huge morale boost to see hunts determined to retain their infrastructure until this temporary ban is repealed. Hunts around the country have shown just how impossible it would be for already overstretched police forces to enforce the legislation.

"The support for hunting in the wake of the ban has been outstanding, and hunts will be looking forward to next season with increased determination.

"The Hunting Handbook, produced by the Alliance in conjunction with the Council of Hunting Associations, has been instrumental in providing a way forward for the hunting community until the Hunting Act is erased from the Statute Book. A new edition will be published soon."

The League Against Cruel Sports, meanwhile, continues its opposition and points to a recent incident in Northern Ireland to show domestic pets are still at risk from hounds as well as foxes.

"Hounds taking part in a hunt in Lurgan viciously mauled an eight-year-old girl's beloved cat to death,"said a spokesman.

"Audrey Spence returned from holiday to learn that hounds from the Iveagh Hunt had got into the garden of her Connaught Park home and killed her daughter's cat Misty."

The distressing spectacle was witnessed by shaken local children, according to the League, and the hunt later apologised.

USPCA chief executive Stephen Philpott said:"The need for a total ban on hunting with dogs has been brutally outlined by the obscene spectacle of a child's pet being torn to shreds in the sanctuary of a garden."

BUMBLEBEES SHOULD NOW be easier to identify thanks to a new guide.

For the first time, 'Field Guide to the Bumblebees of Great Britain and Ireland' uses a three-step way to identify bees, doing away with the need to put them under a microscope.

According to English Nature, the new technique could help an army of naturalists and field workers better monitor bumblebees, especially rare types.

ORGANIC POTATOES ARE now cheaper and come in more varieties than ever before, according to researchers.

A study led by Nafferton Ecological Farming Group at Newcastle University found up to 10 varieties of potatoes which can be grown without using chemical fertilisers or pesticides whilst also being resistant to deadly fungal disease.

The findings were welcomed by the Soil Association at a recent organic farming convention held in Newcastle.

Director Patrick Holden said:"The results from the research are good news for farmers and consumers.

"Organic potato growing can be technically challenging and we hope that these blight resistant varieties will enable UK organic farmers to produce more potatoes and reduce the reliance of imports.

"It is encouraging that the supermarkets are recognising the challenges of growing organic potatoes and have started giving these new varieties a chance on the supermarket shelf."

Professor Carlo Leifert, leader of the Nafferton Ecological Farming Group, said: "Until now it's been hard to find varieties of potato that can be grown organically but can resist blight, and it's taken a lot of investigation to get this far.

"From a European perspective, you can't really find a 'one size fits all' solution to the organic problem. For instance, a potato that's popular with the Swiss for making dishes such as tartiflette and rosti, may not suit what the British consumer wants for baked potato, mash and chips."

TWO PET DUCKS were decapitated by louts who broke into a smallholding in Wales.

The severed heads were left on display at the premises which are run for adults with learning difficulties.

Angry staff at the Castell-Y-Dail Centre, in Newtown, discovered the yobs' handiwork when they arrived for work.

Two cockerels were also stolen in the incident at the Powys County Council-run centre.

"It was a despicable act, " fumed John Evans, spokesman for the council.

The ducks' bodies had been taken away but their heads were left carefully placed on top of the duck shed.

A RARE BUTTERFLY is the subject of a major spring survey across Suffolk.

Butterfly Conservation says the dingy skipper used to be a common butterfly but is now only found at a handful of sites in the county, mainly along forest rides or clearings between Thetford and Bury St Edmunds.

The little butterfly has also declined by a massive 50 per cent across the UK and is now a conservation priority.

Sharon Hearle, regional officer for Butterfly Conservation, said:"We need to survey the dingy skipper to find out where it currently is in Suffolk so that we can work to conserve it."

Rob Parker, county butterfly recorder for Suffolk, added:"Volunteers are needed to help look for the butterfly at various sites - you don't need experience, and you will be shown what to do. If you are interested in helping this lovely butterfly please get in touch."

SEAGULL: noisy cries and a defiant green parrot

SEAGULLS are perfectly designed for life at sea which makes it all the more surprising that so many now choose to live much of their lives inland. Some experts blame this change in lifestyle on the depletion of fish stocks around our coasts but there is no doubt rich pickings are available for those gulls which haunt towns and cities.

Tips and landfill sites are now commonly frequented by seagulls and in most areas their presence is expected as soon as a new one is opened up.

So bad has the problem become that many councils currently view gulls as pests on a par with rats.

In Gloucestershire, one local authority even considered the possibility of constructing huge fake cliffs at a landfill site so that hundreds of gulls would feel more at home there - and stop creating a nuisance by nesting on houses.

But such generosity is rare and in Devon a mother gull and her chicks died of starvation after becoming trapped by netting spread on the roof of a store, something that was supposed to prevent nests being built there.

Seagulls are tough birds that have evolved to survive the worst the elements can throw at them as they ride freezing winds far out at sea.

About 10 species are commonly sighted around Britain, the biggest being the great black-backed gull. Black wing and back feathers instantly mark the great black-backed out, as does its huge body length of up to 65cm.

This gull is an aggressive predator, using its formidable yellow beak to crush and hack to death a variety of prey, from puffins and teal to rabbits and rats.

It will also feed on carrion and take other birds' eggs whenever it can.

Smaller than the great black-backed but similarly voracious is the lesser black-backed whose back and wing feathers are actually greyer in tone.

Roughly the same size as this, at about 52cms body length, is Britain's commonest gull, the herring gull - confusingly, a lot more widespread than the smaller, gentler looking common gull itself.

The herring gull is the gull you are most likely to encounter either on a trip to the seaside or at your local tip.

With its pale grey wings and snowy white body, the herring gull is pretty distinctive, as is its piercing *kyow-yow-yow'* cry.

I was on holiday in Torquay recently and each morning that cry would rouse me in my bed on the sixth floor of an apartment block, usually delivered at full blast by a herring gull cruising past the window.

Interestingly, the only cry that topped it for volume was the startling squawk of a beautiful green parrot which had somehow taken up residence in a tree below.

Gulls and crows tried to frighten this interloper off but it resisted their threats with aplomb.

We offered nuts and other titbits to try to tempt it onto our balcony but nothing worked.

It kept a stiff upper beak and maintained an independent air.

Very British, I thought.

BRITAIN'S COUNTRYSIDE IS being increasingly scarred by rocketing levels of illegal dumping, according to a hard-hitting TV documentary.

In one sequence, 'Dumping on Britain' reveals how tonnes of rubble and waste, including asbestos, are piled two metres high on a nature reserve.

The BBC programme highlights illegal scams used by bogus waste disposal teams and the efforts of investigators to track them down for prosecution.

The one hour documentary shows how illegal dumpers pose as legitimate traders - taking payment for waste disposal - then dump the waste illegally in fields or beauty spots.

Illegal waste disposal is now said to be a new area of organised crime.

Brian Hyams, special enforcement officer for the Environment Agency, said: "Dumping is big business. Rubbish is expensive to deal with legally, which means there is potentially a big profit to be made by unscrupulous individuals prepared to break the law.

"We have come across offenders, for example, who we assess have made more than one million pounds from illegal waste disposal. Rubbish has become part of the new currency of crime.

"This programme not only shows the scams that these individuals might pull, but also the complete disregard that they have for human health, the law and the environment."

-'Dumping on Britain', BBC1, May 4.

CUCKOOS ARE ON a downward spiral because their British host species are also struggling, say experts.

The parasitic birds, which lay their eggs in smaller birds' nests, need to find breeding pipits, warblers or other species when they arrive here each spring from sub-Saharan Africa.

But as UK habitat disappears so do the breeding birds and cuckoos are being left in the lurch.

"The UK's cuckoos are declining in number, largely in England and Wales, something which may be linked to a fall in numbers of key host species like the dunnock and meadow pipit," says the RSPB.

"While they are now on the amber list of conservation concern, their continuing decline over recent years makes them possible candidates for the red list, the highest conservation concern.

"Female cuckoos are genetically disposed towards an individual host species. So a female cuckoo that was fostered by meadow pipits will return to her natal habitat to lay her own eggs in pipits' nests. Some cuckoos prefer wetlands with reedbeds and reed warblers as their 'host', others will favour moorlands with meadow pipits doing the parenting on their behalf.

"Woodland and farmland cuckoos will often choose robins or dunnocks."

HARE COURSERS ARE refusing to accept that their controversial sport is ended for good following the introduction of a ban on hunting with dogs.

Targeting anti-hunt Labour MPs in marginal constituencies is the latest tactic of supporters dedicated to bring back the 'historic pastime' where greyhounds are tested against each other by chasing hares - sometimes with fatal results for the hares.

In a rallying call to members of the National Coursing Club recently, Sir Mark Prescott said:"How many hours did Parliament devote to debating the war in Iraq? The answer is 41 hours. How many have died since that war began? If you believe independent sources, 220,000 men, women and children.

"How many hours did Parliament devote to debating the war in Afghanistan? The answer is 22 hours. How many human beings have died since that war began? If you believe the same independent sources again, it is in excess of 70,000 men, women and children.

"How many hours have Parliament devoted to debating 'Hunting with Dogs'? Answer: 700 hours. How many hares died coursing last year - exactly 169.

"If you told the Man on the Moon that 700 hours of Parliamentary time were devoted to 169 hares and only 63 hours to killing 290,000 human beings, he would scarcely believe you.

"If you then described how, after 700 hours of debate and deep consideration, the Mother of all Parliaments, incorporating presumably the finest brains in the Kingdom, had fine tuned and honed a Bill, to such an extent that it had resulted in it being legal to kill a rabbit but illegal to kill a hare, the Man on the Moon would think you were joking."

A SWAN SITTING on her eggs was shot through the head by a mystery marksman in Scotland.

The bird, whose breeding progress was being followed by delighted locals on a loch at Forres, was found slumped lifeless over her nest in reeds.

A local resident raised the alarm and a group of workmen used a boat to investigate.

The swan is thought to have been killed outright, leaving six eggs and prompting its mate to desert the area.

Police and SSPCA officials believe an airgun was used and have launched an investigation to track down the culprit.

John Beesley, whose house overlooks the loch, said "some mindless idiot" had been to blame.

"People get a lot of enjoyment from watching the swans every year and come to feed them," he added."Now part of that enjoyment has gone."

A BILL WHICH could spell the end for countryside watchdog English Nature has been introduced in the House of Commons for its first reading.

The Natural Environment and Rural Communities Bill is, among other things, set to create new body Natural England, "bringing together the functions of English Nature with parts of the Countryside Agency and Rural Development Service."

Critics say the move is merely a cynical bid by New Labour to silence awkward opinion within English Nature.

447

SPRING LAMBS HAVE borne the brunt of the new law banning hunting with hounds across England and Wales, according to critics of the legislation.

Several farmers are said to have reported an upsurge in attacks on livestock.

Jim Webster, Cumbria president of the Country Land and Business Association, said: "I checked on a Swaledale ewe and her two lambs, which were very much alive and healthy. The next morning I returned to check them to find that one of the lambs had had its head bitten off during the night, undoubtedly by a fox.

"It has happened before, and will undoubtedly happen again, but this time it may continue as I can no longer call in the hunt to solve the problem.

"The powers-that-be have effectively left me with little alternative than to accept that in future I will be losing more stock to these predators, but I am far from happy about the situation.

"If anyone thought that a ban on hunting would prevent cruelty, I would ask them to visit my farm and I will be happy to show them the real evidence."

ANGLERS HAVE NEVER had it so good with many formerly polluted rivers now returned to complete health, say environmentalists.

Dafydd Evans, head of fisheries for the Environ- ment Agency, said:"Rivers that were once lifeless now teem with fish."

The latest edition of 'Reel Life', the Agency's magazine for anglers, tells how trout and grayling are at last returning to once filthy urban waters following extensive clean-up work funded by licence cash.

"It also shows just how much fun angling can be, whether fishing with a friend in the wilds of Wiltshire or seeking out trout in the heart of Huddersfield," added Mr Evans.

AN ELDERLY SEAL is celebrating his 37th birthday with plenty of fish and females at a Cornish animal sanctuary.

The milestone makes Magnus the world's oldest rescued male grey seal.

For years, Magnus had lived at Edinburgh Zoo but, 15 years ago, when the zoo wanted to redevelop his pool for penguins, he was transferred to the National Seal Sanctuary at Gweek.

And despite his advanced age, the old boy still has an eye for the ladies.

"When Magnus arrived we were told he was the laziest seal in Scotland," revealed seal curator Dr Glenn Boyle.

"However, when the breeding season starts each autumn, he is a totally different character.

"With old age upon him, his vision and hearing are now failing. But Magnus knows when it's feeding time and waits in the corner of the pool by the gate.

"If he doesn't receive his fair share of fish, he splashes the water, making feeding time very wet for our Animal Care Team."

THE WORST THREAT to England's dwindling Green Belts comes from the present Government, campaigners claim.

Green Belts are "under attack as never before and the biggest threat is from Government itself," says the Campaign to Protect Rural England.

"Ministers have repeatedly affirmed their commitment to Green Belts so the Government should be their staunchest, most reliable ally," explained Shaun Spiers, CPRE's chief executive.

"Yet a pattern is emerging of sustained attacks on Green Belts across the country. And the biggest pressure is Government policy.

"From the Government's Sustainable Commu- nities Plan to the Aviation White Paper, a major onslaught on Green Belt is underway unlike any seen since national Green Belt policy was introduced 50 years ago. And many local councils — the first line of defence against Green Belt incursion — are meekly following the Government's lead.

"A crucial element of Green Belts is the permanence of their boundaries. Green Belt policy is one of the sharpest tools in the planning toolkit. But its effectiveness is being blunted by the top-down imposition of boundary reviews and careless talk of 'replacing' lost Green Belt land elsewhere.

"This erodes public confidence in planning and fuels land speculation, with damaging consequences for the countryside. Of all planning policies, Green Belt is probably the best known, and best loved by the general public — and it's the envy of other countries. It has been remarkably successful in stopping sprawl and protecting the countryside around our towns and cities, thereby improving quality of life for us all.

"If the Green Belts didn't exist, we'd have to invent them. For millions of people living in our largest towns and cities they are the countryside next door. We want everyone to enjoy them, and for them to be better looked after.

"We should be celebrating this 50th anniver- sary by creating new areas of Green Belt, rather than threatening existing ones."

Mr Spiers warned:"We stand on the brink of massive and unprecedented loss of long- protected Green Belt land. Unlike today, losses in the past were small in scale and usually not a direct result of Government policy.

"It doesn't have to be this way. With political will, Green Belt policy can be strengthened, established Green Belts can be enhanced and new areas of Green Belt can be created. We urge the Government to go beyond fine words about Green Belts, and to pull us back from the brink of their unprecedented destruction. Ministers must provide convincing and positive leadership, to guarantee Green Belt policy even greater success over the next 50 years."

DAY FLYING MOTHS are once again to be an additional quarry at this year's eagerly awaited National Moth Night.

"In 2004, for the first time, participants were encouraged to get out and look for day flying moths, of which there are a number of species, some of which are very scarce. Day-time recording is again being encouraged in 2005," revealed a spokesman for the event on July 9.

National Moth Night, an annual "celebration of moths and moth recording" was launched in 1999.

OSPREY: fatal greed of some hungry fish eaters

SHARP-EYED and deadly, the osprey is a spectacular hunter of unwary fish that make the mistake of swimming too close to the surface.

When a luckless trout or pike rises into view, the osprey plunges down with lightning speed.

It hits the water feet first and will often submerge in its attempt to catch its prey.

When it resurfaces, it needs to frenetically flap its long wings to get airborne again carrying the extra weight.

Once grabbed in an osprey's powerful talons, few fish escape its embrace and most are quickly carried back to a nest or perch to be devoured at leisure.

However, ospreys don't always have it their own way and there is evidence that some have drowned after miscalculating the size of their prey.

Fish weighing up to six pounds are easily taken but anything bigger can drag an osprey to its doom if it fails to release its claws in time.

Ospreys have been enlarging their UK territory lately with nesting forays into England and Wales.

Birdwatchers were delighted when eggs first appeared in Leicestershire and the Lake District within the space of a single month.

Prior to this event, no ospreys had bred in England for 150 years so a measure of excitement was understandable when the mottled white eggs were spotted.

Security measures were soon put in force to protect the nests from egg thieves and vandals - a wise move in the circumstances.

Before 1954, when a pair returned to breed at Loch Garten in Scotland and were given RSPB protection, ospreys had been extinct in Britain for over 50 years as a result of persecution.

Now hopes have been raised that these dramatic predators might gradually become a fixture on less remote stretches of water in England and Wales where more people can study them.

RSPB conservation director Mark Avery said:"*We are delighted that these wonderful fish-eating birds of prey are now breeding again outside Scotland.*

"*This is largely a result of the increasing Scottish population spreading over the border. There are now more than 100 breeding pairs in Scotland, thanks to ongoing conservation work.*"

Ospreys are migrants and come to our shores in March and April after flying all the way from tropical West Africa.

They go back there in October when UK temperatures start to drop. Their navigational skills are extraordinary but, like most birds, ospreys sometimes go slightly off course.

One osprey en route to Scotland caused a flap when it settled exhausted on a Brighton rooftop and had to be rescued from dive-bombing gulls by a fire crew and bird of prey expert.

Taken into protective custody, it was given medical treatment and was soon back on the road to recovery.

Bad news for some unfortunate fish.

SPARE A THOUGHT for deer fawns in the New Forest at this time of year, the Forestry Commission has urged.

New offspring are especially vulnerable to disturbance from horse riders, cyclists, walkers and their dogs, it warns.

New Forest keeper Andy Shore said that the young animals often hid within feet of forest paths and many were at risk unless people took conscious steps to keep them safe.

He said:"Our deer are in terrific shape thanks to the huge quantities of food such as acorns produced in the woodlands last autumn.

"So it's likely to be a good year for babies. With so many young around it is more important than ever that everyone takes care.

"Walkers, cyclists and horse riders should keep to the proper routes. Pet owners need to take care, too, and make sure their animals are not disturbing young deer hidden near the trails.

"We're also urging every dog owner to make certain they know where their pets are at all times. Already this year three deer have been killed by dogs in my area – one was pregnant with two young. Recently, a badger cub has been killed too."

Mr Shore said the golden rule for people out with dogs off the lead was to make sure their pets remained within sight and would unfailingly come to heel when called.

ONCE IT WAS mainly salmon, grouse and deer that lured visitors to Scotland but butterflies may soon prove an equally lucrative tourist attraction.

The country's tourist industry is being made aware of the insects' power to lure visitors in a new project called 'Butterflies mean Business'.

The project, currently centred on Lomond, rural Stirling and the Cairngorms, is being run by the charity Butterfly Conservation Scotland.

Local businesses and people working in tourism are being urged to promote the presence of butterflies to encourage visitors to stay in the area longer or return for another visit.

Project officer Julie Stoneman said:"People love butterflies. All through the summer we have people from further south asking for details of sites where they can observe species like the Scotch argus, the large heath, the pearl-bordered fritillary and the chequered skipper.

"Some of these are very rare elsewhere in the UK. We want to help the local tourist industry reach out and encourage interest not just from elsewhere in Britain but from throughout Europe.

"Butterflies are a colourful aspect of the area's natural heritage.

"They are a resource that can help attract and retain visitors.

"We hope that our project will go some way towards encouraging that."

SKYLARKS COULD BE boosted by a new scheme to persuade farmers to set aside special areas to halt their spiralling decline.

The little farmland birds seem to be on the retreat everywhere but especially in the North West of England where numbers have slumped by a quarter within 10 years.

It is hoped that farmers will help to stop their decline by providing 'skylark plots' - small areas of undrilled land within a winter-sown crop.

Andrew Gouldstone, RSPB conservation manager, said:"A countryside without the beautiful song of the skylark would be a much poorer place.

"Skylark plots are a really simple and yet effective way in which farmers can deliver enormous benefits for these birds within fields of winter cereal.

"To save the skylark, farmers only need to turn off their seed drills for a count of up to two seconds when sowing winter cereals."

Although skylarks traditionally nest and forage in spring-sown cereals, it is thought that the new 'plots' will make winter-sown crops just as helpful to the birds.

MINK COULD BE completely eradicated from Scotland's Western Isles if £3million is poured into wiping them out, experts have revealed.

The first phase of a scheme involving various conservation organisations was begun five years ago to banish the non-native predator from the islands.

Now a second phase is planned.

The mink have become notorious for killing wild birds, local poultry, and raiding fish farms.

David Maclennan, of Scottish Natural Heritage, said:"We are really pleased with the progress that has been made so far and that eradication of mink from the Uists looks likely to be achieved on time.

"If we stopped now, sooner or later mink would again make their way over the Sound of Harris to the Uists and pose the same serious threats.

"We are now working up proposals for the complete eradication of mink from the whole of the Western Isles.

"This will be a major undertaking, expected to cost around £3million."

MOLES ARE FACING extermination as the latest victims of Britain's growing compensation culture.

Council officials are considering gassing dozens of the burrowing creatures at Kearnsey Abbey, Kent, because visitors might trip on mole hills and sue.

Councillor Susan Nicholas explained:"The ground really is quite uneven in parts.

"One person claimed against the council for something that happened in the abbey a few years ago. We have to make every effort to make it safe."

But the RSPCA has condemned the idea as cruel.

A spokesman said:"There is no need to kill moles because somebody might sprain their ankle. This seems like a case of health and safety gone mad."

And The Mammal Society added that killing the moles would not necessarily be the end of the matter.

Other moles would probably just replace them.

AN ANIMAL RIGHTS group has come under bitter attack from officials at the Game Conservancy Trust.

The Trust has slammed the League Against Cruel Sports for its "woefully inadequate understanding of wildlife issues and blatant double standards."

The League recently criticised the new single farm payment scheme - which is encouraging landowners to farm in a more environmentally friendly way - and inferred that shooting estates would benefit from the new subsidies.

But Mrs Teresa Dent, chief executive of the Trust, said:"It is disheartening that the League shows such poor understanding of the countryside and its history.

"The Trust's irrefutable research shows that for the past 30 years it has been shooting estates that have contributed most to the conservation of the countryside.

"But taxpayers' money is certainly not paying to support shooting. The money is being used to support farmland wildlife by encouraging farmers and landowners to grow environmentally friendly crops.

"On our demonstration farm in Leicestershire, through sympathetic farming and good game management, the Trust has reversed a 30-year decline of nine bird species in three years while brown hare numbers increased ten-fold."

Mrs Dent also claimed that while the League was now extremely critical of the use of snares, it openly supported them in its own study of foxes in the 1990s.

A Bill to protect common land in England and Wales from development has now been published.

The Commons Bill "would safeguard and enhance the ancient rights of commoners, allow common land to be managed more sustainably, improve protection from neglect and abuse, and improve registration to ensure all commons have the same amount of protection," said a spokesman.

A NEW ONLINE forum has been created for discussing possible sightings of big cats in Britain's countryside.

A spokesman for the British Big Cats Society, behind the move, said:"We hope the forum will serve as a place for interesting and informative discussions between our members.

"But it is being moderated and we will take action to ban anyone who posts offensive, obscene or inappropriate material."

The Society itself was originally set up to "scientifically identify, quantify, catalogue and protect the big cats that freely roam the British countryside."

The new big cat forum can be located at: www.bigcatforum.siteburg.com

BADGERS HAVE BEEN defended again in the ongoing war of words over the spread of bovine TB.

Cattle movements, not badgers, are the best predictors of the disease, according to a new report.

A paper published in Nature magazine has found that cattle movements "substantially and consistently outweigh all other variables" for predicting the presence of bovine TB amongst cattle.

Dr Elaine King, chief executive of the National Federation of Badger Groups, said:"After 30 years of blaming badgers for spreading bTB, farmers and vets have to face up to the reality that farming itself is to blame for the massive escalation in the disease and its spread all over the country.

"Until DEFRA finally gets a grip on cattle movements, bovine TB will continue to cost taxpayers a fortune in needless compensation payments every year.

"The movement of TB-infected livestock was allowed by MAFF in the wake of foot-and-mouth disease.

"The farming unions claimed credit for MAFF's catastrophic decision.

"As a result, bovine TB has spread to every veterinary division in England and to previously unaffected parts of Wales and Scotland.

"Badgers, deer and other wildlife may yet be shown to play a minor role but the current scientific evidence confirms that DEFRA's new strategy to clamp down on the movement of cattle is going to be effective in controlling bovine TB, provided the measures are properly enforced.

"Farmers and a minority of vets should stop opposing those measures immediately."

WHITE-TAILED SEA eagles deliver an emotional jolt to onlookers more than any other British bird, according to the RSPB.

Spokesman David Sexton said:"The eagles have a profound effect on those who see them. It seems to affect people deep in their soul.

"We had one woman who burst into tears when she saw them. Another couple wrote that it was the best day of their lives.

"Of course, some people just say, 'lovely, fine, thanks very much', but the vast majority seem to experience something they will never forget."

The birds, reintroduced here in the 1970s, took 10 years to nest but are now flourishing in Scotland.

Some 32 pairs are breeding across the Inner Hebrides - from Mull up to Skye - with nest sites no longer closely guarded secrets.

The RSPB is even operating a public viewing hide that looks directly onto one nest on Mull.

THREE FLUFFY CYGNETS were left orphaned by yobs who launched a frenzied attack on both parent swans in North Wales.

The dead adult birds were thought to have been stoned, beaten, and even attacked by the gang's dogs.

The RSPCA, police and local councillors have launched a probe into the incident at Stryt Las Park, Rhos.

All three orphaned youngsters were taken to Stapeley Grange animal sanctuary at Nantwich, Cheshire, to recover from their ordeal.

GOLDCREST: a towering giant in survival stakes

TINY and shy, the goldcrest may be Britain's smallest bird but it is undoubtedly a giant when you consider its survival skills.

No heavier than a 20p coin and less than four inches long, it ekes out an existence in woodland or conifer plantations despite threats from a host of predators.

As mentioned before, even great tits have been known to kill and feed on goldcrests so danger is never far away.

In autumn and winter, native goldcrest colonies are supplemented by migrant goldcrests arriving here from Scandinavia after making perilous trips across the North Sea.

A goldcrest is significantly smaller and lighter even than the blue tit so the thought of it flying across a vast, unforgiving sea to reach us is really quite amazing.

In past centuries, it was thought that goldcrests cheekily hitched lifts on the backs of larger birds but this is obviously untrue.

Goldcrests were also known as 'woodcock pilots' because they often arrived at the same time as migrant woodcocks, appearing to guide them in to the host country.

The goldcrest and its much rarer cousin the firecrest - equally small - are both named after the brightly coloured crests on their heads which they flare in anger or alarm.

After mating, females of both species lay large clutches of lightly spotted white eggs in dainty cup-like nests constructed of moss and cobwebs.

Despite their diminutive size, goldcrests can be quite aggressive and often challenge each other over territory or food.

Insects of various types make up their diet and these are relentlessly pursued from tree to tree.

Goldcrests normally feed on miniscule prey but there are reports of brave individuals attempting to kill large dragonflies - and being comically dragged across the sky in the process.

However, the fact that goldcrests usually manage to find enough to eat in the depths of a freezing winter is a tribute to their remarkable foraging talents.

Like wrens, goldcrests' flitting progress through a tree can be furtive and almost mouse-like.

Often, the first clue to their presence comes from their high-pitched, thin voices as they keep in contact with each other among the branches.

Although rarer, firecrests are said to be easier to spot because their colouring is more dramatic and they tend to feed closer to the ground.

However, when I tramped round the so-called *firecrest trail* at a local wood recently, I failed to pinpoint any.

This was probably less to do with the firecrests themselves and more to do with having a wife and two moaning children in tow.

Faced with that onslaught, who can blame the poor birds for keeping a low profile ?

To be honest, it was a little chilly at the time.

Eventually, I gave in and took my unhappy family home.

BEARS, WOLVES AND lynx could be reintroduced to the British countryside in a controversial Jurassic Park-style scheme at a remote Scottish estate.

Landowner Paul Lister is aiming to bring back the once native predators to his 23,000-acre Alladale Estate in the Highlands.

Mr Lister, 45, revealed:"Our long-term plan is to create the only large-scale, fenced wilderness and wildlife reserve in Europe, similar in style to those already established in southern Africa, such as Shamwari.

"By using carnivores to reduce red deer numbers, there will be a natural regeneration of native plants and trees, including the ancient Caledonian pine forest, along with an increase in the biodiversity of mammal, insect and bird life."

However, ramblers and climbers are said to be worried about the plans, especially the intention to create a huge, 50-mile fence to contain the animals.

Mountaineer Cameron McNeish, who also represents the Ramblers Association in Scotland, said:"I really cannot see this happening. The estate has got Seana Bhraigh, arguably the most remote of all the 284 Munros (peaks over 3,000ft) and also has Carn Ban, which is the most remote of the Corbetts (peaks 2,500ft-3,000ft). With these on his land, he's going to be up against it.

"There is a fair bit of concern locally. Building a 50-mile fence round the estate to keep these animals in makes it more like a wildlife park."

However, three years back, Dutch landowner Paul van Vlissingen asserted that wolves and lynx should be reintroduced to Scotland to control rocketing deer numbers.

OSPREYS ARE CONTINUING their tentative resurgence in Wales with two chicks hatched this year.

Both youngsters appear to be doing well but a third egg failed to hatch.

Gili Armson, manager of the Glaslyn Osprey Project, said:"The adult birds have been treating all three eggs the same and clearly had no idea that one of the eggs was infertile. It is not unusual for this to happen, particularly with a pair that are quite new to breeding like ours.

"Some birds remove infertile eggs out of the nest but birds of prey tend not to do this. The egg will probably get covered up as the birds add more materials to the nest.

"Three chicks would have been nice but we will be more than happy if two healthy chicks fledge from the nest at the end of the season."

The project, which will be open to the public until early September, is part of 'Aren't Welsh Birds Brilliant!' - a partnership between conservation groups.

PHEASANTS ARE BEING culled at a Surrey farm following confirmation of an outbreak of a highly contagious bird virus there.

The birds, being bred for shooting, have apparently fallen victim to so-called Newcastle Disease.

NFU Poultry Board chairman Charles Bourns said:"We support DEFRA's decision to cull the pheasants on the farm as soon as possible. DEFRA have been keeping the NFU informed about this outbreak and we have been advising DEFRA on the issue.

"We urge poultry farmers to be vigilant against any signs of the disease and to implement strict biosecurity measures. Farmers should consult their vets on a vaccination policy as a precaution.

"Poultry farmers should do everything they can to keep their farms clean. This includes strictly limiting and controlling access to poultry flocks, minimising contact between poultry and wild birds, and keeping dogs, cats, rodents and other livestock out of poultry buildings and feed stores."

The Health Protection Agency said that Newcastle Disease did not pose a significant threat to human health.

Chief veterinary officer Debby Reynolds added:"I would like to make it clear that this is not bird flu."

EIGHT DUCKLINGS LESS than a week old were plucked from a potential death trap drain in Shropshire.

Rescuers took four hours to release the frantic birds after a Shrewsbury resident raised the alarm.

The drama unfolded when a householder spotted the distraught mother duck trying to reach the youngsters herself.

Soon the RSPCA had joined members of the public in a rescue operation which eventually saw all ducklings returned to mum unharmed.

DORMICE ARE NOW settling in at a new aristocratic home specially provided for them in Derbyshire.

About 30 of the little mammals - born and raised as part of a captive breeding programme - have just been released at a secret location on the Chatsworth Estate, palatial residence of the Duke and Duchess of Devonshire.

Conservationists hope the move will establish an expanding population of the struggling, native species in the area.

Jill Nelson, chief executive of the People's Trust for Endangered Species, said:"We are very pleased to have found such an excellent reintroduction site for dormice - known to so many as the sleepy character in 'Alice's Adventures in Wonderland'.

"The Devonshire family and the staff at Chatsworth, together with our excellent team of local volunteers, have really helped us to make another important step forward in conserving this endangered and much-loved mammal."

The Dowager Duchess of Devonshire added:"Everyone at Chatsworth is thrilled about the dormouse release taking place on the estate. We hope that this carefully planned and monitored exercise will play a small but significant part in reversing the decline in dormouse numbers."

453

BADGERS ARE NOT to blame for dairy calves being shot, claim conservationists.

According to the NFU, the calves are being shot because of stringent bovine TB movement restrictions - a policy which many farmers say is down to badgers spreading the disease in the first place.

However, badger supporters have always attacked the belief that the burrowing mammals are responsible.

Dr Elaine King, chief executive of the National Federation of Badger Groups, said:"If the NFU is trying to justify killing badgers by pretending that it will save calves, it is grotesquely cynical.

"Research from Oxford University, published in Nature magazine, revealed that cattle movements 'substantially and consistently outweigh' all other factors in predicting outbreaks of TB, including badgers.

"Cattle movements and the weaknesses of the TB testing regime are to blame for the 18 per cent annual rise in bovine TB, not badgers.

"The sooner the Government gets a grip on the spread of bovine TB by cattle, the sooner the £36.2 million annual compensation bill paid by taxpayers to farmers will be reduced."

She also doubted the claims that farmers were all heartbroken over the deaths of calves.

"Every year, around 170,000 calves die in their first month of life, mostly from diseases that could be avoided through better hygiene and management, " she said.

SILVER-STUDDED BLUE butterflies have been released in the UK for the first time in a decade in a bid to save the species from extinction.

Fifty females were freed on Ockham Common, Surrey, by rangers from the Surrey Wildlife Trust.

The silver-studded blue was once common across the UK but, like many butterflies, has declined dramatically over the last 30 years.

It is now very rare and has become confined to small, fragmented heathland areas.

"Silver-studded blues are a sedentary species and only travel an average of 30 metres in their lifetime. Just 1km is their maximum," explained a Trust spokesman.

"Barriers such as pine trees can stop them moving from one area to another.

"This decreases the population and gene pool so relocation programmes are then needed to ensure the survival of the species.

"This release by Surrey Wildlife Trust - made in co-operation with Butterfly Conservation, English Nature and Elmbridge Borough Council - is the first ever to take place in the UK for 10 years and the first ever in Surrey."

EIGHT BOTTLENOSE DOLPHINS, including a calf, were chased and harried by boats into dangerously shallow water off North Cornwall, it has been claimed.

The British Divers Marine Life Rescue and Cornwall Wildlife Trust have jointly condemned the "irresponsible behaviour" of those who harassed the popular creatures in a way which could have resulted in their deaths.

Dave Jarvis, West Cornwall co-ordinator for the rescue group, was nearby at the time and saw the incident unfold.

He said:"The situation, involving bottlenose dolphins which appear to have become almost semi-resident around St Ives Bay, was potentially catastrophic.

"The event was observed by numerous tourists from the beach, some of whom were becoming distressed at the actions of the boats."

BDMLR director Tony Woodley added:"This incident could have quite easily turned into a mass stranding of animals.

"Of course, we all want to be able to see these wonderful animals but it must be done in a responsible manner and in a way which will not harm them.

"Any craft, including jet skis, can cause harassment but we have noticed that this type of incident is dramatically on the increase."

OTTERS, WATER VOLES and great crested newts are just three species being invited to set up home in a new nature reserve in West Yorkshire.

Ward Wildlife Haven has opened to the public at Knottingley after being created as part of the Environment Agency's flood protection scheme.

A simple tree planting ceremony took place with Professor Roy Ward - who gave his name to the site - officially declaring the wetland open.

A WELSH FOREST has gained the backing of Oscar-winning actress Dame Judi Dench.

Dame Judi is backing The Woodland Trust in its "race against the clock" to save Wentwood Forest - one of the largest ancient woodlands in the UK.

A Trust spokesman said the forest, near Newport in South Wales, was fighting for survival from the threat of further commercial forestry.

A substantial part of the forest - 352 hectares - had just come on the open market and the Trust needed to raise at least £1.5 million to secure its purchase and start restoration.

Dame Judi said:"Wentwood Forest is home to rare species like the dormouse. There are over 75 species of birds and 23 species of native butterflies recorded in the area.

"Plants include the wild daffodil, wood anemone and enchanters' nightshade amongst others.

"All these are now struggling to survive. This is our last chance to protect Wentwood Forest and restore it to its former beauty.

"It would be a tragedy if the characteristics of this ancient site were lost forever so please help us by offering your support or making a pledge to our public appeal."

Sue Holden, chief executive of The Woodland Trust, added:"The ancient characteristics are clinging on but we have to act now.

"We need help to save this fantastic national treasure house."

454

BUTTERFLIES: flying into harsher times

BEAUTIFUL and delicate, butterflies have been celebrated for bringing summer colour into our lives since records began but now their annual appearance is threatened as never before.

Despite higher temperatures making Britain more attractive, the relentless destruction of vital habitat is steadily reducing butterfly numbers. Research has shown that three-quarters of those species which might have expanded northwards due to global warming have instead declined - unable to find enough sites to lay their eggs.

According to Butterfly Conservation, native species which tend to stay in the same area have suffered particularly badly, plummeting 89 per cent in numbers compared to a 50 per cent fall among more mobile species.

The depressing findings were based on an in-depth analysis of 1.6 million butterfly sightings by 10,000 amateur naturalists over a four-year period.

Professor Chris Thomas, who helped co-ordinate the research, said:*"Most species of butterflies that reach the northern edge of their geographic ranges in Britain have declined over the last 30 years even though the climate has warmed.*

"This is surprising because climate warming is expected to increase the range of habitats these species can inhabit.

"Climatically suitable areas are available for colonisation but most species have failed to exploit them either because they no longer contain suitable breeding habitats, or because breeding habitats are out of reach."

Greatest losers in the downturn are thought to be the large tortoiseshell, high brown fritillary, wood white, pearl-bordered fritillary, marsh fritillary, large heath, silver-studded blue, duke of Burgundy, dingy skipper, and small pearl-bordered fritillary.

But it is not all bad news and some butterflies are still doing well, especially the Essex skipper, brown argus, holly blue, comma, purple hairstreak, marbled white, white admiral, speckled wood, ringlet, and orange tip.

Among these, the marbled white is thought to have expanded its range by more than 50 per cent and perhaps this estimate is borne out by the fact that I spotted three within an hour on a walk over the summer

The survey also showed that there were currently far more butterflies in the south and east of the country than in the north and west.

Among Britain's few remaining butterfly 'hotspots' are the Chilterns, the North and South Downs, the Cotswolds, Salisbury Plain, the Isle of Purbeck, and Dartmoor.

Besides being physically attractive, butterflies seem to exercise a beguiling hold on Man's imagination and literature is littered with references to them.

Even as far back as the 3rd Century BC, philosopher Chuang Tse is recorded as musing:*"I do not know whether I was then a man dreaming I was a butterfly, or whether I am now a butterfly dreaming I am a man."*

Perhaps he'd been philosophising too hard.

TOURISTS HAVE BEEN blamed for a number of marine wildlife harassment incidents in the South West.

In one of the latest episodes, a colony of seals was repeatedly disturbed by surfers, kayakers, and other boat users at Godrevy Island, off Cornwall.

Volunteers from the Godrevy Seal Group monitored the terrified seals being constantly driven back into the sea by people getting too close.

Spokeswoman Sue Sayer said:"The seals stood no chance of resting or basking in the sun with a continual barrage of visitors.

"The canoers and surfers not only endangered their own lives but they got in the way of legitimate fishing vessels which were seen to change course to narrowly avoid them."

A speedboat was also seen doing high-speed figures of eight near the seals.

"I am concerned that the continued disturbance from pleasure and leisure sea craft will deter the seals from visiting Godrevy and prevent future generations enjoying the wonderful sight of our largest marine mammals at this location," added Ms Sayer.

The seal group wants tourists to adhere to the Marine Code of Conduct which states that all commercial, pleasure or leisure craft should: keep more than 100 metres away from marine life; never move head-on or between marine animals; maintain a steady direction and no wake speed; and avoid allowing people to swim in the water with wild marine animals.

Harassment of seals and other marine animals is a criminal offence carrying a fine of up to £5,000 and six months in prison.

THE GREY PARTRIDGE is being further boosted by an initiative involving over 150 farmers and landowners across parts of southern England.

The Wessex Grey Partridge Recovery Group has been set up by the Game Conservancy Trust in a bid to try and revive grey partridge populations in south Wiltshire, Hampshire and Dorset.

According to the Trust, grey partridges have plummeted from over a million pairs in Edwardian times to just 76,000 pairs now.

Dr Nick Sotherton, director of research for the Trust, said:"A variety of causes have gradually eroded the partridge population, including farming techniques, lack of chick food insects, predation and weather. Setting up regional partridge groups is an ideal way to help the grey partridge at a local level."

In addition, the Trust has launched the Wessex Grey Partridge Trophy which will be presented each year to the farm or estate that contributes most to partridge conservation.

BADGER LOVERS HAVE been celebrating the recent prosecution of eight men, all convicted of attempting to take or injure a badger and sentenced to three months in prison.

The men, mainly from Wigan in Lancashire, were arrested after a successful operation by police and the RSPCA which prevented any badgers being harmed.

Investigators swooped after a 10-month probe which saw the group held at woodland in Skipton, North Yorkshire, last year, along with 13 dogs, tracking devices, and spades.

The defendants were prosecuted at Burnley Magistrates Court.

"This is the largest gang of badger diggers convicted for some time," said RSPCA inspector Ian Briggs.

"They went there on an organised expedition to hunt, take or injure badgers. It was only because of our intervention that they aborted their mission.

"This is a rare set of convictions. There are only perhaps one or two court cases like it a year yet research has shown that 10,000 badgers are killed or injured by diggers a year.

"The RSPCA and the courts take a very dim view of anyone attempting to interfere with a protected species.

"Not only are we concerned about possible injuries to badgers but, in many cases, the dogs can suffer terrible injuries, too."

The men's dogs were also confiscated and made available for rehoming, he added.

TWO PARENT SEAGULLS were blamed for causing a flap in Aberdeen when shoppers thought they were attacking their youngster.

Concerned passers-by reported that the bigger birds were dive-bombing the helpless fledgling outside the St Nicholas Lane shopping centre in the Scottish city.

One man said:"The bigger birds were swooping down onto the baby one and appeared to be attacking it. It looked quite vicious."

However, a spokeswoman for the SSPCA said:"This is nature at work and we recommend that people generally don't interfere. If a baby is seemingly being attacked by two mature birds they are likely to be the parents.

"They swoop down and pretend to feed it but what they are actually doing is agitating the bird and encouraging it to take off. Most fledgling birds spend around 10 days on the ground while learning to fly."

A CULL OF rats living on an island off the Devon coast has paid off, say conservationists, after the first puffin chick in 30 years was spotted there.

Last year's rat crackdown on Lundy proved controversial with animal rights groups asserting the rodents should be allowed to live.

However, bird lovers were alarmed that the voracious creatures were pushing ground-nesting seabirds, such as the puffin and Manx shearwater, to extinction by feasting on their eggs and chicks.

A count in 2000 had found just 10 pairs of puffins remained compared with about 3,500 in 1939.

Before the cull - backed by English Nature and the RSPB - the island was host to 5,000 rats and their numbers were still growing.

Animal Aid, the biggest animal rights group to protest, had claimed it made no sense to wipe out one species on the island to protect another.

RAVENS ARE ROCKETING back to strength after years of persecution, according to the British Trust for Ornithology.

Recent research shows a remarkable resurgence of the birds which are the biggest members of the crow family.

With their powerful, dagger-like beaks and crafty strategies for preying on weak or vulnerable livestock, ravens were detested for years by farmers and landowners.

Thousands were killed but now, it seems, conservationists' pleas to protect the birds appear to be getting through.

"Numbers of raven have increased by 91 per cent since the start of the Breeding Bird Survey in 1994," said a spokesman.

"Two hundred years ago, ravens could be found across the UK, breeding in virtually every county in the country.

"But by the end of the 19th Century, after years of persecution from gamekeepers, this species was restricted to the remote crags and uplands of western and northern Britain.

"However, in the past 10 years, birds have slowly begun to spread eastwards, with breeding pairs now found again in some of our southern lowland counties."

One particular outcome could result, added the spokesman.

"There may yet come a time when captive ravens residing in the Tower of London are again joined by wild birds."

THE RAMBLERS ASSOCIATION has welcomed NHS plans to spend more cash on promoting physical activity, including walking.

However, it warns research shows there is still a long way to go and more resources will be needed to combat Britain's couch potato culture.

The Association says that just 13 per cent of people it questioned in a national survey were advised by a doctor to exercise more, even though over half the British population are overweight or obese.

Nick Milton, the organisation's director of marketing and communications, said:"Walking is one of the best forms of exercise and it can make a major contribution to a healthy lifestyle.

"I would hope that medical practitioners will take serious note of this survey as they are clearly not prescribing walking as much as they could.

"Given the number of people who are overweight in this country and the cost to the NHS of tackling the symptoms of obesity, doctors need to be prescribing walking a lot more if we are to become a healthier nation."

Walking, he added, was the cheapest, most natural and most convenient way to keep fit.

It was also ideal for people starting to exercise after years of inactivity or who have had health problems.

As little as 30 minutes of brisk walking per day is shown to bring major benefits to health.

PLANS ARE BEING drawn up to control or even wipe out giant carnivorous mice eating seabird chicks alive on a British overseas island.

The gruesome activities of the so-called 'super mice' have horrified RSPB researchers.

The house mice, three times bigger than those in the UK, swarm onto their victims under cover of darkness and are thought to kill a million albatross, petrel, and shearwater chicks on Gough Island every year.

The island, a World Heritage base in the South Atlantic, is reportedly the most important seabird colony in the world, serving over 10 million birds.

It is positioned among the Tristan da Cunha islands - a UK Overseas Territory - with the mice thought to have originally come from visiting ships in the 19th Century.

Dr Geoff Hilton, a senior research biologist for the RSPB, said:"Gough Island plays host to an astonishing community of seabirds and this catastrophe could make many extinct within decades. We think there are about 700,000 mice, which have somehow learned to eat live chicks."

Proposals being considered inlude dropping tonnes of poisoned bait onto the island by plane.

A 12ft FEMALE basking shark had a lucky escape when it became trapped in a gill net.

Three divers from Cornwall Wildlife Trust came to the gentle giant's aid, cutting away the net to allow it to swim free.

Steve Adams, the diver who first spotted the creature and got the attention of the others, said: "Initially, we thought the shark was dead and it was a really sad sight. But then we realised that her eyes and mouth were moving and that she was still alive."

It took 30 minutes for the divers to cut the shark free of the net.

Jonathan Smith, another diver involved in the rescue, said:"Once free of the net, the shark was belly-up and it did not appear that she would survive. However, once we turned her the right way up, her recovery was surprisingly fast. Seeing her finally swim off into the blue and capturing it on film was one of the most amazing experiences of my life."

Before spotting the stricken shark, the divers had been carrying out a survey on the eelgrass beds at Roskilly, off Penzance.

GM SUPER-WEEDS ARE springing up in British fields, worrying new research has found.

Fears have been raised that whole tracts of land could now become contaminated by the tough plants.

The study, by the Centre for Ecology and Hydrology, reveals that genes from a GM type of oilseed rape have transferred to two wild cousins in farm trials.

Anti-GM campaigner and commentator Geoffrey Lean said:"So, at long last, the truth is out. What anti-GM campaigners have long predicted - and the biotech industry and its promoters in Government and science dismissed as impossible - has come to pass.

"Modified genes have passed from oilseed rape to the weed called charlock. Meanwhile, evidence is mounting - even in research by biotech giant Monsanto - that GM foods may endanger human health.

"The time has come to call a halt to this disgracefully dishonest charade. The scandal of the herbicide resistant super-weed should be the last nasty GM surprise ever inflicted on the long-suffering British public."

BUZZARD: striking back at a two-legged target

WHEELING and soaring above open country, the buzzard is an expert scavenger of carcasses and hunter of rabbits.

Its large broad wings, circling flight, and brown and white colouring make it easy to recognise as it scans fields or moors for food.

With carrion making up a large part of its diet, dead sheep and lambs are a regular treat but worms are also taken.

Similar in some ways to the rarer red kite, the buzzard's rounded, fan-shaped tail feathers distinguish it from the kite whose tail feathers are slicked into a trailing 'V'.

The buzzard's wingspan is also shorter by about 60cms when compared to the 195cms maximum span of the more majestic kite.

Even so, the buzzard is now thought to be the commonest large bird of prey in Scotland and generally down the western side of Britain.

On a personal level, this was borne out earlier this year when I spotted two within minutes of leaving my car during a trip to Dartmoor.

Although our buzzard rarely leaves its native country, two other species do migrate here.

These are the Scandinavia-based rough-legged buzzard - partial to lemmings as well as rabbits - and, more rarely, the honey buzzard.

This feeds on wasp and bee larvae and occasionally arrives here from the Continent after wintering in Africa.

British buzzards were almost wiped out in the 1950s due to the sheer decimation of rabbits caused by myxomatosis, something which destroyed their main food source during the breeding season.

Illegal shooting of buzzards has always been a problem and most crimes of this nature probably go unrecorded because they happen in remote places and are quickly concealed.

However, the RSPB says that among 37 formally noted shootings of birds of prey one year, 10 victims were buzzards.

Many more are believed to be killed by poisoned bait or die in the jaws of steel spring-traps left on posts or sawn-off tree trunks.

In a way, this makes periodic reports of territorial buzzards attacking ramblers and cyclists all the more excusable.

Even hang-gliders have been threatened by the birds, according to one high-flying enthusiast.

And a jogger in Cumbria recently felt the full force of a particularly vicious attack.

So are buzzards striking back at last in revenge for their persecution ?

I doubt it.

Although the birds are powerful and capable of inflicting terrible wounds, most injuries are minor.

In addition, it later transpired that the jogger-hating buzzard may have escaped from captivity and so had no innate fear of Man.

Still, I'm sure that was of little comfort to the jogger himself who suffered 15 separate slashes to his head courtesy of his attacker's formidable claws and beak.

A passing motorist found the runner dazed, battered, and covered in blood.

He was lucky not to have lost an eye. But at least he lived to tell the tale, unlike so many buzzards.

HEDGEHOGS ARE AT the centre of fresh controversy as plans are finalised to shoot dead any found on an island in the Outer Hebrides.

The British Hedgehog Preservation Society wants supporters to write protest letters about a scheme to blast the prickly mammals on North Uist.

In a letter to its members, the Society urges:"Please write to the SSPCA who have advised this method is acceptable to let them know if you feel it is not."

The latest cull, planned to start on September 26 and last until October 28, is part of an ongoing programme in the Western Isles.

The scheme is aimed at ridding the islands of hedgehogs which are feasting on the eggs of wading birds.

Conservationists fear the hedgehogs' activities could eventually lead to many wader species being wiped out.

Previous culls on the islands since 2003 have seen the shy creatures first located with dogs then given lethal injections.

This time, dogs are expected to track them down again but, with fewer hedgehogs living on North Uist than on neighbouring islands, organisers believe shooting will be more appropriate.

About 1,000 hedgehogs from a population of 5,000 are thought to have already been killed or transported to the mainland for release by concerned animal lovers.

Uist Hedgehog Rescue, an assortment of groups dedicated to saving the animals, has attacked the latest plans as "unethical" and a waste of money.

SEAGULLS HAVE LEFT a Devon grandmother so terrified that she is afraid to leave her house after one launched a vicious attack.

Exeter gran Beryl Walkley's problems started when she saw a gull chick sitting in her back garden and went to investigate.

"I think it was learning to fly," she said."Then I saw the mother or father bird on my roof looking at me.

"Suddenly, it swooped down and attacked with its beak, pecking at my head.

"My head was left bleeding and a neighbour later bathed it for me.

"For a good two weeks afterwards I had seagulls dive-bombing me in the garden. It was extremely frightening."

Even her terrier Sandy was scared, she added.

The RSPCA said it was a shame she had been injured.

However, the birds, thought to be herring gulls, were only following their natural parental instincts and protecting their young.

SHARKS SEEM TO be posing a bigger risk to swimmers off southern English beaches after several incidents over the summer.

Bull and mako sharks - both dangerous to humans - have been spotted in shallow waters by swimmers and surfers this year.

In previous summers, great white sharks have also reportedly been sighted off-shore.

In the latest incident, surfer Luke Goodman, 25, has told how a 6ft bull shark passed beneath his board 30 metres from the beach near Penzance in Cornwall.

His experience - the fifth such sighting recorded in as many weeks - has left experts wondering if global warming could lead to future shark attacks here as more and more sharks visit our waters.

Luke said of the bull shark:"It swam straight under me and I knew what it was immediately as I've been surfing for years and know the differences between sharks.

"I was horrified because I know what those things are capable of. I pulled my legs up behind me and surfed to the shore. I was terrified I'd fall off."

On reaching the shore, he warned others to get out of the water and there was a short panic as people fled the waves.

A spokeswoman at Newquay's Blue Reef Aquarium said bull sharks had never previously been reported north of Spain.

AN ANGRY ADDER has prompted picnicking families to take extra care in Yorkshire after a girl of eight almost died from a bite.

Corinne Kerr had been playing barefoot near a stream close to Osmotherley on the Yorkshire Moors when she stepped on the reptile and was attacked.

She was badly affected and rushed to hospital after her foot swelled and she began to vomit violently.

Her parents maintained a four-day vigil at the hospital in Stockton-on-Tees.

There, doctors administered adrenaline and kept the youngster under close supervision until the poison left her system.

However, Corinne eventually made a complete recovery.

Adders, also known as vipers, are Britain's only poisonous snakes but bites rarely result in death.

The elderly, children, and those weakened by illness, are most at risk of fatalities.

MINK AND OTHER troublesome non-native UK species will be on the agenda for what is expected to be a heated debate.

Anyone with an interest in conservation is being urged to make a note in their diary now for the Earthwatch Balloon Debate: 'Back to Nature - Eradicating Invasive Species from the UK'.

"When non-native species become invasive they can degrade ecosystems and threaten native species,"explained a spokesman for the event.

"Five eminent scientists will make a case against the worst offenders. The audience will be the judge and jury in what is sure to be a hard-fought, eye-opening and emotive debate."

Besides mink, muntjac deer, rhododendron, the Ruddy duck, and the zebra mussel will be debated.

The event will be held at the Royal Geographical Society in Kensington Gore, London, on October 6, starting at 7pm.

DESPITE PLUMMETING IN numbers over recent decades, the red squirrel remains one of Britain's most popular animals.

Forced to flee from most of its traditional strongholds by the march of the bigger American grey squirrel, the red still holds a place in the nation's heart, according to The Wildlife Trusts.

"They're agile, cute and furry, and we're nuts about them," said a Trust spokesman. "Red squirrels are one of the most loved animals in the UK.

"With their distinctive russet fur, tufted ears and twitching tail, a red squirrel is always a captivating sight in the forests of the UK.

"Yet these flashes of red are becoming more and more scarce - the current population is estimated to be only 160,000.

"Red squirrels are at risk from grey squirrels and are usually displaced within 15 years of the arrival of greys. Disease and habitat fragmentation are also key factors in their decline."

This month, however, reds are being boosted with a series of events organised by the Trusts to raise their profile.

Red Squirrel Week runs from September 10 to 18 all over the country and attractions include 'adopting' a red squirrel on Brownsea Island via Dorset Wildlife Trust; becoming a 'friend' of a red through Red Alert North West or Anglesey Red Squirrels; or fans can simply report latest sightings of reds to Cumbria and Northumberland Wildlife Trusts.

BLACKBIRDS ARE DOING best in London, a study of the capital's songbirds has found.

Research has shown that blackbirds are now far more widespread that other once common species such as starlings and sparrows.

Hundreds of volunteers surveyed over 300 of the capital's public green spaces as well as many private gardens.

They found that blackbirds were present at 96 per cent of sites followed by wood pigeons at 93 per cent, crows at 90 per cent, blue tits at 89 per cent, magpies at 86 per cent and robins at 85 per cent.

Collected data forms the basis of the British Trust for Ornithology's 'London Bird Project' which aims to assess the wider wildlife value of the city's current green spaces and looks at how they can be improved.

Sue Gough, research ecologist for theTrust and one of the report's authors, said:"Clinically, tidy parks may look aesthetically pleasing but they certainly aren't the best for birds.

"Having a little extra vegetation makes all the difference and by sacrificing perfectly manicured open spaces we get the added benefit of sharing our space with birds and other wildlife."

More nestboxes, bushes, and strips of grass left uncut are among ideas being considered.

YET MORE TRANQUILLITY will be lost in the countryside if plans to change planes' flight paths get the go-ahead, warn campaigners.

A scheme to amend current flight paths could see more planes flying over eight Areas of Outstanding Natural Beauty as well as the Brecon Beacons National Park, say protesters, angry at proposals from the Civil Aviation Authority.

Paul Hamblin, head of transport policy for the Campaign to Protect Rural England, said: "Government plans to accommodate massive expansion in air travel threaten to wreck the tranquillity of the countryside, as well as its own efforts to tackle climate change.

"These areas, some of our most protected landscapes, are confronting a new threat to their peace and quiet from above. It is a threat which could well spread across the country as the number of flights increase.

"The Civil Aviation Authority seems to have done a serious job of mapping the effects, but concludes that the intrusion will be minimal in the designated areas. We strongly question this view. In any case the huge increase in flights risks damaging the peace and quiet in the countryside outside the National Park and Areas of Outstanding Natural Beauty.

"There is a serious lack of information on the effects of aircraft noise on people in quiet environments, and current standards are too weak as a result."

Deb Wozencraft, liaison officer for the Campaign to Protect Rural Wales, added:"It seems bizarre that in these days of promoting sustainability and encouraging people to enjoy our natural landscape that the issue of increasing air transport has again thrown any progress that we have made into turmoil.

"The predicted increased growth of 42 per cent in air traffic over the Brecon Beacons National Park between now and 2018 will inevitably compromise enjoyment of protected areas and the Welsh countryside as a whole."

A WETLAND AREA proved difficult for breeding birds this year because it was TOO wet, according to the RSPB.

But while the Ouse Washes were too wet , the Nene Washes were too DRY, the Society revealed in a report on its fenland nature reserves in Cambridgeshire.

Graham Elliott, fens area manager, added:"The Nene and Ouse Washes are a great challenge to manage and so influenced by water supply - often outside our control. It took the skill of our reserves' staff to ensure we had a fairly good nesting season, despite too much water on the Ouse Washes and not enough on the Nene Washes."

A SCHEME TO help the public enjoy the autumn colours of Perthshire's forests was launched at Faskally Wood, near Pitlochry.

"Faskally Wood is one of the finest mixed woodlands in Perthshire and is renowned for its brilliant autumn colours," said a Forestry Commission spokesman. "It is also one of the first sites in Perthshire Big Tree Country where access has been improved as part of the three-year £1.9 million Heritage and Access Project.

"The path around tranquil Loch Dunmore, which lies at the centre of Faskally Wood, is now fully wheelchair accessible."

CORMORANT: skilled fish hunter at odds with anglers

QUICK and agile underwater, the cormorant is a voracious hunter of fish, which is why so many anglers have sadly come to detest it.

Mainly a seabird, the cormorant is increasingly deserting its natural habitat around our coasts for easier pickings inland.

Conflict between cormorant and angler is common and many birds are believed to have been killed to protect dwindling fish stocks.

Cormorants also congregate besides rivers or lakes where their acidic droppings can build up and kill off the trees they perch on, infuriating foresters and landowners.

Cormorants' growing unpopularity has prompted a crackdown by the RSPB which says illegal slaughter of the birds must stop.

After one man was fined £250 by Luton magistrates for shooting a cormorant - the first conviction of its type in England - the RSPB appealed to anglers and fisheries managers to give the bird a break.

Julian Hughes, head of the RSPB's species policy section, said: *'Three years of Government-commissioned research have found no evidence that cormorants damage fish stocks at a national level.*

"In those exceptional cases, at a local level, where cormorants have been proved to cause problems, we want to work with fishery managers and anglers to seek lasting solutions. We have no desire to be in court seeing people being convicted for committing these needless crimes."

With its black, blue and bronze feathers offset by a flash of white around the face, the cormorant can be quite a handsome bird.

I often feel there is something almost prehistoric about it, especially when you see it standing stock-still with its wings outstretched, waiting for its feathers to dry.

Those feathers are specially adapted to become waterlogged fast and dispel buoyancy so that a cormorant wastes no time in pursuing its prey.

Cormorants are large birds, as big as geese which they often resemble in flight since their broad wings beat the air at a similar steady pace.

Like geese, they even choose to fly in a similar 'V' formation when a number travel anywhere together But unlike the vegetarian goose, the cormorant has a long, dagger-like beak designed for catching and killing prey after its great webbed feet have powered it within range.

Eels are a favourite food but it will take most fish, setting its menu as wide as possible and thereby putting it on a collision course with anglers and commercial fishermen.

Years ago, some cormorants were kept as pets in Britain and allowed to dive to catch fish for their owners. Today, this practice continues only in Asia where the birds are fitted with throat locks to prevent them eating the fish themselves.

Writer Christopher Isherwood, of 'Goodbye to Berlin' fame, once wrote:*"The common cormorant or shag lays eggs inside a paper bag. The reason you will see no doubt - it is to keep the lightning out."*

Nice line, although shags are a similar but separate species.

Perhaps this is just another example of cormorants being misunderstood. Today, life is definitely no cabaret for a cormorant.

TAWNY OWLS CAN be helped from bird lovers' own beds in a six-month survey starting this October, says the British Trust for Ornithology.

Mike Toms, Trust Garden BirdWatch co-ordinator, explained:"This survey is so easy that it can be done from the comfort of your own bed, listening through an open window or from an armchair on your patio.

"We are asking for volunteers to record when the owls are calling and the type of calls that are heard. For those people unsure what a tawny owl sounds like we have a dedicated 'Owlaphone' that you can call to listen to tawny owls."

The Trust says latest evidence suggests that tawny owls are declining but a better understanding of numbers and distribution is badly needed.

That's why sharp-eared volunteers are being sought across the country to take part in the survey.

"The tawny owl is the most numerous of our five owl species," added a Trust spokesman,"and is the one most likely to be heard in woodland or suburban areas.

"Along with the well-known 'hooting', both sexes also make shrill 'kerr-wick, kerr-wick' calls. Data from the 1989-1991 Breeding Bird Atlas estimated a British population of 20,000 pairs.

"However, this information is now 15 years old and more recent evidence from general bird surveys, aimed largely at day-flying birds, suggest that numbers may have fallen by up to a third since 1994.

"A specific tawny owl survey is needed to establish actual numbers. The best way of estimating numbers of birds that you can't see is by listening out for their distinctive calls and we need help to do this."

A FOX SEEMED to want to brush up on art when it was caught on surveillance cameras in a London gallery.

However, this was no wild visitor on the hunt for rats but a pet called Bandit released by Belgian artist Francis Alys for a film about surveillance called 'Nightwatch'.

The animal is followed by the cameras as it stalks the National Portrait Gallery.

HARES WILL BE centre stage at three October 'workshops' aimed at expanding their habitats.

Farmers and estates managers are being invited to the Brandon Marsh Nature Reserve, Warwickshire, on October 3, the Blackthorn Centre, near Cricklade, Wiltshire, on October 10, and the Fenn Bell Pub, St Mary's Hoo, Kent, on October 12, to learn how they can help the threatened, high-speed mammals in a joint initiative by conservation groups.

POULTRY PRODUCERS, FARMERS' leaders and Government officials have come together to try to reduce mounting panic over a possible bird flu pandemic.

A joint statement issued by the NFU, DEFRA, and the poultry industry is aimed at calming rising fears.

"It is important to underline that the H5N1 strain of avian influenza, reported in southern Europe, is essentially a disease of birds and poultry," says the statement."The risk to human health only arises in persons in very close contact with infected birds.

"The NFU, together with the British poultry industry and the Government are working very closely together to minimise the risk of the disease entering this country.

"The NFU and poultry representative bodies urge the Government to step up its controls at border points. In the event that the H5N1 virus does enter the country we are taking every step to ensure that any outbreak in poultry would be quickly recognised, contained and eradicated.

"The NFU and other poultry bodies have been working closely with DEFRA to develop contingency plans. Each of our organisations has a register of all its poultry members and has communicated on issues of disease control on a regular basis.

"However, we all agree that we should co-ordinate our database, on the location and size of all our commercial enterprises, so that we can issue precautionary messages quickly to all poultry farmers and be fully prepared to manage a disease outbreak.

"The British poultry industry is highly professional and responsible, works under very close veterinary scrutiny and has had strict biosecurity arrangements in place for many years.

"In the event of an outbreak, we would all have particular concerns over the health of poultry farmers, their families and their staff. This concerns around 50,000 people.

"However, poultry businesses and their employees need clear guidance on how to assure worker safety in the event of avian flu. Already a wide range of industry stakeholders have been working on this issue with the Health Protection Agency, Health and Safety Executive, State Veterinary Service, Department of Health and others.

"We are all committed to ensuring that the guidance is available this month.

"The British poultry industry is a real success story, with an annual value at farm level of £1,674 million. We have the second biggest poultry industry in Europe (after France), producing almost 14 per cent of Europe's poultry meat to the highest quality with very strict standards.

"It would be a tragedy if this industry were to be undermined by avian influenza, or by any unfounded scare stories."

UP TO A dozen pilot whales were spotted cruising together just north of Fetlar in the Shetlands.

A day earlier, two minke whales were seen off Uyea Isle, Unst.

The sightings come after a busy summer for wildlife watchers when sperm whales, killer whales, fin whales, basking sharks, porpoises and dolphins were all identified in waters around the islands.

RED KITES, GOLDEN eagles and other birds of prey are still seriously threatened in Scotland, warn conservationists.

Some of Britain's most spectacular predators are falling prey themselves to illegal poisoning, trapping, being shot, or having their nests destroyed.

According to the RSPB, attempts to prosecute people responsible are often hampered by lack of resources for wildlife law enforcement and failure of the courts.

Although some species - such as the buzzard - have made a big fightback after a century of absence from large parts of Scotland, birds of prey continue to face threats from wildlife criminals.

"Recent scientific research commissioned by Scottish Natural Heritage has highlighted the threat to golden eagles from illegal poisoning on grouse moors," said an RSPB spokesman."It is also clear that the effects of persecution are impacting on the whole Scottish golden eagle population.

"Likewise, hen harriers continue to fare very badly on southern and eastern moorlands in Scotland despite the availability of suitable breeding habitats. But they are holding their own in the north and west where grouse moor management is largely absent.

"Red kites - reintroduced successfully in three parts of the country - face an ongoing threat from poisoning, which has certainly damaged the population growth and range expansion at the first reintroduction."

Buzzards were by far the commonest victims of illegal killing, he added, but peregrine falcons, goshawks, long- and short-eared owls, sparrowhawks and kestrels were also dying needlessly.

SLOW DOWN TO save wild animals as nights get darker, Britain's motorists are being urged.

Every year, says the RSPCA, millions of creatures are needlessly killed as drivers rush to and from work.

As it launched a campaign to cut deaths, the Society said the toll included birds, deer, foxes, badgers, rabbits and hedgehogs, as well as domestic pets.

Many victims were left to die but any driver who hit an animal had a moral obligation to look after it, the Society claimed, and could even face criminal charges if he or she did not.

THE BADGER TRUST has welcomed the publication of the Animal Welfare Bill.

Trust director Jack Reedy said: "We are absolutely delighted. The Trust was involved in the consultation process and we are therefore pleased to be associated with a piece of legislation that tackles head on the issue of animal suffering."

FOXHUNTERS ARE GEARING up to renew their battle against the hunt ban with some defiant groups preparing for the new season using birds of prey to kill foxes.

With former Labour sports minister Kate Hoey MP recently named the new chairman of the Countryside Alliance - after her party banned hunting with dogs - many hunts have pledged to carry on as normal, albeit 'within the bounds of the law'.

But attempts to stay within that law while continuing to hunt have been growing increasingly bizarre.

First, mouse hunts were organised in one famous rebuke to the Government and now the coming season is likely to see foxes hunted by horse-borne golden eagles and eagle owls.

Up to 30 hunts are believed to have bought large birds of prey capable of killing foxes as such winged predators are exempt from the Hunting Act.

However, falconry experts are furious about the plans.

Jim Chick, chairman of the Hawk Board, which organises falconry in Britain, said it would completely disassociate itself from the practice.

He said:"This is bringing the sport into disrepute. Firstly there is a welfare issue. Many of the hunts are using people to handle the birds who have just been on a short course. You are not competent to handle a large bird of prey after a short course.

"Secondly, a fox is not a recognised quarry for a bird of prey. It is a large animal and cannot be easily subdued, so there is a big ethical issue over whether they should be used.

"An eagle is possessive and once it has caught a fox it will not let go.

"If the hounds are then brought in they could attack the eagle and a hound could be blinded or killed."

Ms Hoey, MP for Vauxhall in south London since 1989, said rural people had "the right to engage in country sports and other activities without prejudiced legislative assault.

"A true democracy respects the rights of all minorities," she added.

BRITISH BEEF LOOKS set to muscle its way back into more lost international markets following a favourable EU report on BSE prevention measures.

UK beef production first slumped nine years ago when deadly brain illness in humans was linked to ' mad cow' cattle disease.

Export restrictions followed which have slowly been lifted with the latest, positive report set to boost beef farmers further.

The Commission had demanded that BSE cases fall to below 200 cases per million before the ban was lifted, a level reached earlier this year.

A Commission spokesman announced:"This is the beginning of the end, but nothing is automatic about the process.

"There will be a preliminary look at the inspectors' report and then the Commission will, in the next few weeks, prepare a proposal to lift the remaining embargo on British beef in the light of discussions with the member states."

However, it is not all good news.

Earlier this year, our own Government revealed that British beef remained banned in over 80 countries around the world.

DRAGONFLY: savage beauty of a summer killer

MY six year-old daughter saw it first, letting out a cry of fright as it skimmed the surface of the small pond in the garden of her aunt's home - a dazzling, iridescent green dragonfly. More striking than any dragonfly I had ever seen before, it soon began to land at intervals around the edge of the pond and delicately used its ovipositor tail tube to lay eggs.

It had come from nowhere on one of the last hot days of summer and amazed us with its power and beauty.

Despite their fierce reputation, dragonflies are harmless to humans and do not sting, though my daughter could not be reassured and kept well away.

Later, trawling through dragonfly pictures back home, I soon learnt why I had never seen one like it before.

It was a rare species, a brilliant emerald, found only in the Scottish Highlands and parts of the South East.

Larger and more voracious than similarly shaped damselflies, dragonflies range over a much wider area.

While damselflies barely stray from the surface of the nearest pond or lake, mature dragonflies only use water to lay their eggs.

Apart from that, they go wherever prey can be found with butterflies, moths, and assorted other insects all snapped up.

Two huge compound eyes mounted at the front of their long cylindrical bodies give dragonflies a huge advantage, as do their speed, manoeuvrability and powerful jaws. A dragonfly's head is also amazingly mobile and can even be rotated to help it catch and kill its prey.

Several species of dragonfly and damselfly co-exist in this country and it is occasionally difficult to tell them apart at a glance.

But besides its greater size and speed, a dragonfly holds its two pairs of wings in a rigid flight position when at rest.

The weaker damselfly tends to fold back its wings along its abdomen.

Dragonflies are creatures of the summer, warmed by the sun as they shimmer and glitter in pursuit of food.

For all their attractiveness, their life cycle is short, with some species living just six months from egg to death.

Perhaps less than two months of that will be as a flying adult.

Other species may live a few years but, aside from a few final months' flight, most of this time is spent underwater as a predatory larva.

A dragonfly larva is particularly savage, too.

It will eat anything that moves, including tiny fish fry and tadpoles, and can become the scourge of a garden pond.

When maximum growth is achieved after a series of moults, the bloated, ugly larva hauls itself out of the water and clamps itself to a reed or twig.

Then its outer skin splits a final time and the prettier dragonfly emerges.

19th Century writer Dante Gabriel Rossetti marvelled:*"Deep in the sun-searched growths, the dragonfly hangs like a blue thread loosened from the sky."*

Nice image - unless you happen to be a passing butterfly.

RED SQUIRRELS ARE to be saved from extinction in mainland England by a £1million project, it has been revealed.

A spokesman for The Wildlife Trusts said:"The North of England Red Squirrel Conservation Strategy has been developed by a broad partnership of organisations called Red Alert North England, which includes ourselves and the Forestry Commission as well as landowners, businesses, and the local community.

"Conservation efforts will focus on 16 carefully selected Red Squirrel Reserves which offer the species the best chance of survival. It is the biggest ever commitment to red squirrel conservation and will involve hundreds of people and more than £1million.

"Conservationists have carefully selected the designated reserves from the species' last remaining strongholds in the large conifer forests of Northumberland, Cumbria, Yorkshire and Merseyside.

"The woodlands chosen will be managed to get the right mix of trees in terms of species and age structure to support healthy populations of red squirrels, but which are less well-suited to the higher energy demands of the larger grey squirrel. Targeted grey squirrel control will take place in 'buffer zones' surrounding the reserves to protect the red populations."

Mike Pratt, chief executive of the Northumberland Wildlife Trust added: "Public interest in and concern for red squirrels is at an all-time high. More than 30,000 people have reported squirrel sightings to the Trusts as part of our 'Seeing Red' campaign."

VANS THAT SMELL like chip shops are the Forestry Commission's latest wheeze to help its staff go green.

The Commission now has 160 vehicles using 'biodiesel' - "a diesel-like fuel that is refined from vegetable oil, including used cooking oil, and mixed with the usual mineral diesel," explained a spokesman.

"And in the case of one forestry van being used in a trial in northern Scotland, ordinary diesel has indeed had its chips - it's sizzling along nicely on 100 per cent used cooking oil that hasn't even been refined into biodiesel first."

SOME OF THE UK's most environmentally sensitive lakes and streams are recovering from the effects of acid rain, says DEFRA.

A spokesman revealed:"The amount of acidic sulphur in UK waters has generally halved in the last 15 years, according to new research from University College, London. Because of this, acidity in the water is declining and wildlife is starting to recover."

GAME BIRD PRODUCERS have come under attack from animal rights campaigners as potential contributors to a possible bird flu pandemic.

"Migratory birds are being scapegoated by international governments which will not acknowledge the central role of factory farming in such catastrophes," said Animal Aid.

"Whilst the possibility of cooping up the entire UK free range poultry flock hangs in the air, 35 million pheasants will just have been released into the countryside. These birds are purpose-bred for the shooting industry, which uses battery cages, sheds and giant open pens to grow-on the animals before their release when the shooting season starts.

"These purpose-bred birds are as much at risk of catching avian influenza from wild, migratory birds as outdoor poultry flocks. Should they become infected, they will in turn spread the virus. Whilst it is too late to halt this year's release, now is the time for the Government to take decisive steps to prevent shooting estates from unleashing a new generation of game birds into the wild next year. Breeding for next season's birds, which starts in the spring, must not now take place."

The Animal Aid attack comes as the RSPB calls for a month-long EU ban on importing exotic species to be made permanent.

Julian Hughes, head of species conservation for the Society, said:"The trade in imported wild birds is putting many of them at risk and there is no evidence that a ban on bird imports would drive this trade underground.

"It is a dangerous back door route for avian flu to get to the UK, and there are sound conservation reasons for outlawing imports permanently."

He added that the import of wild birds into the EU "is not proven to be sustainable and places our native wildlife as well as the health of humans and livestock at risk."

BEAVERS ARE AT the centre of a legality probe after being reintroduced to England through a Gloucestershire park.

Government officials have confirmed that they are investigating whether the release of beavers at Cotswold Water Park is, in fact, illegal.

Six Eurasian beavers were released into an enclosed reserve at Lower Mill Estate within the park but immediately provoked the DEFRA probe.

Officials are concerned that the animals - once native to Britain before being driven to extinction here - might escape into the wild from their 14-acre enclosure, even though it is protected by electric fences and CCTV.

DEFRA said:"The Eurasian beaver is not a species which is ordinarily resident in Great Britain. The 1981 Wildlife and Countryside Act does not define 'wild' but DEFRA interprets this widely as once an animal is released from captivity it is difficult, if not impossible, to prevent its spread."

The maximum penalty for a conviction if this occurred would be two years' imprisonment and an unlimited fine for landowner Jeremy Paxton.

Derek Gow, who was involved in the beavers' earlier six-month Devon quarantine project, said:"The beavers are now in a big enclosure which is protected by a large fence. There's very little chance of them escaping."

A MASS CULL of rabbits is now underway on remote Lundy Island in the Bristol Channel to prevent the flop-eared munchers causing a second ecological disaster there.

Birdwatchers were delighted when over 40,000 rats were recently exterminated on the island to stop them feasting on bird eggs and chicks, threatening the survival of several species.

But, unknown to many bird fans, the rats were also keeping rabbits in check by eating their young.

Without rats, the rabbit population has rocketed and begun to threaten delicate plant species as well as causing erosion and interference with ancient burial sites.

In a report on the island, English Nature official David Appleton said 14 per cent was now "unfavourable and declining" because of a rabbit population thought to have exploded from a few hundred to tens of thousands.

Animal rights campaigners have called the situation "farcical" and said it proved the danger of meddling with Nature.

EUROPEAN EAGLE OWLS are slowly spreading across parts of the UK, according to an eye-opening documentary shown on BBC 2.

Experts say the powerful predators may be a hazard to our native wildlife as they tend to feast on anything they can overwhelm.

Even hedgehogs and large birds of prey such as buzzards are taken by the birds.

Although numbers of eagle owls here are still very low, the programme asked if we should do anything to discourage their spread.

Some of the first eagle owls to set up in the wild are thought to be escaped pets but these have mated with others which have apparently migrated here from Scandinavian countries.

Livestock, such as lambs and poultry, are also thought to be at risk from the birds.

STARLINGS ARE SET to create quite a breathtaking winter spectacle in Somerset over the next few months, say wildlife watchers.

"Bird lovers should flock to Somerset Wildlife Trust's Westhay Moor nature reserve as millions of starlings have started arriving on Peat Moors," reported a Trust spokesman.

"Some are local but many fly thousands of miles from eastern Europe to enjoy Somerset's milder winter.

"The annual sight of the huge flocks is spectacular, drawing bird enthusiasts from all over the UK and beyond."

The Trust's David Reid confirmed:"The birds have started arriving in flocks of various sizes and congregating at Westhay. Last year we estimated the combined flock numbered around seven million."

Westhay Moor is designated as a National Nature Reserve and has been at the centre of a pioneering wildlife project under the Trust.

Former peat workings have been transformed into a 100 hectare haven at the site.

DEVON AND CORNISH hunt groups may be tracked by a police helicopter to help officers ensure that hunters stay within the bounds of new legislation.

Although it's only one of a number of proposed strategies to monitor hunts, the possibility has caused outrage among hunters who fear a 'spy in the sky' may make horses bolt and throw their riders.

A low-flying helicopter is thought to be responsible for the death of a woman rider in Lincolnshire last year.

However, police say the Devon and Cornwall force's helicopter - based in Exeter - has been fitted with high-powered video equipment which would allow them to gather evidence of illegal fox or deer kills from a safe distance.

Under the new laws, just two dogs at a time are allowed to 'flush' an animal out to where it can be shot.

Wildlife liaison officer PC Roy Adams explained that officers could not follow riders onto private land unless they had a landowner's permission but the chopper would enable them to overcome this obstacle.

Potentially violent clashes between 'pro' and 'anti' groups would also need to be dealt with.

"Although policing hunting is not a priority for the force, safeguarding public safety is," PC Adams said."We take hunting incidents very seriously. We have to make sure the law is complied with."

Any monitoring would be done from above 2,000ft so no horses would be startled, he added.

Countryside Alliance spokeswoman Alison Hawes said that the Assistant Chief Constable of Sussex Police had already recommended that helicopters were not used to shadow hunts in an advisory statement for the Association of Chief Police Officers.

She said:"It goes against the grain of everything we have been told about the way the hunting ban is going to be policed. There is a serious safety concern about helicopters and horses."

Michael Moore, joint Master of the East Devon Hunt, said that using helicopters to police hunts seemed like a terrible waste of money, especially after being told that policing the Hunting Act was not a priority.

A RED KITE is recovering at a wildlife hospital better known for helping hedgehogs after being blasted from the sky.

The bird, hit by a shotgun and felled at Ashley Green, Buckinghamshire, was later transported to St Tiggywinkles Wildlife Hospital at Haddenham.

The fully grown adult victim is being treated for four pellet wounds to its wing and body.

Hospital founder Les Stocker said:"It's extremely unlikely that the kite was shot accidentally because of its size and distinctive appearance.

"The bird suffered pain and distress and is lucky to have been found before its condition worsened. We're very concerned that someone may be deliberately targeting these beautiful and rare birds."

Ashley Green lies in the Chilterns, an Area of Outstanding Natural Beauty which has been at the centre of a national reintroduction programme for the kites.

The birds are often spotted soaring over local towns and villages.

HARVEST MOUSE: biggest challenge for tiny mammal

TINY, shy, and weighing less than a 2p coin, the harvest mouse is facing up to the biggest challenge of its life - warding off extinction.

Changes in agricultural practices, coupled with the attentions of cats and other predators, have pushed this once common mouse to the edge in many parts of the country. Although it is not yet on the critical list like some species, alarm bells have sounded as more and more harvest mouse strongholds vanish.

With its blunt face and small ears, the harvest mouse looks more like a slim, long-tailed vole than a typical mouse.

Head and body measure just two and a half inches but this is doubled by a thin tail of equal length.

The tail itself is prehensile and deployed as an extra foot to help the harvest mouse move swiftly through its normal habitat of tall grass or corn.

In summer, the mouse's main fur is yellowish brown, giving it a better chance of blending in with ripe corn. But in winter, the coat darkens to make the most of shadows and overcast conditions.

Underside fur remains milky white all year round, granting its owner greater anonymity when silhouetted against the sky from below

Grain, seeds, fruit and insects are all part of the harvest mouse's diet and it feverishly hunts for these around the clock, making itself vulnerable to night predators such as owls as well as daytime foes like kestrels.

Most harvest mice are eventually snapped up or die of cold and wet but, by way of redressing the balance, Nature has made them prodigious breeders.

Females may give birth to three litters a year, each litter producing up to eight young.

These are reared in a spherical nest about three inches in diameter made out of tightly woven leaves.

The nest is also sited well off the ground to try to protect the offspring from lurking rats or weasels.

If you are constantly depressed by the failure of British tennis stars at Wimbledon - as I am - , you might divert yourself with the fact that used tournament balls have often been deployed to help harvest mice.

Hundreds of balls were handed to The Wildlife Trusts by the All England Club, providing tough artificial homes for struggling harvest mice in Avon, Glamorgan and Northumberland.

Holes of about 16mm width were drilled into these balls to replicate natural nest entry points before they were attached to stakes at least 75cms off the ground. Commenting on the scheme, Dr Simon Lyster, director general of the Trusts, said: *"The harvest mouse is an excellent indicator of the health of our fields and hedgerows.*

"In recent years it has been under increasing pressure and we hope that specific harvest mouse projects, such as providing artificial nests, will give them the help they need to survive."

Unusually for a big dog, my long-dead labrador Duke seemed to have a nose for hunting harvest mice when he was alive.

On a few occasions he somehow caught them, brought them to me in his soft muzzle, and dropped them gently at my feet - only to watch bemused as they immediately scurried off again.

WILD BOAR HAVE sparked uproar in Devon after up to 100 of the animals were released from a farm by animal activists.

Days before Christmas, the hairy creatures - some weighing more than 400lb - were set free from the Woodland Wild Boar farm in the secluded hamlet of West Anstey.

Farmer Alan Dedames, 38, said that hundreds of metres of fencing had been cut down to allow the boar to escape.

Villagers, besieged by the animals crashing into their hedges and trampling well-kept lawns, have been warned to treat them with respect since they can be dangerous if cornered.

Some of the adults are armed with razor sharp tusks which are used to slash out if they become stressed or angry.

A Devon and Cornwall Police spokesman said:"Motorists in the area are being warned to take care in case the boars stray onto roads. But they do not appear to be dangerous unless provoked."

Christine Pennells, landlady of the local Jubilee Inn, told of her own alarming encounter.

She said:"I was helping two draymen deliver beer. This massive one came from nowhere. It barged the cellar door and got its nose in."

Husband Robert added: "One of our customers saw seven of them walking down the lane on Boxing Day."

The couple are afraid to let their red setter dogs out, fearing the boar would kill them.

Farmer Mr Dedames said attempts are being made to recapture the animals - with some early success - but he thinks many of the boar will be roaming nearby Exmoor for years.

"Ninety per cent of my females are pregnant," he revealed,"and it's a Garden of Eden of nuts, roots and mushrooms out there for them. You have really got a wild boar population in Devon and Somerset now."

A SEAL PUP is recovering at an animal rescue centre after being transported from a Devon beach.

The distressed, underweight pup was spotted on Meadfoot beach in Torquay and was thought to be at risk from dogs.

With the tide coming in fast, an operation was launched to save the animal involving the police, RSPCA, and British Divers Marine Life Rescue.

A BDMLR spokeswoman said:"The pup is now residing at the RSPCA's facility in West Hatch,Taunton, where he is reported as being alert and well but decidedly underweight at 15.8kg and with a question mark over his respiratory system, a classic case of a struggling weaned pup."

BRITAIN'S TALLEST TREE is still in Scotland, according to researchers.

"A BBC team have found that Scotland remains home to the tallest tree - Dughall Mor, a Douglas fir in Reelig Glen near Inverness," revealed a Forestry Commission spokesman.

"Confirmation of this fact came after an investigation was made following a claim that a tree in Wales had grown beyond the height of the Scottish giant.

"The Welsh Douglas fir at Powys Castle was recently measured at a height of 62.5 metres, suggesting it had surpassed the height of the Highland tree, which was measured at 62 metres in 2003. The discovery was made during filming of a new BBC series, 'Trees Which Made Britain', which will be broadcast in Autumn 2006.

"The BBC crew, working with staff from Kew Gardens, travelled north of the border to check the Welsh claim. The crew, together with Jim Patterson of the Tree Register of the British Isles, and Forestry Commission Scotland staff, remeasured Scotland's tallest tree using the latest laser technology. Readings were taken from three locations and gave an average of a few centimetres over 64 metres, reconfirming the tall giant's status as Scotland's, and indeed Britain's, tallest tree."

Inverness Forest district manager David Jardine added:"I am delighted to hear that Dughall Mor, which means 'big dark stranger' in Gaelic, remains the tallest tree in Britain, if not in Europe. This tree is one of a number of very fine trees at Reelig Glen where around 25,000 visitors enjoy the tall trees walk every year."

TALKING TURKEY JUST got easier with a new website launched to help consumers choose the best bird for their table this Christmas.

The NFU website "directs customers to local and regional turkey farmers who produce farm fresh, free range or traditionally reared birds," said a spokesman.

"It contains information on the types of turkey available and which breed would best suit your needs this Christmas. There are also pages on how to cook a traditional roast turkey, recipe tips on using leftovers, plus information on handling raw meat and making sure your bird is properly cooked."

STRANDED SALMON WERE rescued after becoming trapped in a shallow stretch of the River Avon near Salisbury.

Dozens of the fish, some weighing over 20 pounds, were plucked to safety by Environment Agency staff.

"Their migration to upstream spawning grounds was obstructed by an un-opened water hatch leaving them trapped in water little over ankle deep," said a spokesman."Agency fisheries officers netted the salmon in a special operation and released them safely higher up the Avon.

"All the salmon were mature fish in prime breeding condition. The largest weighed more than 22 pounds and measured nearly 3ft from nose to tail.

"Officers also opened the hatch that was causing the obstruction to increase the river flow and encourage the salmon to move up river towards their spawning grounds. A local landowner has been contacted and reminded of the importance of operating the river hatch to assist the safe movement of salmon up the Avon."

CALLS ARE GROWING for the Hunting Act to be amended in Wales where farmers fear widespread slaughter of lambs by foxes next spring.

John Thorley, chief executive of the National Sheep Association, said:"Sheep farmers in Wales have been put in a really ridiculous situation.

"They cannot effectively protect their newborn lambs from foxes, they cannot use a terrier below ground to control foxes if it is to protect livestock - although they can if it is to protect gamebirds - and farmers and hunts can use a maximum of only two dogs to flush a fox to a gun, which is simply ineffective.

"To safeguard our flocks and the future of our farming, we need the law to be amended to allow the use of terriers below ground and allow a greater number of dogs to be used to flush foxes to guns."

Adrian Simpson, South Wales regional director of the Countryside Alliance, added:"All of Wales' hunts are still operating within the law.

"However, there is great concern that within the terms of the Hunting Act 2004, hunts and farmers will be unable to protect newborn lambs from foxes.

"The Welsh Assembly Government have asked for evidence that shows that effective pest control is impossible within the terms of the Hunting Act and we will do all we can and continue as long as is necessary to prove this law is not working."

MARSH HARRIERS AND other birds of prey will be easier to spot in north Kent thanks to construction of a new viewing point aimed at raptor fans.

The RSPB's Capel Fleet viewpoint, near Eastchurch on the Isle of Sheppey, "will give visitors the chance of observing several species of wild birds of prey, including peregrines and barn owls, and will almost guarantee views of Sheppey's speciality, the marsh harrier," said a spokesman.

RSPB site manager Alan Johnson added:"Sheppey is renowned for being one of the very best places in Britain for wild birds of prey. People come from far and wide to try and see them.

"At Capel Fleet, we have created a specially-raised vantage point with parking and disabled access where, given patience, harriers, hawks, owls and falcons can all be seen."

Marsh harriers, which boast a four-foot wingspan, are one of Sheppey's most spectacular species to watch with 2005 marking their best ever year on the island - 35 pairs rearing young in all. The birds are known for their 'sky-dancing' displays in spring and in winter roost communally with up to 20 birds circling the skies together at Capel Fleet.

POP STAR MADONNA has described the moment she decided to give up game bird shooting after a traumatic incident involving a dying bird.

She said:"I was mad for shooting a couple of years ago. I used to go for lessons at the West London Shooting School, and I loved my bespoke outfits and everything. It was so much fun.

"That all changed when a bird dropped in front of me that I'd shot. It wasn't dead. It got up and it was really suffering. Blood was gushing out of its mouth and it was struggling up this hill, and I thought 'Oh God, I did that'. I caused the suffering of this creature."

Her change of heart has been welcomed by animal rights campaigners.

Animal Aid said:"The news that Madonna is giving up pheasant shooting - having witnessed a bird die agonisingly in front of her - is especially good news because her high-profile support for the bloodsport has been responsible for encouraging people to shoot who might never have done so.

"Many additional birds would have suffered and died as a result of her glossy advocacy. We therefore urge Madonna to act, from now on, as a vocal opponent of shooting.

"This means the immediate ending of all production and killing at her own Ashcombe Estate."

Madonna's husband Guy, a keen shooter, has so far shown no desire to follow his wife's example.

His celebrity friends, such as ex-footballer and rising actor Vinnie Jones, are also known to have been invited to the estate for shooting parties.

SEALS ARE BEING secretly shot in Scotland by a giant fish producer to protect salmon stocks, it has been claimed.

According to reports, horrified marine experts have demanded an inquiry after viewing shocking media images of dead and injured seals.

Carcasses are reported to have been found washed up on beaches around Skye and tourists on boat trips claim to have watched injured animals dying from their wounds.

Amsterdam-based firm Marine Harvest claims staff have had to shoot seals to stop them raiding salmon cages at their fish farms.

CORNCRAKES ARE SURGING back in Scotland after conservation measures were launched to stop the shy birds vanishing altogether.

The population in Scotland is now above 1,100 - the highest number recorded by conservationists in 27 years of monitoring the threatened species.

"Figures from the 2005 survey of the birds show an overall total for Scotland of 1,108 calling males, and in the core survey areas a rise from 1,040 in 2004 to 1,082 this year," revealed a spokesman for RSPB Scotland.

"The astonishing success of the bird was particularly pronounced on the Inner Hebrides, with Tiree's population of calling males rising from 260 to 310 birds, and Islay from 10 to 52.

"However, the calling male population in the Outer Hebrides was down 55 birds compared with last year."

With a mere 470 calling males in 1993, the species had been on the brink of extinction in the UK.

HOUSE MARTIN: perilous journey to make a home

LIKE the swallow, the house martin has become a sleek symbol of British summertime although it spends its winter in eastern or southern Africa.

To get here, it makes a perilous journey and many are believed to die from natural causes en route or are trapped or shot by hunters.

The thousands that do make it choose to live in scattered colonies with females raising up to three broods each season comprising four or five chicks each time.

Such fertility obviously increases the odds in favour of the species' long-term survival.

Cliffs are still sometimes chosen as nest sites but most house martins return annually to their favourite buildings and repair old nests or make new ones, usually under the eaves.

A new nest takes about two weeks to build and is constructed from as many as 2,500 individual pellets of mud strengthened by grass.

A superb flyer, the house martin can be told apart from the swallow by its slightly shorter, dumpier physique and small forked tail.

Its white rump and underparts also contrast more vividly with its bluish black back and wings.

Like its more elegant cousin, the house martin eats insects captured on the wing, swooping and twisting in a more frenetic manner than either the swallow or the swift.

Most people welcome the return of house martins to their homes, despite the accompanying noise and mess.

However, some residents do undoubtedly come to hate them. One man seen knocking down a house martin's nest and dumping the contents in a skip became the first person convicted of destroying such a nest at their own home.

The irate householder, from Lincolnshire, was fined £250 after dislodging the nest with a long pole.

Commenting on the case, RSPB spokesman Mark Thomas said:*"Each year we deal with a number of reported incidents involving the alleged destruction of house martin nests.*

"The RSPB believes that many people are unaware that house martins are a protected species and that the destruction of their nests constitutes an offence for which the maximum penalty, in England and Wales, has recently been increased to £5,000 or a six-month prison sentence.

"Obviously the RSPB does not want to see members of the public being convicted of such crimes through ignorance of the law so we have launched a public awareness drive reminding people of the severity of these offences."

I imagine the possibility of being incarcerated or fined should be enough to concentrate minds.

AS EFFORTS CONTINUE to recapture wild boar released by animal activists in Devon, fans of the hairy mammals have only a few more days to voice their support for them.

Similarly, those who detest and oppose the boar's presence in the wild as a danger to ramblers and livestock now only have a limited period to make their views known.

Time runs out for respondents to the Government's consultation document on wild boar on January 6, after which views will no longer be accepted.

Groups and individuals have all been invited to submit their opinions about what should be done about the sizeable creatures which were once native to this country.

As a result, existing colonies of wild boar could eventually be wiped out or allowed to roam free under the same legal protection given to other wild animals.

DEFRA hopes to provide a summary of all responses received within months, by which time any strategy should also be drawn up.

It says it wants "to ensure an acceptable balance between wild boar and the interests of conservation, farming, horticulture, woodland management, infrastructure and human safety as well as the welfare of the boar."

Elsewhere in Europe, numbers of wild boar have rocketed in recent years with many blamed for causing traffic accidents and serious harm to livestock and property.

The animals are widely hunted and even in the UK there is said to be growing enthusiasm among game shooters for the chance to legally take wild boar.

BIRD LOVERS ARE being urged to help the RSPB find out this month if the house sparrow is still the commonest of our garden birds.

"The 2006 Big Garden Birdwatch takes place at the end of January and all you need do to take part is watch the birds in your garden or local park for an hour," said a spokesman.

"Last January, nearly 400,000 people spent an hour watching their local birds, collectively recording over six million birds in more than 200,000 gardens.

"In 2005, the house sparrow was the commonest bird in your gardens, beating the starling into second place.

"The survey is very simple. All you need do is watch your garden or local park for an hour on either Saturday 28 or Sunday 29 January, note down the birds you see and tell us the highest number of each species you see at any one time in the hour - this avoids counting the same birds twice.

"We analyse the results to find out about garden birds in the UK. Your postcode allows us to look at the data by geographical area too."

Results are best submitted online with a special form available on the RSPB website from January 28.

A FEMALE WHALE that made international headlines by swimming through London died due to severe dehydration, muscle damage and reduced kidney function, it was revealed.

The northern bottlenose whale was a young female, probably less than 11 years old and sexually immature, experts said as they published early post-mortem results.

The 17-foot whale, nicknamed Willy before its true gender was known, measured 5.85 metres in length.

A pathologist involved in the post mortem said it was most likely that the whale had become lost in the North Sea and was trying to return to its natural feeding grounds.

It died as experts from the British Divers Marine Life Rescue group escorted it on a barge down the River Thames towards the sea.

Thousands of people had lined the Thames to watch the rescue attempt, carried live on 24-hour news channels.

The spectators cheered as the whale was hoisted onto the barge.

But, sadly, the outcome they wanted - the whale's safe return to the wild - was not to be.

A COW MADE a break for freedom after the trailer carrying it was involved in a road accident in Shropshire.

The animal was among a number of cows being transported near Newport when the Land Rover pulling their trailer reportedly overturned, causing the trailer to tip over, too.

Although the other cows were quickly accounted for, a search was launched for the missing animal after it vanished into local countryside.

But the fugitive seemed to have other ideas about being recaptured and 18 hours after the accident was still on the run.

It was last sighted in the Chetwynd Firs area.

THE LEAGUE AGAINST Cruel Sports claims it was 'pleased' by the massive gathering of hunt supporters over the festive period.

But this was because it felt many of the 300,000-plus people estimated to have attended Boxing Day hunts might have done so because they considered the sport less cruel after recent legislation.

League spokesman Mike Hobday said:"Our impression is that a lot of people turned out but we are not sure if they were supporting the hunts or whether they did not want to be associated with it before but now feel it is legitimate to get involved.

"It was never about stopping people dressing in red coats, having too much to drink and riding around the countryside. We are not killjoys and to that extent we are very pleased they have had a lot of support."

Police turnout had been very low, he admitted, but he was satisfied with the way different forces responded.

Some 250 hunts met over the festive break, many chasing drag lures and dozens using birds of prey in an apparent attempt to kill foxes that way.

Other groups flushed foxes to guns using two hounds, as allowed by the new anti-hunt law.

Meanwhile, the Countryside Alliance has reaffirmed its determination to overturn the law no matter how long it takes.

471

GASSING BADGERS WILL leave a bad taste among shoppers if beef producers persist in calling for the action, it has been claimed.

The Badger Trust issued the warning after the National Beef Association told the Government that it wants farmers to be able to gas badgers with vehicle exhaust fumes.

Trust chairman David Williams said:"The public is supportive of farmers, but not at any price.

"There is even greater public support for animal welfare and nature conservation. Consumers are not going to appreciate the taste of British beef if it is contaminated by the poisonous stench of gassing."

Mr Williams also criticised Robert Forster, NBA chief executive, who said that the slaughter of 30,000 cattle with TB this year "could have been prevented".

He added:"Robert Forster knows full well that the vast majority of the spread of bovine TB is down to the 14 million annual movements of cattle, not badgers.

"The spread of TB could have been prevented years ago, had the National Beef Association and other farming lobbyists not held the Government to ransom over badgers.

"We fully understand that farmers are upset at the spread of bovine TB but the blame for that - as with other animal disease disasters - lies squarely at their own door.

"Bovine TB is a mess of farmers' own making.

"Even in TB hotspots, eight out of nine badgers are not infected with TB.

"Conservationists and the wider public will support farmers in controlling TB through cattle-based measures but the extermination of healthy badgers is simply unacceptable."

THE WOODLAND TRUST is hoping that supporters help it notch up 60 million recycled festive cards this month.

The incredible figure was almost reached last year and officials are certain another push will see the number smashed.

"In January 2005 we collected and recycled 58 million cards - that's 1,150 tonnes of rubbish," said a spokesman.

"Help us reach our target of 60 million in January 2006."

The Trust says that Christmas and New Year cards can be recycled until January 31 at WHSmith and Tesco stores.

This would reduce the amount of waste going to overloaded landfill sites.

"Everyone can take part in the scheme," added the spokesman."It's fun, it's easy and it helps the environment."

DORMICE ARE NOT meant to be eaten, The Mammal Society has stressed - despite viewers of a certain BBC2 TV series getting the distinct impression they are delicious.

"Viewers of the TV drama series 'Rome' may have been taken aback to hear that the Romans ate dormice, " said a spokesman.

"Do not fear, however, for we are not talking here about our own sleepy, Alice in Wonderland dormouse which would have been just a mouthful at a Roman cocktail party.

"No, the Romans ate the so-called edible or fat dormouse 'Glis glis' which is about the same size as a guinea pig - still eaten in Peru.

"Like our native dormouse, the edible species puts on a great deal of fat in the autumn and hibernates for the winter so it is easy to 'store'. The Romans kept these dormice alive in very large pots called dolia which in turn were kept in special dormouse gardens.

"Petronius tells that dormice were glazed with honey and then dipped in poppy seeds. However, the main source of recipes from Classical Roman times is De Re Coquinaria, by Marcus Gavius Apicius.

"This contains around 500 recipes, one of them for 'Glires', a dormouse stuffed with a forcemeat of pork and small pieces of dormouse meat trimmings, all pounded with pepper, pine nuts, asafoetida, fish sauce and broth. The dormouse thus stuffed was put in an earthenware casserole and roasted in the oven, or boiled in the stock pot.

"Although edible dormice are not native to Britain, they were introduced here in 1902 by Lord Rothschild and their population is still based around what was his estate at Tring Park. Both edible and common or hazel dormice are protected under the Wildlife and Countryside Act 1981."

A BABY DEER has been dubbed a "real fighter" as it recovers after breaking three legs.

The muntjac fawn was struck by a car in Buckinghamshire and, at first, it was feared the tiny week-old animal would need to be put down.

However, after vets fitted all three legs with casts, the fawn - named Rudolph - began to rally.

He is now staging an amazing comeback on a diet of goat's milk after being 'fostered' by two human carers.

Two of the legs are thought to be already almost back to normal because the animal is so young.

Les Stocker, who runs St Tiggywinkles Wildlife Hospital at Haddenham where Rudolph was treated, said:"He's a real fighter. We've got high hopes of getting him back into the wild."

COCKLE-EATING BIRDS have been boosted at the River Dee estuary in North Wales after police and Environment Agency Wales pledged to crack down on illegal cocklers.

The site on the Dee Estuary is regulated by the Agency and is currently closed until July this year.

Just last month a large-scale enforcement operation was launched at all access points to and from the fishery in the Mostyn and Flint area.

No offences were detected, said the Agency, although a number of people were spoken to, to make sure they understood the regulations protecting cockles.

RED SQUIRREL: driven out by march of the greys

SMALLER and prettier than its immigrant grey rival, our native red squirrel has had a tough time in recent decades. Driven out of the vast majority of its old stamping grounds, it now hangs on in a few nature reserves within England and Wales while most sizeable colonies are restricted to Scotland.

Bright chestnut with a white underside and almost comically tufted ears, the red squirrel was once a familiar sight in this country.

But introduction of the aggressive grey squirrel from America is thought to be a major cause of its decline with widespread destruction of its preferred habitat - conifer forests - also believed to have played a part.

Recently, however, a raft of conservation efforts have been made to try to protect the red squirrel from potential extinction.

Among these is a bid by a group of woodland experts to ensure that the Scottish Highlands remain a stronghold for years to come.

"Fortunately, as far as we know, the grey squirrel has not moved into the Highlands yet," said group member Ian Collier, a woodland officer with the Forestry Commission. *"However, their spread is relentless so there is no room for complacency.*

"Latest research shows that many of the region's big conifer forests could be key places to conserve healthy numbers of red squirrels. This is because grey squirrels don't like conifer forests but reds seems quite happy in them, especially if they have plenty of Scots pine and Norway spruce trees.

"The smaller, more delicate red squirrel is better adapted to getting the seeds out of pine and spruce cones, whereas the bigger grey squirrel prefers larger foods found on broadleaf trees, such as hazelnuts and acorns.

"Research suggests that conifer forests of at least 5,000 acres stand the best chance of supporting viable numbers of red squirrels and keeping grey squirrels out.

"In some areas it might also be possible to support smaller populations in woodlands of just 500 acres if we manage them the right way and create buffer zones that deter grey squirrels from entering."

I must confess, the last time I spotted a red squirrel outside an English nature reserve I nearly ran it over.

I was learning to drive at the time, doing my first 3-point turn on a quiet, leafy lane as a teenager - so that gives you some idea of how long ago it was.

Road safety's 'Tufty' mascot scooted out from behind the back of the car just as I ruined the manoeuvre by stamping on the accelerator.

It hopped away as I bumped over a grass verge and wrecked a small but beautifully manicured privet hedge.

To this day, I am still a little surprised that my instructor did not knock at the cottage door and apologise for our transgression.

Instead, hissing nervous guidance under his breath, he helped me regain control of the vehicle and we raced off.

We never went there again.

Whether or not Tufty squealed on us I don't know, but he probably thought we were nuts.

THE SPECTRE OF a devastating bird flu outbreak now hangs over British farms even as the ravages of foot-and-mouth are still being felt.

Nine dead swans were examined by health officials as fears of a bird flu outbreak in the UK increased sharply.

However, the birds were later pronounced free of the disease.

The dead swans were located in several regions with their discovery coming as bird flu spread across Europe to reach France, causing deep unease here.

Six ravens at the Tower of London were caged in a bid to cut the risk of them catching bird flu as concerns grow about the disease decimating poultry and wild birds.

Organic poultry farmers in particular - who charge higher prices to recoup costs of allowing birds greater freedom outdoors - are facing financial ruin as their £200million industry braces itself for bad news.

Richard Jacobs, spokesman for Organic Farmers and Growers, said:"This is the last thing we want to see because it would be a potential disaster for the industry."

FEEDING THE BIRDS has landed a wildlife-loving couple in hot water with their local council after complaints from fellow villagers.

For the last eight years, a variety of birds such as sparrows, pied wagtails, thrushes, blackbirds, and starlings have benefited from George and Janine Cope's daily two-hour feeding regime around Kiveton Park, South Yorkshire.

But now their local council has taken a dim view of their activities and issued them with a £50 fixed penalty fine for dropping 'litter' - mostly bread, seeds, and sultanas - which, it says, could attract rats.

The couple are refusing to pay and may face prosecution, a prison sentence or a hefty fine.

Mr Cope, 65, said: "Although we both feed the birds, I am the one named on the ticket and I will go to jail rather than pay. "

Mrs Cope, 42, added:"We are just doing our bit for wildlife and the environment and are being treated like criminals. We are not litter louts. We are bird lovers who respect the environment."

Rotherham Council has labled their feeding "excessive" and said some residents were having problems as a result.

BITTERNS ARE BACK in the heart of London - giving better views than ever to waiting birdwatchers.

Three of the rare birds have returned to the London Wetland Centre.

Anyone who has never seen one of the 'booming' heron-like birds before is invited to the centre's remaining free entry day on February 2.

A spokesman said:"These normally shy and secretive birds have been visiting since 2002. But in the past they have remained hidden. However, this year the birds have moved into smaller areas of reedbed adjacent to the viewing hides."

A MYSTERY BIG cat has been spotted prowling close to Prime Minister Tony Blair's isolated country residence.

The animal, thought to be a puma, was seen loping across a field on the Chequers estate in Buckinghamshire.

Rambler Heather Brown, who lives near Aylesbury, said that she was walking near the Ridgeway Trail when she saw a huge cat padding across the ground about 150 metres away.

Mrs Brown said:"It was the colour of a fox, a brownish sort of colour. As it ran away, it was loping across the field. Foxes and deer trot, this was moving like a cheetah. It was a cat of some kind, and had a long thinnish tail."

After the giant animal had vanished, she met some patrolling police officers and asked if they had also spotted it. She added:"They said they hadn't, but told me I was not the only person to have seen it."

Sightings and rumours of the so-called 'Beast of Bucks' have circulated in the county for years and in 2001 experts confirmed prints found on a local golf course belonged to a puma.

TREES COULD SPRING up nationwide as millions of old mobile phones are handed in under a new scheme.

A joint initiative by The Woodland Trust, Barclays and recycler Cellular Surplus will see donated phones recycled for a fee of £10 per phone for the Trust.

"To the Woodland Trust, £10 is what it costs to purchase land, supply a sapling, plant and care for one native tree," said Kathryn Mintoft, environmental manager for Barclays.

"Alternatively, the money might go towards some of their other activities such as fighting threats to ancient woodland and conserving biodiversity.

"Even recycling a modest fraction of our unused phones could end up making a difference to the environment. Mobile phones can be harmful if they are sent to landfill.

"Over 18 million mobile phones are sold each year in the UK, the majority of which are probably replacement phones. That means there are millions of phones that need recycling."

A ROSES REVOLUTION has got underway with blooms going on sale that smell as good in the vase as they do growing normally.

After 14 years of research, experts have finally developed roses which open out fully after cutting, and retain the glorious smell of uncut flowers.

The two new varieties, peach Juliette and pink Miranda, are said to have looser buds and more petals than existing supermarket roses.

They were cultivated by growers David Austin at nurseries in Shropshire but grown outdoors in Kenya.

Tony Slack, director of licensing for David Austin, said they had achieved the 'Holy Grail'.

He said:"We have finally managed to develop roses that marry all the best qualities of old and new varieties. They arrange themselves beautifully in the vase rather than having straight stems and standing erect, like some other roses."

Veronica Richardson, chief executive of the Flowers and Plants Association, said:"These old-fashioned roses look absolutely wonderful.

"For a long time roses in shops have been bred for their longevity but now people want the scent as well."

A DIRE SHORTAGE of nest sites for garden birds is being highlighted during this month's National Nest Box Week.

And human tidiness has been fingered as a major culprit by the British Trust for Ornithology.

Birds now face a severe "housing crisis", according to a Trust spokesman who added:"Natural nest sites, such as holes in trees and buildings, are fast disappearing as gardens and woods are 'tidied' and old houses are repaired.

"More of the UK is garden than nature reserve and so gardens form an incredibly important habitat for the nation's birds.

"However, with our modern desire for tidy, organised gardens and perfect houses, birds are missing out on the places where they traditionally nest.

"Ivy-covered walls, holes under the eaves of roofs, these are places birds like to nest, but they are rapidly disappearing. So, what can we do to help?

"Launched in 1997, National Nest Box Week highlights the need for people to provide nesting places for the UK's garden birds. The simple act of putting up a box in a suitable place can make the spring for a pair of birds looking to raise a family. Different types of boxes attract different species and, once used, can attract birds year after year."

Jeff Baker, Trust organiser of the event which starts on February 14, added:"Nest boxes are incredibly easy to build or buy and can make a huge difference to the lives of our garden birds. In return you get the enjoyment of watching them raise a family.

"Blue tits love them but, depending on where you are in the country, you could get all manner of species moving in."

FEARS OF A pollution disaster in the English Channel have subsided following a collision between two ships.

A chemical tanker carrying 10,000 tonnes of phosphoric acid collided with a cargo ship around 30 miles north west of Guernsey, with the tanker rupturing and spilling part of its load.

RAF and coastguard teams joined French rescuers to successfully airlift 22 crew members from both vessels to safety.

However, there were fears that the tanker, Ece, could spark an environmental disaster as similar incidents in the past have seen thousands of seabirds, fish, and sea mammals die.

But Fred Caygill, of the Maritime Coastguard Agency, dismissed fears that the chemical released into the sea would devastate the area.

He said:"Phosphoric acid is a corrosive liquid which does not pose a pollution threat. It has dissolved in the sea."

ENGLISH FARMERS WILL begin to receive their first payments from the Single Payment Scheme by the end of this month, Farming Minister Lord Bach has announced.

Some £1.6 billion will be paid directly to farmers and growers, with the bulk of payments completed in March.

Lord Bach said:"I am very pleased to confirm what we said more than a year ago – that full payments will begin in February. I hope this announcement will provide some reassurance to the farming industry.

"The start of these payments signals a milestone in the development of a modern farming industry in this country, one which is no longer driven by subsidies. This new single payment scheme, a key part of the 2003 reforms of the Common Agricultural Policy, rolls 11 old schemes into one.

"It encourages farmers to be more innovative in responding to consumer demand while setting new standards of sustainable agriculture and environmental protection."

DEFRA explained that the Rural Payments Agency will now work hard to establish definitive entitlements by February 14.

Farmers will be informed of their individual entitlements within two weeks of that date.

Johnston McNeill, chief executive of the Rural Payments Agency, added:"Our staff have shown dedication and a lot of hard work in recent months to deliver these payments and it is a great credit to them. Making full payments from February will also deliver major benefits for the future."

THE HEARTACHE AND drama behind Britain's foot-and-mouth catastrophe has inspired a novel.

On February 20, Bluebell Publishing releases 'Following Orders', written by James Drew, to mark the fifth anniversary of an outbreak which devastated livestock herds around the country and drove many farmers to the depths of despair.

FERRETS ARE FUN and just the thing to help youngsters live healthier lives, it has been claimed.

Dad Steve Wise, 42, is trying to rally support for the creatures which have often been criticised as vicious and smelly.

Mr Wise, a former furniture maker from Bourne End, Buckinghamshire, wants to set up his own club of ferret enthusiasts with the aim of helping to keep down the countryside's rocketing rabbit population.

But his beliefs about the ferret effect on unhealthy kids are a little more controversial.

Mr Wise, whose two teenage daughters keep four ferrets between them, is adamant that ferreting is just the thing for getting children out and about.

He said:"The trouble today is that not enough children are getting out. They are not getting fresh air into their lungs.

"As a parent and a ferreter I find this very difficult to understand. Ferreting is a great family day out."

He is hoping that ferret-loving families will become members of his new club.

He added:"It's about making people aware of the ferret. They are not nasty animals."

WOODPECKER: taking knocks and giving a few back

THE drum of beak on wood often announces the presence of a woodpecker long before its distinctive shape is spotted flitting from tree to tree.

As with all woodpeckers, shock absorbers at the front of the skull enable our three native species to drill holes in trees without knocking themselves cold.

Their beaks, too, are extra strong and sharp so they can comfortably excavate nest sites or hack away in pursuit of food.

Prey is usually hidden insects or grubs with woodpeckers using long darting tongues covered in sticky saliva and bristles to catch them.

Stiff tail feathers give woodpeckers additional support as they cling to the rounded trunks of trees with special 'zygodactylous' feet - two toes on each foot pointing forward, the other two backward.

As well as attacking dead or dying trees in the hunt for food, the great spotted woodpecker drums noisily to establish territory.

Both sexes strike resonant branches as much as 15 times per second so those shock absorbers are vital.

A thrush-sized bird, the great spotted has distinctive black, white and red colouring.

It is also the most common British woodpecker, therefore much more likely to be seen.

The green woodpecker - our biggest and most beautiful species - is about the size of a pigeon and boasts a dazzling crimson crown atop lustrous green and yellow plumage. It is also extremely shy and will dart away into cover at the slightest disturbance.

Often, after that, only its curious laughter-like "*yaffle*" cry betrays its whereabouts.

The sparrow-sized lesser spotted woodpecker, meanwhile, is actually the rarest and quietest of the trio.

It looks like a smaller version of the great spotted and spends much of its life hidden from view, feeding in the topmost branches of the forest.

According to the British Trust for Ornithology, the lesser spotted is also the only species showing a consistent decline.

Surprisingly, perhaps, both great spotted and green woodpeckers appear to be doing rather well.

Great spotted numbers rose rapidly in the 1970s, levelled off, and are currently stable - still an achievement when so many other species are plummeting to oblivion.

But green woodpeckers are enjoying an even greater resurgence.

"*Green woodpecker populations have increased steadily since 1966, except for a period of stability or shallow decline centred on the late 1970s,*" revealed a Trust spokesman.

No-one knows why these two species are doing so well but experts suspect both thrive in man-made commercial forests, especially when dead trees are left in place to provide food and nest sites.

So at least some woodland birds are taking the knocks - and giving a few back.

SPIDERS: little lords of their mini-manors

THE discovery of a large colony of unfamiliar red spiders beneath the late Queen Mother's weekend home caused huge excitement at the time.

The mystery spiders were said to be three and a half inches long, venomous, with jaws strong enough to pierce human skin.

Shocked BT engineers retreated when they came across swarms of the unusually aggressive spiders while working beneath the Royal Lodge in Windsor.

Despite initial concerns about a possible threat to the then fragile Queen Mother, entomologists were delighted by the find.

Some believed the spiders could be a completely new species or a fresh strain of an established one such as the woodlice eating woodlouse spider.

Whatever these spiders were, the thought of thousands of them scurrying about in pitch darkness beneath a home would terrify most self-respecting arachnophobes.

But it is quite a fascinating idea for the rest of us.

It also got me thinking of how much we take our more usual species for granted.

Spiders are deadly predators, lords of their own mini-manors, which ruthlessly kill flies and other insects. Craftily setting a snare by spinning a web is a typical method used to catch their prey.

The common house spider - that dark brown species often found trapped in the bath - builds a simple triangular-shaped sheet web, mostly in corners.

After mating with a female, the male of this species dies and is eaten by his mate to provide extra nutrients for their offspring.

What a considerate father.

Elsewhere, the bulbous brown, yellow and white garden spider builds a more intricate wheel-shaped web which can look quite beautiful in the morning sunlight but is a shimmering deathtrap for insects. Females of this species often eat the much smaller male by accident after mistaking him for dinner - a bit unfortunate since he is normally feeling romantic at this point.

Snares, meanwhile, are spurned by the nomadic dark brown wolf spider. This makes no web at all and simply chases and runs its prey down wolf-like in the grass.

The female of this species does not even build a nest at breeding time but carries her eggs on her back in a silken sack.

When her young hatch, they continue clinging to her back for a week or so until strong enough to fend for themselves.

The zebra spider is that little black and white striped spider commonly seen hunting on the walls of your house at the height of summer.

Despite its name, this zebra is actually more like a tiny lion in its ferocity and hunting technique.

First, it slowly stalks its prey then it leaps upon it.

Male zebra spiders perform a frenetic mating dance for females.

Unfortunately, despite their large front eyes, they often mistake each other for a female so courtship can end in a savage fight.

It is not known what the Queen Mother thought of her creepy guests but she had to get used to them - removal work took months.

INDEX

504

INDEX

H

INDEX

INDEX

343, 378
Slimbridge Wildfowl
and Wetlands
Centre 134
sling nets 438
sloe berries 335
sloe gin 335
sloe liqueur chocolates
335
Slough 350
slow down heartbeats
398
slow down to save
animals 463
slow-worm 214, 336
slow-worms 197
Slug Pub 127
slug traps 127
slugs 8, 39,127, 182,
238, 351, 393
slump in pound 313
slump of euro against
pound 134
slurry 240
small food processors
109
Small Mammals: Ecol-
ogy, Survey and
Management 304
small pearl-bordered
fritillary butterfly
455
small shops threat 436
small tortoiseshell but-
terflies 127, 434
small tortoiseshell but-
terfly 235, 236
small-leaved lime 307
small-scale farmers
167
smaller abattoir sec-
tor 73
smallest bird 452
smallest deer 287
smelly letters 326
Smith Square 225
Smith, Alex 56
Smith, Angela 2
Smith, Brian 109
Smith, Chris 31
Smith, Des 134
Smith, Dr Adam 65
Smith, Graham 138
Smith, Guy 88
Smith, Iain Duncan
337
Smith, John 28
Smith, Jonathan 457
Smith, Neil 288
Smith, Nick 362
Smith, Paul 359
Smith, Thorven 64
Smith, Valerie 317
Smithers, Richard 108,

236
smog 195
smolts 209, 228
smooth snakes 197,
399
smorgasbord 84
snail, Vertigo Geyeri
154
snails 8, 39, 49, 332,
393
snake bite panic 459
snake startled golfers
328
snake threat to chil-
dren 321
snake's-head fritillary
435
snakes 21, 48 197,
241, 399
snakes leaflet 336
snakes sunbathing 336
snapdragons 408
snapping turtle 245
snare 78, 349
snared badger 178
snares 245, 263, 387,
451
snares attached to
dragpoles 263
Snares Liaison Group
245
snares petition 231
snaring 110
sniffer dogs 305
sniffing out a solution
27
snipe 5, 161, 305, 317,
347, 386, 399, 415
snipe slump 404
snoozing cow 12
snow goose 259, 379,
419
Snowdonia National
Park 23, 31, 199
snowdrop 196, 236
snowdrops 21, 253
snowy owl 178
snowy owls 179
So, You Own a Wood-
land? 343
soccer fans 222
sodium hyperchlorite
tanks 385
soft ministers 36
soft-hearted golf club
65
software problems 192
soil 438
Soil Association 46,
56, 73, 89, 102,
103, 109, 111, 135,
143, 155, 179 ,
183, 192, 211, 226,
245, 262, 394, 409,

445
soil conditioners 413
soil erosion 402
soil fertility 414
soil importance 402
soil moisture 75
soil physics 186
soil related problems
402
soils guide 258
solar energy schemes
247
solar plexus 26
soldiers slaughtered in
a First World War
battle 62
soldiers taught to
shoot 53
sole pair of choughs
399
Solent 82, 216, 396
Solihull 195
Solway Firth 337
Solway Moss 413
Some Lie Dying 31
Somerfield 41, 87
Somers, Sam 328
Somerset 3, 20, 53,
71, 75, 122, 148,
172, 189, 247, 247,
272, 273, 277, 301,
339, 385, 407, 466,
468
Somerset aquarium 64
Somerset County
Council 251
Somerset farm 366
Somerset Levels 3, 5
Somerset Wildlife Trust
466
sonar studies 148
song thrush 16, 49,
147, 257, 340
song thrushes 78, 119,
185, 223, 241, 311,
332, 351, 407
song thrushes window
strike 389
songbird numbers 286
songbird species 159
songbirds 101, 105,
176, 235, 299, 311,
330, 460
songbirds' singing 347
sonic bat detectors 430
Sotherton, Dr Nick
263, 430, 456
Sound of Harris 450
sous chef 295
South 71
South Africa 208
South African 88
South America 226,
308

South American 147,
302
South American cay-
man 18
South American guard
animal 240
South American na-
tives 431
South Atlantic 457
South Atlantic winds 96
South Church 409
South Coast 36, 144
South Dorset Hunt
kennels 341
South Downs 455
South Downs National
Park 400
South East 42, 46, 65,
73, 79, 146, 179 ,
206, 239, 259, 276,
295, 319, 361, 386,
400, 464
South East Regional
Planning Author-
ity 43
South Finger 134
South Hams 322
South Jason Island 96
South Korea 222
South Korean food 222
South Lakeland Magis-
trates 105
South London 100,
274
South Molton 20
South Staffordshire
Council 414
South Thames
Marshes 206
South Uist 278, 305,
378
South Wales 129
South Wales Police
306
South Warwickshire
328
South West 36, 94,
114, 118, 120, 130,
194, 288, 304, 400,
442, 456
South West beaches
57
South West coast 122
South West Coast
Path 148
South West coasts 196
South West frogs 296
South West Regional
Development
Agency 286, 290
South Yorkshire 31,
47, 70, 229, 263,
311, 321,
South Yorkshire Police

ACKNOWLEDGEMENTS

News stories published here are edited versions of articles previously written by the author between December 1999 and February 2006. Additional information sources, where pertinent, were revealed at the time but have largely been omitted from the main book text to assist with brevity. These sources are now gratefully acknowledged for a second time here:

Aberdeen Evening Express
Aberdeen Press & Journal
Amateur Gardening
Angling News
Auto Express
Bath Chronicle
BBC News
BBC Wildlife Magazine
Birmingham Evening Mail
Bournemouth Daily Echo
Brighton Argus
Bristol Evening Post
British Birds
British Wildlife
Bucks Examiner
Bucks Free Press
Cambridge Evening News
Carlisle News & Star
Channel 4 News
Chester Evening Leader
Country Life
Daily Express
Daily Mail
Daily Post (Wales)
Daily Telegraph
Derby Evening Telegraph
Dorset Echo
Dundee Courier
East Anglian Daily Times

Eastern Daily Press
Economist, The
Edinburgh Evening News
Exeter Express & Echo
Farmers Weekly
Field, The
Financial Times
Gloucester Citizen
Gloucestershire Echo
Grimsby Evening Telegraph
Guardian
Horse and Hound
Hull Daily Mail
Independent
Independent on Sunday
Ipswich Evening Star
ITN News
Journal of Animal Ecology
Lancashire Evening Post
Leicester Mercury
Lincolnshire Echo
London Evening Standard
Manchester Evening News
Nature
Newcastle Evening Chronicle
Newcastle Journal

New Scientist
North West Evening Mail
Northampton Chronicle & Echo
Northants Evening Telegraph
Norwich Evening News
Nottingham Evening Post
Observer
Oxford Mail
Peterborough Evening Telegraph
Plymouth Evening Herald
Portsmouth News
Press Association
Reading Evening Post
Scarborough Evening News
Scotsman
Shooting Times
Shropshire Star
South Wales Argus
South Wales Evening Post
Southern Daily Echo
Sporting Shooter
Sunday Express
Sunday Telegraph
Sunday Times
Tatler
Times